ISBN 978-1-5281-3259-6
PIBN 10922358

English
Français
Deutsche
Italiano
Español
Português

www.forgottenbooks.com

Mythology Photography **Fiction**
Fishing Christianity **Art** Cooking
Essays Buddhism Freemasonry
Medicine **Biology** Music **Ancient**
Egypt Evolution Carpentry Physics
Dance Geology **Mathematics** Fitness
Shakespeare **Folklore** Yoga Marketing
Confidence Immortality Biographies
Poetry **Psychology** Witchcraft
Electronics Chemistry History **Law**
Accounting **Philosophy** Anthropology
Alchemy Drama Quantum Mechanics
Atheism Sexual Health **Ancient History**
Entrepreneurship Languages Sport
Paleontology Needlework Islam
Metaphysics Investment Archaeology
Parenting Statistics Criminology
Motivational

BIENNIAL REPORT

OF THE

ATTORNEY GENERAL

OF THE

STATE OF NORTH CAROLINA

VOLUME 28
1944-1946

HARRY McMULLAN
ATTORNEY GENERAL

GEORGE B. PATTON
HUGHES J. RHODES
W. J. ADAMS, JR.
RALPH MOODY
FRANK P. SPRUILL, JR.
JAMES E. TUCKER
ASSISTANT ATTORNEYS GENERAL

Mr. Patton resigned and was succeeded by Mr. Moody.
Mr. Adams resigned and was succeeded by Mr. Spruill.

LIST OF ATTORNEYS GENERAL SINCE THE ADOPTION
OF CONSTITUTION IN 1776

	Term of Office
Avery, Waightsill	1777-1779
Iredell, James	1779-1782
Moore, Alfred	1782-1790
Haywood, J. John	1791-1794
Baker, Blake	1794-1803
Seawell, Henry	1803-1808
Fitts, Oliver	1808-1810
Miller, William	1810-1810
Burton, Hutchins G.	1810-1816
Drew, William	1816-1825
Taylor, James F.	1825-1828
Jones, Robert H.	1828-1828
Saunders, Romulus M.	1828-1834
Daniel, John R. J.	1834-1840
McQueen, Hugh	1840-1842
Whitaker, Spier	1842-1846
Stanly, Edward	1846-1848
Moore, Bartholomew F.	1848-1851
Eaton, William	1851-1852
Ransom, Matt W.	1852-1855
Batchelor, Joseph B.	1855-1856
Bailey, William H.	1856-1856
Jenkins, William A.	1856-1862
Rogers, Sion H.	1862-1868
Coleman, William M.	1868-1869
Olds, Lewis P.	1869-1870
Shipp, William M.	1870-1872
Hargrove, Tazewell L.	1872-1876
Kenan, Thomas S.	1876-1884
Davidson, Theodore F.	1884-1892
Osborne, Frank I.	1892-1896
Walser, Zeb V.	1896-1900
Douglas, Robert D.	1900-1901
Gilmer, Robert D.	1901-1908
Bickett, T. W.	1909-1916
Manning, James S.	1917-1925
Brummitt, Dennis G.	1925-1935
Seawell, A. A. F.	1935-1938
McMullan, Harry	1938-

LETTER OF TRANSMITTAL

1 December, 1946

To His Excellency
R. GREGG CHERRY, Governor
Raleigh, North Carolina

Dear Sir:

In compliance with statutes relating thereto, I herewith transmit the report of the Department of Justice for the biennium 1944-1946.

Respectfully yours,

HARRY McMULLAN,
Attorney General.

University of North Carolina v. Geo. E. Phillips, et al.
Wesley J. Collier v. Gill, Commissioner of Revenue.
P. P. Johnston v. Gill, Commissioner of Revenue.
State ex rel. Gill, Commissioner of Revenue v. B. P. Saffo, t/a
    Saffo's Confectionery, et al.
Southern Railway Co. v. Gill, Commissioner of Revenue.
Godley Brothers v. Gill, Commissioner of Revenue.
State v. Wilbur Smith.

PENDING BEFORE INDUSTRIAL COMMISSION

Riggsbee v. University of North Carolina.
Robert Farley v. Division of Forestry and Parks, Dept. Conservation and Development.

DISPOSED OF BEFORE INDUSTRIAL COMMISSION

L. O. Hill v. Forsyth County Board of Education.
Jones, Admr. v. University of North Carolina.
Etta Estes v. Board of Buildings and Grounds.
Norman Burgess v. Dept. of Conservation and Development.
Boston Leak v. North Carolina State College.

DISPOSED OF IN NORTH CAROLINA SUPREME COURT

State ex rel. Utilities Comm. v. Atlantic Greyhound Corporation,
    224 N. C. 672
Johnson v. Gill, Commissioner of Revenue, 224 N. C. 638
Gardner v. Board of Trustees, Local Gov. Employees Retirement
    System, 226 N. C. 465.
Ingle v. State Board of Elections, et al., 226 N. C. 454.

DISPOSED OF IN UNITED STATES SUPREME COURT

Williams and Hendrix v. State of North Carolina.
Utilities Commission v. Interstate Commerce Commission.
United States v. Southeastern Underwriters Association.
Inman and Stark v. State of North Carolina.
Harry Weinstein v. State of North Carolina.

DISPOSED OF IN UNITED STATES DISTRICT COURT

Godley Brothers v. Cherry, Governor, et al.

PENDING IN DISTRICT COURT OF APPEALS

Jeannette A. Noel v. Edson B. Olds, Jr., et al (Ackland Will Case)

PENDING BEFORE INTERSTATE COMMERCE COMMISSION

State of North Carolina and Utilities Commission v. Aberdeen
    & Rockfish R. R. Co.

EXHIBIT II

FALL TERM, 1944

State v. Allen, from Wilkes; nonsupport; defendant appealed; venire de novo (new trial); 224 N. C. 530.

State v. Beckwith, from Wake; A.D.W.I. Kill; etc.; defendant appealed; no error (per cur.); 224 N. C. 859.

State v. Biggs, et al., from Guilford; murder first degree; defendants appealed; no error; 224 N. C. 722.

State v. Cody, from Madison; reckless driving; defendant appealed; error and remanded; 224 N. C. 470.

State v. DeBerry, from Forsyth; assault on female; defendant appealed; reversed; 224 N. C. 834.

State v. DeGraffenreid, from Lee; murder second degree; defendant appealed; no error; 224 N. C. 517.

State v. Dunheen, from Guilford; murder first degree; defendant appealed; no error; 224 N. C. 738.

State v. Edwards (Paul), from Johnston; attempted incest—carnal knowledge; defendant appealed; no error; 224 N. C. 527

State v. Edwards (W. L.), from Pitt; manslaughter; defendant appealed; reversed; 224 N. C. 577.

State v. Emery, et al., from Polk; violating liquor laws; defendants appealed; venire de novo; 224 N. C. 581.

State v. Godwin, et al., from Cumberland; A.D.W.I. Kill—conspiracy; defendants appealed; new trial; 224 N. C. 846.

State v. Harrill, from Rutherford; prostitution; defendant appealed; no error; 224 N. C. 477.

State v. Hayden, from Guilford; nonsupport; defendant appealed; new trial; 224 N. C. 779.

State v. Hill, from Guilford; perjury; defendant appealed; no error; 224 N. C. 782.

State v. Inman, et al., from Lee; rape—highway robbery; defendants appealed; appeal dismissed; petitions denied; 224 N. C. 531.

State v. Kirkman, from Guilford; violating liquor laws; defendant appealed; reversed; 224 N. C. 778.

State v. Lewis, from Robeson; assault on female; defendant appealed; no error; 224 N. C. 774.

State v. McLean, from Scotland; burglary first degree; defendant appealed; new trial; 224 N. C. 704.

State v. McMahan, from Yancey; abandonment-nonsupport; defendant appealed; no error; 224 N. C. 476.

State V. Mull, et al., from Burke; robbery with firearms; defendants appealed; no error; 224 N. C. 574.

State v. Ogle, from Madison; reckless driving, etc.; defendant appealed; reversed; 224 N. C. 468.

State v. Oxendine, from Robeson; A.D.W.I. Kill, etc.; defendant appealed; no error; 244 N. C. 825.

State v. Parker, et al., from Johnston; attempt to receive stolen property, etc.; defendants appealed; no error; 224 N. C. 524.

State v. Patterson, from Cherokee; manslaughter; defendant appealed; reversed; 224 N. C. 471.

State v. Pennell, from Caldwell; manslaughter; defendant appealed; new trial; 224 N. C. 622.

State v. Rowell, from Union; murder first degree; defendant appealed; new trial; 224 N. C. 768.

State v. Shook, from Cumberland; A.D.W.I.Kill, etc.; defendant appealed; no error; 224 N. C. 728.

State v. Stewart, from Harnett; operating motor vehicle after license revoked; defendant appealed; no error; 224 N. C. 528.

State v. Stone, from Robeson; manslaughter; defendant appealed; new trial; 224 N. C. 848.

State v. Thompson, et al., from Mecklenburg; murder first degree; defendants appealed; no error; 224 N. C. 661.

State v. Todd, from Cumberland; conviction of murder second degree and judgment thereon set aside by superior court judge for newly discovered evidence; State appealed; appeal dismissed; certiorari denied; 224 N. C. 776.

State v. Wade, from Scotland; rape; defendant appealed; no error; 224 N. C. 760.

State v. Watts, from Columbus; violating liquor laws; defendant appealed; reversed; 224 N. C. 771.

State v. Weinstein, from Wake; larceny and receiving; defendant appealed; no error; 224 N. C. 645.

DOCKETED AND DISMISSED ON MOTION

State v. Alexander, from Durham.
State v. Taylor, from Wake.
State v. Buchanan, from Mecklenburg.
State v. Brooks, from Mecklenburg.
State v. Jones, from Halifax.

SPRING TERM, 1945

State v. Brady, from Randolph; carnal knowledge; defendant appealed; no error (per cur.) ; 225 N. C.

State v. Britt, from Robeson; manslaughter; defendant appealed; no error; 225 N. C. 364.

State v. Brown, from Martin; violating statute regulating seating arrangement in buses; defendant appealed; new trial; 225 N. C. 22.

State v. Clark, from Vance; manslaughter; defendant appealed; new trial; 225 N. C. 52.

State v. Cody, from Buncombe; assault with deadly weapon; defendant appealed; no error; 225 N. C. 38.

State v. Crandall, from Beaufort; A.D.W., etc.; defendant appealed; affirmed; 225 N. C. 148.

State v. Davenport, from Tyrrell; fornication and adultery; defendant appealed; no error; 225 N. C. 13.

State v. Davis, from Rowan; manslaughter; defendant appealed; no error; 225 N. C. 117.

State v. French, from Montgomery; murder first degree; defendant appealed; no error; 225 N. C. 276.

State v. Friddle, et al., from Guilford; breaking and entering-larceny and receiving; defendants appealed; no error; 225 N. C. 240.

State v. Graham, from Bladen; violating liquor laws; defendant appealed; affirmed; 225 N. C. 217.

State v. Harrison, from Guilford; assault with deadly weapon; defendant appealed; new trial; 225 N. C. 234.

State v. Heglar, et al., from Stanly; violating lottery laws; defendants appealed; reversed; 225 N. C. 220.

State v. Hill, from Wayne; A.D.W.I.Kill; defendant appealed; no error; 225 N. C. 74.

State v. Isaac, from Catawba; murder first degree; defendant appealed; new trial; 225 N. C. 310.

State v. King (Cora), from Richmond; larceny; defendant appealed; no error; 225 N. C. 236.

State v. King (Orlie), from Randolph; assault with intent to commit serious injury; defendant appealed; no error (per cur.) ; 225 N. C.

State v. Lord, from Cabarrus; murder first degree; defendant appealed; no error; 225 N. C. 354.

State v. Manning, from Martin; aiding, etc. abortion; defendant appealed; no error (per cur.) ; 225 N. C. 41.

State v. Matheson, from Alexander; murder first degree; defendant appealed; no error; 225 N. C. 109.

State v. Miller, from Anson; contributing to delinquency; defendant appealed; appeal dismissed; 225 N. C. 213.

State v. Mitchell, from Buncombe; practicing palmistry; appeal by State; special verdict; appeal dismissed (per cur.) ; 225 N. C. 42.

State v. Murdock, from Iredell; A.D.W.I.Kill, etc.; defendant appealed; no error; 225 N. C. 224.

State v. Murphy, et al., from Lenoir; assault-robbery; defendants appealed; error and remanded; 225 N. C. 115.

State v. McDaniel, from Guilford; rape; defendant appealed; no error (per cur.) ; 225 N. C.

State v. Parsons, from Caldwell; carnal knowledge; defendant appealed; no error (per cur.) ; 225 N. C.

State v. Perry, from Franklin; A.D.W.I.Kill; defendant appealed; error and remanded; 225 N. C. 174.

State v. Scoggins, et al., from Lee; manslaughter; defendants appealed; no error; 225 N. C. 71.

State v. Smith, from Johnston; arson; defendant appealed; no error; 225 N. C. 78.

State v. Spruill, from Wayne; A.D.W.I.Kill; defendant appealed; new trial; 225 N. C. 356.

State v. Sutton, from New Hanover; A.W.I.Rape; defendant appealed; no error; 225 N. C. 332.

State v. White, from Caldwell; nonsupport; defendant appealed; reversed; 225 N. C. 351.

State v. Williams, from Mecklenburg; manslaughter; defendant appealed; no error; 225 N. C. 182.

DOCKETED AND DISMISSED ON MOTION

State v. Calhoun, from Rockingham.
State v. Walsh, from Caldwell.

FALL TERM, 1945

State v. Barfield, from Scotland; A.D.W.I.Kill; defendant appealed; no error (per cur.) ; 225 N. C.

State v. Bennett, from Guilford; murder second degree; defendant appealed; no error; 226 N. C. 82.

State v. Brooks, from New Hanover; rape-first degree burglary; defendant appealed; no error; 225 N. C. 662.

State v. Cannaday, from Harnett; violating liquor laws; defendant appealed; no error (per cur.) ; 225 N. C.

State v. Cox, from Robeson; violating liquor laws; defendant appealed; no error (per cur.) ; 225 N. C.

State v. Curling, from Washington; A.W.I.Rape; defendant appealed; no error(per cur.) ; 225 N. C.

State v. Dover, from Cleveland; receiving stolen goods, etc.; dedefendant appealed; affirmed (per cur.) ; 225 N. C.

State v. Gordon, from Davidson; fornication and adultery; defendant appealed; reversed; 225 N. C. 757.

State v. Hightower, from Wilkes; murder first degree; defendant appealed; no error; 226 N. C. 62.

State v. Horne, from Gaston; murder second degree; defendant appealed; no error; 225 N. C. 603.

State v. Jackson, from Pender; assault on female; defendant appealed; error and remanded; 226 N. C. 66.

State v. Marsh, from Columbus; trespass-assault; defendant appealed; affirmed; 225 N. C. 648.

State v. Mays, from Lee; murder first degree; defendant appealed; no error; 225 N. C. 486.

State v. Miller, from Wilkes; assault with deadly weapon; defendant appealed; no error; 225 N. C. 478.

State v. Morgan, from Craven; assault on female; defendant appealed; no error; 225 N. C. 549.

State v. McNeill, from Harnett; violating liquor laws; defendant appealed; reversed; 225 N. C. 560.

State v. Peterson, from Sampson; murder second degree; defendant appealed; new trial; 225 N. C. 540.

State v. Petry, from Wake; A. W. I. Rape; defendant appealed; no error; 226 N. C. 78.

State v. Robinson, from Mecklenburg; manslaughter; defendant appealed; new trial; 226 N. C. 95.

State v. Shoup, from Guilford; receiving stolen goods; etc.; defendant appealed; no error; 226 N. C. 69.

State v. Spencer, from Gaston; abandonment-nonsupport; defendant appealed; no error; 225 N. C. 608.

State v. Stevenson, from Columbus; violating liquor laws; defendant appealed; no error (per cur.); 225 N. C.

State v. Stone, from Robeson; murder second degree; defendant appealed; no error; 226 N. C. 97.

State v. Stutts, from Moore; violating liquor laws; defendant appealed; no error (per cur.); 225 N. C. 647.

State v. Talton, from Johnston; manslaughter; defendant appealed; no error (per cur.); 225 N. C.

State v. Vanderlip, from Mecklenburg; abandonment-nonsupport; defendant appealed; reversed (per cur.); 225 N. C. 610.

State v. Williams, from Lee; rape; defendant appealed; no error; 225 N. C. 475.

State v. Wise, from Guilford; murder first degree; defendant appealed; no error; 225 N. C. 746.

DOCKETED AND DISMISSED ON MOTION

State v. Meadows, from Pitt.
State v. Burnett, from New Hanover.
State v. Jestes, from Avery.

SPRING TERM, 1946

State v. Baldwin, from Wake; possessing burglary tools; defendant appealed; no error; 226 N. C. 295.

State v. Bullins, from Rockingham; carnal knowledge, etc.; defendant appealed; new trial as to violating G. S. 110-39; affirmed as to violating G. S. 14-26; 226 N. C. 142.

State v. Carroll, from Caldwell; operating motor vehicle while intoxicated; defendant appealed; new trial; 226 N. C. 237.

State v. Clough, from Davidson; worthless check; defendant appealed; appeal dismissed (per cur.); 226 N. C. 384.

State v. Deaton, from Gaston; murder first degree; defendant appealed; no error; 226 N. C. 348.

State v. Farrar, from Orange; violating liquor laws; defendant appealed; appeal dismissed (per cur.); 226 N. C. 478.

State v. Gardner, from Buncombe; manslaughter; defendant appealed; new trial; 226 N. C. 310.

State v. Gibson, et al., from Caswell; attempted burglary-forcible trespass; defendant appealed; error and reversed as to burglary; no error as to forcible trespass; 226 N. C. 194.

State v. Hart, from Halifax; murder first degree; defendant appealed; no error; 226 N. C. 200.

State v. Herring, from Wayne; rape; defendant appealed; no error; 226 N. C. 213.

State v. Johnson, et al., from Wake; rape; defendants appealed; judgment arrested; 226 N. C. 266.

State v. Jordan, from Dare; burglary second degree; defendant appealed; new trial; 226 N. C. 155.

State v. King, from Lenoir; murder first degree; defendant appealed; no error; 226 N. C. 241.

State v. Lewis, et al.. from Caldwell; A. W. I. Rape; defendants appealed; error and remanded; 226 N. C. 249.

State v. Locklear, from Robeson; burglary second degree; defendant appealed; new trial; 226 N. C. 410.

State v. Malpass, from Columbus; mayhem; defendant appealed; error and remanded; 226 N. C. 403.

State v. Morgan, from Guilford; nonsupport; defendant appealed; judgment arrested; 226 N. C. 414.

State v. Mounce, from Rockingham; receiving stolen goods, etc.; defendant appealed; affirmed; 226 N. C. 159.

State v. McNair, from Forsyth; larceny; defendant appealed; no error; 226 N. C. 462.

State v. Peterson, from Sampson; violating liquor laws; defendant appealed; reversed; 226 N. C. 255.

State v. Presnell, from Buncombe; sale of short-weight butter; defendant appealed; appeal dismissed; 226 N. C. 160.

State v. Setzer, from Caldwell; bigamous cohabitation; defendant appealed; reversed; 226 N. C. 216.

State v. Stewart, from Wake; murder first degree; defendant appealed; no error; 226 N. C. 299.

State v. Taylor, from Wayne; murder second degree; defendant appealed; no error; 226 N. C. 286.

State v. Thomas, from Hoke; receiving stolen goods, etc.; defendant appealed; affirmed (per cur.) ; 226 N. C. 384.

State v. Vaden, et al., from Rockingham; manslaughter; defendants appealed; no error; 226 N. C. 138.

State v. Walker, from Harnett; rape; defendant appealed; no error; 226 N. C. 458.

State v. Witherington, from Wayne; kidnapping; defendant appealed; new trial; 226 N. C. 211.

DOCKETED AND DISMISSED ON MOTION

State v. Parsons, from Caldwell.

SUMMARY

Affirmed on Defendant's appeal	76
New trial or reversed on Defendant's appeal	34
Error and remanded	6
Judgment arrested	2
Appeal dismissed	17
Appeal dismissed on State's appeal	1
	136

FEES TRANSMITTED BY ATTORNEY GENERAL TO STATE TREASURER SINCE FEBRUARY TERM, 1944, THROUGH FEBRUARY TERM, 1946

State v. Herndon	$ 10.00
State v. Dry	10.00
State v. Parker	10.00
State v. Edwards	10.00
State v. Beckwith	10.00
State v. Stewart	10.00
State v. Harrell	10.00
State v. Shook	10.00
State v. Oxendine	10.00
State v. Mull	10.00
State v. Lewis	10.00
State v. Hill	10.00
State v. Manning	10.00
State v. McMahan	10.00
State v. Scoggin, et al	20.00
State v. Parsons	10.00
State v. King	10.00
State v. Davenport	10.00
State v. Davis	10.00
State v. Hill	10.00
State v. Miller	10.00
State v. King	10.00
State v. Graham	10.00
State v. Brady	10.00
State v. Sutton	10.00
State v. Friddle, et al	20.00
State v. Cody	10.00
State v. Murdock	10.00
State v. Curling	10.00
State v. Williams	10.00
State v. Talton	10.00
State v. Cannaday	10.00
State v. Dover	10.00
State v. Horne	10.00
State v. Spencer	10.00

State v. Miller 10.00
State v. Brooks 10.00
State v. Cox 10.00
State v. Barfield 10.00
State v. Marsh 10.00
State v. Stutts 10.00
State v. Shoup 10.00
State v. Bennett 10.00
State v. Petry 10.00
State v. Stone 10.00
State v. Stevenson 10.00
State v. Sawyer 10.00
State v. Vaden, et al 20.00
State v. Bullins 10.00
State v. Mounce 10.00
State v. Presnell 10.00
State v. Gibson, et al 20.00
State v. Parsons 10.00
State v. Baldwin 10.00
State v. Stewart 10.00
State v. Taylor 10.00
State v. Thomas 10.00
State v. McNair 10.00
State v. Farrar 10.00
                                                                                        ———
                                                                                   $630.00

SUMMARY OF ACTIVITIES

STAFF PERSONNEL

During the biennium there were several important changes in the personnel of this office.

Mr. George B. Patton, Assistant Attorney General, resigned to return to private practice on November 15, 1944. He was later made General Counsel for the State Highway and Public Works Commission.

Mr. Ralph Moody, of Murphy, was appointed Assistant Attorney General to succeed Mr. Patton and is now serving in that capacity.

Mr. William J. Adams, Jr., Assistant Attorney General, who had been assigned to the Revenue Department, resigned August 1, 1945, to enter private practice in Greensboro. The vacancy caused by his resignation was filled by the appointment of Mr. Frank P. Spruill, Jr., of Rocky Mount. Mr. Spruill has served during the balance of the biennium in that capacity.

Mr. H. J. Rhodes, as Assistant Attorney General, served throughout the biennium.

Mr. James E. Tucker has continued as a member of the legal staff since 1939.

Mr. Philip E. Lucas, of Burgaw, was appointed as a member of the research staff of the office on April 8, 1946, and was serving in that capacity at the end of the biennium.

The secretarial staff of the office during the biennium was as follows: Mrs. Margaret York Wilson, Miss Elizabeth Flournoy, Miss Ruby Thomas, Miss Elizabeth Kelly, Miss Lillian Turner, and Mrs. Grace H. Baker.

Due to inability to find an available and properly qualified attorney to fill the other position as a research member of the staff, this position remained vacant. There were very few graduates of the law schools during the war period and those who did graduate were promptly taken up by opportunities offered in private practice in this State and elsewhere.

DIVISION OF LEGISLATIVE DRAFTING AND CODIFICATION OF STATUTES

The General Assembly of 1943 adopted Resolution No. 23, creating a commission on statutory revision, consisting of twelve members, being the chairmen and the subcommittees of the Committees on Recodification in the Senate and House of Representatives. The duty of this commission was to serve in an advisory capacity and cooperate with the Attorney General and the Division of Legislative Drafting and Codification of Statutes in a study of the recommendations of the division with respect to desirable clarifying statements and the preparation of such proposed statutes for submission to the General Assembly of 1945. This commission was composed of the following persons:

Senators Irving E. Carlyle, Brandon P. Hodges, D. E. Hudgins, Wade B. Matheny, K. A. Pittman, and Representatives Oscar G. Barker, Frank W. Hancock, Jr., A. I. Ferree, Bryan Grimes, W. I. Halstead, Robert Moseley and Kerr Craige Ramsay.

This commission rendered a valuable service between the 1943 and 1945 sessions of the General Assembly, holding many meetings, and considered in detail the proposed legislative amendments clarifying various obscure sections of the law and correcting conflicting provisions, obvious errors, etc. A bill was presented by the commission to the Legislature, which was enacted as Chapter 635 of the Session Laws of 1945. Although this commission was diligent in attending to the work assigned to it, it was unable to complete the undertaking within the time available for this purpose.

For the continuation and extension of this work, the General Assembly of 1945 enacted Chapter 157, creating the General Statutes Commission, and assigned to it duties as follows:

(a) To advise and cooperate with the Division of Legislative Drafting and Codification of Statutes of the Department of Justice in the work of continuous statutory research and correction, for which the division is made responsible by G.S. 114-9(c).

(b) To advise and cooperate with the Division of Legislative Drafting and Codification of Statutes in the preparation and issuance by the division of supplements to the General Statutes pursuant to G.S. 114-9(b).

(c) To make a continuing study of all matters involved in the preparation and publication of modern codes of law.

Messrs. Robert F. Moseley, I. M. Bailey, Luther E. Barnhart, M. S. Breckenridge, J. Wilbur Bunn, Fred B. Helms, Malcomb McDermott, Henry A. McKinnon and Basil L. Whitener were named as members of the commission.

Mr. Robert F. Moseley was elected chairman.

Mr. Lawrence E. Watt, of Reidsville, was selected as a member of the staff and assigned to duty as Executive Secretary of this commission. Mr. Watt continued in this position until he resigned to run for Congress from the Fifth Congressional District. The place remained open until Mr. Harry W. McGalliard, formerly a member of the staff of this office in the Division of Legislative Drafting and Codification of Statutes, was appointed to carry on this work and continues to serve in that capacity.

This commission will submit, as provided by law, its report to the General Assembly covering its activities during the biennium.

Under the duties assigned to it by Chapter 382 of the Session Laws of 1943, the Division of Legislative Drafting and Codification of Statutes has continued to make a systematic study of the General Statutes of the State, for the purpose of ascertaining what ambiguities, conflicts, duplications and other imperfections in form and expression should be corrected and will submit to the General Assembly its recommendations for such changes as will be suggested. The director of the division, Mr. Clifton W. Beckwith, acts as the Secretary for the General Statutes Commission.

The General Assembly of 1945 enacted Chapter 863, directing the Division of Legislative Drafting and Codification of Statutes of the Department of Justice, under the direction and supervision of the Attorney General, to cause to be published under its supervision cumulative pocket supplements to the four volumes of the General Statutes, which will contain an accurate transcription of all the laws of a general and permanent nature enacted by the General Assembly, and complete and accurate annotations to the statutes, with a cumulative index. This Act made the supplements so published prima facie evidence of the general and permanent laws of North Carolina contained in these supplements.

Acting under authority of this legislation, the Division of Legislative Drafting and Codification of Statutes supervised the publication by The Michie Company of the interim and cumulative pocket supplements of the General Statutes, including the laws of 1945 and annotations thereto. The cumulative pocket supplements to the General Statutes are sold under contract with The Michie Company to subscribers at a cost of $10.00 for each biennium.

LEGISLATIVE DRAFTING

During the General Assembly of 1945, the staff of this office was called upon to prepare a total of 1237 bills, which were at the request of various State and local officials and members of the General Assembly for consideration at that time. This represented a very large proportion of the total number of bills presented to the General Assembly for enactment.

The drafting of this legislation by the members of the staff of this department aids in the codification of these laws in the supplement to the General Statutes, which is later published by The Michie Company. Particular effort is made in the drafting of legislation to fit it in to the existing codification of our statutory law. While the performance of these duties required the cooperation of all the members of this staff and engaged most of the attention of the office during the session of the General Assembly, it was considered by me as well worth the time and effort involved and seemed to be appreciated by the members of the General Assembly, as evidenced by the adoption of Joint Resolution No. 1501, commending the Attorney General and his entire staff for assistance rendered the membership of the General Assembly of 1945.

This work is now required by Article 2 of Chapter 114 of the General Statutes, creating the Department of Justice.

DIVISION OF CRIMINAL AND CIVIL STATISTICS

During the biennium the work of this division has continued under the direction of Mr. Clifton W. Beckwith. A report of its activities has been prepared by the director and will be made a part of this statement. There is included as a part of this Biennial Report a compilation of statistics covering the activities of our criminal courts, other than courts of justices of the peace, and a summarization of civil cases tried in our Superior Court during the biennium.

A RECOMMENDATION

The recommendation is now renewed that the General Assembly, by enactment of a statute, authorize that there be included in each bill of cost, in all civil and criminal cases, a fee of ten cents to be paid to the reporting officer of the superior and inferior courts making the required statistical reports. There is a great deal of opposition to these reports by the reporting officers, as it is felt that they do this work without compensation and often at considerable expense to themselves. In large counties it requires a very substantial portion of the time of one employee to prepare the required reports. If the fee is allowed by law, the reporting officials will feel that they have been reasonably compensated for their time and expense and much better reporting will be obtainable.

STATE BUREAU OF INVESTIGATION

During the latter part of the biennium, Mr. Thomas Creekmore resigned as Director of the Bureau of Investigation and Mr. Walter F. Anderson, the Chief of Police of Charlotte, North Carolina, was appointed to succeed him.

Mr. Anderson came to this bureau with long and valuable experience as a police and investigating officer, having risen from the ranks of the police force of Winston-Salem to become the Chief of Police of that city and later was selected as Chief of Police of Charlotte.

There is included in this Biennial Report the report made by Mr. Anderson as the Director of the Bureau of Investigation. The opportunity for service by this bureau is greatly enhanced by the character of the personnel of the bureau and the fine cooperation which we are now getting from the sheriffs, chiefs of police, solicitors, prosecuting attorneys and other officials. The demands on the bureau for its services far exceed the ability of the limited personnel to respond. I urge that the General Assembly shall give careful consideration to the recommendations of the director of the bureau for the expansion of this service. In the post-war period, it is now evident it will be called upon more and more in criminal investigations requiring the character of service which this bureau offers.

REVENUE DEPARTMENT AND MOTOR VEHICLE DEPARTMENT

During the last biennium the tax collections of the Department of Revenue have far exceeded any year in the history of the State. Under the terms of the statute, G.S. 114-4, Mr. W. J. Adams, Jr., was appointed as Assistant Attorney General assigned to this department. Upon the resignation of Mr. Adams and the appointment of Mr. Frank P. Spruill, Jr., as Assistant Attorney General, this work was continued under his direction.

Mrs. Cornelia McKimmon Trott, who had served as legal assistant in this office, resigned in the last year of the biennium. Later Mr. James E. Tucker, who had served on the staff of this office since 1938, was assigned to work in this department as an employee of the Department of Revenue but under the direction and supervision of the Attorney General, and authorized to act as one of my representatives in that office.

The enormous increase in volume of the collection of taxes for the General Fund and Highway Fund in the Revenue Department has imposed a tremendous burden on the legal staff, which is entirely too much for one lawyer to undertake to perform. All of the work done in this office is under my supervision, but the details must be carried forward by the assistants assigned to the work. There should be at least two Assistant Attorneys General assigned to the work of this department, in conjunction with the work of the Motor Vehicle Department.

RECOMMENDATION

The number of Assistant Attorneys General on my staff is now limited to four. I strongly recommend that the number of Assistant Attorneys General be left to be determined by appropriations made by the General Assembly. Obviously, the work of this office will grow with the expansion of State agencies and no good reason can be found to have a statutory limitation on the number to be provided for this service. The appropriation made by the General Assembly each biennium will determine this question.

The Assistant Attorney General assigned to the Department of Revenue, and the other assistant there who is now classified as a Senior Attorney, likewise provide the legal services needed by the Motor Vehicles Department. The legal work of the Motor Vehicles Department is not comparable to the extent of the legal work of the Department of Revenue, but is very substantial as this department is likewise engaged in the collection of motor vehicle revenues as well as having the supervision of the State Highway Patrol in its activities throughout the State.

During the biennium we have been extremely fortunate in having very little tax litigation, due to the fact that the Commissioner of Revenue, Mr. Edwin Gill, and the staff of the Department of Justice have endeavored at all time to judicially and fairly consider the tax questions which arise with tax-payers. Tax litigation in this State has been very small indeed. It can be anticipated that in the coming years, we may not be so fortunate, as the tax problems become more acute and extensive.

Appreciation is expressed for the fine cooperation and consideration we have received from Mr. Edwin Gill, Commissioner of Revenue, and Mr. T. Boddie Ward, Commissioner of Motor Vehicles, and the members of their staffs.

OFFICE CONFERENCES AND CONSULTATIONS WITH STATE OFFICERS AND DEPARTMENTAL OFFICIALS

Under the provisions of the State Constitution and laws enacted in pursuance thereto, this office has continued to act as the legal advisor for State officials, departments, bureaus and institutions. Throughout the biennium in frequent conferences with State officials and department heads, oral advice has been given and in numerous instances written opinions have been furnished.

Due to changing conditions in the field of public education and with the return of many veterans from service, more than usual demands have been made upon this office for legal services in connection with housing students in our schools and colleges. The problem is extensive and acute throughout this State, as well as elsewhere.

The University of North Carolina at Chapel Hill has found it necessary to erect dormitory space costing $1,000,000 and at State College costing $1,-200,000. Detailed contracts and plans for financing these projects were prepared or supervised in this office.

Appreciation is expressed to Governor R. Gregg Cherry and all other State officials for the cooperation we have received during the biennium, and the assistance given us in the performance of our duties.

ATLANTIC AND NORTH CAROLINA RAILROAD

During the biennium the Attorney General's office has been called upon for legal assistance to the President and Directors of the North Carolina Railroad Company. This railroad continued to be operated by the lessee, the Atlantic and East Carolina Railway Company, during the biennium and as a result of the increase in its gross revenues, has substantially reduced the indebtedness to the State of North Carolina for funds which had been borrowed for its rehabilitation program and otherwise, reference to which is made in the last biennial report of this department.

The future success of the railroad will in a large part depend upon the cooperation of the State and its various departments and agencies. With such help as the State may be able to provide for this company, it is entirely probable that the railroad will continue to be operated successfully and will eventually retire in full the indebtedness to the State. The amount of the State's investment in this road is, in my opinion, fully justified as it remains as an important artery of trade and commerce in the section of the State it serves. Cherry Point Marine Air Station, which is located on its line, is a permanent marine base and provides a substantial source of revenue.

The Port of Morehead City will evidently expand, now that the Standard Oil Company of New Jersey has built large receiving tanks for petroleum products on the Port Authority premises and are distributing petroleum products from that point, a great deal of which moves over rails of the company.

ADVISORY OPINIONS TO LOCAL OFFICIALS

As has been the custom for many years, the office of the Attorney General has continued to furnish advisory opinions to county, city and other local officials, upon numerous questions of administrative law and procedure. The demand for advisory opinions from this office generally originating through attorneys representing these local governments, they have been utilizing this method of determining unsettled administrative practices and questions which arise.

The effort of this office to provide the opinions of local officials has represented a large part of the work of the staff of this office, but an effort has always been made to request that the local legal advisors be first consulted before submitting the questions to this office.

The opinions rendered local officials are very extensive and numerous, to such an extent that it would be impracticable to publish all of them as a part of this report. Digests of these opinions are periodically published in POPULAR GOVERNMENT, the magazine of the Institute of Government of the University of North Carolina, and summaries of these opinions are periodically carried in the press of the State. Digests of opinions of special interest to cities and towns are mimeographed and distributed by the North Carolina League of Municipalities.

STATE BANKING COMMISSION

During the biennium the Attorney General has sat as an *ex officio* member of the State Banking Commission and has participated in the consideration of the many problems confronting this commission.

A report of the activities of this commission will be made through the Commissioner of Banks. Special consideration has been given to the regulations of the small loan business, which was placed under the supervision of the State Banking Commission by an Act of the General Assembly of 1945.

RECOMMENDATION

It is evident that the omitting of lending companies making loans on motor vehicles from the operation of the Act was unfortunate. I join in the recommendation of the Commissioner of Banks that the law should be amended to include all such agencies engaged in making small loans, in order to insure uniformity of practice and prevent the public from being imposed upon by agencies engaged in this business.

TEACHERS' AND STATE EMPLOYEES' RETIREMENT SYSTEM IN NORTH CAROLINA

This department, in keeping with the requirement of the law, has continued to furnish legal services for the Board of Trustees of this System. The increasing work of this System has, as might be expected, added to the legal work of this office extensively. As the System grows and the retirements become more numerous, it is evident that the legal work of this System will make further demands upon us. We have had the finest possible cooperation from the present Director, Mr. Nathan H. Yelton, and his predecessor.

UNEMPLOYMENT COMPENSATION COMMISSION

Although the Unemployment Compensation Commission has its own legal staff, the Attorney General's office from time to time is requested to advice with the attorneys representing this commission. No legal problem of any peculiar difficulty has been presented during the biennium.

STATE BOARD OF PUBLIC WELFARE AND THE STATE COMMISSION FOR THE BLIND

During the past biennium, as theretofore, this office has acted as legal advisor to the State Board of Public Welfare and the State Commission for the Blind. There have been frequent requests for office consultations, and written advisory opinions, some of which are set forth in this report. We acknowledge the fine cooperation we have had from Dr. Ellen Winston, Commissioner of the Board of Public Welfare, and Dr. Roma S. Cheek and her successor, Miss Helen P. Reinhardt, as the executive heads of the State Commission for the Blind.

It is impossible to overstate the work being done by these social agencies for the welfare of needy people of the State. It has been a source of real satisfaction to cooperate with them in all legal problems arising in connection with their responsibilites.

STATE DEPARTMENT OF AGRICULTURE

The State Department of Agriculture has had frequent occasion to call upon this office for legal assistance in problems which have arisen in the performance of their duties, which extend through the confines of the State. The broad powers given to the Commissioner of Agriculture and the State Board of Agriculture, and the expanding functions performed by this important department, touch the lives of all the rural and many of the urban people of the State. Space does not permit detailing of the numerous occasions for rendering legal assistance to this department. We are happy to acknowledge the fine cooperation of the Commissioner of the Agriculture, Mr. W. Kerr Scott, and all members of his staff.

DEPARTMENT OF CONSERVATION AND DEVELOPMENT

The Department of Conservation and Development has grown to be one of the largest State Departments. The extensive functions now performed by this department, including within it the Division of Game and Inland Fisheries and the large personnel required in the enforcement of game and fishing laws and the protection of forests, have given occasion to many calls for legal assistance. An effort has been made to serve all the demands made by this department for legal services and we acknowledge with appreciation the cooperation we have received at the hand of the Director, Mr. R. Bruce Etheridge, and his entire staff. The legal services required by this department require a substantial part of the time of this office.

OTHER STATE DEPARTMENTS AND AGENCIES

During the biennium, this office has had numerous requests for conferences and oral and written advisory opinions to other State departments, agencies and institutions. Among the ones most frequently calling upon us for legal assistance and advice has been the State Board of Alcoholic Control, the Banking Department, the Adjutant General's Office, the Budget Bureau, the State Board of the Elections, the Local Government Commission, the Division of Purchase and Contract; and the recently created boards and commissions, the Hospitals Board of Control, the Veterans Commission, the Recreation Commission and the Medical Care Commission.

During the course of the biennium the staff of the office has had occasion to be called upon by all of the State departments, institutions and agencies for legal assistance and advice. The demands for brevity in this summary exclude a detailed statement of these matters.

INDUSTRIAL COMMISSION AND WORKMEN'S COMPENSATION PAYMENTS

All State employees, except the elected officials, are subject to the provisions of the Workmen's Compensation Act. With the many people now employed by the State, there are numerous accidents arising out of and in the course of employment, some of which are fatal. I am informed that the total amount of Workmen's Compensation claims now being paid by the State are approximately $75,000.00 a year, and the tendency is for a steady increase in these payments.

The State Highway and Public Works Commission has handled the settlement of claims through its own legal staff and these represent probably more than 50% of the claims.

This office, when called upon by the various agencies of the State in case of accidents of this character, has appeared before the Industrial Commission and represented the interest of the State. The increasing number of such cases had made greater demands upon this office than heretofore.

Many claims, I am told, are settled by departments without being brought to the attention of this office. The members of the Industrial Commission have suggested that in all cases, when claims arise, they should be submitted to the Attorney General's Office for advice as to the proper handling. In many instances the claims are brought to our attention only after they are set for hearing before the hearing commissioner.

It is my opinion that in every instance of a claim arising, it should be passed upon from a legal standpoint, in apt time, before an agreement for compensation is entered into.

CRIMINAL CASES OF SPECIAL INTEREST

State v. Williams and Hendrix, 224 N. C. 183, 317 U. S. 287

A series of North Carolina decisions hold that a divorce decree obtained from a North Carolina defendant in a State in which only the plaintiff is domiciled and in which the defendant is not personally served with process and makes no appearance will be treated as void in North Carolina. These decisions were supported by the holding of the United States Supreme Court in HADDOCK v. HADDOCK, 201 U. S. 562, but the constitutionality of the North Carolina rule was challenged in STATE v WILLIAMS AND HENDRIX. The defendants, convicted of bigamous cohabitation in Caldwell County, had obtained in Nevada divorces from their North Carolina spouses on service by publication, had married, and had lived together in North Carolina. Their contention that the Nevada divorce decrees were entitled to full faith and credit under Article IV, Section 1, of the United States Constitution, was rejected by the North Carolina Supreme Court in STATE v. WILLIAMS AND HENDRIX, 220 N. C. 445. A writ of certiorari was granted by the United States Supreme Court and the case was heard by that Court at the October Term, 1942. The United States Supreme Court overruled the decision of HADDOCK v. HADDOCK, 201 U. S. 562, reversed the conviction of the defendants, and remanded the case for further proceedings, 317 U. S. 287. The Supreme Court of North Carolina remanded the case to the Superior Court of Caldwell County for a new trial, 223 N. C. 609. In this prosecution, the State proceeded upon the theory that the plaintiffs in the divorce actions had acquired no bona fide residences in Nevada. The jury accepted the State's contentions and again returned a verdict of guilty. The North Carolina Supreme Court affirmed the conviction. A writ of *certiorari* was granted by the United States Supreme Court and the case was heard by that Court at the October Term, 1944.

The United States Supreme Court affirmed the decision of the North Carolina Supreme Court in STATE v. WILLIAMS AND HENDRIX, 325 U. S. 226. The rule now is that, notwithstanding the full faith and credit provisions of the Federal Constitution, a decree of divorce rendered in one state may be impeached collaterally and denied recognition in another, upon the ground that neither of the parties had a domicil, or residence animo manendi, at the divorce forum; and that notwithstanding the recital in the decree or record from the other state of the findings as to jurisdictional fact of domicil or residence, the court in which the validity of the foreign decree is attacked may go behind the finding of the foreign court as to the jurisdictional fact of domicil, and find that neither of the parties had a bona fide domicil at the divorce forum and that therefore the foreign court had no jurisdiction to render the divorce decree for purposes of its recognition under the full faith and credit provision,—at least where the issue of domicil has not been litigated by a contested hearing at the divorce forum.

State v. Biggs, 244 N. C., 722.

The defendants, Elmer Hardie Biggs, Jr., William Dalton Biggs, and John Edgar Messer, were indicted in the Superior Court of Guilford County upon a charge of first degree murder in connection with the killing of E. J. Swanson. The State contended that William Dalton Biggs and John Messer were engaged in robbing Swanson's store when the killing occurred and that Elmer H. Biggs, Jr., waited for the defendants in an automobile in front of the store while the robbery was being perpetrated. The defendants went to the State of Virginia and were brought back to North Carolina for trial. The first trial resulted in a new trial being awarded by the Supreme Court. See State v. Elmer Hardie Biggs, et al, 224 N. C., 23. On the second trial the defendants were convicted of murder in the first degree as to each defendant, and the defendants appealed to the Supreme Court. The Supreme Court found no error in connection with the trial in the lower court.

State v. DeGraffenreid, 224 N. C., 517

The defendant, Lucille DeGraffenreid, was indicted in the Superior Court of Lee County upon a charge of first degree murder for the killing of Ollie Moore. The deceased, Ollie Moore, et al, attended a party at the home of Leon and Lucille DeGraffenreid. The deceased was asked to leave the house and before his departure was stabbed with a butcher knife. The case was tried three times. In the first trial the defendant was convicted of manslaughter and a new trial was awarded on appeal to the Supreme Court. See State v. DeGraffenreid, 222 N. C., 113.

On the second trial the defendant was convicted of murder in the second degree and her appeal to the Supreme Court ordered a new trial. State v. DeGraffenreid, 223 N. C., 461. On the third trial the defendant was convicted of murder in the second degree, and again appealed to the Supreme Court, and upon this appeal, no error was found in connection with the trial in the lower court.

State v. Inman, 224 N. C., 531

The defendants, Dewey F. Inman and Russell A. Stark, were indicted in the Superior Court of Lee County on charges of rape and highway robbery. The defendants were privates in the United States Army and the Staff Judge Advocate at Fort Jackson, South Carolina, filed a request for the return of the defendants to military control. A trial Judge denied this request and thereafter, before the defendants were arraigned, they entered separate pleas to the jurisdiction of Lee County Superior Court. The trial Judge overruled the defendants' pleas to the jurisdiction of the court and the defendants from this order excepted and appealed to the Supreme Court. After their cases were docketed in the Supreme Court the defendants filed in the Supreme Court a petition or application for a writ of prohibition. The Supreme Court held that the attempted appeal of the defendants from the adverse ruling on their objections to the jurisdiction of the court was premature and denied the application for writ of prohibition. On motion of the Attorney General, the appeal as to both defendants was dismissed and the petition for writ of prohibition was denied.

State v. Weinstein, 224 N. C., 645

The defendant, Harry Weinstein, was indicted in the Superior Court of Wake County on charges of larceny and receiving stolen property, knowing it to be stolen. The first evidence disclosed that the Raleigh Junior Chamber of Commerce conducted a drive through newspapers and radio stations urging citizens to donate their scrap paper, and at a certain date to place scrap paper in bundles in front of their houses for collection. Trucks belonging to the defendant were seen gathering the paper in sections of the City of Raleigh, and this, with other evidence, resulted in the defendant being convicted on both counts in the bill of indictment. The defendant appealed to the Supreme Court from the judgment entered on the verdict entered in the Superior Court. The Supreme Court of North Carolina considered the defendant's exceptions and found no error in the trial of the lower court. The defendant's petition to the Supreme Court of the United States for a writ of certiorari was denied.

State v. John Emery, et als, 224 N. C. 581

The defendants, John Emery, Bill Emery, and LeRoy Turner, were indicted in the Superior Court of Polk County following an indictment containing six counts charging the defendants with violations of the prohibition laws. During the trial in the Superior Court the regular panel of jurors was exhausted and most of the male bystanders were exhausted for the purpose of jury duty. The Sheriff then called from among the bystanders two women of good moral character, freeholders and residents of the County, and they were accepted by the Solicitor as satisfactory jurors. The defendants objected and moved the court to excuse both women from jury service upon the grounds that they were not qualified because of their sex to serve as petit jurors. The defendants' objections were overruled and upon a general verdict of guilty as to each of the defendants, motion was made to set aside the verdict upon the grounds of jury defect. This motion was overruled and from the judgment pronounced upon the verdict, the defendants appealed to the Supreme Court. The Supreme Court held that a jury, as understood at common law and as used in our Constitutions, signifies twelve good and lawful men in a court of justice, duly selected and impaneled in the case to be tried. It was held that women are to be excluded from juries because of their sex, and that aliens and persons under twenty-one years of age are also not competent to serve. A venire de novo was ordered by the Supreme Court.

State v. Henry French, 225 N. C., 276

The defendant, Henry French, was indicted in the Superior Court of Montgomery County upon an indictment charging him with the murder of Duck LeGrand. The evidence disclosed that there was an argument because of damages to French's car, French having struck a telephone pole in going around the car of James Richardson. Duck LeGrand and her husband were in the car driven by Richardson. After a short time the controversy was renewed and French went to his house and came back' with a 'rifle and fired four or five times in the car where Duck LeGrand and her husband were sitting. Duck LeGrand started to get out of the car when the defendant fired again and she fell. The defendant was convicted of murder in the first degree. The defendant appealed from the judgment rendered on the verdict to the Supreme Court, and after considering the exceptions, the Supreme Court found no error in the trial below.

State v. Lord, 225 N. C., 345

The defendant was indicted in the Superior Court of Cabarrus County for the murder of Elder Phifer. The defendant had been keeping company with the deceased, a girl of about seventeen years of age. He became jealous because of her attentions to others, and on the night of October 21, 1944, the defendant saw the deceased at a cafe with another girl and boy. The deceased refused to talk with the defendant and he went to his rooming house and obtained a shotgun. Not finding the deceased anywhere in town, the defendant went to a cotton patch near the home of the deceased, and waited for her. As the deceased approached between twelve and one o'clock in the morning, the defendant came out of the cotton patch and shot the deceased. The jury convicted the defendant of murder in the first degree and from the judgment of death by asphyxiation, the defendant appealed to the Supreme Court. The Supreme Court upheld the verdict and judgment of the trial court and found no error.

State v. Lacy Scoggins, et al, 225 N. C., 71

The defendants, Lacy Scoggins and Newt Thompson, were indicted in the Superior Court of Lee County in connection with the death by drowning of Leonard Hall. The State's evidence disclosed that the defendants, the deceased, and two women were in two boats on a pond; one of the defendants tilted the other boat so that all of its occupants except the deceased were thrown into the water. The deceased refused to give one of the defendants the remainder of the whiskey that was in the boat and thereupon one of the defendants struck the deceased three sharp blows on the head with a paddle, knocking him flat in the boat and apparently rendering him unconscious. Both of the defendants then standing in the water, took hold of the boat in which the deceased was lying and turned it bottom up, throwing the deceased into the pond. The deceased's inert body floated away and no attempt was made to rescue it. The next morning the dead body was recovered and it was determined that death was due to drowning. The defendants were convicted of manslaughter and from the judgment of the Superior Court imposing prison sentence, the defendants appealed to the Supreme Court assigning errors. The Supreme Court of North Carolina considered the defendants' assignments of error and found them to be without substantial merit. No error was found in the proceedings of the trial court.

State v. Bennett, 226 N. C., 82

The defendants, Bennett, Gibson, Salmon, Carroll, Agner, Norris and Thompson, were indicted for the murder of R. L. Beck. It was charged that the murder was committed in the perpetration of the crime of robbery. Prior to the drawing of the jury, the State took a nol. pros. with leave as to Gibson. During the progress of the trial Salmon entered a plea of guilty of murder in the second degree, and at the close of argument of counsel, Agner and Norris entered pleas of guilty of murder in the second degree. The case was submitted to the jury as to Carroll, Thompson, and Bennett; as to each of these the jury rendered a verdict of murder in the second degree. The defendant Bennett appealed to the Supreme Court. The evidence of the State disclosed that all of these persons entered into a conspiracy to hold up and rob the deceased Beck. The defendant Salmon actually fired the gun that killed the deceased; others of the defendants waited in the car which carried Salmon away. Some of the defendants made confessions to the officers which were used in the trial. The assignments of error were numerous and the Supreme Court, after giving careful attention to each of them, failed to find any cause for disturbing the judgment on the verdict against the appellant Bennett. No error was found in the proceedings of the trial court.

State v. Edward Mays, 225 N. C., 486

The defendant was indicted in the Superior Court of Lee County upon a charge of murder in the first degree in connection with the death of one Mattie L. Salmon. The deceased, a woman of about seventy-five years of age, was found dead in her home where she lived by herself. She had been criminally assaulted, and her death was apparently caused by a dress or other clothing placed over her face and being smothered to death. The defendant was suspected and arrested. He made numerous confessions as to how he killed the deceased. The evidence disclosed that the defendant was a native of Abyssinia, and that he had formerly lived as a native of his country in the jungle of that country under very primitive conditions. He and other Abyssinian boys came to Canada and the defendant gradually worked his way to the United States and came to North Carolina where he settled. The jury convicted the defendant of murder in the first degree, and upon appeal, the Supreme Court, after giving all due consideration to the assignments of error, found that they did not disclose any cause for disturbing the verdict. No error was found in the proceedings of the trial court.

State v. Stone, 226 N. C., 97

The defendant was indicted in the Superior Court of Robeson County on a bill of indictment charging him with the murder in the second degree for the killing of T. Willis Edwards. The evidence shows that the prisoner and the deceased were drinking together and upon the prisoner's invitation, went together towards the prisoner's house about 11 p. m. About 3 o'clock A. M., a gunshot was heard in the prisoner's home and two or three minutes later a man was seen leaving the home by the back door. The next morning in the prisoner's home a table was found on which there was a jar and a bottle, both having contained liquor, with two chairs close to the table and a bucket between them containing cigarette butts. The deceased was found dead on his back in the doorway of the room where the table was located. The prisoner's shotgun was between the deceased's legs, one barrel of which contained an empty shell with hammer down and the other hammer cocked. The deceased had a gunshot wound in his breast without powder burns on his body or white shirt. The prisoner made contradictory statements as to the time he left his home and the discovery of the body of the deceased. On the first trial the defendant was convicted of manslaughter, and upon appeal to the Supreme Court, a new trial was awarded. State v. Stone, 224 N. C., 849.

On the second trial the defendant was convicted of murder in the second degree and again appealed to the Supreme Court. The Supreme Court held that its former ruling in the first case to the effect that there was sufficient evidence to be submitted to the jury, was controlling on his appeal, and found no error in the trial below.

State v. Wise, 225 N. C., 746

The defendant was indicted in the Superior Court of Guilford County for the murder of his paramour. The deceased was a married woman, and an adulterous relationship had existed between the deceased and the defendant for some time. On the day that the deceased was killed she and the defendant met at an appointed place and a quarrel arose. The defendant cut the deceased's throat with a knife and struck the deceased about the head and neck with a club. She died from these injuries. The jury found the defendant guilty of murder in the first degree and from the judgment on this verdict the defendant appealed to the Supreme Court. The Supreme Court held that the trial court's instructions as to the various degrees of homicide were correct and that the court had correctly defined malice, deliberation and premeditation. No error was found in the proceedings of the trial court.

State v. Stewart, 226 N. C., 299

The defendant was indicted in the Superior Court of Wake County on a charge of murder in the first degree in connection with the killing of Ernest Jones, Jr. The evidence disclosed that the defendant was searching for a man whom he had seen with his wife. In his search he entered a house and questioned the owner of the house who stated that he did not know where the person whom the defendant was seeking, had gone. The defendant started to leave the house and then turned and demanded of a visitor in the house the same information. Upon receiving a negative reply from the visitor, who was the deceased Ernest Jones, the defendant cursed him and received a reply in kind. The defendant stated that he would shoot the deceased and pulled a pistol from his pocket and shot and killed him. The jury convicted the defendant of murder in the first degree and from the judgment of death by asphyxiation, the defendant appealed to the Supreme Court. It was contended on the appeal in behalf of the defendant that the defendant's intent to kill and the act of killing were simultaneous and, therefore, there was no premeditation and deliberation. The Supreme Court held that in this case there was sufficient evidence of premeditation and deliberation and found no error in the trial below.

State v. Vaden, et al., 226 N. C., 138

The defendants Woodrow Vaden and John Daniel Vaden, were indicted in the Superior Court of Rockingham County upon an indictment charging the defendants with the murder of Carl Bullis. The State's evidence disclosed that there was an affray at a filling station engaged in by all of the defendants; that the fight was stopped, but that thereafter the defendants sought and found the deceased at another filling station. At this filling station other parties induced all of them to shake hands and this apparently settled the controversy. The defendants, brothers, started to leave in their truck when one of them called the proprietor of the filling station and expressed some dissatisfaction about the settlement. The deceased came out of the filling station and the quarrel was renewed. The deceased was armed with a knife and started fighting with one of the defendants, who was armed with a blackjack. While they were fighting another defendant shot from the truck and fatally injured the deceased. The defendants were convicted of manslaughter and appealed to the Supreme Court. The Supreme Court held that the second fight was but a continuation of the first fight, and that the purported settlement of the controversy was not entered into in good faith, and that in reality the defendants had not quit the fight. It was held that the motion to non-suit on the grounds that the State's evidence established the defense of self-defense was properly denied. No error was found in the proceedings of the trial below.

TIDELANDS

During the biennium this office took an active part in supporting legislation in the Congress of the United States, in which it was proposed that the United States should disclaim any title to the lands lying beneath the navigable waters within the several States and within the three mile limit on the coastline. This legislation culminated in the introduction of H. J. 225, which was a Committee Substitute brought out by the Committee on Judiciary of the House.

This legislation was made necessary by the position taken by the Secretary of the Interior, contrary to all former views of himself and other Secretaries of the Interior, who claimed in 1937 that there was some doubt as to the States having the title to the lands lying beneath the ocean within three miles of the coastline of the State of California, and other States.

As a result of this contention, seventeen Resolutions were introduced in Congress for the purpose of disclaiming title to these tidal lands which had been recognized as owned by the States since the founding of the Government. In cooperation with the Attorneys General of all the States of the Union, except one state, and at the request of the Governor and the Department of Conservation and Development, this office supported the enactment of this legislation in Congress.

The resolution was adopted by the House of Representatives by a large majority. Thereafter, the Secretary of the Interior instituted suit in the District Court of the United States in California against an oil company, claiming title to the lands lying seaward of the coastline and within three miles thereof. While the resolution was pending in the Senate, the California suit was discontinued and another suit instituted in the Supreme Court of the United States, as the court of original jurisdiction, by the United States against the State of California, claiming the ownership of such lands. This claim, if established, would affect the ownership of the State of North Carolina of the lands lying within three miles of its coastline and probably the title to the other lands lying under its inland waters.

After H. J. 225 had been adopted by the Senate, it was vetoed by the President of the United States on the grounds that the matter was in litigation in the Supreme Court of the United States and should be left to the court to decide. Congress failed to override the veto.

The California case is now pending in the Supreme Court of the United States but in all probability it may be many years before the questions involved are finally settled.

CIVIL CASES

JOHN J. INGLE V. STATE BOARD OF ELECTIONS, 226 N. C. 454

This was a petition for a mandamus brought by John J. Ingle in the Superior Court of Wake County against the State Board of Elections, asking that the State Board of Elections be required to cause the petitioner's name to be placed on the official ballot as a candidate or nominee of the Republican Party for the office of Associate Justice of the Supreme Court of North Carolina, to be voted on in the general election to be held on November 5, 1946. The substance of the petition was that petitioner had filed notice of candidacy for the office of Associate Justice and that the State Board of Elections had refused to accept his filing fee because he had failed to state for which vacancy on the Court he was seeking the nomination.

The defendant board admitted refusing to place the name of the candidate on the ticket for this position, because the defendant had failed to comply with the requirements of G. S. 163-147, which states that all candidates for Chief Justice and Associate Justice of the Supreme Court shall file with the State Board of Elections, at the time of filing notice of candidacy, a notice designating to which of said vacancies the respective candidate is seeking the nomination; and the statute further provides that all votes cast for any candidate shall be effective only for the vacancy for which he has given notice of candidacy as provided.

The Judge of the Superior Court denied the petition for mandamus and the action of the Judge was affirmed on appeal to the Supreme Court, by the decision reported in 226 N. C., page 454.

GARDNER V. RETIREMENT SYSTEM 226 N. C. 465

This case arose on a petition for mandamus to require the defendant, Board of Trustees of North Carolina Local Governmental Employees' Retirement System, to accept and enroll plaintiff as a member of the Retirement System operated by defendant Board of Trustees. In the Superior Court the case was heard upon the pleadings, and it appeared that the plaintiff was at that time, and had been for a number of years, a member of the Police Department of the City of Charlotte and was a member in good standing in the Law Enforcement Officers' Benefit and Retirement Fund, a retirement system for the benefit of peace officers created and established by Section 143-167 of the General Statutes. The funds for retirement allowances and other benefits under the Law Enforcement Officers' System are primarily obtained from deductions from members' salaries and also from an item of $2.00 additional cost taxed against each person convicted in a criminal case in this State and collected and paid to the Treasurer of North Carolina. Subsequently the City of Charlotte became an employer under the provisions of the Local Governmental Employees' Retirement System as established by Section 128-24 of the General Statutes. The plaintiff as an employee of the City of Charlotte was entitled to be a member of the Local Governmental Employees' Retirement System unless he was excluded from membership by a provision in the act creating the Local Governmental Employees' Retirement System as follows:

"Persons who are or who shall become members of any existing retirement system and who are or who may be thereby entitled to benefits by existing laws providing for retirement allowances for employees wholly or partly at the expense of funds drawn from the Treasury of the State of North Carolina or of any political subdivision thereof, shall not be members."

Unless the plaintiff was excluded by this provision, he was entitled to be a member of both retirement systems. Upon the hearing in the Superior Court, motions were made for judgment upon the pleadings; and the Superior Court judge held that the plaintiff's membership in the Law Enforcement Officers' Benefit and Retirement Fund was of such a nature that any benefits paid under that system were financed from funds drawn from the Treasury of the State of North Carolina even though such funds were collected as costs in criminal proceedings and sent to the Treasurer of North Carolina to be kept in a special fund. Judgment was signed by the Superior Court in favor of the defendant Board of Trustees, and plaintiff appealed to the Supreme Court. The Supreme Court held that the membership exclusion clause of the act creating the Local Governmental Employees' Retirement System should be interpreted to apply to those entitled to benefits from any funds coming into the hands of the State Treasurer by virtue of a State law and was not restricted to membership in a retirement system deriving benefits from the general funds of the State Treasury; that the plaintiff was, therefore, excluded from membership in the Local Governmental Employees' Retirement System. The judgment of the Superior Court was, therefore, affirmed.

P. P. JOHNSON V. EDWIN GILL, COMMISIONER OF REVENUE, 224 N. C. 638

This plaintiff was agent for two Chicago tailoring houses. He maintained a place of business in Charlotte from which he solicited orders for clothes, took measurements, and forwarded orders to his companies. He accepted part of the purchase price at time of order, and his companies collected the remainder when the clothes were delivered by carrier to customer c.o.d. The plaintiff failed to collect any sales or use tax from his customers or to pay any tax to the State. The defendant, Commissioner of Revenue, assessed, and the plaintiff paid under protest and brought this action to recover. The court held (1) that use tax applied to the transaction, (2) that the plaintiff was a "retailer" under the statute, required to collect and remit the use tax, and (3) that the tax on plaintiff could be sustained even as a sales tax because title to the clothes did not pass to customer until c.o.d. delivery in North Carolina, when interstate commerce was at an end.

STANDARD FERTILIZER CO., INC., V. EDWIN GILL, COMMISSIONER
OF REVENUE, 225 N. C. 426

On April 30, 1937, plaintiff entered into a contract with a Pennsylvania corporation for installation of a sprinkler system in its fertilizer plant. Neither the contractor nor the plaintiff paid the excise or use tax imposed by Section 427 of the Revenue Act upon building materials used in this State; nor was any return or report filed as required. Upon discovery of the transaction in 1942, the defendant, Commissioner of Revenue, assessed the tax on the plaintiff, who paid under protest and brought this action to recover. The defendant, Commissioner of Revenue, contended that the three-year statute of limitations in Section 414 applied only where a return had been filed and the assessment was for a "deficiency" in payment of the tax. The Court declined to adopt this view, and decided that the statute of limitations in Section 414 applied to all assessments under the sales tax article, whether a return had been filed or not. Judgment for plaintiff was rendered accordingly.

M. R. GODLEY ET AL. DBA GODLEY BROTHERS v. R. GREGG CHERRY, GOVERNOR, ET AL

This was a suit in equity instituted in the U. S. District Court for the Eastern District of North Carolina, Raleigh Division, seeking to enjoin the State of North Carolina from enforcing Section 115 of the Revenue Act (G. S. 105-47), which levies certain privilege taxes upon dealers in horses and/or mules. The plaintiff contended that the statute was violative of the U. S. Constitution. The matter was heard before a three-judge court in Asheville in accordance with the provisions of Section 266 of the Judicial Code (Section 380, Title 28, USCA). On June 27, 1945, the Court dismissed the suit on the ground that the plaintiffs had an adequate remedy at law in the North Carolina courts. No appeal was taken.

OPINIONS TO GOVERNOR

APPROPRIATION FOR PURCHASE OF PROPERTY
28 December, 1944.

Honorable Charles Ross, Acting Chairman of the State Highway Commission, at your request, has written me under date of December 27, with reference to the allocation of funds for the purchase of a lot in the City of Raleigh opposite the State Capitol for the purpose, at some time in the future, of erecting thereon an office building for the State Highway and Public Works Commission.

The allocation of the sum of $200,000.00 has been requested from the Assistant Director of the Budget under the Appropriation item in the Appropriations Act, Chapter 530, Session Laws of 1943, Title XII, Highway and Public Works, subsection 6, Betterments State and County Roads, and subsection (1), General Betterments. I am advised that the Governor, acting under authority of the Act, has made available for expenditure under this item, a sum more than sufficient for the intended purpose and for the particular purpose for purchasing the site for the proposed building.

I am advised in the letter from the Acting Chairman, Mr. Ross, that the State Highway Commission at a recent meeting passed a resolution expressing the opinion that an enlargement of the offices in Raleigh was necessary in order to provide the proper facilities for the Highway program, and authorized the purchase of the land in question for this purpose, and requested the Director of the Budget to allot from the funds mentioned the sum of $200,000.00.

In a conference with you and Mr. Ross and Mr. Deyton today, I understand that it is the purpose to provide the land for the construction of the building which will house the activities of the State Highway and Public Works Commission, engaged in carrying on its activities, including the betterments of State and county roads, and that without the adequate facilities, this work could not properly be carried on.

In my opinion, the allotment requested may legally be made under the appropriation provided in Article XII of Chapter 530 of the Session Laws of 1943, subsection 6(1), General Betterments.

DOUBLE OFFICE HOLDING; MEMBER OF NORTH CAROLINA
VETERANS COMMISSION
14 March, 1945.

You inquire as to whether or not, in my opinion, membership on the North Carolina Veterans Commission, created by Senate Bill 216 of the present session of the General Assembly, constitutes an office within the meaning of Article XIV, Section 7, of the State Constitution to the extent it would bar a person now holding office from serving as a member of said commission.

I have given careful consideration to this question and I am strongly inclined to the opinion that membership on said commission is not an office within the meaning of the pertinent section of the Constitution, or that if it is an office, it constitutes a commissioner for a special purpose. However, since the courts have not had an opportunity to pass on the question, I cannot be sure that my opinion will be upheld by the court. I hesitate to advise an official of the State to accept membership on a board or commission when the court has not had an opportunity to pass on the status of membership on such board or commission because if such official should accept membership on the commission and such membership should be held by the court to be an office, the official would have vacated his first office.

The court held in the case of Barnhill v. Thompson, 122 N. C. 493, that the acceptance of a second office by one holding a public office operates ipso facto to vacate the first. While the officer has a right to elect which he will retain, his election is deemed to have been made when he accepts and qualifies for the second. The acceptance of the second office of itself is a resignation of the first.

In the case of Whitehead v. Pittman, 165 N. C. 89, our court held, "Where one holding an office or place of profit accepts another such office or position in contravention of this Section of the Constitution, the first is vacated eo instante, and any further acts done by him in connection with the first office, are without color and cannot be de facto.

Of course, one holding an office could be named as an ex officio member of the commission without running afoul of Article XIV, Section 7.

LEASING OF PROPERTY FOR THE NORTH CAROLINA HOSPITALS BOARD OF CONTROL

13 July, 1945

You have inquired as to the proper authority to execute a lease on behalf of the North Carolina Hospitals Board of Control for property to be leased to this board by the Federal Government.

General Statutes 143-48 provides for the creation in the Governor's Office of a division to be known as the "Division of Purchase and Contract," which division shall be under the supervision and control, subject to the provisions of the law, of a Director of Purchase and Contract.

General Statutes 143-49 provides that the Director of Purchase and Contract shall have power and authority and it shall be his duty, subject to the provisions of the article in which the section appears, to do the following things:

"(d) To rent or lease all grounds, buildings, offices, or other space required by any department, institution, or agency of the State Government: Provided, this shall not include temporary quarters for State Highway field forces or convict camps, or temporary places of storage for road materials."

Under this Act the lease of the property made for the benefit of the North Carolina Hospitals Board of Control should be executed on behalf of the North Carolina Hospitals Board of Control by Mr. W. Z. Betts, who is the Director of the Division of Purchase and Contract, and the practice heretofore followed is to have the proper officials of the agency for which the lease is executed also sign it. The title of the North Carolina Hospitals Board of Control is fixed by General Statutes 122-11.8 and on behalf of this board the lease should be signed by its General Business-Manager, Mr. R. M. Rothgeb, whose appointment and authority is fixed by General Statutes 122-11.3.

I would therefore suggest that in the execution of the lease on behalf of the State agency, it should be done substantially as follows:

> "Division of Purchase and Contract
> of the State of North Carolina
> By:..
> Director
> For and on behalf of—the North
> Carolina Hospitals Board of
> Control
> North Carolina Hospitals Board of
> Control
> By:........................ ....
> General Business Manager"

EXTRADITION; FLOYD E. SNOW; EXPENSE IN FELONY CASES PAID BY STATE AND OTHERS BY COUNTY

11 September, 1945

I have reviewed the file in the above matter in which the Sheriff contends that the expense incident to his trip to Florida to return the defendant to the State of North Carolina should be paid by the State, and you inquire as to whether or not this expense should be paid by the State or the county.

Section 15-78 of the General Statutes reads as follows:

> "When the crime shall be a felony, the expenses shall be paid out of the state treasury, on the certificate of the governor and warrant of the auditor; and in all other cases they shall be paid out of the county treasury in the county wherein the crime is alleged to have been committed. The expenses shall be the actual traveling and subsistence costs of the agent of the demanding state, together with such legal fees as were paid to the officers of the state on whose governor the requisition is made. In every case the officer entitled to these expenses shall itemize the same and verify them by his oath for presentation, either to the governor of the state, in proper cases, or to the board of county commissioners, in cases in which the county pays such expenses."

It is apparent from the above section that in felony cases the expense must be paid by the State and in all other cases such expense shall be paid out of the county treasury in the county wherein the crime is alleged to have been committed. The question, therefore, arises as to whether or not in the instant case, the crime constitutes that of a felony or a misdemeanor.

The warrant in the file in this case charges the defendant with obtaining certain sums of money by representing that he had sufficient funds in the bank or had made arrangements for a loan to take care of certain checks issued by him. While the warrant does not state under what section of the statutes the crime is charged, I assume that it is Section 14-106 of the General Statutes, which reads as follows:

> "Every person who, with intent to cheat and defraud another, shall obtain money, credit, goods, wares or any other thing of value by

means of a check, draft or order of any kind upon any bank, person, firm or corporation, not indebted to the drawer, or where he has not provided for the payment or acceptance of the same, and the same be not paid upon presentation, shall be guilty of a misdemeanor, and upon conviction shall be fined or imprisoned, or both, at the discretion of the court. The giving of the aforesaid worthless check, draft, or order shall be prima facie evidence of an intent to cheat and defraud."

It is apparent that the crime in this case is a misdemeanor and that the expense incident to the extradition proceeding instituted to bring the defendant back to Mitchell County will have to be borne by that county.

If the defendant is convicted, I assume that the Court will assess as part of the costs, the expense incident to the extradition proceeding and the county thereby reimbursed for the funds advanced by it.

I certainly agree with Sheriff Honeycutt that he should not be called upon to stand the expense of this trip and should be reimbursed for the same, but since this crime is a misdemeanor the statute clearly requires the county to pay to the sheriff the expense incurred by him in bringing the defendant back to the county.

USE OF SCHOOL BUSES TO CARRY HIGH SCHOOL STUDENTS IN GASTON COUNTY TO VOCATIONAL TEXTILE SCHOOL

2 October, 1945

In conversation with you yesterday, you requested me to furnish you with an opinion as to the authority of the State Board of Education to authorize the use of school buses in transporting high school students to and from the Vocational Textile School, created under the authority of Chapter 360 of the Public Laws of 1941 (found in G. S., Chapter 115, Article 36).

I understand that during previous years the school buses have been used for the purpose of transporting high school students to and from the school and that the question has recently arisen as to whether or not the State Board of Education has the authority to adopt rules and regulations which would permit this service to continue, in view of the fact that the General Assembly of 1945 enacted S. B. No. 385, Chapter 806, creating a Board of Trustees for the North Carolina Vocational Textile School, it having formerly been under the State Board of Education, G. S. 115-255.

It is my understanding that the teachers employed in this Vocational Textile School are paid from State and Federal funds in the same manner as other teachers in vocational schools are paid. It is my understanding further that the students in the high schools to be transported to this Vocational Textile School are pursuing their studies in the high schools in Gaston County and will be given credit for the work done in the Vocational Textile School in the same manner as courses taken in the regular work of the high schools.

G. S. 115-374 provides that the control and management of all the facilities for the transportation of public school children shall be vested in the State of North Carolina under the direction and supervision of the State Board of Education, which shall have authority to promulgate rules and regulations governing the organization, maintenance and operation of school transportation facilities.

Under this broad grant of power, the State Board of Education would have the authority to adopt rules and regulations which permitted the transportation of the public school children or high school students in the schools of Gaston County to and from the Vocational Textile School, to pursue therein a part of the course of study for which credit is given them in their high school work, unless there is some provision in our statute which would prohibit the use of the buses for such purpose. The provision in the statute which has bearing on this question is the following clause in G. S. 115-374:

"The use of the school buses shall be limited to the transportation of children to and from school for the regularly organized school day."

A narrow view of this section might prohibit the transportation of children except on one route trips to and from the school which they regularly attended, but I do not think that this narrow view is necessarily the correct one. It is my opinion that the State Board of Education, in its discretion, would have the power to permit the use of school buses for transporting high school students in the regularly organized school day to and from the Vocational Textile School, between this school and the high schools attended by such students, without violating the provisions of this section.

The policy involved in such a course would be supported by the paragraph in G. S. 115-374 which authorizes the State Board of Education, under rules and regulations to be adopted by them, to permit the use and operation of school buses for the transportation of school children on necessary field trips while pursuing the courses of vocational agriculture, home economics, trade and industrial vocational subject to and from demonstration projects carried on in connection therewith. The courses taken by the high school students in the North Carolina Vocational Textile School could not be properly designated as field trips, but the courses taken in this vocational school are a very essential part of the education of those seeking vocational training in the textile field, which would be denied them if they were not permitted to use this method of transportation between the different schools.

This, however, is a matter for the sound judgment and discretion of the State Board of Education which could, in my opinion, permit or deny the use of the buses for this purpose.

STATE STREAM SANITATION AND CONSERVATION COMMITTEE; CONTINGENCY AND EMERGENCY APPROPRIATIONS

26 October, 1945

I have your letter enclosing to me copy of Senate Bill 378 creating a State Stream Sanitation and Conservation Committee, and a letter from Honorable R. Bruce Etheridge, Chairman of the sub-committee of this Committee, and a letter from Honorable R. G. Deyton, Assistant Director of the Budget. In Mr. Deyton's letter he takes the position that under the Act, contingency and emergency appropriations cannot be made for this activity as the Act contemplates that the Committee shall act through the facilities of the agencies mentioned in the Act. You request my opinion as to whether the Governor and Council of State could lawfully appropriate funds to finance the activities of this Committee.

After a careful study of the Act, I am convinced that the conclusion reached by Mr. Deyton is in part correct. The Act provides in Section 2 that the activities of the State Board of Health and the Department of Conservation and Development shall be coordinated through a Committee designated as a State Stream Sanitation and Conservation Committee. The Act further provides that it shall be the duty of this committee, acting through the facilities of the member agencies to perform the duties imposed upon the Committee. In Section 5 of the Act, it is provided that in the interest of efficient use of the personnel and facilities in execution of surveys, studies and research, the committees are authorized to cooperate with technical divisions of State institutions, and with municipalities, industries, Federal agencies, adjoining states, and others.

No provision is made for any appropriation and in view of the fact that the Act directly requires that the Committee shall act through the facilities of the member agencies in the performance-of-its work, it seems to me that contingency and emergency appropriations could not be made for such activities of the Committee as could be performed through the agencies mentioned. This would exclude the appropriations for engineer and director and a senior sanitation engineer, as well as travel for such officials. The Act provides in Section 4 that the Committee shall elect a chairman and secretary. I would, therefore, think that a contingency and emergency appropriation could legally be made to cover the expense of a secretary, who might also be a stenographer. I would think that a contingency and emergency appropriation might be made for necessary office supplies, travel and per diem of new ex-officio members of the Committee who could not be paid out of any appropriations for the affiliated Departments.

As to the expense in providing an engineer and director and a senior sanitation engineer, if it is found that these are necessary to the proper performance of the work of the Committee and cannot be provided by appropriations available to the State Board of Health or Department of Conservation and Development, or their existing staff, an appropriation could be made legally from the contingency and emergency fund to either the State Board of Health or the Department of Conservation and Development for providing for such of these services as might be found necessary, if their own funds were inadequate for that purpose. The General Assembly contemplates that the work of the Committee shall go forward, and under the contingency and emergency appropriation, funds can be made available to these Departments in order that they can comply with the duties imposed upon them by the General Assembly when the appropriation therefor is inadequate or when no appropriation has been made.

I am returning the correspondence and copy of the Act which you sent me, three extra copies of this letter which you can furnish to the Departments concerned, if you desire to do so.

SALARY INCREASES OF JUDGES AND SOLICITORS

18 October, 1945

In a conference held in your office this morning you inquired if the salary increases for Judges and Solicitors authorized by the 1945 Session of the General Assembly, which are contingent upon the availability of funds, should be paid to said Judges and Solicitors now or whether it will be necessary to wait until the end of the biennium to determine whether funds are available, and if so, to pay the salary increases at that time.

Section 23½ of Chapter 279 of the Session Laws of 1945 (the Appropriations Act) provides for an emergency salary of $10.00 per month to be paid to all full-time school teachers and other State employees. This provision is not applicable to salaries exceeding $3,600.00 per year. This section provides that this emergency salary shall be paid at the end of each fiscal year of the biennium 1945-47 if there are sufficient revenues in the general fund to pay the same. However, this provision is modified by a proviso in this section which requires this emergency salary to be paid monthly during the fiscal year of 1945-46 if the unappropriated surplus in the general fund on June 30, 1945 shall be sufficient to pay the full amount or any amount in multiples of $2.50. It has been determined that the revenues in the general fund on June 30, 1945 were sufficient to pay the full $10.00 emergency salary, and the State employees and teachers are now receiving this full amount.

Chapter 763 of the Session Laws of 1945 reads as follows:

"That on account of the increased cost of traveling, hotel and other expense, the regular and special judges of the superior court are hereby granted, in addition to the salary and expense allowance now paid them, an additional expense allowance of nine hundred fifty dollars ($950.00) per annum, payable monthly, provided such funds shall be available after payment of teachers' and State employees' salaries and emergency salaries under the Budget Appropriation Act for the biennium one thousand nine hundred and forty-five—one thousand nine hundred and forty-seven."

Chapter 764 of the Session Laws of 1945 reads as follows:

"Section 1. That Section seven—forty-four of the General Statutes of North Carolina is hereby amended by striking out the phrase 'forty-five hundred dollars ($4,500.00),' and inserting in lieu thereof the phrase 'five thousand dollars ($5,000.00).'

"Sec. 2. That Section seven—forty-five of the General Statutes of North Carolina is hereby amended by striking out the phrase 'five hundred ($500.00) Dollars' and inserting in lieu thereof the phrase 'seven hundred and fity dollars ($750.00).'

"Sec. 2½. Provided such funds shall be available after payment of teacher's and State employees salaries and emergency salaries under the Budget Appropriation Act for the biennium one thousand nine hundred and forty-five—one thousand nine hundred and forty seven."

In view of these enactments, the question arises whether the availability of funds should be determined at the end of each month or at the end of the biennium. In other words, if after paying the emergency salaries to teachers and State employees in any given month there is available sufficient funds to pay the increased salaries of Judges and Solicitors, should they receive that salary at that time?

Chapter 763, quoted above, was adopted subsequent to the adoption of the Appropriations Act, and it provides that the amount specified therein shall be payable monthly. The same is true of Chapter 764 when it is inserted in the amended section. By requiring these emergency salaries to be paid monthly, the Legislature has evinced an intent to have the availability of funds determined at the end of each month. Thus, if funds are available to pay these emergency salaries to Judges and Solicitors after the payment of the emergency salaries to State employees and teachers at the end of any month, it is my opinion that they should at that time be paid.

I advise, therefore, that these emergency salaries should be paid to the Judges and Solicitors since it appears that funds are available at the present time after the payment of the emergency salaries to teachers and State employees. It is not necessary to wait until the close of the biennium to determine the availability of funds.

PEACE OFFICERS; RAILROAD AND OTHER COMPANY POLICE; APPOINTMENT AND ISSUANCE OF COMMISSION BY GOVERNOR

29 April, 1946.

Reference is made to the letter of F. W. Hoover, General Manager of Government Services, Inc., dated April 19, 1946.

In this letter it is stated that Government Services, Inc. of Washington, D. C,. has entered into a lease contract with the Tennessee Valley Authority under the terms of which Government Services, Inc. will take over the operation of the Authority's village facilities, consisting of various buildings, such as stores, public buildings, schools, hospitals, and approximately four hundred houses at Fontana Dam. It is the purpose of the corporation to develop the area into a recreational project for the pleasure and benefit of tourists expected to visit Western North Carolina.

This corporation considers it necessary to have its Security Officers at Fontana Dam duly commissioned as Corporation Policemen in accordance with the provisions of Sections 3484 and 3485 of Michie's North Carolina Code of 1939. The corporation enclosed a list of men theretofore employed by the Tennessee Valley Authority and commissioned by the Governor's office as State Police and asked that they be given commissions from your office as Corporation Policemen of Government Services, Inc. The corporation asked for advice on this question as to procedure, requirements, and policies of your office inasmuch as they expect to have other persons commissioned in the future. Your Executive Clerk, Mrs. Alma Corbitt, has asked our office if it is proper to issue commissions to these men as Company Police under the statutes provided in our State.

The sections of Michie's Code referred to in the letter and set forth above appear in the General Statutes of North Carolina as Sections 60-83 and 60-84; and for the purpose of this letter, we quote Section 60-83 which is as follows:

"Any corporation operating a *railroad on which steam or electricity is used as the motive power or any electric or water-power company or construction company or manufacturing company or motor vehicle carrier* may apply to the governor to commission such persons as the corporation or company may designate to act as policemen for it. The governor upon such application may appoint such persons or so many of them as he may deem proper to be such policemen, and shall issue to the persons so appointed a commission to act as such policemen. Nothing contained in the provisions of this section shall have the effect to relieve any such company from any civil liability now existing by statute or under the common law for the act or acts of such policemen, in exercising or attempting to exercise the powers conferred by this section." (Underscoring ours.)

While we do not know all of the functions of Government Services, Inc. from the information before us as to its purposes and objects, it does not seem to us that this corporation falls within the category of a corporation operating a railroad propelled by steam or electricity nor does it seem to us that it is an electric or water power company nor can we gather from any information before us that it falls within any category of a construction company, manufacturing company or motor vehicle carrier. It seems to us that the issuance of a commission to these men as police officers is rather serious and particular business, in as much as these men or one of them might kill some individual in the performance of his duties. In such event, it would be highly important that his commission be legal and valid to the end that he might have the protection afforded a police officer in a criminal prosecution. At the present time, this office has grave doubts that Government Services, Inc. is such a type of company as fixed by our statute which would authorize the Governor of our State to issue a commission to any of its employees as special or company police. Under present information, we would advise that such commissions should not·be issued. We are, of course, greatly in sympathy with the work that Government Services, Inc. intends to pursue in our State, and I am sure that we all wish to be of assistance in any way possible. We would suggest that the problem could be solved by having the sheriff of the county appoint these men as deputy sheriffs instead of seeking a commission as special police from the office of the Governor.

If Government Services, Inc. cares to furnish further information as to their powers and objectives which will bring them within the category of corporations set forth in our statute which authorizes the Governor to issue such commissions, then this office will be glad to reconsider this interpretation.

SCHOOLS; LUNCH PROGRAMS; PUBLIC SCHOOLS; NONPROFIT PRIVATE SCHOOLS
27 June, 1946.

You forwarded to me a letter from Honorable Clinton Anderson, Secretary of the United States Department of Agriculture, relating to "The National School Lunch Act," as provided by H. R. 3370, and request my opinion on the following questions:

"1. Has the State educational agency in your State the legal authority and the staff to administer a Statewide school lunch program in accordance with the provisions of H. R. 3370? If not, will you please indicate what agency or agencies you will designate in its stead.

"2. May the State educational agency legally disburse funds to non-profit private schools?"

As to the first question, Chapter 777 of the Sessions Laws of 1945 (Section 115-25.1 of the General Statutes) fully recognizes the authority of the State Board of Education to accept and administer Federal funds and surplus commodities furnished by the Federal Government in grants to provide wholesome and nutritious lunches for the school children of the State. This statute fully authorizes the State Board of Education to cooperate with the Federal authorities, even to advancing certain funds to administrative school units to assist them to fully take advantage of the program.

I am of the opinion that the second question may be answered in the affirmative, in view of Section 143-164 of the General Statutes, which reads as follows:

"*Acceptance of Federal loans and grants permitted.*— The said State of North Carolina, and it several departments, institutions, agencies and commissions, are hereby authorized to accept and receive loans, grants, and other assistance from the United States Government, departments and/or agencies thereof, for its use, and to receive like financial and other aid from other agencies in carrying out any undertaking which has been authorized by the Governor of North Carolina, with the approval of the Council of State."

I am of the opinion that the Governor and Council of State may authorize the State Board of Education to accept and administer funds from the Federal Government in connection with "The National School Lunch Act," to nonprofit private schools.

OPINIONS TO SECRETARY OF STATE

CORPORATIONS; NAME; USE OF "UNITED STATES" AND
"RESERVE" AS PART OF CORPORATE NAME

29 July, 1944

You have requested an opinion as to whether a corporation may be charted under the name of "United States Reserve Credit Corporation."

You delivered to me the proposed charter which shows the objects for which the corporation is to be formed. If I properly interpret this portion of the proposed charter, the use of the terms "United States" and "reserve" is prohibited by Federal statute. Section 585, Title 12, USCA, reads in part as follows:

> "No bank, banking association, trust company, corporation, association, firm, partnership, or person engaged in the banking, loan, building and loan, brokerage, factorage, insurance, indemnity, or trust business shall use the word 'Federal,' the words 'United States,' the words 'Deposit Insurance,' or the word 'reserve,' or any combination of such words, as a portion of its corporate, firm, or trade name or title or of the name under which it does business: . . ."

It is entirely possible that this corporation, if organized, would be conducting a brokerage. If this is true, the use of the term "United States" as part of its corporate name is prohibited by Section 583 of Title 12, USCA. The pertinent provision of that section reads as follows:

> "The use of the word 'national,' the word 'Federal' or the words 'United States,' separately, in any combination thereof, or in combination with other words or syllables, as part of the name or title used by any person, corporation, firm, partnership, business trust, association or other business entity, doing the business of bankers, brokers, or trust or savings institutions is prohibited except where such institution is organized under the laws of the United States, or is otherwise permitted by the laws of the United States to use such name or title, or is lawfully using such name or title on August 23, 1935; . . ."

Of course, if a corporation does not propose to do, and is not organized to do, any of the types of business named in the above section, an entirely different problem would be presented.

STATE LANDS; ENTRIES; DESCRIPTION; ISSUANCE OF GRANT

25 August, 1944

Receipt is acknowledged of your letter of August 18 enclosing papers relative to an entry covering certain lands in Swain County, North Carolina.

Your first question is whether the land covered by the entry may be properly considered as one tract or as three separate and distinct tracts.

G. S. 146-35 provides that every county surveyor, upon receiving the copy of the entry and order and survey for any claim of lands, shall within ninety days lay off and survey the same agreeably to Chapter 146 of the General Statutes, and make thereof two fair plats, the scale thereof and the number of the entry being mentioned on such plats. This section further provides that the surveyor shall set down in words the beginning, angles, distances, marks and water courses and other remarkable places crossed or touched by or near to the lines of such lands and also the quantity of acres. G. S. 146-36 provides that the surveyor shall within one year transmit the plats, together with the warrant or order of survey, to the office of the Secretary of State or deliver them to the claimant, and that the Secretary of State shall, upon receipt of the plats, file one in his office and attach the other to the grant.

From an inspection of the plat prepared by the County Surveyor of Swain County and the description prepared by him, I can see no reason why you should not accept the same as submitted and proceed to issue the grant, if the other provisions of the law have been complied with. I am inclined to the view that the question as to whether the property sought to be acquired should be described as one tract rather than three tracts should be one to be determined by the County Surveyor who makes the survey and prepares the plat.

Your second question is whether there must be a separate entry for each grant issued by the Secretary of State.

From an inspection of the statutes relating to entries and grants, it is my opinion that there must be a separate entry for each grant issued by the Secretary of State. G. S. 146-47 specifically provides that the date of the entry and the number of the survey from the certificate of survey upon which the grant is founded shall be inserted in the grant. You will note that this particular section seems to contemplate only one entry in a grant. There are various other provisions contained in the statutes governing entries and grants which seem to bear out the conclusion reached above.

COMMISSIONER OF AFFIDAVITS; OATH; BEFORE WHOM TAKEN

26 August, 1944

Mr. Abernethy inquired of me over the telephone to determine whether a commissioner of affidavits appointed by the Governor by authority of G. S. 3-1 would have to take and subscribe an oath before a Justice of the Peace in the county or city in which he resides, or would it be sufficient if the commissioner took the required oath before a Notary Public or other officer who, under the laws of the state in which the commissioner resides, is authorized to administer an oath.

It is my opinion that the provisions of the statute, G. S. 3-1, requiring a commissioner of affidavits to take and subscribe an oath before a Justice of the Peace would not exclude the validity of an oath taken before a Notary Public or other officer qualified under the law of the state of residence of the commissioner. It is my opinion that the taking of an oath before a duly authorized officer of the state of residence would meet the requirements of our statute and, when these commissioners have been certified by your office in accordance with Chapter 3 of the General Statutes, they would be duly authorized to perform the duties authorized by law.

SOLICITORS; SECRETARY OF STATE; DISTRIBUTION OF STATE
PUBLICATIONS; OWNERSHIP OF BOOKS

22 June, 1945

You have inquired whether the State publications distributed to Superior Court Solicitors pursuant to G. S. 147-45 remain the property of the State and are to be turned over to the Solicitor's successor in office, or whether they become the private property of the Solicitor, thus making it necessary for a new Solicitor to receive a complete set of publications from your office.

G. S. 147-45 provides that the Secretary of State shall, at the State's expense, distribute to the Solicitors of the Superior Courts one volume of the Session Laws and one volume of the North Carolina Reports, as the same are printed. In my opinion, it was the intent of the law that the publications so distributed should remain the property of the State. In other words, the books belong to the office and not to the individual. Thus, when publications have been distributed to a Solicitor who dies or goes out of office, his successor is entitled to have these books turned over to him upon being inducted into office.

This construction is buttressed by that portion of G. S. 147-45 which provides that Justices of the Supreme Court may retain the Reports furnished them to enable them to keep up-to-date their personal sets of Reports. Thus, the Legislature felt it necessary to specifically provide that Justices could retain their copies of the Reports. No such provision appears as to Solicitors.

Therefore, I am of the opinion that the publications distributed to Solicitors do not become the private property of the person holding the office of Solicitor.

FOREIGN CORPORATIONS; DOMESTICATION; INCIDENTAL AGREEMENT TO
INSTALL ARTICLE SOLD IN INTERSTATE COMMERCE
NOT "DOING BUSINESS"

12 December, 1945

You have referred to me a letter from the Henszey Company of Watertown, Wisconsin, and you request that I give you my opinion as to whether such corporation is doing business within this State so as to be required to domesticate under the provisions of Section 55-118 of the General Statutes.

It appears that the business of the corporation consists of selling equipment such as evaporating plants for evaporated milk. The general manager states that due to the peculiar nature of the product sold, it is necessary that the corporation supervise the installation work. In the installation work local labor is employed. However, all equipment is manufactured in its factory and all sales orders are accepted there.

On the basis of these facts, it is my opinion that the Henszey Company, which is a foreign corporation, is under no obligation to domesticate in this State since, in selling and installing such equipment, it is engaged exclusively in interstate commerce, and is not doing business within this State. An incidental agreement to assemble a product or structure that has been sold in interstate commerce does not destroy the nature of that commerce. YORK MFG. CO. v. COLLEY, 247 U. S. 21.

An examination of leading cases on the subject shows that the courts have extended the protection of the commerce clause to cover, not only a transaction which is purely interstate, but also one which, if viewed separately, is unquestionably intrastate, but is, in fact, a relevant and appropriate part of an agreement in interstate commerce. GENERAL TALKING PICTURES CORP. v. SHEA, 185 Ark. 777; FURNACE CO. v. MILLER, 115 N. Y. S. 625; INTERNATIONAL FUEL SERVICE CO. v. STEARNS, 304 Pa. 157.

As stated in Prentice-Hall, STATE AND LOCAL TAX SERVICE, Section 7377: "A foreign corporation is not 'doing business' within a state when it agrees to assemble and install therein an article sold by it in interstate commerce when the nature of the article is such that it can be properly or efficiently installed or assembled only under the supervision of trained technical experts not ordinarily to be found within the state. . . ."

If, however, the installation of an article or structure is not a mere incident to the interstate contract, but is a distinct and separate activity, the corporation in making such installation would be considered to be doing business within the state. BROWNING v. CITY-OF--WAYCROSS, 233 U. S. 16; GENERAL HIGHWAYS SYSTEM v. DENNIS, 251 Mich. 152.

It appears from the facts stated in the letter from the Henszey Company that the supervision of trained experts, not to be found within this state, is required in making installations of its products. If this is true, such installation work is relevant and appropriate to the interstate sale of the product; and, therefore, such corporation in performing such installation work is not doing business within this State.

CORPORATIONS; OPERATING UNDER ASSUMED NAME

30 May, 1946

I received your letter of May 14, enclosing a letter to you from Mr. W. W. Cohoon, Attorney at Law of Elizabeth City, North Carolina, about which you requested my opinion.

Mr. Cohoon wanted to know whether or not a North Carolina corporation would have a right to do business under an assumed name; that is, a name other than its corporate name, which assumed name did not contain the word "Incorporated" or "Inc." provided he registered same in the clerk's office pursuant to Section 59-87 of the General Statutes, and provided further that the name of the corporation is painted upon the door of its principal place of business as required by law.

I agree with Mr. Cohoon, after making an investigation, that the decisions in this State are silent on this subject and no case involving this question, so far as my investigation reveals, has been passed upon by our Supreme Court.

The general law on this subject seems to be that, in the absence of a statute to the contrary, a corporation may do business under a name other than the name fixed by its charter; in other words, under an assumed name. See 18 C.J.S., title CORPORATIONS, Section 166, page 561; 13 AM. JUR., title CORPORATIONS, Section 132, page 270; 56 A.L.R. 450.

I think the corporation should comply with the provisions of Article 4 of Chapter 59 of the General Statutes as to doing business under an assumed name, although G. S. 59-87 provides that this article shall in no way affect or apply to any corporation created and organized under the laws of this State, or to any corporation organized under the laws of any other state and lawfully doing business in this State.

This may be interpreted as meaning only that a corporation, which by its charter assumes a name, would not have to comply with that article, but if it did business under some name other than its charter name, it might have to do so. The meaning of the statute is not certain as to this. I would, therefore, advise a compliance with the statute if a name other than the corporate name is to be used for carrying on business by the corporation.

OPINIONS TO STATE AUDITOR

LAW ENFORCEMENT OFFICERS' BENEFIT AND RETIREMENT FUND;
PAYMENT OF BENEFIT WHEN HUSBAND AND WIFE HAVE SEPARATED
UNDER DEED OF SEPARATION; CHARLES S. CURRENT, DECEASED

11 January, 1945

I have given careful consideration to the file you turned over to me relative to the estate of Charles S. Current, Deceased. It appears that prior to the death of Mr. Current, he and his wife entered into a separation agreement in which she released all of her right, title, and interest in any of his real and personal property and the question arises as to whether or not she released her interest in his benefit and retirement fund.

Prior to the death of Mr. Current, and, I assume, at the time he became a member of the Law Enforcement Officer's Benefit and Retirement Fund, Mr. Current signed the usual certificate authorizing the Board of Commissioners of the Fund to make payment of the beneficiary and therein named and agreed on behalf of himself and his heirs and assigns that payment to the beneficiary therein named shall be a complete discharge of the claim and shall constitute a release of the fund from any further obligation on account of the benefit. While Mr. Current reserved the right to name some other beneficiary in event that he should survive his wife, by filing with the Board of Commissioners a written designation naming a new beneficiary, I assume that Mr. Current has not designated a beneficiary other than his wife.

I am of the opinion that the deed of separation entered into by Mr. and Mrs. Current does not have the effect of annulling Mrs. Clement's right to the funds accrued and that she, the beneficiary named in the certificate signed by Mr. Current, to wit, his wife, Minnie Belle Current, is entitled to the benefits accruing because of his membership in the Law Enforcement Officers' Benefit and Retirement Fund. I observe from the letter of Mr. Eugene Shaw, administrator of the estate, that he does not care to seriously controvert the claim of Mrs. Current.

However, in view of the fact that the administrator has notified you of at least his interest in this fund, and Mrs. Clement has filed a claim for the fund, it may be best for you to hold the fund until one or the other of the parties has obtained a Court Order establishing his or her claim to the fund.

EMERGENCY (RETIRED) JUDGES; PARTICIPATION IN ADDITIONAL
EXPENSE ALLOWANCE AUTHORIZED BY CHAPTER 763,
SESSION LAWS, 1945

24 October, 1945

I have your letter of October 20 in which you write me as follows:

"Chapter 763, Session Laws of 1945, provides an additional expense allowance of $950.00 to all regular and special judges of the Superior Court. Please advise if the retired judges shall be paid the additional travel allowance under Chapter 763."

Chapter 763 of the Session Laws of 1945 reads as follows:

"That on account of the increased cost of traveling, hotel and other expenses, the regular and special judges of the Superior Court are hereby granted, in addition to the salary and expense allowance now paid them, an additional expense allowance of nine hundred fifty dollars ($950.00) per annum, payable monthly, provided such funds shall be available after payment of teachers' and State employees' salaries and emergency salaries under the Budget Appropriation Act for the biennium one thousand nine hundred and forty-five - one thousand nine hundred and forty-seven."

You will observe that the additional sum provided by this Act is for the "regular and special judges of the Superior Court" and does not include the retired or emergency judges and, therefore, the emergency retired judges would not be entitled to rceive any part of this additional appropriation.

G. S. 7-50 provides that the retired emergency judges named in G. S. 7-51 shall receive their actual expenses incurred while holding any regular or special term of court and in addition they are entitled to receive $50.00 per week to be paid by the county in which any special term is held by them. This is doubtless the reason why the General Assembly did not see fit to include them in the provisions of Chapter 763.

N. C. RECREATION COMMISSION; ADVISORY COMMITTEE; EXPENSES ATTENDING MEETINGS OF COMMISSION

30 October, 1945

I have your letter of October 29 in which you write me as follows:

"Please advise if the Advisory Committee to the North Carolina Recreation Commission (Chap. 757, P. L. 1945, Sec. 6) are entitled to be reimbursed for their travel expenses incident to attending meetings with the Commission."

Chapter 757, creating the State Recreation Commission, Section 6, states that the Governor shall name a Recreation Advisory Committee consisting of 30 members who shall serve for a term of two years. This section provides that the committee shall meet each year with the Recreation Commission at a time and place to be fixed by the Governor. It further states that members of the committee shall serve without compensation. Nothing is said in the Act with reference to the expenses of members of the committee in attending the annual meeting which by law they are required to attend. The Act makes an appropriation of $7,500 for carrying out its purposes.

It is my opinion that the members of the advisory committee would be entitled to their actual expenses in attending the annual meeting of the Commission as necessary implication of the responsibility placed upon them by law of attending this meeting. I believe it was the intention of the General Assembly that out of this appropriation, their actual expenses should be paid.

STATE AUDITOR; DUTY TO INVESTIGATE AND REPORT ON CLAIMS AGAINST THE STATE

13 November, 1945

According to my conversation with you over the telephone, I am returning to you herewith the letter from Mr. Henry Henderson under date of November 8.

G. S. 147-58, Subsection 7, provides that it is the duty of the State Auditor to examine and liquidate the claims of all persons against the State in cases where there is sufficient provision of law for the payment thereof, and where there is no sufficient provision, to examine the claim and report the fact, with his opinion thereon, to the General Assembly.

In the case of BONER v. ADAMS, 65 N. C. 639, the Supreme Court said that the Auditor of the State is not a mere ministerial officer. When a claim is presented to him against the State, he is to decide whether there is a sufficient provision of law for its payment, and if in his opinion there is not sufficient provision of law, he must examine the claim and report the fact, with his opinion, to the General Assembly. There may be some question as to whether or not this statute was intended to embrace a claim of damages sounding in tort, but the statute does not make any distinction between contract and tort claims.

The Supreme Court is construing the constitutional provision authorizing it to hear claims against the State, Constitution, Article IV, Section 9, has held that it would dismiss any claim where the sole question was one of fact, LACY v. STATE, 195 N. C. 284. See other cases cited in the annotation under this constitutional provision.

LAW ENFORCEMENT OFFICERS' BENEFIT AND RETIREMENT FUND; ELIGIBILITY FOR MEMBERSHIP; RAILROAD POLICEMEN; HEALTH OFFICERS; SANITARY INSPECTORS

13 November, 1945

I acknowledge receipt of your letter in which you inquire as follows:

"1. Under the original act creating the Law Enforcement Officers' Benefit and Retirement Fund, were railroad policemen, county and city health officers and sanitary inspectors who had the power of arrest, eligible for membership in the Fund?
"2. Under the act referred to above, as amended by the General Assembly of 1941, it would appear that railroad policemen, county and city health officers, sanitary inspectors would not be eligible to become members in the Fund. Are the railroad policemen, county and health officers and sanitary inspectors who became members of the Fund under the original act permitted to remain as members and receive benefits?"

Section 9 of Chapter 349 of the Public Laws of 1937, paragraph 3, defined "law enforcement officers" entitled to participate "in the Law Enforcement Officers' Benefit Fund" to include "sheriffs, their appointed deputy sheriffs, police officers, prison wardens and deputy wardens, prison camp superintendents, prison stewards, foremen and guards, highway patrolmen, and any citizens duly deputized as a deputy sheriff by a sheriff in an emergency."

This section was amended by paragraph (m) of Chapter 6 of the Public Laws of 1939 to read as follows:

"Law enforcement officers in the meaning of this Act shall include sheriffs, deputy sheriffs, constables, police officers, prison wardens and deputy wardens, prison camp superintendents, prison stewards, prison foremen and guards, highway patrolmen, and any citizen duly deputized as a deputy by a Sheriff or other law enforcement officer in an emergency, and all other officers of this State, or of any political subdivision thereof, who are clothed with the power of arrest."

The 1939 provision answers your first question in the affirmative. That is, that railroad policemen, county and city health officers, and sanitary inspectors *who have the power of arrest*, are eligible for membership in the fund.

The 1941 Act, Chapter 157, does not change the definition of those who are entitled to become members in the fund, so that all classes of officers who have the power of arrest, and eligible under the provisions of the 1937 Act, are still eligible for membership.

It is necessary to impress upon you the fact that only those county and city health officers and sanitary inspectors who have the power of arrest are eligible for membership and I do not know of any General Statute which gives to such officers the power of arrest. However, it is entirely possible that there are Public-Local Acts which have given to these classes of officers the power of arrest or it may be that such officers have been deputized by the sheriff of their respective counties as deputy sheriffs with power of arrest. It, therefore, seems necessary that you determine in each case whether or not a county or city health officer or sanitary inspector has the power to make arrest.

Section 60-82 G. S. provides for railroad police and fully authorizes them to make arrest under the conditions set out in said section.

OPINIONS TO STATE TREASURER

EXECUTORS AND ADMINISTRATORS; SALE OF PERSONAL
PROPERTY BONDS; TRANSFER

5 October, 1944

You have heretofore handed me letter from Kenneth L. Greenfield, administrator of the estate of Lindsay Greenfield, deceased, in which he states that the estate of which he is administrator is the owner of a State of North Carolina highway serial bond and that it is necessary to convert this bond into cash and he desires to have instructions relative to changing the registration of the bond. I assume that Mr. Greenfield, as administrator, contemplates selling the bond at private sale.

G. S. 28-76 provides that whenever an executor or administrator of an estate is of the opinion that the interest of said estate will be promoted and conserved by allowing the personal property belonging to it to be sold at private sale instead of at public sale, such executor or administrator may, upon a duly verified application to the clerk of the superior court, obtain an order to sell it at private sale for the best price that can be obtained and report the sale to the clerk for confirmation if, at the end of ten days from the date of filing the report, no increased bid is filed and it appears that the property has been sold for a fair and adequate price, the sale shall be confirmed by the clerk.

Our Supreme Court, in the case of FELTON v. FELTON, 213 N. C. 194, has held that an administrator may sell notes and choses in action of the estate at private sale without authorization from the court and that the purchaser obtains good title if the sale is made in good faith and for value, and that G. S. 28-76 does not abrogate this common law rule since the statute merely makes the obtaining of an order permissive but not mandatory.

It is my thought that the administrator, in order to protect himself and in order to relieve prospective purchasers from the burden of rebutting the presumption that they may have bought it at under-value, should apply to the clerk of the superior court for an order authorizing the sale of the personal property at private sale and have the sale, when made, confirmed by the clerk of the superior court. When this is done, a copy of the order confirming the sale could be furnished to you, accompanied by authorization from the administrator that the bond in question be transferred to the purchaser and registered in his or her name.

UNIVERSITY OF NORTH CAROLINA; ESCHEATS; FUNDS HELD
BY STATE TREASURER

17 May, 1945.

I have your letter of May 16, in which you write me as follows:

"I have deposited in a special bank account $2,416.62 which is made up of the following items:

"Sir Walter Raleigh Fund	$2,197.09
State Farm Church Bldg. Fund	162.98
Robert E. Lee Memorial Fund	56.55
Total	$2,416.62

"I have had these funds in the bank for a period of more than ten years. There have been no claims against this fund and I am wondering if it would be correct to turn these funds over to the University of North Carolina for the escheat account. Mr. Cates, of the University of North Carolina is anxious to have this turned over to their account. Please advise me if this would be in order."

G. S. 116-25 provides, in part, as follows:

"All moneys now in the hands of the Treasurer of the State represented by state warrants in favor of any person, firm or corporation whatsoever which have been unclaimed for a period of five years shall be turned over to the University of North Carolina."

The funds which you have, above mentioned, do not fall in this category as no state warrants are outstanding for them, so this section would not be applicable.

This is the only section which deals directly with the funds in the hands of the State Treasurer. I do not think you would be justified in turning over to the escheat fund any moneys except by specific authority of legislative enactment. G. S. 116-23 provides for escheat of unclaimed personal property of every kind and sums of money in the hands of any person which shall not be recovered or claimed by the parties entitled thereto *for five years after the same shall become due and payable,* and provides that it shall be deemed derelict property and shall be paid to the University of North Carolina and held by it without liability for profit or interest until a just claim therefor shall be preferred by the parties entitled thereto, if made within ten years. This section is inapplicable as the funds which you hold do not become due and payable until the demand is made for them; in other words, you hold these funds for an indefinite time, subject to a proper demand whenever made. Whether or not this section could be considered applicable to a State official who holds funds of this character may be doubted, as ordinarily statutes are inapplicable to the agents of a sovereign state unless specifically stated. But, in any event, for the reasons stated, I do not think this statute would justify you in the payment of these funds to the University.

It may be that the statute on escheats should be amended at the next Legislature in order that accounts of this character may be cleared and paid over to the escheat fund, but at the present time the statute is insufficient, in my opinion, to justify this course.

OPINIONS TO STATE SUPERINTENDENT
OF PUBLIC INSTRUCTION

SCHOOLS; INSTRUCTIONAL AND JANITORIAL SUPPLIES; FUEL;
TRANSPORTATION SUPPLIES; OWNERSHIP

2 August, 1944.

Receipt is acknowledged of your letter, in which you raise the question as to the ownership of instructional and janitorial supplies, fuel and transportation supplies as between the State Board of Education and county and city administrative units.

It is my opinion that under the provisions of the School Machinery Act of 1939, as now written, the ownership of fuel and instructional and janitorial supplies is vested in the county or city administrative unit at the time of their delivery to such unit.

It is further my opinion that the county or city administrative unit in which ownership is vested should insure this property against loss by fire.

The School Machinery Act, as now written, is not entirely clear as to the ownership of these particular items and it might be advisable to have the next General Assembly clarify the matter to such an extent as to eliminate any question as to ownership.

When we come to consideration of the question of ownership of supplies purchased and used in connection with the transportation system of a particular county or city administrative unit, a different picture is presented. Under the provisions of Section 24 of the School Machinery Act, the control and management of all facilities for the transportation of public school children is vested in the State of North Carolina, under the direction and supervision of the State Board of Education, which has authority to promulgate rules and regulations governing the organization, maintenance and operation of these facilities.

Although county and city administrative units, under certain circumstances, are required to furnish the funds with which to purchase additional buses, title to all the buses is taken and maintained in the name of the State of North Carolina and the State is required to purchase all school buses used as replacements or old buses which were operated by the State during the school year 1940-41.

Although it might be difficult under ordinary circumstances to distinguish between the ownership of fuel and instructional and janitorial supplies, and supplies used in connection with the operation of the transportation of school children, it is my view that the General Assembly in setting up the school transportation system intended that its ownership, management and control should be and remain in the State of North Carolina and should be operated by the State Board of Education. It is, therefore, my opinion that the ownership of transportation supplies is vested in the State and not in the county or city administrative units.

Again let me emphasize that the School Machinery Act as now written is not entirely clear on this question and I would recommend that you take steps to have the General Assembly clarify the Act as to the ownership of this particular type of property.

TEACHERAGE; APPROPRIATIONS THEREFOR BY COUNTIES

16 August, 1944.

I have your letter of August 14 enclosing letter from Mr. G. T. Proffit, Acting Superintendent of Harnett County Schools, in which Mr. Proffit writes as follows:

"At a joint meeting of the Board of Education and the Board of County Commissioners this morning the attorney for the Board of Commissioners raised the question as to the legality of the Board of Education purchasing a building, or buildings, to house the principal and agriculture teacher in Dunn. Dr. Hooper, Chairman of the Board of Education, asked that I write you and get you or the Attorney General to confirm the telephone conversation you had with him recently relative to the legality of this transaction. We would like to have such a letter for our files."

General Statutes 115-157(b) provides as follows: "The capital outlay fund shall provide for the purchase of sites, the erection of school buildings, including dormitories and teachers' homes * * *." This subsection literally provides for the purchase of sites and the *erection* of school buildings, including dormitories and teachers' homes. The authority to purchase the site and erect a dormitory or teachers' home could be considered as authority to purchase one that was already erected if the property purchased would come within the perview of the statute in the use of the terms "dormitories and teachers' homes."

I could not be certain, however, that a court construing this statute would so hold and any opinion I might express would be in anticipation of what the court might decide if the case was presented. There has been no decision of our court construing this language.

There may be some question as to whether or not under the statute a building or buildings to house the principal and the agriculture teacher in a school would come within the purpose of the statute in providing for the erection of dormitories and teachers' homes. In this case there is a contemplated purchase of a piece of property for the use of a specific principal or teacher and would not be what is generally known as a teacherage in which may be housed teachers generally employed in a school. For these reasons, I do entertain some doubt as to the authority to purchase the property contemplated as I understand from Mr. Proffit's letter, but I could not express any conclusive opinion about it.

The only case before our court involving erection of a teacherage is DENNY v. MECKLENBURG COUNTY, 211 N. C. 211, in which it was said that a teacherage would not fall within the authority of the county under the Municipal Finance Act to issue bonds for the erection and purchase of school houses.

SCHOOL LAW; TEACHERS; CONTRACTS; RESIGNATIONS; WHAT NOTICE RE-
QUIRED WHEN DATE OF OPENING POSTPONED; PAYMENT OF SALARIES

18 August, 1944.

I acknowledge receipt of your letter in which you inquire, if the date for
the opening of schools is postponed, if the teachers are required to file their
resignations thirty days prior to the date fixed for the opening, or the date
of the actual opening of the schools.

I have had several inquiries on this question, and I am enclosing herewith a copy of a letter which I have heretofore written, expressing my
views on the question raised by you.

I have heard that in some instances the salaries of teachers will begin
on the date originally fixed for the opening of the school, rather than on
the date to which the opening has been postponed; in such event, I am of
the opinion that, insofar as the teachers are concerned, the date of the opening of the school would be the date on which their salaries began, and not
the date of the actual opening. In other words, if the original opening date
of the school was fixed at September 1, and the teachers' salaries began on
September 1, but the actual opening of the school was postponed until September 18, the teacher would have to resign thirty days before September
1.

SCHOOLS; SALARY SCHEDULE; COUNTY SUPERINTENDENT

26 August, 1944.

Receipt is acknowledged of your letter of June 23, with reference to the
action of the State Board of Education at its meeting preceding that date
with reference to providing additional compensation for Mr. J. C. Manning, of Martin County, for duties performed by him over and above the
regular demands of his office. You state that you are writing to inquire if
the regulation as a general amendment to the salary schedule, applicable
to all similar cases, would in my opinion be legal.

The amendment made at the June 8 meeting is as follows:

"Where a superintendent, with the approval of the State Board of
Education or under its direction, performs duties over and above the
duties of his regular position and where such duties are definitely in
line with the administrative needs of the public schools in an emergency situation, the board may in its discretion increase the salary of
said superintendent for the emergency period."

Following the entry of this amendment in the minutes, the following
resolution appeared:

"Because of the critical illness of Superintendent Edmonson of Beaufort County, the State Board of Education in March approved a plan
by which Mr. James C. Manning, Superintendent of Martin County,
would assist in carrying on the work in Beaufort County during Mr.
Edmonson's illness. On motion of Mrs. McKee seconded by Dr. Massey,
the Board authorized an increase in Mr. Manning's salary of $100 per
month for four months, or a total of $400 for his services in Beaufort
County."

Section 8 of the School Machinery Act provides that the State Board of Education shall fix and determine a State standard salary schedule for teachers, principals and superintendents which shall be the maximum standard state salaries to be paid from State funds for teachers, principals and superintendents. No further detail is given in the statute with reference to this State standard salary schedule or other limitations placed upon the action of the State Board of Education with respect thereto.

In the absence of some limitations on the character of standard salary schedule which might be adopted, I know of no reason why the State Board of Education would not have the authority to include in the schedule the latitude which this amendment proposes. While it might have been desirable to have placed in the resolution a provision limiting the amount of excess salary per month which might be paid under the emergency situation referred to, the lack of this provision would not invalidate, in my opinion, the action taken. It might be added to the resolution if thought desirable at the next meeting of the Board.

I think also it might be desirable by amendment to add to it a provision making the amendment effective as of March 1, 1944, which apparently was intended by the Board as it is proposed to make it applicable to the special work done in Beaufort County by Mr. Manning by arrangement with the Board, beginning in March, 1944.

If it is to be understood that the amendment to the salary schedule was intended to be made effective as of March 1, 1944, then I would be of the opinion that the Board might validly pay the additional compensation of $100 per month for four months, beginning March 1, 1944, to Mr. Manning.

SCHOOLS; LIABILITY OF PARENT FOR ACTS OF MINOR CHILD DRIVING SCHOOL BUS

12 September, 1944.

I have your letter of September 11, enclosing a letter from Mr. F. T. Johnson, Superintendent of the Perquimans County Schools, in which Mr. Johnson writes as follows:

"I have a school girl whose father is willing for her to drive a school bus for the coming year provided you will write me a letter stating that he would not be responsible in case of an accident of the bus which his daughter might be driving. I am sure that no responsibility would attach to a parent who signed the application for his daughter's drivers' permit, but he wants it in black and white."

Under our law the parent of a minor child is not liable for the acts of a child resulting in injuries to another, unless the acts are committed in the presence of the parent. We have in this State a line of cases which hold that a parent may be responsible for the injuries done by a minor child driving what is called "the family automobile" but these cases are based upon the theory that, in driving the family automobile, the child is acting as the agent of the parent. The liability is based upon the theory of the agency rather than the relationship of the parent and child. BOLLINGER v. RADER, 153 N. C. 488; LINVILLE v. NISSEN, 162 N. C. 95; TAYLOR v. STEWART, 172 N. C. 203; BOWEN v. MEWBORN, 218 N. C. 423; HAWES v. HAYNES, 219 N. C. 535.

SCHOOLS; PER CAPITA DISTRIBUTION; INTANGIBLE TAX

2 October, 1944.

Receipt is acknowledged of your letter of September 28, enclosing a letter from Mr. J. W. Wilson, Superintendent of Schools in Mecklenburg County, in which Mr. Wilson refers to a question raised by the auditors as to the payment to the City Schools of Charlotte a per capita distribution of the intangible taxes turned over to the County Schools by the County. More specifically, Mr. Wilson states his question as follows:

"What I want to know is whether the city schools here, after having received directly from the State a share of the intangible taxes, should receive again from the county schools per capita payment on this money."

Section 15 of the School Machinery Act provides, in part, as follows:

"All county-wide Current Expense school funds shall be apportioned to county and city administrative units monthly, and it shall be the duty of the county treasurer to remit such funds monthly as-collected to each administrative unit located in said county on a per capita enrollment basis. County-wide expense funds shall include all funds for current expenses *levied by Board of County Commissioners* in any county to cover items for Current Expense purposes, and including also all fines, forfeitures, penalties, poll and dog taxes and funds for vocational subjects."

You will observe the underscored language in this section. The intangible taxes are not levied by the Board of County Commissioners in any county but are levied under the provisions of Schedule H of the Revenue Act of 1939, as amended, and are distributed under the provisions of Section 715, which provides, in part, as follows:

"The amounts so allocated to each county shall in turn be divided between the county and all municipalities therein in proportion to the total amount of ad valorem taxes levied by each during the fiscal year preceding such distribution."

This section provides further:

"The amounts so allocated to each county and municipality shall be distributed and used by said county or municipality in proportion to other property tax levies made for the various funds and activities of the taxing unit receiving said allotment."

I am of the opinion that our law does not contemplate a per capita distribution to the city administrative unit of the intangible taxes allocated to the county administrative unit by the Board of County Commissioners under the provisions of this statute.

SCHOOLS; SOLICITING TEACHERS AND PUPILS DURING SCHOOL DAYS

16 October, 1944.

I acknowledge receipt of your letter, enclosing a letter from Honorable John A. Oates of Fayetteville, calling my attention to Section 14-238 of the North Carolina General Statutes which prohibits the solicitation or sale of articles of property to teachers and pupils during the school day. In Mr. Oates' letter he states that there is no question in his mind but what this section prohibits soliciting or selling articles to teachers and pupils on the school grounds, but raises the question as to whether or not it is applicable to a merchant who operates an establishment near the school grounds, and then only when the teacher or pupil visits his place of business.

While I think there is considerable merit to the position taken by Mr. Oates, I cannot, because of the penal provision of the statute, construe it otherwise than that it prohibits the solicitation or sale of any article of property to any teacher or pupil either on the school grounds or elsewhere during the school day.

It will be noted that this section can be waived by the merchant obtaining written permission from the superintendent, principal or other person in charge of the school so that a merchant under the circumstances in Mr. Oates' case could request the proper school official to authorize him to make sales during the school day, and if such official does not consider it objectionable, he may authorize such sales.

SCHOOLS; POWER TO SUSPEND OR DISMISS PUPILS

28 October, 1944.

Receipt is acknowledged of your letter enclosing letter from Honorable W. A. Graham, Superintendent of the Kinston Public Schools, in which he raises the question as to whether the principal of one of the schools in the Kinston City Administrative Unit would be authorized to refuse admission to school, under the provisions of C. S. 5563 (G. S. 115-145), of a pupil who has become a mother out of wedlock.

G. S. 115-145 provides:

"A teacher in a school having no principal, or the principal of a school, shall have authority to suspend any pupil who willfully and persistently violates the rules of the school or who may be guilty of immoral or disreputable conduct, or who may be a menace to the school.

"But every suspension for cause shall be reported at once to the attendance officer, who shall investigate the cause and shall deal with the offender in accordance with rules governing the attendance of children in school."

It appears that the question raised in Mr. Graham's letter is one of admission rather than one of suspension. The statute above referred to only authorizes the teacher or the principal to suspend pupils for certain acts and contains no provision relative to admission.

It is therefore my opinion that the principal of a school in the Kinston City Administrative Unit would not be authorized by G. S. 115-145 to refuse admission to a girl who has become a mother out of wedlock.

SCHOOLS; WORKMEN'S COMPENSATION; LIABILITY FOR INJURY TO PUPIL; LIABILITY IN OPERATION OF SCHOOL COMMUNITY CANNERIES

3 November, 1944.

Receipt is acknowledged of your letter of November 1 in which you raise certain questions relative to the liability of school administrative units under the Workmen's Compensation Act in certain instances.

Your first question is raised by a letter from Honorable Lee B. Weathers of Shelby, relative to the liability for injury to a pupil sustained in connection with the operation of a machine used in the course of study of the agricultural class.

Section 22 of the School Machinery Act of 1939, as amended, makes the provisions of the Workmen's Compensation Act applicable to all school employees. However, in order for any liability to arise under the provisions of the Workmen's Compensation Act, it is necessary that there be an employment. BORDERS v. CLINE, 212 N. C. 472.

The Workmen's Compensation Act is to be construed liberally to effectuate the broad intent of the Act to provide compensation for employees sustaining an injury arising out of and in the course of the employment and no technical or strained construction should be given to defeat this purpose. JOHNSON v. ASHEVILLE HOSIERY CO., 199 N. C. 38.

However, the rule of liberal construction cannot be extended beyond the clearly expressed language of the Act. GILMORE v. HOKE COUNTY BOARD OF EDUCATION, 222 N. C. 358.

Where the injury is sustained by a pupil while pursuing his course of study, it is my opinion that no relationship of employer and employee exists, and there would be no liability under the provisions of the Workmen's Compensation Act.

In connection with the second problem, you state that there are approximately two hundred and fifty school community canneries which are built and equipped with public funds, local, county and federal, and you desire to know whether there is any insurance protection to the people of the community who might be injured while at work in the canneries, either by the explosion of a boiler or by damage by some piece of machinery. I assume that you again refer to the provisions of the Workmen's Compensation Act.

From the information I have in connection with the operation of the community canneries, it appears that the people of the community use the canneries for the purpose of canning their own products and, if this is true, again, no relationship of employer and employee is created. Where there is no employment there is no liability under the provisions of the Workmen's Compensation Act. Of course, if the canneries are operated by the school administrative units and persons are employed by such units in connection with their operation, the relationship of employer and employee would be created and liability would arise under the provisions of the Workmen's Compensation Act should an employee sustain an injury arising out of and in the course of his or her employment. The question of liability under the Workmen's Compensation Act must, of necessity, be determined by the facts in each particular case and you can readily see that this office can only go so far as to deal in general principles and would not undertake to anticipate the facts as they might arise in each particular case.

SCHOOLS; SALE OF SCHOOL PROPERTY; APPLICATION OF PROCEEDS OF SALE

11 April, 1945.

I have your letter of April 7, enclosing a letter from Mr. G. H. Arnold, Superintendent of Schools in Thomasville, under date of April 5, in which he writes as follows:

> "I am writing to say that on March 30, 1945 the old Church St. negro school property was sold at public auction for $2700.00. This property was listed in the name of the City of Thomasville. Please advise me as to how this money should be spent.
>
> "We should like very much to use it as capital outlay in the purchase of much needed cafeteria equipment, if permissable."

The letter, as you will note, states that the property was listed in the name of the City of Thomasville. I am not sure as to just what is meant by this statement. If the statement is intended to mean that the title to the property was in the city of Thomasville, the City would have the right to receive the proceeds of sale as in the sale of any other city property. If the title to the property, however, was in the trustees of the Thomasville City Schools or held for the benefit of the city schools, the application of the proceeds of the sale would be controlled by Section 16 of the School Machinery Act. This section provides, in part, as follows:

> "All uncollected taxes which have been levied in the respective school districts for the purposes of meeting the operating costs of the schools shall remain as a lien against the property as originally assessed and shall be collectible as are other taxes so levied and, upon collection, shall be made a part of the Debt Service fund of the special bond tax unit, along with such other funds as may accrue to the credit of said unit; *and in the event there is no debt service requirement upon such district, all amounts so collected for whatever purpose shall be covered into the county treasury to be used as a part of the county debt service for schools . . ."*

The underscored portion of this quotation, I believe, answers the question submitted by Mr. Arnold and would prevent the use of these proceeds as capital outlay to purchase cafeteria equipment.

COUNTY BOARD OF EDUCATION, BLADEN COUNTY

11 April, 1945.

I received your letter of April 9, enclosing a letter of April 6 from Mr. J. S. Blair, Superintendent of the Bladen County Schools.

From this letter and from an examination of Chapter 511 of the Session Laws of 1943 and the provisions of HB 160 of the 1945 session, it appears that in 1943 the Bladen County Board of Education was composed of S. S. Hutchinson, J. Neal Clark and Henry Beatty, each appointed for a term of four years. In 1945, under HB 160, the Board of Education named in the bill were Neal Clark, S. S. Hutchinson and J. S. Melvin.

Section 2 of HB 160 provides that, unless otherwise herein provided, the members of the several county boards of education appointed by this Act shall serve for terms of two years after the first Monday in April, 1945, and until their successors are elected and qualified, "and together with the members of the board of education of the several counties whose terms will not expire on the first Monday in April, 1945, shall constitute the board of education of the respective counties."

S. S. Hutchinson and J. Neal Clark were re-appointed but as the term of Henry Beatty as fixed by the 1943 Act was for four years, it did not expire on the first Monday in April, 1945, and therefore, in my opinion, Mr. Beatty would continue as a member of the County Board of Education of Bladen County.

SCHOOLS; DEBT SERVICE FUNDS; PER CAPITA DISTRIBUTION

13 April, 1945.

I have your letter of April 11, enclosing a letter dated April 7 from Mr. W. E. Abernethy, Superintendent of Schools in Shelby, Cleveland County, in which Mr. Abernethy submits two questions, the first of which is as follows:

"May the Board of Trustees of the Shelby City-Administrative unit use a part or all of our excess debt service funds received on a per capita basis from the county for payment of principal and interest on the two bond issues against our administrative unit?"

In my opinion the answer to this question is yes. I know of no reason why these funds could not properly be used in this way and, in fact, I think it would be a very appropriate use of the funds.

Mr. Abernethy's second question is as follows:

"May we hold in our treasury the excess per capita debt service of $3,864 referred to above to be used later when needed to pay balance and interest on Literary or Special Building Fund loans? Within the next twelve months it will be necessary for us to borrow about $10,000 from the Literary Fund for the purpose of completing four additional classrooms in our High School building to accommodate the twelfth grade beginning with the term 1946-'47."

The School Machinery Act of 1939, General Statutes 115-363, provides, in part, as follows:

"All county-wide debt service funds shall be apportioned to county and city administrative units and distributed at the time of collection and when available shall be expended in the same manner as are county-wide current expense school funds: Provided, that the payments to any administrative unit shall not exceed the actual needs of said units, including sinking fund requirements. The per capita enrollment basis shall be determined by the State Board of Education and certified to each administrative unit: Provided, further, that the debt service apportionment between county and city administrative units shall apply only to debt service for capital outlay obligations incurred by counties and cities prior to July 1, 1937, except in those counties where special legislation has been enacted providing for the issuance of school building bonds in behalf of school districts, and special bond tax units. The provisions of this Act shall not apply to refunding bonds issued for school capital outlay obligations."

As the county-wide debt service funds apportioned to city administrative units are limited to the actual needs of the said units, including sinking fund requirements, under the provisions of the statute which I have just quoted, I fail to understand why there should be a surplus of $3,864 from the per capita allocation of county debt service funds. If, however, these excess funds are paid over to the Shelby City Schools and are available at the time principal and interest on Literary or Special Building Fund loans mature, I would think that they could properly apply these funds for such purpose. There might be, however, a serious question of whether or not, in making allocations and in determining the needs of the debt service fund of the city administrative unit, the county commissioners could take into consideration any such balance on hand and available for debt service purposes.

You will appreciate, I am sure, the difficulties of answering his second question in view of the provisions of the statute. It may be that I do not have a complete picture of the subject and that there are some circumstances connected with the matter which I do not understand.

SCHOOLS; ACQUISITION OF SITES OWNED BY MEMBER OF BOARD

14 April, 1945.

Receipt is acknowledged of your letter of April 12, enclosing a letter from Mr. M. T. Lambeth, Superintendent of the Beaufort County Schools, under date of April 10.

Mr. Lambeth advises that the County desires to purchase some additional land for the school garage and, in that connection, will need a part of a tract of land adjoining the property which they wish to acquire, which part is owned by Mr. C. F. Cowell, Chairman of the Board. He advises that Mr. Cowell is not interested in selling the land and will not do so unless it is necessary to acquire the necessary site. He inquires whether this transaction could be carried out by a lease of the land from Mr. Cowell or through condemnation proceedings.

In my opinion, if the necessary land can be acquired without acquiring the land owned by a member of the Board, it would be much better to do so. If it is absolutely essential to acquire the land owned by Mr. Cowell, who is a member of the Board, it could not be done by lease without violating the provisions of G. S. 14-234, which prohibits a commissioner or director of any trust wherein the State or any county, city or town may be in any manner interested, dealing with himself.

I understand that the County is required to provide the necessary sites and garages for school buses. G. S. 115-85 authorizes the County Board of Education to condemn suitable sites for schoolhouses or other school buildings. In the case of BOARD v. FOREST, 190 N. C. 753, this language was held to authorize the condemnation of additional land for playgrounds adjoining school property. The Court would probably hold, in my opinion, that necessary school garages would be included within the purview of this section. If a condemnation proceeding is instituted by the Board by authority of a resolution, in the passing of which the interested member did not participate, I do not believe that the transaction would be subject to any proper criticism and I do not think it would be a violation of G. S. 14-234. The interested member of the Board would, of course, not participate in any of the deliberations authorizing the condemnation proceeding or the prosecution of it.

SCHOOL DISTRICTS; BOUNDARIES OF SCHOOL DISTRICT NOT AFFECTED BY
ENLARGEMENT OR REDUCTION OF MUNICIPAL CITY LIMITS

18 April, 1945.

I acknowledge receipt of your letter enclosing a letter from Honorable Sam Phifer, Mayor of the Town of Benton Heights, inquiring as to whether or not the merger of the Town of Benton Heights with the Town of Monroe under the provisions of an Act of the 1945 Session of the Legislature, would have the effect of changing the present school district in which Benton Heights is located.

I have given some study to the Act of the Legislature authorizing the merger of the two municipalities involved and I find no provision affecting the Benton Heights School District. I am of the opinion that the merger of the two municipalities will have no effect upon the Benton Heights School District. The School Machinery Act sets up the procedure to consolidate school districts or to enlarge the same.

SCHOOL TEACHERS; NOTICE OF RE-ELECTION TO TEACHERS; NOTICE OF
ACCEPTANCE; FORM OF NOTICE AND METHOD OF GIVING NOTICE

19 April, 1945.

I reply to your letter of April 16, 1945, in which you enclosed a letter from Mr. J. R. Brown, Superintendent of Hertford County Schools, which letter is dated April 13, 1945.

In his letter, Mr. Brown discusses the changes made at the last Session of the General Assembly with reference to giving notice to school teachers of re-election and the notice required by the teacher of acceptance. In a letter written by a member of the staff of this office on April 4, 1945, on this subject, we said:

"Prior to the 1945 amendment, Section 7 of the School Machinery Act provided that teachers and principals should, within ten days after the close of school, give notice of his or her acceptance of employment for the following year. The 1945 amendment rewrote this portion of Section 7 to provide that notice of acceptance should be given within ten days after notice of re-election.

"The purpose of this notice of acceptance is to afford the school authorities a roster of teachers for the ensuing year. Prior to 1945, teachers and principals were required to give notice of acceptance of employment regardless of whether or not such teachers or principals received notice of re-election. Thus in every case, a teacher or principal who did not receive notice of his rejection was required to give notice of acceptance of employment for the following year.

"Since the notice provision was for the convenience of the school authorities, it is my opinion that the effect of the 1945 amendment is to provide a method of obtaining the notice of acceptance of employment if said school authorities so desire. In other words, under the amendment, the school authorities may obtain notice of acceptance of employment if they so desire and this notice may be obtained by giving notice of re-election to the principals and teachers. The reverse is necessarily true. A teacher or principal is required to give notice of acceptance of employment only when he or she receives notice of his or her re-election.

"Thus, the effect of the 1945 amendment is to remove the absolute duty theretofore placed on teachers and principals of giving notice of acceptance of employment and to provide that they shall give notice of acceptance when they receive notice of their re-election."

The 1945 amendment clearly contemplates that the proper school authorities should give a notice of re-election, and places the burden of notice on the school authorities rather than the teacher. Prior to that time, the teacher was required to give a notice of acceptance and apparently no notice of re-election was required.

In his letter, Mr. Brown states as follows: "The clause of written acceptance within ten days after school closes has become void." I doubt if we should say that the clause of written acceptance has become void because written acceptance is still required on the part of the teacher. The existing law simply makes notice from the school authorities a condition precedent to written acceptance on the part of the teacher.

I think the principal question raised in Mr. Brown's letter is his inquiry as to whether or not notice by registered letter before the close of school in case of nonelection of teachers is still necessary.

It is required by Section 115-359 of the General Statutes, as follows:

"It shall be the duty of such county superintendent or administrative head of a city administrative unit to notify all teachers and/or principals now or hereafter employed, by registered letter, of his or her rejection prior to the close of the school term subject to the allotment of teachers made by the state board of education . . ."

I see nothing whatever in any of the other statutes contained in Chapter 115 of the General Statutes nor have I been able to find any amendment that affects the above quoted provision as to notice of non-election, and I am of the opinion, therefore, that Mr. Brown is correct in that notice by registered letter, as above provided, is still in full force and effect.

I think that we might also add that the notice required by the 1945 amendment to be given to the school teacher would be sufficient if contained in a written letter and mailed to the school teacher, and, as a safeguard, it would perhaps be better if the letter was registered to insure receipt of same. You will note that this statute does not say that this type of notice must be written, nor does it say how the notice should be conveyed to the teacher or served. The other statutes, however, in the Chapter where notice is required, speak of the notice being in writing and also speak of it being served or sent by registered mail; and construing these statutes together, I think that the type of notice required by the amendment to Section 115-354 of the General Statutes should be written in form and either personally handed to the teacher or sent by registered mail.

PER DIEM AND EXPENSES FOR MEMBERS OF THE TEXTBOOK COMMISSION

1 May, 1945.

In conference with you today, you have requested my opinion as to the per diem and expenses liable to the members of the State Textbook Commission appointed by the Governor and State Superintendent of Public Instruction under authority of an Act adopted by the last General Assembly, entitled "An Act to provide for the selection and adoption of textbooks in the public schools, to provide for the selection of a Textbook Commission and other related matters." Section 4 of this Act provides that the Governor and Superintendent may appoint a Textbook Commission. The last sentence of the section is as follows:

"The members shall be paid a per diem and expenses as approved by the board."

The "board" as referred to in this section means, as is clear from a reading of the Act, the State Board of Education. Under this provision the State Board of Education is authorized to approve the per-diem and expenses allowed to the members of the commission which, in effect, gives them the right to fix in advance the per diem and the basis of determining the expenses.

I understand that the State Board of Education plans, if so authorized, to fix the per diem at $7.00 per day. In my; opinion, they would have a right to do this under the terms of this Act.

SCHOOL LAW; SPECIAL SUPPLEMENT; EMPLOYMENT OF RECREATION DIRECTOR; PAYMENT OF SALARY FROM SPECIAL SCHOOL TAX; EMPLOYMENT OF DIRECTOR BEYOND REGULAR SCHOOL TERM

2 July, 1945.

In your letter of June 29, 1945, you transmit to this office a letter of June 28, signed by Mr. Paul S. Cragan, Superintendent of North Wilkesboro Public Schools. Mr. Cragan states that on August 15, 1933, a special tax of twenty cents minimum was voted in North Wilkesboro by way of supplement to the regular State school term. There is a public demand for an enlarged program of athletics, and the people desire a recreation program during the summer months. It is proposed by the board of trustees that the recreation director be employed by the school and that his regular teacher's salary plus a supplement be paid during the nine months' school term, and that he be employed by the town and his salary for the three months as recreation director be paid by the town at the same rate. It was the suggestion of the Superintendent that the supplement for nine months and the full salary for three months be paid from the town general fund. The board of town commissioners, however, wish to finance the full cost of the program by a levy from the special twenty cents school tax which was voted.

Mr. Cragan desires to know if it would be legal to use monies derived from such a levy for the support of a community recreation program during the summer months.

I have examined all the laws dealing with the financing of the State school system and I cannot find any Act that will give legal authority for the payment of an athletic director during the summer months. The employment of such a recreation director as a part of the instructional service of the school to my mind places such a director in the same status as a teacher, and under this situation there is no authority for the application of funds for such a purpose above and beyond the regular one hundred and eighty working days as prescribed by law. This is provided by Section 115-350 of the General Statutes and by other laws and regulations governing the schools and the State Board of Education. There is no authority of law for the use of money derived from this tax levy beyond the regular school term, and the payment of these funds during the summer months when the school is not in session to my mind would be an unauthorized act and the diversion or misapplication of these funds.

SCHOOLS; INSURANCE FOR BUILDINGS DESTROYED BY FIRE;
APPLICATION OF FUNDS

10 July, 1945.

You enclosed in your letter of July 3 a letter from Superintendent G. H. Arnold, of the Thomasville City Schools, in which he writes as follows:

"During the school year 1943-44 a fire occurred in the Kern St. Elementary School. The insurance on this building is carried by the county and was collected by the county. There is something like $14,000 remaining in this fund after all damages have been repaired with the exception of installing seats in the auditorium. I should like to ask the following questions:
"1.   Should the money listed above be placed to the credit of the Thomasville City Administrative Unit?
"2·   Could the money be used for other capital outlay purposes?
"3.   Who would be the approving agency for the expending of this fund for such purposes?
"I shall appreciate any information you can give me regarding the above matter."

The first provision in the last paragraph of Section 115-363 of the General Statutes reads as follows:

"Provided, that funds derived from payments on insurance losses shall be used in the replacement of buildings destroyed, or in the event the buildings are not replaced, said funds shall be used to reduce the indebtedness of the special bond taxing unit to which said payment has been made, or for other capital outlay purposes within said unit."

It will be observed that the three purposes for which money derived from losses occasioned by fire may be used are, to replace the building, reduce the indebtedness, or other capital outlay purposes. In your case, the building has been replaced and, since you do not mention any indebtedness of the district, I assume that no such indebtedness exists. This leaves for our consideration the custody of the fund for its use for other capital outlay purposes.

Section 115-83 of the General Statutes imposes upon the board of county commissioners the responsibility to furnish all school buildings, fully equipped, found by the board to be necessary in the maintenance of a nine months school term in the county, and that the county board of education, as to the county administrative unit, and the board of trustees, as to a city administrative unit, shall present such needs and the cost thereof each year to the county commissioners who shall, in turn, have a reasonable time in which to provide funds which upon investigation they find necessary to provide the respective units with buildings suitably equipped. The burden, therefore, of providing funds for capital outlay purposes in city administrative units, as well as county units, rests upon the board of county commissioners. The county has an insurable interest in the building damaged by fire, as the burden is upon it to provide either a new building or the necessary repairs to the old one. But, in my opinion, the sum necessary to replace the old building or to sufficiently repair it is a discretionary matter for the board of county commissioners.

The county capital outlay school fund, unlike the county-wide current expense and debt service fund, is not apportioned on a per capita enrollment basis but is determined by the board of county commissioners, based upon a showing of need by the respective administrative units (see Section 115-363), so that in your case the responsibility and authority to determine the capital outlay needs of the Thomasville City Administrative Unit rests with the board of county commissioners and unless and until the board determines that there is a need within the district for the purposes of capital outlay, I do not think that the $14,000 could be used for capital outlay beyond the replacing or necessary repairs to the building damaged by fire.

Specifically answering your questions, I conclude, first, that since the insurance was placed on the building and the premium therefor paid by the county board of education, the proceeds therefrom should be placed with the county board of education.

Second and third, as to whether or not said fund may be used for other capital outlay purposes is a matter within the discretion of the board of county commissioners. If the board should find that need exists within the district for said fund to be used as capital outlay, the board should so order. But if it does not so find, I am of the opinion that said fund would remain with the county board of education and constitute a surplus which should be reflected in its next budget.

EXPERT WITNESSES; PSYCHIATRIST'S FEES FOR SERVICES PERFORMED FOR THE COURT

30 July 1945

Reference is made to your letter of July 26, 1945, in which you state that it is necessary to secure the services of physicians, surgeons, and psychiatrists for the examination of persons having vocational disability. You particularly refer to the services of psychiatrists and state that there does not appear to be a working guide relative to the matter of compensation or fees to be paid for such diagnostic and treatment services. You refer to the fact that from time to time the services of psychiatrists are secured in the Superior Courts of our state for the purpose of determining the mental conditions of persons charged with crime.

You inquire of this office if the Superior Courts of the state have established any standards for the purpose of determining the amount of compensation to be paid to psychiatrists for the performance of these services, and you further inquire as to the rates of compensation if such standards. exist.

I have conferred with the members of our staff and have also examined the statutes and the only thing that we have been able to find in regard to the matter is a provision in Section 6-52 of the General Statutes of this state which is as follows:

"*Provided further*, that experts, when compelled to attend and testify, shall be allowed such compensation and mileage as the court may in its discretion order."

So far as I know, there has never existed in this state any standards or criteria for determining the amount of compensation to be paid to experts whose services are required by the court. The matter rests entirely within the discretion of the Superior Court Judge, and it has been my experience in some years of active practice, that the Judge simply evaluates the matter on the basis of the type of expert required, the nature of the expert's information, the length of time required in the performance of the services, and the number of miles that the expert was required to travel to and from the court.

I regret, therefore, that we cannot be of any service to you in this matter, and I am sure that you will agree with me that the present law does not contemplate any particular standards other than the discretion and judgment of the Judge of the Superior Court.

SCHOOLS; CAPITAL OUTLAY; LEXINGTON CITY ADMINISTRATIVE UNIT;
CONTRACTS AND SUPERVISION OF EXPENDITURE OF FUNDS

2 August 1945

I have your letter of July 31 enclosing the letter from Mr. Paul F. Evans, County Superintendent in Davidson County, in which he inquires as to whether or not, under the present law, a county board of education has any supervision over the expenditure of capital outlay set up for buildings in the city administrative unit.

This question is answered by the following quotation from G.S. 115-84:

"The building of all new schoolhouses and the repairing of all old schoolhouses over which the county board of education has jurisdiction shall be under the control and direction of and by contract with the county board of education, *provided, however*, that in the building of all new schoolhouses and the repairing of all old schoolhouses which may be located in a city administrative unit, the building of such new schoolhouses and the repairing of such old schoolhouses shall be under the control and direction of and by contract with the board of education or the board of trustees having jurisdiction over said city administrative unit."

The words, "board of education" appearing in the proviso of this section mean the governing body of the city administrative unit and not the county board of education as shown by the reading of the entire section. I have discussed this matter with you and your knowledge of the legislative history of the enactment of this proviso, and I feel that we agree that this construction is correct.

SCHOOLS; EXCLUSION OF PUPILS ON ACCOUNT OF MARRIAGE

17 August 1945

I acknowledge receipt of your letter enclosing a letter from Superintendent Frank B. Aycock, Jr., of the Currituck County Schools, in which he states that there are a number of pupils of the schools of the county who have married and wish to remain as students. Mr. Aycock says that some of the pupils have made quite a nuisance of themselves and that some of the members of the Board have considered the desirability of denying to such pupils the right to attend school. He inquires as to whether or not the County Board of Education would have the right to pass a regulation prohibiting the attendance of such pupils in the public schools of the county.

While Section 115-145 G.S., empowers a teacher in a school not having a principal, or the principal of a school to suspend a pupil who wilfully and persistently violates the rules of the school or who may be guilty of immoral or disreputable conduct, or who may be a menace to the school, I do not think that the mere fact that a pupil is married is sufficient within itself to warrant his or her dismissal, and certainly not when the regulation passed by the County Board of Education is one denying to all married students the right to attend the schools of the county.

However, I am of the opinion that under the provisions of Section 115-145 G.S., the proper official could in any particular case in which it is thought that the conduct of the particular pupil is such as to make his or her presence in the school a menace to the school, such pupil might be dismissed. But if the pupil has been lawfully married the fact of the marriage will not, in my opinion, in itself be sufficient to justify the conclusion that such pupil was a menace to the school.

I can well appreciate the difficulties of the school in which a situation such as exists in your school may produce and the disorganization which might result from it, but in my opinion the dismissal must be considered purely from an individual basis and on the facts of the particular case under consideration.

SCHOOLS; TEACHERS' AGE; COMPULSORY VACCINATIONS

20 August 1945

I acknowledge receipt of your letter enclosing a letter from Superintendent M. H. Bowles, of the Haywood County Schools, raising two questions which he desires to be answered.

Superintendent Bowles first inquires as to whether or not, under the circumstances set out in his letter, he may employ in the public schools of the county, a teacher under 18 years of age.

Section 115-152 G.S., says, "No certificate to teach shall be issued to any person under 18 years of age." In the case of HAMPTON v. BOARD

OF EDUCATION, 195 N. C. 213, the North Carolina Supreme Court in discussing the legal essentials of a valid teacher's contract imposing the liability upon the county, said that a teacher must be at least 18 years of age.

Superintendent Bowles further inquires as to whether or not persons of certain religious faiths may be required to comply with the statutes relating to compulsory vaccination as a condition precedent to entrance into the public schools of the county.

All children of all religious faiths may be required to fully comply with the statutes as to vaccinations for all diseases except that of diphtheria. Section 130-190 G.S., which deals with the subject of immunization of children as to diphtheria, provides in the last paragraph, "This section shall not apply to children whose parent or parents, or guardian are bona fide members of a religious organization whose teachings are contrary to the practices herein required, and no certificates for admission to any public, private or parochial school shall be required of them." As I say, even the children of such religious teachings are exempt only as to the vaccination requirements of diphtheria. There was an Act by the 1945 session of the Legislature which I am satisfied intended to strike out this exemption as to diphtheria but this Act amended a section which does not deal with those who are exempt from the provisions of the section so that I am of the opinion that the 1945 Act is not sufficient to require the vaccination for diphtheria of children whose parents or guardians are bona fide members of a religious organization whose teachings are contrary to the practices provided in the pertinent sections of the statute.

PRIVATE SCHOOLS; EXTENT OF STATE CONTROL OF PRIVATE SCHOOLS; USE OF STATE ADOPTED TEXTBOOKS BY PRIVATE SCHOOLS

27 September 1945

In your letter of September 20, 1945, you enclose letter of R. L. Patton, Superintendent of Schools, in Morganton, N. C., which is as follows:

"Does the law require private schools to get permission from the County Board of Education to operate, and are they required to use the state adopted books? We have two small schools in this County and I would like to know what my duty is toward them."

We have examined the school law of North Carolina as contained in Chapter 115 of the General Statutes and the amendments of the General Assembly of 1945. With reference to private schools, we find only the following:

1. Under the provisions of Section 115-302, all private schools receiving and instructing children of compulsory school age must keep such records of attendance and render such reports of the attendance of such children as are required of public schools. If a private school or a tutor neglects carrying out the duties as to records and attendance, then the attendance of such school shall not be accepted in lieu of attendance at a public school. It should also be noted that the course of instruction of such a school should run concurrently with the term of the public schools in the district and extend for at least as long a term. It would seem to me, therefore,

that unless private schools perform their duty as to reports and attendance, then the general compulsory attendance law of the State and its penalties would be operative.

2. It is provided by Section 115-62 that certain subjects must be taught in elementary schools, such as spelling, reading, writing, grammar, languages and composition, English, arithmetic, drawing, etc. It is further provided in this Section that the State Superintendent of Public Instruction shall prepare a course of study outlining these and other subjects that may be taught in elementary schools, arranging the subjects by grades and classes. The Statute then provides that the Board of Education shall require these subjects in both public and private schools to be taught in the English language and it is declared to be a misdemeanor for any teacher or principal to refuse to conduct his recitations in the English language. After the State Superintendent of Public Instruction has prepared his courses of instructions as outlined above, then it would seem to be the duty of the County Board of Education to require these subjects to be taught in private schools as well as public schools in the English language.

3. It is provided by Section 115-135 that the school committee, with the approval of the County Superintendent, may enter into a contract with a private school regularly conducted for at least six months in the year, sectarian or denominational schools excepted, for instruction of pupils of the district, between the ages of six and twenty-one years, without charge to pupils and free of tuition.

4. It appears to be the function of the State Board of Education to examine into the course of study, certificates and eligibility of teachers of private schools before these schools can be listed as accredited schools and affecting the right of these students to enter a State College.

Other than the references noted above, I have been unable to find any other provisions of law regulating private schools. I do not, of course, consider the question of commercial and correspondence schools. I am unable to find any law whatsoever which gives the State or any of its subdivisions, as related to public schools, the authority to control the selection of textbooks and my answer to the first question of Mr. Patton's is that private schools are not required to use State adopted textbooks. I find nothing in the law that compels private schools to obtain permission from the County Board of Education before such schools can be operated. It may be that some provisions have escaped my attention and if so I will be glad to correct this letter if it should turn out that you remember some provision that I have not incorporated herein.

SCHOOL LAW; PUBLIC HEALTH; HOUSE BILLS NOS. 316, 317, 319; IMMUNIZATION OF CHILDREN AGAINST WHOOPING COUGH, DIPHTHERIA AND SMALL POX; PENALTIES FOR ADMISSION OF CHILDREN TO PUBLIC SCHOOLS WITHOUT IMMUNIZATION OR VACCINATION

29 September 1945

I reply to your letter of September 25, 1945. In your letter you state as follows:

"I should like to know whether children can be required to be vaccinated for small pox, diphtheria, and whooping cough before entering school."

You also enclose letter from Mr. B. H. Duncan, Superintendent of Schools for Ashe County, which is as follows:

"A few parents of my county are refusing to have beginners vaccinated for small pox, diphtheria, and whooping cough as is required by law, before entering school. They insist on sending these children to school in violation of the law. I have instructed all teachers to enroll none of those who have failed to comply with the statutes. I should like advice from you as to what we can do with this problem, and shall be glad to follow your instructions."

I am enclosing to you copy of a letter written to Dr. Carl V. Reynolds, State Health Officer, in which the Act relating to immunization against whooping cough was analyzed by this office. I hope that this letter will be of some service to you.

In regard to whooping cough, the General Assembly of North Carolina for 1945, by House Bill No. 316, added a new article to sub-chapter 3 of chapter 130 of the General Statutes, which new article is designated as "Art. 16A. Whooping Cough." The copy of the letter addressed to Dr. Reynolds enclosed herewith explains the law with reference to this disease. As far as the public schools are concerned, no principal or teacher can permit a child to attend a public, private or parochial school without a certificate of immunization or some other acceptable evidence of immunization against whooping cough. It is the duty of parents, guardians or other persons in loco parentis to see that the child is immunized and the wilful violation of any of this law by parents, guardians or teachers is a misdemeanor. So far as I can see, the only enforcement method available is to prosecute a criminal indictment against the parent, guardian or person in loco parentis and to refuse to permit the child to attend school. The punishment is a fine of not more than $50.00 or imprisonment of not more than thirty days, in the discretion of the court.

Referring to diphtheria, I think that this is governed by Section 130-186 of the General Statutes and Sections following which extend through Section 130-190 of the General Statutes. The pertinent Section is Section 130-190 which provides that a parent or guardian of a child between the ages of six months and twelve months must have the child immunized as to this disease. It further provides that the parents or guardian of any child between the ages of twelve months and five years who has not been previously immunized shall have the immunizing agents administered to the child. Provision is made for this service by the health officer in indigent cases. This Section was amended in 1945 by striking out the fifth paragraph and inserting a new paragraph which requires the physician administering the immunizing agent to give a certificate to the local health or quarantine officer and a copy to the parent, guardian or person in loco parentis. It is further provided in this amendment that no principal or teacher shall allow a child to enter a public school without this certificate or some other acceptable evidence of immunization against diphtheria. A violation of this Section of the diphtheria law is a misdemeanor punishable by a fine of not more than $50.00 or imprisonment of not more than thirty days, in the discretion of the court. I call your attention, however, to the fact that this section does not apply to parents or guardians who are bona fide members of a religious organization whose teachings are contrary to the practice required by the Section and no certificate for admission to public schools is required as to children of such parents.

As to small pox, this disease was formerly covered by Section 130-183 of the General Statutes. This Section was entirely rewritten by the General Assembly of 1945. It now provides that all children in North Carolina must be immunized for small pox before attending any public school. Parents or guardians are required as to children not previously immunized to have the same carried out. There is provision for the performance of this service by the County Health Officer or County Physician, if the person is unable to pay for the services. The physician administering the vaccine must submit a certificate to the local health or quarantine officer and give a copy to the parent, guardian or person in loco parentis. No principal or teacher can permit any child to enter a public school without its certificate of immunization or some other acceptable evidence of immunization against small pox. If a physician certifies that a vaccination would be detrimental to a child's health, then the vaccination can, be postponed until it is found to be no longer detrimental. Wilful violation of any part of the Act on the part of anyone is punishable by a fine of not more than $50.00 or by imprisonment of not more than thirty days.

So far as I can see as to all of these diseases, the only enforcement is by means of a criminal prosecution against the parents or guardian, and, of course, a principal or teacher who allows children to attend the public schools without immunization would be indictable. The principal or teacher can refuse to admit the child until the provisions of the law as to these diseases have been carried out. The violations must be wilful. There does not seem to be any compulsory method by which the public authorities can forcibly seize the child and carry it to a physician for immunization. Criminal indictment and compelling the child to remain out of school are the only methods available.

STATE BOARD OF EDUCATION; ADOPTION OF BASAL TEXTBOOKS FOR
PRIMARY GRADES

4 October 1945

I received your letter of October 2, requesting my opinion as to whether the State Board of Education could adopt for basal use both sets of two level series of readers for the primary grades and buy one-half of the requirements for each level, thus buying no larger total of books than if a single level series were adopted.

G.S. 115-258, under Article 37 of Chapter 115, dealing with textbooks for elementary grades, provides that the State Board of Education is hereby authorized to adopt for the exclusive use in the public elementary schools of North Carolina textbooks and publications, including instructional material, to meet the needs of the schools in each grade and on each subject matter in which instruction is required to be given by law. The statute then provides: "and shall adopt for a period of five years from a multiple list submitted by the Textbook Commission, as hereinafter provided, two basal primers for the first grade and two basal readers for each of the first three grades, and one basal book or series of books on all other subjects contained in the outlined course of study for the elementary grades where a basal book or books are recommended for use . .."

It is my understanding that the State Board of Education has heretofore adopted one basal reader for each of the first three grades and that it is now proposed to adopt, under the authority of the statute, one additional basal reader for each of the first three grades and that the question arises whether, in making this adoption, the State Board of Education could legally adopt for each grade two separate volumes or books on different levels for each of the three grades.

It is my opinion, after a careful study of the statute, that the adoption must be limited to one additional book for each of the three grades, as this is literally, and I think purposely, the intention of the statute. If the adoption could be made of more than one book in each grade, it could be expanded without limitation and evidently the General Assembly purposely provided for two basal books in this adoption for each of the first three grades as it provides for one basal book or series of books for all other subjects contained in the outlined course of study for elementary grades where a basal book or books are recommended for use.

This conclusion is in accord with the letter sent to the publishers by Dr. Clyde A. Erwin, State Superintendent, under date of April 9, 1945, in which he states that the State Board of Education has requested the Textbook Commission to prepare as soon as possible valuation reports of basal books for the following subjects:

"ELEMENTARY
Reading. A series of basal readers for grades 1 through 3; including one pre-primer, one primer, and one reader each for grades 1, 2, and 3."

On June 30, 1945, a letter to the publishers of textbooks contains the same language. I, therefore, could not think that the adoption of more than one additional book would be permitted or authorized by the statute.

SCHOOLS; AUTHORITY OF BOARD MEMBER OVER TEACHERS

8 October 1945

I have your letter of October 4, enclosing a letter of October 1 to you from R. W. Carver, Superintendent of Hickory City Schools.

The individual members of a board of trustees of a city administrative unit have no authority whatever over the teachers in the schools or of the operations of the school. The board members' authority is confined to that which is exercised in meetings of the board in its sessions and, outside of these meetings, an individual board member has no official responsibility.

You are, of course, familiar with the responsibilities and the varied duties of the board of trustees of a city administrative unit as a board and I will not attempt to enumerate these responsibilities, but all of their functions and duties must be exercised in regularly constituted meetings of the board. The same rule would be applicable to the board of trustees of a city administrative unit or to a county board of education as that governing a board of county commissioners. As individuals, they have no authority whatever to act for the county except as a body and when in legal session.

ROCKINGHAM COUNTY v. LUTEN BRIDGE CO., 35 Fed. 301, 66 A.L.R. 735; LONDON v. BOARD OF COMMISSIONERS OF YANCEY COUNTY, 193 N. C. 100; O'NEAL v. WAKE COUNTY, 196 N. C. 184.

The selection of principals and teachers must be made in the manner prescribed by our statute, G.S. 115-354, and the board members in performing the duties prescribed for the board in this section can act only when in legal session.

SCHOOLS; CURRENT EXPENSE FUNDS; BASIS OF ALLOCATION TO CITY ADMINISTRATIVE UNITS

9 October 1945

You have sent me a letter to you from Mr. N. F. Steppe, Superintendent of Public Instruction of McDowell County, in which Mr. Steppe asks you to advise him as to the basis of per capita allotment of current expense funds to city administrative units. He states in his letter that it has been his understanding that the county budget constituted the basis of the appropriation, the county schools and the city schools receiving the same per capita appropriation as to current expense.

Mr. Steppe's statement is, I think, entirely correct. The statute, G.S. 115-363, provides that all county-wide current expense school funds shall be apportioned to county and city administrative units monthly, and it shall be the duty of the county treasurer to remit such funds monthly as collected to each administrative unit located in said county on a per capita enrollment basis.

The illustration used by Mr. Steppe, I think, is apt in describing the procedure for making this allocation. His illustration is as follows:

If in a county there are 2,000 pupils enrolled in the schools of the county administrative unit and the budget as filed by the Board of Education and approved by the Board of Commissioners provides for an appropriation for current expense of $20,000.00, this would be $10.00 per capita. This $10.00 per capita must be paid to the city administrative unit for each student enrolled in such administrative unit and the county would, therefore, have to levy taxes necessary to provide for these payments, less the estimated receipts from fines, forfeitures, penalties, poll and dog taxes and funds for vocational subjects which are included in the current expense.

I think that Mr. Steppe has correctly summarized the law on this subject in his letter, which I am returning. This conclusion is reached by the Supreme Court of this State in the case of SCHOOL TRUSTEES v. BENNER, 222 N. C. 566. In the opinion in this case by Mr. Justice Seawell, Section 178 of Chapter 136 of the Public Laws of 1923 is quoted, which provides:

"The County Board of Education shall allow for current expense, except as otherwise provided herein, the same per capita amount per pupil enrolled for the previous school year to the special charter districts that is allowed to all other schools of the county . . ."

In connection with this the Court says:

". . . However, the principle upon which county-wide taxes were apportioned under the earlier law is fundamentally just and is preserved in the current School Machinery Act, which, after successive amendments . . . reads as follows:

"'All county-wide current expense school funds shall be apportioned to County and City Administrative Units monthly and it shall be the duty of the County Treasurer. to remit such funds monthly as collected to each Administrative Unit located in said county on a per capita enrollment basis . . .' "

SCHOOLS; AGE OF ENROLLMENT; COUNTY BOARD MAY PRESCRIBE REGULATIONS AS TO PROOF OF AGE

11 October 1945

I acknowledge receipt of your letter enclosing a letter from Superintendent J. G. Allen of the Carteret County Schools, in which he sets out in detail certain facts relating to the admission of pupils in the public schools of Carteret County who have not attained the age of six years. Superintendent Allen says that he has reached the following conclusions:

"(1) That the law puts upon the parent the burden of proof as to the beginner's age;

(2) That a beginner should not have been enrolled or kept on the class roll more than one week in the absence of satisfactory evidence of the data of the child's birth;

(3) That, under the circumstances, the parents involved be given two weeks from date to present to the teacher, for the beginner involved, either the child's birth certificate or a satisfactory statement relative thereto by the attending physician;

(4) That it is the duty of the principal to exclude from school beginners whose parents refuse or neglect to furnish satisfactory evidence as to the beginner's age;

(5) That it is lawful to exclude *now* such children as were not 'entitled to enrollment in the public schools' when the current school year opened on Sept. 6, and, therefore, are not now entitled to enrollment even though they have been in attendance from the opening day and even though they may have become 6 years of age since Oct. 1."

Section 115-371 of the General Statutes provides:

"Children to be entitled to enrollment in the public schools for the school year 1939-40 and each year thereafter, must be six years of age on or before October 1 in the year in which they enroll and must enroll during the first month of the school year."

Under the provisions of the quoted section, I agree with Superintendent Allen as to his fourth and fifth conclusions; that is, that it is the duty of the principal to exclude from school beginners whose parents refuse to furnish satisfactory evidence as to the beginner's age and that children who entered school under six years of age prior to October 1, 1945, may now be excluded from the school even though they have become six years of age since October 1.

As to the other conclusions reached by Superintendent Allen, which deal largely with the type of proof necessary to determine the age of the child seeking admission to school, it seems to me that while the requirements and conditions suggested by him are reasonable, it is a matter upon which the County Board of Education should promulgate rules and regulations. I understand that the State Board of Education has not promulgated rules and regulations as to the proof necessary to admit a beginner in school so that under the provisions of Article 6 of Chapter 115 of the General Statutes, the County Board of Education may legislate on this question as this article gives the several county boards general supervision over and power to operate and administer the public school system of the county subject only to rules and regulations adopted by the State Board in conflict therewith.

SCHOOLS; HEALTH; VENEREAL DISEASE; NO AUTHORITY TO REQUIRE WASSERMAN TEST

15 October 1945.

I acknowledge receipt of your letter enclosing a letter from Superintendent Frank B. Aycock, Jr., of the Currituck County schools, in which he inquires as to the authority to require Wasserman tests as a condition precedent to remaining in school and raises the following questions:

"1. May the Board of Education direct that such tests be made on pupils attending school?
2. If the answer to No. 1 is 'no,' may the Board of Health direct that such tests be made when considered advisable by the Health Officer?
3. If the answer to both No. 1 and No. 2 is in the negative, may the Board of Education set up as a requirement for ninth grade health and physical education that the pupil demonstrate his physical fitness and include in this demonstration a health examination and a Wasserman test?"

I am of the opinion that the first question must be answered in the negative. The sections of the General Statutes dealing with the authority of school officials to require evidence of vaccination or immunization of school children are found in Articles 15 and 16 and these sections do not contain any provision for requiring children to subject themselves to a Wasserman test.

I am of the opinion that the Board of Health does not have authority to require all of the children of the school to subject themselves to such a test. The authority of State, county, and municipal health officers in this respect is found in Section 130-206 of the General Statutes and is limited to making examinations of *persons reasonably suspected* of being infected with venereal disease. Under the authority contained in this section, the proper health officials could require Wasserman tests of those pupils who are not reasonably suspected of being infected with venereal disease.

I am likewise of the opinion that the Board of Education could not adopt regulations which in effect would require children to take Wasserman tests but, of course, if the Board had in mind a person reasonably suspected of being infected with venereal disease, such person could be required to submit himself or herself for an examination and be detained until the results thereof are known and require such person to report for treatment until cured.

STATE BOARD OF EDUCATION; ADOPTION OF BASAL TEXTBOOKS FOR PRIMARY GRADES

15 October, 1945.

I have your letter of October 13 in which you enclosed copy of the resolution passed by the State Board of Education at its meeting on October 4, and I note your request that I furnish you a written opinion confirming the oral opinion given by me in the meeting of the State Board of Education, to the effect that the Board had the legal authority to adopt the resolution, which is as follows:

"That the State Board of Education shall adopt the Basic Readers published by Scott, Foresman and Company—*We Come and Go*, pre-primer, bound with *Fun With Dick and Jane*, primer; *Our New Friends*, first reader; Basic Reader Grade II, two parts in one binding, viz. *Friends and Neighbors and More Friends and Neighbors;* Basic Readers, grade III, two parts in one binding, viz. *Streets and Roads and More Streets and Roads;* and that the publisher shall be obligated to supply the two parts·of the second grade Basic Reader in separate bindings and the two parts of the Third Grade Basic Reader in separate bindings, provided that the total cost to the State of the parts bound separately shall not exceed the cost of the single volume for each grade; provided, further, that the purchases of the separate parts for each grade shall be made in accordance with the recommendations of the Textbook Commission."

I do not consider that the adoption made conflicts with the opinion expressed in my letter to you of October 4, 1945, as the publisher had offered bound in one volume each of the books adopted. The fact that the resolution provided that the publisher shall be obligated to supply the two parts of the second grade basic reader in separate bindings, and the two parts of the third grade basic reader in separate bindings, the total cost to the State of the parts bound separately not to exceed the cost of a single volume for each grade, would not violate any provisions of the statutes, in my opinion.

SCHOOLS; TEACHERS; DISMISSAL

29 October, 1945.

You enclosed in your letter of October 22, a letter from Superintendent L. S. Inscoe, of the Nash County Schools, in which he states that one of the teachers in his system obtained a leave from her duties to visit her husband who had recently returned from overseas, but did not come back at the end of the week and notified the principal that she would not be back for a month; and that she did not provide a teacher as substitute. Superintendent Inscoe further states that the principal desires to dismiss the teacher and employ someone else in her place, and inquires as to the authority to dismiss the teacher under the circumstances of this case.

You will find the authority to dismiss teachers under Section 115-143 of the General Statutes which reads as follows:

"The school committee of a district or board of trustees of a city administrative unit, with the approval of the superintendent, may dismiss a teacher for immoral or disreputable conduct in the community or for failure to comply with the provisions of the contract. The superintendent, with the approval of the committee or the board of trustees, has authority, and it is his duty, to dismiss a teacher who may prove himself or herself incompetent or may wilfully refuse to discharge the duties of a public school teacher, or who may be persistently neglectful of such duties. But no teacher shall be dismissed until charges have been filed in writing in the office of the superintendent. The superintendent shall give the teacher at least five days notice, in which time he or she shall have the opportunity to appear before the committee or board of trustees of the district or unit in which the teacher is teaching. And after a full and fair hearing, the action of the committee or board of trustees shall be final; Provided, the teacher shall be given the right to appeal to the county board of education or to the courts."

It will be observed that the responsibility in respect to dismissal of teachers rests upon the school committee and the superintendent and as to whether or not the teacher in the instant case may be dismissed involves to a large extent the exercise of discretion in determining whether or not the teacher has violated the provisions of the section to the extent that she may be dismissed; and since it does require the exercise of discretion, I do not want to venture a specific answer to the question raised by Mr. Inscoe. It seems to me that many things should be taken into consideration to determine whether or not the teacher has violated the terms of her contract or of the section; for instance, it seems to me that the board should take into consideration the length of time required for the teacher to go to and from the camp in which her husband was stationed. I can appreciate the extent to which the orderly conduct of the school would be interrupted by teachers consistently absenting themselves from their duties but I also think a great deal of patience must be shown in cases in which the husband and wife have been separated for a long period of time because of the service of the husband overseas and their natural desire and inclination to be together for a reasonable length of time upon the return of the soldier to this country. But I must repeat that it is a matter in which the school committee and the superintendent should exercise their best discretion and judgment in solving this problem and I do not think that I could unqualifiedly express an opinion unless I were more familiar with all the facts and details in this particular case.

SCHOOLS; DISCIPLINE ON SCHOOL BUSES

1 November, 1945.

I have your letter of October 31st, enclosing a letter from Mr. T. T. Murphy, Superintendent of Schools of Pender County, in which Mr. Murphy states the question has arisen as to the right of a public school teacher who drives a bus to discipline, by inflicting corporal punishment, a child riding on the bus, and the extent to which such corporal punishment could go. Mr. Murphy asks to be advised as to what a regular non-teaching bus driver and a combination teacher and bus driver can do to enforce the rules and regulations on a bus when the children violate the same.

You are familiar with the general rule enforced by our Courts as declared in the case of STATE v. PENDERGRASS, 19 N. C. 365, to the effect that the law confides to school masters and teachers a discretionary power in the infliction of punishment upon their pupils, and will not hold them responsible criminally unless the punishment be such as to occasion permanent injury to the child or to be inflicted merely to gratify their own evil passions. This case has been cited with approval by numerous cases, including the case of STATE v. STAFFORD, 113 N. C. 635.

This discretionary authority of a teacher over the pupils extends to enforcement of rules or discipline of the school on the school grounds, and in my opinion would likewise extend to pupils on a school bus on which the teacher was riding, either as a passenger or as a driver of the bus. The school children while riding on the bus are under the same degree of authority and supervision of the school authorities as they would be while on the school grounds during school hours or in the school rooms.

The rule of law stated by our Court in STATE v. PENDERGRASS would be applicable to the authority of a school teacher in inflicting corporal punishment on a child while riding on a bus, and such punishment must be considered in the light of that decision in determining whether or not the punishment exceeded the authority of the teacher.

In my opinion, a non-teaching bus driver has no authority to inflict corporal punishment on school children while riding on the bus, but that in such cases as might be deemed necessary the conduct of the pupils justifying such punishment should be reported to the principal of the school for such discipline as might be deemed by him necessary. It is my opinion that a non-teaching school bus driver would, however, have authority to require proper conduct on the part of the pupils riding on the school bus, and in the event they persisted in conduct such as to endanger the safety of other pupils riding on the bus or make the presence of such pupils so offending intolerable, the driver of the bus would have the right to require such child to leave the bus, and report the conduct to the superintendent. I do not think the law would permit a non-teaching bus driver to exercise the authority, however, of corporal punishment.

It is my opinion that the school authorities would have the right to adopt and enforce reasonable rules and regulations as to the conduct of pupils riding on the school bus to and from school.

SCHOOLS; ATTENDANCE LAW; EFFECTIVE DATE;
CHAPTER *826*, SESSION LAWS, *1945*

6 November, 1945. ´

I acknowledge receipt of your letter enclosing a letter from Superintendent Frank B. Aycock, Jr., of the Currituck County schools, inquiring as to the effective date of certain of the provisions of Chapter 826 of the Sessions Laws of 1945, which provide that the provisions of the Act shall not apply for the duration of the war and six months thereafter.

I construe the words, "Shall not apply for the duration of the war and six months thereafter," as applied to Chapter 826, to mean that the provisions of the Act shall not be in force until six months after the signing of the peace treaty or six months after the proclamation of the President to the effect that the state of war has terminated, or upon the adoption by Congress of a resolution declaring the war to have terminated. And, of course, as of this date neither of these conditions have taken place.

EDUCATION; COMPULSORY ATTENDANCE LAW; VENUE OR PLACE OF TRIAL

8 November, 1945.

In a letter from J. A. Best, Superintendent of Public Welfare of Wayne County, it is stated that a child of a parent living in another County has been assigned to a school in Wayne County. The child has been reported as being continuously absent from school and the Superintendent of Public Welfare of Wayne County has been asked to prosecute under the school attendance law.

We have been asked to advise if the Superintendent of Public Welfare of Wayne County has the responsibility of prosecuting the parent in a criminal action for failure to comply with the compulsory attendance law under these circumstances.

In our opinion, the order transferring or assigning the child to a school in another County, that is in a County other than the County where the parent lives, does not effect the usual procedure in such cases. It is our thought that if the parent is criminally responsible for failing to comply with the compulsory attendance law that such failure occurred in the County where the parent lives and not in the County where the child attends school. If the parent is prosecuted, the indictment should be obtained and the trial had in the County where the parent lives, and the school authorities in Wayne County should furnish the prosecuting officer with the necessary evidence as to the reports of unlawful absence, which reports constitute prima facie evidence of the violation of the compulsory attendance article, as will be seen from Section 115-306.

I think that the prosecuting officer in the County where the parent lives should be furnished with a proper copy of the order placing the child in the Wayne County school. Your attention is called to the fact that under the case of State vs. Lewis, 194 N. C. 620, that such an indictment must also allege that such child has not attended private schools for the required period since under the compulsory attendance law the parent may send his child to the public schools or provide schools with curricula approved by the County Superintendent of Public Instruction or the State Board of Education.

SCHOOLS; BOARD OF TRUSTEES; RIGHT TO SELECT VICE-CHAIRMAN

23 November, 1945.

I received your letter of November 20, enclosing a letter from Superintendent James E. Holmes, stating that the Chairman of the Board of Trustees of the Leaksville Township Public Schools has been absent on account of illness and inquiring if a vice-chairman could be appointed to act for him during his absence in signing vouchers, etc.

The organization of the Board of Trustees of this district is controlled by the act which created the board which under the school laws became the administrative board of the city administrative unit. This act is Chapter 152, Private Laws of 1925. Section 4 (a) of this act provides that the Board of Trustees of the Leaksville Township Public School District shall have the power to select a chairman from their number whose duty it shall be to preside at all meetings of the Board of Trustees and to select a vice-chairman whose duty it shall be to preside in the absence of the chairman. This act, therefore, authorizes the appointment of a vice-chairman by the Board of Trustees who shall perform the duties of the chairman in his absence, including the signing of vouchers, etc.

I find no other act affecting the creation of the Board of Trustees of the Leaksville Township Public Schools and I assume that this is the one under which the school is organized.

SCHOOLS; OPERATION OF SCHOOL BUS; LIABILITY OF STATE AND COUNTY FOR INJURIES SUSTAINED IN OPERATION

21 January, 1946.

I acknowledge receipt of your letter enclosing a letter from Superintendent Frank B. Aycock, Jr., of the Currituck County Schools, in which he inquires as to the liability of a county board of education for injuries sustained in connection with the operation of a school bus.

The statutory provision for payment for injuries sustained in connection with the operation of a school bus is limited to the liability of the State Board of Education which provides for compensation for children injured under the circumstances provided for in Sections 115-340 to 115-346.

The State nor its agencies, such as the State Board of Education, cannot be sued by a citizen without the State's consent and such consent has not been given by the State or the State Board of Education for injuries sustained in connection with the operation of school busses. See PRUDENTIAL INSURANCE COMPANY v. POWELL, 217 N. C. 494; CHEMICAL COMPANY v. BOARD OF EDUCATION, 111 N. C. 135; GRANVILLE COUNTY BOARD OF EDUCATION v. STATE BOARD OF EDUCATION, 106 N. C. 81.

There is no statute which authorizes county boards of education to assume and pay for injuries sustained in the operation of the school busses of the State and the county is not liable for any damages growing out of tort, being a political subdivision of the State. Further, under the school bus law the control and management of all facilities for the transportation of public school children is vested in the State Board of Education so that there could be no liability on the counties which have no legal responsibility in the operation of the school busses.

I, therefore, advise you that a county board of education is not liable for, nor may it legally pay damages for injuries sustained in connection with the operation of a school bus. Of course, we are not here concerned with the liability of the operator of the bus and I might add that if the injuries were sustained because of the negligent operation of the bus by the driver, such driver might be personally liable to the injured party.

COMMISSIONER OF PUBLIC TRUST; SALE OF ATHLETIC
SUPPLIES TO ATHLETIC ASSOCIATION BY MEMBER
OF SCHOOL BOARD

25 January, 1946.

I acknowledge receipt of your letter enclosing a letter from Superintendent E. S. Johnson of the Washington City Administrative Unit, in which he inquires if a high school athletic association has authority to purchase athletic equipment from a concern partially owned and operated by a member of the Board of School Trustees and pay for the same out of athletic association funds.

The statute applicable to your situation, Section 14-234 of the General Statutes, reads as follows:

"If any person, appointed or elected a commissioner or director to discharge any trust wherein the state or any county, city or town may be in any manner interested, shall become an undertaker, or make any contract for his own benefit, under such authority, or be in any manner concerned or interested in making such contract, or in the profits thereof, either privately or openly, singly or jointly with-another, he shall be guilty of a misdemeanor. Provided, that this section shall not apply to public officials transacting business with banks or banking institutions in regular course of business: Provided further, that such undertaking or contracting shall be authorized by said governing board."

As to whether or not the proposition outlined in your letter is in violation of the quoted section depends upon the facts and circumstances involved. One of the things which should be taken into consideration is whether or not the member of the Board of Trustees is an officer in or the manager of the business or a mere stockholder. In STATE v. WILLIAMS, 153 N. C. 595, in which the defendant was a member of the governing body of the City of New Bern and an officer and manager of the corporation with which the city was trading, the Court upheld the conviction of the defendant but pointed out that it was not passing upon whether or not a person who was a mere stockholder would be guilty. So far as I am able to determine, our courts have not yet held that a mere stockholder would be liable.

If the member of the School Board is an officer or manager of the business and if the high school athletic association is subject to the control of the School Board and purchases made by it are approved by the Board, I think that it would be a violation of the pertinent section of the statute for purchases to be made by the Board from a business owned and managed by one of its members.

On the other hand, if the athletic association is an independent organization and not subject to the jurisdiction of the School Board, and no school funds are used, and purchases are made from the funds of the association without the approval or sanction of the Board, I am of the opinion that the provisions of this section would not be violated, even though the member of the Board was an officer, owner or operator of the business. The latter portion of the pertinent section reads, "Provided further, that such undertaking or contracting shall be authorized by said governing board." so that it is apparent if the board is not required and does not approve the purchases made by the athletic association, neither the offending member or other members of the Board would be in violation of the provisions of the statute.

Because of the severe penalty imposed for the violation of the pertinent section of the statute, this office has followed the policy of advising members of governing boards to refrain from what might be considered as even "appearances of evil" and not to serve on such board if the member in any way has any interest in the financial success of a corporation or business with which the governing board expects to make purchases.

In the Williams case it was also observed that there was no evidence of moral turpitude upon the part of the defendant but that such was not necessary nor was the fact as to whether or not the defendant made any profit on the transaction necessary in order to sustain a conviction but that it was sufficient for a sale to be made by one person interested in the proceeds of the contract of sale or any part thereof.

SCHOOLS; LIABILITY OF COUNTY BOARD FOR TORT; LIABILITY
INSURANCE ON SCHOOL BUSES

11 February, 1946

I acknowledge receipt of your letter enclosing a letter from Superintendent Frank B. Aycock, Jr., of the Currituck County Schools in which he acknowledges receipt of my opinion of January 21 in which I stated that the County School Board and the State School Board were immune to liability arising out of injuries or damages sustained in connection with a school bus collision.

Superintendent Aycock now inquires as to whether or not the County Board of Education could purchase liability insurance on the several school buses and pay the premium on the same.

I see no reason why liability insurance should be purchased by the county board of education as the county is not liable for tort damages and an insurance carrier would only be liable to the extent of the liability of its principal and since the principal is not liable, the insurance company standing in the shoes of the principal would not be liable.

As an alternative, Superintendent Aycock inquires as to whether or not the County Board of Education could require the operators of the several school buses in the county to carry a policy protecting the operators and the public against injuries and damages sustained in their operation and to require the school bus operators to pay the premium on the policy.

Section 115-374 of the General Statutes places the responsibility for the transportation of the school children of the State upon the State Board of Education and not the County Board. The operators of the school buses are employees of the State Board of Education and not the County Board. I am of the opinion that any regulation requiring school bus operators to purchase liability insurance should be adopted by the State Board and not by the County Board and certainly, if a regulation was adopted by the County Board, it would be subject to approval by the State Board. I might point out that since the salary of the school bus operators is so small, it probably would be prohibitive for them to pay necessary premiums to purchase insurance even if required by a local board and approved by the State Board.

SCHOOLS; SALE OF SCHOOL PROPERTY; BY WHOM SALE MADE IN CITY ADMINISTRATIVE UNITS; DISPOSITION OF PROCEEDS OF SALE

19 February, 1946.

I received your letter of January 16, enclosing a letter from Mr. E. S. Johnson, Superintendent of Schools, Washington, North Carolina, in which Mr. Johnson submits to you the following questions:

"The Board of School Trustees of the Washington City Administrative Unit desires to sell two school sites. One site is located within the old special charter district; the other is located in the city unit outside of the old charter district.

"Is it the duty of the Board of School Trustees of the city unit, or the duty of the Board of Education of the county, to institute the sale of this property?

"If this property is sold by the Board of School Trustees, is the money derived from sale to be placed in the hands of the city administrative funds under the head of capital outlay, or is it to be turned over to the county accountant; either way to be used for future budgeting under the head of capital outlay?"

As to the property which is located within the old special charter district of Washington, the title to which was, I assume, taken in the name of the Trustees of the Washington City Schools, the sale would have to be made by the Board of Trustees of the City Administrative Unit after the Board has adopted a resolution authorizing the sale as required by G. S. 115-86, which provides that when, in the opinion of the board, any schoolhouse, schoolhouse site or other public school property has become unnecessary for public school purposes, it may sell the same at public auction, after first advertising said property for the period of time and in like manner as to places and publication in newspapers as is now prescribed for the sales of real estate under deeds of trust. The sale has to be reported to court and remain open for ten days for increase of bids, as required by this section.

The proceeds from sale of this property should be paid to the Treasurer of the Washington City Schools, to be held by the Treasurer for the capital outlay fund of the City Administrative Unit to be expended in accordance with such budgets as may be approved according to law. This is my conclusion about the proper handling of these funds, although there is no express language in the statute dealing with this subject.

G. S. 115-363 provides, in subsection (c), that the proceeds derived from payments of insurance losses shall be used to replace buildings destroyed and, in the event they are not replaced, to reduce the indebtedness of the special bond taxing unit to which said payments are made, or for other capital outlay purposes of the unit. By analogy to this section, I conclude that the funds should be handled in like manner as in the case of the sale of surplus school property.

As to the sale of the school property that is located in the city unit but outside of the old charter district, I would assume, although Mr. Johnson's

letter does not so state, that the title to this property is in the name of
the County Board of Education of Beaufort County. Such being the case,
it is my opinion that the County Board of Education would be the selling
agent, under the authority of G. S. 115-86. In the event of the sale of this
property, the funds should be paid over to the County Treasurer to be held
subject to future budgeting, in the same manner as that above set forth
as to the handling by the City Administrative Unit.

SCHOOLS; TRUCK OWNED AND OPERATED BY THE
COUNTY BOARD OF EDUCATION

20 February, 1946.

I acknowledge receipt of your letter enclosing a letter from Superintendent Frank B. Aycock, Jr., in which he inquires as to whether or not a
truck operated by the county school system for the purpose of repairing
school buildings, small construction jobs and the hauling of coal should
be covered by a public liability insurance policy to protect the county from
damages which might occur in the use of the truck.

I have written Superintendent Aycock several letters on this subject
and I again refer him to letters dated January 21, 1946, and February 11,
1946. I can see no distinction between the truck mentioned in his letter and
those used by the county board of education for other purposes and the
opinions which I expressed in my previous letters are applicable to the
use of the truck in question.

SCHOOLS; LUNCH ROOMS; COMPENSATION
INSURANCE ON EMPLOYEES

28 February, 1946.

I acknowledge receipt of your letter enclosing a letter from Superintendent T. C. Roberson of the Buncombe County Schools inquiring as to whose
duty it is to carry compensation insurance on the employees of the lunch
rooms in the county operated in connection with the Federal lunch room
program.

The situation seems to differ in the several counties of the State. I understand that in some counties the program is sponsored by the County
Board of Education and that the County Board has entered into contracts
with the State Board of Education in the distribution of Federal funds
to such county while in other counties the programs seem to be sponsored
and operated by the local school committee and, in some instances, by the
principal of the school.

I am unable to definitely determine whether the employees of the several lunch rooms are such as would require the county board of education
to secure compensation insurance coverage. However, it is my suggestion
that the county board of education secure compensation insurance covering the employees of the several lunch rooms operating in the county so
that in the event of injury there would be no question as to who would
compensate the injured person. I assume that most of the counties carry
blanket policies on all of their employees and I suggest that this policy

be so worded as to cover the employees of the lunch rooms. Certainly, in furnishing the names of the county employees to the compensation insurance carrier, the names of the employees of all of the lunch rooms should be included. This should not entail very much additional expense to the county but should be paid by the county rather than the State.

TEXTBOOKS; INDEFINITE CONTRACTS

6 March, 1946.

I have your letter of March 5, enclosing the Indefinite Textbook Contract recently tendered Science Research Associates of Chicago, and copies of correspondence relative to this contract. You ask my opinion as to what procedure you should follow in this matter.

It appears from the correspondence that the Science Research Associates are no longer the publishers of the book entitled "Better Rural Living" which was the textbook to which reference is made in the proposed contract, but that it is now published by Albert D. Phillips Company, University Avenue, Chicago. As I understand the matter, you wish to be advised as to whether or not the continuing contract could be offered for this publication to the Albert D. Phillips Company who is now the publisher.

G. S. 115-259 provides that at the expiration of a contract now existing between the State Board of Education and the publisher of any particular book or books, the State Board of Education, upon satisfactory agreement with the publisher, may continue the contract or any particular book or books indefinitely; that is, for a period not less than one nor more than five years.

I understand from the correspondence that the existing contract for this book will expire on May 31, 1946. Under the terms of this statute, it is my opinion that you would have a right to enter into a contract with the present publisher of this book, who happens to be the Albert D. Phillips Company. The statute authorizes the execution of such a contract with "the publisher."

As requested by you, I am returning the correspondence and copy of the contract which you sent me. The contract should be corrected as it refers to the book as "Better Farm Living" rather than the correct title of "Better Rural Living," as pointed out in the letter from Science Research Associates.

SCHOOLS; COUNTIES NOT AUTHORIZED TO FURNISH
BUSSES TO TRANSPORT TEACHERS

20 March, 1946.

I acknowledge receipt of your letter enclosing a letter from Superintendent E. E. Sams, of the Lenoir County Public Schools, in which he states that many of the teachers teaching in the rural districts reside in Kinston because there are no teacherages or other places for teachers to reside near the schools in which they teach. Superintendent Sams inquires as to whether or not the County may purchase and operate station wagons for the purpose of furnishing transportation for teachers to and from the schools in which they teach.

While I greatly sympathize with Superintendent Sams in his problem, I know of no authority whereby a county may purchase station wagons for the purpose of transporting school teachers to and from the schools in which they teach. I.am of the opinion that such authority would have to be given by the Legislature before the county would be justified in expending even surplus funds for this purpose.

SCHOOLS; TUITION FOR OUT-OF-COUNTY PUPIL

20 March, 1946.

I have your letter of March 18 enclosing a letter from Mr. H. M. Roland, Superintendent of Schools in New Hanover County and the City of Wilmington, in which Mr. Roland states that a resident of Wilmington has moved to Pender County and is willing to transport his son to the New Hanover High School at his own expenses, and desires permission for his son to remain in the New Hanover High School until the end of the year. He advises that according to their regulations a nonresident of the County, if accepted, must pay the cost of tuition to the extent of the per capita of the local funds with which the County supplements the State appropriaion, which in his County amounts to approximately $3.00. He states that the parent owns property in New Hanover County and wishes to know if it is possible to send his son to New Hanover High School without the payment of tuition.

G. S. 115-352 provides, in part, that it shall be within the discretion of the State Board of Education, wherever it shall appear to be more economical for the efficient operation of schools, to transfer children living in one administrative unit or district to another administrative unit or district for the full term of such school without the payment of tuition; provided that sufficient space is available in the buildings of such unit or district to which said children are transferred; and, provided further, that the provision as to the nonpayment of tuition shall not apply to children who have not been transferred as set out in this section.

The only other statute relating to this question which I find is G. S. 115-100, which provides as follows:

"The county board of education, with the approval of the.State Board of Education, may transfer from non-local tax territory to local tax districts or city administrative units, an individual family or individual families who reside on real property contiguous to said local tax districts or city administrative units, upon written petition of the taxpayers of said family or families, and there shall be levied upon the property and poll of each individual so transferred the same tax as is levied upon other property and polls of said district or unit: Provided, however, that any transfer to a city administrative unit shall be subject to the approval of the board of trustees."

I find nothing in the statutes which would make it illegal for the Board of Education of the New Hanover County and Wilmington City Schools to require that the nonresident student pay the cost of tuition to the extent of the per capita of local funds which the county supplements the State appropriation, and, if they saw fit to do so, they would have a right to agree to offset against such tuition any school taxes paid by the parent of the pupil in New Hanover County. This, it seems to me, would be a matter of agreement between the County and City authorities and the parent of the pupil.

I would assume that such an arrangement would be made only in rare instances, such as the case here where the student had begun his scholastic year in the Wilmington Schools prior to moving to Pender County and it was desired to finish out the term. It is possible that if this practice was engaged in extensively, it would raise a question as to the authority of the county and city authorities to use the facilities of the county and city schools for purposes other than for the benefit of residents of the county and city. In the event the number of students involved was substantial, I think the provisions of the statute referred to should be complied with.

DEEDS; SCHOOL PROPERTY; REVERSIONS

21 March, 1946.

I have your letter of March 9, 1946, in which you enclose a letter from Mr. T. T. Murphy, Superintendent of Schools in Pender County, in which Mr. Murphy asks if the Pender County Board of Education has authority to sell some real property which it acquired by deed a number of years ago. In the deed the grantors conveyed the land to the grantees "to be occupied and used by the colored people and pupils of said township and said district No. 3 expressly for school purpose and no other, and as soon as the aforesaid . . . fail or their successors in office fail to keep and use said tract of land and the buildings erected thereon for educational purposes and public schools for the aforesaid colored people . . . then this deed of conveyance of said land shall be null and void and of no effect; provided however the said (grantors) shall first pay back to the said (grantees) the aforesaid amount of $10." In the habendum clause the property is granted in "fee simple forever, provided said lot or parcel of land shall be used and occupied as aforesaid mentioned otherwise to revert back to the aforesaid mentioned parties or their legal representatives in the manner prescribed above."

You understand, of course, that I cannot advise you categorically concerning the legal effect of the above quoted language appearing in the deed. I am inclined to the view that this deed creates an estate in fee simple on condition subsequent. If this construction is correct, the failure to use the property for school purposes would probably be a breach of the condition giving the grantors or their heirs the right to re-enter the land. Cf. BLUE v. WILMINGTON, 186 N. C. 321.

Perhaps the legal effect of these conditions appearing in the deed could be determined in a controversy without action should an individual be desirous of purchasing the property covered by the deed. CHURCH v. REFINING CO., 200 N. C. 469.

Schools; Sites; Condemnation Proceedings; Non-Suit May Be Taken by School Board

29 March, 1946

I acknowledge receipt of your letter enclosing a letter from Superinten dent M. T. Lambeth, of the Beaufort County Schools, in which he state that the County Board of Education instituted condemnation proceeding for the purpose of obtaining a school site; that appraisers were appointee and a value placed upon the property far in excess of that which the Boar is prepared to pay for the property; that the School Board now desires t take a non-suit in the proceeding, but that the Clerk of Court has requeste an opinion from this office as to his authority to grant a non-suit.

This is a matter for decision in court, and we would not want to be pu in the position of rendering an opinion which would prejudice either side or appear to be directing the Court as to whether or not it should allow th non-suit. However, it does seem to me that this question is answered in th cases of Light Company vs. Manufacturing Company, 209 N. C., page 56(and In re Baker, 187, N. C. 257. In these cases the Court held that pet: tioners in condemnation proceedings may abandon the proceedings and tak a voluntary non-suit, upon payment of costs, even after the commissioner appointed by the Court have made their appraisal and report, and petitior ers have filed exceptions thereto, provided petitioners abandon the proceed ings before confirmation of the commissioners' report, since the petitioner had not entered into possession of the property and had no right to do s until payment of the appraised value. See also 30 C. J. page 335.

Counties; Authority to Pay Teachers for Lost Time Due to Weather Conditions

15 April, 1946

I have your letter of April 11, in which you enclose me a letter from M A. H. Hatsell, Superintendent of Onslow County Schools, in which M Hatsell requests you to advise him whether or not the Board of Educatio of his County has the authority to pay the teachers out of county funds fo time lost and not made up during the school year.

I know of no authority for the County Board of Education to pay ou county funds to teachers' salaries for time lost and not made up durin the school year. I assume from the question that the teachers have bee paid, or will be paid, for the full length of the school term of 180 days fror State funds, or such funds as may have been voted as a supplement fo this purpose. I find no provision in our statutes which authorizes a boar of county commissioners to make an appropriation of funds to the count board of education to pay for teachers' lost time from schools, in the at sence of which I do not think they would have the legal right to do so.

Special Supplement; Elections; Qualification of Voters; Residence

18 April, 1946.

I have your letter of April 16, enclosing a letter of April 15 from M T. H. Cash, Superintendent of Schools in Forsyth County, in which M Cash states that in the supplement election to be held in Forsyth Count they are not following township lines but school district lines in voting, and that there are some voters who have resided in the County for a year or more but who have moved to another district in the County and do not have a year's residence in the school district at the present time. He inquires as to the right of these voters who have moved their residences to vote in the coming election.

The Constitution, in Article VI, paragraph 2, provides as follows:

"He shall reside in the State of North Carolina for one year and in the precinct, ward or other election district in which he offers to vote four months next preceding the election: Provided, that removal from one precinct, ward or other election district to another in the same county shall not operate to deprive any person of the right to vote in the precinct, ward or other election district from which he has removed until four months after such removal."

The same language is found in the statute, G. S. 163-25.

If the voter has resided in the district to which he has moved for as much as four months, he would be entitled to vote in that district. If he has not resided there for as much as four months, he would be entitled to vote in the district in which he resided for as much as four months.

I trust that this quotation of the Constitution will be sufficient to clarify this matter for Mr. Cash.

SCHOOLS; DATE OF TERMINATION OF PROVISIONS OF SECTION 115-355 G. S.

6 May, 1946.

I acknowledge receipt of your letter enclosing a letter from the secretary of the Board of Education of Gates County in which he calls our attention to Section 115-355 of the General Statutes which reads as follows:

"Provided, further, that for the duration of the present war and for the first school term thereafter, it shall be the duty of the State Board of Education to provide any school in the State of North Carolina having four high school teachers or less and/or four elementary teachers or less not less than the same number of teachers as were allotted to said school for the school year of one thousand nine hundred and forty-four—one thousand nine hundred and forty-five. Provided, further, that in cases where there are less than 20 pupils per teacher in any school a reduction in the number of teachers may be made."

He inquires as to whether or not the pertinent section refers to next school term as the first school term after the duration of the present war.

The war has not yet legally terminated and will not terminate until a peace treaty has been entered into or a proclamation by the President to the effect that the state of war has terminated or upon the adoption by Congress of a resolution declaring the war to have ended, and neither of these conditions have yet taken place so that Section 115-355 will remain in full force and effect until the first school term after the signing of the peace treaty or a proclamation by the President or the adoption of a resolution by Congress declaring the war to have ended.

SCHOOLS; TEACHERS; TERMINATION OF CONTRACT; REFUSAL OF TEACHER TO RECEIVE LETTER GIVING NOTICE OF TERMINATION

5 June, 1946.

Receipt is acknowledged of your letter of June 3, enclosing a letter from Mr. Fred C. Hobson, Superintendent of Schools in Yadkin County, stating that the local committee, the principal and he had decided not to extend the contract of a teacher in a school. The teacher was notified on May 27, which was the last day of school, and requested to resign which she refused to do. Thereupon, Superintendent Hobson wrote her a letter and sent it by registered mail, notifying her of the termination of the contract, this being done on May 27. The teacher refused to accept the letter and the letter was returned with the word "refused" above the signature of the postmaster. Mr. Hobson inquires whether or not the contract is terminated under this precedure.

In my opinion, the required notice was given as provided in the statute, G. S. 115-359, which provides that it shall be the duty of the county superintendent or administrative head of a city administrative unit to notify all teachers and/or principals now or hereafter employed by registered letter of his or her rejection prior to the close of the school term.

The letter having been mailed and offered for delivery to the teacher prior to the close of the school term, the refusal of the teacher to accept the letter would not prevent the termination of the contract from being effective.

As I understand the letter from Mr. Hobson, the registered letter was mailed on the 27th of May, which is all the statute requires and it is not necessary to show that delivery of the letter was made prior to the close of the school year.

EDUCATION; SCHOOL LAW; DISMISSAL OF TEACHERS; APPROVAL OR DISAPPROVAL OF COUNTY SUPERINTENDENT; CONTINUING CONTRACT

19 June, 1946.

There is enclosed with your letter an inquiry from one of the superintendents of schools of a county which states as follows:

"In the discharge of my duty as superintendent of Surry County Schools, I failed to approve the continuing contract of three teachers in Surry County even after the committee had passed on them and submitted their names for approval. Has the superintendent of an administrative unit the authority by law to disapprove a continuing contract of a teacher employed in the particular administrative unit in which the superintendent serves? I shall appreciate a reply at your earliest convenience."

The election of teachers under our law is governed by Section 115-354 of the General Statutes; and from this section, it will be seen that the principals of the districts nominate and the district committees elect teachers for all of the schools of the district subject to the approval of the county superintendent of schools and the county board of education. I think that the election first referred to in the statute governs the situation when the teacher is first employed. This must necessarily be true because later on in this same section it is provided that the teacher's contract shall be a continuing contract from year to year until the teacher or principal is notified as provided in Section 115-359. The last proviso in Section 115-354 was amended by the Session Laws of 1945; and there is enclosed for the use of the superintendent in question a letter written by this office to you, dated the 19 April 1945, which gives the views of this office as to the relative rights and duties between the governing authorities of the school and the teachers as related to notice from the governing authority to the teacher and from the teacher to the governing authority where continuing contracts are in force.

When we consider the means or methods used for the dismissal of a teacher who is holding a position under a continuing contract, it seems to me that there are two ways provided by the law for dismissing a teacher:

(1)   A teacher may be dismissed for cause under the provisions of Section 115-143 of the General Statutes if right of appeal.

(2)   The governing authorities may dispense with the services of a teacher by complying with Section 115-359 by giving the proper notice of rejection prior to the close of the school term. Of course, a teacher may resign by giving not less than thirty days' notice prior to the opening of the school in which the teacher is employed; such notice to be in writing and to be submitted to the official head of the administrative unit.

It is further provided in Section 115-359 of the General Statutes that if a teacher is rejected under the provisions of that section, the rejection shall be subject to the approval or disapproval of the governing authorities of the administrative unit in which the teacher is employed. The converse of the proposition does not seem to be true. Once the teacher is employed and is under a continuing contract and if the committee decides that the teacher shall continue in service under the continuing contract, it does not seem to me that it is necessary nor can I find any provision of law which requires the superintendent of schools to approve or reject such action of the committee. At least, I cannot find any provision in Section 115-354 that can be interpreted in such a manner. I find no provision of law that allows the superintendent of schools to overrule the action of the committee if it is decided that the teacher should continue. I am enclosing a copy of a letter written by this office on the 25 May 1945 on the question of giving notice before the close of the term. This copy is for the use of the superintendent in question.

It seems to me that I am compelled, therefore, to say that in my opinion that the superintendent of a administrative unit does not have the authority under the present school law to disapprove a continuing contract of a teacher employed in the particular administrative unit in which the superintendent serves. I am returning to you the letter written to you by the superintendent in question.

SCHOOL LAWS; CITY ADMINISTRATIVE UNITS;
CHANGING BOUNDARIES

26 June, 1946.

I have your letter of June 18, 1946, in which you enclose a letter from Mr. L. S. Inscoe, Superintendent of Schools in Nash County, containing certain questions upon which you desire for me to advise you. Mr. Inscoe's questions arise upon the following set of facts (I shall draw certain inferences from the facts stated so that my position in the matter will be perfectly clear):

Several years ago the corporate limits of the City of Rocky Mount were extended by legislative enactment but the limits of the City Administrative School Unit of the City of Rocky Mount were not extended with the corporate limits. Within the corporate limits of the City of Rocky Mount, but without the limits of the City Administrative Unit, there is a school known as the Rocky Mount Mills School. This Rocky Mount Mills School is a part of the Nash County Administrative Unit. Within the limits of the Rocky Mount City Administrative Unit a special school tax has been voted by the people, which tax is still being levied and collected.

Arrangements are now being made to transfer the Rocky Mount Mills School from the County Administrative Unit to the Rocky Mount City Administrative Unit. Mr. Inscoe thinks that this is a logical move and one that would be for the best interest of everyone concerned. Because of this proposed transfer of the Rocky Mount Mills School, or the extension of the limits of the Rocky Mount City Administrative Unit to include the same, four questions are asked by Mr. Inscoe. As the school law now stands, I am of the opinion that these questions do not arise; therefore, I shall not attempt to answer them. On the contrary, I shall state what I consider to be the answers to the legal questions involved. My answers are, of course, based upon the facts as I have stated them herein.

It seems to me that the only method of transferring the Rocky Mount Mills School from the County Administrative Unit to the Rocky Mount City Administrative Unit is to extend the limits of the City Administrative Unit. Prior to 1945, the third paragraph of G. S. 115-352 began with the following language:

"City administrative units as now constituted shall be dealt with by the State school authorities in all matters of school administration in the same way and manner as are county administrative units."

G. S. 115-352 appeared as a part of the 1939 Act. By Section 4 of Chapter 970 of the Session Laws of 1945, G. S. 115-352 was amended by adding after the above quoted portion thereof the following proviso:

"Provided, that the State Board of Education may, in its discretion, alter the boundaries of any city administrative unit when in the opinion of the State Board of Education such change is desirable for better school administration."

Under this provision, it seems clear that the State Board of Education has authority to extend the limits of the Rocky Mount City Administrative Unit so as to embrace the territory now included in the Rocky Mount Mills

School. Thus, it seems that the question of transferring the Rocky Mount Mills School from the County Administrative Unit to the Rocky Mount Administrative Unit is a matter for the State Board of Education under the above quoted provision of the statutes.

It appears from Mr. Inscoe's letter that a special school tax is now being levied and collected within the Rocky Mount City Administrative Unit and that this tax has been voted on by the people of this Unit. The question arises, thus, as to the levy and collection of the special tax in the area now comprising the Rocky Mount Mills School if the State Board of Education should extend the limits of the Rocky Mount City Administrative Unit to include this territory. On this point the second paragraph of G. S. 115-361 would seem to be controlling. That paragraph (which was not amended by the 1945 General Assembly) reads as follows:

"Upon a written petition of a majority of the governing board of any district which has voted a supplementary tax, the county board of education, after approving the petition, shall present the same to the board of county commissioners and ask for an election on the question of the enlargement of the boundary lines of any such district so as to include any contiguous territory, and an election in such new territory may be ordered and held under rules governing elections for local taxes as provided in this section: Provided, the local tax rate specified in the petition and submitted to the qualified voters shall be a local tax of the same rate as that voted in the said district to which the territory is to be added. If a majority of the qualified voters in such new territory shall vote in favor of such tax, the new territory shall be and become a part of said district, and the term 'local tax of the same rate' herein used shall include, in addition to the usual local tax, any tax levied to meet the interest and sinking fund of any bonds heretofore issued by the district proposed to be enlarged. In case a majority of the qualified voters at the election shall vote in favor of the tax, the district shall be deemed enlarged as so proposed."

OPINIONS TO COMMISSIONER OF REVENUE

7 July, 1944

You state that a certain taxpayer has for some years made gifts to her sister of amounts in excess of $1,000.00 per year. As I understand it, the donee has no other-income and the taxpayer contends that the amount annually given is not in excess of what is necessary to maintain the donee in the manner in which she has been accustomed to live. The gift tax law provides for an exclusion from tax of gifts not exceeding $1,000.00 in any one calendar year. The taxpayer contends that the portion of the gifts under consideration which exceeds the $1,000.00 exclusion are also entitled to exemption from the gift tax in view of the provision in Revenue Act, Section 600, which exempts from the tax gifts "for charitable, educational, or religious purposes within this State." You desire my opinion upon the taxability of these gifts.

Whether the gifts are taxable depends upon the proper interpretation of the provision exempting gifts "for charitable . . . purposes". What is a charitable purpose?

In Webster's New International Dictionary, under "Charity", there is the following definition: "An eleemosynary gift; a gift, as by grant or devise, of real or personal property to the use of the public or any portion of it (as distinct from specific individuals) for any beneficial or salutary purpose."

The following discussion of charitable purposes appears in 14 C.J.S., page 439:

> "Broadly, a charitable use or purpose may, where neither law nor public forbids, be applied to almost anything tending to promote the well doing and well being of social man, but the use or purpose must be a public, as distinguished from a private, one, for the benefit of the public, at large or of a portion thereof or for the benefit of an indefinite number of persons."
>
> "It is essential to a valid charitable gift that it be for a purpose recognized in law as charitable. To constitute a charitable use or purpose, it must be a public as distinguished from a private one; it must be for the public use or benefit; and it must be for the benefit of the public at large, or of a portion thereof, or for the benefit of an indefinite number of persons."

The status of a gift to poor relations is discussed as follows in 14 C.J.S., page 449:

> "A gift to poor relations or for their benefit is a private gift although it would prevent their becoming a public charge." (Cases cited.)

This paragraph also contains a statement that at common law "dispositions in favor of poor relations are to be ranked among charitable uses whenever they seem to have been treated as such by the testator." One case is cited in support of this proposition (IN RE MOLLER'S ESTATE, 178

N.Y.S. 682). However, I have been unable to find that the Moller case represents the view generally accepted today.

Further, as stated in 10 American Jurisprudence, page 605:

> "Whenever the beneficiary is designated by name he has a right which he can exercise, and his merit alone is to be considered; the bequest is private and not public, and ceases to have the peculiar merit of charity."

The decisions support the general principles quoted from the legal encyclopedias. For example, in MATTER OF BEEKMAN'S ESTATE, 232 N.Y. 371, 134 N.E. 183, a gift was made to the Beekman Family Association, a corporation created for the purpose of educating members of testator's families and of furnishing aid to poor members thereof. The Court held that such a gift was not charitable in scope but was private and personal.

Further, in KENT v. DURHAM, 142 Mass. 216, 7 N.E. 730, it was held that a gift to trustees to be used for the support of testator's children is a private gift. The Court said with relation to public or charitable gifts:

> "That a gift should have this character there must be some benefit to be conferred upon, or duty to be performed towards, either the public at large, or some part thereof, or an indefinite class of persons."

And the Board of Tax Appeals (now the Tax Court) has held under the Federal Gift Tax law that a trust which provided that named relatives of the settlor received specified amounts for college education and that funds not required for that purpose be used for educational aid to young members of a designated church of which the relatives were not members was not charitable within the meaning of the Federal statute (Internal Revenue Code, Section 1004(a)(2)(B)). Although the Federal statute involved in that decision is not the same as the North Carolina statute under consideration, the decision is interesting by way of analogy. *A. H. Crellin*, 46 B.T.A. 1152 (1942).

Since the generally accepted legal definition of a charitable purpose is one which benefits a class rather than particular individuals, it must, in my opinion, be presumed that the General Assembly intended that this meaning be given the words charitable purposes" in Section 600. There is nothing in the gift tax law to indicate that any different or more liberal meaning was intended. I therefore believe that it is entirely reasonable and sound to interpret these words in the light of the meaning generally given them in legal authorities, and therefore that so much of the annual gifts as exceeds $1,000.00 is subject to gift tax.

SALES AND USE TAXES; SALES TO CONTRACTORS WITH DEFENSE PLANT CORPORATION; ALLSTATE ELECTRIC COMPANY, WINSTON-SALEM, N. C.

12 October, 1944

You have referred to me for my opinion your file relating to a proposed assessment against the Allstate Electric Company (hereinafter referred to as the taxpayer) on account of sales made by the taxpayer to Fairchild

Aircraft (a division of Fairchild Engine and Aircraft Corporation) for and on behalf of the Defense Plant Corporation.

You have submitted to me the contract between Fairchild Aircraft and the taxpayer. However, while this contract is helpful in determining the question involved, the contract which is determinative of the question of taxability is that between Fairchild Aircraft and the Defense Plant Corporation and you have not submitted to me this contract. Without the latter contract I cannot give you a definite opinion upon the validity of the assessment. However, I might point out generally the principles involved in this matter in order that both your office and the taxpayer may understand the factors that are determinative of tax liability.

The Defense Plant Corporation is a governmental corporation. All of its stock is owned by the Reconstruction Finance Corporation and all of the stock of the Reconstruction Finance Corporation is owned by the Federal Government. Section 10 of Chapter 8 of the Reconstruction Finance Corporation Act (15 U.S.C. 610) provides that the Defense Plant Corporation shall be exempt from all taxation by a state except that any real property of a corporation shall be subject to ad valorem taxation to the same extent as other real property is subject to such taxation. Thus, it is clear that the Defense Plant Corporation is an agency or instrumentality of the Federal Government.

The State has not jurisdiction to levy a tax directly against any agency or instrumentality of the Federal Government and, hence, the State could not levy a sales tax on sales made directly to the Defense Plant Corporation. FEDERAL LAND BANK v. BISMARK LUMBER CO., 314 U. S. 95, 62 S. Ct. 1. Further, sales made to a true agent of the Defense Plant Corporation would have the same legal status as sales made directly to the Defense Plant Corporation and would be exempt from tax. On the other hand, sales made to a contractor with the Defense Plant Corporation who or which is not a true agent of the Corporation may be subjected to State sales and use taxes even though the burden of the tax is ultimately borne as a reimbursable item by the Defense Plant Corporation. JAMES v. DRAVO CONSTRUCTION CO., 302 U. S. 134; ALABAMA v. KING & BOOZER, 314 U. S. 1.

It is evident from these principles that the controlling factor is the legal relationship between the Defense Plant Corporation and the Fairchild Aircraft Corporation. This relationship arises out of and can be determined only by reference to the contract between these two parties. Thus, it is necessary for this contract to be examined before a final opinion can be rendered.

I might add that in several other states which levy sales taxes sales to contractors with the Defense Plant Corporation are regarded as taxable unless it appears that the same are made to the Corporation directly or through an agent. For example, in Indiana the following regulation has been made (see C.C.H., Interstate Sales Tax Service, page 857-5):

> "Sales by vendors to Defense Plant Corporation through lessee-agents will be considered as sales made to an instrumentality of the Federal Government through its agent and exempt from the provisions of the Gross Income Tax Act where the authority of the lessee-agent .

is clearly defined and specified in the contract with the Defense Plant Corporation."

The following is an extract from an opinion of the Attorney General of Louisiana (C.C.H., Interstate Sales Tax Service, page 857-7K):

> This office has examined contract forms now being used by the Defense Plant Corporation and is of the opinion that under the terms and provisions of this contract, the contractor and not the Defense Plant Corporation is the purchaser and, therefore, the tax on the sale is due."
> "You are advised, therefore, that if the contract in which you are interested was entered into by the X Company with the Defense Plant Corporation, the sale by the dealer is deemed to be a sale to the contractor and is taxable."

Utah has the following provision (C.C.H., Interstate Sales Tax Service, page 862):

> "Sales to contractors who are authorized by the United States Government or an instrumentality thereof to make purchases in the name of the Defense Plant Corporation are deemed to be sales to an agent of the United States Government or the instrumentality thereof and are, therefore, exempt from tax."

A bulletin of the Department of Revenue of Arkansas contains the following ruling (C.C.H., Interstate Sales Tax Service, page 853-4):

> "The Defense Plant Corporation is a federal instrumentality and, therefore, sales to it are exempt from the Gross Receipts Tax. However, sales to persons, firms, or corporations purporting to act for or on behalf of the Defense Plant Corporation will be taxable, unless the billing or invoice is to be made to the Defense Plant Corporation."

If you will make available a copy of the contract between the Defense Plant Corporation and Fairchild Aircraft which existed at the time of the sales made by taxpayer, I can give you a definite opinion upon this matter.

INCOME TAXES;   ETHYL-DOW CHEMICAL COMPANY;   DISALLOWANCE OF INTEREST PAID TO AFFILIATES

20 October, 1944

You have requested my opinion upon the following matter.

You have proposed to make an additional income tax assessment against the Ethyl-Dow Chemical Company (hereinafter referred to as Taxpayer) for the fiscal year ended June 30, 1943, based upon the disallowance of interest which you claim was not allowable under the provisions of Section 318½ of the Revenue Act of 1939, as amended by the General Assembly of 1941. The taxpayer is a foreign corporation which maintains and operates a place and facilites in North Carolina for the extraction of bromine from sea water. One-half of taxpayer's common stock is owned by Ethyl Corporation and one-half by the Dow Chemical Company. Both the Ethyl Corporation and the Dow Chemical Company are foreign corporations. Taxpayer owes a certain sum on first lien notes to the stockholders. This indebtedness was incurred for the construction of the plant in North Carolina and one in Texas. Interest at the rate of 7% per annum is paid to tne creditors and it is this interest which has been disallowed.

Section 318½, as amended by the General Assembly of 1941, contained the following provision:

"If the capital of any such subsidiary or affiliated corporation which is not required to file a consolidated return as above provided is inadequate for its business needs apart from credit extended or indebtedness guaranteed by the parent or affiliated corporation, the commissioner shall, in determining the net income of such corporation, disregard its indebtedness owed to or guaranteed by the parent or affiliated corporation in determining the net income taxable under this article. The capital stock for the purposes of this section shall be deemed inadequate to the extent that additional loans, credits, goods, supplies or other capital of whatsoever nature is furnished by the parent or affiliated corporation."

The contention of the taxpayer is that it is not a "subsidiary or affiliated corporation" within the meaning of Section 318½. This section defines a subsidiary corporation as follows:

"For the purposes of this Section, a corporation shall be deemed a subsidiary of another corporation when, directly or indirectly, it is subject to control by such other corporation by stock ownership, interlocking directors, or by any other means whatsoever exercised bv the same or associated financial interests. whether such control is direct or through one or more subsidiary, affiliated, or controlled corporatiⁿˢ. and a corporation shall be deemed an affiliate of another corporation when both are directly or indirectly controlled by the same parent ccrporation or by the some associated financial interests by stock ownership, interlocking directors, or by any other means whatsoever. whether such control be direct or through one or more subsidiary, affiliated or controlled corporations."

The essential question is whether the taxpayer is controlled by "associated financial interests." If so, it falls within the definition of a subsidiary corporation and the interest was properly disallowed.

At the conference held between the taxpayer's representatives and the Commissioner of Revenue on May 2, 1944, it appeared that the Ethyl Corporation utilizes bromine in making ethylene dibromide for high test gasoline; that Dow Chemical Corporation had gained much experience in the extraction of bromine from sea water; that Ethyl Corporation and Dow Chemical Company sponsored research leading to the formation of the Taxpayer corporation. Taxpayer states that the Ethyl-Dow Chemical Company is operated entirely apart from either of the other corporations; that there are no interlocking directors; no common accounting and management services; but some sharing of technical advice.

Taxpayer contends that Dow Chemical Company and Ethyl Corporation are not to be considered "associated financial interests" since Ethyl Corporation is owned entirely by Standard Oil Company of New Jersey and General Motors, Inc., and the Dow Chemical Company is an independent corporation.

As stated above, taxpayer was organized as a result of common interests of the Ethyl Corporation which needed a supply of bromine but did not think it feasible to conduct its own extraction of that product because of lack of experience and other reasons and the Dow Chemical Corporation which had experience in the manufacture of bromine. The Dow Chemical Corporation did not desire to engage in the construction of the necessary plant and facilities and it was agreed that the Ethyl Corporation would furnish the capital and plant and the Dow Chemical Corporation would operate it. In return for such services, in lieu of a stated annual price or fee, it was decided that a separate company would be formed and that as compensation for Dow Chemical Corporation's services they would receive one-half interest in the new company.

In view of these facts it is my opinion that taxpayer corporation is controlled by "associated financial interests" within the meaning of the statute and that the interest paid is not allowable as a deduction. Taxpayer corporation was formed out of a mutual need and a close association between Ethyl corporation and Dow Chemical Company. The organization and operation of taxpayer corporation have been conducted in the light of the common business interests of these two corporations. Although neither the Ethyl Corporation nor the Dow Chemical Company owns a control of taxpayer and although there are no interlocking directors, it is obvious that Ethyl Corporation and Dow Chemical Company act together in the formulation of the policies and operation of taxpayer corporation.

Furthermore, this is precisely the type of transaction intended to be covered by the quoted provisions of Section 318½. The loan to taxpayer, being used to construct plant facilities, was in the nature of an investment of capital by Ethyl Corporation and Dow Chemical Company. In effect these corporations, through the medium of taxpayer, are using their capital in this state and at the same time ask that this capital be treated as though it had come from outside sources. If this could be done, any parent or affiliated company not doing business in North Carolina could form a subsidiary or affiliated corporation with relatively small capital, and through the device of a loan of its own assets feed it capital at no cost to itself, since the interest is paid to itself, and thus evade its lawful burden of taxation. Section 318½ (and Section 210, relating to franchise taxes) prevents this result.

I, therefore, advise that in my opinion the assessments which you have made are valid.

ESTATE OF CARRIE S. PRINCE; INHERITANCE TAX; JOINT ANNUITY
CONTRACT PURCHASED FOR A SINGLE PREMIUM; AMOUNT INCLUDIBLE
IN ESTATE UPON DEATH OF ONE JOINT ANNUITANT

3 November, 1944

You have requested my opinion upon the following question arising in connection with the above named estate.

The decedent during her lifetime had purchased the following annuity contracts from insurance companies:

(1) A Single Premium Joint and Annuity Contract purchased for a single premium of $5,000 and providing an income of $19.95 monthly, the

first payment due July 2, 1938 and the payments to continue during the joint lifetime of the decedent (born March 19, 1859) and Sarah G. Schwing (born March 2, 1895) and a continuance of the same income for the balance of the lifetime of the survivor of the two. You state that the cost of a single premium straight life annuity providing $19.95 monthly to Sarah G. Schwing computed as of April 9, 1944, (the date of the decedent's death) on the basis of the premium rates then in force would amount to $5,599.29. It is my opinion that this amount is includible in the estate of the decedent which is subject to inheritance taxation in this State in as much as the transaction amounted essentially to a gift to Sarah G. Schwing of $5,599.29, taking effect at the death of the decedent. Section 1 (Third) of the Revenue Act taxes the transfer of property intended to take effect in possession or enjoinment at or after death. The decedent provided by contract that Sarah G. Schwing would receive $19.95 for her lifetime and the value of this provision at the time of the decedent's death was $5,599.29, since that is the amount which would have been required to provide these payments.

(2) A Single Premium Cash Refund Life Annuity purchased on December 1, 1934, for a single premium of $20,000.00 and providing an income of $150.80 monthly, the first payment due January 1, 1935, and the payments to continue during the lifetime of the decedent. The policy was amended by the decedent to provide that the difference between the single premium of $20,000.00 and the total installment payments received by her prior to death was to be used upon her death to purchase a life income for the named beneficiary, Sarah G. Schwing. The refund at death amounted to $3110.40, and it is my opinion that this value should be included in the taxable estate of the decedent since it amounts to a gift by her to Sarah G. Schwing effective at death.

(3) Certain other contracts issued by an issurance company upon payment of a single premium and, based upon the ages of the decedent and Sarah G. Schwing at the time of issuance of the contract, it was provided that a specified monthly annuity would be paid to the annuitants jointly while both were living and to the survivor during the lifetime of the survivor. These contracts are covered by the principles hereinbefore stated and I advise you to include in the taxable estate the values furnished you by the insurance company which are based upon the consideration for a life annuity which the companies would charge to provide a monthly income based on the age of the surviving annuitant equal to one-half of the amount received under each contract and calculated on the rate in effect at the death of the decedent. As stated by the insurance company, the value is calculated only for one-half the actual monthly payments received for the reason that the annuities during the lifetime of both annuitants were payable to them jointly and consequently, upon the death of either annuitant, the survivor thereafter receives one-half share of the decedent in addition to the one-half share of each payment which she received while both annuitants were living.

SALES & USE TAXES;   USE TAX ON RENTAL OF BUSINESS MACHINES;
REPLACEMENT OF MACHINES

30 November, 1944

The following matter has been referred to me for my opinion by Mr. H. DeBerry, Jr., Auditor of the Durham Life Insurance Company.

On June 17, 1937, the Durham Life Insurance Company entered into a contract with the International Business Machines Corporation providing for the furnishing of electric accounting machine service which consists of furnishing certain business machines and devices, giving instruction in their operation, and maintaining them.   Title to the business machines remains in the International Business Machines Corporation and they are rented or leased to the Durham Life Insurance Company (hereinafter referred to as the "taxpayer"), under the contract referred to, at a stipulated monthly charge for each machine.

The taxpayer had leased from the International Business Machines Corporation an alphabetic summary punch machine and paid North Carolina use tax upon this rental.   Pursuant to the replacement provision of the contract hereinafter quoted the taxpayer replaced the alphabetic summary punch machine with an automatic reproducer in order that certain work could be handled more efficiently.   The rental for the automatic reproducer (after having given credit for rent paid in advance) was higher than the rental for the alphabetic summary punch machine.   The International Business Machines Corporation billed the taxpayer for use tax upon the full rental value of the automatic reproducer and the taxpayer contends that this tax was not justified, and that having paid use tax on the rental of the first machine no tax is due upon the rental of the replacement machine.

This contention requires an examination of the transaction in the light of the contract and in the light of the use tax article of the Revenue Act.

The use tax is levied "on the storage, use, or consumption in this State of tangible personal property purchased from a retailer within or without this State on or after July first, one thousand nine hundred and forty-one (1941), for storage, use or consumption in this State at the rate of three per cent of the sales price of such property, regardless of whether said retailer is or is not engaged in business in this State." Revenue Act, Section 802.

Retailers engaged in the business of selling tangible personal property for storage, use or consumption in this State are required to collect the use tax.   Revenue Act, Section 805.   The Act defines tne word "sale" or "selling" as follows:

"(c)   The word 'sale' or 'selling' shall mean any transfer of title or possession, or both, exchange, or barter of tangible personal property, conditional or otherwise, however effected and by whatever name called, for a consideration paid or to be paid, in installments or otherwise, and shall include any of said transactions whereby title or ownership is ultimately to pass notwithstanding the retention of title or possession, or both, for security or other purposes, and shall further mean *and include any bailment, loan, lease, rental or license to use or consume tangible personal property for a consideration paid or to be paid, in installments or otherwise*:   Provided, the provisions of this subsection shall not apply to the lease or rental of Motion Picture Films used for exhibition purposes and for which a tax of three per cent is paid on the total admission for such exhibitions." (Underlining added.)

In view of this statute it is clear that a lease or rental of tangible personal property is, for purposes of the use tax, equivalent to a sale and is therefore subject to the tax unless otherwise exempted. The question then arises whether the replacement of the alphabetic summary punch machine with the automatic producer constituted an independent leasing or rental or whether this transaction must be regarded as merely an extension of the first leasing or rental. The contract between taxpayer and the International Business Machines Corporation contains the following provision regarding replacements:

"Machines and devices, in addition to the above, or to replace any you may have in use, will be furnished you in accordance with the conditions of this contract at the rates prevailing at the time your order for the same is received."

A rental or lease of tangible personal property is an agreement by which one party, for a stipulated sum, permits another party to use the property for a stated period and upon certain conditions. In my opinion a new lease or rental occurred when the alphabetic summary punch machine was replaced by the automatic reproducer. I reached this conclusion because the transaction amounts to the securing of a different type or kind of property at a different price or rental; hence, it cannot be said, in my opinion, that there is a continuation of the first transaction. This is borne out by the contract, which provides that "the charges herein provided for are for the use of the machines and devices and for the services rendered to you hereunder," and gives the lessee "a non-assignable license to use" the machines and devices. Thus, if a new or different machine is secured under the contract, the International Business Machines Corporation charges for the use of the machine and grants the lessee a license to use it, which in addition to any license to use machines already on hand. It therefore seems to me that there is no identity between the leasing of the alphabetic summary punch machine and the automatic reproducer but that they are two distinct transactions.

It is true that the contract between the taxpayer and the International Business Machines Corporation provides for the furnishing of certain machines. However, on the first page of the contract these machines are listed with the monthly charge of each. If an additional machine is used by taxpayer, there would clearly be another rental or leasing. I do not think that this principle is changed by the fact that one machine is discontinued and another is used in its place.

I have carefully considered taxpayer's contentions that the Act does not subject this transaction to tax and that the General Assembly did not intend any such result. I regret that I cannot agree with these contentions.

FRANCHISE TAX; BASE TO BE DETERMINED AS OF END OF CORPORATION'S FISCAL YEAR

20 December, 1944

You request my opinion with regard to the franchise tax liability of the Hickory Chair Manufacturing Company under the following facts.

The taxpayer corporation's fiscal year extends from December 1 to November 30. Due to reasons not apparent here, the corporation on April 7, 1944, sold its real estate plants and equipment, inventories, prepaid insurance and certain other assets at a loss of $198,927.69. On April 12, 1944, it was placed in liquidation by the directors, and on the same day it was ordered that $100.00 per share be paid to stockholders on account in liquidation. Accordingly, $546,800.00 was paid to the stockholders on April 15, 1944. These aforementioned transactions reduced the value of the corporation's surplus and capital stock from $889,922.46, as it was at the end of its fiscal year, to $119,848.97 on June 30, 1944.

The taxpayer contends that in determining its franchise tax base for the year July 1, 1944, to June 30, 1945, the reduced value of capital stock and surplus, i.e., $119,848.97, should be used. The Commissioner of Revenue on the other hand insists that in determining this base the capital stock and surplus should be reported on the basis of its value at the end of the corporation's fiscal year when the value of same was $889,922.46.

Section 210(1) of the Revenue Act is as follows:

"(1) Every corporation, domestic and foreign, incorporated or, by any Act, domesticated under the laws of this State, except as otherwise provided in this article or schedule, shall, on or before the thirty-first day of July of each year, make and deliver to the Commissioner of Revenue in such form as he may prescribe a full, accurate and complete report and statement verified by the oath of its duly authorized officers, containing such facts and information as may be required by the Commissioner of Revenue as shown by the books and records of the corporation as to the close of its last calendar or fiscal year next preceding July thirty-first of the year in which report is due."

Subsection (4) of Section 210 levies the franchise tax and prescribes the rate to be applied after the base has been determined. Section 215 (1) provides:

"(1) Every corporation, domestic or foreign, from which a report is required by law to be made to the Commissioner of Revenue shall, unless otherwise provided, pay to said commissioner annually the franchise tax as required by Sections two hundred ten and two hundred eleven of this Act."

These sections, in my opinion, clearly indicate that the franchise tax return required of a corporation and upon which the tax is based, must reflect the value of its capital stock, surplus and undivided profits as of the close of its last fiscal or calendar year next preceding July 31 of the year 'in which the report is due.

The taxpayer bases his contention on the last sentence of Section 201 of the Franchise Tax Article, which provides "The taxes levied in this Article or schedule shall be for the fiscal year of the state in which said taxes became due." In my opinion this sentence has no reference to the time for valuing a corporation's capital, stock, surplus, and undivided profits for the franchise tax base, but rather, it relates to the time that the franchise taxes, once determined, become due and to the period which they cover.

It is therefore my conclusion that the Commissioner is correct in insisting that the corporation, in determining its franchise tax base, use the valuation of its capital stock and surplus as of November 30, 1943, the end of the corporation's fiscal year.

FRANCHISE TAX; TAXABILITY OF GROSS RECEIPTS FROM SALES OF
POWER TO NAVAL AIR STATION

29 December, 1944

You inquire whether the Roanoke Utilities Company, Inc., is liable for the 6% gross receipts tax, imposed in Section 203 of the Revenue Act of 1939, as amended, on the sales of power to the Naval Air Station. This power is furnished to the Naval Air Station under contract with the United States Government.

Section 203 imposes the 6% gross receipts tax upon every person, firm, or corporation engaged in the business of furnishing power. There is no provision in the Section which would allow a taxpayer to exclude from taxable gross receipts those received from an agency of the Federal Government.

In the absence of any such specific exemption, and in view of the fact that the tax is not levied against the Federal Government, or any agency thereof, but rather, against the person, firm, or corporation furnishing the utility, I conclude that the Roanoke Utilities Company, Inc., has no authority to exclude from its taxable gross receipts those realized from the sale of power to the Naval Air Station.

It has been held by the United States Supreme Court that a tax imposed on a contractor with the Federal Government is not invalid even if the burden of the tax is passed on to, and borne by, the Federal Government. JAMES v. DRAVO CONSTRUCTION CO., 302 U. S. 134; ALABAMA v. KING & BOOZER, 314 U. S. 1.

INTANGIBLES TAX; FEDERAL TRANSPORTATION TAX ACCOUNTS; C.O.D. FUNDS
HELD BY A DEPOSITOR PENDING PAYMENT TO OWNER

15 March, 1945

You inquire whether a transfer company is liable for the payment of the intangibles tax imposed in Section 701 of the Revenue Act upon (1) money on deposit in banks collected by the company as transporation tax for the Federal Government, and (2) money on deposit in banks collected by it as c.o.d charges for shippers.

The transportation tax, imposed in Section 3475 of the Internal Revenue Code, is levied on the person paying transportation charges. Transfer companies in collecting the tax, are acting as agents of the Federal Government, and the money belongs to the Federal Government from the time that it is paid to such agents, who merely hold it in custody until such time as it is remitted to the proper government authority. Section 701 of the Revenue Act provides that the tax levied in that section shall not apply to "deposits of the United States." Therefore, it is my opinion that money collected as transportation tax is not subject to the intangibles tax levied in Section 701.

I think that the situation is different insofar as money on deposit representing c.o.d. charges is concerned. Even though such money is merely held in custody by the transfer company, it has a taxable situs in North Carolina and thus is subject to the intangibles tax. Since such money is deposited in the name of the transfer company the tax must, under the law, be paid by it, even though such money in fact belongs to the shipper. Section 701 imposes the tax upon all money on deposit with any bank or other person, firm, or corporation doing a banking business, whether such money be actually in or out of this State, having a business, commercial, or taxable situs in this State. There is no exemption in the section for money deposited in the name of one but belonging to another.

REVENUE ACT, SECTION 152; LOAN AGENCIES AND BROKERS; LIABILITY FOR TAX OF PERSON PROCURING LOANS FROM THIRD PARTY

29 March, 1945

You have referred to me the letter, with enclosures, of Mr. D. E. Hudgins, Attorney at law, under date of March 22, 1945. This letter raises the question of the liability for the license tax under Section 152 of the Revenue Act (G. S. 105-88) of Mr. Hudgins' client, Mr. W. M. Hubbard, and you request my opinion on this question.

The pertinent facts as stated by Mr. Hubbard are as follows:

Mr. Hubbard, a resident of Texas, is the sole owner and operator of two unincorporated small loan brokerage offices designated as "Hubbard Finance Company" and Guaranty Loan Company," (hereinafter for convenience referred to as "the taxpayer"), respectively. One of these businesses is located in Greensboro and the other in Charlotte. These businesses were commenced in 1944, and Mr. Hubbard paid, without the advice of counsel, the tax levied by Section 152 for the current license year. He now doubts his liability for this tax and requests your views.

The taxpayer has made an arrangement with a Louisiana bank whereby the bank will receive application for and act upon various proposed loans which the taxpayer (claiming to act as agent for the borrower) submits to the bank.

The taxpayer advertises and holds himself out as being engaged in the small loan business. When a borrower applies for a loan, the taxpayer, if he is willing to guarantee the obligation of the bank, procures the execution by the borrower of a document designated "Broker's Contract," by the terms of which the taxpayer is designated as agent of the borrower to procure the loan at a rate not in excess of 6%, and further providing that the borrower shall pay directly to the broker a specified compensation or commission for procuring the loan. This compensation varies with the size of the loan and the risk involved.

After the execution of the broker's contract the borrower signs a regular form note payable to the bank, and at the time of the execution of the note the borrower also signs a sight draft payable and endorsed by the borrower. For convenience to the borrower, the draft is cashed by the taxpayer.

The various drafts and notes which are executed by borrowers during a particular period of time are placed in a large envelope, on the back of which is a sight draft payable to the order of a North Carolina bank with which the taxpayer transacts business. This general draft is sent to the Louisiana bank which, if it approves the various notes, accepts the general draft and thereupon forwards to the North Carolina bank a check to cover the various individual drafts which have been cashed by the taxpayer for the borrowers.

Each of the individual notes is endorsed by the taxpayer, and each individual loan is separately accepted by the Louisiana bank. If the Louisiana bank fails to accept a loan, it returns the note and draft involved to the taxpayer, who thereupon makes demand on the borrower to return the funds in exchange for the cancelled note and draft. In actual practice very few notes are declined, since the Louisiana bank relies largely on the endorsements of the taxpayer.

The broker's contract gives the borrower the option to make payments directly to the bank or to the taxpayer. Actually, nearly all payments are made to the taxpayer in accordance with a statement given to the borrower at the time the note is conditionally accepted. This statement specifies the periodic payments which the borrower must make in satisfaction of the loan, interest and brokerage fees. The loan and interest is repaid in full before any brokerage fee is received by the taxpayer, and the bank never receives more than repayment of the principal of the note plus interest in an amount not exceeding 6%. The funds which are loaned are furnished exclusively by the Louisiana bank, and the taxpayer carries a bank account sufficient only to cash drafts for a short period pending receipt of the remittance of the Louisiana bank covering loans which it has accepted.

All loans are made upon a single personal signature, without additional endorsements or guarantees, and without any form of security.

Completed typical forms used in these transactions have been submitted with the inquiry, and bear out the facts as stated above.

Mr. Hudgins contends that since Section 152 of the Revenue Act (G. S. 105-88) levies a tax upon a company "engaged in the regular business of making loans or lending money," and since the taxpayer does not lend his own money, but that of a third party, there is no tax liability. In other words, it is contended that the taxpayer and the Louisiana bank are entirely distinct; that the taxpayer merely brokers, arranges or negotiates the loans, and does not make them, or engage in the business of lending money.

On Mr. Hubbard's behalf, it is emphasized that the form of this business was not designed to attempt to evade the tax, but was originated in Texas and assumed this form in order to come under a Texas statute covering loan agents, negotiators or intermediaries, which are subject to a lower tax in that State than principals in the loan business.

I have been unable to find any decision of the courts or former opinion of this office throwing any light upon the proper application of the taxing statute to the stated facts. It is therefore necessary to seek the legislative intent in the words of the statute itself.

I have given much thought and consideration to the matter, and it is my opinion that taxpayer is liable for the tax imposed by the statute. My reasons for this conclusion are as follows:

(1) This statute first appeared in the Revenue Acts of the State in the Revenue Act of 1933. While it has been amended in particulars not pertinent to this inquiry, it has in every Revenue Act in which it has appeared carried the title "Loan Agencies or Brokers." While the caption or title of a statute is not, strictly speaking, a part of the statute, and cannot control the text when the text itself is clear, it may be resorted to as an aid to interpretation where the scope of the statute is subject to some doubt. IN RE CHISHOLM'S WILL, 176 N. C. 211; ELLIS v. GREENE, 191 N. C. 761; DUNN v. DUNN, 199 N. C. 535; DYER v. DYER, 212 N. C. 620; STYERS v. FORSYTH COUNTY, 212 N. C. 558; STATE v. KEELER, 214 N. C. 447. Thus, while the caption is not determinative, I believe it may be considered as an element tending to indicate the legislative intent. The term "brokers" has a signification which would include the activity of the taxpayer.

(2) Taxpayer relies on the wording laying the tax on persons, etc., "engaged in the regular business of making loans or lending money", and says that he is not doing either. It is perhaps possible to read these phrases in such a way that, by considering them alone, they support taxpayer's position.

However, the phrase "making loans" does not compel this conclusion, and hence taxpayer's position represents only a possible interpretation, and not the only reasonable interpretation. The verb "make" is one of broad connotation. Among the various meanings assigned this word in Webster's New International Dictionary are the following:

> "To cause to exist, appear or occur, ... to bring to pass; ... to give rise to; ... to cause to be or become; ... to constrain or compel (some action, or some person in respect to action); ... to effect; ... to act or behave so as to produce or gain; ... to cause such action that (one thing) is derived or formed out (of another); ... to form by appropriate action or behavior; ... to prepare or arrange; ... to perform or execute in the appropriate manner."

In the sense of these definitions, I think the taxpayer may reasonably be said to be in the business of making loans in that he arranges, effects, or causes the loans.

(3) The statute also lays the tax on person, etc., "advertising or soliciting such business in any manner whatsoever." The word "such" refers to the business theretofore described in the statute. Thus, even if (as I cannot concede) taxpayer was not himself making loans or lending money, he was advertising for and soliciting such business (i. e., the loan business), and the statute does not condition liability on advertisement or solicitation of *his own* loans. This interpretation is in harmony with the connotation of the word "brokers" in the title.

(4) The taxing statute, in the first paragraph, refers to an office maintained for the "negotiation" of such business and states that the license is

for the privilege of "transacting or negotiating such business." Assuming again that taxpayer's contention that he is not making loans or lending money is correct, he would nevertheless be "negotiating" (i. e., procuring or arranging) such business. This is, in my opinion, an additional indication that brokers are intended to be covered.

(5) The interpretation which I have made is in harmony with what seems to me to be the legislative intent. The statute states that it intends to tax "those persons or concerns operating what are commonly known as loan companies and finance companies" doing the described business. Taxpayer advertises and solicits the small loan business. So far as the borrowers are concerned, he is in the loan business. In spite of the form of the transaction, they look only to him in almost every case. He solicits the loan, arranges and effects the loan, and delivers to them the only money which they receive as a consequence of the loan. He handles all the papers for them, informs them about terms, and receives payments on the loan in practically all cases. I do not think the form of the transaction can alter the fact that essentially and basically, taxpayer is in the business of making loans. The Louisiana bank is too far away to exercise any consideration of or supervision over the loans, and it is evident that they rely entirely on the taxpayer's guaranty of payment.

I am thus unable to agree with taxpayer's position. However, if Mr. Hudgins or his client desire to place before you any further information, or to make any further contentions about the matter in the light of this letter or otherwise, I shall be glad to give further consideration of the matter before advising you finally.

I am sending a copy of this letter to Mr. Hudgins.

INHERITANCE TAX; ESTATE OF R. W. RICE; ILLEGITIMATE CHILD AS
CLASS A BENEFICIARY OF DECEASED FATHER

3 April, 1945

You inquire whether an illegitimate child is a Class A beneficiary of his father for inheritance tax purposes within the meaning of Section 3 of the Revenue Act of 1939, as amended.

It appears from the facts of the case under consideration that the testator had never married but had always recognized the beneficiary as his natural or illegitimate child, and that such child had possibly resided with the testator, his father, for a certain period. There is no evidence that the child had ever been legally adopted by the father.

Section 3 of the Revenue Act defines a Class A beneficiary of a decedent to be "the lineal issue, or lineal ancestor, or husband or wife, ... or step-child ... or child adopted by the decedent in conformity with the laws of this State, or of any of the United States, or of any foreign kingdom or nation ... " of such decedent. It is clear that an illegitimate child is not comprehended within this definition unless such child is to be classed as "lineal issue" of his deceased father.

At common law, illegitimate children were incapable of inheriting. This is the law in North Carolina today except as abrogated by certain statutory provisions authorizing them to inherit property from their mother and from their illegitimate brothers and sisters (G. S. 28-154, 29-1, rules 9 and 10). An illegitimate child cannot claim as heir or distributee of his or her father or through the blood of his or her father unless he or she has been duly legitimated in accordance with G. S. 49-10 or 49-12. Clark, C. J. in ASHE v. CAMP MFG. CO., 154 N. C. 242, states the law as follows: "An illegitimate is 'nullius fillius'—a son without a father—in the eye of the law.... All illegitimates are treated as children without a father of any kind. The law takes no notice of him, for they trace only through the mother, and for the purpose of inheriting property, the illegitimate children of the same mother are legitimates, as between themselves."

. Since under the law an illegitimate child is a "nullius fillius," it follows that such child is not considered the lineal issue of his or her reputed father, but rather, a stranger in blood. Therefore, I conclude that under the facts of the present case, the illegitimate child is not a Class A beneficiary of his or her father within the meaning of Section 3 of the Revenue Act.

In addition to the reasons referred to above, I call your attention to the general rule that the word "issue" when used in a statute, will, or deed shall be construed to mean lawful issue, and will not be extended to embrace illegitimate children unless such construction is necessary to carry into effect the manifest purpose of the legislature, testator, or grantee. 33 Corpus Juris p. 822; LOVE v. LOVE, 179 N. C. 115; DOGGETT v. MOSE-LEY, 52 N. C. 587; HARDESTY v. MITCHELL, 302 Ill. 269; FLORA v. ANDERSON, 67 F. 182; BRISBIN v. HUNTINGTON, 128 Iowa 166; KING v. THISSELL, 222 Mass. 140.

INCOME TAX; EMPLOYEES' TRUST; PREMIUMS PAID FOR LIFE INSURANCE PROTECTION; AMOUNT INCLUDIBLE AS INCOME BY EMPLOYEE

5 April, 1945

You have referred to me a letter from Lucas and Rand, dated March 28, with the request that I give you my opinion on the question raised therein.

A corporation, under an employees' trust plan, purchases retirement income insurance with life insurance protection payable upon the death of the employee participants. You inquire whether the employees in such a case are required under the North Carolina income tax law to report as income that portion of the premiums which represents payments for such life insurance protection.

There is no provision in the North Carolina income tax law or regulations with reference to this specific subject. However, I am advised by the Commissioner of Revenue that the Federal Regulations on this subject will be followed until and unless the Commissioner promulgates a regulation making different provisions.

It is my understanding that under the Federal ruling (Reg. 111, Sec. 29. 165-6) so much of the premiums as is paid by an employer under a trust plan that qualifies under Section 165(a) of the Internal Revenue Code for life insurance protection for an employee constitutes income to the employee for the year or years in which the premiums are paid for such life insurance protection. The cost of such insurance is considered to be the one year term premium for such amount based upon the rates of the company issuing the annuity contract, or, if no one year term policy is issued, the cost of such one year term contract computed by using the same mortality table and rate of interest and rate of loading as was used in determining the rates for the annuity contract. If the trust is one which is not exempt under Section 165(a), any contribution made by an employer for insurance on behalf of an employee must be considered as income to such employee if the employee's beneficial interest is nonforfeitable at the time the contribution is made. (Reg. 111, Sec. 29.165-7.)

The above cited Federal regulations are set forth in full in C.C.H. 1944 Federal Tax Service, Vol. 2, Sections 1150G and 1150H, and I suggest that reference be made to these regulations for a fuller explanation.

I enclose a copy of this letter for the use of Lucas and Rand.

INHERITANCE TAX; CONVEYANCE TO FIRST TAKER FOR LIFE WITH REMAINDER TO "ISSUE"; CHARACTER OF ESTATE CREATED

7 May, 1945

You request that I give you my opinion upon a question which has arisen in construing the terms of a deed made to Walter R. Browne on December 10, 1898. Mr. Browne is now deceased, and, in ascertaining the inheritance tax liability of this estate, it is necessary to determine the nature of the estate which he acquired under the terms of the aforementioned conveyance.

The grantor in the deed conveys certain real property, subject to a life estate reserved for herself, to "Walter R. Browne of the second part, ... for and during the term of the natural life of the said Walter R. Browne and after his death to his isssue...." In the habendum clause these words appear: "To have and to hold unto the said Walter R. Browne of the second part, for and during the term of his natural life and after his death the remainder to his issue absolutely and forever; ... "

The question is whether under this deed Walter R. Browne received a life estate or whether, under the rule in Shelley's case, he received an estate in fee simple.

It would seem that the words of conveyance in this deed represent everything that is necessary for the application of the rule in Shelley's case except that the remainder is limited to the "issue" of the first taker rather than to his "heirs." The question therefore, in my opinion, turns upon whether the word "issue" as used in the deed is a word of limitation or a word of purchase.

The word "issue" per se is not a technical word of either limitation or purchase. 47 Am. Jur. p. 804; 33 C. J. p. 824; 29 L.R.A. (N.S.) 963; DANIEL v. WHARTENBY, 84 U.S. 639. Some courts have held that standing alone it is prime facie a word of limitation equivalent to heirs of the body, while others have declared it to be a word of either purchase or limitation depending upon the grantor's or testator's manifest purpose as expressed in the instrument. Still others have held that it is synonomous with "children," which generally is construed to be a word of purchase.

Etheridge v. Realty Co., 179 N. C. 407; Bobbitt v. Pierson, 193 N. C. 437; SMITH v. SMITH, 130 Ga. 532; PARKHURST v. HARROWER, 142 Pa. 432. The decisions in some states have laid down the arbitrary rule that "issue" when used in a deed is always a word of purchase. McILHINNY v. McILHINNY, 137 Ind. 411; FINDLAY v. RIDDLE, 3 Binn. (Pa) 139.

In FAISON v. ODOM, 144 N. C. 108, the Court considered the question in connection with a will. There the devise was to "Matthew J. Faison ... in trust for the use and benefit of my son Edward, during his life, ... and after the death of my son Edward, to his issue forever." In deciding whether the Rule in Shelley's case had application in this case, the court speaks as follows:

> "There have been cases where it was the manifest intention of the testator that the second taker should take, not from him, but from the first taker; then the words 'children,' 'issue,' etc., as well as the word 'heirs,' have been construed in some jurisdictions as words of limitation, and the Rule in Shelley's case applied. BRINTON v. MARTIN, 197 Pa. St., 618. In the will under consideration there is no manifest intention that Edward Faison should be the root of a new succession and that those in remainder should take as his heirs. In order to bring the rule into operation, the limitation must be to the 'heirs qua heirs' of the first taker. 'It must be given to the heirs or heirs of the body as an entire class or denomination of persons, and not merely to individuals embraced within such class.' 25 A. & E., 650, and cases cited.
> "When the devise is to one for life and after his death to his children or issue, the rule has no application unless it manifestly appears that such words are used in the sense of heirs generally. 25 A. & E., supra, 651, and cases cited.
> "In this will the word 'issue' is evidently used in no such sense, but as a correlative term for children, and this word is not sufficient to indicate a purpose to create an estate of inheritance in Edward Faison. ... "

In BOBBITT v. PIERSON, *supra*, the devise was to Benjamin W. Bobbitt, "for his own use and benefit as long as he lives, and at the time of his death, to go to his issue." The Court upheld the decision in FAISON v. ODOM and held that "issue" as used in the will must be construed to mean children, thus refusing to apply the rule in Shelley's case.

Commenting on the same subject, the Court in FORD v. McBRAYER, 171 N. C. 423, makes the following summary:

> "The cases construing the terms 'issue,' 'issue of the body,' 'bodily issue' are collected in 4 Words and Phrases, p. 3782 et. seq.; and it will also be found from an examination of these and other authorities that there is much difference of opinion as to the method of approaching the construction of the language when used in deeds and wills, some courts holding that the primary meaning of 'issue' is a succession of lineal descendants, and that this interpretation must be given to the term unless a contrary intent appears, while others, when dealing with the rule in Shelley's case, which they are not disposed to extend, and having in mind that the word 'issue' is 'more flexible' than the word 'heirs' (DANIEL v. WHARTENBY, *supra*), and may be applied to those who take by purchase, hold that it must clearly appear that it was the intention to use the term as one of limitation to denote a succession of lineal descendants who are to take by inheritance before that construction will be adopted.
> "The latter view seems to prevail in this State."

A deed in which the word "issue" was used is considered by the North Carolina court in PARRISH v. HODGE, 178 N .C. 133. The conveyance was to Hattie A. Norris, and in the habendum clause were these words: "To have and to hold the aforesaid tract of land to Hattie I. Norris and heirs of her body or issue, to their only use and behoof forever." It was the opinion of the court that "issue" here was intended as synonomous with "heirs of the body" and that the grantee received a fee simple estate. However, that case is readily distinguishable from the case under consideration.

Numerous decisions in this State have reiterated the principle that in construing a deed, as well as a will, such construction should be made of the words of the instrument as is most agreeable to the intention of the maker. COBB v. HINES, 44 N. C. 343; HAYWOOD v. RIGGSBEE, 207 N. C. 685. It is also true, however, that while a will or deed will be construed from its four corners to ascertain and give effect to the intent of the testator or grantor, this intent must be gathered from the language used in the instrument, and the maker will be deemed to have used technical words or phrases in their legal and technical sense unless he indicates in some appropriate way that a different meaning be ascribed to them. WHITLEY v. ARENSON, 219 N. C. 121.

There is no indication in the wording of the deed under consideration that the grantor used the word "issue" as a technical word of limitation or in the sense of heirs generally. Therefore, under the principle laid down in FAISON v. ODOM and BOBBITT v. PIERSON, *supra*, it is to be presumed that the term was employed as a designatio personarum, which would make the Rule in Shelley's case inapplicable.

I therefore conclude that Walter R. Browne took only a life estate under the conveyance.

SALES AND USE TAXES: T. A. LOVING COMPANY; CONTRACTS WITH
FEDERAL GOVERNMENT

9 July, 1945

You have requested my opinion upon the following matter.

T. A. Loving Company, hereinafter referred to as the taxpayer, under contract NOy-6867 entered into, on August 1, 1943, with the Federal Government (represented by the Navy Department), undertook to provide and secure the completion of certain facilities commenced or contemplated under a cost-plus-fixed-fee contract NOy-4957 (which was terminated 31 July 1943) relating to certain work at the U. S. Marine Corp Air Station at Cherry Point and certain outlying fields. An audit of taxpayer's records have raised questions regarding sales and use tax liability upon certain types of purchases. These purchases fell within two different clasifications and you request my opinion upon application of sales and use taxes to each class of purchase.

The classifications and my respective opinions regarding them are as follows:

(1) Purchases from in-state and out-of-state vendors which were assumed by taxpayer and which had by original purchase by contractor NOy-4957

with purchase order forms which had been approved.as tax exempt by the Commissioner of Revenue.

The question here involved is, of course, whether there was a sale from contractor NOy-4957 to taxpayer or whether taxpayer purchased certain materials for use and consumption within the meaning of the use tax law. If there was a sale or purchase, the tax would apply to these transactions.

A determination of this question involves a construction of the agreements and business relations between the parties.

It appears that contract NOy-6867 is a lump sum contract which provides generally that taxpayer "shall furnish the materials for and perform the following work...: to provide and secure completion of facilities commenced or contemplated under a cost-plus-fixed-fee contract NOy-4957...." The contract further provides that the work to be performed by taxpayer includes the furnishing of all labor required to complete the work; the furnishing of all materials which were not purchased under contract NOy-4957 and not delivered prior to August 1, 1943; and the assumption of liability upon and responsibility for all orders for purchase of materials entered into under C.P.F.F. contract NOy-4957 to the extent that the materials covered thereby were undelivered on August 1, 1943. The contract further provides that the Government shall be reimbursed for such materials as are purchased by the contractor by a reduction of the consideration, or the contract price. The effect and intent of these provisions seems to be that as to materials which had been ordered by contractor NOy-4957 on the tax exempt purchase order and which had been delivered to the Navy, the taxpayer would obtain these materials from the Navy at the cost paid for them which would be paid by merely reducing the contract price in an appropriate amount. Since the Navy is not engaged in the business of selling materials and the transaction is an incidental and unusual transaction which was made necessary by the execution of a new contract, it is my opinion that you should not continue this transaction as a sale and should exempt from tax such materials as had been delivered to the Navy under exempt purchase orders.

As to materials ordered by contractor NOy-4957 on the tax exempt purchase order form which had not been delivered at the time taxpayer entered into contract NOy-6867, it is my opinion that there would be no tax for the reason that taxpayer by the contract merely assumes whatever liability existed on the part of contractor NOy-4957 and since the orders were on tax exempt forms no tax liability was created.

(2) The second class of transaction involves purchases from in-state and out-of-state vendors of materials purchased directly by taxpayer under contract NOy-6867 for carrying ont the contract. It is my opinion that materials so purchased are subject to the tax. The contract is a lump sum contract providing that taxpayer shall furnish the materials, therefore, the sales were to taxpayer and not to the Navy and there is no basis for tax exemption.

Taxpayer contends that these sales should be exempt because of a statement made in a letter of the Navy Department dated December 15, 1943 and directed to the officer in charge of Contract NOy-6867. This letter contains a statement to the effect that the contract (which was not executed until the following August) would contain a provision constituting the contractor a purchasing agent of the Government and directing the taxpayer in making purchases to notify its vendors that it was a purchasing agent for the Government. However, this statement is not borne out by the final contract. I am unable to find any provision in contract NOy-6867 which constitutes taxpayer a purchasing agent for the Government with respect to materials purchased thereunder. It is my opinion that the completed contract is controlling on this point and that the preliminary letter would not have the effect of changing this contract. I enclose an extra of this opinion for your use.

TAXATION - INCOME; OPTIMIST PARK, INCORPORATED, DEDUCTIBILITY OF CONTRIBUTIONS TO

6 August, 1945

You have requested my opinion on the following facts:

Optimist Park, Incorporated, was chartered under the provisions of G. S. 55-11 and is to operate a park for boys in a certain portion of the City of Charlotte. The charter of this corporation provides that it has powers and is incorporated for the purposes and objects mentioned in the statute. Its aim is to effectuate its slogan, "Friend of the Boy." In soliciting contributions, this corporation desires to tell prospective contributors that any contribution made to it may be deducted in computing net income for the purpose of income taxation. You inquire if such contributions are deductible.

Subsection 9 of Section 322 of the Revenue Act provides that contributions made to corporations, etc., organized and operated exclusively for religious, charitable, literary, scientific or educational purposes or for the prevention of cruelty to children or animals, no part of the net earnings of which inures to the benefit of any private stockholder or individual, may be deducted in computing net income. It appears that this corporation would not be liable for taxes on the property owned by it. The last sentence of G. S. 55-11 contains this exemption. Under Article V, Section 5, of the North Carolina Constitution, the General Assembly is authorized to exempt from taxation property held for educational, scientific, literary, charitable or religious purposes. The declaration in G. S. 55-11 that the property of corporations chartered under the provisions of that section shall be exempt from taxation is tantamount to a declaration that such corporations are either educational, scientific, literary, charitable or religious, since the Constitution authorizes only property of such corporations to be exempted from taxation. Since statutes are presumed to be constitutional, I am compelled to accept this indirect legislative declaration of the status of corporations chartered pursuant to the provisions of G. S. 55-11. Optimist Park, Incorporated, was chartered pursuant to the provisions of that section; therefore, I advise that in my opinion contributions made to this corporation are deductible in computing net income for income tax purposes.

INHERITANCE TAXATION; PAYMENT BY CORPORATION TO DECEASED OFFICER'S
WIDOW; IF IN PAYMENT OF PAST SERVICES, DEDUCTIBLE AS CORPORATE
EXPENSE AND PART OF GROSS ESTATE OF DECEASED FOR
INHERITANCE TAX PURPOSES

9 August, 1945

You have requested my opinion based upon the following facts.

It appears that the decedent was an officer of a corporation and that after
his death the corporation paid to his widow the sum of $3,000. It appears
further that the corporation proposes to deduct this amount for income tax
purposes as an ordinary and necessary expense under G. S. 105-147. You
desire to know whether the above sum is taxable in the hands of the widow
either as income, gift or inheritance.

The fact that the corporation proposes to treat the payment to the widow
as a deductible expense in calculating the corporation's income taxes indicates that the payment represents the satisfaction of a debt arising from the
decedent's services as an officer of the corporation. Unless the payment
was of this character, it would not be deductible as an ordinary and necessary
business expense by the corporation. On the assumption, therefore, that the
payment represents compensation for the decedent's services, such payment
would be properly payable to the decedent's estate rather than to his widow.
For this reason the sum paid to the widow must be treated, for tax purposes,
as if it actually had been paid to the estate. This means, of course, that the
sum should be included, for inheritance tax purposes, in the decedent's gross
estate.

On the other hand, if the payment to the widow represents a gratuity to
her, rather than compensation for her deceased husband's services, it would
then be subject to the gift tax; and in such case the corporation could not
treat the payment as a deductible expense.

INCOME TAX; BASIS FOR DETERMINING GAIN ON SALE OF STOCK
PURCHASED BEFORE JANUARY 1, 1921

10 August, 1945

You request that I give you my opinion upon the legality of a proposed
income tax assessment for the year 1941 against Mr. Thomas G. Horner.

It appears that the taxpayer, during the year 1941, sold certain stock
which he had acquired prior to January 1, 1921. Taxpayer on his return
determined the market value of the stock as of March 1, 1913, and finding
this amount to be greater than the amount realized from the sale thereof,
reported a loss on the transaction. The Commissioner of Revenue, upon an
examination of the return, disallowed this loss, and proposes an additional
assessment of tax which arises by reason of the fact that the actual cost of
the stock to the taxpayer was used as the basis for determining the gain or
loss. In using the cost basis, a taxable gain was found instead of a loss.

The taxpayer contends that the Commissioner should use as the basis the
fair market value of the stock as of January 1, 1921, instead of the actual
cost thereof.

Section 319 of the Revenue Act contains the following provision:

"For the purpose of ascertaining the gain or loss from the sale or other disposition of property, real, personal, or mixed, the basis shall be, in the case of property acquired before January first, ane thousand nine hundred and twenty-one, the fair market price or the value of such property as of that date and in all other coses the cost thereof. *The cost of such property acquired prior to January first, one thousand nine hundred and twenty-one, would be used in all cases if such cost is known or determinable: ...*"

In view of the above underlined sentence, it is my opinion that the Commissioner is correct in requiring the taxpayer to use the actual cost of the stock as the basis for determining gain or loss. The statute clearly states that if the cost is known or determinable, it *would* be used. I think the word "would" as used here is synonomous with "shall" and thus is used in a mandatory sense.

The taxpayer further contends that the tax imposed upon such portion of the gain realized by the taxpayer as accrued prior to January 1, 1921, the date of the enactment of the State income statute, is unconstitutional. With this I cannot agree.

In NORMAN v. BRADLEY, 173 Ga., 482, 160 S. E. 413, the Court considered this point. Georgia passed an income tax statute in 1929. Thereafter, a taxpayer sold coco-cola stock and realized a profit, all of which was due to increases in value prior to 1929. The Court held that no gain was realized until the sale, and since the sale occurred after the enactment of the income tax law, the gain was taxable. The appeal was dismissed in the United States Supreme Court, sub nom. GLEN v. DOYAL, 285 U. S., 526, 76 L. Ed. 923, "for want of a substantial federal question."

The power to tax such gains was thoroughly considered in MacLAUGHLIN, COLLECTOR v. ALLIANCE INSURANCE CO., 286 U. S. 244, 76 L. Ed. 1083. Here the Court speaks as follows:

"The tax being upon the realized gain, it may constitutionally be imposed upon the entire amount of the gain realized within the taxable period, even though some of it represents enhanced value in an earlier perior before the adoption of the taxing act. COOPER v. UNITED STATES, 280 U. S. 409, 74 L. Ed. 516, 50 S. Ct. 164; compare TAFT v. BOWERS, 278 U. S. 470, 73 L. Ed. 460, 64 A.L.R. 362, 49 S. Ct. 199."

Thus, it is my conclusion that the taxpayer is liable for the payment of the proposed income tax assessment upon the taxable gain as found by the Commissioner.

License Taxes; FHA Loans on Real Estate; Negotiating Loans of Another Person's Money

5 September, 1945

You have referred to me correspondence from————, Attorneys at Law, Charlotte, N. C., relative to ———— Realty & Loan Corporation. It appears that this corporation is in the real estate business, but prior to this time has never engaged in the loan business. It has now been made an approved mortgagee of the FHA. It proposes to make loans for loan correspondents and also to make FHA loans in its own name with its own funds and sell to insurance companies and other loan investment companies. Your inquiry relates to the applicability of G. S. 105-88, and G. S. 105-41.

G. S. 105-41, which is Section 109 of the Revenue Act, applies to a person "who is engaged in the business of soliciting and/or negotiating loans on real estate as agent for another for a commission, brokerage and/or other compensation."

G. S. 105-88, which is Section 152 of the Revenue Act, applies to "every person, firm or corporation engaged in the regular business of making loans or lending money, accepting liens on, or contracts of assignment of, salaries or wages, or any part thereof, or other security or evidences of debt for repayment of such loans in installment payments or otherwise, and maintaining in connection with same any office or other located or established place for the conduct, negotiation, or transaction of such business and/or advertising or soliciting such business in any manner whatsoever." This section does not apply to the "business of negotiating loans on real estate as described in Section one hundred nine of this Act."

It is my understanding that the loans to be made by ——— Realty & Loan Corporation will all be loans on real estate and that no loans will be made on an open or unsecured note. Your inquiry is limited to FHA real estate loans.

It appears that ——— Realty & Loan Corporation will engage not only in the business of lending its own money, but also in the business of negotiating loans of money advanced by other persons.

On the basis of the sections set out above, I am of the opinion that both G. S. 105- 41 and G. S. 105-88 are applicable to this case. I am of the opinion that ——— Realty & Loan Corporation, by engaging in the business of making FHA loans with its own money, brings itself within the definition of a loan agency in G. S. 105-88. The above quoted exception to G. S. 105- 88 relates only to the business of negotiating loans on real estate as defined in G. S. 105-41. An examination of the last quoted section shows that said section applies to the business of soliciting and/or negotiating loans or real estate *as agent for another* for a commission, brokerage and/or other compensation. Thus, I am of the opinion that G. S. 105-41 applies to that part of the corporation's business which consists of making loans for loan correspondents.

I therefore conclude that G. S. 105-41 applies to the corporation's business of making loans with funds belonging to its correspondents and that G. S. 105-88 applies to the corporation's business of making such loans with its own funds.

INCOME TAXES; DEDUCTION OF EXCESS PROFITS PAID TO UNITED KINGDOM

6 September, 1945

You inquire whether the ——— Tobacco Co., Inc., may deduct from its gross income for the year 1942 the amount of income taxes paid to the United Kingdom for the same year by its parent corporation, the ——— Tobacco Co., Ltd.

It appears that the ——— Tobacco Co. is a foreign corporation chartered under the laws of the State of Delaware but is domesticated in this State. It is a subsidiary of the ——— Tobacco Co., Ltd. of London, England. The tax in question was paid by the ——— Tobacco Co. Ltd. on behalf of the ——— Tobacco Co. for the reason that under English law the subsidiary is considered to be a resident of the United Kingdom since it is controlled by a parent company which is a resident there. The ——— Tobacco Co. reimbursed the ——— Tobacco Co., Ltd. for the amount of the tax and contends that the amount of such reimbursement should be allowed as a deduction.

The Department of Revenue refused to allow the deduction in 1942 for the reasons (1) that the English tax was actually levied against the ——— Tobacco Co., Ltd. instead of the subsidiary, and (2) that the tax is an excess profits tax and therefore is one based upon net income which is expressly declared to be not deductible in Section 322, subsection 4, of the Revenue Act.

On August 20, 1945, counsel for the ——— Tobacco Co. submitted to the department a favorable ruling on the allowance of the deduction rendered by the Collector of Internal Revenue in a letter dated July 3, 1945, and requested that the department consider the matter further. An examination of this ruling discloses that the Federal Government has held that the amount claimed is deductible, not as a tax, but as an ordinary and necessary business expense. This ruling arising by reason of the fact that the ——— Tobacco Co. Ltd. has a power of recovery from the ——— Tobacco Co., for taxes paid to the United Kingdom on behalf of the latter company. In justifying the deduction, the Collector makes the following statement in his letter referred to above:

"Any charge, whether for reimbursement of taxes paid by another as in the present case, if such charge is a legitimate business expense, as in the present case (in view of the power of recovery), would be treated as a deductible expense under Section 23(a) and the accrual would be effective at the date when the charge is made by the creditor."

It is my opinion that the Collector is correct in allowing the deduction under the Federal Income Tax Statute since, as he points out, the English tax in this case would have been deductible under the statute if it had in fact been levied against and paid by the ——— Tobacco Co. However, under Section 233 (4) of the North Carolina Revenue Act the tax paid to the United Kingdom would not have been deductible by the ——— Tobacco Co. even though it had been imposed directly against it, since as pointed out above, the section specifically provides that income taxes, or taxes which are in fact based on net income, shall not be deductible. Thus, if the amount is non-deductible as a tax under Section 322(4), it follows that it cannot be deducted as an ordinary and necessary business expense under Section 322(1) of the Revenue Act. To hold otherwise would, in my opinion, defeat the purpose of Section 322(4). Even though the amount paid to the ——— Tobacco Co. Ltd. by its subsidiary be reflected on the books of the latter as an operating expense, it actually represents the tax that has been assessed and paid, and the question of its deduction must be governed by Section 322(4).

I conclude, therefore, that such deduction is not authorized under the State Income Tax Law.

INCOME TAXES; MEANING OF "INTERNAL REVENUE AGENTS REPORT OR
SUPPLEMENTAL REPORT" IN SECTION 334

10 September, 1945

You state that you have denied a refund of taxes paid for the year ended
November 30, 1941, to the Cliffside Mills for the reasons (1) that the claim
for refund was not filed within three years of the date of payment, and
(2) that the taxpayer failed to notify you within thirty days of receipt of
a supplemental revenue agent's report reflecting a change in net income
made by the Federal Government.

The Cliffside Mills contends that the refund should be made since,
although it did not notify you within thirty days of receipt of revenue agents
supplemental report it did notify you within thirty days after such report
was approved by the office of the Commissioner of Internal Revenue in Washington. Stated in other words, it is the taxpayer's contention that when a
taxpayer's reported net income is changed or corrected by the Federal
Government and such taxpayer protests the findings of a local agent in
charge, notice to the Commissioner of Revenue as required in Section 334
of the Income Tax Article, may be delayed until the local agent's report is
approved or disapproved by the final authority of the Bureau of Internal
Revenue in Washington.

The State Department of Revenue has construed Section 334 as requiring
taxpayer to notify the Commissioner of such change in net income within
thirty days after receiving the report of the local agent in charge, whether
or not such report has been finally determined to be correct by the final
authority.

The pertinent portion of Section 334 is as follows: "If the amount of the
net income of any year of any taxpayer under this article, as returned to
the United States Treasury Department, is changed and corrected by the
Commissioner of Internal Revenue or other officer of the United States of
competent authority, such taxpayer, within thirty days after receipt of
Internal Revenue Agent's report or supplemental report reflecting the correct net income, shall make return under oath or affirmation to the Commissioner of Revenue of such corrected net income."

The express wording of the above quoted section seems to strongly support
the position taken by the Commissioner of Revenue. The phrase "Internal
Revenue Agent's report or supplemental report reflecting the correct net
income," in my opinion, clearly has reference to the report prepared by a
local agent in charge, a copy of which is submitted to a taxpayer upon the
completion of the original examination of a taxpayer's return. Had the
statute been intended to refer to any other report of final assessment or reassessment, handed down by the Bureau in Washington upon protest of the
local agent's report by the taxpayer, it would surely have been written to
indicate this. The original report prepared by a local Federal Agent in
charge is designated by the Bureau to be a "revenue agent's report," and,
in transmitting a copy to the taxpayer, it is so called in the letter of trans-
mittal.

Thus, it is my conclusion that the Commissioner of Revenue is correct in
denying the refund in this case since the notification prescribed by Section
334 was not made within the thirty day period.

INCOME TAXES; DEDUCTION OF PREMIUM PAID· BY CORPORATION
FOR ITS OWN BONDS

21 September, 1945

You have requested my opinion as to deductibility of an alleged loss resulting from the cash purchase and retirement by a corporation of its own bonds at a premium. It appears that W. S. Clark & Sons, Inc., of Tarboro, N. C., claimed an income tax deduction on account of a reported or alleged loss resulting from the fact that the corporation during the 1942 and 1943 taxable years called, paid and cancelled, at a premium of 1%, registered debenture bonds previously issued by the same corporation. The amount of the claimed deduction is equivalent to the 1% premium which was paid by the corporation in purchasing and retiring the bonds.

Your request calls directly into issue the correctness of a ruling given by the former Attorney General, A. A. F. Seawell, on January 26, 1937, in the case of Liggett and Myers Tobacco Company, to the effect that, when a corporation purchases its own bonds upon an open market at a premium *and retires them* (instead of reselling them), no deductible loss has been occasioned by the fact that a premium above face was paid. This ruling is further to the effect that no deductible loss arises even in the absence of retirement, if the bonds are not yet resold. Apparently, the ruling is also to the effect that a deductible loss "might" arise only where the corporation buys its bonds on the open market *and resells* them, and that no loss can arise unless and until a resale at less than purchase price.

The corporation in the instant case disagrees with the above ruling and contends that it violates Section 318 of our Revenue Act, which, *inter alia*, provides that if the taxpayer's accounting method does not clearly reflect his income "the computation of net income shall be made in accordance with such method as in the opinion of the Commissioner does clearly reflect the income, but shall follow as nearly as practicable the Federal practice, unless contrary to the context and intent of this article." The taxpayer contends that this section compels the Commissioner to follow the Federal rule with respect to what deductions are allowable, and he cites Section 29.22 (a) 17 of Federal Income Tax Regulations 94 which provides as follows:

"*Sale and Purchase by Corporation of its Bonds.* (1) (a) If bonds are issued by a corporation at their face value, the corporation realizes no gain or loss. (b) If the corporation purchases any of such bonds at a price in excess of the issuing price or face value, the excess of the purchase price over the ·issuing price or face value is a deductible expense for the taxable year. (c) If, however, the corporation purchases any of such bonds at a price less than the issuing price or face value, the excess of the issuing price or face value over the purchase price is gain or income for the taxable year."

I cannot agree that Section 318 of our Revenue Act compels us to allow deductions authorized by Federal regulations. Section 318 refers only to a "method of accounting" designed to reflect clearly the taxpayer's income. It deals only with procedural or administrative, as distinguished from substantive, matters. A directive to accept a method of bookkeeping or accounting does not carry with it any change or adoption of substantive rules of income tax law. I am of the opinion that Section 318 has no effect to determine what deductions are allowable as a matter of substantive right, and that its only purpose is to provide the use of accounting methods which clearly reflect net income as determined under other applicable provisions of the Revenue Act. I am further of the opinion that the allowability of losses as deductions are determinable under the provisions of Section 322 without resort to Section 318. I, therefore, conclude that Section 318 is ineffectual to compel the Commissioner to accept Section 29.22 (a) 17 of the Federal Income Tax Regulation 94 as a correct statement of the law under our Revenue Act.

For the reasons set out above I conclude that the premiums paid by the taxpayer in this case in the purchase and retirement of its own bonds are not deductible.

INCOME TAX; OPA PENALTY AS BUSINESS DEDUCTION

24 September, 1945

You have referred to me a letter from Standard Chair Company of Thomasville, N. C., taxpayer, who claims a deduction consisting of a payment made to the Treasurer of the United States under Section 205(e) of the Emergency Price Control Act of 1942, as amended. It appears that the payment represented a compromise with OPA enforcement attorneys of claims asserted on account of overcharges made by the taxpayer in the course of trade or business. The amount paid was $13,742.70, representing double the amount of overcharges. The full statutory penalty would have been three time the amount of overcharges.

I am of the opinion that the above-mentioned payment is not deductible as an ordinary and necessary business expense under the Revenue Act. Such payment is in the nature of a penalty for a violation of law. The fact that the amount of the penalty was fixed by a compromise agreement, rather than by the court in an action brought by the Price Administrator under the Price Control Act, does not change its character as a penalty. Neither does the fact that the taxpayer's violation was innocent alter the result in any way, for the penalty is incurred under the Price Control Act irrespective of wilfulness or negligence. It is true that the "Chandler Defense" became effective July 1, 1944, allowing a defendant to escape partial liability by showing due care and other things, but this amendment does not aid taxpayer for two reasons: (1) It became effective after taxpayer had incurred the penalty, and (2) it would not affect the character of the penalty actually imposed in any event. Thus, under the Price Control Act the amount paid to the Treasurer of the United States for OPA violations is a penalty, irrespective of the innocent character of the violations and irrespective of the manner in which the amount is fixed and paid.

"Fines and penalties paid by a taxpayer to the government on account of a crime or statutory violation, and penalties paid or incurred by a taxpayer on account of delinquent taxes have been held not deductible, in computing his income tax, as ordinary and necessary business expenses." 27 *Am. Jur., Income Taxes*, Section 98.

In *Commissioner of Internal Revenue v. Longhorn Portland Cement Company*, the U. S. Circuit Court of Appeals, Fifth Circuit, on March 27,

1945, held that statutory penalties were not deductible even though the taxpayer denied his guilt and made a compromise settlement only to avoid expensive litigation.

The reason for this rule is that the penalty is a punishment inflicted by the government for acts violative of fixed public policy, and to permit the violator to gain a tax advantage through deducting his penalty would frustrate the public policy. When a penalty is paid, the violation, in effect, is admited, and the result is the same as it would be in the event the penalty were imposed by the court.

This view is supported by the Federal authorities. The Internal Revenue Office has expressly ruled that payments made to the government by reason of overcharge giving rise to a cause of action under Section 205(e) of the Emergency Price Control Act of 1942 in favor of the Price Administrator, are not deductible (P-H, Sec. 11,086-D). I see no reason why this rule is not equally applicable under our Revenue Act.

For the reasons set out above I conclude that OPA penalties for overcharges, when paid to the government, are not deductible. I expressly refrain from ruling on OPA penalties collected by a consumer.

I am unable to understand taxpayer's statement that, "The Internal Revenue Agent allowed a deduction of $88.05 for overcharges on sales made prior to 1942." There could have been no "overcharges" prior to 1942. It was in January, 1942 that the Price Control Act was passed. If taxpayer · refunded or paid on sales made prior to 1942, he must have done so voluntarily, and it may have been on this basis that Internal Revenue allowed the $88.05 deduction.

INCOME TAXES; DEDUCTION OF PREMIUM PAID BY CORPORATION FOR ITS OWN BONDS

5 October, 1945

This is in reference to your letter of August 29, 1945, in which you request my opinion on the deductibility of an alleged loss arising out of the fact that Carolina Power and Light Company of Raleigh, North Carolina, purchased and retired some of their own bonds at a premium. It appears that this case may be different from others on which this office has given unfavorable rulings to the taxpayers in that the purchase and retirement of the bonds were made by the corporation pursuant to a legal obligation which arose simultaneously with the issuance of the bonds and which was part and parcel of the entire transaction from the beginning. It appears that the bonds were issued upon the written agreement and condition that a certain number, amount or percentage thereof should be retired for cash at a stated premium each year, the identity of the retirable bonds to be determined each year by lot. The point is made that the payment of the premium is thus a legal obligation having the same dignity as interest because it arose at the same time and in the same manner and, as a practical matter, represents interest payable in advance to the holder of the retired bond in lieu of the interest which would accrue if the bond were permitted to mature.

This office has heretofore ruled that a corporation which voluntarily purchases and retires its own bonds at a premium does not sustain a deductible loss. However, it should be observed that such ruling referred to a case in which the purchase and retirement of the bonds at a premium was voluntary on the part of the corporation. It appeared to the Attorney General at that time that if a corporation voluntarily paid a premium, it was unlikely that any real loss would occur. The fact that the corporation voluntarily paid the premium is an indication that the purchase is to the ultimate advantage of the corporation.

In my opinion the same considerations do not hold in a case where the corporation is required either by law or by contractual obligation to purchase and retire its own bonds at a premium. In such case there is no basis for a presumption that the purchase at a premium will result in an ultimate gain or other advantage flowing directly from such purchase. In the case at hand it appears that the taxpayer is under a legal contractual obligation to purchase its bonds at a premium, and that said obligation is co-existent with the issuance of the bonds themselves. It, therefore, appears that the legal duty to purchase these bonds is as binding as the duty to pay the same or to pay interest on the same.

Under these circumstances, I am of the opinion that the previous ruling of this office in inapplicable, and that the premium paid by the taxpayer, under the circumstances related in this letter, represents a deductible loss in the taxable year during which it was sustained.

FRANCHISE TAXES; FOREIGN CORPORATION DOING BUSINESS THROUGH UNINCORPORATED SUBSIDIARY

17 October, 1945

This is in reference to certain correspondence regarding North Georgia Lumber Company, Inc.

North Georgia Lumber Company, Inc. is a Georgia corporation. It does not do any business in this state under its corporate name. However, it does wholly own the Georgia Pipe Company, which is not a corporation, but which is an unincorporated business set up and owned by the Georgia corporation. The Georgia Pipe Company is a small concern which processes and cuts smoking pipe blocks which it supplies to "Briarhouse," another unincorporated company located in Brooklyn, New York, and also wholly owned by North Georgia Lumber Company, Inc., the Georgia corporation.

The North Georgia Lumber Company, Inc., contends that it does not do business in the State of North Carolina; and, therefore, is not subject to the franchise tax. It contends that the Georgia Pipe Company, although owned by a corporation, is not a corporation itself, and carries on its business as a separate firm.

In support of its contention, the North Georgia Lumber Company, Inc. cites a letter purported to have been written by the Hon. Thad Eure, Secretary of State, on July 24, 1945, which is alleged to contain the following language:

"The law of this State does not require the filing with the Secretary of State of date by an unincorporated foreign company which is engaged in business in North Carolina, nor does our statute require a foreign corporation to file with the Secretary of State any corporation data by reason of the operation in North Carolina of such unincorporated subsidiary."

I am not able to say in what connection the aforesaid statement was made by the Secretary of State, or under what circumstances he expressed his opinion. However, I am sure that it was not his intention to exempt a corporation from the statutory requirements simply because the corporation saw fit to carry on its business in this state under some name other than the name of the corporation. Under the facts as set out above it is my opinion that the North Georgia Lumber Company, Inc. is doing business within the State of North Carolina, and is subject to all of the burdens entailed thereby. It is of no consequence that such business is carried on under another name. The Georgia Pipe Company is not a legal entity; neither is it owned by individuals. Inasmuch as it is owned and operated by a corporation, the business performed by it is essentially that of the corporation.

For the reasons stated herein, I advise that the North Georgia Lumber Company, Inc. is subject to the franchise tax imposed by the Revenue Act.

I am sending a copy of this letter to the Secretary of State in order that he may be advised of our position in the matter.

SALES TAX; LENSES AND FRAMES NOT "MEDICAL SUPPLIES"
WITHIN THE MEANING OF SECTION 406(k)

30 October, 1945

You request that I give you my opinion upon the question whether lenses and frames which are to be made into glasses for the eyes are "medical supplies" within the meaning of section 406(k) of the Revenue Act of 1939, as amended; and are, therefore, exempt from the 3% retail sales tax when sold to physicians.

Section 406, subsection (k), exempts from the 3% sales tax "sales of . . . medical supplies to physicians or hospitals or by physicians and hospitals to patients in connection with medical treatments."

Section 406, subsection (r), of the Revenue Act exempts from the 3% sales tax "sales of crutches and sales of artificial limbs, artificial eyes, artificial hearing devices, when the same are designed to be worn on the person of the owner or user, and sales of orthopedic appliances." It seems to me that artificial hearing devices and certain types of orthopedic appliances might be termed medical supplies to as great an extent as, if not greater than, glasses for the eyes. However, the legislature, in specifically incorporating such items as exempt in an entirely different sub-section from the one relating to medical supplies, has indicated, in my opinion, the intent that the term, "medical supplies," as used in sub-section (k), should be construed in a strict sense, and as not contemplating any type of appliance or visual aid such as eyeglasses.

Therefore, I conclude that the 3% sales tax must be collected upon the sale to physicians of lenses and frames, since such items are neither specifically exempt nor intended to fall within the category of "medical supplies," as used in section 406(k).

USE TAX; TAXABILITY OF PHOTOGRAPHIC SUPPLIES SOLD TO
COMMERCIAL PHOTOGRAPHERS

30 October, 1945

You have handed me copy of a letter from Rosenburg, Painter & Navarre, Attorneys of Jackson, Michigan, addressed to B. & H. Photo Company, Charlotte, North Carolina, under date of October 10, 1945. You received this copy from Mr. Victor S. Bryant, Attorney, Durham, North Carolina. The letter purports to be an opinion on the applicability of our sales tax and use tax to a commercial photographer who purchases photographic paper, films, chemicals, and other supplies from wholesale or manfacturing suppliers located outside the state of North Carolina. These supplies are used by the commercial photographer in performing his services in that capacity, and are not offered for resale except insofar as such items constitute an incidental part of the service.

Mr. Rosenburg, who apparently wrote the aforesaid letter, expressed the opinion that B. & H. Photo Company, under the conditions recited above, has no liability for sales or use tax under our Revenue Act. He reached this conclusion apparently on the ground that section 404 under the sales tax Article defines a retail merchant as "every person who engages in the business of buying or acquiring by consignment or otherwise any articles of commerce and selling the same at retail." He points out that this section also provides: "The word 'retail' shall mean the sale of any articles of commerce in any quantity or quantities for any use or purpose on the part of the purchaser other than for resale." He emphasizes the point that our sales tax law does not levy a tax on a service.

It appears to me that Mr. Rosenburg has selected his definitions from the wrong section of our Revenue Act. The tax which your department seeks to impose is not the sales tax, but the use tax. It is, therefore, necessary to look to the use tax Article in order to ascertain whether or not your position can be supported.

Section 802 imposes an excise tax "on the storage, use or consumption in this state of tangible personal property purchased from a retailer within or without this state on or after July first, one thousand nine hundred and forty-one (1941), for storage, use or consumption in this state at the rate of three per cent of the sales price of such property, regardless of whether said retailer is or is not engaged in business in this state." Said section also provides that if sales tax has already been paid, it shall be credited against the use tax imposed by this section.

It seems to be admitted that the commercial photographer sells a service rather than a commodity (although, of course, he may also sell some commodities in the form in which he purchased the same). This is the position which has been taken by the Department of Revenue from the beginning. Mr. Rosenburg emphasizes the same view in his letter. Therefore, it must be concluded that the commercial photographer buys his supplies not for resale, but for use or consumption. The only remaining question is whether or not he has purchased the same from a "retailer" within the meaning of the use tax Article.

Section 801 (g) provides that, " 'Retailer' means and includes every person engaged in the business of making sales of tangible personal property. ... for storage, use or consumption in this state. ... " We must assume that the wholesale or manufacturing suppliers mentioned by Mr. Rosenburg are "engaged in the business of making sales of tangible personal property" when they make sales of photographic supplies to commercial photographers in this state.

For these reasons it seems clear to me that the commercial photographer, under the conditions named above, is liable for the use tax for the reason that he uses in this state tangible personal property which he purchased from a "retailer," as defined in section 801. It, therefore, becomes unnecessary to decide whether or not the wholesale or manufacturing suppliers from whom the commercial photographer purchases his tangible personal property are "retail merchants" or not, for that term describes a person who is subject to the sales tax, with which we are now concerned.

For the reasons stated above I disagree with the opinion expressed by Mr. Rosenburg, and conclude that the use of these supplies is subject to the use tax.

License Taxes; Section 154 Non-Resident Sharecropper Hiring Laborers to Harvest Own Crop Out of State

14 November, 1945

I have received from Mr. Chas. R. Daniel, Attorney, Weldon, N. C., a request for opinion on Section 154 of the Revenue Act, G. S. 105-90. Inasmuch as it is not within the scope of the Attorney General's functions to advise private individuals, I am addressing this opinion to you and sending a copy to Mr. Daniel.

Section 154 provides, in part, as follows:

"Every person, firm or corporation, either as agent or principal, engaged in soliciting, hiring, and/or contracting with laborers, male or female, in this State for employment out of the State shall apply for and obtain from the Commissioner of Revenue a State license for each county for the privilege of engaging in *such business*, and shall pay for such license a tax of five hundred dollars ($500.00) for each county in which *such business* is carried on." (underscoring added.)

Mr. Daniel inquires whether or not the tax imposed by this section is applicable to a share-cropper of Southampton County, Virginia, who comes into Northampton and Halifax Counties, North Carolina, and engages laborers for the sole purpose of harvesting his own crop in Southampton County, Virginia.

In my opinion the Virginia share-cropper under these facts would not be liable for the tax for the reason that he is not engaging in a "business" contemplated by said section.

INCOME TAX; DEDUCTIBILITY OF NET INCOME UNDER SECTION 322 (10)
WHEN BUSINESS IS IN A CITY, BUT NOT A STATE, LEVYING INCOME TAX

19 November, 1945

You inquire whether a resident of this state may, in filing his 1944 income tax return, deduct net income received from a partenership located in Philadelphia. The State of Pennsylvania does not impose an income tax, but the City of Philadelphia imposes a tax on net incomes at the rate of 1½ per cent. This city tax is imposed under authority of an Act of the Pennsylvania State Legislature passed on August 15, 1932, which gives certain cities the power to enact ordinances imposing taxes "on persons, transactions, occupations, privileges, subjects and personal property" within the city limits, except such as are, or will become, subject to a state tax or license fee.

Section 322, subsection 10, of the Revenue Act of 1939, as amended through the year 1943, contained the following provision:

"Resident individuals and domestic corporations having an established business in another State, or investment in property in another State, may deduct the net income from such business or investment if such business or investment is in a State that levies a tax upon such net income."

It is my opinion that the net income taxed by the City of Philadelphia may not be deducted. The partnership is not in a *state* that levies a tax upon net income; and the statute makes no provision for deducting net income when the same arises from an established business located in a *city* imposing a tax upon net income.

TIDEWATER POWER COMPANY; INCOME TAXES; DEDUCTIONS: (1) RETIREMENT OF OWN BONDS AT A PREMIUM UNDER ORDER OF SECURITIES AND EXCHANGE COMMISSION, (2) REIMBURSEMENT OF BONDHOLDER'S TAX, (3) EXPENSE OF VALUATION REPORTS REQUIRED BY UTILITIES COMMISSION

30 November, 1945

You have requested me to review the brief filed by Mr. Louis J. Poisson, Attorney for Tidewater Power Company, and give you my opinion upon the matters therein contained. Mr. Poisson contends that you were in error when you disallowed certain deductions claimed by taxpayer on its returns for several named years. I shall consider these claimed deductions in the order in which they are discussed in the taxpayer's brief. However, I deem unnecessary the repetition of the detailed facts, for it appears sufficient for the purposes at hand to state the facts generally rather than specifically. The specific facts are fully set out in taxpayer's brief, and reference may be made thereto, if necessary.

I

You have tentatively disallowed as a deduction a loss claimed to have been sustained by the taxpayer corporation in the purchase and retirement of its own bonds at a premium. The taxpayer is a public utility. At the time pertinent to the present inquiry, taxpayer was a subsidiary of General Gas and Electric Corporation, a holding company, and was subject to the regulatory powers of the Securities and Exchange Commission, hereinafter referred to as SEC. Under the Holding Company Act the SEC ordered taxpayer to make various changes in its corporate and financial structure. In compliance with this order taxpayer, among other things, retired its first mortgage 5% bonds, 1979. The mortgage provisions required various premiums on retirement prior to certain dates, and these premiums were duly paid in compliance with these provisions.

It is true that this office has repeatedly ruled that where a corporation voluntarily purchases its own bonds on the open market at a premium, no deductible loss is sustained thereby. However, this office has recently expressed the opinion that this rule is inapplicable where the corporation purchases and retires its bonds at a premium as a result of a contractual obligation co-existent with the issuance of the bond.

I am of the opinion that the prior ruling of this office is equally inapplicable in a case where the corporation is required to purchase its bonds at a premium as a result of a valid order of a body of competent jurisdiction. In such case the payment of the premium is no less involuntary than it is when made as a result of contractual obligation; and, unless the purchase at a premium is voluntary on the part of the corporation, there is no reason for the presumption that the corporation suffers no loss by the transaction.

Inasmuch as taxpayer was compelled to purchase its bonds at a premium in order to comply with lawful orders of SEC, I advise that the premium paid represents a deductible loss in the taxable year in which sustained.

It should be observed that under Federal law such premiums are made deductible by regulation without regard to the voluntary character of the purchase. See *Annotation*, 87 L. ed. 801; *Annotation*, 112 A.L.R. 208; 27 *Am. Jur.*, Income Taxes, sections 44 and 107.

II

You have tentatively disallowed as a deduction amounts paid by taxpayer to reimburse bondholders in certain States for bondholder's tax paid by them on the taxpayer's bonds. It appears that this tax is levied on the bondholder only in certain States. In order to level off the cost of the bonds in all States, taxpayer agreed, through the medium of a "tax-free covenant" in the bond indenture, that it would reimburse the amount of the tax in those States where the same was levied. It appears that it was desirable, if not necessary, that the bonds bring a uniform net return in all States, and to achieve this end the taxpayer had the alternative of either reimbursing the amount of the tax in those States or paying a higher rate of interest in those States. The taxpayer elected the former method because it permitted uniformity in interest rates among the various States and because "tax-free covenants" were a customary way of providing an attractive bond issue. ·

It seems clear that the deduction claimed cannot be allowed as the payment of a tax, for two reasons: (1) Tax payer did not actually pay the tax, but simply reimbursed other persons in amounts equivalent to taxes paid by them, and (2) the bondholder's tax was not assessed against this taxpayer, but against the bondholder. The mere fact that a person pays taxes does not entitle him to a deduction at all events. He may not voluntarily assume another person's taxes and thereby entitle himself to a deduction. There must be a legal obligation on the person claiming the deduction to pay the taxes, and this does not mean a contractual obligation voluntarily assumed. See 29 *Am. Jur., Income Taxes*, section 109 and footnotes, together with additional material in pocket parts and annotations there cited.

On the other hand, I am of the opinion that the amounts so disbursed by the taxpayer represent a deductible loss. Inasmuch as the bondholder's tax for which reimbursement is made is an annual matter, it makes little difference in effect whether the loss be described as a capital loss or a current business expense, for in either case the entire amount would be deductible in the income tax year in which paid.

My conclusion that this disbursement would constitute a deductible loss rests principally upon an analogy with those situations in which corporations are deemed to have sustained a deductible loss whenever they issue their bonds. In those cases it is said that the corporation has sustained a capital loss which must be amortized over the life of the bond, and the reason lies in the fact that discount and commissions represent a part of the cost of borrowing capital. *Anno.*, 112 A.L.R. 191; 27 *Am. Jur., Income Taxes*, section 106; *Helvering v. Union Pacific R.R. Co.*, 293 U. S. 282, 79 L. ed. 363 (1934).

I can see no essential difference between discounts and commissions and the tax-free covenant. In each case the money paid or remitted represents the cost of borrowing capital. All, therefore, represent capital losses; but, as stated above, the obligation under the tax-free covenant arises annually, and it is, therefore, immaterial whether it be treated as a capital loss or as an expense, no amortization being necessary as in the case of discounts and commissions.

Therefore, I am of the opinion that the taxpayer's contention that these items are deductible should be sustained. In this view of the matter it is immaterial that the items are neither taxes nor interest.

III

You have tentatively disallowed taxpayer's claim for "amortization deductions of valuation expense." It appears that in 1934 the North Carolina Utilities Commission ordered taxpayer to prepare valuation reports and inventories which taxpayer did, at a cost of approximately $42,000.00; and that thereafter the Commission authorized taxpayer to amortize this cost over a period of ten years. This the taxpayer has done, and it is the annual amortized cost which taxpayer now claims as a deduction.

I am of the opinion that the cost of preparing these reports and inventories represents a capital loss or expenditure. The only question relates to the reasonableness of the period of amortization. If you find that the ten-year period fixed by the Commission is a reasonable allocation of this loss, it is my opinion that the annual amortized portion thereof on that basis should be allowed as a deduction.

BEVERAGE CONTROL ACT;   REFUND OF MALT BEVERAGE TAX PAID FOR
CROWNS OR LIDS LOST IN TRANSIT

30 November, 1945

You inquire whether the Commissioner of Revenue is authorized to refund
the malt beverage tax paid by breweries or bottlers for bottle crowns or lids
which are lost in transit by common carrier between the place of manufacture and the brewery or bottler's.

Under regulations promulgated by the Commissioner, breweries or bottlers
remit to the Department the tax on malt beverages to be sold by them,
which tax is to be evidenced by crowns or lids to be affixed to the bottles or
containers holding the malt beverage. Upon receipt of the tax, the Department sends a release or order to an authorized crown manufacturer which,
in turn, manufactures the tax-paid crowns or lids and sends them to the
brewery or bottler.

The tax on malt beverages, which is evidenced by crowns or lids, is levied
upon the sale of such beverages. The statute requires that the tax-paid
crowns or lids be affixed by each wholesaler or distributor prior to the
delivery of any container thereof to any retailer or other person.

Section 517, subsection (e), provides that "crowns and lids shall be sold
by the Commissioner of Revenue at a discount of two per cent (2%) as sole
compensation for North Carolina crown and lid losses sustained in the
process of production of malt beverages. No compensation or refund shall
be made for tax-paid malt beverages given as free goods, or advertising,
and losses, sustained by spoilage and breakage incident to the sale and
distribution of malt beverages."

It is my opinion that the 2% discount provided for in this section was
intended as the sole compensation allowable for losses of crowns or lids.
Delivery of the crowns or lids to a common carrier constitutes, in contemplation of law, delivery to the person to whom they are destined. Thus, from
the moment of delivery to the common carrier the bottler has legal possession
or control of the crowns or lids, and any loss of the same must be considered
a loss in his hands or the hands of his agent. Inasmuch as the State has
divested itself of possession and control upon delivery to common carrier,
the loss cannot be said to be that of the State.

For the reasons set forth, I am of the opinion that you are not authorized
to make a refund of taxes on account of loss of crowns or lids in transit
per common carrier.

While I do not presume to determine the liability of the common carrier
under the facts in this case, it would seem that taxpayer's remedy, if any,
would be only against the common carrier.

BEVERAGE CONTROL ACT; NO REFUND FOR CROWNS ON UNDERSIZE BOTTLE

22 January, 1946

You have requested my opinion on the following matter.

It appears that the manufacturer of beer through inadvertence attached
to bottles certain crowns of a denomination intended for larger bottles.

The crowns, having been used, were of no further value except on the bottles on which they had been placed. The manufacturer now requests a refund equivalent to the difference between the value of the crowns actually placed on the bottles and the value of crowns of the denomination appropriate for bottles of that size.

It is my opinion that the manufacturer in this case has sustained a crown loss in the process of production within the meaning of Section 517(e) of the Revenue Act. Under the provisions of that section 2% discount at which crowns are sold is the sole compensation for crown or lid losses sustained in the process of production.

Therefore, I am of the opinion that request for refund on these facts must be denied.

INCOME TAXES; THREE-YEAR STATUTE OF LIMITATIONS ON ASSESSMENTS NOT AVAILABLE AFTER NOTICE OF FEDERAL ADJUSTMENTS

7 December, 1945

You have referred to me a written protest with reference to a proposed additional income tax assessment against the Garrou Knitting Mills, and you request that I give you my opinion upon the question involved.

It appears that the Federal government assessed additional income tax against the taxpayer for the year 1940. The Commissioner was notified of the Federal adjustment after more than three years had elapsed from the time that the taxpayer filed its 1940 return. After notification by the Federal agent, the Commissioner examined the 1940 return, and assessed additional tax on August 10, 1945.

The taxpayer contends that since more than three years had elapsed from the time the return was filed until the assessment was made, the Commissioner is barred by the three-year statute of limitations from making the additional assessment. In support of this contention, the taxpayer relies on the decision in *Maxwell v. Hinsdale*, 207 N. C. 37.

It has been the view of this office for many years that, under the provisions of Sections 334 and 335 of the Revenue Act, the State may adjust a taxpayer's return when it learns of a Federal adjustment even after three years from the filing of the original return, the only limitation being that if the taxpayer voluntarily reports the adjustment, the State must make its adjustment within three years from the time when the taxpayer's report of adjustment was due.

I have read the decision in *Maxwell v. Hinsdale*, but, in my opinion, it does not support taxpayer's position. In this case, a refund of taxes overpaid was denied for the reason that the taxpayer failed to apply for refund within the required statutory period. There was a Federal readjustment, but the Court held that the taxpayer was not saved by the provisions of Section 334, since it did not notify the Commissioner of the Federal redetermination within the thirty-day period, as required by the statute. I can see no analogy between the facts in this case and the ones under consideration in connection with the Garrou Knitting Mills assessment. Nor do I find any language in the aforementioned decision which would indicate that the

Commissioner of Revenue is barred from making an assessment at any time after notice of a Federal readjustment.

Therefore, it is my conclusion that the Commissioner was authorized to make the assessment complained of in the protest referred to me.

INTOXICATING LIQUORS; BEER; NON-TAXPAID BEER SHIPPED INTO THIS STATE
11 December, 1945

You inform me that one of your deputies has discovered 400 cases of beer in Davidson County to which the crowns or lids required by G. S. 18-81 have not been affixed. This beer was shipped by truck from New York City to an individual in Davidson County. The beer is now stored in the home of this individual. You intend to indict this individual for the possession of non-tax-paid beer, and you inquire what disposition should be made of the beer. The same question arises as to 64⅓ cases of non-taxpaid beer which has been discovered in a place of business in the same county.

I am of the opinion that you should charge the defendants with the unlawful possession of non-taxpaid beer for the purpose of sale under G. S. 18-32, and with the unlawful possession of non-taxpaid beer under subsection (i) of G. S. 18-81. If the defendants are convicted of the count charging a violation of G. S. 18-32 (the possession of more than five gallons of malt liquor raises a presumption of a violation of that section), the beer will be disposed of by the court under G. S. 18-6. It should be noted that G. S. 18-6 provides for the confiscation of intoxicating liquor transported or possessed illegally. Intoxicating liquor, as used in this section, includes beer. G. S. 18-1.

Davidson County is a county which has not adopted the provisions of the Alcoholic Beverage Control Act. Therefore, the Turlington Act is still in full force and effect therein. STATE v. GRAY, 223 N. C. 120. The only modification of the Turlington Act in dry counties, in so far as beer is concerned, is found in subsection 3 of G. S. 18-1. There it is provided that the Turlington Act shall not make unlawful any acts authorized or permitted by Sections 18-63 through 18-92, the Beverage Control Act of 1939. The Beverage Control Act of 1939 does not authorize or permit the possession, or the possession for the purpose of sale, of beer to which the crowns or lids required by G. S. 18-81 have not been affixed. On the contrary, that Act specifically forbids the possession of such beer.

It would seem, therefore, that the possession of this beer in a dry county would constitute a violation of the Turlington Act and that, under G. S. 18-6, the beer would be subject to disposal by the court.

I am of the opinion that the State would establish a violation of subsection (i) of G. S. 18-81, upon the showing that the defendants did possess the beer and that the crowns required by that section were not affixed to the containers.

INHERITANCE AND INCOME TAXATION; TAXABILITY OF GROWING
CROPS AND INCOME THEREFROM
11 December, 1945

You have requested my opinion as to the taxability of growing crops for inheritance tax purposes upon the owner's death and also as to the taxability of income from growing crops collected by the decedent's personal representative.

In the particular case about which you inquire, a man died intestate on June 19, 1944 while in the midst of farming operations. In reporting for inheritance tax purposes the administratrix did not list the value of the growing crop as an asset of the estate, but did list as deductions outstanding debts which had been incurred in farm operations. You have refused to accept the inheritance tax return on this basis, and have requested me to advise you as to the proper treatment of growing crops for purposes of inheritance and income taxation.

As a matter of common law, it has been held in this State that growing crops (*fructus industriales*), as distinguished from the spontaneous products of the earth (*fructus naturales*), are regarded as personal chattels, and upon death of the owner go to his executor and not to his heir. *Brittain v. McKay*, 23 N. C. 265; *Flynt v. Conrad*, 61 N. C. 190. This principle is now declared by statute, G. S. 28-56, which provides, in substance, that ungathered crops at the owner's death belong to the personal representative as part of the personal assets, and not to widow or heir as part of dower or land unless such intent be manifest in the will.

Inasmuch as ungathered crops are recognized at law as a personal asset of the estate, it seems clear that the value thereof is includible in the estate for inheritance tax purposes.

In connection with the value of an ungathered crop two questions arise: (1) As of what time is a value placed upon the crop for inheritance tax purposes? and (2) In what way is such value determined?

I know of no express provision of the Revenue Act which specifically sets the time as of which an asset must be valued for inheritance tax purposes. However, the inheritance tax is laid upon the transfer of property rather than upon property itself; and it would seem to follow that a value must be determined as of the time the taxable event, i.e., the transfer, occurs, which would be at the death of the person from whom the property passes. Thus, it has been held that such value is to be determined as of the date of the decedent's death, and not as of the date of the distribution of the property. *Shaw v. Bridgers*, 161 N. C. 246; *In Re Davis' Estate*, 190 N. C. 358; *Prentice-Hall Inheritance and Transfer Service*, Vol. I, Sec. 703, and cases cited.

We come now to the second question, relating to the method of valuing an ungathered crop. The answer to this question is somewhat complicated by the answer of the first. For instance, if the determination of value could be delayed until the crops were gathered and converted into money, a value could be ascertained at that time with some degree of mathematical accuracy simply by taking the gross receipts from the sale and deducting therefrom the expenses incurred since the decedent's death in completing the job of cultivating, harvesting and selling; whereas, if value must be determined as of the time of decedent's death, some difficulty is experienced in discovering a reliable and equitable method of determining value.

Growing crops, *as such*, have no value. To the contrary they represent an expense rather than a profit. They have a value not as growing vegetation on the land, but because in the course of nature they will come to fruition and so have a market value, and thus will bring profit from the expenses. 15 *Am. Jur., Crops*, Section 72.

When the asset of a decedent's estate consists of a claim for money, in the form of a note, written contract, oral promise or otherwise, it is said that the property to be valued for inheritance or estate tax purposes is "the right to receive payment." The value of that "right" depends, of course, on the face amount of the claim; but it also depends upon other circumstances, especially those pertaining to the likelihood of payment, time of payment, interest rate, etc. Similarly, I believe it can be said that when the as et consists of an ungathered or growing crop, what must be valued for inheritance tax purposes is not the crop as so much vegetation rooted in the soil, but the *right* to bring that crop to fruition and ultimately to convert it into money.

If the thing to be valued is the right to continue a crop and to convert the same into money, it would seem that the problem is somewhat simplified. While it is not possible to arrive at a value of arithmetical accuracy, it is possible to arrive at a value which has elements of common sense and reason. In my opinion the right to bring a crop to fruition and ultimately to convert the same into money has a value which depends, among other things, upon the probable yield under proper cultivation, the probable value of such probable yield at the time when it will probably be placed on the market for sale, the probable cost of converting the growing crops into the probable yield and ultimately into money (i.e., expense to be incurred *after* decedent's death, not expense already represented in the crop at the decedent's death), the probable loss from the elements of nature, the stage to which the crops have been advanced at the time of the decedent's death and the amount of time which must elapse before any profit can be realized. See *Crow v. Davidson*, 186 Okla. 84, 96 P (2d) 70, 126 ALR 123 (Tort action).

Surprisingly, an exhaustive research has failed to discover any judicial authority upon the proper method of evaluating a growing crop for inheritance tax purposes; and the opinion expressed herein upon that subject is the result of an attempt to work an analogy with the tort cases, in which the courts from time to time have enunciated rules for ascertaining the value of a growing crop in order to determine damages recoverable on account of its distruction. The Federal government seems content to let the matter rest with a regulation adopting the time-honored rule which pegs the value at that amount which would flow from a willing purchaser to a willing seller—a true enough test, but one of no practical benefit.

It seems to me that no absolute rule can be formulated for the evaluation of an ungathered crop. Most of the judicial remarks on the subject have displayed a tendency on the part of the courts to predict the gross income from the crop and the post-death expenses and deduct one from the other. See 15 *Am. Jur., Crops*, Section 72. While this is a good way of predicting the value of crops which have matured and have been harvested and are ready for sale, it fails to take into account the natural growth of the crop and all the contingencies which attend the crop during its cultivation, harvesting and marketing. Thus, while the probable income less expenses is certainly an important element, it is not the sole yardstick by which the value of the growing crop is measured; and, for inheritance tax purposes, such a yardstick would not appear to be adequate for the evaluation of the "right" to bring the crop to fruition, and to receive whatever profit that may be derived out of the transaction.

Therefore, I am of the opinion that this "right" should be valued, for inheritance tax purposes, at whatever it may be worth at the time of the decedent's death, much in the same way a value would be placed on a doubtful monetary claim in favor of the estate. For such things there is no absolute value. Neither is there any absolute yardstick by which such value can be measured. But it seems to me that the difficulties here are not very different in principle from those inherent in any attempt to evaluate property or rights. In the final analysis an evaluation is nothing more than the net result of an appraisal of all the pertinent elements present; and practically all that a rule can do is to enumerate those elements which are sufficiently pertinent to be appraised. While I have suggested some elements or factors which occur to me at the moment, it is not my intention to imply that my enumeration is exclusive, or even indicative of the relative importance of the various elements or factors. These are matters which may vary with each case.

For the reasons set out above, I advise that in my opinion the right to take over a growing or ungathered crop upon the owner's death, and to bring such crop to fruition, is a personal asset of the decedent's estate, the transfer of which by death is taxable under our inheritance tax laws; and, further, that the value of such right for inheritance tax purposes is determinable as of the date of the decedent's death, although in the nature of things it is necessary to look into the future in order to appraise such elements of value as the probable crop yield, the probable income and the probable costs of converting the crop finally into money (but not including expense already incurred by decedent prior to death).

I have not attempted to formulate a rigid rule for determining the value of ungathered crops. In my opinion, such a rule, if it reduces the problem to one of simple mechanics, could not be true. The determination of values should not be circumscribed by too many rules. The problem essentially is one of applying common sense to an unknown quantity. While it would not be technically correct to report an inheritance tax value simply by taking the actual gross income and deducting expenses since death, nevertheless, as a practical matter, I can conceive of this method as reaching a fair and reasonably accurate inheritance tax value under some circumstances, such as where the crops are practically completed at the decedent's death and, therefore, time has eliminated contingencies which are apt to upset predictions of the ultimate income and expenses. I can also conceive of growing crops having, as a practical matter, little or no inheritance tax value, such as where the decedent dies immediately after committing his seeds to the soil, or where the plants have just begun their growth.

In view of the inherent difficulties in the problem of valuing growing or ungathered crops, it would seem the better policy to allow something more than the usual latitude to the executor or administrator who undertakes the task. However, this is an administrative matter for your own determination.

What has been said has nothing to do with that part of Section 7 of the Revenue Act (G. S. 105-9) listing "debts of decedent" as a deduction. The

determination of the value of a specific item of property is an entirely
different question from the ascertainment of the inheritance tax value of
each *distributive* share. In one case, you are placing a value on a particular
piece of property. In the other case you are determining a base on which
the tax is computed. The deduction of the debt does not serve to reduce
the reportable *value* of the particular piece of property. The debt is simply
a deduction which may be taken to arrive at the net taxable distributive
share.

It is important to observe that Section 7 lists *debts* of decedent, not expenses. Thus, a crop expense incurred but not paid at death would be a
debt and, therefore, deductible; but an expense already paid at death would
not be a debt and, therefore, not deductible.

We come now to the taxability of the net income, under Schedule D, which
is finally realized from the matured, harvested and marketed crop.

It is my opinion, under our Revenue Act, that when a person dies, all of
his accrued, but uncollected, income immediately becomes personal assets
of his estate, and that such assets thereafter can never be taxable income.
Thus, where salary is due but uncollected at death, that uncollected salary
constitutes simply a claim in favor of the decedent's estate; and when the
decedent's executor or administrator collects such claim, he is collecting,
not income, but a part of the corpus of the estate. It is not income to the
decedent (if on a cash basis), for he did not receive it; and it is not income
to the executor or administrator, for it did not accrue to the estate as such.
The decedent and his estate, for income tax purposes, are distinct and
separate entities, and what would have been income, if received by the
decedent before death, cannot be income if received by his estate after his
death. Where a person reports on a cash basis, death forecloses all further
income to him; and income to the estate is only that income which accrues
to the estate after decedent's death. *Nichols v. U. S.*, 64 Ct. Cl. 241, 6 AFTR
6592 (1927). See *Prentice-Hall Federal Tax Service*, 1945, Section 15,032,
and cases cited.

On the other hand, it has been held that where the asset in the hands of
the estate realizes, in actual money received, an amount in excess of the
amount which alrealy has been included in the estate for inheritance or
estate tax purposes, such excess represents taxable income, on the theory
that the increase in value took place after death and while the asset was in
the hands of the executor or administrator. See *Prentice-Hall Federal Tax
Service*, 1945, Section 15,032, and cases cited.

In my opinion the above principle is as applicable to a crop as it is to
any other personal asset belonging to an estate. Accordingly, I am of the
opinion that where a growing crop, or the "right to bring a growing crop
to fruition," has been valued for inheritance tax purposes, and thereafter
the gross sum realized from the sale of the matured crop, less the total
after-death cost of cultivating, harvesting and marketing the same, is
greater than the value placed on the growing crop for inheritance tax
purposes, the excess so realized constitutes taxable income to the executor or
administrator for the reason that the personal asset in the hands of the
estate has either increased in value or itself has produced income after the
death of the decedent.

I **am** advised that the opinion I have expressed above is consistent with the administrative policy of the Department and that this policy is one of long standing.

It should be emphasized that in ascertaining net income in such case, the only expenses deductible are those incurred by the estate *after* the decedent's death. The expenses which the decedent paid prior to his death are simply the cost of the personal asset, i.e., the growing crop, which passed to the executor or administrator as a part of the decedent's personal estate. The credit to the estate on account of this asset comes from the fact that in ascertaining net income of the estate, the inheritance tax value of the asset, as well as after-death expenses, are deductible from the gross sum realized from the crop. This is true because the true "gross" income from the crop is only that part of the total receipts which exceeds the inheritance tax value, which, for income tax purposes, was the starting point.

The views expressed in this letter seem to me to be supported both by administrative practice and analogy with personal property other than crops. Strange to say, a careful search of the judicial authorities has failed to reveal any case on the evaluation of crops for inheritance tax purposes and the subsequent treatment of the income for income tax purposes. However, it is believed that the rule announced herein is not only supported by administrative practice and by analogy but also is grounded upon reason.

It may be appropriate to mention here that by an amendment in 1942 to the Internal Revenue Code the Federal government imposes an income tax upon sums received after the decedent's death if such sums would have been income if they had been received by the decedent. In such case the person who receives the sums after the decedent's death places himself in the decedent's shoes for this purpose and treats the sums as if he were the decedent.

INCOME AND INTANGIBLES TAXES; TAXABLE PROPORTION OF DIVIDENDS AND
SHARES MEASURED BY CORPORATION'S NET INCOME FOR PRECEDING
YEAR TAXABLE OTHER THAN IN THIS STATE
[SECTIONS 311½, 322(5), 705]

14 December, 1945

You have presented to me problems which entail an interpretation of Sections 311½, 322 (5) and 705 of the Revenue Act. These problems relate to the taxability of income and intangibles where a corporation has net taxable gains and/or losses inside and/or outside this State. In certain fact situations, hereinafter enumerated, the question arises as to what proportion, if any, of the shares of stock of a corporation is subject to the intangibles tax under Section 705, and as to what proportion, if any, of the cash dividends of a corporation is subject to income taxation under Section 311½ or is deductible under Section 322(5).

But first, it is necessary to dispose of a preliminary question.

Sections 311½ and 322(5) purport to fix the proportion of income from dividends taxable by this State; and Section 705 purports to fix the proportion of the fair market value of corporate shares subject to our intangibles tax. Generally the proportion is measured by the ratio of taxable income in this State to the taxable income in other States, an additional factor in the determination of the intangibles tax under Section 705 being whether or not the corporation pays this State franchise tax on 100% of its capital stock, surplus and undivided profits, or on all its gross receipts.

The general purpose of these sections seems to be to avoid an additional tax on dividends and shares in those cases where the corporation's income has been already taxed by this State; and it would seem that these statutes should be interpreted in the light of this general purpose. There is nothing very mysterious about this purpose. But the administration of it under the language of the statute is complicated by an *apparent* requirement to the effect that, prior to determining the taxability of dividends and shares of stock, it is necessary to determine the corporate income, if any, for the very same year—a practical impossibility because of the fact that the corporate income is not determinable until the close of the present year (if on a calendar year basis) and, as a matter of practice, is not actually determined until the income tax returns are filed later. In brief, the statute at first reading seems to base taxability of dividends and shares upon information which is not known or obtainable until long after the tax is required to be returned and paid.

I cannot believe that such a result was intended. Moreover, I am of the opinion that the statutory language is susceptible of an interpretation which will have the effect of basing the taxable proportion of dividends and shares, not on corporate income earned or loss incurred in the same year for which the dividends and shares are taxable, but on corporate income earned in the preceding year. I base this interpretation upon the theory that the statute refers, not to the year in which the corporate income was *earned*, but to the year in which the corporate income is *paid* or *returnable*. In my opinion there is nothing in the statutory language which militates against this conclusion.

Section 311½ provides that the shareholder who receives dividends shall pay income tax thereon "equalling the percentage of the corporation's income on which it has not paid an income tax to the State of North Carolina for the year in which said dividends are received by the taxpayer." Thus, the corporation's payment of income tax is referred to in the past tense, indicating that the taxpayer who receives dividends bases its taxable proportion on income tax which the corporation has already paid; and, in the nature of things, this payment must have been for taxes on income earned in a prior year, for the corporation cannot compute income earned during any year until the end of that year. Therefore, it is my opinion that when section 311½ refers to the corporation's payment of income tax "for the year in which said dividends are received," it has the same effect as if it had referred to the corporation's return or payment "*in* the year in which said dividends are received," and that the statutory language contemplates the year in which the tax is returnable and due rather than the year in which the taxable income was earned.

In similar vein, Section 322(5) provides that "when only part of the income of any corporation shall *have been assessed* under this Article... only a corresponding part of the dividends received therefrom shall be deducted."

Here, too, the language is couched in the past tense. The income could not "have been assessed" until a year succeeding that in which it was earned, and it seems clear that the statute refers to "this year's assessment on last year's income." Moreover, the statute speaks of dividends "received therefrom." Certainly no dividends can be received from any income except that earned in a year prior to that in which the dividend is declared, for "this year's" income is not even determinable "this year," and, conceivably, there might be a net loss instead of net income.

Section 705, relating to intangibles tax on shares of stock, provides that "there shall be exempt so much of the fair market value of such shares of stock as is represented by the percentage of net income on which tox *is paid* to this State. In my opinion this refers to tax which *is paid* "this year on last year's income," and the same reasons apply here as set forth above in connection with Sections 311½ and 322(5).

My conclusion that Section 705 refers to "last year's income" is not disturbed by the presence of the words "when such income is earned" in the statute. These words appear in the provision that "With respect to corporations which pay to this State a franchise-tax-on-a-part of their stock as is represented by the percentage of net income on which tax *is paid* capital stock, surplus and undivided profits on part of their gross receipts . . . and a tax upon a part of the net income of such corporations . . ., *when such income is earned,* there shall be exempt so much of the fair market value of such shares of stock as is represented by the percentage of net income on which tax is paid to this State." The clause "when such income is earned," as used here, is not restrictive of "there shall be exempt," etc., so as to require the exemption to be based on the income earned in that particular year. To the contrary, the clause "when such income is earned" is restrictive of what precedes it: "with respect to corporations *which pay* . . . a tax upon a part of the net income . . . *when such net income is earned* . . ." If the statute is read in this way, it will be seen that the words "when such income is earned" have the same meaning as the words "*whenever* such income is earned," or the words "if such income is earned." These words merely describe a particular kind of corporation, i.e., the kind that pays us a tax if it earns income; and the word "when" does not tie the exemption to the particular year in which the income was earned. In my opinion the words "when such income is earned," have the same meaning, and were used for the same purpose, as the words "net income, *if any*" appearing six lines earlier in the same Section.

For the reasons set out above I am of the opinion that these statutes contemplate the computation of taxable ratio upon the income which is returnable during the year in which the taxes on dividends and shares accrue.

It should be observed that in 1945, Section 705 was amended so as to add a provision that "In the case of corporations having the same allocation ratios for income and franchise taxes paid to this State, the allocation percentage reported on the franchise returns due in July of each year and received in the year, may be used to determine the portion of the value of the shares of stock of such corporations taxable under this Section." In view of my conclusion that the taxable ratio of shares and dividends is determined upon income *returnable* during the year, it would seem that this 1945 addition is of no administrative value except in those cases where the corporation operates on a fiscal year basis calling for the return of income later than July, for if the corporation files an income tax return prior to July, the necessary information can be obtained from such income tax return. However, the 1945 provision apparently does not compel a result contrary to the one reached under the interpretation I have placed on the statute; and, therefore, its addition to Section 705 seems to be at least harmless.

This disposes of the preliminary question mentioned at the beginning of this letter.

I come now to a consideration of the various fact situations you have presented. A question arises under each fact situation as to the method of determining the taxable ratio of dividends and shares. As stated at the outset, dividends and shares are taxable upon a whole or proportionate basis depending on what part of the corporation's income is not taxed in this State, the general purpose being not to tax that proportion of dividends or shares attributable to or represented by corporate income on which the State has already collected an income tax.

Before entering into a discussion of the individual fact situations, I believe the entire problem will be simplified if I state that a careful consideration of the language of Section 311½, 322(5) and 705 has persuaded me that these statutes intend to reach only that proportion of a dividend or a share of stock which is attributable to or represented by corporate net income not reached by our corporation income tax. In other words, it is my opinion that the answer in each of the fact situations you have presented lies in the answer to the following simple question: Did the corporation earn any net income which was not taxed under the laws of this State? If the answer is "no," then the dividend or share is 100% non-taxable to the holder; and if the answer is "yes," then the dividend or share is taxable to the holder in the same proportion as that particular part of the corporation's net income (i.e., the part not reached by our income tax) bears to the corporation's total income. Using this test, it would follow that (1) where the corporation's entire net income is taxed here, dividends and shares are 100% exempt; (2) where the corporation's net income is taxed partly here and partly elsewhere, the dividends and shares are taxable in the proportion that the income which is taxed elsewhere bears to the total income; (3) where the corporations earns an income, all of which is taxed here but sustains a loss elsewhere, the dividends and shares are 100% exempt; (4) where the corporation sustained a loss here but made a net income elsewhere, taxable there but not here, the dividends and shares are 100% taxable; (5) where the corporation sustains a loss both here and elsewhere, the dividends and shares are 100% exempt.

Having proposed this simple test and having applied the same to five fact situations, let us proceed to an examination and analysis of the statutory language as the same is applicable to these five situations, in order to ascertain whether or not the proposed test is a true one.

(1) *Where the corporation has a net income all of which is taxable
in this State:*

Section 311½ provides that the shareholder "shall pay on the total dividends received an amount equalling the percentage of the corporation's income on which it has not paid an income tax to the State of North Carolina. ... " Where the corporation has paid on 100% of its income, there is no "income on which it has not paid an income tax to the State of North Carolina." Therefore, in such case the shareholder pays no tax.

Section 322(5) clearly provides for a 100% deduction of dividends where 100% of the corporation's income has been assessed by and paid to this State.

Section 705 clearly provides that the intangibles tax on shares of stock shall not apply where the corporation pays this State a franchise tax on its entire capital stock, surplus and undivided profits or entire gross receipts, together with an income tax on all of its net income, if any.

(2) *Where the corporation has a net income, part of which is taxable in this State and part of which is taxable elsewhere:*

Section 311½ provides that the shareholder "shall pay on the total dividends received an amount equalling the percentage of the corporation's income on which it has not paid an income tax to the State of North Carolina. ... " Thus, where the corporation has a net income, a part of which is taxable elsewhere instead of by this State, the ratio of that part to all the net income is the "percentage of the corporation's income on which it has not paid an income tax to the State of North Carolina," and that percentage of the dividend is taxable income in this State under this Section.

Section 322(5) provides that "when only part of the income of any corporation shall have been assessed under this article ... only a corresponding part of the dividends received therefrom shall be deducted." Thus, if part of the corporation's net income is taxed here and part elsewhere, the dividend is deductible only according to the percentage of the corporation's income taxable in this State; which is the converse of saying that the other percentage is taxable income as provided in Section 311½. Therefore, Sections 311½ and 322(5) are consistent and complementary.

Section 705 provides that "with respect to corporations which pay to this State a franchise tax on a part of their capital stock, surplus and undivided profits or part of their gross receipts ... and a tax upon a part of the net income ..., when such income is earned, there shall be exempt so much of the fair market value of such shares of stock as is represented by the percentage of net income on which tax is paid to this State." Thus, where a part of the corporation's net income is taxable here, and a part elsewhere, the share of stock is exempt from the intangibles tax according to the percentage of the corporation's income taxable here; and, of course, the converse of this is that the share is taxable according to the percentage of the corporation's income taxable elsewhere but not here.

(3) *Where the corporation has a net income taxable in this State
but sustains a net loss on business done elsewhere the net
income from which, if earned, would have been taxable elsewhere but not in this State:*

Section 311½ provides that the shareholder "shall pay on the total dividends received an amount equalling the percentage of the corporation's income on which it has not paid an income tax to the State of North Carolina." The word "income" as used here, in my opinion, means "net income," for it is only upon net income that this State levies an income tax. In the situation presented here the corporation sustained a loss elsewhere. Therefore, the entire net income of the corporation was in this State, and there was no "percentage of the corporation's income on which it has not paid an income tax to the State of North Carolina." Accordingly, in this situation Section 311½ provides for no tax on the dividend.

Section 322(5) provides that "when only part of the income of any corporation shall have been assessed under this Article ... only a corresponding part of the dividends received therefrom shall be deducted." In the situation here all the net income of the corporation is taxed here, for there was a net loss, not net income, elsewhere. In this Section too the word "income," in my opinion, means "net income." Therefore, the entire dividend would be deductible under the first sentence in Section 322(5); which is the converse of the proposition that no part of said dividend is taxable under Section 311½.

Section 705, imposing an intangibles tax on shares of stock, provides that "with respect to corporations which pay to this State a franchise tax on a part of their capital, surplus and undivided profits or part of their gross receipts ... and a tax upon a part of the net income of such corporations ..., when such income is earned, there shall be exempt so much of the fair market value of such shares of stock as is represented by the percentage of net income on which tax is paid to this State." In the situation presented the only net income earned by the corporation is that which is earned and taxable in this State, there being net loss instead of net income elsewhere. Thus, the percentage of the corporation's net income taxable here is 100%. Accordingly, the entire value of the share is exempt from the intangibles tax.

(4) *Where the corporation has a net income but no part of the same is taxable in this State because the corporation sustained a net loss on that part of its business the net income from which, if earned, would have been taxable in this State:*

Section 311½ taxes that part of the dividend "equalling the percentage of the corporation's income on which it has not paid an income tax to the State of North Carolina. ...'' In the situation presented here the entire net income of the corporation is non-taxable in this State. Therefore, the dividend would be 100% taxable as income under Section 311½.

Section 322(5) provides for a deduction of dividends in two cases: (1) where all the corporation's income is taxable in this State; and (2) where a part of such income is taxable in this State. In my opinion Section 322(5) does not refer at all to a case where a corporation Section has a net income none of which is taxable in this State. Thus, no part of the dividend in such case would be deductible under Section 322(5); which is the converse of the proposition that such dividend is 100% taxable income under Section 311½.

Section 705 exempts from the intangibles tax "so much of the fair market value of such shares of stock as is represented by the percentage of net income on which tax is paid to this State." In the situation presented here the entire net income was earned out-side the State and is non-taxable here, there having been a net loss on the North Carolina part of the business. Therefore, the "percentage of net income on which tax is paid to this State" is zero. The exemption, being measured thereby, is likewise nothing. Accordingly, the share would be taxable on 100% of its fair market value.

    (5) *Where the corporation does business the net income from which, if earned, would be taxable both in this State and elsewhere, but a net loss is sustained everywhere:*

Section 311½ taxes that part of the dividend "equalling the percentage of the corporation's income on which it has not paid an income tax to the State of North Carolina. ..." In the situation presented here there is no net income anywhere. Therefore, there can be no "percentage of the corporation's (net) income on which it has not paid an income tax to the State of North Carolina." Accordingly, no part of the dividend is taxable under this section.

Section 322(5) provides for a deduction of dividends in two cases: (1) where all the corporation's income is taxable in this State; and (2) where a part of such income is taxable in this State. In the situation presented here there is no net income, for there is a net loss everywhere. Therefore, Section 322(5) is inapplicable; but there is no need for any deduction under this section, for Section 311½, as stated above, does not treat the dividend in such case as taxable income in the first place.

Section 705 provides that "with respect to corporations which pay to this State a franchise tax on a part of their capital stock, surplus and undivided profits or part of their gross receipts ... and a tax upon a part of the net income of such corporation ... *when such income is earned,* there shall be exempt so much of the fair market value of such shares of stock as is represented by the percentage of net income on which tax is paid to this state." In view of the words "when such income is earned," it would seem that the exemption granted in this section is measured by the percentage of corporate income taxed in this State only in those cases where the corporation has earned a net income; and, indeed, this is necessarily so, for there can be no percentage of net income unless such income is earned. At first blush the statute seems to grant the exemption only in cases where a net income has been earned. However, I am of the opinion that this is not so. When the statute is read in the light of the general purpose to tax dividends and shares of stock only to the extent that the corporation's net income escapes our income tax, I am of the opinion that the statute grants the exemption also in a case where no net income at all is earned, and that the statute merely states a rule whereby the exemption may be *measured* in cases where income is earned. It must be conceded that the statute does not contain perfect language to this end; but it seems to me that a full exemption is intended in cases where no net income is earned. The fact that the rule by which the exemption may be measured is applicable only to cases where the corporation earns a net income does not indicate that no exemption at all is granted where a net income is not earned. No yardstick is needed in the latter case, for the exemption runs to the full value of the stock. In order to prove the point, it is necessary only to look to the case of a domestic corporation doing business exclusively in North Carolina.

Certainly it would not be contended that the exemption should be denied just because the corporation in a particular year sustained a net loss instead of earning a net income. I conclude, therefore, that where a net loss is suffered on all the corporation's business, including that in North Carolina, the exemption in Section 705 extends to its shares of stock, to the extent of 100% of their value.

By way of summary, it may bear repeating that in my opinion these statutes seek to tax dividends and stock only to the extent that the corporation has earned a net income which escapes taxation in this State; and that once this principle is fully accepted the answers in the fact situations presented by you become simple and inevitable.

It should be observed that I have repeatedly used the expression "income taxable in this State," and other similar expressions. I have done this only for the purpose of handling the matter more conveniently. The statutes discussed herein refer to "net income on which tax is *paid* to this State" (Section 705), "the income of which shall have been assessed, and the tax on such income *paid*" (Section 322(5)), and "income on which it has not *paid* an income tax in the State of North Carolina." Therefore, I am of the opinion that, in order to make the dividend or share or any part thereof nontaxable or deductible, the corporation must have actually *paid* any income tax on which non-taxability or dividends and shares is asserted.

The opinions herein expressed apply with equal force to domestic corporations and to foreign corporations which do business in this State. They do not apply to foreign corporations which do not do business in this State. The dividends and shares of such corporations are 100% taxable in every case. Section 311½ expressly limits its percentage rule to "corporations paying a tax in this State on a proportionate part of their total income." The deduction granted in Section 322(5) is applicable only where the corporation pays this State on all or a part of its income. Section 705 clearly grants an exemption only with respect to corporations which pay this State a franchise tax on all or part of capital stock, etc., and an income tax on all or part of income, if any. On the other hand, Section 307 clearly includes dividends in "gross income"; and Section 705 clearly lays an intangibles tax on shares of stock. In the absence of express exemption or deduction or specific provision, both taxes are computed on the full amount or value. As to foreign corporations not doing business in this State there is no such exemption, deduction or specific provision, and their dividends and shares are 100% taxable.

I am advised that the opinions herein expressed are not at variance with the administrative practice of the Department of Revenue. The matter was referred to me for a general clarification and restatement.

I am aware of the fact that the application of the law as interpreted herein theoretically may, in some cases, have results not necessarily desired, as in the case of a corporation which does a predominantly North Carolina business and sustains a loss here while earning a nominal net income taxable elsewhere. I am also aware of the fact that the taxability of dividends and shares of a particular corporation may vary between nothing and 100% from year to year. While these are things which are remediable by legislation, they do not in any case justify a casting aside of the language of the statute administratively. We are compelled to accept the law as it is written.

LICENSE TAX; NO COMPENSATION FOR LOSS OF CROWNS WHERE BEER IS SEIZED UNDER PURE FOOD LAWS; SECTION 517(e)

17 December, 1945

You have referred to me a letter from Mr. A. C. Davis, Attorney at Law, Greensboro, North Carolina, who represents the Atlantic Company of Atlanta. It appears that this company claims a loss of crown tax by reason of the fact that a quantity of its beer and ale was seized for destruction under the Pure Food and Drug Act. The company now seeks a refund of tax from the State of North Carolina.

Section 517(e) provides for the sale of crowns and lids at a 2% discount as sole compensation for crown and lid losses sustained in the process of production, and expressly prohibits any compensation or refund on account of losses sustained by spoilage and breakage incident to the sale and distribution of malt beverages.

This office has previously expressed the opinion that there is no express authority in the Revenue Act for any refund or compensation for losses except the 2% discount at which the crowns and lids are sold, and that it is the intent of the statute to allow this 2% discount as sole compensation for losses in the process of productin and to prohibit any compensation or refund at all for losses other than in the process of production.

It would follow that no refund can be allowed where loss of crowns or lids is sustained by reason of a seizure under pure food and drug laws.

Moreover, it would seem that the language of the statute in this case specifically supports this conclusion. If the beer and ale was beneath the legal standards of purity at the time it was bottled, this would be a "loss sustained in the process of production." On the other hand, if the beer lost such quality after being produced, that would be a "loss sustained by spoilage . . . incident to the sale and distribution."

You may advise Mr. Davis in conformity with the views expressed herein.

INCOME TAXES; UNITED STATES CORRECTION OF NET INCOME SECTION 334; WHEN STATUTE OF LIMITATIONS, SECTION 335, BEGINS TO RUN

20 December, 1945

I have read with interest a brief filed by Messrs. Gardner, Morrison and Rogers, attorneys for Dr. James W. Davis, taxpayer. The burden of this brief is to show that the Commissioner of Revenue, under Sections 334 and 335, is barred by the three-year statute of limitations from making any additional assessments for the years 1926, 1927, 1929 to 1937, inclusive, and 1939, on account of corrected net income determined by the United States Government.

I disagree with the conclusion reached by the brief and with the reasoning which leads to that conclusion. It appears to me that taxpayer has misinterpreted both the statute and the prior rulings of this office.

It may clarify the issue if I quote the statutes and designate the various amendments which have been enacted. The original sections were enacted as parts of the Revenue Act of 1927. I have underscored all subsequent amendments and have denoted the year of enactment immediately after each one:

"Section 334 (G. S. 105-159). *Correction and Changes.*

"If the amount of the net income for any year of any taxpayer under this article, as returned to the United States Treasury Department, is changed and corrected by the Commissioner of Internal Revenue, or other officer of the United States of competent authority, such taxpayer, within thirty days after receipt of *Internal Revenue Agent's report or supplemental report reflecting* (1933; formerly, "final determination by the United States Government of") the corrected net income, shall make return under oath or affirmation to the Commissioner of Revenue of such corrected net income. *If the taxpayer fails to notify the Commissioner of Revenue of assessment of additional tax by the Commissioner of Internal Revenue, the Statute of Limitation shall not apply.* (1937) The Commissioner of Revenue shall thereupon proceed to determine from such evidence as he may have brought to his attention or shall otherwise acquire, the correct net income of such taxpayer for the fiscal or calendar year, and if there shall be any additional tax due from such taxpayer, the same shall be assessed and collected; and if there shall have been an overpayment of the tax, the said Commissioner shall, within thirty days after the final determination of the net income of such taxpayer, refund the amount of such excess: *Provided, that any taxpayer who fails to comply with this section as to making report of such change as made by the Federal Gobernment within the time specified shall be subject to all penalties as provided in section 336 of this article, in case of additional tax due, and shall forfeit his rights to any refund due by reason of such change.*" (1935)

"Section 335 (G. S. 105-160). *Additional Taxes.*

"If the Commissioner of Revenue discovers from the examination of the return or otherwise that the income of any taxpayer, or any portion thereof, has been assessed, he may, at any time within three years *(except where the taxpayer has failed to notify the Commissioner of additional assessment by the Federal Department—See Section 334)* (1937) after the time when the return was due, *give notice in writing to the taxpayer of such deficiency. Any taxpayer feeling aggrieved by such proposed assessment shall be entitled to a hearing before the Commissioner of Revenue, if within thirty days after giving notice of such proposed assessment he shall apply for such hearing in writing, explaining in detail his objections to same. If no request for such hearing is so made, such proposed assessment shall be final and conclusive. If the request for hearing is made, the taxpayer shall be heard by the Commissioner of Revenue, and after such hearing the Commissioner of Revenue shall render his decision. The taxpayer shall be advised of his decision and such amount shall be due within ten days after notice is given.* (1933; former precedural provisions not pertinent here). The provisions of this article with respect to revision and appeal shall apply to the tax so assessed. The limitation of three years to the assessment of such tax or an additional tax shall not apply to the assessment of additional taxes upon fraudulent returns. *Upon failure to file returns* and in the absence of fraud the limitation shall be five years." (1937)

The taxpayer contends that the Commissioner of Revenue is barred by the three-year statute from making assessment as to any of the years in question. The gist of his argument seems to be as follows:

(1)   That prior to 1937 the sections quoted above had an inherent "weakness" in that once the statute of limitations was set in motion by the due date of the original or annual return, it continued to run its course, untolled, even though the taxpayer failed to give the required thirty-day notice, and there was no way of stopping the statute, in the absence of fraud.

(2)   That the purpose of the 1937 amendments was to cure this "weakness" by providing that, if the taxpayer should fail to give the required notice, such failure would serve to "toll" the statute in those cases wherein the statute had not already run its full course.

(3)   That the purpose of the 1937 amendments was not to "reopen years already barred," and, if the three years from the due date of the original return had already expired when the thirty-day notice was required, no additional tax could be assessed.

(4)   That if the thirty-day notice is properly given, the statute would continue to run for any unexpired part of the period—even though the unexpired part may be only one day.

(5)   That where the required notice is not given, the statute of limitations is "tolled," not with the "thirty-day letter" or with the "ninety-day letter," but with final determination of liability by the Federal Government, November 3, 1943, by which time all the tax years in question are barred.

(6)   That if the Attorney-General is correct in his interpretation of the statute, the statute "opens up tax years already barred" and "revives causes of action already barred;" and the statute is therefore unconstitutional.

Aside from purely legal reasoning, I can hardly believe that the legislature would consciously enact a statute having the effect attributed to the 1937 amendments by the taxpayer. It happens more often than not that the Federal Government does not get around to correcting the net income of a taxpayer until after three years from the time his return is due and filed. Thus, the taxpayer here would impute to the legislature an intent to bar the State in most cases where net income is corrected by the Federal Government. Under the taxpayer's interpretation the statute is little more than an empty shell, a mere gesture. It requires the filing of the notice *for any year* in which net income is corrected by the Internal Revenue Agent; but taxpayer says, nevertheless, that the Commissioner cannot assess where more than three years have elapsed since th original return. The taxpayer's position is somewhat anomalous. It is hardly to be supposed that the legislature would require the taxpayer to file a corrected return if no tax could possibly be due thereon.

Therefore, it seems to me that the taxpayer's reasoning leads to a wholly unreasonable result.

Moreover, on the basis of legal reasoning the taxpayer's argument fails at the very outset. Without discussion he indulges in the assumption that prior to 1937 the Commissioner was barred *in every case* after the lapse of three years from the due date of the original return; and, in recognition of what he terms a "weakness" in the law prior to 1937, he reads into the 1937 amendments a legislative purpose to remedy this statutory "weakness" by providing for a tolling of the statute *if the period has not already expired.*

In this respect the taxpayer has built his entire argument upon a false premise; and with the failure of the premise his argument loses all validity.

Contrary to the assumption made by taxpayer, the law prior to 1937 did not have the particular "weakness" for which taxpayer seeks a cure in the

1937 amendments. *From the time these statutes were enacted in 1927 this office has consistently held that, where a new or corrected return is required under Section 334, the statute of limitations in question runs, not from the due date of the original return, but from the due date of the new or corrected return.* Therefore, the 1937 amendments could not have had the effect asserted by the taxpayer.

This interpretation of the original statute finds ample support in the language. Section 334 required a "return" of corrected net income. Section 335 provided that the Commissioner could assess at any time within three years from the time a "return" is due. The notice or corrected return is a "return" within the meaning of Section 335, and the Commissioner, since 1927, has clearly had the right to act within three years of its due date in every case.

In view of the consistent rulings of the Attorney General and the compliant administrative practice for ten years to the above effect, it cannot be supposed that the legislature of 1937 acted on any other premise. Therefore, the 1937 amendments necessarily have a purpose which must be construed in the light of the previous administrative application of the statute.

This purpose becomes clear with an understanding of the effect of the statute prior to 1937. Before 1937 the taxpayer was required to file a new return for *any year* for which the Federal Government had determined a corrected or changed net income. The Commissioner of Revenue then had three years from the due date of the new return to make his additional assessment, if any. After three years from the due date of the new return he was barred in every case, except that of fraud, regardless of whether the taxpayer filed his new return or not. In some cases the Commissioner did not discover the Federal correction or change until after three years had passed from the due date of the return. Thus, in 1937 the legislature inserted a provision that, if the new return or notice was not filed as required, the statute of limitations would not apply. The statute of limitations referred to in this 1937 provision is that which otherwise would have run from the due date of the new or corrected return. Thus the Commissioner since 1937 has an unlimited time in which to discover and assess additional income in cases where the required notice is not filed. A positive provision to this effect was placed in Section 334; and a parenthetical exception to the three-year statute, with a reference to Section 334, was inserted in Section 335.

Viewed in this light, the purpose of the 1937 amendments was clear, and the present law has the following effect:

(1)   Where the thirty-day notice is given, as required, the Commissioner is barred after three years from the due date of such notice, but not before in any case.

(2)   Where the notice is not given as required, the Commissioner is never barred, for the statute does not begin to run.

This interpretation does not have the effect of "opening up years already barred." That expression is a misconception and does not meet the question. The statute of limitations does not run against a "year" as such. A "year" as such is never barred. The essence of the matter is that the "cause of action" or the right which accrues in favor of the Commissioner is the right to examine a return and take action on it. It is this right against which the statute runs. True, the old right, i.e., the right to act upon the original return may be barred; but when a new return becomes due under Section 334 a new right arises—a right to act on *this* return. It is not of any importance that the return under scrutiny deals with things which happened more than three years ago. The significant thing is that those things are reportable *now*, and that the Commissioner has a right to examine the report or return and to take action thereon within the statutory period. Certainly this right cannot be barred even before it is born.

The taxpayer disproves the validity of his own position. While he impliedly suggests the theory that it is the *year* against which the statute runs, he nevertheless starts the limitation period with the due rate of the original *return*, which is in the succeeding year. If it is the year, as such, which is barred, the statutory period should be counted from that year rather than from the due date of the return.

I am, therefore, of the opinion that our interpretation of the statute does not have the effect of "opening up years already barred," for no year, *per se* is ever barred. The thing barred, if anything, is the right to act on the original return.

The taxpayer contends that his position is buttressed by the manner in which the 1937 legislature amended Section 335: (1) by leaving unaffected a provision that the three-year statute is inapplicable in fraud cases (implying that such a provision would be unnecessary if the Commissioner could "reopen barred years" anyway), and (2) by inserting a parenthetical provision to the effect that the Commissioner is not barred in three years if no notice is filed under Section 334. The trouble with the taxpayer's argument here is the same trouble which permeates his entire brief: he assumes that the three-year period of the statute of limitations mentioned in the statute is always counted from the due date of the "original" return. Section 335 is not limited in its application to the "original" or annual return. It speaks generally of "the return," and this means any return required by the law, including the return of corrected net income. Under this interpretation the parenthetical exception was appropriately placed in Section 335 by the 1937 legislature; and there was no need to change the provision applicable to fraud cases, for it was wholly appropriate as then worded.

I have carefully reconsidered the case of *Maxwell v. Hinsdale*, 207 N. C. 37, cited by taxpayer in support of his contention that the statute of limitations is always counted from the due date of the original return. I fail to understand how the taxpayer could think that this case supports him in any way, even by analogy or implication. It is not in point. For that matter it is not even near the point. It represents no more than a pronouncement of the clear and unequivocal language of Section 340, which is not involved here. It holds simply what the statute provides, i.e., that to entitle a taxpayer to a revision of tax assessed against him he must apply within three years from (1) the time he filed his return, or (2) the date of notice of assessment of additional tax. In that case the taxpayer waited more than three years after he filed his annual return; *and there was no assessment of additional tax.* Under the provisions of Section 340 he was clearly barred. The statute ran from the filing of his original return in that case because *it was that return which he sought to revise,* and not a new assessment placed on him by the Commissioner.

The *Hinsdale* case is not in point because it deals with a statute of limitations and circumstances which are entirely different from those involved here. Moreover, there is not even any dictum in the opinion which can be turned in the taxpayer's favor. The case upheld a ruling of this office made concomitantly with the rulings under the sections involved here. There is nothing in the *Hinsdale* case repugnant to the position taken here.

In my opinion, there is no merit to taxpayer's contention that the *Hinsdale* case holds that "the three-year statute of limitation plainly refers only to the tax return originally filed by the taxpayer for the year in question and has no application to Federal changes in the Federal income tax return for such year." The "statute of limitations" referred to in that case was the one contained in Section 340, applicable to application by taxpayer for revision and refund. The court was not speaking of the statute which runs against the Commissioner's right to assess, Section 335. Nowhere in the opinion does the court consider the point involved here or even use the expression "original return." On the other hand, the court does refer expressly to the "new return" required under Section 334 and holds that it had nothing to do with that particular case, which was being decided under the express provision of Section 340, which provided for an entirely different "statute of limitations" from the one in Section 334. It is difficult to perceive how the *Hinsdale* case could have been decided any other way.

Under the interpretation we have consistently and continuously placed on these statutes, the taxpayer's conjectures as to "when the statute of limitation is tolled" by failure to give notice become wholly inappropriate, for they are born of his own peculiar interpretation of the statute before and after 1937. We have rejected his interpretation, and under our interpretation the question cannot arise, for there is no "tolling" at any time: the statute does not begin to run until the new return is due; and it does not begin at all if the new return is not filed.

However, taxpayer's position does suggest that he may be confused as to when the new return is due. The statute expressly provides that it is due "within thirty days after receipt of Internal Revenue Agent's report or supplemental report." The taxpayer's argument implies that this provision means thirty days after final determination of net income by the Federal Government. The error of such an interpretation becomes obvious upon an examination of the 1933 amendment, which did away with just those words and substituted the ones now appearing in the statute.

In view of the interpretation we have placed on these statutes, it would seem that no constitutional question arises. The taxpayer's assertion of unconstitutionality is founded on a misunderstanding of our position, and depends upon his theory that we are reviving a right already barred. Under our interpretation no barred right is revived: if the right to act on the original return is once barred, it remains barred; but when a new return is filed, a right arises to act upon it also. That right is a new and different one. There is no question of "years already barred." A year, as such, cannot be barred. Things barred are rights, not years; and the right in question is that which accrues to the Commissioner with respect to the new return. In this view of the matter, I see no need to discuss the validity of the taxpayer's argument on the unconstitutionality of reviving barred causes. For purposes of argument I will simply concede that the general principle asserted by him is correct.

For the reasons stated herein, I advise that in my opinion the taxpayer's position cannot be sustained.

INCOME TAXATION; DEDUCTIBILITY OF PREMIUM ON VOLUNTARY RETIREMENT OF CORPORATE BONDS BEFORE MATURITY

December 31, 1945

You have referred to me a letter under date of December 15, 1945, from Messrs. Ratcliff, Vaughn, Hudson and Ferrell, Winston-Salem, North Carolina, attorneys for Piedmont Publishing Company, taxpayer. It appears that the taxpayer is challenging the correctness of your ruling that the premium paid by it during its fiscal year ended April 30, 1943, upon the retirement of certain outstanding debenture notes prior to maturity was not deductible from gross income.

The taxpayer is aware of the previous rulings of this office to the effect that, when a corporation voluntarily retires its bonds at a premium, such premium is not deductible under our Revenue Act; and the taxpayer further "admits that it was not forced by the terms of the debenture agreement to pay off its debenture notes prior to the maturities stated therein."

However, the taxpayer seeks to lift his case from the rule by contending that two unusual circumstances exist here: (1) "the conditions imposed on the corporation were very stringent, and it was anticipated at the time of execution of the agreement that to be able to operate without having at all times hanging over it the possibility of the former owner taking over operations, the corporation would have to pay off these bonds as soon after the earliest date provided for retirement as was possible"; (2) the indebtedness of the corporation was not decreased, but, on account of the necessity of borrowing new money, including an additional amount to take care of the premium, was actually increased.

I regret that I am unable to agree with taxpayer's contention that these two factors serve to remove his case from the effect of our previous ruling.

His first factor seems to say no more than that it was to the corporation's best interest to retire the bonds. We must assume this to be true in every case; otherwise the bonds would not have been voluntarily retired. In fact, the prior ruling of this office denied the deduction essentially on the ground that the retirement, if voluntary, was presumed to result in a benefit to the corporation rather than a loss or detriment.

The taxpayer's second factor, in my opinion, does not serve to avoid the prior ruling. This factor presumably is advanced to show that retirement of the bonds worked a detriment to the corporation—a position not wholly consistent with that which attends the first factor.

It may be conceded that in actual fact the corporation may, in a given case, be able to show that the voluntary retirement of its bonds ultimately wrought a loss, in that retirement of the bonds was for the best interests of the corporation, and, therefore, the voluntary retirement of the bonds was a mistake, an error of judgment. On the other hand, we cannot assume that a *voluntary* retirement is a bad thing. If it were, it would hardly be done.

Personally I have felt for some time that we should have a rule con. sistent with that of the Federal government, which admittedly is favorable to taxpayer's position. However, the fact remains that the ruling of this office has survived all legislature since 1937, without change; and I hardly see how a reversal of the ruling now could be justified in the light of this history, especially in view of the frequency with which the rule has been applied administratively.

It is true that this office recently has expressed the opinion that the prior ruling is not applicable to cases where the bonds are retired pursuant to contractual or legal obligation. But taxpayer admits "that it was not forced by the terms of the debenture agreement to pay off its debenture notes prior to the maturities stated therein"; and he cites the existence of no other legal obligation to retire said bonds.

For the reasons contained herein, I am compelled to advise that, in my opinion, the premium paid by the taxpayer upon retirement of bonds in this case is not deductible.

INCOME TAXES; LOSSES SUSTAINED FROM BUILDING CONTRACTS EXECUTED IN SOUTH CAROLINA AND FLORIDA

2 January, 1946

You request my opinion upon the following matter. A taxpayer, who is a resident of this state, executes building contracts in South Carolina and Florida, as well as in North Carolina. During the year 1942 he sustained substantial losses in connection with the work performed in South Carolina and Florida, but realized a profit from his operations in North Carolina. You inquire whether such taxpayer may deduct his out-of-state losses in filing his 1942 North Carolina income tax return.

There was no provision in the Revenue Act prior to 1943 which expressly authorized the deduction of losses incurred in connection with a business carried on outside of North Carolina. The Commissioner of Revenue has consistently interpreted the income tax statutes which were in force prior to 1943 as not authorizing a resident individual or a domestic corporation to use an out-of-state loss to reduce taxable income required to be returned to this state. This interpretation, being long continued without change and applying to unamended or substantially re-enacted income tax statutes, is deemed to have received legislative approval and thus had the effect of law. *Helvering v. Winmill*, 305 U. S. 79; *Boehm v. Com. Internal Revenue*, 90 L. Ed. 96.

In 1943 the legislature amended Section 322(10) of the Revenue Act to expressly allow resident individuals, having an established business or investments in a state which does not levy an income tax, to deduct any loss arising from such business or investment from income to be reported to North Carolina. This amendment, of course, is not retrospective and applies only to such losses sustained during the year 1943 and subsequently. The fact that the legislature deemed it necessary to expressly amend the Act to allow such losses clearly indicates that prior to such amendment there was no authority contained in the Act for such an allowance.

I, therefore, conclude that the taxpayer in question has no authority to deduct losses sustained on contracts executed in South Carolina and Florida during the year 1942.

INHERITANCE TAXATION; CERTIFICATION OF SETTLEMENT TO
CLERKS OF COURT UNDER SECTION 20

5 January, 1946

You have referred to me a letter dated December 20, 1945, from Mr. Richard E. Thigpen, attorney for the Estate of Joseph H. Sevier, and you request my opinion on the matters therein set out.

Your request necessitates an interpretation of the following part of Section 20 of the Revenue Act (G.S. 105-22):

"(b) It shall also be the duty of the Clerk of the Superior Court of each of the several counties of the State to enter in a book, prepared and furnished by the Commissioner of Revenue, to be kept for that purpose, and which shall be a public record, a condensed copy of the settlement of inheritance taxes of each estate, together with a copy of the receipt showing payment, or by a certificate showing no tax due, as shall be certified to him by the Commissioner of Revenue."

The taxpayer has remitted to you a sum of money alleged by him to be the correct amount of inheritance tax due by the estate, as computed from the inheritance and estate tax inventory, and has requested you to certify settlement of the tax as contemplated by the paragraph quoted above.

You have declined to certify settlement of inheritance taxes of this estate, assigning as your reason your opinion that the paragraph quoted above refers to final settlement after determination of estate values as provided in Section 26 (G. S. 105-29). The taxpayer takes exception to your ruling and contends that payment of tax along with the inventory within six months, as provided in Section 21 (G. S. 105-23), constitutes a "settlement" within the meaning of the paragraph quoted above, and that you are required by law to certify such settlement to the Clerk of the Superior Court in order that he may allow the executors to make final settlement of the estate in accordance with Section 25 (G.S. 105-28).

I have carefully considered this matter, and have concluded that you are correct in declining to certify settlement of taxes in this case, and that the taxpayer's position cannot be sustained. It is my opinion that the word "settlement" in Section 20(b) of the Revenue Act (G.S. 105-22) means "final settlement," or settlement after final determination of value under Section 26 (G. S. 105-29).

The word "settlement," when used in connection with public transactions and accounts has a well defined meaning. It means *administrative* determination of the amount due. "Final settlement" has exactly the same meaning. Black's Law Dictionary, Third Ed., P. 1613; 57 C. J., *Settlement*, P. 532; and cases cited.

While there may be some kind of determination of the amount of tax due upon the filing of the six-months inventory, there is certainly no *administrative* determination at this time. The amount is merely one which has been submitted by the taxpayer, and the Commissoner of Revenue does not pass at that time upon its correctness. Indeed, Section 21 (G.S. 105-23) expressly refers to the payment of the tax at this time as a "tentative" settlement. There is no such qualifying adjective in Section 20 (G.S. 105-22). It must be presumed that the legislature differentiated consciously, and that Section 20 refers to a final settlement of tax in the absence of qualifying language.

This interpretation is further supported by the language of Section 13 (G.S. 105-15), which provides that heirs and others shall be discharged from liability by paying the taxes, "*settlement* of which they may be charged with." Here the word "settlement" clearly means "final settlement," for the heirs surely would not be discharged from liability upon other than a final settlement. This word must be taken to have the same meaning when used in the related Section 20 (G.S. 105-22), there being nothing to indicate the contrary.

It should also be remembered that from the time this section was added to the Revenue Act in 1923 the Commissioner of Revenue has applied the interpretation now placed on the statute. This consistent administrative practice through all legislatures since 1923 must be accorded great weight, especially in view of the fact that such practice has been applicable to every estate required to file an inventory. The practice by this time has practically the force of law.

Aside from any legal argument, it appears to me that the interpretation urged by the taxpayer would result in the imposition of a rather useless duty upon the Clerk. It seems to me that the primary purpose of the record required by Section 20(b) of the Revenue Act (G.S. 105-22) is to show whether or not the estate is subject to inheritance tax. This purpose would be utterly defeated if the record showed merely "tentative" settlements. If in every case the settlement shown on the record is not a final one, it is of no value, for being subject to change, it cannot be relied upon by any person interested in ascertaining whether the property of the estate is discharged from the tax.

The taxpayer, in support of his contention that your interpretation is incorrect, indulges in the assumption that our courts, "to be sure," would not withhold a final accounting and distribution pending the outcome of litigation over a Federal estate tax liability. While this question need not be decided here, it may be appropriate to remark that I cannot quite as easily indulge in that assumption. Even if the assumption is correct, it may be argued that distribution to the beneficiaries is not necessarily delayed, as a practical matter, by postponement of the final audit by the Clerk of Court. In saying this I am cognizant of Sections 13 (G. S. 105-15) and 28 (G.S. 105-31). But these are matters outside the realm of this opinion, and what I have said is not to be treated as the expression of any opinion.

I cannot agree with the taxpayer's contention that your refusal to certify settlement of taxes to the Clerk causes him to violate G. S. 28-121, providing that the Clerk shall audit an account whether it be filed voluntarily or by compulsion. In my opinion that statute has no application to this case. The Court has already held that the two-year filing limit therein provided has no application where the duties of the fiduciary cannot be completed within that time. *In Re Wachovia Bank and Trust Co.*, 210 N.C. 385. Even if the Clerk did audit what purported to be the final account in this case, in compliance with the statute, he would have to disapprove it because of the fact that settlement of inheritance tax had not been made. Section 25 of Revenue Act (G.S. 105-28). Moreover, G. S. 28-121, requiring the filing of final account within two years and audit thereof by the Clerk, is clearly qualified by G. S. 28-192, which provides that "Nothing in this Chapter shall be construed to affect the discretionary powers, trusts and authorities of an executor or other trustee acting under a will, provided creditors be not delayed thereby nor the order changed in which by law they are entitled to be paid." In any event, I do not think G. S. 28-121 requires a final account or an audit thereof prior to the time it can be properly and completely made; and it cannot be so made until the inheritance tax is paid and receipt from the Commissioner of Revenue is exihibited to the Clerk as required by G.S. 105-28. In this respect G.S. 105-28 is an exception to the requirement of G. S. 28-121.

For the reasons stated herein, I am of the opinion that there has not been a "settlement" of inheritance taxes within the meaning of Section 20 (G.S. 105-22); and, therefore, that your refusal to certify settlement of such taxes was proper.

INCOME TAXATION; DEDUCTION OF EXPENSES UNDER SECTION 322(9½)
ALLOWABLE ONLY AS TO EXCESS ABOVE EXEMPTION

11 January, 1946

You have requested my opinion on paragraph 9½ of Section 322 of the Revenue Act (G.S. 105-147), which provides, in substance, that a taxpayer may deduct amounts actually expended in keeping dependent relatives in an institution:

"Provided, that the deduction authorized in this section shall apply only to actual expenditures in excess of the amounts allowed as personal exemption for dependents under the provisions of subdivision (e) of Subsection 1 of Section 324, and the maximum amount that may be deducted by an individual under the authorization herein stated shall not exceed $800."

In my opinion, this proviso means that

(1) In order to entitle taxpayer to any deduction under this paragraph, his actual expenses for this purpose must equal and then exceed his personal exemption for such dependent, and

(2) The amount of the deduction is the amount actually expended *minus* his personal exemption for such dependent, but

(3) If this difference is more than $800, only $800 may be deducted.

Thus, where a married man living with his wife maintains a son in a mental institution at an actual expense of $800 during the tax year, he would be entitled to his $2,200 personal exemption plus a $600 deduction under Section 332(9½), for $600 is the amount derived by deducting the $200 exemption from the $800 actual expenses.

In order to entitle this same man to the maximum allowable deduction of $800 under this paragraph, his actual expenses must have equalled or exceeded $1,000, for the first $200 would be absorbed by the personal exemption.

I trust that this answers your question.

INCOME TAXATION; GAIN ON SALE BY ADMINISTRATOR DETERMINED ON BASIS OF VALUE AT DEATH, NOT DECEDENT'S COST

12 January, 1946

You have requested my opinion on the following matter.

Mr. "X" prior to January 1, 1921, bought stock at a cost of $5,000. He subsequently died, leaving this stock, which was valued, for inheritance tax purposes, at $7,500. Before distribution of the estate the administrator sold the stock for $10,000. You wish to know how to compute capital gain under these circumstances. You state that you have followed the practice of using the value reported for inheritance tax purpose as the "basis."

In my opinion your practice in using or accepting the inheritance tax value is proper if such value accurately states the true value at the time of the decedent's death.

The increase in value which occurred between the decedent's purchase and his death must be disregarded, for there is no gain or loss until sale; and when the decedent died, the stock, at its then value, became an asset of the estate. The only income chargeable to the administrator is that which accrued after decedent's death. Therefore in my opinion the only gain in the above example would be the difference between the value at death and the sale price.

It would follow, I think, that a loss is ascertainable in the same way.

SALES TAX; SALES LESS THAN 10c DO NOT AFFECT MERCHANT'S LIABILITY

15 January, 1946

I have received a letter dated January 11, 1946, from Mr. C. A. Corbett, 410 S. Wilmington Street, Raleigh, N. C. Mr. Corbett is engaged primarily in the business of buying and selling used clothing, and in connection with this business he sells soft drinks and milk for immediate consumption on the premises. He asks my opinion on whether or not he is liable for sales tax on this latter part of his business. He suggests that he is not liable because he collects from his customers no sales tax on the drinks and the milk, both sales being less than 10c.

The Attorney General can advise only public officers on matters pertaining to their official duties. For that reason I am addressing this opinion to you, and am sending a copy to Mr. Corbett.

It is my opinion that the taxpayer in this case is liable for sales tax upon his total gross sales, even though some of those sales are for less than 10c.

The Sales Tax Article imposes the tax directly upon the retail merchant, and provides that such tax be measured by his gross sales. The fact that the merchant fails to collect the amount of the tax from some or all of his customers on the individual sales does not affect the merchant's liability or the amount of the tax.

The Commissioner of Revenue by regulation has provided that on sales of less than 10c the retail merchant cannot pass the amount on to his customer; but this does not affect the merchant's liability to pay his gross sales.

I believe that Mr. Corbett is misled by the impression that the sales tax is imposed by law upon the consumer. Although the law intended that the tax in appropriate instances shall be passed on to the consumer, such tax is imposed directly and primarily on the retail merchant, whose liability is not affected by what he collects from his customers.

INCOME TAXATION; FOREIGN CORPORATION CANNOT COMPUTE ALLOCATION
FRACTION BY INCLUDING PROPORTIONATE PART OF GROSS RECEIPTS OF
JOINT ADVENTURE IN ANOTHER STATE

24 January, 1946

You have requested my opinion upon the following matter.

McDevitt & Street Company, Charlotte, North Carolina, hereinafter called the taxpayer, is a foreign corporation which is domesticated in this State and is engaged in the contracting business. The taxpayer pays income tax to this State on the basis of the ratio of its gross receipts in this State to its gross receipts within and without the State, as provided in Section 311 (II) (3) of the Revenue Act (G.S. 105-134).

During the taxable year 1942 the taxpayer executed a contract with three other corporations or persons and thereunder entered into a "joint venture" to carry on certain phases of its contracting business in Virginia. The four corporations or persons carried on this "joint venture" under the name of "Grannis, Higgins, Thompson & McDevitt Company." Such "company," though not a corporation, was conducted as a separate business entity. Separate books were kept for said business entity, and the several corporations or persons who owned said business jointly agreed that profits, if any, should be divided and distributed equally among themselves. All "gross receipts" were to flow into the treasury of the "joint venture" and not proportionately into the treasury of each owner corporation or person. It appears that the rights of the several parties to the "joint venture" were similar or analagous to those of the several partners in a partnership.

In arriving at the ratio of gross receipts within this State to gross receipts within and without this State for the taxable year 1942 the taxpayer included in total gross receipts one-fourth of the gross receipts of the "joint venture." This served to reduce the proportion of net income taxable in this State. You have tentatively disallowed the taxpayer's method of determining the apportionment fraction and have proposed to make an assessment of additional income tax. The taxpayer has protested your proposed action, and you request my opinion as to whether or not the assessment is warranted under our law.

It is conceded that if the taxpayer had singly engaged in contracting business in Virginia, the gross receipts from such business would be includible for the purpose of determining the apportionment fraction. But herein lies a difference: where the corporation engages in such business singly, it actually receives the gross receipts of such business—it is the actual recipient; but where the corporation enters into a partnership or "joint venture" with other corporations or persons, it is the partnership, the "joint venture," and not the individual corporate member, which is the recipient. As far as the partner is concerned, he has only a joint interest in the partnership business. The only money actually received by him is the share of the profits which is distributed to him. He has not even the *right* to receive the partnership's gross receipts, or any part thereof, as such. At least to this extent the partnership is a separate entity. I do not think a different result would be effected by designating the business a joint adventure rather than a partnership.

It appears to me that the taxpayer in this case simply entered into an arrangement whereby it received a sum by way of profit, and that this profit was all that it did receive. In view of the fact that the taxpayer did not receive one-fourth or any other part of the "joint venture's" gross receipts, as such, I am of the opinion that no part of such gross receipts are includible in taxpayer's total gross receipts, except those amounts actually distributed to the taxpayer individually.

I am, therefore, of the opinion that your proposed assessment of additional income taxes in this case is proper.

Under the view which I take of this matter it is immaterial that a joint adventure is technically not a legal entity such as can sue and be sued.

(Note: Above opinion subsequently overruled.)

SALES AND USE TAXES; MATERIALS PURCHASED BY CONTRACTOR UNDER LUMP SUM CONTRACT WITH FEDERAL GOVERNMENT

31 January, 1946

You request my opinion upon the liability of the Standard Roofing and Sheet Metal Company for sales and use taxes on account of materials and supplies purchased and used in the performance of a contract entered into with the AAF Overseas Replacement Depot in Greensboro, N. C., which is an agency of the Federal Government,

This office has previously ruled that sales to and purchases by lump-sum contractor engaged in performing construction work for the Federal Government are properly classified as sales to and purchases by the contractor, unless provisions in the contract compel a different conclusion.

The contract under consideration is a "lump sum" type. It provides for the furnishing and installing of five automatic forced warm air heating systems in certain specified buildings used by the AAF Depot at a total cost specified in the contract. Article 1 provides that the contractor shall furnish all the materials necessary and perform the work. Article 10 stipulates that the contractor shall be responsible for all materials delivered and work performed until completion and final acceptance. There is also a provision to the effect that upon the completion of the contract the work shall be delivered complete and undamaged. It is implicit in these and other provisions of the contract that title to the materials purchased and used in the installation work shall not vest in the Federal government until payment is made to the contractor for the completed job.

I am unable to find any provision in the contract which constitutes the Standard Roofing and Sheet Metal Company a purchasing agent for the government with respect to taxable materials purchased and used in the construction work. Therefore, it is my opinion that the contractor is liable for the 3% sales and use tax on materials purchased for use in performing the contract, since such contractor is in this case an independent purchaser. The sales were made to the contractor and not to the AAF Depot, and thus, there is no basis for tax exemption. *Alabama v. King & Boozer*, 314 U. S. 1; *Curry v. United States*, 314 U. S. 14.

INHERITANCE TAX; PAYMENTS TO BENEFICIARIES UNDER FEDERAL SOCIAL SECURITY ACT

31 ·January, 1946

You inquire whether amounts payable under Title II, Section 202, subsections (d) and (g) of the Social Security Act (U.S.C.A. Title 42, Section 402 (d) and (g)) to beneficiaries of a decedent should be included in the estate of such decedent for inheritance tax purposes.

Section 202 (d) of Title II provides for the payment of a stipulated monthly sum to the widow of a decedent covered by the Social Security Act after she has attained the age of sixty-five years. Section 202 (g) provides for the payment of a lump sum to the widow. immediately upon the death of her husbond.

The payments under consideration are made by the Federal government from the Federal Old Age and Survivors' Insurance Trust Fund, which Fund is derived from employment taxes imposed in the Internal Revenue Code upon certain employees and employers. The amount, conditions, and time of the payment of these benefits are expressly regulated by the Social Security Act. The beneficiaries are expressly designated in the Act, and the benefits are paid to them rather than to the estate of the decedent. An individual covered by the provisions of the Act has no power to designate his beneficiaries or to fix the amount which any particular beneficiary will receive at his death. He has no property interest in the Federal Old Age and Survivors' Insurance Trust Fund from which payments to his beneficiaries will be made.

It is my opinion that when a person has no interest in property and no power of disposition over the same, there is no taxable transfer from him when, at his death, such property is transmitted to his beneficiaries. This is the view taken with respect to the benefits in question for Federal estate tax purposes by the Commissioner of Internal Revenue. *C. B. 1940-2 p. 285.*

It is, therefore, my opinion that amounts payable under Title II, Section 202, subsections (d) and (g) of the Social Security Act to beneficiaries of a decedent should not be included in the estate of such decedent for inheritance tax purposes.

INCOME TAXATION; DEDUCTIBILITY OF PAYMENTS TO HOLDERS OF "DEBENTURE BONDS"; HELD HERE TO BE INTEREST RATHER THAN DIVIDENDS

5 February, 1946

You have requested my opinion on the following matter concerning Jewel Cotton Mills, Inc., hereinafter referred to as the taxpayer.

The question is whether or not you should disallow the deductîon by taxpayer of so-called "interest" alleged by him to have been paid during the taxable year 1941 to holders of the taxpayer's "Six Per Cent Debenture Bonds."

Each bond contains a promise to pay $100.00 to the bearer on December 15, 1951, unless earlier retired as therein provided, with interest from December 15, 1941, at 6% per annum, payable semiannually on the fifteenth days of June and December of each year. Payment is secured by all the assets of the taxpayer, "subject only to the priority of the claims of general creditors." The bond takes precedence over the common stock of the taxpayer company, and over any other stock, common or preferred, which may be issued during the life of the bond. Taxpayer can retire each bond after thirty days notice by paying same in full with interest, said retirement to be "as nearly as possible on a pro rata basis." At least 50% of the earnings each year is to be applied to retirement of bonds.

The question here is whether the payments sought to be deducted are "interest," which is deductible, or "dividends," which are not. This, in turn, depends upon whether the instrument is an evidence of indebtedness or a share of stock, i.e., whether the payee is a creditor or a stockholder of the corporation.

I am of the opinion that the debenture bond in question is actually, as its name implies, an evidence of indebtedness. This bond has the essential characteristics of an evidence of indebtedness: a definite obligee, a definite, or ascertainable obligation, a definite time of maturity. On the other hand this bond lacks the usual characteristics of stock: the right to participate in net profits proportionate to the stockholding, the right to participate in management through voting power, the right to share proportionately in the distribution of net assets upon liquidation of the corporation.

In other words, this bond is a definite promise to pay to a definite person a definite amount at a definite time. This promise is not conditioned upon the fortunes of the corporation, but can be enforced in any event. The fact that at least 50% of the annual earnings must be set aside for retirement of bonds does not alter this result.

The authorities in support of the above principles are collected in Prentice-Hall Federal Tax Service 1946, Vol. 2, paragraph 13,004 et seq., and there is no need to list them here.

It is true that the bond in question has one characteristic not wholly consistent with the idea of indebtedness: the bond is made subordinate to the claims of general creditors. However, it seems to be settled that this alone is not sufficient to render the instrument stock in the face of all the other characteristics indicative of the contrary. The U. S. Supreme Court on January 7, 1946 declined to upset a Tax Court ruling to this effect. *John Kelley Co. v. Commissioner of Internal Revenue*, (1946) 90 L. ed. 257.

For the reasons stated herein, I am of the opinion that the debenture bond in question is, by its terms, an evidence of indebtedness rather than stock. I assume that this bond recites the entire contract between the bondholder and the corporation, and that there is no additional contract or understanding which might throw a different light upon the matter. If my assumption is correct, I advise that, in my opinion, the payments in question were interest rather than dividends; and, therefore, are deductible.

INCOME, FRANCHISE, AND LICENSE TAXATION; LIABILITY OF MARKETING
ASSOCIATIONS OR COOPERATIVES FOR TAXES IMPOSED BY REVENUE ACT

6 February, 1946

You have requested me to inquire into the question whether marketing associations or cooperatives are subject to the various taxes imposed by the Revenue Act. This question arose when Farmers Federation Cooperative, Asheville, N. C., requested you to furnish complete information concerning all taxes and license fees payable by it in the operation of the Carolina Farmers Tobacco Warehouses.

The cooperatives in question are those organized under General Statutes, Chapter 54, Subchapter V, or G. S. 54-129 to 54-158, inclusive. G. S. 54-143 provides that these marketing associations shall pay an annual license fee of $10.00, but shall be exempt from all franchise or license taxes. Section 314 of the Revenue Act (G. S. 105-138), paragraph 9, exempts from income tax "marketing associations organized under Subchapter five, Chapter 54 of the General Statutes, Article 19, Section 54-129 *et seq.*"

It seems, therefore, that a marketing association which is duly organized under G. S. 54-129 *et seq.*, and is engaged in business or functions within the scope of its legitimate activity as defined in the statute, is exempt from all franchise, license and income taxes except for an annual $10.00 "license fee."

I have read the charter of Farmers Federation and have compared it with the statutes under which the association was organized; and I observe nothing inconsistent between the two. Therefore, it does not appear, in my opinion, that the charter authorizes any function which would serve to deprive the association of any of the benefits bestowed by the statute under which association was organized. Nor do I think that the operation of a tobacco warehouse is beyond the scope of permissible functions. Therefore, I advise that, in my opinion, the operation of tobacco warehouses does not render a "marketing association," as defined by the statute, liable for income, franchise or license taxes other than the annual $10.00 "license fee."

USE TAX; LIABILITY OF CONTRACTOR FOR USE TAX ON TANGIBLE PERSONAL
PROPERTY USED IN CONSTRUCTION OF PROJECT FOR FEDERAL GOVERNMENT

12 February, 1946

You have requested my opinion on the following matter, which involves the question whether or not McDonald and Wright, herinafter referred to as the taxpayer, is liable for use tax upon certain articles of tangible personal property used in the construction of the Raleigh-Durham Airport, hereinafter referred to as the project. The project was one performed under contract with the Federal Government, the taxpayer being the contractor. The taxpayer is represented by Messrs. Ehringhaus and Ehringhaus, Attorneys at Law, Raleigh, N. C.

It appears that the taxpayer, a Georgia contractor, contracted with the Federal Government for the construction of the Raleigh-Durham Airport. After beginning the project, the taxpayer purchased from dealers, both

within and without this State, for use in carrying out the terms of the contract, i.e., constructing the airport, various articles of tangible personal
property, including gasoline, tires and various other supplies, goods,
materials and equipment durable and otherwise, some of which went into
and became part of the airport buildings, some of which, like gasoline and
oil, were wholly consumed on the project, and some of which were withdrawn from the State after completion of the project because of the fact
that their utility had not been wholly exhausted. Although the particular
articles or material in question here were purchased by the taxpayer after
beginning the project, it is understood that the taxpayer did use on the
project certain articles which had been purchased prior to the beginning of
the project and prior to his coming into the State to begin work on the
project.

You have made an assessment of use tax in this case both as to articles
purchased inside this State and as to articles purchased elsewhere, because
of the fact that the taxpayer has not shown that sales tax has been paid
thereon as provided by Section 802 of the Revenue Act, and thus is not
entitled to the credit therein granted.

The taxpayer challenges your assessment on several different grounds
as follows:

    (1)   That the gasoline purchased and used by taxpayer on this
project is exempt from sales tax and this means that it is also exempt
from the use tax.
    (2)   That tires and other articles not wholly consumed in this State
but used only temporarily in this State are exempt from the use tax.
    (3)   That all of the materials used on this project were "building
materials," as that term is used in the statute, because they or their
use enhanced the value of the property and, therefore, in a sense did
become a part of the "building" or other construction; and that under
a proper interpretation of Section 406(d) of the Revenue Act, with
special reference to the subsequent legislative amendment, all of said
materials are expressly exempt.

These contentions will be considered in this order. All must be considered with reference to the Revenue Act as amended through 1941, as the
events sought to be taxed in this case occurred prior to the effective date of
the 1943 amendments.

I

I cannot agree with the taxpayer that gasoline is exempt from the sales
tax. As a matter of fact, Section 406(a) expressly states that "it is not
the intent of this article to exempt gasoline from the retail sales tax." The
retail sales tax on gasoline is merely satisfied by a *pro tanto* part of the
6c gasoline tax which is levied on such gasoline. Therefore, there is no
exemption here which can be carried forward into the use tax article under
the provisions of Section 803(a). It is my opinion that the use tax attaches
to gasoline which is purchased outside the State for use inside the State
because of the fact that the 6c gasoline tax has not been paid to this State
and there is, therefore, nothing to credit on the sales or use tax.

II

The taxpayer's contention relative to tires and other equipment, the use
of which outlived the project in this State, apparently has reference to

Section 803(e), which exempts from the use tax the storage, use of consumption of

> "(e) Tangible personal property purchased or acquired prior to coming into this State and brought into this State by a person a non-resident thereof for his, her, its or their own use or enjoyment while temporarily in this State."

The assessment which you have made, I understand, is applicable only to those materials which were purchased by the taxpayer after work had been started on the project in this State. Under these circumstances I am of the opinion that the section quoted above is not applicable here for the reason that the materials in question were not purchased by the taxpayer "prior to coming into this State." I am not advertent to any other provision which would exempt these materials. They were purchased for initial use on a project in this State after the purchaser had started work on said project, and they were actually used in this State, both initially and substantially. Under these circumstances, I am of the opinion that such use in this State is not exempt from the use tax, and that the temporary character of the use is not material to this question. __

III

I am unable to agree with the taxpayer that all materials used on this project are exempt as "building materials" under Section 406(d) of the Revenue Act, as amended through 1941.

The gist of the taxpayer's contention seems to be as follows:

That when the relevant part of Section 406(d) was enacted in 1939 it was generally understood that the States could not constitutionally tax *any* materials sold to a contractor with the United States for use in carrying out the terms of the Federal contract, and that it was with this thought that our legislature exempted "building materials" sold to Federal contractors, meaning by the term, "building materials," *all* materials used in Federal construction work, irrespective of the question whether or not such materials entered into or became a part of a building; that subsequently the U. S. Supreme Court decided, in *Alabama v. King and Boozer*, 314 U. S. 1, 86 L. ed. 3, that States could constitutionally tax the sale of such materials to Federal contractors; that our legislature then, in 1943, in the exercise of its newly discovered constitutional power, deleted all reference to the Federal Government so as to tax all such materials when sold to independent contractors with the United States Government.

While conceding the force of the taxpayer's argument, I am of the opinion that the history of this law indicates a quite different interpretation. It appears to me that the following analysis strikes nearer the truth:

In 1937 our legislature enacted Section 427 into the Revenue Act. That section was a "use tax" upon "building materials"; and "building materials" was defined as "tangible personal property ... which shall enter into or become a part of any building or other kind of structure in this State, including all materials, supplies, fixtures and equipment of every kind and description which shall be annexed thereto or in any manner become a part thereof," except certain named materials not pertinent here. Subparagraph (b) of that section exempted from the use tax "such tangible personal property as shall enter into any building or structure erected or constructed under any contract with the Federal Government or any of its agencies. ... "

In 1939 our legislature amended Section 406(d) of the Revenue Act by adding the following:

> "Sales of building material made directly *to the Federal Government or* to State and local governments in this State shall be exempt from the tax on building material levied in this Act, and sales of building material to contractors to be used in construction work for *Federal*, State or local governments shall be construed as direct sales."

In 1943 our legislature amended Section 406(d) by striking out the words underlined above. The effect was to eliminate the exemption as to "building materials" sold to contractors with the Federal Government.

When the legislature created the exemption as to sales of building materials to contractors for Federal construction work, it probably had in mind a line of Federal cases led by *Panhandle Oil Co. v. Mississippi*, 277 U. S. 218 (1937), and *Graves v. Texas*, 298 U. S. 393 (1935). In the *Panhandle* case it was held that a State could not impose a tax, measured by the quantity sold, upon the privilege of selling gasoline to the Federal Government, because in substance and effect such tax on the sale to the Government and, therefore, impeded and burdened the United States in, the exercise of its constitutional powers. In the *Graves* case it was held that a State cannot impose an excise tax on the amount of gasoline withdrawn from storage for sale to the United States. It will be observed that in each of these cases the material, the sale or storage of which was taxed, physically passed to the United States, and that the United States paid an increased price for that very material (i.e., gasoline) in direct proportion to the tax that was laid on it.

If the 1939 legislature, in creating the exemption as to "building materials," intended, as seems likely, to confine such exemption to constitutional necessity as it was then conceived, it would seem that the exemption was intended to cover only those materials which, as part of a building or structure, physically passed to the Federal Government on a "cost-plus-a-fixed-fee" contract, on the theory that only as to these materials was there, in substance and effect, a sale of materials to the United States. Other materials used by the contractor did not actually pass to the Federal Government, and, therefore, the economic burden of the tax on the sale to the contractor was not thought to rest on the Government; and as to these other materials no exemption was granted.

1941 U. S. Supreme Court decided *Alabama v. King and Boozer*, 314 U. S. 1, 86 L. ed. 3, and *Curry v. U. S.*, 314 U. S. 14, 86 L. ed. 9.

These cases overruled the former cases and held that a State could constitutionally impose a tax upon the sale or use of articles sold to or used by a contractor with the United States on a "cost-plus-a-fixed-fee" basis, even though the title to such materials passed to the United States and even though the economic burden of the tax is borne by the United States, if such contractor purchased on his own credit and could not obligate the United States on purchase contracts.

Thus, the Supreme Court in these cases overruled the existing law and held that *even as to building materials*, title to which passed to the Government under the "cost-plus" contract, a State sales or use tax could constitutionally be imposed; and in 1943 our legislature took notice of these decisions by withdrawing the exemption from building materials.

In my opinion the above analysis is the correct one. It tends to show that the legislature originally exempted only "building materials" (i.e., materials which became a part of a building and passed to the Government) because it thought that this was all that the Constitution demanded; and that when the Supreme Court decided that a tax even as to "building materials" was valid, the exemption was forthwith withdrawn.

Aside from any approach to the question of interpretation on the basis of constitutional considerations, it appears to me that the ordinary rules of statutory construction resolve the matter against the taxpayer. The exemption of "building materials" sold to contractors for Federal construction was created by the 1939 legislature. Only two years prior thereto the 1937 legislature had enacted Section 427 of the Revenue Act, which clearly defined building materials as those which became part of a building. It seems clear that the legislature was speaking of the same thing when it created the exemption in 1939. I find nothing to indicate that the legislature meant something different when it used the same term. Furthermore, I am of the opinion that when Section 406(d) speaks of sales to the Government as being exempt from "the tax on building material levied in this Act," it refers primarily to the very tax on building materials imposed by Section 427, which is the only statute which levies a tax (use tax) on building material specifically by that name, the *sales* tax being applicable only because of the fact that it does not exempt building material. Thus, it seems to me that the two sections are tied inextricably together, and that to place different meanings upon the same term would do violence to the statute.

It is of some importance that this interpretation of the statute is the same as that published by the Commissioner of Revenue in a clarifying memorandum immediately after the enactment of the 1943 amendments. No legislative action on the point occurred during the 1945 session of the General Assembly. Therefore, the interpretation placed on the statute by the Commissioner is deemed to have received implied legislative approval.

Conclusion

For the reasons set forth herein, I am constrained to advise that, in my opinion, the taxpayer's position cannot be sustained, and that your assessment of use tax was properly made.

SALES TAXES; CONTRACTOR WITH FEDERAL GOVERNMENT; TAXABILITY
OF BUILDING MATERIALS FOR WHICH BIDS WERE RECEIVED
PRIOR TO APRIL 1, 1943

16 February, 1946.

You request that I give you my opinion upon the liability of the Cleveland Tramrail Carolinas Company, hereinafter referred to as the taxpayer, for a proposed sales and use taxes assessment made on the basis of an audit completed on November 14, 1944, based on purchases made by said taxpayer in the fulfillment of a subcontract for the installation of certain equipment at the Marine Corps Air Station at Cherry Point, N. C.

The principal contract, No. 4957, was between the Federal government and T. A. Loving Company. The original subcontract, which was for a lump sum, was dated January 5, 1943. Since prior to April 7, 1943, the sales tax statute specifically exempted building materials sold to a Federal contractor, it is clear that the taxpayer is not liable for sales or use taxes on building materials purchased under this original subcontract prior to April 1, 1943.

After the work under the original subcontract was commenced, however, it was found necessary to enlarge the scope of the installations agreed upon, and this in turn necessitated the entering into of subsequent agreements between the taxpayer and T. A. Loving Company, which were evidenced by change orders specifying in detail the nature of the additional work and materials to be furnished. Under these agreements, the additional work was to be done and materials furnished for a lump sum, just as was the case in the original contract. It appears that these change orders were dated after April 1, 1943, and, therefore, the question arises whether the additional building materials furnished pursuant thereto were subject to the sales and use taxes.

Counsel for the taxpayer has furnished copies of three letters from the taxpayer addressed to T. A. Loving Company which tend to show that requests for the additional work had been made, and bids therefor had been received, prior to April 1, 1943. Taxpayer's counsel verified this in a letter written under date of August 9, 1945. He pointed out that the paper work in connection with government contracts, such as the change orders under consideration, usually followed by considerable lengths of time the date upon which orders were actually placed and accepted. He also stated that the change orders amounted to nothing more than confirmation of the agreements previously entered into.

The Legislature of 1943 struck out of the law the exemption from taxation of the sales and use of building materials to or by Federal contractors. This amendment was effective April 1, 1943, but the Act in which it was incorporated specifically provided that its provisions did not affect any lump sum or unit price contract which was awarded, or upon which bids were received, prior to April 1, 1943.

Since taxpayer's bids for the additional installation work appear to have been received by T. A. Loving Company prior to April 1, 1943, I am of the opinion that the sales of building materials used in connection therewith are exempted from tax. The fact that the actual change orders executed in connection with the later agreements were made upon dates subsequent to April, 1943, is of no consequence here since the *bids* for the work appear to have been received prior to that date.

It is, therefore, my opinion that you should withdraw the part of the proposed assessment which is based upon (1) sales of building materials entering into the work agreed upon in the original subcontract, and (2) sales of building materials used in connection with the additional work for which bids were received prior to April 1, 1943.

SALES TAX; RESTAURANTS OPERATED IN INDUSTRIAL PLANTS

19 February, 1946.

You request that I advise you whether meals sold in restaurants operated in connection with mills and other industrial plants are subject to the 3%

retail sales tax. Your inquiry, as I understand it, has reference to those restaurants which are operated on a non-profit basis for the benefit of employees only. You state that in some instances these restaurants are operated by the mill or industrial plant itself, while in other instances the mill or industrial plant merely furnishes the space and authorizes other persons to actually operate the restaurant.

The 3% sales tax is imposed upon the sale of meals in cafes, restaurants, cafeterias, and other similar establishments. There is no exemption in the statute in favor of restaurants operated in connection with mills and other industrial plants, and the fact that such restaurants are operated on a non-profit basis and for the benefit of employees only does not, in my opinion, create any exemption in their favor. Charges of some nature are made for meals served therein, and in engaging in this type of service the mill, industrial plant or persons authorized to operate the same are selling taxable merchandise, and are making such sales in competition with other establishments which must collect and remit the tax.

It is, therefore, my opinion that meals sold in such restaurants are subject to the 3% sales tax regardless of the fact that such restaurants are established merely for the convenience of the employees and regardless of the fact that no profit is intended or received.

INCOME TAX; DEDUCTIONS; DEPRECIATION BASIS WHEN
CORPORATION ACQUIRES PROPERTY FROM SUBSIDIARY
ON DISSOLUTION OF LATTER

19 February, 1946.

The Vick Chemical Company of Delaware, successor to the dissolved North Carolina corporation, Vick Chemical Company, has requested refunds of tax as a result of its election to terminate the sixty-month amortization period and recompute net income for back years by spreading the cost of emergency facilities over the shorter period under the provisions of Section 124 of the Federal Internal Revenue Code. While this election is permitted under the Federal law, you have issued a memorandum to the effect that North Carolina accepted the sixty-month period originally as being reasonable; that you still considered it reasonable; and that taxpayers would continue to report depreciation to this State on that basis, irrespective of any election they may make otherwise with the Federal government.

Therefore, unless the taxpayer in this case can show, by adequate evidence, special circumstances which render the sixty-month period so unreasonable as to cause hardship, I am of the opinion that the refunds requested must be denied. Even if some adjusted basis or period were allowed by you and resulted in the necessity of recomputing net income for back years, no refund could be made on account of any changed net income for any taxable year beyond the three-year statute of limitations.

But the principal inquiry you have addressed to me arises out of the fact that the taxpayer, on April 30, 1945, succeeded to all the assets of its wholly owned North Carolina subsidiary of the same name, which on that same day ceased to do business and was dissolved. You ask what basis shall be used by the taxpayer for computing its depreciation deduction on assets acquired in this manner from its wholly owned subsidiary.

Section 322 (8) of the Revenue Act provides, among other things, that

"... The cost of property acquired since January first, one thousand nine hundred and twenty-one, plus additions and improvements, shall be the basis for determining the amount of depreciation. . ."

Section 319 of the Revenue Act states the method for determination of gain or loss from the sale or disposition of property and reads in part as follows:

". . . *Provided*, no gain or loss shall be recognized upon the receipt of a corporation of property distributed in complete liquidation of another corporation, if the corporation receiving such property was on the date of the adoption of the plan of liquidation and has continued to be at all times until the receipt of the property the owner of stock (in such other corporation), possessing at least eighty per centum (80%) of the total combined voting power of all classes of stock entitled to vote, and the owner of at least eighty per centum (80%) of the total number of shares of all other classes of stock (except non-voting stock which is limited and preferred as to dividends."

The Federal Internal Revenue Code expressly provides that the basis to be used for depreciation is the same basis as is used, under the same circumstances, for gain or loss (Section 114). Thus, under the Federal law the gain-or-loss provision relating to liquidation of a corporation (similar to the one quoted above) is expressly made a part of the depreciaton rules by reference.

Although our Revenue Act contains no express provision relating the depreciation section to the gain-or-loss section, I am of the opinion that, construed in the light of each other, their connection with each other is implied. There is no good reason to have one basis for depreciation and another basis for loss or gain under exactly the same circumstances. The special circumstances which would motivate a legislative exception to the "cost" rule in a gain-or-loss case, would likewise, and with the same force, motivate an identical exception in a depreciation case. Whether the taxpayer is computing his gain on the sale of property, or is computing a percentage depreciation, he must have a "basis" or starting point. In most cases that basis will be his cost of acquisition. But in some cases this cost either cannot be ascertained, or is arbitrary, or is not reasonable; and in these cases, such as one where a corporation liquidates and takes over the assets of its subsidiary, it may be feasible and advisable to make an exception to the "cost" rule and name some other basis. Such an exception was made by the 1937 Legislature, which amended Section 319. The effect of this exception, of course, is to give the transferee corporation the "basis" of its transferer for gain-or-loss purposes. I can perceive no reason why the same rule would not be equally applicable for purposes of depreciation. The reason and necessity for the rule are the same in both cases.

Therefore, while our Revenue Act lacks the express language of the Federal Code in this respect, in my opinion there is a clear implication to the effect that under a given set of circumstances the same basis should be used in depreciation cases and in gain-or-loss cases. This intent is implicit in the closely parallel provisions of Sections 319 and 322(8).

Therefore, when the proviso in Section 319 is read as a part of Section 322(S), or rather in its proper relationship with Section 322(8), I am of the opinion that where, as here, a Delaware corporation liquidates and dissolves its wholly-owned North Carolina subsidiary and acquires the latter's assets in a general plan of reorganization, uninterruptedly carrying on the business of its former subsidiary without any apparent change, the Delaware parent corporation should use the basis of its former subsidiary for depreciation purposes as well as for purposes of loss or gain.

... INCOME TAXES; PAYMENTS BY CORPORATION TO WIDOW OF A DECEASED EMPLOYEE

11 March, 1946.

You inquire whether a pension, paid in the form of monthly payments, by Swift & Company to the widow of one of its deceased employees constitutes income to such widow upon which income tax must be computed under the provisions of the North Carolina Income Tax Law for the years 1942, 1943, and 1944.

The definition of gross income from which taxable net income is derived is very broad and includes all income which is not specifically exempted. Section 317, subsection 2, of the Revenue Act provides, however, that the words "gross income" shall not include "the value of property acquired by gift, . . ."

Under the Swift & Company pension plan, monthly payments to widows of certain deceased employees are made on a purely voluntary basis. The corporation reserves the right to change, suspend or discontinue the pension plan at any time. Neither the employees nor their beneficiaries make any contributions whatsoever to the pension fund. Pensions to widows such as the one under consideration can in no sense be deemed to be compensation for services rendered the corporation by such widows. Nor would there be any basis under our law prior to January 1, 1944, upon which Swift & Company, the contributing corporation, might deduct these pension payments from its income required to be reported to this State. In view of these facts, it is my opinion that such pension must be regarded as a gift or gratuity for the years 1942 and 1943, and, therefore, not subject to income tax.

A different situation may exist for the year 1944 and years subsequent. In 1945 the Legislature inserted in the income tax statute certain provisions applicable to pension, profit-sharing, stock bonus, and annuity trusts. These provisions, effective from and after January 1, 1944, clothe certain trusts with an income tax exempt status, and authorize employers making contributions thereto to deduct reasonable amounts of such contributions from gross income. (See Sections 314(10) and 322(13)). Section 318, subsection 5, now expressly states, however, that in the case of trusts which qualify for exemption, employees *or their beneficiaries* shall include in their gross incomes amounts received or made available to them from such trusts within the income year. Thus, if a widow of a deceased employee receives a pension from a trust which qualifies for exemption under Section 314(10) of the Revenue Act, such pension is, since January 1, 1944, no longer treated as a gift to her, but as income upon which tax must be computed.

I have no information as to whether or not the Swift & Company pension plan from which payments are made to the widow under consideration qualifies for exemption under Section 314(10). If such plan is within the exempt class, it is my opinion that payments to such deceased employee's widow during the year 1944 must be reported by her as gross income. If the pension plan is not one which falls within the exempt category, I think that the pension paid the widow must be considered a gift or gratuity to the same extent that it was in the years 1942 and 1943; and, therefore, not a part of gross income for 1944.

INTANGIBLES TAX; BANK DEPOSITS REPRESENTING BENEFITS PAID BY U. S. TO VETERANS, THEIR BENEFICIARIES AND DEPENDENTS

21 March, 1946.

You inquire whether funds on deposit in banks, which represent benefits of various kinds paid to veterans, their dependents, or beneficiaries by the U. S. Government, are subject to the intangible tax imposed in Section 701 of the Revenue Act.

By express provision of Section 454(a) of Title 38, U.S.C.A., payments of benefits made to, or on account of, a beneficiary under any law relating to veterans are exempt from taxation. This statute specifically provides that such benefits are exempt from taxation both before and after receipt of same by the person entitled thereto. In addition to this exemption of general application, the Federal Government has provided for the exemption from taxation of certain specific benefits noted below:

(1)   Section 450(4) of Title 38, U.S.C.A., provides that any benefit payable or paid by the Veterans' Administration shall be included within the exemption set forth in Section 454(a), noted above.
(2)   Section 393 of Title 38, U.S.C.A., provides that any pension paid to a veteran by reason of the fact that his name is placed on the "Army and Navy Medal of Honor Roll" shall be exempt from taxation.
(3)   Section 691(e) of Title 38, U.S.C.A., provides that all mustering-out payments due or to become due to any veteran shall be exempt from taxation.
(4)   Section 816 of Title 38, U.S.C.A., exempts from taxation all payments made to veterans or their beneficiaries under the National Service Life Insurance Act to the same extent that benefits are exempt in Section 454(a).

The Supreme Court of the United States in *Lawrence v. Shaw*, 300 U. S. 245, has held that the immunity from taxation of payments of benefits by the Federal Government to veterans attaches to bank deposits of such veterans which do not represent or flow from his investments, but result from the deposit of warrants or checks received from the government when such deposits are made in the ordinary manner so that the proceeds of the collection are subject to draft upon demand for the veteran's use. In other words, the exemption from taxation extends to such benefits only until they are expended or invested.

The exemptions heretofore noted are contained in laws enacted by the

Congress of the United States. There are in addition to these certain state statutes which grant exemptions in favor of veterans' benefits.

Section 105-344 of the General Statutes exempts from any and all taxes pensions or compensation received by veterans from the government for and on account of wounds or physical disabilities contracted or sustained during the First and Second World Wars.

Section 701 of the Revenue Act, which imposes a tax upon bank deposits, contains this provision: "Deposits representing the actual payment of benefits to World War veterans by the Federal Government, when not reinvested, shall not be subject to the tax levied in this section."

It should be noted that the exemption statutes herein referred to are not applicable to retirement pay received by personnel of the regular Army, Navy and Marine Corps. This office has previously ruled that such retirement pay is subject to state income taxes, and it is my opinion that it is also subject to the intangible tax. Such retirement pay is not a "benefit" or a "pension" within the meaning of the exemption statutes, but, rather, it is considered as compensation for services previously rendered. This is in agreement with the view taken by the Bureau of Internal Revenue with reference to Federal income taxes.

FRANCHISE TAX; INITIAL TAX; COMMISSIONER NOT RESTRICTED   •
TO ORIGINAL AMOUNT OF CAPITAL STOCK

2 April, 1946.

You have requested my opinion on the following matter.

The Port Publishing Company of Wilmington, N. C., hereinafter called the taxpayer, was organized under the laws of the State of North Carolina, and received a charter on September 9, 1944. At that time it was determined that the amount of $20,000 would be issued in capital stock in payment for assets to be transferred to the new corporation. However, on October 1, 1944, an entry was made on the books, debiting stock subscriptions and/or cash with $30,000 and crediting capital stock account so as to increase the capital stock to $50,000. On November 8, 1944, taxpayer filed its initial franchise report. This was within sixty days after date of incorporation in compliance with Section 211 of the Revenue Act, although the capital stock prior to this time had been increased to $50,000. As stated above, this initial report showed a capital stock of $20,000 and payment of franchise tax was tendered on the basis of that amount. The fact that the capital stock had been increased from $20,000 to $50,000 as of October 1, 1944, did not appear to your office until the taxpayer filed its 1945 franchise report indicating a fiscal year beginning October 1. When you discovered this increase you made an additional assessment of initial franchise tax. The taxpayer contends that you had no authority to increase the initial tax, and takes the position that the initial tax in every case is determined on the date of incorporation.

I cannot agree with the taxpayer's contention in this matter. Even in this case the taxpayer implies that the original $20,000 was not issued on the date of incorporation. He says merely that it was "definitely determined that the amount of $20,000 would be issued in capital stock." I see nothing in Section 211 which restricts the computation of the tax either to the amount of stock actually issued and outstanding on the date of incorporation or to any other amount which the incorporators may contemplate on that date. In this case, the very fact that the capital stock was increased is proof that the incorporators' estimate of the amount of stock to be issued was proved to be wrong by the subsequent increase of the stock to $50,000. Under the taxpayer's interpretation of Section 211 a new corporation could avoid payment of tax by the simple device of operating for a few days on a nominal capital. I do not believe that Section 211 was intended to allow such a result. It gives the Commissioner of Revenue authority "to obtain such information concerning the basis for the levy of the tax from such other information he can obtain" and to that end to "require of such corporation to furnish him such a report as may clearly reflect and disclose the amount of its issued and outstanding capital stock, surplus and undivided profits as set out in Section 210 and information as to such other factors as may be necessary to determine the basis of the tax." It is difficult to see how these provisions could have given the Commissioner any broader authority to compute a tax in an appropriate amount.

Therefore, I am of the opinion that under facts in this case the Commissioner is authorized to compute the initial franchise tax on the basis of the increased capital stock of $50,000. As a practical matter, this result seems to be equitable, for the increase was made after the corporation had operated less than one month; and the taxable period after the increase for the purposes of this initial tax seems to have been for a full year.

INTANGIBLES TAXES; BANK DEPOSITS IN OUT-OF-STATE BANKS DEEMED TO
BE "OWNED IN THIS STATE" AND NOT EXEMPT UNDER SECTION 872

2 April, 1946.

You have requested my opinion on this matter.

The Piedmont Fire Insurance Company, 218 S. Tryon Street, Charlotte, North Carolina, hereinafter called the taxpayer, is a North Carolina corporation. It has heretofore filed its annual intangible tax returns, the last one as of December 31, 1944. At that time it had approximately $320,000 on deposit in banks outside the state of North Carolina, and it paid to the State of North Carolina the intangible tax thereon.

Section 872 of the Revenue Act, as amended through 1945, levies a tax on insurance companies measured by gross premiums, and contains the following provision:

"The taxes levied herein, measured by premiums, shall be in lieu of all other taxes upon insurance companies except: fees and licenses under this Article, or as specified in Chapter 58 of the General Statutes of North Carolina, as amended; taxes imposed by Chapter 118 of the General Statutes of North Carolina;. and ad valorem taxes upon real property and personal property owned in this State."

The taxpayer contends that the Section quoted above has the effect of exempting out-of-state bank deposits from the intangible tax because they are not "owned in this state."

I am unable to agree with the contention advanced by the taxpayer. Intangible property, unlike tangible property, has no physical location. Intangible property consists of nothing more or less than a relationship between persons. Therefore, in the case of bank deposits there is a special form of debtor-creditor relationship. It is true that the so-called "bank account" is in a bank outside the state; however, said "bank account" is not itself the intangible property, but merely the evidence of the intangible property, i.e., the evidence of the relationship between two persons.

Because of the fact that intangible property, because of its very nature, can have no physical location, the courts in the absence of some special circumstances, which are not present in this case, have consistently placed the taxable situs of intangibles at the domicile of the owner. It is on this theory that the State of North Carolina has had the constitutional right to tax out-of-state bank deposits owned by North Carolina persons and corporations. If these items of intangible property were not deemed to be within the territorial limits of the state of North Carolina, the State of North Carolina would be prohibited by the Fourteenth Amendment of the Federal Constitution from taxing the same; for a state can levy a tax only on that property which is situated within its boundary. It is my opinion that Section 872 of the Revenue Act was intended to leave undisturbed all North Carolina ad valorem taxes, and that the reference to "real property and personal property owned in this state" is simply descriptive of the state's constitutional limitations. In other words, North Carolina can constitutionally tax only that property which is owned in this state. Therefore it is my opinion that the use of the words "owned in this state" is mere surplusage.

For the reasons stated above it is my opinion that bank accounts owned by a domestic corporation in an out-of-state bank are intangible property "owned in this State" and are subject to the intangible tax which is an ad valorem tax) notwithstanding Section 872 of the Revenue Act.

BEVERAGE CONTROL ACT; WHOLESALER NOT AUTHORIZED TO FURNISH
FREE BEER TO RETAILER AS COMPENSATION FOR PLACING
SIGNS WITHIN LICENSED PREMISES

8 April, 1946.

You request that I advise you upon the following matter.

A wholesale dealer in beer desires to place window signs within a retail dealer's place of business. As compensation for the placing of these signs within the licensed premises, it is the desire of such wholesaler to furnish the retailer with a free case of beer. You inquire whether the furnishing of this type of compensation is authorized, in view of the provisions of Section 506 (a) of the Revenue Act or Beer Regulation No. 5 issued pursuant thereto.

Section 506 (a) provides that it shall be unlawful for any person, firm or corporation engaged in business as a wholesaler of malt beverages to "induce through any of the following means any retailer, engaged in the sale of wine or malt beverages, to purchase any products from such person, firm or corporation . . (2) by furnishing, giving free goods or deals, renting, lending, or selling to the retailer any equipment, fixtures, signs, supplies, money, services, or other things of value, subject to such exceptions as the Commissioner of Revenue shall by regulation prescribe. . . ." Beer

Regulation No. 5 makes certain exceptions to this statute. Paragraph 2 (2) provides that it shall be lawful to furnish to retailers containers of malt beverages sold and delivered. You raise the question whether the furnishing of a free case of beer would come within the meaning of this exception contained in Section 2 (2).

It is my opinion that the furnishing of a free case of beer would clearly come within the prohibitions expressed in Section 506 (a). I have studied the provisions of Regulation No. 5, and I find no authority contained therein which would authorize the furnishing of this type of free goods. I do not think it is the purpose or intent of paragraph 2 (2) of the regulation to authorize wholesalers to distribute malt beverages free of charge in any quantity to retail dealers. This paragraph has reference only to the containers in which beer is handled.

I, therefore, conclude that a wholesaler dealing in beer may not lawfully furnish a retailer with a free case of beer as compensation for the privilege of placing signs within the licensed premises of the retail dealer.

INHERITANCE TAXATION; SECTION 2; EXEMPTION OF PROPERTY PASSING TO NON-PROFIT RELIGIOUS OR CHARITABLE CORPORATIONS LOCATED IN ANOTHER STATE WHICH HAS RECIPROCAL EXEMPTION PROVISIONS

11 April, 1946

Rose C. Harper, in her last will and testament, bequeathed the sum of $5,000 to a church in New Jersey and the sum of $2,000 to a hospital in the same state. You request my opinion as to whether or not such bequests are exempted under our law.

Section 2 of the Revenue Act (G. S. 105-3) exempts:

"(c)   Property passing to religious, educational or charitable corporations, foundations or trusts, not conducted for profit, incorporated or created or administered under the laws of any other state: If such other state levies no inheritance or estate taxes on property similarly passing from residents of such state to religious, educational or charitable corporations, foundations or trusts, incorporated or created under the laws of this state. . ."

Chapter R. S. 54:34-2(b) of the laws of New Jersey exempts from inheritance or estate taxation, bequests of $5,000 or less to similar charities wheresoever incorporated or located. The New Jersey law has always been construed by the Department of Taxation and Finance of that state to permit an exemption of $5,000 to each beneficiary, and not merely an aggregate charitable exemption of $5,000 in the case of each decedent's estate. Charitable bequests in excess of $5,000 are taxed under the New Jersey law at the rate of 5 per cent of the excess.

It is my opinion that a proper construction of our law requires an exemption of any bequest of $5,000 or less to a New Jersey charity. It will be observed that our law exempts the bequest if the state where the charities are located exempts "property similarly passing" from residents of that state to North Carolina charities. If these two charitable bequests had been made by a New Jersey resident to similar charities in North Carolina, they would have been exempted from inheritance taxation under the laws of the

State of New Jersey. In my opinion our law in this respect is intended to be fully reciprocal; and, therefore, I conclude that the charitable bequests in question are exempted from inheritance taxation in this state.

PRIVILEGE TAXES; SECTION 115; LICENSE TAX COMPUTED ON PRECEDING YEAR'S PURCHASES, NOT DIMINISHED BY FEWER PURCHASES IN LICENSE YEAR

12 April, 1946

You have requested my opinion as to the following matter because of the fact that Mr. T. O. Pass, the taxpayer involved, has challenged your interpretation of Section 115 of the Revenue Act, which levies a tax for the privilege of engaging in the business of purchasing horses and mules for resale. This section provides for an annual tax for each location where such business is carried on. The amount of the tax varies according to the number of carloads purchased: $25.00 in case of one carload or less; $50.00 in case of more than one but not more than two; and $100.00 in case of more than two. The section then provides in part as follows:

> "For the purpose of calculating the amount of tax due under the above schedule ... purchases for the preceding license tax year shall be used as a medium for arriving at the amount of tax due for the ensuing year: *Provided, however,* that if during the current license year horses and/or mules are purchased for the purpose of resale in such quantities that would establish liability for a greater tax than that previously paid, it shall be immediately remitted to the Commissioner of Revenue with the license which has already been issued in order that it may be cancelled and a corrected license issued."

The taxpayer, in the year preceding the license year in question, purchased for resale more than two carloads of horses and/or mules; but in the license year in question he purchased less than two carloads. For some reason not pertinent here the taxpayer, instead of paying the tax at the beginning of the license year, waited until the expiration of the license year. At that time he determined that he had purchased, during the license year, not more than two carloads; and he accordingly computed his tax on that basis and remitted $50.00 to the Department. The Department then made an additional assessment of $50.00 on the basis of the preceding year's purchases, which were more than two carloads.

The taxpayer contends that this was error and that the Department can tax him only that amount set out in the schedule opposite purchases of not more than two carloads, that is, $50.00. He bases his argument upon an interpretation of the statute to the effect that the word "medium," as used therein, means "middle"; that the initial calculation of the tax is made on the basis of the preceding year's purchases only as a "middle" or "in-between" amount, and the *exact* amount of the tax is not determined until the business has been done, at the end of the license year, at which time the tax may be found to go on either side of this "middle" point; that is, it may be either more or less; and an adjustment is then made, the taxpayer paying more tax or receiving a refund as the case may be.

At the outset I wish to concede that the taxpayer's argument has some force and a great deal of justice, and it is with much regret that I have been compelled, after careful consideration and prolonged discussion, to express an opinion unfavorable to him. However, we must accept the law as the legislature has given it to us and as we understand it; and in my opinion the statute is not susceptible of the interpretation which the taxpayer has placed upon it.

The taxpayer apparently has made the natural mistake of regarding this tax as a "property tax," i.e., as a tax on so many carloads of horses and/or mules; and he is, therefore, unable to understand why the Department, for this license year, is attempting to levy against him a tax on more carloads than he actually purchased.

But the tax here imposed is not a property tax: it is a *privilege* tax, i.e., a tax which is imposed for the privilege of engaging in business. Like all privilege taxes, this one must be measured by something; and like many privilege taxes, this one is measured by the amount of business which was done during the preceding year. Thus, I think the word "medium" here means "method." In other words, the preceding year's purchases are used as a method or measure for determining the amount of the tax for the ensuing year. In the case of franchise and privilege taxes it is not unusual to measure the tax by the preceding year's business.

So, in my opinion, the tax at the very beginning of the license year is not merely estimated, but fixed, on the basis of the preceding year's business subject to be changed only upon the happening of one thing—an increase in business over that of the preceding year—and then only in the form of an increase in the tax. The fact that the tax cannot be decreased by the performance of less business is implied in the proviso, which specifically calls for additional tax under certain conditions, but omits any mention of a refund or decrease of tax. If the statute was intended to permit a decrease of tax, I believe it would have so provided in express language, just as it does with respect to an increase of tax.

Thus, in my opinion, the tax is not a property tax on so many carloads of horses and/or mules purchased during the license year, but a privilege tax on the privilege of doing business, measured by the *preceding year's* volume of business, but subject to be increased if the business exceeds that of the preceding year.

The most forceful feature of the taxpayer's argument, from a moral standpoint, is that the State will take advantage of a rise in business, but will not give the taxpayer the benefit of a fall. He says, in effect, that, "it's a poor rule that won't work both ways." I cannot fail to see the justice of such criticism. However, it is a rule which (if my interpretation is correct) the legislature in its wisdom has seen fit to enact into law, and administrative power is not effective to change it. I am not able to agree with the taxpayer that the rule is unconstitutional.

Therefore, I advise that the statute required you to assess the tax on the basis of the preceding year's purchases, which were greater than those in the taxable year.

Inasmuch as the taxpayer discussed this matter with me, I am sending him a copy of this letter.

INHERITANCE TAXATION; CONTINGENT REMAINDER CONSTITUTES DEVISABLE INTEREST IN PROPERTY AND IS TAXABLE

19 April, 1946

You have handed to me for examination certain documents and correspondence with the request that I advise you whether or not they indicate a taxable transfer under the provisions of the inheritance tax article of the Revenue Act. I have examined these papers and deduced therefrom certain facts, deemed by me to be essential, which are set out below.

Rowena L. Cocke, a resident of Buncombe County, died some years ago, leaving a last will and testament wherein she bequeathed to her son, Charles Hartwell Cocke, as trustee, certain personal property for the benefit of her daughter, Rowena Cocke, Jr., for life, and then to her issue, if any; and in default of issue, to be applied to the payment of specified legacies, the excess or remainder to be paid to her son, Charles, individually, "or, if dead, then to such person or persons as he shall by will designate." Subsequently, and during the lifetime of his sister, Rowena, Charles H. Cocke died, leaving a last will and testament by which he bequeathed, after payment of debts, "all the rest and residue of my property of every kind to my Beloved Wife, Amy Plank Cocke, absolutely"; and he appointed his wife as successor trustee for his sister under his mother's will.

Other provisions of said will contingent upon the failure of his wife to survive him are not mentioned here because she did survive him, rendering such provisions (including specific instructions as to distribution of his sister's estate) ineffectual.

Charles H. Cocke was survived by both his wife and his sister.

Upon these facts, I am of the opinion that under the will of his mother Charles H. Cocke received a contingent remainder—contingent upon his sister's dying without issue. His sister survived him. Therefore, he died before the happening of the contingency.

But the fact that his death before the happening of the contingency prevented the interest or estate from ever vesting in him does not mean that he did not have something of value in the contingent remainder at the time of his death. A contingent remainder is a valuable interest in property which can be transmitted to another person. Thus, it is well established that a contingent remainder is assignable, or may be conveyed where the contingent remainderman is specified and known. *Beacom v. Amos*, 161 N.C. 357; *Bourne v. Farrar*, 180 N. C. 135; *Hobgood v. Hobgood*, 169 N. C. 485; *Thames v. Goode*, 217 N. C. 639; *Heath v. Corey*, 215 N. C. 721. Moreover, if the contingent remainderman dies before the happening of the contingency (where his death does not render the contingency impossible) his contingent remainder descends under the intestate laws to his heirs and next of kin, and is not defeated by his death. 33 *Am. Jur., Life Estates, Remainders and Reversions*, Sec. 152. Where a contingent remainder would, in case of the contingent remainderman's intestacy descend or devolve upon his heirs or executor or administrator, statute in this State expressly provides that the contingent remainderman may dispose of his contingent interest by will. G. S. 31-40.

I am of the opinion that Charles H. Cocke received, under the will of his mother, a contingent remainder which was transmissable either by the intestate laws or by the terms of his will, and that the provision in his mother's will that, in the event of his death before the contingency, the interest should go "to such person or persons as he shall by will designate," was redundant, for he had the power to bequeath his interest independently of any power to designate the next taker expressed in his mother's will. In this view of the matter it is unnecessary to decide whether or not Charles H. Cocke used language in his will adequate to designate the person who should succeed to his contingent interest. Under the provisions of G. S. 31-40, such interest is considered to be a part of his estate, and passed to his wife under the terms of the will, which gave to her the entire residuary estate. A contingent remainder is an "interest" or "estate" in property which will pass under this residuary clause. *Bourne v. Farrar, 180 N. C. 135.*

Therefore, it seems clear that these facts indicate a transfer of a contingent interest in property by the will of Charles H. Cocke. The only remaining question is whether or not such a transfer is taxable under the inheritance article. It seems to me that the answer to this question is clearly indicated by the following language of Section 1 (G. S. 105-2) :

"A tax shall be and is hereby imposed upon the transfer of any property, real or personal, *or of any interest therein* or income therefrom, *in trust or otherwise,* to persons or corporations, in the following cases: (italics ours)

"*First.* When the transfer is by will or by the intestate laws of this State from any person dying, seized or possessed of the property while a resident of the State."

Therefore, I am of the opinion that the contingent remainder in question was transferred by the will of Charles H. Cocke, and that such transfer is taxable.

It should be observed that the tax is measurable, not by the value of the property itself, but by the value of the contingent interest therein, i.e., by the value of the contingent remainder, which is the thing transferred. Your attention is directed to Section 17 of the Revenue Act. This section need not be, and, by its nature, cannot be applied with exactness. It seems to me that, in valuing the contingent remainder in this case, you should consider any factors deemed by you to be pertinent. The two principal factors, of course, are (1) the strength of the possibility that the estate will actually vest in the transferee, here Mrs. Cocke, and (2) what the value of the estate will probably be if it does vest in the transferee. I realize that this is not a wholly satisfactory way to measure a tax, but it is the best that can be devised under the circumstances.

The attorneys for the estate of Charles H. Cocke contend, among other things, that non-taxability is indicated by the fact that the testator's wife, the present contingent remainderman, has a smaller life expectancy than his sister, at whose death the estate will vest. This argument goes to the value of the contingent interest, under the first factor mentioned above, rather than to the question whether or not the interest is taxable at all. Despite the life expectancy, there is *some* possibility that the wife will survive the sister; thus, the contingent remainder transferred to the wife certainly has some value.

The attorneys for the estate also express concern over the possibility that the entire estate could be exhausted by taxes before it finally came to rest. If this possibility exists, it is purely theoretical. Moreover, the same would be true of any property, or interest therein, which is transferred by will successively from one person to another. It has been seen already that a contingent interest is an interest of some value. It should be remarked also that the thing taxed is the contingent interest, according to its value, not the entire corpus of the property as such.

I believe that the view taken of this matter renders unnecessary any further answer to the distinction which has been drawn between estate taxes and inheritance taxes. Conceding, for purposes of argument, the correctness of the distinction drawn by the estate's attorneys, there is a "receiving" of a present interest in property in this case. The contingent remainder was a valuable and devisable interest which passed to the testator's wife. Therefore, there was an "actual taking" of an interest in property which would render the same subject to an inheritance tax.

I trust that this will be an adequate answer to your question.

INHERITANCE TAXATION; NON-RESIDENT DECEDENT'S INTEREST IN LIMITED PARTNERSHIP IN THIS STATE EXEMPT FROM N. C. INHERITANCE TAX

25 April, 1946

You have requested my opinion based on the following facts.

At her death, Annie S. McCullum, a resident of Danville, Virginia, was a limited partner in the limited partnership known as Mecklenburg Furniture Shops. This partnership was organized and exists under and by virtue of the North Carolina Uniform Limited Partnership Act, G. S. 59-1 et seq., and does business in this state near Charlotte.

Your specific question is whether or not the decedent's interest in the limited partnership, as a limited partner, is subject to the North Carolina inheritance tax upon her death intestate while she was domiciled in Virginia. The taxpayer suggests that this interest is taxable only by Virginia, the domiciliary state.

Regardless of the nature of the property owned by the partnership, whether the same be real estate or personal property, a limited partner's interest in a limited partnership is expressly declared by statute to be personal property. G. S. 59-18. This means, of course, that such interest is intangible personal property. Independently of statute the courts are generally agreed on the proposition that a partner's interest or share in a partnership is intangible personal property, at least when it passes to his personal representative by reason of his death. The representative does not succeed to any right to specific partnership property, for the decedent's interest was simply a chose in action, a right to receive in cash the sum shown to be due him upon an accounting. This right is includible in the decedent's gross estate. McClennen v. Commissioner of Internal Revenue, 131 F. (2d) 165 (1942). See also Blodgett v. Silberman, 277 U. S. 1, 72 L. ed. 749 (1927); 28 Am. Jur., Inheritance, Estate & Gift Taxes, Sec. 109.

A few years ago to have conceded the partner's interest to be intangible personal property would have been equivalent to a relinquishment of all

taxing jurisdiction in this case to the State of Virginia, for the United
States Supreme Court in a line of cases beginning with *Farmer's Loan &
Trust Co. v. Minn.*, 280 U. S. 204, 74 L. ed. 371, 50 S. Ct. 98 (1930), read into
the Fourteenth Amendment a "rule of immunity from taxation by more
than one state"; and, in the case of intangibles, that state was the domiciliary state under the maxim *mobilia sequuntur personam.*

However, the theory that only one state can lay a tax upon the same
property was blasted in *Curry v. McCanless*, 307 U. S. 357, 83 L. ed. 1339
(1939) and the death blow was subsequently dealt in *State Tax Commission
v. Aldrich*, 316 U. S. 174, 86 L. ed. 1358 (1942), which upheld a Utah
inheritance tax upon a nonresident's shares of stock in a Utah Corporation
and expressly overruled *First Nat'l Bank v. Maine*, 284 U. S. 312, 76 L. ed.
313(1932), which had held that only the domiciliary state could tax.

It seems clear now that intangible property can be taxed, not only by
the state of the creditor's domicile, but also by the state of the obligor's
domicile. Intangible property is nothing more than a relationship between
persons. If that relationship receives protection or benefit from more than
one state, it is taxable by both. See *Anno.* 139 A.L.R. 1458.

The interest of a partner in a partnership owes its protection and benefit,
not only to the state of the partner's domicile, but also to the state under
whose laws the partnership was organized and now exists and does business.
Without the protection and authority granted by the latter state the
partner's interest would be valueless and unenforceable. For this protection
and authority the state may ask something in return without running afoul
of the Fourteenth Amendment. See 28 *Am. Jur.*, *Inheritance Tax*, Sec. 109
(pocket parts, 1945); *Anno.*, 144 A.L.R.. 1134; *Re. Bijur Estate*, 127 Misc.
206, 216 N.Y.S. 523 (1926).

Therefore, I conclude that this state may constitutionally impose an inheritance tax upon the transfer, at death, of the share or interest of a
limited partner in a limited partnership in this state, even though such
partner be domiciled in Virginia at the time of his death.

The only remaining question is whether or not North Carolina does impose
an inheritance tax under these circumstances. Section 1 of the Revenue
Act (G. S. 105-2) imposes a tax "upon the transfer of any property, real
or personal, or of any interest therein. . . . "

"*Second* . . .when the transfer is of real property or intangible
personal property within the state, or intangible personal property that
has acquired a situs in this state, and the decedent was a nonresident
of the state at the time of death."

The last paragraph of Section 1 reads as follows:

"*Provided*, however, that nothing in this Article shall be construed
as imposing a tax upon any transfer of intangibles not having a commercial or business situs in this State at the time of his death, and, if
held or transferred in trust, such intangibles shall not be deemed to
have a commercial or business situs in this State merely because the
trustee is a resident or, if a corporation, is doing business in this State,
unless the same be employed in or held or used in connection with some
business carried on in whole or in part in this State."

Inasmuch as an interest in a limited partnership in this State is intangible
personal property, it is my opinion that the provisons just quoted exempt

such interest, when owned by a non-resident, unless it has acquired a business situs within this State. I am not aware of any facts in this case which would give the Virginia resident's interest in the North Carolina partnership a business situs in this State. In my opinion the mere fact that the partnership does business in this State is not sufficient for that purpose. Of course, the intangible property of the partnership, such as its bank account, may have acquired a business situs in North Carolina, and its tangible property actually present in this State has a taxable situs here. But we are not dealing here with the taxability of partnership property, rather with the taxability of a share or interest in the partnership business; and I cannot perceive that this share or interest, as intangible personalty, has acquired a business situs from the mere fact that the business itself is carried on in this State. It has been held that the mere fact that a foreign corporation does business in a State does not give its shares of stock a taxable situs in that State. *Rhode Island Trust Co. v. Doughton*, 270 U. S. 69; *Rotan v. State*, 195 N. C. 295.

For the reasons stated herein, I am of the opinion that, although the recent decisions of the U. S. Supreme Court give North Carolina the constitutional right and jurisdiction to lay an inheritance tax upon the transfer-at-death of a non-resident partner's interest in a North Carolina limited partnership, our Revenue Act by express provision exempts from taxation in such case.

INCOME TAXATION; LABOR ORGANIZATIONS NOT TAXABLE

6 May, 1946.

You have requested me to advise you whether or not, in my opinion, United Tobacco Workers Local 22, a labor union or organization, is liable for payment of income tax. It appears that this is a local unit located in Winston-Salem, North Carolina, affiliated with Food, Tobacco, Agricultural and Allied Workers Union of America. It appears further that this is a local union of the CIO. Its representatives state that the purpose of said union is to engage in collective bargaining for the improvement of wages and working conditions. The income of the organization is derived from initiations, dues, assessments and fines. The funds are expended for maintenance of office and for the purpose of furthering the objectives of the union.

The definition of gross income in Section 317 of the Revenue Act (G. S. 105-141) is sufficiently broad to cover the moneys received by labor unions by way of initiations, dues, assessments and fines. Therefore, such income would be taxable without a specific exemption in the statute.

Section 314 of the Revenue Act (G. S. 105-138) exempts from income taxation, among other things, the following:

"5. Civic leagues or organizations not organized for profit but operated exclusively for the promotion of social welfare."

It is my opinion that this labor union under the facts stated above is an organization not organized for profit but operated exclusively for the promotion of social welfare, and that said labor union is, therefore, exempt from income taxation under our Revenue Act.

I am advertent to the fact that the Federal government and a majority of the states expressly exempt labor organizations by name. However, I do not believe that the failure of our law to contain an express exemption cf this kind necessarily excludes labor organizations from the more general exemptions contained in our Revenue Act. Looking at our Act as a whole, I believe that there is a purpose therein to exempt generally organizations organized and operated exclusively for non-profit purposes; and although labor organizations are not expressly named, others are named such as business leagues, chambers of commerce, merchants' associations, boards of trade, pleasure and recreational clubs, farmers' organizations and mutual associations. It appears to me that a liberal construction of the entire exemption section would embrace labor unions organized and operated under the facts stated above, where no part of the net earnings of which inures to the benefit of any private member.

The conclusion I have reached finds some support in the fact that labor unions have not been required to report their income or pay tax on the same since the inception of the income tax law in this state, a period of approximately twenty-six years. Under these circumstances it appears to me that if labor organizations of the kind described herein are to be liable for income tax, it should be incumbent upon the legislature to enact an express provision to that effect.

INHERITANCE TAXATION; TAXABILITY OF VESTED REMAINDER AFTER DEATH OF LIFE TENANT

8 May, 1946

You have requested my opinion based on the following facts.

Marian Mead died a resident of Buncombe County, N. C., September 8, 1929. An inheritance tax return was duly filed for her estate and a tax of $2,371.91 was paid. By her last will and testament Marian Mead left her property in trust for the benefit of her mother, Mrs. Harriet Mead, for life with remainder in three equal parts, one of which parts was to be held in trust for Mary Hanbury for life, and then for the benefit of the Asheville Foundation for Charitable Purposes. Wachovia Bank and Trust Company was appointed and is now the trustee under the will of Marian Mead. Mrs. Harriet Mead died November 18, 1934. Mary Hanbury died August 3, 1944.

Kate Adams Cooper died a resident of Illinois, July 30, 1917, leaving a last will and testament in which she bequeathed property in trust for Mary Hanbury (the same person named in the will of Marian Mead) for life with the provision that at the death of Mary Hanbury "if she should die without children and there should be anything remaining, the same shall revert to her cousins, Albert Miller Adams and Marian Mead, share and share alike." A court proceeding was instituted in Chicago for a construction of the Kate Adams Cooper will. Wachovia Bank and Trust Company, trustee under the Marian Mead will, was represented in said proceeding. The Superior Court of Cook County, Illinois, on January 24, 1945, entered an order in which the Court found that "under the terms of the will of Kate Adams Cooper the interest of Marian Mead in the trust estate created for the benefit of Mary Hanbury was a vested re-

mainder in and to an undivided one-half interest in said trust estate."
After further hearings a decree to the same effect was entered February
9, 1945, awarding the Mead interest in the Cooper estate to Wachovia
Bank and Trust Company, as trustee under the last will and testament
of Marian Mead. To this decree Albert Miller Adams filed notice of
appeal. However, prior to final determination by the Appellate Court a
compromise with Adams was effected whereby the Mead interest paid
him $4,000, whereupon the controversy was settled, resulting in the receipt
by Wachovia Bank and Trust Company, Trustee, of the amount of $12,-
074.55, less a fee of $1,822.14 to Chicago counsel, or a net amount of
$10,252.41. This amount was received by Wachovia Bank and Trust Com-
pany, as trustee under the will of Marian Mead, which means that said
trustee now holds the same for the equal benefit of the Asheville Foundation
and the two other remaindermen named in the Marian Mead will.

You wish to know whether or not the receipt of this money or property
from the Kate Adams Cooper estate by Wachovia Bank and Trust Company, as trustee under the will of Marian Mead, constitutes a taxable event
for inheritance tax purposes.

Under the facts set out above, it is my opinion that Marian Mead at her
death in 1929 had an interest in the estate of Kate Adams Cooper, who
had died in 1917. Inasmuch as this office has previously ruled that a contingent remainder is a taxable interest in property at the death of the
contingent remainderman prior to the happening of the contingency, the
question whether Marian Mead's interest in the Cooper estate was a vested
remainder, as found by the Cook County Superior Court, or a contingent remainder seems to be of no importance in the determination of the
taxability of Marian Mead's interest in the Cooper estate. Regardless of
whether such interest was vested or contingent, it is my opinion that the
same was taxable at the death of Marian Mead in 1929 under the provisions
of Section 1 of the Revenue Act, which imposes an inheritance tax upon
the transfer of any property, real or personal, "or of any interest therein
or income therefrom in trust or otherwise. ... "

"Second. When the tansfer is by will ... of any property, real
personal or mixed, tangible or intangible, over which the State of
North Carolina has a taxing jurisdiction ... and the decedent was a
resident of the state at the time of death. ... "

Therefore, I am of the opinion that the above facts present simply a
situation in which a resident decedent had an interest in property at the
time of her death which was subject to inheritance tax at that time but
was not taxed at that time because the same was not known to her estate
or to the taxing authorities, said interest being discovered some years
later when money was actually realized from said interest. In my opinion,
when Marian Mead's interest in the Cooper estate became known it was
taxable under our inheritance laws.

INCOME TAXATION; FORGIVENESS OR DISCHARGE OF DEBT NOT
INCOME TO DEBTOR IF GRATUITOUS

11 May, 1946

You have requested my opinion as to whether or not the forgiveness or cancellation of interest by creditor stockholders in favor of a debtor corporation constitutes taxable income to the corporation. You refer to opinions expressed by this office under dates of December 15, 1938, June 12, 1939, and July 25, 1939, all to the effect that a solvent taxpayer who discharges his debts by payment of a sum less than the amount of such debts thereby realizes a taxable gain. These opinions rely principally on U. S. v. KIRBY LUMBER COMPANY, 284 U. S. 1, 76 L. ed. 131 (taxable gain realized when corporation purchases own bonds at a discount), and HELVERING v. AMERICAN CHICLE CO., 291 U. S. 426, 78 L. ed. 891 (taxable gain realized when taxpayer assumed corporation's bonds as part of purchase price of assets, and then acquired bonds for lesser amount). A review of our prior opinions and the correctness of your position is rendered necessary by the fact that, since said opinions were rendered by this office, the situation has been affected by an important United States Supreme Court case, HELVERING v. AMERICAN DENTAL CO., (1943) 318 U. S. 322, 87 L. ed. 785, which held that, under the circumstances there presented, the cancellation of interest by a creditor of a debtor corporation, which had already taken such interest as a deduction when the same had accrued in previous years, was not taxable income to the corporation in the year of such cancellation, but was a gift and, therefore, excluded from gross income by the express provisions of the statute. As you know, our Revenue Act also excludes gifts from gross income. Section 317 (2) (c).

Whether or not the forgiveness, discharge or cancellation of indebtedness results in taxable income to the debtor depends on the particular circumstances. For that reason it is somewhat difficult to state workable rules which may be relied on with assurance. However, since the decision of the United States Supreme Court in HELVERING v. AMERICAN DENTAL CO., supra, certain general principles seem to have been made reasonably clear. One of these principles is that, if the forgiveness, discharge or cancellation is gratuitous, i.e., entirely without consideration, a gift, and not income, results; and this result is not affected by the fact that the debtor-donee may have deducted the item in previous years when it accrued.

The chief difficulty rests in the determination of whether the particular transaction is or is not a gift. In order for the transaction to be a gift, the cancellation must be entirely gratuitous, voluntary and without consideration. There must be a release of something for nothing. Thus, if a debtor renders service for a creditor, who in consideration thereof cancels the debt, the cancellation is income to the debtor, and not a gift. If a debtor purchases his obligations at less than face value, he realizes income. On the other hand, if a shareholder in a corporation which is indebted to him gratuitously forgives the debt, the transaction generally amounts to a gift or, rather, a contribution to the capital of the corporation.

If the forgiveness of debt really amounts to a gift, i.e., if the forgiveness is actually gratuitous, voluntary and without consideration, it is not significant that the motives for the forgiveness were those of business, or even selfish. Neither is it material in such case whether the debtor, in this case a corporation, is solvent or insolvent after the forgiveness, or whether any assets were thereby freed from the claims or creditors.

In the case of the instant taxpayer, Leward Cotton Mills, Inc., it appears that the stockholders forgave certain interests owed to them by the corporation, and that the Federal Agent has recognized the transaction as a gift, and, on that basis, has recommended an adjustment and refund. Of course, you have the privilege of inquiring into the circumstances in order to make your own independent decision as to whether or not the forgiveness of debt was really gratuitous; but I also think you would be justified in accepting the Federal Agent's findings on the question in the absence of any evidence that some consideration passed in the transaction. In the absence of a finding by a Federal Agent, or if there are any circumstances to indicate that the forgiveness was not gratuitous, I am of the opinion that you should make it incumbent upon the taxpayer to establish by competent evidence that no consideration passed from him to the creditor. As a general rule, creditors do not gratuitously forgive the obligations of their debtors; and where forgiveness of debt occurs, it should be scrutinized with more than ordinary care.

What has been said is not necessarily a repudiation of the prior rulings of this office. In the situations then under consideration it was found that taxable income resulted from the transaction. There is no evidence before me now to prove that that conclusion was erroneous upon the facts then presented. Without such evidence it must be presumed that the forgiveness or discharge of debt then under consideration was effected for a consideration of some kind.

It is true that the opinion expressed herein is consistent with Federal regulations upon the subject. However, the rule stated in this opinion springs from a United States Supreme Court interpretation of the Federal statute, rather than from the regulations; and the Federal statute is so like our own in respect of the question material here that the Supreme Court's decision can properly be regarded as authoritative under our statute.

INCOME TAXATION; NO GAIN WHERE STOCK SOLD BY ESTATE AT EXACT VALUE AT DEATH, EVEN THOUGH DECEDENT'S COST WAS LESS

22 May, 1946

You have requested my opinion as to whether or not a taxable gain was realized under the following circumstances.

W. M. Scales purchased or acquired stock in W. M. Scales Leaf Tobacco Company at a cost of $4,000. At his death the Inheritance Tax Division valued this stock at $6,542.79. The personal representative of the Scales estate subsequently sold the stock for exactly this amount. Both decedent and estate were on a "cash basis."

I assume that the value placed upon this stock by the Inheritance Tax

Division represents the true value thereof at decedent's death. In the absence of indications to the contrary, I think you would be justified in accepting it, for income tax purposes, as the true value at decedent's death.

In my opinion, there has been no taxable gain under the above circumstances. The increase in value from the time decedent acquired it up until the time of his death did not represent income to decedent, for he was on a "cash basis" and the stock was not sold. Upon decedent's death the stock became an asset of the estate, valued as of that time. Thus, there was no income to decedent, for he did not actually receive it; and there was no income to the representative of the estate, for he sold the asset at its value when it became an asset of the estate. When the representative of the estate received the stock, with its increased value, he received the increased value, not as income, but as corpus. *Nichols v. U. S.*, 6 AFTR, 6592 and 7101, 64 Ct. Cl. 241, cert. denied 277 U. S. 584; *Safe Deposit & Trust Co. of Baltimore v. U. S.*, 64 Ct. Cl. 697, 6 AFTR 7104.

SALES TAX; SALE OF BUILDING MATERIAL TO CONTRACTOR IS RETAIL SALE

24 June, 1946

You have referred to me a letter from C. S. Lowrimore and Company, Certified Public Accountants, under date of June 17, 1946. Mr. Lowrimore proposes that the following question be submitted to me for an opinion.

"If a manufacturer of mill work, such as door frames, window frames, screen doors, et cetera, sells to a building contractor in wholesale lots under contract, the entire requirements for the completion of the mill work in any building or buildings, and the contractor in turn has sold at retail, the completed structure to the owner. Is this sale by the manufacturer of the mill work subject to the 3% sales tax?"

In my opinion the sale of mill work to the contractor under such circumstances would be a retail sale to the contractor, who under these facts would be the consumer; and such sale, therefore, would be subject to the 3% retail sales tax. I do not consider the sale of the completed building or the completion of the building contract by the contractor as a resale at retail of building materials purchased by the contractor. In my opinion the contractor is simply a purchaser of building materials at retail for the purpose of fulfilling the terms of his contract.

INCOME TAX; GROSS INCOME; GAINS FROM INVOLUNTARY
CONVERSIONS ARE TAXABLE INCOME

25 June, 1946

I have your letter of June 21, 1946, requesting my opinion upon the following matter.

It appears that C. Walker Hodges Dredging Co., Inc., of New Bern, N. C., hereinafter called the taxpayer, lost one of its dredges and received insurance on the same in excess of the depreciated value of the same. This insurance money was set aside to be used for the purchase of a new dredge as soon as it shall become available. The taxpayer wishes to know whether the amount of insurance money received in excess of the depreciated value of the dredge should be reported as income.

The taxpayer's question apparently is prompted by Sec. 112 (f) of the Federal Internal Revenue Code, (P.H. Fed. Tax Service, Par. 10,339), which provides as follows:

> "*IRC., Sec. 112. - - - (f) Involuntary Conversions.*— If property (as a result of its destruction in whole or in part, theft or seizure, or an exercise of the power of requisition or condemnation, or the threat or imminence thereof) is compulsorily or involuntarily converted into property similar or related in service or use to the property so converted, or into money which is forthwith in good faith, under regulations prescribed by the Commissioner with the approval of the Secretary, expended in the acquisition of other property similar or related in service or use to the property so converted, or in the acquisition of control of a corporation owning such other property, or in the establishment of a replacement fund, no gain shall be recognized, but loss shall *be recognized*. If any part of the money is not so expended, the gain, if any shall be recognized *to the extent* of the money which is not so expended (*regardless of whether such money is received in one or more taxable years and regardless of whether or not the money which is not so expended constitutes gain*)."

In the absence of a provision like the one above, gains resulting from involuntary conversions of property would be fully recognized as taxable gains. By this provision Congress has given a measure of relief to persons who are compelled to take a profit without regard to their own wishes. But even this relief is conditional and restricted within narrow limits.

I am unable to find any provision in our Revenue Act similar to the Federal provision quoted above, or any other provision accomplishing a similar purpose. Section 320 in my opinion is not applicable, since it covers "exchanges" of property rather than involuntary conversions. Section 318, providing that the method of finding net income shall follow as nearly as practicable the Federal practice, is not controlling where the Federal practice is "contrary to the context and intent of this article." Moreover, I do not construe Sec. 318 as having the purpose of adopting all provisions of the Internal Revenue Code not contrary to our Revenue Act. It seems, rather, that its purpose is to synchronize the methods of accounting under both Acts. Thus, I do not construe Sec. 318 as being effective to adopt a Federal statute which would work a major change in our substantive law. If the Federal statute required specific legislation to authorize this particular treatment of involuntary conversions, it would seem to follow that our statute, which is not superior in form to the Federal statute before the change, would also require specific legislation to authorize such treatment.

Therefore, I am of the opinion that a gain realized from an involuntary conversion, such as the one described by the taxpayer, must be fully recognized as taxable gain in this State. This means that the taxpayer must include in gross income that part of the insurance receipts which exceeds the depreciated value of the dredge.

In passing, it can be observed that the Federal Goverment also has other provisions giving relief to taxpayers in involuntary conversions. Sec. 117(j) of the I.R.C. allows taxpayers under certain conditions to treat involuntary conversion of property used in trade or business as a sale or exchange of a capital asset, thus giving the benefit of the taxable percentage of income provision and the alternative tax provision of Sec. 117(b), (c) and (d); and Sec. 113 (a) provides relief in the form of a different method of computing cost basis upon the acquisition of the new property in involuntary conversions. Needless to say, these provisions likewise are inapplicable under our Revenue Act. We have no provisions taxing capital gains only partially; Section 319 of our Act fixes the basis in determining gain or loss; and Sec. 322 (8) fixes the basis in determining depreciation. I mention these other provisions only as additional examples of the discrepancy between our statute and the Federal statute. As far as I have been able to determine our Revenue Act gives no special treatment to involuntary conversions as such.

INCOME TAX; DEDUCTIONS; CARRY-OVER LOSSES; DEDUCTIBLE,
PROPORTION DETERMINED BY ALLOCATION RATIO OF YEAR
IN WHICH LOSS SUSTAINED

28 June, 1946

You have requested me to advise you as to my opinion concerning that part of Section 322 of the Revenue Act which allows a deduction of a net economic loss of a prior year or years, otherwise known as the "carry-over" loss deduction.

This deduction is allowed by Sub-section (d) of Section 322. A net economic loss sustained in either or both of the two preceding income years, arising from business transactions or from other allowable losses, may be "carried over" and taken as a deduction in the current income year, subject to certain limitations. One of the limitations is that the net economic loss must be computed without deductions for contributions, personal exemptions, prior year losses, taxes on property held for personal use and non-business interest. Another of the limitations is that net economic loss must be absorbed or reduced first by non-taxable income.

The particular limitation to which you direct my attention is contained in the following provision:

"... except that in the case of foreign corporations, and of domestic corporations or resident individuals eligible for the deduction of a part of net income under the provisions of Sub-section 10 of this Section by reason of having net income earned and taxed in another State, only such proportionate part of the net economic loss of a prior year or years shall be deductible from the income taxable in this State as would be determined by the ratio of net income allocable to this State as compared to all net income received both within and without the State."

You desire my opinion as to how this provision should be applied to a foreign corporation which, during the prior "loss year," would have allocated net income, if it had earned net income, according to an allocation fraction which is different from the allocation fraction computed for the current tax year. For example, a foreign corporation, by use of the statutory "formula," determines its 1944 allocation fraction to be 60% to North Carolina. During that year the corporation sustains a $100,000 "net economic loss." The corporation determines its 1945 fraction to be 70% to

North Carolina. During that year the corporation makes a net income of $200,000.

The example given above presents the possibility of treating a carry-over in several different ways:

(1) Allocate to North Carolina 70% of 1945 income of $200,000, or $140,000, and then deduct the *entire* net economic loss of 1944 in the sum of $100,000, leaving a net income of $40,000 allocable to North Carolina for 1945. This treatment is clearly erroneous, for the statute permits the corporation to carry over only a *proportion* of the 1944 loss, depending on the ratio of income allocable to North Carolina. Therefore, we may dismiss this method summarily.

(2) Carry over into 1945 the entire 1944 loss of $100,000 and deduct it from the entire 1945 net income of $200,000, leaving $100,000, and then allocate to North Carolina 70% (1945 allocation fraction) or $70,000. By this method the proportion of the 1944 loss available as a deduction is determined by the *current* tax year's allocation ratio.

(3) Allocate to North Carolina 70% of the 1945 income of $200,000 or $140,000, and then deduct from that amount 60% of the 1944 loss of $100,000 or $60,000, leaving $80,000 allocable to North Carolina. By this method the proportion of the 1944 loss available as a deduction is determined by the "loss year's" allocation fraction.

Therefore, your question resolves itself into whether the proportion of loss which may be carried over is to be determined by the allocation ratio of the "loss year" or by the allocation ratio of the year in which the deduction is claimed.

There is some support for the argument that the current year's ratio should be used, in that the statute speaks of "the ratio of net income allocable to this State as compared to all net income received both within and without the State," thereby implying the use of a ratio determined in a year in which there actually is or was a net income; which would eliminate the ratio for the "loss year" immediately, and compel the use of the ratio of the current year, in which a net income was earned.

However, I am of the opinion that such an interpretation ignores the subjunctive use of the verb in the expression, "as *would be* determined by the ratio of net income allocable," etc. The use of the subjunctive mood in this instance is, in my opinion, an indication that the statute has reference to a ratio determinable in a year in which no net income was actually allocated to North Carolina because no net income was earned; in other words, a ratio which "would be" determined by allocable net income *if any net income had been earned to be allocated*. It occurs to me that, if the statute had intended reference to a ratio actually determined by allocable net income, it would have employed more direct language to that effect and would have treated the matter in the indicative mood. For instance, the statute might have provided for a deduction of such proportionate part of the net economic loss of the prior year as *is* determined or determinable from the ratio of net income allocable to North Carolina—and the statute might have added, "for the year in which the deduction is claimed." However, it did not.

Therefore, it seems to me that the statute speaks of a ratio determined in a year in which no net income was earned, i.e., the "loss year," and that the ratio of loss to be carried over is that income ratio which would have been determined by the appropriate allocation fraction if any net income ad been made during that year.

This conclusion, in my opinion, is supported by a practical analysis of the matter. The purpose of the statutory formula is to allocate to North Carolina a part of the corporation's net income proportionate with the business done here. Thus, theoretically at least, the allocation fraction states the portion of the corporate business done in North Carolina. This is true irrespective of a net gain or loss. Thus, if the formula attributes 60% of the corporation's business to North Carolina, that means that in a loss year 60% of the loss is attributable to North Carolina business. In this sense that part of the loss is a North Carolina loss. In my opinion, the purpose of the statute is to permit the corporation to carry over against the current year's North Carolina net income a prior year's North Carolina loss. I do not believe that the statute intended to offset a North Carolina net income with a prior year's loss attributable to or suffered in some other State. North Carolina is not concerned with losses which result from business done in another State. In my opinion, the intended function of the statute is to give some measure of relief to taxpayers adversly affected by strict adherence to the principle of annual accounting, by permitting, under some conditions and subject to certain restrictions, some degree of "levelling off" of the good years and the bad; but that North Carolina is concerned with the "levelling off' of such years only insofar as they affect business done in this State. The taxpayer's "net income situation" to which the statute refers is the taxpayer's net economic situation with regard to North Carolina business. That is why the statute allows only a proportionate part of the prior year's loss to be deducted.

To permit a taxpayer to determine the deductible proportion of the prior year's loss by application of the current tax year's allocation ratio does not necessarily bring forward that part of the loss which was attributable to North Carolina business. For example, a foreign corporation with a 1944 allocation ratio of 5% to North Carolina, which carries over a 1944 loss on the basis of a 1945 ratio of 95% to North Carolina, would be reducing North Carolina income by a loss most of which was sustained outside this State. I do not believe that such a result was intended.

For the reasons expressed herein, I am of the opinion that the proportion of the prior year's loss which may be carried over as a deduction is determinable by the allocation ratio which would have been applicable to net income during the year in which the loss was sustained if net income had been earned in that year, and not by the allocation ratio applicable to net income in the year in which the deduction is claimed.

As you know, a net economic loss may be carried over not more than two years; and must be "offset by any income, taxable or non-taxable, of the next succeeding year before any portion of such loss may be carried forward to a second year."

OPINIONS TO COMMISSIONER OF AGRICULTURE

STATE MUSEUM; LIABILITY FOR LOSS OF OBJECTS OF ART LOANED TO THE MUSEUM OR KEPT FOR OTHER STATE AGENCY

21 September, 1944.

Receipt is acknowledged of your letter of September 20, in which you advise that a citizen of Farmville, North Carolina, has a collection of Oriental Art that has been given a maximum value of $15,000, which the owner proposes to lend to the State Art Museum for a period of six years, with the probability that he will make it a permanent gift. The Art Museum, on account of lack of space, has requested that the State Museum find a place to take care of it until such time as they do have space. You inquire as to whether the State would assume any responsibility for loss of material that was loaned.

The State and its departments could not be sued by anyone except with authority of the General Assembly. I know of no law which would authorize a suit for damages which might grow out of the loss of property under these circumstances. In case of bailment with an individual, the bailee would be responsible only for reasonable care, protection and preservation of the property and would not be an insurer.

LIVE STOCK MARKETS; FEE REQUIRED; PAYMENT FOR FRACTIONAL PART OF YEAR

20 November, 1944.

I have your letter of November 18, referring to the remittance made by the Kinston Marketing Company, Kinston, North Carolina, of $10.42 of the $25.00 fee required to be paid by G. S. 106-415.

There is no provision in the statute permitting the payment of a part of the $25.00 fee and, if the company was engaged in the business of operating a live stock market on July 1, it was required to secure the license authorized by G. S. 106-406. The Legislature has made no provision for the payment of a proportional part of the license required.

WEIGH MASTER; TOBACCO; AGRICULTURE

20 February, 1945.

In your letter of January 25th, 1945, you asked several questions concerning public weigh masters and the weighing of tobacco before sale on the warehouse floors.

You inquire first whether a tobacco warehouse operator would come under the provisions of the Public Weigh Master law if he should charge a fee for handling tobacco and not for weighing tobacco. G. S. 81-36 defines weigh master as one who weighs, measures or counts for compensation and issues a certificate of weight for the product. An essential portion of the definition of weigh master is that the Act should be done for compensation. If this element is lacking, the party would not be a Public Weigh Master and the Way Master's Law would have no application.

You also inquire whether a person who weighs tobacco but refuses to issue a certificate of weight is a Public Weigh· Master. As stated in the preceding paragraph, to be a Weigh Master, one must weigh, measure or count for compensation and issue a certificate of weight. In discussing this provision with you recently, we agreed that one would not become a Public Weigh Master unless he issued a certificate of weight. It would appear, therefore, that where no certificate of weight is issued, the person weighing a product would not be a Public Weigh Master within the meaning of that term as used in the present law. I do not believe, however, that a Public Weigh Master could avoid the Weigh Master law by simply refusing to issue a certificate of weight.

When a tobacco warehouse operator weighs, or has his employees to weigh his own tobacco he is not a Public Weigh Master for the reason that no service is performed for which a fee is charged. Therefore, a tobacco warehouse operator may place his own tobacco on the floor for sale without it being weighed by a Public Weigh Master.

The warehouseman is the custodian of tobacco offered for sale during the interim referred to in G. S. 81-43. It is my opinion that the warehouseman is not the custodian of the tobacco beyond the interim referred to in 81-43. The interim ends when the sale is concluded. I do not think that the warehouseman is the custodian of the tobacco after it has been purchased by another.

It is my opinion that the superintendent of weights and measures is not required to enforce the provisions of the Public Weigh Master's Law other than issuing licenses to Weigh Masters.

AGRICULTURE; OLEOMARGARINE LAW; SALE OF COLORED
OLEOMARGARINE TO STATE INSTITUTIONS

12 April, 1945.

In your letter of April 3, 1945, you inquire as to whether or not under ` the present oleomargarine law it is legal for a seller of colored oleomargarine to sell his product to an institution such as the Eastern North Carolina Sanitarium, and whether or not it is legal for such an institution to purchase and serve colored oleomargarine.

Section 106-234 of the General Statutes of North Carolina was amended by rewriting this statute so that the same now reads as follows:

"Sec. 106-234. *Serving of colored oleomargarine prohibited.*—It shall be unlawful to serve in any public dining room, restaurant, cafe, boardinghouse or hotel as a food, oleomargarine which is of a yellow color in imitation or semblance of butter, or when it has a tint or shade containing more than one and six-tenths degrees of yellow, or of yellow and red collectively, but with an excess of yellow over red, as measured in terms of Lovibond tintometer scale, or its equivalent."

The other amendments to the oleomargarine law relate to the enforcement provisions and do not affect the question presented in your letter.

In the above quoted section, it is made unlawful to serve oleomargarine which is of a yellow color in the establishments name in the statute. Except for the above named establishments, it seems to me that it is now legal to sell colored oleomargarine. The only term within the above statute that could possibly give any trouble or raise any question is the term "public dining room." I do not think that a dining room or place where meals are served to patients in such a State institution as the Eastern North Carolina Sanitarium could possibly be classified as a public dining room. To my mind a public dining room is a place open for business and serving prepared meals to those members of the general public or patrons who will pay the rates or prices fixed for such meals. Such a public dining room would fall within that classification of establishments covered by the license tax laws of this State, and I do not think that a dining room or place serving meals in any State institution for the treatment of inmates or patients could possibly fall within this category.

It is my opinion, therefore, that it is legal to sell colored oleomargarine to such an institution mentioned in your letter, and it is also legal for such an institution to purchase and serve colored oleomargarine.

CREDIT UNIONS; SHAREHOLDERS; RIGHT TO OFFSET THEIR SHARES
AGAINST DEBTS OWED CREDIT UNION

28 June, 1945.

In your letter of June 26, 1945, you inquire whether a member of a credit union which is in the process of liquidation may apply his shareholdings in the credit union as part payment on the balance due on a loan.

If a member of a credit union were allowed to apply his holdings therein as part payment on a loan which he had procured from the credit union, it would be tantamount to allowing a shareholder to offset his shares of stock against an indebtedness which he owed to the corporation.

G. S. 54-97 provides, in part, that a shareholder of a credit union shall not be liable for the payment of the credit union's debts for an amount in excess of the par value of the stock which he owns or for which he has subscribed. This section, by implication, provides that the shareholder is liable to the extent of the par value of the shares which he owns or has subscribed for. With this possible liability, I do not believe that a shareholder is entitled to offset his shares against a debt owed the corporation. To allow him to do so would be to grant to him a preference not accorded other shareholders. In addition, since the credit union is in the process of liquidation, the exact value of the shares could not be determined. This conclusion is supported by the general principles relating to the rights and duties of stockholders of corporations. Cf. 14 CORPUS JURIS, CORPORATIONS, § 1628, pp. 1044, 1045; DRUG CO. v. DRUG CO., 173 N. C. 502; WHITLOCK v. ALEXAN-DER, 160 N. C. 465.

AGRICULTURE; SALE OF ARTIFICIALLY BLEACHED FLOUR; REGISTRATION AND
INSPECTION; TRADEMARKS; EXCLUSIVE RIGHT TO USE TRADEMARK

11 July, 1945.

In your letter of July 10, 1945, you call attention to Article 21 of the General Statutes dealing with the registration and sale of artificially bleached flour. You state that a manufacturer or a concern has registered a brand of artificially bleached flour with your agency under the name of "WORLD'S BEST" flour, and that it is the contention of this concern or its representatives that having registered with your Department as a distributor of flour under this brand, that this concern would have priority or exclusive right to this brand or name, and that no other manufacturer happening to have a brand of the same name should be permitted to register and sell in North Carolina.

· You inquire of this office as to what rights a manufacturer or seller of artificially bleached flour would have by virtue of the fact that a particular brand of flour has been registered with your Department.

The laws of our State regulating artificially bleached flour begin with Section 106-210 of the General Statutes and continue through Section 106-219. The Department of Agriculture, acting through the State Chemist, has authority to analyze samples of flour and if the same are found to be artificially bleached, then the same must be appropriately labeled and the manufacturer, dealer or agent who sells same in this State must file a statement with the Department and register the same under the brand name of the flour, if it has such. Inspection fees are charged for every separate brand registered, and there are certain penalties for the violation of the Article. There is nothing in this statute that gives any manufacturer or dealer any priority or exclusive right to the registration of any particular brand name, and there is nothing in this statute which gives any manufacturer or dealer exclusive right to sell any particular registered brand in this State. So far as this Article is concerned, any number of independent manufacturers or dealers can register the same brand with the Department, and if they pay the inspection fees and comply with the Article, so far as this law is concerned, each one would have the right to sell artificially bleached flour under the same brand name.

The exclusive right to trademarks and brands is regulated in this State by Chapter 80 of the General Statutes. Under Section 80-3 of the General Statutes, persons or firms who claim rights with reference to trademarks or brands must register same with the Secretary of State, and if the same are duly registered, then the unauthorized use of such trademarks or brands by persons or firms other than the registrant is made unlawful, and any person who has duly registered a trademark or brand can prevent the unauthorized use of same by another person or firm, and any person or firm unlawfully using a duly registered trademark or brand is liable in damages for such unlawful use. This part of our law is handled by the Secretary of State, and so far as I can see, the Department of Agriculture has nothing to do with the enforcement of our law dealing with trademarks and brands.

I have checked at the office of the Secretary of State and find that the rademark or brand of "WORLD'S BEST" flour was registered in the office of the Secretary of State on April 11, 1919 by Blish Milling Company of Seymour, Indiana. This brand is registered with a design in the shape of a hemisphere, and according to the status of the State's records, it would seem that this firm has the right to use this brand in our State, although I do not wish to be understood as giving a fixed opinion on this angle of the matter without further investigation. I do say, however, that your Department has nothing to do with any exclusive rights or priorities pertaining to a trademark, or brand, and that so far as artificially bleached flour is concerned, it is your duty to accept the registration of any brand and collect the license fees for same, as well as to enforce the inspection provisions of the law.

AGRICULTURE; LIVESTOCK MARKETS; PERMITS; BONDS; TRANSFERABILITY OF PERMITS AND BONDS

29 August, 1945.

I have your letter of August 27, 1945, in which you state that in 1944 a corporation filed an application for a permit to operate a public livestock market. This application was accompanied by a surety bond in the amount of $2,000.00 and by a check for $25.00. The permit was issued for the year ending June 30, 1945. On August 10, 1945, a permit for the year ending June 30, 1946, was issued to this same corporation. It appears that this corporation has now been dissolved and all its property taken over by the president of said corporation. This property has been leased by its present owner to one Roy M. Chipley, who desires to operate it as a livestock market. You inquire if the bond heretofore filed by, and the permit heretofore issued to, the corporation may legally be transferred to Mr. Chipley.

G. S. 106-406 provides that any person, firm or corporation operating a public livestock market within the state of North Carolina shall be required to obtain from the Commissioner of Agriculture a permit authorizing the operation of such market. The application for such permit is to be made on forms furnished by the Commissioner and must show the full name and address of all persons having a financial interest in the market, the names of the officers, manager and person in charge of the market, the name under which the market will operate, and the location at which the market is to be operated. Upon the filing of this application and the giving of bond as required by G. S. 106-407, the Commissioner of Agriculture shall issue a permit authorizing the operation of the market.

I am of the opinion that this permit authorizes the operation of the market at the place and by the person named in the application, and that such permit is not transferable. This conclusion is buttressed by the fact that G. S. 106-407 requires the *operator* of said livestock market to give bond in the penal sum of $2,000.00. Manifestly, a new operator of a livestock market would have to file a bond to cover his activities as an operator and said bond would have to be approved as to him by the Commissioner of Agriculture.

I advise, therefore, that when a livestock market is leased or sold to an

individual who had no interest in said market prior to the leasing or selling of same, the vendee or lessee must file an application, give a bond and
secure a permit before operating a public livestock market in this State.

AGRICULTURE; LIVESTOCK MARKETS; PURCHASE AND RESALE
OF CATTLE FOR IMMEDIATE SLAUGHTER

30 November, 1945.

In your letter of November 20, 1945, you inquire if cattle purchased at a
public livestock market for immediate slaughter may be removed to another
market and there sold at auction to the highest bidder.

Section 106-409 of the General Statutes provides that no cattle except
those for immediate slaughter shall be removed from any public livestock
market unless they are accompanied by a health certificate issued by an
approved veterinarian. This section provides further that cattle removed
for immediate slaughter shall be identified and certain forms shall be filled
out. This section contains the following sentence:

> "Said cattle (cattle intended for immediate slaughter) shall be re-
> sold only to a recognized slaughter plant or the agent of same, or to a
> person, firm or corporation that handles cattle for immediate slaughter
> only, and said cattle shall be used for immediate slaughter only."

The section then provides that no market operator shall allow the removal of cattle in violation of the section. A violation of the section is made
a misdemeanor by G. S. 106-417.

I am of the opinion that when a person buys cattle for immediate slaughter, he would be violating G. S. 106-409 if he offered these cattle for sale at
a public auction, the right to bid at which has been in no way limited. I base
this position on the fact that if the auction sale is not limited, any person,
ordinarily, may become a bidder and a purchaser at such sale. In 5 Am. Jur.,
Auctions, Section 21, page 459, the following appears:

> "Inasmuch as an auction is an open sale, with few exceptions, anyone
> is qualified to become a bidder."

In Section 17, at page 457, of the above cited works, the following appears:

> "Once a bid has been accepted, the parties occupy the same relation
> toward each other as exists between promisor and promisee in an execu-
> tory contract of sale conventionally made. Thereafter, as a rule, the
> seller has no right to accept a higher bid, nor may the buyer withdraw
> his bid."

It would seem, therefore, that when the cattle are sold at public auction
and said auction sale is not limited, there is no way of being certain that the
cattle will be purchased by someone who intends to use them for immediate
slaughter. At such a sale a breeder of cattle or a farmer could become the
highest bidder and under the above authorities the cattle would be sold in
violation of the cited section from the statute. I, therefore, advise that in my
opinion when cattle for immediate slaughter are purchased, it would be a
violation of G. S. 106-409 for the purchaser to resell such cattle at a general
auction sale which has not been in any way limited.

DEPARTMENT OF AGRICULTURE; SEED LAW; ANALYSIS TAGS

4 December, 1945.

I acknowledge receipt of your letter enclosing a letter from the Champion Company of Springfield, Ohio, in which this company states that it is contemplating marketing lawn seed direct to consumers (the cemeteries of the State) and will not make any sales within the State and will maintain no representative or office but that all shipments will be made from Springfield, Ohio.

You inquire as to whether or not this company, under the circumstances set out in their letter, will be required to purchase seed analysis tags as provided for in Section 106-280 of the General Statutes.

Section 106-280 requires a seed analysis tag to be attached to each container of agricultural vegetable seed, weighing ten pounds or more, which is sold, offered for sale, or exposed for sale within this State for planting purposes and provides further that in case the seed is shipped into the State, such tag shall be secured by the person shipping such seed into the State and before shipment is made to an agent, retailer, or *other person*. -- -- --

It is apparent from this section that the Champion Company should be required to obtain a seed analysis tag before making shipment of seed into this State.

DEPARTMENT OF AGRICULTURE; TAX ON FEEDSTUFFS SHIPPED FROM OUT OF THE STATE INTO A MILITARY RESERVATION WITHIN THE STATE

23 January, 1946.

I acknowledge receipt of your letter enclosing a letter from General Mills, Inc., together with the letter from the Fort Bragg Exchange in which it is contended by General Mills and the Exchange that the State of North Carolina is not entitled to collect the North Carolina Feed Tax on shipments of feedstuffs from out of the State to Fort Bragg Exchange on a military reservation within the State of North Carolina.

Assuming that it is proposed to collect a tax on shipments of feedstuff from outside the State of North Carolina to the Fort Bragg Exchange on a military reservation within the State, to be used on the reservation, I do not think that the State may collect such tax since it involves what amounts to a shipment in interstate commerce and would have the same status as if the shipment was being made from the State of Virginia through the State of North Carolina to a consignee in South Carolina. The State of North Carolina has ceded jurisdiction over Fort Bragg, a military reservation, under the provisions of Section 104-7 of the General Statutes of North Carolina to the United States of America. See STANDARD OIL CO. v. JOHNSON, 316 U. S. 481.

This office has on numerous occasions expressed the opinion that the State of North Carolina cannot prohibit the shipment of intoxicating beverages from a distillery located outside of the State to a military reservation located within the State. See JOHNSON v. YELLOW CAB TRANSIT COMPANY, 88 Law Ed. 553. In this case the right to ship intoxicating liquors to Fort Sill, a United States Military Reservation, located within Oklahoma, a dry State, was recognized.

DEPARTMENT OF AGRICULTURE; AUTHORITY TO SET UP AND FINANCE A TOBACCO ADVISORY COUNCIL

2 February, 1946.

I acknowledge receipt of your letter in which you state that it is the purpose of the North Carolina Department of Agriculture to set up within its Division of Markets a North Carolina Tobacco Advisory Council. You enclose a memorandum giving general information relating to the proposed project and inquire as to the legal authority of your Department to set up such a council and finance the same.

I understand from you that the Governor, Commissioner of Agriculture, and the Board of Agriculture have endorsed this proposal and desire that such a council be set up if legal authority can be found to sustain it.

The memorandum proposes that the council shall be composed of the Commissioner of Agriculture and, among others, the Master of the North Carolina Grange, the Executive Secretary of the North Carolina Farm Bureau Federation, the State Director of Extension Service, the Director of Tobacco Research at Duke University, and the presidents of the four tobacco belt warehouse associations and representatives of various other associations interested in tobacco, the Presidents of the North Carolina Bankers Association and North Carolina Merchants Association, respectively, and the President of the Farmers Convention, and five others representing the public at large who are growers of tobacco. That the council shall act in an advisory nature in collecting information and promote and deal principally and primarily with the following subjects:

(a) Research in all its phases as related to the production and use of tobacco;

(b) The improved production of tobaccos through the encouragement of the use of adaptable varieties of certified seed, soil improvement, better methods of fertilization, cultural practices, elimination or retardation of plant diseases and study of entomology as "relating to the production of tobacco;

(c) Improved methods of harvesting, curing, handling, sorting, grading, warehousing, transportation and storage of tobacco; or any phase of marketing, or any services related thereto;

(d) Improving and increasing the foreign markets for the sale of tobacco;

(e) Studies of taxation as relating to tobacco and as affecting the price received by the tobacco farmer for his product, and the consumer in the use of same;

(f) A training program at our schools and colleges to train leadership for all phases of the tobacco program.

The conclusions of the council in an advisory capacity shall be made available from time to time to the public."

Examination of Chapter 106 of the General Statutes, entitled, "Agriculture," reveals that ample authority is contained therein to establish within the Department of Agriculture the proposed agency.

Among other things, Chapter 106 imposes upon the Commissioner and Board the following functions:

"Sec. 106-22 (6). With investigations and experiments directed to the introduction and fostering of new agricultural industries, adapted to the various climates and soils of the state, especially the culture of truck and market gardens, the grape and other fruits."

"Sec. 106-22 (10). With the inducement of capital and immigration by the dissemination of information relative to the advantages of soil and climate and to the natural resources and industrial opportunities offered in this state, by the keeping of a land registry and by the publication of descriptions of agricultural, mineral, forest, and trucking lands which may be offered the department for sale; which publication shall be in tabulated form, setting forth the county, township, number of acres, names and addresses of owners, and such other information as may be needful in placing inquiring home-seekers in communication with landowners; and he shall publish a list of such inquiries in the Bulletin of those who may have land for sale;"

"Sec. 106-22 (12). With the holding of farmers' institutes in the several counties of the state, as frequently as may be deemed advisable, in order to instruct the people in improved methods in farming, in the beneficial use of fertilizers and composts, and to ascertain the wants and necessities of the various farming communities; and may collect the papers and addresses made at these institutes and publish the same in pamphlet form annually for distribution among the farmers of the state. He may secure such assistants as may be necessary or beneficial in holding such institutes."

"Sec. 106-22 (13). The Commissioner shall publish bulletins which shall contain a list of the fertilizers and fertilizing materials registered for sale each year, the guaranteed constituents of each brand, reports of analyses of fertilizers, the date of meeting and reports of farmers' institutes and similar societies, description of farm buildings suited to our climate and needs, reports of interesting experiments of farmers, and such other matters as may be deemed advisable. The department may determine the number of bulletins which shall be issued each year."

Section 106-24 requires the Department of Agriculture to collect, compile, systematize, tabulate and publish statistical information relating to agriculture and to cooperate with the United States Department of Agriculture and the several boards of county commissioners of the state to accomplish such purposes.

Section 106-187 states that it shall be the duty of the Board of Agriculture to investigate the subject of marketing farm products, to diffuse useful information relating thereto and to furnish advice and assist the public in order to promote efficient and economical methods of marketing farm products; authority being given to gather and diffuse timely information concerning the supply, demand, prevailing prices and commercial movement of farm products, including quantities in storage.

Section 106-458 requires the Commissioner of Agriculture to keep statements returned to him from each leaf tobacco market in the State so as to show the number of pounds sold by each market, the number of pounds sold by producers, and the number resold upon each market, and to cause such reports to be published in a bulletin issued by the Agriculture Department and in one or more journals published in the interest of the growth, sale, and manufacture of tobacco in the State.

Comparison of the purposes of the North Carolina Tobacco Advisory Council with the functions and duties of the Commissioner and Department of Agriculture as above outlined, reveals that the purposes of the Council are in many respects identical with the duties and functions now imposed by law upon the Commissioner of Agriculture and the State Department of Agriculture. I am, therefore, of the opinion that there may be set up within the Department of Agriculture the North Carolina Tobacco Advisory Council as one of the mediums through which the Commissioner and the Department may render the services and furnish the information desirable in the advancement of the agricultural program of the State and, in particular, as it relates to tobacco.

If the Board of Agriculture determines that it is necessary to set up the North Carolina Tobacco Advisory Council within the Department, I am of the opinion that the Director of the Budget has authority to provide funds to finance the same. In addition to the appropriation made by the Legislature to the Department there are numerous fees and forfeitures collected which are required by Section 106-6 to be paid into the State Treasury and kept in a separate account as a fund for the exclusive use and benefit of the Department of Agriculture. If there is a surplus within this fund, I am of the opinion that a sufficient sum may be allocated therefrom with which to finance the proposed agency.

CREDIT UNIONS; CLERKS OF THE SUPERIOR COURT; FEES
FOR RECORDING CERTIFICATES OF INCORPORATION
OF CREDIT UNION

19 February, 1946.

In your letter of February 13, 1946, you state that the Treasurer of a Credit Union organized in Winston-Salem informs you that the Clerk of the Superior Court of Forsyth County charged a fee of $7.50 for recording the organization papers. You call attention to the fact that Section 54-78 of the General Statutes provides that the clerk of the Superior Court may charge the same fee for filing a Certificate of Approval, Certificate of Incorporation, and By-Laws that he is now allowed to charge for filing a Certificate of Incorporation of corporation organized under the business corporations laws of the State.

You would like to know if it is a special statute permitting the Clerk of the Superior Court of Forsyth County to charge a fee in excess of $3.00 for filing a Credit Union Organization Papers.

There is such a special statute in Forsyth County which is Chapter 387 of the Session Laws of 1945, and the paragraph with reference to Certificates of Incorporation will be found on page 5361 as follows:

"Corporation Certificate, Certificate of Credit Union, and Certificate of Cooperative Association, recorded, first four pages $3.00, including the Certificate of the Secretary of State, plus 50c for each additional page or fraction thereof. Minimum fee $3.00."

It will thus be seen that a fee of $7.50, allowing $3.00 for the first four pages and 50c for each page or fraction thereafter, would make these Organization Papers of the Credit Union amount to nine pages or at least eight pages and a fraction. I judge that the By-Laws were recorded with the Certificate, and apparently Section 54-78 of the General Statutes contemplates that all of these papers shall be recorded. It is true that the statute uses the word "filed," but filing in this sense and as related to the duties of the clerk of the Superior Court means that a record must be made of these papers in Corporation Book in the clerk's office. You can see this by referring to the chapter of the General Statutes governing clerks of the Superior Court.

I think I have given you the correct legal fees that can be charged; and, of course, you can take the matter up with the Credit Union Treasurer as to the number of pages he had recorded.

AGRICULTURE; FOOD; OLEOMARGARINE; COLORED OLEOMARGARINE; SERVING IN COLLEGE DINING HALLS

23 February, 1946.

I have your letter of February 21, 1946, in which you inquire if it is permissible for Louisburg College to serve colored oleomargarine in its dining rooms. You, of course, have reference only to prohibitions contained in the State statutes on this subject.

G. S. 106-234, as rewritten by Chapter 523 of the Session Laws of 1945, reads as follows:

"It shall be unlawful to serve in any public dining room, restaurant, cafe, boarding house, or hotel as a food, oleomargarine which is of a yellow color in imitation or semblance of butter, or when it has a tint or shade containing more than one and six-tenths degrees of yellow, or of yellow and red collectively, but with an excess of yellow over red, as measured in terms of Lovibond tintometer scale, or its equivalent."

I am of the opinion that by the terms of this Act, the serving of colored oleomargarine is prohibited only in dining rooms, restaurants, cafes, boarding houses and hotels which hold themselves out to the public generally as places at which food for immediate consumption may be purchased. I do not believe that the proscriptive provisions of the Act in question were intended to apply to boarding houses and dining rooms which serve only a select group and are not open to the public either generally or in a restricted sense. Thus, if Louisburg College operates a dining hall for the convenience and benefit of its students only (including, of course, bona fide guests of the students), I am of the opinion that colored oleomargarine may be served therein. Of course, if this dining hall is open to the public as well as to the students at the College, the statute above quoted would prohibit the serving of colored oleomargarine. This ruling is intended to apply only to dining halls operated by colleges for the benefit exclusively of the students and their bona fide guests.

AGRICULTURE; LINSEED OIL; APPLICATION OF INSPECTION LAW TO
OIL SHIPPED INTO STATE AND INCORPORATED IN OTHER PRODUCTS

18 March, 1946.

In your letter of March 14, 1946, you state that there is an impression in some quarters that the inspection fee or tax should not be paid on linseed oil which is shipped into this State and manufactured into other products before being offered for sale; and it has been suggested that there has been some ruling to this effect issued in the past.

You specifically raised a question as to whether or not the inspection fee or tax on linseed oil should be paid when the oil is shipped into this State for incorporation into some other product, such as paint, and is not to be resold as oil.

Our Inspection Law in regard to linseed oil is now contained in Article 32 of Chapter 106 of the General Statutes. I have searched our index cards back to the year of 1931 and have been unable to find any opinion on the Linseed Oil Law that deals with this specific question. I do find that this office issued an opinion on March 24, 1943 which indirectly deals with this question, and I am sending you a copy of this opinion. You will note that the last paragraph of the opinion would indicate that the application of the Act is to be confined to sales and not to purchases made by individuals in this State for the purpose of mixtures or compounds or in other words, working or incorporating the oil into some other product.

You will note that Section 106-285 of the General Statutes says:

"For the purpose of protection of the people of the State from imposition by the fraudulent sale of adulterated or misbranded linseed oil or flaxseed oil as pure linseed oil or flaxseed oils * * *"

You will also note that Section 106-288 deals with the sale of prohibited products; and part of the section is as follows:

"No person, firm or corporation, by himself or agent or as the agent of any other person, firm, or corporation, shall manufacture or mix for sale, sell, offer or expose for sale, or have in his possession with intent to sell under the name of raw linseed oil or boiled linseed oil * * *"

You will note in Section 106-290 that a part of the section is as follows:

"Nothing in this article shall be construed to prohibit the *sale of compound linseed oil*, or imitation linseed oil, or any substance to be used as a substitute for linseed oil, provided * * *" (Underscoring ours.)

You will note in Section 106-291 that a part of the section is as follows:

"Before any raw linseed oil or any boiled linseed oil or any boiled linseed oil with drying agents added or any compound linseed oil or any imitation linseed oil or any other substance used or intended to be used as a substitute for linseed oil shall be sold or offered for sale in this state * * *"

You will note that Section 106-293 as to samples applies to: "Every person who offers for sale or delivers to a purchaser any article named in this article * * *"

You will note that Section 106-295 dealing with seizure or condemnation says: "The oil offered for sale in violation of this article shall be subject to seizure, condemnation, * * *"

You will note that all of these sections deal with the sale or possession of the oil for sale, and this is also true when dealing with compounds and limitations. In addition to all of these sections from which I have quoted above, you will note that the very last section in the article (106-302) allows a dealer to be released from liability when he has a guaranty signed by the wholesaler. It seems to me that the whole sense of the article as gathered from the different sections clearly and emphatically notes that we are dealing with oils shipped into this State to be sold, that is dealers who sell the oil to persons who purchase it as oil. There is no indication in the statute, to my mind, that it should be applied to any person in this State who buys linseed oil or flaxseed oil products to use the same for compounds or mixtures or to incorporate the same into products, which products would later be sold. To my mind, it is only when the oil is brought into this State for the purpose of resale that the article is specifically applicable. I think a person who wishes to use these oils or imitations of same for the manufacture of other products has a right to do so without any inspection or without otherwise complying with the article.

OPINIONS TO BUDGET BUREAU

15 August, 1944.

Receipt is acknowledged of your letter requesting my opinion as to whether or not you would be authorized to pay the necessary and reasonable expenses and per diem to the Commission appointed by Governor Broughton to study the problem of insurance regulation in this State brought about by the recent decision of the Supreme Court of the United States sustaining the indictment of the insurance companies under the Federal anti-trust laws.

In conference with you, I understand that the expenses of this Commission could be paid out of the funds appropriated to the Insurance Department, by proper allocation therefrom.

In view of the fact that this Commission is making a study of the rewriting of our insurance laws, which will have a vital effect on the revenues collected from insurance and otherwise affect the regulations of the insurance business, it is my opinion that the reasonable expenses of this Commission could be paid from the appropriations made by the General Assembly to this Department and that the per diem of the members other than ex officio members could be paid from these funds.

Chapter 530 of the Session Laws of 1943 provides, in Section 4, for the payment of per diem of the members of various commissions and boards and contains this provision:

"All other boards and commissions, including those governing the institutions, but not including such as its members are now serving without compensation, three dollars and fifty cents ($3.50) per day, and five cents (5c) per mile of travel going and returning, and necessary travel expenses."

While this compensation is very low, apparently it would control the amount of per diem which might be paid to the members of this Commission.

EMERGENCY SALARIES; $3,600 LIMITATION; MAINTENANCE ALLOWANCES

12 July, 1945.

I have your letter of July 11, in which you call attention to the provisions of Chapter 279 of the Session Laws of 1945 and the question raised with reference to the emergency salaries which you state as follows:

"The question raised is this—The law says that the $10.00 Emergency Salary shall be paid on all salaries up to and including $3600. Is a man making a $3600 salary, plus full maintenance, entitled to receive the Emergency Salary set out in this law? The same question concerning this problem would arise about a person making a salary plus any maintenance allowances, which added together would be more than $3600. I, frankly, do not know what this answer is, but I would like for you to tell me what you think."

The part of Section 23½ of Chapter 279 upon which the answer to your question depends is as follows:

"The emergency salary shall not apply to salaries exceeding three thousand six hundred dollars a year."

The question, therefore, resolves itself into the problem as to whether or not maintenance provided a State employee is to be, within the purview of this statute, considered as a part of the salary.

While, of course, the employee gets the benefits from the maintenance provided him in connection with his employment by the State, such maintenance, while a benefit and the equivalent of income in some respects, is not, in my opinion, salary in the sense that this word is used in the statute. It is not so clarified in any of the budgetary language, so far as I am advised. Under certain circumstances maintenance would not even be considered as income.

It is my opinion that the emergency salary should be paid to all school teachers and other State employees whose salaries, other than maintenance, do not exceed $3,600.

STATE PROPERTY FIRE INSURANCE FUND; DUTY AS TO ESTABLISHING VALUE OF BUILDINGS

19 October 1945

I acknowledge receipt of your letter in which you state that prior to the enactment of Chapter 1027 of the Session Laws of 1945 (S. B. 359) known as the "State Property Fire Insurance Fund Act," you understood that it was the duty of the Insurance Department to establish the value of all state owned buildings and you inquire as to whose duty it is now to fix such values.

Even prior to the passage of the 1945 Act, there was no statute which specifically required the Insurance Commissioner to establish the value of buildings but I think that such authority was implied from Sections 58-189 and 193 of the General Statutes which required the Commissioner to prepare a schedule of the several properties owned by the State and to procure policies of insurance thereon according to schedules for such amounts as he was able to provide with appropriations for the insurance of State property. I understand that it was the policy of the Insurance Commissioner to discuss the valuation of buildings with the head of each department, institution, or agency of the State and with him jointly determine the valuation to be placed on the buildings of such department, institution, or agency for insurance purposes.

While Section 58-189 was repealed by the 1945 Act, Section 2 thereof provides that upon the expiration of existing fire insurance policies on State owned property, and in making appropriations for any biennium after the next biennium, the Commissioner of Insurance shall file with the Budget Bureau his estimate of the appropriations which will be necessary in order to set up and maintain an adequate reserve to provide a fund sufficient to protect State, institutions or agencies from loss or damage up to 50 per centum of the value thereof. It seems to me that this section certainly impliedly gives to the Commissioner of Insurance the authority and responsibility to determine the value of State owned buildings. It would be observed that the section requires the Commissioner to file with the Budget Bureau his estimate of the appropriations necessary to set up and maintain an adequate reserve and I do not see how the Commissioner could comply with this requirement unless he arrived at a value of the several buildings belonging to the State. It seems to me that the policy followed by the Commissioner prior to the passage of the 1945 Act might well be followed now in arriving at such values.

INSURANCE; STATE SELF INSURANT; BUILDER'S RISK; REPAIRS
OR ANNEX TO OLD STRUCTURE; NEW CONSTRUCTION

29 October, 1945.

You inquire through the Commissioner of Insurance, and direct to this office, as to the necessity of requiring builder's risk insurance in the following instances:

1. As to new construction.
2. When an annex is built to an existing structure.
3. When alterations or repairs are being made to an old building.

You raise these questions because of the probable effect of Chapter 1027 of the Sessions Laws of 1945, commonly known as the "State Self Insurant Act," which prohibits the purchase of fire insurance on State-owned buildings after the expiration of the policies in force at the time of the passage of the act.

If I correctly understand the procedure heretofore followed in letting contracts for the construction of State buildings, the contractor has been required to furnish all of the several kinds of insurance, including a performance bond, except as to builder's risk insurance which was purchased by the State. But since the builder's risk policy is primarily fire insurance risk, I do not think that the State may purchase such insurance either as to new construction or as to an annex or as to repairs being made to an existing building.

As to new construction, including an annex, the performance bond requires the building to be completed according to the terms and conditions and plans and specifications of the contract and the State assumes no responsibility nor is required to accept the building until it is so completed, so that the State looks to the contractor for a completed turnkey job. Any loss by fire before the building is turned over to the State will be borne by the contractor and his bondsman. I can see the desirability of builder's risk coverage, but under the terms of the 1945 Act, I do not think that the State can purchase such coverage and it is a matter between the contractor and his bondsman as to whether or not such risk is purchased.

I am also of the opinion that in view of the 1945 Act, the State may not purchase builder's risk coverage in cases in which old buildings are being repaired. It seems to me that the State's interest in requiring the contractor to purchase builder's risk coverage would be somewhat the same as in requiring indemnity on the part of the contractor against any other kind of loss that might be sustained by the State in connection with repairs to a building; for instance, indemnity against falling walls or undermining the foundation of a building, and in the case of loss occasioned by the negligence on the part of the contractor or his employees, the State would look to the contractor or his bondsman for any damages sustained.

While I am of the opinion that the State may not purchase builder's risk insurance in any of the events inquired about in your letter, I do think that the contractor could furnish such insurance even though it becomes an included item in determining the bids submitted to the State for the particular project.

TRAVEL EXPENSES; MEMBERS, DOMESTIC RELATIONS COMMISSION

23 November, 1945.

I received your letter of November 20 with reference to the opinion furnished by me to Mr. W. E. Church concerning the travel expense of members of the Domestics Relations Commission, created by the last General Assembly, to be paid out of the Contingency and Emergency Appropriation.

After reading your letter, I am convinced that you are correct and I was in error in writing Mr. Church, and that the travel expenses of members of the Commission are limited to $5.00 per day in the State as provided in the Appropriations Act of 1945. The error occurred by reason of the reference to the sections covered by the limitation in the Appropriations Act. The Act provides that the appropriations covered by Sections 1, 2 and 3 are subject to the $5.00 per day limitation, and as these expenses come from the Contingency and Emergency Appropriation, they would be embraced within this limitation.

JUDGES; REGULAR AND SPECIAL; SUPREME COURT JUDGES; INCREASED EXPENSES

6 May, 1946.

A question has arisen about which I have conferred with you, as to the fund from which the increased expenses of regular and special judges of the Superior Court should be paid under Chapter 763 of the Session Laws of 1945; and also the same question as to the increased salaries payable to the Chief Justice and Associate Justices of the Supreme Court under G. S. 7-3.

After giving consideration to the language found in Section 1 of Chapter 763 of the Session Laws of 1945, I am of the opinion that the increased allowance for expenses made to regular and special judges of the Superior Court should be paid from the General Fund of the State and that this Act is, in effect, an appropriation for this purpose, subject to the proviso in the Act that such funds shall be available after the payment of teachers' and State employees' salaries, and emergency salaries under the Budget Appropriation Act of 1945-1947.

As G. S. 7-3 provides that each Justice of the Supreme Court shall be paid an annual salary of $7,500 and in lieu of and in commutation for expenses incident to the attendance upon the court, an amount equal to that allowed each judge of the Superior Court, payable in monthly instalments as a part of his compensation, these two laws must be read together and, in like manner, the appropriation so made for the increased expense allowance for each Justice, of the Supreme Court should likewise be paid from the General Fund and would not have to be paid from the Contingency and Emergency Fund.

PER DIEM AND EXPENSES; TRAVEL EXPENSE; MILEAGE; LUMP SUM ALLOWANCE

7 June 1946

I acknowledge receipt of your letter in which you state that it has been the policy of the Division of Game and Inland Fisheries of the Department of Conservation and Development to make lump sum allowances to game wardens for travel in lieu of the five cents per mile authorized under Article 10, Section 2, Paragraph (b), page 179 of the booklet entitled "Budget and Accounting Procedures—Personnel Classifications and Procedures." I understand that this policy has been followed because it is virtually impossible to keep check on the operators as to the number of miles traveled, and that the allowance is considerably less than the wardens would be entitled to if they were paid on the basis of the five cents per mile. You state that you see no objection to this procedure if it may be legally permitted.

The referred to section states that only actual expenses, and then not in excess of the allowances provided therein, shall be paid, and the paragraph dealing with the per mile charge for the use of personal automobiles on State business reads: "Travel expenses paid for the use of personal automobiles are *limited* to five cents per mile travel."

Therefore, it seems to me that the only concern of your office or of the State Auditor's office is whether or not the payment exceeds five cents per mile actually traveled, and that so long as the lump sum allowance does not exceed the five cents per mile, I can see no objection to the policy followed by the Division of Game and Inland Fisheries in making allowances for travel to their game wardens.

Of course, some way should be devised so that the Department would know that the lump sum allowance does not exceed the five cents per mile actually traveled, and to that end, it is my thought that the game warden could be required to furnish a statement as to the miles traveled up to the number of miles that the payment of five cents per mile would equal the amount of the lump sum allowance.

OPINIONS TO UTILITIES COMMISSIONER

SANITARY DISTRICTS; RATES TO BE CHARGED FOR SERVICES;
JURISDICTION OF UTILITIES COMMISSION

3 April, 1945

You have inquired if the Utilities Commission has authority to fix the service charges or rates to be collected from the residents of a sanitary district for water and sewage services. For the purpose of answering this inquiry, I assume that the sanitary district about which you inquire was formed or created under the general law relating to sanitary districts— Article 6, Chapter 130 of the General Statutes of North Carolina.

Section 130-52 of the General Statutes reads as follows:

"A sanitary district board shall immediately upon the placing into service of any of its works apply service charges and rates which shall, as nearly as practicable, be based upon the exact benefits derived. Such service charges and rates shall be sufficient to provide funds for the proper maintenance, adequate depreciation, and operation of the work of the district, and provided said service charges and rates would not be unreasonable, to include in said service charges and rates an amount sufficient to pay the principal and interest maturing on the outstanding bonds of the district and thereby make the project self liquidating. Any surplus from operating revenues shall be set aside as a separate fund to be applied to the payment of interest on bonds, to the retirement of bonds or both. As the necessity arises the sanitary district board may modify and adjust such service charges and rates from time to time."

The Board referred to in the above quoted section is the Sanitary District Board appointed by the Board of County Commissioners and thereafter nominated and elected as are other county officers, G. S. 130-37.

Under this section, it would seem that authority to fix rates is vested in the Sanitary District Board. I am, therefore, of the opinion that the Utilities Commission does not have the authority to fix service charges or rates to be collected for water and sewage services by a sanitary district.

STATE COMMISSION FOR THE BLIND; RIGHT TO OPERATE PUBLIC UTILITY

25 September, 1945

I have your letter of September 24, in which you advise that the State Commission for the Blind has requested the Utilities Commission to approve its purchase of the Wingate Telephone Company, Union County, North Carolina, and that the Commission has some doubt as to whether this State agency can legally enter into the public utilities field. You advise that the State Commission for the Blind now owns the Fair Bluff Telephone Exchange, the purchase having been made about three years ago without the approval of the Commission.

The State Commission for the Blind was created under the terms of G. S. 111-1. G. S. 111-27 authorizes the Commission, for the purpose of assisting blind persons to become self-supporting, "to carry on activities to promote employment of needy blind persons. . ."

This section has no limitations and it is sufficient authority for the Commission to carry on the activity of operating a telephone exchange.

UTILITIES COMMISSION; AUTHORITY TO REGULATE FRANCHISE AND
NON-FRANCHISE MOTOR CARRIERS: (1) EXCURSION TRIPS, (2) CHARTER
TRIPS, AND (3) CASUAL TRIPS

22 February, 1946

I have receved your letter of February 20, in which you request my
opinion as to authority of the Utilities Commission to regulate franchise
and non-franchise motor carriers as to their respective rights to engage in
(1) excursion trips, (2) charter trips, and (3) casual trips, as to which you
submit examples as follows:

"A holds a franchise certificate authorizing the transportation of
passengers between Raleigh and Greensboro over U. S. Highway 70.
B, oi Raleigh, does not hold a franchise certificate but owns one or more
buses with proper For Hire license tags for transportation of passengers
for compensation. Both of these carriers insist that they have the right
under the law:
"1. To operate an excursion consisting of one or more buses from
Raleigh to Wrightsville Beach over any convenient highways between
said points, whether over the franchise route of another carrier or not.
"2. To hire one of its buses with or without driver to carry a party
from Charlotte to Asheville.
"3. To make a casual trip, as defined in G. S. 62-103 (q) and G. S.
62-104, from Charlotte to Wilmington."
You further state in your letter as follows:

"We are not in agreement among ourselves as to the power, if any,
conferred upon the Utilities Commission to grant or deny such rights or
as to our authority to supervise and regulate trips of this kind by
either class or carriers. We do not find excursion trips or charter
trips mentioned in the Motor Carrier Act, G. S. 62-103 to 62-121.
Neither do we find the term 'contract carrier' mentioned, but G. S.
62-103 (n) and 62-110, and the use of the term 'common carrier' seem
to indicate a purpose to make some distinction between contract carriers
and common carriers.
"In trying to determine what our authority is in the matter here
presented, we have given special consideration to G. S. 62-103 (f), (k),
(n), (o), (p), (q), and (t); 62-104, 62-105, 62-109, 62-110, 20-87 (a),
(c), and (d)."
G. S. 62-105 provides, in part, as follows:

"*Application for franchise certificate.*—Every corporation or person,
their lessees, trustees, or receivers, before operating any motor vehicle
upon the public highways of the State for the transportation of persons
or property for compensation, within the purview of this article, shall
apply to the commission and obtain a franchise certificate authorizing
such operation. and such franchise certificate shall be secured in the
manner following:"

Subsection (j) of this section provides as follows:

"Franchise certficates may be granted to restricted common carriers
as defined herein for any period in the discretion of the commission
not to exceed three years."

Restricted common carriers by motor vehicle are defined in G. S. 62-103 (t)
as follows:

"The term 'restricted common carrier by motor vehicle' means any
person not included in the definition 'common carrier by motor vehicle'
who or which undertakes, whether directly or by lease or other arrangement, to transport passengers or property restricted to any class or
classes of passengers or to any class, kind or commodity or property by

motor vehicle for compensation, whether over regular or irregular routes, and/or 'excursion passenger vehicles' as defined in G. S. 20-38 subsection (q)."

This subsection refers to G. S. 20-38(q) which provides the definition under the Motor Vehicle Act of 1937, as follows:

"(q)   Passenger Vehicles.—(1) Excursion Passenger vehicles.
"Passenger vehicles kept in use for the purpose of transporting persons on sight-seeing or travel tours."

The quoted sections would appear to me to place under the jurisdiction of the Utilities Commission the regulation of both franchise and non-franchise motor carriers with respect to their rights to engage in excursion trips, charter trips, or casual trips under the circumstances stated in your inquiry, unless this authority is negatived by the provision found in G. S. 62-104, which I quote as follows:

". . . provided, further, that nothing in this article shall prohibit a motor vehicle carrier under this article, nor any motor vehicle on which the franchise tax has been paid as provided in the current revenue act, from making casual trips on call over routes established hereunder; provided, that on said casual trips no one shall be allowed to pick up any passenger or property along the route, nor be permitted on the return trip to carry any passengers or property other than those or that included in the original trip; . . ."

The phrase "casual trip" is defined in G. S. 62-103(q) as follows:

"The term 'casual trip' means a trip on call for the purpose of transporting passengers or property to a given destination and return, or either."

The phrase "motor vehicle carrier," not having any statutory definition in the article, would be understood by me to mean any motor vehicle carrier subject to regulation under the article by the Utilities Commission. This quoted provision of G. S. 62-104 means, in my opinion, that any such motor vehicle carrier, or any motor vehicle on which the franchise tax has been paid as provided in the current Revenue Act, is not to be prevented by anything in the Act from making casual trips, as defined, on call over routes established hereunder, which means routes established for franchise carriers by the Utilities Commission upon application and under authority of the Act. This, however, would not mean, in my opinion, that the motor vehicle carriers engaging in this business would not remain subject to the power of the Utilities Commission as to regulation, to the same extent and in the same manner that it is authorized to regulate franchise carriers on regular franchise routes. The quoted phrase would seem to me to mean only that nothing in the article should prohibit the making of casual trips over established routes by the motor vehicle carriers mentioned.

In my opinion, the full authority of regulation given to the Utilities Commission by G. S. 62-109 would be applicable to the motor vehicle carriers for which franchise certificates are granted as restricted common carriers, as defined in G. S. 62-103(t) and G. S. 20-38(q), to which this subsection (t) refers.

The language found in G. S. 62-104, hereinbefore quoted, provided that nothing in the article will prohibit a motor vehicle carrier "under this article" nor any motor vehicle on which the franchise has been paid, as provided in the current Revenue Act, from making casual trips on call over routes established hereunder, would appear to negatively authorize franchise and non-franchise carriers to use their equipment for casual trips, as defined in the statute, over any of the highways of the State, to and from any points in the State, without regard to any established routes over which specific franchises had been granted.

Applying this to the specific illustration which you submit, it is my opinion that such carriers could operate an excursion consisting of one or more buses from Raleigh to Wrightsville Beach over any convenient highways between said points, whether over the franchise route of another carrier or not, or to hire one of its buses with or without a driver to carry a party from Charlotte to Asheville, or to make a casual trip as defined in G. S. 62-103(q) from Charlotte to Wilmington.

Such trips would, however, be subject to regulation by the Utilities Commission, as provided in G. S. 62-109, to the same extent and in the same manner that they might be regulated if operated on regularly scheduled routes.

WATERWAYS; RIGHT-OF-WAY; ACQUISITION BY UTILITIES COMMISSION

20 March, 1946

I have your letter of March 19 enclosing to me a letter from Colonel G. W. Gillette, United States District Engineer, Wilmington, North Carolina, with reference to the acquisition by the Utilities Commission of certain rights-of-way for the Federal Government. On the second page of his letter, Colonel Gillette quotes from General Statutes 104-11, which you state appears to give your Commission authority to acquire the rights-of-way. You request my opinion on behalf of the Commission, as to whether or not you have the authority to proceed as requested by Colonel Gillette. You also inquire, if you have the authority, whether or not this office would handle the matter for you.

Colonel Gillette in his letter requested information as to whether or not your Commission, under the statute G. S. 104-11, could furnish the United States with the necessary agreement to hold and save the Government free from claims for damages resulting from the improvement, and, in the event the Boards of Commissioners experience difficulty in securing the rights-of-way, whether or not your Commission would undertake the acquisition and transfer of a perpetual easement to the United States.

You will observe that the statute, G. S. 104-11, has the proviso that the Utilities Commission is not authorized to enter into an obligation or contract for the payment of any money or proceeds through condemnation, or otherwise, without the express approval of the Governor and Council of State.

I believe, therefore, in the first instance, it would be necessary for the Commission to take this matter up with the Governor and Council of State, as evidently the obligations proposed would involve the payment of money by the State. I know of no appropriation which has been made by the General Assembly from which such funds could be provided, unless it would be from the Contingency and Emergency Fund which, I understand, has been fully committed.

I would be unable to answer the question as to furnishing the legal services necessary to the handling of the matter by this office unless I was fully informed as to the nature and character of the contemplated acquisitions. I have no information whatever about that. I would assume, however, that it would be necessary to employ local counsel to handle the proceedings necessary for condemnation; certainly, if they would involve any large amount of work.

I believe it would be desirable for you to secure from Colonel Gillette full information as to the nature and extent of the rights-of-way and other rights to be acquired, and, thereafter, present the matter to the Governor and Council of State for their consideration. I assure you that I will be glad to cooperate as fully as I can in whatever particulars this office can be of service in this connection.

OPINIONS TO INSURANCE COMMISSIONER

MUNICIPAL CORPORATIONS; CHIEF OF FIRE DEPARTMENT; INSPECTOR OF BUILDINGS; UNSAFE BUILDINGS AND FIRE HAZARDS; PUNISHMENT FOR UNSAFE CONDITIONS AND BUILDINGS.

April 3, 1945

Reference is made to the letter of E. M. Ball, Chief of New Bern Fire Department, dated March 27, 1945, which among other things contains the following paragraph:

"Also at this time, a very grave matter has been called to my attention, which I wish to take up with you. I had a call to inspect a house belonging to Mr. J. L. Hartsfield at 72 Johnson Street of this City. I found the house in very bad condition. There are five families living in this one house, two on the first floor, two on the second floor, and one in the attic. In the attic there are two adults and one child about two or three years old, they use a trap door over the stairs at night to keep the little child from falling down; there is no other door or exit of any kind in this attic. I went to see Mr. Hartsfield about this, and he refused to do anything at all about it, saying, if I condemned the property that he would sue me or the City of New Bern for any rent that he might lose."

You inquire of this office as to the rights of the Inspector or Chief of New Bern Fire Department with reference to this situation.

Section 160-115 of the General Statutes of North Carolina created in the cities and towns of this state, the office of Chief of Fire Department. Section 160-118 of the General Statutes of North Carolina provides that the Chiefs of Fire Departments shall be the local inspectors of buildings for the cities or towns in which they are appointed and provides that such inspectors shall make all inspections and perform such duties as may be required by the law or city or town ordinance or by the Insurance Commissioner. In this same Article of the General Statutes (Article 11, Chapter 160) you will find that under Section 160-151, that among other duties of the inspector are the following:

"Every building which shall appear to the inspector to be especially dangerous to life because of its liability to fire or in case of fire by reason of bad condition of walls, overloaded floors, defective construction, decay *or other causes* shall be held to be unsafe, and the inspector shall affix a notice of the dangerous character of the structure to a conspicuous place on the exterior wall of said building. No building now or hereafter built shall be altered, repaired or moved, until it has been examined and approved by the inspector as being in a good and safe condition to be altered as proposed, and the alteration, repair or change so made shall conform to the provisions of the law."

You will also find in Section 160-152 the following:

"If the owner of any building which has been condemned as unsafe and dangerous to life by any local inspector, after being notified by the inspector in writing of the unsafe and dangerous character of such buildings, shall permit the same to stand or continue in that condition, he shall be guilty of a misdemeanor and shall pay a fine of not less than ten nor more than fifty dollars for each day such building continues after such notice."

Section 160-153 of the General Statutes makes it a misdemeanor for any person to remove any notice which has been affixed to any buildings by the local inspector which notice states the dangerous character of the buildings.

It seems to me that under the situation outlined in the letter that the Chief of the New Bern Fire Department, who is also the inspector for the city, would have the clear right to proceed under the section cited above, and if in his opinion, and acting in good faith in the performance of his duties, he finds that this building justifies a notice of condemnation as heretofore described in the above statute, then I see no reason why he should not proceed to carry out the law and place the notice upon the building. He should, of course notify the owner in writing of the dangerous character of the building as is required by 160-152 of the General Statutes, and if the condition is not altered or changed so that the same is rendered safe, then the inspector should consult the city attorney or other attorney of the city whose business it is to advise and prosecute these matters and to follow the advice of such attorney as to invoking the criminal penalties set forth in Section 160-152.

I am of the opinion that the law requires the Chief of the Fire Department, as inspector, to carry out these duties for the protection, not only of the persons living in the building, but for the protection of the inhabitants of the city at large, and if he acts in good faith in the prosecution of his duties, I am further of the opinion that there would be no legal liability on his part nor on the part of the City of New Bern. I think it is needless to cite a legal authority for the position that municipal officers in carrying out their statutory duties, when acting in good faith, are not liable either criminally or for damages in civil action. What I have here said, of course, would not apply in cases where such official action can be proved to be prompted by a corrupt or malicious motive.

Your attention is also called to Section 6.97 of the North Carolina Building Code. This building code has been adopted as controlling for the construction and condition of buildings in this state and you will find that its adoption was brought about by Section 143-139 of the General Statutes of North Carolina. The section of the code above referred to provides the methods and ways of egress that must be provided in buildings wherein rooms are rented, let, or leased for living or sleeping purposes. This section also provides for additional ways of egress where rooms are let or leased for living purposes and sleeping purposes which must be provided in order to render the building safe. Subsection (c) of this section is to the effect that the regulations of the section shall not apply to buildings used as private dwellings unless such private dwellings exceed three stories in height, but your attention is called to the fact that under Section 2.1 of the code, which contains the definitions used in the code, a dwelling is defined as follows:

" 'Dwelling' means a building occupied exclusively for residence purposes and having not more than two apartments."

I am of the opinion, therefore, that under this definition of dwelling, the house in question could not be defined as a dwelling because it must be exclusively for residence purposes ·and must have not more than two .apartments. It follows, therefore, that Section 6.97 of the Building Code of North Carolina, in my opinion, is applicable to the house described in the letter.

In closing, I would like to call your attention to Article 15 of Chapter 160 of the General Statutes. This Article ·permits cities and towns to pass ordinances whereby unfit buildings can be destroyed or the owners can be compelled to make repairs, alterations, and improvements at a reasonable cost. You will find in Section 160-182 of the General Statutes that whenever a municipality finds that there exists in such municipality dwellings unfit for human habitation due to delapidation, defects increasing the hazards of fire, accidents, or other calamities, etc., that ordinances can be passed whereby such buildings can be condemned or repairs or alterations can be made by compulsion. I am not familiar with the charter of the City of New Bern, and it may be that the charter provides for this type of action. The city attorney will know about this part of the matter, but at any rate, your attention is called to the general law on the subject and your attention is further called to the powers of municipal corporations as contained in 160-200 of the General Statutes which provides in subsection 28 of this section that municipal corporaions have the right:

"To condemn and remove any and all buildings in the city limits, or cause them to be removed, at the expense of the owner or owners, when dangerous to life, health, or other property, under such just rules and regulations as it may by ordinance establish; and likewise to suppress any and all other nuisances maintained in the city." `

The city attorney will know just what steps the city authorities can lawfully take along the lines of compelling alterations or repairs or complete condemnation and removal of the buildings; if, in the opinion of the authorities, such steps are necessary in this case, and if the proper authority to proceed by law is provided in the charter or the statute.

STATE INSURANCE; ONLY STATE-OWNED BUILDINGS, FIXTURES, ETC., THEREIN INCLUDED

May 31, 1945.

I acknowledge receipt of your letter in which you inquire, first, as to whether or not the State, under the provisions of Senate Bill 359, becomes a self-insurer on such property as a patrol cruiser known as the "Croatan" owned by the Department of Conservation and Development; and, second, whether or not the State has become a self-insurer as to certain property owned by the State Board of Health, to-wit:

"40 Motion Picture Projectors and accessories at not more than $300 per unit
55 Microscopes at not more than $190 per unit
48 Fluoroscopes at not more than $600 per unit
all the property of the· North Carolina State Board of Health, and being used in health centers. . . . . ."

Section one of Senate Bill 359 limits the property for which the State becomes self-insurer against fire loss to, "State-owned buildings, fixtures, furniture, and equipment therein, including all such property the title to which may be in any State department, institution, or agency . . . . . ."

It seems to me to be apparent that the cruiser "Croatan" would not be of that type of property for which the State has become a self-insurer and that your department should insure the same against fire hazard as it has heretofore done.

It is my understanding that the property in question owned by the State Board of Health is portable and carried from place to place to be used in the several health centers in the State. Of course, as to whether or not this property is within the purview of Senate Bill 359 depends upon whether or not it is a part of the fixtures, furniture, or equipment located in a building owned by the State of North Carolina. From what I understand the circumstances to be as to this particular property, I am inclined to the opinion that it is not covered by Senate Bill 359 and that insurance against fire hazard should be purchased as has heretofore been done.

INSURANCE; LICENSES FOR INSURANCE AGENTS; GATE CITY AND PILOT LIFE INSURANCE COMPANIES

11 July, 1945

I have your letter of July 5, 1945, with enclosures from Honorable Julius C. Smith, of Greensboro, relating to the above subject.

According to the agreement between the Gate City Life Insurance Company and the Pilot Life Insurance Company and the Jefferson Standard Life Insurance Company, it appears that the Gate City Life Insurance Company has been absorbed by the Pilot Life Insurance Company. From the letter of Mr. Smith, it seems that the capital stock of the Gate City Life Insurance Company is to be cancelled out. The agents of the Gate City Life Insurance Company have procured from you a license, as required by statute. Since the Gate City Life Insurance Company has been absorbed by the Pilot Life Insurance Company, the question now arises whether the licenses heretofore issued to the agents of the Gate City Life Insurance Company are sufficient licenses to authorize these same agents to act as agents of the Pilot Life Insurance Company, or whether new licenses must be procured. These agents procured licenses to act for the Gate City Life Insurance Company for the year commencing April 1, 1945.

It appears that the agreement whereby the Pilot Life Insurance Company absorbed the Gate City Life Insurance Company did not amount to a merger or a consolidation of the two companies. The only method of merging or consolidating two companies is that provided by G.S. 55-165, et seq. COACH COMPANY v. HARTNESS, 198 N.C. 524, 528. To constitute a merger or consolidation under these statutes, the following steps must be taken: (1) An agreement between the corporations to be merged or consolidated must be entered into and this agreement, among other things, must state the method of converting stock in the merging or consolidating corporations into stock of the surviving or consolidated corporation. This agreement may provide, however, for the distribution of cash, property or securities to stockholders of the merged or consolidated corporations in lieu of shares of stock in the surviving or new corporation; (2) This agreement must be submitted to the stockholders of each corporation and be acted upon by them; (3) The notice required by the statute must be given; (4) The agreement must be filed in the office of the Secretary of State, "and shall thence be taken and deemed to be the agreement and act of consolidation or merger of the said corporations" (G.S. 55-165); and (5) This agreement must be recorded in the office of the Clerk of Superior Court of the county where the principal office of the surviving or consolidated corporation is located' and in the office of the Clerk of Court where the original certificates of incorporation of the merging or consolidating corporations are located and in the office of the Register of Deeds in each county where either corporation owns real estate.

From the agreement submitted by Mr. Smith, it appears that steps (1) and (2) above, and possibly step (3), may be considered to have been complied with. However, by checking with the Secretary of State, it appears that step (4) above was not complied with, and thus, step (5) could not have been complied with.

Thus, it follows that the absorbing of the Gate City Life Insurance Company by the Pilot Life Insurance Company does not constitute a merger or a consolidation of those corporations within the meaning of those terms as used in the statute.

Since the term "merger" is used in the agreements between the corporations concerned, I have discussed that phase of the question somewhat in detail, with the idea of showing why, in my opinion, there has been no merger of the Gate City and Pilot Life Insurance Companies. However, even if it be conceded, for the sake of argument, that a merger of the two corporations was accomplished by the agreements, I still find no authority for transferring the licenses of the agents of the Gate City Company to the Pilot Company. When a merger of corporations takes place, the surviving corporation acquires "all the rights, privileges, powers and franchises as well of a public as of a private nature" of the merged corporation, meanwhile retaining all its own rights, etc. (G.S. 55-166). The surviving corporation also acquires all property, real, personal and mixed, of the merged corporation. G.S. 55-166. (This transfer of rights, etc., is accomplished by the filing and recording of the agreement required by Section 55-165. of the General Statutes. G.S. 55-166.) The license issued to an agent of a company is not a right, power, duty or asset of the company; instead, it is a permissive right granted to the agent. As such, the company acquires no transferrable interest therein.

G.S. 58-40 and 58-41 require insurance agents to procure from the Commissioner of Insurance a license for each company which they represent. This construction of these statutes has long been followed by the Insurance Department. From the agreement filed with you, it appears that the agents of the Gate City Life Insurance Company were issued licenses as agents of that company. It appears that these agents will, in the future, represent not the Gate City Life Insurance Company but a new or different company. Therefore, I am of the opinion that new licenses must be procured by these agents.

After studying the agreement and reading Mr. Smith's letter, I can see much merit in his contention that to require these agents to procure new licenses would be unfair. With this idea in mind, I have carefully examined the statutes and I can find no provision which would exempt these agents from procuring new licenses.

INSURANCE; RECIPROCITY IN LICENSING NON-RESIDENT AGENTS

28 July, 1945

I acknowledge receipt of your letter calling my attention to Sections 58-43 and 58-152 of the General Statutes relating to non-resident agents and retaliatory law, and inquiring as to whether or not, under said sections, you may refuse to license a non-resident agent when the home state of the applicant for a non-resident life insurance agent's license will not issue a similar license to a resident of the State of North Carolina.

I am of the opinion that, under the authority vested in you by the two referred to sections, you may refuse to issue license to a non-resident under the circumstances set out in your letter.

INSURANCE; BUILDERS' RISK INSURANCE APPLICABLE TO STATE BUILDINGS

20 August, 1945

I acknowledge receipt of your letter relative to the above subject, stating that Mr. Pollock, of the Budget Bureau, has requested your department to ascertain the extent of liability of the State Property Fire Insurance Fund for loss or damage to buildings owned by the State or under construction in the State in the case of loss or damage during the course of construction or repair.

In order for me to arrive at an opinion on the questions raised in your letter, it will be necessary for me to know the contents of the Builders' Risk Policy and the form and contents of the performance bond furnished by the contractor. I understand from the Budget Bureau that there is probably a provision in the performance bond which requires the State to furnish the Builders' Risk coverage and certainly, I would have to know the wording of this provision before passing upon the questions raised in your letter.

LICENSE TAXES; FEDERAL SAVINGS AND LOAN ASSOCIATIONS; DOMESTICATION AND TAXABILITY

23 October, 1945

This is in reference to your letter of October 15, 1945, in which you inquire as to the status of Home Federal Savings and Loan Association, which has its principal office in Johnson City, Tennessee, but proposes to solicit and make loans in an area in North Carolina embraced within a radius of fiifty miles from its home office. No office is to be maintained in

North Carolina, and all loans are to be closed at the home office. The North Carolina loans will be secured by first lien on real estate in North Carolina. Apparently the North Carolina business will constitute only a minor part of the association's total business.

I assume that this association is a Federal Savings and Loan Association, organized and chartered under the Home Owners' Loan Act of 1933, as amended, 12 U.S.C.A., p. 517, Sec. 1464.

You inquire (1) whether or not this association is a "foreign" association within the scope of G.S. 54-34 *et seq.* so as to require domestication as a condition precedent to doing business in this State, and (2) whether the tax under G.S. 105-73 should be computed on all shares of stock of the association or only on those shares attributable to the business done in North Carolina. I have paraphrased your questions, but believe that this is the substance of your inquiry. I shall discuss these two questions in the order given.

(1) Strictly speaking, a corporation or association chartered under the laws of the United States is neither foreign nor domestic with respect to a particular State, at least in the usual acceptation of those terms. A domestic corporation is one chartered under the laws of the particular State; and a foreign corporation is one chartered under the laws of another State. Before a foreign corporation does business in this State, it must "domesticate" in this State. More specifically, before a foreign savings and loan association does business in this State, it must comply with the provisions of G. S. 54-34 *et seq.*

There seems to be little unanimity of judicial opinion as to whether a federally chartered corporation is domestic or foreign within a given State. 13 *Am. Jur., Corporations*, Sec. 150; *Anno.* 69 A.L.R. 1346; *Anno.* 88 A.L.R. 873. However, it is probable that the diversity of opinion is attributable to the variances in the bases on which the question arose rather than to any actual widespread disagreement. For instance, a Federal corporation may be domestic for one purpose and not for another. Most of the cases seem to have arisen on questions involving jurisdiction of State and Federal Courts, a matter determinable by domicile, residence or citizenship.

I think the particular question at hand is answered, at least inferentially, by *Leggett v. Bank*, 204 N. C. 151, where our court held that the Federal Land Bank of Columbia, having been chartered under federal law, was not a foreign corporation doing business in this State by virtue of any license, express or implied, from North Carolina, but was a corporation which derived its right to do business in this State solely from an Act of Congress; and, therefore, did not come within the provisions of the statute authorizing service of summons on the Secretary of State. The court apparently took the position that a Federally chartered corporation has the right to do business in any State without a license from such State, and that conditions of doing business could not be imposed on such corporation.

I, therefore, advise that the Home Federal Savings and Loan Association is not a "foreign" association within the meaning of G. S. 54-34, and that this and the following sections are not applicable to this association, which may do business in this State as if it were a "domestic" corporation.

(However, it is not a domestic corporation within the meaning of G. S. 54-25 and is not liable for the license tax imposed by that section.)

This conclusion is supported by the language of the statute. Although the Article is designated "Foreign Associations," the body of the statute refers to "association of another state." The fact that a Federal association has its principal place of business in another state hardly would render it an association "of that state." I am of the opinion that an association of another state is an association chartered under the laws of another state and does not include a corporation chartered only under an Act of Congress.

(2) Your second question relates to the amount of tax payable by this association under G. S. 105-73, which applies to "Every building and loan association, domestic or foreign, operating under a charter granted by authority of the laws of this state or any other state, or the United States" for certain stated purposes, and which imposes an annual license tax for the privilege of doing business in the State, said tax being at the rate of "thirteen cents (13c) on each one hundred dollars ($100.00) of liability on actual book value of shares of stock outstanding on the thirty-first day of December of the preceding year" as shown on reports-to-the insurance commissioner.

Inasmuch as this association is an instrumentality of the Federal Government it is free from State taxation except to the extent permitted by Congress. *State v. Minnesota Federal Savings and Loan Association* (Minn. 1944) 15 N. W. (2d) 568. However, in this case Congress has expressly given a limited power of taxation to the States. The Home Owners' Loan Act, 12 U.S.C.A., p. 519-20, Sec. 1464(h) provides, in part:

"and no State, Territorial, County, Municipal or local taxing authority shall impose any tax on such associations or their franchise, capital, reserves, surplus, loans, or income greater than that imposed by such authority on other similar mutual or cooperative thrift and home financing institutions."

This is no less a grant of authority to the State to tax because it is present only by implication or is couched in negative language. *First Federal Savings and Loan Association of Altadena v. Johnson* (1942) 49 Cal. App. (2d) 465, 122 P. (2d) 84.

Thus, it seems clear that North Carolina may impose a tax on Federal savings and loan associations if the same tax is imposed on other similar associations.

I am of the opinion that G. S. 105-73 falls within the scope of the permission granted, for it expressly applies to "Every building and loan association, domestic or foreign, operating under a charter granted by authority of the laws of this state or any other state, or the United States," without distinction or discrimination.

The only quesion left for determination relates to the computation of the tax.

Ostensibly the statute does not draw any line between business done within and business done without the State; and a possible construction of the statute would be to the effect that the statute imposes a tax on the basis of all shares, regardless of the fact that most of said shares may be attributable to business done in another State.

However, I believe that such a construction in this case would work an unconstitutional result. It seems to be settled that a State generally cannot levy on a foreign corporation a franchise tax based on all its capital, without regard for the amount of business done within the State, for this would violate the interstate commerce clause of the Federal Constitution. Such a tax must be apportioned to the business done in the State. *Anno.* 105 A.L.R. 11; *Anno.* 139 A.L.R. 950.

Thus, in *Express Agency v. Maxwell*, 199 N. C. 637, our court, quoting the United States Supreme Court, said:

"A franchise tax imposed on a corporation, foreign or domestic, for the privilege of doing a local business, if apportioned to business done or property owned within the state, is not invalid under the commerce clause merely because a part of the property or capital included in computing the tax is used by it in interstate commerce . . . But in order that the fee or tax shall be valid, it must appear that it is imposed solely on account of the intrastate business; that the amount exacted is not increased because of the interstate business done; that one engaged in exclusively interstate commerce would not be subject to the imposition; and that the person taxed could discontinue the intrastate business without withdrawing also from the interstate business."

Wherever possible a statute will be construed so as to give it a constitutional effect. Therefore, I am of the opinion that G. S. 105-73 imposes a privilege tax on a Federal savings and loan association only in proportion to the business done in this State. I advise, therefore, that Home Federal Savings and Loan Association of Johnson City, Tennessee, is liable for the tax computed at the rate of 13c per $100.00 liability on shares outstanding which are attributable to the business done in North Carolina. While the statute does not provide this expressly, it does state that the tax is for the privilege of doing business in the State; and it must be assumed that the legislature intended to tax within constitutional limitations.

BUILDING RESTRICTIONS; APPLICATION TO COMPLETION OF FIFTH
FLOOR OF BUILDING CONSTRUCTED IN 1922

15 November, 1945

In conference with you, my opinion was requested as to the application of Section 4.26 of the North Carolina Building Code to a hotel which was constructed in Monroe in 1922, circumstances about which you stated were as follows:

This building is of ordinary construction as defined in the Code and was built in 1922 to be used as a hotel and stores. The building was constructed to provide for a basement and five floors. The fifth floor, however, was left unfinished, the partitions, plumbing, etc., never having been installed. It is proposed now to complete the fifth floor for use and occupancy as a part of the hotel. The Building Code, Section 4.26, provides for ordinary construction the building shall not exceed 50 feet when used for public purposes.

Chapter 4 of the Building Code provides in Section 4.21, under the heading "Restrictions as to Height," as follows:

"New Buildings. Except as may be otherwise provided by this code, no building hereafter erected shall exceed in height the limits fixed in this chapter."

Under this heading, Section 4.22 provides, "Alterations. No building shall hereafter be altered so as to exceed the limits of height fixed by this chapter."

It is evident that under these provisions the limitation of height would not be applicable to a building that had been constructed in 1922 unless the other provisions in the Building Code would have the effect of bringing them under these limitations.

Chapter 1, Section 1.11 provides as follows:

"The purpose of the code is to provide certain minimum standards, provisions and requirements for safe and stable design, methods of construction and uses of materials in buildings and/or structures hereafter erected, constructed, enlarged, altered, repaired, moved, converted to other uses or demolished and to regulate the equipment, maintenance, use and occupancy of all buildings and/or structures."

The only words in this section which might have any application would be the words "altered, repaired." I do not think that either of the words would describe what is proposed to be done to the hotel property. This is neither alterations or repairs but merely completion of the building as originally intended.

Neither do I think that Section 1.22 making the Code applicable to alterations affecting the structural strength, fire hazard, exits, lighting or sanitary conditions would be applicable to your situation. Neither do I think that the language of Section 1.23 as to the change of use of the building would be applicable.

It is, therefore, my opinion that the building having been constructed in 1922, the proposed completion of the fifth floor would not bring the building within the provisions of Section 4.26 as to the height limitation.

I understood in conference with you that adequate arrangements would be made for sufficient fire escapes and exits serving all of the floors of the structure would be fully complied with by the owners.

SELF-INSURERS UNDER WORKMEN'S COMPENSATION ACT; ENFORCEMENT OF TAX

15 April, 1946.

I received your letter of April 10, in which you state that you are informed by the North Carolina Industrial Commission that some self-insurers have failed to pay their tax by March 15 and some have failed to report and pay this tax. You inquire of me as to what procedure is to be followed in collecting this liability.

You are correct in your understanding that the self-insurers are required to give bond or deposit securities as a guarantee of the payment of their liabilities under the Workmen's Compensation Act.

G. S. 97-96 provides that whenever an employer has complied with the provisions of G. S. 97-93, relating to self-insurers, the Industrial Commission issues a certificate which can be revoked if the employer has failed to comply with the law.

I have talked with Mr. T. A. Wilson, Chairman, today and he tells me that they always require a bond of the employer or deposit of securities in the case of self-insurers, as authorized by G. S. 97-93. I would assume there would be little difficulty in collecting the taxes due from these insurers. Mr. Wilson said they had never had any trouble, so far as he knew.

STATE PROPERTY FIRE INSURANCE FUND; COVERAGE AGAINST DAMAGE BY LIGHTNING

1 May, 1946.

I acknowledge receipt of your letter in which you state that on August 6, 1945, the Alderman Dormitory was damaged by lightning to the extent of $286.45 and that the insurance companies having policies in force on the University schedule have paid a total of $274.98, leaving a balance of $11.47 as being due from the State Property Fire Insurance Fund as an uninsured portion of the loss.

You inquire as to whether or not Chapter 1027 of the Session Laws of 1945, setting up the State Property Fire Insurance Fund, includes damages caused by lightning as well as by fire.

While the Act makes the State a self-insurer as to fire loss and creates a "State Property Fire Insurance Fund," I am of the opinion that the term "fire insurance" includes lightning.

It is my understanding that fire insurance cannot be purchased separate from lightning insurance nor can lightning insurance be purchased except in connection with a fire insurance policy and that the premium paid in one instance covers both fire insurance and lightning. Section 58-177 of the General Statutes, which prescribes the terms of a fire insurance policy and the form thereof, provides for only one premium and covers insurance against "all direct loss by fire, lightning, and by removal from premises endangered by the perils insured against in this policy, except as hereinafter provided - - - -." And on the back of this form the following description is given:

"Standard fire insurance policy of the State of."

I am satisfied that it was the intention of the proponents of the State Property Fire Insurance Fund Act that the State should become a self-insurer as to all losses included in the usual fire insurance policy and that any loss occasioned by any of those described in the adopted fire insurance policy, on and after the expiration of the insurance then in force, should be paid out of the State Property Fire Insurance Fund.

OPINIONS TO ADJUTANT GENERAL

ESCHEATS; UNCLAIMED FUNDS OF ADJUTANT GENERAL'S OFFICE; CHECKS
OF ADJUTANT GENERAL EQUIVALENT TO STATE WARRANTS

22 June, 1945

In your letter of June 14, 1945, you call attention to the fact that the Adjutant General's office has certain checks drawn on the State Treasurer which have been outstanding for a period of five years and over and have been unclaimed for that period of time. It is further stated that your Department issues its own checks drawn on the State Treasurer in payment of its accounts and that there is some question in your mind as to whether the provision of Section 116-25 of the General Statutes, regulating certain escheats, applies to the checks used in disbursing funds in your Department. Your question is whether or not these funds which have been unclaimed for a period of five years or over, represented by checks issued by your office, which are termed disbursing checks, are subject to the law of escheats as other State warrants covered by this provision of the General Statutes.

The pertinent provision of Section 116-25 is as follows:

"All monies now in the hands of the Treasurer of the State, represented by State warrants in favor of any person, firm, or corporation, whatsoever, which have been unclaimed for a period of five years, shall be turned over to the University of North Carolina."

A subsequent paragraph of this section provides that after the University receives the money the same shall be held subject to claim for a period of ten years after receipt of same and if no claim is filed within that period, then the funds become the property of the University with full and complete ownership.

I am of the opinion that the funds represented by the checks mentioned in your letter are subject to the provisions of Section 116-25 of the General Statutes and that the same should be turned over to the University of North Carolina as other escheats described in that section. It is true that your office issues its own checks and that these checks are signed by the Adjutant General. This method, however, is what is known as a disbursing account system and is used by several other State agencies. It is inconvenient for some of these agencies to issue checks through the normal channels of the State Auditor's office and as an accounting device and as a convenience to these agencies, a disbursing account is set up and these agencies are allowed to issue their own checks which are charged to this disbursing account. At periodic times this account is reviewed by the proper agency of the State and the State Auditor issues one check covering the total sum against the funds held in the office of the State Treasurer. These disbursing account checks are State warrants to the same effect and for the same purposes as if the same had been issued and countersigned by the State Auditor in the normal operation of the State's business. The fact that a different method is devised in disbursing these funds does not change their character nor does it alter the character of the voucher used to effect this purpose. All checks and evidences of indebtedness whereby monies can be lawfully drawn from the State Treasury and which are honored by the State Treasurer in my opinion are State warrants, as the term "State warrant" is a general term and embraces all types of negotiable paper that will be honored by the State.

I am of the opinion, therefore, that these unclaimed funds represented by the checks drawn on your disbursing account should be paid to the University of North Carolina in accordance with the above cited statute.

MUNICIPALITIES; APPROPRIATIONS FOR THE STATE GUARD

6 November, 1945

I understand that you would like to have my opinion as to whether or not municipalities in North Carolina are authorized to make appropriations for the support of the State Guard organized under authority of G. S. 127-111, et seq.

G. S. 127-101 authorizes the appropriations by county commissioners for the various organizations of the National Guard or Naval Militia, and G. S. 127-111, Subsection 6, provides that the North Carolina State Guard shall be subject to the military laws of the State not inconsistent with or contrary to the provisions contained in that Article, with certain exceptions which are not applicable.

The general powers of municipalities are defined in G. S. 160-200 to include the following:

"(4) To appropriate money of the city for all lawful purposes."

The duties of the State Guard as defined in G. S. 127-111 include the duty, subject to the call of the Governor, to execute the law, suppress riots or insurrections, or repel invasions, as is now or may hereafter be provided by law for the National Guard and for the unorganized militia.

I understand, in conference with you, that it has been the practice of various municipalities to make reasonable appropriations to aid the National Guard and State Guard in the carrying on of their organizations, the theory being that the service rendered by such local units as a law enforcing agency in the community, suppressing riots and insurrections, etc., justified the appropriations.

While I cannot be entirely certain about it, I am inclined to the opinion that the courts would uphold reasonable appropriations made by a municipality to aid in the support of the local organization of the State Guard.

ORGANIZATION OF ENLISTED RESERVE CORPS

28 May, 1946

I have before me your letter of May 28, in which you write as follows:

"Sgt. Raymond L. Burke, of the Regular Army, now on duty with the North Carolina Military Area, now located in the Raleigh Building, has inquired of me as to whether or not there is any state law which would have any affect on the organization of the Reserve Association, composed of those enlisted men who have had military service and are now in the Enlisted Reserve Corps of the United States Army. Personally, I am satisfied that there is nothing in our military laws which would have any affect on such an organization, and doubt that there is any law which would prohibit or affect such a military association, unless there be some specific law which deals with organizations in general."

I also have a letter from Sgt. Burke, in which he writes me as follows:

"It has been suggested that an Enlisted Reserve Associations similar to the Reserve Officers Association be organized from members of the Enlisted Reserve Corps.

"At present I am making a survey of the Enlisted Reservists residing in North Carolina with a view of selecting some outstanding leaders to form a basic organization.

"Request I be furnished with information pertaining to the legal requirements which must be met in forming such an organization."

I understand from you and from Sgt. Burke that there is no possible conflict between the contemplated organization and G. S. 127-107, which provides as follows:

"If any person shall organize a military company, or drill or parade under arms as a military body, except under the militia laws and regulations of the state, or shall exercise or attempt to exercise the power or authority of a military officer in this state, wi'hout holding a commission from the governor, he shall be guilty of a misdemeanor."

As I understand it, the purpose of the proposed organization is primarily to promote the enlistments in the Enlisted Reserve Corps. I know of no provision in our law which would prevent such an organization or in any manner attempt to regulate it. I understand it is to be a purely voluntary association for the purpose of promoting the enlistments in the Enlisted Reserve Corps.

OPINIONS TO COMMISSIONER OF LABOR

Education; World War Orphans; Benefits; Limitations

15 September 1944

Receipt is acknowledged of your letter of September 12 in which you state that you have received an inquiry from a beneficiary under our statutes providing educational advantages for children of world war veterans, as to whether the benefits under these statutes could extend beyond the usual four year period.

G. S. 116-145 provides that the scholarship authorized by the section shall not extend for a longer period than four academic years. We have not been able to find a satisfactory interpretation of the word "academic" as used in this particular statute but we have followed the assumption that it is used in the same sense as the term "scholastic." The term "scholastic" year is one of common use and is generally understood to mean a term of nine months and, in the absence of affirmative proof to the contrary, it will be assumed that the scholastic year begins in the Fall and ends in the Spring. See SMITH v. BOARD OF EDUCATION, 113 S. E. 147, 153 Ga. 758.

If the person about which you inquire has already received the benefits for four academic years, he or she would not be entitled to any further benefits under the provisions of the Act.

OPINIONS TO STATE HIGHWAY AND PUBLIC WORKS COMMISSION

STATE HIGHWAY COMMISSION; RESTRICTED USE OF HIGHWAYS

15 February, 1946

I received your letter of February 14, referring to G. S. 20-121 authorizing the State Highway and Public Works Commission to adopt ordinances prohibiting the operation of vehicles upon highways, or imposing restrictions as to weight thereof, for a total period not to exceed ninety days in any one calendar year, when, by reason of deterioration, etc., the highways will be damaged unless the use of vehicles is prohibited or the permissable weights reduced.

You quote the ordinance adopted by the Highway Commission under authority of this statute, the ordinance designated as Section 35, and state that in pursuance thereto the Division Engineer of one of your highway divisions has erected signs on certain highways, restricting the maximum gross load to be carried over such highways to six tons, which has been questioned by the bus companies who hold franchises to operate over these routes. You submit the following question:

> "Does the fact that a bus company holds a franchise to operate over a State highway authorize it to disregard gross load limitations placed in effect by the State Highway and Public Works Commission pursuant to Section 20-121 of the General Statutes of North Carolina?"

Your question is submitted in view of the fact that the State Highway Patrol is interested in the enforcement angle of this problem. I am, therefore, sending a copy of this letter to Honorable T. B. Ward, Director of the Motor Vehicle Division, Department of Revenue.

It is my opinion that the bus company holding a franchise to operate over a State highway does not give it any authority whatever to disregard gross load limitations fixed by statute or put into effect by the State Highway and Public Works Commission pursuant to G. S. 20-121. I can think of no substantial argument whatever which would support the view that such carriers would be authorized to disregard the law in this respect and, in my opinion, it would be as much applicable to a bus company as to anyone else using the highways.

It does seem to me, however, that there may be some question as to whether or not the State Highway and Public Works Commission was acting within its authority when it delegated to the several Division Engineers the right to reduce the maximum gross load of vehicles using the same, as this would be a delegation of authority given to the State Highway and Public Works Commission by the General Assembly of a quasi legislative character, this being upon the principle of the maxim *delegata potestas non potest delegari.* I suggest you might give this feature of the matter your consideration.

OPINIONS TO STATE BOARD OF HEALTH

PUBLIC HEALTH; REGULATION OF MEAT MARKETS; EXEMPTION OF FARMERS

18 July 1944

I have your letter of June 29 which was acknowledged by Mr. Patton on July 10, in which you request that I review the opinion expressed in a letter from Honorable T. W. Bruton, Assistant Attorney General, to Honorable Warren H. Booker, former Director of your division, under date of December 2, 1938, with reference to the exemption of farmers from the provisions of Chapter 244 of the Public Laws of 1937, now General Statutes, Sections 130-264 to and including 130-267.

I have the letter from Mr. Bruton before me and have considered it carefully again as you request. G. S. 130-264 authorizes the State Board of Health to prepare and enforce rules and regulations governing the sanitation of meat markets, abattoirs and other places where meat or meat products are prepared, handled, stored or sold, and to provide a system of scoring and grading such places, and provides that no such meat market or abattoir shall operate which receives a sanitary rating of less than 70%. This section contains this proviso:

"Provided, that this article shall not apply to farmers and others who raise, butcher and market their own meat or meat products."

This proviso seems to completely support the conclusion reached by Mr. Bruton in his letter above mentioned. It may be that the Act should be amended to take care of the situations which you have in mind.

It does not mean, however, that a person whose business is operating a meat market can exempt it from the requirements of the Act because, in addition to operating the market in which meats are bought and sold, such person may be a farmer and incidentally raise some of the meat which may be sold in the market. The statute is intended to take care of a person who is a farmer or who raises and sells only meat which he produces. If, in addition to selling meat which he produces and raises, he also engages in the business of buying and selling other meat and meat products, the statute would be applicable and the regulations adopted by the State Board of Health could be enforced against such business. If, on the other hand, a farmer or person who raised the meat sold only the meat products raised by him in such market, the statute exempts him from its provisions. It could be made applicable only in the event the Legislature should amend the law.

PUBLIC HEALTH; MUNICIPALITIES; DISSOLUTION BY INACTIVITIES; ENFORCEMENT OF SANITARY REGULATIONS

18 August 1944

I acknowledge receipt of your letter in which you set out certain facts relating to the insanitary condition existing in the Town of Bonnie Doone, in Cumberland County. You state that the town was chartered several years ago and a mayor and board of commissioners were elected; that the mayor has since died without being replaced, no election was held on the date on which the last election was supposed to have been held, and that the board is not now functioning.

You state that it is necessary to take some action relating to the water and sewerage in the town, and inquire as to whether or not the Governor, under his emergency powers, could appoint a governing council.

I doubt if the Governor has any authority to appoint a board of commissioners for the Town of Bonnie Doone.

However, the fact that no election was held at the last regularly appointed time does not within itself terminate the offices of the commissioners, and they may continue to serve as de facto commissioners until their successors are elected.

In the case of COMMISSIONERS OF TRENTON v. McDANIEL, 52 N. C. 107, it was held that when the election of the commissioners of an incorporated town was vested in the male citizens thereof, the mere failure for a long time to elect commissioners did not destroy the right, but that it continued as long as there were free male citizens enough to fill vacancies. So that the charter of the town is in no way affected by the failure to elect officers at the appointed time.

In 43 C. J. 173; 19 RCL, 705, it is said that a municipal corporation does not ipso facto become dissolved or disincorporated or lose its existence by misuser or nonuser of its corporate powers, functions and franchises, as by failure to elect officers or by failure of its officers to perform official duties or corporate functions.

It is, therefore, my opinion that the commissioners are still serving as de facto commissioners of the town and may meet and fill the vacancy caused by the death of the mayor, and such mayor and the commissioners may continue to function as the governing body of the town until such time as a regular election is held and their successors named.

I suggest that you take your problem up with the members of the board of commissioners and see if they will not perform the duties required of them as commissioners of the town in respect to its sanitary and health conditions. If they fail to act, it seems to me the only course left open is for legislative action at the coming General Assembly.

SANITARY DISTRICTS; AUTHORITY OF OFFICIALS OF SANITARY DISTRICTS TO ADOPT AND ENFORCE REGULATIONS

18 August 1944

I acknowledge receipt of your letter in which you inquire as to whether or not the officials of a sanitary district created under Section 7077(g) of the Consolidated Statutes have authority to formulate and enforce sanitary rules and regulations in the same manner as municipalities or county boards of health.

Section 130-39 of the North Carolina General Statutes provides:

"When a sanitary district is organized as herein provided, the sanitary district board selected under the provisions of this article shall be a body politic and corporate and as such may sue and be sued in matters relating to such sanitary district. In addition such board shall have the following powers:"

Paragraph 8 provides:

"To formulate rules and regulations necessary for the proper functioning of the works of the district."

Under the provisions of said Section 130-39, I am of the opinion that the governing body of a sanitary district does have authority to adopt and enforce sanitary rules and regulations within the district, but it will be noted from said section that many of the powers granted to the governing body of a district relating to sanitation and health are subject to the approval of the State Board of Health.

VITAL STATISTICS; REGISTRATION DISTRICTS; PAYMENT OF REGISTRATION FEES; BURIAL AND BIRTH CERTIFICATES

18 August 1944

I acknowledge receipt of your letter in which you inquire as to the liability of municipalities for payment of the registrar's fee for the issuance of birth and burial certificates in cases of persons who are not residents of such municipality, but the birth or death takes place in a hospital or other place located within the municipality.

Section 130-71 of the North Carolina General Statutes provides that "for the purposes of this article the State shall be divided into registration districts as follows: Each city, each incorporated town, and each township shall constitute a local registration .district." It is apparent from this section that any incorporated municipality is a separate local registration district.

Section 130-73 provides that the mayor of every incorporated town or city in the State shall appoint a local registrar of vital statistics for his municipality.

Section 130-77 provides that the body of any person whose death occurs in or whose body is found in this State shall not be interred or otherwise disposed of "unless a permit for burial, removal or other disposition thereof shall have been properly issued by the local registrar of the registration district in which the death occurred or the body was found." It is apparent from this section that only the registrar of the local district may issue the burial permit, and in the case of an incorporated town, the local registrar is the registrar of the municipal district, appointed by the mayor.

Section 130-86 provides, in part: "Within five days after the date of each birth there shall be filed with the local registrar of the district in which the birth occurred a certificate of such birth, which certificate shall be upon the form adopted by the State Board of Health. . . . ." This section places the duty upon the local registrar, who is the registrar of the municipality in which the birth occurs, to issue the birth certificate.

Section 130-101 of the North Carolina General Statutes provides:

"Each local registrar shall be paid the sum of fifty cents for each birth certificate and each death certificate properly and completely made out and registered with him. . . . ."
"The compensation of local registrars for services required of them

by this article shall be paid by the County Treasurer for registration work outside of the incorporated municipalities, and by the town or city treasurer for registration work in incorporated municipalities."

I am, therefore, of the opinion that the registration fee provided for in Section 130-101 for the burial permit provided for in Section 130-77, and the birth certificate provided for in Section 130-86, when the death or birth for which such permit or certificate is issued takes place within an incorporated city or town, should be paid by the municipality in which such death or birth occurred, regardless of the residence of the deceased or the person to whom birth certificate is issued.

PUBLIC HEALTH; SANITATION; INNS, HOTELS, RESTAURANTS, ETC.

11 September 1944

Receipt is acknowledged of your letter in which you refer to Article II of Chapter 72 of the General Statutes of North Carolina, Sections 72-8 to 72-29, inclusive, and Article V, being Sections 72-46 to 72-48, inclusive, and request my opinion as to whether you would be justified in following the provisions contained in Article V without reference to those contained in Article II.

The provisions of Article V are contained in Chapter 309 of the Public Laws of 1941 and no reference is made to the prior Acts as contained in Article II. In the preparation and adoption of the General Statutes of North Carolina, it was thought necessary to bring forward both these articles due to the fact that although there might be some conflicts in the subject matter of the two articles, the 1941 Act was in reality only an expansion of broadening of the powers given in the prior Acts as contained in Article II.

It is therefore my opinion that it is necessary to consider the two Acts together and unless there is some irreconcilable conflict between the provisions contained in the two Acts they should both be given effect. The section in the new Act which gives authority to the State Board of Health is contained in G. S. 72-46. This section authorizes, empowers and directs the State Board of Health to prepare and enforce rules and regulations governing the sanitation of hotels, cafes, restaurants, tourist homes, tourist camps, summer camps, lunch and drink stands, sandwich manufacturing establishments, and all other establishments where food is prepared, handled or served to the public at wholesole or retail for pay, or where transient guests are served food or provided with lodging for pay. The section also provides for a system of grading for all establishments covered under the provisions of the section.

Of course, this particular section broadens the coverage contained in G. S. 72-9 which is a portion of Article II. G. S. 72-9 specifically exempts private boarding houses where the majority of the patrons receive boarding accommodations for periods of a week or longer at a time, while G. S. 72-46 makes no specific exemption of boarding houses. It appears to me to be necessary that we consider whether boarding houses are included within the provisions of G. S. 72-46. Boarding houses as such are not specifically mentioned in this section and if they are included they must be included under the following language: "all other establishments where food is prepared, handled and served to the public at wholesale or retail for pay, or where transient guests are served food or provided with lodging for pay." Admittedly, this language would include a boarding house where accommodations are offered to the public at large or where transient guests are served with food or provided with lodging for pay.

The only type of establishment about which I have some doubt is what might be termed a private boarding house where only a limited number of selected guests are accommodated. The 1941 Act contains criminal provisions, and statutes levying taxes or creating criminal offenses are subject to strict construction. STATE v. CAMPBELL, 223 N. C. 828.

It is not the policy of the criminal law to make a person charged with crime the victim of ambiguities and in order for such person to be convicted he must be clearly brought within the coverage of the statute.

It is therefore my opinion that there is a grave doubt as to whether the provisions of the new Act would apply to a private boarding house where a limited number of persons are accommodated and the accommodations are not offered to the public at large.

HEALTH; ARTICLE XIV, OF CHAPTER 130, G. S.; DISEASES COVERED BY SAID ARTICLE XIV

18 September 1944

I have your letter of September 16, 1944, in which you ask what diseases are covered by Article XIV, Chapter 130 of the General Statutes. You inquire specifically as to the meaning of the phrase, in Section 130-176 of the General Statutes, "diseases coming within the meaning of this article."

"Diseases" as used in this article, is not defined. However, in Section 130-173, the following appears: "Whooping cough, measles, diphtheria, scarlet fever, smallpox, infantile paralysis, typhoid fever, typhus fever, Asiatic cholera, bubonic plague, yellow fever, or other disease declared by the North Carolina State Board of Health to be preventible." The same language appears in Section 130-175.

It is my opinion, therefore, that "diseases" as used in Article XIV, of Chapter 130 of the General Statutes of North Carolina, means whooping cough, measles, diphtheria, scarlet fever, smallpox, infantile paralysis, typhoid fever, typhus fever, Asiatic cholera, bubonic plague, yellow fever, or other disease declared by the North Carolina State Board of Health to be preventible.

PUBLIC HEALTH; SCHOOLS; COMPULSORY VACCINATION FOR SMALLPOX

23 October 1944

Receipt is acknowledged of your letter in which you request my opinion as to whether it is necessary that the local board of health take official action in order to authorize the vaccination of school children for smallpox.

G. S. 130-183 provides that the board of health of any town, city or county, shall have authority to require children attending the public schools to present certificate of immunity from smallpox either through recent vaccination or previous attack of the disease. It will be noted that this section vests discretion in the local board of health as to whether children attending the public schools may be required to present certificates of immunity from smallpox.

This statute has been upheld by our Supreme Court in the case of HUTCH-INS v. SCHOOL COMMITTEE, 137 N. C. 68, and MORGAN v. STEWART, 144 N. C. 424. A similar statute has been upheld in the Supreme Court of the United States in the case of JACOBSON v. MOSS, 197 U. S. 10, 49 L. ed. 643.

G. S. 115-139 makes it the duty of teachers, principals, superintendents, and all other governing boards having authority over the maintenance, support and conduct of the public schools, to obey the rules and regulations of the sanitary committee or the board of health for the protection of the health in the district.

It is my opinion that it is necessary that the local board of health take official action before school children may be required to present certificates of immunity from smallpox in order to permit such children to attend school. When the local board of health has taken official action, G. S. 130-183 makes any parent, guardian, school committee, principal, or teacher, guilty of a misdemeanor, punishable by a fine of not less than $10 nor more than $50 for permitting a child to violate the requirement adopted by the local board of health.

PUBLIC HEALTH; SANITARY DISTRICTS; CREATION; BOUNDARIES

25 October 1944

Receipt is acknowledged of your letter in which you raise the question as to the authority of the State Board of Health to reduce the boundaries of a proposed sanitary district without referring the matter to the local authorities for further action.

G. S. 130-33 authorizes the State Board of Health to create sanitary districts under certain conditions without regard for county, township or municipal lines. G. S. 130-34 provides that 51% or more of the resident freeholders within the proposed district may petition the board of county commissioners of the county in which all or the major portion of the proposed district is located, setting forth the boundaries of the proposed sanitary district and the objects it is proposed to accomplish. The board of county commissioners is authorized to act upon the petition and if it is approved the same is to be transmitted to the State Board of Health with the request that the proposed sanitary district be created. G. S. 130-35 provides for public hearing by the State Board of Health and G. S. 130-36 provides that if, after such hearing, the State Board of Health shall deem it advisable to comply with the request of the petition that a district should be created and established for the purpose or purposes described in the petition, a resolution is to be adopted to that effect, defining the boundaries of such district and declaring the territory within such boundaries to be a sanitary district.

The Supreme Court of North Carolina, in the case of IDOL v. HAYNES, 219 N. C. 723, held that the signers of a petition for the creation of a sanitary district are entitled, as a matter of right, to withdraw their names from the petition at any time before action is taken on the petition by the county commissioners on the question of approval and that when their withdrawal reduces the number of signers to less than 51% of the resident freeholders within the proposed district, the board of commissioners is without jurisdiction and its approval of the petition may be enjoined. Of course, this particular case has no bearing on the powers of the State Board of Health and I merely call it to your attention in order to stress the point that a majority of the resident freeholders in the territory sought to be included in a proposed sanitary district must continue their assent in order to justify its creation.

The language used in G. S. 130-36 as to the powers of the State Board of Health is not, to my mind, entirely clear. After the hearing, the State Board of Health is authorized to make the decision as to whether the request of the petition that the district be created- and established should be allowed. If this question is decided in favor of the petitioners, the Board is authorized to adopt a resolution to that effect, defining the boundaries of the district and declaring the territory within the boundaries to be a sanitary district. It is my opinion that the boundaries, as defined by the State Board of Health, should include the same territory as described in the petition. If any other construction should be placed on the language used in the section, it could have the effect of allowing the State Board of Health to establish a sanitary district in a territory where less than 51% of the resident freeholders desire the establishment of such district.

It is my opinion that until the court has given this particular section a construction different from the one outlined above, the State Board of Health should not undertake to change the boundaries of the territory from those outlined in the petition, and if any such change is contemplated, the petition should be denied and a new petition filed containing boundaries which the State Board of Health would be justified in adopting.

BIRTH CERTIFICATES; CHANGE OF RACE

10 November 1944

I acknowledge receipt of your letter, enclosing certain affidavits and inquiring as to whether or not you have authority to change the birth certificates of Henry and Claude Lynch so as to cause said birth certificates to show that said children are of the Indian race rather than the Negro race.

Among other things, Section 130-94 of the North Carolina General Statutes contains this provision:

"No certificate of birth or death, after its acceptance for registration by the local registrar, and no other record made pursuant to this article, shall be altered or changed in any respect otherwise than by amendments properly dated, signed and witnessed: Provided, that a new certificate of birth shall be made by the State Registrar whenever · · · ·
(c) Satisfactory proof is submitted to the State Registrar that there

has been entered in a court of competent jurisdiction a judgment, order, or decree disclosing different or additional information relating to the parentage of a person."

I do not think that you have authority to change birth certificates upon affidavits furnished by third parties. A change in a birth certificate must be done by an amendment to the original certificate.

However, it is provided that a new certificate may be issued upon a judgment or order of a court of competent jurisdiction. It seems to me that in the instant case the interested parties should obtain from a court of competent jurisdiction a judgment, order or decree to the effect that they are full-blooded Indians rather than members of the Negro race, before either amending the old certificate or issuing a new certificate. The latter portion of Section 130-94 provides the machinery for the filing and preservation of the old and new certificates.

LEAVE OF ABSENCE; MILITARY SERVICE; STATE EMPLOYEES

16 November 1944

I have your letter of November 15, in which you write me as follows:

"One of our young women, Miss Isabel Baker, has resigned to join the SPARS. She thinks she is entitled to a leave of absence. Our understanding is that only those persons called to military service by Selective Service Boards or members of the National Guard or Home Guard, are entitled to leaves of absence for military service."

You request my opinion as to whether or not a person volunteering for military duty under the law is entitled to a leave of absence.

Chapter 121 of the Public Laws of 1941 provides that any elective or appointive State official may obtain a leave of absence from his duties for military or naval service, protracted illness, or other reason satisfactory to the Governor, for such period as the Governor may designate. Such leaves shall be obtained only on application by the official and the consent of the Governor.

This statute would be applicable only to State officials and if the status of Miss Baker is that of an employee rather than an official in your department, the statute would not be applicable to her. Independent of the statute, however, it is my understanding that the State departments and agencies have, as a matter of administrative action, been granting leaves of absence to State employees for military or naval service, with the understanding, if possible, that the positions will be held open for them upon their return to civil life. This practice is not confined to persons who are brought into service through Selective Service Boards but would be equally applicable to those who volunteer for service in the armed forces of our country and would, of course, include women who may join the SPARS and other like agencies of the Government. I would not consider that the fact that the service was voluntary rather than through the Selective Service Boards would have any bearing on the subject.

STATE BOARD OF HEALTH; VENEREAL DISEASES; ISOLATION OF PATIENTS

18 November 1944

Receipt is acknowledged of your letter of November 17, in which you quote a regulation adopted by the State Board of Health under the authority of G. S. 130-176, with reference to the isolation of persons infected with a venereal disease, which regulation requires patients to be isolated if considered necessary by a local health or quarantine officer to prevent the spread of the disease in a hospital approved for the treatment of venereal diseases by the State Board of Health, when directed by the local health or quarantine officer.

You inquire as to whether or not it will be necessary to add to this regulation: "regardless of whether or not such hospital is located within the county where the patient resides." You state that this language might be needed in view of the fact that you have only two such hospitals at present."

I do not believe that it is necessary to add the language to the regulation, as the regulation now requires that the isolation be in a hospital approved for treatment of such diseases by your Board and is not confined to a hospital located in the county in which the person is found. I do not think that the language suggested would add anything to the value of the regulation.

MARRIAGE LICENSE ACT; VIOLATION BY REGISTER OF DEEDS; PROSECUTION

27 November 1944

Receipt is acknowledged of your letter of November 24, enclosing copies of letters from the Newport News Health Department, of Virginia, indicating that Mr. J. G. Etheridge, Register of Deeds in Camden County, issued a marriage license without complying with G. S. 51-9, which requires that the applicant shall present to the register of deeds a certificate executed within thirty days, etc., accompanied by the original report from a laboratory approved by the State Board of Health, etc.

A violation of this Act is made a misdemeanor by G. S. 51-13. I, therefore, suggest that the information should be sent by you to Honorable Chester Morris, Solicitor, Currituck, North Carolina, in order that he may determine what action should be taken in this matter.

MERIT SYSTEM COUNCIL; AUTHORITY OVER BONUS PLANS OR SYSTEMS FOR EMPLOYEES OF COUNTY, CITY AND DISTRICT HEALTH DEPARTMENTS

6 December 1944

You inquire of this office as follows:

"Does Section 126-14 of the General Statutes, known as the Merit System Law, authorize the Merit System Council to approve or disapprove bonus systems or plans as applicable to the compensation paid employees of district, county and city health units as well as local welfare boards?"

Section 126-14 of the General Statutes is as follows:

"The merit system council appointed under the provisions of this chapter shall have the authority to establish, maintain and provide rules and regulations, in cooperation with the state board of health and the state board of charities and public welfare, for the administration of a system of personnel standards on a merit rating system with a uniform schedule of compensation for all employees of the county welfare departments and the county, city, and district health departments."

Under this section, the Merit System council is authorized to estabish, maintain and provide rules and regulations, in cooperation with the State Board of Health and the State Board of Charities and Public Welfare for (1) the administration of a system of personnel standards, on a merit rating system, and (2) a uniform schedule of compensation for all employees of the above units. The power conferred by this section relates to the providing of rules and regulations for administration. The State Board of Health and the State Board of Charities and Public Welfare are to cooperate in the rules and regulations established and the compensation system provided must be of a uniform nature as to its schedules.

I am of the opinion that the bonus paid employees of one of these units comes within the definition and meaning of the word "compensation" and that the Merit System Council has the authority to establish by rules and regulations a uniform system or standards with respect to the payment of these bonuses and it follows, therefore, that the Merit System Council can accept or reject any bonus system or plan worked out by city or county authorities upon the grounds that it does not meet the regulations or standards established by the Merit System Council.

In the case of ROBERTS v. MILLS, 184 N. C. 406, page 410, the Supreme Court of North Carolina gives the following definition of a bonus:

"It is not a gift or gratuity, but a sum paid for services. or upon a consideration in addition to or in excess of that which would originally be given."

In this same case it is further stated:

"It has become a very general policy to offer a bonus or *additional compensation* to employees who shall render continuous and efficient service for a specified period of time. This is not a gratuity. or gift, but is an offer on the part of the employer, with whom the offer originates in order to procure efficient and faithful service and continuous employment. . . . ."

It would seem to me, therefore, that it would be the duty of the Merit System Council to set up a uniform system or plan dealing with the payment of bonuses to the employees of these units or to set up reasonable and sufficient standards with which bonus systems or plans of local units would have to comply, and then if such a system is offered by the financial authorities of the local units, to approve or reject this system. Such a bonus system or standard must have uniformity that is required by statute and when distinctions or classifications are made between different groups of employees, there must be a reasonable basis for such distinctions and classifications, and such a system should provide that bonuses should be paid without distinction or discrimination to all persons or employees composing a described class. If a bonus system is submitted by the financial agents of local units, such as counties, cities and towns, and meets the standards or regulations of the Merit System Council, then the Council should approve such a system to the end that it would thereby become a uniform schedule of compensation as provided by the regulations of the Council. In other words, the Council should then by official action make it a part of its own system of regulations as applied to the units in question.

I do not think that the Merit System Council has any right to pass any regulations or standards or in any way control the action of the officials of counties, cities and towns as to any bonus or bonus system provided for employees in other city or county departments. The statutory jurisdiction of the Merit System Council only extends to the agencies and departments named in the statute, and I know of no rule of law or statutory provision that would give the Merit System Council the right to interfere with, approve or disapprove, any form of compensation paid to employees not connected with county, city and district health departments.

I have before me your proposed letter addressed to Dr. Frank T. de Vyver, Merit System Supervisor, and your request for Council action. I note that in your description of the bonus plan you provide that such a system or plan shall cover all employees of all city and county departments. I doubt very much if the Merit System Council has the authority to incorporate this requirement into their regulations or standards, as it seems to me that this would be going beyond the statutory powers conferred upon the Council, and would be an attempt to do indirectly what the Council cannot do directly.

STATE BOARD OF HEALTH; PUBLICATION OF RULES AND REGULATIONS; FILING
WITH SECRETARY OF STATE

4 January 1945

I reply to your letter of January 2, 1945, with reference to your revision of the rules and regulations of the State Board of Health.

You state that under Section 130-176 of the General Statutes you are required to publish the regulations of the State Board of Health in a bulletin. You further state that you have now adopted a revision of all rules and regulations and this has resulted in a large volume of material. You inquire as to whether or not it would be a compliance with the statute to publish this material as a supplement to the North Carolina State Board of Health bulletin, with an entry of this fact in the minutes; you also inquire as to your right to leave off the heading of the bulletin on this pamphlet, and the necessity of sending a copy of the supplement to each of the sixty thousand subscribers of the bulletin.

In our opinion, you should give notice in a regular issue of the bulletin that a pamphlet containing the revised rules and regulations is available and will be furnished to any subscriber upon written application for same. You also have the right to have this revision printed as a supplement to the bulletin and you need not have the regular bulletin heading printed on the supplement. - Section 130-176 of the General Statutes, referred to by you, in my opinion does not in express terms require you to publish a complete recodification or revision of all your rules and regulations in the bulletin. I think that this statute contemplates that you publish each rule or regulation, or amendment thereto, as these rules and regulations and amendments are passed from time to time by the Board of Health. It would be safer, and it would be a substantial compliance with the statute, for you to give notice in the bulletin that a complete revision is available in supplement form and will be furnished on written request. If you do this, I think your Department will be free from criticism on legal grounds.

Your attention is also called to Section 143-195 of the General Statutes, which requires all regulatory and administrative departments of this State to file a complete copy of all rules and regulations with the Secretary of State. This copy should be certified by the Secretary of your Board as being a true and correct copy, and you should also file with the Secretary of State each new rule or regulation, or amendment thereto, as the same is from time to time passed and promulgated by your Board.

PUBLIC HEALTH; H. B. No. 316; EFFECTIVE DATE OF ACT RELATING TO IMMUNIZATION AGAINST WHOOPING COUGH

30 March 1945

In your letter of March 28, 1945, you refer to Article 16-a, Section 130-190.1, of the General Statutes of North Carolina, and you inquire of this office if the enforcement of this Act as to the school requirement should be delayed until 1951, or if a proper construction of the Act requires that all children entering school at the present time must show a proper certificate of immunization against whooping cough.

Subsection (1) of the Act requires all children to be immunized against whooping cough before reaching the age of one year. Subsection (2) requires that any child not previously immunized must be presented to a licensed physician for such immunization. Subsection (3) provides for immunization by the county health officer or county physician for those persons unable to pay for the services of a private physician. Subsection (4) requires the physician administering the doses to submit a certificate to the local health officer with a copy to the parents.

Subsection (5) is as follows:

> "No principal or teacher shall permit *any child* to enter a public, private or parochial school without the certificate provided for in subsection (4), or some other acceptable evidence of immunization against whooping cough." (Italics ours.)

I am of the opinion, however, that the first four subsections of the Act deal with the immunization of children before reaching the age of one year. The expression "such child" appears in Subsection (2) and all of the processes of immunization in the first four subsections seem to be related and to refer to children under one year of age.

I am of the opinion, however, that Subsection (5), which I quoted above, applies to any child entering a public, private or parochial school and, therefore, this subsection is applicable to children now entering school and above one year of age. In other words, this subsection is applicable to all children, entering school at the present time; therefore, no principal or teacher should permit any child to enter the schools described in this subsection without the certificate of immunization. The reference to Subsection (4) in Subsection (5) is merely descriptive of the certificate required. You will note also that the last clause of Subsection (5) permits children to enter the schools upon some other acceptable evidence of immunization against whooping cough. I am of the opinion, therefore, that under this clause certificates or other acceptable evidence of immunization from other states could be accepted and further, that you could provide suitable rules and regulations whereby a principal or teacher could permit a child to attend school upon proper evidence that the child was immune by reason of having had the disease or for any other pertinent reasons that you might see fit to establish by such a policy or regulation.

The section referred to in your letter was declared by the Legislature to be in full force and effect from and after its ratification, and as stated above, it is our opinion that it is now effective as to those children entering school at this time.

PUBLIC HEALTH; APPOINTMENT OF COUNTY HEALTH OFFICERS AS DEPUTY STATE HEALTH OFFICERS; REVOCATION OF APPOINTMENT

4 April 1945

Complying with your request as contained in your letter of March 31, 1945, I am enclosing you a suggested form to be used in revoking the authority heretofore conferred upon local health officers for the purpose of acting as deputy State health officers in the control of communicable diseases.

Of course, I do not contend that you should necessarily use the words in my form, but I think your order of revocation should contain something in substance as set forth in the suggested form.

VITAL STATISTICS; CHANGE OF NAME ON BIRTH CERTIFICATE; CHILD BORN IN WEDLOCK PRESUMED TO BE LEGITIMATE

12 April 1945

I acknowledge receipt of your letter enclosing a copy of a letter from Messrs. McDougle and Ervin, Attorneys at Law, Charlotte, in which they take issue with an opinion expressed by this office relating to the change of the name appearing on a birth certificate, and inquiring as to whether or not this office took into consideration Section 130-94 of the General Statutes when the opinion was written.

I understand the facts in the instant case substantially to be that the mother of the child was married at the time of its birth but had been living separate and part from her husband for a considerable length of time and obtained a divorce from her husband and married another man whom she now claims to be the actual father of her child, notwithstanding the fact in reporting the birth of the child to the registrar she stated that the father of the child was her first husband. I understand that it is the desire of the mother and the present husband that the name of the child appearing on the birth certificate be changed so as to bear the name of the present husband.

In expressing the opinion to your office dated February 2, 1945, to which exception is taken by the attorneys in this case, this office had in mind Section 130-94 G. S. and wrote the opinion in the light of that section as construed by the office.

I know of no provisions in this section to change the name on the birth certificate upon the filing of affidavits with your department. The section specifically provides that, "No certificate of birth or death, after its acceptance for registration by the local registrar, and no other record made in pursuance of this article, shall be altered or changed in any respect otherwise than by amendments properly dated, signed, and witnessed." I cannot construe this to mean that you have authority to amend the birth certificate merely upon the filing of an affidavit. It seems to me that the statute contemplates that the amendment would be in the form of an amendment furnished by one of the officials authorized to issue birth certificates and I am strongly of the opinion that you would not have the authority to change the name on a birth certificate of a child born in wedlock to that of a man whom the mother later marries after having obtained a divorce from the man who was her husband at the time of the conception. or birth of the child. It is a well known principle of law that legitimacy of a child born in lawful wedlock is presumed, WEST v. REDOMOD, 171 N. C. 742. Under the circumstances of this case, there is a strong presumption that the first husband of the mother of the child is its father and in view of such presumption I do not think that you would have authority to change the name of the child upon the filing of affidavits.

It may be that the attorneys have in mind that a new certificate of birth could be issued under authority of paragraph (a) of Section 130-94, which states the conditions upon which a new certificate might be issued. This Subsection reads, "(a) Proof is submitted to the State Registrar that the previously unwed parents of a person have intermarried subsequent to the birth of such person." It does not occur to me that the facts of the instant case come within the purview of this provision for the mother was wed at the time of the conception and birth of the child to a person who is presumed by law to be its father.

As suggested in our previous letters, I am of the opinion that it would be necessary to obtain a court order under the provisions of Section 130-94 specifically authorizing you to amend the birth certificate or to issue a new one before doing so. Such a court order could be obtained in an adoption or some other similar proceeding.

STATE BOARD OF HEALTH; STATUTES; EFFECT OF TWO STATUTES ON THE SAME SUBJECT MATTER PASSED AT THE SAME SESSION; APPOINTMENT OF MEMBERS OF BOARD OF HEALTH OF LOCAL UNITS

17 April 1945

In your letter of April 17, 1945, you call our attention to House Bill 116, passed at the last Session of the General Assembly, and ratified on February

9, 1945. You also call our attention to House Bill 321, which was passed at the last Session of the General Assembly, and ratified on the 21st day of March, 1945.

Both of these bills have the same objective in regard to the registered pharmacists of the State; that is, both bills provide for the appointment of a registered pharmacist as a member of the County Board of Health. These two bills, however, are repugnant and inconsistent with each other as to the time when a meeting shall be held for the appointment or election of members of the County Board of Health, including the appointment of the pharmacists heretofore mentioned. In your letter, you inquire of this office as to which bill should be followed in making these appointments. That is, should the appointments be made under House Bill 116 or under House Bill 321? You inquire generally as to the validity of one bill over the other.

House Bill 116 in its language rewrote the first sentence of Section 130-18 of the General Statutes of North Carolina, so that the first sentence as rewritten reads as follows:

> "The chairman of the board of county commissioners, the mayor of the county town, and in county towns where there is no mayor the clerk of the superior court, and the county superintendent of schools shall meet together on the first Monday in April, one thousand nine hundred and thirty-one, and thereafter on the first Monday of January in the odd years of the calendar, and elect from the regularly registered physicians and dentists or pharmacists of the county two physicians and one dentist or pharmacist, who, with themselves, shall constitute the county board of health."

House Bill 321 deals with other things including the method of appointment of members of district boards of health and county boards of health. In this same bill, Section 130-18 of the General Statutes of North Carolina is completely rewritten, and a definite method of appointment of members of the County Board of Health is provided, including, however, in the appointments a registered pharmacist. That portion of the bill relating to the time of meeting and appointment of members is as follows:

> "The first meeting of the ex-officio members for the election or appointment of public members shall be in the first week in January, one thousand nine hundred and forty-six, and at this meeting one of the public members shall be elected or appointed for a period of four years, one for three years, one for two years, and one for one year; thereafter one member shall be elected each year for a term of four years; . . ."

A registered pharmacist is included in the public members that must be appointed by these ex officio members. As heretofore stated, this bill was ratified the 21st day of March, 1945, while the first bill was ratified on February 9, 1945.

First of all I would like to call your attention to the fact that House Bill 116 in rewriting the first sentence of Section 130-18 of the General Statutes provided for the appointment of a pharmacist and specifically provided that the meeting for making these appointments shall be on the first Monday of January in the odd years of the calendar. The year of 1945 is, of course, an odd year and, therefore, when this law was ratified on February

9, 1945, the first Monday in January in 1945 had already passed in point of time; and under this Act, no appointment of a registered pharmacist could therefore be made on the first Monday in January, 1945. Under House Bill 116, if it is the law and effective, the earliest date on which a registered pharmacist could be appointed on the County Board of Health would be the next odd year or the first Monday in January, 1947. I say this because there is no machinery provided in the Act and there are no words whatsoever providing for a retrospective or retroactive construction of the Act. The Act simply contains a general repealing clause and says that it shall be in full force and effect from and after its ratification.

It is a general law that statutes are to be construed as being prospective in their effect unless the language of a statute clearly and emphatically shows that a retroactive construction or application is intended. In the case of COMMISSIONERS v. BLUE, 190 N. C., at p. 643, our Supreme Court said:

> "There is always a presumption that statutes are intended to operate prospectively only, and words ought not to have a retrospective operation unless they are so clear, strong and imperative that no other meaning can be annexed to them, or unless the intention of the Legislature cannot be otherwise satisfied. Every reasonable doubt is resolved against a retroactive operation of the statute. If all the language of a statute can be satisfied by giving it prospective action, only that construction will be given."

I think it is clear, therefore, that even if we should consider House Bill 116 to be an effective Act, then the earliest time which an appointment could be made which would include a registered pharmacist would be on the first Monday of January, 1947, which is the first odd year since the effective date of the statute.

When we consider House Bill 321, we find, as has already been pointed out, that it is the last expression of the Legislature, having been ratified on the 21st day of March, 1945. While it is true that all acts of the same session of the Legislature upon the same subject matter are to be considered as one act, and must be considered together, under the doctrine of "in pari materia," nevertheless, there are certain exceptions to the rule of statutory construction and these exceptions when they appear must also be followed. In discussing this rule, the Supreme Court of our State in the case of BRAMHAM v. DURHAM, 171 N. C., at p. 198, said:

> "It is a well recognized principle of statutory construction that when there are two acts of the Legislature applicable to the same subject, their provisions are to be reconciled if this can be done by fair and reasonable intendment; but, to the extent that they are necessarily repugnant, the later shall prevail. The position is stated in substantially these terms by Associate Justice Field in U. S. v. TYNEN, 78 U. S., 92 as follows: 'Where there are two acts on the same subject, the rule is to give effect to both, if possible; but if the two are repugnant in any of their provisions, the latter act, and without any repealing clause, operates to the extent of the repugnancy as a repeal of the first'; and in SEDGWICK on STATUTORY CONSTRUCTION, p. 125. quoting from ELY v. BLISS. 5 BEAVAN. it is said: 'If two inconsistent acts be passed at different times, the last is to be obeyed. and if obedience cannot be observed without derogation from the first, it is the first that must give way'."

In addition to the above quoted authority, it should also be stated that House Bill 321 rewrites other sections of the public health law, including the section which is the subject of House Bill 116. As heretofore pointed out, House Bill 321 rewrites all of Section 130-18 of the General Statutes, while House Bill 116 only rewrites the first sentence of that section. When the Legislature passed House Bill 321, it is assumed, and, in fact, there is regular authority for the position, that it is fixed with knowledge of what it had theretofore done in passing House Bill 116; and furthermore, it is also a rule of statutory construction that where a later act revises and rewrites a complete section of a statute or several complete sections, that it operates as a repeal of former statutes relating to the same subject matter. In 59 C.J., p. 919, Section 520 bb., it is said:

> "Where a later act covers the old subject of earlier acts, embraces new provisions, and plainly shows that it was intended, not only as a substitute for the earlier acts, but to cover the old subjects then considered by the Legislature, and to procure the only rules in respect thereto, it operates as a repeal of all former statutes relating to such subject matter. The rule applies not only where the former acts are inconsistent or in conflict with the new act, but also even where the former acts are not necessarily repugnant in express terms, or in all respects, to the new act."

Our Supreme Court has recognized this same principle in the case of WINSLOW v. MORTON, 118 N. C., at p. 491, where it is said:

> "Where a later or revising statute clearly covers the old subject matter of antecedent acts, and it plainly appears to have been the purpose of the Legislature to give expression in it to the whole law on the subject, the latter is held to be repealed by necessary implication."

I am of the opinion, therefore, that House Bill 321, which rewrites all of Section 130-18 of the General Statutes and which is the latest expression of the Legislature on the subject, is the statute under which appointments to the County Board of Health must be made. It should be followed by the officials concerned in making these appointments and the time for making these appointments as expressed in this statute should be in the first week in January, 1946. I think, irrespective of the legal technicalities, that this is also the most favorable construction from the point of view of the North Carolina Pharmaceutical Association, for you will observe that this will place a registered pharmacist on the County Board of Health in January, 1946; whereas, under House Bill 116, sponsored by the Association, it could only hope to place a member on the County Board of Health by the first Monday in January, 1947, which is the first odd year on which a meeting could be held for that purpose. In this connection, attention is also called to the fact that under House Bill 321, provision is made for the appointment of a registered pharmacist on district boards of Health and this was not true of House Bill 116.

It follows from what I have already said that House Bill 116 should be disregarded and House Bill 321 should be followed in all respects.

Public Health; Necessity of Oath of Office for Health Officer and Quarantine Officer; Time of Administering Oath of Office

.. : 9 May 1945

In your letter of May 4, 1945, you call attention to Section 130-169 of the General Statutes, dealing with the oath of office of quarantine officers and health officers acting as quarantine officers. You would like to know if this oath of office should be taken and a certificate submitted to your office each time a health officer is reelected. You call attention to the fact that quarantine officers are elected every four years and health officers are elected every two years, and you ask if it will be proper to have quarantine officers to submit certificates of having taken the required oath every four years and to require this of health officers every two years. In your closing paragraph you ask what would be the situation if a health officer discontinued his position for a period of time and was then reelected.

Under Section 130-168 of the General Statutes, the position of quarantine officer is provided for and his term of office is fixed at four years. It is also provided in the same section that the county health officer may perform the duties of quarantine officer upon making the official oath required, and in such case the office of county quarantine officer shall be coterminous with the office of the county health officer. Section 130-169 of the General Statutes provides for the oath of the quarantine officer and for the certification of the official oath to your office.

Section 130-121 of the General Statutes provides for the election of a county health officer and fixes his term of office at two years. You will recall that I had a conversation with you about the matter of the requirement as to health officers taking an oath of office and I stated to you at that time that I did not find anywhere in the statute any requirement that the health officer must take an oath of office, and I believe it was further stated by a member of your staff that it was not the custom for health officers to take an oath as to the performance of their duties. I have discussed this matter with the members of our office and they have called to my attention Article VI, Section 7, of the Constitution of North Carolina which, among other things, provides as follows:

"Every voter in North Carolina, except as in this article is disqualified, shall be eligible to office, but before entering upon the duties of the office he shall take and subscribe the following oath:" (then follows the oath to support the Constitution of the United States, the Constitution and laws of North Carolina, and to faithfully discharge the duies of office).

It is my opinion, therefore, that under this provision of the Constitution of our State you should require your health officers to take the oath of office. I am further of the opinion that it is necessary for your health officer to also take the prescribed statutory oath of office as quarantine officer where he performs the duties of both positions, and that this oath must be taken each time such health officer is reelected and enters upon the duties of a new term of office. The same thing would apply where you have a quarantine officer performing such duties separate and apart from the health officer. Such individual quarantine officer who is not a health officer should submit his oath of office as required by the statute every four years, no matter how many times he is reelected. If the health officer is also the quarantine officer, I think he should submit both oaths every two years,—that is, his oath as health officer and his oath as quarantine officer, and this should be done, no matter how many times he is reelected and regardless of the number of terms of office.

As to the question in the last paragraph of your letter, if the health officer discontinued his position for a period—I assume that you mean by discontinuance that he has resigned or withdrawn from the service—then upon reappointment or reelection, he would be required to repeat the oath, both of his office and that of the quarantine officer if he was serving in both capacities.

An oath of office only extends and is only applicable to the term of office for which it is administered and new terms of office, no matter if held by the same individual, require the administration of new oaths, as such oaths must be applicable to the duties and acts of the officer for the term in which he is serving. It follows that the obligations of all oaths of office expire with the term of office and likewise they relate to the term of office and not to the individual who may hold only one term or several terms. I would, therefore, advise you to require an oath of office for your health officers and for your quarantine officers beginning with each new term of office, and where the duties of health officer and quarantine officer are combined in the health officer, then he should submit an oath as to his duties as health officer and an oath also as to his duties as quarantine officer for each respective term of office.

VITAL STATISTICS; CONTENTS OF BIRTH CERTIFICATE AS TO ILLEGITIMATE
CHILD; INFORMATION AS TO NAME OF FATHER OR MOTHER

In your letter of May 4, 1945, you call attention to paragraphs 6 and 8 of Section 130-89 of the General Statutes with reference to the contents of a birth certificate of an illegitimate child and especially those items relating to the name of the father and mother. You also enclose a copy of a letter from Dr. W. W. Johnston in which he questions the authority of a physician to give any identifying data on a certificate for an illegitimate child, and it is noted also that Dr. Winston of the State Board of Public Welfare has given some interpretation of the question involved.

Paragraph 6 of Section 130-89 of the General Statutes provides in substance that the word "illegitimate" shall be written across the face of the certificate and "all items on the certificate which would in any way reveal the identity of the father, mother, or illegitimate child itself shall be omitted."

Paragraph 8 of this same section provides that if a child is illegitimate the name of the putative father shall not be entered without his consent but that the particulars contained in paragraphs 9 through 13 as to the putative father may be entered if known and otherwise an entry is made as "unknown." The items contained in paragraphs 9 through 13 are general and relate to the age, birthplace, residence, color and educational attainments of the father.

It should be generally stated as a matter of statutory construction that where there are two statutes on the same subject, or on related subjects, which are apparently in conflict with each other, they are to be reconciled, by construction, so far as may be, on any fair hypothesis, and validity and effect given to both, if this can be done without destroying the intent and meaning of the statute. In the case of BOARD OF AGRICULTURE v. DRAINAGE DISTRICT, 177 N. C. 222, at page 226, the Court quotes from Black's Interpretation of Laws, and says:

> "It is not permissible, if it can be reasonably avioded, to put such a construction upon a law as will raise a conflict between different parts of it, but effect should be given to each and every clause and provision. But when there is no way of reconciling conflicting clauses of a statute and nothing to indicate which the Legislature regarded as of paramount importance, force should be given to those clauses which would make the statute in harmony with the other legislation on the same subject, and which would tend most completely to secure the rights of all persons affected by such legislation."

Along this same subject, it is stated in the case of CECIL v. HIGH POINT, 165 N. C. 431, at page 434, as follows:

> "It is well understood that the law should be construed so as to harmonize the different portions, giving each and every part some significance, if this can be done by fair and reasonable interpretation, and further, that when a statute expresses first a general intent and afterwards an inconsistent particular intent, the latter shall be taken as an exception of the former, and both shall stand."

I do not think that there is any necessary conflict between paragraph 6 and paragraph 8 of this section. You will note in Section 130-86 that it is the duty of the physician, midwife or person acting as midwife to file the required certificate with certain exceptions relating to the situation where such persons are not in attendance when the birth occurs, and that when this information cannot be obtained by diligent inquiry, that the local registrar can secure the information from any person who knows the facts, and it is the duty of the person questioned to answer correctly to the best of his knowledge all such questions and to verify his statement by his signature when requested to do so by the local registrar.

I think, therefore, that the object of paragraph 6 was to prevent the local registrar from compelling any person to give this information as to an illegitimate child, as most persons do not wish to be drawn into a controversy regarding the father of an illegitimate child. I do not find in the vital statistics law where birth certificates are considered as prima facie evidence on the issue of the father of an illegitimate child, and it was evidently the intention of the Legislature to keep the Bureau of Vital Statistics and its officials out of such litigation or bastardy proceedings.

It is also clear to me that the information as to the putative father required by paragraph 8 is an exception to the rule laid down in paragraph 6, and it is considered further that this information should not be construed as information which reveals the identity of the father. Of course, if the father consents, his name can be entered on the birth certificate. You will note that the information contained in paragraphs 9 through 13 is very general in nature and does not necessarily lead to his identity if, in fact, it does at all. If this information is already known to local officials or can be readily ascertained, it was the intention of the statute that the information should be reported, but the local officials cannot compel people to answer as to such questions. This information,—that is, the information in paragraphs 9 through 13—is not entirely worthless, as the officials of the Bureau of Vital Statistics, by the use of this information, can in many instances assist citizens of this State in perfecting and obtaining birth certificates, and especially in those cases where delayed birth certificates are involved. The information is a beginning point when any search for information is required.

I am of the opinion, therefore, that these two statutes should be construed together and that they are not by any means inconsistent, nor is there any conflict between them, and that the information required by paragraphs 9 through 13 should be furnished by the persons named in Section 130-86 of the General Statutes when such information is known or can be reasonably obtained without resorting to any of the compulsive features. There is no reason why the information in paragraphs 9 through 13 should not be furnished as the persons furnishing the information or signing the certificates are acting under a valid statute and are protected from legal liability both civil and criminal when honestly performing their duties. The only thing they cannot do is to enter the name of the father unless he specifically consents thereto.

SANITARY INSPECTIONS; EFFECT OF REPEAL OF SECTION 72-8 BY HOUSE BILL
No. 229 ON DUTY OF STATE BOARD OF HEALTH TO INSPECT PUBLIC
INSTITUTIONS UNDER G. S. 130-3

14 May 1945

In your letter of April 28, you inquire as to whether House Bill No. 229, ratified by the General Assembly March 19, 1945, in any way affected the duty and authority to inspect public institutions imposed upon the State Board of Health by Section 130-3 of the General Statutes.

I have carefully read House Bill No. 229 and I can find nothing in the Act which repeals or amends Section 130-3 of the General Statutes.

Section 72-8, which was repealed by House Bill No. 229, was simply complementary to Section 130-3 and its repeal does not affect the provisions of the latter statute.

In my opinion, you are charged with the duty and have ample authority under the provisions of Section 130-3 to make sanitary inspections of public institutions.

PUBLIC HEALTH; VENEREAL DISEASES; RIGHT TO EXAMINE PERSONS
SUSPECTED OF BEING INFECTED WITH VENEREAL DISEASE

25 May 1945

In your letter of May 24, 1945 you refer to Section 130-206 of the General Statutes and inquire if health authorities or health officers have the right to compel an examination of persons reasonably suspected of being infected with a venereal disease.

The section mentioned in your letter specifically gives the health officials the following powers.

1. To make examinations of persons reasonably suspected of being infected with venereal disease.
2. To detain such persons until the results of the examination are known.
3. To require persons infected with venereal disease to report for treatment to a reputable physician and to continue treatment until cured.
4. When adjudged to be necessary to protect public health, to isolate or quarantine persons infected with venereal disease.
5. It is the duty of all local and State health officials to investigate sources of infection of venereal disease.
6. To cooperate with officers to enforce laws against prostitution.

It is noted that other states have comparable provisions in their health laws and the specific right and authority of health officials to interfere with the liberty of individuals in these respects has been upheld as being constitutional and valid and a proper exercise of the police power of the state for the prevention of disease and as an essential protection to public health. In exercising the power of compelling an examination, the health officials should act upon reasonable information,—that is, the person must be reasonably suspected of being infected with a venereal disease. If the patient is being treated for a venereal disease and he names another person with whom he had relations as the possible source of infection, then I think the courts would say that this is reasonable grounds upon which the health official can proceed in making the investigation and compelling the examination. Of course, a person should not be compelled to submit to an examination upon mere gossip or community rumor. There is a definite type of communication or information that any reasonable person will recognize as being sufficient to authorize action. Any construction of this Act which would not permit a health officer to compel an examination of a person reasonably suspected would nullify the whole venereal disease program. The health authorities then would have their activities limited to the treatment of the known cases, and all efforts to stamp out the source of infection would be in vain.

CRIMINAL LAW; PROSTITUTION AND ASSIGNATION; CRIMINAL LIABILITY OF OWNERS OR MANAGERS OF BUILDINGS USED FOR PROSTITUTION AND ASSIGNATION; AIDING AND ABETTING

11 June 1945

In your letter of June 8, 1945, you state as follows:

"'The following situation has arisen in one city in the state. Certain hotels are used for immoral purposes. Whenever an unmarried couple come to the hotel they are allowed to register. The police department is then tipped off and within a short time the couple is arrested and subsequently tried in court. No action is taken against the hotel which allows this to go on."

Prostitution is defined in Section 14-203 of the General Statutes, and in this same section the term "assignation" is construed to include the making of an appointment or an engagement for prostitution, or an act in furtherance of such agreement or engagement. In Section 14-204 of the General Statutes various acts abetting prostitution are declared to be unlawful, and I quo.e the paragraphs of this section as follows:

"It shall be unlawful:

"1. To keep, set up, maintain, or operate any place, structure, building or conveyance for the purpose of prostitution or assignation.

"2. To occupy any place, structure, building, or conveyance for the purpose of prostitution, or assignation; or for any person to permit any place, structure, building or conveyance owned by him or under his control to be used for the purpose of prostitution or assignation, with knowledge or reasonable cause to know that the same is, or is to be, used for such purpose.

"3. To receive, or to offer or agree to receive any person into any place, structure, building, or conveyance for the purpose of prostitution or assignation, or to permit any person to remain there for such purpose.

"4. To direct, take, or transport, or to offer or agree to take or transport, any person to any place, structure, or building or to any other person, with knowledge or reasonable cause to know that the purpose of such directing, taking, or transporting is prostitution or assignation.

"5. To procure or to solicit, or to offer to procure or solicit for the purpose of prostitution or assignation.

"6. To reside in, enter, or remain in any place, structure, or building, or to enter or remain in any conveyance for the purpose of prostitution or assignation.

"7. To engage in prostitution or assignation, or to aid or abet prostitution or assignation by any means whatsoever."

It is, therefore, plain to me that the managers or operators of any hotel who permit the hotel structure to be used as a place of assignation, or for the purpose of prostitution, or to receive any person or persons in such hotel for these purposes, or permit any person to remain there for such purposes would be guilty of a violation of the criminal law. You will also notice in the last paragraph of the section that it is unlawful to aid and abet prostitution or assignation by any means whatsoever.

Under the facts set forth in your letter, however, it is extremely doubtful if the managers or operators of the hotel in question would be indictable under the criminal law relating to prostitution as above set forth. It seems to me that this hotel is cooperating with the police department, and that the managers or operators of the hotel are not actually receiving persons in the hotel for the purpose of actually carrying through acts of prostitution or assignation, or for the purpose of aiding and abetting in the crimes of prostitution or assignation. In fact, it would seem that they receive these persons for the contrary reason of turning them over to the police department and thus in a measure prevent prostitution and assignation. While it is true that this amounts to a method or form of entrapment which is not looked on with favor by the general public and by normal people, nevertheless, I am compelled to say that under these circumstances there would not be an intentional violation of these acts, and under such circumstances the prosecuting authorities would have the right to take the position that no charges should be preferred against the managers or operators of the hotel. It is a very common thing to use plain clotnes detectives, spies, and agents provocateurs in the suppression of crime.

I am of the opinion, therefore, that unless the hotel operator has a place of assignation and of receiving persons for the purpose of violating the law on prostitution, and does this entirely independent of any agreement or understanding with the police department, the operators or managers would not be guilty of any violation of the criminal law, and in such cases I do not think that prosecution would be in order unless you could prove that he was operating for such purposes independent of any agreement with the police department, or that he merely turned over certain percentages of such persons to the police department and allowed a certain privileged group to use the hotel for such purposes without reporting to the police department. I might add that in the enforcement of the so-called May Act that such agreements exist between the hotels and the authorities in most every case.

PUBLIC HEALTH; GRANTS OF FEDERAL FUNDS TO STATES FOR CONTROL OF TUBERCULOSIS; TITLE TO PROPERTY PURCHASED BY FEDERAL FUNDS; LIABILITY OF STATE FOR NEGLIGENCE OF DRIVER OF MOBILE-UNIT

13 June 1945

In your letter to this office, you call our attention to Section 314 B of the Public Health Service Act, same being Chapter 373, Public Law 410, which was approved July 1, 1944. The specific paragraph mentioned in your letter authorizes the Surgeon General of the United States to use Federal funds in the form of grants in aid to the States, counties and other political subdivisions of States for preventing, treating, and controlling tuberculosis. You further state that part of these funds allotted to North Carolina have been used to purchase mobile x-ray units, which units are installed in and transported by large buses. You ask this office the following questions:

1. Does the title to these buses remain in the United States Public Health Service or are these buses State property with the title vested in the State Board of Health?

2. Assuming that the State does not carry liability insurance on State-owned vehicles, you ask what protection, if any, the driver of such vehicle would be afforded in case of accident.

I am of the opinion that these funds granted to the State by the Federal Government when received in this State become State funds for the designated purposes as contained in the plan or agreement entered into between your department and the Federal Government. The property purchased by these funds belongs to the State and the title to the property, in my opinion, is vested in your agency, the State Board of Health. For a long time there has been contention on the part of the Federal Government that where grants in aid are made to the States and property is purchased by the State in carrying out the purposes for which the grants are made, if the property is devoted to some other purpose than that agreed upon in the plan or agreement between the State and the Government, the Federal Government, even though the State has title to the property, nevertheless the appropriate

agency of the Federal Government in a given case, has the right to supervise and follow the property to the extent of seeing that the property is used
for the purposes for which the money was originally granted. I do not
think, however, that this authority has been tested out in any court, but I
thought I should call this angle of the matter to your attention.

As to your second question, it has been held in many cases that the State
of North Carolina and its agencies are not liable and do not have to respond
in damages because of the injury of any person or property by reason of the
operation of State-owned vehicles and other instrumentalities used by the
State for governmental purposes. I am advised that it has never been the
policy of the State generally to carry liability insurance on State-owned
motor vehicles. You, of course, are familiar with the fact that the employees of the State are covered under the Workmen's Compensation Law
and, therefore, any injury that a driver of such a vehicle receives, which
injury arises out of and in the course of his State employment, would be
compensated for through the instrumentality of that agency.

If a driver of a mobile unit is guilty of negligence and such negligence is
the proximate cause of injury to person or property, the driver himself
would be responsible, personally, for the damages caused by such negligence.
This is expressly held by the Supreme Court of this State in the case of
Miller v. Jones, 224 N. C. 783, where the Court said:

> "The mere fact that a person charged with negligence is an employee
> of others to whom immunity from liability is extended on grounds of
> public policy, does not thereby excuse him from liability for negligence
> in the manner in which his duties are performed, or for performing a
> lawful act in an unlawful manner. The authorities generally hold the
> employee individually liable for negligence in the performance of
> his duties, notwithstanding the immunity of an employer, although
> such negligence may not be imputed to the employer on the principle
> of a *repondeat superior*, when such employer is clothed with govern-
> mental immunity under the rule."

I cannot find any authority in law that would justify the State Board of
Health in carrying personal policies of insurance to protect the drivers of
such mobile units against any liability which they may have personally
because of their own negligence in operating such mobile unit. I do not
think your agency would be authorized in carrying such insurance. If the
driver is personally negligent he ought to be personally responsible in
damages or injuring property or the person of any member of the public.
The personal risk that the driver may be exposed to because of his work
for the State is a hazard or risk common to all people in the pursuit of their
occupations whereby they earn their livelihood and this risk exists for all
people in life whether they work for themselves, a private agency, or a public
agency. The remedy of the driver in such a case is to carry his own liability
insurance. If there are any further questions along this same general
subject, please let us know.

VITAL STATISTICS; BIRTH CERTIFICATES; AMENDING AND PERFECTING; APPLICATION OF TERM "COURT OF COMPETENT JURISDICTION"

11 October 1945

In your letter of October 8, 1945, you call attention to Section 130-94 of the General Statutes which authorizes certain changes in records or certificates of births. You particularly call attention to the terms "the clerk of a court of competent jurisdiction." You would like to know whether or not this term or phraseology includes only courts in North Carolina or if it also includes any court outside the State. The terms or phraseology to which you refer appear in sub-section (b) and you will note also that the words "court of competent jurisdiction" also appear in sub-section (c) of this Section. Both sub-sections deal with the amendment or changing of a birth certificate because of the fact that a judgment, order or decree has been entered by a court of competent jurisdiction disclosing different or additional information relating to the parentage of a person.

Of course these terms within themselves are broad enough to include or bring within their scope an order or judgment affecting the parentage of a person entered by a court of competent jurisdiction anywhere in the nation. I think, however, that these terms must be interpreted and their purpose determined by reference to all of our laws on the subject of vital statistics. The general outline of our system shows that the system is clearly intended to operate in the State of North Carolina and to be so administered. The Statutes dealing with vital statistics do not include any expressed terms in recognition of other systems established in other States. Our law applies to the birth of every child born in this State and it is my thought that in amending or perfecting these birth certificates you are required to take notice of any additional information relating to the parentage of a person as established by the courts of competent jurisdiction in the State of North Carolina and not the decrees and orders entered in courts in other States. I cannot believe that the legislature intended that you and your staff should pass upon the legal technicalities that might be involved as to whether a judgmnt or decree in a court in another State was entered by a court of competent jurisdiction in that State and whether the court in that State actually had jurisdiction over the subject matter of the action in which the judgment, order or decree was entered. It seems to me that if you want to recognize the official acts of other States as affecting birth certificates recorded in this State that there should be express enabling legislation for this purpose and an agreement among the States as to standard forms and methods of proof.

STATE EMPLOYEES; WITNESSES; ATTENDANCE UPON COURT UNDER SUBPOENA; BIRTH CERTIFICATES; CERTIFIED COPIES AS PRIMA FACIE EVIDENCE

8 October 1945

I reply to your letter of October 3, 1945, in which you state that several requests have been made recently for one of the employees of the Vital Statistics Bureau to appear in person at the Wake County Court to testify that certain certified copies of birth certificates were true copies. You further state that you do not receive such requests from other counties and you inquire if it would be possible for you to refuse such requests in the future and let the certified copies serve as the only evidence to be used in the case. You also further state that the attendance of these employees upon the courts means a considerable loss of time on the part of these persons and this loss of time has become a serious problem.

I don't know of any statute or law that relieves state employees from being witnesses in court provided they are served by proper order of the court in the form of a subpoena. The law specifically says that every witness summoned to appear in any of the courts shall appear accordingly and continue to attend from term to term until discharged. In criminal cases the witness must attend until discharged by the court or the prosecuting officer, or the party at whose instance he was summoned. Disobedience as to this subpoena in criminal cases subjects the witness to a forfeiture of $80.00. In a civil case the forfeiture is $40.00. In criminal cases a witness, who has been duly summoned and who fails to appear can be arrested under a capias ad testificandum.

It is provided by Section 8-61 of the General Statutes that the court has the power to issue a subpoena duces tecum for the production of any original papers lodged in any of the public offices of the state, and the person in whose custody the paper belongs can be required to attend court with the original paper.

From what I have said above you will see that the court has the power to require the production of the original birth certificates in your office and could either require you or the Director of the Vital Statistics Bureau to attend and testify as to the record. I am sure that this has become a serious problem with you, and of course, if we knew of any statute or rule of law that would relieve you, we would be glad to inform you to that effect. It would seem that certified copies of birth certificates are only accepted as prima facie evidence of age in certain restricted instances which are set forth in Section 130-96 of the General Statutes. I don't have before me the statutes passed at the 1945 Session of the General Assembly, and know of no statutes which make certified copies of birth certificates as prima facie evidence of age for all purposes both civil and criminal.

If this employee or official is duly subpoenaed by the court we would advise that you obey the subpoena. Your letter indicates that requests have been made for the attendance of such persons without the service of a subpoena. I don't think that any person or employee of your department would have to attend court upon a mere request. The only thing that we could suggest is that when you are requested for such attendance, that you suggest to them that the certified copies should serve the purpose and the presence of witnesses cannot add anything further to what is already certified under seal.

CHAPTER 829 SESSION LAWS OF 1945; (H. B. 229) INSPECTION OF PRIVATE. HOSPITALS, SANITARIUMS; SANATORIUMS AND EDUCATIONAL INSTITUTIONS; DEFINITIONS OF TERMS IN H. B. 229 AND APPLICATION OF ACT

23 October 1945

Your department has asked this office for a ruling as to the application of Chapter 829 of the Session Laws of 1945 to sanitariums, sanatoriums, and educational institutions. I would like to answer this inquiry upon the basis of two situations presented to your department.

From the information laid before me, it appears that a person in Asheville, N. C., owns and operates an institution or home with a capacity of twelve to fifteen patients, all patients with private rooms. At the present time, this person has seven bed-ridden patients who are paralytics. Each patient has his own physician but nursing service is furnished by the home and meals are served by tray. There are three commodes in the house and possibly other sanitary facilities and the prices charged are $35.00 to $40.00 per week per person. Another person in this same City operates a place accommodating about the same number of patients. These patients are all bed-ridden, mostly paralytics, and tray service is likewise furnished to them. There is no dining room at either place and the charges in this latter place are about $45.00 a week. These two institutions take care of chronic convalescents or senile cases. No communicable diseases are admitted.

You inquire of this office if these institutions would fall within the meaning of the terms used in Chapter 829 of the Session Laws of 1945 to the end that the agents of the State Board of Health would be authorized to enter these institutions for the purpose of inspection and examination and if the State Board of Health would be authorized to make rules and regulations covering the sanitation of such establishments and to provide a system of grading therefor.

The act in question is applicable to private hospitals, sanitariums, sanatoriums and educational institutions. In Webster's New International Dictionary, (2nd Edition) a sanitarium is defined as follows:

"A health station or retreat; an institution for recuperation and treatment of persons suffering from physical or mental disorders; a sanatorium."

It appears that the terms "sanatorium" and "sanitarium" are used interchangeably and the two terms are synonymous. The functions and purposes of the two institutions appear to be the same, except that persons making a study of words or semantics say that a sanatorium is sometimes located in a salubrious climate or near springs of mineral water. The objectives, however,, of the two institutions are the same.

In the case of City of Atlanta, et als., vs. Blackman Health Resort, Inc., 113 S. E. 545, 548, the Supreme Court of Georgia considered the meaning of these terms and after quoting the definition given by the dictionary as above set forth, the court said:

"The genus likewise embraces private sanitariums, boarding houses,

or other places of like character where patients are kept and medical
and surgical treatment is given."
A sanitarium is defined in Black's Law Dictionary as follows:

"A health station or retreat; boarding house, or other place where
patients are kept and where medical and surgical treatment is given."

I also cite the following cases as dealing with the definition of these terms
as follows:

SESSIONS V. THOMAS DEE HOSPITAL, 51 Pa. (2d) 229, 234.
INSURANCE CO. V. SMITH, 80 S.W. (2d) 413, 416.
REPUBLIC RECIPROCAL INS. ASSN. V. COLGIN HOSPITAL &
CLINIC, 65 S.W. (2d) 286.

From a review of these definitions, I am of the opinion that Chapter 829
of the Session Laws of 1945 is clearly applicable to these institutions above
described as being operated in the City of Asheville and the State Board of
Health is authorized and empowered to make rules and regulations covering
the sanitation of these establishments, provide a system of grading and the
agents of said Board are entitled to enter and inspect the premises of these
establishments which fall within the meaning of the terms of the bill and
are therefore in my opinion to be classed as sanitariums, sanatoriums or
private hospitals.

The next situation affecting your department arises by reason of a complaint made by a man serving in the armed forces of the United States.
This complaint deals with the sanitary conditions at a certain school in this
State and I am enclosing to you a letter written to this office by Chief Petty
Officer A. H. Parent, a copy of a letter written to Chief Petty Officer Parent
by his wife and also a copy of our letter to Chief Petty Officer Parent. This
information, of course, is furnished you for official use only.

It appears that the school in question is a privately owned military school
in this State and it is our opinion that this school falls within the meaning
of the term "educational institution" as set forth in Chapter 829 of the
Session Laws of 1945. You will note that the law in question deals entirely
with private institutions and therefore this school, in our opinion, is a private educational institution. It is not necessary to cite legal authority for
the meaning of the term "private educational institution." If I am correct
in my assumption, this school is operated as a private venture and an educational institution has been defined in 28 C.J.S. Page 834 as follows:

"One which teaches and improves its pupils; a school, seminary,
college or educational establishment, not necessarily a chartered institution, nor a public or charitable institution altho, in a particular context, it has been held to be a charitable organization."

This term has been construed in many tax statutes and applies to public
or private institutions teaching individuals in elemen ary subjects or institutions belonging to the class or grade denominated as colleges. It also
includes other types of schools teaching specialties, such as physical education, music or business subjects.

We are of the opinion, therefore, that your agents have a right under the
above cited chapter of the acts of 1945 to establish regulations covering the
sanitation of this school and of other schools of like kind privately owned

and operated and that you have a right to grade such schools according to a system or standard. It further follows that your officers and agents have a right to enter these institutions for the purpose of making inspections.

STATUTES; LOCAL ACT AND GENERAL ACT ON SAME SUBJECT MATTER; ARTICLE 2, SECTION 29 OF STATE CONSTITUTION

23 October 1945

In your letter of the 17th you call our attention to House Bill No. 329 enacted at the General Assembly of 1945 and entitled "An act to amend and rewrite sections one hundred and thirty - sixty-six, one hundred and thirty - eighteen and one hundred and thirty - twenty-one of the General Statutes of North Carolina relating to Public Health, and to provide for district or county boards of Health."

You also refer to Chapter 97 of the Public-Local Laws of 1935, the same being entitled "An act relating to the organization of the Cleveland County Board of Health."

You state that the ex-officio members of the Cleveland County Board of Health desire to know which statute should be followed in appointing and organizing the Cleveland County Board of Health, that is, should the Cleveland County Board of Health be appointed and organized under Chapter 97 of the Public-Local Laws of 1935, or should this County Board of Health be organized under Paragraph 1 of Section 130-18 of the General Statutes as the same was re-written and enacted by the General Assembly of 1945. You ask this office to render an opinion on this question.

I shall not attempt to analyze the two methods of organizing the County Board of Health as fixed by each of these two statutes. It is sufficient to say that the method of organization is different and the composition of the two Boards as to types of personnel is also different. First of all, I would like to say that while it is not the function of this office to pass upon constitutional questions for the reason that the constitutional validity of a Statute is a quesion for the courts of the State, nevertheless, I would respectfully suggest that there are grave doubts as to the constitutionality of Chapter 97 of the Public-Local Laws of 1935. Article II, Section 29, of the Constitution of North Carolina limits the power of the General Assembly of this State to enact special legislation with reference to certain subjects and included in these subjects of limitation are local or special acts relating to health, sanitation and the abatement of nuisances. This section and article of the Constitution has been interpreted by our Supreme Court as to the constitutionality of the Public-Local Act which undertakes to create and name the members of the County Board of Health. In the case of Sams vs. Commissioners of Madison, 217 N. C. 284, the County of Madison had a County Board of Health organized under the provisions of Chapter 322 of the Public-Local Laws of 1931. The plaintiff in the case had been appointed by this Board as County physician and quarantine officer and brought suit against the Commissioners to enforce the payment of his salary. The defendant Board of Commissioners denied liability on the ground that the local act of the General Assembly creating the County Board of Health of Madison County violated provisions of Article II, Section 29, of the Constitution of this State and was, therefore, void. In declaring the act to be unconstitutional and therefore void, the Supreme Court said:

"The local act attempting to create a county board of health for Madison County must be held void by reason of its conflict with the constitutional restrictions upon the power of the General Assembly imposed by Art. II, sec. 29, and the persons named as members of the county board of health by this act were thus without power to perform any duty prescribed thereby. Freeman v. Comrs. of Madison County, supra. Nor could validity be given to their acts as de facto òfficers, for the reason that it is found as a fact tha̓t the de jure board of health of Madison County, constituted in accordance with the provisions of the general statute (C. S., 7064), and acting as such, had in April, 1937, elected another person as county physician and quarantine officer for the county, who performed services and was recognized by the board of county commissioners as such. Baker v. Hobgood, 126 N. C., 149, 35 S. E., 253."

' It is important to note that Chapter 97 of the Public-Local Acts of 1935 relating to Cleveland County authorized this Board of Health to elect a County physician and County Health Officer and these officials are by law charged with enforcement of health and sanitary regulations and laws pertaining to the County.

In the case of Board of Health vs. Commissioners of Nash County, 220 N. C. 140, where certain local acts were passed applying to Nash County, giving the County Commissioners the right to approve the appointment of a Health Officer and providing further that if the Health Officer appointed by the Board of Health was disapproved by the Board of County Commissioners, the person so appointed should be ineligible for appointment and within thirty days thereafter the County Board of Health should make another appointment for the approval of the Commissioners. In holding that this act giving the Commissioners the right of approving the appointment of the Health Officer was unconstitutional and therefore void, the Supreme Court said:

"There is no room to doubt that chapters 6 and 193, Public Laws of 1941, are local. By the terms of the statute they apply only to Nash County, one out of the one hundred counties of the State. Chapter 6, section 3, Public Laws of 1941; S. v. Dixon, 215 N. C., 161, 1 S. E. (2d), 521; S. v. Chambers, 93 N. C., 600.
"This court is also committed to the proposition that a law affecting the selection of officers to whom is given the duty of administering the health laws is a law 'relating to health.' Sams v. Comrs. of Madison, 217 N. C., 284, 7 S. E. (2d), 540."

Irrespective of what I have said above, it is plain that Section 130-18 of the General Statutes, as rewritten and enacted by the General Assembly of 1945, lays down and provides a general State policy as to the appointment and organization of the County Boards of Health in all of the Counties of the State. Among other things, paragraph 1, of Section 130-18, provides the following:

"All counties having a separate health depar‍tment shall organize and operate a County Board of Health composed of three ex-officio members, **the same being the Chairman of the Board of County Commissioners, Mayor of the city or town which is the County seat (if there is no such Mayor, then the Clerk of Superior Court of the County) and the County**

Superintendent of Public Instruction;" (then follows the method by which the ex-officio members shall elect the other members of the County Board of Health in each County.)

The only exceptions made in this Section, and in this Paragraph, are those counties having joint City-County Boards of Health authorized by Private-Local or Public-Local Acts. While it is true that the general rule of statutory construction is to the effect that a general act does not repeal a previous special act in the absence of a clear intention so to do and that a special act is not affected by the presence of a general repealing clause in the general act, nevertheless, this rule does not hold or obtain where a special act is in conflict with a state-wide policy on a particular subject. In the case of State vs. Dixon, 215 N. C. 161, 169, the Supreme Court said:

"When the General Assembly, in a public measure, has laid down a controlling principle to be applied uniformly and generally throughout the length and breadth of the State in solving difficulties arising within a par icular field of the law, local measures in contravention of that public measure must yield to the demands of the broader and more fundamental policy when an irreconcilable conflict appears."

It is quite evident that the Supreme Court of this State considers a general law dealing with the appointment of County Boards of Health in all of the Counties of the State to be a matter of State-wide policy for in the case of Sams vs. Commissioners of Madison, Supra, the Court said:

"Furthermore, the act is in conflict with the State-wide policy as contemplated by the Constitution and *established by general laws regulating the composition of county boards of health* throughout the State and the election of county physicians." (Underscoring ours.)

It is clear to me that Section 130-18 are re-written intends to establish a general policy, State-wide in effect as to the method of organizing County Boards of Health, and that this State-wide policy appears as clearly in Section 130-18 as the State-wide policy appeared under the former act providing the method of appointment of organization of County Boards of Health, which was considered in Sams vs. Commissioners of Madison, Supra.

I am of the opinion, therefore, that this question must be answered in favor of the method of appointment and organization of the County Board of Health of Cleveland County, under the provisions of Paragraph 1, Section 130-18 of the General Statutes as re-written and enacted by the General Assembly of 1945. It follows, therefore, that in my opinion the ex-officio members, when they organize the Cleveland County Board of Health on January 1, 1946, should follow the procedure outlined in the State-wide Statute above cited and should disregard Chapter 97 of the Public Local Laws of 1935.

VITAL STATISTICS; NAME OF FATHER OF ILLEGITIMATE CHILD IN BIRTH
CERTIFICATE; ENTERING NAME OF FATHER OF ILLEGITIMATE CHILD
UPON AFFIDAVIT OF MOTHER BEFORE CLERK

1 November 1945

From your letter of October 22, 1945, it appears that you have in your office a birth certificate showing the child as illegitimate. For some reason the mother's name was omitted from the birth certificate. In July 1945 you received an affidavit from the Clerk of the Superior Court of Dare County;

this affidavit was made by the mother of the illegitimate child and states among other things that the name of the father as given in the certificate is correct. You further state that your clerk accepted this statement as coming under the provision of Section 130-94, and you inquire if it was proper to fill in the name of John C. Helms as the father of the child of Iva Whidbee.

In our opinion it was an error for the name of the father of the illegitimate child to be inserted in the birth certificate. It is clearly stated in Section 130-89 that in cases of an illegitimate child the name of the putative father shall not be entered without his consent. An affidavit made by the mother of the illegitimate child and sworn to before the Clerk of the Superior Court is not a judgment, order, or decree, and does not come within the meaning of paragraph (b) of Section 130-94. I think that Mr. Davis, Superintendent of Welfare of Dare County, is correct, and that you should remove this name from the certificate and nothing should appear in the certificate that would indicate that John C. Helms is the father of this child.

VITAL STATISTICS; AUTHORITY FOR ISSUING NEW BIRTH CERTIFICATES; ILLEGITIMATE CHILD; CHANGE OF NAME

1 November 1945

From your letter of October 22, 1945, it appears that Benjamin Franklin Brady was born to Sallie Brady out of wedlock. The father of the child was prosecuted for seduction and found guilty. Some years later the mother married Vollie Gray Webb, and the question has arisen as to the changing of this child's name from Benjamin Franklin Brady to William Lawrence Webb. You further call attention to the fact that in cases like the one described in your letter it is the usual procedure for the foster father to adopt the child and his name is then changed by virtue of Section 48-7 of the Adoption Law which authorizes your Bureau to make such a change and issue a new certificate and thereafter no reference will be made to the old certificate.

In this case instead of following the ordinary adoption proceedings, the foster father, through his attorney, instituted a proceeding under the provisions of Chapter 101 of the General Statutes which authorizes a changing of name upon the filing of a petition before the Clerk of Court and giving certain notices; a decree was obtained changing the child's name to William Lawrence Webb.

You inquire if your Division would be authorized to issue a new birth certificate under the facts in this case.

It seems to us that if such authority exists it would be under subsection (b) of Section 130-94 of the General Statutes which provides that a new certificate of birth shall be made by the state registrar whenever notification is received by the state registrar from the clerk of a court of competent jurisdiction of a judgment, order, or decree disclosing different or additional information relating to the parentage of a person.

I think that your division does have the authority to issue a new birth certificate under the facts disclosed in your letter. I don't think that a narrow interpretation should be given to the word "parentage." For legal purposes persons other than the child's natural parents are included within the meaning of the word or term "parent." Of course, natural parents are included within the term, but in a great many cases a stepfather or stepmother is considered a parent-in-law. See *State* v. *Juvenile Court of Ramsey County*, 204 N. W. 21, (Minn.). Many persons who stand in place of parents are included within the term. These persons are said to have the status of standing in loco parentis. It has been held that a woman who stood in loco parentis to an employee came within the meaning of adopted parent under Workman's Compensation Acts. See *Faber* v. *Industrial Commission*, 185 N. E. 255 (Ill.).

The petition filed before the Clerk of the Superior Court asking for a change of name in this case shows the circumstances as to the natural father of the boy and also shows that Vollie Gray Webb is now standing in loco parentis and exercising parental authority over the boy. In fact this boy thinks that Vollie Gray Webb is his father. Under these circumstances, and giving a liberal construction to the statute, I think the new birth certificate should be issued.

VITAL STATISTICS; CERTIFIED COPIES; COPY OF BIRTH CERTIFICATE FILED WITH REGISTER OF DEEDS.

1 November 1945

In your letter of October 23, 1945, you call attention to Section 130-99 of the General Statutes as to the duties of a local registrar wherein he transmits to the register of deeds of the county a copy of each certificate of births registered by him for the preceding month, retaining a copy for his own use, and sends the original certificate to the Division of Vital Statistics of the State Board of Health. You also call attention to Section 130-88 of the General Statutes as relating to the registration of certain delayed birth certificates. It is provided in this section that after approval as to rules and regulations of the State Board of Health, the registrar shall file the original of the delayed certificate and return the duplicate to the register of deeds for recording.

You inquire of this office if the register of deeds of a county has a right to issue a certified copy of the copy of the birth certificate on file in his office.

It is provided in Section 130-102 of the General Statutes that the state registrar shall upon request supply any applicant a certified copy of the record of any birth or death registered under the provisions of the Vital Statistics Law. This section further provides that any copy of the record of a birth certificate properly certified by the state registrar shall be prima facie evidence in all courts and places of the facts therein stated. It is further provided in Section 130-88 that all copies of birth certificates registered under that section, (delayed birth certificates) properly certified by the state registrar, shall have the same evidentiary value as those registered within five days after birth.

The powers and duties of a register of deeds are fixed by Chapter 161 of the General Statutes. In Section 161-10 a register of deeds is allowed to charge a fee for comparing and certifying the copy of the instrument filed for registration. He is likewise entitled to charge a fee for a copy of any record, or any paper in his office, which fee shall be the same as that charged for registration. It is required in Section 130-99 that the register of deeds keep an index the form of which shall be of the births and deaths that have occurred in the county, and these records shall be open at all times to official inspection.

It is clear that if a copy of a birth certificate is to have any value as evidence it must be certified by the state registrar, since the statutes dealing with the matter plainly say that the certified copy of the state registrar shall be prima facie evidence in all courts and places of the facts therein stated. This is not true as to a copy furnished by the register of deeds, and as pointed out, the official record possessed by the register of deeds is a copy itself of the original and is in the custody of the state registrar. I see no reason why a register of deeds cannot permit a person to have a copy of the copy of the birth certificate registered in his office, but I don't think such a copy has any value as evidence for the specific reason that evidentiary value is only given to the certified copy of the state registrar, and this value is not given to any copy of birth certificates obtained from any copy of certificates filed with the register of deeds.

HEALTH; BEDDING; BEDDING STAMPS; MAILING TO OUT-OF-STATE PURCHASERS; LOSS IN MAILING; LIABILITY

4 December 1945

In a conference with you, you advised me that on August 30, 1945, you received a letter from the Norfolk Mattress Company, Inc., of Norfolk, Virginia, which contained the following:

"We are enclosing certified check for $20.00, for which please rush us North Carolina Law Stamps.
"Thanking you to get these off to us at once, we are."

In reply to the above letter you mailed one thousand bedding stamps by insured parcel post on August 30, 1945. These stamps have never been received by the addressee. You inquire of me if the loss incurred because of the non-delivery of these stamps is the loss of the Health Department or the loss of the addressee or purchaser.

Section 130-272 of the General Statutes, relating to bedding stamps and speaking of the State Health Officer, provides as follows:

"Upon request he shall furnish no less than five hundred said stamps to any person paying in advance ten dollars ($10.00) per five hundred stamps."

In my opinion, the statute contemplates that the sale of said stamps shall take place at the offices of the State Board of Health in Raleigh, North Carolina. This opinion is buttressed by the general authorities on contracts and sales. In 13 CORPUS JURIS-CONTRACTS, Section 116, pages 300, 301, the following appears:

"Where a person makes an offer and requires or authorizes the offeree, either expressly or impliedly, to send his answer by post or telegraph, and the answer is duly posted or telegraphed, the acceptance is communicated and the contract is complete from the moment the letter is mailed or the telegram sent. The request or authorization to communicate the acceptance by mail is implied in two cases, namely: (1) Where the post is used to make the offer, as where a person makes an offer to another by mail and says nothing as to how the answer shall be sent; and (2) where the circumstances are such that it must have been within the contemplation of the parties that according to the ordinary usages of mankind the post might be used as a means of communicating the acceptance."

It would seem under the above authority that by using the mails to order the bedding stamps, the Norfolk Mattress Company, Inc., has, by implication, authorized the North Carolina Department of Health to use the mails in sending the stamps to them. The risk of loss in the mail is a risk which must be borne by the purchaser or contractor.

In 55 CORPUS JURIS-SALES, Section 59, pages 94, 95, the following appears:

"Unless a formal written acceptance is required by the order, an order for goods to be shipped or delivered to the buyer, if not previously withdrawn, is accepted and becomes a binding contract of sale when the goods are shipped or delivered in accordance with the terms of the order, without any formal notice thereof, notwithstanding the order provides for the signing and delivery of a duplicate of the order by the seller."

In OBER v. SMITH, 78 N. C. 313, Mr. Justice Faircloth observes:

"Upon these facts it is our opinion that as soon as the order or proposition of the defendant was accepted, the contract was complete without further notice, and that it was fully performed on the part of the plaintiffs when they delivered the guano in good condition to the steamboat company, when the title vested immediately in the defendant, and that consequently the plaintiff ought to recover."

Therefore, I advise that in my opinion the Norfolk Mattress Company, Inc., in their order for, or offer to buy, stamps through the mails, at least impliedly authorized you to send the stamps by mail, and any loss occurring while the stamps were in transit is the loss of the Norfolk Mattress Company, Inc.

PUBLIC HEALTH; ABATTOIR; RULES AND REGULATIONS OF STATE BOARD OF HEALTH; PENALTY FOR VIOLATION; DEFINITION OF ABATTOIR

15 December 1945

In your letter of December 10, 1945 you refer to Article 24 of Chapter 130 of the General Statutes and also to the rules and regulations promulgated thereunder with reference to meat markets and abattoirs. You state that a person living at the edge of Siler City, who does not raise or own his own hogs, is doing customary slaughtering for farmers and others for which service or business he charges a fixed or set fee. He is conducting this slaughtering business at his home where he has no facilities other than a scalding vat in his backyard.

You inquire of this office if an operation or establishment such as above described is subject to the law and regulations dealing with abattoirs and if this type of business operation or establishment comes within the legal meaning or definition of abattoir.

Section 130-264 of the General Statutes is as follows:

"For the better protection of the public health, the state board of health is hereby authorized, directed and empowered to prepare and enforce rules and regulations governing the sanitation of meat markets, *abattoirs*, and *other places* where meat or meat products are *prepared, handled, stored*, or sold, and to provide a system of scoring and grading such places. No such meat market or abattoir shall operate which receives a sanitary ra ing of less than seventy per cent (70%): Provided, that this article shall not apply to farmers and others who raise, butcher and market their own meat or meat products." (Underscoring ours.)

The State Board of Health is therefore empowered to prepare and enforce rules and regulations governing the sanitation of abbatoirs *and other places* where meat or meat products are prepared, handled or stored. By virtue of Section 130-266 of the General Statutes, any violation of the statutory provisions or of any of the rules and regulations that may be provided under the article is declared to be a misdemeanor; and upon conviction, the violator may be fined not less than ten dollars ($10.00) nor more than fifty dollars ($50.00), or imprisoned in jail for not less than thirty days at the discretion of the court.

The rules and regulations adopted by the State Board of Health on May 4, 1938 pursuant to this article defines abattoir as follows:

"An abattoir is any slaughtering, meat-canning, curing, smoking, salting, rendering, or other similar establishment. (Farmers and others who raise, butcher and market their own meat and meat products are exempted by Section 1, of the Act.)"

Under these rules and regulations, meat is defined among other things to mean and include any part or parts of the edible portion of swine and other animals that are ordinarily slaughtered in abattoirs and sold or used as food for human consumption.

According to Webster's International Dictionary, an abattoir and a slaughter house are synonymous terms. The definition of an abattoir set forth in the rules and regulations includes any establishment in which slaughtering is done, meat canning or any of these operations whether performed individually or in combination. The word "establishment" used in the definition is defined in 30 CJS, p. 1233 as follows:

"In the common understanding of the word, it is most simply defined as meaning something established; hence, an ins itution; an institution, place, building or location;* *more specifically, a fixed place where business is conducted, or a place where the public is invited to come and have its work done*.". (Underscoring ours.)

I am of the opinion, therefore, that the place, establishment and operation carried on by this person comes within the definition of an abattoir as defined in the rules and regulations adopted pursuant to the statute; and, therefore, this person is subject to the rules and regulations governing the sanitation of such abattoirs or places, and a violation of these rules and regulations in past operations or a failure to maintain the sanitary standards required by the rules would be a violation of the criminal law if such violation is established or proven in a court of competent jurisdiction. The fact that the equipment and implements of this person which are used in the slaughtering process are simple; or in other words, the fact that he does not possess the specialized devices used in large and modern abattoirs and slaughter houses would not make any difference. The character of the implements used is not the criterion as to whether the person should or should not comply with the rules and regulations. From your statement of fact, it is plain that this man is in the business of operating an abattoir because he is charging a fixed fee and apparently is holding himself out to the public as being engaged in this business.

The fact that the animals slaughtered by this person are owned and brought to him by farmers does not place him within the exemption set forth in Section 1 of the Act and also in the regulations. The exemption is personal to a farmer who raises, butchers, and markets his own meat. Many exemptions are granted to farmers from taxes or other regulations in dealing with their own products on their own farm such as exemptions relating to the growing and processing of fruits and vegetables and in producing and processing dairy products. The individual described in your letter is not a farmer who is raising, butchering, and marketing his own meat; therefore, he is clearly not protected by the exemption.

VITAL STATISTICS; AUTHORITY OF STATE REGISTRAR TO CONTROL TYPE OF FORMS USED FOR BIRTH CERTIFICATES AND IN THEIR PERFECTION AND PRESERVATION; AMENDMENTS TO BIRTH CERTIFICATES; WITNESSES TO AMENDMENTS; AUTHORITY OF STATE REGISTRAR TO REJECT PROPOSED AMENDMENT TO BIRTH CERTIFICATE

2 January 1946

In your letter you call our attention to Section 130-94 of the General Statutes and especially that portion dealing with the authority of the State Registrar to prepare, print and supply all blanks and forms used in registering, recording and preserving the returns as to birth and death certificates and, any other documents required to be filed and recorded under Sub-Chapter II of Article 9 of Chapter 130 of the General Statutes dealing with vital statistics in the State of North Carolina. You also enclose for purposes of illustration a request made by the register of deeds of one of our counties which request is in the form of a letter written on the county stationery; and there is also enclosed for purposes of illustration another request for amendment or change in a birth certificate which is set forth on a form especially prepared for that purpose by the county in question.

In view of Section 130-94 of the General Statutes and other provisions of the law dealing with vital statistics, you ask two questions which are as follows:

(1) Can the Bureau of Vital Statistics for the purpose of making changes in names, dates of birth, and other information recorded on the birth certificates, accept statements submitted on any type of form other than such forms as may be prepared and supplied by the State Registrar?

(2) In view of the statement in Section 130-94 concerning the witnessing of amendments to birth certificates or the returns, what type of witness is meant?

A third question is also raised in your letter which can possibly be stated as follows:

(3) Is the State Registrar compelled to accept a proposed amendment to a birth certificate or may he use discretion in such a matter; and if not satisfied that the amendment is correct or in good faith, may he reject the proposed amendment?

Directing our attention now to your first question, it appears that our law with reference to vital statistics was first inaugurated in 1913; and one of the original sections of the act is still contained in the law and appears as Section 130-69 of the General Statutes. I quote this section as follows:

> "The state board of health shall have charge of the registration of births and deaths, shall prepare the necessary instructions, forms, and blanks for obtaining and preserving such records, and shall procure the faithful registration of the same in each local registration district as constituted in the succeeding section, and in the central bureau of vital statistics at the capital of the state. *The said board shall be charged with the uniform and thorough enforcement of the law throughout the state,* and shall from time to time recommend to the general assembly any additional legislation that may be necessary for this purpose." (Underscoring ours.)

You will note that in Section 130-70 of the General Statutes the Secretary of the State Board of Health is constituted the State Registrar of Vital Statistics and that the State Registrar has general supervision over the central Bureau of Vital Statistics.

The first sentence of Section 130-94 of the General Statutes is as follows:

> "State registrar to supply blanks; to perfect and preserve birth certificates.—The state registrar shall prepare, have printed, and supply to all registrars all blanks and forms used in registering, recording, and preserving the returns, or in otherwise carrying out the purposes of this article; and shall prepare and issue such detailed instructions as may be required to procure *the uniform observance of its provisions* and the maintenance of a perfect system of registration; *and no other blanks shall be used than those supplied by the state registrar."* (Underscoring ours.)

By virtue of these statutes, I am of the opinion that the Bureau of Vital Statistics, through its State Registrar, has the authority and the duty to prepare and furnish a definite type of form to be used whenever amendments to birth certificates are sought or tendered to the bureau by any official or individual. It is evident that the act contemplates uniform enforcement in all parts of the state and that these primary certificates or documents shall be of the same type and kind to the end that the enforcement of the act will be the same in all parts of the state. In our opinion, the State Registrar has the same authority in preparing and enforcing the use of a form for an amendment as he would have in enforcing the form that is used in the certificate itself. As a result of the amendment, the document does become a part of the certificate. We, therefore, answer your question that if you prescribe a type of form to be used in all parts of the state for an amendment to a birth certificate or amendments to other returns made to your office, you have authority to compel the amendments to be made on these forms; and you may disregard any statements or proposed amendments submitted on any other type of form or on forms other than such forms as are prepared and supplied by the State Registrar.

. In the second question you refer to a portion of Section 130-94 dealing with the witnessing of amendments to birth certificates, death certificates, and other records handled by your·division which is as follows:

> "No certificate of birth or death, after its acceptance for registration by the local registrar, and no other record made in pursuance of this article, shall be altered or changed in any respect otherwise than by amendments properly dated, signed, and witnessed* * *."

You call attention to the fact that the original birth certificate is not signed before a witness, and you would like to know the type of witness that is meant or described in this section.

First of all, I think that it is within the supervisory and regulatory power of the State Board of Health to name and specify the type of witness to an amendment that the board would think proper bearing in mind that accuracy and truthfulness are the things sought in an amendment; and the type of witness should be such a person or official that would guarantee such accuracy and good faith so far as possible. I think that you might consider the persons who sign the certificates or make the certification required in a birth certifica'e as proper witnesses for amendments. You will note that in Section 130-89 of the General Statutes there is set out in Item 24 a list of persons who can make such a certification; and these persons are set forth in their order of importance; and it is required that the most competent person in this order of individuals shall make the certification. I think you could well use this in setting forth your requirements as to witnesses to amendments. I would advise that you set out this matter in the form of a regulation or one of the necessary instructions which the board is authorized to make under the authority of Section 130-69.

As to the third question, we are of the opinion that the State Registrar does not have to make an amendment to a birth certificate, death certificate, or other return theretofore recorded in his office unless he is satisfied that the amendment is accurate, correct, and is made in good faith. The State Registrar is vested with supervisory power and with discretion in handling the records in the central bureau. He is charged with the thorough and efficient execution of the provisions of the law. You will note that a portion of Section 130-94 requires the State Registrar to examine certificates received; and if they are incomplete or unsatisfactory, he may require further information to make the record complete and satisfactory. For example, take the situation where a new certificate of birth is made by the State Registrar. This is done upon proof submitted that previously unwed parents have subsequently intermarried. Or, take the case of a judgment or decree of the court of competent jurisdiction. You will note that satisfactory proof is submitted to the State Registrar. In other words, the State Registrar must be satisfied of the existence of certain things.

This is true likewise as to amendments.. For example, suppose that a person tendered the State Registrar an amendment to a birth certificate properly dated, signed, and witnessed; and a check of the records or birth certificates disclosed certain dates 'of births of sisters or brothers which when compared with the proposed amendments definitely shows that the amendment is untrue, the State Registrar would not have to accept such an amendment. The most vital thing in the records is the date of birth because the age of the individual is predicated upon this information. These dates should not be changed except after careful consideration; and when the State Registrar or those to whom his duties have been delegated are satisfied that the amendment is correct and made in good faith, and not for the mere purpose of establishing an age which would subserve the immediate purposes of the individual tendering the amendment such as draft evasion, increasing age to secure employment or for any other reasons or purposes inconsistent with the truthfulness of the amendment. In fact, this is so important that under Section 130-104 it is made a misdemeanor and a violation of the criminal law to falsify any certificate of birth or death or any other record established by the law.

Before a proposed amendment actually is an amendment, it must be passed upon by the State Registrar; and he must decide that it is entitled to be an amendment. He can send for further information until the proposed amendment becomes satisfactory to him or if it does not become satisfactory, he can finally reject it.

PUBLIC HEALTH; DISTRICT BOARDS OF HEALTH; REGULATIONS OF COUNTY
BOARDS OF HEALTH WHERE DISTRICT BOARDS OF HEALTH ARE
FORMED; UNIFORMITY OF RULES AND REGULATIONS
PROMULGATED BY DISTRICT BOARDS OF HEALTH

24 January 1946

I reply to your letter of January 21, 1946.

In your letter you refer particularly to Chapter 1030 of the Session Laws of 1945 and especially to those paragraphs dealing with district boards of health; and you submit the following questions to this office:

"1. Are rules and regulations as adopted by former county boards of health still applicable in those counties now governed by a district board of health with reference to health matters, or would it be necessary for the district board of health to re-enact the rules and regulations formerly adopted by the several county boards of health in the counties comprising a health district?

"2. If your answer to No. 1 is to the effect that the district board of heal.h must enact rules and regulations to take the place of former rules and regulations adopted by the county boards of health, is it true that until such time as this is done, there are no health rules and regulations in the territory comprising such a district other than state laws and State Board of Health rules and regulations?

"3. Shall the rules and regulations adopted by a district board of health be uniform for every county within the district or can a rule and regulation adopted by the district board of health be made applicable to one county only?"

In answer to your first question, you will recall that this office has already ruled that where district boards of health are organized and become operative under the provisions of Chapter 1030 of the Session Laws of 1945, such district boards of health are the sole health administrative bodies in the respective districts and county boards of health in each county inside of the new district are no longer affected and in fact, superseded by the dictrict organizations. It follows, therefore, as a matter of course that the rules and regulations adopted by the former county boards of health are no longer applicable to those counties now governed by a district board of health. The rules and regulations pertaining to health matters enacted by the different county boards of health depend upon the legal existence and authority of the county boards of health. When this source of authority is therefore nullified, it no longer has any legal existence. The rules and regulations enacted and promulgated by this source of authority likewise have no efficacy or legal existence .The answer, therefor, to your first question is that it is necessary for the district boards of health to re-enact these rules and regulations if they wish them to continue in force or else to enact an entirely new body of regulations applicable to the whole district.

From what I have already said, the answer to your second question is that there are no rules and regulations in effect where a district board of health has been organized but has passed no rules and regulations to take the place of the former rules and regulations adopted by the county boards of health; and as stated in your question, the only thing affecting such a territory is the law of State-wide nature administered by the State Board of Health and the rules and regulations of a general nature promulgated by the State Board of Health.

In answer to your third question, I quote Sub-section 4 of Chapter 1030 of the Session Laws of 1945 which supersedes and is a re-written version of Section 130-66, as follows:

"The rules, regulations and ordinances of the district board of health shall apply to municipalities within a county or counties composing the distric., but the district board of health shall not have power to pass special ordinances covering a municipality only, such authority being implicit in and retained by the governing body of the municipality. The district board of health shall have the immediate care and responsibility of the health interests of its district. It shall meet annually in some city or town in the district designated by it, and three members of the board are authorized to call a meeting of the board whenever in their opinion the public health interests of the district require it. It shall make such rules and regulations, and pay all lawful fees and salaries, and enforce such penalties as in i s judgment shall be necessary to protect and advance the public health."

I think the plain and ordinary meaning of this section is that the rules and regulations of the dis'rict board of health shall be in force and uniform in all portions of the district. The district board of health is supposed to look at problems of a health nature from a district point of view. If the district board of health has to pass an individual and separate set of rules and regulations for each county, then there would be very little use in having a district board of health and it would probably be better to retain the county system. The only difference under such a method would be that you would have one administrative system, but the total effect would be that you would still have a county system because you have to legislate for each county so far as rules and regulations are concerned. I, therefore, answer your third question that in my opinion the rules and regulations of a district board of health should be uniform and applicable in the same fashion and manner in all parts and in all territories of the district irrespective of county lines. I am strengthened in this by a better part of the above quoted statute which specifically says that the district board of health shall not have power to pass such ordinances governing a municipality only as such authority is maintained by the governing body of a municipality.

PUBLIC HEALTH; COUNTY BOARD OF HEALTH; MUNICIPALITIES; CONFLICT
BETWEEN MILK ORDINANCE OF COUNTY BOARD OF HEALTH AND
MILK ORDINANCE OF MUNICIPALITY; EFFECT OF CHAPTER
1030 OF SESSION LAWS OF 1945

13 February 1946

It appears that a conflict has arisen between the requirements of the milk ordinance passed by the county board of health and the milk ordinance which purports to be in force in the City of Kinston. Your statement of the facts in regard to the matter is as follows:

"The City of Kinston has had an old milk ordinance, the requirements of which were less stringent than those of the newest revisions of the U. S. P. H. S. Standard Ordinance, except for the fact that it provided that beginning next January 1 all milk sold in Kinston must be pasteurized. In August 1944, the County Board of Health passed a countywide milk ordinance, using as a basis the latest revision of the U. S. P. H. S. Standard Milk Ordinance. This ordinance made no provision for complete pasteurization, but simply required grading in accordance with sanitary standards. The sanitary inspector has been operating under the county ordinance but was expecting to enforce for the City of Kinston the requirement that all milk be pasteurized beginning next January 1.

"Last week in an alleged move to help out a milk shortage, the city further relaxed its ordinance to permit the sale of Grades B and C raw milk until January 1 of next year and then to require pasteurization only for Grades B and C, permitting Grade A raw to continue to be sold.

"This leaves the situation where the city ordinance permits the sale of Grades A, B and C raw and Grades A, B and C pasteurized and the county board of health ordinance permits the sale of only Grade A raw and Grades A, B and C pasteurized."

It appears, therefore, that the milk ordinance of the City of Kinston has lower requirements and standards than the milk ordinance of the

County Board of Health, the same being the County Board of Health in which the City of Kinston is located. In the case of a conflict of this nature, you would like to know the authority of the county and district boards of health as opposed to the authority of the city to make rules and pass ordinances on this subject. Another way of stating the question would be to ask which milk ordinance prevails in a situation of this nature, the milk ordinance of the county board of health or the milk ordinance of the city?

I think this whole question is answered by the provisions of Chapter 1030 of the Session Laws of 1945. This act amends by re-writing certain sections of the Public Health Law; and your attention is specifically called to Section 2 of this act which constitutes an amendment by re-writing Section 130-18 of the General Statutes of North Carolina. Subsection 2 of this section (p. 1351, Acts of 1945) is as follows:

"The rules, regulations and ordinances of the county board of health shall apply to municipalities within the county but the board of health shall not have the power to pass special ordinances covering a municipality only, such authority being implicit in and retained by the governing body of the municipality. The duties and the responsibilties of the county board of health shall be as set forth in Section one hundred and thirty—nineteen of the General Statutes of North Carolina except as may be modified by the provisions of this section."

I am of the opinion that the above quoted subsection clearly states that the ordinances of the county board of health shall apply to municipalities when in the county; and it is clear that where the county board of health passes an ordinance which is uniform and county-wide in nature, that it is effective inside the corporate limits of a municipality as well as outside of the corporate limits or in other words, in the county at large. The General Assembly of 1945 specifically gave to district and county boards of health the right to pass health ordinances which would be effective and superior to the ordinances of municipalities on such matters provided, as we have said above, the ordinances are uniform and applicable to all sections of the county. The only thing that a county board of health cannot do is to pass an ordinance for a specific municipality, such an ordinance being designated in the statute as a special ordinance. An example of this would be the county board of health's attempting to pass a milk ordinance which would apply in the City of Kinston only. Such an ordinance would be invalid and beyond the power of the district or county board of health, as the case may be.

Under the facts set forth in your letter, we are of the opinion, therefore, that since the County Board of Health has more stringent requirements than the ordinance of the City of Kinston, that the ordinance of the County Board of Health is superior to the ordinance of the City of Kinston and is controlling on the subject of milk regulation. Any conflict between the two ordinances would have to be resolved in favor of the provisions of the ordinance of the County Board of Health.

PUBLIC HEALTH; COMMUNICABLE AND INFECTIOUS DISEASES; REGULATORY
POWER OF BOARD OF HEALTH; PSITTACOSIS; VALIDITY OF
PROPOSED REGULATIONS GOVERNING PSITTACINE BIRDS

18 February 1946

The delay in answering your letter in regard to the proposed amendments
of the Board of Health to the regulations governing and controlling psittacine birds is regretted. I have purposely held the letter without answer
for this length of time because I have been trying to review the legal
authorities and form some definite opinion one way or the other as to the
validity of the proposed amendments before your Board.

I am enclosing a copy of the proposed amendment to Regulation 40 of
the Regulations of the North Carolina State Board of Health governing
the control of communicable diseases. (Supplement No. 1, Volume 60, The
Health Bulletin). There is also enclosed a copy of the Regulations of the
State Board of Health of the State of Florida dealing with psittacine birds
and Regulations of the State Department of Public Health of the State
of California dealing with this same subject. My investigations also disclose
that the boards or departments of health of the States of Georgia and
Michigan have adopted regulations on this same subject, although I do
not know the contents of these regulations. The first copy of these regulations was furnished to me by Dr. Stevick, and this first copy is also enclosed
which I will thank you to have delivered to Dr. Stevick.

Certain infectious diseases must be reported by physicians in this State
according to the provisions of Section 130-173 of the General Statutes.
Any other diseases declared by the North Carolina State Board of Health
must also be reported; and it is provided by Section 130-176 of the General
Statutes that the North Carolina State Board of Health may adopt all
necessary rules and regulations for the management, supervision or control of the diseases coming within the meaning of the article in question.
These rules and regulations are regarded as minimum requirements, and
cities and towns may adopt additional rules and regulations for the control
of the diseases mentioned in the article. A violation of the rules and regulations is made a misdemeanor by Section 130-177 of the General Statutes.

It has been universally held by both courts and textwriters that power
may be delegated to administrative authorities to deal with contagious diseases, and such boards may adopt reasonable regulations for this purpose.
They cannot adopt unreasonable or arbitrary rules and regulations; and
the methods adopted or exercised to prevent the spread of the diseases must
bear some relation to the real danger, and there must exist reasonable
grounds for the necessity of preventing or suppressing the diseases. In the
case of PEOPLE ex rel, BARMORE v. ROBERTSON 302 Ill. 422, 22 A.
L. R. 835, the court said in speaking of the powers of the Board of Health:

"While it is true that the character and nature of such departments
or boards is administrative only, still the powers conferred upon them
by the legislature, in view of the great public interest confided to them,
have always received from the courts a liberal construction, and the

right of the legislature to confer upon them the power to make reasonable rules, by-laws, and regulations has long been recognized by the authorities. When these departments or boards duly adopt rules and by-laws by virtue of legislative authority, such rules and by-laws have the force and effect of law, and are often said to be enforced by authority of the State."

The disease of psittacosis is not mentioned in Section 130-173 of the General Statutes, but I am informed that it has been named as a preventable disease by the State Board of Heal h; and a program for the control of the disease appears in Regulation 40 of the Regulations of the Board of Health concerning communicable diseases. I do not think that the fact that the name of this par.icular disease fails to appear in the list of diseases set forth in the statute makes any difference; as was said by the court in PEOPLE ex rel. BARMORE v. ROBERTSON, supra: •

"Under a General Statute giving to the State Department of Health power to restrict and suppress contagious and infectious diseases, such department has authority to designa.e such diseases as are contag.ous and infectious, and the law is not void for this reason on the ground that it designates legislative power."

The court also said in the same case in substance that legislatures cannot anticipate all the contagious and infectious diseases that may break out in a community and that to limit the activities of the health authorities to those diseases named by the legislature in an act creating the administrative body would very often endanger the health and lives of the people. It was pointed out that there was probably not a legislature in the country that would have named Spanish Influenza as a contagious and infectious disease prior to the terrible epidemic that swept through this country.

Paragraph P of Regulation 40, as the same now appears in your pamphlet of regulations, simply sets forth cer.ain control measures to be used in handling and dealing with birds of the psittacine family and other birds not of this type but which birds have been exposed to psittacosis. The proposed regulations strike out the first four paragraphs of the present regulations and substitute therefor four more paragraphs. Paragraph 1 of the proposed amendment absolutely prohibits the importation into North Carolina all psittacine birds if they are to be offered for sale, barter or as gifts or for public auction. It is further provided that birds imported in violation of the regulations shall be killed and burned immediately after shipment is received by the owner.

Paragraph 2 of the regulations allows shipment of birds into North Carolina for scientific purposes if the birds are grown in aviaries in the United States, and they are certified to be found free of psittacosis by the public health agencies at the point of the shipment.

Paragraph 3 provides that all psittacine birds that have psittacosis or have been exposed to psittacosis known to be or suspected to be infected, shall be killed and burned by the owner or other persons in charge of such birds.

It is provided in Paragraph 4 that no indemnity will be paid or provided for the owner or the person in charge of such birds.

As to your proposed regulation set forth in Paragraph 1, it will be seen that it embodies two propositions: (a) Psittacine birds cannot be imported into the State if offered for sale, etc; and (b) If such birds are imported in violation of the regulations, they shall be killed and burned immediately after shipment is received by the owner or other persons in charge of such birds. I think it should be pointed out that there are already in existence certain Federal regulations on this same subject of psittacine birds and psittacosis (See Code of Federal Regulations, Cumulative Supplement, Book 7, Title 42 in Part 18). I do not know whether the Federal regulations are of such a nature and are so comprehensive that it might be said that the Federal regulations cover the field; and, therefore, that the State regulations of such a nature cannot be enforced.

In 15 C. J. S., Section 59, p. 377, it is said:

> "Quarantine and sanitary regulations established by, or under authority granted by, congress are valid so far, but only so far, as they relate to foreign or interstate commerce. Where congress has exercised its power, all state laws inconsistent with the regulation established by congress are superseded or suspended and cannot be applied; but quarantine regulations of both congress and the states may be sustained where, although they relate to the same subject, they do not cover the identical ground, and the congressional regulation was evidently not intended to supersede the state regulation. A state in the exercise of the police power reserved to it, and in the absence of conflicting regulations by congress, may pass reasonable sanitary and quarantine laws which will be valid, although to a certain extent they necessarily affect interstate and foreign commerce. Of course, quarantine and health laws must have some real relation to the objects named in them in order to be sustained as valid exercises of the police power; and a state cannot, beyond what is absolutely necessary for self-protection, interfere with transportation into or through its territory."

I am told that the incubation period of psittacosis is variable and that birds have been known to develop psittacosis many days after they have been held for the period of time fixed in the Federal Quarantine Regulations. I am also informed that many birds are carriers of the disease although the birds do not appear to have the disease in any active form. It is also said that there is no method or technique for testing the bird for the disease while the bird is still alive. In other words, in order to be sure whether the bird has the disease or not, it is necessary to kill the bird to make the test. The disease of psittacosis (commonly called parrot fever) is apparently easily acquired by human beings who have been associated with psittacine birds, and the mortality rate among human beings is fairly high. There is no known therapeutic agent which is a specific cure for the disease. Apparently the only way to be sure that the disease will not spread among the people of the State is to prevent all birds of the psittacine family from being imported into the State. In this respect, the disease differs from cattle and stock diseases which are usually handled by quarantine regulations whereby the cattle are kept out of a State for a certain length of time and then are admitted. Most diseases of cattle and horses yield to specific treatments and can be specifically tested for the disease while the animal is alive. Examples are glanders and bovine tuberculosis. In all such cases, prohibitions against stock entering the State have been sustained for definite periods of time, but prohibitions against entering the

State for all time have not been sustained. Where it is definitely known that the animals have diseases, of course, the State can exclude such animals from entering its borders. The whole situation as to the control of diseases for livestock is discussed in the case of MCSWEEN v. STATE LIVE-STOCK SANITARY BOARD 65 A.L.R. 508 and note on p. 5251. In as much as other states have regulations to the same effect which exclude such birds from their state, I would advise that this part of your regulation be adopted except I am of the opinion that you should modify this portion of your regulation so as to permit the shipment of such birds through the State of North Carolina when the shipment begins at a point outside of the State and is consigned to another state. In other words, I think you should allow the birds to be shipped through the State of North Carolina to another state if they are sealed and the containers holding the birds are not opened during transit. See Rule 1 of the State of California, copy of which is here enclosed. As to the last part of Paragraph 1 of the proposed amendment, it is impossible for us to say if you have a right to require birds to be killed that have been imported into the State in violation of the regulations. It is true that ordinances have been upheld which authorized the destruction of animals having contagious or infectious diseases.

RANDALL v. PATCH 8 A.L.R. 65, 69
DURAND v. DYSON 111 N.E. 143 (ILL.)
CITY OF NEW ORLEANS v. CHAROULEAU 15 Annotated Cases 46

The statutes and ordinances in the above cited cases provided for compensation when the animals were killed and in other cases no compensation was provided at all; but I call your attention to the fact that it was definitely known by a specific test that the animal had the disease when it was killed or the health authorities had reasonable grounds to believe that the animal had the disease. I frankly do not know what our Supreme Court would say as to your right to compel all psittacine birds to be killed, that is when it is a violation of the proposed regulation. In the absence of a decision of our Supreme Court, this office would not assume any responsibility in such cases.

I see nothing wrong with Paragraph 2 of the proposed amendment, and it seems to me that such paragraph would be a valid regulation.

As to Paragraph 3 of your proposed regulation, you here again propose to kill all psittacine birds already in the State of North Carolina if such birds (a) have psittacosis or (b) have been exposed to psittacosis through birds known to be or suspected to be infec.ed or have been associated with birds known to be or suspected to be infected. I have already explained that we do not know whether the Supreme Court would authorize or uphold a regulation killing all psittacine birds in the State. Of course, I am definitely of the opinion that you have a right to kill a bird if you know that it has psittacosis; and it seems to me that you should have a right to kill them if you can definitely establish the fact that the birds in question have been associated or definitely exposed to other birds known to have had psittacosis. I, however, do not think that that part of Paragraph 3 of the proposed regulation which would require the death of all birds exposed to psit.acosis through birds suspected of having been infected would be valid. I do not think that you can destroy animals or birds upon suspicion. For example in the case of PEOPLE ex rel. BARMORE v. ROBERTSON, supra:

> "A person cannot be quarantined upon mere suspicion that he might have a contagious or infectious disease, but the health authorities must have reliable information upon which they have reasonable ground to believe that the public health will be endangered by permitting the person to be at large."

And, likewise, in the case of birds, I think that you should have something more than mere suspicion; and I think that you should strike out this port.on of the proposed regulation which deals with birds suspected of being infected; and you should insert in lieu thereof some phraseology to the effect of association with birds of which there are reasonable grounds to believe that such birds are infected with psittacosis.

Paragraph 4 of the proposed regulation in my opinion is all right and should be approved, assuming that you have a right to kill such birds.

In conclusion I would suggest that you adopt another paragraph in which you in substance state that no person, firm or corporation residing in, staying in or doing business in the State of North Carolina shall receive, keep, or possess for the purpose of selling any macaws, parrots, etc, and other psittacine birds; that none of the persons or firms as described in the previous clause shall move, sell or transport from a point in the Stat. to another point in the State any such psittacine birds and that no person, firm or corporation residing, doing business, etc., in the State shall purchase from any other person, firm or corporation in the S.ate any macaws, parrots, etc. or other psittacine birds. I suggest that this paragraph be added for the reason that if the court should declare that paragraph 1 of your regulation was unauthorized because of undue burden on interstate commerce or because the Federal regulations are in force and cannot be supplanted by State regulations, then it would seem to me that you would have a right to control and regulate the handling and sale of such birds after they are in the State and are being possessed and have come to rest inside the State.

PUBLIC HEALTH; VITAL STATISTICS; REGISTRATION DISTRICTS; CONSOLIDA-
     TION; TERM OF OFFICE OF LOCAL REGISTRAR

25 February 1946

In your letter of February 20, 1946 you state that it has been customary for the State Board of Health to consolidate all registration areas in a county where there is a full-time health officer, should such health officer be willing to take the appointment as registrar for the entire county. In some cases, you state that the health officer has more than one county in his health jurisdiction and has taken over the appointment as registrar for all of the counties included in the district. You state that consolidations have been, in the past, ordered on the petition of the county commissioners, county medical society, and the county board of health. It has been the custom of the State Board of Health in official session to review such petitions and adopt resolutions for the necessary consolidation. You state that there is a proposed consolidation of Orange, Person, and Chatham counties. You state that a full-time health officer is available and would accept the appointment, and the county commissioners are agreeable to such a change. The commissioners, however, hesi.ate to be formally recorded as in favor of the new arrangements as there are several local registrars who, when their services are discontinued, might raise strenuous objections. It is stated that the county medical society and the county board of health will file the customary petitions.

You inquire if it is necessary under the authority of Section 130-72 that you have pe.itions, as set forth in your letter, before the Board can take action.

You also inquire as to the term of office of local registrars when consolidations are carried out. That is, you want to know if the official term of the local registrars comes to an end or does the term of office of the registrars continue to run concurrent with that of the Governor, irrespective of the consolidation of registration districts. Section 130-72 of the General Statutes is as follows:

"The State Board of Health shall have authority to abolish or consolidate existing registration districts, and or, create new dis'ricts when, in the judgment of the Board, economy and efficiency and the interest of the public service may be promoted, thereby."

I am of the opinion that under the provisions of this statute it is not necessary at all to have the petitions from the county commissioners, county medical society and the county board of health before consolidating registration distric.s. The State Board of Health is required only to act according to its judgment that economy and efficiency of public service are promoted. In doing this, it may act upon its own private investigations or it may act .upon sta.ements from citizens, affidavits, or by means of any of the ordinary channels by which information is conveyed. When a consolida.ion is made, the Board should be in a position to show that economy and efficiency or the interest of the public brought about the change. The sta.ute does not require the petitions of any society, board or group; and it is not quite understood why all this apparently unnecessary petitioning has been resorted to in the past.

As to the term of office of the local registrars when consolidations are brough: about, I think your question is answered by the expressed provisions of Section 130-73 of the General Statutes. The term of office of a local registrar is four years, beginning with the first day of January of the year in which the local registrar is appointed; and until his successor has been appointed and has qualified, unless such office shall sooner become vacant by death, disqualification, opera.ion of law, or other causes. If the registration districts are consolidated and the duties of the local registrars are transferred to a county or district health officer, then and in that event, the terms of office of the local registrars in the consolidated district immediately cease by opera.ion of law. Since the Board has the power to consolidate the registration districts and transfer the duties from the local registrars to the health officers, it follows automatically that the terms of office of the local registrars are terminated by this legal procedure.

PUBLIC HEALTH; MEAT INSPECTION; AUTHORITY OF BOARD OF HEALTH; TO HIRE MEAT INSPECTOR; TERRITORIAL BASIS OF INSPECTION

4 March 1946

You enclose us a letter from a Mr. N. F. Steppe, Superintendent of Public Instruction of McDowell County, from which it appears that the county commissioners of this county have been making an appropriation for a meat inspector for McDowell County. Superintendent Steppe is wondering if this service will be provided by the District Board of Health since the County Board of Health has been abolished. He states that the Chairman of the Board of County Commissioners has requested him to write for an opinion as to whether the County Commissioners can retain this service until such time as the District Health Board can provide for the same, or until the end of this fiscal year. He further states that there is a demand for a meat inspector in the county and that unless the Commissioners are without authority, they would like to continue their system of inspection as heretofore operated.

Upon the basis of this letter, you have presented two questions to this office as follows:

"1. Does the Board of Health have the authority to hire a meat inspector and pay for his services under the authority granted by the Legislature?

"2. In the event it is the responsibility of the County or District Board of Health to do this employing of a meat inspector, will it be possible in the case of Districts for the service to be provided for one County and not made District-wide, and, if so, how under the existing laws?"

The authority of the Board of Health on this subject is derived from Article 24 of Chapter 130 of the General Statutes. I quote Sections 130-264 and 130-265 for the sake of clarity in this letter, as follows:

"For the better protection of the public health, the state board of health is hereby authorized, directed and empowered to prepare and enforce rules and regulations governing the sanitation of meat markets, abattoirs, and other places where meat or meat products are prepared, handled, stored, or sold, and to provide a system of scoring and grading such places. No such meat market or abattoir shall operate which receives a sanitary rating of less than seventy per cent (70%): Provided, that this article shall not apply to farmers and others who raise, butcher and market their own meat or meat products."

"Where municipalities or counties have a system of meat inspection as already provided by law the person or persons responsible for such meat inspection work shall file a copy of all inspection work, reports and other official data with the city or the county health officer, as the case may be, and in municipalities and counties having no organized health department, such person or persons shall file a copy of all inspection work, reports and other official data with the state health officer. The State board of health shall provide or approve the report forms referred to in this section."

It, therefore, definitely appears from the wording of 130-264 that the State Board of Health has the right to prepare and enforce rules and regulations covering sanitation of meat markets, abattoirs, and places where meat products are prepared, handled, stored, and sold. It seems to me that this is a straight out and express grant of authority to the State Board of Health and that it carries with it the power to hire or employ a meat inspector for the obvious reason that the statute says that the Board can enforce the rules and regulations. You will observe, however, that Section 130-265 which is still in force and has not been repealed, so far as I know, allows municipalities and counties having a system of meat inspection of their own to operate this system of inspection subject to the limitation or duty of filing a copy of the inspection work and reports together with other official data with the city or county health officer; and in case of a district, I assume that it would be filed with the District Health Officer or with the State Board of Health.

Under the provisions of Section 106-159, and sections following, of the General Statutes it appears that municipalities and counties have the right to establish and maintain meat inspection located within their corporate limits and within the limits of the county; and it seems to me that this is recognized by Section 130-265 of the General Statutes and that a county should be allowed to hire and operate its own inspection and that this would be so where there is a district system of health in operation. The county inspection, however, it seems to me, is under the supervision of the State Health Officer as he is required to approve the reports filed by the inspector of the county or municipality as the case may be.

In answering your first question, I would say, therefore, that the Board of Health does have the authority to hire a meat inspector and pay for his services under the authority granted by the Legislature subject to the right of the counties or municipalities to operate its own system of inspection provided the municipality or county system files its reports with the proper health officer and subject to his approval. It seems to me that the over-all responsibility still remains with the State Board of Health as provided in Section 130-264.

In answering your second question, it seems to me that you have the authority under the sections that I have already cited and also by virtue of the regulatory power granted to district boards of health under the authority of Chapter 1030 of the Session Laws of 1945 to make uniform rules and regulations for the inspection of meat in a district and that you can also provide that full-time service will not be enforced in all of the district but enforcement will be confined to those counties who provide and maintain a meat inspection system and inspector for their own county. I think you have the authority to make the rules and regulations uniform in the whole district but to limit the enforcement to those counties who co-operate with the State Board of Health and who are willing to pay an inspector for enforcement in their county.

PUBLIC HEALTH; COMPULSORY SCHOOL LAW; EFFECT OF
ISOLATION OR QUARANTINE

20 March 1946

You state that under Regulation 37 of the State Board of Health communicable disease regulations persons with pediculosis may be isolated at home by the local health officer and may not be permitted to enter school without a permit. You state that there are some individuals that have been isolated by the health officer under this Regulation, and the Regulation has been enforced; but the patients in question have remained at home without attempting to remedy the situation. I understand that pediculosis in plain language means the state of being infested with lice or just plain lousy. You s ate that there is nothing in the Regulation that requires the patient to free himself from the infestation.

The health officer would like to know if in this case it would be possible to enforce the School Attendance Act which would mean that the patient would thereby violate the Communicable Disease Regulation unless he did free himself of the condition.

Under the provisions of Section 130-176 of the General Statutes, the State Board of Health has a right to make rules and regulations for governing infectious and communicable diseases; and such rules and regulations have the authority of law if passed within the scope of the statute. Under Section 130-177 a violation of the regulations of the State Board of Health is a misdemeanor and punishable by fine or imprisonment.

Under Regulation 37 dealing with pediculosis, it is provided in subsection I that: "Patients shall be isolated for the duration of the infestation if considered necessary by the local health or quarantine officer to prevent its spread."

It is provided in subsection K of said regulations that: "No person with the infestation shall attend or be employed in any public, private, or parochial school unless a written permit is obtained from the local health or quarantine officer."

Our Compulsory Attendance School Laws are found as Article 42 of the General Statutes in Chapter 115 and begin with Section 115- 302 The State Board of Education has a right to make rules and regulations and to designa.e methods of enforcement. For your reference, there is enclosed a copy of the Compulsory School Attendance Law together with regulations and certain rulings of the Attorney General's office. You will note that on p. 18, as to unlawful absences, the last paragraph on the page, that if any parent or guardian is the cause of the child's non-attendance by keeping said child at home, etc., that the parent or guardian shall be guilty of a misdemeanor; and you will further note that all absences due to the consent or indifference of the parents shall be considered as unlawful absence.

In this case, I would have the health officer to advise this famliy, that is the parents or guardian of the persons involved, the proper means of reli-ving themselves of this infesta'ion of lice; and I would be sure that the proper method of disinfection is made known to them. I would then give them a reasonable time to see that this disinfection is carried out. If they do not do so, I would then report the case to the Compulsory Attendance officer and advise that he indict the parents for failure to send the children to school. I cannot believe the law and regulations on both of these subjects will permit parents to let their children be infected with lice to the state that they cannot go to school and then escape indictment for failure to send the children to school. If they know what to do and willfully refuse to do that which will render the children fit to attend school, then I think they are indictable under the Compulsory Attendance Law and that this should be done. The law does not contemplate foolish things, and it does not contemplate that parents can let their children remain infested with lice and stay out of school.

PUBLIC HEALTH; DISTRICT BOARDS OF HEALTH; SUBSISTENCE AND MILEAGE ALLOWANCE FOR TRAVEL TO AND FROM MEETINGS

21 March 1946

In your letter of March 14, 1946, you inquire of this office as to whether or not it is permissible for District Boards of Health members to receive, in addition to their per diem compensation, a compensation for travel to and from meetings; and if so, what would be the rate of reimbursement.

Section 130-66 of the General Statutes of North Carolina was amended by Chapter 1030 of the Session Laws of 1945 for the purpose of providing a new method or plan of organization for District Health Departments. Subsections (4) and (5) of this section provide for meetings of the District Boards of Health; and, of course, we know from the organization of a District Board of Health that members from some of the counties have to go to one of the counties to a place where it has been designated that the meeting will be held. This results in travel and subsistence expense on the part of those members who do not live in the town or city designated as the meeting place.

It is true that the members are provided with a per diem of $4.00 a day, but we do not think that it was intended to impose a duty on individuals acting in official capacity as members of the District Board of Health to attend these meetings at their own travel and subsistence expense. We are of the opinion, therefore, that the members of the District Boards of Health, when ordered to attend official meetings in the performance of their official duty, are entitled to reasonable subsistence and mileage expenses and that this should be an item in the budget which is set up for the operation of the District Boards of Health. We are further of the opinion that these payments should be made from the appropriations made for the District Boards of Health; and if the present appropriations are not sufficient for that purpose, an amended appropriation can be made to take care of the payments.

In our opinion, the amount of these allowances or reimbursements should be based upon actual expenses. It would be a good method to allow such members to produce and file receipts showing the expense of their travel and their subsistence expenses; and upon inspection and audit of these receipts, these members could then be reimbursed.

I am enclosing you a copy of an opinion in regard to County Superintendents of Public Welfare which illustrates our thought on this same matter as applied to another agency.

PUBLIC HEALTH; PHYSICIANS AND SURGEONS; RELATIONSHIP OF PHYSICIAN
AND PATIENT; HEALTH OFFICER; COMMUNICATIONS
BETWEEN INDIVIDUAL AND HEALTH OFFICER

27 March 1946

In your letter of March 21, 1946, you refer to a letter received by you
from one of the health officers, copy of which is attached to your letter. It
appears that this heal h officer was subpoenaed as a witness in the Superior
Court to testify with reference to syphillis in one of his patients in the
health department. He refused to give the testimony and was then advised
by the judge that the patient was not a private patient and that he would
be bound to answer the questions. As a result of this order of the court, he
answered the questions. The health officer makes the point that patients in
Public Heal h Clinics are treated as individuals and that with respect to
their treatment, they are handled as private patients. They are in some
instances assured that the health officer will treat all information in regard to their case in a confidential manner. This health officer is further of
the opinion that it will not contribute to a good operation of the program
if it should be generally thought that information divulged to the Public
Health physician for purposes of treatment will not be treated in a confidential manner.

You would like to know whether or not patients attending Public Health
Clinics are to be regarded on the same basis as private patients in so far
as the protection of confidential communications is concerned. You would
further like to know if the court has the authority to compel health officers
to make the patient's record available in the courts of the State. You would
like to know further if it is possible for the health officer to give the information as confidential and not bring the matter into public testimony before the court.

You suggest that an additional problem has arisen because of a great
number of divorces. It is beginning to develop that health officers are having
to spend a great deal of time in court testifying as witnesses in these cases,
and they cannot be present in court and attend to their duties in the control
of venereal diseases at the same time. You would like to know what the
rights of the health officers are in this matter of attendance in court.

As to your first question, it is provided by Section 8-53 of the General
Statutes as follows:

> "No person, duly authorized to practice physic or surgery, shall be
> required to disclose any information which he may have acquired in at-
> tending a patient in a professional charac'er, and which information
> was necessary to enable him to prescribe for such patient as a physi-
> cian. or to do any act for him as a surgeon: Provided, that the presid-
> ing judge of a superior court may compel such disclosure, if in his opinion
> the same is necessary to a proper administration of justice."

We do not know, of course, upon what grounds the court based its ruling;
and anything here said is our own opinion without a knowledge of the case
and is not to be construed as a criticism of the judge's ruling. It seems
to us that a true test of the matter is whether or not the person is a patient or in other words, does the relationship of patient and physician exist

between the patient and the health officer. You will note that the statute does not make any distinction between a so-called "private patient" and a so-called "public patient." There is no distinction made in the statute between a person who seeks the aid and assistance of a public health physician and a person who seeks the assistance and medical advice of a purely personal and private physician. If the person is attended by the Public Health physician in a professional character and the information divulged by the person was necessary to enable the Public Health physician to prescribe for him as a physician or to do any act for him as a surgeon, then such evidence or communications between the patient and the physician are privileged communications and cannot be disclosed unless the presiding judge of the Superior Court makes a finding that if, in his opinion, it is necessary to a proper administration of justice that such communications or evidence be disclosed by the physician. You will thus see that this privilege is not an absolute privilege, but it is a privilege that exists unless the judge makes findings that the disclosure is necessary for the proper administration of justice.

While it is true that the relationship of physician and patient is usually created by means of a contract between the parties, express or implied; nevertheless, there are other methods of creating the relationship of physician and patient, and the later decisions are to the effect that the relationship is a consensual one and is created when the patient knowingly seeks the assistance of the physician and the physician knowingly accepts him as a patient. This is true in regards to a physician's action in a public capacity as well as private physicians. In 41 American Jurisprudence, Section 71, p. 191, it is said:

> "A physician is under no obligation to engage in practice or to accept professional employment, but when the professional services of a physician are accepted by another person for the purposes of medical or surgical treatment, the relation of physician and patient is created. The relation is a consensual one wherein the patient knowingly seeks the assistance of the physician and the physician knowingly accepts him as a patient. But the existence of the relation does not need to rest on any express contract between the physician and the person treated. A physician may accept a patient and thereby incur the consequent duties although his services are performed gratuitously or at the solicitation and on the guaranty of a third person. The fact, even, that a third person sends a physician to examine a patient for the purpose of benefiting the third person only, and the patient not at all, may not affect the case, for the patient always has a right to refuse treatment; and when professional assistance is accepted, such acceptance creates the practitioner the physician of the patient and subjects him to the resultant liabilities. * * * The physicians and surgeons of a hospital, public or private, enter into the relation of physician and patient with every patient brought into the hospital as soon as he is brought in."

What I have said above, therefore, also answers your question as to whether the judge has the right to compel the health officer to make the patient's record available to the court. The court does have a right to issue a subpoena compelling the health officer to bring the record to court, and the court does have a right to compel the health officer to testify and explain or disclose the records if the finding is made by the judge that it is necessary for a proper administration of justice. The health officer, of course, when he brings the records to court, should not disclose them or give any information to anybody until the finding is made and the judge orders him to do so.

There is no legal way that I know of that these records and that this evidence may be given to the judge in a private and confidential manner. If the evidence is used at all, it must be used in the trial and become a part of the record of the trial; and the party against whom the evidence is used, under our system of law, must have the right of cross examination.

I regret to say, also, that there is no help that I can give you by way of an opinion on the problem of health officers' being compelled to attend court and testify as witnesses. I have searched our laws relative to witnesses and the attendance of witnesses upon the court, and I cannot find anything that exempts physicians, either private, public, or Public Health physicians, from the obligation and duty to attend court when properly ordered to do so by service of the subpoena. The fact is that all men regardless of professions, races, colors or creeds must attend court and be witnesses when properly ordered to do so. There are no exemptions, and I cannot find anything in the Public Health Law that can be construed even by implication to grant an exemption.

I am sorry that I cannot work out a solution for you in this matter, but there is no solution as long as our law remains as presently written in the statute.

MARRIAGE; PRE-MARITAL EXAMINATION
CERTIFICATES; FORM OF

28 March 1946

I received your letter of March 27, with regard to the question raised by Mr. C .C. Duke, Register of Deeds of Beaufort County, relative to the forms supplied by the State Board of Health for physicians to use in reporting the result of pre-marital examinations. I have carefully considered Form No. 306 which is now being used, a copy of which you sent to me, and the statutes on this subject as amended by the 1945 Act of the General Assembly, Chapter 577. I have considered Mr. Duke's observations on the subject as contained in his letter to me dated March 25, 1946, enclosing a copy of his letter to you of that same date.

My consideration of the matter leads me to suggest that you should adopt two forms of certificates. I think your present form No. 306 ought to be amended by striking out under (a) the words "in the infectious or communicable stage."

The statute now provides in G. S. 51-9 that the applicant shall present to the Register of Deeds a certificate by a regularly licensed physician that no evidence of any venereal disease was found. If you comply with this statute, in my opinion it is necessary to eliminate the words as suggested.

I think you should have another certificate to provide for the exceptions as recognized in G. S. 51-10, which would be substantially in the form shown by the enclosed. If, after considering this, you have any questions about it, I will be glad to go into the matter fully with you.

PUBLIC HEALTH; VITAL STATISTICS; PUBLIC RECORDS; RIGHT OF INSPECTION
AND FURNISHING COPIES OR LISTS

11 April 1946

In your letter you state that the Bureau of Vital Statistics has had frequent inquiries in recent weeks by commercial concerns requesting lists and addresses of new-born children. It is understood that these lists will be used for circularizing the persons in question.

You would like to know if the Bureau of Vital Statistics must comply with such requests under the theory that birth and death certificates are public records and are available to all citizens for any use.

Section 132-6 of the General Statutes of North Carolina deals with the inspection and examination of public records and is as follows:

"Every person having custody of public records shall permit them to be inspected and examined at reasonable times and under his supervision by any person, and he shall furnish certified copies thereof on payment of fees as prescribed by law."

I am of the opinion, therefore, that the law does not compel you to furnish lists of names and addresses of new-born children to any person, firm or corporation. Anyone is entitled to come and look at your records at reasonable times and under your supervision, this inspection to be handled according to the convenience and work that must be performed by your office and its staff. While it is not expressly set forth in the statute, I do not think it would be unreasonable for these persons to make their own private copy of any portion of the record that they desire.

You and your staff are only compelled by law to furnish certified copies of the birth and death certificates as provided by Section 138-102 of the General Statutes, and this will only be done when you are tendered your fees. You are also entitled to the regular fee provided by statute for making a search of your records. I think that a person, firm or corporation could place with you a standing request to furnish them certified copies of all the births pertaining to a certain county, group of counties, etc., provided they tendered you the fees; and you are not compelled to furnish any lists of names or anything outside of certified copies.

MARRIAGE LAWS; HEALTH CERTIFICATES REQUIRED OF
APPLICANTS FOR LICENSES

24 April 1946

You have submitted to this office Form No. 306, which is a certificate of physical examination for marriage license applicants. You have also submitted to this office what I shall call your new Form No. 306, which is a revision of the form now in use. You have also submitted to this office a form which is presently being used, which is designated as Form No. 307, and this is accompanied by a proposed revision of this form, which I shall designate as new Form No. 307. This Form No. 307 is a conditional certificate for marriage license applicants. Under the provisions of Section 51-11 it is the duty of the State Board of Health to design or formulate these certificates which are furnished to the various Registers of Deeds in the State upon request.

Section 51-9 of the General Statutes, dealing with health certificates, was amended at the 1945 Session of the General Assembly by striking out of the section the words "in the infectious or communicable stage." Your proposed new Form No. 306 has been amended to conform with this amendment in the statute. You will also recall that Section 51-10 of the General Statutes, which contains the exceptions in regard to the marriage of diseased persons, has been rewritten entirely. One of these exceptions is to the effect that when an applicant has completed treatment and the physician certifies that he is cured or probated, and that the applicant and the proposed partner have been informed of possible future infectivity, then a certificate can be issued. This condition or exception you have combined in your Form No. 306 for the reason that a person who has received a course of treatment as prescribed by physicians is naturally classed in the category of persons who no longer have a disease. I am of the opinion, therefore, that you are within your rights in combining all of these situations in your proposed new Form No. 306. I see no reason why a third and separate form should be created for the situation where the applicant, although previously infected, nevertheless, at the time of the application he has completed treatment and is cured or probated. Regardless of the fact that the Laboratory report may be positive, nevertheless, both the Register of Deeds and the general public must depend upon the integrity of the physician signing the certificate.

Your proposed Form No. 307 deals with the other exceptions as expressed in Section 51-10. This revision has moved the three exceptions to the front of the certificate and incorporated them in the certificate itself instead of having them printed on the back of the certificate for reference, as provided by the old form. This certificate also contains a form of agreement to be executed by an applicant in conformity with exceptions Nos. 2, 3 and 4, Section 51-10.

In our opinion, these forms,—that is, the proposed revisions—are in conformity with the statute and comply with the law. Persons using these forms, in our opinion, will be using proper and lawful certificates upon which to obtain marriage licenses.

PUBLIC HEALTH; WATER PROTECTION; SYSTEM OF WATER SUPPLY AND SEW-
ERAGE; DUTY OF GOVERNING AUTHORITIES OF CITIES AND TOWNS; AD-
VICE OF THE STATE BOARD OF HEALTH; VALIDITY OF CONTRACT
FOR INSTALLATION OF WATER SYSTEM OR SEWERAGE
SYSTEM WITHOUT ADVICE OF BOARD OF HEALTH;
DEFINITION OF SEWAGE

7 May 1946

Mr. Hubbard of your division has heretofore called our attention to Section 130-110 of the General Statutes which provides in substance that the governing authorities of cities and towns, corporations or firms, shall advise with the State Board of Health in regard to sources of water supply and disposing of drainage or sewage. It is perhaps best that we quote the complete statute which is as follows:

"The state board of health shall from time to time consult with and advise the boards of all state institutions, the authorities of cities and towns, corporations, or firms already having or intending to introduce systems of water supply, drainage or sewerage, as to the most appropriate source of supply, the best practical method of assuring the purity thereof, or of disposing of their drainage or sewage, having regard to the present and prospective needs and interests of other cities, towns, corporations, or firms which may be affected thereby. *All such boards of directors, authorities, corporations, and firms are hereby required to give notice to said board of their intentions in the premises and to submit for its advice outlines of their proposed plans or schemes in relation to water supplies and disposal of sewage, and no contract shall be entered into by any state institution or town for the introduction of a system of water supply or sewage disposal until said advice shall have been received, considered, and approved by the said board.* For the purpose of carrying out the general provisions of this and the preceding sections, every municipal or private corporation, company, or individual supplying or authorized to supply water for drinking or other domestic purposes to the public shall file with the secretary of the state board of health, within ninety days after the receipt of notice from said secretary, certified plans and surveys, in duplicate, pertaining to the source from which the water is derived, the possible source of infections thereof, and the means in use for the purification thereof, in accordance with the directions to be furnished by the said secretary. Failure on the part of any individual, firm, corporation, or municipality to comply with this section shall be a misdemeanor, and upon conviction those responsible therefor shall be fined not less than fifty dollars nor more than one hundred dollars, at the discretion of the court."

It is true that this statute has a penal feature and provides that any individual, firm, corporation, or municipality who fails to comply with the section shall be guilty of a misdemeanor and upon conviction shall be fined not less than fifty dollars nor more than one hundred dollars at the discretion of the court. We were, at first, inclined to the view that if a municipality or other person or firm mentioned in the statute entered into a contract without the advice and approval of the State Board of Health that the contract would be valid, and the only remedy would be a criminal indictment. After some thought about the matter and after consultation among the different members of the staff of this office, we have definitely come to the conclusion that this statute operates upon the formation of the contract; and that a compliance with this statute is a condition precedent to the formation of a valid and binding contract. We are further of the opinion that unless the board of directors, authorities, corporations and firms, and this includes the governing bodies of cities and towns, submit their plans or schemes in relation to water supplies and disposal of sewage to the State Board of Health and obtain the advice of the State Board of Health, consider the same and approve the same, then in that event, there is no contract and there could be no valid contract on the part of any State institution, or town for the introduction of or installation of any water supply or sewage disposal until this is done. This is a remedial statute for the protection of the public, and it is positive and mandatory in its terms. In our opinion, any State institution or town that attempts to enter into a contract without first complying with the provisions of this statute and any State institution or town that does install a water system or sewerage system without same does so in violation of law and is expending public funds without legal permit or sanction. As a situation analogous to what we have discussed above, we would call your attention to the case of RAYNOR v. COMMISSIONERS OF LOUISBURG; 220 N. C. 248. In that case the Town of Louisburg attempted to buy a Diesel engine for its water and power system without submitting the contract for competitive bidding upon due advertisement as required by law. The citizens and taxpayers of the town brought a suit to enjoin the town commissioners from proceeding further without contract, and the Supreme Court of this State held that the taxpayers of the town were entitled to the injunction and that the commissioners of the town should be perpetually restrained from proceeding on the contract without complying with the statute. The Court held that unless the law was complied with, any attempted contract was ultra vires and void. We think that this holding supports our position and that the courts of our State would give as much protection to the people on a contract involving a water supply system or sewerage system which affects the health of the people as it would to the purchase of a Diesel engine which involves at the most only the money contributed by the taxpayers for the support of the town.

It is our opinion, therefore, that funds spent upon any alleged contract without compliance with this section on the part of the State institution or town would be illegal expenditures; and no doubt such expenditures could be enjoined by the taxpayers or any other board or body. The North Carolina State Board of Health is charged with the enforcement not only of this section but with the whole section on public health.

We now call your attention to Section 130-117 of the General Statutes which prohibits the discharge of sewage into a water supply. This section is as follows:

"No person, firm, corporation, or municipality shall flow or discharge *sewage* above the intake into any drain, brook, creek, or river from which a public drinking-water supply is taken, unless the same shall have been passed through some well-known system of sewage purification approved by the state board of health; and the continued flow and discharge of such sewage may be enjoined upon application of any person.

"If any person, firm, or corporation, or officer of any municipality having a sewerage system in charge shall violate the provisions of this section he shall be guilty of a misdemeanor."

You have asked us as to the definition of the word "sewage" as contained in this statute. There are many definitions of the word "sewage"; and for the sake of those who may be interested in this subject, we will cite some cases which may be used for investigation.

CITY OF VALPARAISO v. PARKER, 47 N. E. 330, 331

WINCHELL v. CITY OF WAUKESHA, 85 N. W. 668, 669

SANITARY DISTRICT OF CHICAGO v. CHICAGO MEAT PACKING COMPANY, 241 Ill. Appellate 288

ULMAN v. TOWN OF MT. ANGEL, 112 P. 529, 530; 36 A.L.R. N.S. 140

MORGAN v. CITY OF DANBURY, 35 A. 499, 500
COOPER v. STATE, 48 N. Y. S. (2d) 212, 214

In 57 C. J. (p. 539), sewage is defined as follows:

"Any substance that contains any of the waste products or excremen-
titious or other discharge from the bodies of human beings or animals;
a substance which consists of human excrements and refuse animal
and vegetable matter, which constantly and continuously generates
gases; deleterious matter carried by conduits into a river or other
source of public supply; excreted, as well as waste, refuse, or foul matter carried off in sewers and drains, whether open or closed, by water
flowing therein; something noxious, corrupt, and impure; that which
passes through a sewer; the liquid and solid matter, flowing from
water-closets through the sewer and drain to the river; the refuse and
foul matter, solid or liquid, carried through the sewer by the water
therein flowing, or which a sewer carries off; water polluted by the
filth from the buildings and streets. 'Sewage' is often used to indicate
anything pertaining to sewers, as for example the general drainage
of a city or town by means of sewers."

Our own Court, I think, has defined the term "sewage" as used in this
section; and I think that until some other definition is made by the Court
that your department should follow this definition. In the case of CITY OF
DURHAM v. ENO COTTON MILLS, 144 N. C. 705, the Supreme Court
said:

"We do not think that the dyestuff or the fecal matter from the privies, which was not passed through the defendant's sewer, could be regarded as sewage within the intent and meaning of section 3051. It is
confined, under the facts of the case, to the liquid and solid matter
flowing from the water-closets through the sewer and drain to the
river, and that was our conclusion at the former hearing of this case,
as is apparent from the opinion. Some courts have construed 'sewage' to
mean excreted, as well as waste, refuse or foul matter, carried off in
sewers and drains, whether open or closed, by the water flowing therein. MORGAN v. DANBURY, 67 Conn., 484; WINCHELL v. WAUKE-
SHA, 110 Wis., 101; CLAY v. GRAND RAPIDS, 60 Mich., 451. In
SUTTON v. MAYOR, 27 L.J. (Eq., 1858), 741, the Vice Chancellor
says that, 'in the common sense of the term "sewer" it means a large
and generally, though not always, underground passage (or conduit)
for fluid and feculent matter from a house or houses to some other locality,' usually the place of discharge. Other courts have defined a sewer
to be a closed or covered waterway for conveying and discharging filth,
refuse, and foul matter, liquid or solid, while ditches are drains which
are or may be open and so arranged as to take away surface water.
STATE BOARD OF HEALTH v. JERSEY CITY, 55 N. J. Eq., 116;
7 Words and Phrases, 6457 et seq. Whatever may be the true and
definite meaning of the word, if it has one, either generally or when
ascertained from its use in any given connection, we think the Legislature did not intend, when the word was used in section 3051, that it
should embrace dyestuff and feculent matter other than sewage from
the water-closets in the mill, as the defendant dealth with them, but
only such deleterious matter as was carried by conduits of some kind
into the river or other source of public supply, and would, therefore,
in such large and concentrated quantities, most probably, if not necessarily, pollute the stream at the intake. It seems from the finding of
Judge Ferguson that the defendant, once in each week, 'hauled off and
buried' the excrement from the open privies of its operatives, but it is
also found that not only the dyestuffs, but the feculent matter from the
open privies, are washed into the river by the surface drainage and

contaminate the same. However this may be, we are satisfied that the Legislature did not intend to include within the prohibition of section 3051, under the name of sewage, any matter carried into the supplying watercourse by mere surface washing."

We are of the opinion, therefore, that in the enforcement of this section (130-117), dealing with the discharge of sewage into water supplies, you are confined to the definition that sewage as used in this statute which is liquid and solid matter flowing from the water-closets through sewers and drains; and you will further see that the Court is inclined to the view that the form of the sewer contemplated by the statute is a closed or covered waterway for conveying and discharging filth, refuse and fecul matter.

PUBLIC HEALTH; WATER PROTECTION; PUBLIC WATER SUPPLY; CRIMINAL
ACTION FOR POLLUTION; CIVIL REMEDIES AGAINST PERSONS OF FIRMS
CAUSING CONTAMINATION OR POLLUTION; MUNICIPAL CORPORA-
TION AND STATE AS PARTIES PLAINTIFF

14 May 1946

Your letter on this subject would have been answered sooner but for the fact that there are presented some rather difficult legal problems in connection with the subject of water protection.

It appears that at Lincolnton, North Carolina a local firm has installed sand pumping equipment on a small branch which is the source of raw water for the Town of Lincolnton. Some of this equipment is in the form of a vertical belt-driven pump with a flexible suction hose; this suction hose is set up in the branch approximately 600 feet above the public water supply intake works, and about 100 feet above the backwater of the intake pond; the operation of a flexible suction hose requires that it be moved from place to place by workmen in the stream; a mixture of sand and water is or will be pumped into a bin on the bank and from this bin, water will overflow and drain back into the branch; this pump will have a capacity of from 300 to 400 gallons per minute.

It is stated that in addition to removing the sand that this type of operation is utilized to wash the sand; and as a result, water returning to the stream will carry with it a large proportion of the mud, silt, and other material previously contained in the sand; because of violent agitation connected with the pumping operation, much of this material will become finely divided to such an extent that it will not settle again and will remain in suspension so that it will be picked up by the raw water pumps at the intake works; this matter in suspension with a considerable amount of clay which will be washed into the branch by the returning flow of water from the bin will greatly increase the turbidity of the stream water; the total and combined effects of these operations result in an undesirable increase in suspended matter in the water received at the water treatment plant for the period when sand removal operations are in progress; it is thought that the pumping operations will be intermittent, and this will result in the physical characteristics of the raw water fluctuating according to intermittent operations; this hampers and hinders the proper operation of the treatment plant; all of this will affect the quality of the water because there will be a considerable increase in the bacterial content of the water resulting from a disturbance of the bottom deposits of the stream which deposits provide a more favorable environment for the growth of objectionable types of bacteria than does the flowing water; your department is greatly concerned as to the ill effects that will be caused and the ill effects that the sand removal operation will exert upon the proper condition of the water prior to filtration; it is thought that such operations will cause considerable fluctuation in turbidity of the water entering the plant, and this in turn will require repeated changes in the chemical dosages in order to flocculate the water; under the best conditions, operators have difficulty with rapid changing waters; in the event an operator fails to get the chemical dosage set correctly with the turbid water, the chances are that improperly treated water will pass through the filters; under such conditions, there is not only troublesome and difficult operation but this might well result in an epidemic of water-borne diseases.

You state your question as follows:

"The purpose of this letter, therefore, is to request your opinion regarding the application of Section 7124 of the Consolidated Statutes, a copy of which is enclosed, in preventing situations of this type. In your opinion, is this section of the law sufficiently broad to cover cases as outlined above, and, if so, do you think an injunction should be sought, or should the case be brought to the attention of the Criminal Court?

"The question has also arisen regarding the proper agency to take the action in cases of this kind. We would, therefore, appreciate information in regard to whether the municipality or the State Board of Health should initiate action, or whether joint action should be taken."

Most of our laws dealing with water protection are found in Article 10 of Chapter 130 of the General Statutes under the title of "Public Health." Section 7124 of the Consolidated Statutes mentioned in your letter is contained in this article; and as a part of the General Statutes of North Carolina, it is designated as Section 130-116, and in this letter, all statutory references will be made to the chapter and section numbers of the General Statutes. Section 130-116 of the General Statutes (C. S. 7124) is as follows:

"If any person shall defile, corrupt, or make impure any well, spring, drain, branch, brook, creek, or other source of public water supply by collecting and depositing human excreta on the watershed, or depositing or allowing to remain the body of a dead animal on the watershed, or in any other manner, and if any person shall destroy or injure any pipe, conductor of water, or other property pertaining to an aqueduct, or shall aid and abet therein, he shall be guilty of a misdemeanor."

According to Webster's New International Dictionary, 2nd Edition, corrupt is defined as: "The change from a sound to a putrescent state; to make putrid * * * to change from good to bad; to vitiate; to deprave; to pervert; debase * * * or render impure by alterations or innovations * * *"

Defile is defined as: "* * * To make filthy; to dirty; to befoul * * *"

The statute also uses the words "or make impure" which we think has a commonly accepted meaning; and in this case, it would mean to render the water unwholesome, impure, and unfit for drinking purposes. The statute, of course, mentions certain acts which will constitute a corruption or defilement of the stream such as allowing to remain on the watershed the body of a dead animal, but the statute is not confined to the specific acts of leaving human excreta or the bodies of dead animals on the watershed as the statute specifically says: "or in any other manner." It seems to us, therefore, that the agitation of the bottom of a branch, which is the sole source of water supply, by a pumping operation which results in disturbing the material of the bottom of the branch, results in materials' being suspended in the water, results in washing clay into the branch, increases the bacterial content of the water and interrupts the regular routine of chemical dosages would be defiling, corrupting and making impure this public water supply and would, therefore, be an offense prohibited by this criminal statute. We do not think that some of the citizens of the town will have to die from drinking impure water before a criminal offense will be considered as having been committed. It is to be noted that the statute does not set up any degree or standard of intensity of impurity, defilement or corruption; and I think we should also note that the statute does not condition its effectiveness upon any criminal intention or any mental element. It is a penal statute for the protection of public health, and the doing of the act constitutes the offense irrespective of any intention. No doubt the procuring of sand from the bottom of a branch under ordinary circumstances is a legitimate business, and it is not intended to intimate that the persons or firm operating this sand pumping operation have any wicked designs or intentions.

There is also another statute under which it is possible that an indictment could be maintained in a case such as described in your letter; I refer to Section 143-152 of the General Statutes which is as follows:

"If any person shall in any way intentionally or maliciously damage or obstruct any water line of any public institution or in any way contaminate or render the water impure or injurious, he shall be guilty of a misdemeanor and shall be fined or imprisoned in the discretion of the court."

Your attention is called to the fact that in the case of STATE v. CORBIN, 157 N. C. 619, there is set forth the proper form of indictment to be used when persons are indicted under this section or under Section 130-116 for defiling water supplies. .

If a criminal prosecution should be instituted, in this instance or in any other instance involving the public water supply of a town or city, I am of the opinion that it is not the duty of the agents and officials of the State Board of Health to institute such a criminal prosecution in so far as the above quoted statutes are concerned. There are other statutes in Article 10 of Chapter 130 of the General Statutes which impose on the North Carolina State Board of Health the duty of making rules and regulations for the care and oversight of inland waters and to prevent contamination as well as to secure purifications. Persons failing to comply with these rules and regulations are guilty of a misdemeanor. As an example, see Section 130-109 of the General Statutes which seems to apply to persons, firms or corporations responsible for the management of the water supply. There are also statutes regulating the management and inspection of watersheds and health officers as well as the State Board of Health can furnish rules or instructions to inhabitants or persons residing or owning property on watersheds. Violation of these instructions is made a misdemeanor; and as examples of such statutes, see Sections 130-113 and 130-115. I have examined the rules and regulations of the North Carolina State Board of Health pertaining to watershed areas which have been promulgated from time to time, and I cannot find any regulation that applies to the situation described in your letter.

Under the provisions of Section 130-108 every municipal corporation or agency selling water to the public for drinking and household purposes "shall take every reasonable precaution to protect from contamination and assure the healthfulness of such water * * *" It, therefore, seems to me that a municipal corporation is primarily and specifically charged with the duty of instituting criminal prosecutions against persons or firms who defile, corrupt or render impure public supplies of drinking water. The State Board of Health may make inspections or tests and when properly subpoenaed, its agents should give evidence as witnesses; but I do not think it is the primary duty of the Board of Health to institute such prosecutions where a municipality is concerned. The law contemplates that a municipality shall do some things for themselves and shall look after their public especially in so far as local health and public matters are concerned affecting the daily lives of the inhabitants of such towns; and this duty has not been delegated to the State Administration.

The question of obtaining an injunction to restrain and enjoin the operation of this sand pumping device is not quite as clear cut as the question of criminal indictment. Much depends upon the proof and the attitude of the particular court before whom the matter may be heard. In general, it may be said that acts which endanger the public health or safety of the people may be enjoined. In 43 C. J. S. (Injunctions) Section 124, p. 671, it is said:

> "Acts which are a menace to the public health or safety, or, as sometimes stated in greater detail, acts which are dangerous to human life, detrimental to public health, and the occasion of great public inconvenience and damage, may be enjoined. The power to issue an injunction in these circumstances belongs to the general powers possessed by courts of equity, and is also conferred by some statutes applicable to various situations * * *."

In dealing especially with waters and the protection of water supplies, in 67 C. J. (Waters), Section 146, p. 789, it is said:

> "Injunction is a proper remedy to prevent a threatened pollution of a watercourse, or to stop the further continuance of a nuisance consisting in such pollution, and this remedy is available, although redress might be had by abatement of the nuisance or an indictment, or by action at law. The granting or refusing of an injunction rests in each case on the sound discretion of the court, exercised according to the recognized principles of equity, and plaintiff must not only show the pollution of the stream, but he must further establish facts entitling him to such relief under the equitable principles generally applicable to injunctions."

In the case of MORGANTON v. HUDSON, 207 N. C. 360, the Town of Morganton had condemned a watershed right and joined with the owner of the fee, a lumber company, in seeking an injunction to restrain the cutting and moving of timber trees from a watershed. The Town sought the injunction because the removal of timber from the watershed constituted "a dangerous nuisance and potential infection and contamination of the water supply of said Town of Morganton, and such continued entry and trespass upon plaintiff's said watershed endangers the lives and health of the citizens of the said town." A demurrer was sustained in the plaintiff's appeal, and the Supreme Court decided that the plaintiffs were entitled to the injunction not only because of the removal of valuable timber trees but because such trespass constituted a menace to the health of the inhabitants of the town. This case, as we see it, is a direct authority that an injunction may be obtained in such instances.

In the case of RHYNE v. MFG. CO., 182 N. C., 489, the plaintiff obtained an injunction restraining the defendant company from discharging sewage into a dry ditch where it subsequently flowed over the plaintiff's land and polluted his spring and branch. It was held that the plaintiff was entitled to an injunction, the Court saying that injunctions would be granted in matters involving health; and in reviewing cases where injunctions had been denied, the Court said:

"But so far as we have examined, whenever this principle has been apparently applied with us in cases which threatened serious injury to health and injunctive relief was denied to claimant, it will be found either that there was some defect in the proof offered by plaintiff, or such proof was successfully controverted by defendant, or there were other conditions present which required the application of some other principle than that which the defendant here invokes for his protection."

The cases are all reviewed from all over the United States in a note appended to the case of PENNSYLVANIA RAILROAD COMPANY v. SAGAMORE COAL COMPANY, 39 A. L. R. 882 (Penn.). In this case the Supreme Court of Pennsylvania held that polluted water from a mine cannot be drained into a natural stream to the injury of a public water supply taken from the stream. The court held further that it was a nuisance to pollute any stream from which the public gets its supply of water and that there was no question as to the statute of limitations or prescriptive right involved since there could be no prescriptive right to maintain an obstruction on the highway or pollute a stream to the detriment of the public. In considering the matter, the Court said:

"Is a city as helpless to protect the water supply on which it depends as Sanderson was held to be? Does a great municipality stand on the same ground, when the water supply for its multitudes of people is under consideration, as a single property owner must stand, under Pennsylvania Coal Co. v. Sanderson? . . . Notwithstanding the name of the commonwealth had been put on the record as a plaintiff, at the instance of her attorney general, and notwithstanding the conclusive evidence of the destruction of the water supply for all domestic purposes, on which the borough of Butler had been dependent for many years, the case was disposed of on the narrow ground covered by the rule in Sanderson's Case. The error of the learned judge lies in this treatment of the case."

In the case of CARETTI v. BRORING BUILDING COMPANY, 46 A. L. R. 1, the whole question of obtaining an injunction against the pollution of a stream and a long and extensive annotation appears at the end of the case, beginning on p. 8. This annotation reviews all of the cases in the United States on the question of obtaining an injunction against the pollution of a stream by private persons or corporations. The annotator says on p. 9 as follows:

> "The pollution of a stream by a private individual or corporation has been frequently enjoined where a material and irreparable injury will result from its further continuance, or the right to unpolluted water has been substantially interfered with or threatened, the courts generally taking the view that in such cases a nuisance exists, or will exist unless an injunction be granted."

Your attention is called to two more cases on this subject which are as follows: MERIWETHER SAND & GRAVEL CO. v. STATE, 26 S. W. (2d) 57 (Ark.). In this case, it was specifically held that an injury to a stream by discharging the washings of a gravel plant rendering the stream unfit for use or pleasure of riparian owners and destroying the fish therein would be enjoined by a court of equity, the court saying:

> "It is insisted, however, that the appellees have an adequate remedy at law by an action for damages. In this contention the appellant errs, for the reason that the injury, as shown by the testimony which was accepted by the chancellor, is a continuing and progressive one, and to remit them to their remedy at law would result in unnecessary expense and inconvenience to the litigants, and lead to a multiplicity of suits. 'The remedy at law, to be adequate and complete, and attain the full end and justice of the case, must reach the whole mischief, and secure the whole right of the party in a perfect manner, in praesenti and in futuro.' CONWAY, EX PARTE, 4 Ark. 338. See, also, LAWTON v. HERRICK, 83 Conn. 417, 76 A. 986; PETERSON v. SANTA ROSA, 119 Cal. 387, 51 p. 557. But the appellant says the injury shown is slight, and the resulting damage to it, by reason of the injunction, would be great. In this contention, appellant is concluded by the finding of the court below that the waters of Bodcaw creek have been so polluted as to destroy the fish therein and to render it unfit for the use or pleasure of the riparian proprietors. It would serve no useful purpose to detail the testimony of the several witnesses relative to this question. As before stated, it was conflicting, and we cannot say the chancellor's finding was against its preponderance."

In the case of COMMONWEALTH v. KENNEDY, 87 A. 605, the court held that the pollution of water is the subject of injunctive relief and that the Commonwealth cannot be deprived of its right to secure an injunction because the same situation constitutes a public nuisance, and a criminal prosecution could likewise be maintained.

I am of the opinion, therefore, that if a proper case is shown by the evidence that the stream is being polluted, the water rendered unwholesome and impure, that the chemical dosages are interfered with and that raw water thereby gets into the main pipes without purification and that this situation is of such a nature that there is grave danger of water-borne diseases being propagated or spread, then this, to our way of thinking, constitutes a nuisance and can be restrained and enjoined and an injunction is a proper remedy irrespective of the fact that a criminal prosecution can also be maintained.

We have discussed this question generally, and we do not have in mind any particular firms or persons because we know nothing of the facts or of the merits of the case. The charter of the Town of Lincolnton which is contained in Chapter 369 of the Private Laws of 1899 authorizes the town to provide a sufficient supply of pure water for said town and to provide an adequate water system and water works and sewerage system for said town. (See p. 1013) On p. 1033 of this same volume of Private Laws will be found in Section 52 all necessary powers of condemnation for establishing a water system both within and without the town.

Section 160-234 of the General Statutes gives the governing body of a town power to remove, abate, or remedy everything in the city limits or within a mile of such limits which is dangerous or prejudicial to the public health. We are of the opinion, therefore, that it is the duty of the governing body of the municipality or of interested citizens living in the municipality of Lincolnton to become party plaintiffs and seek an injunction in this matter if they desire to do so. This matter does not involve any particular matter on the city's watershed that the State Board of Health is required by statute to take notice of nor does it involve a matter that is embraced within the regulations of the State Board of Health for the control of residents on watersheds nor does it involve a matter under Section 130-113 which deals more specifically with typhoid fever and cholera. The State could join with the city in seeking an injunction if this was a matter involving sewage under Section 130-117 of the General Statutes. We think, however, that the State does not have the primary duty of seeking the injunction in this case if an application is made and that the Town of Lincolnton and its citizens should seek their own injunction.

SANITARY DISTRICTS; ENLARGEMENT OF DISTRICT

23 May 1946

You inquire through a representative of your office as to whether or not the opinion given by me to Honorable D. Newton Farnell, Attorney for the Bessemer Sanitary District, March 21, 1946, construing Section 130--59 of the General Statutes relating to the enlargement of a special tax district, would be applicable to Section 130-56, prescribing the procedure for the extension of the boundaries of a sanitary district.

When I wrote this letter to Mr. Farnell, I had in mind Section 130--59 but I think that the opinion is as much, if not more, applicable to Section 130-56 than to 130-59, so that I am of the opinion that the procedure suggested in my opinion to Mr. Farnell may be followed if he proceeds under Section 130-56 rather than Section 130-59.

PUBLIC HEALTH; MUNICIPAL CORPORATIONS; AUTHORITY OF CITY OR TOWN TO LEVY TAXES FOR THE SUPPORT OF PUBLIC HEALTH EXCLUSIVE OF AND ASIDE FROM GENERAL-FUND LEVY

18 June 1946

You will recall that you sent us a letter addressed to you from the Director of Public Health of the Wayne County Health Department. In the first paragraph of this letter, the Director requested you to secure an opinion from our office as to whether or not the statutory limit of one dollar per hundred, set up as a maximum expenditure for the general fund, includes expenditures for health; the Director would further like to know if expenditures for health by cities and counties can be made as expenditures for education without regard to the limitation imposed on the general fund. It is stated that this question has arisen in connection with the appropriation of funds by the City of Goldsboro for typhus control.

I have searched our statutes dealing with the subject of public health as related to cities and towns, and I cannot find any statute which gives cities and towns the right to levy taxes for the specific and special purpose of public health matters. It is true that Section 130-31 of the General Statutes, which is in the chapter on public health, gives a city or town the right to employ a municipal physician or a municipal health officer; and in addition, to make regulations, pay salaries and fix and impose penalties for the protection of public health. Nothing is said, however, as to the levy of taxes for this purpose. The section following, 130-32, fixes and describes the duties of the municipal physician or health officer. It is also provided in Section 130-30 that joint city and county health departments "shall have heretofore been created and are existing as joint city and county boards of health," shall have the right to receive funds and that the cities and counties shall have the right to appropriate annually funds for this purpose and to levy special taxes therefor. This, however, does not help us on the question of a city's public health activities when standing alone. I have also examined the charter of the City of Goldsboro and have gone over the private laws of this State covering some thirty years to see if I could find a provision in the charter of the City of Goldsboro that would give the City a right to levy for public health aside from the general fund. I cannot find any such charter provision. If such provision exists which I have overlooked, the city attorney will undoubtedly know of its existence.

When we turn to the chapter on municipal corporations, we find that under Section 160-229 a city has many powers in regard to public health, including the right to contract with hospitals for the care of the sick and afflicted poor of the city within certain limitations therein expressed. Taxes can be levied for this specific purpose, but there is no authority in any of these statutes for a specific levy for public health generally. It is provided in 160-402 of the General Statutes that the governing body of a city or town is limited to one dollar ($1.00) on the one hundred dollars ($100.00) valuation of property in raising revenue for expenses incident to the proper government of the city.

Frankly, I cannot find any authority that allows the city to levy for this purpose at all unless the city includes the expenditure in its budget and undertakes to take care of it out of the general fund which is covered by the one dollar ($1.00) limitation. Expenditures for public health and the power to levy taxes for such a purpose are not on the same basis as education since the requirements for maintaining schools for a certain period of time are governed by other provisions of the Constitution. The situation in regard to counties is different because the counties have a special statute which is Section 130-29 of the General Statutes, and they are thereby authorized to levy a special tax for the preservation of public health. No such statute, as heretofore pointed out, exists in favor of cities. It is also true that cities are authorized to join with other cities and other counties for the purpose of forming a district health unit as provided in Section 160-66 of the General Statutes (Cumulative Supplement of 1945); but here again, cities are not given any specific power to levy any specific tax for this purpose.

So far as I can see, the taxing power of a city for the specific purpose of public health is a matter that has been very much neglected and simply does not exist unless the city includes the item in its budget to be paid by an appropriation from general funds or unless the city has surplus funds or other unincumbered funds which it can devote to this purpose.

OPINIONS TO LOCAL GOVERNMENT COMMISSION

14 March 1945

I received your letter of March 13, with reference to the City of Hendersonville general refunding bonds and water and sewer refunding bonds, dated July 1, 1937, and payable July 1, 1972. I have read the quotation from the resolution of the Board of Commissioners providing for the issuance of the bonds, contained in your letter.

I do not see in the quoted portion of the resolution anything which would authorize the city to proportionally decrease the amount which it was required to annually raise by taxation and from the earnings of the water and sewer system, when, as now contemplated, there is to be a reduction by a refunding operation of a part of the outstanding bonds. In the absence of such a provision in the resolution, I doubt if there would be any authority for the city to decrease the amounts to be provided as required by the resolution until there has been placed in the sinking fund a sum sufficient to retire all of the outstanding bonds.

OPINIONS TO STATE BOARD OF ELECTIONS

ELECTIONS; CREATION OF NEW POLITICAL PARTY; PETITIONERS
MUST BE QUALIFIED VOTERS

15 July 1944

You inquire as to the sufficiency of a petition filed under Section 163-1 of the North Carolina General Statutes, providing for the creation of a new political party, and as to whether or not the burden is on the person or organization presenting the petition to offer evidence satisfactory to the Board that the signers are qualified voters.

Section 163-1 of the North Carolina General Statutes, defining a political party and providing for the creation of a new party, provides that "a political party within the meaning of the Election Laws of this State shall be any group of voters which. . . . .; or any group of voters which have filed with the State Board of Elections, at least ninety days before the State general election, a petition signed by ten thousand *qualified voters*, declaring their intention of organizing a State political party, the name of which shall be stated in the petition, together with the name and address of the State Chairman thereof and also declaring their intention of participating in the next succeeding election. . . . . When any new political party has qualified for participation in an election as herein required, and has furnished to the State Board of Elections the name of such of its nominees as is desired to be printed on the official ballots by the first day of September, it shall be the duty of the State Board of Elections to cause to be printed on the official ballot furnished by it to the counties the names of such nominees."

It will be noted that the petition shall be signed by ten thousand qualified voters. This office has repeatedly expressed the opinion that a qualified voter is one who not only possesses all the qualifications of registering, but is, in fact, a registered voter. I am, therefore, of the opinion that the petition must contain the names of ten thousand registered voters.

It seems to me that one who desires the benefit of the pertinent statute has the duty of going forward and showing that he has complied with the conditions of such statute. The section says: "When any new political party has qualified for participation in an election as herein required, ...". I am of the opinion that the duty is upon the sponsors of the proposed new political party to establish to the satisfaction of the State Board of Elections that the petition filed by it complies with the requirements of the section in that it contains the names of ten thousand qualified voters, before it can require the names of its candidates to be placed on the official ballots.

ELECTIONS; RESIDENCE; QAULIFICATIONS FOR VOTING

27 October 1944

Receipt is acknowledged of your letter of October 27, in which you refer to me for consideration the question asked you on behalf of Mr. L. G. Smith, as to his right to register and vote in Wake County. From your letter it appears that he moved to Wake County from Edgecombe County about nine months ago to become a resident of this County and has not lived in any one precinct as much as four months since he has been in this County, and that he will not have lived in the present precinct in which he now lives for as much as four months preceding the election. He has applied for registration in the precinct in which he now lives and was denied the privilege of registering. You ask my opinion as to whether or not Mr. Smith is entitled to register and vote in Wake County and, if so, in what precinct.

Our fundamental law, the Constitution, Article VI, paragraph 2, provides, in part, as follows:

"He shall reside in the State of North Carolina for one year and in the precinct, ward or other election district in which he offers to vote four months next preceding the election: Provided, that removal from one precinct, ward or other election district to another in the same county shall not operate to deprive any person of the right to vote in the precinct, ward or other election district from which he has removed until four months after such removal."

The same language is found in our statute, G. S. 163-25.

I understand the facts to be from your letter that Mr. Smith has resided in Edgecombe County and in Wake County together for a much longer period than one year, and that the question arises as to his right to register and vote in Wake County only from the fact that he has not resided in any one precinct for as much as four months and will not have resided in any one precinct for as much as four months prior to the election.

G. S. 163-25(e) provides that, if a person removes to another state or county within this State with the intention of making such state or county his permanent residence, he shall be considered to have lost his residence in the state or county from which he has removed.

It is, therefore, clear that under this statute Mr. Smith has lost his right to vote in Edgecombe County, having resided in Wake County for about nine months with the intention of making this County his permanent home and, unless he is permitted to register and vote in some precinct in Wake County, he will be unable to vote anywhere.

An examination fails to reveal any decision of our Court which has construed the language of the Constitution with regard to this particular situation. The general principle followed in all of our decisions dealing with the right of a person to vote is that the Constitution and the statutes are liberally construed with a view of permitting all qualified persons to cast their ballots, rather than to deprive them of such right. In the case of QUINN v. LATTIMORE, 120 N. C. 426, the Court said:

"In construing these provisions of the Constitution we should keep in mind that this is a government of the people, in which the will of the people—the majority—legally expressed, must govern and that these provisions and all Acts providing for elections should be liberally construed, that tend to promote a fair election or expression of this popular will."

Under the constitutional and statutory provisions above referred to, a person who has resided in this State one year and in the ward or other election district in which he offers to vote four months next preceding the election, is stated to possess the qualifications of a voter to register, but with the proviso as follows:

"Provided, that the removal from one precinct, ward or other election district to another in the same county shall not operate to deprive any person of the right to vote in the precinct, ward or other election district from which he has removed until four months after such removal."

Unquestionably, if such person had resided in one precinct in the county for as much as four months, he would have a right to return and register and vote in that precinct, notwithstanding his removal to another precinct in which he had not resided as much as four months prior to the election, and notwithstanding the fact that the voter had never registered or voted in the precinct from which he had moved. It would, therefore, seem that the registration of the voter in the precinct, ward or other election district from which he has moved is not a prerequisite to his right to register and vote later in that precinct or other election district.

The constitutional provision would be capable of being construed in its strictest sense as against the right of the voter to vote in any precinct in the county if he had not resided in one precinct for as much as four months, although he had resided in such county all of his life. The proviso in the Constitution, on the other hand, being liberally construed in favor of the right of the voter to vote, could reasonably be said to mean that the voter is not to be deprived of his vote if his combined residence in all precincts in the county should be four months, and that where a voter has moved from one precinct to another in which he has not resided for the required time, he could return and register and vote in the precinct from which he moved, provided that the residence in such precinct, combined with that in the precinct to which he has moved, by the time of the election amounts to four months.

I would, therefore, prefer to accept this interpretation of the Constitution unless and until the courts have held otherwise. If it should be later decided that the voter was not properly registered in accordance with this view, his vote could be eliminated in any contest in which it might be concerned. If, however, he was denied the right to vote and the question arose and was decided after the election, his right would be lost and could not be restored.

PRIMARY ELECTION; CANDIDATE FOR JUSTICE OF THE SUPREME COURT; DESIGNATION OF VACANCY

18 March 1946

I have your letter of March 18, in which you enclose the Notice of Candidacy filed by Honorable John J. Ingle, of Winston-Salem, for the position of Justice of the Supreme Court. This notice reads in full as follows:

"NOTICE OF CANDIDACY IN PRIMARY ELECTION OF 1946

"STATE BOARD OF ELECTIONS,
RALEIGH, NORTH CAROLINA

"I hereby file my notice as a candidate for the nomination as Justice of Supreme Court in the Primary Election to be held on May 25, 1946. I affiliate with the Republican party, and I hereby pledge myself to abide by the results of said Primary, and to support in the next General Election all candidates nominated by the Republican party.

"Date: 3/15/46   John J. Ingle
                    Candidate sign here
                  Winston-Salem, N. C.
                   Address of candidate

FILING TIME EXPIRES MARCH 16, 1946 AT 6 O'CLOCK, P. M.

"FILING FEES REQUIRED OF CANDIDATES IN PRIMARY

"For United States Senator	$100.00
For Representative to Congress	100.00
For Governor	105.00
For Lieutenant-Governor	7.00
For Secretary of State	66.00
For State Auditor . .	66.00
For State Treasurer ..	66.00
For Attorney General	75.00
For Superintendent Public Instruction	66.00
For Commissioner of Agriculture	66.00
For Commissioner of Insurance . . .	60.00
For Commissioner of Labor	66.00
For Justice of Supreme Court .. .	75.00
For Judge of Superior Court	65.00
For Solicitor	50.00

"NOTICE TO CANDIDATES

"All candidates for these offices must have their Notices of Candidacy, together with the proper filing fee, in the possession of the State Board of Elections by 6 o'clock P. M. on Saturday, March 16th, 1946, to be accepted. This does not mean in the mails at that time and all Notices arriving in the mails after the time expires cannot be accepted. Please do not send currency with this Notice but pay by check or money order."

I note from your letter that at one minute to 6:00 o'clock, P. M., on March 16, 1946, you received this Notice in the mail from Mr. Ingle and at the same time his filing fee of $75.00.

You state that since Mr. Ingle failed to designate in his Notice to which of said vacancies on the Supreme Court he is seeking to be nominated, as is required by Section 163-147 of the General Statutes, you are requesting my opinion as to whether or not you are permitted, after the expiration of the filing time, to contact him to ascertain which vacancy on the Supreme Court he is filing for. You advise that one Republican candidate, in addition to Mr. Ingle, filed his Notice of Candidacy for Justice of the Supreme Court several days prior to the expiration of the filing date and that you called him to ascertain which vacancy he was filing for and he authorized you to designate on his notice that he was filing against Honorable J. Wallace Winborne, whose term of office expires this year.

The two vacancies on the Supreme Court will be caused by the expiration of the terms of office of Justice J. Wallace Winborne and Justice M. V. Barnhill.

G. S. 163-147 provides as follows:

"In any primary when there are two or more vacancies for chief justice and associate justices of the Supreme Court of North Carolina to be filled by nominations all candidates shall file with the state board of elections at the time of filing notice of candidacy a notice designating to which of said vacancies the respective candidate is asking the nomination. All votes cast for any candidate shall be effective only for the vacancy for which he has given notice of candidacy, as provided herein."

As you will observe, the statute requires that *at the time of filing notice of candidacy*, the candidate is required to file designating to which of said vacancies the respective candidate is asking the nomination. The statute further provides that all votes cast for any candidate shall be effective only for the vacancy for which he has given notice of candidacy as provided herein.

The terms of the statute are clear and mandatory and I regret to say that I know of no way for the candidate to later supply the notice which the statute requires shall be given at the time of filing his Notice of Candidacy. No latitude whatever is allowed to the State Board of Elections in permitting a candidate at a later date to comply with this mandatory provision of the law. I regret that I am unable to reach any other conclusion.

OPINIONS TO STATE BOARD OF CHARITIES AND PUBLIC WELFARE

ADOPTION; CONSTRUCTION OF G. S. 110-50; BRINGING OR SENDING CHILDREN INTO THE STATE TO BE ADOPTED

I have your letter of August 3, 1944, in which you ask for my construction of Section 1 of Chapter 226 of the Public Laws of 1931. You inquire more specifically as to the meaning of the phrase "for the purpose of placing him out or procuring his adoption," used in the first sentence of the section referred to above. This section now appears as G. S. 110-50, the first sentence of which reads as follows:

"No person, agency, association, institution or corporation shall bring or send into the state any child for the purpose of placing him out or procuring his adoption without first obtaining the consent of the State Board of Charities and Public Welfare."

It is my opinion that this sentence was intended to prohibit a child from being sent or brought into this State for the purpose of making his home here without complying with the statute. It covers, in my opinion, every case in which a child is brought or sent into this State to remain here with relatives or strangers except where the child is merely visiting in this State and is not to make his home here.

7 September 1944

OLD AGE ASSISTANCE; RECIPROCAL AGREEMENT WITH VIRGINIA

Receipt is acknowledged of your letter of August 1, in which you call my attention to subsection (h), Section 13, Chapter 288 of the Public Laws of 1937, as amended, authorizing the State Board of Charities and Public Welfare to enter into reciprocal agreements with other states relative to providing assistance and services to residents, nonresidents or transients and cooperate with other agencies of the State and Federal Governments in providing such assistance and services. This law is now found as G. S. 108-28(g).

You have furnished me with a copy of the Virginia statute, which is quoted in a letter to you under date of June 23, 1944, from James W. Phil-lips, Director, County and City Organization of the Department of Public Welfare, which is as follows:

"1904 (69). Transfer of dependents. The Commissioner of Public Welfare, subject to the approval of the State Board of Public Welfare and of the Attorney General, is hereby authorized to enter into reciprocal agreements with corresponding state agencies of other states regarding the interstate transportation of poor and indigent persons, and to arrange with the proper officials in this state for the acceptance, transfer and support of persons receiving public aid in other states in accordance with the terms of such reciprocal agreements; provided, that this state shall not nor shall any county or other political subdivision.

of this state be committed to the support of persons who are not in the opinion of said commissioner entitled to public support by the laws of this state.

"This section shall be so interpreted and construed as to effectuate its general purpose and to make uniform the laws of those states which enact it.

"This section may be cited as the Uniform Transfer of Dependents Act. (1940, p. 164)."

"1904 (10). Eligibility for assistance.

"(b) Has resided in this state for at least five years within the nine years immediately preceding the date of application for such assistance, and continuously for one year immediately preceding such application, provided however that this residence requirement may be waived either in part or entirely with respect to persons coming from such states as will enter into reciprocal agreements pursuant to chapter one hundred fourteen, acts of General Assembly of one thousand nine hundred forty (1906 (69)). (1944, c. 346)

"1944 amendment added the proviso."

You inquire as to whether or not, in my opinion, your Board is authorized to enter into a reciprocal agreement with the State of Virginia which would provide that a county could continue old age assistance payments for one year after the recipient moves into the State of Virginia, provided the recipient remains eligible under our statutory requirements. .

G. S. 108-28, of which subsection (g) is a part, provides in subsection (b) that the State Board shall "make such rules and regulations and take such action as may be necessary or desirable for carrying out the provisions of this article. All rules and regulations made by the State Board shall be binding on the counties and shall be complied with by the respective boards of county commissioners and the county boards of welfare."

Under the authority of our statute above quoted and referred to, I am of the opinion that a reciprocal agreement may be legally entered into by your Board with the proper officials in Virginia under authority of the Virginia statutes referred to, providing that each state would continue old age assistance payments for one year after a recipient moves from a county in this State to a county in Virginia, provided the recipient remains eligible to receive old age benefits for that period and, in my opinion, your Board may adopt rules and regulations which would require the county in this State from which such recipient moves to continue the payments to the recipient in compliance with this arrangement.

16 September 1944

CHILD WELFARE; CHILD-CARING CENTER; ESTABLISHMENT;
OPERATION BY COUNTY

Receipt is acknowledged of your letter of September 8 in which you raise the question as to the authority of a county, through its board of county commissioners, to operate a child-caring center.

The General Assembly has power to create counties and to regulate their affairs unless restricted by constitutional provision and counties, being political subdivisions and instrumentalities of the State, perform certain governmental functions within their territorial limits. FREEMAN v. BOARD OF COMMISSIONERS OF MADISON COUNTY, 217 N. C. 209.

The General Assembly alone may increase, modify, or abrogate the powers of counties. MOORE v. BOARD OF EDUCATION OF IREDELL COUNTY, 212 N. C. 499; WILLIAMSON v. CITY OF HIGH POINT, 213 N. C. 96. A county is a body politic and corporate whose powers are exercised by the board of commissioners but the board's exercise of its powers is confined to those powers which are granted by the General Assembly.

I assume that the child-caring center about which you inquire would accommodate children between certain ages, regardless of the financial status of their parents or guardians. If this is true, I am unable to see how the county, through its board of commissioners, would be authorized to establish and operate such an agency or center. It is true that counties are authorized by statute to make certain provisions for the care of its poor and unfortunate and if the proposed center confined its activities to the class of children who would come within the statutory provisions authorizing the care of the poor and unfortunate there might be some basis for saying that the county has authority to establish and operate a center of this kind.

Of course, it is possible that I have overlooked some statute which would grant this authority and, if so, I would be more than glad to change my opinion, as I am convinced that the project the Board-of-County Commissioners of Onslow County has in mind is a progressive and worthy undertaking. In addition to this, there might possibly be some public-local statute applicable to Onslow County which would tend to authorize the establishment and operation of this project. If the county authorities are in position to offer you any further proof as to statutory authorization I will be glad to consider the matter further.

CHILD WELFARE; CRIMINAL LAW; SEPARATION OF CHILD UNDER 6 MONTHS OLD FROM MOTHER

12 October 1944

You state in your letter that a woman in the Marine Corps Reserve, who is a resident of another State, gave birth to an illegitimate child. The mother has resided in the barracks on the Government Reservation prior to and following confinement. The child was born in a Government hospital on the Reservation. Plans are now being made to retain the mother in the Marine Corps service, but the child is to be separated from the mother, and the actual separation will take place on the Reservation. The mother has been advised to contact agencies in her home State for the purpose of plan and care of child, but the question of a temporary boarding placement of the child pending the completion of plans in the home State may involve a placement off the Government Reservation.

Your first question is whether the provisions of G. S. 14-320 (C. S. 4445) will be involved in connection with the placement of the child.

G. S. 14-320 makes it unlawful for any person to separate or aid in separating any child under six months from its mother for the purpose of placing such child in a foster home or institution or with the intent to remove it from the State for such purpose until the procedure outlined in this section has been followed. The section provides that the action must be taken in the county in which the mother resides or the county in which the child was born. I assume that title to the property constituting the Government Reservation referred to in your letter has heretofore vested in the United States Government in fee simple and that the State of North Carolina has ceded its jurisdiction to the Government. If this is true, it is my opinion that the provisions of G. S. 14-320 would not apply to any action taken on the Government Reservation, and that the same rules would apply where the ·child is removed from the Government Reservation to a point outside such Reservation and in the State of North Carolina as would apply to a child who was brought from outside the State of North Carolina into the State. The State of North Carolina would have no more jurisdiction of an action taken on a Government Reservation than it would have of an action taken in another State.

What I have said above would also seem to answer the second question raised in your letter.

ADOPTION LAWS; FILING COPIES WITH STATE BOARD OF CHARITIES AND PUBLIC WELFARE

4 November 1944

Receipt is acknowledged of your letter in which you inquire as to whether a certified copy, instead of the duplicate of a form in an adoption proceeding, may be filed with the State Board of Charities and Public Welfare, under the law as now written.

G. S. 48-1 provides, in part, that the petition for adoption shall be filed in duplicate on standard form to be supplied by the State Board of Charities and Public Welfare, one form to be held in the files of the Superior Court and the other to be sent to the State Board of Charities and Public Welfare.

The word "duplicate" has been defined as that which exactly resembles or corresponds to something else; another, correspondent to the first, hence, a copy, transcript, counterpart.

In 28 C. J. S., p. 590, it is said that the meaning of the word duplicate, in legal phraseology, is the same as that in its use among businessmen and ordinarily embodies primarily the idea of exact identity and being the same as an original having all the legal effect and validity of an original. It is further said that specifically in law it is an original instrument repeated, a document the same as another in essential particulars, differing from a copy in being valid as an original. The term has been held equivalent to and also distinguished from a certified copy.

In STATE v. ALLEN, 35 S. E. 204, 207, it is defined as being the duplicate of anything, an original repeated, a counterpart, a document which is essentially the same as some other instrument. In NICKLE v. LEWIS, 272 N. W. 525, 526, it is defined as being a copy of the original. IN CABLE CO. v. RATHGEBER, 113 N. W. 88, 90, it is defined as an original instrument repeated, the exact repetition of an instrument having all the validity of an original. In WRIGHT v. MICH. CENT. R. CO., 130 Fed. 843, 846, it is said that a duplicate is sometimes defined to be a copy of a thing but though generally a copy, a duplicate differs from a mere copy in having all the validity of an original.

From an inspection of the section of the General Statutes above referred to, it is my opinion that the General Assembly intended to require that two standard form petitions should be signed by the petitioners and filed with the Clerk of the Superior Court at the time the adoption proceeding is instituted, and that one be retained by the Clerk of the Superior Court and the other forwarded to the State Board of Charities and Public Welfare. However, it is my opinion that the court would not be inclined to upset an adoption proceeding solely on the ground that a certified copy of the original petition was forwarded to the State Board of Charities and Public Welfare instead of the duplicate original.

G. S. 48-5 provides that upon making the interlocutory order, the written report of the investigation made by the Superintendent of Public Welfare or representative of the child placing agency shall be forwarded by the Clerk of the Superior Court to the State Board of Charities and Public Welfare. In this instance, the statute requires that the original be forwarded to the State Board. G. S. 48-9 provides that on issuing an order granting letters of adoption, the Clerk of the Superior Court of the county in which the order is issued shall send a copy of such order to the State Board of Charities and Public Welfare and likewise a copy of the revocation of the order to said Board to be held as a permanent record. This section specifically authorizes the use of a copy.

10 November 1944

INSANE PERSONS AND INCOMPETENTS; EUGENICS BOARD; ENFORCEMENT OF ORDERS

I have your letter of November 9, 1944, in which you inquire as to the proper method of enforcing orders of the Eugenics Board.

Section 35-37 of the General Statutes reads as follows:

"It shall be the duty of the board of commissioners of any county of North Carolina, at the public cost and expense, to have one of the operations described in Sec. 35-36, performed upon any mental diseased, feeble-minded or epileptic resident of the county, not an inmate of any public institution, upon the request and petition of the superintendent of public welfare or other similar public official performing in whole or in part the functions of such superin'endent, or of the next of kin, or the legal guardian of such mentally defective person: Provided, however, that no operation described in this section shall be lawful unless and until the provisions of this article shall be first complied with."

This section seems to be the only section of the statutes which deals with the enforcement of orders of the Eugenics Board. It seems that the only method a board of county commissioners could use to enforce an order of the Eugenics Board would be through the courts of the State.

I think there is a great need for some statutory method of enforcing the orders of the Eugenics Board. It may be wise for you to give this some consideration and I will be glad to discuss it with you at some future date.

14 November 1944

ADOPTION LAW; CHILDREN BORN IN WEDLOCK; PRESUMPTION OF
LEGITIMACY; SURRENDER TO CHILD PLACING AGENCY

Receipt is acknowledged of your letter of November 7 in which you state
that during the past year you have been confronted with situations involving children born in wedlock to mothers whose husbands have been in
military service overseas for a period of twelve or more months prior to
the birth of such children. You desire to know whether, in my opinion, the
mother alone would be authorized to sign the surrender or whether it is
necessary that the legal husband of the mother sign such document.

G. S. 48-4 provides that the parents, or surviving parent, or guardian,
of the person or persons having charge of such child, or with whom it may
reside, must be a party or parties of record to an adoption proceeding. This
section contains a proviso to the effect that when the parent, parents, or
guardian of the person of the child, has signed a release of all rights to
the child, the person, agency, or institution to which said rights were released shall be made a party to this proceeding and it shall not be necessary to make the parent, parents, or guardians parties.

G. S. 48-5 provides that upon the examination of the written report of
the Superintendent of Public Welfare or of a duly authorized representative of said agency described hereinbefore, and with the consent of the
parent or parents, if living, . . . the court, if it be satisfied that the petitioner is a proper and suitable person and that the child is a proper subject
for adoption and that the adoption is for the best interests of the child, may
tentatively approve the adoption and issue an order giving the care and
custody of the child to the petitioner. This section contains a proviso to the
effect that when the parent, parents, or guardian of the person of the child
has, in writing, surrendered the child to a duly licensed child placing agency
or the Superintendent of Public Welfare of the county, and has, in writing, consented to the adoption of the child by any person or persons to be
designated by said agency or officer, this shall be deemed a sufficient consent
for the purposes of this chapter and no further consent of the parent, parents, or guardian to a subsequent specific adoption shall be necessary.

The Supreme Court of North Carolina, in the case of IN RE HOLDER,
218 N. C. 136 (1940), said that under the statute in existence at the time
the adoption in that particular case was attempted to be made, required
that the consent must appear within the proceeding itself and must have
reference to the particular proceeding which will culminate in adoption.
The court further said, in discussing the question:

"The court has been careful to preserve the principle of certainty
in adoption proceedings since the laws of inheritance and distribution
of property are directly involved. The social importance of preserving
the integrity of this system is as great as that involved in the benevolent reconstruction of family relations.
"The proceeding is in derogation of the common law and must be
strictly construed. GRIMES v. GRIMES, 207 N.C., 778, 178 S. E. 573."
In the case of WARD v. HOWARD, 217 N. C. 201, 208, the court said:
"We think it unquestionable that the jurisdiction given to clerks of
the superior court in the matter of adoption is, by the statute itself

creating it, made to depend upon the consent of the parent, if living. TRUELOVE v. PARKER, SUPRA. Indeed, regardless of the question of jurisdiction as settled by the wording of the statute itself, it may be doubted whether the State can, through any sort of law, exercise the Spartan privilege of taking a child from the home and custody of a parent and engrafting it into another family without notice to the parent, or proof of the existence of a condition—as of complete abandonment on the part of the parent—that would render such notice unnecessary. Constitution, Article I, section 17."

In the case of TRUELOVE v. PARKER, 191 N. C. 430, the court held that to give a decree of adoption any force or effect, jurisdiction must have been acquired by the court, first, over the person asking to adopt the child, second, over the child and, third, over the parents of the child.

In considering the question you raise, not only are we confronted with the problem as to whether the Supreme Court of North Carolina would uphold the provisions of the adoption statutes authorizing the release by parents to a child placing agency or the Superintendent of Public Welfare, but also whether a release signed by the mother alone would be sufficient to give the court jurisdiction. Under the old English or common law rule, a child born of a married woman was presumed legitimate unless the husband was shown to be impotent or not within the four seas, that is, he was conclusively presumed to be legitimate so long as there remained a possibility that the husband was the father. STATE v. PETTAWAY, 10 N. C. 623; WOODWARD v. BLUE, 107 N. C. 407.

This rather harsh rule has been tempered by the application of a degree of common sense, so that now access or non-access of the husband is a fact to be established by proper proof. The question of legitimacy or illegitimacy of a child of a married woman under the prevailing rule rests upon proof as to the non-access of the husband and the evidence in respect thereto must be left to the jury for determination. RAY v. RAY, 219 N. C. 217.

Courts seem to consistently hold that access between man and wife is always presumed until otherwise plainly proved, and that nothing is allowed to impune the legitimacy of a child short of proof by facts showing it to be impossible that the husband could have been its father. In order to rebut the presumption, it is necessary that competent and relevant evidence be introduced to satisfy the jury that sexual intercourse did not take place at any time when, by the laws of nature, the husband could have been the father of the child. EWELL v. EWELL, 163 N. C. 233.

In the cases which form the basis for your question, the children wree born in wedlock and the presumption that they are legitimate remains until an adjudication is made in a court of competent jurisdiction that they are, in fact, illegitimate, due to the fact that the husbands of the mothers could not have been their fathers. The mothers, in undertaking to sign the surrender affidavit without the joinder of the husbands, are undertaking by that act to declare their children illegitimate. I do not believe the courts would uphold such procedure. It is entirely possible that the husbands of the mothers involved would not desire to repudiate their presumptive parenthood and it certainly appears to me that they could not be eliminated from the picture without notice and without being consulted in any manner.

It is my opinion that where a child is born in wedlock and no adjudication has been made by a court of competent jurisdiction that the husband of the mother is not the father of the child, the husband should join in the execution of the surrender affidavit or should be made a party to the adoption proceedings.

22 November 1944

CHILD-CARING INSTITUTIONS; CORPORATIONS; ORGANIZATION APPROVAL BY STATE BOARD OF CHARITIES AND PUBLIC WELFARE

As requested in your letter of November 21, consideration has been given the provisions of G. S. 110-49, with particular reference to the granting of charters of incorporation formed for the purpose of caring for and placing dependent, neglected, abandoned, destitute, orphaned or delinquent children or children separated temporarily from their parents.

The statute, G. S. 110-49, provides, in part, as follows:

"No individual, agency, voluntary association, *or corportion* seeking to establish and carry on any kind of business or organization in this state for the purpose of caring for and placing dependent, neglected, abandoned, destitute, orphaned or delinquent children, or children separated temporarily from their parents, *shall be permitted to organize and carry on such work without first having secured a written permit from the State Board of Charities and Public Welfare.* The said board shall issue such permit recommending such business or organization only after it has made due investigation of the purpose, character, nature, methods and assets of the proposed business or organization."

The language of this section, and particularly the words I have underscored, in my opinion, mean that no corporation should be formed under the laws of this State for the purposes set forth in this section until its organization has been approved in writing by the State Board of Charities and Public Welfare. I therefore think that it is desirable and necessary for the Secretary of State to refer to the State Board of Charities and Public Welfare any certificates of incorporation filed in his office for the purpose of organizing a corporation to carry on the work provided for in this section, and that the charter should not be granted until the same is approved in writing by this Board.

4 December 1944

ADOPTION PROCEEDINGS; CHANGE OF ENTRIES ON ADOPTION FORMS AFTER ISSUANCE OF FINAL ORDER

In your letter of December 1, 1944, you state that the final order of adoption was issued in a proceeding and it was discovered by the agency placing the child that the date of birth as entered in the adoption forms was inaccurate. You further state that the adoptive parents request that the date of birth as entered on the adoption forms be changed to agree with the date of birth as entered on the birth certificate. You inquire as to how such change can be legally effected since the final order of adoption has been issued.

I have examined the statutory law on the subject of adoption and do not find any particular statute that deals with this question. It is true that G. S. Section 48-5 states in part as follows:

"No party to a completed and final adoption proceeding nor anyone claiming under such a party may later question the validity of the adoption proceeding, by reason of any defect or irregularity therein, jurisdictional or otherwise, but shall be fully bound thereby, save for such appeal as may be allowed by law. Further, no adoption may be questioned by reason of any procedural or other defect by anyone not injured by such defect."

The effect of this clause is to sustain the validity of an adoption proceeding in spite of all irregularities and to finally cut off any objections of any party to a completed and final adoption. This concerns the validity of an adoption and in my opinion does not prohibit a party from seeking to correct clerical errors, mistakes or other omissions of a collateral nature which do not affect the substantive validity of the proceeding.

I further find in G. S. Section 48-5 the following:

"Such order granting letters of adoption shall have the force and effect of, and shall be entitled to, all the presumptions attached to a judgment rendered by a court of general jurisdiction in a common law action."

I am of the opinion, therefore, that a final order of adoption is by this provision made equivalent to and is placed on the same basis as any final order or judgment rendered by a court of general jurisdiction. The same general rules of law in correcting errors and defects in judgments would apply to final orders of adoption.

In McIntosh on NORTH CAROLINA PRACTICE AND PROCEDURE, we find the following:

"A final judgment ends the proceeding as to the matter adjudicated and is presumed to be correct, but where there are clerical errors, or the judgment entered does not express correctly the action of the court, it may be corrected to make the record speak the truth. . . . . In this State it is left to the court to determine by any satisfactory evidence that a mistake was made, and the action of the court is not subject to review. . . . . This is related to the general power of the court to make amendments before and after judgment. It is intended to correct an error in expression, and not an error in decision. . . . . The correction of such errors is not limited to the term of court, nor within the year, but it may be done at any time, upon motion, or the court may on its own motion make the corrections when such defects appear."

I am of the opinion, therefore, that your proper method of making this correction as to the age of the child in question would be to file a motion before the court having jurisdiction of this proceeding, setting forth the facts and requesting that the final order heretofore entered be amended to show the proper age of the child. All interested parties should have notice of this motion, which should be either served on them or they could accept service. The court can then enter an order amending or correcting the final order of adoption in this respect, and upon sending to your office a certified copy of this order making the amendment, you would then be authorized to make all necessary changes as to the date of birth on your adoption forms or the adoption forms held by any other person or persons.

ADOPTION LAWS; SEPARATION OF CHILD UNDER 6 MONTHS OLD FROM MOTHER; FORM OF PETITION; ATTORNEY MAKING APPLICATION FOR MOTHER

5 December 1944

I return copy of petition heretofore submitted by you to this office. You inquire if this petition is a substantial compliance with G. S. Section 14-320, which relates to separating a child under six months of age from its mother; and whether or not an attorney at law can make the application on behalf of the mother.

I am of the opinion that this petition is a sufficient compliance with G. S. Section 14-320, and that it amounts to an application on the part of the mother for authority to separate herself from her child for the purpose of placing the child in a foster home. I am also of the opinion that a duly qualified attorney at law has a right to file this application in behalf of the mother.

A careful reading of G. S. Section 14-320 shows that before a separation of this type can take place, the mother must have the consent of the Clerk of the Court and the County Health Officer of the county in which the mother resides, or of the county in which the child was born. You will note that the statute does not require in express terms that the application of the mother must even be in writing. It does require that the consent of the Clerk of the Court and the County Health Officer must be in writing, and that the Superintendent of Public Welfare shall make a proper investigation, and as the result of the investigation shall make a written report to the Clerk of the Court and the County Health Officer. The proceedings of these public officials must be in writing, but there is no specific requirement that any action taken by the mother shall be reduced to writing.

While the copy of the petition furnished this office is contradictory in some respects, nevertheless it amounts to a sufficient application, since a consideration of the whole petition shows that substantial facts are set forth, an investigation by the Superintendent of Public Welfare is requested, and the written consent of the Clerk of the Court and the County Health Officer is sought in the closing paragraph of the petition. You will note also that this petition purports to have been sworn to by the mother of the child and signed by her, which you will observe in the verification of the oath.

I have before me the separation forms Nos. 1, 2 and 3 as developed and issued by your office, which are excellent forms and it would be better for all applicants to use these forms if possible. This statute, however, does not require the use of any specific form, and in this respect it differs from G. S. Section 48-1, which requires that in matters of adoption the petition for adoption shall be filed in duplicate on a standard form to be supplied by the State Board of Charities and Public Welfare.

I would further like to state that G. S. Section 14-320 is a penal statute, making it a criminal offense for any person to separate or aid in separating any child under six months old from its mother under the conditions expressed in the statute. I am of the opinion, however, that it is proper for the employees or officials of the State Board of Charities to make any investigation or to obtain any report or information from another State as to the situation of the mother, her parents, the situation of the child, or any other pertinent information. It seems to me that you would have this authority under the broad general statutes giving authority and defining the duties of the State Board of Charities and Public Welfare, and that you would also have this authority under G. S. 110-50. At any rate, it seems to me that any report or any information that you obtain about the mother and child from the State of Pennsylvania could not be construed in any way or manner as a violation on the part of you or your employees of G. S. Section 14-320, and that such action could not be construed as aiding in the separation of any child under the conditions therein described.

I hope that this answers your questions as to the form of this petition and other matters that were raised in conference with Miss Mitchell.

ADOPTION LAW; CHILDREN BORN IN WEDLOCK; PRESUMPTION OF LEGITIMACY; RIGHT TO HAVE CHILD DECLARED ILLEGITIMATE

20 December 1944

In your letter of December 16, 1944, you refer to a letter written by this office dated November 14, 1944, in which this office said, in substance, that a child born in wedlock was presumed to be legitimate, and that before a valid surrender affidavit could be executed, the husband of the mother would have to join in the execution of such surrender document.

You now inquire whether a case to establish non-access between man and wife as discussed in this ruling of November 14 would be heard before the Judge and jury in a Superior Court or before the Judge of a Domestic Relations Court.

Frankly, I do not know of any proceeding in the law that is available for the purpose of establishing the mere question of non-access between a husband and wife. The result of establishing non-access would be to declare a child illegitimate and as you know, the law favors legitimacy. For this reason, the presumption that a child born in wedlock is legitimate was established by judicial interpretation. We also have a statute in this State to the effect that children born as the result of a bigamous marriage or from marriages that are annulled are declared to be legitimate. We also have a law which says that no judgment or decree in a divorce proceeding shall have the effect of making children born of the marriage illegitimate. I do not think that just anyone or any party can come into a court and institute a proceeding for the purpose of having a child declared illegitimate. It was held in the case of STATE v. RAY, 195 N. C. 628, that a husband indicted for nonsupport of a child could plead in defense that he was not the father of the child and could thereby raise the question of legitimacy. It is also true that persons claiming under a reputed father in regard to property rights may raise the question of the legitimacy of the child. I know of no case, and have been unable to find one anywhere, which would support the theory that a child can be declared illegitimate in an adoption proceeding or any other proceeding for the mere purpose of dispensing with the consent of the husband of the mother, and also dispensing with notice to him of such a proceeding.

In C. J. at page 953, Section 27, we find the following:

> "One born in marriage will not be allowed to repudiate his own legitimacy. The right to repudiate or to contest his legitimacy generally belongs to the father alone, and can be exercised by him or his heirs only within a fixed time, and only in a direct suit brought for that purpose. If this right is expressly or tacitly renounced by the father, it is extinguished and can never be exercised by anyone. The mother has no right to disavow a child because maternity is never uncertain; she can only contest the identity of the child."

It is true that in the letter of November 14 the language, "no adjudication had been made by a court of competent jurisdiction that the husband of the mother is not the father of the child, ..." was used and this might cause you to think that a proceeding could be brought in court in which non-access could be shown for the express purpose of having a child declared to be illegitimate and thus dispense with the consent of and notice to the presumptive father. This language, however, refers to proceedings brought in court involving the descent of property or other proceedings where the determination of the legitimacy or illegitimacy is directly in issue for the purpose of establishing the status of the parties so the property rights or rights of support and maintenance may be determined. In such a case the reputed or presumptive father is always a party and before the court, and hence, a judgment or decree establishing illegitimacy in such a proceeding is binding on all parties and could be used in an adoption proceeding to dispense with any possible right of consent or notice on the part of the husband of the mother. It was not intended in that letter to convey to your office the impression that you could bring a proceeding of this nature as an aid to an adoption proceeding or that you could raise the question of legitimacy even in an adoption proceeding itself.

It may be that the progress of the law is not in accord with modern social concepts on this question, and it is my opinion that if you desire a remedy whereby such a status can be specifically declared, then you must look to the legislative forum because the present status of the law definitely seeks to uphold legitimacy and seeks to prevent the stigma of illegitimacy in relation to any child. It is, therefore, my opinion that no such proceeding can be maintained for the mere purpose of having a child declared illegitimate and thus facilitate an adoption proceeding. If such a proceeding was attempted, it would not be binding on the presumptive father, and the validity of an adoption proceeding based thereon would be extremely doubtful.

ADOPTION LAWS; CONSENT TO ADOPTION BY SUPT. OF PUBLIC WELFARE, WHERE
CHILD COMMITTED TO CUSTODY BY ORDER OF SUPERIOR COURT

20 December 1944

In your letter of December 16, 1944, you state that you have received an adoption proceeding for registration in which the consent to the adoption has been signed by the Superintendent of Public Welfare acting on the authority of an order from a Judge presiding in the Superior Court. You further state that the report on the proposed adoption shows that the mother of the child is twenty years of age, unmarried, and an inmate of the Farm Colony for Women. You attach to your letter a copy of the order of the Superior Court and you inquire whether or not the Superintendent of Public Welfare has sufficient authority pursuant to the adoption law, and under the circumstances of this case, to consent to the adoption.

I do not think it is necessary to discuss the jurisdiction of a Judge of the Superior Court or the validity of this order, for the reason that the question of the proper party to consent to an adoption proceeding is fixed by G. S. Section 48-5. Under this section the primary right or duty of consent which is necessary to the validity of such proceedings is fixed in the following parties, with priority in the order named:

(1) Parent or parents, if living;
(2) Guardian, if any;
(3) Person with whom such child resides or who may have charge of such child;
(4) A duly licensed child-placing agency, if the parent, parents or guardian of the person of the child has in writing surrendered the child to such agency;
(5) The Superintendent of Public Welfare of the county if the child has been surrendered to such Superintendent-of-Public-Welfare and the parent, parents or guardian have given consent in writing to the adoption of the child.

I cannot find in the statutes dealing with the Juvenile Courts or Superior Courts any authorization which would give such Courts the right to confer on the Superintendent of Public Welfare of the county the right to consent to the adoption proceeding. It seems to me the conditions upon which a Superintendent of Public Welfare of a county can consent to an adoption proceeding are fixed by Section 48-5, and I know of no exception to this statutory rule, and I do not think that an order of the Court finding that a child is neglected and committing the child to the custody of the Welfare Officer for placement can confer any such right of consent in the absence of the surrender of the child to such official by the mother, accompanied by written consent to adoption. As we have heretofore stated in one of our former letters, the consent of the father of an illegitimate child is not necessary, but since the mother in this case is alive, it is my opinion that her consent to the adoption is necessary and vital, or the requisite surrender of the child to the Superintendent of Public Welfare, accompanied by a written consent as to adoption as required by the statute.

It further appears to me that this case would not come within the provisions of G. S. Section 48-10. There is no finding in the order that the parent or parents are unfit to have the care and custody of the child, nor does the order purport to declare the child to be an abandoned child. This section applies to the orders of a Juvenile Court, and I do not find any language in the statute that confers the authority to make such findings upon a Judge of the Superior Court. The statute further provides that if the child is of an age beyond the jurisdiction of a Juvenile Court, that a finding of abandonment can be made by the Court before whom the adoption proceedings are pending. I, therefore, cannot see that this statute is applicable in the case presented by you. It is my thought, therefore, that the consent of the mother is necessary in this case.

ADOPTION LAWS; GRANDPARENTS AS NATURAL GUARDIANS; CONSENT TO · ADOPTION BY NATURAL GUARDIAN WHEN BOTH PARENTS OF MINOR CHILD ARE DECEASED

15 January 1945

In your letter of January 3, 1945, you state that you have a case of a minor child whose parents are dead and that the maternal and paternal grandparents are living. The maternal grandmother cared for the child until she placed him in a foster home several years ago, and the foster parents wish to legally adopt the child. You further state that the maternal grandfather refuses to sign the consent to the adoption. Your question is as follows: "In the event that your interpretation is that all four of the grandparents should participate in the adoption proceedings by signing the consent, will the refusal of the maternal grandfather to sign the consent invalidate the proceeding or could maternal grandfather be made a participant by summons and publication?"

You further state that it has previously been interpreted that where both parents of a child are deceased, the surviving grandparent or grandparents as natural guardians of the child would sign the consent to the adoption. I have carefully examined the holdings of the Supreme Court of North Carolina and have been unable to find any decision that squarely supports the proposition that where a child's parents are dead the grandparents become the natural guardians of the child. There is some authority in other jurisdictions on this question. In 28 C. J., page 1059, Section 6, we find the following:

> "*Who is guardian by nature.* Unless it is otherwise provided by statute, the father or in case of his decease, the mother of an infant is its guardian by nature. And where the father abandons his minor child, the mother becomes the natural guardian. In case of the death of both parents it has been held that the grandfather or the grandmother, when next of kin, becomes the guardian by nature, although some authorities assert that under such circumstances there is no natural guardianship. Under statute, the guardianship by nature is sometimes vested in both parents, their rights being equal, or the right to guardianship is made to depend upon the age of the child, the mother being entitled to the preference when the child is of tender years. In the case of an illegitimate child, the mother is the natural guardian. In case of divorce, the parent to whom custody of the child is awarded becomes its natural guardian. Rights or duties which may belong to the mother as guardian by nature do not devolve on her husband, the minor's stepfather."

In the case of COMMONWEALTH ex rel. STEVENS v. SHANNON, reported in 164 Atlantic, 352 (Penn.), the Court considered this question, and said:

> "(5) Other things being equal, the grandparents or next of kin are entitled to the custody of the minor child because of their inherent common-law rights as natural guardian which are superior to that of a mere stranger. 'Guardianship by nature at common law, according to the early English authorities, was the right of the father, mother and

next of kin, in the order named to the custody of the person of the heir apparent'. 28 Corpus Juris, 1059, citing Coke on Littleton, page 88b, note 12. The principle governing in American jurisdictions is stated in 28 Corpus Juris, 1060, as follows: 'In case of the death of both parents it has been held that the grandfather or the grandmother, when next of kin, becomes the guardian by nature, although some authorities assert that under such circumstances, there is no natural guardianship.' This common-law principle of natural guardianship is one designed to maintain the family structure, and should therefore be applied by the court where not inconsistent with the child's welfare. The rule has also been stated by a learned writer as follows: On the death of the father, guardianship by nature passes to the mother, and, on her death, to the grandfather or grandmother or any other person who is next of kin. Prima facie, the natural guardian is entitled to the custody of the child; but there are exceptions to the rule resulting from the doctrine that the child's welfare must be considered in awarding his custody.' Tiffany, Person's & Domestic Relations (2d Ed.) p. 316, § 148."

In the case of LEHMER v. HARDY, et ux., 294 Fed. 407, The Court of Appeals of the District of Columbia considered this question and held that upon the death of a minor's parents, the paternal grandfather becomes her natural guardian, and by virtue of the fact that he then stands in loco-parentis, he has the right to change or fix the minor's domicile. It is held by all of these authorities that the right of a natural guardian extends to the person of the minor and not to controlling the affairs of the minor's estate. I think that the holding of the Federal Court that upon the death of the parents of a minor the paternal grandfather has prior right as natural guardian is the best holding for the reason that this follows the strong influence of the feudal system which has greatly influenced and controlled the decisions in such matters.

It is my thought that in order to be sure about this matter, it would be better to obtain the consent of the paternal grandparents, the consent of the maternal grandmother, and to make the maternal grandfather a party to the proceeding by publication, under the authority of Section 48-4 of the General Statutes. You will also note that Section 48-5 of the General Statutes enumerates the person or persons authorized to give consent in an adoption proceeding, and says the following: "and with the consent of the parent or parents if living or of the guardian, if any, *or of the person with whom such child resides, or who may have charge of such child.*" (Italics ours.) Inasmuch as the maternal grandmother some years ago placed the child in a foster home, I think that I would go through the formality of having the foster parents to give a formal consent to the adoption because of the phrase in the above quoted statute which is italicized. While it may be to some extent a duplication of effort in that the foster parents probably are the petitioners in this proceeding, nevertheless, after reviewing the question I have come to the conclusion that a person or persons can occupy the dual position of being the petitioners in an adoption proceeding and at the same time be required to give formal consent to the adoption by virtue of the statute that I have quoted above.

On this question I conclude, therefore, that you should get the consent of the paternal grandparents, the maternal grandmother, and make the maternal grandfather a party by publication, and in addition, secure the consent of the foster parents. I advise all of these precautions because it is not clear whether the Supreme Court of this State would follow the doctrine enunciated in other jurisdictions as to grandparents being natural guardians. You cannot take too many precautions on the question of consent to adoption proceedings because we know that in the future many questions involving property rights may arise and the determination of such questions will hinge on the validity of an adoption proceeding.

In your second question it appears that the minor's parents and apparently all four grandparents are dead, but there are several aunts and uncles as well as a sister who has attained her majority. It further appears that the child was committed to the custody of the superintendent of public welfare of the county on the basis of dependency and was later placed by the superintendent in a licensed boarding home. The boarding parents now have filed a petition to adopt the child and the superintendent of public welfare has signed the consent to the adoption. You desire to know what person or persons are required to give consent to this adoption proceeding.

It is noted that in this case you do not state that the Juvenile Court has declared anyone unfit to have the care and custody of such child, nor do you say that the Juvenile Court has found that the child is an abandoned child. Under these circumstances, I fail to see how the order of the Juvenile Court can confer on anyone the right to give consent to an adoption proceeding. I must also say, as in the first case, that I do not know what the Supreme Court of North Carolina would say as to the sister or aunts and uncles being a natural guardian or guardians of the minor. The safest thing to do in this case, as in the first case, is to obtain the consent of the aunts, uncles and sister, and also the formal consent of the boarding parents who desire to adopt the child. Those who will not consent should be made parties by publication, and from your statement of facts you already have the consent of the superintendent of public welfare.

I regret to give an opinion which requires the consent of so many people but in view of the fact that we have no decisions to guide us and the statutory confusion that exists on this subject, there is nothing else to do but to obtain the consent of all parties who might have or assert any legal claim in relation to the status of the child.

PROCEDURE FOR REPLACEMENT WHEN FILING FORMS IN ADOPTION PROCEEDING; REPLACEMENT OF LOST RECORDS IN ADOPTION PROCEEDING; PETITION TO RESTORE CONTENTS OF LOST RECORD

29 January 1945

Reference is made to your letter of January 25, 1945, in which it appears that certain forms in the initial steps of an adoption proceeding have never been received in your office and that the same have been lost or destroyed by some inadvertence. Your inquiry seems to be confined entirely to the consent form and the report of the superintendent of public welfare since, as you state, the Petition and Interlocutory Order are matters of public record. It further appears that this consent form and report of the superintendent of public welfare in this proceeding were evidently lost in the mail between the office of the Clerk of the Court and your office.

I think that you should refer to General Statutes of North Carolina, Section 98-7, which deals with the perpetuating of records that have been destroyed. Under the authority of this section as well as the authority granted by Section 98-14 of the General Statutes, you should cause a petition to be filed before the Clerk of the Court, setting out the contents of the destroyed records and making all persons parties in this proceeding that were parties in the former proceeding,—that is, the adoption proceeding. You must conform to the rule set forth in Section 98-14, which gives you the steps to be followed. Inasmuch as this is an adoption proceeding, the Clerk of the Court has jurisdiction to act on this matter, and after the filing of your petition and upon notice, the same should be heard by the Clerk. If there is no objection made to same, or if objection is made and it is his opinion that the contents of the lost records have been established to his satisfaction, then he should enter an order declaring that the original records have been destroyed and that he finds the contents of the original records to be as set forth in his order or as set forth in the copies of same attached to his order.

Upon this order being entered by the Clerk, the contents of the lost records are considered as having been established for all legal purposes and this can be sent to your office and recorded as in the cases of original orders.

COMPULSORY SCHOOL ATTENDANCE OF DEAF AND BLIND CHILDREN; EFFECT OF
H. B. No. 450, RATIFIED MARCH 10, 1945

4 April 1945

Reference is made to your letter of March 29, 1945, and copy of letter attached from Honorable Ira T. Johnston, Attorney at Law, Jefferson, North Carolina.

Mr. Johnston submits two questions, as follows:

(1) "It will be contended here in Court that a notice by mail is not sufficient notice under the Statutes to parents to comply with the Statute in placing a deaf child in a school for the deaf.

(2) "We need a specific ruling that as to the matter of electing when the two years shall run that parents can keep the child out of school."

As to the first question relating to the manner of serving notice, I am of the opinion that service of notice by mail is not sufficient notice and does not comply with the statute. Section 115-310 of the General Statutes, in providing for this phase of the matter, says:

"Shall in his or their discretion *serve* written notice on such parent." (Italics ours.)

When the statute says that a notice shall be "served," it is my thought that this means that it shall be served by an officer of the State or county authorized to serve process or notices. It is true that a different method of serving notice is provided for serving subpoenas or witnesses and summonses for jurors, which may be done by telephone or by registered mail, but this is specifically provided by statute, and unless the statute specifically authorizes this method for the notice in question, then I think it has to be served by an officer.

As to the second question, which involves the matter of selecting the two years during which the parents can keep the child out of school, I am of the opinion that you do not have to consider this matter at all. In H. B. No. 450, passed at the last session of the General Assembly and ratified March 10, 1945, Section 115-310 of the General Statutes was amended as follows:

"Amend Section 115-310 of the General Statutes by striking out all of said section after the word 'Provided, (1)' in line nine and including the figure (2) in line thirteen."

It would seem therefore, that this last session of the General Assembly has struck out that portion of the law which allowed parents to elect two years between the ages of seven and eighteen years that a deaf child or children may remain out of school. In view of this amendatory legislation, I do not see how this question can now arise. Under the former statute the parents could keep the children out of school at their election for a period of "two years between the ages of seven and eighteen years," and I am informed that the child in question has already been out of school for the two year period. The portion of the statute as to the service of notice applies only to the question of the duty of the parents to send the child to the school. It does not apply to the two years which the parents elect to keep the child out of school.

I have discussed this angle of the matter in order to give the opinion of this office if the question should be pertinent. However, as stated above, I think the amendment entirely disposes of the question.

It should also be brought to your attention that when you discussed this matter with the Attorney General, H. B. No. 450 had not become effective as law, and the informal opinion given to you was based upon the statute before it was amended.

INTERSTATE TRANSFER OF CHILDREN; CHILD BORN IN NORTH CAROLINA TO MOTHER WHO HAS ENTERED THE STATE PRIOR TO OR DURING THE PERIOD OF PREGNANCY

11 April 1945

I have your letter of April 10, in which you request my written opinion as to whether a child born in North Carolina to a woman who had entered the State during the period of pregnancy, or who had become pregnant while living in this State and who did not have a legal settlement in North Carolina, would be regarded as coming under the provisions of Chapter 110, Article 4, Sections 110-50 and 110-51, regarding interstate transfer of children, about which I gave you an informal opinion in a recent conference.

In this connection I have read the comment of Miss Lily Mitchell, Director of the Division of Child Welfare, and the several rulings of this office to which she referred, copies of which were attached to her memorandum. None of these letters, however, seem to have considered this precise question.

After reconsideration of this subject, I am still of the opinion that a woman who had entered the State during the period of pregnancy, or who had become pregnant while living in this State and did not have a legal settlement in North Carolina, would not be regarded as coming under the provisions of Chapter 110, Article 4, Sections 110-50 and 110-51, regarding the interstate transfer of children. It is my opinion that only children who have been born prior to entrance into the State would come within the purview of this section.

ADOPTION LAW; JUDGMENT OF DOMESTIC RELATIONS COURT FINDING
ABANDONMENT OF CHILD BY PARENT AS SUBSTITUTE FOR CONSENT
OF PARENT IN ADOPTION PROCEEDINGS

12 April 1945

In your letter of April 9, 1945, you state that you have received from the Clerk of the Court of one of the counties of this State an adoption proceeding in which the consent of the father has been properly secured and made a matter of record. As a substitute for the consent of the mother to the adoption proceeding there was used an order or judgment entered by the Domestic Relations Court of the county, in which order or judgment it is found as a fact by the Court that the mother abandoned and deserted the child and is unable to provide a fit and suitable home for the child. It was further adjudged that the mother is not a fit person to have the care and custody of the child.

Your question is whether such a judgment is a legal substitute for the consent by the mother required by the provisions of the North Carolina adoption law.

Under the provisions of Section 48-10 of the General Statutes, in cases where a Juvenile Court has adjudged the parent or parents unfit to have the care and custody of the child or has declared the child to be an abandoned child, such parent or parents are declared not to be necessary parties to the adoption proceeding and their consent is not required. If the child is of an age beyond the jurisdiction of a Juvenile Court, then on notice to the parent or parents, the Court in the adoption proceeding is authorized to determine that an abandonment has taken place and then the consent of the parents is not necessary and is not required. It appears that this child is under sixteen years of age and is, therefore, subject to the jurisdiction of the Juvenile Court.

Under the provisions of Article 13 of Chapter 7 of the General Statutes, Domestic Relations Courts exercise all of the jurisdiction of Juvenile Courts and, in fact, in counties where these Domestic Relations Courts are established, they supersede the Juvenile Courts, and all cases pending in the Juvenile Court are transferred to the Domestic Relations Court for final adjudication.

I have been unable to find a decision of the Supreme Court construing Section 48-10 of the General Statutes. All of the cases on the subject deal with the adoption law as it existed prior to the enactment of the present adoption statutes. The decisions of the Court, however, on the former adoption law furnish us with a guide as to what the attitude of the Court might possibly be if called upon to construe the present Act. The case of

WARD v. HOWARD, 217 N. C. 201, deals with an adoption proceeding in which an order of a Juvenile Court was relied upon to sustain the adoption. In that case the Court said:

"The purpose of the Juvenile Court Act was to protect both society and minor children, which form such a large part of it, from the effect of delinquency on the part of the child and neglect on the part of parents and custodians—not any more as to parents than as to others having the care and custody of children. It is in no respect an amendment to the Adoption Law, nor can it be considered as relieving against the stricter provisions of that law, where the Adoption Law itself speaks upon the subject."

Likewise, in the case of IN RE: HOLDER, 218 N. C. 136, the adoption proceeding and its validity depended upon certain adjudications of the Juvenile Court. In that case the Court said:

"One cause of such recurring disappointments seems to lie in the mistaken notion that some of the essential elements of the proceeding may be instituted in the Juvenile Court, or, as in this instance, that some institution or agency to which the child has been committed may take over and exercise functions which the statute leaves exclusively to the parent or guardian. A clear understanding of the limitations of jurisdiction and authority of the various agencies dealing with the custody and welfare of children is imperative."

I am sure that you are already familiar with the fact that our Court has said in numerous opinions that adoption laws are in derogation of common law and must be construed strictly. The Court has also said that adoption laws affect and change the laws governing the inheritance of property and for that reason, all necessary steps required by the statute must be properly taken and the rule is one of strict interpretation.

I frankly do not know what our Court would say, nor how it would construe Section 48-10 of the General Statutes. Until a construction is made, I think that you are entitled to rely upon what the statute says, and where a Juvenile Court acquires jurisdiction over a child and determines that the parent or parents are unfit to have the care and custody of the child, or that the child has been abandoned by its parents, then in such case I think you are warranted in relying upon the statute to the effect that the parent or parents involved are not necessary parties and that their consent is not necessary to the adoption proceeding. I think, however, that such an adjudication by a Juvenile Court or a Domestic Relations Court should be only where the Court has actually acquired jurisdiction over the child for the purpose of administering juvenile law and not for the mere purpose of using the Juvenile Court as an aid to the adoption law and for the mere purpose of dispensing with the consent of a parent or parents.

The thing that causes me considerable concern in this case is the fact that it does not appear from any of the papers before me that any notice was ever served on the mother of the child when the proceedings in the Domestic Relations Court were instituted. It was recited in the judgment that summons was served on Ernest Lee ————, the father of the child, but I do not see anything that indicates that notice was served on the mother. I am, therefore, extremely doubtful if this judgment could be used as a substitute for the consent of the mother. It seems to me that before she would be bound by any adjudication that she had abandoned the child or was unfit to have the care and custody of the child, the mother should have some kind of legal notice in order to deny or dispute this issue if she cared to do so. It is fundamental that before any Court can dispose of the rights of any person the Court must acquire jurisdiction, and while it may be said that in this case the Court had jurisdiction over the child, nevertheless, I cannot see how the Court has acquired any jurisdiction to dispose of the rights of the mother to the child and displace her consent to the adoption proceeding which is mandatorily required by the adoption statute, when she has had no notice. It may be that some other part of the record in the Domestic Relations Court will show that this step was complied with.

I cannot, therefore, say that in my opinion this judgment can be considered as a valid legal substitute for the consent of the mother. I can only say that its validity is a matter of conjecture, and in the absence of a ruling by the Supreme Court, I am extremely doubtful.

TAXATION; PUBLIC WELFARE; ADMINISTRATION EXPENSES OF PUBLIC
WELFARE; COUNTIES; VALIDITY OF TAX LEVY FOR
PUBLIC WELFARE PROGRAM

19 April 1945

In your letter of April 13, 1945, you call attention to the fact that Section 108-38 of the General Statutes has been amended by the General Assembly of 1945 and you ask the following question:

"Are the county commissioners authorized to make a special levy for the county's part of the cost of administering the public welfare program as adopted by the board of county commissioners and the board of public welfare and approved by the State Board of Allotments and Appeal?"

Section 108-38 of the General Statutes is, in part, as follows:

"The State Board of Allotments and Appeal shall annually allocate to the several counties of the State, in accordance with the total amount of benefit payments to be paid in each county for old age assistance therein, the sum provided by the Federal Government under the Social Security Act for payment of administrative expenses. Any amounts in excess of said allotments to the several counties, which are necessary to the proper administration of the public welfare program by the several counties, shall be determined by the State Board of Allotments and Appeal upon budgets submitted to said board by the county welfare boards in each county . . . The State Board of Allotments and Appeal shall, on or before the first day of June in each year, notify the board of county commissioners in each county as to the amount of administrative expenses such county is required to provide, and upon receipt of such notice it shall be mandatory upon each county that it shall be levied within said county to provide for the payment of such part of such county's administrative expenses."

The above quoted portion of this section formerly contained the words "of this article" prior to the last General Assembly. At that time these words were deleted from the statute and the words "of the public welfare program" were substituted for the former term.

In considering the effect of the amendment of 1945, I think we should also consider the portion of Section 108-18 of the General Statutes which is a part of Article 3 of Chapter 108 of the General Statutes, which article is entitled "Division of Public Assistance." In speaking of the whole article and the necessity of levying taxes for the support of the objectives of the article, it is said in this section as follows:

> "*The provisions of this article are mandatory on the State, and each and every county thereof,* and when the levy of any tax is required or directed herein, it shall be understood that the said tax is levied for a special purpose; and full authority is hereby given to the boards of county commissioners of the several counties to levy, impose, and collect the taxes herein required for the special purpose of old age assistance, as defined and provided for in this article." (Italics ours.)

In the portion of the statute last above quoted, you will specifically note that the provisions of all of Article 3 are made mandatory on the State and each and every county, and that, when any tax is to be levied as directed in the article, it shall be understood that the tax is levied for a special purpose. It is clear, therefore, that Section 108-38 has been amended so as to provide for allotments for the administration of the public welfare program and that it is mandatory upon the counties to levy taxes for this purpose. This levy for the public welfare program has now become a part of Article 3 and is, therefore, included in the authority given for the levy as contained in the portion of Section 108-18 above quoted.

You will further note that in the above quoted portion of Section 108-18, the general authority for making such a levy is contained in a clause punctuated with a semicolon and sets off this clause from the concluding clause which contains special authority to levy and collect taxes for the purpose of old age assistance.

It was no doubt considered by the Legislature that it has now become proper to levy taxes for the complete expenses of administering the public welfare program, for the simple reason that the duties of the officials and personnel of the local welfare programs are so connected and are so bound together that it is almost impossible to allocate the amount of time, expense and service applied to each one of the statutory objectives of such programs. I might add that in giving legislative consent for levying taxes for special purposes, the consent can be conferred by a statute general in nature as well as by a more specific statute.

I am of the opinion, therefore, that the State Board of Public Welfare and the commissioners of the various counties should accept this statute, as amended, as a valid statute and should proceed upon this assumption to levy the necessary taxes for the administration expenses of the public welfare program. We should not assume that statutes are unconstitutional and therefore illegal. This is pointed out by our Supreme Court in the case of BICKETT v. TAX COMMISSION, 177 N. C., at page 435, where it is said:

> "It is an elementary principle of law, as held by the U. S. Supreme Court, that no Act can be held unconstitutional unless it is so 'proved beyond a reasonable doubt.' This is quoted with approval in SASH CO. v. PARKER, 153 N. C., 134 (citing cases). All reasonable doubts must be resolved in favor of the constitutionality of legislation. Every

presumption is in favor of the constitutionality of an Act of the Legislature, and all doubts must be resolved in support of the Act.

"The courts may resort to an implication to sustain an Act, but not to destroy it. Statutes are presumed to be valid and every reasonable doubt must be given in favor of their validity. There are many other decisions to the same effect in this Court and in the U. S. Supreme Court. Indeed, they are uniform on this point." (Various cited cases are omitted from quotation.)

Your question is, therefore, answered in the affirmative and, while this is but an opinion, I nevertheless think that the officials should proceed to carry out the will of the Legislature as expressed in its statute and should levy the taxes provided therein.

MEDICINE; PHYSICIANS; PSYCHIATRISTS; REQUREMENT AS TO PSYCHIATRISTS IN REGARD TO MEDICAL LICENSE

30 April 1945

In your letter of April 28, 1945, you state that a well qualified psychiatrist might be interested in a position open in your Department. The duties include inspections of State Hospitals and private mental institutions, clinical examinations of children for psychiatric disorders, promotional work and mental hygiene. You state that this person is a native of Vienna, Austria, and that you understand she cannot receive a license in this country because she did not attend medical schools and receive a medical degree in this country. You would like to know if there would be any legal problem or question which might possibly arise if she became a member of the staff of your Department.

Psychiatry and psychiatric work in this country is considered to be a branch of medicine. It is so defined in the Encyclopedia Brittanica and the National Encyclopedia. It is considered by the Board of Medical Examiners of this State, according to information from the Secretary of the Board, that psychiatrists should be licensed physicians as many mental disorders are caused by physiological or biological conditions, and further, there are many mental disorders that are organic as opposed to functional mental disorders.

I am of the opinion, therefore, that many legal problems could arise that would prove embarrassing both to this person and to your Department if you employ a psychiatrist who is not licensed by the State Board of Medical Examiners, and in addition, it is provided in Section 90-18 of the General Statutes that a person shall be regarded as practicing medicine or surgery within the meaning of this Article who shall diagnose, or attempt to diagnose, treat or attempt to treat, operate or attempt to operate on, or prescribe for or administer to, or profess to treat any human ailment, physical or mental.

It is not required by the laws of this State that a person shall be a citizen in order to practice medicine and an alien can practice medicine in this country if he otherwise meets the requirements of the different States. If you will take this matter up with the Board of Medical Examiners of this State, it is possible that the Board will grant this person a limited license to do the work required by your Department, as the Board is specifically authorized by law to issue limited licenses.

COUNTIES; REAL PROPERTY; POWER TO LEASE

14 May 1945

You have left with me a letter which you received from Louisa deB. Fitz-Simons concerning the right of Cabarrus County to lease its county home to a private individual. The Social Security Board is apparently of the opinion that Cabarrus County does not have legal authority to execute this lease.

With this conclusion, I cannot concur. The authority relied on by the Social Security Board is SOUTHPORT v. STANLEY, 125 N. C. 464. This case deals with the right of a municipal corporation and not a county to dispose of property held for a public purpose. Thus the case is not in point on the question of the right of counties to dispose of property. In addition, this case was decided in 1899 prior to the adoption of Section 160-2, sub-section 6, of the General Statutes. Thus the holding in this case, even as it applies to municipal corporations, has been greatly modified by legislative enactment. The extent to which this case has been modified is best expressed by the Court in ALLEN v. REIDSVILLE, 178 N. C. 513, 524-525. There Allen, J., says:

"Section 2978 [G. S. 160-59] of the Revisal, formerly section 3824 of the Code of 1883, requiring a sale at public outcry, was first enacted (ch. 112, Laws 1872-3), and it received authoritative construction in SOUTHPORT v. STANLEY, 125 N. C., 464, as follows:
" 'The reasonable construction of the statute must be that the town or city authorities can sell any personal property, or sell or lease any real estate which belongs to the town or city as the surplus of the original acreage ceded for the town or city site, or such land as may have been subsequently acquired or purchased; but in no case can the power be extended to the sale or lease of any real estate, which, by the terms of the act of incorporation, is to be held in trust for the *use* of the town, or any real estate with or without the buildings on it, which is devoted to the purposes of government, including town or city hall, market houses, houses used for fire departments or for water supply, or for public squares or parks. To enable the town or city authorities to sell such of the real estate of the town or cities as is mentioned just above, there must be a special act of the General Assembly authorizing such lease or sale.'
"The effect of this decision is that property of the city or town, such as parks, markets, city halls, waterworks, lighting plants, etc., held for the use of the public, are not within the provisions of Rev., 2978 [G. S. 160-59], and cannot be sold thereunder, and that, if sold at all, addition-al authority must be conferred by the General Assembly.
"If there was any doubt of this being the correct view of the SOUTH-PORT CASE, it is put at rest by the unanimous opinion of the Court in CHURCH v. DULA, 148 N. C., 266, in which HOKE, J., speaking for the Court, says: 'This view is not affected in any way by the case of SOUTHPORT v. STANLEY, 125 N. C., 464, to which we were referred by plaintiff's counsel. That decision was to the effect that the general power conferred on the authorities of a town to sell and dispose of town property by section 3824 of the Code of 1883 (Rev., 2978) [G. S. 160-59] does not give the right to sell property held in trust for the

public; for any such purpose there must be an act of the Legislature conferring special power.'

"Under this construction of the statute it became necessary to provide means for selling and leasing property, held for the use of the public, as frequently a sale or lease would be advantageous and would promote the public welfare, and to provide this remedy, section 2916 [G. S. 160-2], subsection 6, was enacted, which deals with the property, which the Court said was not embraced in section 2978 [G. S. 160-59], and thus understood, the two sections mean that under section 2978 [G. S. 160-59] the mayor and commissioners shall have power to sell at auction any property except that held for a public use, and under section 2916 [G. S. 160-2], subsection 6, that they may sell property held for a public use, subject to the approval of the voters.

"The two sections are consistent with each other, and in entire harmony. They were enacted at different times, for different purposes, and deal with different classes of property. The General Assembly evidently thought that in the sale of property, not held for a public use, such as a fire engine which had ceased to be of any value to the town on account of changed conditions, it was a sufficient protection to have a sale at public auction, but that when the property belonged to the other class the approval of the voters, the real owners, should be had.

"There is no reason for reading into the latter section that the sale shall be by public auction, in addition to submitting the question to a vote, and to do so would impose a cumbersome, confusing procedure instead of one that is intelligent and easily understood.

"If the position of the plaintiffs should prevail, the governing body of the town or city would have to offer the property at public sale, at which any one could bid, who could comply with the terms of sale, and after the highest bidder is ascertained the whole question would have to be submitted to a vote, while under the other view the governing body can advertise for bids, can consider the needs of the community, the ability to perform for the present and the future, and can present to the voters a mature plan for their approval or disapproval.

"The second statute, in our opinion, substitutes a vote of the people as to property held for a public use, for a public sale of other property, and the will of the people having been fairly ascertained, as the plaintiffs admit, and emphatically expressed, as to a sale of their own property there is no reason for setting it aside."

Subsections 14 and 15 of Section 153-9 of the General Statutes read as follows: (Counties have power)

"14. To Sell or Lease Real Property.—To sell or lease any real property of the county and to make deeds or leases for the same to any purchaser or lessee.

"15· To Purchase for Public Buildings, and at Execution Sale.—To purchase real property necessary for any public county buildings, and for the support of the poor, and to determine the site thereof, where it has not already been located; and to purchase land at any execution sale, when it is deemed expedient to do so, to secure a debt due the county. The deed shall be made to the county, and the board may, in its discretion, sell any lands so purchased."

These subsections, in my opinion, confer ample authority upon counties to lease any and all property held by them so long as the governing boards act in good faith. The case of VAUGHN v. COMMISSIONERS, 118 N. C. 636, has been considered and the dictum therein is not believed to be controlling.

I am, therefore, of the opinion that Cabarrus County is fully authorized to make the lease in question.

Concerning the third paragraph in the letter which you left with me, I express no opinion.

CLERK SUPERIOR COURT; OLD AGE ASSISTANCE; ENDORSEMENT OF CHECK DUE DECEASED RECIPIENT; SB 91

24 May 1945

I have your letter of May 23, enclosing a copy of my letter to Honorable J. N. Sills, Clerk of the Superior Court of Nashville, under date of May 2, with reference to the above matter.   •

I regret to state that the statute with reference to the handling of the clerk's fees fails to make any exemption in a case of this kind, if the clerk actually collects the check and pays the money out as directed by the statute. I believe, however, that if the clerk does not actually collect the proceeds of the check but merely endorses the check over to the surviving spouse or to the undertaker, it could be reasonably said that the funds did not actually come in his hands under and by color of his office. I can see a difference in a case of this kind in which there is no actual handling of the money by the clerk. To this extent I am glad to modify the letter written to Mr. Sills under date of May 2, and for this purpose I am sending him a copy of this letter.

JUVENILE COURT; ESTABLISHMENT JOINT COUNTY-CITY JUVENILE COURT

11 June 1945

I reply to your letter of June 6, 1945.

In your letter you enclose memorandum prepared by Mr. A. Laurance Aydlett, in which he sets forth a narrative of the usual procedure in establishing such courts. You ask this office to check the memorandum in case there is any further point which might be brought to the attention of the people of Tarboro who are interested in establishing such a court.

Under the provisions of Section 110-44 of the General Statutes, every city in North Carolina having a population of 10,000 or more persons, (census of 1920) must establish and maintain a juvenile court and must bear the expenses of the court. A recorder can act as judge, or a separate judge may be appointed. Provision is made for the appointment of probation officers. The salary of the juvenile court judge is fixed by the governing body of the city and it is authorized to expend such sums from the public funds of the city as may be necessary to carry into effect Article 2 of· Chapter 110 of the General Statutes which deals with the whole subject of juvenile courts. This should be done by proper resolution by the governing body of the city, and the resolution should fix or settle the question as to who should be judge, salary of the judge, probation officers, and salaries for same. Needless to say, the resolution should be passed at a proper legal meeting of the governing authority of the city with sufficient members present for the transaction of business, and Article 2 of Chapter 110 of the General Statutes should be referred to and incorporated in the resolution as being the authority for the establishment of such a court and for the exercise of its jurisdiction.

It is provided also in Section 110-44 that the county and city, that is a city of 10,000 or more population, may agree for the county juvenile court to transact the business of the city, and the city and county can make an agreement for the expense of the joint court, and it would seem that there is considerable latitude as to the form of the agreement in the amount of expenses to be contributed by each for the support of the court. If all matters as to expenses are agreed upon the statute provides that the two governing bodies shall pass a joint resolution electing a judge or an assistant judge for the combined court. All of these things are set forth in the statute and are covered in Mr. Aydlett's memorandum, which I might add seems to be an excellent memorandum on the subject and touches on all of the essential points. I would add, however, that I think that the governing body of the city and the governing body of the county should each pass its own resolution committing the city and the county to the joint program and the authorizing and signing of the agreement by each other, and then a joint meeting should be held and the joint resolution passed as to the judge and the expense of the court to be signed by the proper officials of each unit. Needless to say that all joint resolutions and the agreements between the city and county should be in writing, and if it is possible, to provide for all details as far as possible such as which unit shall furnish the court room, janitor service and such matters.

I would like to add one further thing that is not yet well settled, but it should be considered on the question of the costs of maintaining and operating such a court. As I have already pointed out, the governing body of a city, or each governing body of a joint court is authorized by the Act to expend such amounts as may be necessary to carry the article on juvenile courts into effect. It frequently happens that process, mileage, witness fees, and the question of cost of appeal arise in the conduct of such a court. You will note that under Section 110-26, that the judge may in his discretion authorize the payment of necessary traveling expenses incurred by any witness or person summoned or otherwise required to appear at the hearing of any case. It is best, therefore, to provide for the payment of such fees so that there will not be any misunderstanding. It also frequently arises as to who shall pay the cost when an appeal is taken to the Superior Court. You will note that an appeal is provided by Section 110-40. This question is not well settled; in fact, it has not been settled at all. I think, however, that it is the sense of the whole article on juvenile courts that all cost and expenses of the court shall be maintained and paid by the city, or by the city and county in a joint court. You frequently have conflicts with the clerk of the Superior Court, because when an appeal is made and the same is docketed in his court, he usually wants to charge the normal fee as exacted when appeals are docketed in other phases of the law. I would advise, therefore, that this question be settled before the court is established, as this is proving a source of friction in this state.

CHARITIES AND WELFARE; LICENSING OF ORPHANAGES; ALEXANDER
SCHOOLS, INC.

28 June 1945

I have your letter of June 25, 1945, in which you inquire if the Alexander
Schools, Inc., of Union Mills, North Carolina, is subject to license by the
State Board of Public Welfare in accordance with the provisions of G. S.
108-3, subsection 5.

G. S. 108-3, subsection 5, reads as follows:

, "To grant license for one year to such persons or agencies to carry on
such work as it believes is needed and is for the public good, and is conducted by reputable persons or organizations, and to revoke such license when in its opinion the public welfare or the good of the children
therein is not being properly subserved: Provided, subsection five shall
not apply to any orphanage chartered by the laws of the State of North
Carolina, owned by a religious denomination or a fraternal order, and
having a plant and assets not less than sixty thousand dollars ($60,000),
nor shall it apply to orphanages operated by fraternal orders, under
charters of other states, which have complied with the corporation laws
of North Carolina and have that amount of property."

The Alexander Schools, Inc., was incorporated in 1925. This charter was
amended in 1930. Under the charter, as amended, title to the property used
by this corporation is vested in this corporation. This corporation has varied
powers, including the power to sell or lease, to accept gifts and donations,
and to operate various types of businesses or industries.

Originally, the Board of Directors of this corporation, after the expiration
of the terms of the directors of this corporation appointed in the charter,
were to be appointed subject to the approval of the Home Mission Board of
the Southern Baptist Convention. This provision is the only provision of
the charter, as amended, which places any control or supervision of the
Alexander Schools, Inc., in a religious denomination. This, in my opinion,
does not make a religious denomination the owner of the property of this
corporation. Therefore, I advise that, in my opinion, the provisions of subsection 5 of Section 108-3 of the General Statutes, relating to licenses, is
applicable to this corporation. The fact that the corporation has not been
licensed in preceding years does not alter this conclusion.

JUVENILE COURTS; RESPONSIBILITY OF JUVENILE COURT OF ORIGINAL
JURISDICTION; TRANSFER OF CUSTODY OF CHILD TO JUVENILE
COURT OF ANOTHER COUNTY

3 July 1945

You inquire of this office as to whether or not the Juvenile Court of a
county having original jurisdiction, in case of neglected children who are
made wards of the Court, has the authority to transfer the custody of the
child to the Juvenile Court of another county in which the parent or parents
of the child have subsequently established legal settlement.

Under the provisions of Section 110-24 of the General Statutes, it appears
that a child over whom jurisdiction has been acquired is a ward of the State.

The last sentence of the section is as follows: "It is the intention of this article that in all proceedings under its provisions the court shall proceed upon the theory that a child under its jurisdiction is the ward of the State and is subject to the discipline and entitled to the protection which the court should give such child under the circumstances disclosed in the case."

This statement is approved in the case of STATE v. BURNETT, 179 N. C. 735, at 738, and also in the case of IN RE: COSTON, 187 N. C. 509, at 514. Under Section 110-29 of the General Statutes the Court seems to have wide powers as to the disposition of a child. It is true that under Section 110-21 of the General Statutes, unless a Court order is issued to the contrary or the child is committed to an institution supported and controlled by the State, the jurisdiction of the particular Court shall continue during the minority of the child.

It seems to me, however, that the administrative portions of the statute contemplate that the custody of the child can be transferred from one Juvenile Court to another. For example, under Section 110-33 of the General Statutes, we find that with the approval of the Judge of the Court, a probation officer can supervise a personal probation transferred to his supervision from another Court.

I think, however, the full answer to your question is found in the case of IN RE: COSTON, *supra*, and more especially in the last paragraph of the opinion, where it is said:

"It has been suggested that on a proper perusal of the statute any juvenile court should have the power to examine into and pass upon the conditions of dependent or delinquent children held as wards of the State, but while this may be true as to the administrative features of the law, anl the care and placing of such child, we think, in reference to the adjudication fixing the child's position as a ward of the State, the application to modify or reverse should be made to the original court, to the end that in this respect there should be no conflict or uncertainty as to the status and condition of the child."

I see no reason, therefore, why the custody of a child cannot be transferred to the Juvenile Court of another county in which the parent or parents of the child have subsequently established legal settlement. Of course, if the status of the child as a ward of the State comes into question, then the questions of status will have to be settled by the Court that first acquired original jurisdiction.

STATE BOARD OF PUBLIC WELFARE; ORPHANAGES AND OTHER INSTITUTIONS; POWER OF BOARD TO GRANT LICENSES FOR ORPHANAGES AND OTHER INSTITUTIONS; EXEMPTION OF CERTAIN RELIGIOUS AND FRATERNAL INSTITUTIONS

30 July 1945

Reference is made to your memorandum of June 18, 1945, in which you call attention to certain powers and duties of the State Board of Public Welfare as related to the inspection and licensing of orphanages in this State. You particularly refer to subsections 4 and 5 of Section 108-3 of the General Statutes of this State.

Inasmuch as subsection 5 is applicable to the question raised in your memorandum, for the sake of clarity I will quote this subsection as follows:

"To grant license for one year to such persons or agencies to carry on such work as it believes is needed and is for the public good, and is conducted by reputable persons or organizations, and to revoke such license when in its opinion the public welfare or the good of the children therein is not being properly subserved; *Provided, subsection five shall not apply to any orphanage chartered by the laws of the State of North Carolina, owned by a religious denomination or a fraternal order, and having a plant and assets not less than sixty thousand dollars ($60,000), nor shall it apply to orphanages operated by fraternal orders, under charters of other states, which have complied with the corporation laws of North Carolina and have that amount of property.* (Italics ours.)

You state that the Appalachian School at Penland is conducted under the auspices of the Diocese of Western North Carolina of the Protestant Episcopal Church, and it further appears that perhaps the final authority over this institution is exercised by the Trustees of the Diocese or other administrative bodies or officials of the Diocesan organization.

It appears that this institution or orphanage was organized or established in 1925 and there does not exist any charter for this orphanage in the office or on the records of the Secretary of State. Apparnetly, there is no record of incorporation by a private Act of the General Assembly as is the case of many orphanages in the State. There does exist certain entries on page 77 of the Journal of the Diocese for the year 1941, and on pages 61-65 of the Journal of 1944, but these entries appear to be a result of ecclesiastical action only.

As to the Mountain Orphanage at Black Mountain, it is stated that this orphanage was established in 1904, and is owned and conducted by the Home Mission Committee of the Asheville Presbytery which is affiliated with the Presbyterian Church U. S. It appears that the Home Mission Committee of the Asheville Presbytery is incorporated by virtue of a private Act of the General Assembly, same being Chapter 375 of the Private Laws of 1899. The powers of this religious corporation was set forth in Section 4 of this Act and reads as follows:

"That this corporation under the above name shall exist for the purpose of promoting religion and education in North Carolina and shall be exempt from the payment of the $50 required to be paid by business corporations before a charter is granted by the General Assembly."

You inquire of this office if either or both of these orphanages or institutions come within the scope of the exemption clause contained in subsection 5 of Section 108-3 of the General Statutes. I think the answer to this inquiry depends on whether or not each orphanage must have its own specific charter in order to avail itself of the provisions of exemption set forth in subsection 5. I am of the opinion that a proper interpretation of the statute reveals that the following things must exist in order to claim exemption: (1) The orphanage must be chartered by the laws of the State of North Carolina; (2) the orphanage must be owned by a religious denomination or fraternal order; and (3) the orphanage must have a plant and assets of a valuation of not less than $60,000. The provision as to orphanages operated by fraternal orders under charters of other states has no application here.

It is clear to me that the language of the exemption in subsection 5 requires the interpretation that each orphanage must have its own specific charter. If such is not the case, then there would be no necessity whatsoever for using the language "any orphanage chartered by the laws of the State of North Carolina, * * *." If it had been intended that any orphanage in this state would be entitled to the exemption if it was merely owned by a religious denomination or fraternal order and possessing the necessary amount of assets, then it would have only been necessary to have written the statute as follows: "Provided, subsection 5 shall not apply to any orphanage owned by a religious denomination or fraternal order."

I am strengthening this position by the fact that our information on these institutions shows that all orphanages operated in the State of North Carolina have their own individual and specific charters except the two orphanages concerned in this letter. I think that the purpose of inserting in the statute a requirement that each orphanage should have its own specific charter is that the General Assembly thought that the lines of demarcation as to the application of the exemption should be clearly and definitely drawn and fixed. It is easy to determine the specific institutions involved and to evaluate their assets when they operate under their own specific charter, and the State can thereby determine the ownership of the profit and assets without any confusion. It is not an attempt to establish any State control over ecclesiastical bodies, but it is devised to make certain that the proper exemption will be granted.

It is true that the Mountain Orphanage at Black Mountain operates under the control and auspices of an ecclesiastical body which is incorporated under the laws of the State; however, the orphanage no doubt is only one of the many activities of this religious corporation, and the fact that this larger body is incorporated, does not result in conferring a specific charter for the Mountain Orphanage at Black Mountain as required by the statute.

I am of the opinion, therefore, that both the Appalachian School at Penland, and the Mountain Orphanage at Black Mountain, do not come within the exemption granted in subsection 5 of Section 108-3 of the General Statutes and, therefore, both of these institutions, under their present status, must secure licenses from the State Board of Public Welfare for the operation of these institutions.

If either, or both, of these institutions desire to be brought within the exemption provided in subsection 5, then they should secure charters or certificates of incorporation as non-profit charitable institutions, and as provided by the laws of this State. This they can do by going through the necessary legal procedure and make proper application to the Secretary of State. It will not be expensive and I feel sure that any of the members of these denominations who are lawyers will be glad to perform this service. If this is done, then I advise that you have a right to declare that these organizations are within the scope of the exemption provision, provided of course, that you find that they are owned by the denominations in question and have the necessary amount of assets.

ADOPTION LAWS; RELEASE BY MOTHER OF ILLEGITIMATE CHILD; ACCEPTANCE
BY SUPERINTENDENT OF PUBLIC WELFARE OF COUNTY OTHER THAN
THAT OF RESIDENCE OF MOTHER

1 August 1945

I have your letter of July 27. Under date of March 8, 1943, an opinion
was expressed in a letter to Mr. Albert J. Ellis, Attorney, of Jacksonville,
as follows:

"You inquire as to whether a Superintendent of Public Welfare may
accept an illegitimate child for adoption whose mother is a nonresident
of the county in which the Superintendent of Public Welfare holds
office.

"It is my opinion that the powers and duties'of a County Superintendent of Public Welfare are confined to the county in which such
Superintendent is appointed. This being true, it is my opinion that a
Superintendent of Public Welfare should not undertake to accept a
release or surrender affidavit from the mother of an illegitimate child
where the residence of the mother is in a county other than the county
in which the Superintendent of Public Welfare was appointed."

In your letter of July 27 you submit in the form of questions and answers, the matter of interpretation of the word "residence" as used in this
letter, setting out in substance the questions and answers which we discussed in our conference recently on this subject.

I think you have summarized correctly the questions and answers thereto
as we discussed them. I assure you that all of us in this office appreciate the
opportunity of discussing the problems with you that arise in your office
and that we are always ready to cooperate with you in any way.

ADOPTION; CONSENT; VALIDITY OF COMMON LAW MARRIAGE; VALIDITY AS
AFFECTING CONSENT IN ADOPTION PROCEEDINGS

1 October 1945

In your letter of September 25, 1945, you inquire if the mother's signature to the consent to an adoption of a child born in a common law relationship in another State is sufficient, or if it is necessary for the common law
husband to also sign the consent to the adoption. You further state that the
common law husband has deserted the mother and child and that at the
time of the child's birth the common law husband publicly acknowledged
the common law wife and baby. The couple in question lived in the State of
New York in this common law relationship and the child was born there.

I think the answer to your question depends upon the validity of a common law marriage in the State of New York and the extent of recognition
that the State of North Carolina would give to such a relationship.

To constitute a marriage valid at common law, it was not necessary that
it should be solemnized in any particular form or with any particular rite
or ceremony. It was required, however, that there should be an actual and
mutual agreement to enter into a matrimonial relation, permanent and exclusive of all others, between parties capable in law of making such a contract, and consummated by their cohabitation as man and wife or their

mutual assumption openly of marital duties and obligations. There are some States that still recognize this form of marriage and the general rule is that if a marriage is valid in the foreign country or state where it is celebrated or entered into, then it is valid in all other countries and states, with two exceptions. These exceptions are incestuous marriages and polygamous marriages. The weight of legal authority is undoubtedly to the effect that if a common law marriage is valid in a state where it is entered into, then all other states will recognize the validity of this marriage even tho those states do not recognize common law marriages in their jurisdictions. We have heretofore advised you that North Carolina does not recognize a so-called common law marriage within her own borders. The question as to whether or not this State would recognize and uphold the validity of a common law marriage entered into in a State where such marriages are valid has never been presented to the Supreme Court of this State, so far as I know. For the purposes of this letter, however, I think we can assume that our Supreme Court would follow the weight of legal authority as established by other jurisdictions.

There is some doubt as to whether a common law marriage is valid in the State of New York. Such marriages were recognized at one time in that jurisdiction. In Vernier's "American Family Law," Vol. I, § 26, Page 107, the author lists the State of New York as a State in which common law marriages are valid as late as the year 1929. On the other hand, I find in the encyclopedia under the subject of marriage that the author gives it as his opinion that common law marriages are not now valid in the State of New York and you can see, therefore, that the whole question of validity appears to be in a state of confusion. So far as you are concerned, you might obtain a ruling or statement from the Attorney General of the State of New York on this subject.

The matter is also rendered doubtful due to the fact that many people refer to an illicit relationship as a common law relationship.

If the couple in question has entered into a valid marriage in the State of New York, that is a common law marriage that is recognized by that State, then in my opinion you would have to follow the ordinary rules in obtaining consent to an adoption proceeding and the consent of the father and mother both would be necessary. If common law marriages are not recognized in New York and were not so recognized at the time these people entered into this relationship, then this child is illegitimate and, as we have heretofore ruled, the consent of the mother would be sufficient. You can see that the matter depends on the validity of the relationship in New York and I am extremely doubtful that such relationships have been recognized as valid in the State of New York for a good many years, but I am not sure.

JUVENILE COURTS; TRANSFER OF CUSTODY OF CHILD BETWEEN JUVENILE COURTS; LIABILITY FOR SUPPORT OF CHILD COMMITTED TO CUSTODY

2 October 1945

I reply to your letter of September 25, 1945.

You call attention to a ruling of this office dated July 3, 1945, which was to the effect that in the administration of the juvenile law, the custody of a child could be transferred from one juvenile court to another. You state that you have received from a superintendent of public welfare an inquiry as follows:

"If the Juvenile Court in 'A' county, takes custody of children and they are placed in boarding homes at the expense of that county, and later the parents leave that county and move to 'B' county— can 'A' county transfer these children to 'B' county, giving 'B' county the responsibility of placing these children in boarding homes in 'B' county, and paying for their support?"

You will note that our ruling of July 3, 1945, is based upon several statutes of the juvenile court act, and especially Section 110-33 of the General Statutes which gives a probation officer, with the approval of the judge of the court under which he is serving, the authority to act as probation officer over any person on probation transferred to his supervision from any other court. We also called attention to a statement of the Supreme Court in the case of in re: Coston, 187, N. C. 509, 514.

It is provided in Section 110-29 of the General Statutes that a juvenile court can place a child on probation or commit the child to custody of a relative or other fit person; a child can be committed to the custody of the State Board of Charities to be placed in a suitable institution, society or association; a child can be committed to an institution maintained by the State or any subdivision thereof, or to any suitable private institution or association, approved by the State Board of Charities and Public Welfare. It is provided in Section 110-30 that temporary detention of a child may be carried out in a detention home or the judge may arrange for the boarding of such children temporarily in a private home or homes in the custody of a fit person. This same Section provides that the county in which such child shall reside or may be found shall pay a reasonable sum for the board of such children. In case the child is detained in a detention home maintained by an institution, society or association, the judge shall make an order to pay these expenses in a reasonable amount and they shall be paid by the county commissioners of the county wherein the child resides or is found. It is plain, therefore, that it is the duty of the county wherein the child resides or is found to pay for the temporary board and care of such child, and this is the county of the particular juvenile court that takes jurisdiction of the case. Section 110-34 of the General Statutes appears to be the Section applicable to the expenses of a child when it is committed by the court to the custody of an institution, association, society or person other than its parents or guardian. This seems to relate to the commitment of a more permanent nature and this Section likewise provides that the compensation for the care of such child, when approved by an order of the court, shall be a charge upon the county. This means the county in which the juvenile court is located takes jurisdiction of the child and disposes of the case. This Section also gives the county the right to serve a notice on any parent or person liable for the support of the child to show cause why such parent or person should not pay such sums as the court may direct to cover in whole or in part the cost of support of such child.

I do not find any statutory authority which would allow the juvenile court of one county to send a child to another county and give this latter county the responsibility of placing the child in a boarding home and paying for its support. I am of the opinion that this liability remains with the county in which the juvenile court is located which first assumed jurisdiction over the child. There is no authority of law which would support the transfer of this financial obligation to another county by a mere transfer of the child to such other county under the supervision of a probation officer. The financial liability for the support of the child always remains with the county which assumed jurisdiction over the child. Transfer of administration does not authorize transfer of financial liability.

I think that I should call attention to the fact that the liability of the county in dealing with delinquent juveniles is entirely different from the liability of the county in dealing with the county poor as provided by Article 13 of Chapter 153 of the General Statutes. As you already know, county liability in cases of indigent persons or paupers is entirely determined by legal settlement.

ADOPTION LAW; DISTINCTION BETWEEN VOID AND VOIDABLE MARRIAGES; LEGITIMACY OF CHILDREN

10 November 1945

In a letter sent to you under date of December 20, 1944, in discussing the status of children born as a result of a bigamous marriage, the writer said: "We also have a statute in this State to the effect that children born as the result of a bigamous marriage or from marriages that are annulled are declared to be legitimate."

The above quoted statement is too broad and does not make the proper distinction between void and voidable marriages. Section 51-3 of the General Statutes contains a list of the prohibited marriages in this State. Our Supreme Court has said in numerous cases that of this list of prohibitions, only two of the attempted types of marriage are absolutely void, abbinitio, or from the very beginning. These two are bigamous marriages and marriages between a white person and a negro or indian, within the prohibited degree. All marriages contracted contrary to the other prohibitions of this Section are called voidable marriages, that is, they are valid until annulled or set aside by court decree in an action specifically brought for that purpose. For a discussion of this important distinction, see the case of Parks vs. Parks, 218 N. C. 245, 250.

What I stated in the above quotation from my letter of the 20th of December, 1944, is true in regard to children born as a result of voidable marriages. Such chillren are protected by Section 52-5 of the G. S. and are declared by law to be legitimate. See Taylor vs. White, 160 N. C. 38, 41 and 42.

This rule, however, does not apply to children born of bigamous marriages since such marriages are absolutely void as explained above. Such children would, therefore, be illegitimate and you are advised that in all adoption proceedings involving children born of bigamous marriages, the consent of the mother of such child or children is sufficient, because they are illegitimate. As you know, we have heretofore ruled that the consent of the father is not necessary in adoption proceedings where the child is illegitimate.

OLD AGE ASSISTANCE; ELIGIBILITY; PUBLIC INSTITUTION; LEASE BY COUNTY
OF COUNTY HOME TO INDIVIDUAL FOR NURSING HOME

13 November 1945

Reference is made to lease agreement entered into on the 30th day of June, 1945, between the County of Cabarrus and W. P. Phagan. You have asked us to review this lease for the purpose of determining whether the persons receiving old age assistance and residing in the nursing home operated by Mr. W. P. Phagan would be considered as inmates of a public institution within the meaning of Section 108-21, sub-section (d) of the General Statutes of North Carolina.

The eligibility contents set forth in Article 3 of Chapter 108 of the General Statutes dealing with the recipients of old age assistance contain, among other things, the following as an eligibility requirement:

". . . . is not an inmate of any public institution at the time of receiving assistance. An inmate of such institution may, however, make application for such assistance, but the assistance, if allowed, shall not begin until after he ceases to be an inmate."

It is also provided in sub-chapter one of the social security act, section 303(a), the following:

"Sec. 303. Payment to States; computation of amounts

"(a) From the sums appropriated therefore, the Secretary of the Treasury shall pay to each State which has an approved plan for old-age assistance, for each quarter, beginning with the quarter commencing January 1, 1940, (1) an amount, which shall be used exclusively as old-age assistance, equal to one-half of the total of the sums expended during such quarter as old-age assistance under the State plan with respect to each needy individual who at the time of such expenditure is sixty-five years of age or older and *is not an inmate of a public institution*, not counting so much of such expenditure with respect to any individual for any month as exceeds $40, and (2) 5 per centum of such amount, which shall be used for paying the costs of administering the State plan or for old-age assistance, or both, and for no other purpose." (Italics ours.)

The above quotation is contained in 42 U.S.C.A., Section 303(a) Page 562.

It seems to me that the State old-age assistance plan as well as the State regulations and construction of Statutes should be in conformity with the Federal Act dealing with this subject. See Morgan vs. Department of Social Security, 127 P. (2d) 686 (Wash.). Carmichael vs. Southern Coal & Coke Company, 301 U. S. 495.

It is important, of course, that the recipients of old-age assistance come within the eligibility provisions of the State act not only for proper administration at the State level but also to the end that the administration of the State Act conform to the grant in aid requirements as prescribed by the Social Security Board in the administration of this part of the social security act at the Federal level.

It is understood that any remarks in this letter are addressed to the State agency for its consideration in its own administration problems and that anything herein stated is not to be construed as any attempt to interpret the Federal Statutes or regulations since the Bureau of Public Assistance is responsible for its own administration and interpretations as to conformity.

In our letter to you of May 14, 1945, we set forth fully our reasons to the effect that counties have ample power to lease real estate and it is not necessary to consider again the factor of public ownership. I am of the opinion that all essential legal requirements for a valid lease have been met as to authority, conformity of State law and formal execution.

The consideration expressed in the lease is the sum of $160.00 per month with an option to extend for a second term of five years at a monthly rental of $210.00. It appears that there was a former lease in existence and that the lease under consideration now is a modification of same. Under the former lease, the lessee made certain repairs to the building in the amount of approximately $6000.00. Under the present lease, the lessee is required to maintain the buildings in good condition and it is estimated that to carry out this clause there will be a cost of approximately five or six hundred dollars a year. With this in mind, it seems to me that the rental of the property is sufficient and is reasonable when considered in relation to the rental market and the demand for this type of property.

The duration of the lease is from the first day of July, 1945, until the 30th day of June, 1950, with a clause to the effect that upon written notice not later than the first day of April, 1950, the lease may be extended for an additional period of five years. The lease contains the usual clause of forfeiture for non-payment of rent. I think, however, that we should consider the clause containing the option by the land-lord to terminate the lease, which is as follows:

> "This lease is, however, executed and accepted subject to the condition that if at any time during the term thereof such an emergency should arise that as to make it necessary for the party of the first part to use the premises for county purposes, then in that event the party of the first part may terminate and cancel this lease by giving to party of the second part six months' written notice of such termination."

It seems to me that under this clause the land-lord is the final judge of the type of emergency which would make it necessary for the land-lord to terminate the lease upon six months written notice. Under this clause it seems to me that in spite of the statement of the duration of the lease the practical conclusion to the whole matter is that Mr. Phagan really holds only a six-months lease. It seems to me that this does give the County a large measure of control, which is inconsistent with a private undertaking of this nature and which could be construed as a matter of practice in allowing the county to act in a capacity other than a land-lord.

It is noted that the lease contains provision that the demised premises shall, during the term of this lease, be used exclusively for the purpose of conducting a nursing home. While it is usual in ordinary leases to stipulate as to the type of business that shall be carried on in and about the premises, I think our most usual phrase on this subject is to the effect that the lessee shall make no unlawful use of the premises. So long as the premises are not damaged, it is usually left to the discretion of the lessee as to what use he shall make of the premises.

I am of the opinion that the lease should also contain a clause to the effect that the lease shall constitute the entire contract between the parties and that none of the terms and conditions shall be varied or modified unless such changes or modifications are reduced to writing and made a part of the lease.

The Public Welfare Manual, in defining a public institution in Section 4231, says:

"A public institution is a place of residence which affords shelter or care to a person or persons and is supported or managed, in whole or in part, by or through any public instrumentality, official, or employee acting in an official capacity."

While I am not insinuating that the officials of Cabarrus County are actually converting this nursing home into a public institution, either directly or indirectly, and the comments herein contained are intended as no reflection whatsoever on these officials, nevertheless, I am of the opinion that the clause in the lease pertaining to the use of the property and the clause in the lease pertaining to the forfeiture of the lease upon emergency create conditions which render the demised premises susceptible of being converted into a public institution is a matter of actual practice. While I again state that such is not the case on the evidence before me, nevertheless, in order that there be no question about the eligibility or the recipients of old-age assistance who may reside in this nursing home, it is suggested that the lease be reformed as to the term and as to the use of the premises.

So far as I can see, the other provisions of the lease are in conformity with usual commercial practices in our State.

LEGAL SETTLEMENT; LENGTH OF RESIDENCE; SETTLEMENT OF SINGLE WOMAN
WITH ILLEGITIMATE CHILD; EFFECT OF LIVING IN ADULTERY

7 January 1946

In your letter you state that the Department of Public Welfare of one of the larger counties of the state has been asked to assume responsibility for a child born out of wedlock to a couple who has been living for three years in this county in our state as husband and wife. The facts show that the couple were not married although they posed as man and wife and were accepted as such in the community during their period of residence. The woman was not employed in any occupation, but was supported in the home by the alleged husband. The county contends that, as the woman was unmarried and not self-supporting during the period that she lived in the county in this state, and was really living in fornication and adultery, she has not, therefore, established residence and the county further contends that her legal settlement is in the county in the other state where she had previously resided and claimed as place of residence. You point out that

under our law the child was born out of wedlock and that the legal settlement of the child would follow that of the mother.

You would like to have the opinion of this office in regard to the legal
settlement of this woman based upon the above set of facts.

The law of our state governing legal settlements is found in Section
153-159 of the General Statutes which is as follows:

> "Legal settlements may be acquired in any county, so as to entitle
> the party to be supported by such county, in the manner following, and
> not otherwise:
>
> "1. By one Year's Residence.—Every person who has resided con-
> tinuously in any county for one year shall be deemed legally settled
> in that county.
>
> "2· Married Women to have Settlement of their Husbands.—A mar-
> ried woman shall always follow and have the settlement of her hus-
> band, if he have any in the state; otherwise, her own at the time of
> her marriage, if she then had any, shall not be lost or suspended by the
> marriage, but shall be that of her husband, till another is acquired by
> him which shall then be the settlement of both.
>
> "3· Legitimate Children to Have Settlement of Father.—Legiti-
> mate children shall follow and have the settlement of their father, if
> he has any in the state, until they gain a settlement of their own; but
> if he has none, they shall, in like manner, follow and have the settle-
> ment of their mother, if she has any.
>
> "4· Illegitimate Children to Have Settlement of Mother.—Illegiti-
> mate children shall follow and have the settlement of their mother, at
> the time of their birth, if she then have any in the state. But neither
> legitimate nor illegitimate children shall gain a settlement by birth in
> the county in which they may be born if neither of their parents had
> any settlement therein.
>
> "5· Settlement to Continue until New One Acquired.—Every legal
> settlement shall continue till it is lost or defeated by acquiring a new
> one, within or without the state; and upon acquiring such new settle-
> ment, all former settlements shall be defeated and lost."

Upon the state of facts set forth in your letter this woman not being
married would acquire a legal settlement in the county under subsection
1 of the above-quoted section. In my opinion she would have a legal settlement in the county in this state when she had resided continuously for one
year in that county. You state that she has resided continuously in the
county for three years which of course would make the case much stronger.
The child being illegitimate would have the settlement of its mother according to subsection 4 of the above-quoted section, which is equivalent to
saying that the child would also have legal settlement in the county in
question in this state. I fail to find anywhere in the statute anything that
supports the position that living in fornication and adultery affects the
acquisition of legal settlement. The fact that people live in sin cannot prevent them from becoming residents of the state, or acquiring legal settlements. To my mind the fact that the couple lived in fornication and
adultery has nothing to do with the situation whatsoever. It would be just
as plausible and reasonable to say that because a woman of Anglo-Saxon
descent commits adultery she is thereby changed into an oriental person.
So far our law has not seen fit to combine morals with residence and settlements.

In our opinion the legal settlement of the woman and child are in the county in question in this state.

ADOPTION LAW; ELIGIBILITY FOR ADOPTION; CHILD BORN IN THIS STATE OF NON-RESIDENT MOTHER

8 January 1946

You call attention to the fact that on April 11, 1945, this office issued a ruling concerning the interstate transfer of children wherein it was said that a child born to a mother who came from another state into North Carolina prior to, or during the period of pregnancy, would not be subject to the so-called interstate placement provisions of our law, see Sections 110-50 through 110-56 of the General statutes.

You now give us certain facts as follows:

A non-resident mother came into this state and gave birth to a child; she came to the state a short time before the child was born. The child was placed directly by the mother in the home of a North Carolina couple for adoption and the mother then returned to her own home or residence in another state. You call attention to Section 48-1 of the General Statutes and particularly to that portion which reads as follows:

"Provided, that in every instance when the parent, guardian, or custodian of the child is not a citizen or resident of the state of North Carolina at the time of filing of petition for adoption, or where the child has been brought into the state for the purposes of placement and adoption by a parent, person, agency, institution or association, the provisions of chapter two hundred twenty-six of the Public Laws of one thousand nine hundred and thirty-one (s. 110-50 to 110-56) must be complied with before the child is eligible for adoption."

You also call attention to the fact that on June 30, 1943, we told the Clerk of the Court of Granville County that the provisions of Chapter 226 of the Act of 1931 would apply in the case of a child born in North Carolina to a mother who was then a resident of this state, but who had married and become a resident of another state prior to the filing of the petition for adoption of the child by a North Carolina couple, the child never having left the state.

Your particular question is as follows:

"In the case in point how would we proceed in establishing the eligibility of this child born in North Carolina to a non-resident of the state for adoption in a North Carolina Court so that we may furnish the court with a statement or certificate to the effect that the provisions of Chapter 226, 1931 have been complied with?"

The so-called interplacement law which is really Sections 110-50 through 110-56 of the General Statutes, has now become obsolete, and experience has demonstrated that it has no practical value. The repeal of this entire act, or at least nearly all of its provisions, has been recommended by a person who has made an intense study of our adoption laws and this action will no doubt be approved and recommended by the Committee appointed by the Governor to study all laws dealing with domestic relations. It has been shown beyond a doubt that this type of law does not aid or help solve the problems connected with adoption and often thwarts the purposes of the adoption law. A rigid application prevents children from being adopted into good homes, and it has been demonstrated that the welfare agencies of the different states can be depended upon to work together in a mutual spirit of helpfulness, and that the agencies keep their agreements with each other without the necessity of providing bonds as set forth in Section 110-51, and many other technical requirements in this type of interstate law. I don't think that this office can repeal the act by its interpretation, but I do think that the adoption law should be construed to promote adoption and to give homes to unfortunate children, and the technical application of the interstate placement law should not be construed strictly and its technical scope should not be expanded in an effort to include cases that do not belong within the coverage of such provisions.

The fact remains that the interstate placement law only applies to situations where it is proposed to bring a child from another state into this state for adoption, or where it is proposed to send a child in this state to another state for adoption. As we said in our letter of April 11, 1945, the interstate placement law does not apply to a situation where a woman comes into this state, is pregnant and gives birth to the child in this state; it does apply where a child has already been born out of this state and is brought into this state for purposes of adoption only, as described in Section 110-50. Likewise, the questions of residence and interstate placement do not apply to a child born in this state, although of non-resident parents, and where it is not contemplated that the child will be sent out of the state for the purposes of adoption as described in Section 110-52.

Under the facts set forth in your letter there is simply no place or state of facts under which the application of the interstate placement law should be made. The Granville case or interpretation is not applicable to this case for the reason that the woman in question in that case was a resident of this state and had legal settlement already in this state. She lost the legal settlement through marriage. In this case we knew to begin with that the woman had no legal settlement in this state when she came into the state, and it requires non-residence, plus a bringing in or sending out of the child to bring into play the application of the law.

I am of the opinion, therefore, that under the facts set forth in your letter, the interstate placement law is not applicable and the reference to it in Section 48-1 of the General Statutes does not require its application in this case. If it is thought necessary that any certificate should be made, then a certificate should be made at once to the effect that the child is eligible for adoption, as the Board can do this at once where the parents have not acquired legal settlement, but the child is born in the state.

STATE BOARD OF PUBLIC WELFARE; LICENSE REQUIRED FOR SOLICITING PUBLIC
ALMS; NON-RESIDENT ORGANIZATIONS AND INSTITUTIONS; RESIDENT AND
INTRA-STATE ORGANIZATIONS AND INSTITUTIONS; INDIVIDUAL LICENSE
OF SOLICITOR; DEFINITION OF "LODGE"

9 March 1946

In your letter of February 23, 1946, you submit to us certain questions
arising under Article 5, Chapter 108 of the General Statutes; and more
specifically, the subject of organizations and individuals soliciting public
alms. These questions are as follows:

"1· Does the statute give the State Board of Public Welfare responsibility for granting permits for solicitation to intra-State agencies with the
exceptions listed in 108-90 as well as to agencies chartered or organized outside the State?

"2· Can an agency which is so closely affiliated with an out-of-state
agency that its policies are at least partly determined by the parent organization and a fixed proportion of the funds collected are sent to the
parent organization evade coverage under 108-80 by being chartered in
North Carolina?

"3· Under 108-85 provision is made for licenses to individuals and to organizations, institutions, or associations while 108-86 requires solicitors to
have copies of such licenses. May this be interpreted to mean that whereas
individual solicitors must have licenses, the representatives of licensed organizations conducting well-organized and publicized State-wide campaigns
need not carry individual licenses?

"4· What type of agency is covered under the word "lodge" in 108-90?"

As to your first question, it is provided by Section 108-80 that all organizations, institutions, all associations formed outside of the State for charitable purposes and who, through agents, representatives or by mail, publicly
solicit and receive public donations or sell memberships in the State and
all individual firms or organizations selling merchandise, periodicals, books
with advertising space of any kind upon the representation or upon the
pretense that the whole or any part of the profit derived therefrom shall be
used for charitable purposes are required to file a public statement with the
State Board of Public Welfare setting forth certain information as required by the statute.

There are ambiguities in the statute by construing all the sections together and considering the whole article, and I am of the opinion that the
Act was intended to require all individuals, persons, firms or corporations
soliciting alms for charitable purposes to comply with the act by filing an
application containing the information stated; and this is applicable to
intra-State individuals and associations as well as to foreign organizations,
associations or non-residents. This is the only possible construction of the
article that is consistent with the fact that the statute grants certain exemptions to local organizations. You will note the local organizations or associations can solicit in their counties where they are located. You will also
note that the provisions of the article do not apply to religious, lodge or
other meetings where solicitation is made; and the very last section in the

article (108-90) exempts all churches and religious denominations, lodges, etc., located in, resident in, or having communicants or members resident of the State as well as the employees and representatives of such organizations. There would be no need of these exemptions if the statute is interpreted as not applicable to intra-State individuals, societies, and organizations. One of the dominant objectives of the statute is to protect the public against fraudulent organizations who do not intend to apply their funds solicited to bona fide charitable purposes. The many so-called "rackets" existing in the field of soliciting funds from the public for charitable purposes are well-known and common knowledge. It is hard to see why a statute as broad as this one should be construed as protecting the people of the State against fraudulent schemes of non-resident members or foreign associations and offering the public no protection as against the fraudulent schemes and organizations within the confines of our own State. Such an interpretation is not logical. We are of the opinion, therefore, that this article applies to intra-State agencies; and that such agencies should secure permits for solicitations unless they fall within the exemptions enumerated within the article.

As to your second question, I think that the affiliation of an intra-State organization with an out-of-state agency and to what extent this affiliation determines the control of the policies of the intra-State agency is a question of fact to be found by the State Board of Public Welfare. I think that the State Board of Public Welfare has a right to examine into the internal affairs and connections as well as controls existing between the intra-State agency and the foreign agency. The fact that the intra-State agency has a domestic body, to my mind, is not conclusive; and it seems to me that in enforcing a statute of this type, which is in the nature of a police regulation, the State Board of Public Welfare would have a right to disregard forms and corporate fictions and to examine the actual workings and operations of the two agencies or organizations. If it is further found that the intra-State agency is but a mere branch or representative of the foreign agency, then the Board can so find. If we are correct, however, in our interpretation as to your first question, it seems to me that in the situation presented by your second question, the fact that the organization is of a local nature would still require an application for license; and a license issued if the organization solicits on a State-wide basis. If the organization solicits only in the county of its domestication or home office, it would still require an application and license if it is in fact a representative or an agency of a foreign organization.

As to your third question, I see no reason why the representatives of licensed organizations conducting publicity campaigns and other things aside from actual solicitation should be required to have a copy of the license. The solicitors, of course, under the statute must have such copies.

As to your fourth question, the word "lodge" is defined in the case of ANGE vs. THE SOVEREIGN CAMP OF THE WOODMEN OF THE WORLD, 171 N. C. 40, 41, as follows:

"It had a lodge there, which, according to the accepted definition, means the meeting room of an association as well as the regularly constituted body of members which meets therein, for the transaction of its business or the conduct of its affairs."

In the case of STATE v. NATIONAL ASSOCIATION OF FARMERS AND MECHANICS, 9 P. 956 (Kan.), it is said:

> " 'Lodge,' as used in reference to associations of that name, is defined by Webster to be a secret association such as the Free Masons, Odd Fellows and the like."

There are also a considerable group of insurance societies that have a secret ritual and operate on a large basis such as Woodmen of the World, Modern Woodmen of America, etc. I believe, however, that the definitions given above will be sufficient for the purposes of determining exemptions and for any other purposes in granting or withholding licenses under the article.

STATE BOARD OF PUBLIC WELFARE; COUNTY BOARDS OF PUBLIC WELFARE; MERIT SYSTEM LAW; APPOINTMENTS AND SALARIES OF PERSONNEL EMPLOYED BY COUNTY BOARDS OF PUBLIC WELFARE; EFFECT OF NON-COMPLIANCE WITH MERIT SYSTEM LAW

11 March 1946

In your letter of March 11, 1946 you ask us if the State Board of Public Welfare has any authority to transmit State and Federal funds for public welfare administration and grants-in-aid to counties except and upon the conditions that the appointments and salaries of the personnel in county departments of public welfare are certified by the Merit System Supervisor.

The Merit System Act and the rules and regulations established by the Merit System Council pursuant to the authority granted by the Act are binding upon county boards of public welfare. Section 126-14 of the General Statutes, which is a part of the Merit System Law, provides as follows:

> "The merit system council appointed under the provisions of this chapter shall have the authority to establish, maintain and provide rules and regulations, in cooperation with the state board of health and the state board of charities and public welfare, for the administration of a system of personnel standards on a merit rating system with a uniform schedule of compensation for all employees of the county welfare departments and the county, city, and district health departments."

On May 9, 1941 and on June 24, 1942 this office ruled that the Merit System Law in its coverage extended to all employees of the departments mentioned in the Act and that this extended to all employees of the county welfare departments and the county, city, and district health departments. Copies of these opinions are attached to this letter for the sake of illustrating and defining the scope of coverage of the Merit System Law.

In addition to the interpretations, copies of which have been referred to, the rules and regulations promulgated by the Merit System Council which have the force and effect of law provide in Article XXI under the subject of "Applicability," as follows:

> "All positions other than those hereinbefore exempted in Article I, Definition 8, shall be filled by persons selected on the basis of merit in

accordance with this Rule. This Rule shall apply to all personnel (1) in the North Carolina Unemployment Compensation Commission, (2) in the North Carolina State Commission for the Blind, (3) in the State Board of Charities and Public Welfare, and the County Welfare Boards, and (4) in the North Carolina State Board of Health, and in local health departments."

Under the provisions of Section 103-13 of the General Statutes, a county superintendent of welfare must be appointed according to the rules and regulations of the Merit System. Such a superintendent must take a Merit Examination, and his name must appear on the list of eligibles appearing on the registers as established by the Merit System Council. There is no authority of law to employ any county superintendent of welfare by any other system. The compliance with the Merit System Law and the certification of such a person as eligible by the Merit System Supervisor is a condition precedent to the employment of a county superintendent of welfare. Likewise, all of the employees of the county welfare department must comply with the Merit System Law, take an examination, be established on the registers, and be certified by the supervisor of the Merit System Council before such employees have any legal employment or before the status of employer and employee exists between the county welfare department and such persons. The fact that a county or counties elect to pay all of such salaries from county funds does not change or alter the fact or the rule of law that all of the employees of a county welfare department must be employed and appointed according to the Merit System Law. Any attempted appointments made other than in compliance with the Merit System Law, in our opinion, are void; and such employees have no authority to act or to perform any functions on behalf of the county welfare department nor does any agency or any unit of Government have any legal authority to expend public funds or to pay salaries out of public funds to such persons who are attempting to act as employees of the county welfare department without complying with the Merit System Law and without being certified by the Merit System Supervisor.

It is provided in Section 402 (a) of Title IV of the Social Security Act, dealing with grants to states as aid to dependent children, that a State plan for aid to dependent children, among other things, must:

> "V. Provide such methods of administration (including after January 1, 1940, methods relating to the establishment and maintenance of personnel standards on a merit basis, except that the Board shall exercise no authority with respect to the selection, tenure of office, and compensation of any individual employed in accordance with such methods) as are found by the Board to be necessary for the proper and efficient operation of the plan; * * *"

It is provided in Section 404 of the same title of the Social Security Act that if the Social Security Board finds, after notice and hearing, that there is a failure to comply substantially with any provisions of Section 402(a), then further payments will not be made to the State in the way of grants-in-aid until the Board is satisfied that there is no longer any failure to comply.

I might mention also that under Title I of the Social Security Act the same requirement says that a compliance with the Merit System Law on the part of the State Board of Welfare and the County Board of Welfare is required by the Federal Act with reference to grants to states for old-age assistance. See Section 2(a) of Title I of the Social Security Act as amended. See also subsection 2 of Section 4 of Title I of the Social Security Act.

Under the provisions of Title XI of the Social Security Act the Federal authorities have a right to make rules and regulations for the efficient administration of the Act; and pursuant to this and other powers exercised by the Social Security Board, certain standards for a Merit System of personnel administration in State Public Assistance Agencies has been established by the Board; and by virtue of these standards all positions, such as those that are under discussion in this letter, must be filled on a Merit System basis; and in accordance with standards and procedures set forth in the rules and regulations for the Merit System adopted by the State agencies. In addition to these Federal standards which must be observed as a condition for grants-in-aid, it is provided by our own statute under Section 126-15 as follows:

"Wherever the provisions of any law of the United States, or of any rule, order or regulation of any federal agency or authority, providing or administering federal funds for use in North Carolina, either directly or indirectly or as a grant-in-aid, or to be matched or otherwise, impose other or higher civil service or merit standards or different classifications than are required by the provisions of this chapter, then the provisions of such laws, classifications, rules or regulations of the United States or any federal agency may be adopted by the council as rules and regulations of the council and shall govern the class of employment and employees affected thereby, anything in this chapter to the contrary notwithstanding."

When it comes to the administration of Old-Age Assistance by the Division of Public Assistance, certain powers and duties are given to the State Board of Public Welfare by Section 108-28 of the General Statutes. It is provided that the State Board: "Shall supervise the administration of assistance to the needy aged under this article by the county boards." It is further provided under subsection (b) that the State Board can make rules and regulations and take such action as might be necessary or desirable for carrying out the provisions of the article. The rules and regulations made by the State Board are binding on the counties and must be complied with by the respective boards of county commissioners and county boards of welfare. Under subsection (h) of the same section, the State Board is empowered to receive grants-in-aid from the Federal Government for these purposes and for carrying out the provisions of the article. The same provisions are found in Section 108-57 of the General Statutes, which deals with funds for aid to dependent children. It, therefore, appears that the State Board of Welfare and the Commissioner are charged with the duty of seeing that the administrative funds are properly handled and properly spent.

It is also provided in Section 103-13 as to a county superintendent of public welfare that the county welfare board: "Shall determine the salary to be paid the superintendent of public welfare, in accordance with the Merit System compensation plan, either at the time of his appointment or at such time as they may be in regular or called session for the purpose, and the salary shall be paid by the respective counties from Federal, State, and County funds * * *"

It is provided in Section 108-14 of the General Statutes that the county welfare superintendent is the executive officer of the county welfare board, and he or she must appoint office personnel in accordance with Merit System regulations of the State Board of Charities and Public Welfare and that these salaries shall be paid by the county from Federal, State, and county funds. It is clear, therefore, that as to these employees, including the county superintendent of welfare, that the Merit System compensation plan must be followed as to appointments and as to salaries.

Considering, therefore, the Federal statutes and standards and the State statutes and regulations, we are of the opinion that the State Board of Public Welfare or the Commissioner as administrative agent or officer of the State Board has the right and authority to withhold allotments of State and Federal funds from those county boards of welfare who do not comply with the Merit System Law and its regulations and who do not appoint and pay their personnel including the county superintendent of welfare according to the Merit System Law and regulations and from the registers of eligibles as certified by the Merit System Supervisor. This would especially be true in a case where a county superintendent of welfare is attempting to act under an appointment by the county welfare board when such so-called superintendent of county welfare has not been appointed from the list of eligibles under the Merit System plan and has not been certified by the Merit System Supervisor. In such a case, in our opinion, the person attempting to act is not the de jure county superintendent of welfare. In such a situation, there is really no legal county superintendent of public welfare, and there is no person who has the legal authority to administer the funds at the local level; and there is no one that the State Board of Public Welfare can hold responsible for the administration of the Act as well as the proper expenditure of funds. For this reason alone, the Commissioner of Public Welfare, as well as the Board, would have a right to withhold all grants or allotments of Federal and State funds made to the county welfare board. Where such a situation exists, it is the positive duty of the Board and the Commissioner to withhold such funds and grants until compliance with the Merit System Law and regulations have been established and to the end that the whole State system may be in conformity with the Federal standards and the Social Security Act.

As to those funds and salaries already paid while a county superintendent of welfare has not been appointed according to the Merit System Law and regulations, the Merit System Supervisor has a right to review the payroll for conformity as provided by Article XVIII of the Merit System regulations.

STATE BOARD OF PUBLIC WELFARE; ADOPTION; CONSENT; EFFECT OF FINDING BY JUVENILE COURT UNDER GENERAL STATUTES 48-10; GUARDIAN AD LITEM

13 March 1946

In your letter of February 8, 1946 you enclose copy of a Juvenile Court Order with names deleted, and you ask as to whether or not this Order is sufficient authority under the provisions of Section 48-10 of the General Statutes for the Children's Home Society of North Carolina to place for adoption and consent to adoption of the minor child described therein. You also enclose a copy of another Order of the Court where a guardian ad litem was appointed for the child, and it is your opinion that Order No. 1 was first issued; and the second Order, which is marked Order No. 2, was issued on the same day.

You would like to know if the Order containing the findings of the Juvenile Court is sufficient for the adoptive placement of the baby or you would like to also know if the Order appointing the guardian ad litem should be allowed to stand or should be stricken out for adoptive purposes.

No one can tell to what extent Section 48-10 can be of any use in an adoption proceeding. You will note that Section 48-10 does not confer upon any person or institution the authority to consent to an adoption. It simply cuts off all parental rights in an action or proceeding for adoption and dispenses with consents of parents. In the case of WARD v. HOWARD, 217 N. C. 201, 206 the Supreme Court of North Carolina, in speaking of the relation of the juvenile Court Act to the Adoption Law, said:

> "The purpose of the Juvenile Court Act was to protect both society and minor children, which form such a large part of it, from the effect of delinquency on the part of the child and neglect on the part of parents and custodians—not any more as to parents than as to others having the care and custody of children. It is in no respect an amendment to the Adoption Law, nor can it be considered as relieving against the stricter provisions of that law, where the Adoption Law itself speaks upon the subject."

I think that the best thing to do in this case is for the Judge of the Juvenile Court to make the findings in Order No. 2 provided, of course, he strikes out the clause, "until eighteen years of age." In addition to having this Order signed, I think the Clerk of the Superior Court should appoint a next friend to give or withhold consent as provided in Chapter 787 of the Public Laws of 1945. You will see that this chapter provides that if the Court finds as a fact (the word "Court" here means the Clerk of the Court in adoption proceedings) that there is no person or persons qualified to give legal consent, then the Court can appoint some suitable person or the County Superintendent of Public Welfare of the county to act as next friend and to give or withhold consent in the proceeding.

I suggest, therefore, that you do both of these things; and you will then have made the proceeding as legally proper as possible. Unfortunately our Supreme Court has not given very many, if any, constructions of the present Adoption Law, and there is not much to guide us in the matter. A former interpretation of this office sent to Mr. John Bonner should be modified to accord with the opinion in this letter. At that time, the writer over-looked Chapter 787 of the Public Laws of 1945.

STATE BOARD OF PUBLIC WELFARE; ADOPTION; VALIDITY OF JUVENILE COURT
ORDERS OF STATE OF VIRGINIA AS CONSTITUTING A COMPLIANCE WITH
SECTION 48-10 OF THE GENERAL STATUTES OF NORTH CAROLINA

12 March 1946

You state that the county department of public welfare at Norfolk, Virginia has placed a child who is one of its wards with a couple who subsequently moved into North Carolina. This couple expects to establish residence in North Carolina and to petition for adoption before the clerk of the court of the county in this State in which they have established their residence. The data sent to your agency by the Virginia agency contains a "Commitment for a Dependent Child" filed before the Juvenile and Domestic Relations Court of Norfolk. This Commitment shows that the child was found to be a dependent child and that the welfare of the child required the State to assume guardianship.

You would like to know whether or not this court action in Virginia complies with the provisions of Section 48-10 of the General Statutes to the extent that the Social Service Bureau of the Department of Public Welfare of the City of Norfolk would be authorized to execute a valid written consent for the adoption of this child before a clerk of the court of a North Carolina county.

I have thoroughly read the provisions of the Virginia Code applying to delinquent, dependent, and destitute children; I have also read the chapter in the Virginia Code dealing with Juvenile and Domestic Relations Courts and the adoption laws of the State of Virginia. My research includes all amendments enacted by the 1945 General Assembly of the State of Virginia. I am convinced from reading these statutes that the provision allowing the Department of Public Welfare to give consent to an adoption is intended to apply only to adoption proceedings initiated and concluded in the State of Virginia and entirely within the jurisdiction of that State. It is our further opinion that the Juvenile Court mentioned in Section 48-10 of the General Statutes contemplates a Juvenile Court established in this State. Another grave defect in the matter is the fact that the adjudication in Virginia only goes to the extent of finding that the child is a dependent child. It does not find that the child has been abandoned by its parents or that it is an abandoned child. In my opinion, there is a vast difference between a dependent child and an abandoned child as described in Section 48-10.

I had hoped to give an opinion which would permit the Virginia authorities to give consent, but I am convinced that this cannot be done. If the conditions warrant, I would advise that a guardian ad litem be appointed and the consent given by such guardian as provided by the Acts of 1945.

PUBLIC WELFARE; ADOPTION; CONSENT; EFFECT OF DIVORCE DEGREE ON
CONSENT OF FATHER OR PRESUMPTIVE FATHER

11 April 1946

You state that an adoption proceeding has been had or is in process and that the mother only had signed the consent to the adoption. It further appears that there was a divorce decree entered in January 1944 on the complaint of her husband alleging statutory separation as follows: "Plaintiff and defendant on the 5th day of July 1941 separated on the fault of the plaintiff and they have continued to live apart." The child which is the subject of the adoption was born on October 23, 1943; and according to the statement in your letter is not the child of the husband. The complaint does mention a child which was born in December 1941, and this child resides with the mother; but no mention is made in the complaint of the child which is the subject of this adoption proceeding and which was born in October 1943. The issue as to living separate and apart for two successive years was answered by the jury in the affirmative; and as above stated, the decree was granted in December 1944.

Your inquiry is: Does the divorce decree granted in December 1944 as it stands establish the fact that the child born in wedlock in October 1943 is not the child of the mother's husband?

You further ask: Is the consent of the mother to the adoption of this minor a sufficient consent?

The circumstances related in your letter, of course, indicate that this child is illegitimate; but it is not found by the court, no allegation in the complaint and no adjudication in the judgment that this child is illegitimate. In fact the child seems to have been ignored in the complete divorce proceeding. No adjudication having been made as to the legitimacy or illegitimacy of the child and the child having been born during wedlock or while the status of husband and wife existed between the plaintiff and the defendant in the divorce case, I am compelled to state that the mother's husband is presumed to be the father of the child in accordance with interpretations that this office has heretofore sent you. My answer, therefore, to your first question is that the divorce decree granted on December 1944 does not establish the fact that the child is illegitimate or is not the child of the mother's husband.

It follows, therefore, that the consent of the mother to the adoption of this minor is not sufficient consent standing alone and that the consent of the presumptive father must be obtained for a valid adoption.

JUVENILE COURTS; JURISDICTION; CONTINUING JURISDICTION OF JUVENILE
COURT; MINORITY OF CHILD

16 April 1946

You state in your letter that in 1940 a girl who was of an age within the jurisdiction of the juvenile court was made a ward of the Edgecombe County Juvenile Court until further order of the court. The girl was committed by the Edgecombe County Juvenile Court to one of the orphanages of the State until further order of the court. The superintendent of the orphanage now thinks it advisable that other plans be made for this girl and was on the point of petitioning the Edgecombe County Juvenile Court to rescind the 1940 court order in order to relieve the orphanage of the responsibility and return the responsibility to the Edgecombe County Juvenile Court. It was his thought that the court should plan for the girl during the remainder of her minority which, previous to this time has been interpreted as extending to twenty-one years of age.

It appears that on March 13, 1946, Mr. Clifford Pace, Assistant Director of the Institute of Government, wrote the Judge of the Edgecombe County Juvenile Court a letter in which Mr. Pace gave it as his opinion that the jurisdiction of the juvenile court over a minor ceased to exist when the minor reached the age of 'sixteen and that thereafter the juvenile court could make no further orders with respect to the care and welfare of such minor. A copy of Mr. Pace's letter is enclosed with your letter, and there is also enclosed a copy of a letter written by the clerk of the Superior Court, or in this case, the judge of the juvenile court to the superintendent of public welfare which quotes from Mr. Pace's letter; and closes by saying that in his opinion he no longer has any jurisdiction whatsoever in regard to this matter because she is now over sixteen years of age.

In your letter you raise the question as to the meaning of the word "minor" as used in the juvenile court act with reference to the jurisdiction of the court, and you would like to know whether or not the jurisdiction of the juvenile court over a minor extends or can extend until the minor is twenty-one years of age, assuming that the court acquired jurisdiction at a time when such minor was less than sixteen years of age.

A part of Subsection 3 of Section 110-21 of the General Statutes dealing with the continuing jurisdiction of the juvenile court is as follows:

"When jurisdiction has been obtained in the case of any child, unless a court order shall be issued to the contrary, or unless the child be committed to an institution supported and controlled by the State, it shall continue for the purposes of this article during the minority of the child. The duty shall be constant upon the court to give such child subject to its jurisdiction such oversight and control in the premises as will conduce to the welfare of such child and to the best interest of the State."

In Section 110-23 of the Juvenile Court Article, certain terms are defined; and among other terms, we have the following:

"The term 'child' shall mean any minor less than sixteen years of age. The term 'adult' shall mean any person sixteen years of age or over."

It is our thought that the portion of Section 110-23 above quoted is a definition of child and not of minority and simply measures the number of years of a minor's life which must elapse before the child will be considered an adult for purposes of initial jurisdiction of the court. It is not at all inclusive of the term "minority" itself; and to our way of thinking, it simply marks the dividing line between the age when the court has initial jurisdiction over a minor and when a minor will be considered an adult so as to divest the court of its initial jurisdiction. We do not think that this section intends to divest the juvenile court of jurisdiction once the jurisdiction has been properly acquired nor to prevent the court from exercising jurisdiction until the minor becomes of age, that is twenty-one years of age, when and in such event "minority" in the commonly accepted meaning of the term ceases to exist.

In the case of STATE v. COBLE, 181 N. C. 554, 557, the Court said:

"The jurisdiction of the juvenile court is not to be ousted or denied by reason of the fact that the defendant has now reached the age of sixteen, when it is clear that his age at the time of the commission of the offense, rather than at the time of trial, is to determine his guilt or liability and the tribunal which shall take cognizance of his case. Furthermore, he is not to be tried as a criminal but as a juvenile delinquent; and, under the express provisions of the statute, the jurisdiction of the juvenile court, having once attached, continues for the purposes of correction and reformation *during the minority of the defendant.*" (Emphasis ours.)

In the case of In re Coston, 187 N. C. 509, 511 the Court said:

"From the principles approved in these decisions and in further consideration of the statute and its terms and purpose, it appears that the law has primarily conferred upon these juvenile courts the power to initiate and examine and pass upon cases coming under its provisions. That these powers are both judicial and administrative, and when, having acquired jurisdiction, a juvenile court has investigated a case and determined and adjudged that the child comes within the provisions of the law and shall be controlled and dealt with as a ward of the State, this being in the exercise of the judicial powers in the premises, fixes the status of the child, *and the condition continues until the child is of age,* unless and until such adjudication is modified or revised by a further judgment of the court itself or by the Superior Court judge hearing the cause on appeal as the statute provides." (Emphasis ours.)

It seems to us that it is the general tenor of the authorities that we have examined that the continuing jurisdiction of a juvenile court, assuming that the initial jurisdiction of the court has been properly acquired, extends until the child is twenty-one years of age. In 31 American Jurisprudence, p. 799, Section 31, on the question of continuing jurisdiction, we find the following:

"As a general rule, under statutory provisions in the various states, juvenile courts have continuing jurisdiction over an infant delinquent or offender. The time during which this jurisdiction continues is usually during the minority of the infant, but at least, as the cases hold, it does not cease merely on the adjudication of delinquency and order of commitment. The purpose of a statutory provision declaring that when jurisdiction of the juvenile court has been acquired over the person of a child, such jurisdiction shall continue, for the purposes of the statute, until the child has attained majority, has been said to be to enable the state, under proper circumstances, to take over the custody of delinquent children in order to secure their training and reformation; and the power has been regarded as not dependent wholly upon statutes, it being said that its origin may be traced to that equitable doctrine that 'equity acts upon the person,' and, thus acting, finds no more inviting field for its operation than in the protection of the personal rights of infants. It has been held that a statute providing that when jurisdiction has been acquired under the provisions of the juvenile court law over a child, 'such jurisdiction shall continue for the purpose of this article, until the child shall have attained its majority,' should be construed as meaning that when the juvenile court obtains jurisdiction of a delinquent, its retention of that jurisdiction until the delinquent attains the age of twenty-one is a retention for the purposes of the proceedings in which jurisdiction was obtained, and is not to be construed as excluding the jurisdiction of the criminal courts to proceed against the infant after he attains the age of eighteen on charges of crime committed between that time and his becoming twenty-one years of age."

In 31 Corpus Juris, p. 1111, Section 243, we find the following:

"The duration of the custody or commitment is ordinarily within the discretion of the court, which may discharge him from custody, whenever in the judgment of the court it is to the best interest of the child. However, in some jurisdictions, where a child is entitled to a jury trial, in prosecutions for delinquency, the extent of the punishment is exclusively within the province of the jury, and the court is without authority to fix it. The period of commitment or detention is often regulated by statute, and, in such case, it must comply with that designated. *It ordinarily lasts until the child has obtained his majority*, and this is so, even though the power of the court to commit was limited to children under certain age and the child in question has passed that age. Under some statutes a female minor may be detained until she becomes twenty-one years of age, although she attained her majority and married at eighteen." (Emphasis ours.)

We also make reference to the case of EX PARTE GRACE NICARRAT, 41 S.W. 2(d) 176; 76 A.L.R. 654. There is appended to this case, beginning on p. 657, an annotation of some length which reviews the cases in the United States dealing with the power of juvenile courts to exercise continuing jurisdiction over infants, delinquents or offenders.

In the case of STATE v. PENCE, 262 S.W. 360 (Mo.), the court passed upon a statute giving the juvenile court of that state continuing jurisdiction until the child reached its majority. The word "majority" was used in the Missouri statute, and this is the reverse of our statute which uses the word "minority"; but as we see it, the method of reasoning is the same. In construing the word "majority," the court said:

"However, a majority of the court is of opinion that the quoted statutory language is to be construed to mean that when the juvenile court obtains jurisdiction of a delinquent its retention of that jurisdiction until such delinquent attains the age of twenty-one is a retention for the purposes of the proceeding in which jurisdiction was obtained and is not to be construed as excluding the jurisdiction of the criminal courts to proceed against the youth, after he attains the age of 18, on charges of crime, committed between that time and his attainment of the age of 21."

In the case of EX PARTE CHANDLER, 268 S.W. 749 (Tex.), the court construed the meaning of the word "minority" in a juvenile statute and said:

"The judgment rendered by the trial court is attacked upon the ground that it does not set out the length of time for which applicant is committed to the training school. We find no direction in our statute requiring the court to fix a definite length of time for the commitment of female delinquents, save that it is provided that they shall not be committed for a period beyond minority. The judgment in the instant case directs that applicant be detained in said training school until she shall have reached the age of 21 years, unless the court shall make different disposition of her. We do not think the judgment open to the complaint leveled at it."

It is true that the Supreme Court of North Carolina has not directly passed upon this point, and we are not prepared to say as a matter of technical law and construction that Mr. Pace is wrong in the construction expressed in his letter. The Institute of Government is an excellent agency, and the opinions expressed by the members of its staff are entitled to serious consideration by the various units of our State Government. We, however, are of the opinion that the jurisdiction of the juvenile court, when once properly acquired in this State, continues in the proceeding in which it was acquired until the minor in question reaches his or her twenty-first birthday. It seems to us that our Court has expressed itself along this line of reasoning when it uses the word "majority"; and the word "minority" as used in our statute should be given its usual and accepted meaning which means that period of time that an individual is an infant in contemplation of law or less than twenty-one years of age. We think that this has been the common and accepted construction of the act by the administrative agencies administering and dealing with the act and that these administrative interpretations are entitled to great weight.

We answer your question, therefore, that in the case presented by you, the Juvenile Court of Edgecombe County does have jurisdiction over the girl in question; and, in our opinion, the Judge of the Juvenile Court can enter such orders as he thinks proper for the welfare of the ward.

STATE HOSPITALS; STATE SANATORIUM FOR TUBERCULOSIS; COUNTIES AND
COUNTY COMMISSIONERS; LIABILITY OF COUNTY FOR CHARGES OF
SANATORIUM FOR THE TREATMENT OF INDIGENT PATIENTS

3 May 1946

You enclose a letter from the Superintendent of Public Welfare of Mitchell County, the first two paragraphs of which are as follows:

"There are two adult male patients in Western North Carolina Sanatorium at Black Mountain, North Carolina and three children patients in the North Carolina Sanatorium at Sanatorium, North Carolina from Mitchell County. They are from three different families, two of which are receiving Aid to Dependent Children and the third has been found eligible for such. None of the patients are financially able to pay the fifty cents a day required by the institutions.
"Please get an opinion from the Attorney General whether they would be entitled to such hospitalization without cost to them under Section 131-54 of the General Statutes of North Carolina provided the County Commissioners of Mitchell County refuse to pay as provided in Section 131-60 of the same Statutes."

It seems to me that the principle questions in the letter of the Superintendent of Mitchell County Welfare Department is whether or not the

State of North Carolina is compelled to pay for indigent patients and thus entirely relieve the county of any responsibility in the matter. It is my interpretation of Section 131-54 of the General Statutes that the Directors of the State Sanatorium shall not make any regulation or rule whereby a person shall be excluded from the Sanatorium simply because such person is classified as an indigent patient. You will note that the statute is very careful to say that the patient in such cases is or must be "otherwise properly qualified for admission." I think that the true meaning of this statute is that the Directors of the Sanatorium cannot pass any rule, regulation, or by-law which would exclude the indigent patients in favor of those patients who are able to pay the reasonable value of all charges of treatment. For example, if there is a waiting list of patients, indigent patients cannot be passed over when their turn comes for admission in order that patients who are financially able to pay all charges may be admitted. The statute does not mean that the State of North Carolina has assumed the expenses of treating all indigent patients. You will note that the balance of the statute deals with the collection of charges from those who are able to pay or from persons upon whom patients are legally dependent and which persons are able to pay. There is further provision for bringing suit for collection in the county in which the case shall be tried.

Section 131-60 of the General Statutes gives a city or town or a county the authority, through its governing body, to provide for the treatment of a tuberculous indigent patient provided such patient is a bona fide resident or citizen of the city, town or county in question. The charge for such treatment is limited to not in excess of One ($1.00) Dollar a day per patient. As a matter of fact, I am informed that the actual rate is fifty cents a day for indigent patients. I have been unable to find anywhere in our law any statute that compels a county to pay charges for the treatment of indigent tuberculous persons at the State Sanatorium. A county can enter into such a contract; but so far as I can see, it is not compelled to do so; however, if a county does not wish to pay the regular fees for its indigent patients, I see no reason why the State Sanatorium cannot discharge such patients from such county after they have been received, examined, and given treatment for a minimum period of time as fixed by the regulations of the institution. I am unable to find in the statutes any law which leads me to believe that the fact that the families concerned are receiving Aid to Dependent Children would have anything to do with the situation. The Superintendent of the Mitchell County Welfare Department in his letter states that none of the patients are able to pay the fifty cents a day required by the institutions. He does not say whether the parents or any persons upon whom the children are legally dependent are able to pay the required minimum charges. The two adult male patients at Black Mountain more than likely are liable for their own charges; and if they are unable to pay, then they are actually indigent cases.

My conclusion, therefore, is that the county is not compelled to enter into any agreement or any contract with any of the North Carolina Sanatoria for the payment of charges for indigent patients; but the Sanatoria can admit, examine and exclude such patients of such counties after treating them for a minimum period of time as fixed by their own regulations.

P.S.: In regard to the children from Mitchell County who are at the State Sanatorium located at Sanatorium, North Carolina, I have just talked with the Business Manager of the institution by telephone; and he tells me that a Mr. Yelton brought these children to the Sanatorium and paid their charges for two months in advance in cash. The children were admitted on the 23rd of April, 1946, and the application states that any further charges are to be sent to the mothers of the children in question. The Business Manager states that there is nothing on his records whatsoever to show that Mitchell County has ever agreed to assume any charges in these cases; and the Business Manager states that so far as the records of his office are concerned, the Sanatorium and its officials are not looking to Mitchell County for payment in these cases and that it was understood by the agents of the Sanatorium that the county had not obligated itself in any way. It, therefore, seems to me that it should be understood and agreed upon between the county authorities and the Sanatorium before indigent patients are admitted as to who will assume the obligation.

OPINIONS TO DEPARTMENT OF CONSERVATION AND DEVELOPMENT

GAME LAWS; UNLAWFUL POSSESSION OF GAME; INSPECTION OF
REFRIGERATING PLANTS, ETC.

10 November 1944

Receipt is acknowledged of your letter in which you request my opinion as to whether a game protector, under the authority contained in Section 19, Chapter 486, of the Public Laws of 1935, would have the right to search without warrant freezer lockers rented to individuals for storage purposes.

Section 19 of Chapter 486 of the Public Laws of 1935 provides in part that the Commissioner, all game protectors, deputy game protectors and refuge keepers, shall have the power to enter and search any refrigeration plant, refrigerators and ice boxes of all public refrigerating storage plants, meat shops, hotels, restaurants, or other public eating places in which such officer making such search has reasonable grounds to believe that game taken, killed or stored in violation of the North Carolina game law, has been killed or stored, and which will furnish evidence of violation of such laws. The section further provides that such search may be made without warrant except that no dwelling may be searched without a warrant.

From an inspection of the section above referred to it will be noted that all of the plants, shops, etc., referred to therein are considered strictly as public places, as distinguished from places where the right of private property is to be considered. I assume that when a person rents a freezer locker of the type mentioned in your letter, he acquires a key therefor and that no other person would be allowed to enter or inspect the contents of his locker without his permission. If this is true, we are immediately confronted with two propositions, the first being whether the provisions of the section as written would be broad enough to include individual lockers leased by various persons, and the second question would be whether, conceding that the provisions of the section would be broad enough to include private lockers, the section would be unconstitutional insofar as it authorized a search without a warrant.

Although there might be some question as to whether it was the intention of the Legislature to extend the provisions of the section in question so as to cover the lockers about which you inquire, it is my thought that we should concede, at least for the sake of argument, that such was the intention of the General Assembly. I say this only on account of the ultimate conclusion I am about to reach.

It has never been the policy of this office to declare acts of the General Assembly unconstitutional. The opinions of this office are advisory only and are not binding on the courts and, this being true, unless an act of the General Assembly is clearly unconstitutional, this office would not be justified in rendering an opinion declaring such act to be unconstitutional. The provisions of our Constitution against unreasonable search and seizure are inhibitions upon the power of public officers acting in an official capacity under governmental authority, and these constitutional provisions should receive a liberal interpretation in favor of the citizen, especially in regard to those matters designed to safeguard his liberty and security as to both person and property. The main, if not the sole, purpose of these inhibitions is to place a salutary restriction on the powers of government and to provide against any attempt by legislation or otherwise to authorize, justify or declare lawful any unconstitutional search or seizure.

It has been said in 38 C. J. S., p. 23, that a search without warrant and before arrest for game unlawfully possessed is unlawful under the right of all citizens to immunity from unreasonable search and seizure. It is said in 56 C. J., 1167, that game in the possession out of season of a person may be protected by the constitutional immunity from unlawful search and seizure.

With the above statements and principles in mind, you can readily see that there might be a grave question as to the constitutionality of the provisions of the section above referred to, which authorizes a search without a warrant, where the question of private property enters the picture. It should also be called to your attention that the persons authorized to make the search must have reasonable grounds to believe that game taken, killed or held in violation of the law, is stored in the place proposed to be searched. This does not mean some idea originating in the mind of a game protector that a certain place might possibly have game illegally stored therein, but means that such game protector must have a reasonable basis for his belief.

The idea I am trying to get across is that a game protector would have no right, under the authority contained in this section, to embark upon a tour of exploration without having some tangible evidence in his possession that the place or places to be investigated in reality had game unlawfully stored therein.

There being some doubt as to the constitutionality of the statute, it is my opinion that it would not be advisable to undertake to search a freezer locker, rented by an individual for storage purposes, without his consent until a proper search warrant has been secured. It is my belief that this is a safe and sane course to pursue in cases of this kind.

GAME AND FISH LAWS; REPEAL OF SECTION 5, CHAPTER 278,
PUBLIC LAWS OF 1929

10 November 1944

I acknowledge receipt of your letter, calling my attention to Section 5 of Chapter 278 of the Public Laws of 1929, relating to the necessity of establishing proof as to the identity of sex in the taking of deer, and inquiring as to whether or not said section is now in force.

The referred to section was not carried forward in Chapter 486 of the Public Laws of 1935, which deals with the same subject matter as Chapter 278 of the Public Laws of 1929, and the only section of Chapter 278 of the Public Laws of 1929 carried forward in the North Carolina General Statutes is Section 3, which deals with the question of trappers' license. See Section 113-96, N. C. General Statutes. It, therefore, appears that Section

5 of Chapter 278 of the Public Laws of 1929 has been superseded by Chapter 486 of the Public Laws of 1935, and that said Section 5 is not now in force.

I further call your attention to the fact that that portion of the pertinent section dealing with the sex identity of deer limits the requirement to a period of time of two years from September 1, 1929, so that, notwithstanding whether or not said section has been superseded by the 1935 Act, the section upon which you depend is not now applicable.

OYSTER GROUND LEASES; OYSTER LAND GRANTS

4 May 1945

I have your letter of May 3, enclosing copy of a letter from Mr. John D. Warlick, Attorney at Law, Jacksonville, North Carolina, with reference to the claim of Mr. Warlick's clients for oyster bottoms under grants issued under Chapter 90 of the Public Laws of 1887 and Chapter 298 of the Laws of 1889, which he claims cover a part of the bottom which you have leased to one, Corbett Hansley, under the provisions of Article 16 of Chapter 113 of the General Statutes, as to which you write me as follows:

> "Mr. Warlick claims the two Sidburys inherited the same ground from their father under an old grant and I will thank you to give me a ruling as to whether or not I had authority to lease this land: it was not staked off; not listed on the tax books and certainly not since 1931 nor the taxes paid. It has been my impression for years that State grants have to be entered on the tax abstract of the owners and the taxes kept up, and if these conditions were not complied with the land covered by the grant reverted to the State and became subject to lease by the State."

Grants issued under Chapter 119 of the Public Laws of 1887 were liable for taxation as real estate. See Pell's Revisal, Section 2380. I find no provision in the law which automatically forfeits the title to these bottoms by failure of the holder of the grant to pay taxes. The statute provided (Pell's Revisal 2378) that the grants would be issued by the Secretary of State, provided the holder or holders would make in good faith, within five years of the date of obtaining the franchise, an actual effort to raise and cultivate shell fish on the grounds. It provided that no grant should be made to any one person for more than ten acres, and that no person could hold more than ten acres in any creek, unless the same was acquired through devise, inheritance or marriage.

Chapter 298 of the Public Laws of 1889 created a Shell Fish Commission of Onslow County and it applied only to Onslow County. It is substantially the same law as found in Chapter 90 of the Public Laws 1887 but limited the acreage to be entered by one person to fifteen acres and required the same to be cultivated within three years from the date of the grant.

If the owners of these bottoms have not listed it for taxation, they could be subject to sale for taxation like any other real property, but the mere fact that the property has not been listed for taxation would not vacate the grant. You can find the law on this subject in Pell's Revisal of 1905, Section 2378 through and including Section 2382, taken from Chapter 119 of the Public Laws of 1887. You can probably find this book in the office of the Clerk of the Superior Court.

DEPARTMENT OF CONSERVATION AND DEVELOPMENT; RULES AND REGULATIONS; ERECTION AND USE OF STRUCTURES ON STATE LAKES

22 June 1945

Reference is made to your memorandum of June 13, 1945, directed to the Attorney General, and also to proposals and regulations governing the erection and use of structures on State lakes.

You ask this office to check the regulations as to their legality, wording and intent, and you also inquire as to the responsibility of the State of North Carolina for any accidents that might occur below the high·water mark of the lake on or near the dock of a permittee, and in this connection it is further asked if the responsibility for any accident would be placed upon the permittee, assuming that the permit has been regularly signed, issued and paid for by such permittee.

It is specifically set forth in Section 113-34 of the General Statutes that the Department of Conservation and Development may administer, among other things, State lakes and may segregate the revenue secured through the administration of State lakes and other recreational areas. It is also provided in Section 113-35 of the General Statutes that the Department shall make reasonable rules and regulations of the use by the public of all State lakes under its charge and that such regulations, after having been posted in conspicuous places on or adjacent to such State properties and at the courthouse of the county or counties in which such properties are situated, shall have the force and effect of law, and any violation of any such regulations shall be a misdemeanor punishable by fine of not more than $50.00 or by imprisonment for not exceeding thirty days.

First of all, in regard to the question of the possible liability of the State because of any accident or injury to person or property below the high water mark of the lake or near or on the dock of any permittee, regardless of whether the same occurs above or below the high water mark, I am of the opinion that in the administration of the State lakes and other recreational facilities for the use and benefit of the people of the State, the Department of Conservation and Development and its duly authorized officers and agents are acting in a governmental capacity and there is, therefore, no liability on the part of the State or any of its agencies because of any accidents or injuries to persons or property that may occur as described in your memorandum. The State cannot be sued unless it gives its express consent to be sued in such action by an appropriate statute, and I do not find any law or statute that would allow the State or the Department of Conservation and Development to be sued under such circumstances. This has been clearly established in many cases. See MOODY v. THE STATE'S PRISON, 128 N. C. 12; VINSON v. O'BERRY, 209 N. C. 298; PRUDENTIAL INSURANCE COMPANY OF AMERICA v. POWELL, 217 N. C. 495.

Of course, it is true that an individual officer of a Department may act in a negligent or wanton manner and injure persons or property, and this officer might be held responsible in his individual capacity for such injuries, but this would not affect the immunity enjoyed by the State and the Department of Conservation and Development as its agency. I would approve, however, your Paragraph 14 of the proposed regulations for the reason that I think that the public should know that the State is not liable. However, I would rearrange Paragraph 14 and specifically state that the State and the Department are not liable for any claims of this nature and that so far as the State and the Department are concerned, any and all claims will have to be prosecuted against the permittee only. I would also incorporate a statement to the same effect in the permit as suggested in your memorandum. Any legal responsibility for any accidents or injuries to persons or property which may occur near to or on any such structures or docks are the legal responsibility of the permittee in my opinion.

You will find that Section 146-10 of the General Statutes deals with the erection of piers, docks, etc. upon the waters of State lakes, and you will further find that this section requires that any permit issued "must set forth in required detail the size, cost and nature of such structure, and any person, firm or corporation erecting any such structure, without a proper permit or not in accordance with the specifications of said permit shall be guilty of a misdemeanor. . . . ." I am rather doubtful that the form of your permits as set forth in Paragraph 12 of the regulation complies with this section of the law as it does not seem to me that the permit contains the necessary details as to the size and cost of the structure as is required by the statute, and I would recommend that you examine your regulation again in this respect in the light of the section above cited.

In Paragraph 6 of your regulations you speak of a lease, yet you do not provide any machinery for obtaining leases, nor do you state upon what terms leases will be executed, nor do you reserve any right to revoke any lease for non-compliance with the terms of the laws or of the regulations. It would seem to me that all the regulations enacted for the use of State lakes should be incorporated into any lease, at least by reference to same, and that the State should reserve the right to declare any lease void for any violation of stated conditions. Under the present regulations, it is not clear whether the permittee can assign his permit to some other person or not. It would seem to me that some restriction should be placed upon this possible right of assignment.

I do not find in your regulations any machinery for the revocation of a permit. It would seem to me that you should provide some regulation whereby the Department may serve notice upon a permittee and require him to show cause before the Director why his permit should not be revoked, and in any investigation or hearing before the Director, the decision of the Director should be final. I would suggest, therefore, that you consider regulations providing for the revocation of permits.

I do not find in your regulations any reservation to the Department which would allow its officers and agents to go in and upon such docks, houses or other structures and inspect the same for the purpose of seeing that the regulations are being carried out, and that the permittee is conducting his operation or his use and occupancy in a proper manner. I would suggest, therefore, thàt you reserve the right in your regulations and in your permit for the officials of the Department to make the necessary inspections if the Department so desires, with the right to enter in and upon any and all buildings and structures at reasonable hours.

CONSERVATION AND DEVELOPMENT; STATE LAKES; RIGHT TO ISSUE REGULATIONS GOVERNING THE OPERATION OF BOATS CARRYING PASSENGERS FOR HIRE; ARTIFICIAL LAKES; UTILITIES COMMISSION

24 July 1945

Reference is made to your letter of July 19, 1945, with which you enclosed copy of regulations issued by the Utilities Commission governing the operation of boats and vessels on inland lakes and waters in North Carolina. You further call attention to a letter from Honorable Charles Z. Flack, Chief Clerk of the Utilities Commission, in which it is stated that the Utilities Commission has not interpreted these rulings and regulations to cover the usual boat operations for pleasure on inland lakes since such operation is considered by the Utilities Commission as being within the meàning of the term "common carrier."

You inquire of this office as to whether the Utilities Commission or the Department of Conservation and Development is responsible for the enforcement of these regulations.

The regulations issued by the Utilities Commission are based upon the authority conferred by Sections 62-28 and 62-39 of the General Statutes. If I understand correctly, the present position of the Utilities Commission is that these regulations, so far as its enforcement is concerned, would only apply to regular boats or steamboats operating as common carriers upon a regular route with fixed schedules, and with the regular system tariffs ·or rates for the carriage of passengers or freight. At the present time it does·not seem to be the interpretation of this Commission that these regulations would be enforced by it as to motor launches and pleasure boats·operated for hire or carrying passengers for compensation. You will note that these regulations specifically exempt a boat which is operated by the hirer himself, even though he may take passengers on board, provided, of course, that he does not charge for carrying such passengers.

Section 113-35 of the General Statutes provides as follows:

"The Department shall make reasonable rules for the regulation of the use by the public of such and all State forests, State parks, State lakes, game refuges and public shooting grounds under its charge, which regulations, after having been posted in conspicuous places on and adjacent to such State properties and at the courthouse of the county or counties in which such properties are situated, shall have the force and effect of law and any violation of such regulations shall constitute a misdemeanor and shall be punishable by a fine of not more than fifty dollars or by imprisonment for not exceeding thirty days."

It is further provided in Section 146-8 that all recreation in or upon any of the State lakes may be regulated in the public interest by the State agency having administrative authority over these areas.

I am of the opinion, therefore, that so far as the operation of boats, motor launches and other craft is concerned, the Department of Conservation and Development has the authority to issue reasonable regulations concerning the operation of these boats, and the safety devices which should be affixed to or carried by these vessels or boats. In doing this, the Department should adopt its own rules and regulations and should not attempt to enforce the rules and regulations of any other commission or agency. Such rules and regulations can be made to apply to those persons, firms or corporations who operate such boats for the purpose of carrying passengers for compensation or who lease such boats and either provide a pilot or operator or allow the lessee to operate the boat. Such rules and regulations could only apply to boats or craft operated on State inland lakes, as I do not find any authority which would allow the Department of Conservation and Development to apply such regulations to artificial lakes and ponds and, therefore, before this could be done, the Department would need further enabling legislation. I am further of the opinion that such regulations could be applied to all craft or boats operated by the owner for his own pleasure and that of his guests, even though there would be no element of carrying passengers for hire.

GAME AND FISHERIES; LICENSE TO FISH IN PRIVATE PONDS

31 July 1945

I acknowledge receipt of your letter in which you inquire as to whether or not persons other than the owner of a private lake or pond are required to obtain a license to fish in such lakes or ponds.

Article 14, Chapter 113, of the General Statutes of North Carolina sets out the requirements for and regulates fishing in inland waters. Section 113-154 specifically provides that the provisions of Article 14 shall not "prevent the owners of any land or members of his family under 21 years of age from fishing thereon without a license." While Section 113-155 requires any person to obtain permission of the owner before fishing or attempting to catch fish after being forbidden by the owner of the land, I do not think that persons other than those mentioned in 113-154 may fish in a privately owned lake or pond without first obtaining a license to fish and to otherwise comply with the provisions of Article 14 of said Chapter 113.

SOLICITORS; PRIVATE PROSECUTION; CONTROL OF CASE

22 September 1945

I have your letter of September 18, 1945, in which you inquire if an act was adopted by the 1945 Session of the General Assembly making it mandatory on the judge of recorder's court of Columbus County to transfer a case therein to the Superior Court when a demand for a jury trial is made. If such bill were adopted, you inquire if the request for jury trial can be made only by the prosecuting attorney and the defendant, or can it be made by private prosecution.

The 1945 Session of the General Assembly enacted House Bill No. 353 (Chapter 336, Session Laws of 1945) which provides that in all trials in the recorder's court of Columbus County when a demand for a jury trial is made by either the defendant or the prosecuting attorney, the recorder shall transfer the case for trial to the Superior Court and the defendant shall be required to execute a new and justified bond in such amount as may be fixed by the recorder.

It is my opinion that only the prosecuting attorney may make the demand for jury trial on the part of the prosecution. Of course he may make the demand through private counsel but I do not believe that private counsel is authorized to make such demand when the solicitor objects. In other words, it is my opinion that the solicitor remains in control of the case for the prosecution. Compare State v. Lea, 203 N. C. 13; State v. Carden, 209 N. C. 404. In State v. Lea, supra, Stacy, C. J., Says;

> "The appearance of counsel for the prosecution, other than the solicitor of the district, was a matter which the trial court necessarily had under its supervision. *The solicitor at no time relinquished control of the case, nor does it appear that the assistance of other counsel was not requested or welcomed by him.*" (Italics added.)

GAME LAWS; SALE OR PURCHASE OF GAME FISH; WHAT CONSTITUTES SALE OR PURCHASE

15 October 1945

I have your letter of October 13, 1945, in which you make the following inquiry:

> "I would appreciate very much a ruling in the following case as to whether it is a violation of the State laws involving the sale of game fish:
>
> "A private pond located in Johnston County was drawn down and fished. The owner divided the fish into two lots, one constituted of non-game fish and the other constituted of game fish. The owner auctioned off a string of non-game fish and at the same time held up a string of game fish which were to go as a prize to the highest bidder on the string of non-game fish."

G. S. 113-136 authorizes the Board of Conservation and Development to make certain rules and regulations. This section provides that a violation of these regulations constitutes a misdemeanor. Section 11 of the State-wide Inland Fishing Regulations reads in part as follows:

> "It shall be unlawful in the State of North Carolina for any person, firm or corporation to buy, sell, ship, offer for sale, or possess for the purpose of sale game fish whether taken within or without this State."

I am of the opinion that the establishment of the facts outlined above would be sufficient to sustain a verdict of guilty of selling game fish in violation of the above quoted portion of Regulation No. 11. It seems clear that the string of game fish given as a prize to the purchaser of a string of non-game fish enters into the transaction and becomes a part of the consideration for the amount bid. In other words, it is my opinion that the purchaser in reality is purchasing game fish as well as non-game fish. No doubt the purchaser would not bid as much for the non-game fish if he knew that he would not receive the game fish also.

It would seem, thus, that he is purchasing both game fish and non-game fish. I am of the opinion, therefore, that the circumstances outlined in your letter amount to both a purchase and a sale of game fish.

GAME AND FISHERIES; CHAPTER 160 PUBLIC LAWS 1935; HOUSE BILL NO. 958, 1945 SESSION GENERAL ASSEMBLY

26 October 1945

I acknowledge receipt of your letter enclosing a copy of a letter from Rupert E. West, District Game Protector, in which he inquires as to the responsibility of enforcing the provisions of House Bill 958 of the 1945 session of the Legislature, and further, as to whether or not the requirements in said bill as to box batteries, bush blinds, floating bush blinds, etc., are applicable to skiffs used in transporting hunters to and from the shooting points and blinds.

House Bill 958 (Chapter 1072 Session Laws of 1945) amends Chapter 160 of the Public Laws of 1935 by providing:

> "Any box batteries, bush blind, stationary bush blind, floating bush blind, or any other floating device used in the hunting of wild fowl on the waters of Currituck Sound or its tributaries, shall be at least thirty (30) inches above the water."

While I think the wording of the 1945 Act is broad enough to include any and every kind of floating device, I think that it relates to boats or skiffs only when used in hunting and not to those used exclusively to transport hunters to and from the shooting points or blinds. Of course, if the skiff conveying the hunters to the shooting points or blinds is used from which to hunt or shoot, it would then come within the provisions of the act and would have the same standing as the other devices therein mentioned.

Since the 1945 Act merely adds a new section and in no way changes or alters the 1935 Act, I am of the opinion that the enforcement of the 1945 Act is in the same category as the enforcement of the other provisions of the 1935 Act.

DEPARTMENT OF CONSERVATION & DEVELOPMENT; ABANDONED OIL WELLS; 1945 OIL AND GAS CONSERVATION ACT

1 May 1946

I acknowledge receipt of your letter enclosing the letter addressed to you from Mr. Roderick A. Stamey, President of the Carolina Petroleum Company, together with proposed bond in the sum of $2500.00 and check in the sum of $25.00 for location fee, and plot of the proposed site of the new well.

While I have no personal knowledge of the facts, it is my understanding that this well is to be drilled upon lands not owned by any of the departments of the State of North Carolina but leased by individual property owners. If this is true the State Department of Conservation and Development has no concern as to the authority of the Coastal Plains Oil Company to sublease the same to the Carolina Petroleum Company.

The bond is filed pursuant to Section 113-378 of the General Statutes and seems to comply with the requirements of the section so that I approve the same as to form and legality.

It is not quite clear to me as to the purpose of the $25.00 check. There was no provision in the law prior to 1945 Session of the Legislature which required a "well location fee." The 1945 Legislature enacted Section 113-395 which, among other things, required a fee of $50.00 to be paid before any gas or oil well is drilled. However, this section is not operative until the Governor and Council of State declare the same to be in force after oil has been discovered. See Section 113-382 G. S. Of course, if this section was in force the fee would be $50.00 instead of $25.00. I suggest you contact Mr. Stamey and inquire of him as to the section of the statute under which he has submitted the check for $25.00.

OPINIONS TO COMMISSIONER OF BANKS

BANKS; LIQUIDATION; BOARD OF FINANCIAL CONTROL FOR BUNCOMBE COUNTY; AUTHORITY OF COMMISSIONER OF BANKS TO EXECUTE TRANSFER AS TO SECURITIES SOLD BY BOARD OF FINANCIAL CONTROL

1 July 1944

Receipt is acknowledged of your letter of June 29 enclosing a letter from Lt. Col. Basil A. Wood relative to transfer of a certain note owned by the Board of Financial Control for Buncombe County. Lt. Col. Wood raises the question as to whether you would have the authority, as Commissioner of Banks, to make the transfer in which he is interested.

The Board of Financial Control for Buncombe County was created by virtue of Chapter 253 of the Public-Local Laws of 1931. In Section 1 of the Act, the Board is declared to be a corporation with perpetual succession, the right to use a corporate seal, to sue and be sued, and to purchase or otherwise acquire, hold, manage, control, lease, sell and otherwise dispose of property, real and personal. Section 34 provides for the election by the Board of Financial Control of a liquidating agent to hold office at the pleasure of the Board and who, subject to the supervision of the Board, was to perform the duties and exercise the powers conferred by that portion of the Act dealing with the liquidation of securities.

It appears that the note in question was sold by the liquidating agent of the Board of Financial Control for Buncombe County to L. B. Jackson and Company, a corporation of Asheville, North Carolina. You, as Commissioner of Banks, had no connection with or control over the acts or property of the Board of Financial Control for Buncombe County or its liquidating agent. I am therefore of the opinion that you would have no right, as Commissioner of Banks, to execute any transfer for or on behalf of the Board of Financial Control for Buncombe County.

BANKS AND BANKING; CASHING CHECKS FOR FEES

7 October 1944

I have your letter of October 4, 1944, enclosing a letter from E. B. Stone Finance Company requesting an opinion as to whether there is any law in North Carolina which would prohibit a Finance Company from making a small service charge for cashing payroll checks.

There is no statute in North Carolina which prohibits this practice, nor would this practice constitute dealing in securities so as to make those engaging therein subject to the license required by Section 132 of the Revenue Act. This was the subject of a ruling by this office to Honorable Thomas D. Cooper on 21 July 1944. I am enclosing an extra copy of this opinion for your use.

BANKS AND BANKING; RIGHT OF BANK TO REFUSE TO ACCEPT DEPOSITS

16 October 1944

I have your letter of October 13, 1944, enclosing a letter from Mr. E. C. Guy, President of the Avery County Bank, requesting a ruling from this office on the following question:

"Do we have the right to decline to accept a checking account from an individual, partnership or corporation? Is a bank considered a public service corporation and must we accept accounts from people whom we fear might be crooks?"

There is no North Carolina statute which compels a bank to accept all deposits nor any case in which it has been held that a bank has authority to refuse to accept deposits. We must, therefore, seek an answer to your inquiry in the general law relating to banks and banking.

In 7 C. J., Banks and Banking, Sec. 303, page 628, it is written:

"The chief business of a bank is to receive and lend money. The money received is termed a 'deposit,' although it is not strictly so, as the depositor does not expect to receive the identical thing in return, but another thing of the same kind and of equal value. A bank is not, however, required to keep the deposits of every person who offers money for this purpose, but may decline to do business with those whom, for any reason, it does not wish to serve, and it may close an account at any time by tendering to the depositor the amount due and by declining to receive more."

The same general principle is to be found in 9 C. J. S., Banks and Banking, Sec. 268, pages 548, 549. These general authorities seem to indicate that a bank may refuse to accept deposits.

BANKS; SUSPENSION OF INVESTMENT AND LOAN LIMITATION

25 October 1944

Receipt is acknowledged of your letter referring to an inquiry from the Federal Deposit Insurance Corporation as to the meaning of the words "amply secured" appearing in a proviso to G. S. 53-49, relating to the suspension of investment and loan limitation.

G. S. 53-49 provides:

"The board of directors of any bank, may by resolution duly passed at a meeting of the board, request the commissioner of banks to suspend temporarily the limitations on loans and investments as the same may apply to any particular loan or investment in excess of the limitations of SS 53-46, 53-47, and 53-48 which the bank desires to make. Upon receipt of a duly certified copy of such resolution, the commissioner of banks may, in his discretion, suspend the limitations on loans and investments insofar as they would apply to the loan or investment which the bank desires to make: Provided, however, such loan shall be amply secured and shall be for a period not longer than one hundred and twenty days."

From an inspection of the language used in the proviso as it relates to the remainder of the section, it is my opinion that the words "amply secured" should not be construed to mean that collateral must be specifically pledged to secure the loan. The Commissioner of Banks is authorized, in his discretion, to suspend the limitations as provided in the section if the loan is amply secured and is for a period not longer than one hundred and twenty days. The words "amply secured" as used in the proviso should, in my opinion, be construed to mean that the amount represented by the loan would be collectible by law in event of a failure to pay upon maturity. A loan might not be amply secured even though collateral is specifically pledged to secure its payment. On the other hand, a loan might be amply secured where no collateral is specifically pledged.

BANKS AND BANKING; PROHIBITION AGAINST CORPORATIONS OTHER THAN BANKS ENGAGING IN BANKING BUSINESS

4 November 1944

I have your letter of November 3, enclosing a letter to you from Messrs. Coursolle, Preus and Maag, quoting a statute dealing with the prohibition of the banking business by corporations other than banks, and inquiring if we have a similar statute in this State.

The only statute of a similar character which we have is G. S. 53-127. Of course, under our banking law found in Chapter 53 of the General Statutes, no person, firm or corporation could engage in the banking business except as authorized by this law.

TRUSTS; TRANSFER OF ASSETS; G. S. 36-29; REGULATIONS OF THE BANKING COMMISSION

13 January 1945

I have your letter of January 10, enclosing a letter from Mr. R. W. Barnard, Vice President and Trust Officer of the American Trust Company. He refers to G. S. 36-29 which provides, in part, that no trustee shall, as trustee of one trust, sell property to itself as trustee of another trust, and the order of the State Banking Commission, dated June 28, 1939, containing the following provision:

> "Assets of trusts held by a bank as fiduciary shall not be sold or transferred from one trust to another trust, unless such transfer is expressly authorized by the instrument creating the trust to which the transfer is made, or unless such transfer is approved by the board of directors by unanimous vote at a regular meeting."

Mr. Barnard points out that the regulation of the Banking Commission may be in conflict with the provisions of G. S. 36-29, as to which you ask my opinion.

I am inclined to agree that Mr. Barnard is correct and that the regulation or order of the Banking Commission should be reconsidered, with a view of reconciliation with the statutory provision.

INTEREST FEES; H. B. No. 176; G. S. 14-391; LOANS
ON HOUSEHOLD AND KITCHEN FURNITURE

9 March 1945

I have your letter of March 8 and I have examined, as requested by
you, H. B. No. 176, Section 3, and G. S. 14-391 and 105-88. You inquire
as to whether or not a loan agency or broker licensed under G. S. 105-
88 who is under the supervision of the State Banking Commission after
June 1, 1945, would violate Section 14-391 if he lends on household and
kitchen furniture or assignment of wages are taken as security to loans on
which the fees authorized by Section 3 of H. B. No. 176 are charged.

H. B. No. 176, in Section 3, provides that the loan· agencies defined in
G. S. 105-88 are authorized to charge not in excess of the same fees and
interest that may lawfully be charged by industrial banks on installment
loans. Section 5 of this Act provides that all laws and clauses of laws in
conflict with the provisions of this Act are hereby repealed. If any such
agency makes a loan of the character described in G. S. 14-391, it is my
opinion that such agency could charge the fees authorized by H. B. No.
176, in addition to 6% interest. This Act authorizes these agencies to collect the fees referred to and, to that extent, is in conflict with G. S. 14-391.
As it repeals laws in conflict, I reach the conclusion that these fees could be·
collected in addition to the interest, without violating the law as it will be
from the effective date of H. B. No. 176 on June 1, 1945.

COMMISSIONER OF BANKS; STATE BANKING COMMISSION; PERSONAL
LIABILITY FOR FAILURE TO EXAMINE BANKS

11 April 1945

I received your letter of March 30, in which you wrote me as follows:

"Since January 1, 1945, we have lost four of our experienced State
Bank Examiners. We will need at least one man in addition to our
normal staff to examine the Small Loan Agencies.
"Section 53-117, General Statutes of North Carolina, requires that
the Commissioner of Banks 'shall examine each State bank at least
once each year.' If I should fail to examine any of these banks during
the year, and, after that time, a shortage or other loss should be discovered during a subsequent examination, or otherwise, which might
have been prevented if the required examination had been made,
would I be personally or officially liable for any loss that the bank
might sustain? Would the members of the State Banking Commission
also be liable?"

A consideration of the authorities in this State leads to the conclusion
that in the absence of wilfulness, malice or corruption, the nonperformance
of a judicial act, which involves discretionary powers, will exempt a public
official from personal liability. On the other hand, the nonperformance of
a purely ministerial duty prescribed by statute will render a public official
personally liable to anyone suffering a loss or damage because of such
nonfeasance even if good faith is present. The requirement of Section

53.117 that the Commissioner of Banks "shall examine each State bank at least once each year," appears to be ministerial in nature. However, if circumstances beyond the control of the Commissioner of Banks make performance impossible, then it seems he would be relieved of any personal liability. The same would be true of the Banking Commission.

I am enclosing a copy of a memorandum made in this office on this subject, which may be of interest to you.

It seems to me that in view of this possibility, it would be well to exhaust every reasonable effort to secure the necessary personnel for making an examination of the banks as required by the statute, as the burden might be upon the Commissioner of Banks and the Commission to show that it is impossible to secure the necessary personnel to justify its failure to conduct examinations required by law.

BANKS; DISCOUNTING NOTES OF OFFICERS OR EMPLOYEES

24 April 1945

I have your letter of April 21, enclosing a letter from Messrs. Womble, Carlyle, Martin & Sandridge, in which they write you as follows:

"As you probably know, Wachovia Bank and Trust Company has established a time payment department. In connection with that department, the question has arisen as to whether or not the bank can discount an officer's or an employee's notes given to a bona fide dealer for the purchase of merchandise such as automobiles, refrigerators, ets. Of course, the bank does not propose in any case to lend money directly to the officer or employee. In connection with this question I call your attention to G. S. 53-91, prohibiting any officer or employee of a bank from borrowing any amount whatever from the bank except upon good collateral or other ample security or endorsement, and even then only upon approval by a majority of the board of Directors.

"The situation I propose does not involve a loan to an employee. The loan is made by the bank to the dealer."

G. S. 53-91 provides that no officer or employee of a bank, nor a firm or partnership of which such officer or employee is a member, nor a corporation in which such officer or employee owns a controlling interest, shall borrow any amount whatever from the bank of which he is an officer or employee, except upon good collateral or other ample security or endorsement. The statute requires the approval of the loan by a majority of the board of directors and that a certified copy of the resolution shall be attached to the evidence of indebtedness.

The statute, I believe, would prohibit from doing indirectly what could not be done directly. If the officer or employee of the bank gives his note to another person with the agreement or understanding that the note is to be discounted at the bank with which such officer or employee is connected, I think it would be a violation of this section unless the necessary approval was given. If, on the contrary, the discount of such a note is made at the bank by a customer of the bank who has accepted the note without any agreement, express or implied, that the note would be discounted by the bank, I do not think this section would require the approvals in the form there provided.

On account of the complications which might grow out of these transactions, however, I am inclined to the opinion that it would be desirable for the bank handling such loans to have the form of approval required by the statute given in all cases in which they handle paper executed by officers or employees of the bank. If this is done, there could be no question about it.

INDUSTRIAL BANKS; NOTARIES PUBLIC, ETC.

4 May 1945

I have your letter of May 2, enclosing letter from Honorable Arthur Goodman, Attorney at Law, Charlotte, North Carolina, which I return herewith, asking several questions which are set out herein.

"Is it permissible for an industrial bank to have an acknowledgement of indebtedness to it taken before a person in the bank's employ, who is a Notary Public, and have the fee for such acknowledgement retained by the bank itself?"

A Notary Public can take such acknowledgement provided he is not a party to the instrument, as authorized by G. S. 10-5. Any fees charged by the Notary Public for his service belong to him and whether or not he gives them to the bank depends upon the arrangement between the Notary Public and the bank.

"Is an industrial bank permitted to draw a credit report on someone making a loan and charge the costs for such credit report to the borrower, as part of the expense for granting the loan?"

The fees which an industrial bank can charge are controlled by G. S. 53-141, subsection 3, as amended by the General Assembly of 1945. You have a copy of this law and can furnish Mr. Goodman with it. No other fees could be charged than those authorized by the statute.

"Can an industrial bank fix a small penalty on people who borrow money from the bank if they do not make the payments promptly as set out in the agreement (like the building and loan associations used to do)?"

In my opinion, an industrial bank would have no right to charge any penalty other than legal interest for non-payment of a loan, and any other charges made would be usurious.

"If the industrial bank has the extra expense of sending out a collector to collect on delinquent accounts, can the cost for such service be added to the borrower's account?"

In my opinion, any charges of this character would be unauthorized and usurious.

"Is it possible for an industrial bank in this City to sell investment certificates to the public?"

The sale of investment certificates by an industrial bank are authorized by G. S. 53-141, subsection 2.

"What are the requirements for an industrial bank to a$_{cc}$e$_{pt}$ deposits for a checking account, like the Morris Plan Bank is doing in Charlotte?"

Industrial banks, with approval of the State Banking Commission, are authorized to solicit, receive and accept money or its equivalent on deposit, subject to check. See G. S. 53-141, subsection 7. You can, of course, inform Mr. Goodman as to the procedure to be followed in making an application for this consent.

SMALL LOAN AGENCIES

3 May 1945

You have referred to me the letter of Mr. A. C. Davis of April 23, 1945, and request that I give you my opinion on the following questions therein raised:

"1. Under the law, can the same owners operate a small loan business and an automobile loan business covering loans of $50.00 or more, in the same city under different names and locations? If so, would the automobile loan business come under your supervision?
"2. Under the law, can both a small loan business and an automobile loan business of $50.00 or more be operated by the same owners in the same location, under the same name, but as different departments, keeping separate books and records? If so, would the automobile loan department come under your supervision?"

H. B. 176, enacted by the 1945 session of the General Assembly, placed loan agencies or brokers as defined in G. S. 105-88 under the supervision of the Commissioner of Banks and regulated the fees that may be charged by them.

Section 4½ of this Act provides as follows:

"Sec. 4½. Nothing in this Act shall be construed to apply to any person, firm or corporation engaged solely in the business of making loans of fifty dollars ($50.00) or more secured by motor vehicles."

Section 4½ of the Act contains no qualification or exception based on location, name or method of management. It is unqualified in stating that the provisions of the Act shall not apply to persons, firms and corporations "*engaged solely* in the business of making loans of fifty dollars ($50.00) or more secured by motor vehicles." I find no ground for reading into the statute a qualification or exception that is not there, and conclude that I would not be justified in giving the plain wording of the statute an implied and doubtful meaning. I believe that if the General Assembly had intended that there should be any exceptions or qualifications based on names, locations, or management, they would have been set forth in the statute. It is accordingly my opinion that Mr. Davis' questions should be answered as follows:

It is not unlawful for the same owners to operate a small loan business and an automobile loan business for loans of $50.00 or more in the same city under different names and locations, or to operate said businesses at the same location under the same name but as different departments, but if either of these is done, both businesses would be brought under the supervision of the State Banking Commission, and would be subject to all the provisions of H. B. 176 on and after June 1, 1945.

SMALL LOAN AGENCIES

4 May 1945

I have your letter referring to me for my opinion the questions raised in the letter of Mr. John G. Mills, Jr., dated May 3, 1945. Mr. Mills asks the following questions:

(1) Where one corporation is engaged in the business of financing the purchase of automobiles, refrigerators, washing machines, etc., and is also engaged in the business of an industrial loan agent or broker in the same location, and with the same officers, keeping separate records for each of these aspects or departments of its business, will the operation of the sales financing aspect of the business be subject to the supervision of the State Banking Commission under the provisions of H. B. 176, enacted by the General Assembly of 1945?

It is my opinion that the corporation would be subject to the supervision of the State Banking Commission on both departments of its business. Section 4½ of H. B. 176 exempts from the provisions thereof "any person, firm, or corporation engaged solely in the business of making loans of fifty dollars ($50.00) or more secured by motor vehicles." The corporation would not be engaged solely in this business and would, therefore, not be entitled to the exemption from regulation.

(2) Where there are two separate corporations, one engaged in the business of financing the purchase of automobiles, refrigerators, washing machines, etc., and the other engaged in business as an industrial loan agency, carrying on business at the same location and with the same officers, would the corporation engaged in the sales finance business be exempt from supervision of the State Banking Commission under H. B. 176?

It is my opinion that the corporation engaged in the sales finance business would be subject to regulation under H. B. 176 unless it confined its financing operations solely to loans of $50.00 or more secured by motor vehicles. If it made loans not only on motor vehicles but also on refrigerators, washing machines, etc., it would be subject to supervision in view of the provisions of Section 4½ quoted above. Even if the corporation engaged in the sales finance business would confine its operations to loans of $50.00 or more secured by motor vehicles, it would, of course, be liable for a separate tax under Section 158 of the Revenue Act, since it is a separate or distinct corporation and could not operate under the license tax paid by the corporation engaged in business as an industrial loan agency.

I enclose a copy of this letter and of the opinion to you dated 3 May 1945, so that you may forward them to Mr. Mills.

LICENSING AND REGULATION OF PAWNBROKERS

7 May 1945

You request that I advise you as to the laws which provide for the regulation and licensing of pawnbrokers.

Chapter 91 of the General Statutes outlines certain requirements which must be met by persons, firms, and corporations engaging in business as pawnbrokers. There are provisions for the licensing and bonding of pawnbrokers, by municipal authorities, and there are provisions regulating the manner in which the business must be conducted. Section 91-7 of this Chapter provides that nothing therein shall be construed to relieve any pawnbroker from the penalties incurred under the usury laws of the State. Thus, pawnbrokers are not authorized to charge in excess of the legal rate of interest.

In addition, Section 118 of the Revenue Act of 1939, as amended, imposes a State privilege license on pawnbrokers, and makes provision for the issuance of pledge tickets and the sale of unredeemed articles.

I know of no other statute which relates exclusively to the regulation or licensing of this type of business.

SMALL LOAN AGENCIES

11 May 1945

I have a copy of the letter of Mr. John G. Mills, Jr., to you, dated May 9, 1945, and supplementing his letter to you dated May 3, 1945. My opinion to you under date of May 4, 1945, was based upon a misunderstanding of the facts referred to in Mr. Mills' first letter. I therefore take this opportunity to give you my opinion in the light of the facts in which Mr. Mills is interested and request that both you and he consider this letter to be in substitution for my letter of May 4, 1945.

The questions are as follows:

(1) Where one corporation is engaged in the business of purchasing or discounting from dealers in automobiles, refrigerators, washing machines, etc., notes, chattel mortgages or conditional sales contracts, and is also engaged in the business of making direct loans to borrowers, and both businesses are conducted at the same location and by the same officers, but separate records are kept for each, will the operation of the department purchasing commercial paper be subject to the supervision of the State Banking Commission under the provisions of H. B. 176 enacted by the General Assembly of 1945?

It is my opinion that if the business of purchasing commercial paper is maintained separate and apart from the direct lending business, and distinct and separate records are maintained for each type of business, the business of purchasing commercial paper would not be under the supervision of the State Banking Commission. H. B. 176 intends to regulate only those engaged in the direct lending business and installment paper dealers are specifically exempted from such supervision under the terms of the Act through its reference to the provisions of Section 152 of the Revenue Act to the effect that "nothing in this section shall be construed to apply to . . . installment paper dealers defined and taxed under other sections of this Act." The reference is to Section 148 which taxes installment paper dealers or persons engaged in the business of buying commercial paper.

(2) Where there are two separate corporations, one engaged in the business of buying or discounting from dealers in automobiles, refrigerators, washing machines, etc., notes, chattel mortgages and conditional sales contracts, and the other engaged in business as a direct lending agency, and both carry on business at the same location and with the same officers, would the corporation engaged in discounting commercial paper be exempt from supervision of the State Banking Commission under H. B. 176?

It is my opinion that the corporation engaged in the business of purchasing commercial paper would be exempt from regulation under H. B. 176 if separate records of this business are maintained.

Needless to say, in both the situation outlined in question one and the situation outlined in question two, two privilege licenses would be due to the Commissioner of Revenue, one under Section 148 of the Revenue Act and one under Section 152 of the Revenue Act.

22 May 1945

You inquire whether an officer of a bank, who is allowed by the president of the bank to make personal loans from time to time to individuals who are not in a position to borrow money from the bank, is subject to the supervision of the State Banking Commission as provided in H. B. 176 and the regulations issued thereunder. These loans are all made from the officer's office in the bank.

It is my opinion that the officer is engaged in small loan business as defined in Section 105-88 of the General Statutes and is, therefore, subject to the supervision of the State Banking Commission.

HB 122, Session Laws 1945; Status of State Employees
Returning from Service; Salary, etc.

2 June 1945

I have your letter of May 18, in which you write me as follows:

"You will please find enclosed copy of H. B. No. 122.
"The language in this bill is hard to understand, but it seems to imply that employees of the State of North Carolina who return from military leave shall be reemployed at a salary that would have been paid if they had remained in the services of the State. Your opinion will be highly appreciated."

House Bill No. 122, enacted at the 1945 session of the General Assembly, provides as follows:

"Any employee of the State of North Carolina, who has been granted a leave of absence for service in either (i) the Armed Forces of the United States; or (ii) the Merchant Marine of the United States; or (iii) outside the Continental United States with the American Red Cross, shall, upon return to State employment, if reemployed in the same position and if within the time limits set forth in the leave of absence, receive an annual salary of at least (i) the annual salary the employee was receiving at the time such leave was granted; plus (ii) an amount obtained by multiplying the step increment applicable to the employee's classification as provided in the classification and salary plan for State employees by the number of years of such service, counting a fraction of a year as a year; provided that no such employee shall receive a salary in excess of the top of the salary range applicable to the classification to which such employee is assigned upon return."

This Act is clearly as applicable to employees of the State who have been granted leaves of absence, as provided in the statute, and who return to State employment in the same position, as to employees who are under the Merit System and, upon return, would be entitled to at least the annual salary the employee was receiving at the time the leave of absnce was granted, plus increases as authorized by the statute above quoted.

As to employees who are not under the Merit System, some of the provisions of the Act would not appear to be applicable but I understand from Mr. Deyton, Assistant Director of the Budget, in a conversation with him, that he intends to recognize the principle involved in the Act in determining the salary to be allowed, upon return to service by a veteran. This, I believe, is a very wholesome principle and for which the Budget Bureau has ample authority. It would indeed create an unfortunate condition if a returning veteran should find that his employment status and salary has remained stationary while he has been in the service of our county in time of peril, while his fellow-employees have been advanced.

BANKS; LIMITATION OF LOANS; SUB-
SIDIARY CORPORATIONS

25 July 1945

Receipt is acknowledged of your letter of July 23, enclosing copy of a letter from Mr. J. J. Clark, Assistant Secretary of the American Trust Company at Charlotte, in which Mr. Clark desires to know the application of G. S. 53-48 to loans made to a subsidiary corporation which is not wholly owned by the parent company.

There is nothing in the statute that directly deals with this problem. I think that each case must be considered on its own merits and, if it appears that credit is being extended to substantially the same corporation secured by the same assets, the bank should look through the corporate form and if the subsidiary is controlled by the parent corporation, although not wholly owned, credit should be carefully examined to find out if it conflicts with the spirit and purpose of G. S. 53-48. It might be in some cases that the subsidiary in its own right would be entitled to credit independent of the parent company, and that the limitations provided by the section would not be determined by the combined credits of both corporations. In any case, however, it would require a specific statement of facts in order to reach a satisfactory conclusion and I would not attempt to generalize on the subjects.

BANKS; SUSPENSION OF INVESTMENT AND
LOAN LIMITATIONS

17 September 1945

In a letter from you dated October 17, 1944, you asked for an opinion as to the proper interpretation of the words "amply secured" as used in Section 53-49 of the General Statutes. This request specifically asked whether or not a loan would be considered as amply secured if it was the obligation of a financially strong maker, even though collateral was not specifically pledged. This inquiry originated from the Federal Deposit Insurance Corporation.

In reply to your letter the opinion was expressed, in a letter dated October 25, 1944, that the words "amply secured" should not be construed to mean that collateral must be specifically pledged to secure a loan; that a loan might not be amply secured even though collateral is specifically pledged to secure its payment, but, on the other hand, a loan might be amply secured where no collateral is specifically pledged.

I was furnished with a copy of a memorandum dated April 26, 1945, addressed to Mr. R. N. McLeod, which was handed to me by Mr. Charles Brantley Aycock, representing the FDIC, and in a conference in this office the opinion of this office dated October 25, 1944, was discussed with Mr. Aycock and the opinion expressed by this office was construed by the FDIC as meaning that a note might be considered as amply secured although no security whatever was furnished other than the note evidencing the obligation.

It was not the purpose of the writer of this letter to express the opinion that a note might be considered to be amply secured in case there was no endorsement or security other than the maker's name. It is my opinion that in order to be amply secured, in the sense that these words are used in G. S. 53-49, there should be an endorsement or guarantee by at least one endorser or guarantor with such net worth as may, in the opinion of the Commissioner of Banks, be sufficient and satisfactory, and that the open not of one or more makers, no matter how prosperous they may be, would not be in the terms of the statute "secure"; but I am of the opinion that where the endorsement or guarantee is such as to constitute ample security, the requirements of the statute would be met. Support of this view, I believe, is found in the case of BOYETT v. HURST, 54 N. C. 167, in which our Court holds that a note is not "secured" unless endorsed or guaranteed by someone in addition to the borrower. Endorsers or guarantors are spoken of as being "personal security." The following quotation is from the opinion in this case:

> "Suppose a guardian lends the money of his ward to a person who has property in possession to the value, say of $100,000, and is not at all embarrassed nor engaged in any business of a hazardous nature, and it should so happen that the borrower suddenly fails, the loss will undoubtedly fall upon the guardian; for, *although he took a good note, yet he neglected to take good and sufficient security*, and has not complied with the letter or the spirit of the statute, the policy of which is to require the investment to be *secured by the bond or note of some person* in addition to the borrower."

Regulation No. 2 of the State Banking Commission, adopted on June 28, 1939, in speaking of the need of financial statements, requires that they be given when obligations exceed $500.00 and are unsecured or "secured only by endorsements."

Throughout the law of this State dealing with sureties on the bonds of officials, fiduciaries and others, "personal security" in the nature of guarantees by bonding companies or private individuals is considered sufficient protection even where large amounts are involved, and in none of these cases is it necessary that a lien on specific property be given.

Under the statute the Commissioner of Banks is vested with authority to determine whether or not in a particular case the endorsements provided afford "amply security" for an excess loan and, in my opinion, it is not necessary, in order to make the provisions of the statute applicable, that the loan should be secured by collateral or a direct mortgage on real or personal property.

ESCHEATS; BANK DEPOSIT IN OUT-OF-STATE BANK DUE LIQUIDATED
STATE BANK

25 September 1945

I have your letter of September 24, advising that the Chase National Bank of New York has a balance to the credit of the Peoples Bank, at Union Mills, N. C., in the amount of $56.62, the Union Mills bank having been liquidated by court receivership completed on July 14, 1927. You also state that the Chase National Bank is advertising this account and unless claimed will escheat to the State of New York. You ask my opinion as to whether or not anyone in North Carolina is authorized to receive this deposit.

This deposit should be paid to the University of North Carolina under the provisions of G. S. 116-23, which is as follows:

> "Personal property of every kind, including dividends of corporations, or of joint-stock companies or associations, choses in action, and sums of money in the hands of any person, which shall not be recovered or claimed by the parties entitled thereto for five years after the same shall become due and payable, shall be deemed derelict property, and shall be paid to the University of North Carolina and held by it without liability for profit or interest until a just claim therefor shall be preferred by the parties entitled thereto; and if no such claim shall be preferred within ten years after such property or dividend shall be received by it, then the same shall be held by it absolutely."

COMMON TRUST FUND; AMENDMENT TO INCREASE
LIMIT TO $50,000

28 September 1945

You handed me a letter to you dated August 13 from Mr. Richard G. Stockton, Vice-President and Senior Trust Officer of the Wachovia Bank and Trust Company. In this letter Mr. Stockton refers to the action of the Board of Governors of the Federal Reserve System recently taken, amending the provisions of Section 17 of Regulation F relating to common trust funds, effective September 1, 1945, the most important amendment being to raise the maximum participation from $25,000 to $50,000, and allow seven days in which to make the necessary computations on each valuation date. Mr. Stockton suggests the advisability of the State Banking Commission making the same amendment to Regulation 5 of Order Number 2, to bring about conformity with the Federal Regulations.

I have discussed this matter with Mr. Lawrence E. Watt, of the staff of this office, in which he makes the following comment:

> "Originally this joint investment idea (co-mingling of funds of many trust funds) was for those accounts where money available was 'too small to be invested separately to advantage,' and it seems to me that $25,000 is high enough—but since the Federal Reserve System has raised to $50,000, I believe the State Banking Commission should revise regulations to permit use up to $50,000."

I am inclined to concur in Mr. Watt's views on this subject and I suggest that you take this up at the next meeting of the State Banking Commission for consideration at that time.

BANKS; SUSPENSION OF INVESTMENT AND LOAN LIMITATIONS

2 October 1945

I had a letter from Honorable Francis C. Brown, General Counsel for the Federal Deposit Insurance Corporation, under date of September 25, 1945, in which he quotes from my letter to you under date of September 17 and makes the following comment:

> "We assume, of course, that in all cases the financial condition of the borrower as shown by his financial statement must show his net worth to be in an amount sufficient to discharge the obligation. The statute, authorizing the suspension of the loan limit, requires in addition that the loan be 'amply secured.' This security may be obtained by endorsement, guaranty or a pledge of collateral. We interpret your opinion to require that in addition to the net worth of the maker the obligation be secured by either an endorser or guarantor (not considering the case where collateral is pledged) with sufficient net worth 'to secure' the loan without regard to the net worth of the borrower."

I have not intended to express the opinion that the borrower must show by his financial statement that his net worth is an amount sufficient to discharge the obligation. My opinion on this question was not requested and I have not attempted to go into that at all. I would assume that the Commissioner of Banks, in exercising the discretion vested in him by the statute, would necessarily take into consideration the financial ability of the borrower to discharge the obligation and that sole reliance would not be placed in the security offered by the borrower.

I do not think that the statute, as stated by Mr. Brown, requires "in addition" that the loan be amply secured, if by "in addition" he means that the borrower would have to show by a financial statement that he, independent of the security offered, was financially able to discharge the obligation. The last sentence quoted in the extract from Mr. Brown's letter is not the view held by me as to that matter. I do not think it is in all cases necessary to require that the security offered by the borrower is in itself independent of the financial strength of the borrower sufficient to discharge the obligation. I believe that the Commissioner of Banks would be justified in considering the paper as a whole and the strength of the maker and the security offered in reaching his conclusion.

BANKS; LOANS TO DIRECTORS; G. S. 53-91

4 October 1945

I have your letter of September 28, enclosing a letter from Mr. W. P. Rainey, Vice President of the Wachovia Bank & Trust Company. In this letter from Mr. Rainey, he inquires as to whether or not G. S. 53-91 would be applicable to a loan made to a club signed by various members of the club, each signer guaranteeing a specified amount of the loan, some of the signers being officers of the Wachovia Bank & Trust Company. Attached to his letter is a copy of the agreement proposed, which shows that the Old Town Club, Incorporated, which would borrow the money, is a corporation. The loan, if made, as I understand it, would be made to the corporation, the individuals who sign it as guarantors being members of the club.

The Statute, G. S. 53-91, provides that no officer or employee of a bank, nor a firm or partnership of which such officer or employee is a member, or a corporation in which such officer or employee owns a controlling interest, shall borrow any amount whatever from the bank of which he is an officer or employee except upon good collateral or other ample security or endorsement, and no such loan shall be made until the same has been approved by a majority of the board of directors and a resolution duly entered, etc., as set out in the statute.

The question submitted, therefore, would turn upon whether or not the officers signing the agreement, or other officers of the Wachovia Bank and Trust Company, own controlling interest in the Old Town Club, Incorporated. If these officers do not own a controlling interest in this corporation, then it would not seem to me that this statute would be applicable. By these officers, I mean all the officers or Directors of the Wachovia Bank & Trust Company, whether they are proposed as guarantors of the contract or not. If the officers, including Directors of the Wachovia Bank & Trust Company, own a controlling interest in the Old Town Club, Incorporated, then the statute would be applicable.

BANKS; DEPOSITS; PAYMENT OF DEPOSIT WITHOUT SURRENDER OF PASS BOOK

5 October 1945

You request my opinion as to whether or not a bank is permitted to pay a deposit to the administrator of a deceased depositor when the pass book has been lost and cannot be presented by the administrator.

It is my understanding that the deposit in the instance about which you inquire was with an industrial bank and that there had been issued a pass book showing a deposit to the deceased depositor's credit, containing the provision that the deposit could be withdrawn only upon presentation of the pass book.

A pass book constitutes an admission of the bank's indebtedness to the depositor and is ordinarily regarded as prima facie but not conclusive evidence of the existence of a contract and state of accounts between the parties. A pass book, however, is not negotiable and its possession constitutes no evidence of the right to withdraw money thereon. See 9 CORPUS JURIS SECUNDUM, 553, citing McCASKILL v. CONN, SAVINGS BANK, 13 L.R.A. 737; SMITH v. BROOKLYN SAVINGS BANK, 54 Am. Rep. 653.

A pass book is mere evidence of the ownership of the deposit and if the depositor is alive and can establish his identity as the depositor with the bank in which it is made, he would be entitled to withdraw the deposit after due notice, notwithstanding the rules of the bank that required that the pass book be presented at the time of the withdrawal. The loss of a pass book would not result in forfeiture of the depositor's right to his deposit, and, if it could be established that the pass book had been lost or destroyed and could not be presented, the bank would be protected in paying the deposit to the depositor.

The same would be true as to the payment to the executor or administrator of a deceased depositor, if the administrator or executor is entitled to collect, receive and administer all the personal estate, including deposits, of the deceased. It is not necessary for the bank to have a surrender of the pass book in order to get a sufficient and valid receipt acquitting it of liability for the deposit, if it is satisfied as to the identity of the depositor or his personal representative withdrawing the deposit.

CORPORATIONS; DIRECTORS; BY-LAWS FIXING THE QUALIFICATIONS OF DIRECTORS

27 October 1945

I have your letter of October 23rd in which you submit the following question asked you by Mr. John A. Kramer, Cashier of The Bank of Edenton, Edenton, North Carolina:

> "Please advise me if a bank's by-laws can legally require more stock for qualification of a director than the statutes of North Carolina call for. That is the case here. It looks to me that if this can be done a few large stockholders can absolutely dictate the running of a bank even though they hold a minority of the stock."

Our statute, G. S. 55-48, provides that a corporation may, by its certificate of incorporation or by-laws, determine the number of shares a stockholder must own to qualify him as a director.

This, I believe, fully answers the question submitted by Mr. Kramer.

BANKS; BANK ON GOVERNMENT RESERVATION—CHERRY POINT—CLOSING ON SATURDAYS

7 November 1945

I have your letter of November 6 enclosing a letter from Mr. J. D. Murray, Assistant Vice President, First Citizens Bank and Trust Company, of Cherry Point, North Carolina. Mr. Murray advises you that beginning November 1 all Naval and Marine Corps activities on that base are closing on Saturdays, including the Post Office and depot, and that they have been ordered by General T. J. Cushman, the commanding officer, to operate their bank on a five-day week. He enclosed copy of the paragraphs 3 and 6 of their contract with the United States Navy, showing that their operation was subject to the orders of the commanding officer on the base.

Mr. Murray further advises that they can remit for any cash letters which come into the bank on Friday and that they will get no mail of any description on Saturday and there will be nothing held over to inconvenience anyone. He requests your advice as to whether or not as a bank he would be authorized to close on the days as ordered by the commanding officer.

There is no provision in our statutes which requires banks to be open at any specific times and it is my understanding that no rule or regulation of this character has been adopted by the State Banking Commission. The reason for banks maintaining regular schedules of openings on all days of the week except Sundays and holidays is to avoid any possibility of liability under the Negotiable Instruments Law.

G. S. 103-4 prescribes the dates for legal holidays in this State. Section 103-5 G. S. provides that where the day or the last day for doing an act required or permitted by law to be done falls on Sunday or on a holiday the act may be done on the next succeeding secular or business day. G. S. 53-77 provides that the Governor with the approval of the Council of State, may proclaim other days as banking holidays. There are other statutes which refer to banks keeping open for the transaction of business on all secular or business days. G. S. 53-54, for instance, provides that nothing in that section would be construed to compel a bank which by law or custom is entitled to close at 12 o'clock noon on Saturday or for the whole or part of any legal holiday, to keep open for the transaction of business or to perform any of the acts or transactions aforesaid on any Saturday after regular banking hours or on any legal holiday except at its option.

Under the circumstances stated by Mr. Murray, however, the bank would be compelled to obey the directions of the commanding officer and I cannot see that he has any alternative about it; inasmuch as no mail will be received on Saturdays the possibility of any liability would be largely eliminated. It is impossible for me to foresee every conceivable case in which a situation might arise under the Negotiable Instruments Law in which some act would be required to be performed by the bank on the Saturday on which it is closed and I could not, therefore, attempt to express any opinion as to what the results would be in such a situation. It would seem, however, that the bank, in order to continue its operation at Cherry Point, would be in a position to have to take any chances which are involved in such a situation. I do not mean to say that there would be any liability but I could not say that there would not be any to arise by reason of such circumstances.

INTANGIBLE TAXES; SECTION 704; LIABILITY
OF FINANCE COMPANIES

14 February 1946

You request that I give you my opinion upon the question whether finance companies are liable for the intangible taxes, imposed in Section 704 of the Revenue Act, upon notes and other evidences of debt held by such companies in connection with the transaction of their loan business.

Section 704 imposes a tax upon "all bonds, notes, demands, claims, and other evidences of debt however evidenced, whether secured by mortgage, deed of trust, judgment, or otherwise, or not so secured, having a business, commercial or taxable situs in this State. . ." I think it is clear that notes and other evidences of debt held by finance companies fall within this classification of taxable items.

There is no exemption from the tax expressed in the Intangible Tax Article in favor of finance companies. Therefore, it is my opinion that such companies are liable for the payment of the tax levied in Section 704 upon notes and other evidences of debt held by them.

As you know, banks and certain similar institutions are exempt from the payment of the tax imposed in Section 704. Although I am in no position to say for certain why a distinction was drawn between finance companies and banks in this respect, I think that a possible explanation might be in the fact that banks lend money belonging to the general public which has been placed with them on deposit, while finance companies lend their own money.

INDUSTRIAL LOANS; OUT-OF-STATE LENDERS; INTERSTATE COMMERCE

14 May 1946

I received your letter of April 18, sending me an advertisement in post card form issued by the State Finance Company, Kansas City, Missouri, in which they offer to make personal loans by mail with charges of 3% per month on loans of $100 or less, etc. You state that you understand that this is a legalized company in Missouri and you would like to know whether or not they have a right to do business by mail in North Carolina and charge the rates as shown on the enclosed advertisement.

This State would recognize the validity of a contract made in accordance with the laws of another State, under the circumstances stated by you, if it was entered into in good faith and not for the purpose of evading the usury laws of this State.

You do not state, however, whether or not under the laws of Missouri the lender in that State is authorized to charge the rates of interest advertised in this manner. If these charges are authorized by the State of Missouri and the contract was entered into in good faith by mail and not for the purpose of evading our usury laws, it would probably be recognized as valid in this State; but if such was not the case, the borrower would be entitled to plead usury against the collection of the note and interest.

I have also considered the question as to whether or not such method of doing business would be subject to regulation by the State Banking Commission or subject to taxation by the Commissioner of Revenue.

A study of this question leads me to the conclusion that where the business is done entirely by mail and the company has no agency or office in North Carolina and carries on no local function except the solicitation by mail, this business is not subject to taxation or regulation in this State.

BANKS; LIMITATIONS ON LOANS; FOREIGN LOANS GUARANTEED BY INTER-
NATIONAL BANK FOR RECONSTRUCTION AND DEVELOPMENT,
AUTHORIZED BY ACT OF CONGRESS APPROVED
JULY 31, 1945, P. L. 171 79TH CONGRESS

20 May 1946

I received your letter of May 11, enclosing to me the questionnaire submitted to you by the National Association of Supervisors of State Banks, in
which they ask the following questions:

"(1) Do the State laws and regulations permit State banks and
trust companies to invest in the direct obligations of the International
Bank?
"(2) Do the State laws and regulations permit State banks and
trust companies to invest in obligations of foreign issuers guaranteed
by the International Bank?
"(3) If the securities are eligible for such investment, what limitations do the State laws or regulations impose on the amounts that a
bank may hold?"

The first and second questions, I assume, would be answered "yes," as
it is pointed out that the questions do not cover the investment of trust
funds by our banks but applies only to their own investments of their own
funds.

The third question, in my opinion, should be answered that such investments would be subject to the limitation provided by G. S. 53-48, as these
loans would not come within the exemption provided by this statute.

ESCHEAT OF DERELICT BANK DEPOSITS

31 May 1946

In response to an inquiry addressed to you from Mr. W. W. Woodley, Jr.,
Vice President of the Durham Bank & Trust Company under date of May
27, 1946, and inquiries received from other banks, you have requested me
to advise you as to the proper construction of our statute, General Statutes
116-24, providing for the escheat of certain unclaimed bank deposits to the
University of North Carolina. The statute referred to reads as follows:

"All bank deposits in connection with which no debits or credits have
been entered within a period of five years, and where the bank is unable to locate the depositor or owner of such deposit, shall be deemed
derelict property and shall be paid to the University of North Carolina
and held by it, without liability for profit or interest, until a just claim
therefor shall be preferred by the parties entitled thereto; and if no
such claim shall be preferred within ten years after such deposit shall
be received by it, then the same shall be held by it absolutely. The
receipt of the University of North Carolina of any deposit hereunder
shall be and constitute a release of the bank delivering over any deposit coming within the provisions of this section from any liability
therefor to the depositor or any other person."

This statute was first enacted by Chapter 400 of the Public Laws of 1937
and at that time the statute was limited to bank accounts of $5.00 or less.

In 1939 the law was amended by Chapter 29, which struck out the limitation of $5.00 and now, as you will observe, the statute applies to all bank deposits in connection with which no debits or credits have been entered within a period of five years, and where the bank is unable to locate the depositor or owner of such deposit.

This answers the question submitted to you by Mr. Woodley as to what size balances come under the law.

The second question submitted by Mr. Woodley was as follows:

• "Would an interest credit made semi-annually be construed as credit activity in the account?"

The statute, as you will observe, applies to those accounts in connection with which no debits or credits have been entered within a period of five years. It is my opinion that interest credits made on a savings account or an interest bearing account would constitute credits within the meaning of this statute. It is my understanding that there are some savings accounts which are not interest bearing, on account of the size of the accounts. The statute would apply to checking accounts and non-interest bearing savings accounts but would not, in my opinion, apply to interest bearing accounts as, in accordance with the contract, credits would be made to the account for interest accruals at stated periods.

The question is also asked as to whether or not the statute would apply to certificates of deposit issued by a bank.

In my opinion it would not apply to certificates of deposit issued by a bank, as this is not the character of deposit which comes within the purview of the statute.

The statute does not apply in any case to a deposit unless (1) there have been no debits or credits entered within a period of five years, and (2) the bank is unable to locate the depositor or owner of such deposit.

Debits of service charges or intangible taxes charged against such accounts, in my opinion, do not amount to debits within the meaning of the statute, as these are involuntary on the part of the depositor.

The statute, as you will observe, does not apply in any case in which the bank is able to locate the depositor or owner of such deposit. The account may be inactive for more than five years but, if the bank is able to locate the depositor or owner; that is to say, is able to know who the depositor is and where he or she can be found, the statute is inapplicable. It is intended to apply only to those accounts in which the owner of the account is unknown to the bank and cannot, after exercise of reasonable effort, be located by the bank. There are, doubtless, many accounts in banks which have been inactive for a period of more than five years, as to which the bank knows who the depositors are and where the depositors can be found. In such cases, the statute is entirely inapplicable.

You request my advice as to what steps should be taken by the bank in order for it to determine whether or not it can locate the depositor or owner of the deposit.

The statute leaves this to the good faith and cooperation of the banks and does not establish any standard for determination of this question.

All that is required is that the bank shall make such reasonable effort as it considers fair to enable it to determine whether or not it can ascertain the name and location of its depositor, and whether or not the depositor can be found. Having made a reasonable effort in good faith to determine this question, this matter is left in the sound judgment of the bank.

The statute provides that after the deposit is turned over to the University of North Carolina, if no claim is preferred within ten years after such deposit has been received by the University, then the same shall be held by it absolutely.

The Board of Trustees of the University of North Carolina has adopted a resolution, which is a part of the minutes of the Board, agreeing to waive the ten-year provision of this statute in all instances, and in any case in which the owner of a deposit is found, it will promptly return the money to the owner or to the bank from which it received the deposit.

The resolution of the Board of Trustees and the action of the administrative officials of the University leave the question of identification of the depositor, and the right of the return of the money, to the bank from which the deposit was received. I am advised by the Escheats Officer of the University that they will enter into an arrangement with all the banks by which the bank, having paid a deposit over to the University, may pay the depositor the amount of the deposit at any time that he should appear, and that the Escheat Fund of the University will honor any draft made upon it for a refund to the bank. In this way the bank could discharge its liability to the depositor without taking the matter up otherwise than by making a draft on the University.

The Board of Trustees of the University of North Carolina, which includes the three branches of the University—the Woman's College at Greensboro, the Chapel Hill unit and the·State College at Raleigh, have adopted a resolution providing that the funds derived from all escheat sources, including bank deposits, shall be created into an endowment fund and invested for the purpose of providing loan funds to worthy students at the University. No part of the money is used by any of the three institutions for the operating costs of the institutions and, therefore it will at all times be available for the refund of any deposits which are afterwards claimed by a depositor whose whereabouts has been ascertained.

I am, therefore, of the opinion that there would be no practical question of procedural due process involved in the application of the statute as to any bank that complies with it, as the refund of the deposit will always be made by the bank or the University to a depositor who later appears and claims the deposit.

In my opinion, the statute is constitutional and it is expressly authorized by Article IX, Section 7, of the Constitution, which provides as follows:

"The General Assembly shall provide that the benefits of the University, as far as practicable, be extended to the youth of the State free of expense for tuition; also, that all the property which has heretofore accrued to the State, or shall hereafter accrue, from escheats, unclaimed dividends, or distributive shares of the estates of deceased persons, shall be appropriated to the use of the University."

The Supreme Court of the United States, in the case of ANDERSON NAT'L BANK v. LUCKETT, 88 L. ed. 692, has held that the escheat of bank deposits, provided by state laws, is applicable to national banks as well as to state banks. There is no discrimination, therefore, between state and national banks.

OPINIONS TO DIVISION OF PURCHASE AND CONTRACT

PURCHASE OF MAPS FOR PUBLIC SCHOOLS

30 August 1944

Receipt is acknowledged of your letter of August 29, in which you advise that there was presented to the Board of Award at a recent meeting the matter of negotiating for and supplying maps for the public schools of the State. You state that the Board was advised of a previous attempt to call for bids and contract for maps, which had not proven entirely satisfactory, and that the Textbooks Division of the State Board of Education has advised that an offer has been received from three map companies who allow a discount of 10% from the standard list prices if purchased and distributed through the State agency.

You further advise that the Board of Award authorized you to present this matter to me for an opinion to determine whether, under the laws of the State, this Division could authorize and approve a negotiated contract for maps for the public schools of the State of North Carolina, without public bidding.

G. S. 115-372 provides that it is the duty of the local authorities to purchase all supplies, equipment and materials in accordance with contracts and with the approval of the State Division of Purchase and Contract.

The powers and duties of the Division of Purchase and Contract are defined in G. S. 143-49, which includes the duty to canvass all sources of supply and to contract for the purchase of all supplies, materials and equipment required by the State Government, or any of its departments, institutions or agencies, under competitive bidding in the manner provided in G. S. 143-52.

Since the purchase of the maps for the local school boards is made by virtue of the requirement of G. S. 115-372, it would not necessarily follow that in the making of these contracts the requirement as to competitive bidding, which is prescribed as to State purchases, would be applicable. It is to be noted, however, that under G. S. 143-54(a) maps, books, pamphlets and periodicals purchased for the use of the State Library, or any other library in the State supported in whole or in part by State funds, are not required to be purchased in the manner provided by the Act creating the Division of Purchase and Contract.

It is my opinion, therefore, that you would be authorized to approve the contracts for the purchase of the maps for use of the public schools under a contract of the type referred to without the necessity of inviting bids, if, in the opinion of the Board of Award, such contract was desirable and proper.

TAXATION-GASOLINE; EXEMPTION; USE FOR PUBLIC SCHOOL TRANSPORTATION

8 February 1945

Referring to my letter to you under date of January 19, 1944, in reply to your letter of January 15, 1944, in which I expressed the opinion that the purchase of gasoline from any available source of supply authorized by your department would be within the meaning of Chapter 119 of the Public Laws of 1941, authorizing the invoicing of gasoline sold to the county boards of education less the gasoline tax, you inquired in conference today whether or not this authority would include purchases from filling stations as well as from bulk plants.

It is my opinion that such purchases would be included, both from filling stations and bulk plants.

PURCHASE OF FURNITURE AND EQUIPMENT FOR NURSES' HOME, STATE HOSPITAL AT RALEIGH

29 May 1945

In conference with you, Mr. Rothgeb and Mr. R. P. Pearce, Business Manager of the State Hospital at Raleigh, today with reference to the contract for the purchase of furniture and equipment for the Nurses' Home which has been constructed at the State Hospital in Raleigh, a question was presented by the Federal Works Agency through a letter from Mr. O. T. Ray, Division Engineer, as to the approval of the contract for the purchase of this furniture and equipment by the Division of Purchase and Contract and the Board of Awards thereof.

Under the Act creating the Division of Purchase and Contract, the purchase of this furniture and equipment, in my opinion should be made by the Division of Purchase and Contract after having proceeded as required by the statute. I understand that the North Carolina Hospitals Board of Control advertised for bids on this furniture and equipment and opened the bids and awarded the contract, under competitive bidding, to the lowest bidder at a price that was satisfactory.

In my opinion, if the Board of Awards of the Division of Purchase and Contract shall fully review this transaction and if they find that the requirements of the law have been complied with as to the advertisement for competitive bids on this furniture and equipment, they could validly ratify, confirm and approve the action taken by the North Carolina Hospitals Board of Control in this behalf and validate the contract made for the purchase of this furniture and equipment, as awarded in this competitive bidding. When so approved, the contract entered into for the purchase of this furniture and equipment would be valid.

UNIVERSITY OF NORTH CAROLINA; CHAPEL HILL; MILK SUPPLY; LETTING CONTRACT

3 October 1945

You have submitted to me the forms to be used by the University of North Carolina Purchasing Department, at Chapel Hill, requesting bids on the milk supply for the University dining halls and other agencies. These forms indicate that bids will be requested on an annual basis and state in complete detail the terms and provisions of the contract to be entered into with the successful bidder, including specifications of the milk to be purchased.

Section 5 of the contract deals with the price and provides that proposals for bids shall be based on the current average wholesale milk price paid to producers prevailing at the time the contract will go into effect, and provision is made for adjusted average wholesale price during the life of the contract.

G. S. 143-54 provides that unless otherwise ordered by the Director of Purchase and Contract, with the approval of the Advisory Budget Commission, the purchase of supplies, materials and equipment through the Director of Purchase and Contract by State institutions shall not be mandatory in case of perishable articles such as fresh vegetables, fresh fish, fresh meat, eggs and milk, and that these articles may be purchased directly by the departments, institutions and agencies and shall, wherever possible, be based on at least three competitive bids. This section further provides that whenever an order or contract for such articles is awarded by departments, institutions and agencies of the State Government, a copy of such order or contract, together with a record of the competitive bids upon which it was based, shall be forwarded to the Director of Purchase and Contract.

The furnishing of milk over the period of time contemplated by the contract with the University is such that I think the basis upon which proposals are invited is fully justified under existing circumstances. With my knowledge of the situation existing at Chapel Hill, I agree with the conclusion reached by them that this is not a case in which bids on the basis of competitive prices of milk would be possible. The method adopted for determining the prices, it seems to me, would be entirely fair.

GASOLINE TAX; EMERGENCY PURCHASES EXEMPT IF MADE UNDER
SPECIFIC AUTHORITY

7 May 1946

You have referred to my opinions of January 19, 1944, (incorrectly stated as "1945" in letter of Mr. C. D. Douglas) and February 8, 1945, to the effect that the purchase of gasoline during the emergency by a county board of education from any available source, including a filling station, if made pursuant to specific authority given in each instance by your office, is equivalent to a purchase under a State contract within the contemplation of G. S. 105-449, and, therefore, exempt from the gasoline tax. You ask whether or not the exemption applies to such purchases if made prior to February 8, 1945, the date of my most recent opinion on this matter.

The controlling factor is not the date of my opinion, but whether or not the particular purchase complies with the statute as interpreted in my opinion. Therefore, it is my opinion that if a purchase of gasoline was made at any time after the effective date of the statute (1941) from a filling station or any other available source pursuant to and in compliance with specific authority granted to the county board of education by your office, such purchase was exempt as a purchase under a State contract, even if made before February 8, 1945, or before January 19, 1944. Thus, if the dealer in such case has already paid the tax, and has otherwise complied with G. S. 105-449, he is entitled to a refund.

OPINIONS TO STATE BOARD OF EDUCATION

TEACHERS SALARIES; PAYMENT ON MONTHLY BASIS DISCRETIONARY,
WITH STATE BOARD

16 August 1944

Receipt is acknowledged of your letter of August 15 in which you write me as follows:

"The question has been raised, under section 3 of Chapter 358, Public Laws of 1939, as amended by acts of the General Assemblies of 1941 and 1943, as to whether or not the State Board of Education has discretionary authority in requests from local administrative school units for the payment of teachers' salaries in twelve equal monthly installments, provided, of course, that all requirements of the law have been met.

"We shall appreciate it very much if you will furnish us an opinion showing whether the State Board of Education's authority is discretionary or mandatory under the law referred to in this letter."

The statute to which you refer is a part of Section 3 of the School Machinery Act, and reads as follows:

"Salary warrants for the payment of all State teachers, principals, and others employed for the school term shall be issued each month to such persons as are entitled to same. The salaries of superintendents and others employed on an annual basis shall be paid per calendar month: Provided, that teachers *may* be paid in twelve equal monthly installments in such administrative units as shall request the same of the State Board of Education on or before October first of each school year." (Emphasis added)

The general rule of statutory construction is that words will be given their usual and ordinary meaning unless a statute clearly indicates that some other and different meaning was intended. The word "may" appearing in the statute is one of permission and is not a mandatory expression such as "shall."

Under the provisions of the statute quoted, the use of the word "may" in my opinion leaves it within the sound discretion of the State Board of Education as to whether or not salaries will be paid in twelve equal monthly installments. It is conceivable that a different construction could be placed upon the statute but I believe that the opinion above expressed is a better view.

SCHOOL LAW; INJURY TO CHILD NOT RIDING SCHOOL BUS;
COVERAGE UNDER WORKMEN'S COMPENSATION LAW

9 May 1945

Reference is made to your letter of May 5, 1945, in which you enclose a letter from Mr. O. P. Johnson, Superintendent of Duplin County Schools. In Mr. Johnson's letter it is stated that a school bus of Duplin County had left or failed to take on a small girl and her father overtook the bus in his automobile. The children in the bus notified the driver that he had left the child and the driver, not knowing that the child's father had parked back of the bus, started backing the bus slowly to get back to a lane. The child started to get out of the car and the bus backed into the door of the car when the child had one foot on the ground. This forced the automobile door shut and the child suffered a rather severe cut on her knee and possibly broken bones in her knee.

Upon this state of facts, Mr. Johnson inquires that since the child was not injured while riding in the school bus, if the case would be within the jurisdiction of the Industrial Commission.

As Mr. Johnson has correctly stated, the claim would not be covered by Section 115-341 of the General Statutes since this only authorizes payment for injuries received by a school child while such child is riding on a school bus to and from the public schools of the State.

As to the jurisdiction of the North Carolina Industrial Commission, I cannot see anything in the statement of facts before me that would bring the case within the Workmen's Compensation Act, which is the law administered by the Industrial Commission. It is fundamental that before any person can be covered under the Workmen's Compensation Act, the relationship of employer and employee must exist between the individual injured and the employer of that individual. This is set forth in Chapter 97 of the General Statutes, wherein you will find the term "employer" defined and the term "employee" defined, and you will also see that the person injured at the time of the injury must be engaged in employment or performing services under a contract of hire. It is manifest that this injured child was not an employee of the county board of education or of any of the public school authorities of the State of North Carolina, and I am not aware of any provision of law that would bring the injury of this child or its relationship to any of the authorities within the scope of the Workmen's Compensation Act. I have been unable to find any amendment made by the General Assembly of 1945 that attempts to deal with this subject as related to school children. My answer, therefore, is that the provisions of the Workmen's Compensation Act as administered by the North Carolina Industrial Commission have no application to this case.

I am sure that the circumstances under which the child was injured appeal strongly to the sympathies of the members of this office, and if there was any statute whatsoever which would give us the slightest foundation by means of liberal construction to provide the relief in this situation, we would gladly make such an interpretation. As the law now stands, I do not know of any remedy which could be invoked in favor of the child. The only way the situation can be handled is for the Representative of the County to introduce a bill at the next session of the General Assembly to provide for reimbursement in this specific case.

• STATE BOARD OF EDUCATION; RIGHT TO ACT AS SELF-INSURER; STATE SCHOOL BUSES

31 May 1945

I acknowledge receipt of your letter calling my attention to Section 115-377, G. S., which authorizes the State Board of Education in its discretion to purchase fire insurance coverage on school buses or act as self-insurer, and inquiring as to whether or not in my opinion the State Board of Education may adopt the policy of acting as self-insurer and set aside a reserve fund to cover any loss which might be sustained by fire.

While it seems to me that Section 115-377 is sufficient within itself to authorize the State Board of Education to act as self-insurer on account of loss by fire to State-owned school buses, that authority has been greatly strengthened by Senate Bill 359, enacted into law by the recent session of the General Assembly, in which the State adopted a general policy of becoming self-insurer as to State-owned buildings and equipment therein. I am of the opinion that you have ample authority to act as self-insurer upon the adoption of a proper resolution by the State Board of Education.

You further inquire concerning setting aside a reserve fund to cover any loss that might be sustained. Senate Bill 359 fully recognizes this policy and provides that as to the property for which the State becomes a self-insurer, at least the sums of money necessary to provide insurance coverage should be set aside as a "State property fire insurance fund." I think that your Board would be fully justified in setting aside as a reserve fund out of the moneys appropriated to it, a sum at least equal to the average amount paid during the past ten years for insurance premiums, out of which any loss sustained by reason of fire to the school buses may be paid.

SCHOOL LAW; INJURY TO CHILD NOT RIDING ON BUS; AMENDMENT OF 1945—H. B. 557

4 June 1945

A reference to the file in this matter shows that on May 5, 1945, you wrote this office a letter enclosing a letter signed by Mr. O. P. Johnson, Superintendent of Schools of Duplin County. Mr. Johnson's letter was dated May 1, 1945. In response to your letter this office on May 9, 1945, sent you an opinion to the effect that the State Board of Education had no legal authority to pay the claim mentioned in Mr. Johnson's letter which arose by reason of an injury to a school child by a school bus under the circumstances related in the Superintendent's letter.

On May 29, 1945, Mr. Johnson wrote you another letter in regard to this claim, in which he made an amendment to the statement of facts, this amendment being in substance that the child was standing on the ground when the accident happened and that the operator of the school bus backed the bus so far as to wedge her between the fender of her father's car and the school bus and thus caused the injury to the child's knee. On May 31, 1945, you wrote this office a letter which is the subject to this reply and enclosed both letters received in your office from Mr. Johnson, the Superintendent of Schools. You ask if the information furnished by Mr. Johnson in his letter of May 29, 1945, in any wise changes the opinion which this office furnished you on May 9, 1945.

The authority of the State Board of Education to pay compensation for injuries arising because of the operation of school busses is conferred under Article 49, Subchapter XXI, of Chapter 115 of the General Statutes. The section of this article which describes the type of accident or the conditions under which injuries are sustained that may be compensated is 115-341 of the General Statutes. This section was amended by the General Assembly of 1945, the amendment being incorporated in H. B. 557, and more particularly in Section 3 of this bill, so that the section as revised now reads as follows:

> "The State Board of Education is hereby authorized and directed to pay out of said sum provided for this purpose to the parent, guardian, executor, or administrator of any school child, who may be injured and/or whose death results from injuries received while such child is riding on a school bus to and from the public schools of the State, or from the operation of said bus on the school grounds or in transporting children to and from the public schools of the State, medical, surgical, hospital, and funeral expenses incurred. on account of such injuries and/or death of such child in an amount not to exceed the sum of six hundred and no one-hundredths dollars ($600.00)."

It is to be noted that this statute permits compensation under three situations, which are as follows:

1. A school child who may be injured: "While such child is riding on a school bus to and from the public schools of the State."
2. A school child who may be injured: "From the operation of said bus on the school grounds."
3. A school child who may be injured by reason of the operation of a school bus "in transporting children to and from the public schools of the State."

It is plain that the General Assembly intended by using the phrase "in transporting children to and from the public schools of the State," to widen the scope and to create more liberal and additional grounds upon which the State Board of Education could pay claims for injuries to school children arising out of the operation of the school busses of the State. The first authorization as given above takes care of the situation where the child is a passenger on the bus and manifestly deals with the situation where the children are riding inside the bus. The second authorization given above deals with accidents on the school grounds and appears to be broad enough to cover injuries received by children both inside and outside of the busses, although this question is not now before us. The third authorization added by the General Assembly of 1945 was intended to take care of the situation where school children are injured when a bus is used in transporting children to and from public schools of the State and causes an injury to a school child outside of the bus so long as the proximate cause of the injury is the operation of the bus in transporting children to and from the schools.

This is the only interpretation that is reasonable and possible for this amendment as the other situation when the children are passengers has been provided for and has existed in the statute for some time.

I am of the opinion, therefore, that when a child is injured after it has been a passenger on a bus, and the injury occurs after it leaves the bus but because of the operation of the bus, that the State Board of Education is authorized to pay such claim. I am also of the opinion that if a child is injured immediately before it gets on a bus and while it is attempting to become a passenger on the bus for the purpose of being transported to school, that under this third addition to the statute the State Board of Education is likewise authorized to pay such a claim. I think that two things must appear before such a claim is authorized: (1) The school bus must be used in transporting children to and from the public schools of the State, and such a use must be in progress at the time the accident occurs; and (2) The proximate cause of the injury must flow from and arise because of the use and operation of the bus at the time the accident occurs. For example, if a child gets off a bus and starts across the road in front of same and the driver does not observe the child and strikes it, then the Board would be authorized to compensate such claim. As another example, if a child was attempting to become a passenger on a bus, in order to go to or from school, and is injured by the bus in such an effort, then I think the Board is authorized to compensate the parent or guardian for injuries sustained as provided by the Act. This would not mean that the Board would be authorized to pay any claim because of an injury arising from the action or negligence of some independent agency. For example, if a child alights from a bus and is struck by an automobile driven by some person traveling on the highway, then I do not think the Board would be authorized to pay such claim.

In view of the amendment of 1945, it is my opinion that the Board is authorized to pay the claim in this case. When I wrote the letter sent from this office on May 9, 1945, I did not know about or have before me the amendment of 1945 as contained in Section 3 of H. B. 557. A proper interpretation of this amendment will allow the payment of this claim, and you should disregard our letter of May 9, 1945, as the same is not controlling in this matter.

SCHOOLS; TRANSPORTATION OF SCHOOL CHILDREN FROM ONE SCHOOL TO ANOTHER FOR LUNCHES

6 September 1945

I acknowledge the receipt of your letter in which you state that the Moore County Board of Education has requested permission from the State Board of Education to use two school busses at Carthage, two at Aberdeen, and two at Robbins to transport 100 school children at each place from the high school building to the elementary school building for lunch for 180 school days during the school year 1945-46. In making the request for the use of these busses, the Moore County Board of Education proposes to appro-

priate enough county funds to pay all the expenses of this extra transportation, including a $5,000 insurance policy on the life of each child involved,
and the driver, and damages to the school busses in case of accident.

You inquire as to whether or not the State Board of Education has authority to grant the request of the Moore County Board of Education.

It is my understanding that the State Board of Education desires to permit the use of the. school busses by the Moore County Schools if it may
legally do so and in conference with the transportation committee, consisting of Honorable H. E. Stacy, Honorable J. A. Pritchett, and Honorable
Santford Martin, I was impressed with the idea that the legal members
of the committee are of the opinion that the State Board does have such
authority.

Sections 115-374, 115-375 and 115-376 of the General Statutes, place
squarely upon the State Board of Education the responsibility for the
operation of the school busses of the State and authorizes it to promulgate
rules and regulations governing the organization, maintenance, and operation of the school transportation facilities, and to establish routes to be
followed by such school busses. But it seems to me that the primary purpose of the use of school busses is to transport children to and from their
respective schools except as enlarged by the pertinent sections. It is so
enlarged by authorizing the Board to adopt rules and regulations to permit
the use of school busses for the transportation of school children on necessary field trips while pursuing the course of vocational agriculture, home
economics, trade and industrial vocational subjects and to and from demon-
strations carried on in connection therewith, and authorizes the Board, when
ordered by the Governor, to furnish sufficient school busses to transport
members of the State Guard to and from authorized places of encampment.
The statute is silent as to whether or not pupils may be transported from
one school to another even within the same system, and it can be argued with
considerable merit that the statute limits the transportation of pupils from
their homes to the school in the morning and from the school to their homes
in the afternoon, except as otherwise provided in the statute.

Section 115-381 provides that local school trustees or committees, when
they deem it necessary, may "as a part of the functions of the said public
schools," provide cafeterias and places where meals may be sold, and operate
or cause the same to be operated for the convenience of teachers, school
officers and pupils of the school. It may, therefore, be argued with some
merit that the transportation of children as proposed by the Moore County
Board of Education from one of the schools in the town to another for
lunches is as much a function of the schools in furthering the health program
of the schools as is the transportation of the pupils on field trips while pursuing the course of vocational subjects is a furtherance of the training of
the minds of the children. This section was incorporated in the law by the
1939 Session of the Legislature and the sections governing the use of the
school busses have been amended several times since 1939 but the General
Assembly has not seen fit to provide for the use of the school busses to
transport children from school buildings in which there are no lunch rooms
or cafeterias to school buildings having such services.

Since the pertinent sections do not specifically authorize or prohibit the transportation of pupils from one school building to another in the same system but located in different sections of the municipality, I cannot categorically answer your question yes or no, since the Court has not had an opportunity to pass upon it.

Even though I am inclined to the opinion that the Legislature intended to restrict the use of the busses to one round trip transportation of children to and from school except as otherwise provided in the statute, it is possible that our Court might hold that the State Board of Education could adopt rules and regulations and fix bus routes so as to enable the Board to comply with the Moore County request and on the terms outlined by it. I certainly do not see how the Board could be charged with acting in bad faith if it grants the request of the Moore County School Board when it proposed that the county will take care of every expense and every risk that might be incurred by the State in permitting the use of the busses. However, I call your attention to the fact that the authority of the County Board to enter into such an arrangement with the State Board raises another serious question and since the State Board of Education is called upon to pass upon the county board budgets, you might consider now as to whether or not the State Board would approve the budget providing funds to indemnify the State against any such loss.

SCHOOLS; $300,000.00 REVOLVING FUND; AID FOR SCHOOL LUNCH ROOM PROGRAM

18 September 1945

I acknowledge receipt of your letter calling my attention to Senate Bill No. 264 which makes available a revolving fund of $300,000.00 to be administered by the State Board of Education to assist those counties and city administrative units participating in the federal lunch room program. You raise certain questions in connection therewith and enclose rules and regulations adopted by the Board, one of which is to the effect that the Controller, with the approval of the Attorney General, shall prepare the necessary legal papers to be used in carrying out the provisions of the Act. You also enclose proposed resolutions to be adopted by the boards of county commissioners and county boards of education and city administrative units.

In the first place, let me say that the provisions of the Act must be assumed by administrative officials to be constitutional. In BICKETT v. TAX COMMISSION, 177 N. C. 44, the Court said:

> "When a legislative act has been duly ratified by the law making department of the government, it is not merely *prima facie* law, but it is 'the law' unless repealed by that body itself, or declared unconstitutional by some tribunal vested with judicial power to declare it unconstitutional upon the application of some party interested who shall show beyond a reasonable doubt in the minds of such tribunal that his interest in the matter in controversy was protected by the Constitution, and has been infringed by the statute. This State has always refused to give veto power to the Governor. The Tax Commission cannot veto or deny the validity of an act of the Legislature. They should obey it unless enjoined by the court."

I shall, therefore, for the purposes of this letter, assume that each and every provision of the pertinent Act of the Legislature is constitutional.

There is an abundance of authority in the Act for advancing funds to county boards of education for the purpose of assisting the public schools of the respective counties to provide low-cost lunches as sponsored by the Federal Government. There is likewise ample authority for county boards of commissioners and county boards of education to enter into agreements with the State Board of Education as to the repayment of such advances and to pledge the full faith and credit of the county to that end. The Act provides that the State Board of Education shall have a lien on all federal funds received by the State Board of Education for payment to county boards of education in anticipation of which advances have been made by the State Board of Education. I, therefore, think it is altogether proper and within the purview of said Act that the county boards of education participating in the fund shall adopt resolutions providing that the State Board shall have a lien upon any federal funds coming into the hands of the State Board and belonging to the county boards, and to authorize the State Board of Education to credit such sums on any advances made by the State Board to any county board of education.

I suggest that your proposed resolution, paragraph No. 2, be amended so as to authorize the State Board of Education to credit any funds coming into its hands from the Federal Government for use in the lunch room program against any claim which the State Board may have for funds advanced to the county. Of course, any resolution pledging the faith and credit of the county or otherwise assuming any obligation on the part of the county, other than for purposes provided for in the county budget, will have to be passed upon by the county board of commissioners.

I also suggest that the certificate certifying the adoption of resolutions and giving the book, page, etc., should be signed by the clerk to the county board of commissioners or clerk to the county board of education rather than by the county attorney, since the clerk is the keeper of the minutes and not the county attorney.

I regret to say I find but little, if any, authority in the Act applicable to city administrative units. While I am convinced that the Legislature had in mind rendering the same assistance to city administrative units as to county administrative units, it is not clearly so stated in the Act. For instance, Section 2, which provides that the State Board shall have a lien on federal funds, refers to the county boards of education and the tax levying authorities of the counties and does not mention city administrative units; and Section 4, which authorizes the pledging of the full faith and credit, is applicable only to counties and not to cities or city administrative units.

I am sure that it would be contrary to the intention of the Legislature to deprive city administrative units of the assistance provided for in the Act and that the benefit of any doubt should be resolved in their favor and that, if possible, machinery should be set up to enable them to participate in the fund. To do this, it seems to me that the application for funds and agreements to pledge federal funds due city administrative units to the State Board to apply against funds advanced by it should be a joint one on the part of the county board of commissioners, the county board of education and the city administrative unit. In other words, in so far as possible, the county authorities will have to act on behalf of the city administrative units but I do not think that this necessarily means that funds advanced by the State Board out of the revolving fund would have to go through the county officials but may be sent direct to the city administrative unit.

I, therefore, suggest that agreements be entered into between the State Board of Education, the city administrative units, county boards of commissioners and county boards of education, agreeing for the particular city unit to participate in the fund and to pledge its interest in any federal funds to the State Board as a credit against funds advanced by the State Board to the city units.

SCHOOLS; BUDGET; DEBT SERVICE BUDGET; WHAT TO INCLUDE

28 September 1945

I have your letter of September 24, in which you advise that Mr. B. L. Smith, Superintendent of the Greensboro City Schools, has presented the City School Funds Budget for Greensboro City Schools for 1945-1946, containing the usual sections of Current Expense, Capital Outlay and Debt Service, and that he has set up items in the Debt Service Budget amounting to $4,375.00, as follows:

"Treasurer	$2,400.00
Asst. to Treasurer	1,500.00
Office Expense	350.00
Audit	125.00
	$4,375.00"

You state that these items are not usually carried in the Debt Service Budget but in Current Expense and you state that it is your understanding that the Debt Service Budget or fund is strictly for the payment of bonded indebtedness, including principal, interest, commissions and fees, and that the items listed above should be included in the Current Expense Fund. You submit the following questions:

"1. Should debt service include any item other than bonded indebtedness, including principal, interest, commissions and fees?
"2. Have we acted within the bounds of good practice in requesting that items under General Control be placed in the Current Expense Budget?"

G. S. 115-157(c) provides that the debt service fund shall provide for payment of all loans due the State, the interest and principal on bonds, payments to the sinking fund, payment of district indebtedness for schools assumed by the county, apportionment to districts voting bonds or to districts borrowing from the county board of education and all other indebtedness which is payable during the fiscal year for which the budget is prepared.

G. S. 115-158 provides, in part, as follows:

"The county board of education shall set forth in the budget the amount of the interest and installments on all loans due the State, and of all interest and installments on bonds and other evidences of indebtedness that may fall due. This shall be a separate item in the budget, and the commissioners shall levy annually a tax sufficient, clear of all fees, commissions, rebates, delinquents and the cost of collection to repay the same; and if the taxes are not collected when the repayments fall due, the commissioners shall borrow the money and place the amount to the credit of the county board of education."

The items included by Mr. Smith in his budget in the Debt Service Fund appear to be apportionments of the expense of the Treasurer, Assistant to the Treasurer, Office Expense and Audit. I do not find in the statute any authority to charge any of these items under the Debt Service Budget or fund.

In G. S. 115-356 there is listed items included under the head of General Control, which is a part of the current expense of the school under subsection 1.f., the following: Audit of school funds. This is, therefore, the legislative classification of this expense as a part of current expense.

I regret that I cannot agree that the classification of the budget by Mr. Smith is authorized.

OPERATION OF SCHOOL BUSSES; MINORS; LIABILITY OF STATE OR COUNTY; LIABILITY OF PARENT OF MINOR DRIVING BUS

5 October 1945

I have your letter of October 3, enclosing a letter from Mr. Charles C. Erwin, Superintendent of Schools for Rowan County, in which Mr. Erwin submits several questions, as follows:

"Is the State liable for damage done by a school bus driven by a minor?
"Is the County liable for damages (property) done by a school bus driven by a minor?
"Can a citizen sue the State and recover damages done by a school bus?
"Can a citizen sue the County and recover damages done by a school bus?"

The only liability of the State for injuries in connection with the operation of school busses is that provided by statute found in Article 49 of Chapter 115 of the General Statutes, providing compensation for children injured from the operation of school busses under the circumstances provided in Sections 115-340 to and including 115-346, with which, of course, you are entirely familiar.

That the State cannot be sued by a citizen without its consent is well established under our law. PRUDENTIAL INS. CO. v. POWELL, 217 N. C. 495, and cases cited therein. As the State has not authorized any individual to bring suit against it on account of injuries by accident in the operation of school busses, no such actions would lie.

The same rule would be applicable as to a suit against the State Board of Education which, under the Constitution and laws of the State, has the responsibility for the operation of busses as an agency of the State. CHEMICAL CO. v. BOARD OF AGRICULTURE, 111 N. C. 135. There is now no provision in our law authorizing suits against the State Board of Education which is not by statute declared to be a corporation, as it was formerly. GRANVILLE COUNTY BOARD OF EDUCATION v. STATE BOARD OF EDUCATION, 106 N. C. 81.

Under the law, the control and management of all facilities for the transportation of public school children is vested in the State of North Carolina, under the direction and supervision of the State Board of Education (G.S. 115-374). This being the case, there could be no liability on the counties, as the counties have no legal responsibility whatever for the operation of the school busses.

These additional questions are also submitted:

"Is a parent liable for property damages done by a school bus driven by a minor?
"Can a citizen sue the parent of a minor and recover damages done by a school bus driven by his son?"

The parent of a minor driving a school bus would not be liable for any property damage or personal injury done by the school bus in this operation. A parent is not liable for the torts of his child solely on the grounds of relationship. BRITTINGHAM v. STADIEM, 151 N. C. 299. A parent is not liable for the torts of his minor son in the absence of a showing of the approval thereof by him or that the son was his agent. LINVILLE v. NISSEN, 162 N. C. 95; TAYLOR v. STEWART, 172 N. C. 203; BOWEN v. MEWBORN, 218 N. C. 423.

I believe this answers all of the questions submitted.

DISCHARGED SERVICEMEN; RIGHT TO CLAIM POSITIONS AS TEACHERS AND PRINCIPALS; RIGHTS OF INCUMBENT TO COMPENSATION FOR DISCHARGE FROM POSITION

11 December 1945

Receipt is acknowledged of your letter of December 7, enclosing two letters from Mr. J. J. Pence, Superintendent of Scotland County Schools, under dates of November 7 and 20.

It appears from Mr. Pence's letters that a former principal of a school in his county has been discharged from the Army and has requested that his job be given back to him and this has been done, making the position available to him on November 12, 1945. It also appears that in the absence of the soldier, his position had been filled by a teacher who had signed a contract in May, 1945, for the 1945-1946 term and this person taught in the schools in July and August, 1945. It seems from Mr. Pence's letters that the party who signed the contract has been relieved from his position and Mr. Pence asks the following question in his letter of November 20:

"Does King, who has been teaching since Page has been in the Army and who signed a contract for the term 1945-46 and taught two months have any rights under this contract to ask for salary for the remaining seven months and will the State Board provide any money for such cases?"

Under the Federal Act, the State and local governments are not required to restore positions to returning veterans but the Act recommends that this be done, as, of course, the Federal Government would have no power to pass legislation compelling states to be bound by such provisions. It is, however, my understanding that all State and local agencies of government are complying with the recommendations as a matter of sound public policy and in justice to our returning veterans. As the principal is not an officer entitled to a leave of absence under the North Carolina statute, the provisions of that statute would not be applicable to this present situation.

Whether or not a person who lost his position, by reason of a returning veteran, would be entitled to claim for compensation for the balance of the contract term, would depend upon whether or not at the time the contract was made there was any agreement, express or implied, that upon a return of the veteran he would resign and make the position available to the returnee. If no such agreement was entered into and the person whose position is taken insists upon his legal rights to demand compensation for the unexpired portion of the contract, this will, in turn, depend upon whether or not, after making a reasonable effort, he is unable to find other employment which he is able to perform and whether or not in such employment he could or should receive as much or more compensation than he would have in the teaching position. In other words, in order to recover in such an action, the claimant would have to establish the fact that after making reasonable efforts, he was unable to find other employment and by reason of such fact suffered financial loss.

Before the Board of Education of Scotland County could voluntarily pay such person for the unexpired period of the contract, it would have to ascertain whether or not he was able to secure other employment and to what extent, if any, he suffered financial loss on account of same. In these times, in which there is such a shortage of manpower and when there are so many positions available to people who seek employment, it is doubtful that such person could establish the essential fact that he was unable to secure other employment, but this would be a question for a court or jury, or for the Board of Education of Scotland County, if they attempted to pass upon the question.

If such compensation is provided to the person who has been relieved of his position by judgment of the court or voluntary action of the County Board of Education, I know of no provision in the law which would permit such payments to be reimbursed by the State Board of Education. The law is simply silent on this subject.

The question necessarily involves an indefinite answer, as the facts in any particular case would have to be fully developed before anyone could have any complete or final opinion about it. In other words, each case would have to stand on its own bottom.

Schools; Expenditure of Fines, Forfeitures, Penalties, Dog Taxes and Poll Taxes

26 February 1946

I have your letter of February 23, in which you state that you have a request for information relating to objects and items of local administrative unit budgets which can be supplemented without vote of the people. You request me to answer three questions. Your first question is as follows:

"1. For what purposes may local funds be used to supplement items and objects of local unit budgets without a special supplementary school tax?"

G. S. 115-356 provides as follows:

"The objects of expenditure designated as maintenance of plant and fixed charges shall be supplied from funds required by law to be placed to the credit of the public school funds of the county and derived from fines, forfeitures, penalties, dog taxes, and poll taxes, and from all other sources except state funds: Provided, that when necessity shall be shown, and upon the approval of the county board of education or the trustees of any city administrative unit, the state board of education may approve the use of such funds in any administrative unit *to supplement any object or item of the current expense budget, including* the supplementing of the teaching of vocational subjects; and in such cases the tax levying authorities of the county administrative unit shall make a sufficient tax levy to provide the necessary funds for maintenance of plant, fixed charges, and capital outlay: . . ."

The underscored portion of the above quoted part of this section refers to the current expense budget which is provided for in G. S. 115-157. Subsection (a) of this section reads as follows:

"(a) The current expense fund shall include (1) Expenses of general control—per diem of board of education, salaries of superintendents, attendance officer, and clerical assistants, travel and communication, office supplies and expense, and other necessary expenses of general control; (2) instructional service—salaries of teachers, principals, and supervisors, and any other necessary items of instruction; (3) operation of school plant—wages of janitors and other employees, fuel, water, light and power, janitors' supplies, expenses for care of grounds, and other necessary expenses of operation; (4) maintenance of plant—upkeep of grounds, repair of buildings, repair and replacement of heating, lighting and plumbing equipment, instructional apparatus, furniture, and other equipment, and other necessary expenses of maintenance; (5) fixed charges—rent, insurance and other necessary fixed charges; (6) auxiliary agencies—replacement of and repair of library books, transportation of pupils, and other necessary auxiliary activities."

The underscored portion of the above quotation from G. S. 115-356 provides that the funds mentioned can be used to supplement any object or item of the current expense budget when necessity has been shown, and with the approval of the county board of education or the trustees of any city administrative unit and the State Board of Education. If such application of these funds is made, the section requires that the tax levying authorities of the county administrative unit shall make a sufficient tax levy to provide the necessary funds for maintenance of plant, fixed charges and capital out-lay. *Revenue derived from tax sources must be confined to maintenance of plant, fixed charges, capital outlay, and debt service unless supplements are voted by the people.*

The budgets for all city and county administrative units, under G. S. 115-363, must be approved by the tax levying authorities. This section provides that the tax levying authorities in such units may approve or disapprove the supplemental budget, in whole or in part, and, upon approval being given, the same shall be submitted to the State Board of Education which shall have authority to approve or disapprove any object or item contained therein. This, therefore, means that in addition to the approval of the county board of education or board of trustees of the city administrative unit and the State Board of Education, such an expenditure must likewise be approved by the tax levying authorities who would have to levy the taxes to take the place of the fines, forfeitures, etc., if used for some other purpose than maintenance of plant and fixed charges.

Your second question is as follows:

"2. Are funds derived from fines, forfeitures, and penalties permitted to be used in supplementing salaries of teachers up to an amount equal to collections from said sources?"

In the event that necessity shall be shown, as required by the statute, and the required approvals are secured as set forth in answer to your first question, the funds derived from fines, forfeitures and penalties could be used in supplementing salaries of teachers up to the amount equal to the collection from said sources. The statute, however, very clearly indicates that the primary purpose to which such sources of revenue should be devoted are maintenance of plant and fixed charges and I would assume that it would require a strong showing of necessity to divert these funds from such application, in order to convince the above mentioned authorities which would have to approve the same.

Your third question is as follows:

"3. When a supplementary tax is levied, must the funds secured from said supplementary tax levy be distributed per capita to all races, or has the Board of Education discriminating power with reference to the allocation of funds with regard to races based on needs?"

It is my opinion that when a supplementary tax is levied under the quoted provisions of G. S. 115-356, or under the local supplement provisions of G. S. 115-361 and 115-362, the funds derived therefrom would have to be distributed without discrimination on account of race or any other cause, but this does not necessarily mean that the funds in every instance would have to be distributed upon the per capita enrollment basis. It may well be that in most instances this would be necessary in order to avoid any semblance of discrimination, but circumstances might exist which would justify another reasonable method of application of these funds. There is no provision in the statute which provides that the avails from such sources of revenue should be distributed on a per capita basis, but, under the supreme law of the land, no discrimination should be made against any schools on account of race.

SCHOOLS; SUPPLEMENTS; ABC FUNDS

16 April 1946

Receipt is acknowledged of your letter of April 15, enclosing a letter from Mr. J. Edward Allen, Superintendent of Warren County Schools, who requests an opinion as to whether or not ABC funds paid to a county could be used to supplement objects and items in the current expense budget of the county schools.

This question has not heretofore been presented to this office. G. S. 115-356 provides, in part, that the objects of expenditures designated as maintenance of plant and fixed charges shall be supplied from funds required by law to be placed to the credit of the public school funds of the county and derived from fines, forfeitures, penalties, dog taxes and poll taxes, *and from all other sources except state funds.*

This section further provides that when necessity shall be shown, and upon approval of the county board of education or the trustees of any city administrative unit, the State Board of Education may approve the use of such funds in any administrative unit to supplement any object or item of the current expense budget, including the supplementing of the teaching of vocational subjects.

The Alcoholic Beverage Control Act of 1937, in G. S. 18-59, provides that the net earnings of the ABC stores shall be paid quarterly into the general fund of each respective county wherein the stores are operated.

There is no specification in the law as to what purposes the earnings from the ABC stores shall be expended by the county except as provided in this section, which directs that the earnings shall be paid into the general fund.

I am of the opinion that under the authority contained in G. S. 115-356, in the event the board of county commissioners should see fit to make the appropriation of a part of the ABC revenue for the purpose, the county board of education or the board of trustees of the city administrative unit, with the approval of the State Board of Education, could use these funds to supplement any object or item in the current expense budget, as the statute G. S. 115-356 provides that the revenue from fines, forfeitures, etc., and "from all other sources except state funds" could be used for this purpose under such conditions.

SCHOOLS; COUNTY TAX LEVIES FOR VOCATIONAL EDUCATION

28 May 1946

I acknowledge receipt of your letter in which you inquire as to whether or not the tax levying authority of a county may levy for vocational subjects without first submitting the question to a vote of the people.

Article 34 of Chapter 115 of the General Statutes authorizes and empowers the State Board of Education to cooperate with the Federal Government in the teaching of vocational education in agriculture and trades and industries and to appropriate money for such purposes. This article likewise authorizes the several counties of the State to cooperate with the State Board of Education; and Section 115-247 reads as follows:

"The county board of education, board of county commissioners, or the board of trustees of any city administrative unit may cooperate with the state board of education in the establishment of vocational schools or classes giving instruction in agricultural subjects, or trade or industrial subjects, or in home economics subjects, or all three subjects, and may use moneys raised by public taxation in the same manner as moneys are used for other public school purposes: Provided, that nothing in this article shall be construed to repeal any appropriations heretofore made by any of said boards for said purposes."

While it is true that in 1933 the State took over the operation of the schools of the State, including the payment of the salaries of public school teachers, the State did not make any provision for the payment of the county's part of the salaries or other expenses incident to the promotion and teaching of vocational education. Prior to the adoption of the 1933 act the burden of providing teachers rested upon the counties so that the wording of Section 115-247 authorized the county commissioners to levy a tax and appropriate funds for the teaching of such subjects the same as for other public school purposes. While it may be argued that since the counties have been relieved of the burden of providing for the salaries of public school teachers, the wording of Section 115-247, "and may use moneys raised by public taxation in the same manner as moneys are used for other public school purposes," is no longer in force and effect since the counties do not now levy for salaries for public school teachers. But I think that since the 1933 act made no provision whatsoever for the payment of the salaries of vocational education teachers the authority granted in Section 115-247 is still in force.

Again, we find in Section 115-356, which among other things provides for the distribution of fines, forfeitures, penalties, dog tax and poll taxes, and other sources other than state funds, it is specifically provided that such funds may be used to supplement the teaching of vocational subjects. And also that the tax levying authorities in any county administrative unit, with the approval of the State Board of Education, may levy taxes to provide necessary funds for teaching vocational agriculture and home economics and trades and industries which are supported in part from Federal vocational educational funds.

I am, therefore, of the opinion that subject to the approval of the State Board of Education, the several boards of county commissioners of the State may levy a tax and appropriate such sums as they may deem necessary to provide for the teaching of vocational agriculture, home economics, trades and industrial vocational subjects which are supported in part from Federal vocational educational funds.

You call my attention to Section 115-362 which authorizes the Boards of County Commissioners to levy a tax among other purposes "to employ additional vocational teachers." I do not think that this section means that an election must be held before any teachers of vocational education may be employed but is applicable only to teachers other than those whose salary is paid in part by Federal vocational educational funds.

Schools; Workmen's Compensation; Basis of Payment

12 June 1946

I received your letter of June 11, in which you wrote me as follows:

"We have before us a workmen's compensation case in which a school teacher received most of her pay from the State; yet a substantial sum was received from local funds in the form of a supplement. In determining the amount of workmen's compensation benefits to which this employee is entitled, does the law require that we figure the salary on the basis of the amount received from the State or on the basis of the total compensation of both state and local funds?"

G. S. 150-370, as amended by the last General Assembly, provides that the State shall be liable for compensation on the basis of the average weekly wage of such employees as defined in the Workmen's Compensation Act, whether all of said compensation for the nine months school term is paid from State funds or is in part supplemented by local funds.

I believe this answers your question, and that the basis of compensation will be the average weekly wage from both State and local funds for the employees covered as provided in G. S. 115-370 (1945 Supplement).

Schools; Use of School Busses to Transport Members of the Cast of THE LOST COLONY

25 June 1946

I acknowledge receipt of your letter, in which you state that a request has been made to the State Board of Education to permit one of its school busses at Manteo, in Dare County, to be used for the purpose of transporting members of the cast of THE LOST COLONY to and from the theater at Manteo.

I agree that Section 115-374 of the General Statutes contains no direct authority for the use of school busses for the purpose mentioned in your inquiry. I think that the primary purpose of the pertinent section of the statute is to assure the availability of school busses at all times for the transportation of school children during the nine months school term without hindrance or delay, and to assure this, the use of busses for other purposes which might or could interfere with the transportation of school children is restricted. Strong argument can be advanced to the effect that the limitations prescribed in Section 115-374 are applicable only during the regular nine months term, since during vacation period the busses are not used by the school authorities for the purposes mentioned in the statute but are stored or are in the process of reconditioning.

The Roanoke Island Historical Association was established under the provisions of Chapter 953 of the Session Laws of 1945 and authorizes the appointment of a governing body and appropriates a sum not exceeding $10,000.00 a year to aid in the production of the historical drama, THE LOST COLONY, and the State Auditor is required to make an annual audit of accounts of the association and report to the General Assembly at each of its regular sessions. The Roanoke Island Historical Association, therefore, is at least a quasi governmental agency.

The school busses are owned by the State and the contemplated use in the instant case is by at least one of its quasi governmental units and I understand that it is the custom of one State agency to favor another with the use of its property when such use will not interfere with the use for which it was originally acquired. The use of a school bus in the instant case could not interfere with the transportation of school children since the schools will not be in session during the period of the contemplated use.

The Governor has expressed considerable interest in this matter and it is his desire, if possible, to permit the proposed use of at least one of the school busses assigned to Dare County. It is the thought of the Governor and this office that a contract might be entered into between the State Board of Education and the Board of Directors of the Roanoke Island Historical Association permitting the use of a school bus for the desired purpose, upon such terms and conditions as might be prescribed by the State Board of Education, such contract to provide for a reasonable rental and require the lessee to provide the necessary liability insurance, both as to public liability and collision, and to otherwise assure the State that the bus will be returned at the end of the agreement in as good condition as at the time of the agreement.

It seems to me that the section limiting the use of school busses is subject to the construction that it applies only during the nine months school term and, if this is true, there is no prohibition in the pertinent section against the use of a school bus during the vacation season by some other agency of the State. I am inclined to the opinion that the State Board of Education could enter into the proposed agreement without doing serious violence to the restrictive provisions of Sections 115-374. But it should be kept in mind that Sections 115-374 through 115-376 of the General Statutes places upon the State Board of Education the responsibility for the operation of the school busses of the State, and authorizes it to promulgate rules and regulations governing their organization, maintenance and operation and, even though it be conceded that a school bus may be used for the purpose mentioned in your letter, it is still within the province of the State Board of Education to determine whether or not such use is expedient or advisable or interferes with the proper administration of the public school system.

SCHOOLS; APPROPRIATIONS; SCHOOL BUSSES; SALE OF DISCARDED BUSSES

28 June 1946

You inquire as to whether or not funds received from the sale of old school busses and fire insurance recoveries on school busses should be placed in the general nine months school fund account or the special account for the purchase of school busses.

The General Assembly, by Chapter 530 of the Session Laws of 1943, created a special fund for the purchase of school busses and it is my under-·

standing that no general nine months school funds are now used for that purpose, but that all busses, including replacements, are purchased from the special fund.

It seems to me and I am of the opinion that the funds in question should be credited to the special school bus account to aid in replacing the busses from which the funds so deposited were received.

OPINIONS TO STATE COMMISSION FOR THE BLIND

COUNTIES; LEASE OF PROPERTY

15 March 1945

I received your letter of March 15 and, as requested, I have prepared a lease from the Board of Commissioners for Cabarrus County to the North Carolina State Commission for the Blind for the county-owned property located two miles from Concord at the intersection of Charlotte Street and Charlotte Highway 29A, which I enclose.

This lease recites the resolution adopted by the Board of Commissioners for Cabarrus County authorizing the execution of the lease. In your letter you state that you wish me to advise you whether or not the Board of Commissioners for Cabarrus County would have the legal authority to execute this lease for the purposes therein recited.

The statute, G. S. 153-9(14), authorizes the Board of Commissioners to rent any property belonging to the county. This section, in my opinion, furnishes ample authority for the Commissioners to make this lease.

AID TO THE BLIND; PERSONS ENTITLED THERETO—OLD AGE ASSISTANCE, AID TO DEPENDENT CHILDREN

20 November 1945

I received your letter of November 19, in which you write me as follows:

"The question has been raised with our Agency as to whether a county should instead of making an Aid to the Blind grant to a needy individual who is blind and eligible to receive Aid to the Blind, give, in lieu thereof, to such person Old Age Assistance, General Relief or Aid to Dependent Children.

"Both the Federal Congress and the North Carolina Legislature have taken cognizance of the complicated problems of blindness by establishing special category of financial assistance to needy blind people. This category, as you know, is administered by County Welfare Departments under the supervision of the Commission for the Blind through caseworkers who are skilled in the problems of adjustment to blindness, restoration of vision, the teaching of Braille, and in occupational therapy crafts.

"In order to carry out the intention of the North Carolina Legislature, is it your opinion that under North Carolina law, needy blind people should be given Aid to the Needy Blind rather than being placed on General Relief, Old Age Assistance, or Aid to Dependent Children programs, in as much as the special services needed by blind individuals and intended for them by the North Carolina Legislature are not available through any other relief program?"

Recognizing the necessity for special consideration, care and treatment of persons who are blind or who are likely to become blind, the General Assembly in 1935 enacted Chapter 53, which was amended by Chapter 124 of the Public Laws of 1937, which provides for the creation of the North Carolina State Commission for the Blind which is charged with the supervision of the administration of assistance to needy blind and authorizes the commission to adopt rules and regulations necessary for the carrying out of the provisions of that chapter.

Under the authority of this Act, special care and attention is given to blind people of the State with the view of rehabilitation so that whenever possible, notwithstanding the handicap of loss of vision, they may be returned to useful and productive lives. Various provisions of the law found in Chapter 111, Sections 13 to 29, deal with this subject.

G. S. 111-21 provides that no aid to needy blind persons shall be given under the provisions of this article to any individual for any period with respect to which he is receiving aid under the laws of North Carolina providing aid for dependent children or relief for the aged. Under the Old Age Assistance Act, G. S. 108-21, a person is not eligible unless he has not sufficient income or other resources to provide a reasonable subsistence compatible with decency and health. Under the Aid to Dependent Children Act, dependent Children are defined in G. S. 108-49 as those who have no adequate means of support. Under our system no person is entitled to receive Old Age Assistance, Aid to Dependent Children, or Aid to the Needy Blind who is receiving assistance from any other of such funds.

It is the purpose of the law, in my opinion, to provide aid for the needy blind in all cases in which persons are eligible or entitled to receive it under the terms of the act found in Article 2 of Chapter 111, G. S. A person entitled to this relief could not be deprived of same because of having been placed upon the rolls for receipt of Old Age Assistance or Aid to Dependent Children. If the person who is on the roll for Old Age Assistance or Aid to Dependent Children is found to be eligible and entitled to Aid for the Needy Blind, such person should be removed from the roll of those entitled to Old Age Assistance or Aid to Dependent Children and furnished the relief provided under the law for Aid to the Needy Blind which is a specialized service and relief provided for the unfortunate people falling within this classification.

STATE COMMISSION FOR THE BLIND; AUTHORITY TO PRESCRIBE STANDARDS OF EMPLOYMENT OF CASE WORKERS

5 December 1945

I have your letter of December 4, in which you request my advice as to whether or not the North Carolina State Commission for the Blind has the authority to establish objective standards for personnel to be qualified in the administration of Aid to the Needy Blind, provided by Article 2 of Chapter 111 of the General Statutes, and if such standards so established would be binding on the boards of county commissioners and all agencies charged with the duty of administering that article. You refer particularly to the qualifications of case workers handling the Aid to the Blind program under the legal supervision of the State Commission for the Blind, administered locally by county welfare departments as the agents of the county commissioners.

G. S. 111-13 provides as follows:

"The North Carolina State Commission for the Blind shall be charged with the supervision of the administration of assistance to the needy blind under this article, and said commission shall establish objective standards for personnel to be qualified for employment in the administration of this article, and said commission shall make all rules and regulations as may be necessary for carrying out the provisions of this article, which rules and regulations shall be binding on the boards of county commissioners and all agencies charged with the duties of administering this article."

In my opinion, this statute definitely gives the North Carolina State Commission for the Blind the right to establish objective standards for personnel to be qualified for employment in the administration of Aid to the Blind, and that these standards as provided in the statute, when established, are binding on the boards of county commissioners and other agencies charged with the administration of this law.

VOCATIONAL REHABILITATION; DISBURSEMENTS UNDER THE BARDEN-LAFOLLETTE REHABILITATION ACT BY THE STATE COMMISSION FOR THE BLIND

14 May 1946

You have discussed with me the exception taken by the Federal Vocational Rehabilitation auditors for disbursements on rehabilitation clients who have not been living in North Carolina for one year, during the period between December 1, 1943, and March 17, 1945, the date of the enactment of Chapter 698 of the Session Laws of 1945, these disbursements having been made under the Barden-LaFollette Rehabilitation Act. After giving this matter careful consideration, I am of the opinion that under the law you are authorized to make these disbursements to which exceptions have been taken on account of residence and in my opinion the exceptions should be withdrawn by the Federal auditors, which I hope will be done. These expenditures did not in any way violate any North Carolina law.

OPINIONS TO THE GREATER UNIVERSITY

Education; World War Orphans; Benefits

12 July 1944

Receipt is acknowledged of your letter of July 8 in which you state that a young lady, who is a prospective student in your institution, attended Peace Junior College in Raleigh and was able to transfer sufficient academic credits to graduate from the University of North Carolina in three years. During the time she attended the University of North Carolina at Chapel Hill, she received the full benefits under the statute authorizing educational advantages for children of World War veterans. She now desires to enter your institution for the study of textiles. You desire to know whether, in my opinion, this young lady would be eligible for further benefits under the statute authorizing educational advantages for children of World War veterans and, if so, for what period of time.

G. S. 116-145 provides that the scholarship authorized by the section shall not extend for a longer period than four academic years. It appears from your letter that the young lady in question has only received the benefits from the scholarship for three academic years, as contemplated by the statute, and if this is true it appears to me that she would be entitled to a scholarship in your institution for one additional academic year. I have not been able to find a satisfactory interpretation of the word "academic" as used in this particular statute but I assume that is is used in the same sense as the term "scholastic." The term "scholastic year" is one of common use and is generally understood to mean a term of nine months and, in the absence of affirmative proof to the contrary, it will be assumed that the scholastic year begins in the Fall and ends in the Spring. SMITH v. BOARD OF EDUCATION, 113 S. E. 147, 153 Ga. 758. It would necessarily follow that the term "academic year" as applied to your institution would be the term which begins in the Fall and ends in the Spring.

You raise the further question as to whether your institution would be required to provide a room for this young lady. You state that the institution has always furnished male students with dormitory rooms but that you do not maintain dormitories for girls. We have heretofore adopted the view that a State educational institution would only be required to furnish a student with the facilities furnished by the institution and that the institution would not be under obligation to make cash expenditures for items not furnished by the institution. If you furnish rooms for any girl students you would be required to furnish these accommodations to the young lady in question but if you do not furnish such rooms to girl stdents I do not believe you would be required to pay for the room and board of the young lady elsewhere.

EXCHANGE OF CONE PROPERTY ON FRANKLIN STREET FOR HIGH SCHOOL PROPERTY ON PITTSBORO ROAD

14 August 1944

I acknowledge receipt of your letter setting out certain facts relating to a proposed exchange of properties between the county board of education of Orange County -and the University of North Carolina, and enclosing memorandum from you to President Graham, the original deed, and copy of contract between the University and the County Board of Education.

You inquire as to the sufficiency of the reversionary clause in the deed and inquire as to the proper procedure for exchange of the two tracts of land.

I am of the opinion that the reversionary clause contained in the deed is sufficient to cause the property described in said deed to revert back to the University upon the abandonment of the property by the Board of Education of Orange County for the purposes specified in the deed and contract. Assuming that the proposed agreement is satisfactory to both parties, it occurs to me that the better procedure to follow is for the County Board of Education, after having been duly authorized by the proper resolution, to execute and deliver to the University a sufficient deed and setting out therein that the County Board of Education has determined to abandon said property for the uses specified in the original deed and contract.

When this has been done, it seems to me that the University could convey the other tract to the County Board of Education on the same terms and conditions as that upon which the original tract was conveyed.

I observe that in the deed used in conveying the Pittsboro Road tract to the County Board of Education, the conveyance was made by the University of North Carolina through its Board of Trustees. In view of Sections 143-147 to -150, I am of the opinion that conveyances made on the part of the University of North Carolina should be executed by the proper officials of the Board of Trustees and by the Governor and Secretary of State, after its approval by the Council of State.

WORKMEN'S COMPENSATION; SUBDIVISION OF STATE HAS NO AUTHORITY TO WAIVE STATUTE REQUIRING CLAIM TO BE FILED WITHIN ONE YEAR

15 August 1944

I acknowledge receipt of your letter, enclosing a letter and other documents from Mr. John C. Lockhart, Assistant Controller and Business Manager of the Woman's College of Greensboro. In expressing an opinion on the question raised by you, I am assuming the facts to be that the employee, William A. Man, sustained minor injuries on or about April 22, 1943, from which symptoms of hernia developed but an operation was not advised by the surgeon; that the employee did not at that time, nor has he since filed a claim for compensation but continued at his work until recently, when he was re-examined by a surgeon, who now recommends an operation for hernia. I further assume that no compensation has been paid to the employee and no claim has been filed by him with either his employer or the North Carolina Industrial Commission.

You inquire as to whether or not the College should now tender and pay for an operation for hernia alleged to have been sustained by the employee on April 22, 1943.

Section 97-24 of the North Carolina General Statutes provides: "The right for compensation under this article shall be forever barred unless a claim be filed with the Industrial Commission within one year after the accident. . ."

It appears from the facts in this case that more than one year has elapsed since the injuries were sustained by this employee; therefore, his claim is barred by statute.

I do not know of any authority for the College to waive the requirement that the claim must be filed within twelve months from the date of the injury.

I observe that the notice of the accident was filed with the North Carolina Industrial Commission by the College on Form 19, but no mention is made of any claim being filed with either the College or the Commission. In construing the twelve months' requirement the Court held, in the case of HARDISON v. HAMPTON, 203 N. C. 187, that this section is deemed to have been complied with when a claim is filed with the employer and the report of the accident and claim is filed with the Commission by the employer, so that if your employee filed with the College a written claim for compensation or medical services within the twelve months' period, and a report of it was made to the Industrial Commission, it seems that under the case of HARDISON v. HAMPTON the employee has complied with the statute and is entitled to an operation.

STATE LICENSING BOARD FOR CONTRACTORS; DISTRIBUTION OF SURPLUS FUNDS

5 March 1945

I have your letter of March 3, 1945, in which you inquire if it would not be wise to have the laws amended so as to permit the payment of surplus funds of the State Licensing Board for Contractors to the Controller of North Carolina State College of Agriculture and Engineering. The idea occurred to you because the Engineering School of the Greater University is located at North Carolina State College of Agriculture and Engineering in Raleigh.

As originally adopted, the law requiring the distribution of surplus funds of the Licensing Board for Contractors provided that such surplus should be paid over, share and share alike, to the University of North Carolina and to North Carolina State College of Agriculture and Engineering for the use of their Engineering Departments. As a result of the consolidation act (1931, c. 202) the Engineering School of the Greater University is concentrated at the North Carolina State College of Agriculture and Engineering at Raleigh.

In preparing the manuscript for the General Statutes of North Carolina, the Division of Legislative Drafting and Codification of Statutes recommended a change in the law governing the distribution of these surplus funds. This recommendation was adopted by the General Assembly and the statute now provides that the surplus funds shall be paid over to the Greater University of North Carolina for the use of its Engineering Department. G. S. 87-7.

As the law now reads, and since the Engineering Department of the University is at North Carolina State College of Agriculture and Engineering in Raleigh, it is my opinion that these funds may legally be paid directly to the North Carolina State College of Agricuulture and Engineering. This is the apparent intent of the law and would be in strict compliance with the letter thereof.

Under this interpretation, I do not believe that an amendment to the law is necessary.

ESCHEAT; DISPOSITION OF PROCEEDS PAID ADMINISTRATOR IN FOREIGN STATE ON CLAIM FOR WRONGFUL DEATH OCCURRING IN THIS STATE

21 April 1945

In your letter of April 3, 1945, you enclose a letter from Mr. Henry V. Charbonneau, and from his letter, it appears that Frank Bonenfant was born in the State of New Hampshire about thirty-five years ago and his parents are unknown. He was brought up by Mr. and Mrs. Frank D. Bonenfant and assumed their name but was never adopted. He married a lady from Lowell, Massachusetts, and in the year 1943, he was in the Army and stationed in Florida. His wife went to visit him in December of that year, and on December 16, 1943, he and his wire were on their way to Lowell on the Atlantic Coastline Railroad and were both killed in a collision of trains which occurred near the Town of Rennert in Robeson County, North Carolina. Apparently, Frank Bonenfant has no next of kin. At least, none can be found.

Mr. Charbonneau is the duly appointed administrator of the estate of Frank Bonenfant, and after the expiration of one year after the date of the accident, he settled the claim for the wrongful death of Frank Bonenfant for the sum of $5,625. The funds in his hands are claimed by the administrator of the estate of the wife of Frank Bonenfant on the ground, that she survived her husband by several minutes. The Commonwealth of Massachusetts claims that this amount escheats to that State because there are no heirs at law or next of kin. The persons who reared Frank Bonenfant have brought suit against the estate for board and lodging and also alleged the breach of a contract to make a will. The administrator has petitioned the Court of Massachusetts for instructions as to how the distribution of this money should be made and has named the University of North Carolina as a party in this petition because, as he states, the statutes of this State pertaining to wrongful death may have helped him in obtaining a settlement.

You inquire of this office if the University of North Carolina has any rights in the distribution of these funds by reason of the law of escheat.

I have examined the statutes and the legal authorities in regard to the subject of escheat and so far I have been unable to find any authority upon which the University of North Carolina could base a claim to share in the distribution of these funds.

It is not clear from Mr. Charbonneau's letter whether Frank Bonenfant was a resident of the State of Massachusetts or not. Apparently, he was a resident of the State of Massachusetts since his marriage to Grace M. Brown of that State. At any rate, he was not a resident of the State of North Carolina, and letters of administration were granted to Mr. Charbonneau in the State of Massachusetts.

It seems to me that this claim against the railroad for his wrongful death is a type of property right when reduced to settlement or payment that would be handled and administered by the laws of the State of Massachusetts. If the administrator in Massachusetts had brought suit in that State, it no doubt could have been maintained by reason of the North Carolina statute which grants a right of action for a wrongful death, but the administration of the proceeds of funds derived from such an action or claim would be administered by the laws of the State of Massachusetts for the reason that the claim and the property derived therefrom in the form of money would be determined by the laws of the State in which the decedent was domiciled. In 12 C. J., page 476, § 71, it is said:

"Under the fiction of law that movables are present at the domicile of the owner, no matter what their actual location may be, the law of his domicile governs their distribution and disposition in case of his death intestate. It should be observed in this connection that the law of domicile which is meant is the law as it existed at the time of the owner's death, unaffected by any change which thereafter may have been made."

While it is true that a claim of this sort is not in existence during the lifetime of a decedent and it is not strictly treated as assets of his estate so far as the laws of this State are concerned, nevertheless, I can find no authority which would compel the courts of the State of Massachusetts to follow the statute of North Carolina as to distribution of the funds.

In the case of HALL v. RAILROAD, 146 N. C., p. 345, the facts were that the decedent was a resident of the State of Virginia and was killed in the State of North Carolina on a railroad in this State. The action for his wrongful death was brought in this State and our Court said in the opinion as follows:

"Our statute would control the distribution of the fund, whether the statutes of the two States are alike or not; so that it is immaterial to consider the similarity of the two enactments, even if there were evidence of it. We have held in the last cited case [HARTNESS v. PHARR] that the fund must not only be distributed according to the law of this State, but by an administrator appointed here, and that is conclusive against the plaintiff's right to recover in this action."

I have cited this case because the facts are the reverse of those contained in your letter on this question in that although the decedent in both cases was killed in North Carolina, yet the suit in the case cited was brought in this State and the claim, which is the subject of your letter, was prosecuted in another State.

It is also the accepted holding of the Supreme Court of this State that personal property of the estate of a deceased domiciled in another State will be disposed of according to the law of the State of the domicile, which is expressly held in the case of McGEHEE v. McGEHEE, 189 N. C., p. 561.

In 30 C.J.S., p. 1167, § 3, the author discusses the law as to escheat and the property subject to escheat, and says:

> "Personal property does not escheat in the ·original and technical sense of the term; but the doctrine of escheat is, in effect, applied to personalty as well as to realty. The doctrine extends to intangible as well as to tangible property, and generally to all rights of property of any nature whatever. However, to be subject to escheat, the property ordinarily must have its situs within the territorial limits of the particular State."

I am of the opinion, therefore, that the situs of this claim, or any funds paid as a result of the claim, follows the domicile of the decedent, and therefore would be distributed according to the laws of the State of Massachusetts; and further, that the laws of the State of North Carolina governing escheats do not have any extraterritorial effect, and that the University of North Carolina does not have any valid claim to share in the distribution of these proceeds.

SOIL CONSERVATION; PER DIEM COMPENSATION AND EXPENSE ALLOWED SUPERVISORS

6 July 1945

You call my attention to Senate Bill 215, being Chapter 481 of the Session Laws of 1945, which amends Chapter 393 of the Public Laws of 1937, known as the Soil Conservation Districts Law, and inquire as to whether or not, under the provisions of the 1945 Act, you may approve a payment of per diem and expenses of soil district supervisors in attending the State Association of Supervisors and a supervisor who visits an area not in a district for the purpose of encouraging the people in such area to organize a district.

The 1945 amendment reads: "Each supervisor shall receive as compensation for his services the sum of $3.00 per diem for each meeting of the supervisors, not exceeding four meetings per year, and shall also be entitled to expenses, including traveling expenses, necessarily incurred in the discharge of his duties."

It thus appears that the number of days for which you may pay a per diem is limited to four but I do not think that the limitation as to the payment of expenses is so limited. The Act prescribes the duties to be performed by a supervisor and I am of the opinion that he is entitled to expenses, including travel expenses, necessarily incurred in the discharge of those duties. Though only expenses necessary in the performance of their duties may be paid to the supervisors, the question as to whether the expenses in the given case are proper and are incurred in the performance of the official duties of the supervisor is one which must be determined by you as Director of the State Agricultural Extension Service in compliance with the provisions of the State Budget Act so that if you find that in order for a supervisor to officially perform the duties imposed upon him it is necessary that he attend a State Association of Supervisors, the necessary expenses might be paid. If the supervisor who went into an area not in a district, went there for the purpose of performing the duties imposed upon him by the Act or by his superior in the furtherance of the soil erosion program, I think that he would be entitled to his necessary travel expenses. I again call your attention to the fact that the number of per diems which may be paid is limited to four.

UNIVERSITY OF NORTH CAROLINA

20 August 1945

I acknowledge receipt of your letter in which you inquire as to whether or not a contract may be made on behalf of the State of North Carolina by the "Board of Trustees of the University of North Carolina."

Section 116-3, G. S., provides that the Trustees of the University shall be a body politic and corporate, to be known and distinguished by the name of "University of North Carolina" and by that name shall have perpetual succession and a common seal. I am, therefore, of the opinion that any contracts entered into by the University of North Carolina should be done in the name of "University of North Carolina."

You further inquire as to whether or not it is necessary to obtain the consent of the Supreme Court before the University can be sued.

The second paragraph of Section 116-3 of the General Statutes specifically provides that the University shall be capable in law to sue and *be sued in all courts whatsoever.*

I am, therefore, of the opinion that it will not be necessary for one having cause of action against the University to first obtain the consent of the Supreme Court before bringing action against it.

UNIVERSITY OF NORTH CAROLINA, CHAPEL HILL; APPLICATION OF MUNICIPAL
ORDINANCES; RIGHT OF TRUSTEES TO MAKE REGULATIONS

3 December 1945

I received your letter of November 29 with reference to the operation of motor vehicles on Cameron Avenue through the campus of the University at Chapel Hill and the application of ordinances of the Town of Chapel Hill to this area.

As stated in your letter, it is my view that the ordinances of the Town of

Chapel Hill regulating the parking, speed and other uses of motor vehicles on the streets and highways in Chapel Hill, would not be applicable to Cameron Avenue or other places on the campus of the University as this would not be a public street or highway or public parking place.

You inquire with regard to the regulations concerning parking, parking areas, and other desirable regulations governing the operation and use of motor vehicles, whether the University Board of Trustees would have any authority to prescribe regulations which would be enforceable at law and if the present law is insufficient for this purpose, whether the Legislature would have the power to pass a law delegating to the Board of Trustees of the University a right to make such regulations and prescribing that a breach of the same would constitute a misdemeanor and prescribing punishment.

The only statute which I find having a bearing on this subject is G. S. 116-10 which provides that the Trustees shall have the power to make such rules and regulations for the management of the University as they may deem necessary and expedient, not inconsistent with the Constitution and laws of the State. Under this statute the Board of Trustees could make rules and regulations for the purpose of controlling the use of Cameron Avenue by motor vehicles and the parking of motor vehicles elsewhere on the campus, but I do not think that the violation of such rules and regulations as they may prescribe constitute crime enforceable by indictment. There is nothing in the statute which prescribes that such a result would follow the violation of any regulation adopted by the University.

It is my opinion, however, that the General Assembly could constitutionally delegate to the Trustees of the University authority to adopt rules and regulations for the management of matters of this character and prescribe that a violation of such rules and regulations so adopted would constitute a misdemeanor and prescribe the punishment therefor.

It is conceivable that the Trustees of the University might adopt rules and regulations forbidding the parking of motor vehicles except in certain designated areas and that a violation of such regulations might be indictable as a criminal trespass under G. S. 14-134. I doubt, however, that the Trustees of the University would want to take this method of enforcing parking ordinances although I think it is possible they could legally do so.

VETERANS; PUBLIC LAW 346; TUITION CHARGES

11 March 1946

You have advised me that you have a request from the Veterans Administration that you submit evidence clearly setting forth the fact that the nonresident tuition charges to all veterans enrolled at the University of North Carolina at Chapel Hill, at the North Carolina State College of Agriculture and Engineering of the University of North Carolina, and at the Woman's College of the University of North Carolina, under the provisions of Public Law 346, 78th Congress, are legal. You state that this request comes as a requirement under the Veterans Administration Instructions No. 6, issued April 17, 1945, by the Administrator of Veterans Affairs, which reads as follows:

"Institutions which have non-resident tuition may, if they so desire, charge for each Veteran enrolled under Part VIII such customary tuition and incidental fees as are applicable to all non-resident students, provided that the charges are not in conflict with existing laws or other legal requirements. Managers will secure evidence from the institutions or proper official that such charges are legal."

I have carefully examined the provisions of the Constitution and laws of the State of North Carolina with reference to this matter and I have carefully examined the resolutions adopted by the Executive Committee of the Board of Trustees of the University of North Carolina at a meeting held in Raleigh on this date, with reference to the charges of the tuition under consideration, and, in my opinion, the policy of charging the Federal Government the out-of-State tuition rate for all veterans of World War II enrolled at the University of North Carolina at Chapel Hill, North Carolina State College of Agriculture and Engineering of the University of North Carolina, and the Woman's College of the University of North Carolina, as prescribed in these resolutions, is legal and fully authorized by the Constitution and laws of this State.

OPERATION OF STORE BY STATE COMMISSION FOR THE BLIND ON STATE COLLEGE CAMPUS

13 May 1946

I received your letter of May 9 enclosing to me a request from the officers of the Veterans Trailer Camp on State College campus for the establishment by the State Commission for the Blind of a grocery store on the College campus to serve married former servicemen who are now in school. You request my opinion as to whether or not the establishment of a grocery store under the conditions stated would be in conflict with our laws, particularly Chapter 122 of the Public Laws of 1939, known as the Umstead Act, which is now G. S. 66-58.

G. S. 111-27 authorizes the officials in charge of various State and municipal buildings to permit the operation of vending stands by needy blind persons on the premises of any State, county or municipal property under their respective jurisdictions, provided such operators shall be first licensed by the North Carolina State Commission for the Blind and provided further that in the opinion of the Commission or officials having control and custody of such property such vending stands may be properly and satisfactorily operated on such premises without undue interference with the use and needs thereof for public purposes. This statute in my opinion would authorize the proposed operation on the campus of State College under the conditions and upon compliance with the terms of the statute.

I have examined G. S. 66-58, commonly known as the Umstead Act, which does not in my opinion in any way prevent the operation of such a store by an operator licensed by the State Commission for the Blind. This statute deals only with the sale of merchandise by a State institution, its employees or an agency of such employees.

I am returning herewith a letter to you under date of May 8 from Mr. Earl A. Carter, Mayor, and others.

OPINIONS TO RETIREMENT SYSTEM

RETIREMENT SYSTEM; APPLICATION OF S. B. No. 143 TO PRIOR SERVICE
AND TO MEMBERSHIP SERVICE

30 March 1945

I reply to your letter of March 28, 1945.

You state in substance that when the Retirement System was established as of July 1, 1941, the State assumed the obligation of all prior service and that no member was entitled to participate in the System as to that part of his compensation in excess of $3,000. S. B. No. 143, referred to by you, amends Subsection (6) of Section 135-1 of the General Statutes by allowing participation up to $5,000. This Act or amendment was passed during the 1945 session of the General Assembly.

Your question is whether or not this Act extending participation on the part of a member up to $5,000 (1) applies to prior service, and (2) whether or not it is compulsory for a member to make up or pay in the additional contribution between $3,000 and a salary since July 1, 1941 up to $5,000. You also inquire as to the power of the Board of Trustees to establish a rule making it optional with a member as to whether or not such member should pay in this difference covering the period from July 1, 1941 up to the April, 1945, pay-roll.

The amendment referred to in your letter as S. B. No. 143 is as follows:

"(6) 'Member' shall mean any teacher or State employee included in the membership of the system as provided in Sections 135-3 and 135-4: Provided that no member shall be entitled to participate under the provisions of this chapter as to that part·of the compensation in excess of five thousand dollars ($5,000.00) received by such member during any year and this shall apply to all creditable service."

I am of the opinion that S. B. No. 143 applies to all prior service since the provision extending the participation to $5,000 is specifically made applicable by the statute "to all creditable service." Subsection (12) of Section 135-1 defines creditable service as "prior service plus membership service for which credit is allowable as provided in Section 135-4." Membership service is defined as service a teacher or State employee rendered while a member of the Retirement Service. The amendment in S. B. No. 143, therefore, clearly embraces prior service and membership service as these two types of service are the component parts of creditable service.

Subsection (6) of Section 135-6 defines the power of the Board of Trustees as to rules and regulations and is as follows:

"Subject to the limitations of this chapter, the Board of Trustees shall, from time to time, establish rules and regulations for the administration of the funds created by this chapter and for the transaction of its business. The Board of Trustees shall also, from time to time, in its discretion, adopt rules and regulations to prevent injustices and inequalities which might otherwise arise in the administration of this chapter."

I am of the opinion, therefore, that the participation of a member to the extent of $5,000 is retroactive and applies to that period of time beginning July 1, 1941 and extending up to the April, 1945, pay-roll.. But I am also of the opinion that under the section of the law that I have quoted above with reference to rules and regulations, the Board of Trustees has the power to establish a regulation which would make a retroactive application of this amendment optional with the member. In other words, I think that the Board of Trustees, for example, can by regulation establish a time limitation whereby those members who wish to pay in or make up the additional part of their contribution for those salaries in excess of $3,000 and up to $5,000 can do so, and those who do not wish to make the additional contribution would not have to do so. Such a regulation should be uniform and should apply equally to all members affected thereby. The establishment of such a regulation would be within the discretion of the Board of Trustees.

The amendment is effective as to all members whose salaries exceed $3,000 and extend to $5,000, beginning with the pay-roll of April, 1945, and this, of course, is mandatory and there is no discretion in applying the statute to this feature of the contribution.

MUNICIPAL RETIREMENT SYSTEM; EXECUTIVE OFFICER OF CITY OR TOWN SERVING AS MEMBER OF THE BOARD OF TRUSTEES

19 April 1945

In your letter of April 16, 1945, you call attention to subsection 2, Section 7, of House Bill No. 275 and ask if there is any constitutional or legal prohibition against a full-time executive officer of a city or town participating in the system serving as members of the Board of Trustees of the Local Governmental Employees' Retirement System.

Section 128-28 of the Retirement System Law for counties, cities and towns as contained in the General Statutes, provides in substance that the Board of Trustees of the Teachers' and State Employees' Retirement System of North Carolina shall be responsible for the general administration of the retirement system for counties, cities and towns. Section 135-6 of the General Statutes provides for the Board of Trustees of the State Retirement System and fixes the duties of this board. The members of this board are appointed by the Governor of North Carolina and are confirmed by the Senate; that is, all members are appointed in this manner other than the two *ex officio* members. The members are appointed at first for a term of two years, three years and four years, and at the expiration "of these terms of office" the appointment shall be for a term of four years. This section further provides that each member or trustee other than the *ex officio* members shall, within ten days after appointment, "take an oath of office." There are many other indications in this statute which strongly suggest that the members or trustees of this board are officers and that the position is that of an office.

The amendment pointed out in your letter, which is pertinent to this question, is as follows:

"The board shall consist of the Board of Trustees of the Teachers' and State Employees' Retirement System and two other persons to be appointed by the Governor; one a full-time executive officer of a city or town participating in the retirement system, and one a full-time officer of the governing body of a county participating in the retirement system, these to be appointed for a term of two years each. At the expiration of *these terms of office*, the appointment shall be for a term of four years." (Italics ours.)

I think it would be very hard, if not impossible, to find an executive officer of a city or town and a full-time officer of the governing body of a county who is not holding a definite public office; in fact, the very words denote such a situation, and, while I am not at this time giving you an opinion that a member of the Board of Trustees of the State Retirement System, which is likewise the Board of Trustees for the Municipal Retirement System, is a public officer and that such a position is an office, nevertheless these statutes contain such duties and such phraseology that I think that it is highly advisable that these two positions—the full-time executive officer of the city or town and the full-time officer of the governing body of a county—should remain vacant and that at this time no appointments should be made to the Board of Trustees of the Municipal System of this type of member. In my opinion, if these positions remain vacant, it will not affect the legality of the decisions of the Board of Trustees, its regulations and its duties. The board can take legal action with four members and it already consists of seven members, so there is no reason why the board cannot function in a legal manner without these appointments. If you do proceed to have these appointments made, there is grave danger that such officials would vacate their offices which they hold with a city or town, as the case may be, if such member should qualify by taking the oath of office as a member of the Board of Trustees, and I know that you do not want to bring about this result.

RETIREMENT SYSTEM; RETURN OF ACCUMULATED CONTRIBUTIONS;
REGULAR INTEREST

24 May 1945

Reference is made to your letter of May 8, 1945, in which your specific question is whether or not the Board of Trustees of the Teachers' and State Employees' Retirement System could make a legal rule which would permit the return of the accumulated contributions with interest based on the earnings being made by the Retirement System instead of 4%. You call attention to certain statutes containing definitions which bear upon this question, and you further state that your investment experience shows that you are earning a return of 2.58 on invested funds of the Retirement System. You also call attention to Chapter 719 of the Session Laws of 1943 relating to the power of the Board of Trustees to adopt rules and regulations to prevent injustices and inequalities in the administration of the law governing the Retirement System. This chapter appears as the last sentence in paragraph (6) of Section 135-6 of the General Statutes.

When a member ceases to be a teacher or State employee, other than by death or retirement, the member's benefit rights are governed by paragraph (6) of Section 135-5 of the General Statutes, which is as follows:

"(6) Return of Accumulated Contributions.—Should a member cease to be a teacher or state employee except by death or retirement under the provisions of this chapter, he shall be paid such part of the amount of the accumulated contributions standing to the credit of his individual account in the annuity savings fund as he shall demand. Should a member die before retirement the amount of his accumulated contributions standing to the credit of his individual account shall be paid to his estate or to such persons as he shall have nominated by written designation, duly executed and filed with the board of trustees."

The term "accumulated contributions" is a defined term and its definition appears in paragraph (15) of Section 135-1 of the General Statutes and is as follows:

"(15) 'Accumulated contributions' shall mean the sum of all the amounts deducted from the compensation of a member and accredited to his individual account in the annuity savings fund, together with regular interest thereon as provided in § 135-8."

The term "regular interest" appears in this definition, and this term is likewise defined in the statute and appears as paragraph (14) of Section 135-1 of the General Statutes, and in this definition interest is to be compounded annually at a rate determined by the Board of Trustees in accordance with Section 135-7 of the General Statutes, Subsection two. The above paragraph is as follows:

"(14) 'Regular interest' shall mean interest compounded annually at such a rate as shall be determined by the board of trustees in accordance with § 135-7, subsection two."

Paragraph (2) of Section 135-7 gives the formula for determining regular interest and fixes a minimum of three per centum and a maximum of four per centum. This paragraph is as follows:

"(2) Regular Interest Allowance.—The board of trustees annually shall allow regular interest on the mean amount for the preceding year in each of the funds with the exception of the expense fund. The amounts so allowed shall be due and payable to said funds, and shall be annually credited thereto by the board of trustees from interest and other earnings on the moneys of the retirement system. Any additional amount required to meet the interest on the funds of the retirement system shall be paid from the pension accumulation fund, and any excess of earnings over such amount required shall be paid to the pension accumulation fund. Regular interest shall mean such per centum rate to be compounded annually as shall be determined by the board of trustees on the basis of the interest earnings of the system for the preceding year and of the probable earnings to be made, in the judgment of the board, during the immediate future, such rate to be limited to a minimum of three per centum and a maximum of four per centum, with the latter rate applicable during the first year of operation of the retirement system."

Your question more specifically deals with the right of the Board of Trustees to return accumulated contributions to qualified beneficiaries by returning to such beneficiary upon ceasing to be a member of the System the exact amount of deductions from salary plus the actual earnings on investment, or in other words, the power of the Board of Trustees to substitute actual earnings on investments in lieu of regular interest as defined in the statute. As a possible authority for this course of action, you cite Chapter 719 of the Session Laws of 1943, which is as follows:

"The board of trustees shall also, from time to time, in its discretion, adopt rules and regulations to prevent injustices and inequalities which might otherwise arise in the administration of this chapter." ,

Of course, it should also be noted that the Board of Trustees has the statutory power to establish rules and regulations for the administration of the funds created by the Retirement Act. The terms "injustices and inequalities" are very broad and general terms, but I think that we should carefully note that rules and regulations designed to prevent injustices and inequalities are confined to matters of administration, and I cannot conceive that this particular language would authorize the Board of Trustees to set aside or annul those duties and things which the statute in specific terms requires the administrative body to do. If the Board of Trustees of the Retirement System can change the requirements and definition of "regular interest" after such term has been specifically spelled out in the statute and after the statute requires that regular interest shall accompany deductions when a member ceases to be a teacher or State employee, then I see no reason why the Board of Trustees could not change the amount of funds that a member receives when he or she retires, or in one particular case reduce the amount of benefits received on retirement of one individual and in another case increase the amount of benefits received by another individual, all contrary to and above or below the formula specifically fixed by the statute. This form of reasoning carried to its logical end would allow the Board of Trustees, if it so desired, to nullify the whole statute, and in the hands of a Board composed of men less careful and less attentive to their duties than the present Board, could lead to very harmful results and loss of confidence in the System.

The Act of 1943 cited by you applies to matters of administration in which the Board of Trustees has discretion. It was never intended by this Act that the Board of Trustees could substitute its judgment and its policy in lieu of the specific requirements of the statute, and especially when the statute carefully describes in detail what shall be done in a certain situation. This is true, no matter how reasonable and meritorious the proposed policy or regulation of the Board may be. In such case, the only remedy is to change the written law.

I am of the opinion, therefore, that your Board of Trustees does not have the authority to make a regulation or rule that would permit the return of the accumulated contributions with interest based on the earnings made by the Retirement System instead of regular interest. There is much merit and justice in your position, but it is a matter for legislative action.

The definition of regular interest allowance as contained in paragraph 2 of Section 135-7 allows the Board of Trustees some discretion and latitude in determining the rate that shall be established between the minimum of three per centum and the maximum of four per centum. The financial plan of the System as contained in Section 135-8 clearly shows that judgment and discretion are to be used in arriving at the beneficial objectives of the Retirement System. When these statutes are construed in connection with the statute pointed out by you (paragraph 6 of Section 135-6), then I am of the opinion that the Board of Trustees does have the power and authority to adopt a suitable rule or regulation defining regular interest at the three per centum minimum as the regular interest contained in the definition of accumulated contributions, and that this minimum of three per centum as defined in regular interest shall be the standard or amount used in computing the accumulated contributions to be paid to those beneficiaries who cease to be a teacher or State employee other than by death or retirement. It is manifestly an injustice and inequality for persons who withdraw from the System, to be paid the maximum amount of regular interest when they do not continue to remain as members and contribute to the general fund and invested reserves. To allow such persons the maximum amount of regular interest is a discrimination against those members who continue to remain in service until their time of retirement. By adopting a rule or regulation fixing the definition of regular interest at the minimum of three per centum for those persons who are paid accumulated contributions upon withdrawal, you do not depart from the limitations fixed by the statute.

NORTH CAROLINA LOCAL GOVERNMENTAL EMPLOYEES' RETIREMENT SYSTEM; ADMINISTRATION; STATE CONTROL OVER LOCAL GOVERN- MENTAL EMPLOYEES' RETIREMENT SYSTEM

2 July 1945

In your letter of June 20, 1945, you call our attention to Section 128-28, as amended by Chapter 526 of the Session Laws of 1945, and you especially call our attention to Subsection 7 of the amendment. Your question is: Does the Board of Trustees of the North Carolina Local Governmental Employees' Retirement System have the authority for the general administration and responsibility of this Retirement System, independent of any other State agency?

Article 3 of Chapter 128 of the General Statutes provides in detail for a Retirement System for the employees of counties, cities and towns. This Retirement System is known as the "North Carolina Local Governmental Employees' Retirement System." Those municipal units desiring to have their employees covered under the Act may do so voluntarily, and all benefits under the Act are financed by a fund which is accumulated by means of contributions paid into the fund from the salaries of municipal employees; likewise, the counties, cities and towns make payments by way of employer contributions. The State Treasurer is custodian of the funds and payments are made by him upon vouchers signed by two persons designated by the Board of Trustees. The Board of Trustees has the authority to select the depository for the funds. These vouchers are not handled through the office of the State Auditor, and so far as I can see, the use of State funds is nowhere contemplated by this Act. All employees and all expenses are paid out of the funds furnished by the municipalities. The Board of Trustees of the Teachers' and State Employees' Retirement System also acts as the Board of Trustees for this municipal system, plus certain members who represent the counties, cities and towns.

Prior to the General Assembly of 1945, it was provided in Section 128-28 of the General Statutes that all of the provisions of Section 135-6 of the General Statutes would apply to the administration of this municipal system. The result of this was, of course, that the administration of the system was then subject to the approval of the Director of the Budget. At the Session of the General Assembly of 1945 Section 128-8 was amended by striking out this whole section and rewriting the section by means of adding fifteen paragraphs, and among other things, paragraph or sub-section 7 provides in part as follows:

"The compensation of all persons engaged by the board of trustees, and all other expenses of the board necessary for the operation of the retirement system, shall be paid at such rates and in such amounts as the board of trustees shall approve."

I am of the opinion, therefore, that in the administration of the North Carolina Local Governmental Employees' Retirement System the Board of Trustees is vested with authority to generally administer this Act in behalf of the counties, cities and towns, and that the responsibility for this administration on the part of the Board is independent of any other State agency or State control. In my opinion, the Board of Trustees of this Retirement (municipal) System has the sole responsibility for fixing the salaries of employees and the payment of any and all other expenses, and such payments are not subject to the approval of the Director of the Budget of this State. I am further of the opinion that in purchasing any supplies or making any contracts for purchases whatsoever, the Board of Trustees of the Municipal Retirement System is not bound by any regulation of the Division of Purchase and Contract, and all of the statutes contained in Article 3 of Chapter 143 of the General Statutes dealing with State purchases and contracts in my opinion are not applicable to the Board of Trustees while transacting business for the benefit of the Municipal Retirement System.

I do not think of any other of our State agencies that might be involved, but to my mind the Municipal System is governed by its own Board of Trustees, furnishes its own finances, and is separate and independent of State laws, regulations and controls other than those specified in its own organic statute.

1 November 1945

Sometime ago you inquired of this office as follows:

"Please examine Section 18 of Chapter 390, Public Laws 1939, as amended by Chapter 357, Public Laws 1941, and let me know if the provisos in that Section removing the City of Greensboro, Mt. Airy, Pitt County and others from the requirement of a vote of the people to set up such a retirement system is constitutional."

Your inquiry was made during the Session of the General Assembly and we advised you over the telephone as to our opinion in the matter. For the purpose of closing our records, however, I am sending you this letter. You, of course, realize that it is not the duty or function of our office to pass upon the constitutionality of statutes. Anything that we may say is advisory only, since the courts of the state are the proper agencies to pass upon constitutional questions and make binding decisions in such matters.

It has been said by our Supreme Court and also by the Supreme Court of the United States that a statute will not be declared unconstitutional unless it is clearly in conflict with the constitution, and those who attack on constitutional grounds must show beyond a reasonable doubt that such conflict exists. I think that public officials administering statutes have a right to proceed under those statutes until they are declared unconstitutional.

Under the authority of the case of *Bridges v. Charlotte*, 221 N. C., 472, we think that the provisions of the statute removing the City of Greensboro, Mount Airy, and Pitt County, as well as certain other municipalities from the requirements of the vote of the people in order-to-set up a retirement system and provide the necessary contributions to finance the retirement system, is constitutional.

TEACHERS' AND STATE EMPLOYEES' RETIREMENT SYSTEM; EMPLOYEES OF THE DEPARTMENT OF AGRICULTURE PAID IN PART BY FEDERAL GOVERN-MENT; DEDUCTIONS OF EARNABLE COMPENSATION

20 December 1945

Reference is made to your letter in which you state that the Department of Agriculture of the State of North Carolina carries on its payroll certain employees whose salaries are paid partly by Federal funds and partly by State funds. These employees are hired by the State, and their total salaries are certified by the Budget Bureau although they are paid from both State and Federal sources.

You inquire of this office if these employees should be permitted to make contributions to the Retirement System on the basis of their total salary regardless of the source of payment.

I have talked with Mr. A. R. Powledge of the Division of Audits and Accounts of the Department of Agriculture, and he tells me that there are certain employees in the Division of Markets, Warehouses, Tobacco and Test Farms who are paid from State and Federal sources as mentioned in your letter. He further states that in these cases this method of payment has been worked out and agreed to between the Department of Agriculture and the appropriate agency of the Federal Government, as a matter of convenience to the government in handling accounts. For example, one employee at a test farm is paid $800.00 by the Federal Government. This is matched by the State of North Carolina by buying supplies for the test farm in the amount of $800.00. He states that the government preferred to use this method for the reason that the government would thereby discharge its obligation by issuing one check into payment of one account. That is, from the government's point of view, the whole thing would be closed in one transaction; whereas, if the government bought the supplies, there would be a great number of checks and entries.

Earnable compensation is defined in Paragraph (15) of Section 135-1 of the General Statutes; and under the provisions of Section 135-8, each employer is to deduct 4% (four per cent) of this earnable compensation from the salary of each member and from every payroll for each and every payroll period. While it is true that the salary items in question are paid by Federal voucher, which is not cleared through the auditor's office; nevertheless, it seems to me that these items should be considered as a part of the total salary of this class of employees and that deductions should be made and paid into the Retirement System on these items. Mr. Powledge states that such employees have a definite classification, and a definite salary under the State System, including a definite salary range. He further states that if this arrangement with the government did not exist, the employees in question would receive the same total salary paid by the State in entirety. I am of the opinion, therefore, that where this arrangement with the government exists and the Federal payment is made as a means of convenience to the government and to aid the government in the simplification of its accounting proceedures, then the deductions should be based on total salary regardless of source. It should be clearly understood that this opinion is confined to such a situation and specifically to the situation where the State makes corresponding expenditures as an aid to the simplification of government payments and accounting. It should be definitely understood that this does not apply to every case where a State employee has his salary supplemented by Federal funds.

TEACHERS' AND STATE EMPLOYEES' RETIREMENT SYSTEM

31 December 1945

You state that it is one of the requirements of the Retirement System Law that a member who makes application for retirement, either service retirement, or disability retirement, must be employed at the time of filing application. The circumstances upon which your inquiry arises is stated in your letter of November 15, 1945, as follows:

"This letter is written to you in connection with application for disability retirement filed on March 19, 1943, from Mrs. Addie Belle Perry, R.F.D. No. 1, Spring Hope, N. C. Mrs. Perry was under contract to teach school in Franklin County for the school year 1942-43. However, during the summer of 1942 her physical condition became progressively worse and she was notified by her doctor that she would not be able to begin teaching on the opening day of school, September 5, 1942. At this time, she was advised by her physician that it would be advisable for her to obtain a substitute until November 1 and on November 1 the applicant presented to her employer a certification from her physician stating that she would not be able to do any teaching at all. At this juncture this teacher tendered her resignation, and another teacher was employed in her stead. You will thus see that she was not employed as a teacher when on March 19, 1943 she filed her application for disability retirement. It occurred to us that your office might possibly construe this case as being one in which the applicant was technically employed. Due to circumstances entirely beyond her control, it was physically impossible for her to be employed at the time of filing her application, since she entertained the hope that she would be able to return to her employment and this hope did not materialize."

You inquire of this office if, under these circumstances, this applicant should be considered technically employed, and should she, therefore, be granted disability retirement as provided by the terms of the Teachers' and State Employees' Retirement System Act. The benefits allowed under the Retirement System are set forth in Section 135-6 and subsection (4) and paragraphs following of this same section contain the conditions for the allowance of disability retirement.

Subsection (6) of Section 135-6 is as follows:

"Subject to the limitations of this chapter, the board of trustees shall, from time to time, establish rules and regulations for the administration of the funds created by this chapter and-for- the transaction of its business. The board of trustees shall also, from time to time, in its discretion, adopt rules and regulations to prevent injustices and inequalities which might otherwise arise in the administration of this chapter."

I am of the opinion that it is a matter for the Board of Trustees to pass suitable rules and regulations to prevent this type of injustice or inequity, and that if, in the discretion of the Board of Trustees, they desire to adopt a regulation or rule that would take care of this situation, then I think they have the power to do so. Such a rule or regulation should not be passed for special cases, but should be uniform and broad enough to cover this and other cases of a like kind.

TEACHERS' AND STATE EMPLOYEES' RETIREMENT SYSTEM; NORTH CAROLINA
RURAL REHABILITATION CORPORATION; COVERAGE OF EMPLOYEES
UNDER THE RETIREMENT SYSTEM FOR TEACHERS
AND STATE EMPLOYEES

31 December 1945

This is in reply to your inquiry which originated because of a letter written to your agency by Mr. W. Carey Parker, Secretary-Treasurer of the North Carolina Rural Rehabilitation Corporation.

In his letter Mr. Parker called attention to the fact that he is an employee of the North Carolina Rural Rehabilitation Corporation, and that this corporation was organized by the North Carolina Emergency Relief Administration and was chartered in 1934 under the laws of this state as a benevolent, non-profit corporation. He further states that under the terms of the charter the assets of the corporation are to become a part of the general funds of the State of North Carolina in the event the corporation is dissolved.

The affairs of the corporation are administered by a Board of Directors and its Executive Committee. The directors are elected at the annual meeting of the stockholders. Mr. Parker, as Secretary-Treasurer, actively manages the affairs of the corporation subject to the approval of the directors and the Executive Committee of the Board of Directors. It appears at the present time that Mr. Parker is the only state employee of the corporation. No profits can inure to the benefit of any stockholder, and the stockholders and directors receive no compensation for attending meetings and performing their duties.

Section 137-31 of the General Statutes is as follows:

"The North Carolina rural rehabilitation corporation, a non-profit corporation, organized by the members of the commission of the North Carolina emergency relief administration, and chartered by the State to serve as a social and financial instrumentality in assisting to rehabilitate individuals and families by enabling them to secure subsistence and gainful employment from the Soil and co-ordinated and other enterprises in order to restore them as self sustaining citizens and thereby reduce the burdens of public relief for the needy and unemployed, is hereby recognized and designated as an agency of the State of North Carolina and of the North Carolina emergency relief administration and its successor within the powers and limitations of its charter for the carrying out of said objects and purposes."

All of the powers and duties of the corporation are set forth in Article 2 of Chapter 137 of the General Statutes. Apparently, the funds of the corporation are not paid out of the State Treasury, nor do any of the financial transactions come within the purview of the law creating the budget bureau and the laws governing the State Auditor's office.

Subsection (5) of Section 135-1 of the General Statutes defines an employer under the Teachers' and State Employees' Retirement System as follows:

" 'Employer' shall mean the state of North Carolina, the county board of education, the city board of education, the state board of education, the board of trustees of the University of North Carolina, the board of trustees of other institutions and agencies supported and under the control of the state, or any other agency of and within the state by which a teacher or other employee is paid."

An employee under this system is defined in Subsection (4) of Section 135-1, as follows:

" 'Employee' shall mean all full-time employees, agents or officers of the state of North Carolina or any of its departments, bureaus and institutions other than educational, whether such employees are elected, appointed or employed: Provided, that the term 'employee' shall not include any justice of the Supreme Court or any judge of the superior court."

There is nothing in the Chapter dealing with the State Teachers' and State Employees' Retirement System which specifically requires that the payments which are the earnable compensation of an employee shall be made in any specific manner. It seems to me that the North Carolina Rural Rehabilitation Corporation comes within the definition of employer as defined above, and that it certainly falls within the clause "or any other agency of and within the state by which a teacher or other employee is paid."

In dealing with the question as to how funds are handled by which employees are paid, this office ruled on the 21st of April, 1944, as follows:

> "The fact that the funds prior to July 1, 1943, were handled through the Wachovia Bank & Trust Company rather than the Treasurer of the State of North Carolina would not change my views due to the fact, as above pointed out, that the contracts specifically provide that the expenditures and reimbursements are to comply with the administrative procedure established by the college in cooperation with the Treasurer of the State of North Carolina. The fact that the funds were not handled through the office of the Treasurer of the State of North Carolina should not be held to deprive this particular group of employees of the benefits to which they would otherwise be entitled under the provisions of the Retirement Act."

I am of the opinion that this employee of the North Carolina Rural Rehabilitation Corporation should be covered under the Retirement System of Teachers and State Employees, and should be considered a member of this system. It is my thought that this employee comes within the definition of employee in that Act, and that the employer comes within the definition of employer as defined in that Act. It is not a question entirely free from doubt and perhaps the best solution would be to present the matter to the Board of Trustees and if the Board of Trustees decide that this employer should be covered under the Act, then they should pass a resolution declaring the same to be done and stating that this person is entitled to membership in the Retirement System from the date of its establishment.

NORTH CAROLINA LOCAL GOVERNMENTAL EMPLOYEES' RETIREMENT SYSTEM;
METHOD OF FINANCING; AMOUNT OF SALARY OR EARNABLE
COMPENSATION OF AN EMPLOYEE UPON WHICH
DEDUCTION IS BASED

17 January 1946

You state that a question has arisen as to whether or not the last Legislature passed a law setting the maximum amount of $3600.00 for the members participating in the North Carolina Local Governmental Employees' Retirement System. It is further stated by you that it was the intention of the City of Charlotte at the time they considered entering the system that this maximum of $3600.00 was in existence and would be the basis upon which employee compensations were made or deducted. You call attention to the fact that $5000.00 is the maximum amount for participation of members of the Teachers' and State Employees' Retirement System; and you inquire of this office if there is any section of law creating the maximum of $3600.00 as a basis for member contributions in the North Carolina Local Governmental Employees' Retirement System.

Your questions answered by the provisions of Article 3 of Chapter 128 of the General Statutes. Sub-section (19) of Section 128-21 of the General Statutes is as follows:

"Earnable compensation shall mean the full rate of the compensation that would be payable to an employee if he worked the full, normal working time, including any allowance of maintenance or in lieu thereof received by the member."

The first sentence of Paragraph (a) of Sub-section (1) of Section 128-30 of the General Statutes is as follows:

"Each participating employer shall cause to be deducted from the salary of each member on each and every payroll of such employer for each and every payroll period four per centum (4%) of his earnable compensation."

I have examined, read, and reread the whole act on this subject and on this system. The answer to your question is that contributions must be based upon the full amount of the salaries of the member employees. There is no limitation fixed by statute on this particular subject; and the statute is written in mandatory language that four per cent (4%) of a member's earnable compensation must be deducted by the employer, and there is no limitation on the amount. Deductions, therefore, must be based upon the full amount of salaries or other forms of earnable compensation. The Board of Trustees has no authority to change this by regulation because this is definitely fixed by statute, and regulations cannot qualify or nullify statutes when they definitely cover a subject.

LOCAL GOVERNMENTAL EMPLOYEES' RETIREMENT SYSTEM; DEFINITION OF EMPLOYEE; PRIOR SERVICE; NURSES EMPLOYED BY CITY OF CHARLOTTE BUT PAID BY CHARLOTTE COOPERATIVE NURSING ASSOCIATION

18 January 1946

I reply to your letter of January 11, 1946.
Your question is stated as follows:

"All nurses now on the City of Charlotte payroll who were employed prior to July 1, 1937 came under the supervision of the City of Charlotte Health Department but received their compensation from the Charlotte Cooperative Nursing Association, funds for which were put up by the local merchants and clubs.
"Are these nurses, who now wish to become members of and participate in the North Carolina Local Governmental Employees' Retirement System effective February 1, 1946, entitled to credit for prior years service for the time served under the Charlotte Cooperative Nursing Association?"

Prior service is defined in Sub-section 6 of Section 128-21. In Sub-section 5 of this same section, service is defined by reference to Sub-section 3 of the same section which defines employee. An employee under this section is defined as follows:

" 'Employee' shall mean any person who is regularly employed in the service of and whose salary or compensation is paid by the employer as defined in subsection two of this section, whether employed or appointed for stated terms or otherwise, except teachers in the public schools and except such employees who hold office by popular election as are not required to devote a major portion of their time to the duties of their office. *In all cases of doubt the board of trustees shall decide who is an employee.*"

If the Board of Trustees of the Local Governmental Employees' Retirement System shall find as a fact that these nurses were actually employed by the City of Charlotte or one of its administrative agencies and that the City of Charlotte fixed the amount of salary, the conditions and terms of service, and the right to control and direct the service and to terminate the contract of employment, then I do not think that the source of funds or the matter of payment by means of an arrangement with the Charlotte Cooperative Nursing Association would affect the situation; and the nurses would be considered as employees of the City of Charlotte even though paid from a source of funds other than the treasury of the City of Charlotte. I do not find anything in the act that says that the funds by which an employee of a unit is paid must come from the unit's particular treausry or must be tax money or any other type of funds. Conceivably, the City could hire and put many public health nurses on its payroll, and they would be paid by the Rockefeller Foundation of any one of a great number of humanitarian and philanthropic organizations.

On the other hand, if the Board of Trustees shall find as a fact that the nurses were actually employed, paid, and controlled by the Charlotte Cooperative Nursing Association; that the services of the nurses were merely loaned to the City, and that the nurses were, therefore, at all times employees of this Nursing Association, then, of course, such service could not be counted or be valid as prior service. It all depends upon how the Board of Trustees acts upon the facts presented to them. In my opinion this is one of the cases of doubt in which the statute specifically requires the Board of Trustees to decide the matter.

LOCAL GOVERNMENTAL EMPLOYEES' RETIREMENT SYSTEM; PERSONS OUT OF
SERVICE ON LEAVE OF ABSENCE; PERSONS OUT OF SERVICE DRAWING
WORKMEN'S COMPENSATION BENEFITS; RIGHT TO MAKE CON-
TRIBUTION COVERING PERIOD OF ABSENCE; LIABILITY
OF EMPLOYER FOR MATCHING CONTRIBUTION

18 January 1946

You ask this office to give you an opinion upon the following questions:

"(1) After entrance of the City of Charlotte into the North Carolina Local Governmental Employees' Retirement System, are people who are out on compensation or leave of absence entitled to make up their contributions to the Retirement System upon return to duty or during their absence in order to get continuous service?

"(2) Is the City of Charlotte liable for a matching contribution?"

An examination of Article 3 of Chapter 228 of the General Statutes which contains the statutes authorizing the North Carolina Local Governmental Employees' Retirement System discloses that there is no statutory authority whereby an employee as a matter of right can make up his contributions for periods of non-service time because of leave of absence caused by injuries compensated under Workmen's Compensation. There is, likewise, no statute that would compel the employer (the City of Charlotte in this case) to match contributions paid in to cover such periods of absence.

The Board of Trustees of the Retirement System in question has the authority to adopt rules and regulations for the administration of its business and to prevent injustice and inequality which may otherwise arise in the administration of the law. I think the Board of Trustees could establish a system by rules and regulations whereby the persons described in your letter could make up these contributions covering the periods of time represented by their absence from service; but it would have to be done by mutual agreement and consent between the employer and the employee because under the present law the employer cannot be compelled to match contributions under such circumstances. In no case, should it be done or should such contributions be permitted unless it is agreed between the employer and employee that both types of contributions will be made; that is, the employer will make his contribution covering such periods of time as well as the employee. Such a rule or regulation should also fix the earnable compensation basis upon which these contributions will be based. I think that the Board of Trustees should consult the actuary of the system and obtain his opinion as to the effect of such a regulation upon the plan of financing the system before final adoption of same.

LOCAL GOVERNMENTAL EMPLOYEES' RETIREMENT SYSTEM; TEACHERS' AND STATE EMPLOYEES' RETIREMENT SYSTEM; TRANSFER OF MEMBERSHIP FUNDS, AND CREDITS FROM ONE SYSTEM TO ANOTHER

18 January 1946

You inquire of this office if a member of the Teachers' and State Employees' Retirement System goes to work for a local unit that is participating in the North Carolina Local Governmental Employees' Retirement System and desires to become a member of that system, can transfer his funds already accumulated with the Teachers' and State Employees' Retirement System and permit him to become a member of the Local Governmental Employees' Retirement System, or vice versa?

Both of these retirement systems are creatures of statute, and all powers and duties executed by the Board of Trustees in each system must have statutory sanction. There is no statutory authority that permits an exchange of members from one of these systems to another; and there is, likewise, no statutory authority that says that the governing authorities of one system must recognize the membership service accumulated in another system. There is no sanction of law saying that prior service recognized by one system shall be recognized as prior service in another system.

The answer to your question is that these transfers cannot be made under the present status of the law governing both systems.

LOCAL GOVERNMENTAL EMPLOYEES' RETIREMENT SYSTEM; CONTINUITY OF
SERVICE OF VETERANS DISCHARGED AT ONE TIME AND RETURNING
TO EMPLONMENT A PERIOD OF TIME LATER

18 January 1946

In your letter, you ask us to answer the following question:

"Upon entrance of the City of Charlotte into the North Carolina
Local Governmental Employees' Retirement System, a few ex-service
men were discharged at one date and returned a period of time later.
Do they have continuous prior years service credit for this lapse of
time between time of discharge from military duty and return to duty
with the City of Charlotte?"

I think your question is answered by a portion of Section 128-26 of the
General Statutes which is as follows:

"(1) Under such rules and regulations as the board of trustees
shall adopt each member who was an employee at any time during the
year immediately preceding the date of participation of his employer,
and who becomes a member during the first year thereafter, shall file
a detailed statement of all service as an employee rendered by him to
his employer prior to such date of participation for which he claims
credit.
"(2) The board of trustees shall fix and determine by appropriate
rules and regulations how much service in any years is equivalent to
one year of service, but in no case shall more than one year of service
be creditable for all service in one calendar year.
"(3) Subject to the above restrictions and to such other rules and
regulations as the board of trustees may adopt, the board of trustees
shall verify, as soon as practicable after the filing of such statements
of service, the service therein claimed."

If the Board of Trustees of the Local Governmental Employees' Retirement System wish us to regard this as the equivalent of prior service, then
I think it is a matter for them to consider by way of formulating and passing an appropriate regulation. While I am not altogether sure that such
a regulation, which would make the period of time described in your letter
the equivalent of prior service, is invalid, I am by no means certain that it
is valid. You will note that prior service is defined in Section 128-21; and
in this same section, the word "service" is defined; and the word "employee" is also defined. It seems to me that in order for a period of time
to be counted as prior service, there at least should be some time during
this period in which some service is performed for the employer. I would
suggest that if you pass such a regulation counting such periods of time as
prior service that you make the validity of such prior service dependent or
conditioned upon approval of the next General Assembly.

LOCAL GOVERNMENTAL EMPLOYEES' RETIREMENT SYSTEM; PRIOR SERVICE; STATUS OF PERSONS INJURED AND RECEIVING WORKMEN'S COMPENSATION BENEFITS

18 January 1946

You state that there are some employees or persons of the City of Charlotte who were injured at line of duty and are now receiving compensation in the form of benefits paid by virtue of the Workmen's Compensation law. This situation existed before the entrance of the City of Charlotte into the North Carolina Local Governmental Employees' Retirement System.

You inquire of this office if these employees should be given a continuous prior service credit during the period of time while out on compensation.

Your question is answered by the provisions of Section 128-26 of which section I quote a portion as follows:

"(1) Under such rules and regulations as the board of trustees shall adopt each member who was an employee at any time during the year immediately preceding the date of participation of his employer, and who becomes a member during the first year thereafter, shall file a detailed statement of all service as an employee rendered by him to his employer prior to such date of participation for which he claims credit.

"(2) The board of trustees shall fix and determine by appropriate rules and regulations how much service in any year is equivalent to one year of service, but in no case shall more than one year of service be creditable for all service in one calendar year.

"(3) Subject to the above restrictions and to such other rules and regulations as the board of trustees may adopt, the board of trustees shall verify, as soon as practicable after the filing of such statements of service, the service therein claimed."

It is a question for the Board of Trustees by the regular rules and regulations to determine this question. If the individual in question was out of service or did not perform any services for the City for a whole calendar year or for the majority of the time in the calendar year, then I do not think that I would count this time as continuous service in my regulation. On the other hand, if the individual in question worked and performed services for the City of Charlotte for the majority of the time of the calendar year, then I think I would count such service as continuous. It is a question for the Board of Trustees to determine how much service in any year is equivalent to one year of service. I think we should also remember that when we enlarge prior service, we are creating greater liability against the funds of the system.

LOCAL GOVERNMENTAL EMPLOYEES' RETIREMENT SYSTEM; ELIGIBILITY FOR MEMBERSHIP OF PERSONS WHO HAVE CEASED TO BE MEMBERS OF THE LAW ENFORCEMENT OFFICERS BENEFIT AND RETIREMENT FUND

30 January 1946

In your letter of inquiry you call attention to the definition of membership in the Local Governmental Employees' Retirement System as set forth in Section 128-24 of the General Statutes. You further call attention to the fact that we have heretofore ruled that persons who are members of the Law Enforcement Officers Benefit and Retirement Fund cannot at the same time be members of the Local Governmental Employees' Retirement System.

You inquire as to the eligibility of a person for membership in the Local Governmental Employees' Retirement System who has formerly been a member of the Law Enforcement Officers Benefit and Retirement Fund and has withdrawn from that system.

The rules and regulations of the Law Enforcement Officers Benefit and Retirement Fund, as adopted on June 29, 1945, contained the following sections as to membership and withdrawing from membership of that retirement system:

"(4) Should the contributions of any member be more than months in arrears, or should a member cease to be a law enforcement officer, or should he withdraw his contributions, or die or retire under the provisions of the Fund, he shall thereupon cease to be a member; except that a member who ceases to be a law enforcement officer and does not withdraw his contributions may, by notifying the Board, maintain his membership for not more than one year after ceasing to be a law enforcement officer, but during such absence from service no contributions shall be paid and no benefit other than that provided for under Section 5, Subsections (9) and (10), of these Rules and Regulations be payable.

"(5) Anything in these Rules and Regulations to the contrary notwithstanding, any member who ceases to be a law enforcement officer to enter the service of the United States in a time of war and who becomes a law enforcement officer within six months of his honorable discharge from such service, is allowed credit for a pension from the Courts Account equal to the same pension to which he would be entitled had he remained a contributing member at the same salary which he was receiving at the time of entering such service. If he so desires, he may pay monthly contributions while in the Armed Forces on the Basis of his rate of contributions at the time of entering such service; or he may, within six months of being honorably discharged from such service, make up contributions for the period of absence in such service."

It seems to me that if a person has been a member of the Law Enforcement Officers Benefit and Retirement Fund and has legally and properly ceased to be a member as provided by the rules and regulations of that retirement system, then and in that event I see no reason why such person would not be eligible to become a member of the Local Governmental Employees' Retirement System, assuming, of course, that he is employed by an employer covered under the Local Governmental Employees' Retirement System and that he is an employee as defined in such system.

If you have occasion to deal with such situations, I would recommend that you have the executive secretary or proper officer of the Law Enforcement Officers Benefit and Retirement Fund to certify to you that the persons in question have ceased to be members of the Law Enforcement Officers Benefit and Retirement Fund. I do not think that you should accept any persons as members of the system or receive any contributions until your retirement system is protected by such a certificate or letter of information.

ELIGIBILITY OF MEMBERS OF THE CHARLOTTE POLICE DEPARTMENT TO BELONG
TO BOTH THE LAW ENFORCEMENT OFFICERS RETIREMENT SYSTEM AND THE
LOCAL GOVERNMENTAL EMPLOYEES' RETIREMENT SYSTEM

11 February 1946

You have already received a letter from Mr. John D. Shaw, Attorney for
the City of Charlotte, setting forth the five propositions or procedures which
we agreed to follow in order to determine the question of whether or not the
policemen of the City of Charlotte are eligible to belong to the Local Governmental Employees' Retirement System and at the same time belong to
the Law Enforcement Officers' Retirement System.

As I recall at the meeting, I was to confer with the Attorney General; and
we were to decide the question as to whether we would advise the trustees
of the North Carolina Local Governmental Employees' Retirement System
if they had the power and authority to agree to those propositions as em-
bodied in Mr. Shaw's letter. We have discussed the matter, and the Attorney General and myself are of the opinion that under the provisions of
Section 128-28 of the General Statutes, as amended, and especially under
Subsection (6) of said section, the Board of Trustees of the Local Governmental Employees' Retirement System has the legal authority and power
to enter into an agreement to follow the procedures set forth in Mr. Shaw's
letter. We, therefore, advise further that the Board of Trustees should adopt
a resolution incorporating these procedures and agreements set forth in
Mr. Shaw's letter; and they should further incorporate in the resolution a
statement to the effect that if. a decision from the Supreme Court decides
that the policemen of the City of Charlotte are, and at all times were,
eligible to belong to the North Carolina Local Governmental Employees'
Retirement System, then in that event, the policemen of the City of Charlotte shall be entitled to be members of said system with all rights as to prior
service, membership service, rights to retirement, and any or all other
beneficial rights of said system.

I am sending a copy of Mr. Shaw's letter and this letter to the Honorable
Charles M. Johnson, Chairman of the Board of Trustees for his information.
I am also sending a copy of this letter to Mr. John D. Shaw for his information. Please have the Board of Trustees pass on this matter as soon as
reasonably convenient.

RETIREMENT SYSTEM; PRIOR SERVICE; BOARD OF COSMETIC ART

12 February 1946

You state in your letter that in 1943 the North Carolina State Board of
Cosmetic Art was placed under the direction of the Budget Bureau. Apparently since the Board of Cosmetic Art was placed under the Budget Bureau, the salaries of their inspectors and agents approved by the director of
the budget, its budget made subject to the approval of the director of the
budget, and all fees and collections turned over to the State Treasurer, it

has been considered to be a bona fide State agency and no question arises as to its status since 1943.

You inquire of this office as to the status of the North Carolina State Board of Cosmetic Art prior to the year of 1943 and in especially to July 1943, your particular question being as to whether or not this Board should be considered as a State agency at such prior time; and the answer to this question also answers the question as to whether three persons who are full-time employees of the Board would be entitled to prior service under the Teachers' and State Employees' Retirement System.

An examination of our Public Laws discloses that the first act to regulate the practice of Cosmetic Art in this State appears as Chapter 179 of the Public Laws of 1933. This basic act was amended in 1935, 1941 and in 1943. Certain rather sweeping amendments were made as to the fiscal control and management of the Board. At all times, however, the Board has had certain regulatory powers as to registration, granting certificates of registration, and as to the revocation of these certificates for statutory reasons. The Board has at all times exercised certain statutory powers granted to them by the Legislature of North Carolina; and in this respect, there has been delegated to them certain sovereign powers of the State.

We answer your question, therefore, that in our opinion this Board has at all times been an agency of the State of North Carolina and that its full-time employees are entitled to prior credits as authorized and provided by Chapter 135 of the General Statutes, the same being the law setting up the Teachers' and State Employees' Retirement System.

TEACHERS' AND STATE EMPLOYEES' RETIREMENT SYSTEM;
ELIGIBILITY FOR PRIOR SERVICE

8 March 1946

Reference is made to your letter of March 1, 1946 in which you state the following:

"Under Section 3, Membership, of Chapter 25, Public Laws 1941, the question has arisen as to when a teacher is eligible for prior service credit. Is it necessary for a teacher or a State employee to be em. ployed between 1936 and 1941 and also during the year 1941-1942 to be eligible for prior service credit? This question is giving this office a good deal of concern and we will appreciate very much the clarification of this section of the law by you.

"For example, a teacher was employed during the years 1936 to April 15, 1941 and is not employed any more until September, 1944. Would this person be entitled to credit for prior service?"

To be eligible for prior employment, one must be a member of the Re. tirement System. Membership is fixed by Section 135-3 of the General Statutes. Creditable service under the Retirement Act is made up of prior service plus membership service. Creditable service is defined in Section 135-4 of the General Statutes. Your attention is called to subsection (1) of Section 135-4 which fixes the conditions under which prior service is al. lowed. These conditions are (a) the member must be a teacher or State employee at any time during the five years immediately preceding the establishment of the System, and (b) the member must become a member of the System during the first year of operation of the Retirement System. The date of the establishment of the System is fixed by Section 135-2, and you will see in the last sentence of the first paragraph of this section that the Retirement System is established as of the first day of July, 1941. There is no statute that I have been able to find that defines or explains the term "first year of operation." It is true that Section 135-13 of the General Statutes provides that no benefits can be paid under the Act nor can any compulsory retirement be allowed until the end of one year following the date of the establishment of the System; but, in my opinion, the first year of operation begins with the date of the establishment on July 1, 1941 and extends to July 1, 1946. The System was actually operating, collecting contributions, the trustees had organized, the office employees were functioning; and it seems to me that this would be the first year of operation regardless of the fact that retirements and payments of benefits were postponed until one year after the date of establishment.

Your attention is further called to the fact that after a person becomes a member, it is apparent that such person remains a member unless he dies, withdraws his accumulated contributions or is absent from service more than five years in any period of six consecutive years after becoming a member.

Applying these statutes to the situation set forth in your letter, it appears that this teacher was employed during the years of 1936 to April 15, 1941. She, therefore, became a member of the System by virtue of subsection (3) of Section 135-3. She retained her membership in the System because she was not absent for a period of more than five years in a period of six consecutive years, appearing from your letter that she was employed again in September 1944. Having retained her membership by. virtue of this saving clause although deductions and contributions were not made, she has the right of being a member of the System during the first year. Such a membership preserves to a person the legal status of being a member regardless of the fact that no contributions or deductions are made; and by virtue of this saving clause, I am of the opinion that the conditions relating to prior service have been met by this person, and she is entitled to credit for her prior service if the Board of Trustees shall find that her verified statement of service is correct.

TEACHERS' AND STATE EMPLOYEES' RETIREMENT SYSTEM; BIBLE TEACHER IN SCHOOLS OF CITY OF CHARLOTTE; ELIGIBILITY FOR MEMBERSHIP

11 April 1946

You enclosed with your letter a copy of a letter received from H. P. Harding, Superintendent of Charlotte City Schools. Mr. Harding states in substance that Bible teachers in Charlotte are paid from funds that are contributed by the Missionary Union of the Protestant Churches of the City. These funds cover all the salaries of the Bible teachers. Money is collected and turned over to the treasurer of the School Board, and the salary checks are sent out from the office of the administrative unit. The checks are signed by the treasurer of the Board. It is stated that the School Board assumes no financial responsibility for the course, but credit is given for the work towards graduation. Mr. Harding also states that the course has been given for a period of twenty years.

You would like to know whether or not the Bible teachers employed by the City of Charlotte in their schools would be eligible for membership in the Teachers' and State Employees' Retirement System.

In a letter dated June 1, 1945, written to the Chairman of the Board of Trustees of the Goldsboro Graded Schools in discussing the subject of Bible teachers in public schools, the Attorney General said:

> "Under the statute, it is definitely the responsibility of principals to nominate the teachers and they are elected only in the manner provided by law. This would be applicable as much to the teacher who became a member of the staff of the school under the circumstances petitioned for as any other teacher. Such teacher would also be entitled to the benefits of the Teachers' and State Employees' System, and, in case of injury by accident arising out of and in the course of employment, would be entitled to Workmen's Compensation. Provision is made, as you know, for sick leave for teachers, which might likewise be involved in such an arrangement. Such teacher would, of course, have to have a certificate and comply with all other requirements of law to become a member of the teaching force of the school. The State Board of Education is given the authority to approve all school budgets and, if such an arrangement is made, it should be dealt with in the budget and approved by the State Board of Education, G. S. 115-363, 115-365. * * * From what has been said, we see that the matter of receiving donations from a group of people to be applied and used for the purpose of paying the salary of a teacher in the public schools is not supported by any express provisions of the statute and, if done, would involve the complications connected with the retirement, sick leave, liability for Workmen's Compensation and certainly the approval of the State Board of Education as a part of the budget of the school. I find no case which throws any light upon this question and you will appreciate, I am sure, that I cannot furnish you any categorical answer to it."

If the funds donated by the Missionary Union of the Protestant Churches of the City are added into the School Budget as other funds and the Bible teachers are regularly employed and paid as other teachers, I am of the opinion, therefore, that such teachers are eligible to be members of the Teachers' and State Employees' Retirement System; and as said by the Attorney General, the school system of the City of Charlotte will have to assume the liability of contributing to the Retirement System on behalf of such teachers; and such teachers are entitled to the benefits of sick leave coverage under Workmen's Compensation and all the other privileges of any other teacher.

TEACHERS' AND STATE EMPLOYEES' RETIREMENT SYSTEM; MEMBERSHIP
SERVICE; CONTRIBUTIONS COVERING TIME SPENT IN MILITARY SERVICE

21 May 1946

You state that Mr. J. P. Jenrette was employed at Burgaw, Pender County, as a teacher from 1935-1938. He was also employed from 1938 to May 1941, at a salary of $135.00 per month at Washington, North Carolina. You did not say whether the Washington, North Carolina, employment was in State service or not, but for the sake of answering your letter, I will assume that it was also in State service. You further state that this man was employed by the Department of Agriculture in a temporary capacity from July 1941 to February 1942. He entered the Navy in March 1943, and served until February 2, 1946. I assume that this temporary employment with the Department of Agriculture was with the Department of Agriculture of our State and not for the Department of Agriculture of the United States. However, you state that Mr. Jenrette has no membership service to his credit, but that your inquiry pertains to whether or not he will be permitted to make payment for the time he was in military service so that he will not lose credit for the time that he has been away toward retirement.

I cannot see that Mr. Jenrette is entitled to any prior service because he cannot meet the conditions of Section 135-4 of the General Statutes in that he was not a member and did not become a member during the first operation of the Retirement System. It is also doubtful that he has had any five years immediately preceding the establishment of the system in which he was employed in State service for that length of time, that is creditable State service. I thought I had better comment on this fact in spite of the fact that you say he has no membership service to his credit.

It is true that teachers and State employees who have previously established prior service in the system, and who entered the armed services of the United States after September 16, 1940, and prior to February 17, 1941, and who return to the service of the State after they have been honorably discharged from the armed services, shall be entitled to full credit for all prior service. See subsection (6) of Section 135-4 of the General Statutes. I don't see, however, that this can help Mr. Jenrette because he never at any time had any prior service.

Since Mr. Jenrette was not a member before he went into the service, we cannot give him the advantage of subsection (3) of Section 135-3 of the General Statutes which allows any member to be absent for at least five years in a period of six consecutive years.

You are also familiar with the fact that subsection (e) of Section 135-8, provides that a member, that is a person who has the status of a member, can have a leave of absence for military services, and upon his return can make his contributions and bring his account up to date, but I cannot see where Mr. Jenrette can avail himself of this provision. I would like to help this man in any way possible, but I cannot find anything in the retirement law for his relief because he has never been a member of the service until now, as I assume he now is a member or you would not be making this inquiry.

Local Governmental Employees' Retirement System; Eligibility of Employees of Board of Light and Water Commissioners of Concord, North Carolina

31 May 1946

In your letter of May 21, 1946 you refer to Chapter 71 of the Private Laws of 1905 creating the Board of Light and Water Commissioners of Concord, North Carolina; and you inquire of this office whether or not the employees of this Board are eligible to participate in the North Carolina Local Governmental Employees' Retirement System as employees of the City of Concord.

A reference to Chapter 71 of the Private Laws of 1905 shows that the Board of Light and Water Commissioners of the City of Concord was created by an act which amends the charter of the Town of Concord. The mayor of Concord is ex-officio chairman of this Board, and the aldermen of the City of Concord appoint the commissioners constituting the Board and fill all vacancies occurring in the membership of the Board. The Board's right to hold property is stated in this language:

"And said Board of Commissioners shall, for the City of Concord, take and hold the land, real estate, rights, franchises and property of every kind now owned by said City of Concord or that may hereafter be purchased, for the purpose of operating and maintaining a system of water works and lights for said City."

The Board has a right to issue and sell bonds and operates as a corporation. Many cities and towns have a mere department that performs these same functions, and I am forced to the conclusion that the City of Concord has merely incorporated into a board what is usually carried on in a separate department of the municipal government.

In the case of HUNTER v. THE RETIREMENT SYSTEM, 224 N. C. 359, the Wilmington Public Library was created by a private act. The Board of Aldermen of the City of Wilmington elected the trustees who controlled and operated the library, and likewise filled all vacancies in the library's Board of Trustees. The trustees appointed by the city councilmen f Wilmington executed absolute authority and control over the library, its ersonnel, payment of salaries and policies of operation. In holding the ibrary to be a mere agency of the City of Wilmington and that its employees ere entitled to participate in the City of Wilmington's Retirement System, he Supreme Court said:

"The law under which the library is created makes its establishment mandatory upon the city government, and the city is obeying the mandate of the law when it pursues the method it has pursued in establishing and operating the library. The Wilmington Public Library as created and operated is but an agent of the council of the city of Wilmington to carry out the mandate of the law. The library is entirely dependent upon city government for its functioning and very existence. Since the Wilmington Public Library is but an agent of the City of Wilmington, under its complete control, it follows that the employees of the library are employees of the city."

I am of the opinion that the Board of Light and Water Commissioners

of the City of Concord is a mere appendage or agency of the City of Concord. It was created for the express purpose of performing certain specific
municipal functions for the City, that is the operation of the city's Water
System and Light System. These functions are ordinarily operated in most
cities and towns as a mere department of the municipal government. I am
of the opinion, therefore, that the employees of the Board of Light and
Water Commissioners of the City of Concord are entitled to participate in
the North Carolina Local Governmental Employees' Retirement System and
that the City of Concord, if it becomes an employer under this System,
should make the deductions from the salaries of these employees and should
pay the funds necessary to match these deductions according to the law
creating the Retirement System here under consideration. In reporting the
employees of the Board of Light and Water Commissioners of the City of
Concord, they should be reported as if they were on the direct payroll of
the City of Concord.

TEACHERS' AND STATE EMPLOYEES' RETIREMENT SYSTEM; DISABILITY
RETIREMENT BENEFITS; TIME WHEN DISABILITY RETIREMENT
BENEFITS TO MEMBERS BEGIN TO BE PAID; POSSIBILITY OF
RETROACTIVE PAYMENT OF BENEFITS

6 June 1946

Your inquiry refers to Section 135-5 of the General Statutes, and more
particularly to subsection (3), (4) et seq., dealing with disability retirement
benefits. You would like to know if disability retirement benefits can be
paid retroactively to the date of the beginning of the disability which brought
about the eligibility for the benefits.

This might be stated in another way, and that is, after it has been adjudicated or adjudged that a member is entitled to retire because of disability,
can that member be paid retirement allowances from the date the actual
disability began, or must the retirement allowance be paid from the date
that it is determined that the member is entitled to disability retirement.

You will see from subsection (3) of Section 135-5 of the General Statutes
that after a member has had ten or more years of creditable service upon
application, he may be retired by the Board of Trustees for "not less than
thirty and not more than ninety days next following the date of filing such
application, on a disability retirement allowance." It is also provided that
the Medical Board after a medical examination of such member, shall certify that the member is mentally or physically incapacitated for the performance of his duty, and that such incapacity is likely to be permanent.

You will see under subsection (4) of this same section that "Upon retirement for disability a member shall receive a service allowance etc." It is
plain, therefore, that the retirement allowance because of disability cannot
be paid until after the member retires. In the preceding section it is shown
that he must make his application and can then be retired "not less than
thirty and not more than ninety days next following the date he filed such
application." Retirement allowances, therefore, can only be paid after

retirement. The disability which produces the retirement may have existed for some considerable period prior to the actual time of filing the application and the adjudication that the member is entitled to disability retirement benefits. There is no provision of law that authorizes or allows your Board of Trustees to pay such benefits retroactively to the date of the beginning of the disability. In fact, if your Board did so, it would be making payment of benefits over a period of time when such person had not retired and had not even filed an application for benefits.

I am of the opinion, therefore, that you can only pay such benefits after the application has been allowed and it has been determined that the member is entitled to disability retirement allowances.

TEACHERS' AND STATE EMPLOYEES' RETIREMENT SYSTEM; SERVICE MEMBERSHIP SERVICE; LEAVE OF ABSENCE FOR MILITARY SERVICE; ELIGIBILITY FOR PRIOR SERVICE

6 June 1946

From a letter of Mr. R. Bruce Etheridge, Director of Conservation and Development, enclosed with your letter, it appears that Mr. F. H. Claridge has now returned to the Department of Conservation and Development from Military Service and took up his duties as Assistant Forester on January 15, 1946. It appears that he was absent from June 6, 1933, to August 1, 1937. During this period he was on leave of absence from the Department as Director of the North Carolina Civilian Conservation Corps. He was under the supervision of the State Forester of the State Department, but was paid from Federal funds. He now desires to pay into the retirement fund the amount necessary to cover his military absence.

You would like to know if it is in accordance with the retirement system law for this man to be credited with prior service or is his service between the dates above-stated, or in other words, you would like to know if you would be permitted to recognize the leave of absence and give credit for the four years that Mr. Claridge was serving in the employment of the Federal Government. The conditions under which the prior service is allowed to be credited to the service account of a member of the Teachers' and State Employees' Retirement System are set forth in Section 135-4 of the General Statutes. Nothing but actual service for the state can be allowed. There is no system or plan in the statute whereby a person can be granted a leave of absence for prior service, and in fact such a concept of prior service has never been contemplated. All that can be credited to the account of the member is actual service in behalf of the State of North Carolina.

As you know, creditable service under this system is composed of two types of service: (a) membership service, and (b) prior service. You will find under subsection (10) of Section 135-1 of the General Statutes that prior service is service rendered prior to the date of the establishment of the system, and you will find in subsection (11) of this same section that membership service is service rendered the state as a state employee after the establishment of the system or, that is, while one is a member of the retirement system.

It is true that subsection (e) of Section 135-8 allows the person who has a leave of absence for Military Service to make up his contributions after he returns to state service on the basis of the salary he was receiving when the leave of absence was granted. This applies, however, only to a leave of absence *after the person becomes a member of the system*. There is no provision of law which permits the Board of Trustees to allow a member to make up or fill in gaps in his prior service record.

I am sorry that I cannot give you a favorable opinion on such a case as this and I have examined the law with particularity in order not to do this man an injustice. I am of the opinion, however, that his request in this matter cannot be legally allowed, and you are so advised.

TEACHERS' AND STATE EMPLOYEES' RETIREMENT SYSTEM; RIGHT OF MEMBER PREVIOUSLY SEPARATED FROM SERVICE TO DEPOSIT CONTRIBUTIONS COVERING PERIOD OF ABSENCE; RIGHTS OF MEMBER UPON RE-EMPLOYMENT AFTER ABSENCE FROM SERVICE

12 June 1946

You will recall that some time ago you left your file containing the records of your office on the case of Miss Amanda Davenport, and you asked us to review the file and advise you concerning the case.

In her letter to the Retirement System, dated October 26, 1945, Miss Davenport states that she resigned from the service of the Unemployment Compensation Commission on October 1, 1942 in order to accept a position with the United States Employment Service. Her services for the U.S.E.S. were to be and were performed in the State of North Carolina. Miss Davenport states that she did not withdraw her accumulated contributions from the treasury of the Retirement System and that she remained with the U.S.E.S. until October 1, 1945 at which time she was again re-employed by the Unemployment Compensation Commission of North Carolina; and, of course, she is now again covered by the Retirement System Act and is again a member of the System. She states that she has applied to the Federal Government for a refund of any money that she has paid into the Federal Retirement System, and she wants to use any refund that she may be granted from the Federal Retirement System in the form of contributions to the State System in order to make up the three years that she was absent from the State System.

The file indicates some considerable correspondence on this question. Miss Davenport makes a point that at the time she left State Employment, she was on the promotional register of the State Merit System; (See Chapter 126 of the General Statutes) and she is of the opinion that the position offered her by the U.S.E.S. should be considered as a mere promotion and a transfer because she was employed; and her promotions and transfers are governed by the rules and regulations promulgated by the Merit System Council. She states that she was advised by her supervisor of the Unemployment Compensation Commission that it would be necessary for her to submit a letter of resignation in order to accept the position with the Employment Service; and according to this advice, she submitted the letter of resignation which merely stated her intention to accept the position of interviewer with the U.S.E.S. She further states that she was advised by Dr. W. R. Curtis that she should let her accumulated contributions remain with the State System and that she would be able then to pay up her contributions when she returned to State service. She contends that her resignation from State service was only a technical one since her accumulated sick leave was transferred to the U.S.E.S.; and there are other indications that her change in status should be considered as a mere transfer. She makes a further point that the Employment Service, under the law, is a division of the Unemployment Compensation Commission; and, therefore, they are one and the same organization. It is further contended that she had full re-employment rights as is shown by her reinstatement by the Unemployment Compensation Commission at the top of her grade as interviewer which reinstatement was approved by the Assistant Director of the Budget. This perhaps summarizes the most important contentions made by this employee as to why in her opinion she should be allowed to pay up the contributions covering the period of her absence from the State System.

Subsection (e) of Section 135-8 of the General Statutes authorizes the Board of Trustees to accept monthly contributions of a member who is on leave of absence because of military service or for any other purpose which would tend to increase the efficiency of the service of the member to his or her employer.

Subsection (4), Section 135-3 of the General Statutes (Chapter 799, Session Laws of 1945) provides in substance that those employees of the State who were taken over and required to perform services for the Federal Government on a loan basis and by virtue of an executive order of the President of the United States effective on January 1, 1942, should still be deemed to be members of the Retirement System during the period of Federal service; and that after cessation of the Federal service and within a period of six months after such cessation, such person, if employed again by the State, should be considered as a member of the System and should be allowed to deposit contributions for the period of time during which they were absent from State service.

Other than the two types of situations mentioned above, I do not know of any law or statute that will allow Miss Davenport to make contributions covering the period of her absence from State service. It may be true that she looks upon the matter from her point of view as a mere transfer; but the fact remains that she submitted a resignation and separated from the service of the Unemployment Compensation Commission. After that time, she was employed by a Federal agency, and she was paid Federal funds by means of Federal salary vouchers. It is true that there is a law on the statute books saying that the State Employment Service is a part of the Unemployment Compensation Commission, but this law has been superseded by the executive order of the President transferring all the functions of that division to the Federal Government; and this appropriation of State agency by the President under his war powers has for the time being dispensed with the State Employment Service entirely. The fact that Miss Davenport was employed under the State Merit System and that this same Merit System was recognized by the U.S.E.S. is, of course, not controlling. The U.S.E.S. recognizes the registers of the State Merit System as a voluntary act and was not compelled to do so for the simple reason that the overall authority controlling the U.S.E.S. was the War Manpower Commission.

I have been unable to find any statute or law that would allow me to advise the Board of Trustees that they could agree with Miss Davenport's contentions in this matter. If it is said that such an opinion is highly technical, then I must say in reply that the whole Retirement System Act is nothing but a system of technicalities. In fact, any law is technical; and in this respect, the Retirement System Act does not deal in technicalities to any greater extent than the Unemployment Compensation Law or the Laws and regulations governing the Merit System and the U.S.E.S.

It is with great regret that I cannot agree with these contentions as I am personally acquainted with Miss Amanda Davenport; and in my opinion, she is a good employee and a competent person. I am compelled, however, to say that under the present status of the law, she cannot deposit contributions with the Board of Trustees for the period of her absence when she was employed by the U.S.E.S.

OPINIONS TO DEPARTMENT OF MOTOR VEHICLES

V. P. LOFTIS COMPANY. MOTOR VEHICLES; REGISTRATION OF VEHICLES
USED BY N. C. OWNER IN 2 OR MORE STATES

13 July 1944

You have requested my opinion upon the following matter.

V. P. Loftis, trading as V. P. Loftis Company, has his residence and principal place of business in Charlotte, North Carolina. Mr. Loftis is engaged in the contracting business. He maintains a division office in Charleston, South Carolina, which was established in 1942. The division office is under the supervision of a manager living in Charleston and several persons are employed at the Charleston office. A warehouse is maintained in Charleston in connection with the office for the storage of equipment. Some projects and jobs are carried through by the Charleston office as a unit and the Charleston manager shares in the profits of such projects and jobs. All drafts are paid by the Charlotte office where general supervision of the whole business of V. P. Loftis Company is centered.

In 1942 V. P. Loftis Company purchased from a Charlotte motor company a number of Ford dump trucks. These trucks were licensed in North Carolina for the last quarter of 1942 and then driven to Charleston where they have since been under the supervision and control of the South Carolina office. Subsequently these trucks were used on projects in Florida and Georgia and in April 1944 were driven to a project being performed by the V. P. Loftis Company at the Winston-Salem airport. Before the trucks were moved into North Carolina at this time, South Carolina licenses were obtained for them.

You were of the opinion that V. P. Loftis Company was liable for North Carolina license tags on account of its use of these trucks on the Winston-Salem airport project. However, V. P. Loftis Company contends that these trucks had acquired a business situs in South Carolina and were lawfully entitled to be operated in this State under the South Carolina licenses that had been acquired for them. You request my opinion upon which view is correct.

General Statutes, Sec. 20-50, provides that "every owner of a vehicle intended to be operated upon any highway of this State and required by this article to be registered shall, before the same is so operated, apply to the Department for and obtain the registration thereof, the registration plates therefor, and a certificate of title therefor, and attach the registration plates to the vehicle, except when an owner is permitted to operate a vehicle under the registration provisions relating to . . . non-residents. . . ."

General Statutes, Sec. 20-38 (s), defines "non-resident" as "every person who is not a resident of this State."

General Statutes, Sec. 20-38 (t), defines "owner" as follows:

"(t) *Owner.*—A person who holds the legal title of a vehicle or, in the event a vehicle is subject to an agreement for conditional sale or lease thereof, with the right of purchase upon performance of the conditions stated in the agreement and with the immediate right of possession vested in the original vendee or lessee; or, in the event a mortgagor of a veh.cle is entitled to possession, then such conditional vendee or lessee or mortgagor shall be deemed the owner for the purpose of this article."

General Statutes, Sec. 20-83, which relates to the registration of non residents, provides as follows:

"Sec. 20-23. *Registration by non-residents.*—(a) Nonresidents of this state, except as otherwise provided in this article, will be exempt from the provisions of this article as to the registration of motor vehicles for the same time and to the same extent as like exemptions are granted residents of this state under laws of another state, district or territory; Provided, that they shall have complied with the provisions of the law of the state, district or territory of their residence relative to the registration and equipment of their motor vehicles, and shall conspicuously display the registration plates as required thereby, and have in their possession the registration certificates issued for such motor vehicles, *and that nothing herein contained shall be construed to permit a bona fide resident of this state to use any registration plate or plates from a foreign state, district or territory, under the provisions of this section.* The commissioner shall determine what exemptions the non-resident vehicle operators of the several states, districts or territories, are entitled to under the provisions of this section, and ordain and publish rules and regulations for making effective the provisions of this section, which rules and regulations shall be observed and enforced by all the officers of this state whose duties require the enforcement of the automobile registration laws, and any violations of such rules and regulations shall constitute a misdemeanor." (Italics added.)

The effect of the statutes referred to above is to require of every owner (in this case V. P. Loftis, trading as V. P. Loftis Company) intending to operate a vehicle upon the highways of this State to secure proper registration for the same unless exemption from registration is granted by General Statutes, Sec. 20-83, relating to the registration of non-residents. If the trucks in question are legally to be treated as trucks of a resident of North Carolina, they are clearly subject to registration when used in this State. If, however, they are to be legally treated as the trucks of a non-resident, V. P. Loftis Company contends that they are exempt from registration under the reciprocity agreement between this State and the State of South Carolina.

You will note that General Statutes, Section 20-50, requires registration by the owner of the vehicle and that General Statutes, Section 20-38(t) would define the owner of the trucks in question as V. P. Loftis Company since the legal title to them is in V. P. Loftis Company. Since registration is required of the legal owners of vehicles it seems clear that the references to "non-residents" and "residents" mean resident owners or non-resident owners as the case may be. It is not disputed that V. P. Loftis is a resident of North Carolina and since he owns the business he is a resident owner of the vehicles. Therefore, in my opinion, V. P. Loftis Company is not entitled to the reciprocity provisions provided for by General Statutes, Section 20-83.

I should like to point out that the motor vehicle laws of this State do not provide that vehicles having a commercial or business situs in another state may be treated as non-resident vehicles.

I, therefore, find no basis in the law for treating the vehicles in question as non-resident vehicles.

SEIZURE OF LICENSE PLATES TO FORCE PAYMENT OF LICENSE FEES DUE IN PRIOR YEARS

26 July 1944

You inquire whether the Commissioner of Motor Vehicles has authority summarily to take possession of license plates issued to commercial vehicles in order to enforce the payment of license fees due by the owners of such vehicles for operations in prior years. You state that on occasions due to error on the part of rate clerks or to other things, such vehicles are rated lower than is proper and the correct amount of the license fees for such year is not ascertained until the next license year.

Section .27(a) of the Motor Vehicle Act (G. S. Sec. 20-63) authorizes the Commissioner of Motor Vehicles to seize any registration plate which he believes is being illegally used. If the operator has paid all tax due for the current year, it is my opinion that his registration plates are not being illegally used within the meaning of this statute merely because he owes additional license fees for a prior year.

I, therefore, conclude that payment of these back taxes must be enforced in some other way than by seizing license plates which have been issued for the current year.

FEDERAL TAX ON TRANSPORTATION OF PROPERTY; SHIPMENTS TO STATE EXEMPT

15 August 1944

You inquire whether federal tax on amounts paid for the transportation of property imposed in Section 3475 of the Internal Revenue Code is applicable to shipments made to or from the State of North Carolina.

Subsection (b) of Section 3475 of the Internal Revenue Code contains the following language, which is effective on and after June 1, 1944:

"(b) *Exemption of Government Transportation.* The tax imposed under this section shall not apply to (1) amounts paid for the transportation of property to or from the government of a state, territory of the United States, or political subdivision thereof. . . ."

This provision, in my opinion, exempts from the tax any amount paid by the State itself for the transportation of property, and also any amount paid by a shipper for the transportation of property to the State. I would like to point out, however, that I have no authority to render official opinions on the applicability of Federal laws, and for the reason I suggest that you procure a ruling on this question from the office of the U. S. Collector of Internal Revenue in Greensboro, North Carolina.

MOTOR VEHICLES; PENALTY FOR OPERATING A "FOR HIRE" TRUCK
WITH PRIVATE LICENSE; CONTINUOUS OFFENSE

20 March 1945

You request that I give you my opinion upon the following question.

Party "A" is operating his truck with private license and is apprehended for performing a "for hire" operation. He is cited to purchase "for hire" license and in accordance with the citation pays a $25.00 penalty and the "for hire" license fee, but refuses to accept the "for hire" license plate, preferring to continue to operate on the private license plate. If this party is again apprehended operating for hire, should the penalty and "for hire" license fees be collected again, or does the fact that he has paid the prescribed license for a "for hire" operation preclude the department from collecting further "for hire" fees?

Section 50 of the Motor Vehicle Act of 1937 (G. S. 20-86), provides that "any person, firm, or corporation operating vehicles for hire without having paid the tax prescribed *or* using private plates on such vehicles shall be liable for an additional tax of twenty-five dollars ($25.00) for each vehicle in addition to the normal fees prescribed for 'for hire' vehicles." (Italics added.)

In view of the above provision, it is my opinion that the Department of Motor Vehicles is not authorized to collect the regular annual "for hire" license fees more than once for each vehicle regardless of whether or not the proper license plates are displayed on the same. However, if an operator continues to use private plates on a vehicle, which should carry "for hire" plates, I think he may be required to pay the $25.00 penalty each time he is apprehended in the act of using such illegal plates. You will note that the statute quoted above makes illegal the operation without having paid the "for hire" tax *or* the "for hire" operation with the use of private plates. In my opinion, the law contemplates that a vehicle must carry the type of tag prescribed for the particular operation in which it is engaged. Thus, the fact that the operator has been apprehended once and, as a result, paid the penalty, does not entitle him to continue to evade the law for the remainder of the license year, but each violation of the law would constitute a separate and new offense.

STATE HIGHWAY PATROL; AUTHORITY IN MAKING ARRESTS; HB 765

29 March 1945

House Bill number 765, enacted at the last General Assembly, ratified on March 21, 1945, provides that members of the State Highway Patrol, in addition to the duties, power and authority hereinbefore given, shall have the authority throughout the State of North Carolina of any police officer in respect to making arrests for any crimes committed in their presence and shall have authority to make arrests for any crime committed on any highway and shall have the right of any peace officer in making arrests when called upon by the sheriff of any county or chief of police of any municipality.

It seems to me that it would be desirable that members of the Highway Patrol, in making arrests when called upon by the sheriff of any county or chief of police of any municipality, should have some written request from the sheriff or chief of police. The statute does not require that this written request be made but if the member of the Highway Patrol had the request in writing, he would have evidence of his authority which would protect him in the event he received any injury while engaged in the performance of his duty, under the Workmen's Compensation Laws or the Officers' Benefit and Retirement Fund. If the officer at the time of making the arrest requested by the sheriff or chief of police does not have time to get the request in writing, he could get it after the service had been performed so that he would have a sufficient written record of the transaction.

I believe that you would find that if such policy was followed, any question as to the authority of the patrolman in making the arrest under such circumstances would be removed, to the advantage of your department and the patrolman concerned.

STATE HIGHWAY PATROL; DUTY OF JAILER TO RECEIVE PERSONS ARRESTED
BY PATROLMEN; COMMITMENTS TO JAIL

4 April 1945

You have referred to me the letter dated March 23, 1945, from Lt. W. B. Lentz, which requests my opinion upon the following questions:

(1) Is the sheriff of a county, or any other person acting as a jailer, required to place in the jail any person arrested by a State Highway Patrolman and brought to the jail by the patrolman, when the person has been arrested for a criminal offense committed in the presence of the patrolman?

(2) Is it necessary for the patrolman to secure a commitment before the arrested person can be placed in jail, and when is it necessary to present a commitment when placing an arrested person in jail?

G. S. 15-46 is as follows:

"Sec. 15-46. *Procedure on arrest without warrant.*—Every person arrested without warrant shall be either immediately taken before some magistrate having jurisdiction to issue a warrant in the case, *or else committed to the county prison*, and, as soon as may be, taken before such magistrate, who, on proper proof, shall issue a warrant and thereon proceed to act as may be required by law. (Rev., s. 3182; Code, s. 1130; 1868-9, c. 178, subc. 1, s. 7; C. S. 4548)" (Italics added.)

State Highway Patrolmen are given the power to arrest for certain offenses by G. S. 20-188, and when an arrest is made by a Highway Patrolman within the scope of the power thus granted, it is my opinion that it is the duty of the county sheriff or jailer, or other person in charge of the county jail, to receive and place in custody the person arrested by the Highway Patrolman in either of the following instances:

(a) Where a commitment has been issued directing that the person arrested be placed in jail; or

(b) Where the arrest has been made under circumstances that make it impossible for the patrolman to immediately take the arrested person before a magistrate for the issuance of a warrant and the obtaining of a commitment.

I call your attention to the enclosed copy of an opinion to your office under date of November 23, 1942, which, on pages two and three, discusses the power of a patrolman to have an arrested person confined in jail pending the time when it is possible to have the warrant and commitment issued.

You will note that when a patrolman arrests a person without warrant, it is the duty, if possible, to take the arrested person immediately to some magistrate or judge in order that a warrant may be issued and that the arrested person may have an opportunity to post bail, or, failing that, that he may be committed to jail under a commitment. However, if the arrest is made at a time and place where the arrested person cannot be taken before a magistrate, the officer is authorized to take the person to jail, where it is the duty of the jailer to receive him, pending the earlist time at which the patrolman may secure the issuance of the warrant and commitment. These matters are more fully discussed in the letter referred to.

MOTOR VEHICLES; FRANCHISE HAULERS; CREDIT FOR VEHICLES DESTROYED BY FIRE OR COLLISION ON PURCHASE PRICE OF NEW LICENSES

24 July 1945

You stated that a franchise hauler had a portion of the vehicles owned by him destroyed by fire or collision during the year 1944. Upon the destruction of these vehicles the owner purchased new vehicles and purchased new licenses for them. At that time the unexpired portion of the cost of the original license could have been allowed as a credit on the cost of the new licenses under G. S. 20-100. You inquire if you may now allow that owner this deduction.

I am of the opinion that the deduction should be allowed. Sections 20-100 and 20-64 make provision for the credit of the unexpired portion of the license on a destroyed vehicle on the purchase price of a license for a vehicle replacing such destroyed vehicle or for a transfer of licenses. Under these sections I am of the opinion that the Commissioner may allow this credit *nunc pro tunc.*

MOTOR VEHICLES; LICENSES; REFUNDS WHEN LICENSES ARE USED ONLY A PORTION OF THE YEAR

1 August 1945

In your letter of July 30, 1945, you request my opinion on the following matter.

A carrier secures a for hire license at the beginning of the year and pays a full year's fee therefor. Within three months the vehicle for which license was purchased is sold to a non-resident who immediately takes the vehicle to the State of his residence and therein procures a license. The vendor of the vehicle removed the license plate and returned the same to the Department, with a request for refund because the license was not used for the entire year for which purchased. You inquire if the Department is authorized to make this refund.

G. S. 20-94 and 20-95 provide for deferred payments for licenses and for licenses for less than a year. G. S. 29-94 has no application to the present question, as the license was paid in full. G. S. 20-95 does not, in my opinion, authorize the purchase of a license for less than a year when the purchase is made at the beginning of the license year. That section only authorizes a purchase of licenses for less than a year, when the purchase is made after the beginning of the year. This section, therefore, has no application to the present question.

I have found no other section of the General Statutes relating directly to this matter. Therefore, I advise that the refund should not be made.

OSCAR MACY HARRELL, WALLACE, N. C.

10 August 1945

You have requested my opinion under Section 12 (b) of the Uniform Drivers License Act, G. S. 20-17, paragraph (b).

It appears that the above named driver was convicted on May 1, 1944, in the General County Court at Kenansville for illegal transportation of intoxicating liquors and that you suspended his license for one year from that date under the authority of Section 11 of the aforesaid Act. On September 28, 1944, said driver was convicted of operating a motor vehicle while said suspension was still in effect. You thereupon revoked his license for a period of one year from May 1, 1945, which was the expiration date of the suspension period.

I am of the opinion that your second action in this case should have been a suspension rather than a revocation. Section 12 (b) of the Uniform Drivers License Act provides that if the Department receives a record of the conviction of any person upon a charge of operating a motor vehicle while the license of such person is suspended or revoked, it shall immediately *extend the period of such first suspension or revocation for an additional like period.* In my opinion this means that the original period is extended and that the character of your first action is not changed. Thus, if your original action is a suspension, your second action would be an additional period of suspension. Please observe that the statute does not provide that the Department shall immediately "suspend or revoke" for an additional like period, but that the Department shall immediately "extend the period of *such first suspension or revocation* for an additional like period."

MOTOR VEHICLE LAW; RECISSION OF REGISTRATION PLATES ISSUED TO TAXICAB
OPERATING IN TOWNS WHEN NO CERTIFICATE OF CONVENIENCE
AND NECESSITY HAS BEEN ISSUED

18 September 1945

This letter is supplementary to the one on the same subject which I wrote to you under date of August 29, 1945. That letter was an attempt to answer your inqiury as to the power of the Department to cancel registration licenses issued to taxicab operators under the following two situations:

(1) An operator in an unincorporated town secured a license and then moved into an incorporated town and is operating in the latter place without a certificate of convenience and necessity from the governing body thereof.

(2) An operator rented a room in an unincorporated town for the purpose of making the place his motor vehicle registration address, although he actually maintained his place of living in an incorporated town. After obtaining his license he began operating his taxicab in an incorporated town without a certificate of convenience and necessity from the governing body thereof.

In my attempt to answer your inquiry I assumed that in each of the aforesaid cases the principal operation of the taxicab *at the time the license was issued* was to be in a city or town which has a governing body, and that the license was issued on the false premise that the principal operation would be elsewhere than such city or town.

On the basis of my assumption of additional facts, as stated above, I reached the conclusion that the Department had authority to cancel the license on the theory that when a license has been issued which in the first instance should never have been issued, it is within the inherent power of the issuing authority to rescind its unwarranted action in issuing the license.

It appears now that my assumption of additional facts was not entirely correct. At any rate you have now presented for my consideration a situation contrary to the assumption which I made. You now inquire whether or not the Department has the authority to cancel or rescind an operator's license where such operator obtained his license lawfully upon a truthful statement that his principal operation was in a certain incorporated town, and then subsequently removed his place of operation to another incorporated town from which he has not received a certificate of convenience and necessity.

If the operator actually obtained a certificate of convenience and necessity from the incorporated town in which he conducted his principal operation, and on the basis of such certificate obtained his license from the Department, such license would be lawfully issued and, moreover, would grant a privilege to operate anywhere within the state of North Carolina. Under these circumstances the reasoning of my previous letter to you would be inapplicable because of the fact that the conclusion reached therein was based upon the inherent power of the Department to undo an act which it had no legal authority to do from the beginning. In the case which you now present for my consideration the act was lawful and warranted in the beginning, and the power of the Department to rescind or cancel the license would depend entirely upon a specific power to revoke licenses.

Inasmuch as the Statute does not expressly provide for revocation under these circumstances, it is my opinion that the Department has no power in this case to revoke or rescind the operator's license. It appears to me that in cases like this the only remedy lies in such action as the incorporated town or city desires to take by way of an ordinance regulating the matter.

DRIVERS LICENSE ACT; REVOCATION OR SUSPENSION OF LICENSE ON
CONVICTION OF TEMPORARY LARCENY OF AUTOMOBILE

21 September 1945

I have before me the file on Earl Craven, 922 Lexington Avenue, Greensboro, North Carolina. It appears that on August 18, 1945 you issued your official notice of revocation to this driver, stating that you were revoking his license as of June 18, 1945 because of the fact that he was convicted in the Superior Court of Guilford County of the larceny of an automobile.

The report which was received from the Guilford County Superior Court revealed that this driver pleaded guilty and was convicted of temporary larceny. This fact has been subsequently confirmed by the driver's attorney, Z. H. Howerton, of Greensboro.

An examination of the Uniform Drivers License Act, particularly of Sections 11 and 12, persuades me that revocation of license in this case was not proper. It is true that Section 12 provides for mandatory revocation upon conviction of any felony in the commission of which a motor vehicle is used. However, G. S. 20-105 provides that temporary larceny of an automobile is a misdemeanor rather than a felony. I am unable to find that conviction of a single misdemeanor, as such, constitutes ground either for suspension or revocation; and I am unable to fit this case into any of the other grounds specifically mentioned as grounds for revocation or suspension.

For the reasons stated above I am of the opinion that a driver's license cannot be revoked or suspended on the ground that a driver has been convicted of temporary larceny.

It is probable that your Department inadvertently overlooked the word "temporary" in the report from Guilford County. If this driver had been convicted of larceny, the revocation would have been proper.

MOTOR VEHICLES; SPEED LIMITS IN EFFECT FROM AND AFTER •
NOVEMBER 1, 1945

31 October 1945

You have requested me to summarize and clarify the North Carolina speed laws which will be in effect on and after November 1, 1945, the date on which the Emergency War Powers Proclamation Number XVI, issued by the Governor, becomes effective.

The applicable statute is G. S. 20-141. This statute, as amended by the aforesaid proclamation, makes it unlawful to drive any vehicle on a highway

(1) at a speed greater than 50 miles per hour, or

(2) at a speed greater than is reasonable and prudent under the conditions then existing.

The 50 miles per hour speed limit is an absolute maximum under any conditions and in any type of vehicle. The mere fact of exceeding that limit is a violation in itself without further proof of conditions or type of vehicle.

The second violation named, i.e., driving a vehicle at a speed greater than is reasonable or prudent under the conditions then existing, is a question of fact which depends on the circumstances in each case. However, the statute helps in determining this question by providing that where no special hazard exists the following speeds shall be lawful, but any speed in excess thereof shall be *prima facie* evidence that the speed is not reasonable or prudent (and, therefore, unlawful):

(1) 20 m.p.h. in a business district (any vehicle)

(2) 25 m.p.h. in a residential district (any vehicle)

(3) 35 m.p.h. for motor vehicles designed, equipped for, or engaged·in transporting property; and 30 m.p.h. for such vehicle with trailer attached; except: 40 m.p.h. for ¾-ton trucks and 45 m.p.h. for ½-ton or pickup trucks

(4) 45 m.p.h. for all vehicles (other than trucks described in (3) above) when operating other than in a business or residential district

Thus, the only *absolute* maximum speed named in the statute is 50 miles per hour, applicable to any vehicle under any conditions. All of the other so-called "speed limits" are speeds which are deemed lawful under the specific conditions named where no special hazard exists, and are "limits" only in the sense that if a person drives at a greater speed, that fact constitutes *prima facie* evidence that his speed was "greater than was reasonable and prudent under the conditions then existing," and, therefore, unlawful. The violation in such case consists, not in exceeding the *prima facie* speed limit, but in driving at a speed "greater than is reasonable and prudent under the conditions then existing;" and the fact that a person exceeds the *prima facie* speed limit does not *necessarily* mean that he has violated the statute, for he may be able to show affirmatively that his speed, though greater than the *prima facie* speed limit, nevertheless was reasonable and prudent under the conditions then existing. I shall make no attempt to explain under what circumstances a speed above the *prima facie* limit would be reasonable and prudent.

I realize that patrolmen may have some difficulty under these circumstances in determining when a speed under 50 miles per hour is unlawful, for it depends in each case on whether or not such speed is **"greater than is** reasonable and prudent under the conditions then existing." I think **a pa-**trolman *ordinarily* would be justified in making arrests whenever the *prima facie* limit has been exceeded, for while that fact *per se* does not constitute a violation, it does make out a *prima facie* case in court and throws on **the** defendant the burden of overcoming the presumption by showing affirmatively that his speed was reasonable and prudent under the conditions then existing. However, this observation should not be taken to mean that a patrolman would be justified in making arrest in every such case, without an appraisal of the conditions then existing. He should remember that a speed under 50 miles per hour is not unlawful unless it is "greater than is reasonable or prudent under the conditions then existing."

Subsection (c) of section 20-141 provides that the fact that the speed of a vehicle is lower than the specified *prima facie* limits does not relieve the driver of a motor vehicle from the duty to decrease speed when approaching and crossing an intersection, when approaching and driving around a curve, when approaching the crest of a hill, when travelling upon any narrow or winding roadway, or when any special hazard exists with respect to pedestrians or traffic or by reason of weather or highway conditions, and speed shall be decreased to the degree necessary to avoid colliding with any person, vehicle, or other conveyance on or entering the highway.

Subsection (h) of section 20-141 provides that no motor vehicle shall be driven at such a slow speed as to impede or block the normal and reasonable flow of traffic except when reduced speed is necessary for the safe operation of a vehicle or is in compliance with law.

The speed limitations set forth herein are, by virtue of section 20-145 of the General Statutes, made inapplicable to: (1) vehicles operated with due regard for safety under the direction of the police in the chase or apprehension of violators of the law or of persons charged with or suspected of any such violation; (2) fire department or fire patrol vehicles when travelling in response to a fire alarm; and (3) public or private ambulances when travelling in emergencies. This exemption, however, does not protect the driver of any of such vehicles from the consequence of a reckless disregard for the safety of others.

It is noted that local authorities, within their respective jurisdictions, and the State Highway and Public Works Commission within certain areas under certain road conditions may alter the *prima facie* speed limits.

MOTOR VEHICLES; LICENSING REQUIREMENTS OF VEHICLES OWNED BY THE RFC AND LEASED TO PRIVATE OPERATORS

15 January 1946

You request my opinion upon the following matter. A North Carolina franchise carrier is leasing a group of trucks and trailers from the Reconstruction Finance Corporation for the period beginning January 1, 1946, and ending July 1, 1946. The lease provides for a stipulated rental fee to be paid monthly during the lease. According to information furnished by the lessee, the rental agreement does not contain a provision which would give the lessee an option to purchase the vehicles at the termination of the lease.

On the basis of the above facts you inquire (1) whether the lessee can be considered the owner of the vehicles for the purpose of licensing; and (2) whether the United States Government would be required to procure licenses for such vehicles if it is determined that said lessee is not the owner for the purpose of licensing such vehicles.

Section 20-52 of the General Statutes provides that every owner of a vehicle subject to registration shall apply to the Department of Motor Vehicles for the registration thereof and the issuance of a certificate of title therefor. The term "owner," as the same is used in the Motor Vehicle Act, is defined in G. S. Section 20-38 (t) as follows:

> "Owner.—A person who holds the legal title of a vehicle or, in the event a vehicle is subject to an agreement for conditional sale or lease thereof, with the right of purchase upon performance of the conditions stated in the agreement and with the immediate right of possession vested in the original vendee or lessee; or, in the event a mortgagor of a vehicle is entitled to possession, then such conditional vendee or lessee or mortgagor shall be deemed the owner for the purpose of this article; except that in all such instances when the rent paid by the lessee includes charges for services of any nature and/or when the lease dose not provide that title shall pass to the lessee upon payment of the rent stipulated, the lessor shall be regarded as the owner of such vehicle, and said vehicle shall be subject to such requirements of this article as are applicable to vehicles operated for compensation."

It is my opinion that under the wording of this section the Reconstruction Finance Corporation is the "owner" of the vehicles under consideration. The statute in clear terms provides that when the lease does not provide that title shall pass to the lessee upon payment of the rent stipulated, the lessor shall be regarded as the owner of the vehicle. There is no provision in this contract of lease for passage of title to the lessee nor is there an option to purchase at the end of the rental period.

The Reconstruction Finance Corporation is an agency of the United States Government. Since it is the owner of the leased vehicles, I am of the opinion that the Department of Motor Vehicles has no authority to require that licenses be procured for such government-owned vehicles. Section 20-51 of the General Statutes specifically provides that no certificate of title need be obtained for any vehicle owned by the United States Government.

MOTOR VEHICLES; EARTH MOVERS; "SPECIAL MOBILE EQUIPMENT"

18 January 1946

You have requested my opinion upon whether or not certain vehicles are subject to the requirement of registration and certificates of title under the Motor Vehicle Act of 1937 (G. S. 20-38 et seq.). This Act applies to all vehicles intended to be operated upon any highway of this State except those specifically exempt by G. S. 20-51; and this, in my opinion, means intended to be operated *at all*. Inasmuch as it is conceded that the vehicles in question are to be operated, at least incidentally or to some extent, upon the highways, the only question to be determined is whether or not such vehicles are specifically exempt under G. S. 20-51. This depends on whether or not they constitute "special mobile equipment" as defined in G. S. 20-38 as follows:

> "(bb) Special Mobile Equipment.—Every vehicle not designed or used primarily for the transportation of persons or property, but incidentally operated or moved over the highways, such as farm tractors, road construction or maintenance machinery, ditch-digging apparatus,

well-boring apparatus and concrete mixers. The foregoing enumeration shall be deemed partial and shall not operate to exclude other vehicles which are within the general terms of this section."

The vehicles in question are the "13-yard Model F Bottom-Dump Euclid," and the "Model F Rear-Dump Euclid." Advertising folders showing pictures of these vehicles have been submitted. These vehicles are generally known as "earth movers," or "earth-hauling machines." They are designed primarily to move very heavy loads of earth, including rock, over short distances. They apparently are designed for the purpose of moving earth in connection with road construction, and it is for this purpose that they are actually used in the present case. The only operation on the highway in this case consists of moving earth from one point to another on the highway, as a part of the construction of such highway, and of moving from one construction job to another. The "bottom-dump" vehicle resembles a tractor with a huge trailer-hopper attached, although the tractor portion also has some characteristics of a truck, as, for instance, two front wheels which are of truck size and form and which are in line with the rear wheels. The "rear-dump" vehicle closely resembles the usual dump truck.

It is conceded that the "bottom-dump" vehicle exceeds the maximum allowable size provided in G. S. 20-115, and that the "rear-dump" vehicle exceeds both the maximum size and weight provided in G. S. 20-115; and it is further conceded that each vehicle, as a prerequisite to operation on the highways, must have a special permit under G. S. 20-119.

The question in this case does not lend itself to an easy answer. However, after a thorough consideration of the matter, I am of the opinion that the vehicles in question are "special mobile equipment" within the meaning of the definition contained in G. S. 20-38.

The Motor Vehicle Act of 1937, as amended, has the general purpose of regulating by registration only those vehicles which are designed for use or are used on the public highways. There seems to be no intent to require registration of any vehicle which is neither designed for use nor actually used on the highways.

Reading this general purpose into the definition of "special mobile equipment," such definition would embrace any vehicle "not designed or used primarily for the transportation of persons or property" *over the public highways,* "but incidentally operated or moved over the highways." In other words, the statute, in speaking of a vehicle not designed or used primarily for the transportation of persons or property, in my opinion, means transportation over the highways. In this view of the matter the question in this case resolves itself into whether or not these vehicles are designed or used primarily for the transportation of property over the highways.

It is true that the actual use of these vehicles in this particular case is necessarily upon the highways, for it is the highway in every instance which is being constructed with the use of the vehicles; and, so, it may be said that, technically, the vehicles are used primarily to transport property, i.e., earth, over the highway.

On the other hand, such an interpretation, in my opinion, would impart to the word "transportation" a scope not contemplated by the usual and ordinary acceptation of that word; and I do not believe that the legislature intended it in that way.

The vehicles in question perform a job similar to that performed by a grading machine. While the earth or rock moved by these vehicles may properly be called "property," this "property" merges with the very highway upon which the vehicle is operated and loses its identity therein. The primary purpose is not to transport the "property" as such, but to level off or otherwise change the structure and contour of terrain. The same general purpose is accomplished by scoops, graders, drags, bulldozers, steam shovels, and various other kinds of machinery which take dirt from one place and leave it in another.

The vehicles in question are actually used by the owner in this case primarily for the purpose of road construction, and perform the task of moving earth from one spot to another in the pursuit of that purpose. Under these circumstances I am of the opinion that such vehicles are "not . . . . used *primarily* for the transportation of . . . . property."

The only remaining question is whether or not such vehicles are "*designed* . . . . primarily for the transportation of . . . . property."

These vehicles are designed primarily to do the sort of thing for which they are actually used in this case, i.e., the moving of earth from one place to another. While the primary purpose of such operation in every case may not be the structural change of the earth's surface, it can hardly be said that they are primarily designed for use on the highway. The nature of the load carried seems to indicate a short haul, and one not necessarily over the highways. Earth, unless it has some intrinsic value because of characteristics which render it adaptable to a specialized use, ordinarily is not moved over long distances. Earth, used simply as a space filler, is moved usually from one place to another in the same vicinity; and the removal of earth as a space filler does not necessarily contemplate use of the highway. At any rate, I am of the opinion that such an operation is not "primarily" one of transporting property over the highways.

My opinion that these vehicles are not designed primarily for transportation of property on the highways has been influenced by the fact that they are of a size or weight, or both, which prohibits their operation on our highways, and, I am advised, on the highways of other States.. While not necessarily controlling, this fact does lend some validity to the conclusion that they are designed for non-highway use, especially when taken in conjunction with the other characteristics of the vehicles.

For the reasons stated above, I am of the opinion that these vehicles are "special mobile equipment" within the meaning of the statute; and, therefore, that they are exempt from registration.

MOTOR VEHICLES; SUSPENSION OF LICENSE FOR FAILURE TO SATISFY JUDGMENT CONTINUES UNTIL JUDGMENT IS SATISFIED OR PROOF OF ABILITY TO RESPOND IN DAMAGES IS GIVEN

29 January 1946

You have requested my opinion as to when an operator's license may be restored to a person whose license has been suspended under G. S. 20-198 for failure to satisfy a judgment or to post liability insurance.

I believe that your question is answered by the following portion of G. S. 20-198:

"... the said operator's license and all of the registration certificates ... shall be forthwith suspended ... and shall remain so suspended and shall not be renewed, nor shall any motor vehicle be thereafter registered in the name of the said person, firm or corporation while any such judgment remains unstayed, unsatisfied and subsisting and until every such judgment is satisfied or discharged, or until the said person gives proof of his ability to respond in damages, as hereinafter required, for future accidents."

Proof of ability to respond in damages may be established by execution of a bond or posting liability insurance in the amounts required (G. S. 20-199).

"Satisfaction" of judgment is had under G. S. 20-199 when such judgment is for an amount in excess of the statutory requirements for insurance and the statutory amounts ($5,000—$10,000 personal injury, and $1,000 property damage) have been credited on the judgment.

If the person whose license was suspended under G. S. 20-198 in 1939 has failed, both to satisfy the judgment and to give proof of ability to respond in damages as required by the law, I am of the opinion that you cannot renew or restore his license, and that you cannot do so as long as his failure continues.

UNIFORM DRIVER'S LICENSE ACT; APPLICATION TO FEDERAL EMPLOYEES

30 April 1946

You have referred to me a letter written by R. L. Prince, Investigator of the Alcohol Tax Unit, Internal Revenue Service, Treasury Department. Mr. Prince wishes to know whether or not an employee of the Federal government is required to have a North Carolina driver's license while he is engaged in official business.

While our law contains no specific exemption in this case, the Supreme Court of the United States has held that a state does not have the constitutional power to require Federal employees to comply with the Uniform Driver's License Act in the operation of an automobile in conduct of Federal business. JOHNSON v. MARYLAND, 254 U. S. 51.

Needless to say, if the employee uses the automobile to any extent for personal reasons or for any reason other than the conduct of Federal business, he will immediately become liable to secure a state driver's license. The above decision of the Supreme Court grants immunity from the Driver's License Act only where the Federal employee is engaged strictly and exclusively in the operation of the vehicle for the prosecution of Federal business.

MOTOR VEHICLE LAWS; INSPECTORS; OFFICIAL OATHS

4 May 1946

You have requested me to advise you whether or not, in my opinion, your Motor Vehicle Inspectors will be required to take an oath of office upon their appointment and transfer from the State Highway Patrol, even though they have already taken such an oath as patrolmen.

I have been unable to arrive at a satisfactory answer to this question. It would seem that the safest course to follow would be to have each Inspector take such an oath. Certainly no harm could result therefrom.

MOTOR VEHICLES; LICENSE OVER $400; NO DEFERMENT BEYOND JUNE 1

8 May 1946

You have requested my opinion upon a question arising under G. S. 20-94, which provides, in substance, that in the case of a license of more than $400.00, half of such amount may, if the Commissioner is satisfied of the financial responsibility of the owner, be deferred until June 1 in any calendar year upon the execution of a draft on a bank for said half of the amount plus a carrying charge of one-half of 1%.

You wish to know whether you have the authority under this statute to defer payment of any part of such license fee beyond June 1 in any calendar year. It is my opinion that you do not.

RE: HARLEE ARMISTEAD BANGLE

17 May 1946

You have handed me your file in the above case with the request that I advise you what action you should take at this point. From the file it appears that the Superior Court has rendered judgment declaring the Department's revocation of license wrongful and ordering that the same be restored immediately. The hearing in Superior Court was conducted under and by virtue of G. S. 20-25, which allows an appeal from the Commissioner's action to the Superior Court judge. At the hearing the Department was represented by H. J. Hatcher, Director of the Highway Safety Division of your Department.

In view of the fact that our first knowledge or notice of this matter comes after an adverse decision in the Superior Court, it would seem the better course to arrange a conference between this office and yours, at which time all the questions involved may be discussed fully. I hardly think the information contained in the file provides in itself a sufficient basis for the rendition of an opinion by this office.

OPINIONS TO MERIT SYSTEM COUNCIL

MERIT SYSTEM COUNCIL; CONTRACTS; EXECUTION; AUTHORITY TO ENTER
INTO WITH MUNICIPAL CIVIL SERVICE COMMISSIONS

27 July 1944

I acknowledge receipt of your letter, enclosing the proposed contract between the North Carolina Merit System Council, the North Carolina State Board of Health, and the Civil Service Commission of the City of High Point, and inquiring as to the legal right of the Council to enter into said contract, and by whom such contract should be executed on behalf of the Council.

Chapter 378 of the Public Laws of 1941, creating and setting up the Merit System Council, is silent on the questions raised by you. However, I am inclined to the opinion that the North Carolina Merit System Council does have authority to enter into the proposed contract and I, therefore, approve the same as to form and legality. While it is not the duty of this office to pass upon the policy, and I do not raise that question here, it does occur to me that in entering into the enclosed contract you will be adopting a policy which should be followed with other governmental units under similar facts and circumstances existing in the High Point case. In other words, I do not think that the statute contemplates that you should enter into a contract with one unit of the government which you would not enter into under similar facts and circumstances with other municipal units.

I am of the opinion that the North Carolina Merit System Council should pass a resolution formally approving the contract and authorizing its execution by its Chairman and Secretary.

VETERANS; EMPLOYMENT BY AGENCIES UNDER THE N. C. MERIT SYSTEM
WHILE RECEIVING RETIREMENT PAY

7 August 1944

I have your letter of August 5, 1944, in which you ask the following question:

"Will you kindly advise as to whether it is forbidden by Federal law for a veteran who is drawing retirement pay to be employed by any of the agencies under the supervision of the N. C. Merit System?"

I have been unable to find any Federal statute or regulation which prohibits veterans drawing retirement pay from being employed by agencies under the supervision of the North Carolina Merit System. Title V, Section 62, of the F. C. A., which prohibits double office holding, exempts therefrom retired enlisted men of the Army, Navy, Marine Corps or Coast Guard, and retired officers of the same services when they have been retired because of injuries received or incapacity incurred in line of duty, or when such officers are appointed by the President, by and with the consent of the Senate. The prohibition contained in Executive Order No. 10 (6098) would not apply to employment by North Carolina agencies under the Merit System.

VETERANS; PREFERENCE RATING OF TEN PER CENT FOR VETERANS OF WORLD
WAR II IN EXAMINATIONS FOR STATE POSITIONS; PREFERENCE OF
VETERANS IN STATE EMPLOYMENT AND IN
PROMOTIONS AFTER EMPLOYMENT

23 January 1945

I reply to your letter of January 18, 1945.

In your letter you refer to Chapter 8 of the Public Laws of 1939, which
is known as the Veterans' Preference Act, and the same is carried forward
in the General Statutes of North Carolina as Section 128-15. In 1943, the
General Assembly of North Carolina passed another Act relating to Veterans' preferences which made the Act of 1939, applicable to all persons
who have served, or are now serving, or shall serve in any branch of the
Armed Services during the present war; and the Act of 1939 was likewise
made applicable to the widows of such veterans and the wives of the disabled veterans of the present war. For the sake of reference I think these
statutes should be quoted, and they are as follows:

"s. 128-15. *Preference for veterans in employment*· Hereafter in all
examinations of applicants for positions with this state or any of its
departments or ins..itutions, a preference rating of ten per cent shall
be awarded to all the citizens of the state who served the state or the
United States honorably in either the army, navy, marine corps, or
nurses' corps in time of war.

"All departments and institutions of the state, or their agencies,
shall give preference to such unemployed veterans as enumerated in
this section in filling vacant positions in construction or maintenance of
public buildings and grounds, construction of highways, or any other
employment under the supervision of the state or its departments, institutions, or agencies: Provided, that the provisions of this section
shall apply to widows of such veterans and to the wife of any disabled
veteran."

"s. 128-15.1 *Section 128-15 applicable to persons serving in the present war*.—All the provisions for preference rating and preference of
employment to citizens who served the state or the United States, honorably in either the army, navy, marine corps or nurses' corps in time
of war and to the widows of such veterans and the wives of disabled
veterans provided in Section 128-15 are hereby specifically made applicable to men and women who have served, are now serving, or shall
serve in any branch of the armed services or the nurses' corps during
the present war, and are honorably discharged from such service, and
to the widows of such veterans and.the wives of disabled veterans of
the present war."

In your letter you state as follows: "The question at issue at the moment
concerns the adding of 10 points to examination grades given to men who
are now veterans; but who at the time of their examinations were not
veterans." I assume, therefore, that you are dealing with a case of an individual whose name now appears on an eligible list by virtue of an examination given pursuant to the provisions of Chapter 126 of the General
Statutes of North Carolina which established the Merit System Council
and authorized such examination; such an individual I assume was not a
veteran at the time of taking the examination, nor at the time his grade

was computed and the eligible list prepared on which his name appears, but such individual is now a veteran by reason of services in the present war, which is sometimes called World War II.

I have read these statutes very closely and also note the contention in your letter that such individual should have the status of a veteran at the time of his examination before the 10 points can be added to the final examination grade. In my opinion these veterans' preference laws are remedial in nature, formulated and designed to give a veteran a favorable chance in employment in consideration of the fact that he has performed services, and perhaps risked his life, in the defense of this Nation. It is an accepted rule that such laws should receive a liberal construction and in doubtful cases the advantage in interpretation should be given the beneficiary that the Legislature had in mind when the statute was drafted.

The Act of 1939 referred to in your letter does not fix any definite time when the 10 points or ten per cent shall be awarded or taken into consideration in computing the final examination grade. It simply says that in examinations persons who have served honorably in the Armed Forces shall have ten per cent added to their grade, and that in all State employment such persons shall have the preference. I further call your attention to the fact that the Act of 1943 (Section 128-15.1 of the General Statutes) which makes the Act of 1939 applicable to persons serving in the present war says that the Act of 1939 is "hereby specifically made applicable to men and women *who have served, are now serving, or shall serve*, in any branch of the armed services or the nurses' corps during the present war, and are honorably discharged from such service, and to the widows of such veterans and the wives of disabled veterans of the present war." When we consider, therefore, that Chapter 8 of the Public Laws of 1939 does not fix any definite time when the ten per cent shall be awarded or added to the final examination grade, and we consider the further fact that the Act of 1943 makes the Act of 1939 applicable to persons "who have served, are now serving, or shall serve in any branch of the armed services etc.," then I am of the opinion that men who are now veterans, but who at the time of their examinations under the Merit System were not veterans, are entitled to have the ten per cent or 10 points at this time added to their final examination grade, and that their standing on the eligible list should be readjusted accordingly. I am further of the opinion that this should be done under suitable rules and regulations promulgated by the Merit System Council prescribing reasonable forms and proper modes of proof showing that the person has the status of a veteran.

What I have said above should be construed in harmony with the other provisions and regulations of the Merit System. For example, I am of the opinion the construction that I have given above would only apply to such examinations as are still current under the provisions and regulations of the Merit System Law. It would not apply to those eligible lists which have become invalid and void in the passing of time, or because the same has been declared invalid or void by the Merit System Council or the Merit System Supervisor. You would not, therefore, have to take into consideration those examinations where the eligible list is closed and no longer has any validity or effectiveness; my rule would only apply to current examinations and to eligible lists current when the application for recomputation of the final examination grade is made.

When an appointing agency calls upon you for a list of eligibles to fill a vacancy, I think you have a right to furnish this appointing agency your current eligible list for the positions involved, and when the appointing agency employs an eligible from this list, then in my opinion the position so filled by the appointing agency would not be affected by the fact that subsequently the eligible list was again readjusted by any applications of veterans for recomputations. In other words, when the appointing agency fills a position from the current eligible list, then the position so filled cannot be vacated or affected by the fact that you are again required to adjust the list even though subsequent adjustment would place a veteran among the first three eligibles and with a higher grade than the persons already employed. Both you and the appointing agency have the right to rely on the status of the eligible list as it was at the time you certified it to the appointing agency.

I would like to give this further opinion in regard to the employment of veterans where their names appear on eligible lists maintained under the provisions of the Merit System Law; it is my thought that where a veteran's name appears among the first three eligibles certified to the appointing agency, then it is the duty of the appointing agency to employ the veteran as I think this is the clear meaning of the Act of 1939; if more than one veteran's name appears among the first three eligibles on the list, then it is the duty of the agency to employ or give preference to one of the veterans. I call to your attention, however, that this applies only to original employment. In my opinion it does not apply to any eligible list maintained for purposes of promotion inside the agency. On a promotional register it is my thought that all eligibles are governed by the same rules, both civilians and veterans, and the preference is not applicable. The preference is only applicable to employment and not promotion after employment.

In the last above paragraph I have assumed that the veteran has already received his ten per cent, either at the time of the examination, or by readjustment after the examination. If a person has formerly been employed by an appointing agency, has received military leave, and served in the Armed Forces and has returned to his old position, then it is my thought that he can have his recomputation made and his grade adjusted as a veteran, and this adjusted grade should be taken into consideration when promotions are to be made inside the agency from the promotional register maintained for that purpose. In this connection the veteran has not had the advantage of the ten per cent until this agency gives it to him, and he is entitled to have it considered for promotion, while in the above paragraph the veteran had already attained his ten per cent and it had been worked into his final grade.

I am sorry to give you an opinion that will no doubt cause you some administrative difficulties, but I don't think that administrative exigencies and difficulties should prevail over a liberal interpretation according to the spirit of the Act.

DOUBLE OFFICE HOLDING; MEMBER, MERIT SYSTEM COUNSEL;
MEMBER, N. C. VETERANS COMMISSION

5 July 1945

Reference is made to your inquiry over the telephone in which it was stated that Mr. Maynard, a member of the Merit System Council, has been appointed by the Governor of this State as a member of the North Carolina Veterans Commission, created by Senate Bill 216 of the session of the General Assembly of 1945.

You wish to know if this would affect Mr. Maynard's status as a member of the Merit System Council, or, in other words, if this will constitute double office holding so that upon acceptance of the appointment on the North Carolina Veterans Commission, a vacancy would be created in the Merit System Council.

On the 15th of April, 1941, in regard to a member of the Merit System Council, this office ruled as follows:

"From the above opinions and the wording of the statute quoted, it is my opinion that perhaps the courts would hold that membership on the Merit System Council would be considered an office within the meaning of the constitutional provision which prohibits multiple office holding."

On the 14th of March, 1945, this office rendered an opinion to the Governor of North Carolina on the question of whether membership on the North Carolina Veterans Commission constitutes an office within the meaning of Article XIV, Section 7, of the Constitution of this State. In this opinion it was stated in substance that the courts had not passed upon this question; therefore, we were hesitant to advise an official of the State to accept membership on a board or commission when the courts had not had an opportunity to pass upon the status of the membership. We further stated that if a person did accept membership on such commission and such membership should be held by the court to be an office, the official would vacate his first office.

Inasmuch as the laws of this State provide that a person who attempts to hold two offices may be amerced in the form of a monetary penalty, I think the safest thing for Mr. Maynard to do if he intends to continue to serve as a member of the North Carolina Veterans Commission, is to submit his resignation as a member of your Council and thus put the matter beyond all doubt.

MERIT SYSTEM LAW; REGULATIONS; REVISION OF ARTICLE 5,
SECTION 6, PARAGRAPH 1.

9 August 1945

In your letter of August 6, 1945, you state that you are revising the Merit System Rule and inquire of this office if any legislative action has been taken that would require a revision of Article 5, Section 6, paragraph 1, of the Merit System Rule. You further state that you are of the opinion that persons who have served with the Overseas Red Cross Unit should be taken care of in this paragraph.

I have examined the laws of the 1945 session of the General Assembly and I do not find any new Acts or amendments to old Acts that would affect or necessitate any revision of Article 5, Section 6, paragraph 1, of the Merit System Rule. You are, of course, familiar with the fact that Chapter 8 of the Laws of 1939 provided certain veterans' preferences and these are referred to in the paragraph in question of your Rule. This section is carried forward in the General Statutes as Section 128-15. You are also familiar with the fact that Chapter 168 of the Laws of 1943 made all the provisions of Chapter 8 of the Laws of 1939 applicable to the veterans of the present war, or World War II. This is carried forward in the General Statutes as Section 128-15.1. This latter section, dealing with World War II, is not referred to in paragraph 1 of the Rule in question and it might be that in your revision you would want to make some reference to the veterans of World War II as being included within the scope of the preference.

I am sorry that I have been unable to find where persons who served with the Overseas Red Cross Unit are entitled to a veterans preference as provided by the Rule in question. No doubt the persons serving overseas in this particular unit deserve to have such a preference but I cannot find any statutory authority that would warrant this action. I am hoping that I have overlooked something and that you can give me a reference that will clear up the matter. It is possible that you are thinking of House Bill No. 122, passed at the session of 1945, which included members of the armed forces of the United States, the Merchant Marine of the United States and American Red Cross Units serving outside the continental United States. The effect of this statute, however, is to give these persons who have been granted leaves of absence for service in these units the advantage of any salary increases granted to their position when they return to State employment. You will recall that they are to receive upon their return their annual salary, plus the step increment multiplied by the number of years of such service. So far as I can see now, the veterans preferences referred to in Article 5, Section 6, paragraph 1, and as contained in the above cited statutes, applies only to members who served in the actual armed forces of the United States and does not apply to Red Cross personnel serving outside the United States. I am hoping, however, that you can show that I am wrong.

Except for the matters above mentioned, I do not find anything else that should be incorporated in your revision in this respect.

VETERANS PREFERENCE IN MERIT SYSTEM EXAMINATIONS; STATUS OF
WIDOWS PREFERENCE ESTABLISHED BEFORE RE-MARRIAGE

24 September 1945

In your letter of September 18, 1945, you state that an employee of one of the agencies subject to the Merit System Law was the widow of a veteran, and according to Section 128-15 of the General Statutes, received ten points as the widow of a veteran on all of her examination grades. This employee is also on the promotional registers for several positions. You state that this employee has re-married and under a former ruling she will not receive a preference as the widow of a veteran on any examinations that she may take hereafter.

You inquire of this office if the Merit System Council should take away or nulify the preference she has already been given on the promotional examinations she has already taken?

I have always had my doubts about the applications of the status on veterans preferences to promotional examinations. While the matter is not free from doubt, nevertheless, it has always seemed to me that the preferences should apply to examinations for original positions and original appointments, and not to examinations for promotions if the person involved has already been employed and has acquired a permanent status. You do not raise this question and, therefore, I am not expressing any opinion on this point.

Referring again to your original question, I agree with you that the employee in question lost her status as the widow of a veteran after her re-marriage and is not entitled hereafter to any further-preference as the widow of a veteran should she take further merit examinations. This point was settled by a letter written to you by Mr. Adrian J. Newton on May 2, 1939, in response to your letter of April 21, 1939. Mr. Newton cited cases to sustain the point in question and which was the subject of your letter of that date.

I am of the opinion that the employee in question is entitled to retain the preferences granted to her by your Council and which were given her on promotional examinations while she still had the status of a widow of a veteran. Assuming that she was entitled to these preferences because of her status when they were granted, then I do not think the fact that she re-married would divest her of these preferences to which she was rightfully entitled when they were granted. Her re-marriage or change of status would only operate prospectively as applied to future examinations. This change of status in my opinion should not be construed or applied in a retroactive or retrospective manner. It is true that certain statutes, by express declaration in the statute, can be applied in a retroactive manner, but the law does not favor such applications and such interpretations except in certain fields and then only when the statute itself calls for such an application in plain and unequivocal language.

I am of the opinion, therefore, that the employee in question should retain the preferences which were proper and legitimate when granted to her.

MERIT SYSTEM LAW; INTERPRETATION OF SECTION 126-6 OF THE G. S.; AR-
TICLE VI OF MERIT SYSTEM RULES; DURATION OF REGISTERS

7 November 1945

In your letter of November 3, 1945, you quoted Section 126-6 of the G. S., which is a Section of the merit system law, as follows:

"All persons having successfully passed merit examinations under the merit rating system now in effect and are shown on the register as eligible for employment, shall not be required to take further examinations as provided herein and shall have their names placed on the new registers of those eligible for employment to be established under this act."

You further stated in your letter as follows:

"It is my understanding that this Section of the Law refers to those people who were on the registers established for the Unemployment Compensation Commission in 1939, and that there is nothing, therefore, in this Section of the Law which would make Article 6 of the Merit System Rule illegal."

Section 126-6 of the merit system law, which is now a part of the G. S. under this same designation, was passed at the 1941 session of the General Assembly. Prior to the passage of this act, a merit system was in existence and was applicable to certain agencies by virtue of regulations and in conformity with certain standards of the social security board. Employees of these agencies had already taken the merit system examination and were actually employed under that system prior to the passage of the merit system law of 1941. Prior to 1941 the system existed by regulations and had no statutory basis; for example, the original unemployment compensation law passed by the extra session of 1936, among other things, provided in section 11(d) "all positions shall be filled by persons selected and appointed on a non-partisan merit basis." It further provided that the commission should provide for the holding of examinations to determine the qualifications of applicants for the position so classified.

When the General Assembly of 1941 passed the present merit system law, it was known that a merit system already existed and certain employees had already passed examinations and were on the registers of eligible persons for appointments. It was not thought that these persons should again take another examination, hence Section 6 of Chapter 126 of the G. S. was inserted in the bill which provided that those persons who had already passed a merit examination under a merit rating system "now in effect" should not be required to take a further examination when the new merit system council began to function and to establish registers for the agencies included in that act. The words "now in effect" meant the system in effect in 1941, prior to the passage of the bill, and the words "further examinations as provided herein" meant the examinations provided by the merit system council established in the 1941 act. The act further provided that these persons who had theretofore successfully passed the examination should have their names placed on the new registers established under the 1941 act and should not be required to take further examination.

In our opinion, this Section was included to take care of a specific situation and in no wise has anything to do with nor does it invalidate article 6 of the merit system rule which provides for the establishment of registers containing the names of eligible persons and also provides and fixes the duration of these registers and the manner in which they may be declared exhausted or extended.

We are of the opinion, therefore, that the merit system council has a right to declare registers to be normally ended, exhausted or extended according to the provisions of this rule.

VETERANS' PREFERENCE; RATING IN STATE EXAMINATIONS; APPLICATION TO MEMBER OF STATE GUARD

17 November 1945

In your letter of November 15, 1945, you call attention to House Bill No. 33 of the General Assembly of 1939, which is now incorporated in the General Statutes as Section 128-15. This section awards to veterans of certain organizations a preference rating of ten per cent in examinations for positions.

You inquire of this office if this statute is applicable to a member of the State Guard, who served in that organization in time of war, to the end that such person can be awarded the preference rating of ten per cent on a State examination, or merit system examination.

The first paragraph of Section 128-15 is as follows:

"Hereafter in all examinations of applicants for positions with this state or any of its departments or institutions, a preference rating of ten per cent shall be awarded to all citizens of the state who served the state or the United States honorably in either the army, navy, marine corps, or nurses' corps in time of war."

This same section is specifically made applicable to veterans of World War II by Section 128-15.1 which was passed by the General Assembly of 1943.

The State Guard exists by virtue of authority contained in Section 127-111 of the General Statutes, and is designated as "North Carolina State Guard," and is composed of men of the unorganized militia on a voluntary basis; although this organization is subject to the rules and regulations of the War Department, it is primarily a State organization and is financed and paid according to State law. The preference rating in the statute above-quoted is awarded to citizens of the State who serve the State or the United States in either the army, the navy, marine corps, or nurses' corps in time of war. It is plain that the State Guard does not fall within the units named in this statute since the units named therein are component parts of the Armed Forces of the United States, and the preference is limited to those citizens of the State who served in these units. It is also evident that when we read the second paragraph of this same section that the preference is to be given to veterans because the language in part is as follows:

"All departments and institutions of the state, or their agencies, shall give preference to such unemployed *veterans* as enumerated in this section * * *." (Italics ours).

No doubt the patriotic men who gave their time and energy in serving in the State Guard should be entitled to this preference, but the present statute does not bring them within its scope and meaning, and if such preference is desired for members of the State Guard the remedy is by legislation.

3 January 1946

I reply to your letter of December 31, 1945.

I have gone through the Session Laws of 1943 carefully, and I do not find any law dealing with the status of state employees on military leave. In 1941 an act was passed granting leaves of absence to certain state and county officials for military purposes; but so far as I know, this act was never applied to employees. It was only for the "brass hats."

You are, of course, familiar with the act that gives veterans a preference in state employment and an additional ten per cent in examinations. In 1943 this was made applicable to veterans of World War II. It has always been my general understanding that the State of North Carolina has no statute that guarantees to veterans their former state employment. As you already know, such returning rights exist in the agencies affiliated with the Merit System Council by reason of regulations but not by any statute.

You refer to House Bill 122, Laws of 1945 (Chapter 220, Session Laws of 1945). This is simply a guarantee that a veteran who does return to state employment shall be entitled to all of the salary increases applicable to his classification and which increases were granted during his absence in military service.

At present, I am unable to find any law that corresponds to the description in your letter, but there are so many laws that it is extremely difficult to be familiar with all of them.

If you have any more definite information, I will be glad to look thoroughly again.

MERIT SYSTEM COUNCIL; VETERAN'S PREFERENCE RATING OF 10% ON EXAMINATIONS; APPLICATION TO UNITED STATES MERCHANT MARINE AND RED CROSS OVERSEAS SERVICE

15 January 1946

In your letter of January 12, 1946 you call attention to House Bill 122, Chapter 220 of Session Laws of 1945, dealing with the United States Merchant Marine and the Red Cross Overseas Service; and you then state the question for interpretation as follows: "I am wondering if persons having rendered service in the above mentioned capacities would be entitled to Veteran's Preference on our examinations?"

House Bill 122 or Chapter 220 of the Session Laws of 1945, mentioned in your letter, is as follows:

"Any employee of the State of North Carolina, who has been granted a leave of absence for service in either (1) the Armed Forces of the United States; or (2) the Merchant Marine of the United States; or (3) outside the Continental United States with the American Red Cross, shall, upon return to State employment, if reemployed in the same position and if within the time limits set forth in the leave of absence, receive an annual salary of at least (1) the annual salary the employee was receiving at the time such leave was granted; plus (2) an amount obtained by multiplying the step increment applicable to the employee's classification as provided in the classification and salary plan for State employees by the number of years of such service, counting a fraction of a year as a year; provided that no such employee shall receive a salary in excess of the top of the salary range applicable to the classification to which such employee is assigned upon return."

This act does not confer authority for granting leaves of absence for military service, but the act speaks of a situation where leave has already been granted. It seems to me that the above quoted act deals better with the question of salary, and it fixes what the salary shall be or furnishes a formula for fixing the salaries of persons in the organizations mentioned in the statute when and if they return to the service of the State. I can see nothing in the statute that deals with the Veteran's Preference rating of ten points in your examinations given under the Merit System. The basic statute under which the ten-points' preference is given is Section 128-15 of the General Statutes, and this ten-points' preference is granted to all the citizens of the State "who serve the State or the United States honorably in either the Army, Navy, Marine Corps, or Nurses Corps in time of war." In 1943 the General Assembly passed another section making this basic statute applicable to the veterans of World War II, and this appears in the General Statutes as Section 128-15.1. In this latter section, the ten-points preference granted in Section 128-15 is made applicable to those persons of World War II "who served the State or the United States, honorably in either the Army, Navy, Marine Corps or Nurses Corps in time of war and to the widows of such veterans and the wives of disabled veterans*". You can readily see that the Merchant Marine service and the Red Cross Overseas Service are not mentioned in these preference statutes. I do not know of any rule or statutory construction that would allow us to take the services mentioned in Chapter 220 of the Session Laws of 1945 out of that chapter and move them over into Sections 128-15 and 128-15.1. The types of services designated in each of these statutes must be considered in the frame of reference in which each of these types appears. I am sure we all appreciate the splendid services performed by the Merchant Marine of the United States, and we have all read of the voyages to Murmansk and all other heroic accounts of these men; and the same can be said of the Red Cross Service overseas. This does not authorize us, however, to exceed the bounds of statutory constructions; and if the persons serving in the branches of service mentioned in your letter desire the benefits of a preference rating, they will have to have the Legislature of North Carolina to enact a law to such effect.

I am compelled to say that in my opinion that persons serving in the United States Merchant Marine and the Red Cross Overseas Service are

not at the present time entitled to any Veteran's Preference under the laws
of the State of North Carolina.

MERIT SYSTEM COUNCIL; PUBLIC HEALTH; INSPECTORS IN ENFORCEMENT OF
MATTRESS OR BEDDING LAW; COVERAGE OF EMPLOYEES OF BOARD OF
HEALTH UNDER MERIT SYSTEM LAW

19 April 1946

In your letter of April 17, 1946 you call attention to an act of the General Assembly made effective March 22, 1937 entitled: "An Act to Improve the Sanitary Conditions of the Manufacture of Bedding." This act now appears in our General Statutes as Article 25 of Chapter 130 and begins with Section 130-268. This act deals with the sterilization and renovation of mattresses and bedding and also deals with the manufacture and sale of same. In Section 130-272, there is provided an enforcement fund which is accumulated from the sale of adhesive stamps. The monies collected from the sale of stamps is put into a "Bedding Law Fund," and all money in this fund must be expended solely in salaries and expenses of inspectors and other employees who devote their time to the enforcement of this particular law. It is further provided that expenses connected directly with the enforcement of the article, including certain attorneys' fees for prosecutions, may be paid out of this fund.

Your particular question arises under the enforcement of the Merit System Law; and you would like to know whether these bedding inspectors paid out of this "Bedding Law Fund" are such employees as are subject to the Merit System Law, the same being Chapter 126 of the General Statutes.

Section 126-1 of the General Statutes provides for the appointment of Merit System Council to be composed of citizens of recognized standing and interested in the impartial selection of government personnel "for the Unemployment Compensation Commission, the State Board of Health, the State Board of Charities and Public Welfare, and the State Commission for the Blind." There is an additional section which brings local units of the Board of Health and local units connected with the Welfare Department within the scope of coverage of the act.

It is provided in Section 126-4 of the General Statutes, among other things, as follows:

"All applicants for positions in the agencies or departments affected by this chapter shall be subjected to an examination by the Merit System Council which shall be competitive and free to all persons meeting requirements prescribed by said council."

It is further provided in Section 126-10 of the General Statutes, which is a part of this same Merit System Law, as follows:

"All original appointments to permanent positions shall be made from officially promulgated registers for a probationary period of six months."

It should also be mentioned that under Section 126-2 of the General Statutes, the supervisor of merit examinations is charged with the duty of preparing rules and regulations for all employees of the affected departments; and a portion of the statute is as follows:

"The Merit System Council appointed under the provisions of this chapter is authorized to appoint a supervisor of merit examinations, * * * and who shall, after his appointment, * * * prepare rules and regulations, job specifications, and *prepare and give examinations for and to all employees and applicants for employment and/or promotions of the agencies or departments affected by this chapter.*" (Emphasis ours.)

The act is a comprehensive act and gives the Merit System Council power to make regulations, set up registers of employees, fill vacancies; and the whole tenor of the act shows clearly that all employees of the agencies affected by the act must be employed under this system. There is nowhere in the act any expression or indication that the employees of the affected agencies or any particular group or departmental section of employees can be exempt from the operations of the act simply because they are paid certain designated funds. In other words, there is no exemption from the act on any basis pertaining to source of funds. It is true that the last section in the chapter recites that the act was passed primarily to bring about conformity between these agencies and the rules and regulations of the Federal Social Security Board; and more particularly in situations involving the use of grant-in-aid funds. There is nothing, however, in the coverage provisions of the laws limiting the application of a chapter specifically to employees performing services in departments specifically financed by grant-in-aid funds.

I am of the opinion, therefore, that your question must be answered to the effect that these bedding inspectors being employees of the health department are subject to the Merit System Law, rules and regulations of the Council, and Merit System examinations as a method of selection and appointment.

OPINIONS TO STATE BOARD OF ALCOHOLIC CONTROL

Alcoholic Beverages; Sale and Transportation into United States
Naval Auxiliary Air Station on Leased Property

12 October 1944

Receipt is acknowledged of your letter of October 10, transmitting an inquiry from Schenley Distillers Corporation with reference to the shipment of alcoholic beverages to the United States Naval Auxiliary Air Station at Manteo. You advise that they have raised the point that this particular station is located on land·leased to the Navy Department and under the full jurisdiction of the Navy Department.

Unless the State of North Carolina has ceded jurisdiction to the Navy Department over this Naval Auxiliary Air Station, shipment of alcoholic beverages into this reservation would be in violation of North Carolina law. See PENN DAIRIES v. MILK CONTROL COMMISSION, 87 L. ed. 749. The fact that the Station is under the control of the naval authorities would not oust the criminal jurisdiction of the State of North Carolina and any shipment of alcoholic beverages into this territory, in violation of the North Carolina statute, would be indictable.

This situation is to be distinguished from that dealt with in the case of JOHNSON v. YELLOW CAB TRANSIENT CO., 88 L. ed. 553, Advance Sheet No. 10, decided on March 13, 1944, in which the Supreme Court of the United States held that cession by a state to the United States of general power to govern a military reservation within its borders leaves the state without power to control liquor transactions upon the reservation.

I have not checked to ascertain whether or not the State has ceded jurisdiction over the Naval Auxiliary Air Station at Manteo but assume that it has not done so. You can get the information about this at the Governor's Office, where there is a complete record of all the territory over which the State has ceded jurisdiction to the Federal Government.

The above statement answers your other letter of October 10, in which you inquire if this office has a record of the various military posts and reservations located in North Carolina over which the State has ceded its jurisdiction. We do not have that list in this office but it can be obtained at the Governor's Office.

State A. B. C. Board; Senate Bill No. 72; Compliance Bond

12 May 1945

I acknowledge receipt of your letter enclosing the proposed bond required under the provisions of Senate Bill No. 72, enacted into law by the 1945 Session of the General Assembly.

I have carefully examined the form of this proposed bond and I am of the opinion that it complies with the provisions of the pertinent statutes and I approve the same as to form and legality, except as to two minor respects.

In the third paragraph, I think that the reference to the statute should read as I have indicated in pencil by striking out the hyphen between the figures "9" and "1" and inserting a dot, and by striking out the words, "as amended in —— enacted by the North Carolina General Assembly, 1945 Session." The reason for this is that Senate Bill No. 72 is in the form of new subsections to Section 18-49 and Senate Bill No. 72 constitutes the subsections and, of course, does not amend subsection one.

In the fourth paragraph I suggest changing the words, "an adequate" to "this."

WINES; HOUSE BILL 877; SECTION 18-93 G. S.; ADOPTING RULES AS TO STANDARDS; IDENTITY OF WINE, ETC.

12 May 1945

I acknowledge receipt of your letter enclosing a letter from Honorable Stewart Berkshire, Deputy Commissioner, Commissioner of Internal Revenue, in which he inquires as to the effect Section 18-109 of House Bill 877, ratified March 19, 1945, has upon Section 18-93 G. S.

Section 18-93 G. S. provides, "The 'Standards of Identity for Wine' and the regulations relating to 'Labeling and Advertising of Wine' promulgated by the Federal Alcohol Administration of the United States Treasury Department, and known respectively as Regulation Number Four, Article II, and Regulation Number Four, Articles III and VI, are hereby adopted by North Carolina."

Section 18-109 of House Bill No. 877 provides in part, "Powers of State Board of Alcoholic Control. The State Board of Alcoholic Control is authorized and empowered:

"(1) To adopt rules and regulations establishing standards of identity, quality and purity for the wines described in Section eighteen - sixty-four (b) and in Article five, Chapter eighteen, of the General Statutes."

I construe House Bill 877 as authorizing and empowering the State Board of Alcoholic Control to either adopt as a part of its regulations the provisions of Section 18-93 or it may entirely depart therefrom and may adopt rules and regulations not consistent with Section 18-93. But, until the State A. B. C. Board adopts rules and regulations as prescribed in Section 18-109, Section 18-93 G. S. would remain in full force and effect.

It seems to me that in order to clarify the matter, the State Board of Alcoholic Control should either adopt Section 18-93 or such other rules and regulations as it deems necessary under the circumstances.

WINE; HOUSE BILL 877; REGULATIONS; SIZE, SHAPE OF CONTAINERS

5 June 1945

Pursuant to our recent conversation relative to amending the rules and regulations adopted by the State Board of Alcoholic Control under authority of House Bill No. 877, I suggest the following changes to meet objections which have been raised.

I suggest that Paragraph C of Part 9, be amended by adding at the end, the following:

"Quart, one-half of a gallon, and one gallon."

That Paragraph B of Part 10, be amended by adding at the end the following:

"Provided that all licensees having on hand as of April 12, 1945, standard wines, shall have until the first day of January, 1946, in which to dispose of such wines or obtain the approval of such wines by the Board."

WINES; FORTIFIED AND SWEET MAY NOT BE SOLD IN DRY COUNTIES

8 June 1945

You inquire as to whether or not a winery may sell wines containing more than 14 per cent alcohol reckoned by volume, to a hospital located in a dry county.

Two classes of wines containing more than 14 per cent alcohol are authorized to be sold under certain conditions in the State. Section 18-95, G. S., prohibits the sales of fortified wines at any place in the State except through county-operated Alcoholic Beverage Control stores; and Section 18-96 defines fortified wines as, "any wine or alcoholic beverage made by fermentation of grapes, fruit, and berries and fortified by the addition of brandy or alcohol or having an alcoholic content of more than 14 per cent absolute alcohol reckoned by volume." Section 18-97 provides in part, "that nothing herein contained shall be construed to permit any person to order and receive by mail or express any spiritous liquors." It is apparent from these sections that fortified wines may be sold in the State only through alcoholic beverage control stores so that if the wine in question is a fortified wine, it may not be sold by a winery to any person, firm, or corporation in a dry county.

Section 18-99 authorizes the sale of a sweet wine containing more than 14 per cent alcohol reckoned by volume in hotels, grade A restaurants, drug stores, and grocery stores in any county in which the operation of alcoholic beverage control stores is authorized by law. Sweet wine is defined by Section 18-99 as one, "made by fermentation from grapes, fruit, and berries to which nothing but pure brandy has been added which brandy is made from the same type of grapes, fruit, or berries which is contained in the base wine to which it is added, and having an alcoholic content of not less than 14 per cent and not more than 20 per cent of absolute alcohol reckoned by volume." It would be observed that the sale of this type of wine is limited to those counties in which alcoholic beverage control stores are operated as authorized by law. If the wine in question is a sweet wine, this section prohibits its sale except in so-called wet counties and such wine may not be sold in dry counties.

The above referred to sections do not deny the right of a person, firm, or corporation residing in a dry county to purchase wines containing more than 14 per cent and transport the same or have it shipped to him by an alcoholic beverage control store unless such wine is purchased and possessed for the purposes of sale.

Section 18-97 provides in part, "it shall be unlawful for any person to purchase on order and receive by mail or express from any such alcoholic beverage control store fortified wines in quantities not in excess of one gallon at any one time."

WINE; SUB-STANDARD; 1945 ACT; FORM OF WARRANT; PROCEDURE

20 September 1945

Pursuant to the request of Mr. Batts, I am enclosing herewith a proposed form of charges to be preferred in warrants against persons charged with the violation of the sub-standard wine act. It will be observed that the offender will be charged with the illegal possession, illegal possession for the purpose of sale, and sale, and for violating the rules and regulations of the Board. The more I have studied the 1945 Act, the more I am convinced that a charge of illegal possession will be sustained by our court, but I think it best in all cases to obtain evidence of actual sale if possible.

Paragraph 3 of Section 1, of the 1945 Act, empowers your Board to test wines possessed or offered for sale or sold in the State and to make an analysis thereof or to determine in any other manner whether such wines meet the standards set up by your Board. This section likewise empowers you to confiscate and destroy any wines not meeting the standards. It will be observed that this section is applicable to those who possess as well as sell sub-standard wines, but it occurs to me if those in possession of this wine refuse to permit your agents to take charge of and destroy the wines, that you not resort to force but apply to the Court in a civil action for an order authorizing you to seize the wine and destroy it. I have discussed this phase of the matter with Mr. Batts.

I also think that your Board should adopt a regulation specifically barring from possession or sale, wines branded sub-standard and make it a violation of your regulations for a person to possess or sell wines branded sub-standard.

BEER AND WINE; SHIPMENT OF WINE FOR SACRAMENTAL PURPOSES

19 October 1945

I acknowledge receipt of your letter enclosing a letter which inquires as to the statutes relating to the shipment of wines to residents of this State for sacramental purposes.

Section 18-21 of the General Statutes answers your question and provides:
"It is lawful for any ordained minister of the gospel who is in charge of a church and at the head of a congregation in this State to receive in the space of ninety days, a quantity of vinous liquor not greater than five gallons, for use in sacramental purposes only, and it shall be lawful for him to receive same in one or more packages or one or more receptacles."

INTOXICATING BEVERAGES; 20 PER CENT WINES; SALE TO MERCHANT IN
SMOKY MOUNTAIN NATIONAL PARK

5 December 1945

I acknowledge receipt of your letter enclosing a letter from Mr. Harry
Marlowe, wholesale dealer, Bryson City, North Carolina, and inquiring as
to whether or not sale of 20 per cent wines may be made by Mr. Marlowe to
a merchant operating a store within the Smoky Mountain National Park.

Under the provisions of Section 403-1, Title 16, USCA, the United States
accepted sole and exclusive jurisdiction of the lands within the Great Smoky
Mountains National Park, acquired from the State of North Carolina and
the State of Tennessee as authorized by the Legislatures of said States on
March 18 and April 12, 1929, respectively, so that the status of the Great
Smoky Mountains National Park, insofar as it relates to the shipment into
or sale on of intoxicating beverages, is the same as that of military reservations over which the State of North Carolina has ceded jurisdiction.

I have heretofore expressed the opinion that a common carrier may
accept shipments of intoxicating beverages from outside of the State and
transport the same into the State through dry counties to a Government
Reservation over which the State of North Carolina has ceded its jurisdiction to the Federal Government. I suggest, however, that inquiries should
be made of the authorities in control of the Great Smoky Mountains National Park as to whether or not there are any Federal regulations restricting the shipment into or sale within the Park.

INTOXICATING BEVERAGES; SALE OF ON AIRPLANES OPERATED OVER ROUTES
CROSSING STATE OF NORTH CAROLINA

3 January 1946

I acknowledge receipt of your letter enclosing a letter from the Distilled
Spirits Institute in which they inquire as to the legality of the sale of
alcoholic beverages on airplanes operated on routes which cross the State
of North Carolina.

Chapter 18 of the General Statutes of North Carolina prohibits the sale
of all alcoholic beverages which contain more than 14 per centum of alcohol
by volume in any place except county-operated A. B. C. stores. The only
exception to this is as to sweet wines made by fermentation of grapes, fruit
or berries to which nothing but pure brandy made from the same type of
grape, fruit or berry is added and having an alcoholic content less than 14
per centum nor more than 20 per centum of absolute alcohol reckoned by
volume which may be sold in Grade A restaurants, hotels, drug stores and
grocery stores in counties in which Alcoholic Beverage Control Stores are
authorized by law. Beer containing one-half of one per centum of alcohol
by volume but not more than 5 per centum, and unfortified wines of not
less than 5 per centum and more than 14 per centum may be sold only by a
person, firm or corporation which has been a bona fide resident of the State

of North Carolina for at least one year and who has been licensed as required by the statute.

I, therefore, conclude that no alcoholic beverage of any kind may be sold on an airplane while passing through the State of North Carolina unless it be the right to sell beer or wine of not more than 14 per centum and then only by a person or corporation which has been a resident of the State of North Carolina for one year and who has been licensed under the provisions of Chapter 18 of the General Statutes.

BEER AND WINE; TRANSPORTATION OF WINE FOR SACRAMENTAL PURPOSES

21 March 1946

I acknowledge receipt of your letter in which you inquire as to whether or not under the present Statutes wine may be shipped in the State of North Carolina for sacramental purposes when such wine has not been placed on the approved list by the State Board of Alcoholic Control.

The original Turlington Act provided in Section 18-2 of the General Statutes that wine for sacramental purposes may be manufactured, purchased, sold, bartered, transported, imported, exported, delivered, furnished and possessed as provided by Title II of "The Volstead Act." Section 18-21 of the General Statutes reads

> "It is lawful for any ordained minister of the gospel who is in charge of a church and at the head of a congregation in this State to receive in the space of ninety consecutive days the quantity of vinous liquor not greater than five gallons, for use in sacramental purposes only, and it shall be lawful for him to receive same in one or more packages or one or more receptacles."

I find nothing in Chapter 903 of the Session of Laws of 1945 which requires wines used solely for sacramental purposes to be on the approved list of the State Board of Alcoholic Control. This Act seems to deal with the shipment of wines in the State for the purposes of re-sale.

I am therefore of the opinion that wines for sacramental purposes may be shipped in the State to an ordained minister as provided in Section 18-21, above quoted.

OPINIONS TO UNEMPLOYMENT COMPENSATION COMMISSION

UNEMPLOYMENT COMPENSATION COMMISSION; AUTHORITY TO PAY
READJUSTMENT ALLOWANCES TO FORMER MEMBERS OF THE
ARMED FORCES OUT OF THE UNEMPLOYMENT
COMPENSATION FUND

22 August 1944

Receipt is acknowledged of your letter of August 22, in which you write me as follows:

"I call your attention to the Service Men's Readjustment Act of 1944 (Chapter 268—Public Law 346), and I would like to especially direct your attention to Title V of this Act (See page 316 U. S. C. A. Congressional Service of 1944, Issue No. 5). You will see under Chapter 11 of this title, Section 1100 that the Administrator of Veteran's Affairs is authorized to administer the title and is authorized to enter into compacts or agreements with Unemployment Compensation Agencies for the purpose of filing claims for readjustment allowances and also paying such allowances to the veterans or former members of the armed forces.· You will also see in Section 1100(d) where the Secretary of the Treasury is authorized to repay any agency administering this portion of the Act those amounts or allowances paid by the agency and properly certified. There are other sections that deal with the administration of the Act by means of a State agency.

"Your attention is now called to Section 9(a) of the Unemployment Compensation Law of North Carolina which deals with the handling and administration of the unemployment compensation fund, and further in this connection, your attention is called to Section 11(k) and Section 11(L) of the Unemployment Compensation Law of this State which sections set forth the powers of this agency to enter into reciprocal agreements with agencies of other states or of the Federal Government.

"The Unemployment Compensation of North Carolina proposes under the terms of the above-cited Federal statute to pay out of its fund Service Men's Readjustment Allowances, and also proposes to enter into an agreement to administer that part of the so-called G. I. Bill.

"Will you please advise us on two questions as follows:

"1. Does the Unemployment Compensation Commission of North Carolina have the power and authority to enter into an agreement or compact with the Administrator of Veteran's Affairs for the purpose of paying readjustment allowances to former members of the armed forces as contemplated in Title V of the so-called G. I. Act?

"2. Does the Unemployment Compensation Commission of North Carolina have the power and authority to pay the above allowances out of (benefit account) the unemployment compensation fund above referred to subject to reimbursements as provided in Title V of the so-called G. I. Act?

"I will appreciate your early answer to these questions to the end that we may arrange if possible to administer this part of the Act for the benefit of the veterans of this state and as a service to the Administrator of Veteran's Affairs."

Under our Unemployment Compensation Act, G. S. 96-6, which provides for the setting up of the Unemployment Compensation fund in which there shall be maintained three separate accounts: (1) a clearing account, (2) an unemployment trust fund account, and (3) a benefit account, in subsection (c) the following provision is made:

> "*Withdrawals.*—Moneys shall be requisitioned from the state's account in the unemployment trust fund solely from the payment of benefits and in accordance with regulations prescribed by the commission . . . Upon receipt thereof the treasurer shall deposit such moneys in the benefit account and shall pay all warrants drawn thereon by the state auditor requisitioned by the commission for the payment of benefits solely from such benefit account."

G. S. 96-4 makes elaborate provisions for reciprocal arrangements with "appropriate and duly authorized agencies of other states or the Federal Government, or both," with regard to various things and the following provisions are made:

> "(B)   Potential rights to benefits accumulated under the unemployment compensation laws of one or more states or under one or more such laws of the Federal Government, or both, may constitute the basis for the payment of benefits through a single appropriate agency under terms which the Commission finds will be fair and reasonable as to all 'affected interests and will not result in any substantial loss to the fund;
> "(C)   Wages or services, upon the basis of which an individual may become entitled to benefits under an unemployment compensation law of another state or of the Federal Government, shall be deemed to be wages for insured work for the purpose of determining his rights to benefits under this act, and wages for insured work, on the basis of which an individual may become entitled to benefits under this act shall be deemed to be wages or services on the basis of which unemployment compensation under such law of another state or of the Federal Government is payable, but no such arrangement shall be entered into unless it contains provisions for reimbursements to the fund for such of the benefits paid under this act upon the basis of such wages or services, and provisions for reimbursements from the fund for such of the compensation paid under such other law upon the basis of wages for insured work, as the Commission finds will be fair and reasonable as to all affected interests; and
> "(D)   Contributions due under this act with respect to wages for insured work shall for the purposes of Section Fourteen of this Act be deemed to have been paid to the fund as of the date payment was made as contributions therefor under another state or Federal unemployment compensation law, but no such arrangement shall be entered into unless it contains provisions for such reimbursements to the fund of such contributions and the actual earnings thereon as the Commission funds will be fair and reasonable as to all affected interests.
> "(2)   Reimbursements paid from the fund pursuant to clause (C), of paragraph (1) of this subsection shall be deemed to be benefits for the purpose of Sections Three, Seven, and Nine of this act. The Commission is authorized to make to other states or Federal agencies and to receive from such other state or Federal agencies, reimbursements from or to the fund, in accordance with arrangements entered into pursuant to paragraph (1) of this subsection."

Under the Service Men's Readjustment Act of 1944, Chapter 268, Public Law 346, known as the G. I. Bill, under Title V, provision is made for the payment of Unemployment Compensation benefits to discharged veterans who are unable to find employment, and, in Chapter XI—ADMINISTRATION, it is provided that the Administrator of Veteran's Affairs is authorized to administer Title V and, in so far as possible, utilize existing facilities and services of Federal and State departments or agencies on the basis of mutual agreements with such departments or agencies. This section provides that allowances paid by the cooperating agencies shall be repaid upon certificate of the Administrator, and that the Secretary of the Treasury, through the Division of Disbursement of the Treasury and without the necessity of audit and settlement by the General Accounting Office, shall pay monthly to the departments, agencies or individuals designated the amount so certified. Other provisions are made under which prompt reimbursement can be made to the State agency administering the Act under agreement with the Administrator of Veteran's Affairs.

Under the quoted provisions of the North Carolina Act, I am of the opinion that your Commission has the power and authority to enter into an agreement or compact with the Administrator of Veteran's Affairs for the purpose of paying readjustment allowances to former members of the armed forces, as contemplated in Title V of the G. I. Act.

I am also of the opinion that your Commission has the authority, under the provisions of our law above quoted, to pay the allowances out of the benefit account of the Unemployment Compensation fund maintained under our law to be reimbursed as provided in Title V of the so-called G. I. Act.

UNEMPLOYMENT COMPENSATION LAW; STATUTES; RETROACTIVE APPLICATION OF SECTION 96-10(a) OF THE GENERAL STATUTES

12 June 1945

Prior to his leaving the service of the Agency, Dr. W. R. Curtis, former Director of the Unemployment Compensation division of the Agency, orally requested the writer for a ruling as to the application of the Unemployment Compensation law upon a statement which is substantially as follows:

Newnan's Market of Reidsville, North Carolina, was an employer under the Unemployment Compensation law for the years of 1941 and 1942. The employer did not know of his liability for contributions to the Unemployment Compensation fund of this State. According to a statement of employer's manager, a Deputy Collector of Internal Revenue stated to the employer that the employer should pay the full 3% tax to the Federal Government for the years in question and the Collector of Internal Revenue would allocate to the State its part of the tax for the Unemployment Compensation fund. The employer in good faith, and at the proper time, paid the Federal Government the full 3% tax for the years in question based upon the wages paid his employees. Subsequently, the employer's records were checked by a field representative of the Commission and the employer for the first time was informed that he should have paid 2.7% of the tax to the State Unemployment Compensation fund, and that this would have been certified to the Federal Government for offset against the Federal levy as provided by the Internal Revenue Code. Thereafter, the employer paid the Unemployment Compensation fund the full amount of the principal and filed claim for refund with the Federal Government as provided by the Internal Revenue Code. The employer did not pay any interest on the principal of taxes due the Commission and has always contended that under these circumstances he did not owe any interest to the Commission and thereafter, the employer filed a notice with the Commission in the nature of a demand for a hearing before the Commission to determine his liability for the interest in question and to date the interest has not been paid and no hearing has yet been conducted by the Commission.

In 1943, Section 96-10(a) of the General Statutes was amended so that the last sentence in said paragraph read as follows:

"If any employer, in good faith, pays contributions to another State, prior to a determination of liability by this commission, which contributions were legally payable to this State, such contribution, when paid to this State, shall be deemed to have been paid by the due date under the law of this State if paid by the due date of such other State."

You will note that this part of the paragraph as it existed in 1943 does not contain any reference to a payment to the United States; and in 1945 the General Assembly further amended this paragraph so as to place the payment made to the United States under the Federal Unemployment Compensation Act on the same basis as a payment made in good faith to another state. The question, therefore, is whether or not the Commission is authorized to give the employer the benefit of this portion of paragraph (a) of Section 96-10 of the General Statutes in a situation where the payment of a tax was made to the United States before this statute was passed by the General Assembly of North Carolina.

Ordinarily, the rule of statutory construction is that statutes and amendments thereto are deemed to be prospective in their effect and application and are not construed to have retroactive application unless the language in the statute clearly and unequivocally shows that the statute was designed to have such construction and application. This rule, however, is not followed so closely in remedial and procedural statutes, nor is it of universal application in tax statutes where the amendment is designed to give the taxpayer some relief with reference to interest and penalties. A statutory provision exacting payment of interest for delinquency in the payment of taxes does not make the interest a part of the tax but merely only pertains to the remedy employed to compel the payment of the tax when due. It does not require citation of authority to support the position that interest and penalties so far as taxation is concerned are the creatures of legislative power and the Legislature has the right to reduce or abolish either or both of these incidents of taxation.

In the case of HENRY v. McKAY, 3 Pac. (2d) 145, 77 ALR, 1025, the Supreme Court of Washington had before it a case in which an interest rate of 12% was charged on delinquent county taxes and the statute was subsequently amended and among other things contained in the amendment, the rate of 12% was stricken out and a rate of 10% inserted. The Court held that this amending statute governed the computation of interest prior to its effective date on taxes which theretofore had become delinquent, saying that the true rule as to amendments made to tax legislation was that:

"Where a section of a statute is amended, the original ceases to exist, and the section as amended supersedes it and becomes a part of the statute for all intents and purposes as if the amendments had always been there."

And the Court further said in substance that where a statute changed the time at which tax installments may be deemed delinquent and the rate of interest chargeable upon delinquent taxes, it referred to all taxes payable by the provisions of the Act and this by reference made the statute applicable to taxes imposed under an original Act as well as to those imposed subsequent to its amendment.

It is also interesting to note that the Court of Appeals of Kentucky, in the case of UNEMPLOYMENT COMPENSATION COMMISSION OF KENTUCKY v. CONSOLIDATION COAL COMPANY, 152 S. W. (2d) 977, held that where the Legislature of Kentucky amended the Unemployment Compensation law relating to refunds so that the period of refund was extended to two years instead of the prior term of one year, this two year extension should be construed retroactively and, therefore, authorized refunds which had been barred by the former period of one year.

In the present case, I think the 1945 amendment is exactly analogous to the situation where the Legislature by enactment extends the time for the payment of a tax or says in statutory language that the tax heretofore delinquent shall not be deemed to be delinquent under certain conditions. I am of the opinion, therefore, that the employer in this case is entitled to avail himself of the present statute and its amendments and that it would be within the law for the Commission to hold or rule that under these circumstances the employer was not indebted to the Commission in any sum whatsoever because of interest. I do not think that this ruling does any violence to the Unemployment Compensation law, and you will note that such a holding is not the same thing as saying that a tax theretofore paid under a valid and existing provision of the law should be refunded. This ruling, therefore, does not conflict with the last sentence of paragraph (e) of Section 96-10, which says:

"Provided, that nothing in this section or in any other section of this chapter shall be construed as permitting the refund of moneys due and payable under the law and regulations in effect at the time such moneys were paid."

I have before me Interpretation No. 31, issued by your agency, and it appears that the last sentence in this Interpretation is in conflict with the ruling given in this letter. The determination spoken of in this paragraph of the Interpretation had specific reference to a determination as to contributions and was not dealing specifically with a question where interest itself is in dispute and there is no question as to contributions. In the present case the only thing in dispute is the payment of interest and the right to compel the payment of same. No adjudication has been made by the Commission although the employer has filed the necessary statutory motion for a hearing and an administrative adjudication. Any ruling made by the Commission must of necessity now be entered since the effective date of the 1945 amendment. I am of the opinion, therefore, that the last sentence or any other sentences in the Interpretation conflicting with the holding in this opinion should be modified and that where interest has not been paid and there is a dispute as to the validity of the interest, the Commission does have a right to give effect to an amendment affecting the matter since the dispute arose. Of course, if the interest had already been paid, then under the provision of the Act above quoted, no refund could be made.

UNEMPLOYMENT COMPENSATION LAW; LIMITATION OF RIGHT TO BRING SUIT OR INSTITUTE PROCEEDINGS; MEANING OF TERMS "SUIT" OR "PROCEED-INGS"; COMMENCEMENT OF SUIT OR PROCEEDINGS

10 July 1945

In your letter you quote Section 96-10(i) of the General Statutes, which is as follows:

"No suit or proceedings for the collection of unpaid contributions may be begun under this chapter after five years from the date on which such contributions become due; provided, that this subsection shall not apply in any case of willful attempts in any manner to defeat or evade the payment of any contributions becoming due under this chapter."

You inquire as to the difference in meaning between the term "suit" and the term "proceedings." Referring to these terms, you inquire as follows:

1. "Are they to be considered the same under the Unemployment Compensation Act, or can the Unemployment Compensation Commission bring a suit within one time under this provision, and bring proceedings at another time under this provision?"
2. "Are the two so joined together in the paragraph that they are to be considered of the same effect in the administration of the law?"
3. You call attention to the administrative proceeding of determining liability whereby a Claims Deputy makes up a transcript of evidence and the Chairman rules upon the basis of this transcript, and you ask: "Is this a proceeding as mentioned in the paragraph, and will such proceeding, when brought before a Claims Deputy, stop the running of the statute of limitations as set out in this paragraph?"

The Unemployment Compensation Law (Chapter 96 of the General Statutes) provides three general methods for the compulsory collection of contributions or taxes. These methods are:

1. Under the provisions of 96-10(b) of the General Statutes, after due notice, the Commission may maintain a civil action in the Superior Court for the recovery of delinquent taxes and this is handled, and the proceedings therein are the same, as in any other action instituted in our courts of general jurisdiction.

2. Under the provisions of the same section and subsection, if delinquent taxes are not paid within thirty days after the due date, and after due notice and reasonable opportunity for hearing, the Commission may

certify according to an appropriate form the amount due to the Clerk of the Superior Court of the county in which the taxpayer resides or has property, and when this certificate is docketed and indexed it has the effect of a judgment of the Superior Court. Duplicates of the certificate are certified to the Sheriff and have the same force and effect as an execution issued upon a judgment.

3. Under the provisions of Section 96-4(m) and subsections following, the Commission after due notice has the right and power to hold and conduct hearings for the purpose of determining the status and liabilities of employers and employing units. It also has the right to determine the amount of contributions, if any, that may be due by an employer, and the decision of the Commission when docketed in the office of the Clerk of the Superior Court becomes a judgment. This is a regular administrative determining of liability, and findings of fact made by the Commission are conclusive when supported by competent evidence. Provision is also made for judicial review of the decision by the courts.

The above quoted statute was passed by the General Assembly of 1945, and prior to that time it would seem there was no limitation on the right of the Commission to institute suits or proceedings for the collection of delinquent taxes. The form and words contained in the above quoted statute are similar to the form and words as contained in limitations prescribed by the Internal Revenue Act wherein the United States sets certain limitations on its right to collect income taxes, excess profits taxes, etc. This type of limitation has been passed upon by the Federal Courts and there are many cases on the subject, but one of the leading cases is the case of SEAMAN v. BOWERS, 297 Fed. 371 (Circuit Court of Appeals, Second Circuit), and I think that this case answers nearly all of your questions. In that case the Court had before it a limitation statute of the Revenue Act of 1921, the pertinent parts of which are as follows:

"No suit or proceeding for the collection of any such taxes due under this Act or under prior income, excess profits, or war profits tax Acts, ... shall be begun, after the expiration of five years after the date when such return was filed, but this shall not affect suits or proceedings begun at the time of the passage of this Act. . . ."

It was contended by counsel for the Government that "proceeding" and "suit" mean the same thing and that both meant an action or proceeding in court as distinguished from executive action or administrative proceedings to collect taxes. In collecting its taxes, the Government uses an administrative or executive proceeding known as a "warrant for distraint," and this proceeding is the equivalent of the summary judgment used by the Unemployment Compensation Commission. In disposing of this argument, the Court said:

"Cases are cited by both sides as to the meaning of the word 'proceeding' in various connections, and counsel for the collector invokes the principle of ejusdem generis in support of the argument, in effect, that 'suit' and 'proceeding' mean the same thing.

"We think it unnecessary to go beyond the statute to ascertain the meaning of 'proceeding.' In our view, it was clearly the legislative intent to set up the statutory limitation against the collection of the tax whether by administrative action or by law suit.

"To enforce the collection of the tax on action or suit by or on behalf of the government in the courts is far less usual than procedure by way of warrant for distraint or other executive action. Certainly, where the taxpayer has property which may be levied upon, the executive method is more speedy and summary and the one to which resort is most usually had. It would, indeed, be strange if there were no statutory limitation in respect of proceedings by the collector, such as this, and yet a statutory limitation in regard to suits brought by or on behalf of the government."

This same construction or interpretation was applied by the District Court of South Dakota in the case of NEW YORK AND ALBANY LIGHT-ERAGE COMPANY v. BOWERS, INTERNAL REVENUE COLLECTOR, 4 Fed. (2d) 604.

It is clear, therefore, from the interpretations contained in these cases that so far as suit or proceedings are concerned, the five year limitation applies to both and it is equally clear that the word "proceedings" covers any executive or administrative method for the compulsory collection of taxes, such as the summary judgment heretofore mentioned or an administrative hearing by the Commission. It is equally clear that in collecting its taxes the Unemployment Compensation Commission has a choice of remedies,—that is, it may bring a suit in court or it may use its administrative proceedings, and I am of the opinion that the method of collecting by summary judgment is a proceeding, and likewise the method of collecting by hearing before the Commission is a proceeding within the meaning of the above quoted statute. I am further of the opinion that the five year limitation is binding upon the Commission and will bar the right of the Commission to compel the collection if either of the three methods is used unless the same are instituted within the five year period. In this instance, the word "suit" and the word "proceedings" are not synonymous and their application is not confined to suits in court, but to the contrary, the word "proceedings" brings within its meaning and scope all executive or administrative methods for the compulsory collection of taxes as provided by the law.

Of course, one of the vital questions that will arise in the future is the question when a proceeding is commenced or begun so that it tolls or stops the running of the statutory limitation. As to a suit in court, we know that the statute provides that it is commenced or begun when the summons is issued. As to hearings held by the Commission wherein decisions are made on transcripts furnished by Deputies as provided by Section 96-4(m) of the General Statutes, I am of the opinion that such a hearing or proceeding would be deemed to be commenced or begun when the taxpayer is notified of the hearing,—that is, when the taxpayer receives notice of the hearing. You will note from a reading of the statute that the Commission does not have any right or power to exercise jurisdiction until "after due notice." It is possible that the Court would say that after the taxpayer receives notice the date of beginning would relate back to the date of the notice,—that is, the date the same was issued, but to be on the safe side,

I think you should consider the date that the taxpayer receives the notice as the date when the proceeding is begun.

I think that this same reasoning would also apply in your collection of taxes by summary judgment. You will note in that statute that you cannot issue—that is, you cannot docket—a summary judgment until "after due notice and reasonable opportunity for hearing." There is some disposition of the courts to say that a proceeding of this type is not begun until after all of the days of notice have expired. See NEW YORK AND ALBANY LIGHTERAGE case, *supra*. I think, however, that I would contend that a proceeding is begun when the taxpayer receives the notice.

UNEMPLOYMENT COMPENSATION LAW; COVERED SERVICES; STATUTORY SCOPE OF COVERAGE; INCLUSION OR EXCLUSION OF COMMISSION SALESMEN OF CEMETERY LOTS; INCLUSION OR EXCLUSION OF COMMISSION AGENTS OF BALTIMORE SALESBOOK COMPANY

15 November 1945

Sometime ago you sent to our office a transcript of evidence and other papers in the matter of J. U. Shoff Sales Company of Kannapolis, North Carolina, (Employer No. 65-13-002). At the same time, you also sent to our office a transcript of evidence and exhibits in the matter of Baltimore Salesbook Company, 3132 Frederick Avenue, Baltimore, Maryland, (Employer No. 51-60-154) and Arthur Reid, 113 Reynolds Building, Winston-Salem, North Carolina. Both of these records deal with persons who have certain working relationships with the employing units involved and are compensated on a commission basis. Both groups performing these types of service are salesmen and the evidence and exhibits contain an explanation of the circumstances under which these parties work and perform their services.

In your letter, yau stated in substance that the Unemployment Compensation Commission desired that we should review these records and give the Commission an opinion as to whether or not these persons should be counted as persons performing services covered under the Unemployment Compensation Law. If these persons are performing services covered under the Act, the result would be that these persons would be counted in determining liability under the Act, and in case the Commission decided that the employing units involved were employers, then the Commission would assess taxes or contributions based upon the commissions paid to these salesmen.

We will first consider the case of J. U. Shoff Sales Company of Kannapolis, North Carolina, designated by your employer number 65-13-002.

In connection with the above matter which is now before the Commission to determine the status of these salesmen, attention is called to the fact that an opinion has already been issued in this case which is designated as Opinion Number 529, and signed by the Chairman of the Commission. Exceptions to the ruling of the Commission, which are attached to the record, were filed by Counsel for the J. U. Shoff Sales Company, and I assume that the matter is still before the Commission to be heard upon the exceptions.

In this case, the liability of the employing unit concerned is at issue in the record for the years of 1943 and 1944. Contributions have been paid by J. U. Shoff Sales Company for the year of 1943 under circumstances to indicate that the same were paid under protest. The employing unit refused to pay for the year 1944, and as a result of the protest, a hearing was held which resulted in the present record. Briefly, it appears that this employing unit continuously carries two persons on its payroll who occupy the status of employees, and their relationship with the employing unit is not contested. Admissions in the record show that if the individuals selling cemetery lots on commission basis are determined to be engaged in employment under the Act, then the employing unit would be an employer and liable for payroll taxes for the years in question. The status of the salesmen selling cemetery lots is decisive of the question of the employing unit's liability, it appearing from the record that there are at least eight of these salesmen for the years in question or the number of these salesmen, plus the regular employees, add up to the required number to establish liability for the years in question.

It briefly appears that J. U. Shoff Sales Company is a partnership engaged in the business of selling cemetery lots under a contract between it and the Carolina Cemetery Park Corporation. The Cemetery Park Corporation fixes the price of the lots; the salesmen are not paid any salary, or compensation for their services except on a commission basis; no salesman has a drawing account, or obtains any advances; no directions are given to the salesmen as to the manner in which they shall sell the lots, and the salesmen are not confined to any particular territory or limitation in that respect; they have no fixed hours of work and are free from all control or direction in the performance of their acts of salesmanship. Cemetery lots are practically all sold in the homes of prospects; in fact, it appears that a great many of the salesmen have merely furnished tips as to prospects rather than making the actual sale. The only qualifications of a salesman is that he shall be honest and not make any false representations, and the sale of the lots is restricted to members of the white race. The salesman is furnished with a kit containing maps of the cemetery and certain sales materials. J. U. Shoff Sales Company hires the salesmen and has the right to terminate the relationship. No part of the sales work is performed in the office of the J. U. Shoff Sales Company, and these salesmen are not required to submit any reports. Most of the salesmen are engaged in other businesses such as real estate, ministry, working in textile mills, selling cars, vacuum cleaner business, electrical business, insurance business, teaching school, and one is the Secretary of the Merchants Association of Kannapolis and has been so for years. A salesman by the name of C. D. Blake was engaged full time as a salesman, and perhaps one or two others were engaged in this same type of work on a full-time basis. There is no evidence that J. U. Shoff Sales Company held any meetings, maintained field supervisors, or maintained any of the usual administrative machinery used in promoting and conducting sales and in operating a cohesive sales force.

We now call attention to the fact that on the 27th day of June, 1940, the

Unemployment Compensation Commission issued an option in the matter of W. Halberstadt and W. F. Halberstadt, trading as, Montlawn Sales, Raleigh, North Carolina. The record and evidence in that case is hereby referred to for the purpose of showing the conditions under which the cemetery lots salesmen performed their services as outlined in that case. The Commission adjudged and determined that the cemetery lots salesmen in the Halberstadt case were not engaged in services covered under the Act; that the salesmen were customarily engaged in independently established trades, occupations, professions, or businesses, and that they were free from control, both under their contract of service and in fact.

On July 18, 1942, the Unemployment Compensation Commission of North Carolina rendered another decision wherein cemetery lots salesmen were considered by the Commission as to their status under the Act. This was the case of Providence Memorial Association, 616 Commercial Bank Building, Charlotte, North Carolina. Reference is made to the record and evidence in that case for the purpose of showing the plan of operation of the cemetery lots salesmen and their similarity of operation as contained in the Montlawn case. In the Providence Memorial Association case, the Commission determined that the cemetery salesmen in question were free from control or direction in the performance of their services; that the services were outside the usual course of the business for which such service was performed and was performed outside of all the places of business of the Memorial Association; that the cemetery lots salesmen were customarily engaged in independently established trades, occupations, professions, or businesses.

On January 28, 1942, the Commission again had before it the question of the status of salesmen of cemetery lots and whether or not the type of services performed by these individuals should be considered as covered services under the Act. This was the case of Guilford Memorial Park, Inc. of High Point, North Carolina. It was adjudicated in this hearing by the Commission that the cemetery lots salesmen were not performing services within the meaning of the Act, and that these salesmen met all of the tests or requirements of exclusion as contained in Section 96-8 (g) (6) (A) (B) (C) of the General Statutes. (See page 10 of the pamphlet of the Unemployment Compensation Law).

It thus appears that since the days the Commission has been organized in the early part of the year 1937 up until the present time, or for a period of nearly nine years, it has been the accepted ruling and decision of the Unemployment Compensation Commission that salesmen of cemetery lots met the conditions of exclusion set forth in the Act, and are not engaged in covered services under the Unemployment Compensation Law. The firms above named, or employing units, have relied on these opinions, and as a result have not paid any taxes or contributions based on the services performed by these commission salesmen of cemetery lots.

We are of the opinion that if the Unemployment Compensation Commission should now hold that such cemetery lots salesmen are engaged in services covered under the Act, that the Commission could not now go behind their decisions and tax those firms or corporations which they have heretofore held to be not liable for such taxes. The principle or law of res judicata has become established in administrative proceedings and administrative law. See an article entitled, "Administrative Res Judicata" in 40 Illinois Law Review, May-June, 1945, page 56, page 83. See also an article entitled "Res Judicata in Administrative Law" in 49 Yale Law Journal, 1250. In the case of *George H. Lee Company* v. *Federal Trade Commission*, 113 F. (2d), 583, 586, the Court said:

> "Unless a question which a court or an administrative board has power to decide is to be regarded as conclusively settled as between the parties by the formal decree of the court or the final order of the board, there can be no end to a controversy except as the result of the financial disability of one of the parties."

There is also another rule of administrative law, which in our opinion, is applicable to this situation, and that is: "The settled construction of a statute by an administrative body indicating the method of its application to specific cases, which embodies the practical interpretation of the statute by the department or agency charged with its administration is entitled to great weight with the courts unless there are very cogent reasons for rejecting it. A uniform, long continued, and undisputed administrative construction is not usually disturbed unless for very compelling reasons, and unless the construction is found by the court to be entirely unwarranted by law and outside of the scope of the statute under which the administrative body is acting." See Chapter 28, Federal Administrative Law by Von Baur. See also Chapter 16 of Hart's Introduction to Administrative Law, the chapter being entitled, "Conclusiveness of Administrative Determinations."

In the case of *United States* v. *Philbrick*, 120 U. S. 52, 59, the Court said:

> "A contemporaneous construction by the officers upon whom was imposed the duties of executing these statutes is entitled to great weight; and since it is not clear that the construction was erroneous, it ought not now to be overturned." See also *United States* v. *Hill*, 120 U. S. 169.

The doctrine of stare decisis is also beginning to be applied to the decisions of administrative tribunals, especially where these administrative tribunals are performing quasi judicial functions. We should not lose sight of the fact that in the performance of its quasi judicial duties, the Unemployment Compensation Commission of North Carolina is a judicial tribunal. In the case of the *Prudential Insurance Company of America* v. *Unemployment Compensation Commission*, 217 N. C. 495, 501, Mr. Justice Barnhill in his opinion said:

> "The legislature has conferred upon the Unemployment Compensation Commission the right and power to determine the rights, status and liabilities of an employer under the terms of the Act. * * * It would seem, therefore, that by express legislative mandate, the Unemployment Compensation Commission is the proper forum for determining the very question the plaintiff here seeks to present. *In certain respects the Unemployment Compensation Commission is a judicial tribunal and the declaratory judgment act expressly provides that*

rights, status, and other legal relations may be determined by the courts within their respective jurisdictions." (Italics ours).

In the case of *National Labor Relations Board* v. *Mall Tool Company*, 119 F. (2d) 700, 702, in speaking of the duty of administrative bodies to follow former precedents, the Court said:

"Consistency in administrative rulings is essential, for to adopt different standards for similar situations is to act arbitrarily."

While it is true under the so-called (A) (B) (C) statute of the Unemployment Compensation Law, the Commission has a certain discretion as to whether certain types of services fall within or without the statutory standards, nevertheless, it has been held in many cases that this discretion must be exercised in a reasonable manner and must not be arbitrated. We are of the opinion, therefore, that the Commission in this case should follow the precedents or rulings heretofore established, and for the Commission to now hold that such cemetery lots salesmen are engaged in covered services would result in a ruling inconsistent with its former rulings, contrary to its former precedents, and might lead to the position of lack of uniformity in taxation or discrimination in taxation, since former employing units have been held to be free of taxation under like circumstances. It would also, in our opinion, place the Commission in a position where it might be charged that it was acting in an arbitrary manner and had abused its discretion since it has applied the rule of exclusion to three employing units in former cases which resulted in these units not being taxed, whereas, now it purposes to tax an employing unit on practically a similar situation.

We think in this case that the Commission should follow the principle of administrative consistency, and that this should be done because the Commission has established the rule of exclusion which has existed over a period of nine years, and that this principle should be followed unless the courts reverse the Commission. It is true that Supreme Courts, including the Supreme Court of the United States, overrule decisions, but a decision overruling former decisions is never applied retroactively, and is never applied so as to result in discrimination or so as to establish a lack of uniformity.

Irrespective of what we have said about long settled practice in administrative construction, and in fact, irrespective of anything we have said above, we are of the opinion that under the facts shown in the record of J. U. Shoff Sales Company, the rules of exclusion have been met and that these cemetery lots salesmen are not engaged in services covered under the Unemployment Compensation Law. The employing unit does not maintain the administrative supervision, the suggestive sales literature, nor does it have the cohesive machinery of a regular or typical sales organization which results in control or which indirectly indicates that some sovereign or dictatorial power is lurking in the background.

In our opinion, the test as to the service being outside of the places of business of the employing unit has been fully met and that the salesmen concerned, or at least a sufficient number, are engaged in independently established trade, occupations, professions, or businesses.

It is for the members of the Commission to be satisfied that the rules of exclusion as to this type of service apply or do not apply. We cannot substitute ourselves for the Commission in the exercise of this discretion, but we do say that in our opinion, that if we were serving as Commissioners, we would be satisfied that the rules of exclusion do apply, and that the cemetery lots salesmen in this case are not engaged in employment and are not performing services covered under the Act.

We now consider the case of the salesmen of the Baltimore Salesbook Company designated as your employer number 51-60-154. To our mind, the record does not disclose any liability whatsoever on the part of Arthur Reid, the state agent of the company, and we will, therefore, not discuss any liability with respect to this individual.

It appears that Arthur Reid in the year of 1921 or 1922 became the first representative of the Baltimore Salesbook Company in North Carolina. He subsequently took up other lines of business in sales work, but appointed certain jobbers around over the State of North Carolina to whom the Baltimore Salesbook Company shipped direct and billed the jobber direct, or made drop shipment to the jobber's customers under his name and billed the jobber. A list of these jobbers appears on page fourteen of the record and it is quite apparent that they are all engaged in businesses of their own, no doubt long established, some of them being corporations; and it seems to us that the jobbers mentioned in the record do not enter into the determination to be made in this case. They buy goods outright and sell outright. There are, however, certain commission salesmen who do enter into the determination of this case, and if these commission salesmen are engaged in covered services under the law, then the Baltimore Salesbook Company would be an employer as defined under the Unemployment Compensation Law. There is a possibility that this employing unit is an employer under the law for it appears in the record that it has paid contributions on one full time employee located at Charlotte. Irrespective of this question, the Commission does have before it the question of whether it will assess contributions or payroll taxes on the commissions paid the salesmen of the Baltimore Salesbook Company, and it is to this question that we address our attention since the fact that it may be an employer, either by election or by other means of establishing such a status, can be readily determined as a matter of record by the Commission. It appears that an agent of the Commission or field representative made an examination sometime prior to the hearing and thought that the salesmen met the rules of exclusion. It appears that the employing unit in question does not give any instructions as to how the salesmen should carry on their duties, has no field managers or supervisors, and are selected by the employing unit principally upon the basis of honesty and good character. The state agent has never terminated the relationship with any of these salesmen. There is no written contract; there is no course of training; the salesmen are not required to work any regular number of hours; there are no advancements, drawing accounts, or payments of expenses; the salesmen do not have the right to collect money from customers. A list of the salesmen is found on page fifteen of the record. The salesmen are paid by a monthly commission check sent to them by the Baltimore Salesbook Company. No manuals are distributed and the salesmen have no right to extend credit. No attempt is made to see whether the salesman is working or not, or where he may be in the state; the salesmen do not occupy any of the office space or any building space furnished by the Baltimore Salesbook Company; no courses of instruction are given to the salesmen, but inquiries are answered as to proper prices. The record contains a series of affidavits showing that these salesmen are engaged in handling other lines, engaged in other work, and occupations, and those men engaged exclusively in sales work carry many other items with other companies, and also carry the lines of Baltimore Salesbook Company as a non-competing line.

The definition of employment in the Unemployment Compensation Law is found in Section 96-E (g) (1), and is as follows:

"'Employment' means service, * * * performed for remuneration or under any contract of hire, written or oral, express or implied."

The rules for determining the inclusion or exclusion of services under the Unemployment Compensation Law are as follows:

"Services performed by an individual for remuneration shall be deemed to be employment subject to this chapter unless and until it is shown to the satisfaction of the commission that:

"(A)   Such individual has been and will continue to be free from control or direction over the performance of such services, both under his contract of service and in fact; and

"(B)   Such service is either outside the usual course of the business for which such service is performed, or that such service is performed outside of all the places of business of the enterprise for which such service is performed; and

"(C)   Such individual is customarily engaged in an independently established trade, occupation, profession, or business."

Much could be said as to whether the services performed by these salesmen is actual employment under the first above quoted section of the Act; that is, whether or not these salesmen are performing service under a contract of *hire*, whether the same be a written or oral contract, or an express or implied contract. In passing upon the question as to whether services are covered under the Unemployment Compensation Law, it is the duty of the Commission to first ascertain if the person involved is performing services under a contract of hire since a contract of hire has a definite technical meaning. Persons must first be found to be engaged in employment under a contract of hire before the Commission then proceeds to apply the so-called (A) (B) (C) clause and then determine if the type of service should be included or excluded even though it is performed under a contract of hire. Perhaps not much attention has been paid to this method of determination, but that this is the correct procedure to follow is pointed out in the case of *Broderick, Inc.* v. *Riley*, 157 Pac. (2d) 954, 958 (Wash.). See also the case of *Singer Sewing Machine Company* v. *Industrial Commission*, 134 Pac. (2d) 179, and the case of *Singer Sewing Machine Company* v. *Industrial Commission*, 151 Pac. (2d) 694.

Irrespective of whether these salesmen are engaged in a contract of hire, we are of the opinion that as disclosed by the evidence in this record, the salesmen in question satisfy the exclusion requirements contained in the so-called (A) (B) (C) clause, and are not engaged in service covered under the Act. What we have said above in regard to the cemetery lots salesmen applies with equal force to this situation. We are aware of the fact that there are many cases decided by many Supreme Courts holding that commission salesmen are engaged in services subject to the various unemployment compensation laws. Many of these laws contain similar provisions to the Unemployment Compensation Law of this state. See:

Electrolux Corporation v. *Board of Review*, 28 Atl. (2d) 207 (N. J.)
Schomp, et al. v. *The Fuller Brush Company*, 19 Atl. (2d) 780
Globe Grain and Milling Company v. *Industrial Commission, et al.*, 97 Pac. (2d) 582.
Mulhausen v. *Bates*, 114 Pac. (2d) 995.

On the other hand, under other circumstances, commission salesmen have been held to be not covered under these same unemployment compensation acts. See:

Fuller Brush Company v. *Industrial Commission*, et al., 104 Pac. (2d) 201.
Coppedage v. *Riley*, 157 Pac. (2d) 979.

The cases of *Unemployment Compensation Commission* v. *Jefferson Standard Life Insurance Company*, 215 N. C. 479, and *Unemployment Compensation Commission* v. *National Life Insurance Company*, 219 N. C. 576, hold that life insurance agents under the circumstances outlined in those cases were engaged in services subject to the Act. It is pointed out in these cases that the test of coverage is not the master and servant relationship, and that the statute contains its own definition and its own standards of coverage which are very broad and conclusive. It is pointed out on page 485 of the opinion in the Jefferson Standard case that the soliciting agents were subject to a high degree of control by reason of their written contracts; that some of their services were performed in the office of the company, and that the company maintained an integrated, cohesive, sales administrative organization. In fact, we think it can be generally said in all cases where commission salesmen have been held to be covered by the Act, the organization of procedure, sales meetings, suggestions, manuals, and other sales procedures which are prevalent in our modern type of business, were so applied and used that the commissions and courts in passing upon the relationship could not get away from the position that the employing unit or employer actually controlled the salesmen with the same force and to the same extent as if the salesmen were working directly under some agent of the company in an office or building of the company. We do not mean to say that there are not many cases in which commission salesmen should not be covered under the Unemployment Compensation Law of this state, for no doubt there are many cases where they should be covered and rightly so. We are of the opinion, however, that under the facts and circumstances disclosed by the record in this case, there is no integrated organization or salesmanship plan, supervision, or suggestion that brings this case within the scope and coverage of the statute. It is for the Commission to decide in its discretion and judgment whether or not the conditions imposed by the (A) (B) (C) clause have been met and whether or not the employing unit has sustained the burden of meeting these conditions. The Commission may decide that these salesmen are covered, but if we were sitting as Commissioners, we would be of the opinion that this record does not present the clear-cut case which demands the coverage of these salesmen under the Act, and that in our opinion payroll taxes or contributions should not be assessed from the commissions paid the salesmen in this case.

UNEMPLOYMENT COMPENSATION LAW; EMPLOYER; SEPARATE EETABLISH-
MENTS; SCOPE OF COVERÁGE

16 April 1946

In your letter of April 11, 1946, you call our attention to Section 96-8(f) (8) of the General Statutes of North Carolina pertaining to contractors and sub-contractors; and you submit to us a state of facts as follows:

"Employing unit A has only three persons in its employ. Employing unit A is a bulk station operator of oil company B. Prior to the passage of Section 96-8(f) (8) as of March 13, 1945, oil company B was responsible for the contributions on the wages paid by employing unit A to its employees. Since the passage of such amendment above-referred to, employing unit A becomes a liable employer even though it does not have but three persons in its employ and becomes liable by reason of its contractual relationship with oil company B. Employing unit A, who has now become an employer, also owns a grocery store in which three persons are employed. Employing unit A, therefore, in both the bulk station and the grocery store, only employs six persons; is employing Unit A, who has now become an employer, liable for contributions on the wages paid to the persons in its employ in the grocery store?"

The section above referred to pertains to contractors and sub-contractors and was passed at the 1945 Session of the General Assembly. Prior to that time, the so-called sub-contractors' clause existed in another form in our Unemployment Compensation Law; but for our purposes, it is unnecessary to discuss the statutory history of this provision.

First of all, I call your attention to the fact that the present provision is incorporated in the definition section of the Unemployment Compensation Law; and as now written, this provision is set forth in its terms as one of the sections defining an "employer." If any person, firm or corporation, coming within the definition of an employing unit, becomes an employer under the Unemployment Compensation Law, such employer is required by the act to report and pay contributions upon all of the wages paid to his employees for the performance of services. Because an employer has separate establishments or separate branches engaged in different kinds of work or activity is no reason why any particular branch is exempt from coverage under the Law. You will note that a portion of Section 96-8 and particularly a portion of Subsection (e) of such section is as follows:

"All individuals performing services within this State for any employing unit which maintains two or more separate establishments within this State shall be deemed to be employed by a single employing unit for all the purposes of this chapter."

It is further noted that under the provisions of 96-9 of the General Statutes, contributions are based upon and paid "with respect to wages for employment."

There is no exemption in the statute or in the Unemployment Compensation Law because an employer has separate establishments or because the employees of a certain establishment are engaged in work different from the employees in another establishment belonging to the same employer. The only exception to this statement are those services contained in the exemption clauses of the act which are found in Section 96-8(g) (8). Of course, if one of the separate branches of an employee's activities fell within these exemptive clauses, then that branch would not be covered because of their type of service or employment.

In the case put by you, however, the employer becomes an employer under the sub-contractors clause. He has three employees in his bulk station connected with his oil company. He also has a grocery store in which he has three employees. I assume for purposes of this question that this employer has two separate branches, that is three employees for the oil business and three employees for the grocery store. The answer to your question, therefore, is that this man being an employer, all of his employees are covered under the Unemployment Compensation Law of this State. The fact that he is an employer brings under coverage the three employees in the grocery store just the same as the three employees in the bulk oil station. The status of employer once having been fixed, covers all employees in all branches and types of service or industry operated by that employer. The employees in the grocery store are not engaged in employment or in performing services falling within the exemptive clauses heretofore mentioned.

In this respect, the Unemployment Compensation Law differs from our Workmen's Compensation Act. You will note under Section 97-2 (a) of the Workmen's Compensation Act that coverage is based upon five or more employees "regularly employed in the same business or establishment." You will thus see that coverage there is based upon the number of employees in each establishment of an employer; and it is specifically so stated in the statute. It seems to me that this situation which is perhaps valid in Unemployment Compensation laws because different businesses have different accident risks, has been studiously avoided in our Unemployment Compensation Law for the reason that unemployment in one branch of an employer's business is just as bad and just as serious as unemployment in another branch of an employer's business.

From what we have said above, employer A shoull report and pay contributions on all of his employees in all of his establishments; and this necessarily includes the employees in the bulk station and in the grocery store.

OPINIONS TO STATE PROBATION COMMISSION

CRIMINAL LAW; CRIMINAL PROCEDURE; SUSPENSION OF SENTENCE AND PROBATION; VALIDITY OF JUDGMENT

6 June 1946

You enclosed with your letter a copy of a judgment entered by Judge Lacy S. Collier of the Recorder's Court of Cumberland County, Fayetteville, North Carolina. From this transcript of judgment it appears that the defendant, M. P. Suttle, was either convicted or plead guilty, to a charge of failing to send his children to school. He was sentenced to work under the supervision of the State Highway and Public Works Commission for a period of one month. The sentence was suspended and the defendant, under the terms of the suspension, was placed on probation for a period of two years under the supervision of the North Carolina Probation Commission. The defendant was required to perform the usual conditions of probation which are set forth on the judgment and numbered (a) through (j) and in addition thereto he was required to perform as a special condition of probation an order requiring him to keep his minor children in school.

You further state that you have no information as to whether or not the defendant had been fined $25.00 for this offense and failed to pay the fine before being given the thirty days suspended sentence and being placed on probation. You inquire of this office, whether in our opinion, this judgment is valid. Apparently, the defendant did not appeal from this judgment, and as you know, he is presumed to have accepted the terms of the suspension and probation. In *State* v. *Miller*, 225 N. C., 213, 215, the court said:

> "But the order suspending the imposition or execution of sentence on condition is favorable to the defendant in that it postpones punishment and give him an opportunity to escape it altogether. When he sits by as the order is entered and does not then appeal, he impliedly consents and thereby waives or abandons his right to appeal on the principal issue of his guilt or innocence and commits himself to abide by the stipulated conditions. *He may not be heard thereafter to complain that his conviction was not in accord with due process of law.*" (Emphasis supplied.)

I think that this question must pertain to the compulsory school law and especially to the penalty statute as set forth in Section 115-305 of the General Statutes. This particular section is as follows:

> "Any parent, guardian, or other person violating the provisions of this article shall be guilty of a misdemeanor, and upon conviction shall be liable to a fine not less than five dollars nor more than twenty-five dollars, and upon failure or refusal to pay such fine, the said parent, guardian or other person shall be imprisoned not exceeding thirty days in the county jail."

You no doubt have a question in your mind as to the validity of this judgment because the transcript or copy does not show that the fine was imposed and that the defendant failed or refused to pay the fine. Since the defendant has not raised any question about the legality of the judgment, and as he is the party provided by law with the right of appeal, and he has not seen fit to exercise this right, it does not seem to me that the Probation Commission should question the judgment which appears to be regular upon its face. It is true that the judgment does not recite that the fine was imposed and that the defendant refused or failed to pay it, and I don't think that we have a right to assume that the Judge of the Recorder's Court acted without regard to the statute and in an illegal manner. In fact, the contrary is true as a strong presumption of law; it seems to me that the true law is that it is presumed that all necessary proceedings were taken in the court to support the validity of the judgment.

As I understand the law the Supreme Court itself does not presume invalidity or illegality of the proceedings in the court below unless the same appears on the record. In fact the contrary is true as a condition necessary to the validity of an order or judgment, or if sufficient evidence is necessary to support a finding and these things do not appear of record, the presumption is that such condition was complied with, or that the court had sufficient evidence before it upon which to base its findings.

I am of the opinion, therefore, that the Probation Commission should not place itself in the position of a party to a criminal proceeding and seek to attack a judgment of court or refuse to carry out the order of probation on such a judgment as the enclosed judgment. It may be that cases might arise in the future in which the judgment would be completely void on its very face, and that such a question should be raised, but I don't see that type of judgment in the matter now under consideration.

OPINIONS TO BOARD OF EXAMINERS OF PLUMBIN AND HEATING CONTRACTORS

STATE BOARD OF EXAMINERS OF PLUMBING & HEATING CONTRACTORS; IS-
SUANCE OF LICENSE; NOT REQUIRED UNDER FACTS
IN LETTER AUGUST 4, 1944

12 August 1944

I acknowledge receipt of your letter of August 4 in which you state cer tain facts relating to the application of Mr. M. R. Buchanan of High Point North Carolina, for license to engage in both 'the professions of plumbin and heating contracting. I understand that your Board was founded i June 1931 and at that time Mr. Buchanan did not hold a license from th Revenue Department and was required by your Board to make applicatio and pass the required examination of the Board for license as a plumb ing contractor; that he successfully passed the examination as a plumbin contractor but did not take the examination and was not licensed as a heat ing contractor; that during the intervening years he has practiced the pro fession of plumbing contracting but has not engaged in the profession o heating contracting.

I further understand that Mr. Buchanan now makes application to you Board to be licensed as a heating contractor, claiming that he should no be required to take the examination but should be given a license under th provisions of Section 12 of your regulatory Act, stating that while he di not hold a license from the State Department of Revenue prior to th formation of your Board, he did hold a license from the City of High Poin as both a plumbing and heating contractor.

You inquire as to whether or not Mr. Buchanan is now entitled to b licensed to engage in the profession of heating contracting in addition t plumbing contracting.

Section 12 of Chapter 52, Public Laws of 1931, creating the State Boar of Examiners of Plumbing and Heating Contractors, provides, in part "All persons now engaged in the plumbing or heating business and holdin a State license shall receive his or their license or renewal thereof to er gage in said business without examination, upon payment of an annua license fee of $50.00." I am of the opinion that the license referred to i said section is the license required by the State Department of Revenue.

This section was repealed by Section 8 of Chapter 224 of the Public Law of 1939, so that it appears that there is no provision in the law now fo a person to be given a license by your Board unless and until the appli cant has taken the necessary qualifying examination. However, even if i could be argued that Mr. Buchanan held a license from the City of High Point as a heating contractor prior to the formation of your Board an therefore could have qualified under the provisions of the original Sectio 12 of the 1931 Act, I do not think that he comes within the requirement o said Section 12 as it requires an applicant to not only be engaged in th profession but to hold a State license. Under the facts set out in your letter Mr. Buchanan did not hold a State license but a license issued by the City of High Point.

Under the facts and circumstances set out in your letter, I do not think that your Board is required to license Mr. Buchanan to engage in the profession of heating contracting until he has successfully passed the qualifying examination.

OPINIONS TO LIBRARY COMMISSION

LIBRARIES; SPECIAL ELECTIONS; PETITIONS; TIME OF HOLDING ELECTION

6 February 1946

You have referred to this office a letter from Miss Edith M. Clark of Salisbury, in which she submits for approval the following petition for a special election for libraries:

"We the undersigned registered voters of Rowan County who voted in the last election for Governor, respectfully petition the Board of County Commissioners of Rowan County to submit the question of the establishment and support of a free public library to the voters at a special election for that purpose; that a special tax be levied of not more than five cents (5c) nor less than three cents (3c) on the one hundred dollars ($100.00) of the assessed value of the taxable property of Rowan County; and that said election be held as soon as possible."

In connection with this petition three questions arise. These questions are:

1. Is the petition in proper form?
2. Is the statement in the petition as to the amount of tax to be levied sufficiently definite or should a certain rate be named?
3. May this question be submitted to the voters of Rowan County as a part of a special election to be held in Rowan County to determine whether bonds for another and separate project shall be issued?

There is no statutory form which must be followed in drafting a petition to be presented to the Board of Commissioners of a county requesting said Board to call a special election. The above quoted petition is, in my opinion, sufficient and would in all respects be proper. The petition states that it is directed to the Board of Commissioners of Rowan County; that it is to be presented to said Board for the purpose of requesting that a special election be held to determine whether public libraries shall be established and supported and that the question of whether a tax shall be levied shall be determined at the election. This I believe is all that the law requires.

G. S. 160-65, as rewritten by Chapter 1005 of the Session Laws of 1945, reads in part as follows:

"If a majority of the qualified voters at said special election vote in the affirmative, the governing body of the voting unit shall establish the library and may levy, and cause to be collected as other general taxes are collected, a special tax in the amount requested by the petition, which shall not be more than five cents (5c) nor less than three cents (3c) on the one hundred dollars ($100.00) of the assessed value of the taxable property of such unit."

This sentence provides for the collection of a special tax in the amount requested by the petition which shall not be more than five cents nor less than three cents on the one hundred dollars of the assessed value of the taxable property of the unit in which the election is held. While it would probably be better to name a specific amount in the petition, I am of the opinion that the naming of a maximum and a minimum amount of taxes

.o be collected (the amounts stated in the statute) is a sufficient compliance
vith the statute. The petitioners, by using a maximum and a minimum,
have expressed a willingness to vest in the governing board the discretion
to determine just what rate of tax shall be levied so long as the maximum
and minimum are observed. I am of the opinion, therefore, that the petition
is not objectionable on this point.

G. S. 160-65, as rewritten, provides that the governing board of the unit
in which the election is held "may submit the question of the establishment
and support of a free public library to the voters at a special election *for
that purpose.*" This section also provides that there shall be a new registration of the qualified voters before the special election is held. In my
opinion the statute contemplates a special election called for the purpose
of voting on the question of establishing free public libraries. I do not believe, therefore, that this question should be submitted to the voters at a
special election called for the purpose of determining some other issue.
Of course, the special election called for determining whether free public
libraries should be established and supported may be called on the same
day that some other special election is being called. If so, it is my opinion
that the same election officials may conduct the election. However, there
should be a new registration of the qualified voters for the election on the
question of establishing and maintaining free public libraries.

In other words, two special elections may be held on the same day and
under the control of the same election officials but the question of establishing free public libraries should not be voted on at a special election called
for some other purpose.

I have discussed this matter with Honorable Kerr Craige Ramsey, County
Attorney for Rowan County, and he assures me that he is in complete
accord with the opinions herein expressed.

OPINIONS TO COMMISSIONER OF PAROLES

CRIMINAL LAW; PENALTY FOR OPERATING MOTOR VEHICLE DURING
PERIOD OF REVOCATION OF LICENSE

30 August 1944

I acknowledge receipt of your letter in which you state that on October 28, 1943, a defendant was convicted of transporting liquor and sentenced to twelve months on the roads, suspended on payment of a fine of $500.00 and cost and refrain from the operation of a motor vehicle for twelve months. That pursuant to this judgment the Department of Motor Vehicles suspended the driver's license for a period of one year from the date of conviction.

You further state that at the March Term, 1944, of the Superior Court the defendant tendered a plea of guilty of driving an automobile during the period of the suspension of his license and was sentenced to twelve, months on the road.

You inquire as to whether or not the Commissioner of Paroles may release from prison the defendant upon his contention that the sentence is an illegal sentence in that the maximum prison sentence authorized by law for the offense of which he was convicted is six months.

I assume that the defendant was not committed to the roads for violation of the conditions of the suspended sentence entered in the first case, but that he was committed for punishment growing out of the second case. Section 20-28 of the North Carolina General Statutes provides:

"Any person whose operator's or chauffeur's license has been suspended or revoked, as provided in this article, and who shall drive any motor vehicle upon the highways of this State while such license is suspended or revoked, may be guilty of a misdemeanor and upon conviction shall be punished by imprisonment for not more than six months, and there may be imposed in addition thereto a fine of not more than five hundred dollars ($500.00)."

It, therefore, appears that the maximum sentence which may be imposed under the pertinent section is six months in prison in addition to a fine.

Of course, your Department has authority to commute the sentence of a prisoner, irrespective of whether the sentence is a valid one or not, and therefore, has authority to commute the sentence in this case, in which the prisoner has been sentenced for a longer period of time than the statute provides.

Of course, if the defendant was committed for violation of one of the conditions imposed in the original judgment, the court has ample authority to impose the twelve months' sentence provided for in the judgment. And in the present case, even if your Department commuted his sentence to six months, there is no reason why the defendant could not be brought into court for violation of the condition of the judgment in the first case and sentenced to an additional twelve months.

CRIMINAL LAW; TERMS OF SENTENCE; CONCURRENT SENTENCES
AND CUMULATIVE SENTENCES

10 April 1945

In your letter you state that at the August Term, 1943, of Aurora Recorder's Court three sentences were imposed against the defendant, Raymond Bettard. You enclose a copy of the commitment in each case, and inquire of this office as to whether or not these sentences run concurrently or consecutively.

An examination of the certified copies of the commitments shows that in each case the sentence imposed was twenty-four months, and in each case the sentence was ordered to commence on August 3, 1943. Each commitment is dated the 3rd day of August, 1943.

In the case of STATE V. DUNCAN, 208 N. C. 316, 317, the defendant was convicted of two counts in a consolidated indictment, one count being murder in the second degree and the second count being manslaughter. He was sentenced by the court to imprisonment in the State's Prison on each verdict for a term of not less than fifteen nor more than twenty years. In construing this sentence the Court said:

> "It is not ordered in the judgment that one term shall commence at the expiration of the other. The terms of the sentences on both convictions are concurrent. In re: Black, 162 N. C., 467, 78 S. E., 273, it is
>
> said: 'It seems to be well settled by many decisions and with entire uniformity that where a defendant is sentenced to imprisonment on two or more indictments on which he has been found guilty, sentence may be given against him on each successive conviction; in the case of the sentence of imprisonment, each successive term to commence at the expiration of the term next preceding. It cannot be urged against a sentence of this kind that it is void for uncertainty; it is as certain as the nature of the matter will admit. *But the sentence must state that the latter term is to begin at the expiration of the former; otherwise, it will run concurrently with it.*'" (Italics ours).

There is nothing in the commitments before me to indicate that the court ordered any one of these sentences to commence at the expiration of any of the other sentences and I am, therefore, of the opinion that the three sentences run concurrently, and when the defendant or prisoner has served one sentence, he has, therefore, served them all.

OPINIONS TO BOARD OF COSMETIC ART

19 May 1945

You inquire whether or not a registered cosmetologist who becomes engaged in another line of work may renew his or her certificate or registration upon payment of the required registration fee at the end of three years and not furnish the renewal certificate as to physical fitness, and continue in such other work for three years, pay the $5.00 fee, furnish the physical certificate, and have his or her certificate renewed.

The pertinent part of Section 82-25 G. S., reads, "Any registered cosmetologist who retires from the practice of cosmetic art for not more than three years may renew his or her certificate upon payment of the required registration fee and by furnishing to the secretary of the board certificate of physical fitness."

I construe this to mean that at the end of the first three years the registered cosmetologist may have his or her certificate of registration renewed upon the payment of the registration fee and by furnishing to the secretary of the board a renewal certificate of physical fitness. If such person merely pays the fee at the end of the three years and does not furnish the certificate as to physical fitness, he or she may not require the board to renew his or her registration certificate upon the payment of the registration fee and furnishing of the certificate of physical fitness. Such person can only obtain a renewel of his or her certificate by meeting the requirements of the examining board through a new examination.

SALARIES OF MEMBER OF STATE BOARD BARBER EXAMINERS AND EXECUTIVE SECRETARY; EMERGENCY SALARY

23 July 1945

I have your letter of July 21, in which you request an opinion as to whether or not the members of the State Board of Barber Examiners and its Executive Secretary are entitled to the $10.00 emergency salary.

The General Assembly of 1945 enacted House Bill No. 267, which was ratified on March 19, 1945, which amended G. S. 86-7 fixing the salary of the Secretary of the State Board of Barber Examiners at $3,600.00 a year, and amended G. S. 86-8 which fixed the salary of each member of the Board of Barber Examiners at $3,600.00 a year. This is the regular salary fixed by law for the Executive Secretary and members of the Board now in effect.

The General Assembly enacted the emergency salary law found in Chapter 279 of the Session Laws of 1945. Section 23½ provides "an emergency salary not in excess of $10.00 per month to all full time public school teachers and employees and all other State employees." This section recites the conditions under which the emergency salaries are to be paid and how the amount of it is to be determined. It provides that this emergency salary shall not be paid to employees of any special operating fund if the revenues of the general fund are insufficient to provide the emergency salary for public school teachers and employees and other general fund employees.

It further provides that the Director of the Budget is authorized and empowered to allocate out of the agriculture fund, the highway fund and other special operating funds employing personnel, amounts sufficient to pay the emergency salary as provided in this section.

In my opinion, this Act contemplates that the emergency salary shall be paid to all State employees whose salaries do not exceed $3,600.00 per year, whether or not the salaries paid are fixed by statute or fixed by other means provided under the law as to salaries of State employees. This being an emergency salary, it is to be considered in addition to any regular salary, however fixed, whether by statute or other means. Such being the case, I am of the opinion that the members of the Board of Barber Examiners and its Executive Secretary are entitled to the emergency salary to the same extent as other State employees.

OPINIONS TO INDUSTRIAL COMMISSION

WORKMEN'S COMPENSATION ACT; STATE'S LIABILITY FOR COMPENSATION
VOCATIONAL AGRICULTURE; HOME ECONOMICS; TRADES AND
INDUSTRIAL EMPLOYEES OF SCHOOLS

9 November 1945

I have your letter of November 8, in which you call my attention to the provision found in G. S. 115-370 of the State School Law as follows:

"and such local units shall likewise be liable for workmen's compensation of school employees employed in connection with teaching vocational agriculture, home economics, trades and industrial vocational subjects, supported in part by State and Federal funds, which liability shall cover the entire period of service of such employees."

And you also call my attention to the fact that the General Assembly of 1945 enacted H. B. 557, Section 11, effective on and after ratification, which provides as follows:

"The State shall also be liable for workmen's compensation for all school employees employed in connection with the teaching of vocational agriculture, home economics, trade and industries, and other vocational subjects supported in part by State and Federal funds, which liability shall cover the entire period of service of such employees."

You state that the original words as set forth in the first quoted paragraph were not specifically repealed, but the bill did have a repealing clause, and that the Industrial Commission desires to be advised whether or not the 1945 Act repeals the quoted provision appearing in the law prior to that time.

It is my opinion that the 1945 provision above quoted repealed the prior provision above quoted, as the two are entirely inconsistent, and the 1945 Act repealed all laws and parts of laws in conflict therewith, so that there is both an implied and a specific repeal of the provision theretofore existing as to this subject.

OPINIONS TO STATE HOSPITALS AND INSTITUTIONS

REFORMATORIES; STONEWALL JACKSON; COMMITMENT OF
OFFENDERS; AGE LIMIT

28 September 1944

You state in your letter of September 27 that a Taylor boy was up in juvenile court in Winston Salem in July and that at the time he lacked two or three days of reaching his sixteenth birthday. It further appears that he was committed to your institution at the time but that about the time he was ready to be brought to your institution an appeal was taken to the superior court and that the matter will not be heard in the superior court until the October Term. You desire to know whether, in my opinion, this boy should be received by your institution if the judgment of the juvenile court is affirmed in the superior court.

Under the provisions of the statutes creating and governing the procedure in juvenile courts, the juvenile court was authorized at the time the court first acquired jurisdiction of the Taylor boy to commit him to your institution. G. S. 110-40 provides that an appeal may be taken from any judgment or order of the juvenile court to the superior court having jurisdiction in the county by the parent or, in case there be no parent, by the guardian or next friend of any child whose case has been heard by the juvenile court. The section further provides that the appeal shall be taken in the manner provided for appeals to the superior court and that written notice of such appeal shall be filed in the juvenile court within five days after the issuance of the judgment or order of the court. Except for the appeal to the superior court the Taylor boy would have already been in your institution and the question of his age would not have arisen.

G. S. 134-10 authorizes judges of the superior courts, recorders, or other presiding officers of the city or criminal courts of the State to sentence to your institution all persons under the age of 16 years convicted in any court of this State of any violation of the criminal laws. The jurisdiction of the juvenile court is not ousted or denied by reason of the fact that the defendant reaches the age of 16 after the institution of the proceeding in the juvenile court. STATE v. COBLE, 181 N. C. 554.

On appeal from the juvenile court to the superior court it seems that the judgment of the juvenile court is reviewed by the judge of the superior court. STATE v. BURNETT, 179 N. C. 735.

In the case of IN RE HAMILTON, 182 N. C. 44, 47, the court, citing the case of STATE v. BURNETT, held that the supervision and oversight of the superior courts should be exercised in an orderly way by appeal from the juvenile court where such is provided by statute and otherwise by appropriate writ where no appeal is available.

If, in the case of the Taylor boy, the judge of the superior court, upon reviewing the proceedings in the juvenile court, should affirm the order of the judgment of the juvenile court committing the boy to your institution, it is my opinion that you should receive him in spite of the fact that he may have reached the age of 16 years during the pendency of his appeal. I might add that it is my view that when a commitment is presented to you, issued by a proper court, it is your duty to accept the person named in the commitment. Of course, if the judge of the court in which the case arose had no authority under the statute to commit the person named in the commitment to your institution, you should call the matter to the attention of the court in order that you might be relieved of the custody and control of the person named in the commitment and if the court should refuse to modify the judgment the matter should be called to the attention of this office in order that we might take steps to have the judgment of the court reviewed by the Supreme Court of this State.

DEAD BODIES; DISPOSITION WHEN NOT REQUESTED BY BOARD OF ANATOMY

28 September 1944

I have your letter of September 27, 1944, in which you inquire as to what disposition should be made of bodies of persons dying while inmates of Caswell Training School. You state that the Board of Anatomy has all the bodies it needs for this, and perhaps next, year.

Sections 90-211 through 90-216 of the General Statutes provide in general that the bodies of persons who have died while inmates of state and local institutions shall, upon request, be delivered to the North Carolina Board of Anatomy. If the Board of Anatomy has an adequate supply of cadavers, I assume that no request will be made for additional ones. If no request is made by the North Carolina Board of Anatomy for the bodies of deceased inmates, the bodies should be disposed of in the same manner that they were prior to the creation of the North Carolina Board of Anatomy in 1943.

From your letter, it appears that the method of disposition heretofore has been burial, except where the family claims the body. In my opinion, this course should be pursued in the future where there is no request by the Board of Anatomy that the bodies be delivered to them.

CRIMINAL LAW; SENTENCE; COMMITMENT; INDUSTRIAL FARM COLONY FOR WOMEN; PAROLE; REVOCATION

17 October 1944

Receipt is acknowledged of your letter enclosing file relative to one Mildred Eastwood.

It appears from the file that the defendant was tried in the Granville Recorders Court on September 18, 1942, on a charge of prostitution and was sentenced to not less than 12 months nor more than 2 years in the Industrial Farm Colony for Women. The commitment was issued on September 18, 1942, and on March 19, 1943, the defendant escaped. On April 15, 1943, the defendant was paroled by the Governor with the right reserved to revoke the parole at will for any cause satisfactory to the Governor and without evidence. On or prior to the 26th day of September, 1944, the defendant was arrested and placed in jail and her parole was revoked by the Governor. Following the revocation of the parole she was again placed in your institution. An attorney for the parents of Mildred Eastwood now demands her release. On yesterday I wired you as follows:

"IN MY OPINION YOU SHOULD HOLD MILDRED EASTWOOD UNTIL COMPLETION OF SENTENCE OR UNTIL RELEASED BY ORDER OF COURT OR GOVERNOR. LETTER FOLLOWS."

G. S. 134-45 provides that if a paroled inmate of your institution violates her parole and is returned to the institution, she may be required to serve the unexpired term of her maximum sentence, including the time she was out on parole, or any part thereof, in the discretion of the board of directors, or she may be paroled again if the board of directors shall so recommend.

The maximum sentence of Mildred Eastwood was 2 years and at at the time of her escape she had only served from September 18, 1942, until March 19, 1943. Upon the revocation of her parole, she, in my opinion, could be required to serve the remainder of her maximum term of 2 years.

The Supreme Court of North Carolina has held, in the case of STATE v. YATES, 183 N. C. 753, that where a prisoner has accepted a conditional pardon from the Governor and has obtained his freedom, the breaking of the condition after the term would have otherwise expired affords no legal excuse why he should not be re-committed to serve out the balance of his sentence.

If the attorney for the parents desires to test the legality of the imprisonment of Mildred Eastwood, he has the right to do so by means of an application for a writ of habeas corpus. I am still of the opinion that you should hold Mildred Eastwood until the completion of her maximum sentence unless released by an order of court entered on a habeas corpus proceeding or until the Governor, on recommendation of your board of directors, grants her another parole.

CRIMINAL LAW; COURTS; JUSTICES OF THE PEACE; COMMITMENT OF DEFENDANTS TO INDUSTRIAL FARM COLONY FOR WOMEN

18 October 1944

Receipt is acknowledged of your letter in which you raise the question as to whether you are authorized to accept women committed to your institution by a justice of the peace.

G. S. 134-43, in providing for commitments to your institution, seems to include the superior court or any inferior court. In the first part of the section, it is also provided that women 16 years of age and older, belonging to certain classes, may be committed by any court of competent jurisdiction to your institution.

This office, on January 4, 1937, in a letter to Miss Elsa Ernst, Superintendent of the Industrial Farm Colony for Women, expressed the view that commitments might be properly made by the mayor's court and other courts inferior to the superior court where the defendants were convicted of the specified crimes enumerated in G. S. 134-43. Of course, the court of a justice of the peace is an inferior court but as the maximum punishment which may be imposed by a justice of the peace in a criminal case is 30 days, I would seriously doubt the wisdom of undertaking to accept such prisoners in your institution.

CASWELL TRAINING SCHOOL; ACCEPTANCE OF GIFTS FOR USE OF INMATES

17 April 1945

I acknowledge receipt of your letter, in which you state that the Veterans Administration wishes to turn over to the Caswell Training School each month the sum of approximately $8.00 each for two of the inmates of your institution. You inquire as to the authority of the institution to accept this money.

Section 116-126 of the General Statutes authorizes your institution to acquire and hold all such property as may be devised, bequeathed or conveyed to it, and I am of the opinion that you may accept the sums mentioned from the Veterans Administration to apply toward the expense of the two inmates, William and Bernice Canady.

HOLIDAYS; DEMURRAGE CHARGE

22 May 1945

I acknowledge receipt of your letter in which you inquire as to whether or not the Norfolk and Southern Railway Company may require the payment of demurrage on a carload of carrots placed on your siding on the afternoon of March 31. You state that you do not think that this demurrage should be charged since one of the days for which the charge was made was Easter Monday, a holiday.

Section 103-4 G. S., does designate Easter Monday of each year as a legal holiday but insofar as it affects the performance of duties incident to one's business, it does not have the same effect as Sunday. In the case of STATE v. MOORE, 104 N. C. 743, it was said that this section merely declares certain days of each year shall be public holidays and does not purport to prohibit persons from pursuing their usual avocations on such dates. See also LATTA v. CATAWBA ELECTRIC CO., 146 N. C. 285.

I am, therefore, inclined to the opinion that you may be required to pay demurrage on the carload shipment for Easter Monday.

INSANE PERSONS AND INCOMPETENTS; PERSONS COMING INTO THIS STATE WITH MENTAL DISEASES; DOMICILE; MARRIED WOMEN

1 June 1945

I have your letter of May 29, 1945, in which you inquire if a person who comes into this State in an unsound mental condition can establish a residence in this State. You also inquire if the residence or domicile of a married woman is that of her husband.

G. S. 122-39 provides that, "no person who shall have removed into this

State from another State shall be deemed a resident or a citizen of this State, and no length of residence in this State of a person who was insane at the time he moved into this State shall be sufficient to make that person or [sic] citizen or resident of North Carolina within the meaning of this chapter." Thus, if a person was of unsound mind when he came into this State, he cannot acquire a residence herein.

You understand, of course, that I am not in a position to advise as to whether the person about whom you inquire was of unsound mind upon her entry into this State.

The rule in North Carolina is that the domicile of the husband is *prima facie* the domicile of the wife. IN RE ELLIS' WILL, 187 N. C. 840. However, it is still possible for a wife to acquire a separate domicile from that of her husband. ARRINGTON v. ARRINGTON, 102 N. C. 491; MILLER v. MILLER, 205 N. C. 753.

It is impossible for me to advise categorically on the facts you state in your letter whether the domicile of the person about whom you inquire is that of her husband or whether she has acquired a separate domicile.

HOSPITALS FOR THE INSANE; DISCHARGE OF PATIENTS; PATIENT DIS-
CHARGED AS IMPROVED; SUBSEQUENT DISCHARGE IF CURED

23 July 1945

I have your letter of July 18, 1945, in which you state that a patient was discharged as improved from that Hospital more than eleven years ago. The Clerk of the Court of Guilford County has requested the Hospital authorities to issue a discharge as completely recovered for this person. You inquire if the Hospital authorities have authority to issue such a discharge.

The provisions of the statute providing for the discharge of patients from State hospitals are found as Sections 122-66, 122-67, and 122-68 of the General Statutes. In my opinion these statutes do not contain any provision which would authorize you at this late date to issue a discharge as requested by the Guilford County Clerk of Court. From the facts in your letter it appears that this patient was discharged from the Hospital approximately eleven years ago. This discharge, in my opinion, terminated the authority of the Hospital to take any action in connection with this patient. I, therefore, advise that you should not issue the discharge requested.

Of course, the patient could be restored to her rights upon the finding of a jury as provided by statute.

INSANE PERSONS AND INCOMPETENTS; CASWELL TRAINING SCHOOL; DIS-
CHARGE OF INMATES FOR BEST INTERESTS OF SCHOOL

21 August 1945

I have your letter of August 15, 1945, in which you inquire if an inmate f The Caswell Training School may be discharged because his remaining at the school will not be for the best interests of the school. You refer to Section 5904 of the Consolidated Statutes but state that the recent law leaves you in doubt as to the effect at the present time of that section.

G. S. 5904 now appears as Section 116-136 of the General Statutes. That section provides that any pupil of The Caswell Training School may be discharged or returned to his or her parents or guardian when, in the judgment of the directors, it will not be beneficial to such pupil or will not be for the best interests of said school to retain the pupil therein.

I find no provision in the 1945 laws relating to hospitals for the insane which in any way affects this section. I therefore advise that, in my opinion, this section is still legal and valid anl may be used in proper cases. As you know, the Session Laws of 1945 have not yet been printed but I have consulted the index in the office of the Secretary of State and do not find therein any provision modifying this section.

North Carolina State School for the Blind and Deaf; Superintendent's Duty; Pupil Lice-Infected

8 October 1945

I acknowledge receipt of your letter in which you state that one of the pupils of the school, after having been sick for some two weeks, was examined by Dr. Haywood who discoverel that she was completely covered with crab lice and that her illness was due to the poison from the bites of the lice. I further understand that the pupil was sent home but will return to you after Christmas. You also state that because of the condition prevailing in the home she will probably return to you in the same condition as when she left. You inquire as to your duty in the matter.

I suggest that you call the attention of the County Welfare officials to the matter and report the case to the County Health authorities and request them to take the necessary steps to remedy the condition existing in the home.

Insane Persons and Incompetents; Caswell Training School; Age of Persons Admitted

I have your letter of October 17, 1945, in which you inquire if persons over twenty-one years of age may legally be committed to Caswell Training School. You refer to Section 5898 of the Consolidated Statutes of 1919.

Section 5898 of the Consolidated Statutes was rewritten by Chapter 34 of the Public Laws of 1923. As rewritten, this section appears as Section 116-129 of the General Statutes. It now reads as follows:

"There shall be received into the Caswell Training School, subject to such rules and regulations as the board of directors may adopt, feeble-minded and mentally defective persons *of any age* when in judgment of the offcer of public welfare and the board of directors of said institution it is deemed advisable. All applications for admission must be approved by the local county welfare officer and the judge of the juvenile court or the clerk of the court of the county wherein said applicant resides." (Italics added).

G. S. 116-130 contains regulations relating to the application for the admission of minors. G. S. 116-131 outlines the procedure for the admission of adults.

It seems clear, therefore, that the law as now written contemplates that adults may be admitted to Caswell Training School.

STATE SCHOOL FOR THE BLIND AND DEAF, RALEIGH;
FREE TEXTBOOKS

31 October 1945

I have your letter of October 29 in which you refer to G. S. 116-124.1, providing that North Carolina School for the Deaf at Morganton, North Carolina, shall have the right and privilege of participating in the distribution of free textbooks and in the purchase and lental system operated by the State of North Carolina in the same manner as any other public school in the State. You inquire whether or not the Legislature intended to make the free books available for the deaf negro children in the State School for the Blind and Deaf at Raleigh.

While evidently it was an oversight, unfortunately the Legislature did not include in this Act the State School for the Blind and Deaf at Raleigh, so that the use of free textbooks could be extended to the negro deaf children in the school here at Raleigh. I have no doubt whatever that if this matter is called to the attention of .the General Assembly at its next meeting, it will include your institution in the statute to the same extent as the school at Morganton. I wish it were possible to construe the statute as including your institution.

EXTRADITION; ESCAPEES OF STONEWALL JACKSON MANUAL TRAINING
AND INDUSTRIAL SCHOOL; WILLIAM ROGERS

23 January 1946

I have your letter of January 21, 1946, in which you request assistance in having William Rogers, an escapee of Stonewall Jackson Manual Training and Industrial School, extradited from Virginia.

This boy was admitted to the above named Institution on October 16, 1944, from Lee County. He was committed by the Juvenile Court because it was found that he was not obedient to the commands and wishes of his parent. On October 3, 1945, Rogers escaped from the Institution and was later apprehended in Richmond, Virginia, where he is now being held.

I am of the opinion that the extradition laws do not apply to a case of this kind and, therefore, you cannot secure the return of this person by resort thereto. Generally, extradition applies only when the person fleeing the bounds of the demanding State is charged with a crime and has fled the State prior to the prosecution, and cases in which a person convicted of crime has escaped from confinement or broken the terms of his bail, probation or parole. G. S. 15-59, 15-60, and 15-77.

From the facts outlined in your letter, I conclude that this particular individual was not at the time of the hearing in the Juvenile Court, nor is he now, charged with the commission of a criminal offense. In addition, it appears that detention under the statutes creating and regulating Stonewall Jackson Manual Training and Industrial School is not imprisonment as a punishment for crime. IN RE: WATSON, 157 N. C. 340.

There is a statute authorizing the apprehension of escapees from correctional and penal institutions established by the laws of North Carolina. G. S. 153-184. This section, however, merely authorizes sheriffs and peace officers in this State to take into custody such escapees and to cause their return to the institution from which they escaped. It does not provide that an escapee shall constitute a criminal or an extraditable offense.

G. S. 122-23 and G. S. 122-27 relate to escapes from hospitals for the mentally disordered. They have no application to escapees from Jackson Training School.

G. S. 153-220 applies only to county institutions.

There are other statutes applicable to named institutions, but Jackson Training School is not among those covered thereby. See: G. S. 134-46, Industrial Farm Colony for Women; G. S. 134-64, Reformatories or Homes for Fallen Women; and G. S. 134-31 to 134-35, State Home and Industrial School for Girls.

There seems to be a hiatus or interstice in the law relating to Jackson Training School on this particular point. This may be a matter which you desire to discuss with members or a committee of the General Assembly. As the law is now written, I advise that in my opinion there is no legal authority under which William Rogers may be extradited from Virginia on the facts outlined in your letter.

DEAF AND BLIND; COMPULSORY ATTENDANCE; G. C. 115-309, 310, 311

4 February 1946

I have your letter of January 30, 1946, in which you refer to G. S. 115-309, 115-310, and 115-311, regulating the compulsory attendance of deaf and blind children at institutions for the same. You point out that deaf and blind children between the ages of six and eighteen years are required to attend school for a term of nine months in each year by G. S. 115-309, as amended by the 1945 Session Laws.

G. S. 115-310 makes the parents, guardians or custodians of deaf children between the ages of seven and eighteen years guilty of a misdemeanor if they fail to send such children to some school for instruction after notice has been served on such parents, guardians or custodians directing such children to be sent to school. G. S. 115-311 contains a similar provision relating to blind children. You suggest that these two sections conflict with Section 115-309 because that section fixes the age for cumpulsory attendance at from six to eighteen years, while these sections provide criminal penaltended to require blind and deaf children six years of age to attend school but that no criminal penalties would attach to the parents, etc., for failing to send such children before they became seven years of age. In other words, the Legislature has declared that it favors the policy of requiring blind and deaf children six years of age to attend school, but that it will not imties for parents, etc. for failing to send children between the ages of seven and eighteen years.

This is perhaps a matter which you desire the Legislature to act upon. However, I do not feel that the statutes as now written conflict with each other. It is my opinion that the Court would say that the Legislature inpose criminal penalties upon parents, etc. for the failure to send such children to school.

SCHOOLS; COMPULSORY ATTENDANCE OF BLIND AND DEAF CHILDREN

—————20 February 1946

I have your letter of February 18, 1946, in which you request the opinion of this office as to what person is under a duty to institute proceedings against parents, guardians, etc., of deaf and blind children for failure to send such children to schools for the deaf and blind.

G. S. 115-302 through 115-308 relate to the compulsory attendance of pupils in the public schools of the State and do not apply to the attendance of deaf and blind children. G. S. 115-309 through 115-312 are the specific sections regulating the compulsory attendance of deaf and blind children in schools for the deaf and blind. G. S. 115-312 places the duty upon the County Superintendent to report the names and addresses of guardians, parents, or custodians of deaf, dumb, blind, and feeble-minded children to the principal of the institution provided for each. The County Superintendent referred to is, in my opinion, the County Superintendent of Public Welfare. This opinion is based upon the use of the term "County Superintendent of Public Welfare" in G. S. 115-306 which is a part of the same chapter of the 1923 Public Laws. Upon receipt of this report of the County Superintendent of Public Welfare, I am of the opinion that the duty rests upon the principal of the institution to institute the legal proceedings necessary and required. This seems to be the intent and meaning of G. S. 115-312 when it provides for the report of the County Superintendent to the principal of the institution.

INSANE PERSONS; INCOMPETENTS; NONRESIDENTS; TRANSFER FROM HOSPITALS TO STATE OF RESIDENCE; COSTS AND EXPENSES

4 March 1946

I have your letter of February 27, 1946, in which you advise that several nonresidents of this State have been admitted to the State Hospital. It is the desire and intention of the Hospital authorities to send these nonresident patients to the State of their residences. You inquire if the expense of conveying these patients is to be borne by the Hospital authorities or by the counties from which the patients were committed.

G. S. 122-63 contains the following provision:

"If the state of the mentally disordered person's residence shall not provide for the removal of the said person from this State to the state of his residence or citizenship within a reasonable time, the superintendent of the State hospital shall cause him to be conveyed directly from the State hospital to the state of which he is a citizen or resident and delivered there to the superintendent of the proper state hospital. The cost of such proceedings and conveyance away from the State shall be borne by the county in which the person shall have been adjudged to be mentally disordered."

From the above quoted provision can be seen that the primary duty of paying the cost of conveying any nonresident patients rests upon the States of their legal residences. Our Legislature, however, is not in a position to impose obligations upon other States. If the other States do not make provision for conveying these nonresident patients thereto, this burden falls upon the counties in which the persons have been adjudged to be mentally disordered. The statute seems to be specific and clear on this point. I do not believe that the counties of the State will refuse to assume this obligation once the statute has been called to their attention.

CASWELL TRAINING SCHOOL; ADMISSIONS UNDER COURT ORDER

18 March 1946

I have your letter of March 15, in which you state that at your institution you have reached the saturation point as to admissions and that occasionally there comes a court order in which the judge orders you to admit some individual when there is no vacancy. You state that your policy is to especially note any court order and honor it at the first vacancy, which is often long delayed because of the few vacancies. You request me to advise you whether or not your policy in this respect is correct.

The law does not require any public official to do the impossible and, if it is physically impossible for you to admit the person as directed by a court order, I think you should at once make a full and ample explanation to the committing judge of the circumstances which makes it impossible for you to comply with the order. Of course, the patient should be admitted at the earliest possible date thereafter. You should always be well fortified in your statement as to the impossibility of admitting the patient without overcrowding your institution.

I personally realize he fact that your institution is and has been for a long while greatly overcrowded and this has received recognition by the Legislature in the priority which they have already proviled in the building program. I hope the situation may be relieved at some early date.

HOSPITALS FOR INSANE; ORDINANCES; MOTOR VEHICLES; SPEED REGULATIONS

15 April 1946

Please excuse the delay in replying to your letter of March 30, 1946. We have been exceptionally busy in the preparation and presentation of cases in the Supreme Court and the opportunity to write you has not presented itself prior to the present time.

You inquire if the Board of Directors of the State Hospital at Raleigh is authorized to limit to fifteen miles per hour the speed at which automobiles shall be operated within the State Hospital grounds. You intend to post signs on the grounds and to appoint persons to enforce the speed limit once it is established.

G. S. 122-16 confers upon the Board of Directors of the State Hospital at Raleigh authority to enact ordinances for the regulation and deportment of persons in the buillings and grounds of the Institution and for the suppression of nuisances and disorder. When this ordinance is adopted it shall be recorded in the proceedings of the Board and printed and one copy shall be posted at the entrance to the grounds and not less than three copies posted at various places within the grounds. A violation of any ordinance is a misdemeanor punishable by fine of not more than $50.00 or imprisonment for not more than thirty days. The Board may prescribe penalties for the violation of the ordinance adopted and may sue and recover such penalties in the court of a Justice of the Peace.

The Board of Directors as used in this section means the unified Board of Directors. G. S. 122-8.

By G. S. 122-33 the Superintendent of the State Hospital is authorized to appoint special policemen to enforce the ordinance adopted by the Hospital authorities and such special policemen shall have the right to arrest without warrant any person violating any of the State laws or the ordinances of the Hospital.

It is my opinion that this grant of authority is broad enough to permit the adoption and enforcement of the ordinance about which you inquire.

INDIANS; PROVISIONS FOR CARE OF BLIND AND DEAF INDIAN CHILDREN

28 May 1946

In your letter you state as follows:

"Section 116-109 of the General Statutes carries a statement that this school shall admit all white blind children and all negro blind and deaf children who are residents of this State. In-as-much as no reference is made to the Indian race, will you kindly tell us our obligation with regard to accepting an Indian child? If in your opinion we are obligated to receive an Indian child, should the child be enrolled at the white school or at the colored school?"

It has been the legislative policy of this State to not only provide for separation of white and colored races in State institutions but also persons of Indian descent. Apparently this question of segregation of races has not been left to the discretion of the boards of directors of institutions but has always been incorporated in a statute where segregation had been provided for. For example, in the State Hospital in Morganton, you will find under the provisions of Section 122-3 that members of the Eastern band of Cherokee Indians can be admitted to that hospital. Under the provisions of Section 122-5 of the General Statutes you will find that the insane and inebriate Indians of Robeson County and all of the insane and inebriate Croatan

Indians of the other counties shall be cared for in the hospital for the insane in wards separate and apart from the white patients. You will also see that under the provisions of Section 122-83 provision is made for the criminal insane whereby white patients are sent to the State Hospital at Raleigh, colored patients are sent to the State Hospital at Goldsboro; and if the alleged criminal is an Indian from Robeson County, he is sent to the State Hospital at Raleigh. Nothing is said in this section about the Eastern band of Cherokee Indians living both on and off of the government reservation in the Western part of the State. There are other statutes on this subject, but I have cited these to show you that so far as the admission of patients to State institutions is concerned, the matter is strictly one of legislative policy as expressed in statutes.

I am enclosing you a copy of a ruling issued by this office on June 20, 1938 at the instance of Mrs. W. T. Bost, who was at that time Commissioner of the State Board of Charities and Public Welfare of this State. She desired to know if two deaf Indian girls residing in Western North Carolina could be admitted to the North Carolina State School for the Deaf. You will see from reading the copy of this opinion that the State School for the Deaf only admitted white deaf children. Nothing was said about Indians. In my opinion, this ruling is equally applicable in your case. It is true that you can admit white and colored children both, but it is likewise true that nothing is said in the statute about your authority to admit Indian children.

We are of the opinion, therefore, that you do not have authority to admit an Indian child to your school; therefore, it is unnecessary for us to answer your second question as to whether or not if such child was admitted should it be enrolled in the white or colored school. It is our thought that if you desire to have blind and deaf Indian children admitted to your school, you should seek legislative authority for this purpose as it does not now exist.

OPINIONS TO DEPARTMENT OF ARCHIVES AND HISTORY

TEACHERS' & STATE EMPLOYEES' RETIREMENT ACT

9 March 1945

I have your letter of March 8, in which you write me as follows:

"Toward the end of the fiscal year after an employee of the Department of Archives and History has reached the age of sixty-five, it is customary for the Secretary of the Department to write that employee a letter, asking that he or she remain on the pay roll for one additional year, and, if deemed advisable, a new letter of like content is written each year thereafter. Under the law, if such a letter were not to be written before the end of some fiscal year before the employee should have reached his or her seventieth birthday, what would be the effect upon that employee's status? Would he or she automatically have to retire? Also, what would be the effect if the head of the Department were to write a letter to such an employee, stating that the request that he or she continue on the Department's pay roll would not be renewed?"

G. S. 135-5 provides, in part, as follows:

"(b) Any member in service who has attained the age of sixty-five years shall be retired at the end of the year unless the employer requests such person to remain in the service and notice of this request is given in writing thirty days prior to the end of the year."

The provision I have quoted is the only one in the Act which specifically deals with the matter of retirement at the age of sixty-five. There is nothing in this provision which attempts to deal with the situation which you describe, in which an employee is requested to remain on the payroll for an additional year, and, therefore, I am unable to answer your question, when such action has been taken by the employing agency for which no provision is made in the statute.

G. S. 135-6(6) authorizes the board of trustees, subject to the limitations of the chapter, from time to time, to establish rules and regulations for the administration of the funds created by the chapter and for the transaction of its business. The board of trustees is also authorized, from time to time, in its discretion, to adopt rules and regulations to prevent injuries and inequalities which might otherwise arise in the administration of this law.

I have discussed your question with Major Baxter Durham, Director, who tells me that it is the practice to permit the employing agency to request an employee to stay on from year to year and when such request is made it will be recognized; that if the request is made for the employee to remain one year, the employee would automatically go off unless the request was renewed for the next succeeding year.

STATE DEPARTMENT OF ARCHIVES AND HISTORY; POWER TO DONATE FUNDS TO UNOFFICIAL HISTORICAL BODY

25 May 1945

In your letter of May 21, 1945 you ask if your Department would be authorized to make a contribution to the North Carolina Council for the Social

Studies. You enclose a copy of the constitution of this organization and you have also explained in conversation the nature of the work of the organization concerned.

The powers and duties of the State Department of Archives and History as contained in Chapter 121 of the General Statutes have been rewritten and superseded by Senate Bill No. 52, passed at the last session of the General Assembly. Paragraph 4 of Section 121-5, as rewritten, in regard to the expenditure of funds is limited as follows:

"To control the expenditure of such funds as may be appropriated for the department, subject to the provisions of the Executive Budget Act;"

The Department has specific power to accept gifts, bequests and endowments, but there is no corresponding specific power on the part of the Department to make gifts and donations. The Appropriation Act of 1945 as supported by the basic budgetary estimates does not contain any item for this purpose. It is true that Senate Bill No. 52 does contain the following language:

"To cooperate with and assist, in so far as practicable, historical and other organizations engaged in activities in the fields of North Carolina Archives and History."

While this is very broad language, nevertheless I think that before a State agency or department can make a donation or render direct financial assistance to an unofficial organization from funds allotted the department and derived from tax sources of the State, then such grant of authority should be plain and unequivocal so that no factor or interpretation would ever be involved.

Paragraph 4 of Section 121-4, as rewritten, does, however, allow you some authority in the specific field of assistance to such organizations. It is one of the duties of the Department:

"To have materials on the history of North Carolina properly edited, published as other State printing, and distributed under the direction of the department."

If you are, therefore, satisfied that the data and materials of the North Carolina Council for the Social Studies contain necessary materials on the history of North Carolina, and that these materials are of such historical significance as to come within the scope of your Department, then I am of the opinion that in your discretion you can make reasonable expenditures to have this data and materials published, and that you can thus be of aid and assistance to this organization in that manner without exceeding the duties and authority as contained in the organic act establishing your Department.

I have carefully read the opinion of this office dated November 15, 1935, which authorized you to make an allowance for the excavation of an Indian mound in Randolph County. This opinion is based upon the interpretation that implements and objects recovered by excavation come within the meaning of the term "historical data." While I do not disagree with this opinion, nevertheless, I do not think it has definite application to the question presented in your letter.

HISTORICAL MATERIALS ACQUIRED BY DEPARTMENT OF ARCHIVES AND HISTORY; SALE OR TEMPORARY LOANS OF SAME

18 May 1946

I received your letter of May 15, in which you write me as follows:

"In 1933 the State Department of Archives and History (then the State Historical Commission) purchased the manuscript Minutes of Meherrin Baptist Church, 1933-1874. It has been suggested that the item might well be transferred to the custody of the Wake Forest Collect Library where there is a large collection of North Carolina Baptist materials, and this matter will be considered at the next meeting of the Executive Board of this Department on May 28. It will be appreciated if, before that meeting, you will let me know whether the law authorizes such a transfer."

I have examined the provisions of Chapter 121 of the General Statutes, with regard to the State Department of Archives and History, and particularly G. S. 121-2 which provides, in part, that it is the duty of the department to have collected from the files of old newspapers, court records, church records, private collections and elsewhere, historical data pertaining to the history of North Carolina, and the territory included therein, from earliest times. There is nothing in this section, defining the duties of the department, which authorizes the department to make any gift of or sale of the historical materials acquired, and I think the general purpose of the law is that such historical materials as are acquired shall be preserved by the department.

I believe, however, that if the department should determine that the Minutes of Meherrin Baptist Church, referred to, could best serve the historical purposes for which they were acquired by a temporary loan of such materials to the Wake Forest College Library, with a written agreement that the title to such materials would remain in the department and be subject to recall at any time they may see fit to do so, the department would be justified in taking such action. I do not think that the law would authorize the unconditional transfer of the materials to anyone.

OPINIONS TO BOARD OF CORRECTIONS

INDUSTRIAL FARM COLONY FOR WOMEN; COMMITMENTS CONTRARY
TO THE STATUTE

16 April 1945

I have your letter of April 14, in which you call attention to G. S. 134-43 with reference to commitments to the Industrial Farm Colony for Women, and particularly that part of this section which provides that no woman who has been adjudged epileptic or insane by a competent authority or is of such low mentality or is so markedly psychopathic as to prevent her from profiting by the training program of the institution shall be admitted.

You state that judges generally, and recorders court judges in particular, seem not to consider that part of the statute at all and quite often women are delivered to the institution by a sheriff or a police officer who cannot be handled at all without locking them in a cell; that Mrs. Jimison, the Superintendent, is most generous in her consideration of the women sent her, but these occasional women offset her entire program and demoralize the entire institution; that apparently the judge has sent the women to rid the community of a menace. You inquire as to what would be the proper steps for Mrs. Jimison to take in cases of this kind. She wants to abide by the law, to be helpful to the women, and to cooperate as best she can with the county officials. She has asked you to take the matter up with me in order that some policy may be worked out whereby she can form some policy of procedure.

If the woman committed has been adjudged epileptic or insane by competent authority, I believe the proper course would be for the Superintendent to refuse to accept the person and notify the court, giving the reason therefor and citing the record of the court in which adjudication had been made. The statute definitely says that such person shall not be admitted to the institution. There would be no difficulty in determining who are the people who come within this category.

As to women "of such low mentality or . . . so markedly psychopathic as to prevent her from profiting from the training program of the institution," this has reference to a mental condition about which the presiding judge might have one opinion and the Superintendent or the Directors of the institution another opinion. It is my thought that the Superintendent would not have a right to refuse to accept a person upon these grounds, as the commitment of the court would be an expression of a contrary determination of this fact.

I believe, however, it would be desirable for you, as Commissioner of Correction, to get out a circular letter and send it to all of the judges of the Superior and inferior courts, calling attention to the provisions of the statute and asking for their cooperation in keeping from the institution the type of women that the statute says shall not be admitted. I believe in this way you may secure a reasonable cooperation from the courts and judges. It might well be that you could suggest to the various judges that if they were in doubt as to the mental condition of the person committed, your psychiatrist would examine the person to determine whether or not she is such a person as should be committed to the institution. It may be practical to work out a plan of this kind in doubtful cases.

OPINIÓNS TO RECREATION COMMISSION

NORTH CAROLINA RECREATION COMMISSION; STATE RECREATION
ENABLING ACT

14 May 1945

I acknowledge receipt of your letter in which you call my attention to the new State Recreation Enabling Act introduced by Representative Sellers of Alamance County, and inquiring why in defining what units of government municipalities included, there was eliminated "school districts" and as to whether or not under the new Enabling Act, a school district may take advantage of any of the provisions thereof.

Mr. Sellers discussed this Act with this office on several occasions before it was introduced and it was his specific request that the term "school district" be eliminated from the term "municipality." This seemed advisable since there is no machinery set up in an ordinary school district for the levying and collection of taxes. Since this act specifically eliminates school districts, it does not have any effect or bearing upon the authority of school districts to maintain recreation facilities in existence prior to the passage of the 1945 Act.

SCHOOLS; PLAYGROUNDS; SCHOOL PROPERTY; CONTROL; RECREATION
COMMISSION; USE OF SURPLUS FUNDS

20 October 1945

I have before me your letter of October 18 to Mr. Clifton Beckwith of this office with reference to the recreation plans contemplated at Elizabeth City, in which you advise that the community has established a legal Recreation Commission set up by the Mayor and Council with a Legal Ordinance; that the local school board owns four acres of land adjacent to the school property, a part of which is now used as a playground for school children; and that the Recreation Commission wishes to build a stadium on this property and the school board is willing to have the stadium built; and the question is, can the school board deed this land to the Recreation Commission and allow the Commission to build a stadium and control its use?

There is no authority for a school board to convey the property to the Recreation Commission except as authorized by G. S. 115-86, which permits the sale when the property is unnecessary for school purposes, but requires it to be made at public sale to the highest bidder, and this would, of course, exclude the type transaction which you contemplate.

Your next question is, can the school board let the Commission use the area and the Commission have complete control? There is likewise in my opinion an absence of any authority for a school board in this matter to surrender its responsibility over school property. I know of no statute which would include any authorization of this type of transaction.

The next question is, could the Town Council, from surplus money, use some of it in the aid of the Recreation Commission in building a stadium? To furnish any opinion upon this question we would have to have a full statement of all the facts, including information as to ownership and location of the site on which the stadium is to be built.

Under Chapter 1052 of the Session Laws of 1945, the expenditures for the erection of a stadium as a part of a public playground would be undoubtedly public expense for which a municipality would be authorized to expend any surplus funds which it might have, and the expenditure of which would not involve any tax levy or the creation of any debt. Before this is done, however, it would require a full understanding as to what funds were involved and whether or not such funds in legal contemplation constitute what is known under our law as surplus funds.

I would, therefore, recommend that before any action is taken with respect to this matter, that detailed consideration be given to the problem by the city Attorney, and we will be glad to confer with him on any questions involved upon which he might desire our opinion.

OPINIONS TO TEACHERS COLLEGES

COLLEGE STUDENTS; RIGHT OF A COLLEGE TO DECLINE TO ADMIT OR
DISMISS A STUDENT

26 October 1944

I have your letter of October 24, in which you present a question as to the right of your College to dismiss a student or refuse to register a student who is found by the College officials to be without promise as a teacher, or whose social and moral behavior is such as to be considered injurious to the College.

You quote from pages 13, 14 and 39 of your current catalogue, making provision for the dismissal or right to refuse to register any student whose social and moral behavior, whether on or off the campus, is such as would be considered injurious to the College, and the regulation providing that the College may refuse to re-register any student whose past record is such as to indicate moral or scholastic unfitness for the teaching profession, or for any other reason is adjudged without promise as a teacher.

With reasonable limits, the governing board of your institution has a right to make rules and regulations of this character and the courts would not afford relief against the enforcement of such rules unless it could be shown that the board acted arbitrarily and for a fraudulent purpose. In other words, if the Board of Trustees in good faith enforced the regulations quoted from your catalogue, the courts would not, in my opinion, in anywise interfere with them in doing so. See 11 CORPUS JURIS, page 997, title Colleges and Universities, and cases cited.

WATER SYSTEM; LIABILITY OF COLLEGE FOR ABANDONED SYSTEM

22 January 1945

I received your letter of January 19 and have considered the facts set forth. I understand that you have secured an entirely new and ample source of water, independent of the old system.

I believe it would be advisable for you to have a meeting of all the persons who are now using the water from the old system and ascertain what their claims and contentions are with respect to the right to use the same free of charge, and, in such meeting, see what plan could be worked out between the persons who are using the system to continue it, and what price, if any, they would be willing to pay the College for its property used in connection with it. It may be that these persons would be willing to pay a fair price for the system and would make an offer of this character. When purchasing the system, they would have a right to sell rights to tap it to other persons who might want to use it.

The deed from J. R. Bryson and wife is an unconditional deed conveying the right to the State Board of Education and their successors in office to this property. After conference with the parties who are now using the water supply, I believe it would be well to confer with J. R. Bryson and ascer_ tain what his position would be with reference to the sale of the interest of the College in the property, and ascertain what his contentions would be. The deed was made to the State Board of Education and their successors in office, the words "heirs and assigns" being stricken out of the deed, but, notwithstanding this, I think that the State Board of Education could convey its rights under the deed if it had any value which could be sold, as the instrument indicates that the intention was to convey it in fee simple.

If it is ascertained that there is no marketable value in the water supply system, it would seem to me that the thing we should do would be to give notice to all interested parties that it will be abandoned and, thereafter, leave it to such arrangements as may be made by those concerned.

VETERANS, WORLD WAR II; REEMPLOYMENT RIGHTS UNDER FEDERAL AND STATE LAW

26 February 1945

It appears that an employee of Western Carolina Teachers College gave up his employment because he expected to receive a commission in the armed forces of the United States. The employee in question did not receive the commission at that time but accepted a position with another State agency and remained with this agency for approximately two years. This person, however, has received recently a commission as a Captain in the army. You further state that the Board of Trustees feels that the position of this former employee should now be filled in order to meet the needs of returning soldiers and that the former employee in question insists that he has a claim on his former position with Western Carolina Teachers College.

You inquire of this office if the Board would be within its rights, under either Federal or State law, to proceed to employ a man for the position.

The Selective Training and Service Act, 50 U.S.C.A. Appendix, Section 308, provides that ex-service men shall be restored to their positions when employed by the United States Government or employed by a private employer. With respect to State employment or employment of political subdivisions of the State, it says the following in Paragraph (C), subsection (b), Section 308:

"If such position was in the employ of any state or political subdivision thereof, it is hereby declared to be the sense of the Congress that such person should be restored to such position or to a position of like seniority, status and pay."

This whole section is applicable to the position a person leaves when inducted into the services, and you will further note that Congress does not undertake to say that the State or an agency of the State *shall* restore such person to the position, but merely recommends that such person should be restored. It is extremely doubtful if the Congress has any right to compel a State to restore such person to his former employment, and in recognition of this fact, Paragraph (C) is simply written as a recommendation. Therefore, so far as the Federal law is concerned, it is my opinion that you do not have to restore this person to his former position with the College.

I do not know of any State law which compels you to restore this person to his former position. Section 128-15 of the General Statutes of North Carolina provides that a preference shall be given to veterans in all State employment or any other employment under the supervision of the State or its departments, institutions or agencies. We have always given a liberal construction to veterans' laws in this respect, but it seems to me that this statute applies where you already have applicants for the position in ques- tion and some of these applicants are veterans. The section does not under- take to fix reemployment rights or the right of a veteran to return to his former position.

Irrespective of any application of Federal or State law, it appears that this man left your employment and worked for approximately two years with another State agency, and apparently he left the employment of that agency and went into the army. If he has any reemployment rights under the Federal or State law, it would be with that State agency and not with Western Carolina Teachers College. The duty of reemployment would be with that agency, whether the duty is moral or legal.

I am of the opinion, therefore, that you have a right to fill this position now and that the former employee in question does not have any claims of reemployment against Western Carolina Teachers College.

EDUCATIONAL INSTITUTIONS; FAYETTEVILLE STATE TEACHERS COLLEGE;
FIRE INSURANCE COVERAGE; NEWBOLD BUILDING

6 August 1945

I acknowledge receipt of your letter relative to insurance policies on the addition to the Newbold Training School on the campus of the Fayetteville State Teachers College.

I am afraid that I cannot answer the questions raised by you unless I had more information at hand. I would like to see the contract or a copy thereof, between the Federal Government and the State relative to the construction of the addition to the Newbold Building and, in particular, as to any refer- ence to requiring the State to carry fire insurance.

As you know, the 1945 Session of the Legislature enacted into law what is known as the State Self-Insurer Act, which provides that the State can- not purchase insurance after the expiration of policies then in force on any buildings, the title to which is in the State of North Carolina or any of its institutions, departments, or agencies, so that the State would bear the same relation to the Federal Government that would an insurance company if a policy of insurance was in force. In other words, the State now stands in the shoes of a fire insurance company as to all State-owned property covered by the 1945 Act.

Your letter indicates that the title to the property is in the Federal Gov- ernment and I am wondering just how the transfer of the title to the lot on which the building is erected was made and as to the conditions in the in- strument of conveyance.

STATE INSURANCE FUND; FAYETTEVILLE STATE TEACHERS COLLEGE; NEWBOLD BUILDING

23 August 1945

Since the Act of the 1945 Session of the Legislature making the State of North Carolina a self insurer applies only to property, the title to which is in the State of North Carolina, I do not think that that portion of the Newbold Training School Building erected on property owned by the United States Government is covered by said fund. In view of the provisions of the contract dated May 27, 1943, between the United States of America and the Fayetteville State Teachers College, requiring the lessee to procure and maintain for the benefit of the government such insurance covering the risk to which the leased property is exposed as is customarily carried in connection with similar facilities located in the same or comparable area, sufficiently to protect the government's financial interest in the leased property, I am of the opinion that insurance coverage should be secured in the same manner and to the same extent as was in force prior to the adoption of the 1945 Act of the Legislature.

I am forwarding a copy of this letter to the Honorable William P. Hodges, Insurance Commissioner for the State of North Carolina.

The Council of State met yesterday and I discussed the matter of acquiring the Federal Government's building and site and it was the sentiment of the Council of State that your Board should contact the Federal officials and get the best offer possible and then submit it to the Council of State for action. I called Mr. Emanuel but he was out of town, attending Court, and I did not know that the Council of State was going to meet until just a few minutes before it did meet.

I suggest that your committee take this matter up with our representatives in Washington and ascertain the best proposition the Government will make to enable the State to acquire title to the property in question and I assure you that I shall be glad to cooperate with you in this respect.

STATE INSTITUTIONS; ELIZABETH CITY STATE TEACHERS COLLEGE; STATE NOT LIABLE INJURIES SUSTAINED BY PERSONS RIDING ON ON STATE VEHICLES

30 October 1945

In response to my letter to you of October 20, you make further inquiry as to whether or not you may purchase out of the appropriation made by the Legislature to your institution for insurance purposes, fire and theft coverage on motor vehicles owned by the institution and whether or not you may purchase insurance protecting pupils riding upon such vehicles for any injuries sustained by them.

Chapter 1027 of the 1945 Session Laws does not prohibit purchasing fire or theft insurance covering motor vehicles belonging to a State-owned institution, but I do not think that your institution may purchase any form of insurance protecting pupils riding on such vehicles from injuries sustained in the event of accident. As I stated to you in my letter of October

20, no suit can be maintained against your institution for negligence in the operation of the motor vehicles owned by it and so there would be no occasion to purchase liability insurance. Of course, the operator of the truck might be liable in case of negligence on his part, but this is a matter in which he would be interested and if he desires liability insurance it would be up to him to purchase and pay for such coverage.

EDUCATION; EAST CAROLINA TEACHERS COLLEGE; RESIDENT AND NON-RESIDENT TUITION; RESIDENCE OF STUDENT HERETOFORE STATIONED
IN THIS STATE IN THE MARINE CORPS

19 March 1946

You state that on January 16, 1946 a young man enrolled as a student; and for the purpose of the records, he gave his home address as Mound City, Illinois; and he gave the same address for his parents or guardians. At that time, he paid out-of-state tuition. You further state that the college catalog sets forth that for a student to be exempt from out-of-state tuition, he must be one whose parents or guardian are residents of the State at the time of his first enrollment in college or that the student whose parents reside outside of the State must himself have established residence in the State at least six months before he entered the college.

This student has now recently informed you that he was stationed in this State in the Marine Corps for the past seventeen months and is about to receive his discharge. It is the contention of this student that he should be exempt from out-of-state tuition for the reason that he has been in the State for the past seventeen months.

You would like to know if a person in military service stationed at a regular Marine or Army base within the State thereby establishes residence which would exempt him from payment of out-of-state tuition when he is enrolled in a State institution.

The question of residence is a difficult matter because so much depends on the mental element, such as a person's intentions or purposes. On the question of acquiring residence in this State by military personnel for the purpose of obtaining a divorce, we made an interpretation, a part of which reads as follows:

"The word 'residence' has, like the word 'fixtures' different shades of meaning in the Statutes, and even in the Constitution, according to its purposes and context. In the case of Discount Corp. vs. Radecky, 205 N. C. 163, the Court, in discussing the meaning of the word 'residence,' said:
'The term "residence" has no fixed meaning which is applicable to all cases, its definition in a particular case depending upon the connection in which it is used and the nature of the subject to which it pertains.'
"Residence, in its true sense, means the place of a person's abode, dwelling or habitation. It is made up of fact and intention. There must be the fact of abode and the intention of remaining. In the case of Watson v. Railroad, 152 N. C. 215, 217, the Court, in discussing the meaning of the word 'residence,' said:
'Probably the clearest definition is that in Barney v. Oelrichs, 138

U. S. 529: "Residence is dwelling in a place for some continuance of time, and is not synonymous with domicil, but means a fixed and permanent abode or dwelling as distinguished from a mere temporary locality of existence; and to entitle one to the character of a 'resident,' there must be a settled, fixed abode, and an intention to remain permanently, or at least for some time, for business or other purposes." To same effect Coleman v. Territory, 5 Okl. 201: "Residence indicates permanency of occupation as distinct from lodging or boarding or temporary occupation. 'Residence' indicates the place where a man has his fixed and permanent abode and to which, whenever he is absent, he has the intention of returning." In Wright v. Genesee, 117 Mich. 244, it is said: "Residence means the place where one resides; an abode, a dwelling or habitation. Residence is made up of fact and intention. There must be the fact of abode and the intention of remaining." And in Silvey v. Lindsay, 42 Hun. (N.Y.) 120: "A place of residence and the common-law acceptation of the term means a fixed and permanent abode, a dwelling-place for the time being, as contradistinguished from a mere temporary local residence." '

"With the above definitions in mind, it is my opinion that where a person from another state enters the armed forces of the United States and is sent to a military reservation in North Carolina, and after arriving in this State, such person resides on the military reservation and has no intention of making the State of North Carolina his home, he would not become a resident of the State of North Carolina within the meaning of the divorce statute, which requires six months residence in the State of North Carolina before the institution of a divorce action. On the other hand, if a person in the military service comes to the State of North Carolina with the intention of making North Carolina his home, and resides outside the military reservation to which he is attached, it is my opinion that he would be a resident of the State of North Carolina within the meaning of the divorce statute."

You will note that the above interpretation makes two things applicable as tests: (a) the intention of the person when he came into the State and (b) the fact that he resided off of the military reservation if he is engaged in military service. I think the fact of residing off of the reservation was added as a precaution and as showing such person had established his residence in this State because he had independent quarters or a household separate and apart from the quarters provided on the military post or reservation. The fact that the man has been in this State for seventeen months is not of itself conclusive. It seems to me that you should apply the rule that was applied in the divorce case; and that there should be not only the intentions to be a resident of the State, but there should be independent or a separate establishment or household as evidence of that residence which exists off of the military reservation.

Taxation; Exemption

7 June 1946

In response to your request, I have looked into the question of the right of the Board of County Commissioners of Watauga County to exempt from taaxtion real property belonging to Miss Florence Boyd.

You will understand, of course, that the right to exempt property from taxation is controlled by statutes in effect in this State and neither the Board of County Commissioners nor the Attorney General would have any right to exempt any property from taxation unless authorized by the statute. The Board of County Commissioners is charged with the duty of assessing and valuing all property listed for taxation and may adjust valuations in accordance with the true value of the property at the appropriate time.

I understand that this is rural property owned by Miss Florence Boyd and that, during the time she has owned it, she has maintained a home for crippled children on the property, until the buildings were destroyed by fire.

The statute exempts from taxation real property belonging to anl actually and exclusively occupied by Young Men's Christian Associations and other similar religious associations, orphanages or other similar homes, hospitals and nunneries not conducted for profit but entirely and completely as charitable institutions.

I understand that a store was conducted on the property at which merchandise was sold to the public.

It seems from what you stated that Miss Boyd was engaged in fine, charitable work but, unfortunately, she had not confined the use of the property exclusively for the purpose of maintaining a home for crippled children, although she generously supported crippled children in her home from her own means and from other available sources.

In order to be sure that the property is entitled to exemption, it would be necessary for her to have it deeded to a non-profit, non-stock corporation which would be chartered for the purpose of operating a home for crippled children or some other type of home. A home for crippled children which had been incorporated as above indicated, would come within the exemption provided by the above statute and the property would be entitled to exemption from the first tax listing date after its incorporation.

OPINIONS TO VETERANS COMMISSION

ADMINISTRATORS; APPOINTMENTS; VETERANS PRESUMED DEAD
BY THE WAR AND NAVY DEPARTMENTS

5 March 1946

I have your letter of March 2, 1946, in which you write as follows:

"Questions are arising in the minds of the Clerks of Court in the State as to the necessary proof to be required for appointment of administrators for members of the armed forces who have been missing in action and have been declared officially dead by the War and Navy Departments.

"Is a statement from the War and Navy Departments stating the member of the armed forces is presumed to be dead, sufficient evidence for the Clerks to act in the appointment of an administrator etc? If this is not sufficient proof, what is required?"

By Section 28-29 of the General Statutes it is provided that upon application for letters of administration the Clerk must ascertain by affidavit of the applicant or otherwise that the person whose estate is to be administered is dead and that he died intestate. Our statutes do not specify the type of evidence which is required to be presented as a basis for the Clerk's finding of death. It may be that in a particular case the Clerk of Court will be convinced of the death of the person whose estate is to be administered by a statement from the War or Navy Department to the effect that such person is presumed to be dead. I, of course, cannot advise as to whether the Clerk will be so satisfied in any given case. It would be wise to remember that a grant of letters of administration upon the estate of a living person is void for lack of jurisliction. SPRINGER v. SHAVENDER, 118 N. C. 33.

There is a common-law presumption that a person is dead from his continued absence for seven years. This presumption is in effect in North Carolina, but it is a presumption of fact which may be rebutted. CHAMBLEE v. BANK, 211 N. C. 48. Whether the action of a Clerk in appointing an administrator of the estate of a person who has been continuously absent for seven years would be valid if the party subsequently should be found, is a question which has not been settled in North Carolina. In SPRINGER v. SHAVENDER, 116 N. C. 12, 18-19, the following appears:

"Should a case be presented where administration had been granted not upon false information of a person's death, but upon a presumption of law arising from his absence without being heard from for seven years, a different question might be presented. Whether the acts of an administrator who proceeded honestly upon a presumption, to which the law gave the force of a fact, will not be held, because of such presumption, to be valid, as in some courts has been the decision, where an executor performed a part of his imposed trust under a will afterwards ascertained to be a forgery, we need not now determine. To exclude a conclusion, it may be best, however, to announce that should such a case arise, the question whether it is to be governed by or distinguished from the ruling in that before us, is an open one. Such a case would raise the point whether the presumption of law that one is dead

does not confer jurisdiction over a living person's estate, when it could not possibly be acquired in the absence of such presumption." ,
The general authorities indicate that if it appears in evidence that the absent person within the seven years encountered some specific peril or within that period came within the range of some impending or immediate danger which might reasonably be expected to destroy life, the Court or jury may infer that life ceased before the expiration of the seven years. DAVIE v. BRIGGS, 97 U. S. 628; 16 AM. JURISPRUDENCE, *DEATH*, Section 27, page 25; 25 C.J.S., *DEATH*, Section 10, page 1068.

I regret that I cannot be more specific and definite but the law itself is indefinite. I am of the opinion, however, that the Clerk would have jurisdiction to appoint an administrator if he is satisfied of the death of the person whose estate is to be administered, and I believe that the communication from the War or Navy Department, that such person is presumed to be dead, would be evidence to be considered. If it should be established that the missing person is actually alive, the action of the Clerk would be void.

ADMINISTRATORS; APPOINTMENTS; VETERANS PRESUMED
DEAD BY THE WAR AND NAVY DEPARTMENTS

8 March 1946

Thank you for your letter of March 7, 1946, directing my attention to Chapter 731 of the Session Laws of 1945, which deals with the above subject. When I wrote to you on March 5, 1946, I did not take this chapter into consideration. However, I am of the opinion that the views expressed in that letter are legally correct. The only effect of Chapter 731 is to give artificial weight to the declaration of the Federal Department or agent that a particular person is presumed to be dead. With this statute in existence, I believe that Clerks of the Superior Courts will be more willing to appoint administrators for the estates of persons who have not been officially declared dead.

Thus, when an application for letters of administration is made, a Clerk of the Superior Court will be aided in his determination of whether the person is dead by the legislative declaration that a written finding of presumed death is *prima facie* evidence of the death. In other words, the effect of Chapter 731 is to give to a written finding of presumed death an additional weight as evidence.

If the person for whose estate an administrator has been appointed should return, the act of the Clerk in appointing the administrator would be void despite the adoption of Chapter 731.

VETERANS; CHILDREN OF; EDUCATIONAL ADVANTAGES FOR CHILDREN

29 April 1946

I have considered at some length the five specific questions raised in your letter regarding educational advantages provided by our Statutes for children of World War veterans, and I submit the following observations:

1. A reading of Paragraph 1 of General Statutes 116-145 in connection with General Statutes 116-146 would seem to indicate that our Legislature intended to create two classes of beneficiaries under these two sections.

General Statutes 116-146 is based on Chapter 370 of the Public Laws of 1931 and its benefits are restricted to "Any child in North Carolina who is drawing compensation from the United States Government. . .and who has not attained the age of twenty-one years."

This was the original act granting educational advantages to children of World War veterans and it not only applies to a limited class of children, but carries with it a definite limitation as to age; while General Statutes 116-145 is based on later enactments of the sessions of 1937, 1939, 1941 and 1943 as set out in the editor's note following this section, and the benefits and advantages of General Statutes 116-145 are extended to "Any child who has been a resident cf North Carolina for two years and whose father . . .," without regard to the age of such child.

Here the class of beneficiaries who may qualify is considerably broadened as compared with General Statutes 116-146, and under General Statutes 116-145 there is no age limitation imposed; so, just as you suggest, the word "child" in this connection may be reasonably considered as designating only the required relationship to the veteran without regard to the age of the child. This interpretation, it seems to me, would not result in an unreasonable discrimination between beneficiaries under General Statutes 116-145 and General Statutes 116-146.

2. In regard to the residence requirements under General Statutes 116-145, we find that the provision as to two years residence, which now appears in Paragraph 1 of General Statutes 116-145, was taken from Chapter 242 of the Public Laws of 1937, while the language immediately following the words ". . . the legal termination thereof . . ." appearing alter in lines 10 and 11 of Paragraph 1 of General Statutes 116-145, came in by way of amendment through Chapter 54 of the Public Laws of 1939. Here I feel that the purpose of this amendatory act was to extend the application of the article so as to include additional beneficiaries, by liberalizing the classification of veterans whose children might participate; and I do not feel that it was the legislative intent to change the requirements as to two years residence in the state so as to accept children of mere temporary residence. No such interpretation is made necessary by the language of the Statutes and to place such a construction upon the act would result in an unjustified discrimination in this respect among beneficiaries in the same classification.

3. I am inclined to agree with your conclusion that the benefits extended by Paragraph 1 of General Statutes 116-145 are now available without regard to the financial status of the applicant. It seems clear that the obvious intent of Chapter 534 of the Public Laws of 1943 was to add ". . . room and board and all necessary fees . . ." to the benefits available under General Statutes 116-145 (Section 1 of Chapter 242 of the Public Laws of 1937), and although Paragraph 2 of General Statutes 116-145 was not expressly repealed by Chapter 534 of the Public Laws of 1943, it appears

that it was in effect superseded, as the 1943 amendment makes available under Paragraph 1 of General Statutes 116-145, without regard to financial status, substantially all the benefits theretofore available under Paragraph 2 of General Statutes 116-145 to ". . . children needing financial assistance." This, it seems to me, was the obvious legislative intent, and it is difficult to see why an applicant should now undertake to qualify under Paragraph 2 of General Statutes 116-145, since the same benefits are now generally available under Paragraph 1 of General Statutes 116-145 irrespective of financial need.

4. The same reasoning as under Item 3 would seem to support your conclusion as to General Statutes 116-145 to the effect that applicants designated in General Statutes 116-147 are qualified to receive the benefits set out under Paragraph 1 of General Statutes 116-145, without regard to financial need. Any other interpretation would result in discrimination among applicants without any apparent justification.

5. In regard to the statutory limitation on the number of scholarships available to children of veterans qualifying under the terms of General Statutes 116-147, I am of the opinion that not more than five scholarships may be granted in any one year to the particular class of beneficiary set up under this section. This, I believe, is in line with your own interpretation of this section, and also in accord with the existing administrative practice as I understand it.

I am further of the opinion that these educational benefits were intended for the actual children of veterans, and that the existing statutes could not properly be construed to include illegitimate children, stepchildren, or adopted children.

OPINIONS TO NORTH CAROLINA COLLEGE
FOR NEGROES

NORTH CAROLINA COLLEGE FOR NEGROES; GRADUATE COURSES; EXTENT OF
PARTICIPATION IN EXPENSES ATTENDING OUT-OF-STATE COLLEGE

27 April 1945

I have your letter of April 24, in which you advise that a good many of the people who are making applications for this summer desire to attend universities in California, Washington and other far western states; that they can secure similar courses at universities which are nearer but their preferences are to attend those far western universities. You inquire what is the power of the committee in dealing with such problem and, specifically, is the committee compelled to grant their requests, should the committee grant any part of the requests, or should the application be denied.

The answers to your questions are found in the language of the statute, which is now General Statute 116-100. This section, taken from Chapter 65 of the Public Laws of 1939, provides that the Board of Trustees of the North Carolina College for Negroes is authorized and empowered to establish from time to time such graduate courses in the liberal arts field as the demand may warrant, and the funds of the said North Carolina College for Negroes justify. A similar provision is made for the Negro Agricultural and Technical College at Greensboro as to graduate and professional courses in agricultural and technical lines as the need for same is shown and the funds of the State will justify, and establish suitable departments therein.

The next paragraph of the section reads, in part, as follows:

"In the event there are negroes resident in the state properly qualified who can certify that they have been duly admitted to any reputable graduate or professional college and said graduate or professional courses are not being offered at the North Carolina College for Negroes, then the board of trustees of the North Carolina College for Negroes when said certification has been presented to them by the president and faculty of the North Carolina College for Negroes, may pay tuition and other expenses for said student or students at such recognized college *in such amount as may be deemed reasonably necessary* to compensate said resident student for the additional expense of attending a graduate or professional school outside of North Carolina. . . . It is further provided that the student applying for such admission must furnish proof that he or she has been duly admitted to said recognized professional college. In the case of agricultural or technical subjects such students desiring graduate courses should apply to the Agricultural and Technical College at Greensboro, North Carolina. The general provisions covering students in the liberal arts field as stated in this section shall apply. In no event shall there be any duplication of courses in the two institutions."

The italicized portion of the above quoted part of the section leaves the amount to be awarded to the out-of-State student in the discretion of the trustees, by providing such amount as may be deemed reasonably necessary to compensate said resident student for additional expenses of attending a graduate or professional school outside of North Carolina. This would mean that if, in the opinion of the Board of Trustees, it was not reasonably necessary for the student to incur the expenses of traveling to a far western state to secure the educational opportunity which is desired, the board would not be compelled to allow the costs of travel or any other item of expense which was not deemed reasonably necessary. In other words, if in the opinion of the Board of Trustees the student could obtain the advantages sought at some other institution at less expense and the additional expense incurred in travel or otherwise was not reasonably necessary, the trustees could refuse to allow such items of expense and thereby, I believe, control within reasonable limits the expenditures which could be made by the student.

If the student insists upon attending some distant institution and incurring more expense than is deemed reasonably necessary by the Board of Trustees, it would be within the discretion of the board to allow such part of the expense as they deemed reasonably necessary over and above what it would cost the student if the student attended a North Carolina institution, the statute providing compensation for the "additional expense of attending a graduate or professional school outside of North Carolina." The statute, therefore, I believe, provides a satisfactory answer to your first questions.

You also advise as follows:

"The University of North Carolina maintains a School of Nursing Education. It is not on the graduate level. We have applications from trained nurses who have not finished high school but who desire to secure the B. S. degree in Nursing Education. We do maintain such a school here. As I understand it, the funds entrusted to our care were for graduate work. What is the province of the committee in such cases as these? I would be very glad to have your official ruling on the matter so that the committee can govern itself accordingly."

The provisions of the statute, G. S. 116-100, relate entirely to providing for graduate courses in your institution and in the Negro Agricultural and Technical College at Greensboro and provide for out-of-State graduate courses when not offered in this State. As the School of Nursing Education at the University of North Carolina is not on a graduate level, I am of the opinion that the provisions of this section would have no application and your conclusion about this is, I think, entirely correct.

EMINENT DOMAIN; RIGHT OF CITY OF DURHAM TO CONDEMN PROPERTY
OF NORTH CAROLINA COLLEGE FOR NEGROES

28 May 1946

I received your letter of May 25 enclosing copy of a letter from the City of Durham Planning Department, under date of May 22, in which they state that the City proposes to widen and relocate the present right of way of Alston Avenue, abutting the College property, in connection with which they propose acquiring by purchase or condemnation a strip of land varying from 48.65 feet to 50.35 feet in width and 472.4 feet in length across the property owned by the State of North Carolina for the North Carolina College for Negroes.

You state in your letter that the acquisition of this property would be a great sacrifice and that the College could not afford to lose the strip of land. You mention the fact that the proposed condemnation would take only about 5 feet from the opposite side of the street.

You request my advice as to whether or not the City would have a right to condemn State property for this purpose. You ask also whether the Board could collect money for any purchase which they may grant, and also whether the Board has a right to refuse to give the land.

In the case of YADKIN COUNTY v. HIGH POINT, 217 N. C. 462, our Supreme Court expressed themselves on this subject, as follows:

"The power of eminent domain, as general understood, extends only to the right to condemn private property for public uses. WISSLER v. POWER CO., 158 N. C., 465, 74 S. E., 460; JEFFRESS v. GREEN-VILLE, 154 N. C., 490, 70 S. E., 919. It is for the General Assembly to say whether in the particular case or under certain conditions, the power shall be enlarged to embrace public property and property devoted to a public use as well as private property. 10 R.C.L., 198. The authorities are to the effect that a general authorization to exercise the power of eminent domain will not suffice in a case where property already dedicated to a public use is sought to be condemned for another public use which is totally inconsistent with the first or former use, R. R. v. R. R., 83 N. C., 489; 20 C.J., 602. In such a case a specific legislative grant or one of unmistakable intent is required. VERMONT HYDROELECTRIC CORP., v. DUNN et al., 95 Vt., 144, 112 Atl., 223, 12 A.L.R., 1495; MINNESOTA POWER & LIGHT CO. v. STATE, 177 Minn., 343, 225 N. W., 164; CITY OF ALBUQUERQUE v. GARCIA, 17 N. Mex., 445, 130 Pac., 118; VILLAGE OF RIDGEWOOD v. GLEN ROCK, 15 N. J. Misc., 65, 118 Atl., 698. Especially insistent are the cases where the property sought to be condemned for a second public use is owned by an agency of the Government, or a subdivision thereof, and by it devoted to a state purpose. CITY OF ST. LOUIS v. MOORE, 269 Mo., 430, 190 S. W., 867.

"It will be noted that the county property here sought to be condemned is already devoted to a public use. Its condemnation for a second inconsistent public use, which is necessarily destructive of the first, may not be accomplished except under legislative authority given in express terms or by necessary implication. FAYETTEVILLE STREET RY. v. R. R., 142 N. C., 423, 55 S. E., 345. Admittedly, the city; of High Point is without such authority here. SELMA v. NOBLES, 183 N. C., 322, 111 S. E., 543."

Under the authority of this decision, it is my opinion that the City of Durham could not condemn the property of the North Carolina College for Negroes for a purpose which would be inconsistent with purposes for which it was acquired. This property being owned by the State of North Carolina, no action could be instituted by the City of Durham against the State for the purpose of condemning this property, as the State cannot be sued without consent given by the General Assembly and no consent has been given in a matter of this kind.

I, therefore, think that the Board would have a right to make a reasonable charge for the land which would be taken for the purposes proposed, against which would be offset any special benefits which would accrue by reason of the widening of the street, if any such benefits would accrue to the College. No conveyance of this property could be made except by the Governor and Council of State, upon recommendation of the Board of Trustees of the College. It would naturally follow that the Board would have a right to refuse to give the land to the City.

OPINIONS TO STATE BOARD OF MEDICAL EXAMINERS

MEDICINE; CRIMINAL LAW; CITIZENSHIP; CONVICTION
OF FELONY IN ANOTHER STATE

30 April 1945

In your letter of April 28, 1945, you enclose a copy of a letter written to you by a proposed applicant for license to practice medicine in this State, which shows that this person was previously licensed in the State of Maryland and was convicted of the crime of abortion and conspiracy in the State of Maryland, and as a result thereof the Medical Board of that State revoked his license.

You ask whether or not this man's citizenship is in order for your Board to consider him as an applicant.

I cannot find anything in the state dealing with the practice of medicine in this State, which is Article I of Chapter 90 of the General Statutes, which requires an applicant for license to be a citizen. You will remember that on the 2d of February, 1945, this office ruled at the instance of your Board that an alien could practice medicine in this country if such alien otherwise complied with the requirements of your Board as to obtaining license. So far as I can see, the person in question is a citizen. The conviction of such person an a felony charge in the State of Maryland would not operate to deprive him of his citizenship in this State, and he was not convicted in any Federal Court, there would not be any question of a Federal nature to complicate the situation. I am assuming, of course, and I am answering this letter on the basis that abortion is a felony in the State of Maryland as it is in the State of North Carolina.

I am of the opinion, therefore, that the proceedings in Maryland did not operate to deprive this person of his citizenship insofar as he is a citizen of the United States and of the State of North Carolina.

LICENSES; CHANGE OF NAME BY MARRIAGE AFTER ISSUANCE OF LICENSE

9 October 1945

I have your letter of September 25, 1945, attaching copy of a letter from Jane Gregory Marrow, M.D., whose license was issued last June to her under the name of Lucy Jane Gregory, and who now desires to substitute the name, Jane Gregory Marrow, by reason of her recent marriage. Dr. Marrow enclosed with her letter a certified copy of her marriage certificate. She states that she wants this matter settled in order that she might use the name, Jane Gregory Marrow, both professionally and in private life.

There is nothing necessary to be done by Dr. Marrow to enable her to use her new name either professionally or in private life. Upon her marriage to Mr. Marrow she immediately acquired her new name by operation of law, and she is entitled to use such new name not only in private life, but also professionally. The fact that her license is in her maiden name does not affect her right in this respect as long as there is sufficient identification of person.

Aside from the fact that Dr. Marrow need take no action to accomplish what she desires, I know of no way in which she could have her license changed to carry her married name. Moreover, there would be the practical difficulty in regard to the issuance date stated on the certificate. If the original issuance date is used, the certificate could not very well recite her married name, for she was not married on that date. If the certificate carried a subsequent date, it would not state the truth, for the reason that the license was not issued on that date. It seems to me that the only other alternative might be the issuance of a new and different kind of certificate, reciting all of the facts, including the fact of original issuance and the fact of subsequent marriage. However, I know of no authority by which this can be done.

APPLICATIONS FOR MEDICAL LICENSE; REFUSAL BY BOARD; REMEDY OF APPLICANT

21 November 1945

I have your letter of November 19 in which you write me as follows:.

"Please advise me what recourse, if any, a physician may have when the State Board of Medical Examiners refuses him a license by endorsement of credentials and refuses him permission to take the regular examination for licensure. I have in mind a case in which the board refused an applicant because he was not a graduate of a grade A medical school."

In order to express any opinion about the particular case which you have in mind, I would have to have full information about it. The Statute, G. S. 90-9, provides it shall be the duty of the board of medical examiners to examine for license to practice medicine or surgery, or any of the branches thereof, every applicant who complies with the provisions set out in this section. In the event the board should refuse to provide an examination for anyone entitled to it under the provisions of this law, the applicant would have the right to compel the board to provide an examination by a writ of mandamus.

G. S. 90-12 provides that the Board of Medical Examiners may, whenever in its opinion the conditions of the locality where the applicant resides are such as to render it advisable, issue a limited license. This, however, is entirely at the discretion of the board and, in my opinion, if the board refused to grant it, the applicant for such limited license would have no redress.

APPLICATIONS FOR MEDICAL LICENSES; GROUNDS UPON WHICH THEY MAY BE REFUSED

29 November 1945

I have your letter of November 27th, supplementing your letter of November 19th on the above subject, in which last letter you write me as follows:

"Please refer to our correspondence on April 28 and 30, 1945, in reference to Luther R. Fultz.

"Fultz now requests permission to take the regular State Board of Medical examination. The board has refused this permission on the grounds that he was convicted of criminal abortion in the State of Maryland and that his licensure would not be in the best interest of medical service to the citizenship of the state. This action was taken after, but not necessarily because of a resolution adopted by the Richmond County Medical Society as follows: 'Resolved to recommend to the State Board of Medical Examiners that Luther R. Fultz not be granted the privilege of taking the State Board examination.'

"Please advise if in your opinion the board is justified in its refusal to grant permission for examination."

G. S. 90-11 provides that every person making application for a license to practice medicine or surgery in the State shall be not less than twenty-one years of age and of good moral character before any license can be granted by the Board of Medical Examiners.

Under this section the Board of Medical Examiners of the State of North Carolina would have the right to refuse to permit a person to take the examination who is found by the board not to be a person of good moral character. The fact that an applicant had been convicted in another State of criminal abortion would be very strong evidence to be considered by the Board upon the question of the moral character of the applicant. This circumstance or any other of which the Board may have knowledge could form the basis of such a determination. The applicant, however, should be given notice and opportunity for hearing before such determination is made.

APPLICANTS FOR MEDICAL LICENSE; REQUIREMENTS AT TO MEDICAL EDUCATION; CLASS A AND CLASS B MEDICAL SCHOOLS

4 December 1945

I have your letter of December 3, in which you state that an applicant for a license to practice medicine in this State has been refused, the applicant being a graduate of a medical college classified by the American Medical Association as a grade B school. The board refused licensing by endorsement of credentials of the applicant and refused permission to take the regular examination because of inadequate qualifications of the applicant. You state that this practice has been followed consistently by the board except in perhaps one or two cases, which may have been permitted by oversight. You inquire whether or not the board is authorized to take this position.

The statute dealing with this subject is found in General Statutes, Chapter 90, Article 1. Section 90-6 provides that the Board of Medical Examiners is empowered to prescribe such regulations as it may deem proper governing applicants for license, admission to examinations, the conduct of applicants during examinations, and the conduct of examinations proper.

G. S. 90-9 provides that it shall be the duty of the Board of Medical Examiners to examine for license to practice medicine or surgery, or any of the branches thereof, every applicant who complies with the following provisions:

"He shall, before he is admitted to examination, satisfy the board that he has an academic education equal to the entrance requirements of the University of North Carolina, or furnish a certificate from the superintendent of public instruction of the county that he has passed an examination upon his literary attainments to meet the requirements of entrance in the regular course of the state university. He shall exhibit a diploma or furnish satisfactory proof of graduation from a medical college in good standing requiring an attendance of not less than four years, and supplying such facilities for clinical and scientific instruction as shall meet the approval of the board; but the requirement of four years attendance at a school shall not apply to those graduating prior to January the first, nineteen hundred."

G. S. 90-10 provides for preliminary and final examinations and repeats the requirement that the applicant shall furnish satisfactory evidence of a medical school in good standing, and supplying such facilities for anatomical and laboratory instruction as shall meet with the approval of the board.

These statutes vest in the board the authority to determine whether or not the medical college is in good standing and provides for anatomical and laboratory instruction which is considered as necessary by the board.

I am not informed as to what is required to meet the classification of medical colleges made by the American Medical Association or what constitutes grade A or grade B schools. The State Board of Medical Examiners would undoubtedly have the authority to act under the statutes cited to determine whether or not such institution had the required facilities for providing the education necessary, in their opinion, for admission to practice. If the board has determined that the grade B college is not in good standing or does not supply such facilities for clinical and scientific instruction as meets its approval, then it would have a right to refuse to issue the license by comity or to provide an examination for the applicant.

OPINIONS TO MEDICAL CARE COMMISSION

25 September 1945

In your letter to me of August 28 you asked for an interpretation of the words "cost of hospital care" as used in General Statutes 131-119. You state that you are unable to decide whether the cost referred to in the law means an average cost of hospitalization, some arbitrary established cost, or some modification of the actual cost.

The word "cost" as used in this section, in my opinion, is to be taken in its ordinary and established meaning and I do not think that for your purposes it is necessary to further define it. It is my thought that all the Commission would need to know was that the cost of the hospitalization of the indigent person was as much or more than the amount contributed from the State fund and that the balance of the expense or cost of the patient in the hospital was to be provided by the county or city having responsibility for the care of such indigent patient, or from some other sources, whatever the cost might be. It would probably be that the hospital itself would accept an amount less than the actual cost to them of the indigent patient, and that would meet any requirements, so far as the State Commission is concerned, under the terms of this section.

You also requested an interpretation of the words appearing in this same section, "or owned and operated by charitable, non-profit, non-stock corporations."

These words mean, in my opinion, the hospitals in which no individual stockholder can under any possible circumstances receive any profits or earnings of the corporation. If it has this quality, it would be considered as a charitable, non-profit corporation. The law provides for the organization of non-stock corporations, which are corporations which do not issue capital stock but has a membership elected as may be prescribed by its charter or by-laws. In the event you have any particular instance to pass upon, it would be well to submit us a copy of the charter of the corporation in order that you might be advised as to its legal character.

At your request, I have studied the question as to when the appropriation of $500,000.00 made in Section 131-119 will become available. I have sent you a copy of Section 23½ of Committee Substitute for House Bill No. 11, the general Appropriations Bill of 1945. If after studying this and the language found in Section 131-119 any further advice from me is necessary, I will be glad to discuss this with you and the Assistant Director of the Budget, Mr. Deyton.

You also ask my opinion about the language in the second paragraph of Section 131-122, which provides as follows:

> "Provided that no action shall be taken under this provision of this section, other than the work of the Commission, until a survey has been made and a report submitted to the Governor and Medical Care Commission by the Rockefeller Foundation or some other accredited agency with experience in the field of surveying large areas in connection with medical education and medical care. . ."

You state that you have been unable to secure a survey to be made by the Rockefeller Foundation or any other accredited agency, but that you can get individuals from the Rockefeller Foundation, and perhaps some other organization, who would help in the work.

I believe that this statute requires that the survey be made by the Rockefeller Foundation or some other "accredited agency" and I do not believe that the provisions of the statute would be met by merely having individuals from these organizations to do the work. The statute contemplates that the organization itself should have the responsibility for the survey. I hope you can arrange it so that this can be done. I am enclosing you a copy of Section 131-122.

EXPANSION OF MEDICAL SCHOOL OF THE UNIVERSITY OF NORTH CAROLINA

27 December 1945

I have your letter of December 22, in which you write me as follows:

"It is respectfully requested that your interpretation be given for the guidance of this Commission as to Statutes 131-122 of Chapter 1096, Session Laws of 1945.

"Does the limitation apply to all or only a part of Section 131-122?

"What is the extent of duties as prescribed in Statutes 131-122, of the 'Rockefeller Foundation or some other accredited agency with experience in the field of surveying large areas in connection with medical education and melical care?."

G. S. 131-122 reads as follows:

"Expansion of Medical School of the University of North Carolina. In order to carry forward the State-wide plan of hospital and medical care, the Board of Trustees of the University of North Carolina, by and with the approval of the Governor and the North Carolina Medical Care Commission, is hereby authorized and empowered to expand the two-year Medical School of the University of North Carolina into a standard four-year medical school. The North Carolina Medical Care Commission is authorized and directed to make a complete survey of all factors involved in determining the location of the expanded medical school, giving especial attention to the advantages and disadvantages of locating said school in one of the large cities of the State, and shall render a report of their findings to the Governor and Board of Trustees of the University of North Carolina.

"Provided that no action shall be taken under *this provision* of this section, other than the work of the Commission, until a survey has been made and a report submitted to the Governor and Medical Care Commission by the Rockefeller Foundation or some other accredited agency with experience in the field of surveying large areas in connection with medical education and medical care. The report of such agency is to be submitted to the Governor and the Medical Care Commission in a reasonable time in advance of the report of the Governor and the Commission to the Board of Trustees." (Italics supplied).

After giving this matter the careful consideration that its importance deserves, I am of the opinion that the survey referred to in the last paragraph, to be made by the Rockefeller Foundation or some other accredited agency, is intended to refer to the survey as to the location of the expanded medical school which is referred to in the last sentence of the first paragraph.

Under the last sentence of the first paragraph in the section, the North Carolina Medical Care Commission is authorized and directed to make a complete survey of all factors involved in determining the location of the expanded medical school, and, as a second requirement of this sentence, the Medical Care Commission is required to render a report of its findings to the Governor and the Board of Trustees of the University of North Carolina. Immediately following this sentence is the proviso sent up as an amendment on the floor when the bill was under consideration in the Senate, which says that no action shall be taken under this provision of this section, which is, in my opinion, a reference to the immediately preceding sentence in the section. The first sentence authorized and empowered the Board of Trustees of the University, with the approval of the Governor and the Medical Care Commission, to expand the two-year medical school into a standard four-year medical school. The provision of the second sentence, as above noted, is with reference to a complete survey and a report to the Governor and the Board of Trustees.

· It seems to me that the reference to the survey in the last sentence of the first paragraph of the section and the reference to a survey in the proviso, both relate to a survey as to location as the two sentences are connected by a direct reference as well as one immediately following the other.

Under the section as a whole, however, the Medical Care Commission and the Governor are required to approve the action of the Trustees of the University of North Carolina in expanding the Medical School and if, in the opinion of the Medical Care Commission, it is desirable to secure the opinion of the agency making the survey under the last paragraph of the section as to need or other factors in connection with the expansion of the medical school, there is nothing in the Act which would prevent the Medical Care Commission from requesting this special agency to include in its survey the question of need or any other factors which would be desired by the Medical Care Commission, or the members thereof, in aiding them in their decision as to approval of the action of the Board of Trustees of the University in expanding the medical school.

OPINIONS TO HOSPITALS BOARD OF CONTROL

INSANE PERSONS AND INCOMPETENTS; TRANSFER OF RESIDENTS OF THIS
STATE FROM HOSPITALS WITHOUT THE STATE TO HOSPITALS WITHIN
THE STATE; AUTHORITY OF HOSPITAL TO HOLD PATIENTS
PRIOR TO ACTION OF CLERK

21 August 1945

I have your letter of August 13, 1945, in which you ask for my construction of Section 122-63.1 of the General Statutes of North Carolina. You specifically ask if the Superintendent of a Hospital in this State has authority to retain a resident of this State who, while outside of this State, was found to be mentally disordered and was committed to a Hospital in some other State and is transferred directly to a Hospital in this State as provided for in the above cited section.

I agree with you that the law is not entirely clear on this point. However, it is my opinion that when a resident of this State is found to be mentally disordered while outside of the State, and is committed to a Hospital in another State and transferred directly to a Hospital in this State, the Superintendent of the Hospital to which he is transferred has the same authority over this patient upon admittance to the Hospital as he has over any other patient committed to the Hospital. I realize that this would mean that the Superintendent would be holding the patient before legal commitment papers have been issued by a clerk of court in this State. While this is not to be desired, it seems to me that we must so construe G. S. 122-63.1 or have that section become meaningless in many cases. I do not believe that the General Assembly intended for a mentally disordered resident of this State to be brought into this State from a Hospital outside of the State and then be discharged until he can be again apprehended and a legal commitment issued. The section, you will note, provides that the patient shall be transferred directly to the proper State Hospital in this State. Until some patient applies to, and is released by, a court of competent jurisdiction, I think it is wise that the Superintendents of the various Hospitals hold these patients even prior to the issuance of the commitment. I do not believe that any liability would be incurred by such action.

I regret that I cannot be more specific, but the law itself is in an uncertain state.

HOSPITALS FOR THE INSANE; INSANE PERSONS AND INCOMPETENTS; RIGHT
OF HOSPITAL AUTHORITIES TO MAKE SPINAL FLUID TESTS TO DE-
TERMINE IF PATIENT IS INFECTED WITH VENEREAL DISEASE

16 October 1945

You have inquired if the Hospital authorities are permitted to make spinal fluid tests to determine whether persons committed to said institutions are infected with venereal diseases, and to determine, when persons are infected, whether the central nervous system has become affected by the disease. You also inquire if the local health officers have authority to make this test on patients of the State Hospitals when the authorities at the Hospital do not object.

The statutes regulating the hospitals for the mentally incompetent in this State do not specifically authorize the physical examination of persons committed to said hospitals. Of course, the right to make an examination must necessarily be implied from the general nature of the treatment required of these institutions. This generally implied power would probably be broad enough to include the right to make a spinal fluid test. However, since we are acting upon implied rather than express powers, it is my opinion that it would be wise to refrain from making such tests unless the patient consents thereto. If the patient consents to the test, he would be estopped to later raise any objection. If he does not consent, and the test is made against his will, some difficulties, both practical and legal, may arise. It would seem wise, therefore, to make this test only when the patient consents. I am informed that this is the policy followed by the State Board of Health and by the United States Army.

This office has heretofore ruled in a letter to Honorable Adam Younce, Greensboro, that health officers have authority to make spinal fluid tests. I am enclosing a copy of this opinion for your use. You will note that the opinion expressed in the letter is modified by the policy which has been adopted by the State Board of Health. This is found in a postscript to the letter.

As stated above, it seems to me that this policy adopted by the Board of Health would be a wise one for you to follow.

INSANE PERSONS AND INCOMPETENTS; OPERATIONS ON INMATES OF STATE HOSPITALS; CONSENT OF PATIENT AND NEXT-OF-KIN

23 October 1945

In conference with you last week, my attention was directed to an opinion of this office to Dr. J. F. Owen, written on January 20, 1943, relating to the above subject. This opinion considered what now appears as Article 22 of Chapter 130 of the General Statutes (130-242, 130-243). These sections create a board of consultation which is to give its approval to the performance of operations on inmates of State hospitals. You have inquired if these sections contain the exclusive method of acquiring consent for the performance of an operation or whether the consent of the patient and his or her next-of-kin will be sufficient without complying with the provisions of these sections.

It is my opinion that these sections were adopted to fill a hiatus or interstice which existed in the law theretofore. A reading of the sections discloses that they were intended to apply in situations where, for any reason, the consent of the patient and his next-of-kin could not be procured. I am, therefore, of the opinion that the hospital authorities would be justified in rendering surgical treatment to inmates when necessary and when the proper consent has been secured, without complying with the provisions of the above quoted sections. This construction makes the sections in question complementary and enabling rather than exclusive and restrictive.

NORTH CAROLINA HOSPITALS BOARD OF CONTROL; RIGHT TO CONSTRUCT AND OPERATE PSYCHIATRIC HOSPITAL

30 November 1945

I have your letter of November 27th, in which you request my opinion as to whether any provision is now made by law by which a psychiatric hospital could be constructed in connection with the four year medical schools at Duke and Wake Forest which would either be operated by the two medical schools or operated by the State in connection with these institutions.

There is no appropriation made by the General Assembly which would authorize the construction of such a psychiatric hospital. The only provision made by law of this character with which I am familiar is the one provided for the construction of a hospital in connection with the four year medical school of the University of North Carolina, with the provisions of which I am sure you are familiar. In the absence of such legislation no appropriation or expenditure of the character mentioned by you could be male, and there are no funds from which any such allocation could be provided.

DEAD BODIES; AUTOPSIES; INMATES OF HOSPITALS; PERFORMANCE OF AUTOPSIES ON BODIES OF

8 May 1946

I have your letter of May 3, 1946. You inquire as to the right of the Hospital authorities to perform autopsies on the dead body of an inmate of a State Hospital. Your inquiry relates to the granting of consent for the performance of such autopsies by North Carolina Board of Anatomy, the surviving spouse or next of kin of the deceased, and the deceased himself.

The last paragraph of G. S. 90-212 provides that whenever an inmate of a State Hospital, etc. dies, his body may be embalmed and delivered to the North Carolina Board of Anatomy but said body shall be surrendered to the husband or wife of the deceased or to any other person within the second degree of consanguinity upon demand at any time within ten days after death upon the payment to said Board of the actual cost to it of embalming and preserving the body.

G. S. 90-213 makes it unlawful to hold an autopsy on any dead human body subject to the provisions of Article 14 of G. S. 90, without first obtaining the consent, in writing, of the Chairman of the Board of Anatomy or his agent. This section does not prevent a person from making a testamentary disposition of his or her body after death.

G. S. 90-218 provides that the superintendent or other administrative head of an institution maintained by the State may authorize a post-mortem examination of the dead body of any inmate of such institution.

G. S. 90-220 provides that no such authorization shall be given without first securing the written consent of the deceased person's spouse or one of the next of kin or nearest known relative.

If the decedent had sufficient mental capacity to make a will and he did so and authorized an autopsy to be performed on his body after death, the Hospital authorities could act upon this testamentary disposition without regard to the statutory provisions outlined above. Since, however, we are concerned with the bodies of mentally disordered persons, it becomes obvious that this provision will be of little help in solving the problem with which we are now faced.

Although the general law (25 C.J.S.—DEAD BODIES, Section 3) is to the effect that no particular formality is required in directing the disposition of one's remains, and that such directions may be parol, I am of the opinion that this general rule is abrogated in this State by the provisions of G. S. 90-212, which provide that the body of an inmate of a State Hospital shall be surrendered to the surviving spouse or next of kin upon demand made within ten days after the death of the inmate. This position is buttressed by the fact that the General Assembly specifically inserted a provision preserving the right to make a testamentary disposition of one's body.

The rights granted by Articles 14 and 15 of Chapter 90 of the General Statutes do not accrue until the death of the inmate. Thus, it is my opinion that the surviving spouse or next of kin cannot waive his right to claim the body of a deceased inmate of a State Hospital in advance of the death of such inmate. Such a waiver would be merely an attempt to dispose of an expectancy or possibility. On the contrary, our statute specifically provides that the body of the deceased inmate shall be surrendered to the spouse or next of kin upon demand within ten days after death. This right accrues to the spouse or next of kin upon the death of the decedent and may be extinguished by consent to the autopsy by such spouse or next of kin at any time after the death of the decedent. In other words, it is my opinion that the right must accrue before the waiver or surrender of the right would be effective, and the right does not accrue until the death of the inmate.

This same reasoning would, in my opinion, apply to the consent which is to be given by the Board of Anatomy under G. S. 90-213, and the authorization of the superintendent of the Hospital under G. S. 90-218, and the consent of the next of kin under G. S. 90-220.

I advise, therefore, that in my opinion, where there is no testamentary disposition of the body, the State Hospital authorities must apply the statutes as of the time of the death of the inmate. All consents or waivers must be secured after the death of the decedent to be effective. The only way in which the authorities can avoid the holding of the dead body for the ten days specified in G. S. 90-212 is to secure a waiver of rights or a consent to the performance of the autopsy after the death of the decedent and before the expiration of the ten days. Of course, insofar as the rights of the

Board of Anatomy are concerned, its consent may be given at any time after the death of the decedent. This consent, however, will be no protection until the rights of the surviving spouse or next of kin have been waived, or have been extinguished by the lapse of time.

MISCELLANEOUS OPINIONS NOT DIGESTED

18 July 1944

I have your letter of June 27 which was acknowledged in my absence by Mr. Patton. I note that you wish to be advised as to whether or not, under Chapter 752 of the Session Laws of 1943, the allotments by the Governor and Council of State from the Contingency and Emergency Fund would be confined to the present biennium or whether the Act is one that continues to authorize such allotments in future bienniums.

There is nothing in the Act which confines the authority given to the Governor and Council of State to the present biennium. Section 1 provides that the Governor and Council of State may, in their discretion, allot from the Contingency and Emergency Fund such amounts, not exceeding $2,-000.00 per annum, as may be deemed essential to supplement the revenue and income from the North Carolina State Art Society, Incorporated, in paying the necessary administrative expenses of the same. I am, therefore, of the opinion that under this Act the Governor and Council of State would be authorized, in future bienniums, to make such allocations as are authorized by this Act.

CONSTITUTIONALITY OF CURATIVE STATUTES

16 March 1945

I have been requested to submit to you a memorandum in regard to the constitutionality or curative statutes. I think the subject has particular reference to a bill introduced in the General Assembly by Senator Rose of Cumberland County dealing with the validation of certain irregular sales under executions. In the short time that I have, I can only deal with the subject in a general manner.

It should first be stated that curative Acts relating to defects in acknowl-edgments, probates, probate of wills, and many other subjects have generally been held to be constitutional by the Supreme Court of this State and by the highest appellate Courts of other states. It is only when third parties have acquired rights which will be impaired by the Act which is intended to cure the defective execution, probate, etc., that such Acts are held to be invalid. We may say, therefore, that curative Acts are constitutional and valid, but in their application to particular cases they may be invalid. Per-haps the best statement on this subject is contained in Volume 1 of American Jurisprudence, Section 133, which is as follows:

"A curative statute, in so far as it applies to the parties to instruments or persons standing in no better position, does not come within the constitutional prohibition of legislation that impairs the obligation of contracts or divests vested rights. The statute in this aspect merely seeks to do justice by carrying out the intention of the parties. Any other view would concede a vested right to do a wrong, inasmuch as it would permit the party to take advantage of the defect or omission and escape his just obligation. The act, then, does not defeat any 'rights' of the parties, but merely changes a rule of evidence so as to permit

proof of the contract evidenced by the instrument. Persons whose
rights accrue subsequent to the statute must be deemed to have acted
in contemplation thereof, and are not in a position to attack its validity
by claiming that their rights are beyond its control; but innocent third
persons who acquired rights before the enactment of the statute are
in a different situation. They are protected by the principle of our
constitutional law which finds expression in the provisions inhibiting
the legislature's impairing of contracting obligations or divesting of
vested rights. As to such persons, the statute is inoperative."

In dealing with the question of validating irregularities of execution
sales and judicial proceedings, we find the following in 12 C. J. Section 791,
page 1093:

"The legislature may cure judicial acts which are void through irregularity in procedure. Thus the legislature may cure irregularities
in the time or place of the sitting of the court, or defects in returns of
sheriffs to levies of execution; it may validate acts of a sheriff in improperly selling land under execution; it may legalize judgments entered on an unauthorized waiver of summons by a defendant; and it
may make valid and effective unsigned records of a court. But where
the court in which the proceedings were had possessed no jurisdiction,
its acts cannot be validated. And, in like manner, prior defective judicial proceedings may not be validated where the effect would be to
confirm actions resulting from fraud, or to divest vested rights, or, it
would seem, where there was an absolute lack of notice to the losing
party."

The Supreme Court of North Carolina is in accord with the doctrine laid
down in these reference works.

In the case of VAUGHT v. WILLIAMS, 177 N. C., page 80, the Supreme
Court of North Carolina quotes with approval Cooley on Constitutional
Limitations (7th Ed.), 531, as follows:

" 'If the thing wanting or which failed to be done, and which con_
stitutes the defect in the proceedings, is something the necessity for
which the Legislature might have dispensed with by prior statute, then
it is not beyond the power of the Legislature to dispense with it by
subsequent statute. And if the irregularity consists of doing some
act, or in the mode or manner of doing some act which the Legislature
might have made immaterial by prior law, it is equally competent to
make the same immaterial by a subsequent law.'
" 'In general, statutes curing defects in acts done or authorizing the
exercise of powers which act retrospectively are valid, provided the
Legislature originally had authority to confer the powers or authorize
the acts. The Legislature may legalize conveyances made by executors, administrators, guardians, or other persons in similar positions of
trust, which are irregular because of some omission or lack of power
on the part of such trustee.' " 8 Cyc., 1023.

Quoting again from VAUGHT v. WILLIAMS:

"This principle has been fully recognized in this State, and acts vali_
dating probates and curing defects in other instruments which would
have made them inoperative have, as between the parties, been fre_
quently sustained. Tatom v. White, 95 N. C., 458; Gordon v. Collett,
107 N. C., 363; Barrett v. Barrett, 120 N. C., 129, and other cases, 6
R.C.L., 321.

"Speaking of certain curative acts, then under consideration, Justice
Walker says, in Weston v. Lumber Co., 160 N. C., 268: 'The statutes are

highly remedial and should be liberally construed, so as to embrace all
cases fairly within their scope. It is constructive legislation; we are
saving titles, and not destroying them. It has been said that "such
acts are of a remedial character, and are the peculiar subjects of legislation. They are not liable to the imputation of being assumptions of
judicial power." ' "

The following cases sustain the validity of curative statutes:

WESTON v. LUMBER CO.,	160 N. C. 263;
FIBRE CO. v. COZAD,	183 N. C. 611;
TATOM v. WHITE,	95 N. C. 460;
SLUDER v. LUMBER CO.	181 N. C. 72;
BARRETT v. BARRETT,	120 N. C. 131.

In the case last above cited the Court said:

"The Legislature has power to pass, repeal or modify the laws regulating the manner of executing, proving or recording conveyances, and
the exercise of such power to cure defective compliance with former statutes cannot be an interference with vested rights as between the parties
to such instruments. It only becomes so when third parties have acquired rights which will be impaired by the act which is intended to
cure the defective execution, probate, or registration. . . . . It is competent for the Legislature to decide what mode of probate shall be
valid, and when it does so it can affect past as well as future probates,
except that the rights of third parties, claiming prior to the validating
act, cannot be divested. Retrospective legislation is not necessarily
invalid."

While I have not had time to find a case dealing with execution sales, it
is submitted, however, that such sales and their requirements have been
created and fixed by statute, just as the requirements of probates and acknowledgments, and the Legislature, therefore, has the right to cure by; subsequent statute a failure to comply with a former statute in that respect,
subject always to the vested rights of third parties acquired before the effective date of the validating statute. The application of curative statutes
to execution sales does not seem to have ever been questioned. As an example, you will find such statutes dealing with executions in our General
Statutes, Sections 1-331, 1-332 and 1-335.

TEACHERS' AND STATE EMPLOYEES' RETIREMENT SYSTEM; MUNICIPAL
RETIREMENT SYSTEM OF WINSTON-SALEM; RIGHT OF EMPLOYEE
TO PARTICIPATE IN STATE SYSTEM AND
MUNICIPAL SYSTEMS

10 April 1945

You state that by virtue of the provisions of Chapter 296 of the Public
Local Laws of 1939, the governing body of the City of Winston-Salem was
authorized to establish a Retirement Fund for the employees of the City of
Winston-Salem. You further state that the voters of the City of Winston-
Salem sometime ago authorized the levy of a tax up to twenty cents with
which to supplement the salaries paid to teachers in the local schools. It
is now proposed by virtue of the Public-Local Act above cited to establish

a Retirement Fund for the employees of the City of Winston-Salem, and some of the teachers in the public schools of Winston-Salem who are also members of the State Retirement System, would like to participate in the Winston-Salem System, with contributions on the part of the City and on the part of the teachers being based upon that part of the teachers' salaries paid from the local System.

Your questions are as follows:

(1) Are such teachers employees of the City of Winston-Salem within the terms of Chapter 296 of the Public-Local Laws of 1939, and, if so, are they eligible to participate in the proposed Winston-Salem Retirement System?

(2) Will participation by a teacher in the public schools of the City of Winston-Salem in the State Retirement System preclude the teacher's participation in the Winston-Salem System?

The coverage provisions,—that is, those provisions descriptive of the membership in the Winston-Salem System,—are found in Section 2 of Chapter 296 of the Public-Local Laws of 1939, and are as follows:

. "That the governing body of the City of Winston-Salem may establish, by ordinance, a Retirement Fund which provides for the payment of benefits to employee members of the Winston-Salem Employees' Retirement Fund . . . ."

And in the third paragraph of Section 2 the following appears with reference to membership in the Fund:

"Membership may be compulsory for such officers and employees of the City of Winston-Salem as shall be so designated in the ordinance. The City of Winston-Salem and such members shall contribute jointly to the Winston-Salem Employees' Retirement Fund in such proportion as shall be stated in the ordinance, in order to meet the liabilities accruing against such Fund because of personal service rendered to said City by such members after the establishment of such Fund . . . ."

It seems to me that the above Public-Local Act intended to limit its coverage to officers and employees of the City of Winston-Salem. It is true that the phrase, "as shall be so designated in the ordinance" is used in the statute, but it appears that this phrase is used to allow the City of Winston-Salem to designate the type and kind of officers and employees who may have the benefit of membership in the Retirement Fund. Such persons so designated must still be "officers and employees of the City of Winston-Salem" and I can see nothing in this sentence that authorizes the governing authority of the City of Winston-Salem to make a definition of employment or of employee above and beyond the generally accepted definition of such terms. To have the benefit of the Retirement System established under this Act, a person must belong to that group designated as officers and employees of the City of Winston-Salem and beyond that, such person must be in the classification and group designated in the ordinance. I think it is unnecessary, for the purposes of this letter, to discuss the legal meaning of the word "employee" or to make any interpretation of the word "officers."

The public school system of the State and the status of school teachers is fixed by Chapter 115 of the General Statutes. When you speak of the teachers in the public schools of Winston-Salem, I assume you speak of the teachers of the public schools in that city administrative unit, as I understand that all special charter districts have been abolished. Section 115-8 of the General Statutes defines a city administrative unit. Beginning with Section 115-352 and extending through 115-382 of the General Statutes, there is fixed by law and organization of schools in county and city administrative units, their administrative officers, and the method of employing school teachers as well as their dismissal. The method for city administrative units will be found in Sections 115-353, 115-354, and 115-359. It is the duty of the governing body of a city administrative unit to cause written contracts, on forms to be furnished by the State, to be executed by all teachers and principals. As I see the matter, therefore, without discussing details or statutes, the school teachers in the schools of the City of Winston-Salem do not enter into any contract of employment whatsoever with the City of Winston-Salem, but to the contrary, they enter into a contract with the board of trustees or other governing body of the city administrative unit, which is an entity and organization separate and apart from the municipality of Winston-Salem. Attention is also called to the fact that the boundaries of a city administrative unit are not necessarily co-equal or limited by the corporate limits of a city, as in many cases the boundaries of a city administrative unit extend beyond and take in other taxpayers and territories than those within the city limits. The fact that a tax has been voted with which to supplement salaries paid to teachers in the local schools does not detract from what I have already said. This is all explained in the case of BRIDGES v. CHARLOTTE, 221 N. C. 472, at pages 480 and 481. In that case the Court said:

"From those cases, as well as from the reasoning of the matter, we gather a clear impression that whatever may be the limitations of a municipality with respect to its ordinary government under Article VII. Section 7, they do not apply to it as an authorized agency in connection with the public school system; and that they do not, in fact, apply to any agencies as school administrative bodies, some of which, indeed, have no municipal functions to becloud the issue. In many city administrative units, the boundaries of the unit do not coincide with the city limits."

This is made clear also in the concurring opinion of Justice Barnhill, where he states on page 385 of this same case as follows:

"Any local administrative agency, with the approval of the tax-levying authorities within the agency and the State School Commission. in order to operate schools of a higher standard than those provided by the State support, may supplement any object or item of school expenditure, including an extended term not exceeding a total of 180 days. The tax levy to provide the funds with which to supplement must first be approved by the electorate. The amount raised by taxation becomes a part of the total allotment for operational expenses and must be budgeted and approved by the State School Commission. Section 17. The funds of the unit, including the part raised by local taxation, is audited by the school authorities, section 20(2), and are disbursed under the regulatory provisions of the statute.

"Hence, it appears that the State supported school within the local administrative unit, as thus supplemented, does not, by virtue of the supplement, become a separate school entity. It remains an integrated part of the State School System. The discretion vested in the local authorities is the discretion to provide or not to provide higher standards, including an extended term. The 'school of higher standards,' once established, remains a part of the State-wide system under the general supervision of the State School Commission until the special levy is revoked or changed by an election. Section 17."

In examining the cases decided under the Workmen's Compensation Law, I think you will find that in no instance has a school teacher been regarded as an employee of a city. There are several cases involving the question of liability as between the State and the County Board of Education, or the governing authority of the city administrative unit, but I have been unable so far to find a case where it has been held that a teacher is an employee of a corporate municipality. It seems to me that at the present time the teachers are employed by the governing authority of the city administrative unit acting as an administrative agency of the State of North Carolina and as an agency which is a component part of the whole public school system of the State, and such teachers do not hold any contracts of employment and are not under any contractual obligations to or with the governing authority of the City of Winston-Salem, which is a governmental system separate and apart from the school system, irrespective of the fact that citizens and property owners of the City may vote to tax themselves to supplement salaries of school teachers or for the purpose of extending the term of school.

I am of the opinion, therefore, that the teachers mentioned in your letter are not employees of the City of Winston-Salem within the terms of Chapter 296 of the Public-Local Laws of 1939. If you have certain teachers whose salaries are paid entirely from local funds, I am still of the opinion that they are not employees of the City of Winston-Salem within the meaning of the Public-Local Act mentioned above.

As to your second question, I do not find anything in Chapter 135 of the General Statutes which authorizes the Retirement System for teachers and State employees which would prevent participation by a teacher in the public schools of the City of Winston-Salem in the Winston-Salem Retirement System because such teachers are covered by and are members of the State Retirement System. Of course, when I say this, the opinion I have given above as to the right of such teachers to be members of the Winston-Salem System at all must be taken into consideration. The only persons specifically excluded from the State Retirement System,—that is, persons who might come within the coverage provision,—are State Highway patrolmen, who have become members of the Law Enforcement Officers Benefit and Retirement Fund, which you will see by reading Section 135-3.1 of the General Statutes. Incidentally, your attention is called to Section 135-8 of the General Statutes dealing with the State Retirement System, which requires city administrative units to pay contributions into this System where the salary is paid in part from State funds and part from local funds, or where the entire salary is paid from county or local funds.

If you should decide, therefore, that irrespective of what is here said, school teachers of Winston-Salem schools are entitled to participate in the Winston-Salem System, then I know of no statute or law that would cause such teacher or teachers to forfeit their rights in the State Retirement System, and likewise there is no law that would relieve the city administrative unit from contributions to the State System or would relieve such teachers from deductions from their salaries for payment into the State System.

VENEREAL DISEASE EDUCATION INSTITUTE; CONTRACT FOR PRODUCTION OF MOVING PICTURE FILM; METHOD OF LETTING

25 April 1945

Receipt is acknowledged of your letter of April 24, in which you advise that your Institute, an agency supported by the United States Public Health Service and the North Carolina State Board of Health, with an additional annual gift from the Smith Reynolds Foundation, is interested in making a contract with a motion picture concern for the production of a picture to be used in the educational work of your organization. I understand from your letter that the money to pay for the cost of this film will be paid to you by the State of Georgia from money allotted to it by the United States Public Health Service and that, in consideration of this payment, the State of Georgia will have a right to use the film in that State.

You inquire whether or not you can negotiate a contract with the producer without offering this job through competitive bidding, and whether or not the contract would have to be let through the Division of Purchase and Contract.

I have conferred with you and Mr. W. Z. Betts in the office today about this matter.

General Statutes 143-49, defining the powers and duties of the Director of Purchase and Contract, provides in subsection (c) as follows:

"(c) To purchase or contract for all telephones, telegraph, electric light power, postal and any and all other contractual services and needs of the State Government, or any of its departments, institutions, or agencies; *or in lieu of such purchase or contract to authorize any department, institution or agency to purchase or contract for any or all such services.*"

Under the italicized portion of this subsection, I am of the opinion that the Director of Purchase and Contract would have the authority to authorize your Institute to enter into the contract for the production of the film without letting this contract at public bidding. The requirements of our statute, 143-53, as to competitive bidding, applies only to the purchase of supplies, materials and equipment involving an expenditure in excess of $2,000.00. This section, however, requires that regardless of the amount of the expenditure, it is the duty of the Director of Purchase and Contract to solicit bids direct from reputable sources of supply. These provisions, however, are not applicable to the contracts for services such as contemplated in the proposed motion picture production contract. G. S. 143-49, which relates to this matter, requires that the contracts be made by the Director of Purchase and Contract or by the agency, with his authority, as provided in subsection (c) above quoted.

MUNICIPALITIES; WAR MOBILIZATION AND RECONVERSION ACT OF 1944; ·
ADVANCES TO MUNICIPALITIES NOT A DEBT

7 September 1945

You have requested my opinion whether or not advances made to counties, cities and towns under the provisions of Title 5 of the War Mobilization and Reconversion Act of 1944, which authorized the Federal Works Administrator to make advances of funds to non-federal public agencies to assist in plan preparation of their public works, could be accepted by counties, cities or towns in this State, and if such advances would constitute debts within the meaning of the Constitution and laws of this State.

The Act, as recited on page 4 of the regulations adopted, authorizes assistance in the form of loans or advances of federal funds for plan preparation for specific public works and the regulations provide, in Section 4(b), that an advance shall not be required to be repaid until funds become available to the public agency to construct the specific public work for which the advance was made, and, therefore, until such funds are available, an advance shall not be deemed by the United States to be a debt or obligation within the meaning of any constitutional, statutory or other debt limitation.

Section 12 of the regulations provides, with respect to repayment of advances, as follows:

"Each advance made for plan preparation shall be repaid in full without interest by the applicant out of the first funds that become available to it from any source for the construction of the specific public work so planned."

By the terms under which the advances may be made as recited, no obligation exists on the part of the local government to repay the advance until funds become available to the public gaency to construct the specific public work for which the advance was made. This, in practical effect, means that if the advancee never made available the funds for the construction of the project, there would never be any obligation whatever to repay the money.

It would also mean that if, in order to construct the project, it would be necessary to raise funds by the issuance of bonds, supported by a vote of the people and approval of the Local Government Commission, no obligation to repay the money would arise until all such conditions had been complied with; in other words, it is an obligation which would arise in the future if the conditions referred to exist and, if they do not exist, there would be no obligation to repay the money. If such conditions do arise, then all statutory and constitutional provisions must be complied with prior to the time the funds will become available for such purpose.

There is no law which prohibits a county, city or town from accepting funds under these circumstances and, in my opinion, they could lawfully

Trustees of the University of North Carolina; Power to Accept the William Hayes Ackland Memorial Building for an Art Gallery or Museum

30 October 1945

I am advised in a letter received from you under date of October 16, that the attorneys representing Rollins College have filed a brief in which they challenge the right of the Board of Trustees of the University of North Carolina to accept, if designated for this purpose by the Court, the William Hayes Ackland Memorial Building which, under the terms of the will, is to be in the form of a gallery or museum to include an apse for the interment of the testator's remains, to be known as the William Hayes Ackland Memorial, the building to be substantially in accordance with plans for such a museum which had been submitted to the testator by Duke University.

The right of the Trustees of the University of North Carolina to accept the designation by the Court as the Southern University best suited to carry out the general charitable purposes of the testator is challenged by the attorneys for Rollins College upon the basis that the Trustees of the University have no authority to accept the trust, as its provisions require that the remains of the deceased shall be interred on the campus of the University.

As a second position, they contend that the designation of the University of North Carolina should not be made because the University could not be subject to suit to enforce the provisions of the trust in the event there was any violation on its part of any of the conditions thereof.

In support of the position of the attorneys for Rollins College, they refer to a letter of the present Attorney General dated June 28, 1939, directed to Mr. L. B. Rogerson, Assistant Controller of the University. This letter merely states the proposition that the University of North Carolina is an instrumentality of the State and as such, is not subject to the payment of Social Security taxes imposed by the Federal Government. This letter has no bearing upon the question which we are presently considering.

In order to answer this contention fully, it is necessary to consider the applicable provisions of our Constitution and the laws of this State. The Constitution provides in Article IX, Section 6, that the General Assembly shall have the power to provide for the election of Trustees of the University of North Carolina in whom, when chosen, shall be vested all the privileges, rights, franchises and endowments thereof in any wise granted to or conferred upon the Trustees of said University; and the General Assembly may make such provisions, laws and regulations from time to time as may be necessary and expedient for the maintenance and management of the said University.

Under the Authority of this constitutional provision, the General Assembly has provided in General Statutes, 116-3, as follows:

"The trustees of the university shall be a body politic and corporate, to be known and distinguished by the name of the 'University of North Carolina,' and by that name shall have perpetual succession and a common seal; and by that name shall be able and capable in law to take, de-

mand, receive, and possess all moneys, goods, and chattels that shall be
given for the use of the university, and to apply the same according to
the will of the donors; and by gift, purchase, or devise to receive, possess, enjoy, and retain forever any and all real and personal estate and
funds, of whatsoever kind, nature, or quality the same may be, in special trust and confidence that the same, or the profits thereof, shall be
applied to and for the use and purpose of establishing and endowing
the university, and shall have power to receive donations from any
source whatever, to be exclusively devoted to the purposes of the maintenance of the university, or according to the terms of donation.

"The corporation, by its corporate name, shall be able and capable in
law to bargain, sell, grant, alien, or dispose of and convey and assure
to the purchasers any and all such real and personal estate and funds
as it may lawfully acquire when the condition of the grant to it or the
will of the devisor does not forbid it; and shall be able and capable in
law to sue and be sued in all courts whatsoever; and shall have power
to open and receive subscriptions, and in general may do all such things
as are usually done by bodies corporate and politic, or such as may be
necessary for the promotion of learning and virtue.

"In addition to these powers, the board of trustees shall succeed to
all the rights, privileges, duties and obligations by law, or otherwise,'
enjoyed by or imposed upon the University of North Carolina, the
North Carolina State College of Agriculture and Engineering, and the
North Carolina College for Women, prior to March 27, 1931."

It is contended by the attorneys for Rollins College that this broad grant
of authority to the Trustees of the University would not include the authority to accept any gift which would authorize the Trustees of the University to accept the execution of the trust created by the Ackland will which
would include in it the direction that the remains of testator should be transferred to the apse which is a part of the building for permanent interment
in a marble-sarcophagus beneath a recumbent statue.

I cannot agree with any such contention. Although the General Assembly
has authority to make laws and regulations necessary to and expedient for
the maintenance and management of the University, the General Assembly
has apparently never found it necessary and expedient to prohibit the University of North Carolina from accepting a gift or other benefit merely because, as an incident to the gift or benefit, the remains of the donor are to be
buried on the campus of the University—for no statute or regulation to
that effect has ever been enacted. On the contrary, it is specifically provided in Section 116-3 of the General Statutes of North Carolina, quoted
above, that the Trustees of the University who are made and constituted a
body corporate by the name of the University of North Carolina shall have
power to receive all moneys, goods, chattels and donations given for the use
of the University "and to apply the same according to the will of the donors"
or "according to the terms of the donation."

The United States Circuit Court of Appeals for the District of Columbia
(*Noel v. Olds*, 138 Fed. (2d) 581) has already ruled that the motive or desire of Mr. Ackland to perpetuate his name by the inclusion of an apse and
recumbent statue in his proposed museum "was minor and insignificant compared with the larger purpose," which larger purpose was to benefit the
cause of art in the South through the erection, maintenance, operation and
enlargement of an art museum on the campus of a Southern University. The

provision in Section 116-3 of the North Carolina General Statutes as quoted above that donations, etc. may be received by the University and used according to the will of the donors or the terms of the donations would seem clearly to contemplate and authorize compliance with incidental details of a will, such as the provision in the Ackland will for an apse and burial of the remains of the testator, to the end that the larger gift or primary purpose would be fully served and not permitted to fail because of any lack of authority to comply with "minor and insignificant" conditions attached to the gift by the donor.

The terms of the North Carolina statutory provisions referred to in the brief of Rollins College, as well as other provisions of North Carolina law, have been carefully examined and no language has been found which would preclude the University from accepting any gift which it might deem worthy of acceptance. Certainly the provisions of Section 116-3 would not prohibit, and in my opinion they specifically authorize and permit, the Trustees to accept the designation of the Court for carrying into full effect the trust created under the Askland Will. The Trustees of the University have heretofore adopted resolutions specifically accepting the responsibility for carrying the trust into effect, and under the statute, G. S. 116-3 they have full and ample authority to do so.

The position stated is fully supported by the decision of the Supreme Court of North Carolina in the case of BREWER v. UNIVERSITY, 110 N. C. 26, from which the following is quoted:

> "The defendant has ample power and authority and it is capable in all pertinent respects to take, receive, have, own and possess property, both real and personal, to be used for, applied and devoted to the purposes for which it is created, as the donors thereof may direct by will or otherwise. Constitution, Art. IX, sec. 6; The Code, secs. 2610, 2630.
>
> "It was therefore competent for the testatrix named to make the bequest mentioned to the defendant for the particular purpose specified in connection therewith. The defendant has and holds the fund charged with a trust for that purpose, and not for its general business purposes. The fund cannot be applied or made subject to the payment of its debts, whether the same be reduced to judgment or not. *The defendant is charged with it only for the purpose to which the donor devoted it.*" (Italics added.)

The second position taken by the attorneys for Rollins College, that the University of North Carolina and the Board of Trustees thereof will not be subject to suit to enforce the provisions of the trust in the event there was any failure upon their part to carry it into effect, is not supported by the statute and decisions of this State.

It is expressly provided in G. S. 116-3, heretofore quoted, that the Trustees of the University shall be a body politic and corporate, known as the University of North Carolina, and that "the corporation, by its corporate name, shall be able and capable in law to sue and be sued in all courts whatsoever."

It is true, of course, that, as stated in the opinion rendered by the Attorney General in a letter dated November 2, 1933, the statute authorizing a suit against the University of North Carolina would not authorize a suit against the University in tort, but would extend only to actions ordinarily incidental in its operation, citing MOODY v. STATE'S PRISON, 128 N. C. 12; CAR-PENTER v. RAILROAD, 184 N. C. 400.

This is not any authority, however, for the position that the Board of Trus-tees of the University and the University would not be liable to be sued for its failure to carry out the terms of trust which, by the same statute, G. S. 116-3, it is fully authorized and empowered to accept and carry out "ac-cording to the will of the donors." A failure or refusal of the Trustees of the University to carry out the terms of a trust of this character which it had formerly accepted would, of course, not be an action in tort but a suit to enforce the observance of obligations assumed under authority of the statute, which would definitely and clearly come within the authorization of the statute permitting the University to sue and be ,sued. To take any other view would give no meaning to the statute which has been quoted above and will do violence to the specific provisions of the law.

DEMOCRATIC EXECUTIVE COMMITTEE; QUORUM; NOTICE OF
SPECIAL MEETING

16 January 1946

I have your letter of January 15, in which you inquire as to the number of members of a Democratic Executive Committee required to be present to legally transact business. You state that your Executive Committee con-sists of twenty-two members.

The Democratic Plan of Organization provides in Section 14 for the organization of county executive committees, composed of the chairmen of the several precinct committees, and that a majority of the said precinct chairmen in person or by proxy, in the person of some active Democrat of the precinct in which an absent chairman resides, shall constitute a quorum. This means, therefore, that you would have to have at least twelve members of your Executive Committee present, in person or by proxy, at any meet-ing in order to legally transact business.

You also inquire as to what is the legal requirement as to the calling of a meeting of the County Executive Committee by the county chairman, other than a regularly scheduled meeting.

Section 8 of the Democratic Plan of Organization provides that all Dem-ocratic Executive Committees shall meet at such times and places as the chairmen of the respective counties may appoint and designate in his call. Under this provision, the chairman may call a meeting at such time as he may designate, as to which reasonable notice would have to be given.

UNAUTHORIZED PRACTICE OF OPTOMETRY; FITTING CONTACT LENSES

25 April 1946

In conference with you today and your counsel, Mr. Oscar G. Barker of Durham, North Carolina, you requested me to advise you whether or not the fitting of contact lenses by a person, firm or corporation which is not li-censed to practice optometry or medicine under Article 6 of Chapter 90 of the General Statutes of North Carolina, would be a violation of this Act.

The practice of optometry is defined by G. S. 90-114 to be the employment of any means, other than the use of drugs, medicines, or surgery, for the measurement of the powers of vision and the adaptation of lenses for the aid thereof, and this section provides that in such practices as therein defined, the optometrist may prescribe, give directions or advice as to the fitness or adaptation of a pair of spectacles, eyeglasses or lenses for another person to wear for the correction or relief of any condition for which a pair of spectacles, eyeglasses or lenses are used, or to use or permit or allow the use of instruments, test-cards, test types, test lenses, spectacles or eyeglasses or anything containing lenses, or any device for the purpose of aiding any person to select any spectacles, eyeglasses or lenses to be used or worn by such mentioned person.

G. S. 90-115 makes it unlawful for any person to practice optometry unless he has first obtained a certificate of registration and filed the same, or a certified copy thereof, with the clerk of the superior court of his residence. This section states that, within the meaning of Article 6, a person shall be deemed as practicing optometry who does or attempts to sell, furnish, or replace a lens, frame, or mounting or furnishes any kind of material or apparatus for ophthalmic use, without a written prescription from a person authorized under the laws of the State of North Carolina to practice optometry, or from a person authorized under the laws of the State of North Carolina to practice medicine.

Contact lenses may be described as a device that fits in contact with the eye, used to improve vision. It consists of a plastic or glass lens, or a water lens, which is intended and does perform the same service for correction of vision as glass lenses mounted on frames, or other devices for improving vision.

It seems evident to me that any person engaged in the practice of fitting or adjusting contact lenses on a person would be engaged in the practice of optometry or medicine, and, unless licensed as provided by Article 6 of Chapter 90, would be violating the provisions of this article.

You requested my advice also as to whether or not such practice could be engaged in by a lay body or corporation which had associated with it a licensed optometrist or physician.

G. S. 90-125 provides that it shall be unlawful for any person licensed to practice optometry under the provisions of this article to advertise, practice, or attempt to practice under a name other than his own, except as an associate of or assistant to an optometrist licensed under the laws of this State; and that it shall likewise be unlawful for any corporation, lay body, organization, group, or lay individual to engage, or undertake to engage, in the practice of optometry through means of engaging the services, upon a salary or commission basis, of one licensed to practice optometry or medicine in any of its branches in this State. This section further provides that it shall be unlawful for any optometrist licensed under the provisions of this article to undertake to engage in the practice of optometry as a salaried or commissioned employee of any corporation, lay body, organization, group, or lay individual.

The reference to this statute, I believe, fully answers your question.

OFFICE DIGEST OF OPINIONS

BEER AND WINE: ISSUANCE OF LICENSE MANDATORY

25 May 1944

It is mandatory upon the governing body of a town or county, in the absence of a local act to the contrary, to issue beer and wine licenses to applicants who meet the requirements of the pertinent statutes.

DOUBLE OFFICE HOLDING: MEMBER, BOARD OF COUNTY COMMISSIONERS; .
MEMBER, LOCAL SCHOOL BOARD

29 May 1944

One person cannot serve as a county commissioner and at the same time serve as a member of a local school board as both positions are offices within the meaning of the provision of the North Carolina Constitution prohibiting double office holding.

ELECTIONS: BALLOTS; PRINTING NAMES; TITLES OR DEGREES

25 May 1944

The title of 'M. D." following the name of a person, being the initials standing for "medical doctor," is a designation of a profession in which the person is engaged, and there is no authority for placing such initials after a person's name on an election ballot as they constitute no part of the legal name of the person.

EXECUTION: SERVING CIVIL PROCESS; PROCESS AGENT OF UNEMPLOYMENT
COMPENSATION COMMISSION

26 May 1944

A process agent of the Unemployment Compensation Commission has the same authority in making a levy on personal property that a sheriff has; therefore, as to buildings other than dwellings, the officer may demand entrance for the purpose of levying on property contained therein, and upon being refused admittance he may forcibly enter. He should not use any more force or do any more damage than is necessary to gain entrance. The officer may not break into a dwelling house without the consent of the owner for the purpose of executing civil process.

JUSTICES OF THE PEACE: FORFEITURE OF OFFICE

24 May 1944

When a justice of the peace absents himself from his township and does not return thereto for the period of six months, he thereby forfeits his office and if he presumes to ace thereafter, unless reelected or reappointed, he is guilty of a misdemeanor.

MUNICIPALITIES: POLICEMAN MUST BE QUALIFIED VOTER OF TOWN

24 May 1944

A policeman is an officer of the town in which he serves and must, therefore, be a qualified voter therein. Thus, a nonresident of a town is not qualified to be a policeman in the town.

VITAL STATISTICS: LOCAL REGISTRAR; AUTHORITY TO ISSUE CERTIFIED COPIES

24 May 1944

A local registrar of vital statistics is not given authority to issue certified copies of the certificates in his possession. However, both the registrar of deeds of the county and the State Registrar are authorized to issue such copies, and if issued by the State Registrar, the certified copy is prima facie evidence in all courts and places of the facts stated therein.

CHIROPRACTORS: LICENSE; PRACTICE WITHOUT LICENSE

29 June 1944

Any person who practices chiropractic in this State without first having obtained a license is guilty of a violation of the criminal laws of the State. The fact that no fees are to be charged for the services is immaterial.

COURTS: CANCELLATION OF TERMS; GOVERNOR

26 June 1944

The local bar of the county has no right to cancel a term of the Superior Court of the county provided for and set out in the statute. However, the 1943 General Assembly set up a uniform method for the cancellation of terms of the Superior Court by the Governor.

CRIMINAL LAW: MUNICIPAL ORDINANCE

17 June 1944

It is provided by general statute that anyone who violates a municipal ordinance shall be guilty of a criminal offense, and the same officers would be authorized to swear out or serve warrants in connection therewith as in any other violation of a criminal statute of the State.

FINES & FORFEITURES: DISPOSITION; FEES OF MAGISTRATE

29 June 1944

When a defendant is bound over to a recorder's court by a magistrate and fails to appear, the magistrate is not entitled to his fees out of the bond when it is declared forfeited.

INSANE PERSONS & INCOMPETENTS: HOSPITALS FOR THE INSANE; ADMISSION; FEEBLE-MINDED

23 June 1944

Neither the State Hospital at Raleigh nor the State Hospital at Morganton is authorized to accept a patient who is an idiot or who is feeble-minded.

INTOXICATING LIQUORS: SALE TO INDIANS

23 June 1944

There is no North Carolina statute which makes any distinction between the sales of intoxicating liquors to Indians and sales to any other persons.

MUNICIPALITIES: APPOINTMENT OF SPECIAL POLICE; CHIEF OF POLICE MAY

DEPUTIZE CITIZEN TO ASSIST IN ARREST

29 June 1944

While only the governing body of a municipality may name city police, the chief of police may deputize a citizen to aid him in making an arrest or in serving legal process.

MUNICIPALITIES: COMMISSIONERS; VACANCIES; FILLING OF VACANCIES

26 June 1944

In case of a vacancy after election in the office of municipal commissioner, the remaninig commissioners are authorized to fill the same until the next election.

TAXATION: LEVY FOR THE CONSTRUCTION OF AN AIRPORT

14 June 1944

A special tax may not be levied for the construction and maintenance of an airport without a vote of the people as the construction and maintenance of an airport is not a necessary expense.

TAXATION: SALES TAX

22 June 1944

The proceeds of the sale of Coca-Cola through a vending machine owned by an American Legion Post is subject to the North Carolina sales tax even though the proceeds are used entirely for charitable purposes. It is sales *to* certain charitable or religious organizations that are exempt from the sales tax rather than sales *by* such organizations.

BEER & WINE: LICENSE; NONRESIDENTS

12 June 1944

A person desiring to sell beer and wine must apply for a license, and the application must contain, among other things, a statement that the applicant is a citizen and resident of North Carolina. Therefore, a person who is a subject of a foreign country is not authorized to receive a license to sell beer and wine in North Carolina.

BEER & WINE: POSSESSION NOT ILLEGAL

15 June 1944

There is no law in North Carolina which prohibits one from possessing twelve cases of beer. The purpose of possession is immaterial. However, if the beer is possessed for the purpose of sale, the possessor should procure a license before offering it for sale.

COUNTIES: OFFICERS; LEAVES OF ABSENCE

6 June 1944

The county commissioners are authorized to grant a leave of absence to any county official, whether elective or appointive.

COUNTIES: MONUMENTS; DONATIONS

7 June 1944

While a county may become a member of any memorial association or organization for perpetuating the memory of the soldiers and sailors who fought in World War I or who fought in the War between the States and may make contributions out of the general fund to such associations or organizations, the law at this time does not authorize contributions toward the construction of memorials for perpetuating the memory of soldiers and sailors of the present war.

COURTS: JUSTICE OF THE PEACE; REMOVAL FOR CRIME

9 June 1944

When a justice of the peace is convicted of an infamous crime, or of corruption and malpractice in office, he becomes disqualified to hold or enjoy any office of honor, trust or profit under this State.

INTOXICATING LIQUORS: STORAGE IN AND WITHDRAWAL FROM STATE WAREHOUSE

14 June 1944

Alcoholic beverages may be stored in the State supervised warehouse solely for the convenience of delivery to ABC boards of the State, and such beverages may not be stored in nor removed from such warehouse except by the interested ABC boards.

MUNICIPALITIES: PLANNING BOARDS

14 June 1944

While the statutes authorize cities and towns to create Planning Boards for the purpose of making studies of the resources, possibilities and needs of cities and towns, there is no authority for the establishment of a county or joint county-city Planning Board.

MUNICIPALITIES: TAXATION

10 June 1944

A city may legally impose a privilege tax on bakeries distributing their products within the corporate limits even though the places of business of the bakeries are located outside of the city and county.

MUNICIPALITIES: USING SURPLUS FUNDS

14 June 1944

Surplus funds of a city may be expended for public purposes whether a necessary expense or not.

STATE BONDS: DESTRUCTION OF SURRENDERED BONDS

9 June 1944

The State law requires surrendered State bonds to be listed as to number, date, amount and purpose for which issued and then destroyed by fire in the presence of the Governor, the Treasurer, the Auditor, the Attorney General, the Secretary of State and the Superintendent of Public Instruction.

TAXATION: LIABILITY OF CORPORATION CARRYING ON DREDGING OPERATIONS IN NAVIGABLE WATERS OF STATE UNDER CONTRACT WITH FEDERAL GOVERNMENT

5 June 1944

A corporation engaged in dredging work in navigable waters of North Carolina under a contract with the Federal Government is liable for the bidders' and project taxes imposed by the Revenue Act. The fact that the work is being done under a contract with the Federal Government and in navigable waters affords no exemption.

BANKS: JOINT BANK ACCOUNTS

10 July 1944

Under the laws of North Carolina an estate by the entirety or a joint tenancy in a bank account is not recognized. However, it is possible for two persons by express agreement to deposit money in a joint bank account with provision that upon the death of either, the whole account shall be paid to the survivor.

BEER & WINE: HOURS OF SALE; APPLICATION OF LAW TO ALE

5 July 1944

The North Carolina statute which prohibits the sale of beer between 11:30 P. M. and 7:30 A. M. also prohibits the sale of ale between those hours.

BEER & WINE: ON PREMISES LICENSES

1 July 1944

When a person obtains an "on premises" license to sell beer, he is authorized thereby to sell beer for consumption off the premises. The "on premises" license includes the "off premises" license.

COUNTIES: LIABILITY FOR INJURIES SUSTAINED BY INDIVIDUAL FALLING IN PUBLIC BUILDING

7 July 1944

When an individual sustains injuries from a fall in a county-owned agricultural building, the county is not liable for the injuries so sustained nor does it have authority to make contributions toward compensating the individual for hospital expenses incurred or for loss of time.

CRIMINAL LAW: JURORS; ALTERNATE JURORS

8 July 1944

The North Carolina statutes make provision for a thirteenth or alternate juror who is to sit with the regular petit jury during the trial and upon the sickness, disqualification or discharge of a juror, the thirteenth or alternate juror becomes one of the jury and serves in all respects as though selected as an original juror. This statute has been held constitutional by the Supreme Court of North Carolina.

DOUBLE OFFICE HOLDING: MEMBER OF DURHAM CITY & COUNTY BOARD OF HEALTH; MEMBER, BOARD OF DIRECTORS NORTH CAROLINA RAILROAD; CHAIRMAN DRAFT BORD

10 July 1944

Being chairman of a draft board does not constitute the holding of an office within the meaning of the term "office" as used in the provision of the North Carolina Constitution prohibiting double office holding. Being a member of a county-city board of health does constitute the holding of an office. Being a member of the Board of Directors of the North Carolina Railroad does not constitute the holding of an office. Therefore, since only one of the above positions is an office, one person may hold all three.

DOUBLE OFFICE HOLDING: MEMBER OF GENERAL ASSEMBLY; TOWN CLERK & TREASURER

7 July 1944

The positions of town clerk and treasurer and member of the General Assembly are both offices within the meaning of the provisions of the North Carolina Constitution prohibiting double office holding; therefore, one person may not hold both positions.

FINES & FORFEITURES: DISPOSITION; CLERK'S FEES

5 July 1944

Since the law requires the clear net proceeds of all fines and forfeitures to be turned over to the county school fund, the clerk of Superior Court has no authority to deduct a commission before turning over such fines and forfeitures to the school fund.

MUNICIPALITIES: TAXICABS; REGULATION OF TAXICABS OPERATED WITHIN MUNICIPALITY WHEN OFFICE LECATED WITHOUT MUNICIPALITY

6 July 1944

When taxicabs are operated within a municipality, they are subject to regulation by the municipality even though their office is located outside the municipality. This authority is granted by an Act of the General Assembly of 1943.

STATE EMPLOYEES: RIGHT TO PARTICIPATE IN POLITICAL ACTIVITIES

5 July 1944

There is no State statute which prohibits or restricts the activities of State, county or municipal employees in political campaigns or elections. However, some of such employees may be paid in part from federal funds and may be subject to the federal law known as the "Hatch Act."

TAXATION: GIFT TAXES; GIFTS TO POOR RELATIVES

7 July 1944

Gifts to a taxpayer's sister in excess of $1,000.00 per year are subject to gift taxes. The gift tax law exempts such gifts only when not in excess of $1,000.00 in any one calendar year, and the exemption in the tax law of gifts for charitable purposes does not apply to gifts to an individual for his own personal use. To be exempt as a gift for charitable purposes, the gift must be for the use of the public or a portion of it as distinct from individuals.

CRIMINAL LAW: CONCEALED WEAPONS; MAYOR

17 July 1944

The mayor of a city has no right to carry a concealed weapon. While the statute prohibiting the carrying of concealed weapons exempts certain officers from the operation thereof, a mayor of a city is not one of them.

CRIMINAL PROCEDURE: EXTRADITION; COSTS

12 July 1944

When the crime for the commission of which a person is being extradited is a felony, the expenses of the extradition shall be paid out of the State Treasury on the certificate of the Governor and the warrant of the Auditor. In all other cases, the expenses of extradition shall be paid out of the county treasury of the county in which the crime is alleged to have been committed.

CORPORATIONS: OFFICERS; OWNERSHIP OF STOCK

18 July 1944

While it is true that the president of a corporation must be a stockholder in the corporation, there is no requirement, in the absence of such a requirement in the by-laws, that the vice president or secretary of a corporation shoull be stockholders therein.

DOUBLE OFFICE HOLDING: MAYOR-MEMBER, COUNTY BOARD OF EDUCATION

12 July 1944

The positions of mayor of a city and membership on the county board of education are both offices within the meaning of the provision of the North

Carolina Constitution prohibiting double office holding; therefore, one person may not hold both positions at once.

Double Office Holding: Town Policeman-Alderman

17 July 1944

The positions of town policeman and alderman are both offices within the meaning of the provision of the North Carolina Constitution prohibiting double office holding; therefore, one person may not hold both positions at one time.

Elections: Filling Vacancies in Candidates for County Office and Member of House of Representatives

17 July 1944

In the event that any person nominated in any primary election as a candidate of a political party for a county office or for the House of Representatives shall die, resign or for any other reason become ineligible or disqualified between the date of such primary election and the ensuing general election, the vacancy shall be filled by the executive committee of the party affected thereby in the county wehrein such vacancy occurs.

Intoxicating Liquors: Possession and Sale of "Home Brew"

11 July 1944

The manufacture, possession, sale and transportation of the ordinary variety of "home brew" is prohibited by the North Carolina statutes.

Municipal Corporations: Necessary Expenses; Acquisition of Freezer-Lockers to Be Installed in Municipal Market Building

18 July 1944

Since the acquisition and installation of individual freezer-lockers to be rented to citizens of the municipality is not a necessary expense, a municipal corporation cannot contract a debt therefor without a vote of the people authorizing the same. This result is not changed by reason of the fact that such freezer-lockers are to be installed in a market house, the erection and maintenance of which is a necessary expense.

School Law: Compulsory Attendance Officer; Salary; Taxation

10 July 1944

The county board of education of a county may employ a special attendance officer whose salary is to be paid from fines, forfeitures, and penalties or other local funds. Thus, if the fines, forfeitures and penalties are not sufficient to pay the salary of such officer, the board of education is authorized to include in the school budget an amount sufficient to cover the salary of such officer.

SCHOOLS: LOCAL COMMITTEES; RESIDENCE

17 July 1944

Members of a district school committee appointed pursuant to G. S. 115-354 must reside within the territorial limits of the school district. This conclusion is not affected by the fact that some of the pupils attending the schools in the district may come from an adjoining county.

TAXATION: MUNICIPAL CORPORATIONS; RAILROADS

13 July 1944

A municipal corporation may not levy a license, franchise or privilege tax on railroads. Such a tax is prohibited by Section 202 of the Revenue Act which imposes a franchise tax on railroads and specifically provides that "no county, city or town shall levy a license, franchise, or privilege tax on the business taxed under this section." ·

BANKS AND BANKING: JOINT BANK ACCOUNTS

24 July 1944

Although under the law of this State, an estate by the entirety or a joint tenancy in a bank account is not recognized, it is possible for two persons, by express agreement, to deposit money in a joint account with the understanding that upon the death of either the whole account shall be payable to the survivor. However, even if there is such a survivorship agreement, the portion contributed to the account by the decedent would be includable in his estate for inheritance tax purposes. The bank may, upon notice to the Commissioner of Revenue, allow the survivor to withdraw as much as 80% of the deposit and retain the remainder to cover any inheritance tax that may be assessed.

CORONERS: VACANCIES; APPOINTMENT FOR UNEXPIRED TERM

22 July 1944

When a coroner who was elected in 1942 for a four-year term dies, the County Commissioners appoint someone to fill the vacancy who holds office for the remainder of the four-year term and not just until the 1944 general election.

DOUBLE OFFICE HOLDING: CHIEF OF POLICE; TOWNSHIP CONSTABLE

21 July 1944

The positions of Chief of Police and Township Constable are both offices within the meaning of that term, as used in the provision of the North

Carolina Constitution prohibiting double office holding. Therefore, one person may not hold both at the same time.

MOTOR VEHICLES: SEIZURE OF LICENSE PLATES TO FORCE PAYMENT OF LICENSE FEES DUE IN PRIOR YEARS

26 July 1944

The Commissioner of Motor Vehicles is authorized to seize any registration plate which he believes is being illegally used. If the operator has paid all tax due for the current year, the registration plates are not being illegally used, within the meaning of this statute, merely because he owes additional license fees for a prior year. Therefore, the Commissioner may not seize license plates to force payment of license fees due for prior years.

MUNICIPAL CORPORATIONS: NECESSARY EXPENSES; PUBLIC HOSPITALS

26 July 1944

Since the North Carolina Supreme Court has held that the building, maintenance, and operation of a public hospital is not a necessary expense, a municipal corporation has no authority to levy a tax to maintain and operate a hospital without a vote of the people.

MUNICIPAL CORPORATIONS: ORDINANCES; REQUIRING CONSENT OF ADJOINING LAND OWNERS BEFORE ISSUANCE OF BUILDING PERMIT

19 July 1944

A municipal corporation is without authority to enact an ordinance which requires the consent of all the owners of land adjoining the land on which the building is to be erected before a building permit is issued.

MUNICIPAL CORPORATIONS: POLL TAX; RECOVERY

26 July 1944

The Constitution of North Carolina provides that cities and towns may levy a capitation tax which shall not exceed $1.00. However, where more than $1.00 has been levied and collected and the procedure as to payment under protest is not followed, the taxpayer is not entitled to recover even though he has paid an amount in excess of that authorized by law. By a 1943 statute, the governing body of any city or town may refund any money paid through clerical error or by a tax illegally levied and assessed upon the taxpayer's making demand in writing for the remission and refund within two years of the date the same was due to be paid.

MUNICIPAL CORPORATIONS: SALE OF REAL ESTATE

26 July 1944

Where property is acquired by a city, at tax foreclosure sale, the city may recall the property to the former owner or other person formerly having an interest in said property at private sale for an amount not less than its interest therein. If the property was not acquired at a tax foreclosure sale the sale must be made to the highest bidder at public outcry after 30 days notice.

TAXATION: TAX ON LAUNDRIES

22 July 1944

A municipal corporation may levy a license tax on laundries operating within the municipal limits. This tax is to be levied under the municipal corporation's general power to tax trades and professions and not under the Revenue Act.

TAXATION: LOAN AGENCIES; CASHING CHECKS FOR PROFIT

21 July 1944

There is no statute in the laws relating to banks and banking which either authorizes or prohibits the carrying on of the business of cashing checks for profit by a loan agency. The loan agency would not be required to procure a security dealer's license to engage in such business.

BANKS: AUTHORITY TO ACT AS SURETY

10 May 1944

A bank organized under the laws of North Carolina has no authority to act as surety on a bond or to engage in the surety business, except such as is necessary to and in connection with the conduct of its own affairs as a bank or trust company.

CONSTABLES: JURISDICTION

10 May 1944

The powers and duties of a constable are county-wide, and are not restricted to the township in which he is elected.

CRIMINAL LAW: ABANDONMENT AND NON-SUPPORT; STATUTE OF LIMITATIONS

10 May 1944

The abandonment of children by the father is a continuing offense and is not barred by any statute of limitations until the youngest child shall arrive at the age of eighteen years.

DOUBLE OFFICE HOLDING: MAYOR OF TOWN; CHIEF OF POLICE

1 May 1944

One person may not hold the office of mayor of a town and at the same time be chief of police of the town. Both positions are offices within the provision of the North Carolina Constitution prohibiting double office holding.

ELECTIONS: RESIDENCE

10 May 1944

Persons living in trailer camps on government owned reservations do not thereby acquire voting residence.

ELECTIONS: REGISTRAR ACTIVE ON BEHALF OF ONE OR MORE CANDIDATES

8 May 1944

When the registrar of an election uses his influence on behalf of one or more candidates during the voting hours, he violates the terms and conditions of his oath and may be removed from office. The election, however, would be a valid election.

JUSTICES OF THE PEACE: WITNESS' FAILURE TO APPEAR

1 May 1944

When a witness is duly summoned and fails to appear at a trial before a justice of the peace, he shall forfeit and pay eight dollars ($8.00) to the party at whose instance he was summoned and shall further be liable to such party for all damage sustained by such non-attendance. The non-attending witness may also be guilty of contempt.

MUNICIPALITIES: AUTHORITY TO ISSUE BEER LICENSE TO APPLICANTS WHO LIVE WITHIN A RADIUS OF ONE MILE OF THE CORPORATE LIMITS

8 May 1944

In the absence of a public-local act to the contrary, the governing body of a municipality has no authority to issue or refuse to issue a license for the sale of wine or beer in any territory outside of the corporate limits.

MUNICIPALITIES: CONTRIBUTIONS TO PUBLISH HISTORY OF CITY AND COUNTY

9 May 1944

A municipal corporation has no authority to make contributions for the publication of a history of the municipality and the county.

TAXATION: COSTS; FEES FOR ATTORNEY

1 May 1944

While a taxing unit may pay its attorney a commission or fee of more than five dollars ($5.00) for the collection of delinquent taxes, no more than the statutory attorney's fee of five dollars ($5.00) may be assessed against the delinquent taxpayer.

CHILD WELFARE: JUVENILE COURTS; JURISDICTION

16 May 1944

When the juvenile court acquires jurisdiction of a juvenile and awards the custody of said juvenile to a person, the court's jurisdiction is not exhausted, but it may change its order and award the custody of the child to some other person.

COUNTIES: SALARY OF JANITOR OF COURTHOSE OFFICES

15 May 1944

In the absence of a local act to the contrary, a county should furnish janitor service for the upkeep of the various offices within the courthouse.

MUNICIPALITIES: DEPOSIT RECEIPT FOR WATER ACCOUNT; INTEREST RATE

15 May 1944

When a customer makes a deposit with the water department of a municipality and receives a receipt therefor, the receipt, in the absence of a local statute or special agreement, draws interest at the rate of six per centum per annum.

MUNICIPALITIES: SALE OF POWER LINE

18 May 1944

A municipality has no authority to sell a municipally owned public utility without the approval of a majority of the qualified voters of the municipality.

MUNICIPALITIES: TAXICABS; LIMITING NUMBER OPERATING IN CITY

19 May 1944

A municipality has no right under the general law to restrict the number of taxicabs which may be operated within the corporate limits of the municipality, if the operators are in a position to comply with the other provisions of the general law regulating taxicabs.

PROBATE & REGISTRATION: VERIFICATION OF COMPLAINTS

15 May 1944

Those military officers authorized by the 1943 Session Laws to take acknowledgments of instruments permitted or required to be registered, may also take affidavits for the verification of pleadings in divorce and other civil actions.

Public Health: Venereal Diseases; Quarantine; Application of Law to Minors

20 May 1944

The quarantine and isolation laws relating to venereal diseases are applicable to minors. However, if a minor under sixteen is to be prosecuted criminally for a violation of such laws, the juvenile court has exclusive jurisdiction.

Schools: Liability for Injury Received in Athletic Contest

15 May 1944

The board of trustees of a city school is not liable for, nor does it have authority to pay, medical and other expenses incurred by a student because of injuries received in a practice athletic contest.

Taxation: Second-Hand Clothing Dealers

22 May 1944

There is no State privilege tax upon the business of selling second-hand clothes except the regular sales tax. Counties may not collect a privilege tax for engaging in such business, but municipalities may levy and collect such a tax.

Taxation: Poll Tax

24 May 1944

Cities and towns are authorized to levy a capitation or poll tax of not more than one dollar on every male inhabitant of the city or town who is over twenty-one and under fifty years of age. Taxes so levied and collected may be used for any purpose permitted by law.

Double Office Holding: Chairman, School Board; Member, County ABC Board

18 August 1944

The positions of chairman of a local school board and membership on a county ABC board are both offices within the meaning of the provision of the North Carolina Constitution prohibiting double office holding. Therefore, one person may not hold both positions at once.

Elections: Expenses of Absentee Registration and Voting

15 August 1944

The expenses incurred by the cunty board of elections in carrying out the requirements of the 1943 Absentee Registration and Voting Act must be borne by the county. Likewise, the expenses incurred by the State Board of Elections in administering this Act must be borne by the State.

HOSPITALS FOR THE INSANE: INMATES; DISPOSITION OF LEGACY TO INMATE

2 August 1944

When an inmate of a State Hospital for the Insane is made a legatee in a will, the legacy should not be paid directly to the inmate but to a guardian who is to be appointed by the clerk of the superior court of the county in which said inmate resided at the time he became insane. This appointment may be made upon the certificate of the superintendent of the hospital sworn to and subscribed before the clerk of the superior court, a notary public or the clerk of a court of record of the county in which the hospital is situated.

MARRIAGE LAWS: MARRIAGE OF FIRST COUSINS

7 August 1944

Under the laws of North Carolina first cousins are permitted to marry. Marriages between persons of closer kin than first cousins are void.

MARRIAGE LAWS: PROXY MARRIAGES NOT RECOGNIZED

7 August 1944

Marriage by proxy is not permitted in North Carolina, but if such marriage is celebrated in a State recognizing proxy marriages, it would probably be recognized in this State.

PROCESS: CHIEF OF POLICE MAY NOT ISSUE

8 August 1944

A chief of police of a municipal corporation has no authority to issue warrants nor to administer oaths to affidavits in search warrants. The chief of police may sign the affidavit for the issuance of a search warrant, but he must make the same before some person authorized to administer oaths.

TAXATION: CIGARETTE VENDING MACHINES

18 August 1944

While a municipal corporation may levy and collect an operator's occupational license tax on cigarette vendors, it may not levy and collect a license tax for the operation of each individual cigarette vendor located within the municipal corporation.

TAXATION: EXEMPTION; AMERICAN LEGION PROPERTY

18 August 1944

The North Carolina Law provides for an exemption from taxation of buildings with the land actually occupied belonging to the American Legion or post of the American Legion used exclusively for lodge purposes, together with such additional adjacent land as may be necessary for the convenient use of the buildings thereon.

TAXATION: SALES TAX; SALES TO CHURCHES

17 August 1944

The Revenue Act exempts from sales tax sales of tangible personal property to churches when such tangible personal property is purchased for use in carrying on the work of the church.

TAXATION: SALES TAX; SALES OF RUGS

11 August 1944

A person who desires to sell in North Carolina home-made rugs made in South Carolina must procure from the Commissioner of Revenue a license issued for the sum of one dollar. In addition to this license, every retailer is required to collect and remit to the Commissioner of Revenue each month a tax equal to 3% of the amount of gross sales realized from such business.

WORKMEN'S COMPENSATION: RIGHT OF STATE TO WAIVE STATUTE REQUIRING

CLAIM TO BE FILED WITHIN ONE YEAR

15 August 1944

A subdivision of the State of North Carolina has no authority to waive the statutory requirement that a claim for injury under the Workmen's Compensation Act must be filed within twelve months from the date of the injury.

CORONERS: VACANCIES IN OFFICE

23 August 1944

When a vacancy occurs in the office of coroner, it is to be filled by the action of the county commissioners and their appointee serves for the unexpired term and not just until the next general election in the county.

CRIMINAL LAW: OPERATING MOTOR VEHICLE WHILE OPERATOR'S

LICENSE REVOKED

30 August 1944

Any person who operates a motor vehicle upon the highways of the state after his driver's license has been revoked is guilty of a misdemeanor and upon conviction he may be imprisoned for six months and fined not more than five hundred dollars.

DEADLY WEAPON: CARRYING CONCEALED IN HALLWAY OF APARTMENT HOUSE

23 August 1944

The statutes of North Carolina make it a criminal offense for a person to carry a concealed weapon off of his own premises and a person carrying such a concealed weapon in the hallway of an apartment house in which he has an apartment is carrying the weapon off of his premises.

DOUBLE OFFICE HOLDING: TOWN COMMISSIONER; MEMBER COUNTY BOARD OF HEALTH

28 August 1944

The positions of town commissioner and member of the county board of health are both offices within the meaning of the provision of the North Carolina Constitution prohibiting double office holding; therefore, one person may not hold both at once.

ELECTIONS: CANDIDATE MUST FILE IN PRIMARY

28 August 1944

In a county to which the state primary law is applicable, the executive committee of a political party may not name a nominee for a county office and have his name placed on the general election ticket. Such a nominee must be selected by the voters in a primary.

INTOXICATING LIQUOR: POSSESSION OF LIQUOR UPON WHICH THE FEDERAL TAX HAS BEEN PAID

24 August 1944

It is not a violation of any North Carolina statute for a person to possess in a dry county two pints of liquor on which the state tax has noe been paid so long as the federal tax has been paid and so long as the liquor is not possessed for the purpose of sale.

INTOXICATING LIQUORS: POWERS OF COUNTY A.B.C. BOARDS

30 August 1944

While the statutes authorize county A.B.C. boards to expend not less than 5% and not more than 10% of the total profits for law enforcement purposes, the county A.B.C. boards have no authority to expend any part or all of this sum to employ a teacher for the purpose of putting into effect an educational program on alcoholism.

JUSTICES OF THE PEACE: TAKING ACKNOWLEDGMENTS OF DEEDS TO BE REGISTERED IN SOME OTHER COUNTY

29 August 1944

While a justice of the peace is authorized to take the acknowledgment of a deed or other instrument which is to be recorded in another county, before such instrument can be recorded in such other county it must have attached thereto a certificate of the clerk of the superior court of the justice's county stating that the justice was; at the time of taking the acknowledgment, an acting justice of his county and that the justice's signature is genuine.

MARRIAGE: HEALTH CERTIFICATE; OSTEOPATH; RIGHT TO ISSUE

24 August 1944

A duly licensed osteopath is a "licensed physician" as that term is used in the marriage laws and, therefore, the register of deeds may issue a marriage license upon the certificate of such osteopath that an examination discloses that the parties to the proposed marriage have no venereal disease in the infectious or communicable stage.

MOTOR VEHICLES: DRUNKEN DRIVING; APPEAL FROM CONVICTION; SUSPENSION OF DRIVER'S LICENSE

29 August 1944

When a defendant is tried for operating a motor vehicle while under the influence of intoxicating beverages, is convicted, and appeals, the department of motor vehicles may (if from its records or other satisfactory evidence, it is shown that defendant operated a motor vehicle while under the influence of intoxicants) suspend the operator's license pending the appeal. The defendant, however, may apply to the department of motor vehicles for a hearing on the matter and the department may rescind its order, extend the suspension if the facts so warrant, or revoke the license.

MOTOR VEHICLES: SUSPENSION OF DRIVER'S LICENSE

29 August 1944

The Department of Motor Vehicles has authority to suspend the license of any operator or chauffeur, without preliminary hearing, upon a showing by its records or other satisfactory evidence that the licensee has been convicted of illegal transportation of intoxicating liquors. The Department shall, however, afford the licensee an opportunity for hearing to be held in the county in which the licensee resides, unless the Department and the licensee agree that the hearing may be held in some other county.

MUNICIPALITIES: AIRPORTS; USE OF SURPLUS FUNDS TO IMPROVE

29 August 1944

A municipal airport is not a necessary expense and an appropriation therefor may not be included in the annual budget of the municipality without a vote of the people. However, when a municipality has a surplus which it secures from the sale of municipal property, this surplus may be used for enlarging and maintaining an airport.

MUNICIPALITIES: SALE OF PROPERTY

21 August 1944

While the statute authorizes the mayor and commissioners of a town to sell town property at public outcry, after 30 days notice, to the highest bidder, and apply proceeds of the sale as they think best, they do not have authority to sell or lease any real estate which is to be held in trust for the use of the town. Nor may they sell real estate with or without the buildings on it which is devoted to the purposes of government, including town or city halls, market houses, houses for fire departments, or for water supply or for public squares or parks. Before they can sell such property the town authorities must have special authorization by the general assembly.

MANAGERS: WATER AND STREET SUPERINTENDENT

29 August 1944

A water and street superintendent is an employee of a town and not an officer. Therefore, a person residing outside the corporate limits may be employed as a water and street superintendent.

PHOTOGRAPHERS: LICENSE REQUIRED

22 August, 1944

An individual who has obtained a state and city photographer's license is not privileged to engage in the business of photography unless and until he has met the requirements of the North Carolina Board of Photographic Examiners. However, the statute creating the Board of Photographic Examiners provides that it shall apply only in cities or towns having a population of more than 2,500 and that it shall not apply to photographers whose product is retailed at a unit price not exceeding 10c per picture.

REVENUE ACT: SAFETY DEPOSIT BOXES RENTED JOINTLY

28 August 1944

When a safety deposit box is rented in the joint names of a husband and wife and one spouse dies, the statute requires that the box be opened in the presence of the clerk of the superior court or his representative. The surviving spouse is not authorized to open the box in the absence of the clerk or his representative.

SALES TAX: SALES TO CHURCHES; REFUNDS

31 August 1944

Effective July 1, 1943, sales to churches became exempt from sales tax. Therefore, as to any such sales which occurred after July 1, 1943, on which the churches inadvertently paid taxes, an application for refund may be made to the Commissioner of Revenue on a form prescribed by him, stating the facts with respect to such purchases and the amounts thereof. Churches seeking refunds should obtain the consent of the merchants from whom the property was purchased that the refunds may be paid directly to the churches instead of to the merchants. This is necessary since, under the law, the sales tax is levied against and collected from the merchant and ordinarily sales tax refunds are made to the merchants.

SCHOOLS: COUNTY BOARD OF EDUCATION; VACANCIES; HOW FILLED

25 August 1944

Vacancies in the membership of the board of education in the various counties shall be filled by action of the county executive committee of the political party of the member causing such vacancy until the meeting of the next regular session of the General Assembly, and then for the residue of the unexpired term by that body.

TAXATION: LISTING REAL ESTATE AND IMPROVEMENTS THEREON SEPARATELY; LIEN

22 August, 1944

The North Carolina statutes provide that when land is owned by one party and the improvements thereon by another, the parties may list their interests separately or in the name of the owner of the land and the lien for the taxes on the improvements shall be a lien on both the real property and the improvements, or vice versa.

CRIMINAL LAW: GAMBLING; JURISDICTION OF JUSTICE OF PEACE

6 September 1944

The statutes provide that if any person shall play at any game of chance at which any property, money, or other thing of value is bet, whether the same be in stake or not, both those who play and those who bet thereon shall be guilty of a misdemeanor, punishable in excess of a justice's jurisdiction. Therefore, a justice of the peace does not have final jurisdiction of the offense of gambling.

CRIMINAL PROCEDURE: SEARCH WARRANTS; SERVICE ON SUNDAY

7 September 1944

While the statute provides that it shall not be lawful for any sheriff, constable, or other officer to execute any summons, capias, or other process on Sunday, unless issued for treason, felony or misdemeanor, it would seem that a search warrant issued pursuant to the North Carolina statutes prohibiting the possession or sale of intoxicating liquors could be served on Sunday. If the person signing the affidavit to the search warrant is not under oath, facts discovered by reason of the issuance of the warrant are not competent as evidence.

DOUBLE OFFICE HOLDING: MEMBER COUNTY BOARD OF HEALTH; COUNTY HEALTH OFFICER

1 September 1944

The positions of county health officer and member of the county board of health are both offices within the meaning of Article XIV, Section 7, of the North Carolina Constitution, prohibiting double office holding. Therefore, one person may not hold both positions at once.

ELECTION LAWS: ABSENTEE BALLOT; SOLDIER SERVING TERM IN DISCIPLINARY BARRACKS

6 September 1944

When the application for an absentee ballot is regular upon its face, the applicant is entitled to the ballot and entitled to vote the ballot despite the fact that he is serving a term in the disciplinary barracks for violation of the aws of the United States.

MOTOR VEHICLES: SPEED LIMIT

5 September 1944

Since the adoption of the North Carolina Emergency War Powers Proclamation No. 2, issued by the Governor on May 6, 1943, it is unlawful for a rivate individual to operate a motor vehicle at a speed in excess of 35 miles er hour.

MUNICIPALITIES: MAYOR; AUTHORITY TO MAKE ARRESTS

6 September 1944

While the mayor of a municipality is by virtue of statute constituted an nferior court, he has no right as such mayor nor as such court to make an rrest. Of course, he has the same right of arrest as a private citizen, to-vit: where he is present at any riot, rout, affray, or other breach of the eace, if necessary in order to suppress the same and also to arrest a person vho commits a felony in his presence.

MUNICIPAL TAXATION: JEWELRY COMPANY SELLING MERCHANDISE IN
CAR PARKED ON STREET

6 September 1944

While there is no provision in Schedule B of the Revenue Act relating to privilege taxation of persons engaged in selling jewelry, a municipal corporation, under its general authority, may classify the occupation of selling jewelry as one subject to taxation. A person parking on the streets of a town displaying, selling and collecting for jewelry sold would be sufficiently engaged in activity within the town to be subject to the tax.

TAXATION: EXEMPTIONS

1 September 1944

When a buliding located within a county would be exempt from taxation except for the fact that a part of the building is used in such a way as to be in competition with private enterprise, the tax levying authorities have authority, after placing a valuation on the building, to pro rate the valuation' so as to require the payment of taxes only on that portion of the building which would not be exempt.

TAXATION: MUNICIPALITIES; TAX LIST

5 September 1944

When a municipality has set up machinery for the listing of taxes and taxes have been listed by the citizens, the municipality has no authority to disregard such listings and adopt the listings of the same property by the county. However, municipalities, except those situated in more than one county, are required to accept the valuations fixed by the county authorities as modified by the State Board of Assessment.

TAXATION: MUNICIPALITIES; POLL TAX

5 September 1944

The Machinery Act of North Carolina provides for the levy by the board of county commissioners in each county of a poll tax of $2 on every male inhabitant over 21 and under 50 years of age. Cities and towns may levy a poll tax not exceeding $1.

ALCOHOLIC BEVERAGES: TRANSPORTATION INTO NAVAL AIR STATION

12 October 1944

Only where the State has ceded jurisdiction over a Naval Air Station to the Navy Department may alcoholic beverages be shipped into the reservation without violating the statutes of North Carolina. The mere fact that the station is under the control of the Naval authorities does not oust the criminal jurisdiction of the State.

CLERKS OF SUPERIOR COURT: ASSISTANTS

4 October 1944

By statute an assistant Clerk of the Superior Court is as fully authorized and empowered to perform all the duties and functions of the office of clerk as the clerk himself, and all of his acts, orders and judgments are entitled to the same faith and credit as those of the clerk.

EXECUTORS AND ADMINISTRATORS: PAYMENT OF LEGACIES TO CLERK

7 October 1944

The representative of a decedent may at any time after 12 months from the date of letters testamentary or administration pay into the office of the Clerk of the Superior Court any monies belonging to the legatees. or distributees of the estate of his testator or intestate. The payment discharges the representative and the sureties on his official bond to the extent of the amount so paid.

GAME LAWS: TRANSPORTING GAME INTO THIS STATE WHICH HAS BEEN LEGALLY KILLED IN ANOTHER STATE

28 September 1944

It is unlawful to possess, transport, purchase, or sell any dead game animals or birds, or parts thereof, during the closed season in North Carolina, even though such animals or birds, or parts thereof, were taken or killed without the State of North Carolina and in the open season for such birds or animals where taken or killed.

SALES TAX: DEVELOPING FILMS

28 September 1944

The charge made by photographers for developing films is a service charge and does not represent a sale of tangible personal property. Such charges are not subject to the sales tax. However, if the photographer makes printed pictures from the developed negative and sells the printed pictures to customers, the sales tax is due and should be collected.

SALES AND USE TAX: PAINT BOUGHT WITHOUT THE STATE FOR USE ON CONTRACT JOB WITHIN STATE

30 September 1944

When a contractor agrees to furnish a completed job of painting for a lump sum, he is liable for the 3% tax on the purchase price of the paint which he purchases, whether within or without the State, for use on the job.

SALES AND USE TAXES: SALES IN NORTH CAROLINA BY OUT-OF-STATE FIRM SELLING THROUGH AGENTS

12 October 1944

When an out-of-State firm sells merchandise in North Carolina through salesmen, the 3% use tax on sales made within the State should be collected and remitted to the State.

TAXATION: AUCTIONS

26 September 1944

There is no tax imposed on the owners of real estate who sell the same at auction, unless such persons are engaged in the business of selling property at auction. The tax is levied on persons engaged in the business of conducting auction sales of real estate for profit, and not upon the owner who is selling at auction.

TAXATION: REAL PROPERTY OWNED BY DEFENSE PLANT CORPORATION

10 October 1944

Real property located in North Carolina which is owned by a defense plant corporation is subject to ad valorem taxation.

BANKS: RIGHT TO REFUSE TO ACCEPT DEPOSITS

16 October 1944

A bank is not required to keep deposits for every person who offers money for this purpose, but may decline to do business with those whom, for any reason, it does not wish to serve, and it may close an account at any time by tendering to the depositor the amount due and by declining to receive more.

DOUBLE OFFICE HOLDING: CHIEF OF POLICE; CONSTABLE; FIRE CHIEF

16 October 1944

The position of township constable, fire chief, and chief of police are all officers within the meaning of the provision of the North Carolina Constitution prohibiting double office holding. Therefore, one person may hold only one such position at any one time.

ELECTIONS: ABSENTEE VOTING; OATH; ADMINISTRATION BY NOTARY PUBLIC WHO IS A CANDIDATE

23 October 1944

A notary public who is also a candidate in the general election is disqualified to administer oaths to persons desiring to vote by means of absentee ballots.

ELECTIONS: CONVICTION OF FEDERAL OFFENSE NO BAR TO VOTING

18 October 1944

While a person who has been convicted or confessed his guilt in open court of a crime punishable by imprisonment in the State's penitentiary may not vote in North Carolina unless his citizenship has been restored, a person who has been convicted of a federal offense in a federal court and sentenced to the federal prison is not thereby deprived of his privilege to vote.

ELECTIONS: REGISTERING AND VOTING AS AN INDEPENDENT

6 October 1944

While the statutes do not authorize the registration and voting of an independent in a primary election, they do provide for the registration and voting of an independent in a general election.

ELECTIONS: SPLITTING TICKET FOR PRESIDENT AND VICE PRESIDENT

21 October 1944

A voter cannot vote for the nominee for President of one party and for the nominee for Vice President of another party. When a voter marks the Presidential ballot, he is either voting for the Democratic Presidential electors or for the Republican Presidential electors. The names of these electors are not printed on the ballot, but are represented by the candidates of their party.

SCHOOL LAW: AGE WHEN CHILDREN MAY BE ENROLLED

2 October 1944

To be entitled to enroll as a student in the public schools for the first year course, a child must be six years of age on or before October first of the year in which he desires to enroll and must enroll during the first month of the school year.

SCHOOLS: SALE OF COUNTY SCHOOL PROPERTY

6 October 1944

Before a County Board of Education may sell a county schoolhouse, schoolhouse site, or other county school property at private sale, it must first sell the property at public auction after notice. Then, if the Board finds that the price offered is inadequate, it may reject the bid and sell at private sale if the price received at said private sale is greater than the amount offered at the public sale.

AUCTIONEERS: LICENSES

14 November 1944

The North Carolina statutes provide that no person or partnership shall receive a license to conduct an auction sale of furs, glassware, chinaware, gold, silver or jewelry unless such person, or a member of the partnership, is and has been for a period of one year a resident of North Carolina, and has been for six months a resident of one of the counties for which he seeks a permit. However, a nonresident may allow his goods to be sold by a resident of this State who complies with the above conditions.

CLERK SUPERIOR COURT: VACANCIES

17 November 1944

When a vacancy occurs in the office of the clerk of the superior court, a judge of the superior court appoints someone to fill the vacancy until the next election, at which time someone is elected to fill the vacancy for the unexpired term of the former clerk.

CONSTABLES: FILLING VACANCIES

17 November 1944

When a person has been a constable for a number of years but fails to file as a candidate for the office within the proper time, a vacancy occurs at the expiration of the term which the constable was serving. When the vacancy occurs, the county commissioners appoint to fill the same until the next election of constables.

GRAND JURY

12 November 1944

In North Carolina a defendant in a criminal action may be tried without a bill of indictment where the offense is a misdemeanor, but where the offense is a felony a common law grand jury must return a true bill.

MILITARY PERSONNEL: SURRENDER TO MILITARY AUTHORITIES

18 November 1944

Upon written demand by the commanding officer, the courts are authorized to surrender a soldier for trial to military authorities in cases of felonies and in cases of misdemeanors.

MOTOR VEHICLES: SIRENS

14 November 1944

While the statute authorizes the use of sirens on police and fire department vehicles, it does not authorize their use on the personal vehicles of volunteer firemen.

Municipal Police Officers: Arrest Outside of Corporate Limits

16 November 1944

In the absence of a public-local act, a municipal police officer does not have authority to make an arrest in a misdemeanor case outside the corporate limits of the city.

Names: Change of

8 November 1944

Before a person can change his name under the North Carolina statute, he must be a resident of this State. Where a resident of another state enters the armed services of the United States and is sent into North Carolina on a military mission and has no intention of making North Carolina his home, he is not eligible to institute a proceeding to change his name in the county in which he is located under military orders.

Taxation: Sales Tax; Sales to Educational Institutions

14 November 1944

Under the North Carolina Sales Tax Act, sales to educational institutions are exempt therefrom only when they are educational institutions principally supported by the State of North Carolina and the personal property is purchased for use in carrying on the work of such institutions.

Beer & Wine: Possession of Beer

1 December 1944

Under North Carolina statutes, a person is not forbidden to possess any amount of beer which he may legally acquire. Such possession will raise no presumption against the possessor, but he may not sell the beer without complying with the statutes relating to license, etc.

Counties & Cities: Appropriations for Civil Air Patrol

7 December 1944

By an Act of the 1943 General Assembly, counties and cities are authorized to make appropriations from their general funds to local organizations of official state and federal governmental agencies engaged in the war effort, so long as none of this appropriation is used to pay the compensation of members of such agencies. This Act would authorize contributions to the Civil Air Patrol. However, the Act does not apply to thirteen counties.

Garnishment of Wages: Taxes; Open Accounts

4 December 1944

For the collection of private debts, garnishment proceedings may be used, but salaries or wages for personal services earned within 60 days next preceding the order of garnishment are exempt and cannot be collected by this process if it appears that these earnings are necessary for the use of a family supported wholly or in part therefrom. In addition, the debtor would be entitled to his personal property exemption of $500.

As to taxes, no garnishment is allowed for state taxes when the salary is at a rate of less than $200. As to county and city taxes, no garnishment is allowed exceeding 10% of each instalment of salary or wage.

INEBRIATES: COMMITMENT TO STATE HOSPITAL; PAYMENT OF EXPENSES BY COUNTY

9 December 1944

When an inebriate is committed to the State Hospital and said inebriate is indigent, the actual cost and expense of restraint, care and treatment shall be borne by the county from which he is committed. The county is liable, however, only for board and clothing.

MARRIAGE: HEALTH CERTIFICATES

1 December 1944

The North Carolina statute requires that when an application is made for marriage license, an original report from a laboratory approved by the State Board of Health must accompany the health certificate of a regularly licensed physician. Under this law, a telegram from a laboratory would not be considered as an original report.

MUNICIPALITIES: CONTRIBUTION TO MUSIC CLUBS

7 December 1944

A municipality has no authority to make contributions to a music club which is sponsoring public school music.

PRISONS: JAILER

27 November 1944

In the absence of a public-local act, the sheriff has the care and custody of the jail of his county and he is the keeper thereof unless he appoints someone else as keeper.

TAXATION: AMERICAN LEGION PROPERTY

2 December 1944

The North Carolina statutes exempt from taxation buildings, with the land actually occupied, belonging to the American Legion or Posts of the American Legion or any benevolent, historical or charitable association used exclusively for lodge purposes by said association, together with such additional adjacent land as may be necessary for the convenient use of the buildings thereon. However, if taxes were due and had become a lien on the property prior to its acquisition by such organizations, such taxes may be collected.

TAXATION: MUNICIPAL TAXES; UNIMPROVED PROPERTY

30 November 1944

When a municipality levies ad valorem taxes on property, it should collect such taxes and the property owner is not relieved from the payment thereof because of the fact that no municipal improvements have been made which would benefit such property.

TAXATION: LANDLORD AND TENANT; LEVY UPON UNDIVIDED CROPS FOR TAXES OF SHARE CROPPERS

30 November 1944

Under the North Carolina law, levy cannot be made upon the crop for the taxes and debts of the share cropper after the crop has been harvested but while it is still in the hands of the landlord. The reason for this rule is that both the possession and title are deemed to be in the landlord under the North Carolina statutes.

SOIL CONSERVATION ACT: DRAINAGE DISTRICTS; CONTROL OF PESTS

11 December 1944

There is no authority under the Soil Conservation District laws which would justify the organization of soil conservation districts for the purpose of drainage alone, nor for the control of crop pests. There are, however, separate statutes providing for drainage districts and crop pest control.

DOUBLE OFFICE HOLDING: EFFECTIVE DATE OF CONSTITUTIONAL AMENDMENT

AFFECTING NOTARIES PUBLIC

11 December 1944

The constitutional amendment permitting notaries public to hold another public office became effective as of December 1, 1944, at 4:00 P. M.; consequently, a notary public may now serve as solicitor of a municipal police court.

NOTARIES PUBLIC: REVOCATION OF COMMISSION

29 December 1944

General Statutes 10-1 gives to the Governor ample authority to revoke the commission of a notary public.

SALARIES AND FEES: ASSIGNMENT OF SALARIES BY TEACHERS

11 December 1944

A county superintendent of schools is not required to recognize an assignment of future wages by a teacher.

AD VALOREM TAXATION: VETERANS' BONUSES AND PENSIONS; PROPERTY PURCHASED WITH BONUS OR PENSION FUNDS

13 December 1944

Funds received by a veteran of World War I from the Federal Government as bonus or pension are exempt from ad valorem taxation while on deposit in a bank to the veteran's credit, but this exemption does not apply to property purchased by the veteran with such funds.

GAME LAWS: JURISDICTION OF JUSTICE OF THE PEACE; REVOCATION OF HUNTING LICENSE; AFFECT OF APPEAL

14 December 1944

A first offense in violation of game laws or regulations is a misdemeanor within the jurisdiction of a justice of the peace, but a second offense is not within such jurisdiction. An appeal upon a conviction and judgment involving the revocation of a hunting license has the effect of staying the revocation pending the outcome of the appeal, the revocation being a part of the judgment.

TAXATION: QUADRENNIAL REASSESSMENTS

14 December 1945

A board of commissioners by proper resolution finding as a fact that present valuations throughout the county are fair and uniform may adopt the present valuations as fixed by the last quadrennial revaluation.

COUNTIES: COUNTY ATTORNEY; TAX ATTORNEY

15 December 1944

In the absence of a public-local act to the contrary, a county has the right to employ a county attorney and a tax attorney, and the question of consolidating the duties of the two is a matter entirely within the discretion of the board of county commissioners.

ARRESTS: BREAKING INTO DWELLING TO MAKE ARREST WITH AND WITHOUT WARRANT

15 December 1944

An officer armed with a warrant may forcibly enter a dwelling to serve the same if he has reasonable grounds to believe that the person for whose arrest the warrant calls is concealed therein.

An officer without a warrant may forcibly enter a house, admission having been demanded and refused, if a felony or other infamous crime has been committed and there is reasonable grounds to believe that the guilty person is concealed therein.

MARRIAGE: PROXY MARRIAGE; MAY NOT BE CELEBRATED IN NORTH CAROLINA

16 December 1944

Marriage by proxy may not be celebrated in this State, but it is entirely possible that if such contract of marriage was celebrated in a state in which such marriage is recognized, it would be likewise recognized in North Carolina.

MUNICIPALITIES: CONDEMNATION OF UNSAFE BUILDINGS

16 December 1944

Municipalities have authority to condemn and remove any and all buildings in the city limits or cause them to be removed, at the expense of the owners, when dangerous to life, health or other property, under proper rules established by ordinance.

SALES & USE TAXES: GLASSES ORDERED FROM OPTICAL COMPANY BY PHYSICIAN PRESCRIBING FOR PATIENTS

20 December 1944

A physician prescribing glasses for a patient and ordering glasses from an optical company for sale by him to the patient is not justified in collecting 3% of the price charged such patient for the glasses, as the taxable transaction is the sale from the optical company to the physician.

SCHOOLS: RIGHT TO REGULATE SECRET SOCIETIES

22 December 1944

The proper school authorities have the right to exclude from extracurricular activities students who belong to secret societies or organizations prohibited by school regulations.

SCHOOLS: TEACHERS' CONTRACTS; RESIGNATION

22 December 1944

Under the School Machinery Act, principals and teachers desiring to resign must give to the official head of their administrative unit at least thirty days' notice in writing prior to the opening of their school. A violation of this provision may deprive the offender of the right to teach in a public school of North Carolina for a period of one year.

FINES & FORFEITURES: CLERK SUPERIOR COURT; FEES AND COMMISSIONS

27 December 1944

A clerk of the superior court is not justified in deducting any fees or commissions from amounts collected or paid into his office on fines, forfeitures or penalties.

ARREST OF FUGITIVES

28 December 1944

A police officer does not have the right to arrest and hold without bond a North Carolina citizen on a justice of the peace warrant from another state. As a matter of law, it is only in cases of capital felony that a police officer has any right to hold any person without privilege of bond.

CRIMINAL LAW: PROSECUTING WITNESS; MAY NOT APPEAL

27 December 1944

Under our law a prosecuting witness has no right to appeal in a criminal action before a justice of the peace in which the defendant is acquitted. However, in case the prosecution is found to be frivolous and the prosecuting witness was assessed the costs, he may appeal to the superior court on the question of the payment of such costs.

CRIMINAL LAW: SALE OF CIGARETTES TO MINORS

28 March 1945

It is a violation of our criminal laws for any person to sell or give away cigarettes, or tobacco which may be used as a substitute for cigarettes, to any minor under the age of 17 years, or to aid or abet in such sale.

It is also unlawful for any person to assist any such minor in obtaining cigarettes, or tobacco to be used as a substitute therefor.

ELECTION LAWS: PERSON CONVICTED OF MISDEMEANOR NOT DISFRANCHISED

28 March 1945

A person convicted of a misdemeanor is not thereby deprived of the right to vote or run for office in North Carolina, as our Constitution provides for such forfeiture only in case the offense involved is one which may be punished by confinement in the State Prison.

ELECTION LAWS: RESIDENCE QUALIFICATIONS OF ELECTOR

8 January 1945

The question of residence of an elector is one to be determined by the registrar and judges of election of the precinct, and depends upon their determination of the intentions of the elector in respect to relinquishing or retaining his place of residence in the precinct.

JURORS: SPECIAL VENIRE; FEES WHEN SUMMONED TO ANOTHER COUNTY

13 January 1945

All special venire jurors are entitled to compensation for mileage and time, to be paid by the county to which they are summonsed at the rate now provided by law for regular jurors in the county of their residence.

MUNICIPALITIES: POWER TO GRANT EXCLUSIVE FRANCHISE; TAXICABS

4 January 1945

A municipal corporation is without authority to grant a franchise giving the exclusive right or privilege to operate taxies in the city limits nor would the payment of a compensating tax for what would amount to a special monopolistic privilege remove the constitutional objections.

MUNICIPALITIES: TOWN CONSTABLE, CHIEF OF POLICE MUST BE RESIDENTS OF TOWN

4 January 1945

In the absence of a PublicLocal Act to the contrary, the governing body of a town may name a chief of police as well as a constable for the town, but such appointees must be qualified voters and residents of the town.

OFFICIAL BONDS: COUNTY OFFICERS ON FEE BASIS

8 January 1945

In the absence of a Public-Local Act to the contrary, a board of county commissioners is not authorized to pay the premiums on the official bonds of a sheriff who is on a commission or fee basis.

TAXATION: EXEMPTION OF NON-PROFIT GOLF CLUB

12 January 1945

A board of county commissioners is without authority to relieve a non-profit Golf Club from payment of ad valorem taxes assessed and levied by a county or city.

WILLS: EXECUTION BY MINORS IN ARMED FORCES

16 January 1945

Under North Carolina law, the will of a minor who is in the armed forces cannot be admitted to probate.

WILLS: PROBATE W~~HERE~~ W~~ITNESSES~~ ARE DEAD

5 January 1945

A will may be admitted to probate in North Carolina when both subscribing witnesses are dead, upon proof of the handwriting of the testator and both witnesses, when the Clerk of the Superior Court is satisfied that the witnesses subscribed to the will in the presence of the testator.

GAMBLING: DISPOSITION OF MONEY CONFISCATED

9 March 1945

Money confiscated by a court because it was being used in gambling under provisions of General Statutes 14-299 should be placed in the general fund of the county in which the confiscation occurred and the court cannot properly order other disposition to be made of such confiscated money. Constitutionality of G. S. 14-299 not judicially determined.

MARRIAGE LAWS: ABANDONMENT

14 March 1945

A husband who leaves this State and goes to another state solely for the purpose of obtaining a divorce, after wrongfully abandoning his wife in this State, may be indicted for such abandonment and extradited and tried in the courts of North Carolina.

MARRIAGE LAWS: CONVICTION OF CRIME DOES NOT EFFECT THE RIGHT TO MARRY

3 March 1945

There is no state statute which denies to a person, who has been convicted of a felony and who may have lost his citizenship, the right to marry, if not otherwise disqualified.

MOTOR VEHICLES: PENALTY FOR OPERATING "FOR HIRE" VEHICLES WITH PRIVATE LICENSE

20 March 1945

Any one operating vehicles for hire without having paid the tax prescribed, or using private license plates on such vehicles for hire, shall be liable to an additional tax of $25.00 for each vehicle so used, and each additional use of such vehicle in such manner shall constitute a separate offense.

OFFICERS: LEAVE OF ABSENCE FOR SERVICE IN ARMED FORCES

14 March 1945

A state or county official may obtain a leave of absence and accept a temporary officers commission in the United States armed forces without vacating his civil office and without violating the constitutional provision against dual office holding.

School Teachers: Place of Listing Taxes

5 March 1945

School teachers should list their personal property for taxation in their county of legal residence; that is, the county in which they have their permanent home.

Taxation: Poll Tax; Release of Members of Armed Forces from Payment

17 January 1945

The board of county commissioners is the proper authority for a member of the armed forces to apply to for release from payment of poll tax levied against him.

Sales Tax: Liability of Church Owned College

12 March 1945

Only those educational institutions which are principally supported by the State are entitled to exemption from the 3% sales tax.

Name of Persons: Change Under Statute; Residence of Applicant

22 January 1945

In order to have a name changed under Chapter 101 of the General Statutes, the applicant must be a legal resident of the county in which the proceeding is instituted.

Name of Person Cannot Be Changed by Private Act of General Assembly

8 February 1945

Our State Constitution provides that the General Assembly shall not have power to pass any private law to alter the name of any person. The proper procedure must be under the general statutory law provided for this purpose.

Bail Bond: Approval by C.S.C. Under Order of Court

2 February 1945

An order of court in respect to a bail bond may designate the approval of the clerk or some other officer of the court, as a prerequisite thereto.

CONCEALED WEAPONS: CONFISCATION

24 February 1945

Under our law, it is mandatory that a weapon carried concealed be confiscated by the court upon conviction of the defendant, irrespective of the ownership of the weapon.

COUNTY BOARD OF EDUCATION: VACANCY—HOW FILLED

2 February 1945

If any candidate for membership on a county board of education shall die, or resign, or for any reason become ineligible between the date of his nomination and election by the General Assembly, the vacancy may be filled by the county executive committee of the political party of such candidate.

COUNTY COMMISSIONERS: CHAIRMAN REFUSING TO PUT QUESTION

12 February 1945

The chairman of a board of county commissioners cannot destroy the right of a majority of the board to take action by refusing to submit the question to a vote. Upon the refusal of the chairman to put the motion, the proponent could put it himself and the action of a majority would constitute the action of the board.

ELECTION LAWS: POLL TAX NOT A PREREQUISITE TO VOTING

13 February 1945

The poll tax in this State is levied solely as a source of revenue, and has no bearing on a person's right or qualification to vote.

ELECTION LAWS: RESIDENCE QUALIFICATIONS

26 February 1945

The question of whether a person is a member of a particular voting precinct within the meaning of the election laws is one to be determined by the registrars and judges of election, and the facts must be determined by them.

ELECTION LAWS: TEMPORARY REMOVAL FROM COUNTY

7 February 1945

A person does not lose his citizenship or right to vote and hold office in a county when he leaves the same temporarily but retains the intention of returning to his home county when circumstances permit.

INCOME TAX: RETIREMENT PAY OF ARMY OFFICER

9 February 1945

The retirement pay of a retired army officer does not come within the exemption provisions of Sec. 317 of the Revenue Act of 1939, as amended, and his retirement pay is subject to N. C. income tax, as the exemption applies only to persons on active duty with the armed forces.

MARRIAGE LAWS: PRE-MARITAL REQUIREMENTS

13 February 1945

Assuming that no disqualification exists, the only formal premarital requirements for marriage in North Carolina are a health certificate, and a marriage license issued by the register of deeds of the county in which the ceremony is to be performed.

MARRIED WOMEN: PRIVATE EXAMINATION NO LONGER REQUIRED

24 February 1945

All the requirements heretofore existing in our statutes as to taking the private examination of married women have been eliminated by H. B. No. 55, which was passed by the General Assembly of 1945. Although this Act was ratified on Feb. 7, 1945, it expressly provides that all instruments executed after Nov. 7, 1944, shall be valid without private examination.

POLL TAXES: SERVICEMEN'S EXEMPTION

1 February 1945

Members of the armed forces and the Merchant Marine of the United States are relieved from all poll taxes which such persons were required to list prior to induction, including those levied prior to 1939, if such taxes are unpaid by the serviceman.

PHYSICIANS: ALIEN'S RIGHT TO TAKE STATE MEDICAL BOARD EXAMINATION

2 February 1945

There is no constitutional or statutory ground for denying to an unnaturalized alien the right to be examined by the State Medical Board and to receive license to practice as a physician upon proof of qualification.

TOWN COMMISSIONERS: VACANCIES—HOW FILLED

24 January 1945

In case of a vacancy after election in the office of town commissioner, the remaining members of the board may appoint a successor to serve for the unexpired term.

TAXATION: LIEN FOR TAXES AFTER PAYMENT BY OTHER THAN OWNER

19 February 1945

A person who pays taxes on property to which he does not hold title, without securing an assignment of the tax sale certificate, is not entitled to a lien on the property against which the taxes were assessed, as the law makes no provision for the preservation of the lien under such circumstances.

COUNTIES: LEASE OF COUNTY PROPERTY

15 March 1945

A board of county commissioners has authority under our statutes to rent any property belonging to the county.

CRIMINAL LAW: LEGALITY OF GAMBLING DEVICES

20 March 1945

Punch boards, slot machines, pin ball machines and other gambling devices cannot be operated in this State without violating the state law.

DIVORCE: MEMBER OF ARMED FORCES MAY OBTAIN DIVORCE

24 March 1945

All other requisites being met, a member of the armed forces may obtain a divorce in this State without being present in person.

ELECTIONS: SERVICEMAN'S RIGHT TO FILE AS CANDIDATE

7 March 1945

A member of the armed forces otherwise qualified has a clear right to file as a candidate for public office, but it would be necessary that he personally sign the filing statement. If elected, he would be entitled to qualify just as any other person, but as this would require his personal presence it might involve practical difficulties.

MOTOR VEHICLES: DISPLAY OF LICENSE TAG

9 February 1945

The display of a motor vehicle license tag on the windshield of the vehicle does not comply with the regulations of the Commissioner of Motor Vehicles on this point, nor does the display of a license plate covered or partially covered by the paper cover in which it came meet the requirements of the statute.

MUNICIPALITIES: EXTENSION OF CORPORATE LIMITS

13 February 1945

The only provision for the extension of the corporate limits of a municipality is by an act of the General Assembly, which may provide for the extension upon a vote of the people, or may by the terms of the act itself extend the corporate limits.

MUNICIPALITIES: FURNISHING WATER AND ELECTRICITY TO OUT OF TOWN CUSTOMERS

8 February 1945

A town may furnish water and electricity to out of town customers, at rates agreed upon, where such service is available, but cannot be compelled to take on undesired customers, nor those for which there are no available facilities.

MUNICIPALITIES: POLICE JURISDICTION --

13 February 1945

In the absence of a public-local act or charter provisions to the contrary, a policeman has no authority to make arrests outside the corporate limits of the municipality in which he is serving as a policeman.

MUNICIPALITIES: POOL ROOMS

13 February 1945

Municipalities, under our law, have authority to license, prohibit and regulate pool and billiard rooms and dance halls, and in the interest of public morals provide for the revocation of such licenses.

MUNICIPALITIES: REGULATION OF BUSINESS HOURS

12 February 1945

A municipality has no right to regulate opening and closing hours of restaurants.

MUNICIPALITIES: SALE OF BEER AND WINE NEAR CHURCHES

13 February 1945

It is unlawful to sell or dispense beer and wine within fifty feet of a church in an incorporated town, or a town having police protection, while religious services are being held in such church, or to sell or dispense the same within three hundred feet of a church located outside the corporate limits of a town while religious services are in progress.

TAXATION: AD VALOREM; EXEMPTION OF PRIVATE CORPORATIONS

16 January 1945

A municipality is without authority in North Carolina to exempt the personal property of private corporations from taxation, or to furnish water without charge as an inducement to such corporations to operate in the municipality.

LOAN AGENTS: INTEREST RATES

30 April 1945

In considering whether the amount to be paid by the borrower exceeds the maximum legal interest rate, it is immaterial that a loan agent does not stipulate the exact rate of interest to be charged, but leaves the borrower to determine the amount of interest to be paid.

MUNICIPALITIES: DISSOLUTION

27 April 1945

Under the American doctrine, a municipal corporation, when once created by an act of the General Assembly, can be dissolved only by an act of the General Assembly.

MOTOR VEHICLES: FARMERS' LICENSES; LUMBER AS FARM PRODUCT

26 April 1945

The motor truck license marked "Farmer," and issued at a lower rate than that for a private hauler, does not authorize the use of such farm truck in the hauling of lumber, which does not come within our statute's definition of "farm products."

SALE OF COUNTY PROPERTY AT PRIVATE SALE

20 April 1945

In the absence of fraud or collusion, sale of county property by a board of county commissioners at private sale would in all respects be binding.

MUNICIPAL ELECTIONS: WRITING IN NAMES ON BALLOTS

20 April 1945

Municipal election ballots should provide space for voter to write in the names of any persons for whom he desires to vote other than the ones whose names appear on the official ballots.

MUNICIPAL ELECTIONS: NO STATE-WIDE PROVISION FOR PRIMARIES

19 April 1945

There is no state-wide statute authorizing primary elections for municipalities, and in the absence of specific charter provisions authorizing such primaries, they may not legally be held.

DIVORCE: RESIDENCE REQUIREMENTS, AND SEPARATION AS GROUNDS

17 April 1945

Under our law, in order to obtain a divorce on grounds of separation, a person must have been a resident and citizen of this state for six months immediately preceding the institution of the divorce action, and the parties must have lived separate and apart for two years immediately preceding the institution of the action.

POLL TAX: MAXIMUM AMOUNT WHICH CITY OR TOWN MAY LEVY

17 April 1945

Cities and towns in North Carolina may levy a poll tax not to exceed one dollar on every male inhabitant over twenty-one and under fifty years of age.

TAXICABS: BONDS AND INSURANCE

16 April 1945

The governing body of a city or town may fix the amount of insurance or surety bond required of taxicab operators, provided the amount of this bond or insurance shall not exceed $10,000.00 for each taxicab operated.

PARTY AFFILIATION OF CANDIDATE IN PRIMARY ELECTION

14 April 1945

In a primary election under our law, a person registered as a Republican could not file as a Democratic candidate, or vice versa. An aspirant to office must be affiliated with the political party whose candidate se seeks to be.

EFFECTIVE DATE OF N. C. LAWS

11 April 1945

Acts of our General Assembly shall be in force only from and after thirty days after the adjournment of the session at which they were passed, unless otherwise expressly provided. There is no provision in our law which excludes Sundays and holidays in determining the date upon which a law becomes effective.

QUALIFIED VOTERS

11 April 1945

The words "voter" and "elector" mean the same under our law. The term "qualified voter" implies not simply that the person is eligible to be a voter, but as well and necessarily that he is registered as such in the manner prescribed by law. The fact of registration is essential.

MUNICIPAL ELECTIONS: ABSENTEE VOTING NOT ALLOWED

4 April 1945

Our state law provides for absentee voting in general elections only, which does not include municipal elections.

BEER & WINE: PROHIBITING SALE ON SUNDAY

4 April 1945

Section 18-107 of the General Statutes provides that the governing bodies of municipalities shall have the power to regulate and prohibit the sale of wine or beer from 11:30 P. M. on each Saturday until 7:00 A. M. on the following Monday.

ELECTION LAWS: RESIDENCE REQUIREMENTS OF CANDIDATES

'4 April 1945

In order for a person to be eligible to hold a city office, he must be a resident of the city and a registered voter therein. The question of residence is one to be determined by the registrars and judges of election, upon the facts, and the question of qualification for office would have to be determined by an appropriate proceeding, if it were contested.

DUTY OF JAILER TO RECEIVE PERSONS ARRESTED BY HIGHWAY PATROLMEN

4 April 1945

State Highway Patrolmen are given power to make arrests for certain offenses by G. S. 20-188, and when an arrest is made by such patrolman within the scope of the power thus granted, it is the duty of the person in charge of the county jail to receive and place in custody the person so arrested, either where a commitment directing that such person be placed in jail has been issued, or where the arrest has been made under circumstances making it impossible for the patrolman to immediately take the arrested person before a magistrate for the issuance of a warrant and the obtaining of a commitment.

AUCTIONEERS OF SILVERWARE AND GLASSWARE

5 May 1945

A resident of another state or county may not lawfully conduct auction sales of silverware or glassware in North Carolina.

BUSINESS NAMES: "ARMY" AND "NAVY" EXCLUDED

11 May 1945

In North Carolina, it is unlawful for anyone to use the words "Army" or "Navy" or either or both in the name or as part of the name of any mercantile establishment in this State which is not in fact operated by the United States Government or a duly authorized agency thereof.

COUNTY COURT HOUSE: CUSTODY & CONTROL

4 May 1945

The custody and control of the county court house is vested in the board of county commissioners.

CRIMINAL LAW: USE OF CRIMINAL PROSECUTION TO ENFORCE CIVIL CLAIM

8 May 1945

Our courts will not ordinarily permit the use of the criminal docket for the purpose of collecting civil claims, but in legal theory a defendant who has violated the criminal law is not to be relieved of criminal responsibility on account of civil liability.

ELECTIONS: ABSENTEE BALLOTS

7 May 1945

No absentee ballots, civilian or military, are permitted in municipal elections in North Carolina.

ELECTIONS: "WRITE-IN" CANDIDATES

4 May 1945

Under our Australian Ballot law, if an elector desires to vote for a person whose name does not appear on the ticket, he can substitute the name by writing it in with a pencil or ink in the proper place and making a cross mark in the blank space at the left of the name so written in, and the name so written in will be treated like any other name on the ballot.

ELECTION LAWS: RESIDENCE AS TEST OF RIGHT TO VOTE

3 May 1945

The right of a former resident living out of this State for over a year to vote in North Carolina depends upon whether he intended to change his residence from this state. This is a question to be determined by the proper election officials.

ELECTION LAWS: REGISTRATION REQUIREMENT IN MUNICIPAL ELECTIONS

1 May 1945

Persons registered to vote in a special election, but not registered for a general municipal election, must register with the proper officials for the general municipal election in order to be entitled to vote therein.

INTOXICATING LIQUOR: SHIPMENT OF WHISKEY 'INTO N. C. PROHIBITED

8 May 1945

Under North Carolina law, it is illegal to ship any quantity of intoxicating liquor into this state, whether tax paid or not, except through a state agency under our alcoholic control statutes. A person is permitted to transport in his personal possession into this state tax paid whiskey not in excess of one gallon, provided the container is unopened.

MUNICIPAL CORPORATIONS: RIGHT TO ENGAGE IN MERCHANDISING

4 May 1945

There is no provision in the general law authorizing a municipal corporation to engage in the mercantile business, and in the absence of specific charter provisions, such an activity would not be justified.

MUNICIPAL CORPORATIONS: REGULATION OF THEATERS

14 May 1945

A municipality has the right to regulate, restrict and prohibit theaters and shows of any kind by ordinances, uniform in their application, and this would include the right to prohibit shows being held on Sundays, even when sponsored by a volunteer fire department or other civic organization.

PAWNBROKERS: USURY LAWS

7 May 1945

The statutes providing for the licensing and bonding of pawnbrokers in North Carolina specifically states that they shall be subject to our usury laws. Thus, pawnbrokers are not authorized to charge in excess of the legal rate of interest.

PARTITION PROCEEDINGS: ATTORNEYS AND COMMISSIONS FEES

1 May 1945

In a partition proceeding, the clerk of the superior court may allow an attorney's fee and a commissioner's fee to a person serving in both capacities, subject to the approval of the judge of the superior court.

SCHOOLS: USE OF SCHOOL PROPERTY FOR CIVIL AND FRATERNAL PURPOSES

2 May 1945

It is the policy of this state to encourage the proper use of school buildings for civil and community meetings, subject to rules and regulations adopted by local boards of education with the approval of the State Board of Education; and, there is no legal reason why such rules and regulations should not provide for such use by fraternal organizations.

WINE: 1945 STATE-WIDE WINE ACT; APPLICATION AS TO "ON PREMISES CONSUMPTION"

1 May 1945

The statute governing the "on premises consumption" sale of wine is state-wide in its application, and restricts the issuance of "on premises" license to bona fide hotels, cafeterias, cafes and restaurants in which prepared food is customarily sold, and which have a grade A rating from the State Board of Health.

COURTS: MAYORES PROCESS NOT RETURNABLE BEFORE J. P.

14 May 1945

In the absence of a public-local act to the contrary, and no recorder's court having been established in the jurisdiction, it is as much a part of a mayor's duty to act in his judicial capacity as it is to perform any of his other official functions; and there is no general authority by which he could issue warrants and other legal process, and make the same returnable before a justice of the peace.

CRIMINAL LAW: JUSTICES OF THE PEACE; PRABABLE CAUSE

15 May 1945

It is the duty of a justice of the peace, when probable cause is shown in a criminal prosecution for violation of the motor vehicle laws in which he does not have final jurisdiction, to bind the case over to the Superior Court in those counties in which there are no courts of intermediate jurisdiction.

HEALTH: VENEREAL DISEASES

25 May 1945

Under our state laws, the health authorities have the following powers, among others:

1. To make examinations of persons reasonably suspected of being infected with venereal disease;

2. To detain such persons until the results of the examinations are known;

3. To require persons infected with venereal disease to report for treatment and to continue such treatment until cured;

4. When necessary in the public interest, to isolate or quarantine persons venereally infected;

5. To investigate sources of venereal infection;

6. To cooperate with officers in the enforcement of laws against prostitution.

JUSTICES OF THE PEACE: PRACTICE OF LAW DEFINED

22 May 1945

Our statutes define the practice of law to be "performing any legal service for any other person, firm or corporation, with or without compensation, specifically including the preparation of deeds, mortgages, wills, trust instruments, reports of guardians, trustees, administrators or executors." Thus, any justice of the peace performing any of these or similar services, with or without compensation, would be violating the law.

MARRIED WOMEN: LEGAL NAMES

29 May 1945

At marriage the wife takes the husband's surname, with which should be used her own given name; and she may use the title "Mrs." to distinguish her from her husband and to show that she is a married woman. This is the proper legal usage, and should be observed in all business transactions.

MOTOR VEHICLES: "HIT AND RUN"

21 May 1945

Our statutes require the driver of a vehicle involved in an accident resulting in damage to property, or injury or death to any person, to immediately stop such vehicle at the scene of the accident and give his name, address, operator's or chauffeur's license number and the registration number of his vehicle to the driver or occupants of any vehicle involved in the collision.

MUNICIPAL CORPORATIONS: REGULATION OF PARKING OF GASOLINE TRUCKS

15 May 1945

A municipality may, by proper ordinance, prohibit the parking of gasoline trucks on its streets except for business purposes and in cases of breakdown.

MUNICIPALITIES: TOWN CLERK—QUALIFICATIONS

14 May 1945

The position of town clerk is an office, and before any one may hold a municipal office, he must be a qualified elector of the municipality, and as residence is one of the qualifications of a voter, a person living outside the corporate limits of a municipality may not properly serve as town clerk, in the absence of a public-local act to the contrary.

NEWSPAPERS: FALSE INFORMATION

14 May 1945

It is unlawful and punishable as a misdemeanor for any person in North Carolina to state, deliver, or transmit by any means whatever to any newspaper for publication therein any false and libelous statement concerning any person or corporation, and to thereby secure the publication of the same.

DOUBLE OFFICE HOLDING: JUDGE RECORDER'S COURT—TOWN ATTORNEY

15 June 1945

Since holding the position of town attorney does not constitute the holding of an office, one person may at the same time be town attorney and judge of a recorder's court without violating the proscriptive provisions of the North Carolina Constitution relating to double office holding.

JUSTICES OF THE PEACE: DISMISSING CASES AT REQUEST OF PROSECUTOR

.25 June 1945

The dismissal of a warrant in a criminal case once the warrant has been sworn out is within the sound discretion of the Justice of the Peace and no criminal case should be dismissed merely because the person who swore out the warrant requests that the prosecution be discontinued and the warrant withdrawn. Manifestly it would be wrong to permit a prosecuting witness to use the criminal docket as a means of collecting a debt.

MARRIAGE: VOID MARRIAGES; PROCEEDINGS TO DECLARE VOID

19 June 1945

A marriage contracted by a person who has a living spouse from whom he has not been divorced is void and not voidable in North Carolina. Legally it is not necessary that a void marriage be so declared by a court before the parties thereto may marry a second time. However, a suit to declare such a marriage void *ab initio* will be entertained by the courts of this State.

MUNICIPALITIES: CONTRIBUTIONS TO MEMORIAL TO PERSONS SERVING IN WORLD WAR II

14 June 1945

In the absence of a Public-Local Act, a municipality has no authority to make contributions toward the erection of a permanent memorial to persons serving in World War II.

PHYSICIANS AND SURGEONS: RIGHT OF ALIEN TO PRACTICE MEDICINE

22 June 1945

There is no requirement in the North Carolina statutes that an applicant for a license to practice medicine must be a citizen of this State.

POOL ROOMS: MINORS

16 June 1945

Municipal corporations are authorized by statute to fix the age at which minors may be allowed to play in or frequent pool rooms. The general law makes it unlawful for the keeper of a pool room to permit any minor to enter or remain therein where the keeper has been notified by the parents or guardian of such minor not to allow him to enter or remain therein.

PUBLIC OFFICES: CONVICTION OF FELONY; RESTORATION TO CITIZENSHIP

25 June 1945

The position of chief of police of a municipal corporation is an office and a person who has been convicted of a felony is not eligible to hold such office unless his citizenship has been restored in the manner prescribed by law. Once his citizenship is restored, however, such person is as eligible to hold office as a person who has never been convicted of any offense.

SALES TAX: APPLICATIONS TO OPERATORS ON INDIAN RESERVATIONS

19 June 1945

Persons trading with Indians on the Indian Reservation are not subject to sales tax on so much of their business as is carried on with the Indians. That portion of the business which is not carried on with Indians is subject to the sales tax.

TAXATION: PERSONAL PROPERTY TAX EXEMPTIONS; ESTATES

25 June 1945

The personal property exemption of $300.00 from taxation is extended to each household to be distributed among the members of a household as they see fit and to single persons not residing with persons on whom they are dependent. This exemption does not extend to an administrator or an estate as such.

TAXATION: PROPERTY OF A. B. C. BOARDS

27 June 1945

The property of County A. B. C. Boards is subject to county taxation. The fact that a part of the net profits realized from the A. B. C. business is earmarked by statute for the county furnishes no legal basis for holding such property tax exempt.

SALE OF REAL ESTATE OF WARD LYING IN TWO COUNTIES: APPROVAL BY JUDGE

6 July 1945

A petition for the sale or mortgaging of a ward's real propertly may be filed in the Superior Court of the county in which all or any part of the real estate is situated. No sale or mortgage shall be made until approved by the Judge of the Judicial District in which the petition was filed.

CRIMINAL LAW: CONCEALED WEAPONS; CONFISCATION; DESTRUCTION

6 July 1945

Under our statute, the only legal disposition that can be made of a pistol in a case in which a defendant has been convicted or has entered a plea of guilty of carrying a concealed weapon is the destruction of the same, and the trial judge is under the mandatory duty to enter an order for such destruction.

POOL ROOMS: MUNICIPAL ORDINANCE PROHIBITING POOL PLAYING BY MINORS

9 July 1945

Under our law, municipal corporations are granted authority to license, prohibit and regulate pool and billiard rooms, and under this grant of statutory authority, a municipal ordinance forbidding minors to play pool in pool and billiard rooms could be sustained. Further, under our statute, it is unlawful for the keeper or owner of a billiard room to allow minors to enter or remain therein where the owner or keeper has been notified by the parent or guardian of the minor not to allow him to enter or remain in such billiard room; this statute is violated only where the parent or guardian of the minor has notified the keeper or owner not to permit the minor to enter.

GAME WARDENS: SEARCH AND SEIZURE

11 July 1945

Under our State law, game wardens have no authority to search an automobile without having first procured a search warrant.

BEER AND WINE: RIGHT OF COUNTY ABC BOARD TO SELL UNFORTIFIED WINE

14 July 1945

County ABC stores have no authority to possess or sell unfortified wines.

CITIZENSHIP

16 July 1945

A person does not lose his citizenship or right to vote in North Carolina because of conviction of crime unless he was convicted of an offense which was a felony under our law.

MUNICIPALITIES: PARKING LOTS

16 July 1945

The governing authorities of all cities and towns of North Carolina have the power to own, establish, regulate, operate and control municipal parking lots for parking of motor vehicles within the corporate limits. They are likewise authorized in their discretion to make a charge for the use of such parking lots.

COLLECTING AGENCIES

· 20 July 1945

There is no law in North Carolina which requires agencies collecting delinquent accounts on a commission basis to collect their fee or any part of it from the client. That is entirely a matter of contract between the collecting agency and the client.

DEATHS: REPORTING DEATHS TO CORONER

20 July 1945

We have no statute which specifically requires hospitals or doctors to report deaths to the county Coroner, but when it appears that a person has died as a result of a criminal act or default of some person, the Coroner should be notified. This, however, is a duty imposed upon all citizens of the State and is not a special duty imposed upon doctors or hospitals.

CONSTABLES: APPOINTMENT; RESIDENCE; QUALIFICATION

21 July 1945

Under our law, a person must be a resident of the township in which he is appointed constable before such appointment will be valid.

MUNICIPAL POLICE: RIGHT TO ARREST PERSON OUTSIDE OF CORPORATE LIMITS

30 July 1945

A municipal police officer has no right to pursue and arrest a person beyond the municipal limits for a breach of the peace committed in his presence inside the corporate limits whether or not a warrant has been issued.

DIVORCE: NO WAITING PERIOD

31 July 1945

Assuming that a divorce proceeding is in all other respects regular, the judgment or divorce decree is legal and effective immediately upon the signing of the same by the trial judge and upon being filed in the office of the Clerk of the Superior Court. In North Carolina, no so-called "waiting period" is required.

OFFICERS: AGE REQUIREMENT

31 July 1945

Under Section 1, Article VI, of our State Constitution, a person must be at least 21 years of age to be eligible to hold office.

FISHING LICENSE: FISHING IN PRIVATE PONDS

31 July 1945

Only the owner of a private fishing pond or members of his family under 21 years of age are exempted from the requirement of obtaining a fishing license before fishing therein.

FORTUNE TELLING: AUTHORITY OF CITY TO PROHIBIT

2 August 1945

In this State, municipal corporations have no authority to prohibit the practice of palmistry or fortune telling.

LICENSE TAX: ITINERANT PHOTOGRAPHERS

3 August 1945

Under our laws, cities and towns are not authorized to levy a license tax on itinerant photographers.

INTOXICATING LIQUORS: POSSESSION OF MORE THAN ONE GALLON IN WET COUNTY AS PRIMA FACIE EVIDENCE

8 August 1945

In this State, the possession of more than one gallon of intoxicating liquor in a county operating under the provisions of the ABC Act, constitutes prima facie evidence that such liquor is possessed for the purpose of sale.

SCHOOLS: MARRIAGE AS GROUNDS FOR BARRING OR DISMISSAL OF PUPILS

17 August 1945

The mere fact that a pupil is married is not sufficient within itself to warrant the barring or dismissal of such pupil from a public school in North

Carolina. However, under the provisions of our law, the proper school official could bar or dismiss a pupil in any particular case in which it was thought that the conduct of the particular pupil was such as to make his or her presence in the school a menace to the school, but the question must be considered purely on an individual basis and on the facts of the particular case under consideration.

DETECTIVES

21 August 1945

It is unlawful in North Carolina for persons' licensed or representing themselves as detectives to engage in the business of collecting claims, accounts, bills, notes or other money obligations for others, or to engage in the business known as a collection agency.

CRIMINAL WARRANTS: ATTORNEY SIGNING NAME OF CLIENT

23 August 1945

Our statute requires that the complainant in a criminal warrant be examined under oath. A person cannot be examined under oath through his attorney; therefore, it is not proper for an attorney to make out a warrant and sign another person's name thereto as complainant.

CRIMINAL LAW: PIN BALL MACHINES

27 August 1945

In this State, it is unlawful to possess, sell, manufacture or operate those devices usually described as pin ball machines, whereby a plunger shoots balls into an arrangement of lights, slots or holes in such a way as to register a varying score; and this is so even though such devices be represented as a game of skill and nothing is promised to or received by the player.

CRIMINAL LAW: POSSESSION OF LOTTERY TICKETS

28 August 1945

The mere possession of any tickets, certificates or orders used in the operation of any lottery shall be prima facie evidence of violation of our statute prohibiting lotteries.

VOID MARRIAGES

3 August 1945

Under North Carolina law, the following marriages are void: marriages between a white person and a negro or Indian, or between a white person and a person of negro or Indian descent to the third generation, inclusive, or between a Cherokee Indian of Robeson County and a person of negro descent to the third generation, inclusive, or between any two persons nearer of kin than first cousins, or between a male person under 16 years of age and any female, or between the female person under 14 years of age and any male, or between persons either of whom has a husband or wife living at the time of such marriage, or between persons either of whom is, at the time, physically impotent or is incapable of contracting from want of will or understanding; neither may double first cousins marry. However, no marriage followed by cohabitation and the birth of issue shall be declared void after the death of either of the parties for any of the causes stated above, except for that one of the parties was a white person and the other a negro or Indian, or of negro or Indian descent to the third generation, inclusive, and for bigamy.

CRIMINAL LAW: CARRYING A CONCEALED WEAPON

27 August 1945

The statute prohibits the carrying of a weapon by any person ". . . concealed about his person." That is, concealed near, in close proximity to him and within convenient reach so that he could promptly use it is prompted to do so by any violent motive. This being the case, a pistol carried in the closed glove compartment of an automobile is a violation of this provision of our law.

PHRENOLOGISTS AND FORTUNE TELLERS: MUNICIPAL LICENSES

5 September 1945

Under our laws, counties, cities and towns may levy a license tax on the practice of phrenology and on the practice of fortune telling, but the amount of such tax must not be unreasonable.

INCOME TAX: COMPENSATION TO VETERANS ON ACCOUNT OF PHYSICAL DISABILITY INCURRED IN ARMED SERVICE

5 September 1945

In cases where compensation is received by a disabled veteran from the Federal Government by reason of injuries sustained while in the armed forces and, consequently, based on physical disability, such compensation is not subject to State income tax.

SPECIAL ELECTIONS: ABSENTEE BALLOTS

5 September 1945

Under our election laws, absentee voting is not authorized in municipal elections or in special elections but is expressly restricted to general elections.

SCHOOLS: AGE OF ADMISSION OF CHILD

5 September 1945

The school laws of this State provide.that children, in order to be entitled to enrollment in the public schools of the State, must be six years of age or before October 1st of the year in which they enroll, and must enroll during the first month of the school year.

JUSTICES OF THE PEACE: DISPOSITION OF CASES OF PROBABLE CAUSE

7 September 1945

A justice of the peace acting as a committing magistrate in any case in which he does not have final jurisdiction, is charged with the responsibility either to find probable cause and bind the accused over to the proper court, or, if no probable cause is found, to dismiss the case. This is within the sound discretion of the magistrate, but his action in dismissing the case would not be a bar to indictment or other prosecution against the accused.

MUNICIPAL TAX RATE: EXPENSE OF PUBLIC CEMETERIES

15 September 1945

Municipalities are authorized by our law to acquire property in fee simple and to use property now owned by them in fee simple or otherwise for the purpose of establishing and maintaining new cemeteries. The governing boards of municipalities are, therefore, authorized to appropriate tax funds for these purposes.

BEER AND WINE: CLOSING HOURS

20 September 1945

The governing bodies of all municipalities in North Carolina are vested with full power and authority to regulate and prohibit the sale of beer and wine from 11:30 P. M. on each Saturday until 7:00 A. M. on the following Monday.

MUNICIPAL BUILDING CODES NOT APPLICABLE TO STATE CONSTRUCTION PROJECTS

21 September 1945

The State of North Carolina, in the construction of buildings or other projects for State purposes, within municipal limits, is not bound by or subject to municipal building codes or fees imposed thereunder.

MUNICIPALITIES: CONTRACTS IN EXCESS OF $1000; ADVERTISEMENT FOR BIDS

21 September 1945

Our statutes require the governing body of any municipality in North Carolina to advertise for bids for construction or repair work, supplies,

material or equipment involving the expenditure of public funds in the
amount of $1000 or more.

PIN BALL MACHINES

22 September 1945

A pin ball machine which operates on the coin-in-the-slot principle and
does not give exactly the same score or tally each time it is played is illegal
and its operation or possession is illegal.

MERCHANDISE SALES STIMULATOR MACHINES: LOTTERY LAWS

24 September 1945

Our courts have very broadly construed our laws prohibiting any form of
lottery or game of chance in which a person, for a consideration gets an opportunity to win merchandise or other property as decided by some form
of chance, and it is a violation of our law to use a device described as a "Merchandise Sales Stimulator Cabinet," in which a ball is dropped in a slot and
finally comes to rest on one of various numbers; thus, through an element
of chance, entitling the player-customer to certain articles of merchandise
identified with such numbers, and the circumstance that each player-customer
purchases a regular item of merchandise at its regular price as a prerequisite to playing the machine for an additional prize does not change the unlawful character of the machine nor remove the unlawful elements from its
operation.

MUNICIPALITIES: RIGHT TO OPEN, CLOSE OR ALTER STREETS

25 September 1945

Municipalities in North Carolina have direct authority, in their discretion, to open new streets, change, widen or extend and close any street or
alley that is now or may hereafter be open. Such action by a municipality,
however, could in proper cases be the basis for claims for compensation for
the taking or injury of private property.

MUNICIPAL TAX RATE

25 September 1945

Under our laws, the governing bodies of cities and towns have the right
to fix municipal tax rates during the month of August of each year, provided the tax rate so fixed does not exceed $1.00 on each $100.00 of value of
taxable property.

MARRIAGE LICENSE: LENGTH OF TIME FOR WHICH VALID BEFORE CEREMONY

27 September 1945

A marriage license issued under North Carolina laws authorizes the proper
officials to perform the ceremony within sixty days after the date of issuance

as set forth in the license, and it is also necessary that the license be returned by the person performing the·ceremony to the issuing register of deeds within sixty days of the performance of the ceremony.

RESIDENCE: HOW ACQUIRED IN NORTH CAROLINA

27 September 1945

Two elements must concur in order for a non-resident to establish residence in North Carolina. There must be the actual physical presence, plus the intent to remain for an indefinite length of time; a fixed or permanent abode or dwelling as distinguished from a mere temporary locality of existence.

CRIMINAL PROCEDURE: BAIL; WHO MAY TAKE

10 September 1945

At any time before final judgment, any person lawfully committed to jail may submit a justified bond in an amount and form approved by the proper authority, and the sheriff, deputy sheriff, jailer or other person having the prisoner in custody is authorized to accept such bond and release the prisoner.

VETERANS: REGISTRATION AND CERTIFICATION OF DISCHARGES; FEES

27 October 1945

In this State, each register of deeds is required to keep a book in which to record discharges from the armed forces of the United States and such discharges must be recorded without charge when presented to the register of deeds.

The register of deeds must also furnish without charge certified copies of such discharges upon request of members of the armed forces.

COUNTY COMMISSIONERS: AUTHORIZED TO MEET COST OF RECORDING VETERANS' PAPERS

Boards of county commissioners are authorized to appropriate from the general fund an amount sufficient to cover the additional expense of recording and certifying veterans' records.

TORRENS LAW: LAND LOCATED IN MORE THAN ONE COUNTY

2 October 1945

Adverse claims arising against land registered under the Torrens Law subsequent to the date of the original decree of registration should be filed in the county in which the certificate of title was issued. Suit to enforce such a claim should be instituted in the county where the land lies.

CONVEYANCES: PRIVATE EXAMINATION OF WOMEN; REGISTRATION BY CLERK

31 October 1945

Although it may be surplusage whenever an instrument is presented for probate, the Clerk of the Superior Court should adjudge a certificate showing the private examination of a female party thereto to be sufficient and order the instrument to be recorded. The fact that the private examination may not be necessary would not justify the clerk in striking out that portion of the instrument.

SEARCH WARRANTS: DEFECTS IN WARRANT DO NOT AFFECT ADMISSIBILITY OF EVIDENCE OBTAINED THEREBY

30 October 1945

If the necessary affidavit is made, the fact that a search warrant does not, in other ways, comply with the provisions of a statute authorizing such warrants, does not affect the admissibility of evidence obtained as a result of a search thereunder.

TRUSTEES: BONDS

29 October 1945

Unless the instrument creating the trust specifically requires it, there is no requirement under our law for a trustee who is a resident of the State to give bond for the faithful performance of his duties. In case of a non-resident trustee, a bond is required.

CORPORATIONS: DIRECTORS' QUALIFICATIONS

27 October 1945

Under North Carolina law corporations may, through its certificate of incorporation or its by-laws, fix the number of shares a stockholder must own in order to be eligible as a director.

DIVORCE: WIFE'S SUPPORT

26 October 1945

Upon the issuance of a decree of divorce from the bonds of matrimony, all rights arising out of the marriage cease and either party may marry again unless otherwise barred by law. Thus, although a judgment for alimony obtained prior to the divorce is not affected thereby, a wife could not maintain a separate action for support after the granting of the divorce.

TRADEMARKS: TRADE NAMES

26 October 1945

Our law does not contemplate that the name of a business should be registered as a trade-mark; a trade-mark is intended to apply to the product of its business, not to its name.

SPECIAL SCHOOL ELECTIONS

25 October 1945

The board of county commissioners has general supervisory authority over a special school election and the only function of the county board of elections in such case is in connection with the preparation and distribution of the ballots.

USE OF "ARMY" AND "NAVY" IN TRADE NAME

19 October 1945

It is unlawful for anyone in North Carolina to use the word "Army" or "Navy" in any trade name of any establishment not actually operated by the United States Government or an agency thereof.

LICENSE TAXES: PEDDLER-PRODUCER

17 October 1945

A person who sells articles produced by himself is not liable to our State Peddler's License Tax but this exemption does not include articles which are assembled by the seller from component parts not produced by him.

FRANCHISE TAX: FOREIGN CORPORATION OPERATING IN NORTH CAROLINA THROUGH UNINCORPORATED SUBSIDIARY

14 October 1945

A foreign corporation doing business in North Carolina through an unincorporated subsidiary is subject to all the tax burdens and liabilities incident to doing business in this State.

ADOPTION: SUMMONS BY PUBLICATION; CONSENT

16 October 1945

Under our law it would be possible to make parents parties to an adoption proceeding by publication of summons but the necessary consent of such parents cannot be obtained by publication as consent is a positive and voluntary act and cannot be presumed from mere silence.

RE-ADOPTION

16 October 1945

Our statutes do not provide for re-adoption and consequently consent of the natural parents to a second adoption is necessary.

ADOPTION: CONSENT OF PARENTS

16 October 1945

The consent given by a child's parents for its adoption by designated parties cannot be assigned or transferred so as to authorize an adoption by other than the originally named parties.

GAME LAWS: SALE OR PURCHASE OF GAME FISH

15 October 1945

It is unlawful in North Carolina for any person, firm or corporation to buy, sell, offer to sell or possess for the purpose of sale any game fish either taken within or without this State.

PREDATORY GAME ANIMALS AND BIRDS

12 October 1945

The Board of Conservation and Development is authorized to issue permits for the killing of such birds or animals as may become seriously injurious to property. And it is lawful to take or kill without such permit any bird or animal actually committing or about to commit depradations.

GAME LAWS: FEDERAL MILITARY RESERVATION

11 October 1945

State game laws are not in force on a Federal military reservation within this State and the question of whether a hunting license is required for hunting thereon is a matter for the Federal authorities to determine.

SCHOOLS: FINES AND FORFIETURES FROM MUNICIPAL COURTS

11 October 1945

All fines and forfeitures from the courts of North Carolina go into the county school fund and are distributed to county and city administrative units on a per capita basis. This includes fines and forfeitures collected by municipal courts.

SCHOOLS: AGE OR ENROLLMENT

11 October 1945

In order to be entitled to enrollment in our public schools, a child must have attained the age of six years on or before the first day of October of the year in which such child enrolls and the enrollment must be during the first month of the school year.

MOTOR VEHICLES: SPEED LIMITS

31 October 1945

On and after the expiration of the war time provision on November 1, 1945, 50 miles an hour is the absolute maximum legal speed limit for motor vehicles in North Carolina. The only exceptions to this limitation are police cars in pursuit of law violators; fire equipment traveling in response to fire alarms; and ambulances traveling in emergencies.

SALES TAX: EYE-GLASS LENSES AND FRAMES

The three per cent State sales tax applies to sales to physicians of lenses and frames used for eye glasses since such items are not specifically exempted by statute nor do they come within the definition of medical supplies.

DOUBLE OFFICE HOLDING: POLICEMAN AND DEPUTY SHERIFF

26 October 1945

Police officers and deputy sheriffs are both officers within the meaning of the Constitutional provision against dual office holding.

WILLS: MINORS; VETERANS

2 October 1945

Under our law a will executed by a minor who dies after attaining his majority may not be probated as a valid testamentary disposition of property. Minor veterans are no exception to this rule.

CONSTITUTIONALITY OF STATUTES

1 November 1945

It has been held by our Supreme Court and by the Supreme Court of the United States as well, that a statute will not be declared unconstitutional unless it is clearly in conflict with the Constitution, and those who attack a law on statutory grounds must show beyond a reasonable doubt that such conflict exists.

LICENSE TAX: SOLICITORS FOR FARM PAPERS AND OTHER PUBLICATIONS

1 November 1945

Our Revenue Act imposes no license or privilege tax on persons soliciting subscriptions to a farm paper or other periodical. Such a tax would be contrary to the provisions of the Constitution of the United States.

BIRTH CERTIFICATE: ILLEGITIMATE CHILD; ENTERING NAME OF PUTATIVE FATHER

1 November 1945

In the case of an illegitimate child, the name of the putative father shall not be entered upon the birth certificate without his consent.

DETECTIVE AGENCY: PRIVILEGE TAX

1 November 1945

Under our Law, every person operating a detective agency or engaging in "secret service work," and every person employed in such work, is required to procure a state privilege license before engaging in such business.

SCHOOLS: DISCIPLINE ON SCHOOL BUS

1 November 1945

The discretionary authority of a teacher over pupils extends to pupils on school bus on which the teacher is riding, either as a passenger or as driver, nd this authority includes the right to inflict corporal punishment in proper ases. However, a non-teaching bus driver has no authority to inflict corporal unishment on pupil passengers.

PUBLIC HEALTH: MASSAGE

3 November 1945

In North Carolina there is no state board before which one must qualify efore engaging in practice as a masseuse. A person so employed is not en- aged in the practice of medicine nor included under our definition of "chiro- ractic." However, a masseuse, as such, is subject to a state license tax.

POLL TAX: EXEMPTION OF SERVICEMEN

5 November 1945

Our exemption of servicemen from the payment of poll tax extends to such ervicemen only for such time as they are in service and, if such persons ere not actually in service at the last listing date, they would be liable to he tax. This exemption is also limited in all cases to the next listing period fter the ending of the existing state of war.

Notaries Public: Expiration of Commission; Power to Act Before Renewal

6 November 1945

A notary public holds office for two years from the date of appointment, excluding the first and including the last day. The two year period runs from the date of appointment but a notary public must qualify as required by statute before he can legally perform notarial duties.

Divorce: Insanity

6 November 1945

Before a divorce may be obtained in North Carolina on grounds of insanity, it must be shown by the plaintiff, among other things, that the husband and wife have lived separate and apart for ten consecutive years without cohabitation and by reason of the incurable insanity of one of them; and that the insane spouse has been confined in an institution for the insane for ten consecutive years.

Criminal Law: Abortion

6 November 1945

It is a felonious offense to procure or in any manner bring about an abortion unless such abortion is necessary to preserve the life of the mother. This is the only exception under our law.

Marriage: Age Requirements

6 November 1945

Under North Carolina law, all male persons sixteen years or more of age, unless otherwise barred, may lawfully marry, and all female persons over fourteen and under sixteen years of age, unless otherwise barred, may marry with the written consent of one parent or a person standing *in loco parentis*. All female persons sixteen years of age or over may legally marry unless otherwise barred.

Bail: Who May Fix

6 November 1945

There is no authority under our law for a sheriff or deputy sheriff to fix or approve bail for a prisoner except in case of a capias issued to such officer by the clerk of the superior court after an indictment has been found.

Bail: Who May Fix

6 November 1945

In North Carolina when a person is charged with a crime but has not been committed to prison, bail may be fixed by any justice of the Supreme Court or judge of the Superior Court in all cases, and also by a justice of the peace or chief magistrate of any incorporated city or town in all except capital cases.

BAIL: WHO MAY FIX

6 November 1945

After a person has been committed to prison in North Carolina, and before trial, a justice of the Supreme Court or a judge of the Superior Court may fix bail in all cases, and a justice of the peace or chief magistrate of any incorporated city or town may fix or approve bail in all but capital cases.

MOTOR VEHICLES: MUNICIPAL TAXATION

6 November 1945

Under our law no county or municipality may levy any license or privilege tax in excess of $1.00 per year upon the use of any motor vehicle licensed by the State. In addition to this $1.00 tax, cities or towns may levy a tax not in excess of $15.00 per year upon each vehicle operated as a taxicab in such city or town.

VETERANS: MINOR SPOUSES OF VETERANS

7 November 1945

Under our law a veteran and his minor spouse may execute a valid instrument of conveyance whenever such instrument is necessary to procure for the veteran any benefit to which he may be entitled under the laws of the United States.

PARTNERSHIPS: BUSINESS UNDER ASSUMED NAME

7 November 1945

Persons engaged in business in North Carolina under an assumed name or designation other than the real name of the individuals owning or conducting such business, are required to file in the office of the clerk of the superior court of the county in which such business is conducted a certificate setting forth the name under which such business is conducted, and the real name and home address of the persons owning the same.

BANKING HOURS

7 November 1945

There is no provision in our statutes which requires a bank to be open at any specific time. The reason for banks maintaining regular hours on all days except Sundays and holidays is to avoid the possibility of liability under the negotiable instrument law.

BANKS: BRANCHES ON MILITARY RESERVATIONS

7 November 1945

A bank operating a branch on a federal military reservation in this State would be compelled to obey the directions of the commanding officer in regard to opening and closing hours, and bank holidays.

EDUCATION: COMPULSORY ATTENDANCE LAW; VENUE

8 November 1945

In case of prosecution of a parent under our compulsory school attendance law, the indictment should be obtained and the trial held in the county where the indicted parent resides, even though the delinquent child attends school in another county.

PRIVATE EXAMINATION OF MARRIED WOMEN ABOLISHED

8 November 1945

The private examination of married women has been abolished in North Carolina in cases where it was heretofore required, and no longer exists as a legal requirement.

UNCONTESTED DIVORCE ACTION

8 November 1945

The provisions of our law to the effect that uncontested cases in which no answer has been filed may be tried at any term after the time for filing an answer has expired, applies to uncontested divorce actions and, in effect, abolishes the requirement of waiting ten days after the time for filing answer expired.

VETERANS: RETURN TO FORMER EMPLOYMENT WITH THE STATE

9 November 1945

The so-called G. I. Bill of Rights guarantees to returning servicemen their former jobs, and, while this Federal Act is not binding on the State of North Carolina, it is the policy of the State to follow this provision of the Federal law as far as it is possible to do so.

LIQUOR: DISPOSITION OF CONFISCATED LIQUOR

9 November 1945

Our law requires that all confiscated or contraband liquor be held until the termination of the trial, and in case of acquital, the liquor is to be returned to the established owner. In case of conviction or failure to appear for trial, the liquor, if non-tax paid, is to be destroyed. In case of tax paid liquor so seized and held, the Board of County Commissioners is authorized to distribute such tax paid liquor to hospitals for medicinal purposes or to sell it to A. B. C. stores within the state, the proceeds going into the school fund.

TAXICABS: MUNICIPAL FRANCHISES

9 November 1945

A municipal corporation may legally refuse to issue a franchise for the operation of a taxicab if, in the judgment of the governing board, the public convenience and necessity does not require it, or if the applicant or operator does not comply with reasonable terms laid down by such governing board as a condition to the granting of such franchise.

TAXICABS: MUNICIPAL REGULATIONS

9 November 1945

A municipality is not authorized to grant an exclusive franchise for the operation of taxicabs, nor may it impose unreasonable or arbitrary conditions upon the granting of franchise for the operation of taxicabs.

MARRIAGE LAWS: VOID AND VOIDABLE MARRIAGES

10 November 1945

Our Supreme Court has said that in North Carolina only two types of attempted marriage are absolutely void from the beginning, these being igamous marriages and marriages between a white person and an Indian r a Negro within the prohibited degree. Other prohibited marriages are erely voidable as distinguished from absolutely void, and are valid until et aside by court decree in a proper action.

CHILDREN OF VOIDABLE MARRIAGE LEGITIMATE

10 November 1945

Children born of a marriage which is voidable but not absolutely void, are eclared by North Carolina law to be legitimate.

MUNICIPALITIES: USE OF SIDEWALK FOR RAILROAD SIDING

13 November 1945

A municipality has the right under our law to permit the use of a public idewalk for the running of a spur track in the city if it finds it desirable nd in the public interest to do so. This does not mean, however, that the ity would not, in proper cases, be liable for damages sustained by an abuting property owner by reason of such use of a sidewalk.

PUBLIC SCHOOLS: LIABILITY OF SCHOOL AUTHORITIES FOR INJURY TO STUDENT

13 November 1945

Under North Carolina law, school authorities are not liable in damages on account of alleged negligence resulting in injury to a student, as authorities such as county boards of education, superintendents of schools and the like are engaged in a governmental function in discharging their official duties, and as governmental agents of the State, cannot be held liable in tort.

TOWN COMMISSIONER NOT REQUIRED TO BE PROPERTY OWNER

13 November 1945

We have no general statute requiring a person to own property or pay taxes in order to be eligible to serve on a Board of Town Commissioners.

DOUBLE OFFICE HOLDING

14 November 1945

Membership on a municipal zoning commission does not constitute office holding within our constitutional prohibition against double office holding and the same person could serve on such a zoning commission and could legally hold office as a member of a Board of Adjustments at the same time. This, however, might result in some conflict of interest between the two positions.

LAW ENFORCEMENT OFFICER: WITNESS FEES

15 November 1945

A law enforcement officer who receives a salary or compensation for his services from any source other than from the collection of fees, shall receive no fee as a witness for attending any court within the territorial jurisdiction in which such officer has authority to make an arrest.

STATE GUARD: VETERANS' PREFERENCE

17 November 1945

The veterans' preference rating of ten per cent on examinations under our State Merit System does not apply to members of the North Carolina State Guard.

CLERK OF SUPERIOR COURT: FEES FOR TRANSCRIPT OF RECORD ON
APPEAL TO SUPREME COURT

17 November 1945

A Clerk of the Superior Court is required to charge the statutory fee of ten cents per copy sheet in case of transcript of record on appeal to the

Supreme Court, irrespective of whether he actually prepares such transcript or merely certifies it. His responsibility is the same in either instance.

INTOXICATING LIQUORS: TRANSPORTATION TO FEDERAL MILITARY RESERVATION OVER WHICH THE STATE HAS CEDED JURISDICTION

19 November 1945

Under our laws intoxicating beverages may be legally consigned and delivered by railway or other common carrier to individuals located on a Federal Military Reservation to which the State has ceded jurisdiction, but the shipment and delivery must be made directly to the Reservation, and may not be delivered to the consignee en route.

ESTATES BY ENTIRETY: EFFECT OF DIVORCE

20 November 1945

A decree of absolute divorce converts an estate by the entirety into a tenancy in common, and the interest of either tenant thereupon becomes subject to execution under a judgment against such tenant.

FIREWORKS: REGULATION

20 November 1945

Our State law authorizes the governing bodies of cities and towns to regulate or prohibit the sale of fireworks within their limits, but this authority does not extend to Boards of County Commissioners.

MOTOR VEHICLES: REVOCATION OF LICENSE UPON CONVICTION IN ANOTHER STATE

21 November 1945

Our Department of Motor Vehicles is authorized to suspend or revoke a North Carolina drivers license upon receiving notice of such driver's conviction in another state of any offense which, if committed in North Carolina, would constitute grounds for suspension or revocation.

HUSBAND AND WIFE: HUSBAND'S LIABILITY FOR HOSPITAL FEES OF INSANE WIFE

21 November 1945

A husband, if living, or his estate in case of his death, is liable under North Carolina law for the actual cost of the care and treatment of an insane wife while an inmate of the State Hospital, and no statute of limitation would run against the State's claim.

HUSBAND AND WIFE: WIFE'S INSANITY; YEAR'S SUPPORT

21 November 1945

A wife's insanity does not impair her right to a distributive share in her husband's estate, nor her right to a year's support.

DOUBLE OFFICE HOLDING: CONSTABLE AND TAX LISTER

28 November 1945

A constable and tax lister are both officers coming within our constitutional prohibition against double office holding, and a person qualifying for one while holding the other vacates the office first held.

TAXICABS: MUNICIPAL REGULATIONS AS AFFECTING STATE INSTITUTIONS

28 November 1945

Municipal corporations have authority to fix rules and regulations governing the licensing and use of taxicabs within such municipalities and officials of a State institution have no authority to change the schedule of rates fixed by a municipal board.

MEDICAL LICENSES: QUALIFICATIONS OF APPLICANT; GROUNDS FOR REFUSAL

29 November 1945

Every applicant for a license to practice medicine or surgery in North Carolina must have attained the age of twenty-one years and be of good moral character before such license can be granted by the Board of Medical Examiners. The qualifications of applicants is a question to be determined by the Board of Medical Examiners and the applicant is entitled to notice and a hearing before an unfavorable decision is rendered against him.

ELECTIONS ON COUNTY A. B. C. STORES: SUFFICIENCY OF PETITIONS

30 November 1945

Our law provides that a petition to a County Board of Elections for the purpose of calling a county election on A. B. C. stores must be signed by at least fifteen per cent of the registered voters in the county who voted in the last election for governor. Thus, a petition signed before the last election for governor could not be used thereafter as a basis for calling a county election on liquor control.

MUNICIPALITIES: ZONING ORDINANCES

· 30 November 1945

A municipality in North Carolina may adopt a zoning ordinance prohibiting the storing of fertilizer in designated sections within the city limits.

LIVE STOCK: SALE FOR IMMEDIATE SLAUGHTER

30 November 1945

Livestock purchased for immediate slaughter may not be resold in North Carolina except to a recognized slaughter plant or to a person, firm or corporation that handles live stock for immediate slaughter only.

NORTH CAROLINA INDUSTRIAL FARM COLONY (DOBBS FARM)

30 November 1945

Our law authorizes the commitment of women to the North Carolina Industrial Farm Colony (Dobbs Farm) in case of conviction or submission to a misdemeanor charge.

MARRIAGE: JUSTICE OF THE PEACE ACTING AS DEPUTY REGISTER OF DEEDS NOT DISQUALIFIED TO PERFORM CEREMONY

3 December 1945

The prohibition in our law which bars a Justice of the Peace who is also Register of Deeds from performing a marriage ceremony does not extend to a Justice of the Peace who is also serving as a Deputy Register of Deeds.

RECORDER'S COURT: AGE REQUIREMENT OF DEPUTY CLERK

4 December 1945

The Deputy Clerk of a Recorder's Court is a public officer under our law and one of the requirements of a public officer in this State is that in order to hold office, a person must have attained the age of twenty-one years.

DOUBLE OFFICE HOLDING: SOLICITOR OF RECORDER'S COURT AND NOTARY PUBLIC

4 December 1945

While a Solicitor of a Recorder's Court and a Notary Public are both officers in North Carolina, an amendment to our State Constitution adopted at the last election specifically exempted Notaries Public from the prohibitory provisions of Article XIV, Section 7 of our Constitution relating to double office holding, so that the same person may not legally hold both positions at the same time.

DEPARTMENT OF AGRICULTURE: SEED LAW; ANALYSIS TAGS

4 December 1945

Our law requires that a seed analysis tag be attached to every container of vegetable seed weighing ten pounds or more which is sold or offered or exposed for sale in this State for planting purposes, and, further, that in case such seed is shipped into this State, the shipper shall secure such tags before shipment is made.

DEPUTY CLERKS OF SUPERIOR COURT: AGE REQUIREMENT

4 December 1945

A Deputy Clerk of Superior Court in North Carolina, being a public officer, must, as one of the qualifications, be at least twenty-one years of age.

MUNICIPALITIES: NECESSARY EXPENSES; PUBLIC BATH HOUSES

4 December 1945

The construction and operation of a public bath house by a municipality is not such an exercise of the governmental function as would justify the levying of taxes without special authorization of the General Assembly and a vote of the people. Neither can surplus funds be used for such a purpose without special authorization from the General Assembly.

VETERANS: CERTIFIED COPIES OF DISCHARGE

6 December 1945

A Register of Deeds is under legal obligation to furnish free of charge to any veteran applying therefor as many certified copies of such veteran's discharge from service as the veteran may require.

DOUBLE OFFICE HOLDING: NOTARY PUBLIC AND JUSTICE OF THE PEACE

6 December 1945

The offices of Justice of the Peace and Notary Public are each specifically exempted from the prohibitory provisions of Article XIV, Section 7 of the State Constitution in respect to double office holding.

REVALUATION OF PROPERTY: POSTPONEMENT

6 December 1945

Under an act of the 1945 General Assembly, Boards of County Commissioners may, in their discretion, defer or postpone revaluation and reassessment of real property for the years 1945 and 1946.

MUNICIPAL CORPORATIONS: WATER SYSTEMS; PURCHASE OF EXISTING SYSTEM

10 December 1945

There is no North Carolina Statute which requires a municipality to purchase a privately owned water system operating within the city limits, but it would have authority to do so if it were found to be proper to make such purchase.

INTOXICATING LIQUORS: BEER; NON TAX PAID BEER IN "DRY" COUNTY;
DISPOSITION OF CONFISCATED LIQUORS

11 December 1945

In a North Carolina county which has not adopted the Alcoholic Beverage
Control Act, the Turlington Act is still in force and under this Act the
possession of non tax paid beer in such a county is unlawful and the beer
subject to confiscation and disposal by the court.

MUNICIPAL CORPORATIONS: TAXATION; DUTY OF MUNICIPALITY TO ACCEPT
VALUATION SET BY COUNTY

12 December 1945

Under our law, all cities and towns not situated in more than one county
are required to accept the tax valuations fixed by the county authorities as
modified by the State Board of Assessments.

FEDERAL TAX STAMP: DEED FROM STATE OF NORTH CAROLINA DOES
NOT REQUIRE

12 December 1945

No Federal Internal Revenue Stamps are required to be attached to
a deed of conveyance made by the State of North Carolina.

UNEMPLOYMENT COMPENSATION: BENEFITS EXEMPTED FROM TAXATION

12 December 1945

In North Carolina, a municipal corporation cannot legally use garnishment for the purpose of collecting or subjecting unemployment benefits to
the payment of taxes.

COUNTIES: AUTHORITY TO SELL PROPERTY WITHOUT PUBLIC SALE

13 December 1945

Under our law, counties are authorized to lease or sell real property and
make deed to any purchaser, and it is not required that all such sales be
public sales.

COUNTIES: AUTHORITY TO DONATE CITE TO SCHOOL DISTRICT

13 December 1945

Where a county has property available for a school cite, it may donate
such property to a school district instead of providing funds for the purchase of other property.

MEMBERSHIP ON CUONTY BOARD OF HEALTH

13 December 1945

The circumstance that a person is a medical doctor would not bar him from appointment as a member of a county board of health as being "one who shall be a public spirited citizen," even though such appointment should result in having two physicians on the board.

PUBLIC HEALTH: ABATTOIR; RULES OF STATE BOARD OF HEALTH

15 December 1945

Anyone customarily engaged in the slaughtering of livestock for others and charging a fee therefor is subject to the rules and regulations of the State Board of Health governing the operation of such business, and a violation of such rules and regulations would constitute a violation of our criminal law.

TAXATION: AD VALOREM; RELEASE OF SEPARATE PARCELS

15 December 1945

Under North Carolina law, when a lien of taxes of any taxing unit for any year attaches to two or more parcels of real estate owned by one tax payer, the lien may be discharged at any time before advertisement upon payment of the taxes for such year upon the parcel sought to be released, with interest and penalties thereon, plus a proportionate part of the personal property, dog and poll taxes owed by the tax payer for the same year, with interest and penalities thereon, and a proportionate part of the costs prescribed by law.

EMERGENCY WAR POWERS OF GOVERNOR EXTENDED

10 December 1945

Our 1945 General Assembly extended the emergency war powers of the Governor so as to cover the duration of the then existing state of war and a six months period thereafter.

CLAIMS AGAINST THE STATE

17 December 1945

There is nothing in our law which prohibits an individual from having a Bill introduced in our Legislature to compensate him for a loss incurred or to satisfy a claim against the State.

GOVERNOR: VETO POWER

17 December 1945

The Governor of North Carolina does not have the veto power.

Beer and Wine: Sale of Unfortified Wine

17 December 1945

Unfortified wine containing not less than five nor more than fourteen per cent absolute alcohol, reckoned by volume, may be sold in any county in North Carolina in which such sale is not prohibited by a Public Local Act or by action of the local governing bodies under the authority of the Legislature.

Intoxicating Liquor: Bringing Into North Carolina from Out of the State

18 December 1945

Under our law, a person may purchase legally outside of this State and bring into this State for his own personal use not more than one gallon of intoxicating liquor.

Executors and Administrators: Bonds of Executors

20 December 1945

In North Carolina, a resident executor is not required to give bond unless the will itself requires him to do so, except where he obtains an order to sell real estate for the payment of debts, or unless he marries a woman who is an executrix.

Veterans: Local Agencies Financed by Counties, Cities or Towns

20 December 1945

Our Statutes authorize counties, cities and towns to make appropriations out of the general funds to establish and maintain local veterans' service agencies in order to carry out the provisions of the Act creating the North Carolina Veterans' Commission.

Fees of State Highway Patrolmen

27 December 1945

All fees for arrest or service of process that may be taxed in the bill of costs for the various courts of the State on account of the official acts of members of the State Highway Patrol shall be remitted to the general fund of the county in which said cost is taxed.

Motor Vehicle Laws: Owner Permitting Operation of Car by Person Under Influence of Intoxicating Liquors

21 December 1945

If the owner of a motor vehicle knowingly permits a person under the influence of intoxicating liquor to operate a motor vehicle, the owner is guilty of a criminal offense under North Carolina law.

ATTORNEYS AT LAW: DRAWING DEEDS FOR CONVEYANCE OF OWN PROPERTY BY PERSON NOT AN ATTORNEY AT LAW

29 December 1945

There is no provision of our law which prohibits the owner of property from drawing a deed disposing of his own property, even though such owner is not an attorney at law. This right, however, does not extend to any transaction in which such person is not the actual owner of the property conveyed.

TAXATION: EXEMPTION OF FARM PRODUCTS

31 December 1945

In North Carolina, all farm products, both those considered as money crops and otherwise, owned by the original producer or held by him for any cooperative marketing or growers' association are exempt from taxation for the year following that year in which such products were grown, but not for any year thereafter.

INTOXICATING LIQUORS: TAXPAID LIQUOR; "DRY" COUNTY; POSSESSION; TRANSPORTATION; POSSESSION FOR THE PURPOSE OF SALE

15 December 1945

When an individual leaves his home in a "dry" county, going to another point in said county, carrying in his automobile taxpaid liquor, he is guilty of the illegal transportation of liquor and the illegal possession of liquor. The possession of the liquor will, by reason of the presumption created by the Statute, support a verdict and judgment for the illegal possession of liquor for the purpose of sale.

BAD CHECK LAW; PROCURING OF THE ISSUANCE OF WORTHLESS CHECKS FOR THE PURPOSE OF ENFORCING COLLECTION OF DEBT

28 December 1945

The procuring of the issuance of worthless checks for the purpose of securing the payment of small loans at usurious interest rates constitutes a violation of the Small Loan Law of this State, and anyone engaged in the practice of making small loans and procuring the issuance of worthless checks as security therefor, would not only be criminally liable under the Small Loan Law but would also be liable for the State tax imposed upon persons engaged in the small loan business.

Furthermore, such person procuring the issuance of worthless checks under such circumstances, knowing the same to be worthless when drawn, would be subject to indictment as having aided and abetted the issuance of a worthless check.

MUNICIPAL CORPORATIONS: SALE OF REAL PROPERTY

3 January 1946

In North Carolina a municipal corporation is authorized to sell its real property at public outcry to the highest bidder after thirty days notice and this method of disposing of real estate or other property of a municipality must be followed. This rule does not apply, however, to property held in trust by a municipal corporation for public purposes, which can be sold only as authorized by a secial act of the Legislature, or to public utilities, which can be sold only after a vote of the people.

TAXICABS: MUNICIPALITIES REQUIRING CABS TO OPERATE FROM TAXI STANDS

3 January 1946

A municipal corporation in North Carolina may require taxicabs to operate from taxi stands.

MUNICIPALITIES: POLICE OFFICER MAY NOT ARREST OUT OF CORPORATE LIMITS; EXCEPTION

3 January 1946

In the absence of a Public Local Act to the contrary, a municipal police officer does not have authority in North Carolina to make an arrest outside of the corporate limits. The only exception to this rule is the case of hot pursuit of a violator of the prohibition law, in which case the officer may press the pursuit beyond the corporate limits and even into another county and make the arrest.

INTOXICATING BEVERAGE; SALE ON AIRPLANES FLYING OVER STATE

3 January 1946

With the exception of beer or wine with not more than 14% alcoholic content, sold by a licensed retailer, no alcoholic beverage of any kind may lawfully be sold in any airplane passing over or through the State of North Carolina.

SCHOOLS: RESIGNATION NOTICE OF TEACHERS OR PRINCIPALS

8 January 1946

In North Carolina school teachers or principals desiring to resign are required to give at least thirty days notice prior to the opening of the school in which they are employed. This notice must be given to the official head of the respective administrative unit.

DOUBLE OFFICE HOLDING: CHAIRMAN OF BOARD OF ELECTIONS AND
, PUBLIC ADMINISTRATOR

9 January 1946

A public administrator is not the holder of a public office within our constitutional prohibition against holding more than one public office at the same time.

MUNICIPAL ORDINANCES: WATER RATES; MINIMUM CHARGES

10 January 1946

The authority granted municipalities by our statutes to fix and enforce water rates carries with it the authority to fix a minimum charge to be paid by all consumers.

AUCTIONEERS: DEPUTY SHERIFF ACTING AS AUCTIONEER

11 January 1946

There is no such public office under our statutes as public auctioneer, and no authority for the appointment of such an official by a board of county commissioners. Therefore, a deputy sheriff acting as auctioneer would not be guilty of double office holding.

COUNTIES: EXTRADITION; ATTORNEY FEES FOR APPEARANCE IN ANOTHER STATE

14 January 1946

There is no authority under our law for a board of county commissioners to pay the fee of an attorney who represents the State of North Carolina in an extradition hearing in another state, even though he appears at the request of a district solicitor of North Carolina.

MERIT SYSTEM COUNCIL: VETERANS' PREFERENCE RATING; MERCHANT MARINE AND RED CROSS

15 January 1946

Persons serving in the United States Merchant Marine or the American Red Cross Overseas Service are not entitled to any veterans' preference under the laws of the State of North Carolina.

RURAL ELECTRIFICATION LINES: EXEMPTION FROM TAXATION

16 January 1946

There is no authority under North Carolina law for the taxation of electric lines owned by municipalities, even though they may serve rural districts, and these properties, like any other municipal property used for governmental purposes, are exempt from taxation.

DOUBLE OFFICE HOLDING: PENALTY; CHIEF OF POLICE AND DEPUTY SHERIFF

19 January 1946

A Chief of Police and a deputy sheriff are both holders of a public office within our constitutional prohibition against double office holding, and a person presuming to hold both offices at the same time would be subject to a forfeiture of $200.00.

TAXATION: COSTS IN CRIMINAL CASES; CREDIT OF COSTS AGAINST TAX ACCOUNT OF CLAIMANT

21 January 1946

In the absence of a local act, it is unlawful for a board of county commissioners to pay any person who is indebted to the county for taxes any money payment out of county revenue on account of costs in a criminal case when the person to whom such costs are due owes the county for taxes.

VITAL STATISTICS: DUTY OF STATE REGISTRAR TO FURNISH CERTIFIED COPY OF BIRTH CERTIFICATE WITHOUT CHARGE

21 January 1946

Under our law, the State Registrar is required to furnish, within three months of the birth and without charge, a certified copy of all birth certificates to the mother of each child or to the person standing in the place of the parents.

COURTS: JURY; EXEMPTION OF MEMBERS OF FIRE DEPARTMENT

21 January 1946

All active members of a fire department, either paid or volunteer, are exempt from jury duty in North Carolina.

SCHOOLS: LIABILITY OF STATE AND COUNTY IN CONNECTION WITH OPERATION OF SCHOOL BUS

21 January 1946

Neither the State nor any of its agencies can be sued by a citizen without the State's consent, and such consent has not been given in connection with injuries arising out of the operation of school busses.

SCHOOLS: CLAIMS ARISING OUT OF INJURIES IN CONNECTION WITH OPERATION OF SCHOOL BUSSES

21 January 1946

Liability of of the State under claims arising out of injuries resulting from the operation of school busses is confined to the statutory authority given the State Board of Education to pay compensation in certain cases of injury suffered by children as a result of operation of school busses.

SCHOOLS: OPERATION OF SCHOOL BUSSES; COUNTY BOARD OF EDUCATION; LIABILITY

21 January 1946

A County Board of Education is not liable for, nor can it legally pay damages for injuries sustained in connection with the operation of school busses.

DEPARTMENT OF AGRICULTURE: STATE TAX ON FEED STUFFS SHIPPED FROM OUTSIDE OF THE STATE INTO A MILITARY RESERVATION WITHIN THE STATE

23 January 1946

This State cannot collect a feed tax on shipments of feed stuffs from outside the State into a military reservation within this State to which the State has ceded jurisdiction to the Federal Government.

GAME LAWS: EXEMPTION OF TENANT OR SHARE CROPPER FROM LICENSE REQUIREMENT

7 January 1946

In North Carolina, a tenant or share cropper can legally hunt on the land which he rents without a State hunting license.

TAXATION: PENALTY FOR FAILURE TO LIST PERSONAL OR REAL PROPERTY

7 January 1946

In the application of penalties under our tax laws there is no distinction drawn between late listing of personal and real property and failure to list at all. The penalties apply equally in either case. Neither is there any distinction in this respect between real or personal property; and in each case, the aplication of the penalties is mandatory whenever the terms of the Statutes have been violated.

ADOPTION LAWS: CHILD OF NON-RESIDENT MOTHER IN THIS STATE

8 January 1946

A child born in North Carolina of a non-resident mother who came into this State prior to or during pregnancy would not be subject to the so-called interstate placement provisions of our law.

CRIMINAL LAW: PERMIT ISSUED BY ANOTHER STATE TO CARRY CONCEALED
WEAPON

24 January 1946

North Carolina does not recognize permits or licenses, issued by other
states, to carry concealed weapons; our courts taking the view that such
permits or licenses are valid only within the territorial limits of the state
issuing them.

CRIMINAL LAW: COSTS; JUSTICE OF THE PEACE. FRIVOLOUS AND MALICIOUS
PROSECUTION; RIGHTS OF APPEAL FROM ORDER TAXING PROSECUTING
WITNESS WITH COSTS

25 January 1946

Where, upon a finding by a Justice of the Peace that there is no probable
cause in a criminal action, or that the prosecution is frivolous and malicious,
an order is issued taxing the prosecuting witness with the costs, the prose-
cutor has the right of appeal to the Superior Court from such other order,
upon the questions of whether he shall pay the costs, or whether the prosecution was frivolous and malicious. Pending the final outcome of such
appeal, the costs need not be paid.

MOTOR VEHICLES: SUSPENSION OF LICENSE FOR FAILURE TO SATISFY
JUDGMENT; DURATION OF SUSPENSION

29 January 1946

It is not lawful for the Department of Motor Vehicles to restore or renew
an operator's license which has been suspended for failure to satisfy a
judgment until is satisfied or discharged, or until the operator has given
proof under the statute of his ability to respond in damages for future
accidents.

ELECTIONS: SPECIAL ELECTIONS; BOND ISSUE; TIME FOR HOLDING

2 February 1946

Under our law, no special bond election may be held within one calendar
month before or after a regular election.

BEER & WINE: CANCELLATION OF LICENSE; EFFECT

2 February 1946

Whenever any license for the sale of beer or wine issued by a municipality,
a board of county commissioners, or the Commissioner of Revenue has been
revoked, it is unlawful to re-issue a license for said premises to any person
within a term of six months after such revocation.

DEPARTMENT OF AGRICULTURE: AUTHORITY TO ESTABLISH AND FINANCE A TOBACCO ADVISORY COUNCIL

2 February 1946

If the Board of Agriculture determines that it is necessary to set up a Tobacco Advisory Council within the Department of Agriculture as one of the mediums through which the department and the commissioner may properly function, such a council may be legally established and the director of the budget has authority to provide funds to finance it.

ALCOHOLIC BEVERAGES: SALE BY CHARTERED CLUBS

2 February 1946

There is no provision under our law by which a club, chartered or otherwise, can legally sell alcoholic drinks to its members or to the public.

STATE EMPLOYEES: VACATION

4 February 1946

State employees are allowed vacation leave at the rate of one day for each full month worked during the fiscal year. This vacation leave is not cumulative and must be used, if at all, before January first of the succeeding year.

STATE EMPLOYEES: SICK LEAVE

4 February 1946

State employees are entitled to ten days sick leave per year, and this sick leave is cumulative from year to year. No employee is entitled to any pay for sick leave not used, and all rights in respect to sick leave terminate on resignation or dismissal.

TAXICABS: OPERATING PERMITS; ISSUANCE TO FELONS

6 February 1946

Our statutes give to the governing bodies of municipalities the right to refuse to issue, in their discretion, permits for the operation of taxicabs to persons who have been convicted of a felony.

SCHOOLS: CREATION OF NEW CITY ADMINISTRATIVE UNIT

12 February 1946

Under our School Machinery Act, the only way a new city administrative unit can be legally created is by specific authority through an act of the General Assembly.

MUNICIPAL CORPORATIONS: PUBLIC CONTRACTS IN EXCESS OF $5,000; DIVISION OF CONTRACTS INTO INTEGRAL PARTS

12 February 1946

Our statutes require that all public contracts in excess of $5,000 entered into by municipalities shall be advertised and awarded upon proposals submitted upon the terms of such advertisement, and no bill or contract shall be divided for the purpose of evading this provision of our law.

PHYSICIANS & SURGEONS: CITIZENSHIP NOT REQUIRED AS PREREQUISITE TO PRACTICE

12 February 1946

There is no citizenship requirement as a prerequisite to the practice of medicine in North Carolina.

PUBLIC OFFICERS: STATE HIGHWAY PATROL; DUTY TO REFER CASES ON INTOXICATING LIQUOR TO STATE COURTS

12 February 1946

All state and local law enforcement officers, including State Highway Patrolmen, are required by law to refer all cases involving intoxicating liquor to a state court in the jurisdiction where the case arises. Failure to do so amounts to malfeasance in office and subjects the officer to indictment and a fine of $100.

CORONERS: REMOVAL OF BODIES BEFORE NOTIFICATION OF CORONER

12 February 1946

The bodies of persons who have been killed accidentally may legally be removed from the scene of such accident and prepared for burial, as there is no general provision in our statutes requiring that the coroner must be notified before any dead body can be removed. The coroner's duties in this respect are chiefly confined to persons killed by the criminal act or default of another, and there is no necessity of an inquest if the coroner is satisfied that the death was not the result of foul play or criminal negligence.

MUNICIPALITIES: PURCHASE OF HOUSES FROM THE FEDERAL GOVERNMENT FOR RESALE

12 February 1946

We have no statute specifically authorizing a municipality to invest public funds in the purchase of houses from the Federal Government or other sources for the purpose of resale, rental, or lease; nor is there any legal means by which a municipality could purchase such houses for resale, rental or lease other than through a duly constituted housing authority.

MUNICIPALITIES: HOUSING AUTHORITIES; SALE OF HOMES TO VETERANS

12 February 1946

A duly constituted housing authority would have the right to sell houses exclusively to veterans who provide vacant lots on which to place them, as the service of veterans during wartime is such a public service as to include them in the constitutional eexmption from the rule against exclusive emoluments and privileges.

PUBLIC HEALTH: CONFLICT BETWEEN MILK ORDINANCE OF THE COUNTY BOARD OF HEALTH AND A MUNICIPALITY

13 February 1946

In case of any conflict between a county-wide milk ordinance passed by a county board of health and a milk ordinance passed by a municipality within such county, the provisions of the county ordinance are controlling, and any difference between the two must be resolved in favor of the county ordinance.

INTOXICATING LIQUOR: SALE OF CONFISCATED VEHICLE SUBJECT TO OPA CEILING PRICE

14 February 1946

In cases where an OPA ceiling price exists on a vehicle confiscated for violation of our liquor laws, such sale price is valid and binding even as to such sale of such confiscated vehicle by an ABC board or other state or local governmental agency.

LICENSE TAX: SCHEDULE B; VETERANS EXEMPTION

14 February 1946

A board of county commissioners, upon proper application, may exempt from the state peddlers tax disabled veterans of the second world war who have been residents of North Carolina for twelve months or more, and cities and towns are prohibited from imposing any peddlers tax upon a veteran so exempt. This exemption, however, does not extend beyond the limits of the county in which it is granted.

MUNICIPALITIES: TAXICABS; EXCLUSIVE FRANCHISES

14 February 1946

In North Carolina, a municipality is not authorized to issue exclusive franchises for the operation of taxicabs within such municipality, but may, in its discretion, refuse to issue franchises to taxicab operators when the public convenience and necessity does not require the operation of such a cab.

ELECTIONS: NOTARIES PUBLIC SERVING AS REGISTRARS

14 February 1946

While the recent amendment of Art. XIV, Section 7 of our State Constitution exempts Notaries Public from the prohibition against holding more than one public office, it does not declare that Notaries Public are no longer to be considered public officers. Therefore, Notaries Public as public officers still come under the provisions of the statute prohibiting any public officer, except a Justice of the Peace, from serving as an election official.

MUNICIPALITIES: TAXICABS; REGULATION

14 February 1946

In North Carolina, cities and towns have the power to license, regulate and control drivers and operators of taxicabs within the city or town limits, and to regulate and control operators of taxicabs operating between cities and towns to points not incorporated within a radius of five miles of such city or town.

MAYOR'S COURT: AUTHORITY TO IMPOSE JAIL SENTENCE; AUTHORITY TO SUSPEND SENTENCE

14 February 1946

A mayor's court may, in cases over which it has jurisdiction, sentence a defendant to jail for a period of thirty days to be worked under the supervision of the State Highway Commission. Such a court also has inherent authority to suspend its sentences.

MUNICIPALITIES: TOWN CONSTABLE ACTING AS TAX COLLECTOR

14 February 1946

A town constable may legally serve also as town tax collector without violating the constitutional prohibition against holding more than one public office.

TAXATION: AD VALOREM; EXEMPTION; DATE ON WHICH OWNERSHIP DETERMINES TAXABILITY

16 February 1946

In North Carolina, all property subject to ad valorem tax shall be listed and assessed in accordance with its ownership and value as of the first day of January of each year.

SCHOOLS: APPOINTMENT OF LOCAL COMMITTEE; INCREASING MEMBERSHIP

16 February 1946

Our statutes require that the County Board of Education bi-biennially during the month of April, or as soon thereafter as practicable, appoint a local school committee for each of the several districts, each such committee to consist of not less than three nor more than five persons for each district, to serve for a term of two years. After such a committee has been appointed, its number cannot legally be increased, although the County Board of Education is authorized to fill any vacancy on such a local committee.

MARRIAGE: AGE

16 February 1946

Under our statutes, the legal minimum age for marriage is sixteen years. However, if either party is under eighteen years of age, formal consent of the parent or person standing in the place of the parent must be obtained.

MARRIAGE: AGE; WAITING PERIOD

16 February 1946

In North Carolina there is no State-wide requirement as to any waiting period between the application for and the issuance of a marriage license, but in the counties of Dare, Tyrrell, Washington, Martin, Beaufort, Hyde, Pamlico, Camden, Currituck, Chowan, Gates, Pasquotank, Perquimans, Hertford and Bertie, no Register of Deeds may issue a license to any two persons, both of whom are nonresidents of North Carolina, unless application for such has been on file in the office of the Register of Deeds for at least forty-eight hours.

MORTGAGES: HOUSEHOLD AND KITCHEN FURNITURE; COMBINATION
RADIO-PHONOGRAPH

19 February 1945

A combination radio-phonograph is such an article of household furniture as to require the joinder of the wife in the execution of a mortgage thereon; further, such an article of furniture could be claimed and set aside as part of one's personal property exemption under our State Constitution.

EXECUTORS & ADMINISTRATORS: NONRESIDENT CORPORATIONS AS FIDUCIARIES

20 February 1946

A corporation created under the laws of another state or by any foreign government is not eligible to qualify in this state as executor, administrator, guardian, or trustee under the will of any person domiciled in this State at the time of death.

DUCATION: COUNTY BOARD OF EDUCATION; RIGHT TO DETERMINE SCHOOL IN WHICH CHILD IS ENROLLED

20 February 1946

Under our school law, a county board of education has the right to designate the schools in the county administrative unit which the various children, residing in the county administrative unit, shall attend, subject to the right of the State Board of Education to transfer pupils from one district r unit to another in the interest of economy and convenience in the operation f the schools.

EDUCATION: COUNTY BOARD OF EDUCATION; AUTHORITY TO DETERMINE SCHOOLS TO WHICH CHILDREN OF DIFFERENT RACES ARE TO BE ADMITTED

20 February 1946

It is a proper function of a county board of education to determine the racial status of a child for the purpose of assignment to the proper school within the county administrative unit.

COURTS: COUNTY RECORDER'S COURTS; AUTHORITY TO APPOINT VICE-RECORDER

20 February 1946

A board of county commissioners, as the governing body of a county, has the authority to appoint an assistant or vice-recorder to serve in a county recorder's court.

DEPARTMENT OF AGRICULTURE: INSPECTION OF BAKERIES

20 February 1946

Our bakery inspection law applies only to regular bakeries, as the term is commonly known and used, and does not include the right to inspect hotels, restaurants and other places producing their own bakery products specifically for sale with meals served in dining rooms or restaurants directly connected with the establishments making such bakery products.

MUNICIPAL CORPORATIONS: CEMETERIES; RIGHT TO ACQUIRE

21 February 1946

Our statutes authorize municipalities to purchase and hold land within or without the corporate limits but not exceeding fifty acres for the purpose of a cemetery. The use of public funds for the perpetual care of such cemeteries is also authorized.

ELECTIONS: DEPUTY SHERIFF MAY NOT SERVE AS REGISTRAR

22 February 1946

A deputy sheriff is a public officer and may not legally serve as a registrar or judge of election.

MUNICIPALITIES: RIGHT TO CONSTRUCT POST OFFICE FOR RENTAL PURPOSES

22 February 1946

A municipality has no legal authority to construct a building to be rented as a post office, as this is no responsibility of the municipality and public funds could not legally be expended for such purposes.

SCHOOLS: SUPPLEMENTS; ELECTION PROCEDURE

23 February 1946

There are three major preliminary steps required in order to obtain an election on the question of a local supplement in a county administrative school unit:

First, there must be a petition of the district committee;

Second, there must be approval by the county board of elections;

Third, the approval by the tax levying authority of the county and the State Board of Education. After these requirements have been met, then the county board of education must request the board of county commissioners to call and provide for the election.

CLERK OF SUPERIOR COURT: VACANCY; APPOINTMENT; ELECTION TO FILL VACANCY FOR UNEXPIRED TERM

25 February 1946

A clerk of superior court who is appointed to fill a vacancy and then elected in other than a regular election year, is not elected for a four year term but for the unexpired term, and if he is to continue to serve, must stand for reelection and be reelected at the next succeeding general election.

MINORS: LIMITATION AS TO ENTERING DANCE HALLS WHERE BEER AND WINE ARE SOLD

25 February 1946

North Carolina cities and towns have authority to license, prohibit, and regulate pool and billiard rooms and dance halls in the interest of public morals, and an ordinance regulating or prohibiting the attendance of minors at dance halls where beer and wine are sold would come within this authority.

NAME: RESUMPTION OF MAIDEN NAME BY WOMAN AFTER DIVORCE; FOREIGN DIVORCES

27 February 1946

Our statute authorizing a divorced woman to resume her maiden name applies only to women who are divorced in this state; however, such divorced woman could file a petition and have her name changed under the general statutes providing for the change of names of individuals. Under these statutes the divorcee could have her name changed to her maiden name.

WEAPONS: PISTOLS; PERMITS TO CARRY; NON-RESIDENT'S RIGHT TO CARRY IN AUTOMOBILE

1 March 1946

There is no law in North Carolina which authorizes the issuance of a permit to carry a pistol, and non-residents as well as residents are subject to indictment for carrying a weapon concealed about the person when off their own premises.

ADMINISTRATORS: APPOINTMENTS; PERSONS REPORTED DEAD BY WAR AND NAVY DEPARTMENTS

5 March 1946

A Clerk of Superior Court has authority to appoint an administrator if he is satisfied of the death of a person whose estate is to be administered, and official communication from the War or Navy Department would be evidence to be considered by the Clerk in reaching his conclusion as ot death. However, should it later develop that the person is actually alive, the action f the clerk would be void.

MARRIAGE: DEGREE OF KINSHIP; DOUBLE FIRST COUSINS MAY NOT MARRY

5 March 1946

Our statutes prohibit marriage between persons nearer of kin than first ousins, and specifically provides that double first cousins may not marry.

TRADEMARKS: REGISTRATION; EFFECT

6 March 1946

Under North Carolina laws, the registration of a trademark in this State rotects the owner in the use of the registered name or trademark within his State but not beyond our boundaries.

TAXATION: AD VALOREM; PERSONAL PROPERTY TAX FOR PRIOR YEARS DOES
NOT ATTACH TO SUBSEQUENTLY ACQUIRED REAL PROPERTY

9 March 1946

Under our law personal property taxes listed for a prior year do not attach to and become a lien on real property subsequently acquired.

REGISTER OF DEEDS: VACANCIES; PERIOD FOR WHICH APPOINTMENT MADE

9 March 1946

When a vacancy occurs in the office of Register of Deeds, the Board of County Commissioners is required to fill the vacancy by appointment of a successor for the unexpired term. Such appointee would not have to stand for re-election until the expiration of the unexpired term of his predecessor.

BOARD OF COUNTY COMMISSIONERS: DUTY TO PROVIDE AND MAINTAIN
NECESSARY COUNTY BUILDINGS

14 March 1946

Our statutes place upon the several boards of county commissioners the responsibility of providing and maintaining necessary county buildings, and such boards are indictable for failure or refusal to keep and maintain in good and sufficient repair a county courthouse.

COUNTY HOME: INMATES; DISCIPLINE

14 March 1946

A board of county commissioners has no authority to transfer an unruly inmate of the county home to the county jail. Such an inmate would be liable to indictment for violation of the criminal law, but the extent of the board of county commissioners' right to discipline him would be to exclude him from the home.

DOUBLE OFFICE HOLDING: REGISTRAR; MEMBER OF TOWNSHIP PUBLIC
SCHOOL COMMITTEE

15 March 1946

A member of a township public school committee, being a public office holder, cannot serve as registrar in an election .

SCHOOLS: CITY ADMINISTRATIVE UNITS; ALTERATION OF BOUNDARIES

1 April 1946

The State Board of Education is authorized to alter the boundaries of any city administrative unit when the board is of the opinion that such change is desirable in the interest of an improved administration of the school.. However, a vote of the residents within the new territory would be necessary before any supplementary school tax could be imposed on them.

MUNICIPALITIES: EXTENSION OF CORPORATE LIMITS

3 April 1946

The corporate limits of a municipality can be extended by an act of the legislature without a vote of the people, although it is customary for the question to be submitted to a vote of both the residents of the proposed new territory and of those residing within the old boundaries.

BEVERAGE CONTROL ACT: WHOLESALER FURNISHING FREE BEER TO RETAILER AS COMPENSATION FOR ADVERTISING SPACE

8 April 1946

A wholesaler dealing in beer may not lawfully furnish a retailer with free beer as compensation for the privilege of placing advertising signs on the licensed premises of the retailer.

JUSTICES OF THE PEACE: DELIVERY OF BOOKS AND PAPERS TO CLERK OF SUPERIOR COURT

12 April 1946

When a vacancy exists in the office of a justice of the peace from death or other cause, such former justice of the peace, if living, or otherwise his personal representative, shall deliver to the clerk of Superior Court all official dockets, records, papers and books for delivery by the clerk of Superior Court to the person succeeding such justice of the peace.

ENTRIES: SUBMERGED LAND

12 April 1946

Under our statutes, land covered with navigable waters are not subject to grant, except to a limited extent for the purpose of providing wharves.

STATE HOSPITALS FOR INSANE: ORDINANCES; MOTOR VEHICLES; SPEED REGULATIONS

15 April 1946

The board of directors of the State Hospital for the Insane at Raleigh has statutory authority to enact and enforce ordinances regulating conduct n the hospital premises, and the violation of any such ordinance is a misdeaeanor. This authority is broad enough to include an ordinance fixing the peed limit of motor vehicles on hospital property at fifteen miles per hour.

ELECTIONS: PERSON FILING FOR JUDGE OF RECORDER'S COURT AND
JUSTICE OF PEACE

15 April 1946

Our State Constitution specifically exempts justices of the peace from the prohibitoin against holding more than one public office at the time, so that there is nothing in our law to prevent a person from running for the office of justice of the peace and judge of a recorder's court at one and the same time.

REPORT OF THE DIRECTOR OF THE BUREAU OF INVESTIGATION TO THE ATTORNEY GENERAL FOR THE BIENNIUM JULY 1, 1944 TO JULY 1, 1946

The State Bureau of Investigation was established on July 1, 1939. This report covers the sixth and seventh years of its activities.

During a great part of 1944 and 1945 while our nation was at war the Bureau operated with only five agents for field duty. In May, 1946 one of its agents who had been in military service returned for duty with the Bureau. Also in May, we employed one additional agent and in June another agent was employed making now available for field duty eight agents.

During the war years our facilities for firearms identification were interrupted, since our ballistics expert was on leave of absence in the service of the United States Army. He has now returned and we are able to furnish qualified expert service to law enforcement in this State, not only in ballistics examination but also in the problems involving questioned documents. The Bureau is called upon from time to time to include comparison of handwriting, typewriting and printing, erasures and alterations, obliterations, secret writings, comparison of papers, inks, and writing instruments, which we are now able to render to law enforcement and State agencies by having on our Staff a qualified expert in this field of police science.

The requests received by the Bureau for chemical analyses are conducted by Dr. Haywood M. Taylor, Pathologist and Toxicologist of Duke University. The requests for this type service includes the examination of blood, vital human organs, liquids, and foods, as well as other materials. Such examinations are valuable in cases of poison, rape, murder, hit-and-run driving, and other crimes. Dr. Taylor has rendered a most valuable service to our Bureau and to the progress of law enforcement in this State.

We now have six fingerprint experts who have a thorough knowledge of the various methods of obtaining latent fingerprints and are prepared to do this work in the field at the scene of crime. In the small police departments and rural areas where they do not have fingerprint experts our men have been able to render valuable service to these law enforcement agencies. These men are also skilled in photography in criminal investigations and they have been able to make photographs at the scene of the crime before time has permitted physical changes and this has proved exceedingly beneficial to the solicitors in prosecuting cases where major crimes have been committed.

The Bureau is now sending to each law enforcement agency including police, sheriffs, State Highway Patrol, and Federal Bureau of Investigation a Weekly Bulletin keeping all law enforcement agencies informed on the crimes committed in all parts of the State so that a department who may arrest an individual with property believed to have been stolen, will have knowledge of where it was stolen so that immediately the agency can be notified. In this manner we are serving as a clearing house for the various agencies and they send to us items they want included on the Weekly Bulletin which goes out to all law enforcement agencies in the State each week.

All assistance and service rendered by the State Bureau of Investigation is without cost to local law enforcement agencies throughout the State, since provision is made by the Legislature for this purpose.

In this reconstruction period law enforcement in this State will be faced with many problems in using the experiences of the past to guide us in our planning for the future. We believe there will continue to be an increase in crime. The services of the State Bureau of Investigation can be not only of great service to the other law enforcement agencies of this State but to the citizenship who are the ones who suffer in the taking of life, the theft and destruction of property. It shall be our aim and purpose to cooperate fully and actively assist the other law enforcement agencies in giving the very best possible protection to life and property of all the citizens of North Carolina.

On behalf of the Staff, may we express our genuine appreciation for the splendid cooperation rendered by the administrative officers, judges, solicitors, law enforcement officers, and law abiding citizens of the State of North Carolina.

The following classification of crime has been adopted by the Bureau and all cases received and investigated have been assigned thereunder:

CRIME CLASSIFICATION

A. Assault..
               1. Simple Assault
               2. A.D.W. with Intent to Kill
               3. Assault with Intent to Commit Rape
               4. All Others

B. Burglary-Breaking
   and Entering
               1. First Degree (occupied)
               2. Second Degree (unoccupied-safecracking)

E. Embezzlement-
   Fraud
               1. Embezzlement
               2. Forgery
               3. Worthless Checks
               4. Extortion
               5. All Others

H. Homicide..
               1. First Degree Murder
               2. Second Degree Murder
               3. Manslaughter
               4. Suspicious Death

L. Larceny
               1. Auto
               2. All Others

R. Robbery.
S. Sex Offenses
               (person)
               1. Rape
               2. Abortion
               3. Adultery and Fornication

      4. Bastardy
      5. Bigamy
      6. Buggery
      7. Incest
      8. Prostitution
      9. Seduction
    10. All Others

M. Miscellaneous.   1. Arson
      2. Bribery
      3. Buying or Receiving Stolen Property
      4. Conspiracy
      5. Perjury
      6. Possession Burglar Tools
      7. Trespass
      8. Unlawful Use or Possession Explosives
      9. Weapons
    10. Abandonment and Non-support
    11. Escape
    12. Abduction
    13. Poisoning
    14. Resisting Arrest
    15. Riot
    16. Anonymous Letters
    17. Pure Food and Drug Laws
    18. Prohibition Laws
    19. Motor Vehicle Laws
    20. Gambling and Lottery
    21. Parole Violation
    22. Probation Violation
    23. Election Laws
    24. All Others

The following statement shows new, old, and miscellaneous cases investigated and closed for each month during the period from July 1, 1944 to July 1, 1945:

| | NEW CASES | | OLD CASES | | MISCELLANEOUS CASES |
	Investigated	Closed	Investigated	Closed	Investigated and Closed
July	22	15	8	4	22
August	37	20	10	3	22
September	21	11	9	2	23
October	23	16	12	3	12
November	27	11	14	8	10
December	19	12	13	7	13
January	25	13	10	4	15
February	25	14	11	7	5
March	24	19	8	4	11
April	25	12	11	8	10
May	22	13	9	7	10
June	34	16	6	3	12
Totals	304	172	121	60	165

The following statement shows new, old, and miscellaneous cases investigated and closed for each month during the period from July 1, 1945 to July 1, 1946:

| | NEW CASES | | OLD CASES | | MISCELLANEOUS CASES |
	Investigated	Closed	Investigated	Closed	Investigated and Closed
July	18	7	12	4	12
August	27	14	10	4	10
September	23	13	5	1	16
October	23	11	8	5	13
November	25	15	4	1	12
December	21	12	6	1	11
January	18	5	10	4	15
February	21	7	6	2	12
March	28	14	7	3	14
April	30	14	4	2	.13
May	26	16	8	2	12
June	31	19	9	2	13
Totals	291	147	89	31	153

TOTAL TYPES OF CRIMES INVESTIGATED IN VARIOUS COUNTIES:

	1944-45	1945-46
Assault	14	6
Burglary	121	137

Embezzlement	19	12
Homicide	46	39
Larceny	16	28
Robbery	7	10
Sex Offenses	15	14
Miscellaneous	56	45
	304	291

TOTAL REQUESTS FROM LAW ENFORCEMENT AGENCIES:

	1944-45	1945-46
Sheriff's Departments	150	134
Police Departments	91	108
Highway Patrols	14	11
Solicitors	21	19
Judges	0	0
Executive Departments	5	9
Coroners	4	1
Miscellaneous	19	9
	304	291

TOTAL REQUESTS RECEIVED FROM EACH JUDICIAL DISTRICT:

District	1944-45	1945-46
First	23	7
Second	20	6
Third	18	20
Fourth	23	38
Fifth	10	13
Sixth	21	31
Seventh	17	18
Eighth	17	6
Ninth	18	13
Tenth	11	26
Eleventh	9	2
Twelfth	12	7
Thirteenth	50	22
Fourteenth	5	5
Fifteenth	15	29
Sixteenth	14	14
Seventeenth	3	12
Eighteenth	6	7
Nineteenth	1	3
Twentieth	2	3
Twenty-first	9	9
	304	291

July 1, 1944 to July 1, 1945

The following statement shows the number of requests received by counties and the classification of the types of crime investigated therein:

Counties	Assault	Burglary	Embezzle-ment	Homicide	Larceny	Robbery	Sex Offenses	Misc.	Totals
Alamance		1	1	2				1	5
Alexander				1					1
Alleghany	1							1	2
Anson		7						3	10
Ashe		1	1	1				2	5
Avery									0
Beaufort		1	1						2
Bertie						1		1	2
Bladen	1	2		1				1	5
Brunswick									0
Buncombe								1	1
Burke	1			3	2		2		8
Cabarrus									0
Caldwell									0
Camden	1				1		3		5
Carteret		4					1	1	6
Caswell		1							1
Catawba				1					1
Chatham		3						1	4
Cherokee									0
Chowan		1	1		1				3
Clay									0
Cleveland									0
Columbus		1		3		1	1	2	8
Craven				1			2		3
Cumberland	1		1	1				1	4
Currituck		1			1				2
Dare		1		1				1	3
Davidson		4		3		1		2	10
Davie	1								1
Duplin	1	5		1	3	1			11
Durham									0
Edgecombe		1						3	4
Forsyth						1			1
Franklin	1	5	1				1		8
Gaston		1						1	2
Gates		1							1
Graham								1	1
Granville		1	1						2
Greene									0
Guilford				1					1
Halifax		3							3
Harnett		1	1					1	3
Haywood									0
Henderson								1	1
Hertford		5							5
Hoke			1					1	2
Hyde									0
Iredell				1					1
Jackson									0
Johnston		2		4	2		1	1	10
Jones									0
Lee				1			1	1	3
Lenoir		1		1					2

Embezzlement	Homicide	Larceny	Robbery	Sex Offenses	Misc.	Totals
				1		3
						0
						0
						6
						2
1					2	3
						0
						1
					1	5
			1		2	5
				1	1	3
					1	4
					2	2
	1				1	3
						0
	1					3
	3	1				7
						2
					1	1
1					1	1
					1	1
1	1				2	11
4	6	1		1	2	23
					2	6
						0
						0
						0
						5
	1					9
					1	3
					1	1
1	1	1	1			6
		1				1
						1
						0
					1	1
	1					3
1	3		1		3	10
						3
1						2
	1	1				4
						3
					1	1
					3	3
						1
						0

July 1, 1944 to July 1, 1945

The following statement shows the number of requests received by counties and from what sources requests were made:

Counties	Sheriff's Depts.	Police Depts.	Highway Patrol	Solicitors	Judges	Executive Depts.	Coroners	Misc.	Totals
Alamance	3	2							5
Alexander	1								1
Alleghany	2								2
Anson	9			1		•			10
Ashe	4			1					5
Avery									0
Beaufort		2							2
Bertie	1							1	2
Bladen	5	1							6
Brunswick									0
Buncombe	1								1
Burke	5	2							7
Cabarrus									0
Caldwell									0
Camden	1			3				1	5
Carteret	3	2	1						6
Caswell	1								1
Catawba			1						1
Chatham	4								4
Cherokee									0
Chowan		3							3
Clay									0
Cleveland									0
Columbus	2	1		2		2			7
Craven			1	1			1		3
Cumberland	2	1	1						4
Currituck				3					3
Dare	2								2
Davidson	2	8		1					11
Davie	1								1
Duplin	3	7		1			1		12
Durham									0
Edgecombe	1	2						1	4
Forsyth		2							2
Franklin	2	2	1					2	7
Gaston		1						1	2
Gates			1						1
Graham				1					1
Granville		1						1	2
Greene									0
Guilford	1								1
Halifax		3							3
Harnett		2		1				1	4
Haywood									0
Henderson								1	1
Hertford			3						3
Hoke	1		1						2
Hyde									0
Iredell		1							1
Jackson									0
Johnston	4	4				1			9
Jones									0
Lee	3								3
Lenoir	1	1							2

Counties	Sheriff's Depts.	Police Depts.	Highway Patrol	Solicitors	Judges	Executive Depts.	Coroners	Misc.	Totals
ncoln	1	1							2
acon									0
fadisou									0
fartin		6							6
lcDowell	2								2
fecklenburg		2		1					3
litchell									0
fontgomery	2								2
foore	1	4							5
ssh	5								5
ew Hanover	2	1							3
orthampton		3		1					4
nslow			1	1					2
range	3								3
amlico									0
asquotank	1	2							3
ender	6			1					7
erquimans	4								4
erson	1								1
tt								1	1
olk	1				1				2
andolph	11								11
ichmond	13	5						5	23
obeson	4	2							6
ockingham									0
owan									0
utherford									0
ampson	5								5
cotland	4	5							9
tanly	1	1							2
tokes								1	1
urry	6			1					7
wain			1						1
ransylvania		1							1
yrrell									0
nion	1								1
ance	1	2							3
Vakc	1	2	2	1	1	1	1	2	10
Varren	1	2							3
Vashington	1	1							2
Vatauga	4								4
Vayne		2						1	3
Vilkes	1								1
Vilson	1	1			1				3
adkin	1								1
ancey									0

July 1, 1945 to July 1, 1946

The following statement shows the number of requests received by counties and the classification of the types of crime investigated therein:

Counties	Assault	Burglary	Embezzlement	Homicide	Larceny	Robbery	Sex Offenses	Misc.	Totals
Alamance		12	1	1	1		1	1	17
Alexander					1				1
Alleghany									0
Anson		1							1
Ashe				1					1
Avery									0
Beaufort			1					1	2
Bertie		7							7
Bladen	1								1
Brunswick									0
Buncombe							1	2	3
Burke		1		2	1	1		1	6
Cabarrus	1	1							2
Caldwell				1					1
Camden			1						1
Carteret		7		1				2	10
Caswell									0
Catawba			1						1
Chatham		5		1					6
Cherokee									0
Chowan				1					1
Clay									0
Cleveland									0
Columbus									0
Craven									0
Cumberland				2				1	3
Currituck									0
Dare				1					1
Davidson			1	1				1	3
Davie	1							1	2
Duplin		16		1				3	20
Durham									0
Edgecombe		1						1	2
Forsyth							1		1
Franklin		1		3	1			1	6
Gaston		1		1				1	3
Gates									0
Graham							1		1
Granville		3			1				4
Greene		1							1
Guilford				3				1	4
Halifax		3	1						4
Harnett		3		1			1	1	6
Haywood									0
Henderson				1					1
Hertford		1							1
Hoke									0
Hyde									0
Iredell				3					3
Jackson									0
Johnston		7	1			1		1	10
Jones					2				2
Lee		13				1	1		15
Lenoir		3		1		1	1	1	7

Counties	Assault	Burglary	Embezzlement	Homicide	Larceny	Robbery	Sex Offenses	Misc	Totals
inroln		1						1	2
lacou								2	2
ladison									0
lartin									0
lcDowell									0
lecklenburg						1		1	2
litchell									0
lontgomery		1		1		1		1	4
loore		5	1		2			2	10
ash									0
ew Hanover									0
orthampton								1	1
nslow					1				1
range		1				1	1	1	4
anlico									0
asquotank		1							1
ender	1	3	1		1				6
erquimans									0
erson		1							1
itt									0
olk								1	1
ndolph		8		1	5	1		2	17
ichmond		1		2	1		2	1	7
obeson		8		1					9
ockingham			2		1				3
owan		1						1	2
utherford	1	3			1				5
ampson				2			1		3
cotland		1		1	2				4
tanly									0
tokes									0
urry	1	2			3				6
wain									0
ransylvania									0
yrrell					1				1
nion									0
Vance		1						2	3
Wake		1		4	2		2	3	12
Warren		4							4
Washington				1				1	2
Watauga		3				1			4
Wayne		1							1
Wilkes		1			1			1	3
Wilson			1					1	2
Yadkin		2				1	1	3	7
Yancey									0

Counties	Sheriffs' Depts.	Police Depts.	Highway Patrol	Solicitors	Judges	Executive Depts.	Coroners	Misc.	Totals
Alamance	6	11							17
Alexander	1								1
Alleghany									0
Anson			1						1
Ashe	1								1
Avery									0
Beaufort		1				1			2
Bertie	5	2							7
Bladen	1								1
Brunswick									0
Buncombe	1			1				1	3
Burke	2	4							6
Cabarrus		2							2
Caldwell	1								1
Camden				1					1
Carteret	7	1		1			1		10
Caswell									0
Catawba		1							1
Chatham	3	3							6
Cherokee									0
Chowan			1						1
Clay									0
Cleveland									0
Columbus									0
Craven									0
Cumberland		2	1						3
Currituck									0
Dare				1					1
Davidson	1	2							3
Davie	1			1					2
Duplin	7	10	1			2			20
Durham									0
Edgecombe		1		1					2
Forsyth		1							1
Franklin	3		2					1	6
Gaston	2	1							3
Gates									0
Graham	1								1
Granville	1	3							4
Greene	1								1
Guilford	1	3							4
Halifax	1	2						1	4
Harnett	3	3							6
Haywood									0
Henderson	1								1
Hertford	1								1
Hoke									0
Hyde									0
Iredell	3								3
Jackson									0
Johnston	2	6	1			1			10
Jones	2								2
Lee	6	9							15
Lenoir	4	2						1	7

Counties	Sheriffs' Depts.	Police Depts.	Highway Patrol	Solicitors	Judges	Executive Depts.	Coroners	Misc.	Totals
Lincoln		2							2
Macon						1		1	2
Madison									0
Martin									0
McDowell									0
Mecklenburg		1		1					2
Mitchell									0
Montgomery	4								4
Moore	4	6							10
Nash									0
New Hanover									0
Northampton	1								1
Onslow	1								1
Orange	2	1				1			4
Pamlico									0
Pasquotank	1								1
Pender	6								6
Perquimans									0
Person	1								1
Pitt									0
Polk		1							1
Randolph	8	9							17
Richmond	5	1		1					7
Robeson	3	6							9
Rockingham		2				1			3
Rowan		1		1					2
Rutherford	3	1		1					5
Sampson				3					3
Scotland	1	1	2						4
Stanly									0
Stokes									0
Surry	5		1						6
Swain									0
Transylvania									0
Tyrrell	1								1
Union									0
Vance	1	1		1					3
Wake	2	2		4		1		3	12
Warren	2	2							4
Washington	2								2
Watauga	4								4
Wayne		1							1
Wilkes	1		1					1	3
Wilson	1					1			2
Yadkin	6			1					7
Yancey									0

The following statement shows the volume of work performed by the Technical Division for each month during the period from July 1, 1944 to July 1, 1945.

	1944						1945						
	July	*Aug.*	*Sept.*	*Oct.*	*Nov.*	*Dec.*	*Jan.*	*Feb.*	*Mar.*	*April*	*May*	*June*	*Totals*
Fingerprint Examinations	7	12	4	6	6	2	9	11	6	6	8	14	91
Firearms Examinations	4	2	1				2	2					11
Document Examinations	1		2				2						
Medico-Legal Examinations	1	1	6	2			1		1	2			14
Psychological Tests	3	6	8	1			1	1	2	3			25
Microscopic Examinations													0
Photography Ultra-Violet Ray	10	18	11	12	17	16	18	23	16	22	17	22	202
Examinations													0
Sound Equipment													0
Totals	26	39	32	21	23	18	33	37	25	34	25	36	349

FROM JULY 1, 1944 TO JULY 1, 1945

	Sheriffs' Depts.	Police Depts.	Highway Patrol	Solicitors	Judges	Exec. Depts.	Coroners	Misc.	Totals
Fingerprint Examinations	52	33	4					2	91
Firearms Examinations	9								1
Document Examinations	1	4						1	6
Medico-Legal Examinations	8	3	2					1	14
Psychograph Tests	7	14	1	3					25
Microscopic Examinations									0
Photography Ultra-Violet	52	38	8			4		100	202

Examinations		0
Sound Equipment ...		0

Totals	129	92	15	3		4		106	349

The following statement shows the volume of work performed by the Technical Division for each month during the period from July 1, 1945 to July 1, 1946.

	1945						1946						
	July	*Aug.*	*Sept.*	*Oct.*	*Nov.*	*Dec.*	*Jan.*	*Feb.*	*Mar.*	*April*	*May*	*June*	*Totals*
Fingerprint Examinations	6	6	6	5	6	12	7	11	7	13	20	7	106
Firearms Examination		1		1				1	1	1	1	2	8
Document Examinations							2		1	1	7		11
Medico-Legal Examinations			2				1	3		1	2	2	11
Psycholgraph		1	1	1			2			2			o
Microscopic Examinations													u
Photography	17	23	17	18	26	29	22	35	30	34	38	38	327
Ultra-Violet Ray Examinations													
Sound Equipment													-
Totals	28	31	26	25	33	41	34	51	39	52	68	50	473

FROM JULY 1, 1945 TO JULY 1, 1946

	Sheriffs'	Police Depts.	Highway Patrol	Solicitors	Judges	Exec. Depts.	Coroners	Misc.	Totals
Fingerprint Examinations	50	51	5						106
Firearms Examinations	4	2	2						8
Document Examinations	3	4				4			11
Medico-Legal Examinations	8	3							11
Psychograph Tests	2	7							9
Microscopic Examinations									0
Photography	56	53	7	2		3		206	327
Ultra-Violet Examinations				1					1
Sound Equipment									
Totals	123	120	14	3		7		206	473

BRIEF SUMMARY OF IMPORTANT CASES
INVESTIGATED

July 1, 1944 to July 1, 1946

State v. A. J. Van Andel & L. S. Blackburn, Asheboro
Foundry & Randleman Bargain House Victims—
Breaking &Entering

On January 31, 1946 the Asheboro Foundry was broken into and a complete acetylene torch outfit was stolen. The same night the Randleman Bargain House was entered and a safe weighing about 700 pounds was carried away. The safe contained $1,000.

Through an investigation by Sheriff W. M. Bingham of Randolph County, assisted by S. B. I. Agents, it was determined that A. J. Van Andel and Leon S. Blackburn, white, of High Point, committed these crimes. The stolen safe and acetylene torch were found in a woods about 15 miles from Vass. The torch was used to open the safe and get the $1,000.

Blackburn was arrested on March 5, 1946 near his home in High Point, admitted his guilt, and involved Van Andel. He also confessed in detail to other similar crimes committed by him and Van Andel in St. Pauls, Asheboro, and Randleman.

After an extensive search for Van Andel in several states he was finally arrested on March 20, 1946 by the F. B. I. in Columbia, S. C. and brought back to Asheboro by an S. B. I. Agent and Deputy Sheriff M. W. Millikan.

Van Andel and Blackburn were tried and convicted in Randolph County Superior Court in April, 1946. Judge Hoyle Sink, presiding, sentenced Van Andel to serve 16 to 20 years in State Prison and Blackburn to serve 11 to 16 years.

State v. James E. Dyson
Avery Atwood, Victim—Robbery

About 9:30 p. m., May 17, 1945, Avery Atwood of Thomasville was held up and robbed of $450 to $500 cash at his gasoline station in Thomasville.

Investigation by Chief of Police E. R. Richardson of Thomasville assisted by S. B. I. Agents resulted in the positive identification of James E. Dyson of High Point as being one of the two men who robbed Atwood. Dyson was arrested at his home on June 4, 1945. When questioned by officers he denied all guilt of robbing Atwood. However, he was tried in Davidson County Superior Court, found guilty and sentenced to serve five years in the State Prison.

The second man who participated in the robbery of Atwood, James F. Prevost, was not identified until July, 1945 when he was arrested on suspicion, identified by Atwood and others and confessed that he and Dyson robbed and assaulted Atwood.

State v. John T. Barnes
Howard Barrett, Victim—Arson

The home of Howard Barrett, Negro, in Wilson County was destroyed by fire on the night of September 29, 1946. At the time of the fire eight people were sleeping in the house; however, all escaped without injury. An investigation by Deputy Sheriff W. L. Green of Wilson County determined that the fire was of incendiary origin.

Deputy Sheriff arrested two suspects; John T. Barnes and Fred Carr, both Negroes, and brought them to Raleigh office of the S. B. I. for a lie detector test. Both Barnes and Carr agreed to submit to the test. As a result, Barnes confessed his guilt stating that he set fire to the house because of a quarrel he had with his father-in-law the night before the fire. The examination showed Fred Carr to be innocent.

State v. Claude Chalmers
Dan M. Bass, Victim—Murder

Between 11 and 12 o'clock on the night of February 8, 1946 Dan M. Bass, Negro, age 57, was robbed and killed at his small store located on U. S. Highway 421 one mile south of Bonlee in Chatham County. Two Agents of the S. B. I. assisted Sheriff G. H. Andrews and his deputies of Chatham County in investigating the murder. As the result of the investigation, it was learned that Claude Chalmers, a Negro living about two miles from the Bass store was at the Bass store a few hours before the robbery and that since that time he had been spending money in Siler City and in the community where he lives, paying his grocery bill, buying a cook stove, and other items. He was held for investigation.

Sheriff Andrews and Deputy Sheriff W. R. Farrar interviewed Chalmers and Chalmers confessed that he killed Bass with an axe during a quarrel with Bass. After killing Bass he took his pocketbook, carried it near his home and hid it in the woods. He went with officers and showed where he hid the pocketbook which was found to contain $88.

He was tried in May, 1946 in Chatham County Superior Court, a plea of accessory before the fact charging murder was offered by the defense and accepted by the State. Judge Allen H. Gwynn, presiding, sentenced Bass to serve life imprisonment.

State v. Lacy Salmon, Raymond Bennett, Henry H. Agner,
Sam Thompson, Clarence Norris and Herbert E. Carroll
R. L. Beck, Victim—Murder

On the night of June 9, 1944, R. L. Beck, a blind man and known bootlegger living near High Point, was shot by robbers at his home and died in the hospital on June 10, 1944. Investigation of this murder was made by Sheriff John Story and his deputies of Guilford County, assisted by S. B. I. Agents. The shooting of Beck took place while being robbed.

An extensive investigation resulted in the arrest of Herbert E. Carroll, Sam Thompson, Henry H. Agner, Raymond Bennett, Clarence Norris, and

Lacy Salmon all charged with conspiracy to rob and the murder of R. L. Beck.

They were tried in June, 1945, in Guilford County Superior Court, all found guilty of second degree murder and each sentenced by Judge J. H. Clement to serve not less than 25 nor more than 30 years in the State Prison.

State v. William David White
Mrs. Bryant, Victim—First Degree Burglary

On October 10, 1944 Highway Patrolman B. F. Dixon of Murfreesboro brought to the S. B. I. in Raleigh William David White, Negro, whom he had arrested on suspicion of having entered in the nighttime the home of a Mrs. Bryant of Murfreesboro. White denied having entered Mrs. Bryant's home and Patrolman Dixon requested S. B. I. to make a psychographic examination of White. White agreed to the examination which was made. As a result of the examination he made a confession but stated that he was drunk at the time of entering the Bryant home.

On October 17, 1944 he was tried in Hertford County Superior Court, convicted of first degree burglary and sentenced to life imprisonment.

State v. Wilson Ferebee, Dennison Revels & Charles Ferebee
Darden Brothers, Victim—B & E & Larceny

The Darden Brothers Department Store in Hertford was entered on November 14, 1944 and about $55 in cash, stamps, a flash light, and pistol were taken. On the same night the Reed Oil Company of Hertford was entered and an unsuccessful effort made to open the safe. On November 10, 1944 the Wilson Reed Grocery Store in Hertford was entered and $100 in cash stolen.

The S. B. I. assisted Sheriff J. E. Winslow of Perquimans County in his investigation of these cases. The investigation resulted in the arrest of Wilson Ferebee, Dennison Revels, and Charles Ferebee, all Negroes, who confessed guilt in all three cases. Wilson Ferebee told officers if they would take him to his home he would show them where he hid the pistol stolen from Darden Brothers. Highway patrolman Charles Payne and Thomas Miller, a Hertford Police Officer, took Ferebee home. Upon entering the home several Negroes jumped on the officers and seriously injured them and took Miller's gun from him. Wilson Ferebee made his escape but later gave himself up.

They were tried in April term, 1945, Perquimans County Superior Court and found guilty. Judge J. J. Burney, presiding, sentenced Wilson Ferebee to serve eight to eleven years in State Prison, Revels to serve five to eight years; and Charles Ferebee, 15 years old minor, was remanded to the custody of the Clerk of Superior Court.

State v. William Pender
Thomas Dixon, Victim—Arson

On September 25, 1944, a barn and contents valued at $5,000 belonging to Thomas Dixon of Elm City was destroyed by an incendiary fire. As the result of an investigation by Deputy Sheriff W. L. Green of Wilson County, William Pender was arrested by Green, confessed to burning the barn and implicated Cary Pender and Ronas McGee. Deputy Green, after questioning Cary Pender and McGee, was doubtful of the guilt of these two men and requested the S.B.I. to make a lie detector test of William Pender, Cary Pender, and Ronas McGee. All three agreed to take the test which resulted in establishing the innocence of Cary Pender and Ronas McGee and a confession by William Pender that they were innocent, that he alone was guilty of burning the barn.

State v. Howard Miller
Marvin Faulkner, Victim—Murder

About 4 a. m., February 18, 1946, Marvin Faulkner, Negro, was shot and fatally wounded with a shotgun at his home in Asheboro. An Agent of the S.B.I. assisted Chief of Police Clarence Lovett of Asheboro in his investigation of the shooting. A fired 12-gauge shotgun shell was found at the scene of the shooting.

Investigation developed the fact that Howard Miller, Negro, was seen near the home of Faulkner after midnight the night of the shooting. Miller was arrested and after considerable questioning admitted shooting Faulkner. Miller stated that about 8 p. m., February 17, 1946 when passing Faulkner's home, Faulkner was sitting on his front porch with a shotgun. He got up and said he was going to kill Miller because he had been running around with Faulkner's girl friend. Miller ran away, went home, got his shotgun, and returned to Faulkner's home. After Faulkner again threatened to kill him, Miller shot him. Faulkner's gun was found at the scene of the shooting. A single barrel shotgun, 12-gauge, was taken from Miller's home by officers who fired a test shell from it. The test shell was compared with the shell found at the scene of the crime, and it was found that both were fired from Miller's gun.

Miller was tried at the June, 1946 term of Randolph County Superior Court, tendered a plea of manslaughter which was accepted by the Solicitor. Miller was sentenced by Judge Hoyle Sink, presiding, to serve seven to ten years in State Prison.

State v. Bruce C. Sherrin, Jr.
Martha Goldston, Victim—Bigamy

On October 11, 1945 Bruce C. Sherrin, Jr. married Martha Goldston of Goldston, Chatham County, and later it was found that he had a living wife from whom he was not divorced. A warrant was issued in Wake County for his arrest on a charge of bigamy. Sherrin could not be found and the S.B.I. was requested to locate and arrest him. After considerable investigation, he was arrested by an officer of the Roanoke, Virginia Police Department and brought back to Raleigh on November 16, 1945 by agents of the S.B.I.

When his case was called for trial in Wake County Superior Court in

November, 1945 he entered a plea of nolo-contendere. Judge R. Hunt Parker, presiding, after hearing the evidence, sentenced Bruce C. Sherrin, Jr. to serve not less than two nor more than three years in the State Prison.

State v. Jack Napier, Grady Carver & Wade Treece
Gulf, Sinclair, & Texaco Oil Companies
Victims—Breaking & Entering

On February 22, 1945 the Gulf, Sinclair, and Texaco Oil Companies in Asheboro were entered and about 4,950 gallons of gas and 805 gallons of kerosene coupons were stolen. The S.B.I. assisted Deputy Sheriff M. L. Johnson of Randolph County in his investigation of these crimes.

The investigation resulted in the arrest and confessions of Jack Napier, Grady Carver, Wade Treece, George Edwards, and U. B. Blalock. All except U. B. Blalock were tried and found guilty. Napier, Carver, and Treece were sentenced to serve three to five years in State Prison. George Edwards was released on probation. U. B. Blalock was found to be A.W.O.L. from the U. S. Army and was turned over to Fort Bragg Military Police. Blalock while being transferred from Fort Bragg to Maxton-Laurinburg Base struck an army officer, was court martialed, and sentenced to serve five years at hard labor in Fort Leavenworth, Kansas.

State v. Burnett Williams
Kathleen Hall and Joe Dowdy, Victims,
Rape and Robbery

About 5:30 p. m. on March 4, 1945, Joe Dowdy and Kathleen Hall while in a car parked on the Pumping Station Road about three miles from Sanford were held up and robbed, and Kathleen Hall raped by a negro man.

At the request of Sheriff A. G. Buchanan of Lee County and Chief of Police Paul Watson of Sanford, agents of the S.B.I. assisted them in their investigation of this crime. Dowdy was able to give a full description of the Negro and as a result officers arrested Burnett Williams, a 24-year-old Negro, who fitted in every way the description given by Dowdy. When Williams was searched at the Police Station he had on a pair of rubber boots and in one of them was found a lady's wrist watch of yellow gold which was identified by Miss Hall as being the watch taken from her by the Negro who raped her. At the point of a gun Williams forced Dowdy to get into the trunk of the car and then Williams locked the trunk, carried Miss Hall a short distance to some woods, raped her, then took her back to the car, put her in the trunk with Dowdy and locked them in it. They remained there until early next morning when Williams let them out but tied them up with a rope and left about 5:00 a. m. They freed themselves, went to a nearby farmhouse and were able to secure transportation to Sanford where they reported the crime. Both Dowdy and Kathleen Hall positively identified Williams. Dowdy's car, which had been left at the scene of the crime, was thoroughly examined for latent prints by an S.B.I. fingerprint expert. A piece of glass which apparently was broken from the car door was found just behind the back seat and on it was found a good latent fingerprint and it was found to be the left thumb print of Burnett Williams.

Williams was tried in Lee County Superior Court on March 30, 1945 and the jury after deliberating for fifteen minutes found him guilty of rape. Judge C. E. Thompson, presiding, sentenced Williams to death in the gas chamber. He was duly executed on October 26, 1945.

State v. Edward Johns
James Hanna, Victim—Murder

On September 16, 1944, about 10 p. m., James Hanna, white, age 23, and Edward Johns, Negro, age 23, met each other on a street in Laurinburg, bumped into each other, and immediately started fighting. During the fight Johns stabbed Hanna with a dagger resulting in his death. While being taken to a hospital Johns made good his escape.

Chief of Police C. R. Cook requested assistance of the S.B.I. in locating and arresting Edward Johns. Wanted notices were mailed to officers throughout North Carolina and adjoining states. On October 1, 1944 Chief of Police Cook and three Laurinburg officers arrested Johns while asleep at a point about two miles from Laurinburg. After Johns' arrest a detailed statement was obtained from him, and Chief Cook and S.B.I. Agent proceeded to make a further complete investigation, interviewing numerous possible witnesses.

The case against Johns was called for trial in Scotland County Superior Court in September, 1944, and the State accepted a plea of manslaughter. Judge F. Don Phillips, presiding, sentenced Edward Johns to serve a term of seven to ten years in the State Penitentiary.

State v. Henry Bond & Harry Land
C. H. Jenkins Motor Co., Victim—Breaking & Entering & Auto Theft

On the night of December 7, 1944, the C. H. Jenkins Motor Co. of Williamston was broken into and a large safe moved from the main office to the garage where the hinges were sawed off in an unsuccessful effort to enter the safe. However, the thieves did steal a 1940 model Oldsmobile sedan from the garage.

At the request of Chief of Police C. R. Mobley of Williamston S.B.I. fingerprint experts carefully searched the office and safe for latent prints. They found, lifted, and photographed several good palm prints on the safe. The stolen car was located by Highway Patrolman W. E. Saunders, but no latent prints of value were found on it. Officers arrested as a suspect Harry Land, a 19-year-old Negro, who denied entering the Jenkins Motor Co. but admitted other breaking and enterings and implicated Henry Bond, a Negro, in these other cases. Bond was arrested for investigation. His palm prints were compared with the latents found on the Jenkins Motor Co. safe and they proved identical; whereupon, he admitted entering the Jenkins Motor. Co., sawing the hinges from the safe and stealing the automobile. He implicated Harry Land, Julian Willard, and William H. Rogers. All are Negroes and only Bond and Land have been arrested.

Land and Bond were tried in Martin County Superior Court in March, 1945 and found guilty. Judge W. H. S. Burgwynn, presiding, sentenced Bond to serve not less than six nor more than ten years in State Prison.

Land was sentenced to not less than three nor more than five years in Central Prison.

State v. Albert Hager, Clyde Queen & Martha Moore
C. E. Kellum, Victim—Robbery

On August 25, 1945 about 6 p. m. C. E. Kellum while milking a cow in his barn located near the High School in Biscoe was robbed of his billfold containing $200 and a watch by two white men who threw him to the ground and tied him up with a rope.

The S.B.I. assisted Sheriff Earl D. Bruton of Montgomery County in his investigation of the robbery. The investigation resulted in casting suspicion upon Albert Hager, Clyde Queen, and Martha Moore, 19 years of age and a friend of C. E. Kellum. The watch stolen from Kellum was sold by Albert Hager to a man named Clyde Keaton. The watch was recovered from Keaton. The suspects, Hager, Queen, and Moore, were arrested and after questioning confessed their guilt.

They were tried in Montgomery County Superior Court and convicted. Albert Hager and Clyde Queen were sentenced to serve seven to ten years, and Martha Moore was sentenced to serve twelve months in Central Prison.

State v. Willie Bell, Lon Harris, James Park, and Ralph Clark
Emma McGee, Victim—Murder

On Sunday, May 13, 1945, the body of Emma McGee was found not far from her home in Davidson County in a vacant field with several stab wounds in her neck and chest. She was dead when found. The S.B.I. assisted Chief of Police W. R. Lanning of Lexington in his investigation of the death of Emma McGee.

As a result of the investigation, Willie Bell, Lon Harris, James Park, and Ralph Clark were picked up for questioning. As a result they were charged with murder. They were all drinking and gambling in the home of Lon Harris. Emma McGee came to the Harris home in a drunken condition, a quarrel ensued resulting in the death of McGee by being stabbed by Lon Harris and Willie Bell. All assisted in disposing of the body. All parties involved are Negroes.

In Davidson County Superior Court in June, 1945, Willie Bell was convicted of second degree murder and sentenced to 12 to 18 years; Lon Harris second degree murder, sentenced to 12 to 15 years; James Park and Ralph Clark convicted of manslaughter and each sentenced to five to seven years.

State v. Lee S. Taylor
Myers Theatre, Victim, Breaking & Entering & Safe Robbery

During the night of July 31, 1944, the Myers Theatre in Rich Square was broken into and a wall safe in the office was broken open and robbed of $65. Chief of Police Frank Outland of Rich Square investigated the case and arrested Samuel Lee Taylor, colored, as a suspect. He brought Taylor to the Raleigh office of the S.B.I. for a lie detector test. Taylor agreed to the test. As a result of the test, Taylor confessed he broke into the Myers Theatre office safe and robbed the safe.

State v. Dr. Leon R. Meadows
State of N. C. Eastern Carolina Teachers College, Victim
Embezzlement & Misapplication of State Funds

At the request of State Auditor George Ross Pou and direction of Governor J. M. Broughton, the S.B.I. assisted the State Auditor's office in making an investigation of the handling of receipts and disbursement of funds at the Eastern Carolina Teachers College, Greenville. A very intensive and extensive investigation over a period of many weeks was made. As a result, Dr. Leon R. Meadows, President of E.C.T.C. was indicted on charges of embezzlement and misapplication of state funds.

At a special term of Pitt County Superior Court on March 23, 1945, after a trial lasting eight weeks, the jury could not agree and Judge Clawson Williams ordered a mistrial. Meadows was again placed on trial in June, 1945, and after a trial lasting several weeks, he was found guilty of embezzling $3,000 and also guilty of false pretenses. Judge J. Paul Frizzell sentenced Meadows to serve two years for embezzlement and one year for false pretense, the sentences to run consecutively. Appeal taken to State Supreme Court, but lower court sentence was affirmed.

State v. Edward Bill Mays
Mrs. Mattie L. Salmon, Victim—Rape & Murder

Mrs. Mattie L. Salmon, white, age 76, was raped and murdered the night of June 16, 1945 at home on Route No. 2 in Lee County. She was living alone at the time of the crime, her nearest neighbor living about 400 yards from her home.

Sheriff A. G. Buchanan and his Deputy D. F. Holder of Lee County requested S.B.I. assistance in investigating the murder. Photographs of the victim and scene of the crime were taken. Investigation by officers resulted in casting suspicion upon Edward Bill Mays, Negro, 50 years old, who lived about two miles from the Salmon home, because of his having been seen on numerous occasions at night near the victim's home. He was arrested and confined in Central Prison in Raleigh for safekeeping. Mays, when questioned by officers, made a complete confession of having raped and murdered Mrs. Salmon by stuffing part of her dress down her throat and in her mouth causing suffocation. He admitted that on many other occasions he had been to Mrs. Salmon's home and unsuccessfully tried to get into her house for the purpose of raping her.

In making this investigation officers found foot tracks leading from a tract of woods to the victim's home and going away from her home in the same direction that they approached it. The left shoe track showed that there was a piece nailed on the outside of the shoe, and when Mays was arrested a shoe identical to this was found on his left foot. A plaster cast had been made of the shoe track and when the shoe taken from Mays was compared with it, it was found to be identical.

• Mays was tried in Lee County Superior Court on July 18, 1945 and the jury after deliberating twenty minutes found him guilty of first degree murder and sentenced by Judge W. H. S. Burgwyn to die in the gas chamber. He was duly executed on November 2, 1945.

State v. Thomas Gurganus and Thomas Bowen
D. Q. Smith Store, Victim—Breaking & Entering

The general merchandise store of D. Q. Smith in Willard, N. C. was broken into on November 17, 1945 and a quantity of merchandise was stolen. The side door of the store was broken open with an axe and several panels removed from the door. On one of these panels several good latent fingerprints were found. An investigation by Sheriff J. T. Brown of Pender County and an S.B.I. Agent resulted in the arrest of Thomas Bowen, colored, who confessed he assisted Thomas Gurganus, colored, in breaking into and robbing the Smith Store. Bowen then went with Sheriff Brown and S.B.I. Agent to Willard and showed them where the stolen merchandise was hidden and it was all recovered. Gurganus was arrested and admitted his guilt.

They were tried at the January, 1946 term of Pender County Superior Court, convicted and sentenced to from five to ten years and placed on probation during good behavior.

State v. Hosea Parker
H. S. Taylor Store, Victim
Breaking and Entering and Safe Robbery

A store operated by H. S. Taylor in Hookerton was broken into and the safe broken open by the use of several axes and 23 $100 bills stolen. This method of breaking in a safe was used in about 10 other safe robberies recently investigated by the S.B.I.

A fingerprint examination at the scene of the above crime failed to secure any latent prints suitable for identification. However, several good shoe prints were found on the floor around the safe and they were photographed for possible identification.

Sheriff H. K. Cobb and deputies of Greene County arrested Hosea Parker, Negro, on the highway between Hookerton and Snow Hill as he was walking away from his car which had turned over. Deputy Sheriff Fred Carraway searched Parker and took from his person 23 $100 bills. When questioned by Sheriff Cobb and S.B.I. Agent, he denied robbery of the Taylor Store. The shoes he had on compared identically with the shoe prints found in front of the safe. Parker confessed he robbed the Taylor Store safe. He also confessed to 17 store and safe robberies.

The S.B.I. had made fingerprint examinations at the scenes of most of these crimes and it was noted that no satisfactory fingerprints were ever developed. When Hosea Parker was arrested, it was found that he had destroyed his fingerprints apparently with some kind of acid; however, palm prints were taken from Hosea Parker and these compared with palm prints found at the scene of some of the crimes and resulted in an identification being made in several of the cases. This evidence was used against Hosea Parker in Superior Court trials.

He was tried in Greene County Superior Court, convicted, and sentenced by Judge Leo Carr to serve 18 to 23 years. He was tried in Lenoir County Superior Court on two counts of breaking and entering, was convicted and sentenced by Judge C. Everett Thompson to serve five years on each count, the ten-year sentence to begin at the end of his previous sentence in Greene County. H is still to be tried in Duplin County on four counts and in Bertie County on three counts.

State v. Eula Shipley
White Troy, Victim—Murder

White Troy, Negro, of Columbus County, on September 4, 1944, was found in a dying condition laying in a wagon drawn by two mules. Troy was taken to a hospital where he died a few hours later from a severe blow on the back of his head causing a fracture of the skull.

Investigation by Sheriff H. D. Stanley of Columbus County assisted by S.B.I. Agents resulted in casting suspicion on Eula Shipley who was arrested and placed in jail in Elizabethtown in Bladen County. Sheriff Clark of Bladen County questioned Shipley who confessed to robbing and killing Troy. He repeated his confession in the presence of Sheriff Stanley and two S.B.I. Agents. He stated he got on Troy's wagon shortly after Troy left his home asking Troy for a ride. While driving through the woods, he picked up a piece of plank from the wagon, hit Troy across the back of the head, took his pocketbook and jumped from the wagon.

He was tried in Columbus County Superior Court in November, 1944, entered a plea of guilty of second degree murder and was sentenced by Judge O. K. Nimmocks, presiding, to serve 23 to 25 years in State Prison.

State v. J. W. Andrews
Miss Cary May Wade, Victim—Assault with
Deadly Weapon with Intent to Rape

Miss Mary May Wade of Charlotte while at Wrightsville Beach was assaulted about 12:15 a. m., August 31, 1944, on a street in Wrightsville Beach and her throat severely cut by a Negro man. Investigation by Chief of Police M. S. Faircloth of Wrightsville and Deputy Sheriff C. P. Snow resulted in the arrest of J. W. Andrews, a 20-year-old Negro, who steadfastly denied guilt. Faircloth and Snow brought to the S.B.I. for laboratory examination the following articles taken from Andrews: a pocket knife, one shoe, a handkerchief, a shirt, and a pair of pants. Upon examination, all except the pants were found negative for human blood. Stains on the pants were positive for human blood.

With his consent, a lie detector test was made on Andrews which indicated guilt. Andrews made a confession, and at his trial in New Hanover County Superior Court entered a plea of secret assault with intent to kill and was sentenced by Judge Henry L. Stevens, presiding, to serve 20 years in State Prison.

CRIMINAL STATISTICS

REPORT OF
DIVISION OF CRIMINAL AND CIVIL STATISTICS

The first of the following tabulations presents a general summarization of all criminal cases reported by clerks of the superior courts of the 100 counties for the two-year period from January 1, 1944, to January 1, 1946, as required by Chapter 315 of the Public Laws of 1939.

The second tabulation covers criminal cases reported by clerks of the various courts of record below the superior court.

The third tabulation covers divorce cases reported from the superior court for the five-year period from 1941 through 1945, the figures being presented by counties arranged alphabetically within the twenty-one judicial districts, and also in such a way as to reflect the county, district and state totals, together with the type of divorce and the percentage of cases in each county, based on population.

FIRST JUDICIAL DISTRICT
IN SUPERIOR COURT

Column group headers: **JANUARY 1, 1944—DECEMBER 31, 1944** (Convictions / Other Dispositions) and **JANUARY 1, 1945—DECEMBER 31, 1945** (Convictions / Other Dispositions). Each sub‑section has White, Negro, Indian, Unclassified columns each split into M and F.

Offense	44 Conv W‑M	W‑F	N‑M	N‑F	I‑M	I‑F	U‑M	U‑F	44 Oth W‑M	W‑F	N‑M	N‑F	I‑M	I‑F	U‑M	U‑F	45 Conv W‑M	W‑F	N‑M	N‑F	I‑M	I‑F	U‑M	U‑F	45 Oth W‑M	W‑F	N‑M	N‑F	I‑M	I‑F	U‑M	U‑F
Assault	11		10								1						4	1	4	2					4		2	2			2	
Assault and Battery			4	1															1									1				
Assault with deadly weapon	2		1						1		1				1		2		15						1		2	1				
Assault on female	1		1														1		4						1		1					
Assault with intent to kill																			6	1												
Assault with intent to rape																			2													
Assault—Secret																																
Drunk, drunk & disorderly	7	1	1						7		1						5		1						1		1					
Possession—illegal whiskey	1																															
Possession for sale—sale											1														2		3					
Manufacturing—possession of material for																																
Transportation																																
Violation liquor laws	11		6						4								18		6				1									
Driving drunk	8		3						11		2						2		2						16	2	2				2	
Reckless driving	1								7		3								2													
Hit and run	1																															
Speeding	1								1								1						1									
Auto license violations									5																							
Violation Motor Vehicle laws	1		8																						1						1	
Breaking and entering	1								4		2						2		9													
And larceny	1								1		1								6													
And receiving	4		11						2		2						11		4													
Housebreaking																			1													
And larceny																			5													
And receiving																			6													
Storebreaking			2																													
And larceny																																
And receiving																																

Offense	Counts
Larceny by trick & device	3
Larceny of automobile	
Temporary larceny	
Murder—first degree	
Murder—second degree	
Manslaughter	
Burglary—first degree	
Burglary—second degree	
Abandonment	
Abduction	
Affray	
Arson	
Bigamy	
Bribery	
Burning other than arson	
Carrying concealed weapon	
Contempt	
Conspiracy	
Cruelty to animals	
Disorderly conduct	
Disorderly house	
Disposing of mortgaged property	
Disturbing religious worship	
Violation of election laws	
Embezzlement	
Escape	
Failure to list tax	
Food and drug laws	
Fish and game laws	
Forcible trespass	
Forgery	
Fornication and adultery	
Gaming and lottery laws	
Health laws	
Incest	
Injury to property	
Municipal ordinances	
Nonsupport	
Nonsupport of illegitimate child	
Nuisance	

FIRST JUDICIAL DISTRICT—(Continued)
IN SUPERIOR COURT

JANUARY 1, 1944—DECEMBER 31, 1944

Offense	CONVICTIONS								OTHER DISPOSITIONS							
	White		Negro		Indian		Unclassified		White		Negro		Indian		Unclassified	
	M	F	M	F	M	F	M	F	M	F	M	F	M	F	M	F
Official misconduct																
Perjury										1						
Prostitution in																
Rape	2								2	1	1	1				
Receiving stolen goods			1													
Removing crop				1							1	1				
Resisting officer	2		1													
Robbery			1													
Seduction																
Slander																
Trespass			5						1	1	1					
Vagrancy									1							
Worthless check									1							
False pretense																
Carnal knowledge, etc.			1						1		2					
Crime against nature																
Slot machine laws																
Kidnaping																
Revenue act violations	2		4						1							
Miscellaneous									1	2	33	2			2	
Totals	67	1	94	3					60	2	33	2			2	

Convictions 165
Nolle pros 58
Aquittals 40
Other dispositions 1

JANUARY 1, 1945—DECEMBER 31, 1945

Offense	CONVICTIONS								OTHER DISPOSITIONS							
	White		Negro		Indian		Unclassified		White		Negro		Indian		Unclassified	
	M	F	M	F	M	F	M	F	M	F	M	F	M	F	M	F
Official misconduct																
Perjury	2		1							1						
Prostitution in																
Rape									2		2					
Receiving stolen goods	1		2						1		1					
Removing crop	1															
Resisting officer			2	1					3							
Robbery			6													
Seduction																
Slander																
Trespass	2		1						1		1					
Vagrancy			1													
Worthless check																
False pretense																
Carnal knowledge, etc.																
Crime against nature																
Slot machine laws																
Kidnaping									1							
Revenue act violations			2						1	1						
Miscellaneous																5
Totals	91	3	122	8				3	49	1	22	6				5

Convictions 227
Nolle pros 48
Aquittals 35
Other dispositions ....

Second Judicial District

SECOND JUDICIAL DISTRICT
IN SUPERIOR COURT

Offense	JANUARY 1, 1944—DECEMBER 31, 1944 CONVICTIONS White M	White F	Negro M	Negro F	Indian M	Indian F	Unclassified M	Unclassified F	OTHER DISPOSITIONS White M	White F	Negro M	Negro F	Indian M	Indian F	Unclassified M	Unclassified F	JANUARY 1, 1945—DECEMBER 31, 1945 CONVICTIONS White M	White F	Negro M	Negro F	Indian M	Indian F	Unclassified M	Unclassified F	OTHER DISPOSITIONS White M	White F	Negro M	Negro F	Indian M	Indian F	Unclassified M	Unclassified F
Assault	5		16						4		18						1		9						2		4					1
Assault and battery																																
Assault with deadly weapon	3		18	3					1		7	1				3	4	1	17	5					3		9	4				
Assault on female			6						1		4						3		9						5		1	3				
Assault with intent to kill	2		7	1			1		3	1	1						2		9	2					4		5	3				
Assault with intent to rape	1		1								1						1		8						1							
Assault—secret			1	1					1										5						8		1					
Drunk—drunk & disorderly	13	1	4	1					28	1	5				3		7	3	5				1				3	1				2
Possession—illegal whiskey			1	1					4										1								1					
Possession for sale—sale	1								1																		1					
Manufacturing—possession of material for			1																													
Transportation	2		6	1					2	1	1				1		2		9	1					6		1					
Violation liquor laws	4		2						1	1							1		1						4		1					
Driving drunk	2		3						6	1	1						2		4				1		1		2					
Reckless driving			2						1		2								1						1							
Hit and run			2						2		1						2		1						1							
Speeding																																
Auto license violations																																
Violation motor vehicle laws	5		3	1			1		4		5						2		5						5	1	1	1				
Violation motor vehicle laws	4		7														7		4								3					
Breaking and entering	8		10						1								2		10						3		2					
And larceny	3																2		2								2					
And receiving											6				1		10		4								1					
Housebreaking	9		1																													
And larceny	1	5	7	1																												
And receiving			1																								5					
Storebreaking																																
And larceny																																
And receiving																																

Larceny by trick & device	3	4				1		1		6	1				3		1
Larceny of automobile		3				7		1		1					1		1
Temporary larceny																	
Murder—first degree	1	1	2			1	3			1					3		1
Murder—second degree	1	1				2	2								1		1
Manslaughter	2						2								5		1
Burglary—first degree															1		
Burglary—second degree		2					2			1							
Abandonment																	
Abduction																	
Affray	2	2				1	2			1					1		1
Arson		2	1			2	2								1		
Bigamy							1			1							
Bribery																	
Burning other than arson	1	1				1									1		
Carrying concealed weapon																	
Contempt							1										
Conspiracy																	
Cruelty to animals	2					2									1		1
Disorderly conduct	2	4				2	3	2							3		
Disorderly house																	
Disposing of mortgaged property																	
Disturbing religious worship																	
Violation of election laws																	
Embezzlement	2	1				1	1			1					1		
Escape																	
Failure to list tax																	
Food and drug laws	2																
Fish and game laws	5	2	2			1				2					1		
Forcible trespass	9	1	1			2				4					1		
Forgery											1						
Fornication and adultery															1		
Gaming and lottery laws	2					2	2								1		
Health laws																	
Incest																	
Injury to property	1	1				1	1			1					1		1
Municipal ordinances						1	1			1					1	2	1
Nonsupport	4					1				1							
Nonsupport of illegitimate child						1	1			1					1		

SECOND JUDICIAL DISTRICT—(Continued)
IN SUPERIOR COURT

JANUARY 1, 1944—DECEMBER 31, 1944

Offense	CONVICTIONS								OTHER DISPOSITIONS							
	White		Negro		Indian		Unclassified		White		Negro		Indian		Unclassified	
	M	F	M	F	M	F	M	F	M	F	M	F	M	F	M	F
Nuisance									1							
Official misconduct																
Perjury																
Prostitution	5	2							4	4						
Rape	1		3								3					
Receiving stolen goods			3													
Removing crop																
Resisting officer			1	1												
Robbery	1		8								10					
Seduction																
Slander															1	
Trespass	1		2						1		1					
Vagrancy			1						1	5	5					
Worthless check									3							
False pretense	2		1						1		1					
Carnal knowledge, etc.	1		1								1					
Crime against nature	1															
Slot machine laws																
Kidnaping																
Revenue act violations			4	2					4		7					
Miscellaneous															2	
Totals	120	16	176	18			2		102	17	118	7			11	

Convictions _____ 332
Nolle pros _____ 167
Acquittals _____ 65
Other disposition _____ 20

JANUARY 1, 1945—DECEMBER 31, 1945

Offense	CONVICTIONS								OTHER DISPOSITIONS							
	White		Negro		Indian		Unclassified		White		Negro		Indian		Unclassified	
	M	F	M	F	M	F	M	F	M	F	M	F	M	F	M	F
Nuisance												1				1
Official misconduct																
Perjury																
Prostitution	1									4		1				
Rape			3													
Receiving stolen goods																
Removing crop																
Resisting officer			1								3					
Robbery			3						1		3					
Seduction									1							
Slander																
Trespass									1		3				1	
Vagrancy									1	4	1					
Worthless check			4	1					1		1					
False pretense	1		1						1		1				1	
Carnal knowledge, etc.																
Crime against nature																
Slot machine laws																
Kidnaping																
Revenue act violations											2					
Miscellaneous								1								
Totals	87	7	159	9			1		64	9	71	11			8	2

Convictions _____ 263
Nolle pros _____ 97
Acquittals _____ 48
Other disposition _____ 20

Third Judicial District

THIRD JUDICIAL DISTRICT
IN SUPERIOR COURT

Offense	JANUARY 1, 1944—DECEMBER 31, 1944																JANUARY 1, 1945—DECEMBER 31, 1945															
	CONVICTIONS								OTHER DISPOSITIONS								CONVICTIONS								OTHER DISPOSITIONS							
	White		Negro		Indian		Unclassified		White		Negro		Indian		Unclassified		White		Negro		Indian		Unclassified		White		Negro		Indian		Unclassified	
	M	F	M	F	M	F	M	F	M	F	M	F	M	F	M	F	M	F	M	F	M	F	M	F	M	F	M	F	M	F	M	F
Assault	2																															
Assault and battery			1														1		5						2			2				
Assault with deadly weapon	8		13						2		4						13		12						2		3	2				
Assault on female	1																2		4													
Assault with intent to kill	1		7																2													
Assault with intent to rape			4								3								6						1		2					
Assault—secret			2														3		1						3							
Drunk—drunk & disorderly	1																		1													
Possession—illegal whiskey																	1		1	1												
Possession for sale—sale																	2		1													
Manufacturing—Possession of material for			1																1													
Transportation																																
Violation liquor laws				1															1						1		1					
Driving drunk	11		3						4		1	1					5		5													
Reckless driving	3		1														2		1													
Hit and run			5														2		1								1					
Speeding	1		2						1								2		1													
Auto license violations																																
Violation motor vehicle laws																	1		3						1		1					
Breaking and entering	2		9								1						5		5						1		8					
And larceny	2		8						1		4						2		4						1							1
And receiving											1						2		2													
Housebreaking																			1													
And larceny																																
And receiving																																
Storebreaking																																
And larceny																																
And receiving																																

Offense	Figures
Larceny of automobile	1, 1, 16, 1, 1
Temporary larceny	2, 1
Murder—first degree	4, 1, 1, 1, 1
Murder—second degree	2, 1, 3, 1, 2
Manslaughter	5, 1
Burglary—first degree	1
Burglary—second degree	
Abandonment	
Abduction	1, 1
Affray	1
Arson	2, 1, 1, 1, 2
Bigamy	1
Bribery	
Burning other than arson	1
Carrying concealed weapon	
Contempt	
Conspiracy	2, 2
Cruelty to animals	
Disorderly conduct	1, 1, 1, 2
Disorderly house	
Disposing of mortgaged property	
Disturbing Religious worship	
Violation of election laws	
Embezzlement	1
Escape	
Failure to list tax	
Food and drug laws	
Fish and game laws	1, 2
Forcible trespass	
Forgery	1
Fornication and adultery	
Gaming and lottery laws	8, 2, 2
Health laws	1, 2, 1
Incest	1
Injury to property	
Municipal ordinances	
Nonsupport	1, 3, 2, 1

THIRD JUDICIAL DISTRICT—(Continued)
IN SUPERIOR COURT

	JANUARY 1, 1944—DECEMBER 31, 1944																JANUARY 1, 1945—DECEMBER 31, 1945															
	CONVICTIONS								OTHER DISPOSITIONS								CONVICTIONS								OTHER DI POSITIONS							
	White		Negro		Indian		Unclassified		White		Negro		Indian		Unclassified		White		Negro		Indian		Unclassified		White		Negro		Indian		Unclassified	
Offense	M	F	M	F	M	F	M	F	M	F	M	F	M	F	M	F	M	F	M	F	M	F	M	F	M	F	M	F	M	F	M	F
Nonsupport of illegitimate child																																
Nuisance																																
Official misconduct			1																													
Perjury											1																					
Prostitution																			1								1					
Rape	1		1						1								1										1					
Receiving stolen goods	1		3						1		2								1						1							
Removing crop																									2							
Resisting officer			1								1						6		1						1		1					
Robbery																	6															
Seduction																																
Slander																																
Trespass																			1								1					
Vagrancy																																
Worthless check																	1		1													
False pretense	1		1						1		1						2		5						1		1					
Carnal knowledge, etc.	1		2						1	1							2								2							
Crime against nature			2																													
Slot machine laws																																
Kidnaping																																
Revenue act violations																	2								2							
Miscellaneous			1													1									2							1
Totals	53	6	114	2					18	1	35	3				1	98	2	107	2					34		30	2				1

Convictions 175
Nolle pros 34
Acquittals 19

Convictions 209
Nolle pros 36
Acquittals 28

Fourth Judicial District

FOURTH JUDICIAL DISTRICT
IN SUPERIOR COURT

Offense	1944 Convictions White M	White F	Negro M	Negro F	Indian M	Indian F	Unclassified M	Unclassified F	1944 Other Dispositions White M	White F	Negro M	Negro F	Indian M	Indian F	Unclassified M	Unclassified F	1945 Convictions White M	White F	Negro M	Negro F	Indian M	Indian F	Unclassified M	Unclassified F	1945 Other Dispositions White M	White F	Negro M	Negro F	Indian M	Indian F	Unclassified M	Unclassified F
Assault	7		8	1					7	1	3				1		6		8						6		2				2	
Assault and battery	1																															
Assault with deadly weapon	21		17	1					2	2	2				2		23		21						8		8				4	
Assault on female	2		3						1		1						3		7				1		2		2					
Assault with intent to kill			12						4		1				1		7		7					1			1					
Assault with intent to rape	2										4				1		3								2							
Assault—secret	1																															
Drunk—drunk & disorderly	4		1			1											5		2				2		1							
Possession—illegal whiskey	1										1								1	2							1					
Possession for sale—sale																											1					
Manufacturing—possession of material for	1																															
Transportation											1						3		3						1		1					
Violation liquor laws	8		5	1					4		1						9		1	1					3	2	1					
Driving drunk	5		4						3								17		3						2		1					
Reckless driving	3								3								5		2								1					
Hit and run	1								1								1		1						1		1				1	
Speeding	1																															
Auto license violations	3		1						1		1						1								2							
Violation motor vehicle laws	2		8														2		1						1		3					
Breaking and entering	3		12												1		5		1						1		11	2			4	
And larceny	3								1		5								9	1					1							
And receiving																																
Housebreaking	5		8														7		5						2		1					
And larceny			1																													
And receiving																									2							
Storebreaking																			1						2							
And larceny																																

Offense																			
Larceny by trick & device	20						1				2	7				1			2
Larceny of automobile	6			3					3	1	1	2	2	4	1				1
Temporary larceny																			
Murder—first degree	1	2			1				1		2	1	1		1				
Murder—second degree	2			2						3	4		1						
Manslaughter	8			3			1		3		7	1	7		1			1	4
Burglary—first degree																			
Burglary—second degree	5			5				1				6		4					
Abandonment																			
Abduction								1											
Affray	2			1								1							
Arson	2											2							
Bigamy	2	1		1			1			1									1
Bribery															1				
Burning other than arson	1										1								
Carrying concealed weapon	1											1							
Contempt																			
Conspiracy																			
Cruelty to animals	1			1					1										
Disorderly conduct				1					1										
Disorderly house																			5
Disposing of mortgaged property																			
Disturbing religious worship																			
Violation of election laws											2								
Embezzlement	1			1								1	1					1	
Escape							5			1									
Failure to list tax	7			1		11			7		1		1		1	1			4
Food and drug laws	1			7															
Fish and game laws																1			
Forcible trespass																1			
Forgery	10	3		3					3			2	3	3	1	10		1	
Fornication and adultery	2			1					1		1	1		1					
Gaming and lottery laws											1	1				2			
Health laws																			
Incest	1						1												
Injury to property	1												1						
Municipal ordinances	1												1	1					
Nonsupport	5			1			7					7	5	5		5			

FOURTH JUDICIAL DISTRICT—(Continued)
IN SUPERIOR COURT

JANUARY 1, 1944—DECEMBER 31, 1944

Offense	Convictions White M	Convictions White F	Convictions Negro M	Convictions Negro F	Convictions Indian M	Convictions Indian F	Convictions Unclassified M	Convictions Unclassified F	Other Dispositions White M	Other Dispositions White F	Other Dispositions Negro M	Other Dispositions Negro F	Other Dispositions Indian M	Other Dispositions Indian F	Other Dispositions Unclassified M	Other Dispositions Unclassified F
Nonsupport of illegitimate child																
Nuisance																
Official misconduct																
Perjury	3		2						1							
Prostitution	1		2	1					1		1					
Rape	2		6													
Receiving stolen goods												1				
Removing crop																
Resisting officer			1						1		2					
Robbery	6		8	1					3		3				2	
Seduction	1								1							
Slander	1															
Trespass			1								1					
Vagrancy	1								1		1					
Worthless check	1										1					
False pretense									2						4	
Carnal knowledge, etc.																
Crime against nature																
Slot machine laws																
Kidnaping																
Revenue act violations	10	1	1	1					2							
Miscellaneous										3					3	
Totals	181	7	140	13			1	1	68	3	55	5			34	

Convictions............ 343
Nolle pros............. 113
Acquittals............. 50
Other disposition...... 2

JANUARY 1, 1945—DECEMBER 31, 1945

Offense	Convictions White M	Convictions White F	Convictions Negro M	Convictions Negro F	Convictions Indian M	Convictions Indian F	Convictions Unclassified M	Convictions Unclassified F	Other Dispositions White M	Other Dispositions White F	Other Dispositions Negro M	Other Dispositions Negro F	Other Dispositions Indian M	Other Dispositions Indian F	Other Dispositions Unclassified M	Other Dispositions Unclassified F
Nonsupport of illegitimate child	2		2	2							1					
Nuisance																
Official misconduct									1							
Perjury																
Prostitution			2	2					2		1					
Rape	1		2													
Receiving stolen goods	1															
Removing crop																
Resisting officer	1								1							
Robbery	3		4								4					
Seduction	1															
Slander																
Trespass	2		1													
Vagrancy	1		1												1	
Worthless check																
False pretense																
Carnal knowledge, etc.			2						1							
Crime against nature											2					
Slot machine laws																
Kidnaping	1															
Revenue act violations	2		1						5		1					
Miscellaneous								5	5	3	71	2				
Totals	167	1	135	11			10		71	5	71	2			25	

Convictions............ 324
Nolle pros............. 125
Acquittals............. 41
Other disposition...... 8

Fifth Judicial District

FIFTH JUDICIAL DISTRICT
IN SUPERIOR COURT

JANUARY 1, 1944—DECEMBER 31, 1944

Offense	CONVICTIONS								OTHER DISPOSITIONS							
	White		Negro		Indian		Unclassified		White		Negro		Indian		Unclassified	
	M	F	M	F	M	F	M	F	M	F	M	F	M	F	M	F
Assault	2															
Asslt and battery			1	1			12	1		1						
Asslt with deadly weapon	7		7						2	1	6					
Asslt on female	1		5													
Asslt with intent to kill	1	1	4								1					
Asslt with intent to rape	2															
Asslt—secret		1	4													
Drunk—drunk & disorderly	1															
Possession—illegal whiskey			1	1												
Possession for sale—sale	1		1													
Manufacturing—Possession of material for																
Transportation																
Violation liquor laws	5		11	3					3		1				1	
Driving drunk	16		7								2				1	
Reckless driving	1		2								1				2	
Hit and run	2															
Speeding									1							
Auto license violations																
Violation motor vehicle laws	12		20													
Breaking and entering	4		6						2		4					
And larceny	1															
And receiving			13								2					
Housebreaking									1							
And larceny																
And receiving																
Storebreaking																
And larceny																

JANUARY 1, 1945—DECEMBER 31, 1945

Offense	CONVICTIONS								OTHER DISPOSITIONS							
	White		Negro		Indian		Unclassified		White		Negro		Indian		Unclassified	
	M	F	M	F	M	F	M	F	M	F	M	F	M	F	M	F
Assault	2	1														1
Asslt and battery			4								2	1			1	
Asslt with deadly weapon	7		14	3			3		2		1					
Asslt on female	1		4	1					2		2					
Asslt with intent to kill	5		4						1		2					
Asslt with intent to rape	3		1						1							
Asslt—secret	1								2						3	3
Drunk—drunk & disorderly	6		7	1			2				1					
Possession—illegal whiskey									1	1	1					
Possession for sale—sale				1					1							
Manufacturing—Possession of material for							1		2							
Transportation	1		1													
Violation liquor laws	3	1	4	1					5		2	1				
Driving drunk	12	1	5				2	1	3		2					
Reckless driving	6		1				1		1							
Hit and run			5	1					1		1					
Speeding																
Auto license violations																
Violation motor vehicle laws	1		13						1							
Breaking and entering	9		4				2				6	1				
And larceny	6								2	1					2	
And receiving																
Housebreaking																
And larceny																
And receiving																
Storebreaking																
And larceny																

Offense																										
Larceny by trick & device																										
Larceny of automobile	1						1																			
Temporary larceny																										
Murder—first degree		3	1									1														
Murder—second degree		2																								
Manslaughter	2			1																						
Burglary—first degree																										
Burglary—second degree																										
Abandonment	4	1	1		1	2		1																		
Abduction																										
Affray								1																		
Arson							2																			
Bigamy	1						1	1																		
Bribery																										
Burning other than arson	1		1				1																			
Carrying concealed weapon	1	1					1																			
Contempt																										
Conspiracy								1		1																
Cruelty to animals															12											
Disorderly conduct																										
Disorderly house	1																									
Disposing of mortgaged property																										
Disturbing religious worship																										
Violation of election laws																										
Embezzlement	2				1		1		1																	
Escape																										
Failure to list tax							1																			
Food and drug laws							2																			
Fish and game laws		1				1	1							1												
Forcible trespass	1	1				3	2																			
Forgery						1	1	1							15											
Fornication and adultery						1	1																			
Gaming and lottery laws	1			1		1	1																			

FIFTH JUDICIAL DISTRICT—(Continued)
IN SUPERIOR COURT

	JANUARY 1, 1944—DECEMBER 31, 1944																JANUARY 1, 1945—DECEMBER 31, 1945																
	CONVICTIONS								OTHER DISPOSITIONS								CONVICTIONS								OTHER DISPOSITIONS								
	White		Negro		Indian		Unclassified		White		Negro		Indian		Unclas.		White		Negro		Indian		Unclassified		White		Negro		Indian		Unclassified	
Offense	M	F	M	F	M	F	M	F	M	F	M	F	M	F	M	F	M	F	M	F	M	F	M	F	M	F	M	F	M	F	M	F
Health laws																																
Incest	1																								1							
Injury to property																																
Municipal ordinances																																
Nonsupport	4		1														3		3						1							
Nonsupport of illegitimate child			1	1							1	1					1		4													
Nuisance			3								1																					
Official misconduct																																
Perjury																																
Prostitution																																
Rape															1		1		1						1		1	2			1	
Receiving stolen goods																																
Removing crop																																
Resisting officer	1		1														1										3					
Robbery																	1		12												1	
Seduction																	1								1						1	
Slander	1																1															
Trespass			1						1										1						1		1					
Vagrancy	1								1								1	3	1						1	1	1					
Worthless check									1								1								1		1					
False pretense																	1															
Carnal knowledge, etc.	1		2								1								2													
Crime against nature			2																2													
Slot machine laws																																
Kidnaping																																
Revenue act violations																																
Miscellaneous	1		1						1		1						1		114						1	2	44	5			1	
Totals	94	2	117	11			40	1	17	1	34	4			4		95	7	114	10			14		39	2	44	5			16	

Convictions _____ 265
Nolle pros _____ 45
Acquittals _____ 14

Convictions _____ 270
Nolle pros _____ 69
Acquittals _____

Sixth Judicial District

SIXTH JUDICIAL DISTRICT
IN SUPERIOR COURT

	JANUARY 1, 1944—DECEMBER 31, 1944																JANUARY 1, 1945—DECEMBER 31, 1945																
	CONVICTIONS								OTHER DISPOSITIONS								CONVICTIONS								OTHER DISPOSITIONS							
	White		Negro		Indian		Unclassified		White		Negro		Indian		Unclassified		White		Negro		Indian		Unclassified		White		Negro		Indian		Unclassified	
Offense	M	F	M	F	M	F	M	F	M	F	M	F	M	F	M	F	M	F	M	F	M	F	M	F	M	F	M	F	M	F	M	F
Assault	2																1		2						3							
Assault and battery			3						1			1					2		24	2							1					
Assault with deadly weapon	5		8						1								7		1						3		2					
Assault on female	6	1	3						1								5		8						1		1					
Assault with intent to kill	10		8						2		1						2		5						1		1					
Assault with intent to rape	1		1						1		1														6		1					
Assault—secret	1		1																1													
Drunk—drunk & disorderly	1		1								1						3		1						1							
Possession—illegal whiskey	2		2						2		1						2		5						1		1					
Possession for sale—sale	2	1	2														2		10	2												
Manufacturing—possession of material for	1							1									1		7													
Transportation	3		1						2		1						1		1													
Violation liquor laws			4														1		1													
Driving drunk	12		1						2		2						5		5						1							
Reckless driving	1	1	1										1				2		8				1		2							
Hit and run	2		1						1								1		1													
Speeding	1								1		1						2								1							
Auto license violations	1																2		1								1					
Violation motor vehicle laws	1								1								1		6								2					
Breaking and entering	3		3						1		3						4		19		1				8		4					
And larceny	5		5						1								1															
And receiving																																
Housebreaking			3																1													
And larceny	3																2															
And receiving																																
Storebreaking			3														2		1													
And larceny																																
And receiving																																
Larceny	4	1	11	1					4			1					8	1	13													

Offense									
Larceny & [steal]ing	1	7		2		6	1	5	1
Larceny from the person									
Larceny by trick & device									
[Larceny] any of automobile								5	
Temporary larceny	2	2	5	2				4	1
Murder—first dee[degree]	1	1			1	2	2	1	1
Murder—second degree	2			1			4	3	
Manslaughter		1				3			
Burglary—first degree							1		
Burglary—second degree	1					1			
Abandonment	2	1		2	2	2	4	1	
Abduction									
Affray									
Arson	2	3		2	2	1	3	1	1
Bigamy	1	1		1		1	1		
Bribery									
Burning other than arson	1	1		1			1		
Carrying concealed weapon	1						1		
Contempt									
Conspiracy									
Cruelty to animals						6			
Disorderly conduct	1						1	1	1
Disorderly house						1			
Disposing of mortgaged property									
Disturbing religious worship									
Violation of election laws						2	4		
Embezzlement									
Escape						1			
Failure to list tax									
Food and drug laws									
Fish and game laws									
Forcible trespass	1	1					2	2	
Forgery	2	2		1	1	1	6	1	2
Fornication and adultery				1		1	1	2	
Gaming and lottery laws						1			
Health laws									1
Incest									
Injury to property		1		1		1	1		
Municipal ordinances							1		

SIXTH JUDICIAL DISTRICT—(Continued)
IN SUPERIOR COURT

JANUARY 1, 1944—DECEMBER 31, 1944

Offense	CONVICTIONS White M	White F	Negro M	Negro F	Indian M	Indian F	Unclassified M	Unclassified F	OTHER DISPOSITIONS White M	White F	Negro M	Negro F	Indian M	Indian F	Unclas. M	Unclas. F
Nonsupport	3		1						2							
Nonsupport of illegitimate child																
Nuisance																
Official misconduct									1							
Perjury	1	7							1	1						
Prostitution	1															1
Rape																
Receiving stolen goods																
Removing crop																
Resisting officer		1														
Robbery	4		9													
Seduction																
Slander																
Trespass	1		1						1							
Vagrancy		3								1						
Worthless check			2							1						
False pretense	1								4							
Carnal knowledge, etc.	1								1							
Crime against nature																
Slot machine laws																
Kidnapping																
Revenue act violations	1								1							
Miscellaneous									1		3					
Totals	**92**	**16**	**90**	**5**			**7**		**35**	**2**	**29**	**4**	**1**		**1**	

JANUARY 1, 1945—DECEMBER 31, 1945

Offense	CONVICTIONS White M	White F	Negro M	Negro F	Indian M	Indian F	Unclassified M	Unclassified F	OTHER DISPOSITIONS White M	White F	Negro M	Negro F	Indian M	Indian F	Unclas. M	Unclas. F
Nonsupport	4		1						2		2				1	
Nonsupport of illegitimate child			3													
Nuisance	2															
Official misconduct																
Perjury	1															
Prostitution																
Rape			2								1					
Receiving stolen goods																
Removing crop																
Resisting officer	2		5						1		1	1				
Robbery			7								1					
Seduction																
Slander																
Trespass																
Vagrancy																
Worthless check	1															
False pretense	1		1						1	1						
Carnal knowledge, etc.																
Crime against nature																
Slot machine laws																
Kidnapping																
Revenue act violations									2							
Miscellaneous									2	2	33	3			7	
Totals	**95**	**1**	**171**	**6**	**1**		**2**		**68**	**2**	**33**	**3**			**7**	

Convictions _____ 210
Nolle pros _____ 46
Acquittals _____ 25
Other disposition _____ 1

Convictions _____ 276
Nolle pros _____ 64
Acquittals _____ 43
Other disposition _____ 6

Seventh Judicial District

SEVENTH JUDICIAL DISTRICT
IN SUPERIOR COURT

	JANUARY 1, 1944—DECEMBER 31, 1944															JANUARY 1, 1945—DECEMBER 31, 1945								
	CONVICTIONS								OTHER DISPOSITIONS							CONVICTIONS							OTHER DISPOSITIONS		
	White		Negro		Indian		Unclassified		White		Negro		Indian		Unclas.	White		Negro		Unclassified			White	Unclassified	
Offense	M	F	M	F	M	F	M	F	M	F	M	F	M	F	M	M	F	M	F	M	F		M	M	F
Assault	1		1						2																
Asslt and battery	5		15																					3	
Asslt with deadly weap n	1		3	2							1				1										
Asslt on ‗	5		6																					1	
Assault with intent to kill	1																								
Assault with intent to rape																									
Assault—secret ‗									2																
Drunk—drunk & disorderly	3		6	3							2	1													
Possession—illegal ‗	4										1														
Possession for sale—sale																									
Manufacturing—possession of material for																									
Transportation																									
Violation liquor laws			1																						
Driving drunk	4								1		2													2	
Reckless driving	3																								
Hit and run	1																								
Speeding		1																							
Auto license violations																									
Violation motor vehicle laws	1		3																						
Breaking and entering			6																						
And larceny																									
And receiving																									
Housebreaking	1																								
And larceny	5		17								1														
And receiving																									
Storebreaking			6																						
And larceny																									
And receiving																									

Offense																
Larceny by trick & device												2			1	
Larceny of automobile								6		6		6				
Petty larceny												1				
Murder—first degree			1			1			3		1	2				
Murder—second degree	2		2			2		12	4		1					
Manslaughter								1				1				
Burglary—first degree	1							1				1				
Burglary—second degree								1		2					2	
Abandonment			1			1					2					
Abduction												1				
Affray			1				2									
Arson											2	1				
Bigamy	1								3				1			
Bribery								2			1					
Burning other than arson			1													
Carrying concealed weapon											1	2				
Contempt											2					
Conspiracy					1											
Cruelty to animals	1							1				1				
Disorderly conduct			1			1					1				1	
Disorderly house																
Disposing of mortgaged property																
Disturbing religious worship																
Violation of election laws					1											
Embezzlement												2				
Escape														2		
Failure to list tax												1				
Food and drug laws														2		
Fish and game laws												1				
Forcible trespass	3															
Forgery	10									1		2	1			1
Fornication and adultery	9	7								1		2	2			4
Gaming and lottery laws	1	2							10			1				
Health laws																
Incest													1			
Injury to property												1				1
Municipal ordinances	2			1												
Nonsupport	1															1
Nonsupport of illegitimate child	1											3	1			

SEVENTH JUDICIAL DISTRICT—(Continued)
IN SUPERIOR COURT

JANUARY 1, 1944—DECEMBER 31, 1944

Offense	CONVICTIONS								OTHER DISPOSITIONS							
	White		Negro		Indian		Unclassified		White		Negro		Indian		Unclassified	
	M	F	M	F	M	F	M	F	M	F	M	F	M	F	M	F
Nuisance																
Official misconduct			1													
Perjury	1															
Prostitution																
Rape	1		3	2							1					
Receiving stolen goods																
Removing crop																
Resisting officer	1		1													
Robbery			5													
Seduction	1															
Slander																
Trespass			1								1	1				
Vagrancy			1													
Worthless check									1							
False pretense	3														2	
Carnal knowledge, etc.	1															
Crime against nature																
Slot machine laws																
Kidnaping																
Revenue act violations									2							
Miscellaneous			1					1								
Totals	89	11	140	11				1	20	2	17	3			13	

Convictions _____ 252
Nolle pros. _____ 44
Acquittals _____ 8
Other disposition _____ 3

JANUARY 1, 1945—DECEMBER 31, 1945

Offense	CONVICTIONS								OTHER DISPOSITIONS							
	White		Negro		Indian		Unclassified		White		Negro		Indian		Unclassified	
	M	F	M	F	M	F	M	F	M	F	M	F	M	F	M	F
Nuisance																
Official misconduct			1													
Perjury																
Prostitution																
Rape			2												1	
Receiving stolen goods															1	
Removing crop																
Resisting officer			1													
Robbery	27		18								7				2	
Seduction																
Slander															2	
Trespass			1													
Vagrancy			1													
Worthless check																
False pretense	3								1						1	
Carnal knowledge, etc.	1														1	
Crime against nature	1															
Slot machine laws																
Kidnaping																
Revenue act violations																
Miscellaneous	3		1													
Totals	165	8	157	8				9	26	3	21	1			25	1

Convictions _____ 347
Nolle pros. _____ 62
Acquittals _____ 10
Other disposition _____ 5

Eighth Judicial District

EIGHTH JUDICIAL DISTRICT
IN SUPERIOR COURT

JANUARY 1, 1944—DECEMBER 31, 1944 / JANUARY 1, 1945—DECEMBER 31, 1945

Offense	1944 Convictions White M	F	Negro M	F	Indian M	F	Unclass M	F	1944 Other Dispositions White M	F	Negro M	F	Indian M	F	Unclass M	F	1945 Convictions White M	F	Unclass M	F	1945 Other Dispositions White M	F	Unclass M	F
Assault	4								2	1	1	1									2	1		
Assault and battery	9		13	1																				
Assault with deadly weapon	1								1		5	1									6			
Assault on female	7		19	1					1		4	1									2			
Assault with intent to kill	2		2						3		1										4			
Assault with intent to rape																					1			
Assault—secret	21		1								1													
Drunk—drunk & disorderly	1		1						1		1													
Possession—illegal whiskey			3						1		1													
Possession for sale—sale									1		1													
Manufacturing—possession of material for			1						1		1													
Transportation	1								2	1	1													
Violation liquor laws	8		8						5	2	2													
Driving drunk	2		1				1		6		5													
Reckless driving	1		3						1		1													
Hit and run	2		4								1													
Speeding			1								1													
Auto license violations	2								1		1													
Violation motor vehicle laws	3		2						2		1													
Breaking and entering	6		3				1																	
And larceny	1								1		1													
And receiving	1		5																					
Housebreaking	1		4																					
And larceny	2																							
And receiving	1		7						5		3													
Storebreaking	18																							

Offense	No.
Larceny by trick & device	1
Larceny of automobile	11
Petty larceny	37
Murder—first degree	4
Murder—second degree	3
Manslaughter	5
Burglary—first degree	1
Burglary—second degree	
Abandonment	2
Abduction	
Affray	1
Arson	7
Bigamy	5
Bribery	
Burning other than arson	
Carrying concealed weapon	
Contempt	
Conspiracy	
Cruelty to animals	
Disorderly conduct	3
Disorderly house	3
Disposing of mortgaged property	
Disturbing religious worship	
Violation of election laws	
Embezzlement	1
Escape	
Failure to list tax	1
Food and drug laws	
Fish and game laws	
Forcible trespass	1
Forcible trespass	1
Forgery	16
Fornication and adultery	4
Gaming and lottery laws	
Health laws	
Incest	2
Injury to property	
Municipal ordinances	
Nonsupport	6

EIGHTH JUDICIAL DISTRICT—(Continued)
IN SUPERIOR COURT

	JANUARY 1, 1944—DECEMBER 31, 1944																JANUARY 1, 1945—DECEMBER 31, 1945															
	CONVICTIONS								OTHER DISPOSITIONS								CONVICTIONS								OTHER DISPOSITIONS							
	White		Negro		Indian		Unclassified		White		Negro		Indian		Unclassified		White		Negro		Indian		Unclassified		White		Negro		Indian		Unclassified	
Offense	M	F	M	F	M	F	M	F	M	F	M	F	M	F	M	F	M	F	M	F	M	F	M	F	M	F	M	F	M	F	M	F
Nonsupport of the child																	1															
Nuisance																		4														
Official misconduct																			1													
Perjury		7	1				1		1		1	1				1			1													
Prostitution	3		1							3							2	2	1						1	5						
Rape	5		1								2								5						3							
Receiving stolen goods	2		1														2		1						2							
Removing crop	1	1	1	2							2						2								1							
Resisting	7	1	10	1			1	1	5	1	2					1	3		20				2		1		7					
Seduction									5	1	2				1				20													
Slander	2	1																														
Trespass	2	1	2								1						4								1	1	4					
Vagrancy																	1										1					
Worthless chk	14		1								1						4	1														
False pretense	6	1									3						7								1							
Carnal knowledge, etc	2	1									3						2	1	2						1		1					
Crime against nature	1	1		1													1		1													
Slot machine laws																									1							
Kidnaping				1																												
Revenue act violations	6	1	1	2					4		1	1					4	1	2	1	1				3		1					
Miscellaneous																															2	
Totals	251	30	152	19	5		17	2	61	9	59	9			5		210	22	219	23	1		16		89	10	62	22	4		2	

Ninth Judicial District

NINTH JUDICIAL DISTRICT
IN SUPERIOR COURT

	JANUARY 1, 1944—DECEMBER 31, 1944																JANUARY 1, 1945—DECEMBER 31, 1945																
	CONVICTIONS								OTHER DISPOSITIONS								CONVICTIONS								OTHER DISPOSITIONS							
	White		Negro		Indian		Unclassified		White		Negro		Indian		Unclassified		White		Negro		Indian		Unclassified		White		Negro		Indian		Unclassified	
Offense	M	F	M	F	M	F	M	F	M	F	M	F	M	F	M	F	M	F	M	F	M	F	M	F	M	F	M	F	M	F	M	F
Assault	8	2	15		9	2	2	2	4		2				1		10		6		2	1	2									
Assault and battery	1			1		1																1										
Assault with deadly weapon	18	2	22	1	10	1	3	2	5		3		1				17		8	2	8	1		1	2				3	1	1	
Assault on female	4		2		7		1										5		5		1				8				1			
Assault with intent to kill	3		7				4										2		2													
Assault with intent to rape			2																													
Assault—secret			2								1						5	1	1			1										
Drunk—drunk & disorderly	4		1	1	2		1		1		2		1				1		3		2		1									
Possession—illegal whiskey	3		3		3	1											2		2								1					
Possession for sale—sale	1		10		2				1		2		1				2															
Manufacturing—possession of material for	1		3		4												5	1	1		1		1		1		1					
Transportation			1												2		1		1					1	3							
Violation liquor laws	1		4	1	3		1		2	1	3				1		5		1	1	1											
Driving drunk	11		4		3		1		4	1							6		1				2	1								
Reckless driving	4		2				1		2		2						1		3	1												
Hit and run			2				1		1																							
Speeding	3				1				1								1		1		1		1									
Auto license violations	1																															
Violation motor vehicle laws	2		5		2		1		4		2		1				15	1	1		1				1	1	1		1			1
Breaking and entering	25	1	17		5		1		8		5						8		19		6		6		1		3		1			
And larceny							1										3		16		3		3	1	1				1			
And receiving																																
Housebreaking																																
And larceny																																
And receiving																																
Storebreaking																																
And larceny																																

Larceny by trick & device					1		1
Larceny of automobile					1	1	
Temporary larceny					1		
Murder—first degree			1	1	1	1	1
Murder—second degree			2		1		
Manslaughter							
Burglary—first degree							
Burglary—second offe	1			1	1		
...							
Abduction							
Affray							
Arson							
Bigamy	1						
Bribery							
Burning of other than ars o							
Carrying ... weapon	1			1			
Contempt							
Conspiracy							
...lty to animals							
Disorderly conduct							
Disorderly h us o							
Disposing of mortgaged property	1						
Disturbing rel igus worsh'p							
...ion of ele tion laws							
Embezzlement							
Escap s	2					1	
Failure to list tax							
F d and drug laws	1						
Fish and game laws	4						
Forcible trespass	1						
Forgery	2			2	2	1	1
Fornication and adultery	1						
Gaming and lery laws	1	1					
Incest	1						
Injury to property	1	1			1		1
Municipal ordinances							
Nonsupport	1						
Nonsupport of illegitimate child							

NINTH JUDICIAL DISTRICT—(Continued)
IN SUPERIOR COURT

Offense	1944 CONVICTIONS White M	F	Negro M	F	Indian M	F	Unclas. M	F	1944 OTHER DISPOSITIONS White M	F	Negro M	F	Indian M	F	Unclas. M	F	1945 CONVICTIONS White M	F	Negro M	F	Indian M	F	Unclas. M	F	1945 OTHER DISPOSITIONS White M	F	Negro M	F	Indian M	F	Unclas. M	F
Nuisance																																
Official misconduct																																
Perjury																																
Prostitution																																
Rape			10	2	1		1								1		4		2	1	1	1	1	1					1		
Receiving stolen goods											1																					
Removing crop					2						1																					
Resisting officer	7	3	2	2					2								5		1	2		1							1		
Robbery	1																5		1			1					1		1		
Seduction																													1		
Slander															1	3		2			1								1		
Trespass				1					2	1			1																
Vagrancy			1														2		1		1						1		1		
Worthless check	2																														
False pretense	1		2								1				1		2														
Carnal knowledge, etc.															1		2		1						1						
Crime against nature																			1												
Slot machine laws																															
Kidnaping					1																										
Revenue act violations																															
Miscellaneous	6	2					1		6		1		1		2	1		1	1		1			1	1				15		1
Totals	159	11	193	14	73	6	22		55	8	37	1	9	2	13	146	3	135	9	50	6	12	1	22	1	9	1	15	1	1

Convictions_____ 478

Convictions_____ 362

Tenth Judicial District

TENTH JUDICIAL DISTRICT
IN SUPERIOR COURT

JANUARY 1, 1944—DECEMBER 31, 1944

Offense	Conv. White M	White F	Negro M	Negro F	Indian M	Unclas. F	Other Disp. White M	White F	Negro M	Negro F	Indian M	Indian F	Unclas. M	Unclas. F
Assault	2		1											
Assault and battery	7		32	1			7		9	1				1
Assault with deadly weapon	3		17						1	1			1	
Assault on female	1	1	2				3		2	1				
Assault with intent to kill	3		8				2		2					
Assault with intent to rape			2				1		1					
Assault—secret		1	1				1							
Drunk—drunk & disorderly	2		2				1		1					
Possession—illegal whiskey	7		4											
Possession for sale—sale	2		2						2					
Manufacturing—possession of material for														
Transportation	1													
Violation liquor laws	2		2						1					
Driving drunk	19		3				12	1	3				2	
Reckless driving	5	1	3				6		2				1	
Hit and run	1		2											
Speeding	2						1							
Auto license violations	3													
Violation motor vehicle laws														
Breaking and entering	2		7				5							
And larceny	5		4					4						1
And receiving														
Housebreaking		1						1						
And larceny			4											
And receiving														
Storebreaking														
And larceny														
And receiving														

JANUARY 1, 1945—DECEMBER 31, 1945

Offense	Conv. White M	White F	Negro M	Negro F	Indian M	Indian F	Unclas. M	Unclas. F	Other Disp. White M	White F	Negro M	Negro F	Indian M	Indian F	Unclas. M	Unclas. F
Assault	3		1	1												
Assault and battery	5	3	6	2	1	1			2	1	7					
Assault with deadly weapon	10	3	21	2	1				7		8					
Assault on female	3	3	8						3							
Assault with intent to kill			1													
Assault with intent to rape	1		1													
Assault—secret									1		4					
Drunk—drunk & disorderly	11		2	1					2		1					
Possession—illegal whiskey	5		5													
Possession for sale—sale	6		2	2					2							
Manufacturing—possession of material for																
Transportation	1		2	1					1		3					
Violation liquor laws											3					
Driving drunk	33		6						15		3					
Reckless driving	16		13						6	1						
Hit and run	1		2													
Speeding	2		1						1							
Auto license violations																
Violation motor vehicle laws	5		4						2							
Breaking and entering	4		3						1	2						
And larceny	5		3						1							
And receiving	2		2													
Housebreaking	2		15				15									
And larceny			1				1				1					
And receiving																
Storebreaking	14		6								6					
And larceny	15		7						1		7					
And receiving	31	2	29						4	4	8	1				

	C1	C2	C3	C4	C5	C6	C7	C8	C9	C10	C11	C12
Larceny by trick & device	6	1	1				3		5		3	
Larceny of automobile		2							5			
Temporary larceny												
Murder—first degree	3	1	1				5	1	1	1		
Murder—second degree		1	4				5		1	4	1	
Manslaughter	3	2				1	2				5	
Burglary—first degree		1										
Burglary—second degree	3			1			2		3		2	1
Abandonment							1					
Abduction	1	3				2	1		2		1	
Affray						1	1					
Arson	1	2				1					1	
Bigamy	1								2			
Bribery	1											
Burning other than arson	1									1		
Carrying concealed weapon		4	1	4		1	1		3	1		
Contempt												
Conspiracy	4					2	7	2		2		
Cruelty to animals	4		1	1		4	1	4	3			
Disorderly conduct	3									1		
Disorderly house												
Disposing of mortgaged property						1						
Disturbing religious worship												
Violation of election laws	2		1			1	2			1		
Embezzlement		2					3	5			2	
Escape												
Failure to list tax												
Food and drug laws												
Fish and game laws												
Forcible trespass	1					2						
Forgery	3	3	1	8		10	10		3	2	
Fornication and adultery	2	2				19	19		2	14		1
Gaming and lottery laws						1	2	2			2	
Health laws				1		1					1	
Incest												
Injury to property	2	4	2	2		1	4		4	1	2	1
Municipal ordinances			2			1	2		2		1	1
Nonsupport	6	5	1		1	1	12		5	2	1	1
Nonsupport of illegitimate child						1	1			2	2	2

TENTH JUDICIAL DISTRICT—(Continued)
IN SUPERIOR COURT

Offense	1944 Conv White M	F	Negro M	F	Indian M	F	Unclas M	F	1944 Other White M	F	Negro M	F	Indian M	F	Unclas M	F	1945 Conv White M	F	Negro M	F	Indian M	F	Unclas M	F	1945 Other White M	F	Negro M	F	Indian M	F	Unclas M	F
Nuisance	2		2						3								2	1								3						
Official misconduct	1	1																														
Perjury			1																1													
Prostitution	4		5	2					3	1	3							8	1						3	3	1	2				
Rape	1		1						2								2		3						1		1					
Receiving stolen goods	1		7						4		15	6			7																	
Removing crop									1										1								2					
Resisting officer	1		2							1	1						10	2	1	1					1							
Robbery	2		3						1		1						2	2	8								2					
Seduction																																
Slander									1								4		3						2	1	1					
Trespass			1						2	1	1														6		1					
Vagrancy											1														2		1					
Trespass									2	1	1						4		3						6		1					
Vagrancy			1								1														1							
Worthless check			1						1																2		1					
False pretense	1		1	1					2		1						1		8	2					1							
Carnal knowledge, etc.	2								2		1						1															
Crime against nature									4																							
Slot machine laws																																
Kidnaping																																
Revenue act violations																																
Miscellaneous	4								6		5	12			1		5		3						5	1	3					
Totals	140	7	22	8			3		106	8	94	12	1		14		280	24	220	10		2	3		101	17	69	4				

Convictions 382
Nolle pros 155
.... 79

Convictions 539
Nolle pros 111
Acquittals 75

Eleventh Judicial District

ELEVENTH JUDICIAL DISTRICT
IN SUPERIOR COURT

JANUARY 1, 1944—DECEMBER 31, 1944 / JANUARY 1, 1945—DECEMBER 31, 1945

Offense	1944 CONVICTIONS White M	W F	Negro M	N F	Indian M	I F	Unclas M	U F	1944 OTHER DISP. White M	W F	Negro M	N F	Indian M	I F	Unc M	U F	1945 CONVICTIONS Negro M	N F	Indian M	I F	Unclas M	U F	1945 OTHER DISP. White M	W F	Negro M	N F	Indian M	I F	Unc M	U F
Assault	6																1	1					1	1						
Aslt and battery	5		13	4					3		1						6	2					1		1					
Assault with deadly w ap n	2		1									2					2	1					1		1	1				
Aslt on female	3		8														6													
Aslt with aslt to kill			1														2													
aslt with aslt to rape																														
Assault—Secret	7	1							4			2																		
Drunk—Drunk and Dsly	1																													
Possession—illegal whiskey	1																													
Possession for sale—sale																														
Manufacturing—possession of material for	2								1		2						2	2							1					
Transportation	13	2	11	5					1		2	1											3							
Violation liquor laws	8		2						2		2						5						2							
Driving drunk	13		4						2		1	1					3													
Reckless driving	3		2						2														1							
Hit and run	1								1																					
Speeding	2																													
Auto license violations									1		1						2													
Violation motor vehicle laws	1		1														3													
Breaking and entering									1																					
And larceny	1								1		2	2																		
Housebreaking	6		3																											
And larceny																														
And receiving			26	1																										
Storebreaking	5		3						4	1	3						2													
And larceny	19		10						4	1		3					3													
And receiving	14	2	25	8																										
Larceny																														

Offense							
Larceny of automobile	2						2
Temporary larceny	2	1	1				
Murder—first degree	1	1	2				
Murder—second degree			2				
Manslaughter	3	1	3	4	3	2	1
Burglary—first degree	1	2	1			5	
Burglary—second degree							
Abandonment	1						
Abduction							
Affray	1	1				6	
Arson	1	1					
Bigamy	1			1	1	1	
Bribery							
Burning other than arson	1			1			
concealed weapon						4	
Conspiracy							
Cruelty to animals	1		2				
Disorderly conduct	1	2					
Disorderly house							
Disposing of mortgaged property			2				
Disturbing religious worship							
Violation of election laws					1		
Embezzlement	3	1				3	1
Escape		2				3	
Failure to list tax							
Food and drug laws							
Fish and game laws						8	1
Forcible trespass						8	1
Forgery	3	1					
Fornication and adultery	3	2					
Gaming and lottery laws	2	6	2		1		
Health laws	4						
Incest							
Injury to property	3	1			1	1	
Municipal ordinances			1				
Nonsupport	8	1	16	2			
Nonsupport of illegitimate child			1				
Nuisance	1	1	1	1			

ELEVENTH JUDICIAL DISTRICT—(Continued)
IN SUPERIOR COURT

Offense	JANUARY 1, 1944—DECEMBER 31, 1944																JANUARY .., 945—1 DECEMBER 31, 1945																
	CONVICTIONS								OTHER DISPOSITIONS								CONVICTIONS								OTHER DISPOSITIONS							
	White		Negro		Indian		Unclassified		White		Negro		Ind'an		Unclas. sified		White		Negro		Indian		Unclassified		White		Negro		Indian		Unclassified	
	M	F	M	F	M	F	M	F	M	F	M	F	M	F	M	F	M	F	M	F	M	F	M	F	M	F	M	F	M	F	M	F
Official misconduct																																
Perjury			1																													
Prostitution																																
Rape	1										1								1						1							
Receiving stolen goods			2								1						3		3	1					2							
Removing crop			1																													
Resisting officer		1																														
Robbery	2		7						1								8															
Seduction																			4	1												
Slander									1								1									1						
Trespass									1		1						1															
Vagrancy	12	4	3						1		1						1	3														
Worthless check	22									1																						
False pretense	1																															
Carnal knowledge, etc.	1		1								1						2		1													
Crime against nature			2														1		1													
Slot machine laws																																
Kidnaping																																
Revenue act violations	1	7							1									2	1							1						
Miscellaneous	7		4									1					2	2							29	5	12	3				
Totals	190	24	154	21					38	2	20	4					197	16	154	18					29	5	12	3				

Twelfth Judicial District

TWELFTH JUDICIAL DISTRICT
IN SUPERIOR COURT

Offense	JAN 1, 1944 – DEC 31, 1944 CONVICTIONS White M	F	Negro M	F	Indian M	F	Unclas. M	F	OTHER DISPOSITIONS White M	F	Negro M	F	Indian M	F	Unclas. M	F	JAN 1, 1945 – DEC 31, 1945 CONVICTIONS White M	F	Negro M	F	Indian M	F	Unclas. M	F	OTHER DISPOSITIONS White M	F	Negro M	F	Indian M	F	Unclas. M	F
Assault	6																6	1	3														
Assault and battery			2						3																1							1	
Assault with deadly weapon	11		14									1			1		23	1	19	4					3			1					
Assault on female	4		21	4					1	1	1	3					7		5														
Assault with intent to kill	2		6						1								6	1	6	1					2								
Assault with intent to rape	1		4								1	3					7		5									1					
Assault—secret	1																										1						
Drunk—drunk & disorderly	42	5	11	4					3		3				3		21	1	5						1								
Possession—illegal whiskey										1									1	2					1								
Possession for sale—sale																																	
Manufacturing—possession of material for																	1		1														
Transportation	5	1																															
Violation liquor laws	7		5	2					3	1	1	1							5				1										
Driving drunk	7								3																								
Reckless driving	1						2		5		1						4	1	4														
Hit and run	3		1					1	1								9		4						3	1	2	1					
Speeding	3	1	2								1						2		4						4								
Auto license violations			1																						1								
Violation motor vehicle laws									1																								
Breaking and entering	9		6						1		2						1								1								
And larceny	9		2						1								22		2						4		5						
And receiving	16		37						1								11		10								2	1					
Housebreaking	5		5														34	1	43						1								
And larceny																																	
And receiving																																	
Storebreaking																																	

Offense	Count
Larceny by trick & device	2
Larceny of automobile	10
Temporary larceny	1
Murder—first degree	1
Murder—second degree	1
Manslaughter	2
Burglary—first degree	1
Burglary—second degree	
Abandonment	7
Abduction	
Affray	1
Arson	
Bigamy	7
Bribery	
Burning other than arson	
Carrying concealed weapon	
Contempt	2
Conspiracy	
Cruelty to animal	1
Disorderly conduct	3
Disorderly house	2
Disposing of mortgaged property	
Disturbing religious worship	
Violation of election laws	
Embezzlement	4
Escape	
Failure to list tax	
Food and drug laws	
Fish and game laws	
Forcible trespass	5
Forgery	8
Fornication and adultery	3
Gaming and lottery laws	10
Health laws	
Incest	
Injury to property	1
Municipal ordinances	3
Nonsupport	4
Nonsupport of illegitimate child	2

JANUARY 1, 1944—DECEMBER 31, 1944

Offense	Conv White M	Conv White F	Conv Negro M	Conv Negro F	Conv Indian M	Conv Indian F	Conv Unclas M	Conv Unclas F	Other White M	Other White F	Other Negro M	Other Negro F	Other Indian M	Other Indian F	Other Unclas M	Other Unclas F
Nuisance										1						
Official misconduct																
Perjury		4	3						1							
Prostitution	2						1		1	1					1	
Rape	2		6	4							1					
Receiving stolen goods																
Removing crop			1													
Resisting officer	3		6								2					
Robbery	4								1		3					
Seduction																
Slander																1
Trespass				1											2	
Vagrancy	1	7														
Worthless check																
False pretense			4												1	
Carnal knowledge, etc	2		1								1					
Crime against nature	5		5													
Slot machine laws																
Kidnaping	2															
Revenue act violations		1										1				
Miscellaneous	3	1	2	1			2		3	1	3	1				
Totals	287	29	238	29			5	1	42	8	34	10			10	1

JANUARY 1, 1945—DECEMBER 31, 1945

Offense	Conv White M	Conv White F	Conv Negro M	Conv Negro F	Conv Indian M	Conv Indian F	Conv Unclas M	Conv Unclas F	Other White M	Other White F	Other Negro M	Other Negro F	Other Indian M	Other Indian F	Other Unclas M	Other Unclas F
Nuisance																
Official misconduct																
Perjury																
Prostitution	1	3							1	1	1					
Rape	5		5						2							
Receiving stolen goods																
Removing crop																
Resisting officer	2		1						6		1					
Robbery	8		4						2							
Seduction																
Slander									3	2						
Trespass																
Vagrancy	1	1		2					3	2						
Worthless check	9	8														
False pretense	3	1	1						2		1					
Carnal knowledge, etc	1		1													
Crime against nature	3		1						2							
Slot machine laws																
Kidnaping																
Revenue act violations	1								1	1						
Miscellaneous	4	2	2	25				1	79	12	30	9			3	7
Totals	336	31	186	25				1	79	12	30	9			3	7

Convictions 589
Nol pros 63
Acquittals 38
Other disposition 4

Convictions 579
Nol pros 50
Acquittals 61
Other disposition 26

Thirteenth Judicial District

THIRTEENTH JUDICIAL DISTRICT
IN SUPERIOR COURT

Offense	JANUARY 1, 1944—DECEMBER 31, 1944							JANUARY 1, 1945—DECEMBER 31, 1945						
	CONVICTIONS				OTHER DISPOSITIONS			CONVICTIONS			OTHER DISPOSITIONS			
	White	Negro	Indian	Unclassified	White			White	Negro	Indian	White	Negro	Indian	Unclassified
			F	M	F	M	F							F
Assault														
Assault and battery						1								
Assault with deadly weapon						2								
Assault on female						1								
Assault with intent to kill						1								
Assault with intent to rape						2								
Assault—secret														
Drunk—drunk & disorderly						1								
Possession—illegal														
Possession for sale—sale														
Manufacturing—possession of material for														
Transportation														
Violation liquor laws														
Driving drunk														
Reckless driving														
Hit and run														
Speeding														
Auto license violations														
Violation motor vehicle laws														
Breaking and entering														
And larceny														
And receiving														
Housebreaking														
And larceny														
And receiving														
Storebreaking														
And larceny														
And receiving														
Larceny														

Offense									
Larceny of automobile	4							2	2
Temporary larceny	2	8	2		1	4		1	
Murder—first degree	2	1	1		4	1		1	1
Murder—second degree		2			1				1
Manslaughter	2	2		1	3	3			
Burglary—first degree	1								
Burglary—second degree	2	2		1	1	2		1	
Abandonment	2				1	1			
Abduction					1				
Affray	2	1	1		1	2			1
Arson	1								
Bigamy		2	1		2	1			
Bribery					1				
Burning other than arson	1	1							
Carrying concealed weapon					1				1
Contempt									
Conspiracy									
Cruelty to animals	1		1		1				
Disorderly conduct									
Disorderly house									
Disposing of mortgaged property									
Disturbing religious worship									
Violation of election laws									
Embezzlement									
Escape				1	2	1			
Failure to list tax					1	1	1		
Food and drug laws									
Fish and game laws	2								
Forcible trespass	1								
Forgery	2	2			4	1	1		
Fornication and adultery			1						
Gaming and lottery laws	1	1							
Health laws	1	1	1				1		
Incest									
Injury to property							1		1
Municipal ordinances					1				
Nonsupport	4	1		1	2	4		2	2
Nonsupport of illegitimate child		1			1	1			

THIRTEENTH JUDICIAL DISTRICT—(Continued)
IN SUPERIOR COURT

	JANUARY 1, 1944—DECEMBER 31, 1944																JANUARY 1, 1945—DECEMBER 31, 1945															
	CONVICTIONS								OTHER DISPOSITIONS								CONVICTIONS								OTHER DISPOSITIONS							
	White		Negro		Indian		Unclassified		White		Negro		Indian		Unclas.		White		Negro		Indian		Unclassified		White		Negro		Indian		Unclassified	
Offense	M	F	M	F	M	F	M	F	M	F	M	F	M	F	M	F	M	F	M	F	M	F	M	F	M	F	M	F	M	F	M	F
Nuisance																																
Official misconduct																			1													
Perjury	3		1	1														1	5										1			
Prostitution																		1							1							
Rape	3		3						1			1					3		4						2		2	2				
Receiving stolen goods											1																1					
Removing crop			2		1																											
Resisting officer	1		1	1	1				1		1						1		1						1		1	1				
Robbery	17		4						1		1						12		6								1					
Seduction																																
Slander																									1							
Trespass	2		3						1		1	1													1							
Vagrancy				1							1	1					1															
Worthless check									1		1																1					
False pretense			1						1		1						1								2							
Carnal knowledge, etc.																			1						4							
Crime against nature			1																								5					
Slot machine laws																																
Kidnaping																																
Revenue act violations																																
Miscellaneous	2	1	2	1																					1	2	2	1				
Totals	133	7	126	9	2				38	1	27	6	2		2		100	7	110	8	5				65	2	41	9	3			

Convictions..........282

Convictions..........230

Fourteenth Judicial District

FOURTEENTH JUDICIAL DISTRICT
IN SUPERIOR COURT

JANUARY 1, 1944—DECEMBER 31, 1944

Offense	CONVICTIONS White M	CONVICTIONS Negro M	CONVICTIONS Indian	CONVICTIONS Unclassified	OTHER DISPOSITIONS Unclassified F
Assault		5			
Assault and battery		52			
Asslt with deadly weapon		4			
Assault on female					
Assault with intent to kill		12			
Assault with intent to rape		4			
Assault—secret					
Drunk—drunk & disorderly		3			
Possession—illegal					
Possession for sale—sale					
Manufacturing—possession of material for					
Transportation					
Violation liquor laws		2			
Driving drunk		5			
Reckless driving		3			
Hit and run		4			
Speeding		2			
Auto license violations					
Violation motor vehicle laws					
Breaking and entering					
And larceny					
And receiving					
Housebreaking					
And larceny					
And receiving					
Storebreaking					

JANUARY 1, 1945—DECEMBER 31, 1945

Offense	CONVICTIONS White M	CONVICTIONS White F	CONVICTIONS Negro M	OTHER DISPOSITIONS White M	OTHER DISPOSITIONS White F	OTHER DISPOSITIONS Negro M	OTHER DISPOSITIONS Negro F	OTHER DISPOSITIONS Indian M	OTHER DISPOSITIONS Indian F	OTHER DISPOSITIONS Unclassified
Assault										
Assault and battery	10		1	3	2					
Asslt with deadly weapon	1									
Assault on female	38	2	53	14		19	12			
Assault with intent to kill	13		3	7		2	5			
Assault with intent to rape	5		14	3		7	1			
Assault—secret	2		2							
Drunk—drunk & disorderly				10	4	1				
Possession—illegal										
Possession for sale—sale										
Manufacturing—possession of material for										
Transportation										
Violation liquor laws										
Driving drunk										
Reckless driving										
Hit and run										
Speeding										
Auto license violations										
Violation motor vehicle laws										
Breaking and entering										
And larceny										
And receiving										
Housebreaking										
And larceny										
And receiving										
Storebreaking										

Offense																					
Larceny by trick & device	4																				4
Larceny of automobile	2																				
Temporary larceny	3	1				3				5											
Murder—first degree	1	3				15				2			3							4	
Murder—second degree	2	12				3				4			2							1	
Manslaughter		3								5			3								
Burglary—first degree	1	1				1				4			1		1		1				1
Burglary—second degree	10	2				5	4	1		16			4				8			4	
Abandonment	1					1				1							1				
Abduction	2	2				1		1		1											
Affray	1	1								1			2								
Arson	4	1				1				1					1					1	
Bigamy																					
Bribery							1										2				
Burning other than arson	1									4	1						7				
Carrying concealed weapon	1					3		2													
Contempt						1															
Conspiracy																					
Cruelty to animals	1	1				2		3		3							3				
Disorderly conduct																					
Disorderly house																					
Disposing of mortgaged property	1																				
Disturbing religious worship	1																				
Violation of election laws																					
Embezzlement	4	5			1	2		1		4							6			2	
Escape	1																				
Failure to list tax																					
Food and drug laws																					
Fish and game laws																					
Forcible trespass	1	1				3		2		2										2	
Forgery	3	3	3			5	1	10		10							1			2	
Fornication and adultery	1	18				1	22	1		1					1		1			1	
Gaming and lottery laws		11																			
Health laws																					
Incest	1	1			1	1		1		1										1	
Injury to property	1	1				9				24	7		1				2	1		2	
Municipal ordinances	2	2				2		1		3							9			7	
Nonsupport	10	1			1																
Nonsupport of illegitimate child	1																				

FOURTEENTH JUDICIAL DISTRICT—(Continued)
IN SUPERIOR COURT

JANUARY 1, 1944—DECEMBER 31, 1944

Offense	CONVICTIONS White M	White F	Negro M	Negro F	Indian M	Indian F	Unclassified M	Unclassified F	OTHER DISPOSITIONS White M	White F	Negro M	Negro F	Indian M	Indian F	Unclassified M	Unclassified F
Nuisance									1							
Perjury				1												
Prostitution			1						1	4	1	1			1	
Rape	2		2						1		2					
Receiving stolen goods			7						1						1	
Tobacco crop																
Resisting officer			1						1		2					
Robbery	9		9						6		9	3			2	
Seduction																
Slander	3	1														
Trespass	2								2	1						
Vagrancy															1	
Worthless check	1		1						4	1						
False pretense																
Carnal knowledge, etc.	1		1						5							
Crime against nature	1		1													
Slot machine laws									2							
Kidnaping																
Revenue act violations									1		1					
Miscellaneous	2	1	1						1	17	98	2			2	
Totals	222	14	282	59		1	2		161	17	98	21			98	1

Convictions 580

JANUARY 1, 1945—DECEMBER 31, 1945

Offense	CONVICTIONS White M	White F	Negro M	Negro F	Indian M	Indian F	Unclassified M	Unclassified F	OTHER DISPOSITIONS White M	White F	Negro M	Negro F	Indian M	Indian F	Unclassified M	Unclassified F
Nuisance																
Perjury																
Prostitution	2	3	1						1	4	1	2			2	
Rape	4	2	7						3		4				2	
Receiving stolen goods									1		1					
Resisting officer	6								1							
Robbery	12	1	15						2		12					
Seduction	1								1		1					
Slander																
Trespass	2		3						2		1				1	
Vagrancy	2								1							
Worthless check	2		3						1							
Carnal knowledge, etc.	1		2								1					
Crime against nature	1										1					
Slot machine laws	1															
Kidnaping																
Revenue act violations	2	1							2	1	1	1			1	
Miscellaneous	2						2		2	29	109	23			108	1
Totals	448	26	331	72			2		206	29	109	23			108	1

Convictions 879

Fifteenth Judicial District

FIFTEENTH JUDICIAL DISTRICT
IN SUPERIOR COURT

JANUARY 1, 1944—DECEMBER 31, 1944

Offense	Convictions White M	White F	Negro M	Negro F	Indian M	Indian F	Unclas. M	Unclas. F	Other Dispositions White M	White F	Negro M	Unclas. F
Assault	6		2	1					2			
Assault and battery	17	1	9	4					11	2	2	
Assault with deadly weapon	7		5	1					3		1	
Assault on female	2		1						1			
Assault with intent to kill	1		1						1			
Assault with intent to rape												
Assault—secret	15	3	2						5		2	
Drunk—drunk & disorderly	32	2	11	3								
Possession—illegal whiskey	6		1									
Possession for sale—sale												
Manufacturing—possession of material for	9		4						1			
Transportation	2		2						1			
Violation liquor laws	4	2	1						1	1		
Driving drunk	68		13						24			
Reckless driving	11								11		1	
Hit and run	2		1						1			
Speeding	1		2									
Auto license violations	5		1									
Violation motor vehicle laws	2								1			
Breaking and entering	4		16	1					2		1	
And larceny	15	1	7									
And receiving	6		11									
Housebreaking												
And larceny			1						1			
And receiving												
Storebreaking												

JANUARY 1, 1945—DECEMBER 31, 1945

Offense	Convictions White	Negro M	Negro F	Indian M	Indian F	Other Dispositions White	Negro M	Negro F	Indian M	Unclassified M
Assault		1								
Assault and battery		2					3	1		
Assault with deadly weapon							1			
Assault on female										
Assault with intent to kill										
Assault with intent to rape		1								
Assault—secret		1								
Drunk—drunk & disorderly										
Possession—illegal whiskey		3								

Larceny by trick & device										3				
Larceny of automobile							1	1		1			2	
Temporary larceny														
Murder—first degree		1					3	1		3	4		1	2
Murder—second degree										4				2
Manslaughter			1	1			4	1		4	1		4	2
Burglary—first degree														
Burglary—second degree		1												1
Abandonment										2		2		
Abduction										1	1	1		
Affray				2						6		6		
Bigamy														
Bribery														
Burning other than arson														3
Carrying concealed weapon		1	1							3		3	1	
Contempt														
Conspiracy											1	1		
Cruelty to animals														1
Disorderly conduct				1										
Disorderly house										1				
Disposing of mortgaged property														
Disturbing religious worship														
Violation of election laws		1					1							2
Embezzlement													1	1
Escape														
Failure to list tax														
Food and drug laws														
Fish and game laws		1			1			2		2	1	2		2
Forcible trespass								3		3	1	3		3
Forgery	1						2	2		2	1	2		13
Fornication and adultery														6
Gaming and lottery laws								1						
Health laws														
Incest														
Injury to property		1					1			1		1	2	1
Minucipal ordinances														10
Nonsupport				3			9	3		9	4	9	4	10
Nonsupport of illegitimate child		1					4			4	1	4	1	2

FIFTEENTH JUDICIAL DISTRICT—(Continued)
IN SUPERIOR COURT

JANUARY 1, 1944—DECEMBER 31, 1944

Offense	Conv White M	Conv White F	Conv Negro M	Conv Negro F	Conv Indian M	Conv Indian F	Conv Unclas M	Conv Unclas F	Other White M	Other White F	Other Negro M	Other Negro F	Other Indian M	Other Indian F	Other Unclas M	Other Unclas F
Nuisance																
Official misconduct		1														
Perjury	1									1						
Prostitution	1															
Rape	2		3						2		1					
Receiving stolen goods	9	1							1							
Removing crop																
Resisting officer	1		1													
Robbery	1								1		2					
Seduction	7															
Slander																
Trespass	1	1	3	1						1		1				
Vagrancy	1								4	1		1				
Worthless check							1		1							
False pretense	1		1						1		1				1	
Carnal knowledge, etc.	2		1													
Crime against nature																
Slot machine law																
Kidnaping																
Revenue act violations																
Miscellaneous	4	2	1	1					4							
Totals	344	22	157	16			2		111	8	23	4			2	

Convictions _____ 541
Nolle pros _____ 120
Acquittals _____ 23
Other disposition _____ 5

JANUARY 1, 1945—DECEMBER 31, 1945

Offense	Conv White M	Conv White F	Conv Negro M	Conv Negro F	Conv Indian M	Conv Indian F	Conv Unclas M	Conv Unclas F	Other White M	Other White F	Other Negro M	Other Negro F	Other Indian M	Other Indian F	Other Unclas M	Other Unclas F
Nuisance																
Official misconduct																
Perjury																
Prostitution																
Rape	3		3	1					1		1					
Receiving stolen goods																
Removing crop																
Resisting officer	4		1													
Robbery	5	1	1						4		1					
Seduction																
Slander																
Trespass	1	1	1						1							
Vagrancy	1		1						1							
Worthless check																
False pretense	4		1						2		1					
Carnal knowledge, etc.	1		2						2		2					
Crime against nature	4															
Slot machine law																
Kidnaping																
Revenue act violations																
Miscellaneous	3		2						2							
Totals	309	7	113	17					80	6	18	7				

Convictions _____ 446
Nolle pros _____ 93
Acquittals _____ 12
Other disposition _____ 6

Sixteenth Judicial District

SIXTEENTH JUDICIAL DISTRICT
IN SUPERIOR COURT

Offense	JANUARY 1, 1944—DECEMBER 31, 1944																JANUARY 1, 1945—DECEMBER 31, 1945																
	CONVICTIONS								OTHER DISPOSITIONS								CONVICTIONS								OTHER DISPOSITIONS							
	White		Negro		Indian		Unclassified		White		Negro		Indian		Unclassified		White		Negro		Indian		Unclassified		White		Negro		Indian		Unclassified	
	M	F	M	F	M	F	M	F	M	F	M	F	M	F	M	F	M	F	M	F	M	F	M	F	M	F	M	F	M	F	M	F
Assault	4	1	2				1		1								8								1	1	1	1			1	
Assault and battery																																
Assault with deadly weapon	20		10	2					7	1	5	1			1		20		5	2			5	1	6	1	2				1	
Assault on female	5		4						2		1						10		3	1					1	1						
Assault with intent to kill			3														1															
Assault with intent to rape	3								1								1	6									1					
Assault—secret																		4								2						
Drunk—drunk & disorderly	13	2					1		1								34	4	5	2			4		4	2						
Possession—illegal whisky																	2															
Possession for sale—sale																																
Manufacturing—possession of material for	1														1		5															
Transportation																	2								2							
Violation liquor laws	43		4	1					7	1	2				1		29	1	8	3					2		1	2				
Driving drunk	64		4				2		4								70		6						5							
Reckless driving	9		2						3		2				1		5		2				1		5	1	2				1	
Hit and run	2										1						2								1							
Speeding	2		1						1																							
Auto house	4		1						1								1		1						1							
Violation motor vehicle laws	2								1								11		3				1									
Breaking and entering	1		2						2								8		4				3		6		1				2	
And larceny	10		4						1		1	1					19		5													
Aid receiving			1																													
Housebreaking																																
And larceny																																
Aid receiving																																
Storebreaking																																

Offense								
Larceny from the person	1		1					2
Larceny by trick & device	4							
Larceny of ...								
Murder—first degree	5	4	·	1	3	1	1	
Murder—second	2	2	1		4			
Manslaughter		1						
Burglary—first degree								
Burglary—second degree	2			2	2			
Abandonment								
Abduction	3	1			1			
...	2	1	1	2	2			
Arson	1							
...By				1				
Bribery								
Burning other than arson	3							
...rying concealed ...pon				1	1			
Contempt								
...ty to animals	1							
Disorderly conduct	2							
Disposing of mortgaged property	1							
Disturbing rel...								
...n of election laws								
Embezzlement	1					1		
Escape						4		
Failure to list tax				10				
Food and drug laws						1		
Fish and game laws								
Forcible ...ss	1	1						
Forgery	15	1		2				
Fornication and adultery	2			3				2
Gaming and lottery laws								
Health laws	2			1				
Injury to property				11				
...al ordinances	14							22
Nonsupport								2

SIXTEENTH JUDICIAL DISTRICT—(Continued)
IN SUPERIOR COURT

	JANUARY 1, 1944—DECEMBER 31, 1944																JANUARY 1, 1945—DECEMBER 31, 1945															
	CONVICTIONS								OTHER DISPOSITIONS								CONVICTIONS								OTHER DISPOSITIONS							
	White		Negro		Indian		Unclassified		White		Negro		Indian		Unclassified		White		Negro		Indian		Unclassified		White		Negro		Indian		Unclassified	
Offense	M	F	M	F	M	F	M	F	M	F	M	F	M	F	M	F	M	F	M	F	M	F	M	F	M	F	M	F	M	F	M	F
Nonsupport of illegitimate child	1		3						1								1		3													
Nuisance																																
Official misconduct																																
Perjury																									1	1						
Prostitution	5	2	2	1					1									7							3	1						
Rape	4		2	1													1	1							1						2	
Receiving stolen goods			1												1		6								3	1						
Removing crop	2																															
Resisting officer	7								1								10		6						1	1	2					
Robbery																	6								1	3		2				
Seduction		1																										1				
Slander																																
Trespass																	1						1									
Vagrancy	1								1								2	4					1									
Worthless check	1		1						1								2						1				1					
False pretense											1																					
Carnal knowledge, etc.																	1										1					
Crime against nature																																
Slot machine laws																																
Kidnaping																	1															
Revenue act violations																											1					
Miscellaneous	284	15	71	13			7		79	7	24	3			5	3	354	41	78	13			26	1	68	19	15	3			9	

Convictions_____ 390

Convictions_____ 513

513

Seventeenth Judicial District

SEVENTEENTH JUDICIAL DISTRICT
IN SUPERIOR COURT

JANUARY 1, 1944 – DECEMBER 31, 1944

Offense	Convictions White M	White F	Negro M	Negro F	Indian M	Indian F	Unclas. M	Unclas. F	Other Dispositions White M	White F	Negro M	Negro F	Indian M	Indian F	Unclas. M	Unclas. F
Assault	1		1						6							
Assault and battery																
Assault with deadly weapon	15		5	1					11							
Assault on female	3								3							
Assault with intent to kill	2								3							
Assault with intent to rape	1								1							
Assault—secret																
Drunk—drunk & disorderly	5		1						3							
Possession—illegal whiskey	3		1													
Possession for sale—sale																
Manufacturing—possession of material for	3															
Transportation																
Violation liquor laws	37	1	2						9		2					
Driving drunk	74		4						6							
Reckless driving	15		1						2							
Hit and run	1															
Speeding	1															
Auto license violations	2								5	1						1
Violation motor vehicle laws	40		3						9							
Breaking and entering	1															
And larceny	5															
And receiving	1															
Housebreaking																
And larceny	1		5													
And receiving																
Storebreaking	1															

JANUARY 1, 1945 – DECEMBER 31, 1945

Offense	Convictions White M	White F	Negro M	Negro F	Indian M	Indian F	Unclas. M	Unclas. F	Other Dispositions White M	White F	Negro M	Negro F	Indian M	Indian F	Unclas. M	Unclas. F
Assault	7	1	4						4	2						
Assault and battery									9	2	1					
Assault with deadly weapon	24	1	7	1					4							
Assault on female	5		1													
Assault with intent to kill									2							
Assault with intent to rape																
Assault—secret	6								1							
Drunk—drunk & disorderly	4															
Possession—illegal whiskey	1															
Possession for sale—sale																
Manufacturing—possession of material for	4								1							
Transportation	3		5						2							
Violation liquor laws	39	1	2						3							
Driving drunk	53	1	2						5							
Reckless driving	14								1							
Hit and run	2								2							
Speeding	3															
Auto license violations	47		5						12							
Violation motor vehicle laws	3								3							
Breaking and entering	1		1													
And larceny	1															
And receiving									2							
Housebreaking	1								6							
And larceny	5															
And receiving																
Storebreaking										1						

Larceny of ...															1	2
...ly larceny																2
Murder—first degree			1													
Murder—second degree																
Manslaughter																
Burglary—first degree				1	1							1			5	
Burglary—second degree			2	1	1										3	
Abduction				4							2					
Aff ... ga																
At ... n					1							1			5	
Bigamy					3										3	
Bribery																
...g ... ber than ars n																
Carrying concealed weapon					1										5	
Contempt																
Conspiracy																
Cruelty to animals															3	3
Disorderly conduct						3							1		1	1
...lly house													1		1	
Disposing of mortgaged property																
Disturbing religious worship																
Violation of ...tion laws																
Embezzlement					1										1	
Escape																
...ure to list tax													1		6	5
Food and drug ...ws													3		2	
Fish and game ...ws													3		11	
...ale trespass												2	5		5	
Forgery																
Fornication and adultery															1	
Gaming and lottery laws																
Health laws																
Inst															8	8
Jury to property													1		5	5
...tal ordinances																
...support																
N ...t of illegitimate child																

SEVENTEENTH JUDICIAL DISTRICT—(Continued)
IN SUPERIOR COURT

Offense	JANUARY 1, 1944—DECEMBER 31, 1944																JANUARY 1, 1945—DECEMBER 31, 1945																
	CONVICTIONS								OTHER DISPOSITIONS								CONVICTIONS								OTHER DISPOSITIONS							
	White		Negro		Indian		Unclassified		White		Negro		Indian		Unclassified		White		Negro		Indian		Unclassified		White		Negro		Indian		Unclassified	
	M	F	M	F	M	F	M	F	M	F	M	F	M	F	M	F	M	F	M	F	M	F	M	F	M	F	M	F	M	F	M	F
Nuisance																																
Official misconduct																																
Perjury	4	6															4	4														
Prostitution			2						1	1															2							
Rape			2						3								3								3		1					
Receiving stolen goods																																
Removing crop																																
Resisting officer	4	1							1								6															
Robbery																			4						1		1					
Seduction																	1	1														
Slander									1																1	3						
Trespass									1																4							
Vagrancy	2								2								2															
Worthless check									3																							
False pretense									1																							
Carnal knowledge, etc.	1																								2	1						
Crime against nature	1																															
Slot machine laws																																
Kidnaping									1																							
Revenue act violations									4								3	1														
Miscellaneous	7														1										1							
Totals	204	21	38	1					104	5	6				3		137	16	41	1					101	24	6					

Eighteenth Judicial District

EIGHTEENTH JUDICIAL DISTRICT
IN SUPERIOR COURT

Offense	JANUARY 1, 1944—DECEMBER 31 1944																JANUARY 1, 1945—DECEMBER 31, 1945															
	CONVICTIONS								OTHER DISPOSITIONS								CONVICTIONS								OTHER DISPOSITIONS							
	White		Negro		Indian		Unclassified		White		Negro		Indian		Unclassified		White		Negro		Indian		Unclassified		White		Negro		Indian		Unclassified	
	M	F	M	F	M	F	M	F	M	F	M	F	M	F	M	F	M	F	M	F	M	F	M	F	M	F	M	F	M	F	M	F
Assault	7	1	1						7								5	2	2	2					3							
Assault and battery	9		13	1					4			1					24	2	2				2		3			1			1	
Assault with deadly weapon	13								8								7		12				1		1							
Assault on female	4		1						2			1					2						1		3							
Assault with intent to kill		1	1				1		1								1		1						2							
Assault with intent to rape	3		2														22															
Assault—secret	22	1	4														1		2				3		1							
Drunk—drunk & disorderly	2	1																														
Possession—illegal whiskey	1																															
Possession for sale—sale																																
Manufacturing—possession of material for	3		1						1								6		1													
Transportation	6		4	3					1		2				2		6	1	3				1		6		1					
Violation liquor laws	28	2	14	1			2		4		2						35		17				1		5		1	1				
Driving drunk	33		7						4		2						42		3				1		2							
Reckless driving	8		1														7		2													
Hit and run			1														1		1													
Speeding	3								1										1						1							
Auto license violations	2		4								2						4		1						1		2					
Violation motor vehicle laws	7		3						3		2						24	4	6						2							
Breaking and entering	48		2	1													4		1													
And larceny	6		1														4															
And receiving																																
Housebreaking																																
And larceny																																
And receiving																																
Storebreaking	1																															
And larceny	1																															

EIGHTEENTH JUDICIAL DISTRICT—(Continued)
IN SUPERIOR COURT

JANUARY 1, 1944—DECEMBER 31, 1944

Offense	CONVICTIONS White M	F	Negro M	F	Indian M	F	Unclassified M	F	OTHER DISPOSITIONS White M	F	Negro M	F	Indian M	F	Unclassified M	F
Nuisance																
Official misconduct																
Perjury																
Prostitution		3														
Rape									1							
Receiving stolen goods	3										2					
Removing crop																
Resisting officer	7		3													
Robbery																
Seduction																
Slander																
Trespass			1													
Vagrancy																
Worthless check									1		2					
False pretense	1															
Carnal knowledge, etc.																
Crime against nature																
Slot machine laws	1															
Kidnaping																
Revenue act violations	4	1	1	1												
Miscellaneous												1				
Totals	315	14	88	13			5		62	4	20	1				

JANUARY 1, 1945—DECEMBER 31, 1945

Offense	CONVICTIONS White M	F	Negro M	F	Indian M	F	Unclassified M	F	OTHER DISPOSITIONS White M	F	Negro M	F	Indian M	F	Unclassified M	F
Nuisance																
Official misconduct																
Perjury																
Prostitution			1							1						
Rape	2	1	1	1					1							
Receiving stolen goods	1	1														
Removing crop																
Resisting officer	3		1	1												
Robbery																
Seduction																
Slander																
Trespass	2		1													
Vagrancy	15															
Worthless check	4								1	1						
False pretense			1													
Carnal knowledge, etc.	1															
Crime against nature																
Slot machine laws																
Kidnaping																
Revenue act violations	2	1	1						1							
Miscellaneous									1							
Totals	311	17	77	5			13	1	53	2	6	1			2	

	1944	1945
Convictions	435	424
Nolle pros	64	52
Acquittals	21	11
Other disposition	2	1

Nineteenth Judicial District

NINETEENTH JUDICIAL DISTRICT
IN. SUPERIOR COURT

Offense	1944 Conv. White M	White F	Negro M	Negro F	Indian M	Indian F	Unclas. M	Unclas. F	1944 Other White M	White F	Negro M	Negro F	Indian M	Indian F	Unclas. M	Unclas. F	1945 Conv. White M	White F	Negro M	Negro F	Indian M	Indian F	Unclas. M	Unclas. F	1945 Other White M	White F	Negro M	Negro F	Indian M	Indian F	Unclas. M	Unclas. F
Assault	2								1								6	1	1	1												
Assault and battery																																
Assault with deadly weapon	13		2	1													23		3	1					8	1	3					
Assault on female	11		2						6		1						7		2						5		2	1				
Assault with intent to kill	9		5						1	1							3			1					5		3					
Assault with intent to rape	5											1					1		1						2							
Assault—secret																																
Drunk—drunk & disorderly	19	1							5	2							25	3	1						5							
Possession—illegal whiskey	1																4	1							1							
Possession for sale—sale																																
Manufacturing—possession of material for	3								1																							
Transportation	3																7	1	1						1							
Violation liquor laws	12																								1							
Driving drunk	19		2						8		1						23	2	1						3							
Reckless driving	2																3	1							2							
Hit and run	1																1															
Speeding																																
Auto license violations	1								1																							
Violation motor vehicle laws			1						1	1							5		4													
Breaking and entering	2								1								4								1							
And larceny	3																															
And receiving																																
Housebreaking									1																							
And larceny	1		1						2																							
And receiving	37		8														13		20						1		1	1				
Storebreaking																															1	
And larceny																																

Offense					
Larceny by trick & dev.	25		7		
Larceny of automobile.					
Jury					
Murder—first degree.	1	2			1
Murder—second degree.	1				1
Manslaughter.	2		5	1	
Burglary—first degree.			1		
Burglary—second degr e.	1				
Abandonment	6			2	
Abduction					
Affray.					
Arson.		1		1	
Bigamy.	1				1
Bribery.					
Burning other than arson.			1		
Carrying ...led weapon.	1				2
Conspiracy.					
...ty to animals.					
Disorderly conduct.	1			1	
...ly house.	2	2			
Deposing of mortgaged property.					
Disturbing religious worship.					
Violation of ...on laws.					1
Embezzlement.	3			1	
Escape.	3			1	
Failure to list tax.					
Food and drug laws.					
Fish and game laws.				1	
Forcible trespass.	33		1		
Forgery.	7	3		1	
Fornication and adultery.	1	1		1	
Gaming and lottery laws.			1		
Health laws.	2	1	3	1	
Incest.					
Injury to property.	3	1		3	
Municipal ordinances.					
Nonsupport.	6			2	
Nonsupport of illegitimate child.	3			3	1

NINETEENTH JUDICIAL DISTRICT—(Continued)
IN SUPERIOR COURT

JANUARY 1, 1944—DECEMBER 31, 1944

Offense	Convictions White M	White F	Negro M	Negro F	Indian M	Indian F	Unclas M	Unclas F	Other Disp. White M	White F	Negro M	Negro F	Indian M	Indian F	Unclas M	Unclas F
Nuisance									1							
Official misconduct																
Perjury		2	1	2												
Prostitution																
Rape	6								6	1						
Receiving stolen goods			1						1							
Removing crop									7	3	3					
Resisting officer	2		1						2			2				
Robbery	7		4													
Seduction										1						
Slander	1	1	1						2	1						
Trespass																
Vagrancy									1							
Worthless check	2		2						1							
False pretense	2															
Carnal knowledge, etc.																
Crime against nature																
Slot machine laws	2															
Kidnaping																
Revenue act violations									4	1					2	2
Miscellaneous	5	3			1				20	11	8	5				
Totals	290	21	58	3	1											

JANUARY 1, 1945—DECEMBER 31, 1945

Offense	Convictions White M	White F	Negro M	Negro F	Indian M	Indian F	Unclas M	Unclas F	Other Disp. White M	White F	Negro M	Negro F	Indian M	Indian F	Unclas M	Unclas F
Nuisance																
Official misconduct																
Perjury																
Prostitution									1							
Rape	4		2						1							
Receiving stolen goods									1							
Removing crop	3		3													
Resisting officer	3		2													
Robbery	10		1						8		1					
Seduction									1							
Slander																
Trespass	3	1														
Vagrancy																
Worthless check	2		2						2							
False pretense									1		1					
Carnal knowledge, etc.	1								1							
Crime against nature																
Slot machine laws																
Kidnaping																
Revenue act violations	4	1	1						12	1	1	1				
Miscellaneous	253	20	72	8			1		83	8	33	6				
Totals	253	20	72	8			1									

1944
Convictions 373
Nolle pros 82
Acquittals 32
Other disposition 2

1945
Convictions 354
Nolle pros 76
Acquittals 41
Other disposition 3

Twentieth Judicial District

TWENTIETH JUDICIAL DISTRICT
IN SUPERIOR COURT

Offense	1944 Conv White M	F	Negro M	F	Indian M	F	Unclass M	F	1944 Other White M	F	Negro M	F	Indian M	F	Unclass M	F	1945 Conv White M	F	Negro M	F	Indian M	F	Unclass M	F	1945 Other White M	F	Negro M	F	Indian M	F	Unclass M	F
Assault	22	1	2						19	4	1		1				21	6		1	2				9	3						
Assault and battery																																
Assault with deadly weapon	24		4						9	1			1				12		1		2				7	1	1					
Assault on female	2								4																	1						
Assault with intent to kill	1																															
Assault with intent to rape	1																															
Assault—secret		1							10		1																					
Drunk—drunk & disorderly	17		1		1												7															
Possession—illegal whiskey	6								1								2															
Possession for sale—sale	1																															
Manufacturing—possession of material for	2																3															
Transportation	4																2															
Violation liquor laws	57	12	1						31	8							52	7	1		4	1			17	2	2					
Driving drunk	112		1		1				63						5		98				1				20	1	2					
Reckless driving	27		1		1				13								16		1						3							
Hit and run	1								1																							
Speeding					1				3																							
Auto license violations	4		1														4															
Violation motor vehicle laws	5		4						2								5				1											
Breaking and entering	4	1															4		1		1				5	1						
And larceny																	1															
And receiving	1								4									4							1							
Housebreaking																									1							
And larceny	4								4																							
And receiving																																
Storebreaking																																
And larceny																																
And receiving																																
Larceny	23	1	7		5				30	5							21		4		3				8	2						
Larceny & receiving									1																							

Offense									
Larceny by trick & device	4		1			4		3	
Larceny of automobile									
Temporary larceny	2	1		1					
Murder—first degree		1		1		4	3		
Murder—second degree	3								
Manslaughter	3	1			1		1		
Burglary—first degree									
Burglary—second degree	10	1	4		15		1		18
Abandonment	14	1			2	2			
Abduction					5	1			
Affray					1				
Arson									
Bigamy									
Bribery									
Burning other than arson	23	1	1		11				3
Carrying concealed weapon								7	1
Contempt								16	7
Conspiracy									
Cruelty to animals	2				2	1	2		
Disorderly conduct					2				2
Disorderly house					1				
Disposing of mortgaged property	1								
Disturbing religious worship									
Violation of election laws									
Embezzlement	2				2		2		
Escape					1				
Failure to list tax									
Food and drug laws	2				2				
Fish and game laws	1	2							
Forcible trespass	4	1	1		4	6		7	4
Forgery	2	3			8				
Fornication and adultery					1		1		1
Gaming and lottery laws									
Health laws									
Incest	1				1				
Injury to property									
Municipal ordinances	18	3	1		10				3
Nonsupport		3						17	
Nonsupport of illegitimate child								1	

TWENTIETH JUDICIAL DISTRICT—(Continued)
IN SUPERIOR COURT

Offense	1944 CONV White M	F	Negro M	F	Indian M	F	Unclas M	F	1944 OTHER White M	F	Negro M	F	Indian M	F	Unclas M	F	1945 CONV White M	F	Negro M	F	Indian M	F	Unclas M	F	1945 OTHER White M	F	Negro M	F	Indian M	F	Unclas M	F
Nuisance	2	1															6	1	1						4	2	1					
Official misconduct											1																					
Perjury																1																
Prostitution		1							1									5							1							
Rape	4																3															
Receiving stolen goods																	4															
Removing crop																																
Resisting Officer	14		1						3		1						6													1		
Robbery	4								1	2																						
Seduction	2								3								1													1		
Slander																																
Trespass																	2										2					
Vagrancy	2						1										1															
Worthless check	1								2								1		1													
False pretense																																
Carnal knowledge, etc									1																							
Crime against nature									1																							
Slot machine law	3								19																							
Kidnaping																	1								1							
Revenue act violations																									1							1
Miscellaneous	5								5								10			2	18		1		2							
Totals	444	22	36		16	1	1		295	32	7		3	2	6		197	36	12	2	18		1		104	17	9		1	1		

Convictions	520	Convictions	466
Nolle pros	296	Nolle pros	127
Acquittals	22	Acquittals	5
Other disposition	27	Other disposition	2

Twenty-first Judicial District

TWENTY-FIRST JUDICIAL DISTRICT
IN SUPERIOR COURT

Offense	JANUARY 1, 1944—DECEMBER 31, 1944																JANUARY 1, 1945—DECEMBER 31, 1945																
	CONVICTIONS								OTHER DISPOSITIONS								CONVICTIONS								OTHER DISPOSITIONS							
	White		Negro		Indian		Unclassified		White		Negro		Indian		Unclassified		White		Negro		Indian		Unclassified		White		Negro		Indian		Unclassified	
	M	F	M	F	M	F	M	F	M	F	M	F	M	F	M	F	M	F	M	F	M	F	M	F	M	F	M	F	M	F	M	F
Assault	15		7														12		1	1					1							
Assault and battery	21		11	2					2								28	2	26	2					8		3					
Assault with deadly weapon	7		4												1		10		6						2	1					1	
Assault on female	6		5												2				5													
Assault with intent to kill			5								2						1								2	1						
Assault with intent to rape									1								1															
Assault—secret	20		8					1	1		1						41	1	6	1							1					
Drunk—drunk & disorderly	5		5						1								6		5	1												
Possession—illegal whiskey																			1													
Possession for sale—sale	1																1															
Manufacturing—possession of material for	1		2														1		2						1							
Transportation									4		3				2		6		1						3	1	3					
Violation liquor laws	36		13	1					6		2				2		11		4						4						1	
Driving drunk	51		4				1		5						1		49		5						1							
Reckless driving	11		1						5								15		5						4			1				
Hit and Run	3		1														2															
Speeding									1						1		4		1						1							
Auto license violations	3		4														4		1													
Violation motor vehicle laws																	2															
Breaking and entering	1								1								47		5													
And larceny	15		7																						1						1	
And receiving								1	1																							
Housebreaking	3								1								8		1						1						1	
And larceny																																
And receiving	3								1								28															
Storebreaking																																
And larceny																																
And receiving																																
Larceny	9		8	1					3		2						28	1	6						6	2	1					
Larceny & receiving	13	1	1						1		1				1		3	1	2						2		1	1				
	1								1						1		2	1	2													

Offense	
Larceny by trick & device	7
Larceny of automobile	
Temporary larceny	
Murder—first degree	1
Murder—second degree	2
Manslaughter	1
Burglary—first degree	7
Burglary—second degree	
Abandonment	4
Abduction	
Affray	1
Arson	
Bigamy	
Bribery	
Burning other than arson	3
Carrying concealed weapon	3
Contempt	
Conspiracy	
Cruelty to animals	1
Disorderly conduct	1
Disorderly house	2
Disposing of mortgaged property	
Disturbing religious worship	
Violation of election laws	
Embezzlement	1
Escape	5
Failure to list tax	
Food and drug laws	
Fish and game laws	
Forcible trespass	1
Forgery	1
Fornication and adultery	1
Gaming and lottery laws	2
Health laws	
Incest	
Injury to property	2
Municipal ordinances	3
Nonsupport	2
Nonsupport of illegitimate child	4

TWENTY-FIRST JUDICIAL DISTRICT—(Continued)
IN SUPERIOR COURT

Offense	JANUARY 1, 1944—DECEMBER 31, 1944																JANUARY 1, 1945—DECEMBER 31, 1945															
	CONVICTIONS								OTHER DISPOSITIONS								CONVICTIONS								OTHER DISPOSITIONS							
	White		Negro		Indian		Unclassified		White		Negro		Indian		Unclassified		White		Negro		Indian		Unclassified		White		Negro		Indian		Unclassified	
	M	F	M	F	M	F	M	F	M	F	M	F	M	F	M	F	M	F	M	F	M	F	M	F	M	F	M	F	M	F	M	F
Nuisance	1																1															
Official misconduct																																
Perjury																	1															
Prostitution			1															1	2							1						
Rape											1						1									1						
Receiving stolen goods			2																													
Removing crop																			3													
Resisting officer	1		1														5															
Robbery			1						3						1		1															
Seduction	2														1																	
Slander									3																							
Trespass			1						2		1						2															
Vagrancy			1						2		1								1								2					
Worthless check																									1							
False pretense									1																2							
Carnal knowledge, etc.																	3		1						3							
Crime against nature																																
Slot machine laws																																
Kidnaping			1								1														2							
Revenue act violations									1						2		4		1						2	1						
Miscellaneous	12														1			11	112	6					47	6	15	2				
Totals	278	4	107	3			3		35		16	1			16		355	11	112	6					47	6	15	2				4

1944		1945	
Convictions	395	Convictions	484
Nolle pros.	32	Nolle pros.	36
Acquittals	27	Acquittals	29

ALPHABETICAL LIST OF CRIMES IN SUPERIOR COURTS

	1944 Convictions	1944 Other Dispositions	1945 Convictions	1945 Other Dispositions
Assault	223	102	226	79
Assault and battery	56	24	28	12
Assault with deadly weapon	605	198	818	225
Assault on female	148	49	170	57
Assault with intent to kill	213	59	155	72
Assault with intent to rape	52	26	73	31
Assault—secret	23	2	24	11
Drunk—drunk and disorderly	319	93	333	68
Possession—illegal whiskey	117	23	110	16
Possession for sale—sale	38	8	85	28
Manufacturing—possession of material for	45	7	69	17
Transportation	32	12	53	18
Violation liquor laws	391	129	324	90
Driving drunk	652	260	696	230
Reckless driving	184	109	237	90
Hit and run	51	11	57	18
Speeding	33	17	26	9
Auto license violations	42	26	4	0
Violation motor vehicle laws	81	23	140	53
Breaking and entering	234	69	263	59
And larceny	292	62	280	89
And receiving	149	15	214	20
Housebreaking	20	6	13	1
And larceny	128	12	97	16
And receiving	48	8	54	17
Storebreaking	20	2	18	4
And larceny	36	5	37	3
And receiving	61	11	69	22
Larceny	727	253	757	257
Larceny and receiving	210	67	154	67
Larceny from the person	52	25	71	27
Larceny by trick and device	7	2	2	1

	1944 Convictions	1944 Other Dispositions	1945 Convictions	1945 Other Dispositions
Larceny of automobile	189	32	164	28
Temporary larceny	5	1	32	2
Murder—first degree	100	65	12	32
Murder—second degree	47	10	106	27
Manslaughter	135	56	172	60
Burglary—first degree	21	13	5	2
Burglary—second degree	20	0	21	4
Abandonment	90	45	139	58
Abduction	3	5	3	8
Affray	64	7	30	18
Arson	26	15	19	16
Bigamy	85	24	64	20
Bribery	1	1	1	3
Burning other than arson	5	2	20	3
Carrying concealed weapon	84	38	86	23
Contempt	3	1	1	0
Conspiracy	10	6	3	12
Cruelty to animals	3	4	6	2
Disorderly conduct	74	28	57	33
Disorderly house	23	11	6	2
Disposing of mortgaged property	4	4	2	4
Disturbing religious worship	5	5	5	3
Violation of election laws	0	0	1	0
Embezzlement	39	27	53	29
Escape	25	5	47	4
Failure to list tax	8	41	2	5
Food and drug laws	1	0	0	0
Fish and game laws	7	5	11	3
Forcible trespass	104	8	151	16
Forgery	205	26	218	40

ALPHABETICAL LIST OF CRIMES IN SUPERIO

	1944	
	Convictions	Other Dispositions Co
Fornication and adultery	63	44
Gaming and lottery laws	81	16
Health laws	12	4
Incest	6	5
Injury to property	41	22
Municipal ordinances	4	9
Non-support	151	63
Non-support of illegitimate child	26	9
Nuisance	11	13
Official misconduct	0	0
Perjury	4	10
Prostitution	92	44
Rape	30	23
Receiving stolen goods	107	52
Removing crop	6	3
Resisting Officer	67	19
Robbery	168	83
Seduction	5	10
Slander	1	3
Trespass	38	31
Vagrancy	34	33
Worthless check	39	14
False pretense	57	38
Carnal knowledge etc.	26	19
Crime against nature	26	13
Slot machine law	9	19
Kidnaping	5	6
Revenue act violations	2	1
Miscellaneous	159	102
Totals	7,945	2,908

Convictions	7,945	Convictions
Other dispositions	2,908	Other dispositions
Total	10,853	Total

GRAND TOTAL

FIRST JUDICIAL DISTRICT
INFERIOR COURTS

JANUARY 1, 1944—JANUARY 1, 1946

Offense	CONVICTIONS								OTHER DISPOSITIO						
	White		Negro		Indian		Unclassified		White		Negro		Indian		Unclassified
	M	F	M	F	M	F	M	F	M	F	M	F	M	F	M
Assault	100	6	171	27			2		22	3	37	18			
Assault and battery	3		5	1					1		1				
Assault with deadly weapon	14		45	13					4		15	1			
Assault on female	2		12						2		4				
Assault with intent to kill			2						1		2				
Assault with intent to rape									1		1				
Assault—secret															
Drunk—drunk & disorderly	196	25	357	25			6		12		1				
Possession—Illegal whiskey	29	1	39	1					7		10	1			1
Possession for sale—sale	16	1	37	6			1		2		2	1			
Manufacturing—possession of material for	1		1												
Transportation	5		2						6		3				1
Violation liquor laws	6		8				1		2		1	1			
Driving drunk	120	2	50				3		15	1	6				
Reckless driving	114	2	86	3			4		19		15				
Hit and run	13	1	10	2					1		3				
Speeding	303	15	214	6			9		4		1				
Auto license violations	119	16	171	13			6	1	13		6	1			
Violation motor vehicle laws	163	7	236	4			11		5		5				
Breaking and entering	3		1						1		4				
And larceny									2		10				
And receiving															
Housebreaking	1														
And larceny															
And receiving															
Storebreaking											1				
And larceny															
And receiving															
Larceny	21	6	61	4					18		28	6			
Larceny & receiving			16												
Larceny from the person			1								1				
Larceny by trick & device															
Larceny of automobile	4		2						14		1				
Temporary larceny	6		1							1					
Murder—first degree									1		1	1			
Murder—second degree									1		1				
Manslaughter									1		2				1
Burglary—first degree															
Burglary—second degree									1						
Abandonment	2		1												
Abduction															
Affray	34		35	20					7		7	4			
Arson									2						
Bigamy															
Bribery															
Burning other than arson			1												
Carrying concealed weapon	7	1	26	3					2		1				
Contempt	4	2	2												
Conspiracy															
Cruelty to animals	1		1												
Disorderly conduct	44	5	54	15					8	1	2				
Disorderly house		1	1												
Disposing of mortgaged property	2		1						2						
Disturbing religious worship															
Violation of election laws															
Embezzlement									2						

FIRST JUDICIAL DISTRICT
INFERIOR COURTS

JANUARY 1, 1944—JANUARY 1, 1946

Offense	CONVICTIONS								OTHER DISPOSITIONS							
	White		Negro		Indian		Unclassified		White		Negro		Indian		Unclassified	
	M	F	M	F	M	F	M	F	M	F	M	F	M	F	M	F
pe.	1															
re to list tax																
and drug laws	9		1													
and game laws	2		3													
ible trespass	1		4								1					
ery			1						3		14					
cation and adultery	3	3	5	4					1			1				
ing and lottery laws	27	1	71	8			2		4		15					
lth laws	1	2	3	4							3					
st																
ry to property	31	3	25	4			1		3		4					
nicipal ordinances	596	105	94	8							5					
support	21		32				1		3		4					
nsupport of illegitimate child			4								2					
sance	4		3	3												
cial misconduct																
ury																
stitution	16	16	7	6					2	8		1				
e									1		2					
eiving stolen goods			11	3					3		4		1			
moving crop																
sisting officer	35	1	25	3							2					
bbery			1						1		6					
luction																
nder																
spass	21	4	22	2			1		17		12	3				
grancy	7	13	5						1		6					
rthless check	24		8						9		2					
se pretense	3		5	1			1		4		3	2				
rnal knowledge etc.									3		2					
me against nature																
t machine laws	4															
lnaping																
venue act violations																
scellaneous	58	16	62	8					9	4	3	4				
Totals	2802	255	2043	197			49	1	243	18	262	16			3	

Convictions	5348
Bound over to superior court	133
Other dispositions	439
Total	**5920**

JANUARY 1, 1944—JANUARY 1, 1946

Offense	CONVICTIONS								OTHER DISPOSITIONS							
	White		Negro		Indian		Unclassified		White		Negro		Indian		Uncsifi
	M	F	M	F	M	F	M	F	M	F	M	F	M	F	M
Assault	90	4	193	40					48	3	76	12			1
Assault and battery	14		13	1					3		5	2			
Assault with deadly weapon	44	5	180	25					22	7	78	16			
Assault on female	37		89						14		36				
Assault with intent to kill			2						6	2	11				
Assault with intent to rape															
Assault—secret	2								1						
Drunk—drunk & disorderly	386	65	501	71					30	2	13	1			
Possession—illegal whiskey	28		53	7					10		11	1			
Possession for sale—sale	18		30	6			1		3		6				
Manufacturing—possession of material for	21		15						12		4				
Transportation	6		9						1		5				
Violation liquor laws	62	4	191	12			3		15	1	29	6			
Driving drunk	201	3	114	3					24		5				
Reckless driving	75	1	64				1		46	2	22				
Hit and run	6		4						2						
Speeding	500	39	114	4			1		29	4	2	1			
Auto license violations	92	6	90	2					9		5				
Violation motor vehicle laws	305	19	196	5			6		25	1	16				
Breaking and entering	2		2						14		40	2			
And larceny									1		13				
And receiving											1				
Housebreaking				3											
And larceny			1								1	1			
And receiving															
Storebreaking															
And larceny															
And receiving															
Larceny	48	3	107	41					32	3	58	7			1
Larceny & receiving	13	2	15	3					8		8	1			
Larceny from the person			2								3	2	1		
Larceny by trick & device			1												
Larceny of automobile															
Temporary larceny	1		1												
Murder—first degree									5		12	1			
Murder—second degree															
Manslaughter	1								1		2				
Burglary—first degree											2				
Burglary—second degree											2				
Abandonment	12	1	14	2					5	3	11	2			
Abduction															
Affray	33	4	38	28					9		8	8			
Arson									1		6				
Bigamy											1	1			
Bribery															
Burning other than arson															
Carrying concealed weapon	9		25						7		7				
Contempt															
Conspiracy															
Cruelty to animals	3		3						2		3				
Disorderly conduct	50	15	103	43					6	2	12	6			
Disorderly house	1			1							1				
Disposing of mortgaged property											1				
Disturbing religious worship			1						1		2				
Violation of election laws															
Embezzlement			2								2				

SECOND JUDICIAL DISTRICT
INFERIOR COURTS

JANUARY 1, 1944—JANUARY 1, 1946

| Offense | CONVICTIONS | | | | | | | | OTHER DISPOSITIONS | | | | | | | |
| | White | | Negro | | Indian | | Unclassified | | White | | Negro | | Indian | | Unclassified | |
	M	F	M	F	M	F	M	F	M	F	M	F	M	F	M	F
...e	1		2	1							4					
...e to list tax									1							
...and drug laws																
...nd game laws	7										1					
...ble trespass	5		9									1				
...ry	1		2						9		3					
...cation and adultery	1	1	9	7					2	2	6	6				
...ng and lottery laws	37		114	5					5		3					
...h laws	6	2	29	23						1	3	2				
...y to property	6		18	2					3		9	4				
...cipal ordinances	17	1	4	1					5	2						
...upport	34		50	1					13	2	25					
...upport of illegitimate child	8		14						6							
...nce	25	2	26	3					1		2					
...al misconduct																
...ry																
...itution	8	12							2	3	1	1				
									2		2					
...iving stolen goods	7		8	1					2		1	3				
...oving crop			1													
...ting officer	15	2	22	3					2		1					
...ery	2	1							6	1	16					
...ction									1							
...ier									1		1	1				
...pass	12	1	39	3					10		7	7			1	
...ancy	3	8	32						2	1	4	1				
...thless check	26	1	4						12		4				2	
...pretense	1		2						9		9					
...al knowledge, etc									2		5					
...e against nature									1							
...machine laws																
...aping									3							
...ence act violations																
...ellanous	37	12	31	7					13	2	7	1			1	
Totals	2715	214	2725	360			12		505	49	635	95			6	

Convictions	6030
Bound over to superior court	224
Other dispositions	1066
Total	7320

THIRD JUDICIAL DISTRICT
INFERIOR COURTS

JANUARY 1, 1944—JANUARY 1, 1946

Offense	CONVICTIONS								OTHER DISPOSITION						
	White		Negro		Indian		Unclassified		White		Negro		Indian		Uncsifi
	M	F	M	F	M	F	M	F	M	F	M	F	M	F	M
Assault	125	8	176	42					26		39	16	1		2
Assault and battery															
Assault with deadly weapon	34	4	205	25			2		21	2	65	13			2
Assault on female	18		104				1		7		26				1
Assault with intent to kill	1		1						1		3				
Assault with intent to rape															
Assault—secret															
Drunk—drunk & disorderly	751	27	454	20			27		30	3	6	2			1
Possession—illegal whiskey	22		46	6					2		12	4			
Possession for sale—sale	30	1	71	13					6	1	19	1			
Manufacturing—possession of material for	4		27	1					3		4				
Transportation	21		23						5		11				
Violation liquor laws	6		36	5					4		3	1			
Driving drunk	177		223				1		45	5	23	1			1
Reckless driving	95		118						50	4	44				2
Hit and run	2		8								1				
Speeding	184	6	106				2		27	2	13	2			3
Auto license violations	29	2	69	1					6	1	9				1
Violation motor vehicle laws	61	4	175	5			1		7	1	14	1			1
Breaking and entering									2		8				
And larceny			2						4		9				
And receiving									4		1	1			
Housebreaking															
And larceny															
And receiving															
Stout breaking															
And larceny															
And receiving															
Larceny	24	1	82	15					26	4	42	8			
Larceny & receiving	1		13	1					2	1					
Larceny from the person									1						
Larceny by trick & device															
Larceny of automobile	2		5						6		6				
Temporary larceny			5												
Murder—first degree											3				
Murder—second degree															
Manslaughter											1				
Burglary—first degree															
Burglary—second degree															
Abandonment	5	1	14						7		5	1			
Abduction															
Affray	8		41	2					1	2	15				
Arson									2						
Bigamy															
Bribery															
Burning other than arson	1		1								1				
Carrying concealed weapon	7	1	25	2					5		2				1
Contempt															
Conspiracy															
Cruelty to animals			1								2				
Disorderly conduct	34	2	128	38			5		5		20	6			
Disorderly house											1	1			
Disposing of mortgaged property			2								1				
Disturbing religious worship			4								2				
Violation of election laws															
Embezzlement			1								2				

THIRD JUDICIAL DISTRICT
INFERIOR COURTS

Offense	CONVICTIONS								OTHER DISPOSITIONS							
	White		Negro		Indian		Unclassified		White		Negro		Indian		Unclassified	
	M	F	M	F	M	F	M	F	M	F	M	F	M	F	M	F
...pe			3													
...ure to list tax			44													
...l and drug laws																
...and game laws	1										1					
...ible trespass	3	1	10								1					
...gery	1								1		3					
...ication and adultery	2	2	13	10							2	2				
...ing and lottery laws	43		59						10		3					
...lth laws	2	1	2													
...est											1					
...ury to property	24	2	37	7			1		7	1	8	2				
...nicipal ordinances	18	6							11	2	1					
...nsupport	38		35						17		14					
...nsupport of illegitimate child	1		2								7					
...isance	6	2	4	1												
...cial misconduct																
...jury											1					
...stitution	2	3	5	6							1	1				
...pe																
...ceiving stolen goods	2		6						3		4	1				
...moving crop																
...sisting officer	9		8	3					2	1	1				1	
...bbery		1	1						2		1		1			
...duction									1		2					
...nder																
...espass	19	2	23	1					7		7					
...grancy	15		22						2		1				1	
...orthless check	27	1	20						7							
...lse pretense	1	1	4						1		2					
...rnal knowledge, etc											2					
...ime against nature									2		1					
...ot machine laws																
...dnaping									1	1						
...venue act violations																
...iscellaneous	31	8	33	4			1		18		20	4				
Totals	1887	87	2500	208			41		797	32	495	68	2		16	

Convictions	4723
Bound over to superior court	97
Other dispositions	913
Total	5733

FOURTH JUDICIAL DISTRICT
INFERIOR COURTS

JANUARY 1, 1944—

Offense	CONVICTIONS								OTHER DISPOSITIONS						
	White		Negro		Indian		Unclassified		White		Negro		Indian		Unclassified
	M	F	M	F	M	F	M	F	M	F	M	F	M	F	M
Assault	138	12	168	41	2			2	58	5	49	25			3
Assault and battery															
Assault with deadly weapon	133	10	416	53					74	6	62	24	1		
Assault on female	73		101					1	28		27				3
Assault with intent to kill			3						13	5	4				
Assault with intent to rape	2								1		1				
Assault—secret											2				
Drunk—drunk & disorderly	451	21	281	34	25	6	2		18	2	12	2			1
Possession—illegal whiskey	118	5	72	10	2		2		11	2	12	2			1
Possession for sale—sale	24	3	76	29					3	1	13	7			1
Manufacturing—possession of material for	39		54	2					5		2		1		1
Transportation	35	1	31	2	2				5	2	4				
Violation liquor laws	209	8	183	34					21		33	13			
Driving drunk	527	10	411	2	2			2	46		22	1			
Reckless driving	194	3	89	3	2			1	69	5	23				
Hit and run	12		9						5		3				
Speeding	114	2	19	1				2	2						
Auto license violations	71	5	30	1	3				3		2				
Violation motor vehicle laws	59	20	127	9	3			2	26	1	11	2			
Breaking and entering	3		3						5	1	14	5			
And larceny			3						1		6				
And receiving															
Housebreaking															
And larceny									4		3				
And receiving															
Storebreaking									6						
And larceny															
And receiving															
Larceny	86	5	125	16	1			2	51	3	64	9			
Larceny & receiving															
Larceny from the person											1				
Larceny by trick & device															
Larceny of automobile									6		4				
Temporary larceny	2		3												
Murder—first degree											1				
Murder—second degree									3		1	1			
Manslaughter									2						
Burglary—first degree															
Burglary—second degree															
Abandonment	45	1	34	2				1	18	2	13				1
Abduction									1						
Affray	48	3	57	31	1				6	1	6	6			
Arson											2				
Bigamy											2				
Bribery															
Burning other than arson															
Carrying concealed weapon	30		56	4					7	1	5	1			
Contempt															
Conspiracy									4						
Cruelty to animals	7		4						4						
Disorderly conduct	26	4	43	23				1	16	1	2	6	1		
Disorderly house	2		1	2											
Disposing of mortgaged property			2	1					2		1				
Disturbing religious worship			8								3				
Violation of election laws															
Embezzlement	1								2		3	1			

FOURTH JUDICIAL DISTRICT
INFERIOR COURTS

Offense	CONVICTIONS								OTHER DISPOSITIONS							
	White		Negro		Indian		Unclassified		White		Negro		Indian		Unclassified	
	M	F	M	F	M	F	M	F	M	F	M	F	M	F	M	F
...e.	13	......	11	1	...	....	.....	......	2	......	1	......	...	...	......	......
...e to list tax	......	..	......	..	......	......	......	......	......	......	......	......	......	......	......	......
...and drug laws	......	......	......	..	......	......	......	......	......	......	......	......	......	......	......	......
...and game laws	4	......	.. ...	2	......	......	......	......	3	......	1	......	....	..	......	......
...ble trespass	6	......	13	......	......	......	......	......	1	......	......	1	......	......	......	......
...ry	......	......	......	......	......	......	......	......	1	......	1	......	......	......	......	......
...tation and adultery	15	16	27	21	......	....	.. ...	......	4	5	10	7	......	......	......	......
...ing and lottery laws	12	......	59	8	......	......	......	......	5	......	14	7	......	......	......	......
...ch laws	1	1	1	1	......	......	.. ..	......	1	......	2	......	......	......	......	......
...t	......	......	......	......	......	......	......	.. ..	2	......	......	......	......	......	......	......
...y to property	27	......	19	5	......	......	......	......	12	1	6	......	......	......	......	......
...icipal ordinances	9	1	... ...	......	......	......	......	1	3	1	......	......	......	......	......	......
...upport	64	......	48	......	......	......	......	1	25	1	9	......	......	......	2	......
...upport of illegitimate child	7	......	18	......	......	......	......	......	1	......	2	......	......	......	......	......
...ance	......	......	......	......	.. ...	......	......	......	......	......	......	......	......	......	......	......
...al misconduct	.. ..	......	.. ...	......	......	......	......	......	......	.. ...	......	......	......	......	......	......
...ry	......	......	......	......	.. ....	......	......	......	.. ...	.. ....	......	......	.. ..	......	......	......
...itution	8	24	25	23	...	....	......	1	3	3	2	1	......	......	......	......
...	.. ..	......	.. ...	.. ...	......	......	...	..	6	......	3	......	.. ..	......	......	......
...iving stolen goods	2	......	7	......	......	......	......	....	2	......	11	1	......	......	......	......
...ioving crop	1	......	1	1	......	......	......	......	5	......	2	......	......	.. ...	......	......
...sting officer	24	......	12	2	......	......	......	......	1	......	3	......	......	......	......	......
...bery	......	......	1	......	......	......	......	.. ..	7	......	12	1	......	......	......	......
...ction	2	......	......	......	......	......	......	....	1	......	......	......	......	......	......	......
...der	......	......	......	1	......	......	.. ...	....	.. ..	......	1	......	......	......	......	......
...pass	51	4	26	5	......	......	...	....	17	2	6	3	......	1	.. ...	...
...rancy	5	6	7	......	......	....	. ..	......	3	......	1	......	......	......	......	......
...thless check	25	......	7	......	......	......	......	......	5	......	2	......	......	......	......	......
...e pretense	1	......	1	......	......	......	.. ..	......	12	......	6	......	.. ..	......	.. ...	......
...hal knowledge, etc	......	......	1	......	......	......	......	......	6	......	4	......	......	......	......	......
...ne against nature	.. ...	......	......	......	......	....	. ...	......	2	......	......	..	......	......	......	......
...machine laws	2	......	......	......	......	......	......	.. ..	......	......	......	......	......	......	......	......
...naping	1	......	......	......	......	......	.. ...	......	3	......	......	......	......	......	......	......
...enue act violations	......	......	.. ...	......	......	......	....	......	......	......	......	......	.. ..	......	......	......
...cellaneous	47	15	32	8	......	.. ...	2	2	32	5	16	......	......	...	1	......
Totals	˙076	150	˙325	378	46	6	23	2	391	56	28	126	2	1	14	2

Convictions	6036
Bound over to superior court	187
Other dispositions	1233
Total	**7456**

FIFTH JUDICIAL DISTRICT
INFERIOR COURTS

	JANUARY 1, 1944—														
	CONVICTIONS								OTHER DISPOSITIONS						
Offense	White		Negro		Indian		Unclas-sified		White		Negro		Indian		Un-si
	M	F	M	F	M	F	M	F	M	F	M	F	M	F	M
Assault	26	1	40	13			4		5		5				
Assault and battery															
Assault with deadly weapon	26	1	105	15			3		22	1	30	10			
Assault on female	8		14					.	3		4				
Assault with intent to kill															
Assault with intent to rape															
Assault—secret															
Drunk—drunk & disorderly	186	1	144	3			23		1		6				
Possession—illegal whiskey	9		15	5							1				
Possession for sale—sale			15	4			2						1		2
Manufacturing—possession of material for			3	1			3								
Transportation	6		8												
Violation liquor laws	26	3	103	76					7	2	17	7			
Driving drunk	113	6	41	1			15		11	2	1				
Reckless driving	50	2	41				15		17	3	9				7
Hit and run	1	1							1						
Speeding	39	2	17				19		1						
Auto license violations	5		25	2			6								
Violation motor vehicle laws	43	1	52	4			3		2						1
Breaking and entering											3				
And larceny											1				
And receiving															
Housebreaking															
And larceny															
And receiving															
Storebreaking															
And larceny															
And receiving															
Larceny	17	1	77	5			1		7		28	4			
Larceny & receiving			3						1						
Larceny from the person															
Larceny by trick & device															
Larceny of automobile			1												
Temporary larceny	1		2												
Murder—first degree															
Murder—second degree															
Manslaughter											1				
Burglary—first degree															
Burglary—second degree															
Abandonment	12		11				5		3		1				
Abduction	27		18	8				1							
Affray															
Arson															
Bigamy															
Bribery															
Burning other than arson															
Carrying concealed weapon	6		31	1			1		2		2				
Contempt															
Conspiracy															
Cruelty to animals		1							1						
Disorderly conduct	7		9	3			1				6				
Disorderly house			1	1											
Disposing of mortgaged property															
Disturbing religious worship			3												
Violation of election laws															
Embezzlement															

FIFTH JUDICIAL DISTRICT
INFERIOR COURTS

Offense	CONVICTIONS White M	White F	Negro M	Negro F	Indian M	Indian F	Unclassified M	Unclassified F	OTHER DISPOSITIONS White M	White F	Negro M	Negro F	Indian M	Indian F	Unclassified M	Unclassified F
JANUARY 1, 1944—JANUARY 1, 1946																
...			7	1					1							
to list tax			1													
ad drug laws																
d game laws	2								1							
e trespass	3	1	3													
...																
ition and adultery	1	1	1	1								1				
g and lottery laws	10		36					1	2		3					
laws			13	22					1							
to property	8		5						2							
pal ordinances	2		11				4									
)port	6		14				1		2		1					
)port of illegitimate child	1										1					
ce	2		1	1												
misconduct																
...																
ution	1	1	4	4								1				
ing stolen goods	1		2													
ng crop																
g officer	2		3	1							1					
...																
n																
...																
...	9		21	1					2	1	1	1				
)y	3	23	15	9					1	2	1					
ss check	5		6				3		1							
retense			1						1							
knowledge, etc											1					
gainst nature																
chine laws	1															
ing									1							
e act violations																
neous	14	3	11	2			3		5	1	6					
otals	879	49	984	154			113	1	104	12	132	23			10	

Convictions _____ 1960
Bound over to superior court _____ 18
Other dispositions _____ 263

Total _____ 2241

SIXTH JUDICIAL DISTRICT
INFERIOR COURTS

JANUARY 1, 1944—J

Offense	CONVICTIONS								OTHER DISPOSITIONS						
	White		Negro		Indian		Unclassified		White		Negro		Indian		Un-sif
	M	F	M	F	M	F	M	F	M	F	M	F	M	F	M
Assault	35	9	33	11			12	1	11	5	11	6			
Assault and battery															
Assault with deadly weapon	65	10	189	66			11		51	6	68	11			8
Assault on female	49		116				1		33		36				1
Assault with intent to kill	1		2	1			1		3		9	1			
Assault with intent to rape									1						
Assault—secret											4				
Drunk—drunk & disorderly	588	71	551	54	1		1	2	69	10	23	6			1
Possession—illegal whiskey	66	2	25	2	1		18	1	5		3				2
Possession for sale—sale	29	3	61	25	8		10	1	4		3	1			2
Manufacturing—possession of material for	33	2	21	1			1		3		1				
Transportation	27		17	1	1		6		3		1				
Violation liquor laws	27	6	52	24			1	1	7		2	3			
Driving drunk	179	3	87		4		20		31	1	2				9
Reckless driving	223		104	1	2		17		36	3	8				10
Hit and run	4	1	8						4		3				1
Speeding	207	6	51		1		107		11		1				18
Auto license violations	57	1	36		1		2		7						2
Violation motor vehicle laws	243	8	188	7			10		18		8		1		1
Breaking and entering			2				3		3		6				
And larceny			1						11		12				1
And receiving															
Housebreaking															
And larceny															
And receiving															
Storebreaking															
And larceny															
And receiving															
Larceny	33	5	108	15			3	2	15	6	48	11			13
Larceny & receiving	6		4						3		1				
Larceny from the person			1						4	1	13				
Larceny by trick & device											1				
Larceny of automobile	2		1						7		6				1
Temporary larceny	4		10												1
Murder—first degree															
Murder—second degree															
Manslaughter									1						
Burglary—first degree															
Burglary—second degree															
Abandonment	21	3	28	4					14	1	10				1
Abduction															
Affray	19	1	35	11			2		6	1	8	3			
Arson															
Bigamy											1				
Bribery															
Burning other than arson	1														
Carrying concealed weapon	15		44	3			6		6		9				
Contempt															
Conspiracy															
Cruelty to animals	8		2						3						
Disorderly conduct	29	7	87	32			2		14	3	9	4			
Disorderly house	2	9	3	4					2	1					
Disposing of mortgaged property			1						4						
Disturbing religious worship			1						1						
Violation of election laws															
Embezzlement			1								2				

SIXTH JUDICIAL DISTRICT
INFERIOR COURTS

Offense	CONVICTIONS								OTHER DISPOSITIONS							
	White		Negro		Indian		Unclassified		White		Negro		Indian		Unclassified	
	M	F	M	F	M	F	M	F	M	F	M	F	M	F	M	F
e.	2	1	3													
e to list tax.	2		1													
ind drug laws.																
nd game laws.	4														2	
le trespass.	16	2	2b	13			2	1	2	1	2				4	
y.	1		1				1				1	2				
ation and adultery.	4	4	11	12			1	3	3	1		1				
g and lottery laws	44		82	2					3		11					
i laws.			6	6							1					
											1					
to property	24	3	23	5			3		5	1	16	1			2	
ipal ordinances.	24	2	21	2					9	1	1					
pport.	33		33				3		18		13				1	
pport of illegitimate child.	1		12						1		1					
nce.	17	7	3				5		5		1				2	
l misconduct.																
y.															1	
ution.	33	112	62	25			2	4	10	10	9	8			3	1
											2					
ing stolen goods.			5				1				3					
ng crop.			1						2							
ig officer.	7	1	9	2			2		2						1	
y.							1		8		19					
on.															1	
									3							
is.	7	2	6	4			1	1	7		2				1	
cy.	14	56	35	47			2	4	7	6	7	8			1	
ess check.	21	1	8				1		2	1	2					
retense.	1								1							
knowledge, etc.											3					
igainst nature.	2								1		1					
chine laws.	4	1	3						1		1					
ing.									1	1						
e act violations.			1													
aneous.	25	5	30	4			1		21	1	10	3			8	3
otals.	687	344	284	87	18		260	21	06	62	415	69	1		99	4

Convictions 6041
Bound over to superior court 141
Other dispositions 1015

Total 7197

SEVENTH JUDICIAL DISTRICT
INFERIOR COURTS

JANUARY 1, 1944—J

Offense	CONVICTIONS								OTHER DISPOSITIONS						
	White		Negro		Indian		Unclas-sified		White		Negro		Indian		Unc sifi
	M	F	M	F	M	F	M	F	M	F	M	F	M	F	M
Assault	28	2	44	10					4	3	7	1			
Assault and battery	104	9	135	10					37	3	20	4			
Assault with deadly weapon	79	2	240	72					40	5	82	21			
Assault on female	28		32						14		11				
Assault with intent to kill	2		1						6		10	4			
Assault with intent to rape									1		1				
Assault—secret															
Drunk—drunk & disorderly	1330	122	772	76					38	10	10	1			
Possession—illegal whiskey	47	6	68	28					8	1	17	8			
Possession for sale—sale	9	1	24	12					6		3				
Manufacturing—possession of material for	9		29						1		1				
Transportation	13		12						5	1	1	1			
Violation liquor laws	13	1	26	3					5		9	3			
Driving drunk	144	7	60	1					30	3	7				
Reckless driving	93	2	73	1					33		14				
Hit and run	8		8				1		3		1				
Speeding	385	21	94				1		16	1	3				
Auto license violations	47	5	55	3					3		5				
Violation motor vehicle laws	133	11	119	5					22	1	6				
Breaking and entering	4		6						2		7				
And larceny			3						2		7				
And receiving			1						11		15				
Housebreaking															
And larceny															
And receiving															
Storebreaking															
And larceny															
And receiving															
Larceny	72	6	110	28					63	5	81	15			
Larceny & receiving	7		21	2					2	3	4				
Larceny from the person									4		15	3			
Larceny by trick & device	1		5												
Larceny of automobile	2		1						14		15				
Temporary larceny	6		7								1				
Murder—first degree									1		1				
Murder—second degree											5				
Manslaughter									2		1				
Burglary—first degree									1		2				
Burglary—second degree									1		1				
Abandonment	25	1	12	1					7		2	1			
Abduction															
Affray	50		45	25					8	1	10	1			
Arson									1						
Bigamy									2	2	1	1			
Bribery															
Burning other than arson															
Carrying concealed weapon	21		45	4					6		3				
Contempt															
Conspiracy															
Cruelty to animals	2		2						1		3				
Disorderly conduct	159	31	314	65					23	5	22	10			
Disorderly house			1								1				
Disposing of mortgaged property			3												
Disturbing religious worship			2								2				
Violation of election laws															
Embezzlement	1								3		4				

	JANUARY 1, 1944—JANUARY 1, 1946															
	CONVICTIONS								OTHER DISPOSITIONS							
Offense	White		Negro		Indian		Unclas-sified		White		Negro		Indian		Unclas-sified	
	M	F	M	F	M	F	M	F	M	F	M	F	M	F	M	F
:ape	2		4	1							1					
lure to list tax																
d and drug laws									1							
h and game laws	3		1													
cible trespass	11	1	12	2							3	1				
gery									6	3	4					
nication and adultery	19	13	12	11					2	2	8	7				
ning and lottery laws	70	5	97	3					18		28	1				
lth laws	1	1	19	27						2	4	3				
est											1					
ry to property	20	2	44	6					13		8	2				
nicipal ordinances	272	42	60	2					43	10	7					
support	70	2	48						20		7					
support of illegitimate child			7								3					
isauce	48	22	41	4					3	3	4					
cial misconduct									1							
jury																
stitution	5	6	3						1	2	1					
e									7		3					
eiving stolen goods			4						11		7					
oving crop											1					
sting officer	20	1	14	2					2		3					
pery			1						7		18	2				
ction	1															
der									2							
pass	42	12	45	4					7	2	8					
rancy	27	8	32	5					12	6	4					
thless check	33	1	19						12		1					
e pretense	2		7						10		2					
al knowledge, etc	1															
c against nature								1	3							
machine laws																
aping											1					
nue act violations																
ellaneous	107	26	19	2					8	2	1	2				
Totals	3576	369	780	15			1		615	76	339	92				

Convictions _____ 7141
Bound over to superior court _____ 230
Other dispositions _____ 1092

Total _____ 8463

EIGHTH JUDICIAL DISTRICT
INFERIOR COURTS

JANUARY 1, 1944—JANUARY 1, 1946

Offense	CONVICTIONS								OTHER DISPOSITIONS							
	White		Negro		Indian		Unclassified		White		Negro		Indian		Unclassified	
	M	F	M	F	M	F	M	F	M	F	M	F	M	F	M	F
Assault	111	16	73	32		1	11	4	78	14	38	23	1		2	
Assault and battery							2								2	2
Assault with deadly weapon	113	6	339	80			27	5	'24	14	198	57	1		18	3
Assault on female	132		366				15		147		219				19	
Assault with intent to kill	1		13						8	3	18	2			1	
Assault with intent to rape	1		1						2		2				1	
Assault—secret	3			1							1					
Drunk—drunk & disorderly	2360	149	1660	100	3		103	14	95	4	33	3			7	
Possession—illegal whiskey	59		68	17			15	4	5		8	4			2	
Possession for sale—sale	15	3	32	8			2		9	2	8	7				
Manufacturing—possession of material for	38		23				1		9		3				1	
Transportation	38		32	4			5		7		5	4			3	
Violation liquor laws	48	7	110	30			17	5	19	1	30	17			7	1
Driving drunk	370	8	132	2			45		124	2	20				8	
Reckless driving	255	6	169	5			56	1	80	2	30	3			16	
Hit and run	19	2	15				3		18		14				3	
Speeding	1631	106	356	5	1		256	21	62	5	15				10	
Auto license violations	36	6	29				3		5	1	16				2	
Violation motor vehicle laws	389	26	273	18	1		138	11	66	4	37	2			13	
Breaking and entering	1	1	2	1					3		6	2			3	
And larceny	1								4							
And receiving	1		3						2		5					
Housebreaking	1		2				1				2	1				
And larceny																
And receiving	1		2								10					
Storebreaking			1						3		1					
And larceny									1		1					
And receiving			1						18		7					
Larceny	29		33	5			6		17	1	18	3			5	
Larceny & receiving	30	8	100	44	1		7	2	38	3	47	18			11	1
Larceny from the person	1		1								11					
Larceny by trick & device	1								5	1	3					
Larceny of automobile	3		6	2					55		14				4	
Temporary larceny	4		4	2			1		6		3				1	
Murder—first degree																
Murder—second degree	1										8	1				
Manslaughter									1		2					
Burglary—first degree											1					
Burglary—second degree	1		2						2							
Abandonment	21	1	18	1			5	1	27	2	11				3	1
Abduction									1							
Affray	93	6	89	32			10	1	43	4	32	11			4	1
Arson											1					
Bigamy									7	5	3	3			1	1
Bribery																
Burning other than arson																
Carrying concealed weapon	46	1	73	7			10		10		13				3	
Contempt							1									
Conspiracy									1	1						
Cruelty to animals	2								3		1					
Disorderly conduct	237	46	252	124			26	9	62	15	46	22			7	
Disorderly house				1											1	
Disposing of mortgaged property	1															
Disturbing religious worship	1		1													
Violation of election laws																
Embezzlement			1						4		4					

EIGHTH JUDICIAL DISTRICT
INFERIOR COURTS

Offense	Convictions White M	F	Negro M	F	Indian M	F	Unclassified M	F	Other Dispositions White M	F	Negro M	F	Indian M	F	Unclassified M	F
	JANUARY 1, 1944—JANUARY 1, 1946															
:cape	6	3	15	2	...	...	8	2	1	...	...	...	...	...	...	...
ulure to list tax	...	...	...	...	...	...	...	...	...	...	...	...	...	...	...	...
)od and drug laws	...	...	...	...	...	...	...	...	...	...	...	...	...	...	...	...
sh and game laws	10	...	...	...	...	...	...	...	13	...	1	...	...	...	...	...
)rcible trespass	6	1	21	4	...	...	...	...	...	...	3	...	...	...	...	...
)rgery	..	...	...	...	...	...	...	...	27	1	3	...	...	...	2	...
)rnication and adultery	26	30	25	23	...	...	5	4	12	13	27	18	...	...	2	2
aming and lottery laws	75	1	156	3	...	...	16	...	7	...	35	2	...	...	6	...
ealth laws	2	2	1	5	...	...	2	...	2	6	5	2	...	...	3	...
icest	...	...	...	...	...	...	...	...	...	...	1	...	...	...	...	...
jury to property	50	4	54	6	...	...	10	1	43	3	29	8	...	...	14	...
unicipal ordinances	13	25	79	5	...	1	23	3	14	1	18	...	...	...	2	...
onsupport	47	...	66	...	...	...	10	...	60	...	36	...	...	...	8	...
onsupport of illegitimate child	3	...	12	...	...	...	...	...	2	...	4	...	...	...	...	...
uisance	10	6	10	...	...	...	...	...	4	1	5	2	...	...	...	...
ficial misconduct	...	...	...	...	...	...	...	...	...	...	...	...	...	...	...	...
rjury	...	...	...	...	...	...	...	...	...	...	...	...	...	...	...	...
ostitution	66	105	26	35	..	...	12	8	31	32	9	7	...	...	8	5
ape	..	...	..	...	...	...	...	...	5	...	6	...	...	...	1	...
eceiving stolen goods	1	...	9	...	...	...	2	...	7	...	3	2	...	...	2	...
moving crop	...	...	1	...	...	...	...	...	1	...	1	...	...	...	1	...
sisting officer	89	5	42	9	...	...	5	...	18	...	7	...	...	...	2	...
bbery	.	1	7	...	...	...	...	...	7	1	30	2	...	...	11	...
luction	...	...	...	...	...	...	...	...	1	...	1	...	...	...	...	...
nder	..	...	...	...	...	...	...	...	...	1	...	...	...	...	...	...
espass	34	3	22	2	...	...	5	...	27	10	5	6	...	...	7	1
grancy	33	17	29	10	...	...	1	1	98	21	167	11	...	...	9	2
orthless check	28	1	9	...	...	...	26	1	28	...	2	...	1	...	3	...
lse pretense	...	...	6	...	...	...	...	...	3	4	6	...	...	...	1	1
rnal knowledge, etc	...	.	...	...	...	...	...	...	2	...	3	...	...	...	...	...
ime against nature	..	.	...	...	...	...	...	...	5	...	1	...	...	...	...	...
t machine laws	3	1	2	...	...	...	...	...	...	...	...	...	...	...	...	...
dnaping	...	...	...	...	...	...	...	...	...	...	...	1	...	...	...	...
venue act violations	2	...	...	...	...	...	...	...	...	...	...	...	...	...	...	...
scellaneous	60	17	44	2	...	...	12	...	37	5	20	8	...	...	10	1
Totals	759	320	824	127	6	2	303	98	620	183	1379	252	3	...	256	26

```
Convictions ................................................. 13339
Bound over to superior court ............................... 418
Other dispositions ......................................... 3301
                                                           ——
Total ...................................................... 17058
```

NINTH JUDICIAL DISTRICT
INFERIOR COURTS

JANUARY 1, 1944—JANUARY 1, 1946

Offense	CONVICTIONS								OTHER DISPOSITION						
	White		Negro		Indian		Unclassified		White		Negro		Indian		Unc-sif
	M	F	M	F	M	F	M	F	M	F	M	F	M	F	M
Assault	197	23	219	36	53	2	9		78	13	41	14	12	2	5
Assault and battery															
Assault with deadly weapon	12		84	15	30	1	18	1	14	1	23	2	13	1	14
Assault on female	11		8		10		1		2		3				
Assault with intent to kill	1								1	1	2		6		
Assault with intent to rape											1				
Assault—secret													1		
Drunk—drunk & disorderly	513	32	472	22	177	12	133	3	17	1	8		1		2
Possession—illegal whiskey	56		27	4	14	7	8		3		3		2		1
Possession for sale—sale	11	1	18	1	17	1	3		1		2	1	3		
Manufacturing—possession of material for	6		4		29	1			2		4		8		1
Transportation	36	1	10	2	3		3		7						2
Violation liquor laws	78	10	262	67	20	4	34	3	25	7	22	4			2
Driving drunk	224	6	111	2	27	1	25		25	1	11		3		7
Reckless driving	179	5	97	1	17		6		52	5	12	1	3		3
Hit and run	3		4		3				1						
Speeding	158	36	99	2	7		33		12		4				
Auto license violations	134	23	93	3	38	1	12	1	6	1	3	1	3		
Violation motor vehicle laws	62		127	3	13	2	20	1	8		4		1		1
Breaking and entering					1						7		8		2
And larceny					1						3	1	5	1	
And receiving															
Housebreaking															
And larceny															
And receiving															
Storebreaking															
And larceny	1														
And receiving															
Larceny	65	6	116	22	17	3	11		18	7	28	2	2	1	4
Larceny & receiving			5		2								1	4	
Larceny from the person															
Larceny by trick & device															
Larceny of automobile															
Temporary larceny	1		1						1						
Murder—first degree									1						
Murder—second degree															
Manslaughter															
Burglary—first degree													1		
Burglary—second degree															
Abandonment	9	1	6	2	2		2		6	1	4		1		3
Abduction									1						
Affray	11	5	30	11	5	2	11		6		8		2		2
Arson															
Bigamy									1						
Bribery															
Burning other than arson															
Carrying concealed weapon	30	1	67	3	16		5		10		4	1	3		
Contempt															
Conspiracy															
Cruelty to animals	1	1			1		1		1		2				
Disorderly conduct	25	2	10	3					9	2	5		1		
Disorderly house									1	1	1				
Disposing of mortgaged property	2								2						1
Disturbing religious worship			8		1		2						1		1
Violation of election laws															
Embezzlement											1				1

NINTH JUDICIAL DISTRICT
INFERIOR COURTS

Offense	CONVICTIONS								OTHER DISPOSITIONS							
	White		Negro		Indian		Unclassified		White		Negro		Indian		Unclassified	
	M	F	M	F	M	F	M	F	M	F	M	F	M	F	M	F
Escape	5		1													
Failure to list tax																
Food and drug laws																
Fish and game laws	2		1		1				1							
Forcible trespass	8	2	5		2				10	1						
Forgery																
Fornication and adultery	7	4	15	10			2		9	9	2	2	2			1
Gaming and lottery laws	56		50	7	1	1	13		6		1	1			1	
Health laws	2		2						1							
Incest																
Injury to property	9	1	13	1	6		1		4	2	4	2	8			
Municipal ordinances	21		11		1	2	3		4		2					
Nonsupport	35		24		6	1	3		13		11		1		3	
Nonsupport of illegitimate child			7				2				1		1			
Nuisance	5	2			1	1			6	2						
Official misconduct																
Perjury	2															
Prostitution	23	67	1		1	1	2		2	5						
Rape												1				
Receiving stolen goods			6						1		4	1				
Removing crop	1		3						1							
Resisting officer	20	2	14	2	8		1		3	1	2	1			1	
Robbery																
Seduction													1			
Slander	2	2							10		5				2	
Trespass	17		27	2	9	1	5		10		5	2			2	
Vagrancy	6	1	5				1		3	2	4		1			
Worthless check	19		8		2		5		2		1		1	1		
False pretense	3		4						6	2	1					
Carnal knowledge, etc									2							
Crime against nature																
Slot machine laws																
Kidnaping					1											
Revenue act violations																
Miscellaneous	51	15	38	13	15	4	12		18	2	12	2	9		8	
Totals	420	249	211	337	558	43	387	9	112	67	258	38	104	10	8	2

Convictions	6021
Bound over to superior court	51
Other dispositions	908
Total	6980

Offense	CONVICTIONS								OTHER DISPOSITIONS							
	White		Negro		Indian		Unclassified		White		Negro		Indian		Unclassified	
	M	F	M	F	M	F	M	F	M	F	M	F	M	F	M	F
ault	36	4	47	9					7		9	2			3	1
ssault and battery	252	33	423	45			4	2	78	11	64	16				
ssault with deadly weapon	141	11	518	120			5		73	10	149	47			8	
ssault on female	29		53						17		10					
ssault with intent to kill	2		2						4		7	2				
ssault with intent to rape									1		6					
sault—secret									2	1	3					
runk—drunk & disorderly	2494	215	1002	161			6	1	52	5	15	4				
ossession—illegal whiskey	195	9	222	61			5		20	1	40	22			3	
ossession for sale—sale	79	2	76	17			2		13	1	8	8			2	
Manufacturing—possession of material for	20		44	4			1		1	2	4	2				
ransportation	21		12	1					2		3	1			2	
iolation liquor laws	8	2	5	2					2	1		1				
riving drunk	304	7	118				4		40		8					
eckless driving	489	13	231	4	1		8		116	6	52	3			3	
it and run	25	1	27	1					13	1	4				1	
peeding	1791	83	505	9			11		21	2	5					
uto license violations	283	35	331	16	1		5		24	3	39				2	
Violation motor vehicle laws	36	3	61						8	3	3				1	
reaking and entering	1		3						2		8					
And larceny	4		3				2		4		10					
And receiving			1													
ousebreaking									1		1					
And larceny									9	1	21				1	
And receiving																
torebreaking									5							
And larceny	4	1	1						39		48					
And receiving									1							
arceny	89	9	211	44			3		70	13	93	21			7	
arceny & receiving			5													
arceny from the person	2								5	2	11	1			1	
arceny by trick & device											4					
arceny of automobile			7						1	1	1					
emporary larceny	1	1	9						1		1					
Murder—first degree									1		9					
Murder—second degree											1					
anslaughter									8		8				1	
urglary—first degree											4					
urglary—second degree																
bandonment	30	2	13				1		5	2	1	1			2	
bduction			1								2					
ffray	115	6	92	39			3		21		20	9			1	
rson											1					
igamy									3							
ribery																
urning other than arson																
arrying concealed weapon	46	1	109	13					8		8	1				
ontempt	3		1	2				1			1					
onspiracy	3															
ruelty to animals	1		2													
isorderly conduct	216	96	230	126					39	14	23	13			1	
isorderly house	1		3	3					1	1						
isposing of mortgaged property	1		3						2		1					
isturbing religious worship			1						3							
Violation of election laws																
mbezzlement	2		1						5		3					

TENTH JUDICIAL DISTRICT
INFERIOR COURTS

	JANUARY 1, 1944—JANUARY 1, 1946															
	CONVICTIONS								OTHER DISPOSITIONS							
Offense	White		Negro		Indian		Unclassified		White		Negro		Indian		Unclassified	
	M	F	M	F	M	F	M	F	M	F	M	F	M	F	M	F
Escape	22	11	26	19			1		4		1	1				
Failure to list tax																
Food and drug laws																
Fish and game laws	12		1						4							
Forcible trespass	54	6	39	7					12	1	2					
Forgery	1		1						18		11	2				
Fornication and adultery	25	37	33	39					3	3	5	6			2	
Gaming and lottery laws	196	1	224	7			1		28		14					
Health laws	19	2	9	4	1		2		3	1	1					
Incest											4					
Injury to property	108	11	77	12			3		23	5	16	2	1			
Municipal ordinances	1642	218	189	24			5		109	20	27	3			3	
Nonsupport	119	1	98				4		51		28	1	1		4	
Nonsupport of illegitimate child	3		32		1		2		1		9					
Nuisance	12	22	9	10			1		4	13	1	2				
Official misconduct																
Perjury									1							
Prostitution	8	18	2	11					2	7	1					
Rape									1		5					
Receiving stolen goods	4	1	2								3					
Removing crop	1		1						1							
Resisting officer	46	10	47	15			2		10	5	5	2				
Robbery			1						14		17	1				
Seduction									1							
Slander		2		2					1			1				
Trespass	59	7	48	13			1		11	6	10	5				
Vagrancy	22	29	4	7					14	4	3	3				
Worthless check	22	3	5				1		3		1				1	
False pretense	6		14	2					10	1	13				1	
Carnal knowledge, etc.											3					
Crime against nature									4	1	2					
Slot machine laws	1								1							
Kidnaping									5							
Revenue act violations				1												
Miscellaneous	119	144	95	42			5		49	11	35	14				
Totals	9229	1057	5629	915	4		88	4	1110	159	920	197	2		50	1

Convictions	16929
Bound over to superior court	358
Other dispositions	2093
Total	19380

Offense	CONVICTIONS								OTHER DISPOSITIONS							
	White		Negro		Indian		Unclassified		White		Negro		Indian		Unclassified	
	M	F	M	F	M	F	M	F	M	F	M	F	M	F	M	F
ult..	183	49	144	111			1		64	23	36	44				
ult and battery																
ssault with deadly weapon	137	30	702	229					68	16	168	112	1			
ult:on female	178		638						73		108					
ssault with intent to kill			3	1					6		8	1				
ssault with intent to rape									4		1					
ssault—secret																
runk—drunk & disorderly	1851	169	781	158			1		15	2	1					
ossession—illegal whikey																
ossession for sale--sale	1		1						1							
Manufacturing—posses- on of material for																
ransportation																
iolation liquor laws	354	21	365	236					45	9	27	22				
riving drunk	286	9	67	1					21	1	4					
eckless driving	260	27	112	5					415	67	135	6			1	
it and run	6	1	1							1	2					
peeding	144	59	224	3					2							
uto license violations	394	47	200	10					11	1	11	4				
iolation motor vehicle laws	87	3	45	2					3		2					
reaking and entering											4					
And larceny																
And receiving																
ousebreaking	1		1						3		3					
And larceny											1					
And receiving		2									34	5				
torebreaking	1								3	1	3					
And larceny											3					
And receiving	2	2							34	1	62	1				
Larceny	83	20	210	60					113	10	133	29				
Larceny & receiving	1															
Larceny from the person	1								1		1					
Larceny by trick & device																
Larceny of automobile			1						4		3					
Temporary larceny									2							
furder—first degree											3	1				
furder—second degree											1					
Manslaughter									18	7	10	1				
urglary—first degree											1					
urgl r—second degree									4		11					
Abandonment		3		3						4	1	1				
Abduction												1	1			
Affray	2		3	4					2				3			
Arson											1					
Bigamy	2								2		4					
Bribery																
Burning other than arson																
Carrying concealed weapon	18	2	32	4					5		1					
Contempt	1															
Conspiracy																
Cruelty to animals			1													
Disorderly conduct	2	1		1												
Disorderly house		2		1							5					
Disposing of mortgaged property	10		2	2							1		1			
Disturbing religious worship											4					
Violation of election laws																
Embezzlement	1		3	1					8	5	8					

ELEVENTH JUDICIAL DISTRICT
INFERIOR COURTS

	JANUARY 1, 1944—JANUARY 1. 1946															
	CONVICTIONS								OTHER DISPOSITIONS							
Offense	White		Negro		Indian		Unclassified		White		Negro		Indian		Unclassified	
	M	F	M	F	M	F	M	F	M	F	M	F	M	F	M	F
:ape			8	1												
lure to list tax																
)d and drug laws	2															
h and game laws	3															
·cible trespass	7	1														
gery	2	1							14	2	3	1				
·nication and adultery	8	8	38	37					5	5	2	2				
ning and lottery laws	197	6	368	56					36	1	12	1				
.lth laws	1	7	23	36						1		1				
est									1							
ary to property	50	7	97	44					13	4	11	7				
nicipal ordinances	196	31	170	11					10		3	1				
isupport	101	2	198				1		89	1	70					
isupport of illegitimate child			2						1		1					
sance	213	50	158	103					23	17	29	24				
cial misconduct																
jury												1				
stitution	93	111	11	11					10	7						
ie									3		6					
eiving stolen goods	4		29	2					12		3					
noving crop																
isting officer	17		14	6					1		1					
·bery	1		1						13	1	18	1				
iction									2							
ider																
ipass	23	6	60	7					9	1	9	3				
rancy	20	42	26	10					8	12	6					
thless check	1															
e pretense	5		3						21		5					
nal knowledge, etc									2		1					
ue against nature									2		3					
machine laws																
naping																
enue act violations																
cellaneous	68	13	62	28					12	3	11	4			1	
Totals	611?	732	3104	1184			3		122?	209	399	278	1		2	

Convictions 13,141
Bound over to superior court 465
Other dispositions 2,245

15,851

JANUARY 1, 1944—J

Offense	Convictions White M	F	Negro M	F	Indian M	F	Unclassified M	F	Other Dispositions White M	F	Negro M	F	Indian M	F
Assault	103	64	200	70			1		134	25	50	36		
Assault and battery											1			
Assault with deadly weapon	245	19	254	138			7		129	19	118	53		
Assault on female	254		125				3		110		94			
Assault with intent to kill	2		3	1					23	2	23	10		
Assault with intent to rape	1								8		10			
Assault—secret									3		1			
Drunk—drunk & disorderly	2855	293	517	172	3		27	1	72	14	10	3		
Possession—illegal whiskey	90	2	38	18			3		8		5	4		
Possession for sale—sale	42	6	111	93			5		12	4	32	27		
Manufacturing—possession of material for	7		2				1							
Transportation	14		16				1		8	1	6			
Violation liquor laws	235	12	139	44					38	4	21	9		
Driving drunk	1897	153	197	71			9		108	6	12	1		
Reckless driving	517	30	186	3			6		162	43	84	5		
Hit and run	63	5	33	1			1		34	1	7			
Speeding	1843	73	338	5			57	1	16		7			
Auto license violations	520	65	228	28			13		70	3	40	1		
Violation motor vehicle laws	114	2	45				1		13	2	4			
Breaking and entering	9		3						51	1	37	1		
And larceny														
And receiving	1								18	1	34			
Housebreaking														
And larceny	2													
And receiving	1		2	1					65	1	57	2		
Storebreaking														
And larceny														
And receiving														
Larceny	98	15	143	38			1		76	9	56	20		
Larceny & receiving	78	15	116	25			1		63	13	52	17		
Larceny from the person			1	2	2				13	1	32	9		
Larceny by trick & device	1	2	4						6	1	3			
Larceny of automobile	4		3						50	2	10	2		
Temporary larceny	1								1		1			
Murder—first degree									1	1	6	4		
Murder—second degree									1		1			
Manslaughter	1			1					37	1	20	5		
Burglary—first degree														
Burglary—second degree									5		5			
Abandonment	83	15	33	6			7		44	4	12	1		
Abduction									3		1			
Affray	211	26	143	95			2		105	11	57	33		
Arson									1		3	1		
Bigamy									6	6	4	2		
Bribery														
Burning other than arson														
Carrying concealed weapon	41	3	72	6					14		9	5		
Contempt	1													
Conspiracy									17		4			
Cruelty to animals	4		2						4					
Disorderly conduct	354	101	308	231			8		87	32	46	32		
Disorderly house	2	9	4	3					2	1	1	5		
Disposing of mortgaged property	4		3						1	1				
Disturbing religious worship									2		2			
Violation of election laws														
Embezzlement	11		9						19	1	7	1		

JANUARY 1, 1944—JANUARY 1, 1946

Offense	Convictions								Other Dispositions							
	White		Negro		Indian		Unclassified		White		Negro		Indian		Unclassified	
	M	F	M	F	M	F	M	F	M	F	M	F	M	F	M	F
ape	39	14	30	18			1		1		3	1				
lure to list tax																
d and drug laws																
1 and game laws	10															
cible trespass	34	2	24	3					7	3	5	2				
gery									30	2	8	1			3	
nication and adultery	51	50	118	113			2		24	11	14	10			1	
ning and lottery laws	220	2	62	24			8		47	1	20	7			2	1
lth laws	14	16	46	51			1	1	1	8	5	11				
est									2		2	1				
iry to property	89	8	50	15					49	4	11	6			1	
nicipal ordinances	581	62	218	19			10	1	54	8	30	1			2	
isupport	276	4	102	4			7		116	3	25	2			10	
isupport of illegitimate child	9		26	1			1		14		7				2	
sance	4	2	4						10	3	5	4				2
cial misconduct																
jury									2							
stitution	34	65	9	16			2		11	16	4	7			1	
ie									5		10					
eiving stolen goods	14		9	6			1		30	1	8	1				
noving crop											1					
isting officer	60	2	30	12					17	3	9					
bery	1		2						41		22	1			2	
ction											1					
der	3	3							1	6						
pass	50	9	30	7			1		32	9	13	3			1	
rancy	77	170	40	101			7		40	43	22	22			3	1
thless check	42	1	10				3		6		2				2	
e pretense	23	25		2					25	8	14	2			3	
al knowledge etc											5					
e against nature	1		1						12		10					
machine laws	6	1	1						1							
aping									2		1	1			1	
nue act violations																
ellaneous	338	381	200	135			9	2	319	49	86	20			9	
Totals	11988	1725	5516	1579	3		207	6	2736	290	1328	400			101	4

Convictions	21,027
Bound over to superior court	754
Other dispositions	4,205
Total	**25,986**

THIRTEENTH JUDICIAL DISTRICT
INFERIOR COURTS

JANUARY 1, 1944—JANUARY 1, 1946

Offense	CONVICTIONS								OTHER DISPOSITIONS						
	White		Negro		Indian		Unclas-sfied		White		Negro		Indian		Unc- sifi
	M	F	M	F	M	F	M	F	M	F	M	F	M	F	M
Assault	149	13	139	47	5				30		20	8			
Assault and battery	12		17	4					3		1	1			
Assault with deadly weapon	101	6	188	77	4				46	3	62	16			
Assault on female	45		55				1		20		8				
Assault with intent to kill	3		2								6	2			
Assault with intent to rape											3				
Assault—secret	1		1						1		1				
Drunk—drunk & disorderly	170	95	1098	93	22	1			27	6	6	1			
Possession—illegal whiskey	55	2	75	18	2						7				
Possession for sale—sale	22	3	33	14					2		6	2			1
Manufacturing—possession of material for	15		10	2	6						1				
Transportation	23		30		1				1		1		1		
Violation liquor laws	63	3	115	21			2		17	5	11	4			
Driving drunk	349	10	109	1	4				20		2				
Reckless driving	229	8	103	3					27	1	10				
Hit and run	8	1	5						2						
Speeding	497	20	104	1	1		3		12	1					1
Auto license violations	197	20	128	7	1				16	1	7				
Violation motor vehicle laws	555	6	149	6	1		1		61	1	6	1			1
Breaking and entering	1		6	1					8	2	10	1			2
And larceny	1		2						3	1	8				
And receiving	1		3						16			1			
Housebreaking															
And larceny															
And receiving															
Storebreaking															
And larceny															
And receiving															
Larceny	40	4	74	15	5				18	2	24	7			
Larceny & receiving	22	1	38	7					3		15	1			
Larceny from the person			3						1		4				
Larceny by trick & device			1						1		1				
Larceny of automobile	6		8						7		2				
Temporary larceny	5		4						2						
Murder—first degree									1						
Murder—second degree															
Manslaughter									5		1				
Burglary—first degree															
Burglary—second degree											2				
Abandonment	31	3	15						7		5				
Abduction											3				
Affray	25	1	43	13					2		1	3			
Arson									2				2		
Bigamy	1		1						2	2	2	1			
Bribery															
Burning other than arson															
Carrying concealed weapon	33	4	55	7	1				6	1	4				1
Contempt	1														
Conspiracy			1												
Cruelty to animals	1								1		2				
Disorderly conduct	16	2	40	9					5		1				
Disorderly house	1		1	2	1				1						
Disposing of mortgaged property	2		2						2		1				
Disturbing religious worship	1		8		1	1					3		1		
Violation of election laws															
Embezzlement									4		1				

THIRTEENTH JUDICIAL DISTRICT
INFERIOR COURTS

JANUARY 1, 1944—JANUARY 1, 1946

Offense	CONVICTIONS White M	F	Negro M	F	Indian M	F	Unclassified M	F	OTHER DISPOSITIONS White M	F	Negro M	F	Indian M	F	Unclassified M	F
:ape.	3		6													
lure to list tax.																
od and drug laws.																
h and game laws	20		2													
rcible trespass.	16	2	9	2					1	3	2					
rgery.									7	4	3					
rnication and adultery	8	12	12	22					6	5	1	4				
ming and lottery laws	91	2	71						6		1					
alth laws	2		4	10			1				1	3				
est.									1		1					
ury to property	20		16	3					9		4					
inicipal ordinances	14	1	4	2					2		1	1				
nsupport	60	3	49						17		10					
nsupport of illegitimate child	2		6						4		1					
iisance	3	3	1								1					
icial misconduct																
rjury																
stitution	1	8	4	7					2	2						
pe.									1		4					
ceiving stolen goods	10		6	1					2		4	1				
moving crop	2								3		1					
sisting officer	35	4	34	11					5		2	3				
bbery	1		1						12		3	1				
duction									3		1					
nder										1						
espass	27	1	22	1					13		7	5				
igrancy	5	4	4	10					3		1					
orthless check	13	2	2	1					5							
lse pretense	6	2	8						1		5					
rnal knowledge, etc.			1								2					
ine against nature											1					
t machine laws																
idnaping																
evenue act violations																
iscellaneous	67	10	74	15	1		1		14	2	6	3				
Totals	4621	265	2999	433	56	2	9		499	43	311	70	4		6	

Convictions	8,385
Bound over to superior court	122
Other dispositions	811
Total	9,318

	JANUARY 1, 1944—JANUARY 1, 1946															
	CONVICTIONS								OTHER DISPOSITIONS							
Offense	White		Negro		Indian		Unclassified		White		Negro		Indian		Unclassified
	M	F	M	F	M	F	M	F	M	F	M	F	M	F	M
Assault	282	63	135	62			1		96	30	45	32			
s a aud battery	3			2					1		1				
s au with deadly weapon	147	17	271	171			1		183	21	366	196			
Assault on female	81		131				1		100		113				
a with intent to kill									2		2				
Assault with intent to rape									3		5				
Assault—secret															
Drunk—drunk & disorderly	1 0356	1131	2387	506			2	19	121	37	38	9			
Possession—illegal whiskey															
Possession for sale—sale	1		1								1				
Manufacturing—possession of material for															
Transportation	1														
Violation liquor laws	367	28	47	106					69	12	28	28			1
Driving drunk	271	27	102	2					69	3	11				
Reckless driving	201	7	123	3			1		41	2	24	3			1
Hit and run	60	6	42						41	1	17	1			
Speeding	1431	112	178	8					27	1	9	1			
Auto license violations	300	15	125	6			5		24		7	1			1
a n motor vehicle laws	123	7	97	2					9		9				
rea ng and entering	1		2						4		6				
And larceny									2		1				
And receiving	1								11	1	4				
Housebreaking									1						
And larceny	1								24	1	77	13			
And receiving															
Storebreaking	2								42		112	2			
And larceny									14		2				
And receiving															
Larceny	133	25	215	73					200	30	181	57			
Larceny & receiving	34	12	39	9					21	10	25	13			
Larceny from the person									9	6	17	4			
Larceny by trick & device															
Larceny of automobile	14	1	5						66	1	25	1			
Temporary larceny	6		4								1				
Murder—first degree				1					11	2	33	8			
Murder—second degree															
Manslaughter									6	1	8				
r ary—first degree									1		2				
r ar —second degree									1		2				
Abandonment	14	2	5						6		3				
Abduction															
Affray	149	29	71	70			1		41	7	18	16			
Arson									1		3	1			
Bigamy	1								3	7	4	1			
Bribery															
rn n other than arson															
Carrving concealed weapon	63	8	97	9					21		15	2			
n em t			1												
Conspiracy															
r el to animals	1								1		1				
r er conduct	242	88	170	154					43	22	27	16			
Disorderly house		2	2	6								4			
Disposing of mortgaged property	1								3						
Disturbing religious worship			1								1				
a n of election laws															
Embezzlement	2		1						15		12				

FOURTEENTH JUDICIAL DISTRICT
INFERIOR COURTS

Offense	CONVICTIONS								OTHER DISPOSITIONS							
	White		Negro		Indian		Unclassified		White		Negro		Indian		Unclassified	
	M	F	M	F	M	F	M	F	M	F	M	F	M	F	M	F
ape		3	11													
lure to list tax																
od and drug laws																
h and game laws																
rible trespass	21	2	17						2		1			1		
gery		1		1					14		4	3				
nication and adultery	16	15	26	27					6	4	2	4				
ming and lottery laws	10	5	127	45					9		40	13				
alth laws	1		3	2												
est																
ury to property	70	8	58	25					38	3	26	10				
uicipal ordinances	58	36	205	34					76	9	25	7				
nsupport	47	1	18				1		23	1	8					
nsupport of illegitimate child	1															
iisance	4	1														
icial misconduct																
rjury																
ostitution	40	48	24	25					7	6		6				
pe									5		9					
ceiving stolen goods	7		16	1					10	2	26	2				
moving crop																
sisting officer	60	5	16	5					11	2	4	2				
bbery	2								32	3	80	1				
duction																
un er		1							8	5						
espass	57	7	27	4					28	8	12	3			1	
grancy	26	38	13	22					15	5	18	3				
orthless check	25	8	2						3	3	1	1				
lse pretense	7	4		1					13	3	6					
nal knowledge, etc																
ime against nature	1		3						4		5	1				
ot machine laws																
idnaping	3								2							
venue act violations	3								2							
iscellaneous	284	236	84	28				1	64	33	29	5				
Totals	5030	2002	5602	1410			2	31	1700	282	1552	70			5	

Convictions	24.677
Bound over to superior court	1.188
Other dispositions	2.821
Total	**28 686**

FIFTEENTH JUDICIAL DISTRICT
INFERIOR COURTS

Offense	CONVICTIONS								OTHER DISPOSITIONS						
	White		Negro		Indian		Unclassified		White		Negro		Indian		Unc sifi
	M	F	M	F	M	F	M	F	M	F	M	F	M	F	M
Assault	112	33	35	14			2		28	3	11	5			3
Assault and battery	2														
Assault with deadly weapon	149	24	188	108			8		96	11	46	20			7
Assault on female	111		97				3		88		47				7
Assault with intent to kill	2		3						3		2				
Assault with intent to rape									2						
Assault—secret															
Drunk—drunk & disorderly	1176	65	410	34	1		43		25	2	4	1			3
Possession—illegal whiskey	120	9	39	9			2		12	1	5	3			
Possession for sale—sale	18		44	9							1				
Manufacturing—possession of material for			2												
Transportation	13		5				1				1				
Violation liquor laws	97	7	68	16			3		2		1	1			
Driving drunk	462	8	79	1			4		26	1	4				2
Reckless driving	241	6	58	1			10		83	6	15				5
Hit and run	33	1	18				1		6		1				
Speeding	954	40	122				39	1	16		1				
Auto hoense violations	113	9	38	1			12		4		1				1
Violation motor vehicle laws	52	2	23	1			1		7		1				
Breaking and entering		1	2						7		13	1			
And larceny											1				
And receiving	3		3						12		8	1			
Housebreaking	1		1								1				
And larceny															
And receiving															
Storebreaking															
And larceny															
And receiving															
Larceny	48	4	40	13			2		27	2	9	3			
Larceny & receiving	68	7	92	15			6		45	4	32	6			5
Larceny from the person		1													
Larceny by trick & device		1	5												
Larceny of automobile															
Temporary larceny	2		17												1
Murder—first degree									2		3				
Murder—second degree															
Manslaughter									4						
Burglary—first degree															
Burglary—second degree									1						
Abandonment	55	9	7	1			4		11	1	3				3
Abduction															
Affray	34	6	18	8					1						
Arson												1			
Bigamy			1						1	2		2			
Bribery															
Burning other than arson															
Carrying concealed weapon	55	3	36	2			5		7		3				
Contempt															
Conspiracy									2	1					
Cruelty to animals	2								1						
Disorderly conduct	29	13	12	15			1	2	5	1	1	1			3
Disorderly house	2	2													
Disposing of mortgaged property	5	2													
Disturbing religious worship	2		2						2	1					
Violation of election laws															
Embezzlement	2								1	1		1			

FIFTEENTH JUDICIAL DISTRICT
INFERIOR COURTS

Offense	JANUARY 1, 1944—JANUARY 1, 1946															
	CONVICTIONS								OTHER DISPOSITIONS							
	White		Negro		Indian		Unclassified		White		Negro		Indian		Unclassified	
	M	F	M	F	M	F	M	F	M	F	M	F	M	F	M	F
	5	3	13	3												
to list tax																
nd drug laws																
d game laws																
e trespass	32	1	20	6			1		10						1	
r	2	1	1						12	2					1	
ition and adultery	32	26	13	13			1		7	7	2					
g and lottery laws	199		126	8			3		9		11				5	
laws	2	1	3	1												
to property	24	3	8				2		12		2	1			1	
pal ordinances	118	3	24	1			2		4		1					
port	114	4	32				6		49		8				1	
port of illegitimate child	1		2						1		2				2	
ce	5	3	1							1						
misconduct																
r	3															
ution	1	6														
	1								2		1					
ing stolen goods	1	1	8				1									
ing crop																
ng officer	39	3	17	2			1		4							
y	1								7		10					
on									1							
		1							1	1						
s	32	5	8	5			2		10	1	4					
cy	34	27	25	2			1		12	2		1				
ess check	12	3	4						5		1					
retense	5	2	4						6	2						
knowledge, etc									2							
gainst nature									1							
chine laws	4															
ing																
e act violations	1															
aneous	65	15	17	3			2		15	2	1	2				
otals	'698	259	1791	294	1		169	3	697	55	257	51			51	

Convictions 7.313
Bound over to superior court 135
Other dispositions 976

Total 8.424

SIXTEENTH JUDICIAL DISTRICT
INFERIOR COURTS

JANUARY 1, 1944—J

Offense	CONVICTIONS								OTHER D.SPOSITIONS						Un si
	White		Negro		Indian		Unclassified		White		Negro		Indian		
	M	F	M	F	M	F	M	F	M	F	M	F	M	F	M
Assault	176	47	78	31			3		55	14	20	11			
Assault and battery	2														
Assault with deadly weapon	209	37	239	89			3		103	20	65	27			
Assault on female	189		130				2		47		23				
Assault with intent to kill	3		2						3						
Assault with intent to rape									3		4				
Assault—secret											5				
Drunk—drunk & disorderly	1055	239	1046	139	1		75	1	157	11	25	6			2
Possession—illegal whiskey	61	2	12	2					7		5				
Possession for sale—sale	34	1	12	2					4			1			
Manufacturing—possession of material for	15		3	1					1						
Transportation	24		13	1			1		7		1				
Violation liquor laws	219	5	155	52			6		24	3	11	9			
Driving drunk	386	12	81	3			4		38		2				
Reckless driving	255	8	62						71	3	13				
Hit and run	27		8						9		1				
Speeding	352	7	51				4		10	1	5				
Auto license violations	57	8	29	2					11	1	1				
Violation motor vehicle laws	174	7	56	2			6		21		6				
Breaking and entering	2	1	4						32		23	1			
And larceny	3		1						7	2	10				
And receiving	1								2		1				
Housebreaking															
And larceny															
And receiving									1						
Storebreaking															
And larceny															
And receiving															
Larceny	74	8	58	11			1		48	6	31	9			
Larceny & receiving	13	1	15						11	2	7	1			
Larceny from the person	1	1	2	1					10		9	6			
Larceny by trick & device															
Larceny of automobile	10								9		5				
Temporary larceny	6		1						2						
Murder—first degree			1						25	1	11				
Murder—second degree															
Manslaughter									7		2				
Burglary—first degree															
Burglary—second degree									2						
Abandonment	82	7	18				1		33	3	3				
Abduction									1						
Affray	99	25	48	36			2		28	5	12	1			
Arson															
Bigamy		1							7	1	3	1			
Bribery															
Burning other than arson															
Carrying concealed weapon	38	1	38	2			1		2		6				
Contempt	1														
Conspiracy									4						
Cruelty to animals	1								2						
Disorderly conduct	5	1		1					3	2					
Disorderly house	2	13							1	2					
Disposing of mortgaged property	4	1	1						1		1				
Disturbing religious worship			10						1						
Violation of election laws															
Embezzlement	1		1						4	7	5				

SIXTEENTH JUDICIAL DISTRICT
INFERIOR COURTS

Offense	CONVICTIONS								OTHER DISPOSITIONS							
	White		Negro		Indian		Unclassified		White		Negro		Indian		Unclassified	
	M	F	M	F	M	F	M	F	M	F	M	F	M	F	M	F
e......	6	1	7	1					1							
e to list tax......																
and drug laws......																
ind game laws......																
ble trespass......	8		6						7	1	2	1				
y......	2								8	5	7	1				
ation and adultery......	18	18	16	18					5	6	4	5				
ig and lottery laws......	74		88	3					9	1	3					
n laws......	5	3	3	6					1	1		1				
to property......	33	2	22	1					18	2	4	1				
ipal ordinances......	48	1	1						8							
ipport......	182	4	48				4		56	2				0		
ipport of illegitimate child......	16		17						5		5					
nce......			1	1						1						
d misconduct......																
y......									1							
tution......	36	37	15	16					8	11	6	3				
1	1								5		3					
ving stolen goods......	8		2						4		5	1				
ving crop......																
ing officer......	49	3	10	3					4		4	1				
ery......	4		1						2	1	6					
tion......	1		1						6		2					
er......	2	4							1	1		1				
ass......	34	6	21	6					13	5	6	2				
ncy......	16	58	13	7					8	23	3					
hless check......	32	1	3						10	1	1					
pretense......	2								5	1	5					
l knowledge, etc......									5		3					
against nature......	2								5							
achine laws......	4															
iping......									1							
ie act violations......																
illaneous......	88	19	28	15			2		37	10	4	3				
Totals......	7257	590	2472	452	1		115	1	1047	156	389	96			11	

Convictions 10.988
Bound over to superior court...... 287
Other dispositions...... 1.412

Total 12.087

SEVENTEENTH JUDICIAL DISTRICT
INFERIOR COURTS

Offense	JANUARY 1, 1944—JAN														
	CONVICTIONS								OTHER DISPOSITION						
	White		Negro		Indian		Unclassified		White		Negro		Indian		Unclassified
	M	F	M	F	M	F	M	F	M	F	M	F	M	F	M
Assault	69	11	4	2					6		4				
Assault and battery															
Assault with deadly weapon	6		4	1											
Assault on female	1		1								1				
Assault with intent to kill															
Assault with intent to rape															
Assault—secret															
Drunk—drunk & disorderly	184	6	21	2											
Possession—illegal whiskey															
Possession for sale—sale	7														
Manufacturing—possession of material for			1												
Transportation			1												
Violation liquor laws	5														
Driving drunk	6		2						1						
Reckless driving	5		1						1						
Hit and run	1														
Speeding	4														
Auto license violations	12		1	2											
Violation motor vehicle laws															
Breaking and entering									1		1				
And larceny															
And receiving															
Housebreaking															
And larceny															
And receiving															
Storebreaking															
And larceny															
And receiving															
Larceny				1					3		1				
Larceny & receiving			1												
Larceny from the person															
Larceny by trick & device															
Larceny of automobile															
Temporary larceny															
Murder—first degree															
Murder—second degree															
Manslaughter															
Burglary—first degree															
Burglary—second degree															
Abandonment	4														
Abduction															
Affray					1										
Arson															
Bigamy															
Bribery															
Burning other than arson															
Carrying concealed weapon			1												
Contempt															
Conspiracy															
Cruelty to animals															
Disorderly conduct	1	1													
Disorderly house															
Disposing of mortgaged property															
Disturbing religious worship															
Violation of election laws															
Embezzlement															

SEVENTEENTH JUDICIAL DISTRICT
INFERIOR COURTS

JANUARY 1, 1944—JANUARY 1, 1946

Offense	CONVICTIONS								OTHER DISPOSITIONS							
	White		Negro		Indian		Unclas- sified		White		Negro		Indian		Uni·las- ·if; d	
	M	F	M	F	M	F	M	F	M	F	M	F	M	F	M	F
be																
re to list tax																
and drug laws																
and game laws																
ble tresapss	4															
ry																
ication and adultery	4	1														
ng and lottery laws			3													
h laws																
t																
y to property																
cipal ordinances	2															
upport	3		1													
upport of illegitimate child																
ance	1		5	2												
al misconduct																
ry																
itution																
iving stolen goods	3															
oving crop																
sting officer	4	2	1													
bery									1							
ction																
der																
pass	1		2													
ancy									1							
thless check																
e pretense																
ial knowledge, etc																
ie against nature																
machine laws			1													
aping																
enue act violations																
ellaneous	3	2														
Totals	330	23	50	11					14		7					

Convictions 414
Bound over to superior court 7
Other dispositions 14

Total 435

EIGHTEENTH JUDICIAL DISTRICT
INFERIOR COURTS

JANUARY 1, 1944—JA

Offense	CONVICTIONS								OTHER DISPOSITION						
	White		Negro		Indian		Unclassified		White		Negro		Indian		Un sif
	M	F	M	F	M	F	M	F	M	F	M	F	M	F	M
Assault	61	12	23	11					24	7	12	5			
Assault and battery									1						
Assault with deadly weapon	76	11	54	15					49	11	24	14	1		
Assault on female	14		10						7		4				
Assault with intent to kill															
Assault with intent to rape									3						
Assault—secret															
Drunk—drunk & disorderly	171	6	62	9					13	1	2	1			
Possession—illegal whiskey	14		1	2											
Possession for sale—sale	2														
Manufacturing—possession of material for	4														
Transportation	8		1	1					1						
Violation liquor laws	173	11	75	20			1		35	2	16	5			5
Driving drunk	214	10	24	1					18	1	3				
Reckless driving	73		18	1					19	2	4				
Hit and run	3								1		1				
Speeding	136	4	18						11		1				
Auto license violations	99	18	17	2					7		3				
Violation motor vehicle laws	17	1	3						5		1				
Breaking and entering	2		1						1	1	1				
And larceny									14		5	2			
And receiving															
Housebreaking															
And larceny															
And receiving									1						
Storebreaking															
And larceny															
And receiving															
Larceny	37	5	26	7			1		40	5	10	6			
Larceny & receiving	2														
Larceny from the person															
Larceny by trick & device															
Larceny of automobile									2		1				
Temporary larceny			1						2						
Murder—first degree									1						
Murder—second degree															
Manslaughter															
Burglary—first degree															
Burglary—second degree															
Abandonment	19	2	3						4	1	1				
Abduction										1					
Affray	11	2	4	1					4		4				
Arson															
Bigamy									1	1	1	1			
Bribery															
Burning other than arson															
Carrying concealed weapon	22	2	12						6	1	1				
Contempt	1			1							1				
Conspiracy									3						
Cruelty to animals															
Disorderly conduct		1	1	1					1	2					
Disorderly house		2		1											
Disposing of mortgaged property		1							2	1					
Disturbing religious worship	2								1						
Violation of election laws															
Embezzlement									1						

EIGHTEENTH JUDICIAL DISTRICT
INFERIOR COURTS

JANUARY 1, 1944—JANUARY 1, 1946

Offense	CONVICTIONS								OTHER DISPOSITIONS							
	White		Negro		Indian		Unclassified		White		Negro		Indian		Unclassified	
	M	F	M	F	M	F	M	F	M	F	M	F	M	F	M	F
e to list tax	7	1							1							
nd drug laws																
nd game laws	1		4													
le trespass	12	4	7	1					5	1						
ry									5							
ation and adultery	16	25	4	1					7	9	1					
g and lottery laws	23		19						2	1	5	1				
laws	3	1		1					1	1		1				
to property	6		2						3			1				
cipal ordinances	1								1							
pport	36	2	8	1					9	1	5					
pport of illegitimate child	2		2						2		1					
nce																
l misconduct																
ry																
itution	6	8							2	2						
									4		2					
ving stolen goods	3	1	2	1					7		1					
ving crop																
ting officer	26	2	5	1					1							
ery	1								1							
ction									3							
er	1								3	4						
ass	6	2	6	2					6	3	1	2				
ancy	4	6	1						1							
hless check	5	2		1					2		1					
pretense	3	1							5							
al knowledge, etc																
e against nature																
machine laws	8	2									1	1				
aping																
u act violations																
ellaneous	40	12	11	3					16	4	2	1				
Totals	1371	157	425	85			2		365	63	117	40			6	

Convictions	2040
Bound over to superior court	56
Other dispositions	535
Total	2631

TWENTIETH JUDICIAL DISTRICT
INFERIOR COURTS

JANUARY 1, 1944—J

| Offense | CONVICTIONS | | | | | | | | OTHER DISPOSITION | | | | | | Un si |
| | White | | Negro | | Indian | | Unclassified | | White | | Negro | | Indian | | |
	M	F	M	F	M	F	M	F	M	F	M	F	M	F	M
Assault	28	2							2	2					
Assault and battery															
Assault with deadly weapon	1								3		1				
Assault on female															
Assault with intent to kill															
Assault with intent to rape															
Assault—secret															
Drunk—drunk & disorderly	888	29	8	4	1				141	3	1				4
Possession—illegal whiskey	12	1													
Possession for sale—sale	2														
Manufacturing—possession of material for															
Transportation	8								3						
Violation liquor laws	3								2						
Driving drunk	39	1	1						5						
Reckless driving	22		1						3						
Hit and run	1														
Speeding	22														
Auto license violations	25	7							3						
Violation motor vehicle laws	34	2	1						5						
Breaking and entering															
And larceny									7						
And receiving															
Housebreaking															
And larceny															
And receiving															
Storebreaking															
And larceny															
And receiving															
Larceny	12								3	2	1				
Larceny & receiving															
Larceny from the person															
Larceny by trick & device															
Larceny of automobile															
Temporary larceny															
Murder—first degree									1						
Murder—second degree															
Manslaughter															
Burglary—first degree															
Burglary—second degree															
Abandonment															
Abduction															
Affray	16								3		1				
Arson															
Bigamy															
Bribery															
Burning other than arson															
Carrying concealed weapon	3														
Contempt															
Conspiracy															
Cruelty to animals															
Disorderly conduct	10	6		1					2		1				
Disorderly house									1						
Disposing of mortgaged property															
Disturbing religious worship															
Violation of election laws															
Embezzlement	1														

TWENTIETH JUDICIAL DISTRICT
INFERIOR COURTS

JANUARY 1, 1944—JANUARY 1, 1946

| Offense | CONVICTIONS | | | | | | | | OTHER DISPOSITIONS | | | | | | | |
| | White | | Negro | | Indian | | Unclassified | | White | | Negro | | Indian | | Unclassified | |
	M	F	M	F	M	F	M	F	M	F	M	F	M	F	M	F
...ape																
...lure to list tax																
...od and drug laws																
...h and game laws																
...rcible trespass																
...rgery									1							
...rnication and adultery																
...ming and lottery laws	22								1							
...alth laws																
...est																
...ury to property	9								7							
...unicipal ordinances	39	1	3						7	2						
...nsupport	2								1							
...nsupport of illegitimate child																
...isance																
...ficial misconduct																
...rjury																
...ostitution	3	2								1						
...pe																
...ceiving stolen goods																
...moving crop																
...sisting officer	2															
...bbery																
...duction																
...nder	1															
...eapss																
...grancy	6	5							2	1						
...orthless check	2								1							
...lse pretense									1							
...rnal knowledge, etc																
...ime against nature																
...ot machine laws																
...idnaping																
...evenue act violations																
...iscellaneous	5		1						1							
Totals	121	56	15	5	1				205	11	5				4	

Convictions	1,295
Bound over to superior court	10
Other dispositions	215
Total	1,520

TWENTY-FIRST JUDICIAL DISTRICT
INFERIOR COURTS

JANUARY 1, 1944—JANUARY 1, 1946

| Offense | CONVICTIONS | | | | | | | | OTHER DISPOSITIONS | | | | | | |
| | White | | Negro | | Indian | | Unclas-sified | | White | | Negro | | Indian | | Unc sif |
	M	F	M	F	M	F	M	F	M	F	M	F	M	F	M
Assault	114	21	39	19					23	3	6	6			
Assault and battery	1														
Assault with deadly weapon	92	13	84	19					50	5	25	2			
Assault on female	116		116						34		7				
Assault with intent to kill	1								1		2	3			
Assault with intent to rape			1						4						
Assault—secret	1														
Drunk—drunk & disorderly	1755	50	355	35					24		8	1			
Possession—illegal whiskey	25		9	1					1			1			
Possession for sale—sale	7		4						2			1			
Manufacturing—possession of material for	13		8												
Transportation	5	1	6	1					1		1				
Violation liquor laws	132	2	32	24					11	1	1	3			
Driving drunk	229	1	52						17		5				
Reckless driving	19.	2	53	1					42	1	17	2			
Hit and run	18	1	10	1					4						
Speeding	294	4	93	1			3		3	1					
Auto license violations	153	14	84	3					4		4				
Violation motor vehicle laws	35	1	15						3						
Breaking and entering	4								8		2				
And larceny			1						13	1	6	1			
And receiving	1								53	2		7			
Housebreaking															
And larceny											1				
And receiving															
Storebreaking															
And larceny															
And receiving															
Larceny	40	6	13	1					27		9	1			
Larceny & receiving	28	2	16	3					26		8	3			
Larceny from the person	1								6	1	6	2			
Larceny by trick & device	1														
Larceny of automobile	2								28		3				
Temporary larceny	3		2						2		1				
Murder—first degree									3		4	3			
Murder—second degree															
Manslaughter									7	1					
Burglary—first degree											1				
Burglary—second degree															
Abandonment	24	3	2	1					5	2	2				
Abduction															
Affray	49	5	16	7					20	3	7	4			
Arson									2						
Bigamy									3						
Bribery															
Burning other than arson															
Carrying concealed weapon	38	2	15						4		3				
Contempt	1														
Conspiracy	2	1													
Cruelty to animals	5								2						
Disorderly conduct	50	5	25	15					2		1	3			
Disorderly house	1	1									1				
Disposing of mortgaged property	1														
Disturbing religious worship	1		7												
Violation of election laws									3						
Embezzlement	1	1							3			1			

TWENTY-FIRST JUDICIAL DISTRICT
INFERIOR COURTS

JANUARY 1, 1944—JANUARY 1, 1946

Offense	CONVICTIONS								OTHER DISPOSITIONS							
	White		Negro		Indian		Unclassified		White		Negro		Indian		Unclassified	
	M	F	M	F	M	F	M	F	M	F	M	F	M	F	M	F
ape.	12															
lure to list tax																
od and drug laws																
h and game laws																
rcible trespass	4		3	1												
rgery									10	7	2					
rnication and adultery	2		1	1					2	1	1	1				
ming and lottery laws	36		13	3					5		2					
alth laws	1									1						
est									1							
ury to property	39	3	8	4					11		3	1				
nicipal ordinances	10		5						3		2					
nsupport	65	3	20	1					29	1	5					
nsupport of illegitimate child	4		12						2		5					
isance	7	1	4	1							3					
cial misconduct																
rjury																
stitution	1	3														
pe									6		1					
ceiving stolen goods	1								3	1	1					
moving crop																
sisting officer	28	1	9	1					1	1						
bbery									11							
duction																
ander	1								1	1						
espass	49	3	25	2					9	6	1					
graucy	23	5	18	3					1		3	9				
orthless check	8	1							2							
lse pretense	1		2						3							
rnal knowledge, etc.	1								6		3					
ime against nature									2							
ot machine laws	3															
idnaping			2	2					2							
evenue act violations																
iscellaneous	'286	26	70	9					20	7	6	3				
Totals	3001	1?2	24?	160				3	568	53	172	49				

Convictions	5.493
Bound over to superior court	219
Other dispositions	623
Total	**6.335**

ALPHABETICAL LIST OF CRIMES IN INFERIOR COURTS

Crimes	From July 1, 1944 to July 1, 1946 Convictions	Dispos. Other
Assault	7,318	1,448
Assault & Battery	1,201	248
Assault with Deadly Weapon	7,565	2,081
Assault on female	4,011	1,167
Assault with intent to kill	62	235
Assault with intent to rape	6	71
Assault—secret	9	26
Drunk—drunk and disorderly	54,554	1,058
Possession—illegal whiskey	2,392	205
Possession for sale—sale	1,454	251
Manufacturing—possession of material for	531	371
Transportation	572	161
Violation liquor laws	5,180	645
Driving drunk	9,205	723
Reckless driving	5,913	1,350
Hit & Run	547	209
Speeding	14,655	209
Auto license violations	5,053	419
Violation motor vehicle laws	5,131	274
Breaking & entering	72	849
And larceny	7	108
And receiving	5	152
Housebreaking	11	13
And larceny	2	185
And receiving	9	182
Storebreaking	4	178
And larceny	7	108
And receiving	5	152
Larceny	3,115	1,930
Larceny & receiving	962	508
Larceny from the person	23	219
Larceny by trick and device	23	26
Larceny of automobile	86	862
Temporary larceny	118	29
Murder—first degree	2	161
Murder—second degree	1	26
Manslaughter	3	171
Burglary—first degree	0	128
Burglary—second degree	3	23
Abandonment	376	345
Abduction	55	15
Affray	2,369	661
Arson	0	36
Bigamy	7	105
Bribery	0	0
Burning other than arson	3	1
Carrying concealed weapon	1,496	239
Contempt	16	2
Conspiracy	17	28
Cruelty to animals	58	40
Disorderly conduct	4,495	775
Disorderly house	98	36
Disposal of mortgaged property	60	32
Disturbing religious worship	69	35
Violation of election laws	0	0
Embezzlement	45	146
Escape	368	23
Failure to list tax	48	1
Food and drug laws	2	1
Fish and game laws	103	24
Forcible trespass	552	101
Forgery	21	275
Fornication and Adultery	1,291	349
Gaming and lottery laws	4,521	485
Health laws	455	82
Incest	0	19
Injury to property	1,448	310
Municipal ordinances	6,656	473
Non-support	2,295	930
Non-support of illegitimate child	242	96
Nuisance	897	143
Official misconduct	0	0

ALPHABETICAL LIST OF CRIMES IN INFERIOR COURTS

Crimes	From July 1, 1944 to July 1, 1946	
	Convictions	Other Dispos.
Perjury	5	6
Prostitution	1,559	299
Rape	2	115
Receiving stolen goods	231	200
Removing crop	14	20
Resisting officer	1,094	157
Robbery	35	472
Seduction	5	29
Slander	26	39
Trespass	1,202	464
Vagrancy	1,439	690
Worthless check	549	152
False pretense	173	242
Carnal knowledge, etc.	4	67
Crime against nature	8	54
Slot machine laws	52	6
Kidnaping	6	25
Revenue act violations	8	2
Miscellaneous	4,026	1,056
Totals	168,341	26,180

	ABSOLUTE					SEPARATION					GRAND TOTAL					5 yr tot.	One Divorce for No. of Population given below	
	1941	1942	1943	1944	1945	1941	1942	1943	1944	1945	1941	1942	1943	1944	1945		1941	1945
BEAUFORT																		
White																		
Colored																		
Total	50	37	39	36	71						50	37	39	36	71	233	728	513
CAMDEN																		
White	1	3	4	2	2						1	3	4	2	2	12		
Colored			2	2	3								2	2	3	7		
Total	1	3	6	4	5						1	3	6	4	5	19	5,440	1,088
CHOWAN																		
White	4	2	3	4	5						4	2	3	4	5	18		
Colored	7	6	9	9	8						7	6	9	9	8	39		
Total	11	8	12	13	13						11	8	12	13	13	57	1,052	890
CURRITUCK																		
White	5	1	15	6	4						5	1	15	6	4	31		
Colored	1		6	4	1						1		6	4	1	12		
Total	6	1	21	10	5						6	1	21	10	5	43	1,117	1,341
DARE																		
White	2	8									2	8				10		
Colored		1										1				1		
Total	2	9	0	0	0						2	9	0	0	0	11	3,020	0
GATES																		
White	2	1	1	1	1						2	1	1	1	1	6		
Colored	2	2	2	2	1						2	2	2	2	1	9		
Total	4	3	3	3	2						4	3	3	3	2	15	2,515	5,030
HYDE																		
White	3	2	2	2	1						3	2	2	2	1	10		
Colored			1	1	3								1	1	3	5		
Total	3	2	3	3	4						3	2	3	3	4	15	2,620	1,965
PASQUOTANK																		
White	53	45	56	78	65				1		53	45	56	79	65	297		
Colored	28	38	41	33	34	1					29	38	41	33	34	174		
Total	81	83	97	111	99	1			1		82	83	97	112	99	472	250	207
PERQUIMANS																		
White	4	5		8	8						4	5		8	8	25		
Colored	2	3	4	5	3						2	3	4	5	8	17		
Total	6	8	4	13	11						6	8	4	13	11	42	1,628	888
TYRRELL																		
White	1	6			1						1	6			1	8		
Colored		3		1								3		1		4		
Total	1	9		1	1						1	9		1	1	12	5,556	5,556
DISTRICT 2 **EDGECOMBE**																		
White	15	21	21	19	14					1	15	21	21	20	14	91		
Colored	15	14	19	26	11						15	14	19	26	11	85		
Total	30	35	40	45	25					1	30	35	40	46	25	176	1,638	1,966

	ABSOLUTE					SEPARATION					GRAND TOTAL					5 yr tot.	One Divorce for No. of Population given below	
	1941	1942	1943	1944	1945	1941	1942	1943	1944	1945	1941	1942	1943	1944	1945		1941	1945
MARTIN																		
White	12	21	18	15	19						12	21	18	15	19	85		
Colored	10	29	15	29	38						10	29	15	29	38	121		
Total	22	50	33	44	57						22	50	33	44	57	206	1,186	458
NASH *																		
White	28	21	17	9	1						28	21	17	9	1	76		
Colored	7	7	8	2							7	7	8	2		24		
Total	35	28	25	11	1						35	28	25	11	1	100	1,588	55,608
WASHINGTON																		
White	4	5	8	8	8	1					5	5	8	8	8	34		
Colored	1	7	4	5	9						1	7	4	5	9	26		
Total	5	12	12	13	17	1					6	12	12	13	17	60	2,053	724
WILSON																		
White	2		3	5	3						2		3	5	3	13		
Colored																		
Total	2		3	5	3						2		3	5	3	13	25,109	16,739
DISTRICT 3 **BERTIE**																		
White	8	5	4	2	1						8	5	4	2	1	20		
Colored	10	23	17	9							10	23	17	9		59		
Total	18	28	21	11	1						18	28	21	11	1	79	1,455	26,001
HALIFAX																		
White		35	40	32	39			1				35	41	32	39			
Colored		15	14	30	31							15	14	30	31			
Total	48	50	54	62	70			1			48	50	55	62	70	285	1,177	807
HERTFORD																		
White	12	9	5	2	4						12	9	5	2	4	32		
Colored	15	16	16	17	17						15	16	16	17	17	81		
Total	27	25	21	19	21						27	25	21	19	21	113	716	921
NORTHAMPTON																		
White	7	11	8	5	4						7	11	8	5	4	35		
Colored	13	23	17	17	16						13	23	17	17	16	86		
Total	20	34	25	22	20						20	34	25	22	20	121	1,414	1,414
VANCE																		
White	22	23	27	28	26					1	22	23	27	28	27	127		
Colored	18	10	12	24	24						18	10	12	24	24	88		
Total	40	33	39	52	50					1	40	33	39	52	51	215	749	587
WARREN																		
White	5	4	10	8	5						5	4	10	8	5	32		
Colored	8	4	5	9	16						8	4	5	9	16	42		
Total	13	8	15	17	21						13	8	15	17	21	74	1,780	1,102
DISTRICT 4 **CHATHAM**																		
White	15	14	12	14	12		1				15	15	12	14	12	68		
Colored		2	10	12	7							2	10	12	7	31		
Total	15	16	22	26	19		1				15	17	22	26	19	99	1,648	1,301

	ABSOLUTE					SEPARATION					GRAND TOTAL					5 yr tot.	One Divorce for No. of Population given below	
	1941	1942	1943	1944	1945	1941	1942	1943	1944	1945	1941	1942	1943	1944	1945		1941	1945
HARNETT																		
White	33	45	49	33	36						33	45	49	33	36	196		
Colored	2	2	5	4	13						2	2	5	4	13	26		
Total	35	47	54	37	49						35	47	54	37	49	222	1,263	902
JOHNSTON																		
White	51	45	53	47	54			1			51	45	54	47	54	251		
Colored	5	1	7	6	9						5	1	7	6	9	28		
Total	56	46	60	53	63			1			56	46	61	53	63	279	1,139	1,012
LEE																		
White		12	19	12	23							12	19	12	23	66		
Colored		1	9	3	6							1	9	3	6	19		
Total		13	28	15	29							13	28	15	29	85	0	646
WAYNE																		
White	72	77	63	66	75		1				72	78	63	66	75	354		
Colored	17	34	52	54	66				1		17	34	52	55	66	224		
Total	89	111	115	120	141		1		1		89	112	115	121	141	578	655	413
DISTRICT 5																		
CARTERET																		
White	24	31	32	20	40			3		3	24	31	35	20	43	153		
Colored	2	3	2	7	4	1					2	4	2	7	4	19		
Total	26	34	34	27	44	1		3		3	26	35	37	27	47	172	703	389
CRAVEN																		
White	24	39	55	32	64					1	24	39	55	32	65	215		
Colored	8	15	26	23	17						8	15	26	23	17	89		
Total	32	54	81	55	81					1	32	54	81	55	82	304	978	381
GREEN																		
White	8	8	6	10	9						8	8	6	10	9	41		
Colored	4	5	16	12	9						4	5	16	12	9	46		
Total	12	13	22	22	18						12	13	22	22	18	87	1,545	1,030
JONES																		
White	8	5	7	2	7						8	5	7	2	7	29		
Colored	1	0	1	0	1						1	0	1	0	1	3		
Total	9	5	8	2	8						9	5	8	2	8	32	1,214	1,365
PAMLICO																		
White	4	7	5	4	7						4	7	5	4	7	27		
Colored	0	1	3	2	3						0	1	3	2	3	9		
Total	4	8	8	6	10						4	8	8	6	10	36	2,426	970
PITT																		
White	32	51	69	50	65						32	51	69	50	65	267		
Colored	17	57	16	45	58						17	57	16	45	58	193		
Total	49	108	85	95	123						49	108	85	95	123	460	1,249	497

DIVORCES

	ABSOLUTE					SEPARATION					GRAND TOTAL					5 yr tot.	One Divorce for No. of Population given below	
	1941	1942	1943	1944	1945	1941	1942	1943	1944	1945	1941	1942	1943	1944	1945		1941	1945
DISTRICT 6																		
DUPLIN																		
White	9	19	13	33	9						9	19	13	33	9	83		
Colored	6	7	16	17	6						6	7	16	17	6	52		
Total	15	26	29	50	15						15	26	29	50	15	135	2,649	2,649
LENOIR																		
White	46	63	75	109	89	1					47	63	75	109	89	383		
Colored	10	19	40	44	32						10	19	40	44	32	145		
Total	56	82	115	153	121	1					57	82	115	153	121	528	723	340
ONSLOW																		
White	3		46	26	29						3		46	26	29			
Colored	0		2	1	0						0		2	1	0			
Total	3	14	48	27	29						3	14	48	27	29	121	5,979	618
SAMPSON																		
White	13	32	28	33	21						13	32	28	33	21	127		
Colored	0	0	10	6	14						0	0	10	6	14	30		
Total	13	32	38	39	35						13	32	38	39	35	157	3,649	1,355
DISTRICT 7																		
FRANKLIN																		
White	14	21	11	7	7						14	21	11	7	7	60		
Colored	3	4	4	6	1						3	4	4	6	1	18		
Total	17	25	15	13	8						17	25	15	13	8	78	1,787	3,797
WAKE																		
White	149	129	143	145	165				1		149	129	143	146	165	732		
Colored	17	40	82	64	69						17	40	82	64	69	272		
Total	166	169	225	209	234				1		166	169	225	210	234	1004	659	468
DISTRICT 8																		
BRUNSWICK																		
White	16	10	17	17	16						16	10	17	17	16	76		
Colored	5	7	9	2	3						5	7	9	2	3	26		
Total	21	17	26	19	19						21	17	26	19	19	102	815	901
COLUMBUS																		
White	37	33	55	60	74				1	1	37	33	55	61	75	261		
Colored	2	13	10	17	17						2	13	10	17	17	59		
Total	39	46	65	77	91				1	1	39	46	65	78	92	320	1,170	496
NEW HANOVER																		
White	88	150		171	219						88	150		171	219			
Colored	14	45		66	50						14	45		66	50			
Total	102	195	282	237	269						102	195	282	237	269	1085	469	178
PENDER																		
White	7	9	8	10	10						7	9	8	10	10	44		
Colored	0	5	5	10	8						0	5	5	10	8	28		
Total	7	14	13	20	18						7	14	13	20	18	72	2,530	983

	ABSOLUTE					SEPARATION					GRAND TOTAL					5 yr tot.	One Divorce for No. of Population given below	
	1941	1942	1943	1944	1945	1941	1942	1943	1944	1945	1941	1942	1943	1944	1945		1941	1945
DISTRICT 9																		
BLADEN																		
White	6	3	8	22	6						6	3	8	22	6	45		
Colored	2	1	2	1	1			1			2	1	3	1	1	8		
Total	8	4	10	23	7			1			8	4	11	23	7	53	3,394	3,879
CUMBERLAND																		
White	61	41	59	35	22	1					62	41	59	35	22	219		
Colored	6	8	28	59	47						6	8	28	59	47	148		
Total	67	49	87	94	69	1					68	49	87	94	69	367	872	859
HOKE																		
White	4	7	3	10	7						4	7	3	10	7	31		
Colored	0	2	5	5	5						0	2	5	5	5	17		
Total	4	9	8	15	12						4	9	8	15	12	48	3,734	1,244
ROBESON																		
White	50	56	43	66	78						50	56	43	66	78	293		
Indians	3	8	2	0	2						3	8	2	0	2	15		
Colored	2	4	12	9	7						2	4	12	9	7	34		
Total	55	68	57	75	87						55	68	57	75	87	342	1,397	883
DISTRICT 10																		
ALAMANCE																		
White	2	11	4	4	6						2	11	4	4	6	27		
Colored	3	3	0	0	1						3	3	0	0	1	7		
Total	5	14	4	4	7						5	14	4	4	7	34	11,485	8,203
DURHAM																		
White	147	136	191	164	210					1	147	136	191	164	211	849		
Colored	30	53	92	67	111						30	53	92	67	111	353		
Total	177	189	283	231	321					1	177	189	283	231	322	1202	453	249
GRANVILLE																		
White	5	5	2	11	10						5	5	2	11	10	33		
Colored	3	7	16	20	18						3	7	16	20	18	64		
Total	8	12	18	31	28						8	12	18	31	28	97	3,667	1,048
ORANGE																		
White	18	11	25	17	29						18	11	25	17	29	100		
Colored	2	1	14	16	10						2	1	14	16	10	43		
Total	20	12	39	33	39						20	12	39	33	39	143	1,153	591
PERSON																		
White	8	2	16	7	11						8	2	16	7	11	44		
Colored	2	1	5	6	7						2	1	5	6	7	21		
Total	10	3	21	13	18						10	3	21	13	18	65	2,502	1,390
DISTRICT 11																		
FORSYTH																		
White	174	152	161	187	179	2	6		2	5	176	158	161	189	184	868		
Colored	100	151	187	175	164						100	151	187	175	164	777		
Total	274	303	348	362	343	2	6		2	5	276	309	348	364	348	1645	458	363

DIVORCES

	ABSOLUTE					SEPARATION					GRAND TOTAL					5 yr tot.	One Divorce for No. of Population given below	
	1941	1942	1943	1944	1945	194.	1942	1943	1944	1945	1941	1942	1943	1944	1945		1941	1945
ALLEGHANY																		
White	6	.....	3	5	10						6	.....	3	5	10	24		
Colored																		
Total	6	.....	3	5	10						6	.....	3	5	10	24	1,390	834
ASHE																		
White	14	8	10	.....	25						14	8	10	.....	25	57		
Colored	.....	1	1	.....	1						.....	1	1	.....	1	3		
Total	14	9	11	.....	26						14	9	11	.....	26	60	1,618	871
DISTRICT 12 **DAVIDSON**																		
White	53	45	52	75	80			1	1	1	53	45	53	76	81	308		
Colored	0	2	10	15	12						0	2	10	15	12	39		
Total	53	47	62	90	92			1	1	1	53	47	63	91	93	347	1,007	573
GUILFORD																		
White	156	174	145	168	243					1	156	174	145	168	244	887		
Colored	25	23	41	38	53						25	23	41	38	53	180		
Total	181	197	186	206	296					1	181	197	186	206	297	1067	850	518
DISTRICT 13 **ANSON**																		
White	9	8	16	10	20						9	8	16	10	20	63		
Colored	4	8	6	2	8						4	8	6	2	8	28		
Total	13	16	22	12	28						13	16	22	12	28	91	2,187	1,015
MOORE																		
White	22	21	13	28	26	1					23	21	13	28	26	111		
Colored	16	10	2	9	15						16	10	2	9	15	52		
Total	38	31	15	37	41	1					39	31	15	37	41	163	794	755
RICHMOND																		
White	40	41	42	60	67		1				40	42	42	60	67	251		
Colored	4	0	2	6	8						4	0	2	6	8	20		
Total	44	41	44	66	75		1				44	42	44	66	75	271	836	490
SCOTLAND																		
White	21	15	23	16	34					1	21	15	23	16	35	110		
Colored	1	4	5	4	18						1	4	5	4	18	32		
Total	22	19	28	20	52					1	22	19	28	29	53	142	1,056	438
STANLY																		
White	50	23	23	37	46				1		50	23	23	38	46	180		
Colored	2	2	1	1	4						2	2	1	1	4	10		
Total	52	25	24	38	50				1		52	25	24	39	50	190	631	656
UNION																		
White	30	22	28	20	26			1	.....	1	30	22	29	20	27	128		
Colored	2	3	6	3	8						2	3	6	3	8	22		
Total	32	25	34	23	34			1	.....	1	32	25	35	23	35	150	1,221	260

	ABSOLUTE					SEPARATION					GRAND TOTAL					5 yr tot.	One Divorce for No. of Population given below	
	1941	1942	1943	1944	1945	1941	1942	1943	1944	1945	1941	1942	1943	1944	1945		1941	1945
DISTRICT 14																		
GASTON																		
White	189	188	192	258	279			2	1		189	188	194	259	279	1109		
Colored	5	9	13	19	16						5	9	13	19	16	62		
Total	194	197	205	277	295			2	1		194	197	207	278	295	1171	451	296
MECKLENBURG																		
White	311	354	333	482	555	2	3	5		2	313	357	338	482	557	2047		
Colored	31	61	56	78	86						31	61	56	78	86	312		
Total	342	415	389	560	641	2	3	5		2	344	418	394	560	643	2359	441	236
DISTRICT 15																		
ALEXANDER																		
White	12	5	7	3	10						12	5	7	3	10	37		
Colored	1	0	0	1	2						1	0	0	1	2	4		
Total	13	5	7	4	12						13	5	7	4	12	41	1,034	1,121
CABARRUS																		
White	152	119	124	140	144						152	119	124	140	144	679		
Colored	0	19	16	5	4						0	19	16	5	4	44		
Total	152	138	140	145	148						152	138	140	145	148	723	390	401
IREDELL																		
White	36	24	70	41	54						36	24	70	41	54	225		
Colored	10	13	20	11	13						10	13	20	11	13	67		
Total	46	37	90	52	67						46	37	90	52	67	292	1,291	203
MONTGOMERY																		
White	14	4	10	6	9			1			14	4	11	6	9	44		
Colored	0	2	0	1	0						0	2	0	1	0	3		
Total	14	6	10	7	9			1			14	6	11	7	9	47	1,162	1,808
RANDOLPH																		
White	45	31	38	65	74						45	31	38	65	74	253		
Colored	1	0	0	0	2						1	0	0	0	2	3		
Total	46	31	38	65	76						46	31	38	65	76	256	968	586
ROWAN																		
White	45	68	65	63	93	1					46	68	65	63	93	335		
Colored	0	2	2	3	0						0	2	2	3	0	7		
Total	45	70	67	66	93	1					46	70	67	66	93	342	1,504	744
DISTRICT 16																		
BURKE																		
White	45	41	63	50	91						45	41	63	50	91	290		
Colored	2	1	3	4	5						2	1	3	4	5	15		
Total	47	42	66	54	96						47	42	66	54	96	305	821	402
CALDWELL																		
White	43	43	57	55	78	3				1	46	43	57	55	79	280		
Colored	3	2	7	3	5						3	2	7	3	5	20		
Total	46	45	64	58	83	3				1	49	45	64	58	84	300	730	426

DIVORCES

	ABSOLUTE					SEPARATION					GRAND TOTAL					5 yr tot.	One Divorce for No. of Population given below	
	1941	1942	1943	1944	1945	1941	1942	1943	1944	1945	1941	1942	1943	1944	1945		1941	1945
CATAWBA																		
White	59	86	74	102	107					1	59	86	74	102	108	429		
Colored	3	7	4	6	3						3	7	4	6	3	23		
Total	62	93	78	108	110					1	62	93	78	108	111	452	833	465
CLEVELAND																		
White	53	70	66	90	89		1				53	71	66	90	89	369		
Colored	2	3	7	5	15						2	3	7	5	15	32		
Total	55	73	73	95	104		1				55	74	73	95	104	401	1,055	558
LINCOLN																		
White	21	14	22	20	19						21	14	22	20	19	96		
Colored	7	3	3	5	5						7	3	3	5	5	23		
Total	28	17	25	25	24						28	17	25	25	24	119	863	1,007
WATAUGA																		
White	10	13	11	9	10						10	13	11	9	10	53		
Colored	0	1	0	0	0						0	1	0	0	0	1		
Total	10	14	11	9	10						10	14	11	9	10	54	1,811	1,811
DISTRICT 17																		
AVERY																		
White	0	13	5	10	3						0	13	5	10	3	31		
Colored	0	0	0	0	0						0	0	0	0	0	0		
Total	0	13	5	10	3						0	13	5	10	3	31	0	4,520
DAVIE																		
White	10	13	6	11	7						10	13	6	11	7	47		
Colored	2	1	0	1	4						2	1	0	1	4	8		
Total	12	14	6	12	11						12	14	6	12	11	55	1,242	1,355
MITCHELL																		
White	2	7	7		3	1					3	7	7		3	20		
Colored	5	0	0		1						5	0	0		1	6		
Total	7	7	7		4	1					8	7	7		4	26	1,997	3,995
WILKES																		
White	18	28	40	30	45		1				18	29	40	30	45	162		
Colored	0	1	2	4	1						0	1	2	4	1	8		
Total	18	29	42	34	46		1				18	30	42	34	46	170	2,389	934
YADKIN																		
White	11	9	7	1	8						11	9	7	1	8	36		
Colored	0	0	1	2	0						0	0	1	2	0	3		
Total	11	9	8	3	8						11	9	8	3	8	39	1,877	2,582
DISTRICT 18																		
HENDERSON																		
White	26	21	49	71	49	1					27	21	49	71	49	217		
Colored	1	1	1	6	5						1	1	1	6	5	14		
Total	27	22	50	77	54	1					28	22	50	77	54	231	930	482

	ABSOLUTE					SEPARATION					GRAND TOTAL					5 yr tot.	One Divorce for No. of Population given below	
	1941	1942	1943	1944	1945	1941	1942	1943	1944	1945	1941	1942	1943	1944	1945		1941	1945
McDOWELL																		
White	19	21	18	19	22	1					20	21	18	19	22	100		
Colored	1	0	3	1	7						1	0	3	1	7	12		
Total	20	21	21	20	29	1					21	21	21	20	29	112	1,095	792
POLK																		
White	2	3	8	9	17						2	3	8	9	17	39		
Colored	0	1	0	3	4						0	1	0	3	4	8		
Total	2	4	8	12	21						2	4	8	12	21	47	5,937	565
RUTHERFORD																		
White	44	48	48	34	65						44	48	48	34	65	239		
Colored	0	0	1	2	5						0	0	1	2	5	8		
Total	44	48	49	36	70						44	48	49	36	70	247	1,035	651
TRANSYLVANIA																		
White	20	12	12	10	19						20	12	12	10	19	73		
Colored	0	0	0	1	2						0	0	0	1	2	3		
Total	20	12	12	11	21						20	12	12	11	21	76	612	582
YANCEY																		
White	9	16	14	17	15						9	16	14	17	15	71		
Colored	0	0	0	2	1						0	0	0	2	1	3		
Total	9	16	14	19	16						9	16	14	19	16	74	1,911	1,075
DISTRICT 19																		
BUNCOMBE																		
White	224	212	280	319	426		1	2	6	3	224	213	282	325	429	1473		
Colored	15	9	9	22	39						15	9	9	22	39	94		
Total	239	221	289	341	465		1	2	6	3	239	222	291	347	468	1567	455	232
MADISON																		
White	26	14	14	22	29						26	14	14	22	29	105		
Colored	0	0	0	0	1						0	0	0	0	1	1		
Total	26	14	14	22	30						26	14	14	22	30	106	866	750
DISTRICT 20																		
CLAY																		
White	5	2	1	2	3						5	2	1	2	3	13		
Colored	0	0	0	0	0						0	0	0	0	0	0		
Total	5	2	1	2	3						5	2	1	2	3	13	1,281	2,135
CHEROKEE																		
White	9	19	12	28	17		1				9	20	12	28	17	86		
Colored	1	0	0	1	2						1	0	0	1	2	4		
Indians	0	0	0	0	0						0	0	0	0	0	0		
Total	10	19	12	29	19		1				10	20	12	29	19	90	1,881	990
GRAHAM																		
White	15	4	11	7	5			1		1	15	4	11	8	6	44		
Colored	0	0	0	0	0						0	0	0	0	0	0		
Total	15	4	11	7	5			1		1	15	4	11	8	6	44	427	1,069

DIVORCES

	ABSOLUTE					SEPARATION					GRAND TOTAL					5 yr tot.	One Divorce for No. of Population given below	
	1941	1942	1943	1944	1945	1941	1942	1943	1944	1945	1941	1942	1943	1944	1945		1941	1945
HAYWOOD																		
White	26	17	44	41	67						26	17	44	41	67	195		
Colored	0	0	1	0	1						0	0	1	0	1	2		
Total	26	17	45	41	68						26	17	45	41	68	197	1,338	511
JACKSON																		
White	16	18	11	10	15						16	18	11	10	15	70		
Colored	1	0	1	1	0						1	0	1	1	0	3		
Indians	0	0	0	1	0						0	0	0	1	0	1		
Total	17	18	12	12	15						17	18	12	12	15	74	1,139	1,291
MACON																		
White	11	21	13	10	23					2	11	21	13	10	25	80		
Colored	0	0	2	0	0						0	0	2	0	0	2		
Total	11	21	15	10	23					2	11	21	15	10	25	82	1,443	635
SWAIN																		
White	28	7	20	21	25						28	7	20	21	25	101		
Colored	0	0	0	1	0						0	0	0	1	0	1		
Indians	0	0	0	2	2						0	0	0	2	2	4		
Total	28	7	20	24	27						28	7	20	24	27	106	434	451
DISTRICT 21 **CASWELL**																		
White	3	4	4	3	1						3	4	4	3	1	15		
Colored	5	3	3	2	3						5	3	3	2	3	16		
Total	8	7	7	5	4						8	7	7	5	4	31	2,504	5,008
ROCKINGHAM																		
White	69	50	57	48	74				1		69	50	57	49	74	299		
Colored	15	8	7	13	15						15	8	7	13	15	58		
Total	84	58	64	61	89				1		84	58	64	62	89	357	689	650
STOKES																		
White	10	2	4	6	7						10	2	4	6	7	29		
Colored	2	0	0	3	1						2	0	0	3	1	6		
Total	12	2	4	9	8						12	2	4	9	8	35	1,888	647
SURRY																		
White	20	30	31	53	31	1					21	30	31	53	31	166		
Colored	0	0	0	2	1						0	0	0	2	1	3		
Total	20	30	31	55	32	1					21	30	31	55	32	169	1,989	1,305

INDEX

A

D

H

N

T

U

V